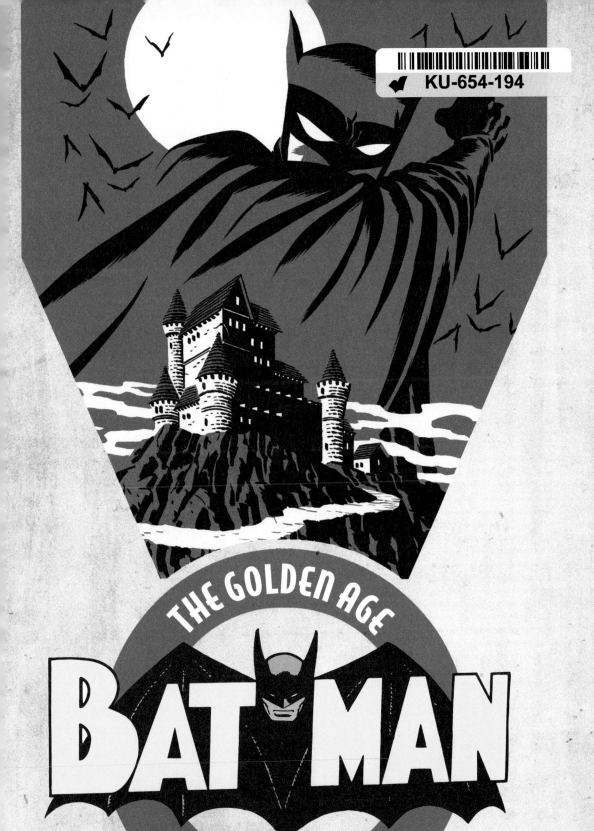

THE GOLDEN AGE
BAT MAN
VOLUME ONE

BILL FINGER
WRITER
WITH **GARDNER FOX, WHITNEY ELLSWORTH**

BOB KANE
ARTIST
WITH **SHELDON MOLDOFF,
JERRY ROBINSON, GEORGE ROUSSOS**

MICHAEL CHO
COVER ARTIST

BATMAN created by **BOB KANE** with **BILL FINGER**.

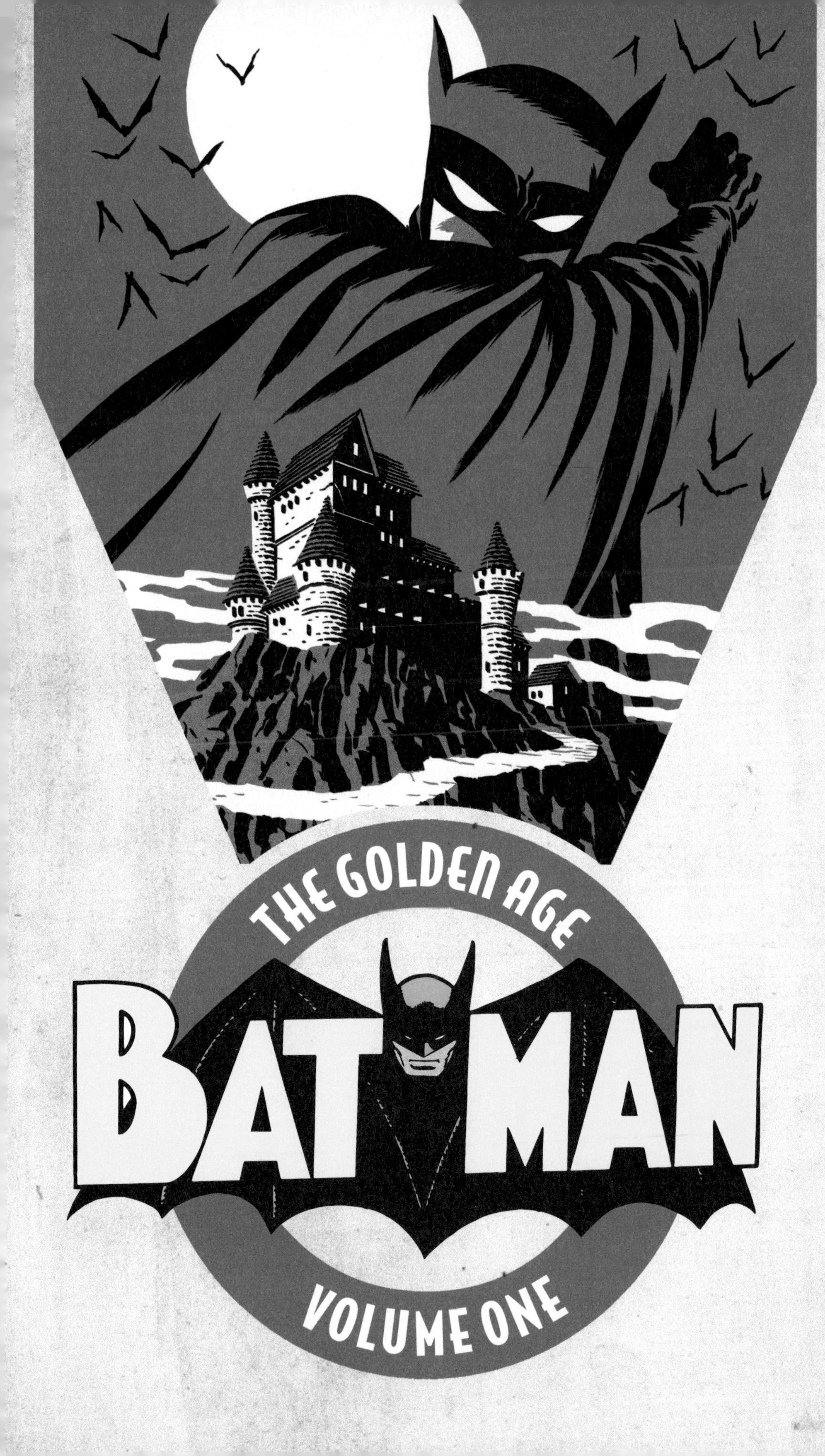

THE GOLDEN AGE

BATMAN

VOLUME ONE

WHITNEY ELLSWORTH Editor – Original Series
JEB WOODARD Group Editor – Collected Editions **PAUL SANTOS** Editor – Collected Edition
STEVE COOK Design Director – Books **LOUIS PRANDI** Publication Design

BOB HARRAS Senior VP – Editor-in-Chief, DC Comics

President **DIANE NELSON**
Co-Publishers **DAN DIDIO** and **JIM LEE**
Chief Creative Officer **GEOFF JOHNS**
Senior VP – Marketing & Global Franchise Management **AMIT DESAI**
Senior VP – Finance **NAIRI GARDINER**
VP – Digital Marketing **SAM ADES**
VP – Talent Development **BOBBIE CHASE**
Senior VP – Art, Design & Collected Editions **MARK CHIARELLO**
VP – Content Strategy **JOHN CUNNINGHAM**
VP – Strategy Planning & Reporting **ANNE DEPIES**
VP – Manufacturing Operations **DON FALLETTI**
VP – Editorial Administration & Talent Relations **LAWRENCE GANEM**

ALISON GILL Senior VP – Manufacturing & Operations
HANK KANALZ Senior VP – Editorial Strategy & Administration
JAY KOGAN VP – Legal Affairs
DEREK MADDALENA Senior VP – Sales & Business Development
JACK MAHAN VP – Business Affairs
DAN MIRON VP – Sales Planning & Trade Development
NICK NAPOLITANO VP – Manufacturing Administration
CAROL ROEDER VP – Marketing
EDDIE SCANNELL VP – Mass Account & Digital Sales
COURTNEY SIMMONS Senior VP – Publicity & Communications
JIM (SKI) SOKOLOWSKI VP – Comic Book Specialty & Newsstand Sales
SANDY YI Senior VP – Global Franchise Management

BATMAN: THE GOLDEN AGE VOLUME 1

Published by DC Comics. Compilation, cover and all new material Copyright © 2016 DC Comics. All Rights Reserved. Originally published in single magazine form in DETECTIVE COMICS 27-45, BATMAN 1-3, NEW YORK WORLD'S FAIR COMICS 2. Copyright © 1939, 1940 DC Comics. All Rights Reserved. All characters, their distinctive likenesses and related elements featured in this publication are trademarks of DC Comics. The stories, characters and incidents featured in this publication are entirely fictional. DC Comics does not read or accept unsolicited submissions of ideas, stories or artwork.

DC Comics, 2900 West Alameda Ave., Burbank, CA 91505
Printed by RR Donnelley, Salem, VA, USA. 7/8/16. First Printing.
ISBN: 978-1-4012-6333-1

Library of Congress Cataloging-in-Publication Data is Available.

*All stories by **BILL FINGER** and all art by **BOB KANE** except where noted.*

DETECTIVE COMICS #27 May 1939
"The Case of the Chemical Syndicate"
Cover art by Bob Kane
8

DETECTIVE COMICS #28 June 1939
"Frenchy Blake's Jewel Gang"
Cover art by Fred Guardineer
15

DETECTIVE COMICS #29 July 1939
"The Batman Meets Doctor Death"
Cover art by Bob Kane
Writer: Gardner Fox
22

DETECTIVE COMICS #30 August 1939
"The Return of Doctor Death"
Cover art by Fred Guardineer
Writer: Gardner Fox
Inkers: Bob Kane and Sheldon Moldoff
33

DETECTIVE COMICS #31 September 1939
"Batman Versus the Vampire, Part One"
Cover art by Bob Kane
Writers: Gardner Fox with Bill Finger
Inkers: Bob Kane and Sheldon Moldoff
44

DETECTIVE COMICS #32 October 1939
"Batman Versus the Vampire, Part Two"
Cover art by Fred Guardineer
Writer: Gardner Fox
Inkers: Bob Kane and Sheldon Moldoff
55

DETECTIVE COMICS #33 November 1939
"The Batman Wars Against the Dirigible of Doom"
Cover art by Bob Kane
Writer: Gardner Fox
Inkers: Bob Kane and Sheldon Moldoff
66

DETECTIVE COMICS #34 December 1939
"Peril in Paris"
Cover art by Creig Flessel
Writer: Gardner Fox
Inkers: Bob Kane and Sheldon Moldoff
79

DETECTIVE COMICS #35 January 1940
"The Case of the Ruby Idol"
Cover art by Bob Kane
Inkers: Bob Kane and Sheldon Moldoff
90

DETECTIVE COMICS #36 February 1940
"Professor Hugo Strange"
Cover art by Bob Kane
Inkers: Bob Kane and Jerry Robinson
103

DETECTIVE COMICS #37 March 1940
"The Spies"
Cover art by Bob Kane
Inkers: Bob Kane and Jerry Robinson
116

DETECTIVE COMICS #38 April 1940
"Introducing Robin, the Boy Wonder"
Cover art by Bob Kane and Jerry Robinson
Inkers: Bob Kane and Jerry Robinson
129

BATMAN #1 Spring 1940
Cover art by Bob Kane and Jerry Robinson
142

"The Legend of the Batman–
Who He Is and How He Came To Be!"
Inkers: Bob Kane and Sheldon Moldoff
"The Joker" *
Inkers: Bob Kane and Jerry Robinson
"Professor Hugo Strange and The Monsters"
Inkers: Bob Kane and Jerry Robinson
"The Cat" *
Inkers: Bob Kane and Jerry Robinson
"The Joker Returns"
Inkers: Bob Kane and Jerry Robinson

DETECTIVE COMICS #39 May 1940
"The Horde of the Green Dragon!"
Cover art by Bob Kane and Jerry Robinson
Inkers: Bob Kane and Jerry Robinson
198

DETECTIVE COMICS #40 June 1940
"Beware of Clayface" *
Cover art by Bob Kane and Jerry Robinson
Inkers: Bob Kane and Jerry Robinson
211

DETECTIVE COMICS #41 July 1940
"A Master Murderer" *
Cover art by Bob Kane and Jerry Robinson
Inkers: Bob Kane and Jerry Robinson
224

BATMAN #2 Summer 1940
Cover art by Bob Kane and Jerry Robinson
237

"Joker Meets Cat-Woman" *
Inkers: Jerry Robinson and George Roussos
"Wolf, The Crime Master" *
Inkers: Bob Kane and Jerry Robinson
"The Case of the Clubfoot Murderers"
Inkers: Bob Kane and Jerry Robinson
"The Case of the Missing Link"
Inkers: Jerry Robinson and George Roussos

NEW YORK WORLD'S FAIR COMICS #2 1940
"Batman and Robin Visit the New York World's Fair"
Cover art by Jack Burnley
Inkers: Bob Kane and George Roussos
290

DETECTIVE COMICS #42 August 1940
"The Case of the Prophetic Pictures!"
Cover art by Bob Kane and Jerry Robinson
Inkers: Bob Kane and Jerry Robinson
304

DETECTIVE COMICS #43 September 1940
"The Case of the City of Terror"
Cover art by Bob Kane and Jerry Robinson
Inkers: Bob Kane, Jerry Robinson, and George Roussos
318

DETECTIVE COMICS #44 October 1940
"The Land Behind the Light"
Cover art by Bob Kane, Jerry Robinson, and George Roussos
Inkers: Bob Kane, Jerry Robinson, and George Roussos
332

BATMAN #3 Fall 1940
Cover art by Bob Kane and Jerry Robinson
346
"The Strange Case of the Diabolical Puppet Master"
Inkers: Jerry Robinson and George Roussos
"The Ugliest Man in the World"
Inkers: Jerry Robinson and George Roussos
"The Crime School for Boys!!"
Inkers: Jerry Robinson and George Roussos
"The Batman vs. the Cat-Woman"
Inkers: Jerry Robinson and George Roussos
"The Batman Says"
Writer: Whitney Ellsworth
Artist: Jerry Robinson

DETECTIVE COMICS #45 November 1940
"The Case of the Laughing Death!"
Cover art by Bob Kane, Jerry Robinson, and George Roussos
Inkers: Bob Kane, Jerry Robinson, and George Roussos
400

*These stories were originally untitled and are titled here for reader convenience.

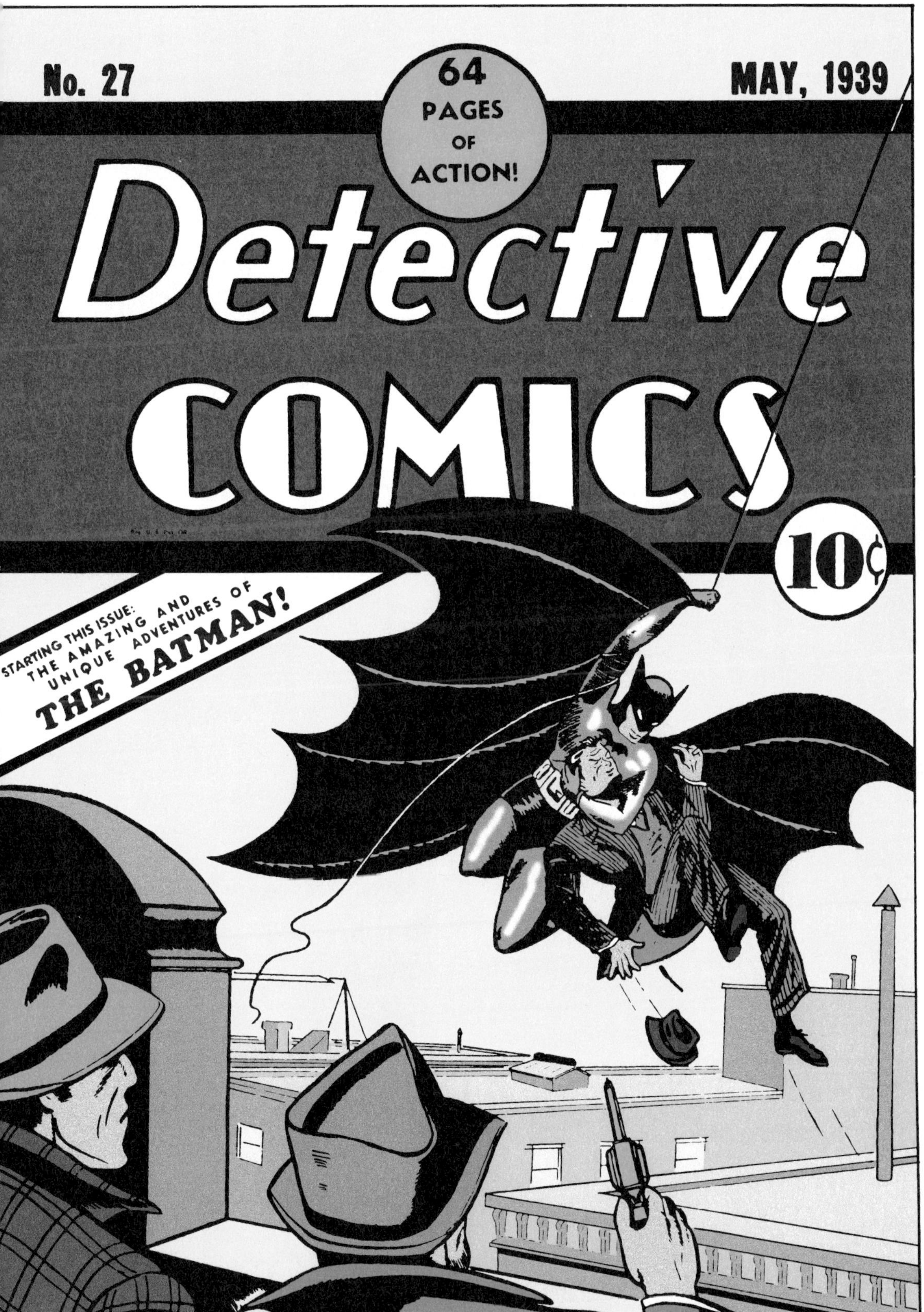
No. 27
64 PAGES OF ACTION!
MAY, 1939
Detective
COMICS
10¢
STARTING THIS ISSUE: THE AMAZING AND UNIQUE ADVENTURES OF
THE BATMAN!

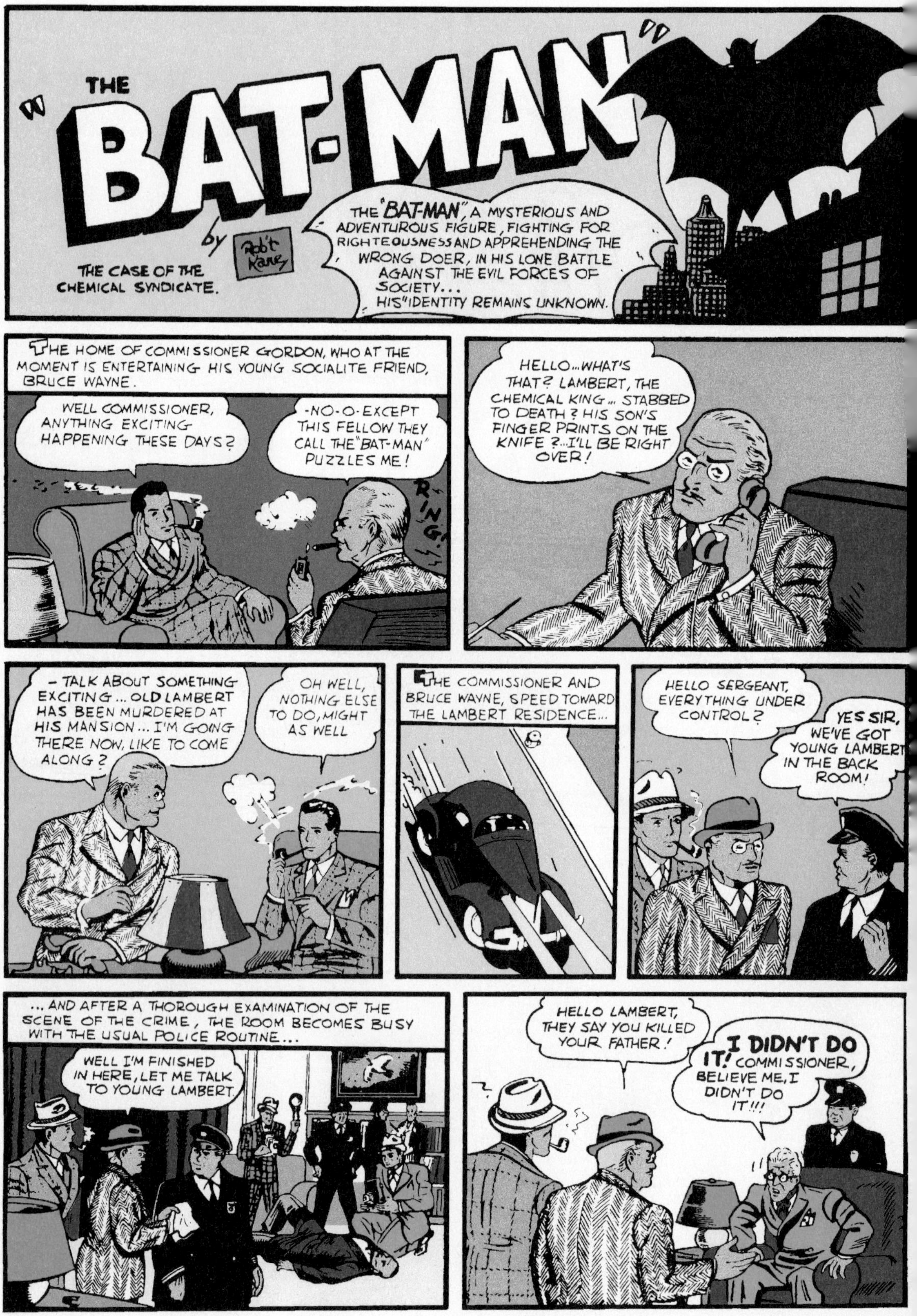

"THE BAT-MAN"
by Rob't Kane
THE CASE OF THE CHEMICAL SYNDICATE.
THE "BAT-MAN", A MYSTERIOUS AND ADVENTUROUS FIGURE, FIGHTING FOR RIGHTEOUSNESS AND APPREHENDING THE WRONG DOER, IN HIS LONE BATTLE AGAINST THE EVIL FORCES OF SOCIETY... HIS IDENTITY REMAINS UNKNOWN.
THE HOME OF COMMISSIONER GORDON, WHO AT THE MOMENT IS ENTERTAINING HIS YOUNG SOCIALITE FRIEND, BRUCE WAYNE.
WELL COMMISSIONER, ANYTHING EXCITING HAPPENING THESE DAYS?
-NO-O-EXCEPT THIS FELLOW THEY CALL THE "BAT-MAN" PUZZLES ME!
R-I-N-G!
HELLO...WHAT'S THAT? LAMBERT, THE CHEMICAL KING... STABBED TO DEATH? HIS SON'S FINGER PRINTS ON THE KNIFE?...I'LL BE RIGHT OVER!
- TALK ABOUT SOMETHING EXCITING... OLD LAMBERT HAS BEEN MURDERED AT HIS MANSION... I'M GOING THERE NOW, LIKE TO COME ALONG?
OH WELL, NOTHING ELSE TO DO, MIGHT AS WELL
THE COMMISSIONER AND BRUCE WAYNE, SPEED TOWARD THE LAMBERT RESIDENCE...
HELLO SERGEANT, EVERYTHING UNDER CONTROL?
YES SIR, WE'VE GOT YOUNG LAMBERT IN THE BACK ROOM!
... AND AFTER A THOROUGH EXAMINATION OF THE SCENE OF THE CRIME, THE ROOM BECOMES BUSY WITH THE USUAL POLICE ROUTINE...
WELL I'M FINISHED IN HERE, LET ME TALK TO YOUNG LAMBERT.
HELLO LAMBERT, THEY SAY YOU KILLED YOUR FATHER!
I DIDN'T DO IT! COMMISSIONER, BELIEVE ME, I DIDN'T DO IT!!!

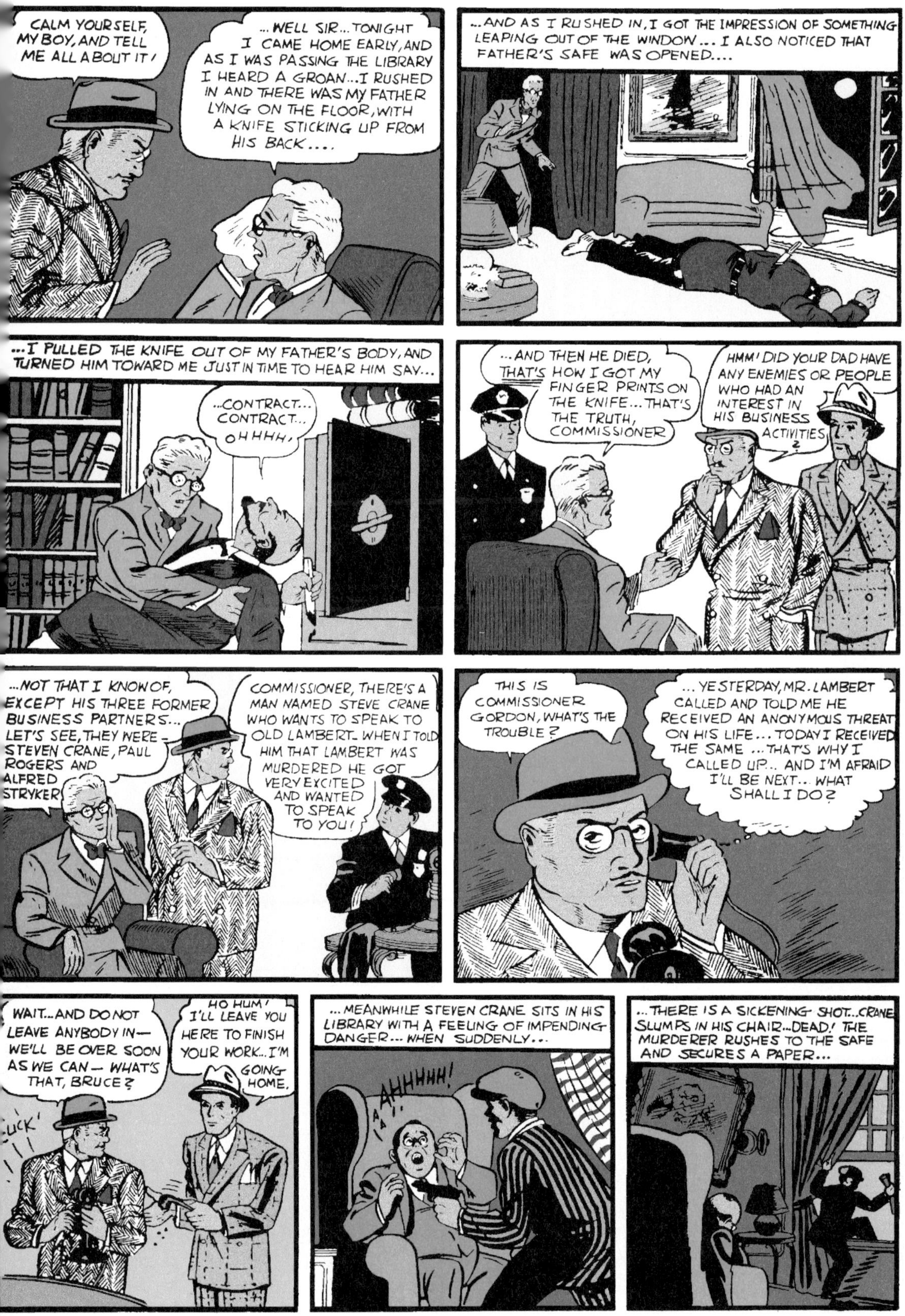
CALM YOURSELF, MY BOY, AND TELL ME ALL ABOUT IT!
...WELL SIR...TONIGHT I CAME HOME EARLY, AND AS I WAS PASSING THE LIBRARY I HEARD A GROAN...I RUSHED IN AND THERE WAS MY FATHER LYING ON THE FLOOR, WITH A KNIFE STICKING UP FROM HIS BACK....
...AND AS I RUSHED IN, I GOT THE IMPRESSION OF SOMETHING LEAPING OUT OF THE WINDOW... I ALSO NOTICED THAT FATHER'S SAFE WAS OPENED....
...I PULLED THE KNIFE OUT OF MY FATHER'S BODY, AND TURNED HIM TOWARD ME JUST IN TIME TO HEAR HIM SAY...
...CONTRACT... CONTRACT... OHHHH.
...AND THEN HE DIED, THAT'S HOW I GOT MY FINGER PRINTS ON THE KNIFE... THAT'S THE TRUTH, COMMISSIONER
HMM! DID YOUR DAD HAVE ANY ENEMIES OR PEOPLE WHO HAD AN INTEREST IN HIS BUSINESS ACTIVITIES?
...NOT THAT I KNOW OF, EXCEPT HIS THREE FORMER BUSINESS PARTNERS... LET'S SEE, THEY WERE - STEVEN CRANE, PAUL ROGERS AND ALFRED STRYKER
COMMISSIONER, THERE'S A MAN NAMED STEVE CRANE WHO WANTS TO SPEAK TO OLD LAMBERT. WHEN I TOLD HIM THAT LAMBERT WAS MURDERED HE GOT VERY EXCITED AND WANTED TO SPEAK TO YOU!
THIS IS COMMISSIONER GORDON, WHAT'S THE TROUBLE?
...YESTERDAY, MR. LAMBERT CALLED AND TOLD ME HE RECEIVED AN ANONYMOUS THREAT ON HIS LIFE... TODAY I RECEIVED THE SAME ...THAT'S WHY I CALLED UP... AND I'M AFRAID I'LL BE NEXT... WHAT SHALL I DO?
WAIT...AND DO NOT LEAVE ANYBODY IN— WE'LL BE OVER SOON AS WE CAN— WHAT'S THAT, BRUCE?
HO HUM! I'LL LEAVE YOU HERE TO FINISH YOUR WORK...I'M GOING HOME.
...MEANWHILE STEVEN CRANE SITS IN HIS LIBRARY WITH A FEELING OF IMPENDING DANGER... WHEN SUDDENLY...
AHHHHH!
...THERE IS A SICKENING SHOT...CRANE SLUMPS IN HIS CHAIR...DEAD! THE MURDERER RUSHES TO THE SAFE AND SECURES A PAPER...

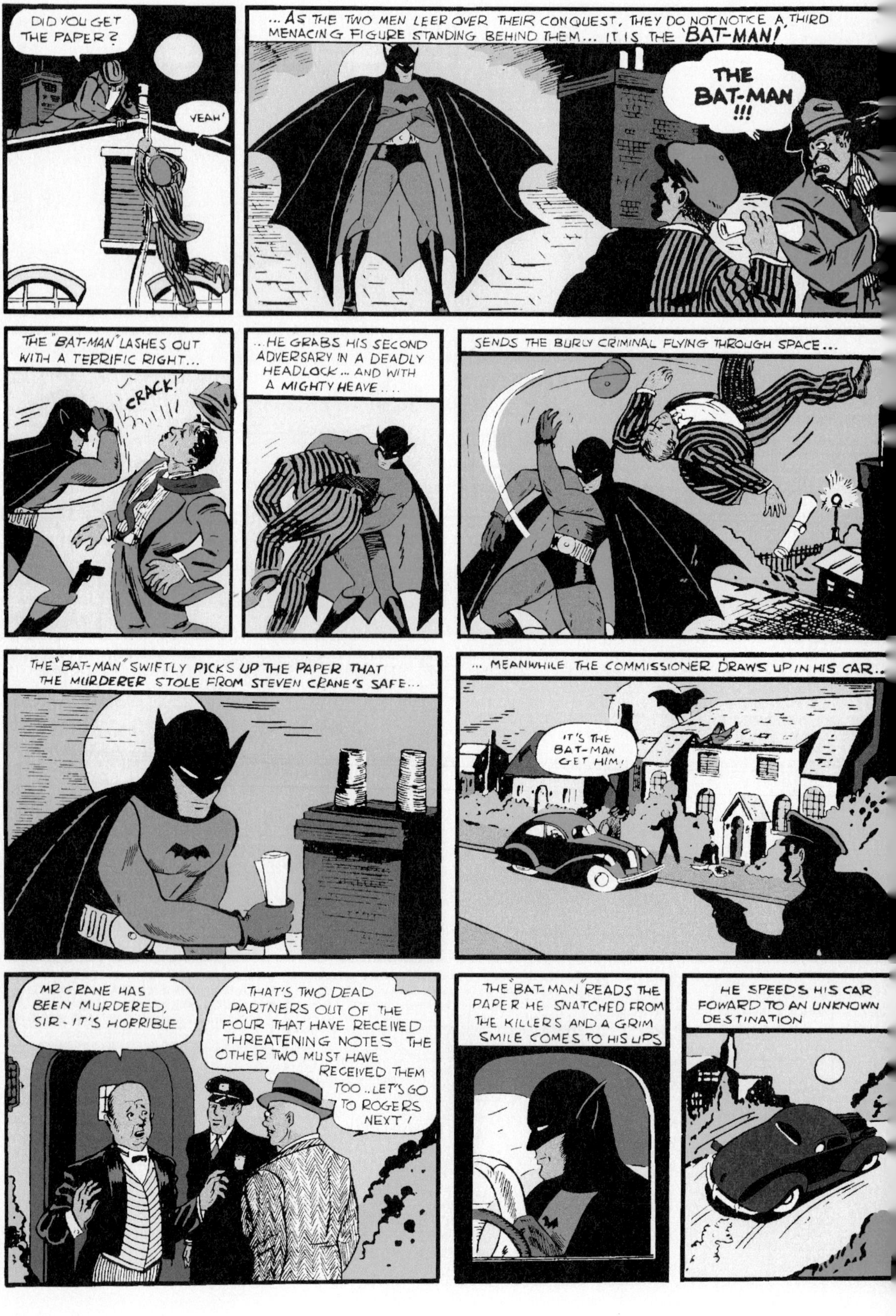
DID YOU GET THE PAPER?
YEAH'
...AS THE TWO MEN LEER OVER THEIR CONQUEST, THEY DO NOT NOTICE A THIRD MENACING FIGURE STANDING BEHIND THEM... IT IS THE 'BAT-MAN!'
THE BAT-MAN !!!
THE "BAT-MAN" LASHES OUT WITH A TERRIFIC RIGHT...
CRACK!
...HE GRABS HIS SECOND ADVERSARY IN A DEADLY HEADLOCK... AND WITH A MIGHTY HEAVE....
SENDS THE BURLY CRIMINAL FLYING THROUGH SPACE...
THE "BAT-MAN" SWIFTLY PICKS UP THE PAPER THAT THE MURDERER STOLE FROM STEVEN CRANE'S SAFE...
... MEANWHILE THE COMMISSIONER DRAWS UP IN HIS CAR...
IT'S THE BAT-MAN GET HIM!
MR CRANE HAS BEEN MURDERED, SIR - IT'S HORRIBLE
THAT'S TWO DEAD PARTNERS OUT OF THE FOUR THAT HAVE RECEIVED THREATENING NOTES THE OTHER TWO MUST HAVE RECEIVED THEM TOO.. LET'S GO TO ROGERS NEXT!
THE "BAT-MAN" READS THE PAPER HE SNATCHED FROM THE KILLERS AND A GRIM SMILE COMES TO HIS LIPS
HE SPEEDS HIS CAR FOWARD TO AN UNKNOWN DESTINATION

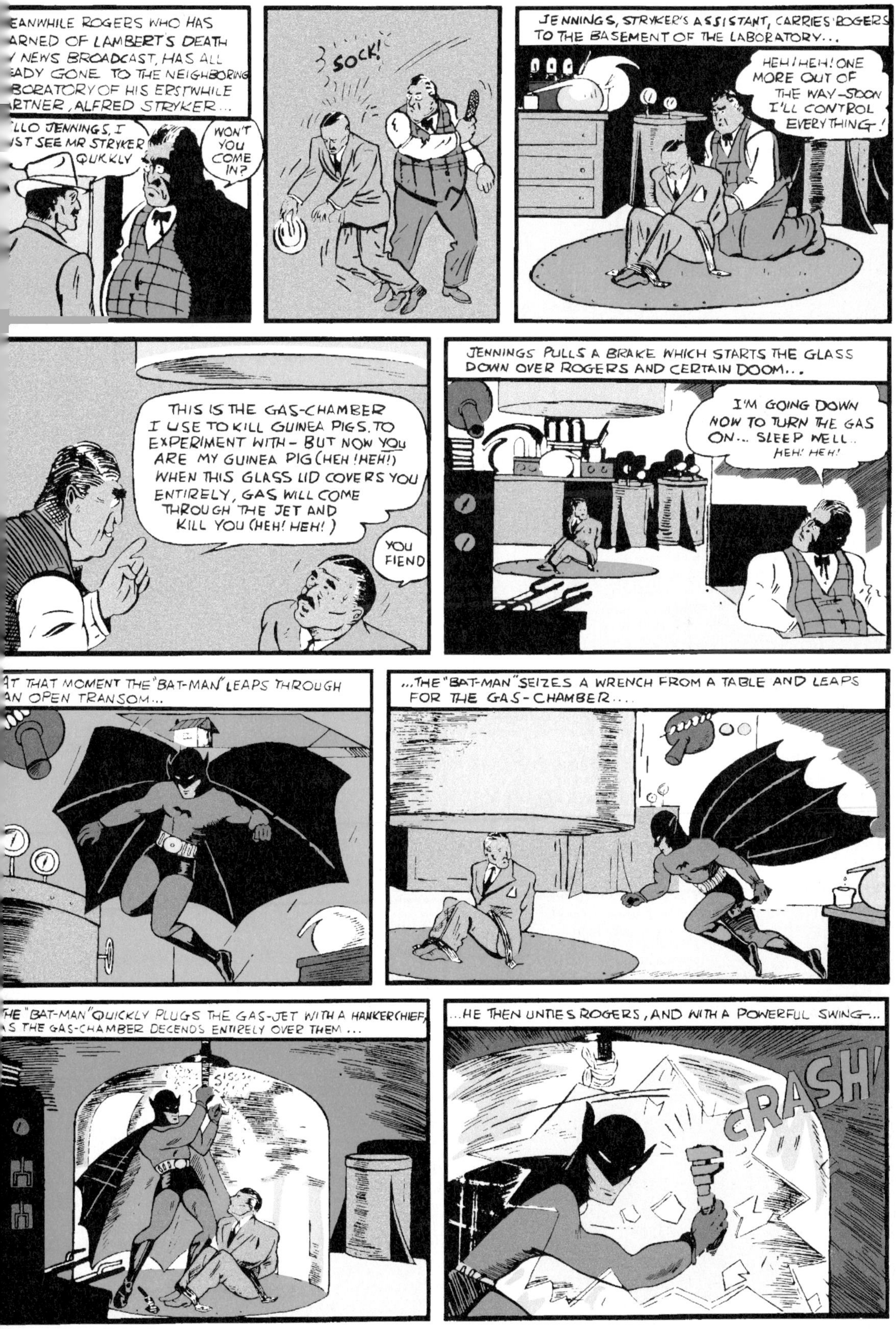
EANWHILE ROGERS WHO HAS ARNED OF LAMBERT'S DEATH Y NEWS BROADCAST, HAS ALL EADY GONE TO THE NEIGHBORING BORATORY OF HIS ERSTWHILE RTNER, ALFRED STRYKER...
LLO JENNINGS, I UST SEE MR STRYKER QUKKLY
WON'T YOU COME IN?
SOCK!
JENNINGS, STRYKER'S ASSISTANT, CARRIES ROGERS TO THE BASEMENT OF THE LABORATORY...
HEH! HEH! ONE MORE OUT OF THE WAY-SOON I'LL CONTROL EVERYTHING!
THIS IS THE GAS-CHAMBER I USE TO KILL GUINEA PIGS. TO EXPERIMENT WITH - BUT NOW YOU ARE MY GUINEA PIG (HEH! HEH!) WHEN THIS GLASS LID COVERS YOU ENTIRELY, GAS WILL COME THROUGH THE JET AND KILL YOU (HEH! HEH!)
YOU FIEND
JENNINGS PULLS A BRAKE WHICH STARTS THE GLASS DOWN OVER ROGERS AND CERTAIN DOOM...
I'M GOING DOWN NOW TO TURN THE GAS ON... SLEEP WELL.. HEH! HEH!
AT THAT MOMENT THE "BAT-MAN" LEAPS THROUGH AN OPEN TRANSOM...
...THE "BAT-MAN" SEIZES A WRENCH FROM A TABLE AND LEAPS FOR THE GAS-CHAMBER....
HE "BAT-MAN" QUICKLY PLUGS THE GAS-JET WITH A HANKERCHIEF, S THE GAS-CHAMBER DECENDS ENTIRELY OVER THEM ...
...HE THEN UNTIES ROGERS, AND WITH A POWERFUL SWING-...
CRASH!

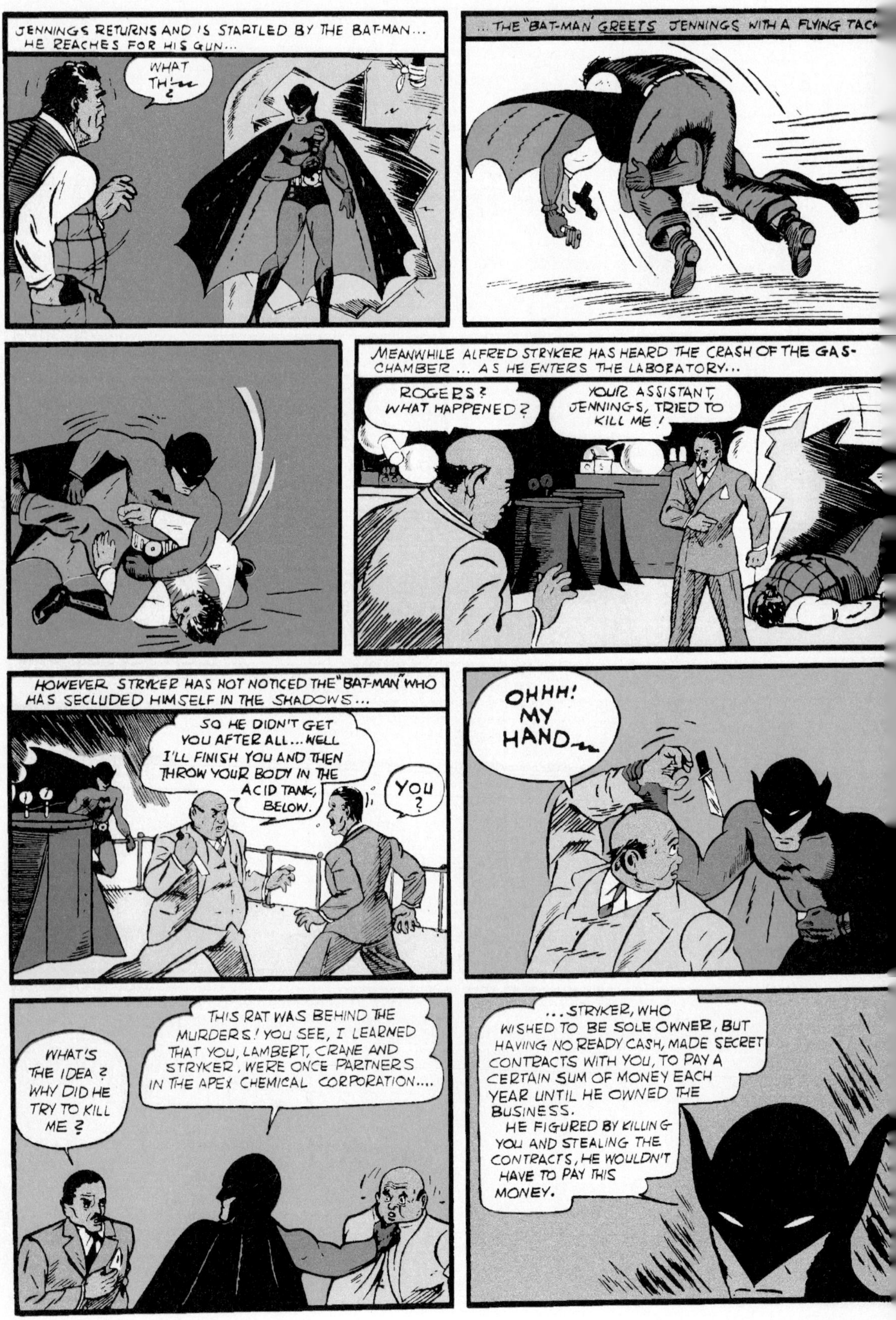

JENNINGS RETURNS AND IS STARTLED BY THE BAT-MAN... HE REACHES FOR HIS GUN...
WHAT TH'--?
...THE "BAT-MAN" GREETS JENNINGS WITH A FLYING TAC
MEANWHILE ALFRED STRYKER HAS HEARD THE CRASH OF THE GAS-CHAMBER ... AS HE ENTERS THE LABORATORY...
ROGERS? WHAT HAPPENED?
YOUR ASSISTANT, JENNINGS, TRIED TO KILL ME!
HOWEVER STRYKER HAS NOT NOTICED THE "BAT-MAN" WHO HAS SECLUDED HIMSELF IN THE SHADOWS...
SO HE DIDN'T GET YOU AFTER ALL... WELL I'LL FINISH YOU AND THEN THROW YOUR BODY IN THE ACID TANK, BELOW.
YOU?
OHHH! MY HAND--
WHAT'S THE IDEA? WHY DID HE TRY TO KILL ME?
THIS RAT WAS BEHIND THE MURDERS! YOU SEE, I LEARNED THAT YOU, LAMBERT, CRANE AND STRYKER, WERE ONCE PARTNERS IN THE APEX CHEMICAL CORPORATION....
...STRYKER, WHO WISHED TO BE SOLE OWNER, BUT HAVING NO READY CASH, MADE SECRET CONTRACTS WITH YOU, TO PAY A CERTAIN SUM OF MONEY EACH YEAR UNTIL HE OWNED THE BUSINESS.
HE FIGURED BY KILLING YOU AND STEALING THE CONTRACTS, HE WOULDN'T HAVE TO PAY THIS MONEY.

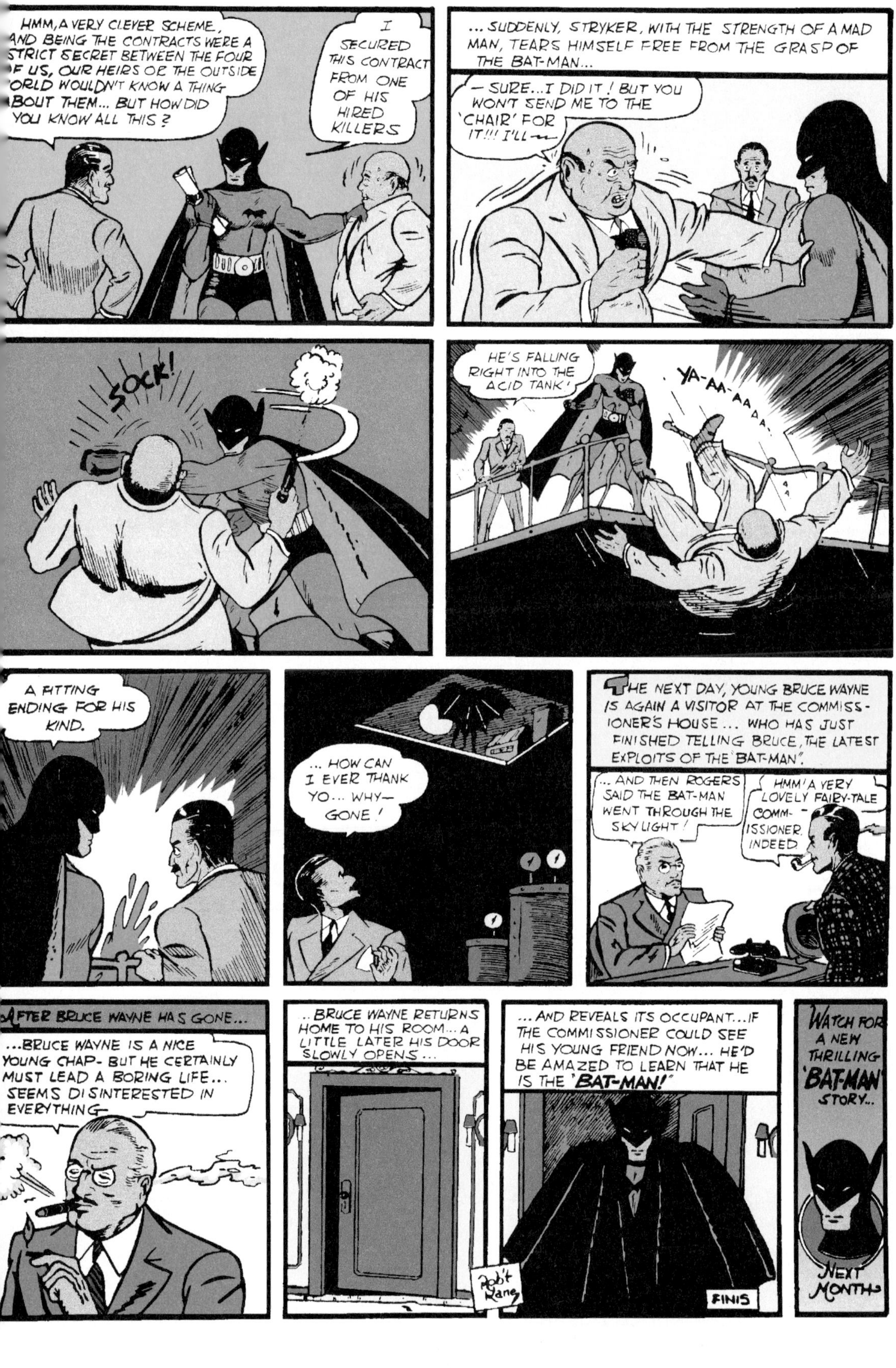
HMM, A VERY CLEVER SCHEME, AND BEING THE CONTRACTS WERE A STRICT SECRET BETWEEN THE FOUR OF US, OUR HEIRS OR THE OUTSIDE WORLD WOULDN'T KNOW A THING ABOUT THEM... BUT HOW DID YOU KNOW ALL THIS ?
I SECURED THIS CONTRACT FROM ONE OF HIS HIRED KILLERS
... SUDDENLY, STRYKER, WITH THE STRENGTH OF A MAD MAN, TEARS HIMSELF FREE FROM THE GRASP OF THE BAT-MAN...
— SURE... I DID IT ! BUT YOU WON'T SEND ME TO THE 'CHAIR' FOR IT!!! I'LL—
SOCK!
HE'S FALLING RIGHT INTO THE ACID TANK !
YA-AA-AAAA...
A FITTING ENDING FOR HIS KIND.
... HOW CAN I EVER THANK YO... WHY— GONE !
THE NEXT DAY, YOUNG BRUCE WAYNE IS AGAIN A VISITOR AT THE COMMISSIONER'S HOUSE ... WHO HAS JUST FINISHED TELLING BRUCE, THE LATEST EXPLOITS OF THE 'BAT-MAN'.
... AND THEN ROGERS SAID THE BAT-MAN WENT THROUGH THE SKYLIGHT !
HMM 'A VERY LOVELY FAIRY-TALE COMMISSIONER, INDEED
AFTER BRUCE WAYNE HAS GONE...
... BRUCE WAYNE IS A NICE YOUNG CHAP- BUT HE CERTAINLY MUST LEAD A BORING LIFE... SEEMS DISINTERESTED IN EVERYTHING
... BRUCE WAYNE RETURNS HOME TO HIS ROOM... A LITTLE LATER HIS DOOR SLOWLY OPENS ...
... AND REVEALS ITS OCCUPANT... IF THE COMMISSIONER COULD SEE HIS YOUNG FRIEND NOW... HE'D BE AMAZED TO LEARN THAT HE IS THE "BAT-MAN!"
Rob't Kane
FINIS
WATCH FOR A NEW THRILLING 'BAT-MAN' STORY... NEXT MONTH

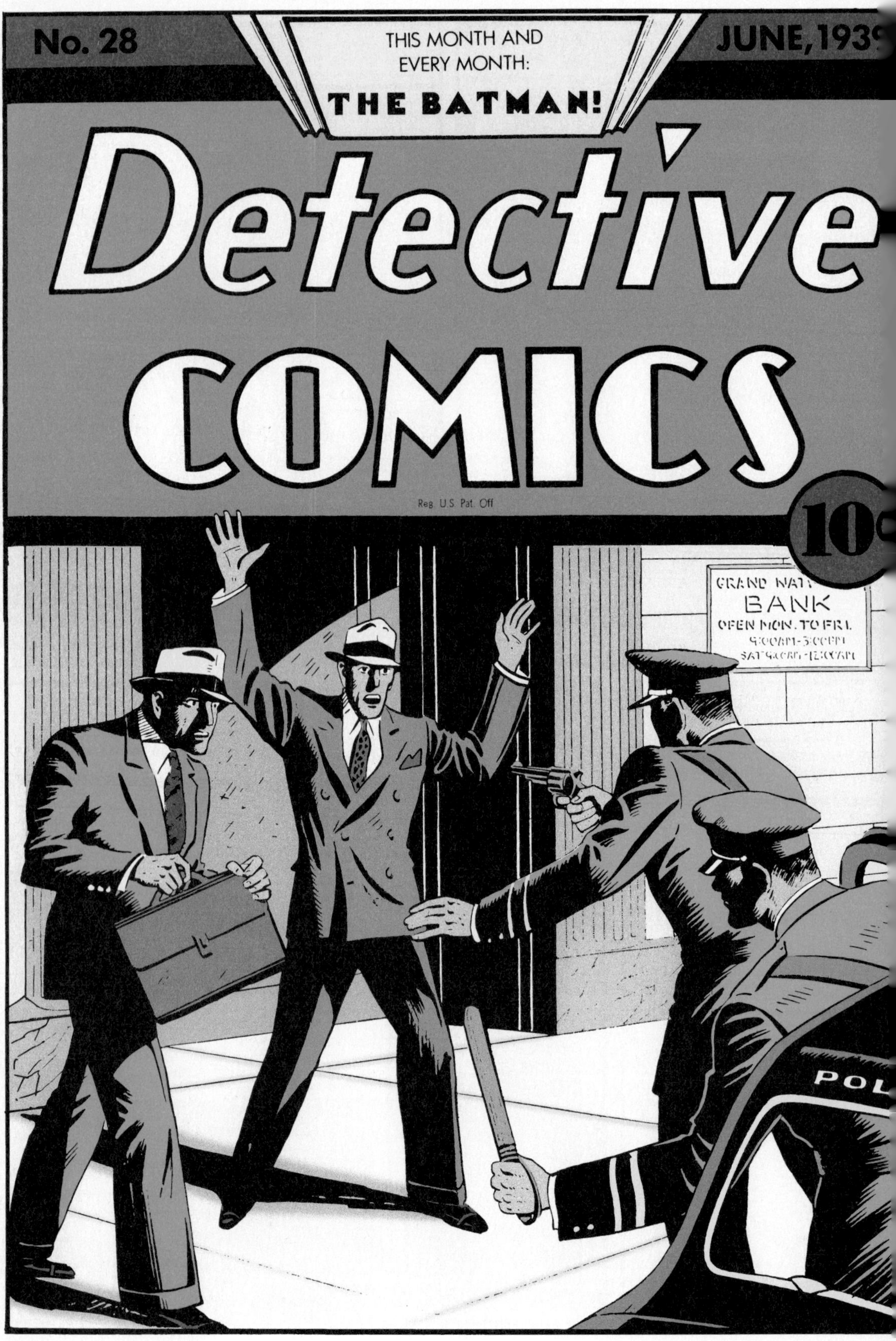
No. 28
THIS MONTH AND
EVERY MONTH:
THE BATMAN!
JUNE, 1939
Detective
COMICS
Reg. U.S. Pat. Off
10¢
BANK
OPEN MON. TO FRI.

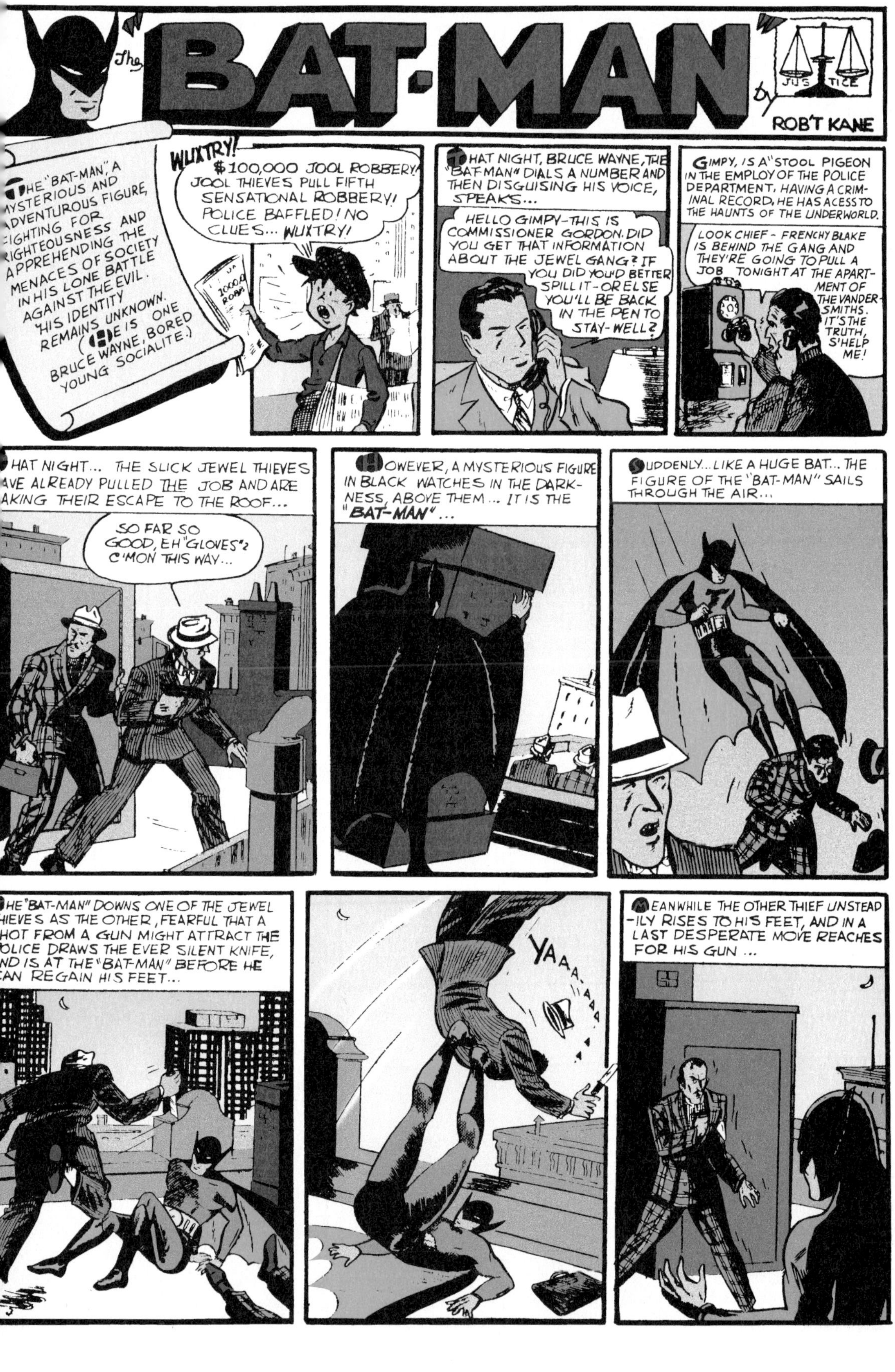

The BAT-MAN by ROB'T KANE
JUS TICE
THE "BAT-MAN," A MYSTERIOUS AND ADVENTUROUS FIGURE, FIGHTING FOR RIGHTEOUSNESS AND APPREHENDING THE MENACES OF SOCIETY IN HIS LONE BATTLE AGAINST THE EVIL. HIS IDENTITY REMAINS UNKNOWN. (HE IS ONE BRUCE WAYNE, BORED YOUNG SOCIALITE.)
WUXTRY! $100,000 JOOL ROBBERY! JOOL THIEVES PULL FIFTH SENSATIONAL ROBBERY! POLICE BAFFLED! NO CLUES... WUXTRY!
THAT NIGHT, BRUCE WAYNE, THE "BAT-MAN" DIALS A NUMBER AND THEN DISGUISING HIS VOICE, SPEAKS...
HELLO GIMPY-THIS IS COMMISSIONER GORDON. DID YOU GET THAT INFORMATION ABOUT THE JEWEL GANG? IF YOU DID YOU'D BETTER SPILL IT-OR ELSE YOU'LL BE BACK IN THE PEN TO STAY-WELL?
GIMPY, IS A "STOOL PIGEON" IN THE EMPLOY OF THE POLICE DEPARTMENT, HAVING A CRIMINAL RECORD, HE HAS ACESS TO THE HAUNTS OF THE UNDERWORLD.
LOOK CHIEF - FRENCHY BLAKE IS BEHIND THE GANG AND THEY'RE GOING TO PULL A JOB TONIGHT AT THE APARTMENT OF THE VANDERSMITHS. IT'S THE TRUTH, S'HELP ME!
HAT NIGHT... THE SLICK JEWEL THIEVES AVE ALREADY PULLED THE JOB AND ARE AKING THEIR ESCAPE TO THE ROOF...
SO FAR SO GOOD, EH "GLOVES"? C'MON THIS WAY...
HOWEVER, A MYSTERIOUS FIGURE IN BLACK WATCHES IN THE DARKNESS, ABOVE THEM... IT IS THE "BAT-MAN"...
SUDDENLY... LIKE A HUGE BAT... THE FIGURE OF THE "BAT-MAN" SAILS THROUGH THE AIR...
HE "BAT-MAN" DOWNS ONE OF THE JEWEL HIEVES AS THE OTHER, FEARFUL THAT A HOT FROM A GUN MIGHT ATTRACT THE POLICE DRAWS THE EVER SILENT KNIFE, ND IS AT THE "BAT-MAN" BEFORE HE CAN REGAIN HIS FEET...
YAAA-AAA
MEANWHILE THE OTHER THIEF UNSTEAD-ILY RISES TO HIS FEET, AND IN A LAST DESPERATE MOVE REACHES FOR HIS GUN...

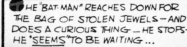

THE "BAT-MAN" REACHES DOWN FOR THE BAG OF STOLEN JEWELS — AND DOES A CURIOUS THING ... HE STOPS — HE "SEEMS" TO BE WAITING ...

THE BODY OF THE MAN THAT WENT OVER THE ROOF HAS ATTRACTED THE POLICE. THEY "SEEM" TO "SURPRISE" THE "BAT-MAN" WHO "DROPS" THE BAG OF JEWELS.

IT'S THE "BAT-MAN"!

SO SORRY, GENTLEMEN, BUT I'M AFRAID I HAVE TO GO NOW... GOOD NIGHT!

TO THE HORRIFIED EYES OF THE POLICE, THE "BAT-MAN" DIVES OFF THE ROOF..

...HE TURNS A COMPL[E]T[E] SOMERSAULT IN MID-A[IR] AND...

...LANDS ON HIS FEET ON THE PENTHOUSE ROOF BELOW!

HE QUICKLY DRAWS A TOUGH SILK ROPE FROM HIS BELT AND TWIRLS IT ABOVE HIS HEAD

LASSOING A FLAGPOLE JUTTING OUT O[F] A NEARBY BUILDING

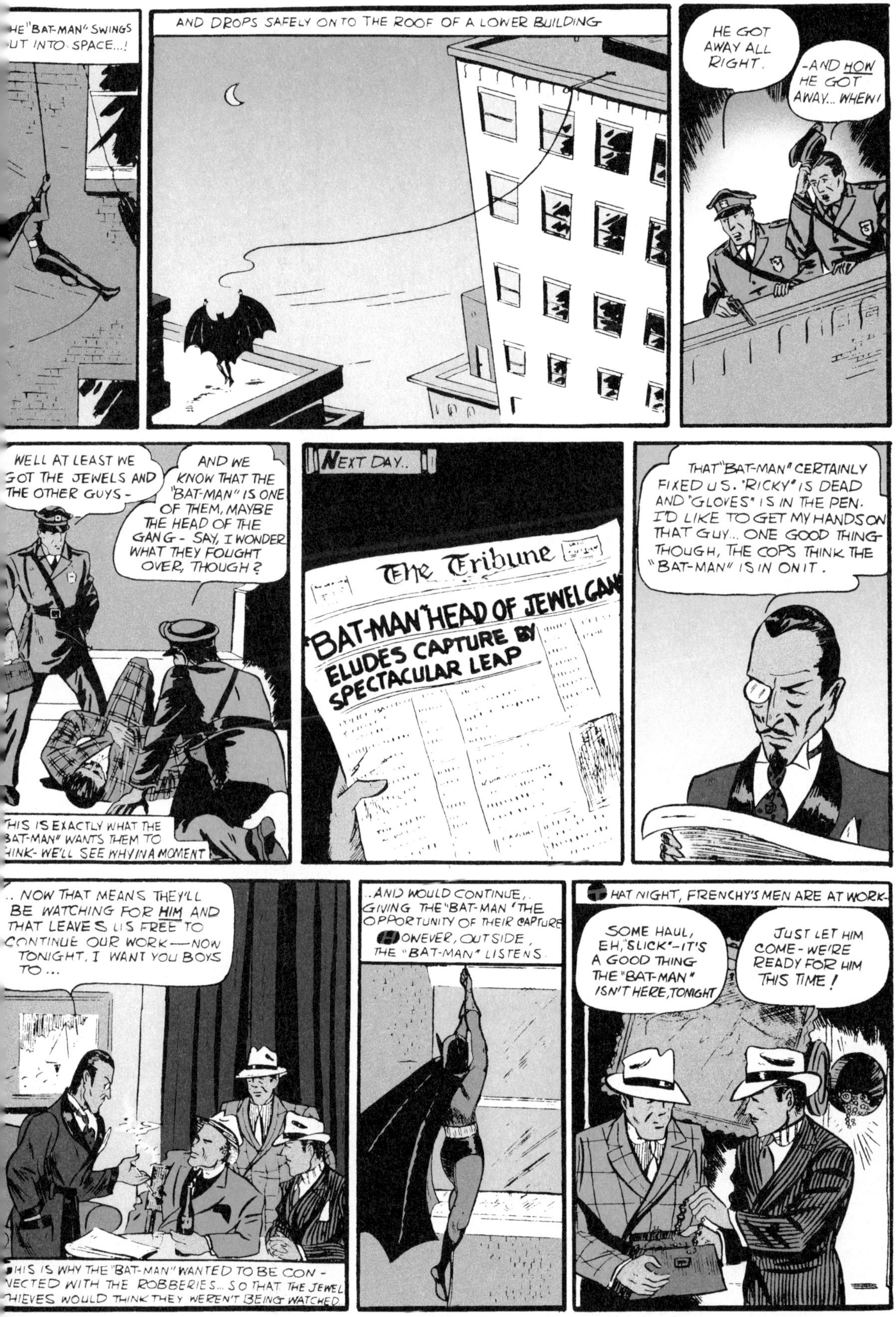

HE "BAT-MAN" SWINGS
UT INTO SPACE...!
AND DROPS SAFELY ON TO THE ROOF OF A LOWER BUILDING
HE GOT AWAY ALL RIGHT.
-AND HOW HE GOT AWAY... WHEW!
WELL AT LEAST WE GOT THE JEWELS AND THE OTHER GUYS -
AND WE KNOW THAT THE "BAT-MAN" IS ONE OF THEM, MAYBE THE HEAD OF THE GANG - SAY, I WONDER WHAT THEY FOUGHT OVER, THOUGH?
HIS IS EXACTLY WHAT THE
BAT-MAN" WANTS THEM TO
HINK- WE'LL SEE WHY IN A MOMENT
NEXT DAY..
The Tribune
"BAT-MAN" HEAD OF JEWEL GAN
ELUDES CAPTURE BY SPECTACULAR LEAP
THAT "BAT-MAN" CERTAINLY FIXED US. "RICKY" IS DEAD AND "GLOVES" IS IN THE PEN. I'D LIKE TO GET MY HANDS ON THAT GUY... ONE GOOD THING THOUGH, THE COPS THINK THE "BAT-MAN" IS IN ON IT.
.. NOW THAT MEANS THEY'LL BE WATCHING FOR HIM AND THAT LEAVES US FREE TO CONTINUE OUR WORK — NOW TONIGHT, I WANT YOU BOYS TO...
HIS IS WHY THE "BAT-MAN" WANTED TO BE CON-
NECTED WITH THE ROBBERIES... SO THAT THE JEWEL
HIEVES WOULD THINK THEY WEREN'T BEING WATCHED.
..AND WOULD CONTINUE,. GIVING THE "BAT-MAN" THE OPPORTUNITY OF THEIR CAPTURE
HOWEVER, OUTSIDE, THE "BAT-MAN" LISTENS.
THAT NIGHT, FRENCHY'S MEN ARE AT WORK-
SOME HAUL, EH, "SLICK"-IT'S A GOOD THING THE "BAT-MAN" ISN'T HERE, TONIGHT
JUST LET HIM COME - WE'RE READY FOR HIM THIS TIME!

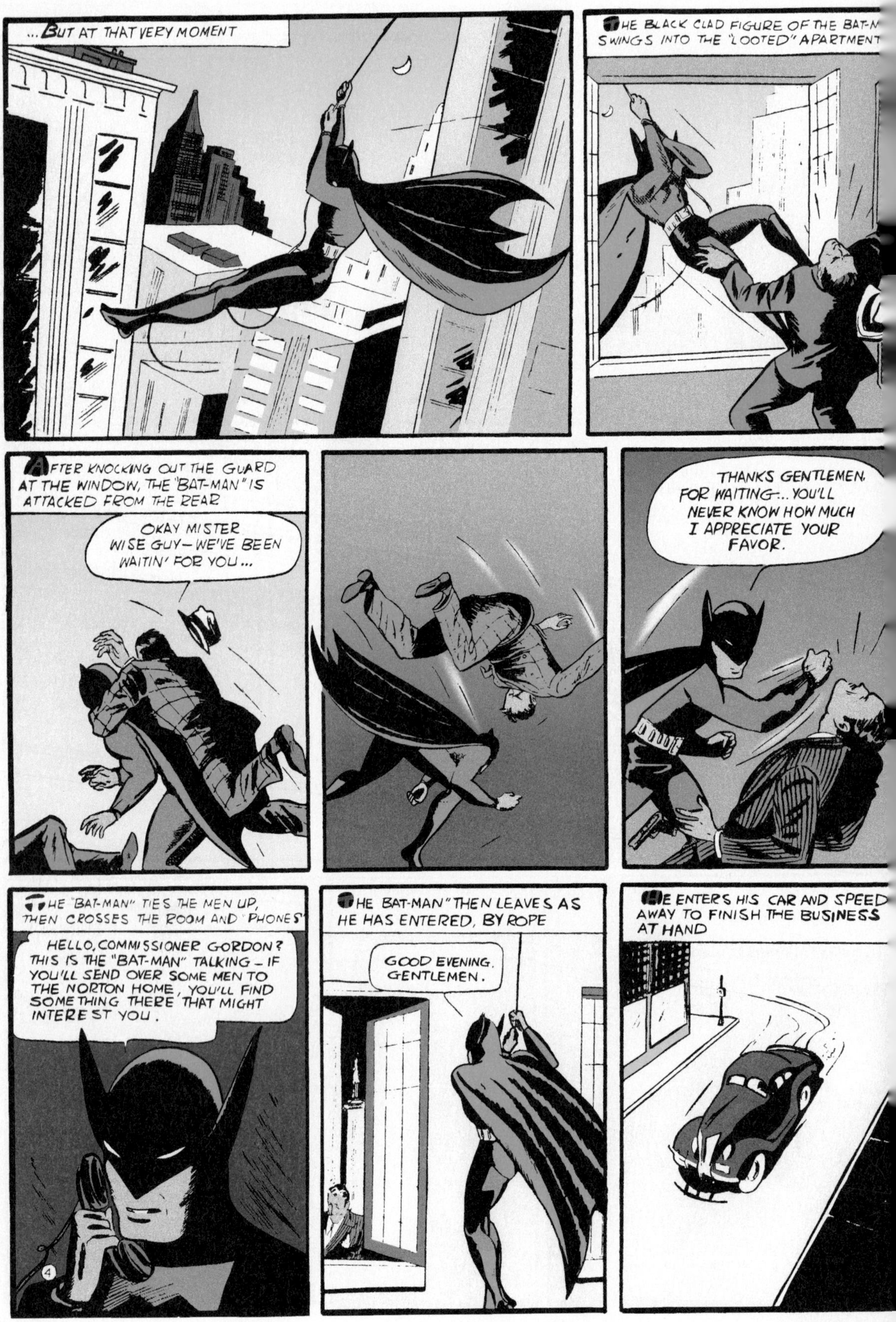

...BUT AT THAT VERY MOMENT
THE BLACK CLAD FIGURE OF THE BAT-M
SWINGS INTO THE "LOOTED" APARTMENT
AFTER KNOCKING OUT THE GUARD AT THE WINDOW, THE "BAT-MAN" IS ATTACKED FROM THE REAR
OKAY MISTER WISE GUY—WE'VE BEEN WAITIN' FOR YOU...
THANKS GENTLEMEN. FOR WAITING...YOU'LL NEVER KNOW HOW MUCH I APPRECIATE YOUR FAVOR.
THE "BAT-MAN" TIES THE MEN UP, THEN CROSSES THE ROOM AND "PHONES"
HELLO, COMMISSIONER GORDON? THIS IS THE "BAT-MAN" TALKING - IF YOU'LL SEND OVER SOME MEN TO THE NORTON HOME, YOU'LL FIND SOMETHING THERE THAT MIGHT INTEREST YOU.
4
THE BAT-MAN" THEN LEAVES AS HE HAS ENTERED, BY ROPE
GOOD EVENING. GENTLEMEN.
HE ENTERS HIS CAR AND SPEED
AWAY TO FINISH THE BUSINESS AT HAND

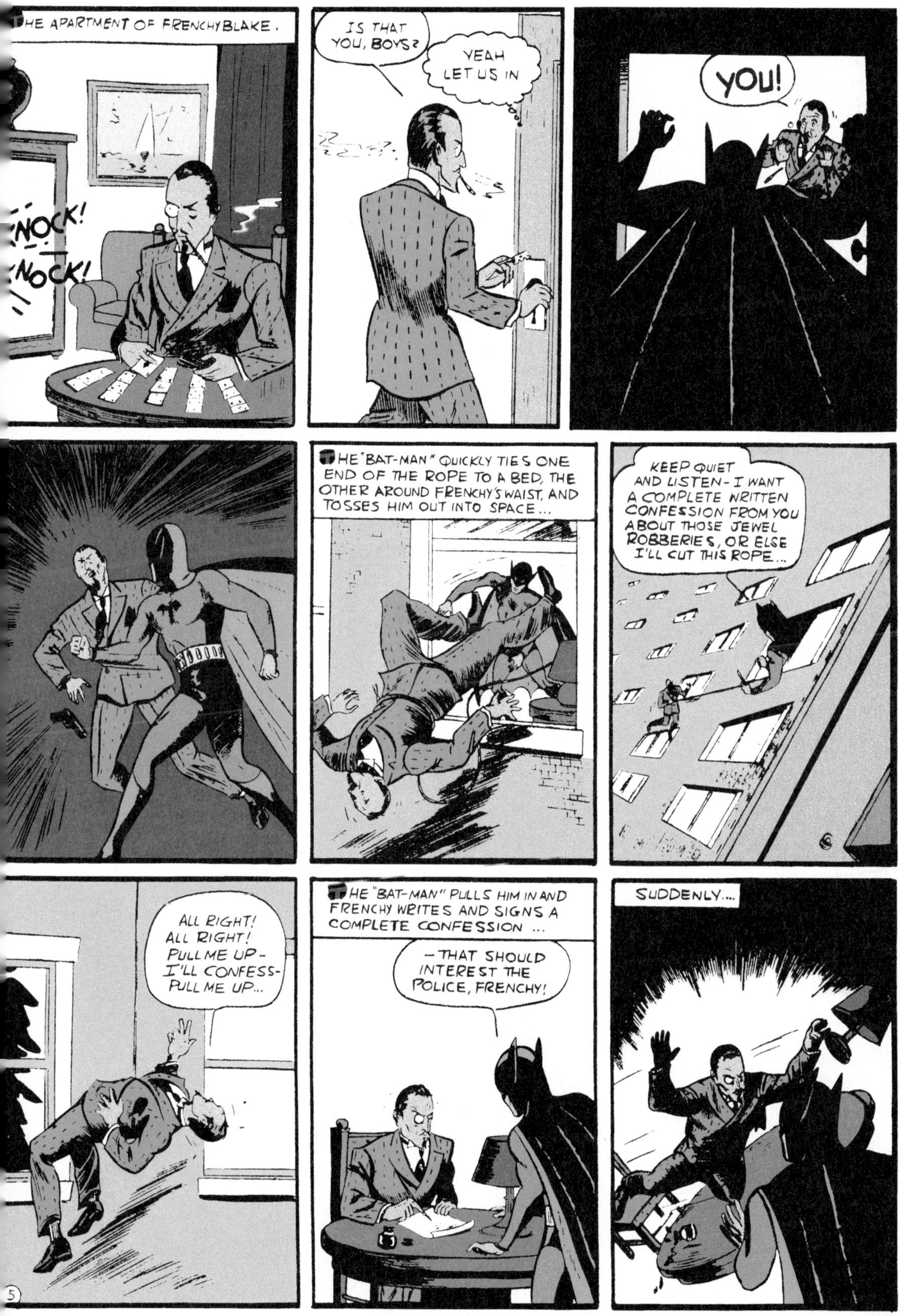
THE APARTMENT OF FRENCHY BLAKE.
KNOCK!
KNOCK!
IS THAT YOU, BOYS?
YEAH LET US IN
YOU!
THE "BAT-MAN" QUICKLY TIES ONE END OF THE ROPE TO A BED, THE OTHER AROUND FRENCHY'S WAIST, AND TOSSES HIM OUT INTO SPACE...
KEEP QUIET AND LISTEN- I WANT A COMPLETE WRITTEN CONFESSION FROM YOU ABOUT THOSE JEWEL ROBBERIES, OR ELSE I'LL CUT THIS ROPE...
ALL RIGHT! ALL RIGHT! PULL ME UP- I'LL CONFESS- PULL ME UP...
THE "BAT-MAN" PULLS HIM IN AND FRENCHY WRITES AND SIGNS A COMPLETE CONFESSION ...
-THAT SHOULD INTEREST THE POLICE, FRENCHY!
SUDDENLY....
5

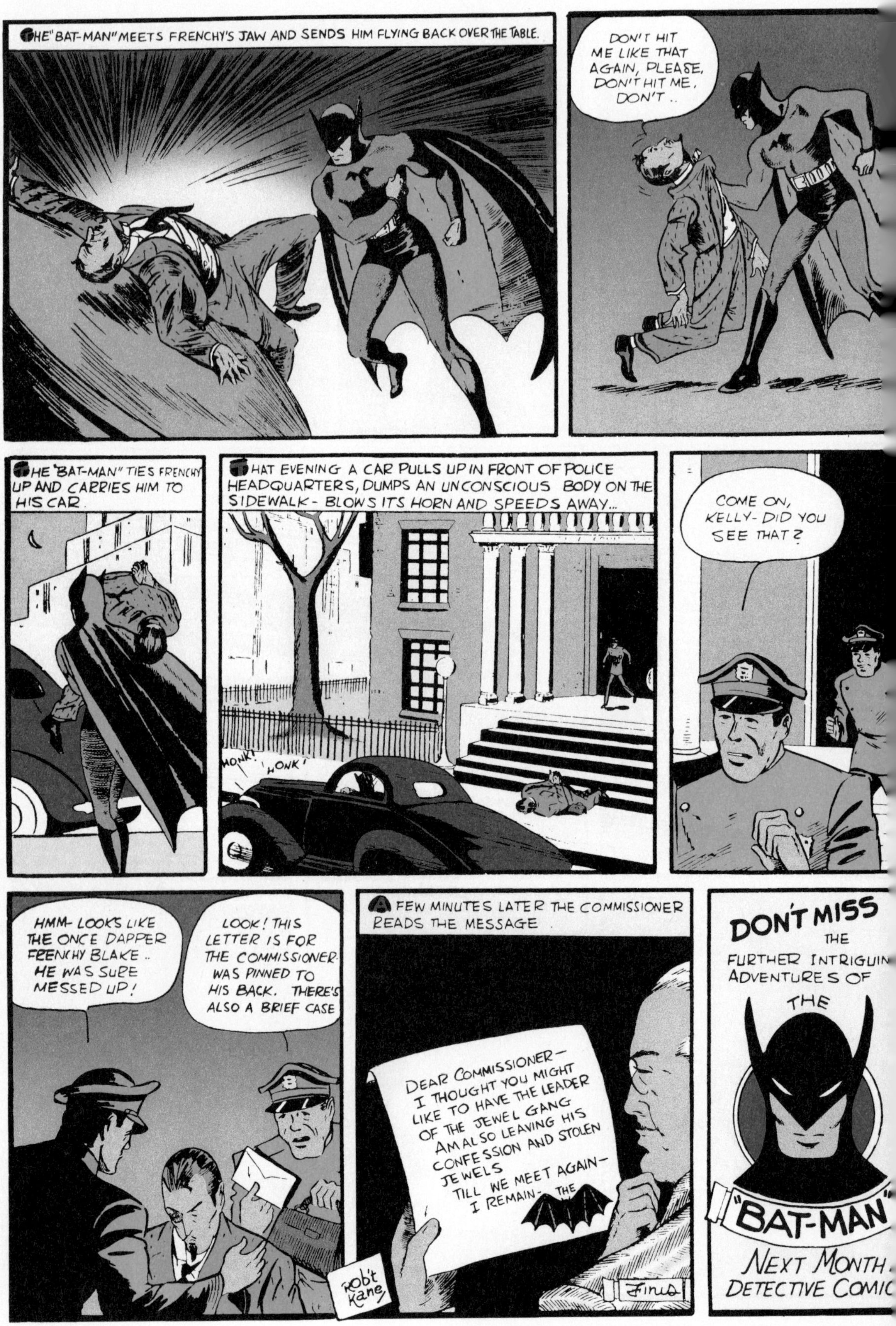
THE "BAT-MAN" MEETS FRENCHY'S JAW AND SENDS HIM FLYING BACK OVER THE TABLE.
DON'T HIT ME LIKE THAT AGAIN, PLEASE, DON'T HIT ME, DON'T ..
THE "BAT-MAN" TIES FRENCHY UP AND CARRIES HIM TO HIS CAR.
THAT EVENING A CAR PULLS UP IN FRONT OF POLICE HEADQUARTERS, DUMPS AN UNCONSCIOUS BODY ON THE SIDEWALK - BLOWS ITS HORN AND SPEEDS AWAY...
HONK! HONK!
COME ON, KELLY- DID YOU SEE THAT?
HMM- LOOKS LIKE THE ONCE DAPPER FRENCHY BLAKE .. HE WAS SURE MESSED UP!
LOOK! THIS LETTER IS FOR THE COMMISSIONER- WAS PINNED TO HIS BACK. THERE'S ALSO A BRIEF CASE
Rob't Kane
A FEW MINUTES LATER THE COMMISSIONER READS THE MESSAGE.
DEAR COMMISSIONER— I THOUGHT YOU MIGHT LIKE TO HAVE THE LEADER OF THE JEWEL GANG AM ALSO LEAVING HIS CONFESSION AND STOLEN JEWELS TILL WE MEET AGAIN- I REMAIN- THE
Finis
DON'T MISS THE FURTHER INTRIGUIN ADVENTURES OF THE "BAT-MAN" NEXT MONTH DETECTIVE COMIC

No. 29
64 PAGES OF Thrill-Packed ACTION!
JULY, 1939
Detective COMICS
Reg. U.S. Pat. Off.
10¢
Another thrilling episode of THE BATMAN in this issue
BOB KANE

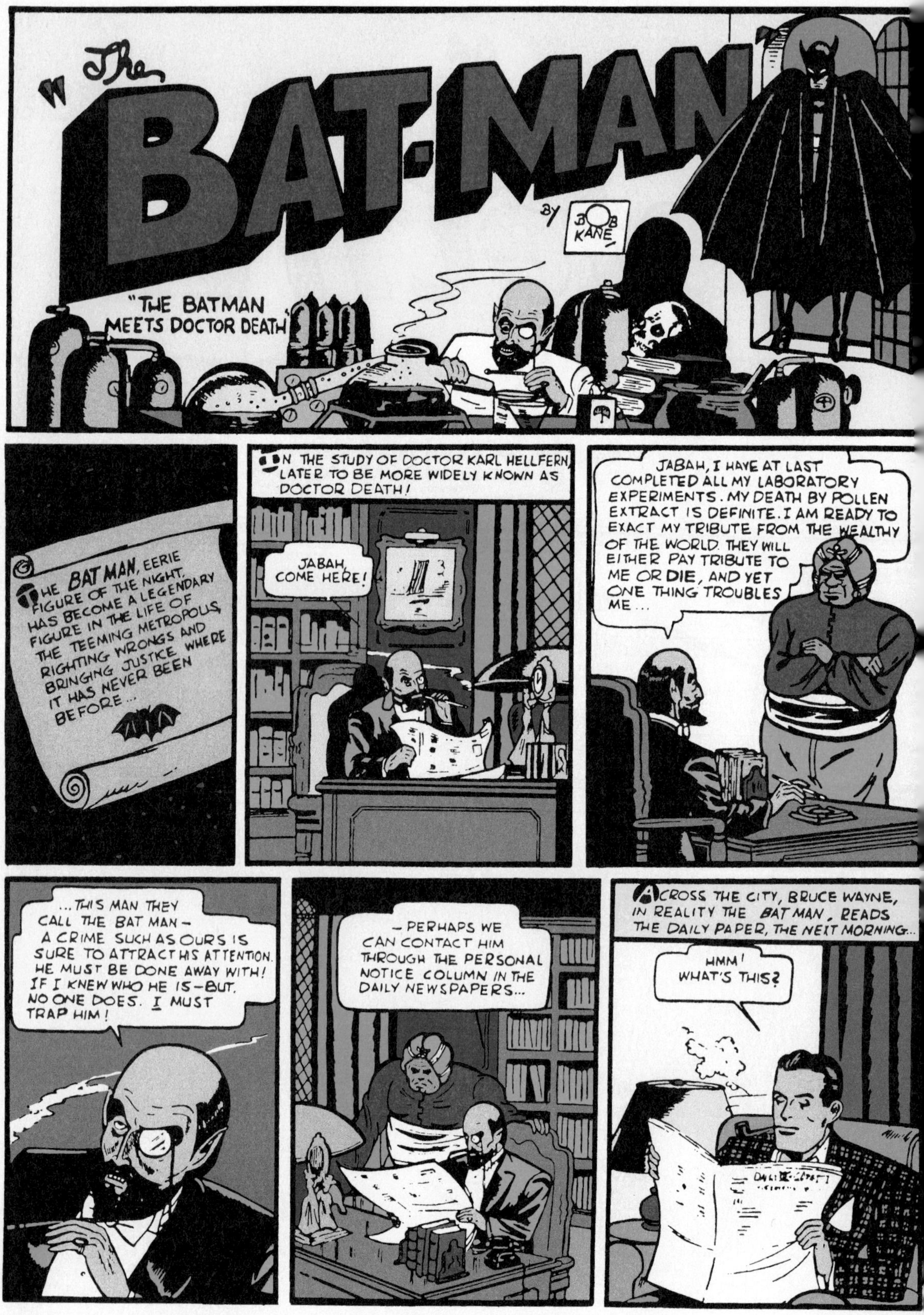
"The BAT-MAN"
BY BOB KANE
"THE BATMAN MEETS DOCTOR DEATH"
THE BAT MAN, EERIE FIGURE OF THE NIGHT, HAS BECOME A LEGENDARY FIGURE IN THE LIFE OF THE TEEMING METROPOLIS, RIGHTING WRONGS AND BRINGING JUSTICE WHERE IT HAS NEVER BEEN BEFORE...
IN THE STUDY OF DOCTOR KARL HELLFERN, LATER TO BE MORE WIDELY KNOWN AS DOCTOR DEATH!
JABAH, COME HERE!
JABAH, I HAVE AT LAST COMPLETED ALL MY LABORATORY EXPERIMENTS. MY DEATH BY POLLEN EXTRACT IS DEFINITE. I AM READY TO EXACT MY TRIBUTE FROM THE WEALTHY OF THE WORLD. THEY WILL EITHER PAY TRIBUTE TO ME OR DIE, AND YET ONE THING TROUBLES ME...
...THIS MAN THEY CALL THE BAT MAN - A CRIME SUCH AS OURS IS SURE TO ATTRACT HIS ATTENTION. HE MUST BE DONE AWAY WITH! IF I KNEW WHO HE IS-BUT, NO ONE DOES. I MUST TRAP HIM!
-PERHAPS WE CAN CONTACT HIM THROUGH THE PERSONAL NOTICE COLUMN IN THE DAILY NEWSPAPERS...
ACROSS THE CITY, BRUCE WAYNE, IN REALITY THE BAT MAN, READS THE DAILY PAPER, THE NEXT MORNING...
HMM! WHAT'S THIS?

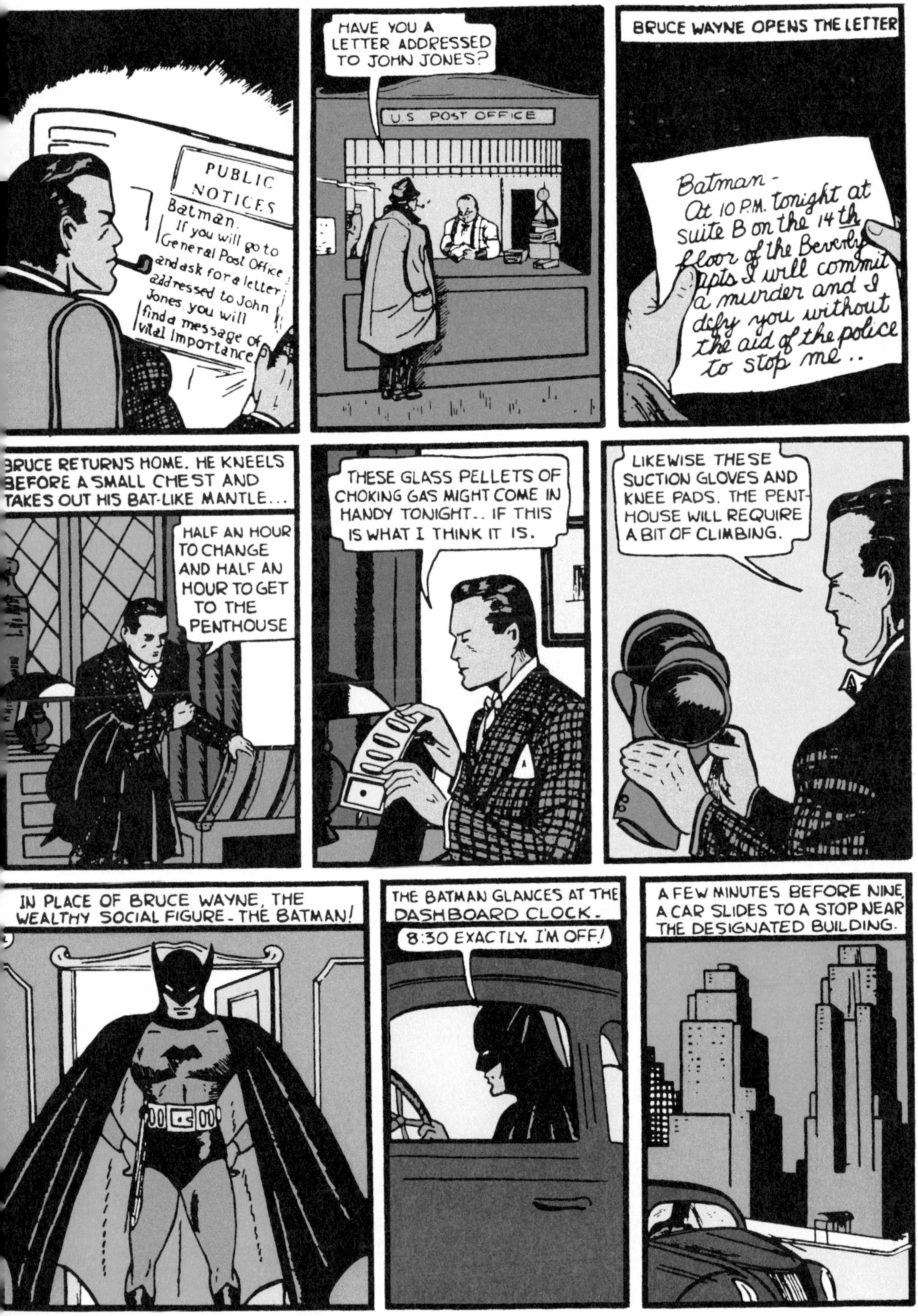
PUBLIC NOTICES
Batman: If you will go to General Post Office and ask for a letter addressed to John Jones you will find a message of vital importance.
HAVE YOU A LETTER ADDRESSED TO JOHN JONES?
U.S. POST OFFICE
BRUCE WAYNE OPENS THE LETTER
Batman - At 10 P.M. tonight at suite B on the 14th floor of the Bevrly apts I will commit a murder and I defy you without the aid of the police to stop me..
BRUCE RETURNS HOME. HE KNEELS BEFORE A SMALL CHEST AND TAKES OUT HIS BAT-LIKE MANTLE...
HALF AN HOUR TO CHANGE AND HALF AN HOUR TO GET TO THE PENTHOUSE
THESE GLASS PELLETS OF CHOKING GAS MIGHT COME IN HANDY TONIGHT.. IF THIS IS WHAT I THINK IT IS.
LIKEWISE THESE SUCTION GLOVES AND KNEE PADS. THE PENT-HOUSE WILL REQUIRE A BIT OF CLIMBING.
IN PLACE OF BRUCE WAYNE, THE WEALTHY SOCIAL FIGURE - THE BATMAN!
THE BATMAN GLANCES AT THE DASHBOARD CLOCK.
8:30 EXACTLY. I'M OFF!
A FEW MINUTES BEFORE NINE, A CAR SLIDES TO A STOP NEAR THE DESIGNATED BUILDING.

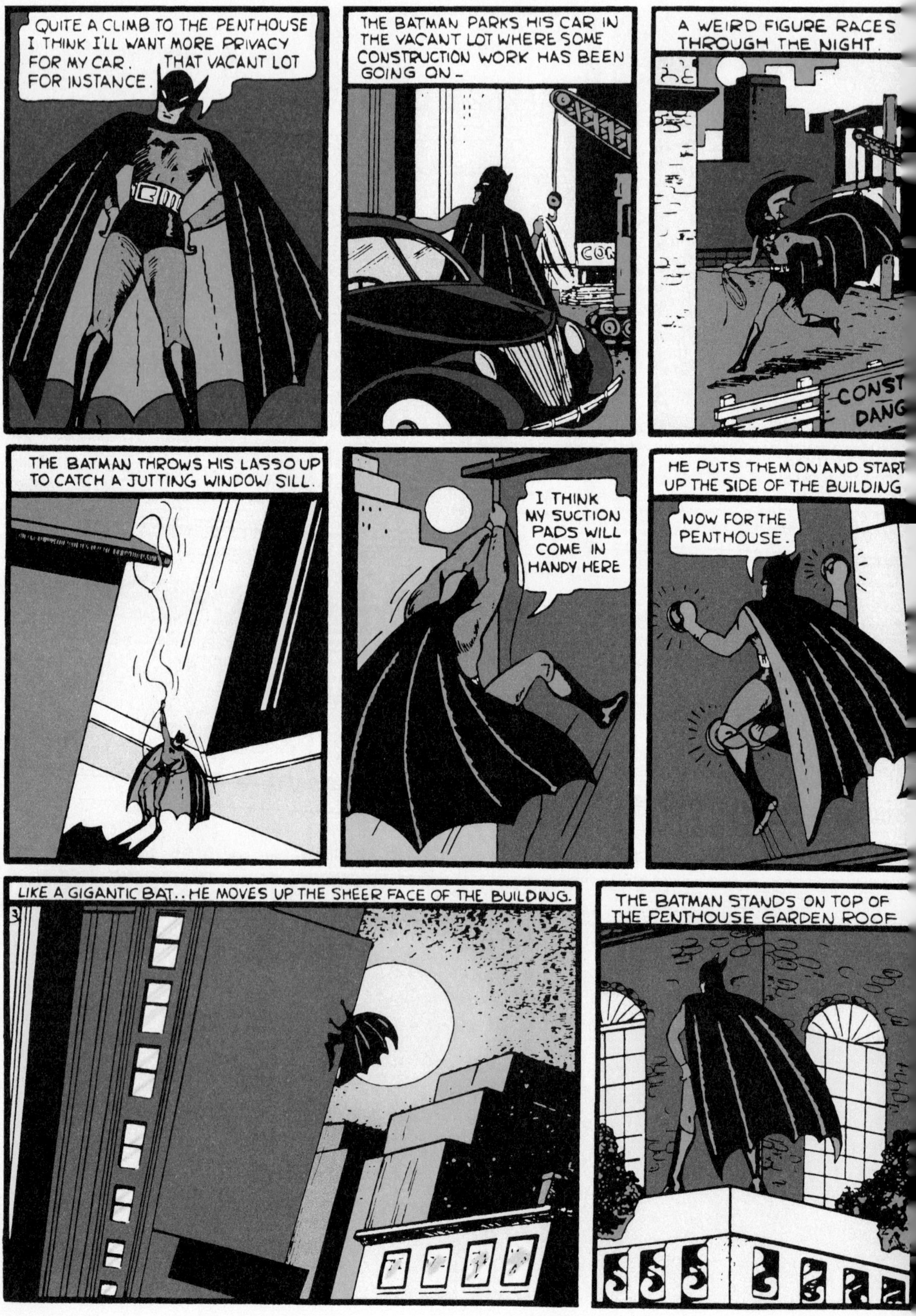
QUITE A CLIMB TO THE PENTHOUSE I THINK I'LL WANT MORE PRIVACY FOR MY CAR. THAT VACANT LOT FOR INSTANCE.
THE BATMAN PARKS HIS CAR IN THE VACANT LOT WHERE SOME CONSTRUCTION WORK HAS BEEN GOING ON–
A WEIRD FIGURE RACES THROUGH THE NIGHT.
THE BATMAN THROWS HIS LASSO UP TO CATCH A JUTTING WINDOW SILL.
I THINK MY SUCTION PADS WILL COME IN HANDY HERE
HE PUTS THEM ON AND START UP THE SIDE OF THE BUILDING
NOW FOR THE PENTHOUSE.
LIKE A GIGANTIC BAT.. HE MOVES UP THE SHEER FACE OF THE BUILDING.
THE BATMAN STANDS ON TOP OF THE PENTHOUSE GARDEN ROOF

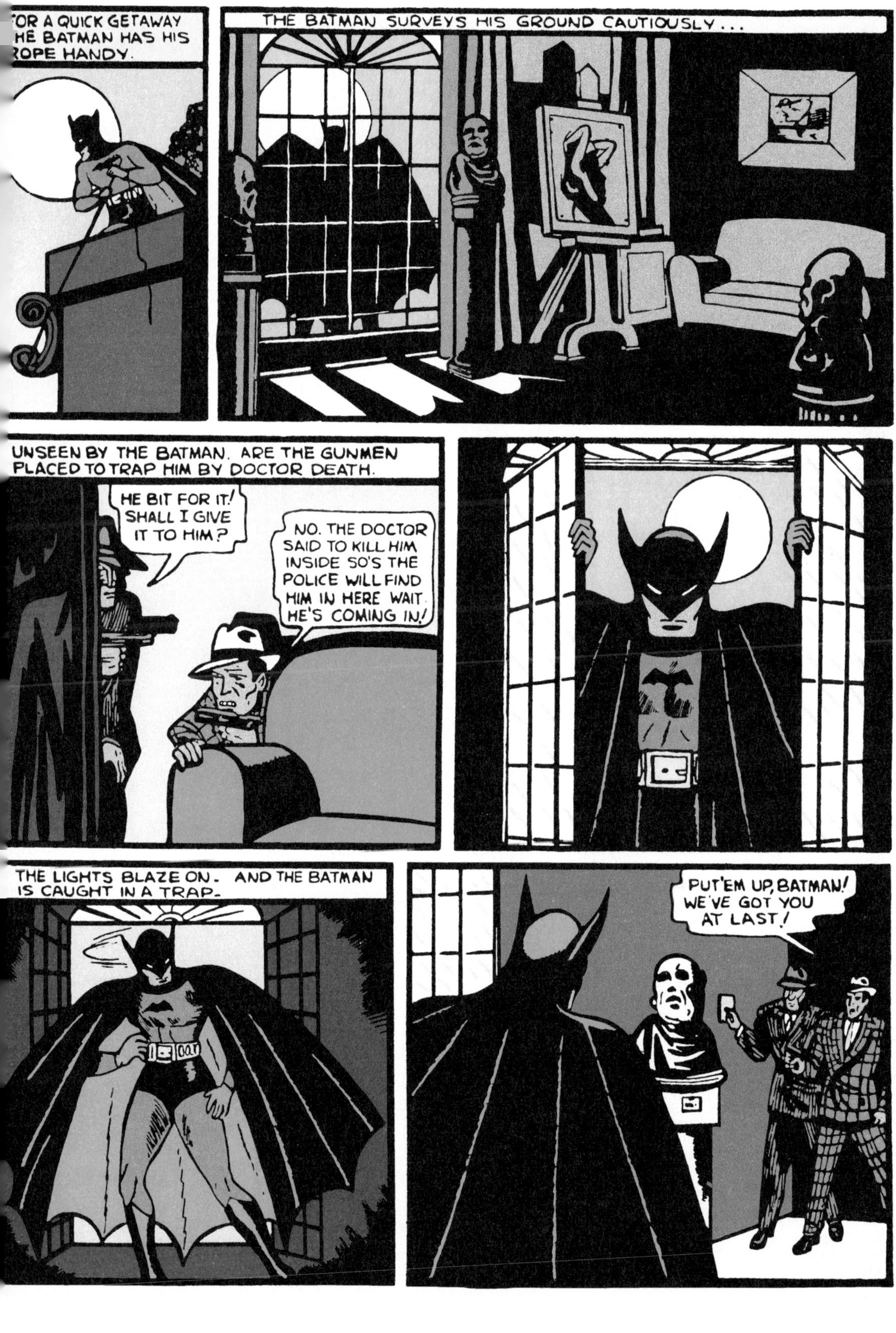
FOR A QUICK GETAWAY THE BATMAN HAS HIS ROPE HANDY.
THE BATMAN SURVEYS HIS GROUND CAUTIOUSLY...
UNSEEN BY THE BATMAN. ARE THE GUNMEN PLACED TO TRAP HIM BY DOCTOR DEATH.
HE BIT FOR IT! SHALL I GIVE IT TO HIM?
NO. THE DOCTOR SAID TO KILL HIM INSIDE SO'S THE POLICE WILL FIND HIM IN HERE WAIT. HE'S COMING IN!
THE LIGHTS BLAZE ON. AND THE BATMAN IS CAUGHT IN A TRAP.
PUT'EM UP, BATMAN! WE'VE GOT YOU AT LAST!

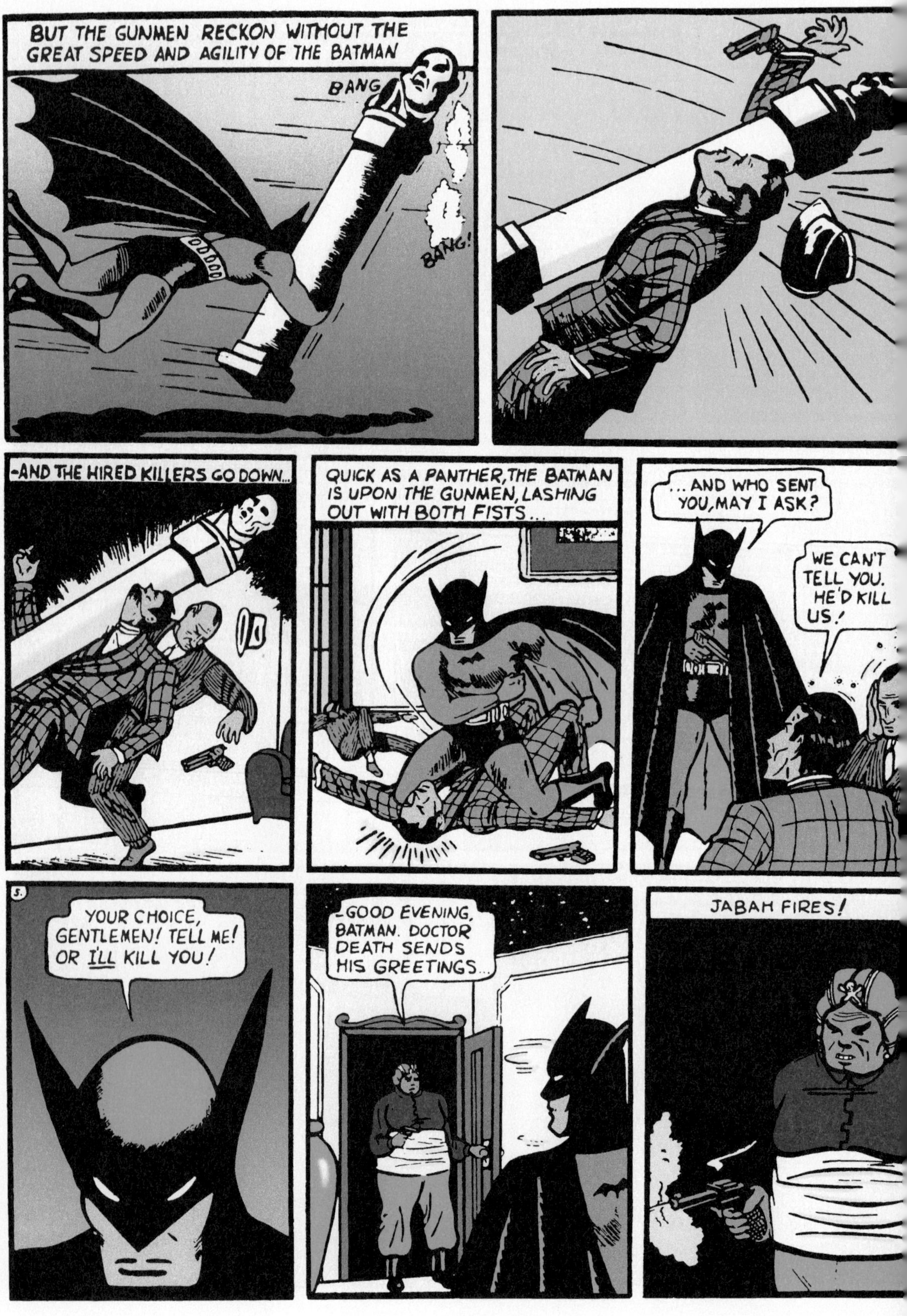
BUT THE GUNMEN RECKON WITHOUT THE GREAT SPEED AND AGILITY OF THE BATMAN
BANG
BANG!
-AND THE HIRED KILLERS GO DOWN...
QUICK AS A PANTHER, THE BATMAN IS UPON THE GUNMEN, LASHING OUT WITH BOTH FISTS...
...AND WHO SENT YOU, MAY I ASK?
WE CAN'T TELL YOU. HE'D KILL US!
YOUR CHOICE, GENTLEMEN! TELL ME! OR I'LL KILL YOU!
-GOOD EVENING, BATMAN. DOCTOR DEATH SENDS HIS GREETINGS...
JABAH FIRES!

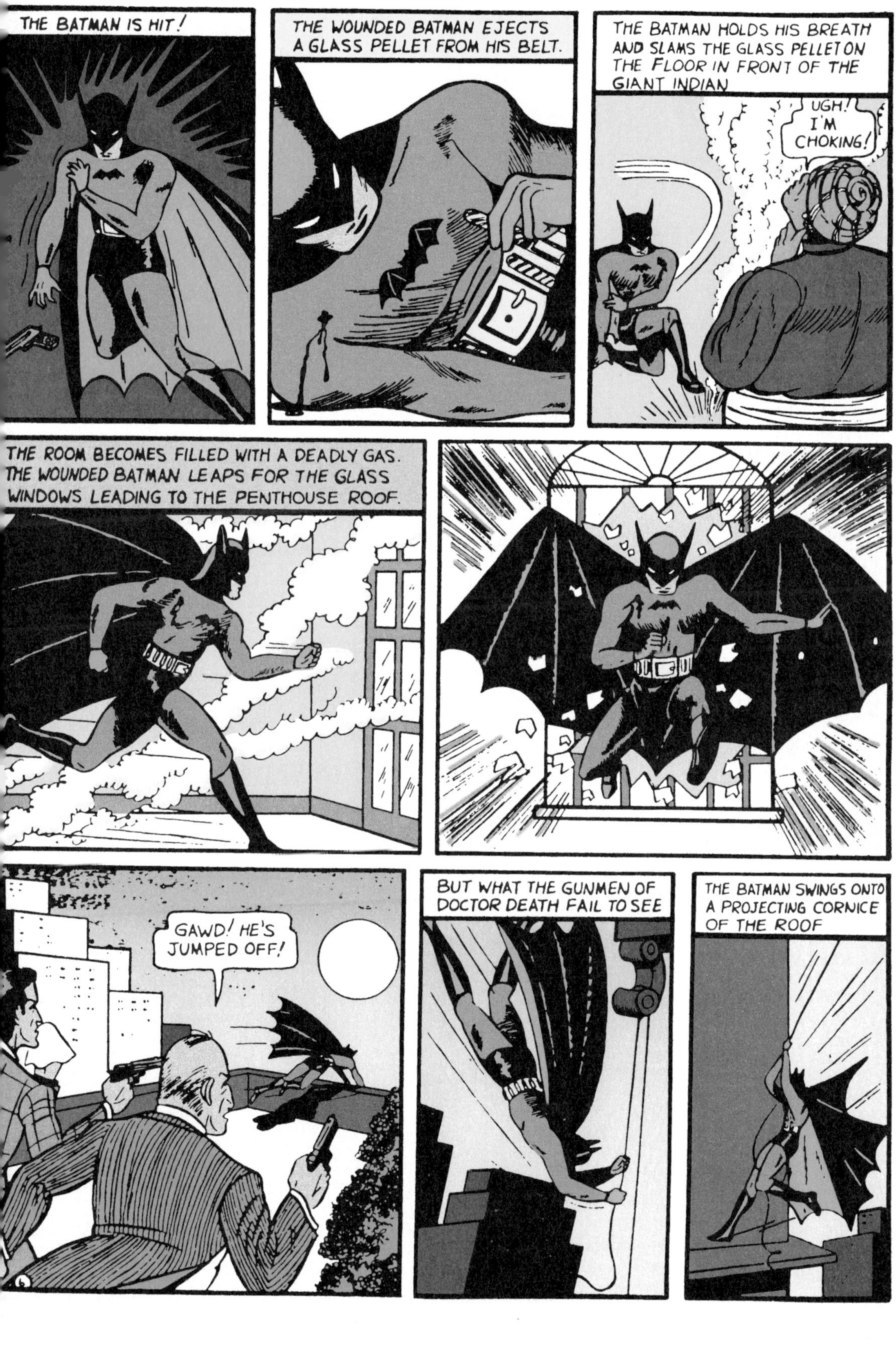
THE BATMAN IS HIT!
THE WOUNDED BATMAN EJECTS A GLASS PELLET FROM HIS BELT.
THE BATMAN HOLDS HIS BREATH AND SLAMS THE GLASS PELLET ON THE FLOOR IN FRONT OF THE GIANT INDIAN
UGH! I'M CHOKING!
THE ROOM BECOMES FILLED WITH A DEADLY GAS. THE WOUNDED BATMAN LEAPS FOR THE GLASS WINDOWS LEADING TO THE PENTHOUSE ROOF.
GAWD! HE'S JUMPED OFF!
BUT WHAT THE GUNMEN OF DOCTOR DEATH FAIL TO SEE
THE BATMAN SWINGS ONTO A PROJECTING CORNICE OF THE ROOF

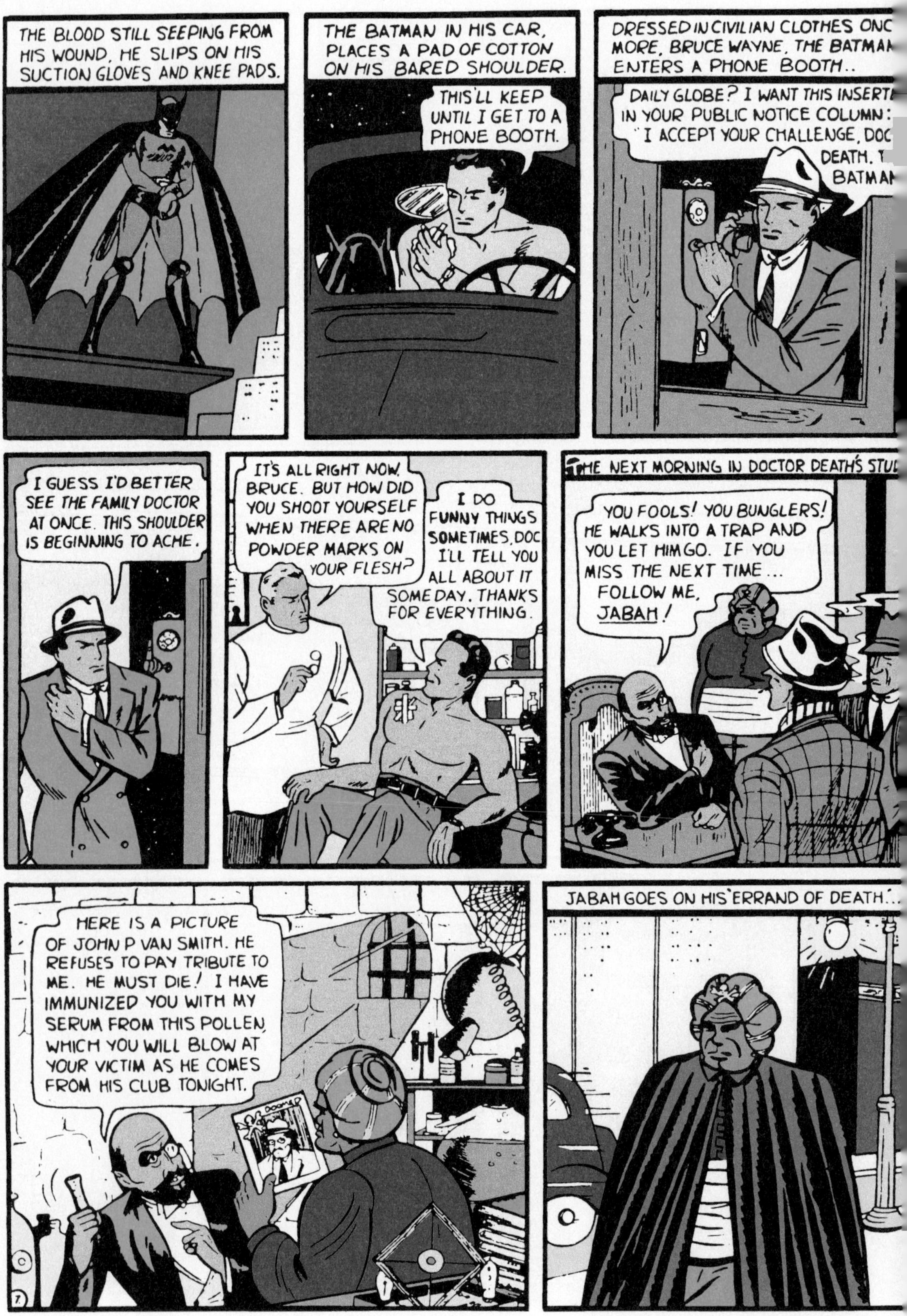
THE BLOOD STILL SEEPING FROM HIS WOUND, HE SLIPS ON HIS SUCTION GLOVES AND KNEE PADS.
THE BATMAN IN HIS CAR, PLACES A PAD OF COTTON ON HIS BARED SHOULDER.
THIS'LL KEEP UNTIL I GET TO A PHONE BOOTH.
DRESSED IN CIVILIAN CLOTHES ONC MORE, BRUCE WAYNE, THE BATMAN ENTERS A PHONE BOOTH..
DAILY GLOBE? I WANT THIS INSERT IN YOUR PUBLIC NOTICE COLUMN: "I ACCEPT YOUR CHALLENGE, DOC DEATH. BATMAN
I GUESS I'D BETTER SEE THE FAMILY DOCTOR AT ONCE. THIS SHOULDER IS BEGINNING TO ACHE.
IT'S ALL RIGHT NOW, BRUCE. BUT HOW DID YOU SHOOT YOURSELF WHEN THERE ARE NO POWDER MARKS ON YOUR FLESH?
I DO FUNNY THINGS SOMETIMES, DOC. I'LL TELL YOU ALL ABOUT IT SOME DAY. THANKS FOR EVERYTHING.
THE NEXT MORNING IN DOCTOR DEATH'S STU
YOU FOOLS! YOU BUNGLERS! HE WALKS INTO A TRAP AND YOU LET HIM GO. IF YOU MISS THE NEXT TIME ... FOLLOW ME, JABAH!
HERE IS A PICTURE OF JOHN P VAN SMITH. HE REFUSES TO PAY TRIBUTE TO ME. HE MUST DIE! I HAVE IMMUNIZED YOU WITH MY SERUM FROM THIS POLLEN, WHICH YOU WILL BLOW AT YOUR VICTIM AS HE COMES FROM HIS CLUB TONIGHT.
DOOMED
JABAH GOES ON HIS "ERRAND OF DEATH"...

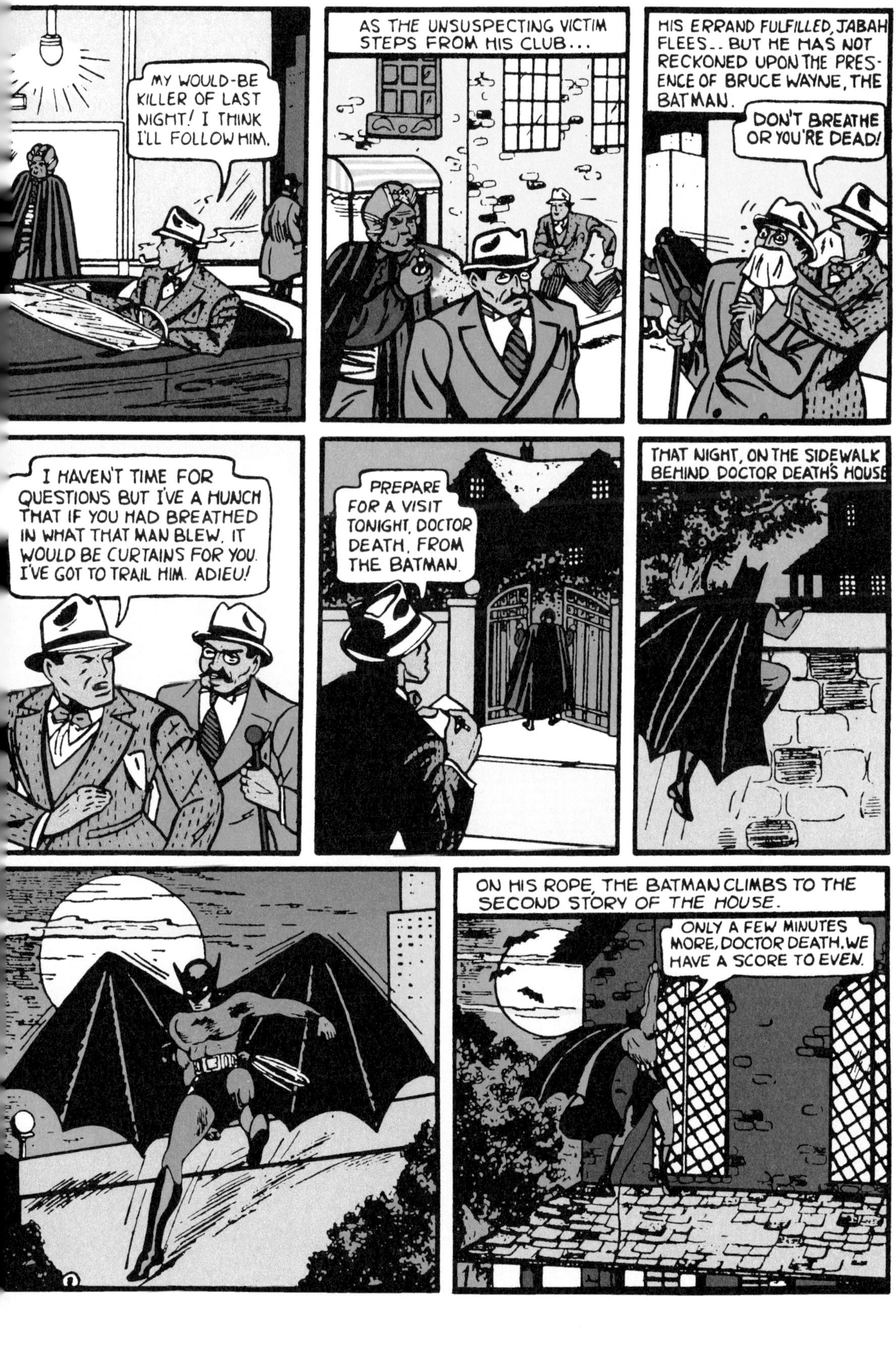
MY WOULD-BE KILLER OF LAST NIGHT! I THINK I'LL FOLLOW HIM.
AS THE UNSUSPECTING VICTIM STEPS FROM HIS CLUB...
HIS ERRAND FULFILLED, JABAH FLEES.. BUT HE HAS NOT RECKONED UPON THE PRESENCE OF BRUCE WAYNE, THE BATMAN.
DON'T BREATHE OR YOU'RE DEAD!
I HAVEN'T TIME FOR QUESTIONS BUT I'VE A HUNCH THAT IF YOU HAD BREATHED IN WHAT THAT MAN BLEW, IT WOULD BE CURTAINS FOR YOU. I'VE GOT TO TRAIL HIM. ADIEU!
PREPARE FOR A VISIT TONIGHT, DOCTOR DEATH. FROM THE BATMAN.
THAT NIGHT, ON THE SIDEWALK BEHIND DOCTOR DEATH'S HOUSE
ON HIS ROPE, THE BATMAN CLIMBS TO THE SECOND STORY OF THE HOUSE.
ONLY A FEW MINUTES MORE, DOCTOR DEATH. WE HAVE A SCORE TO EVEN.

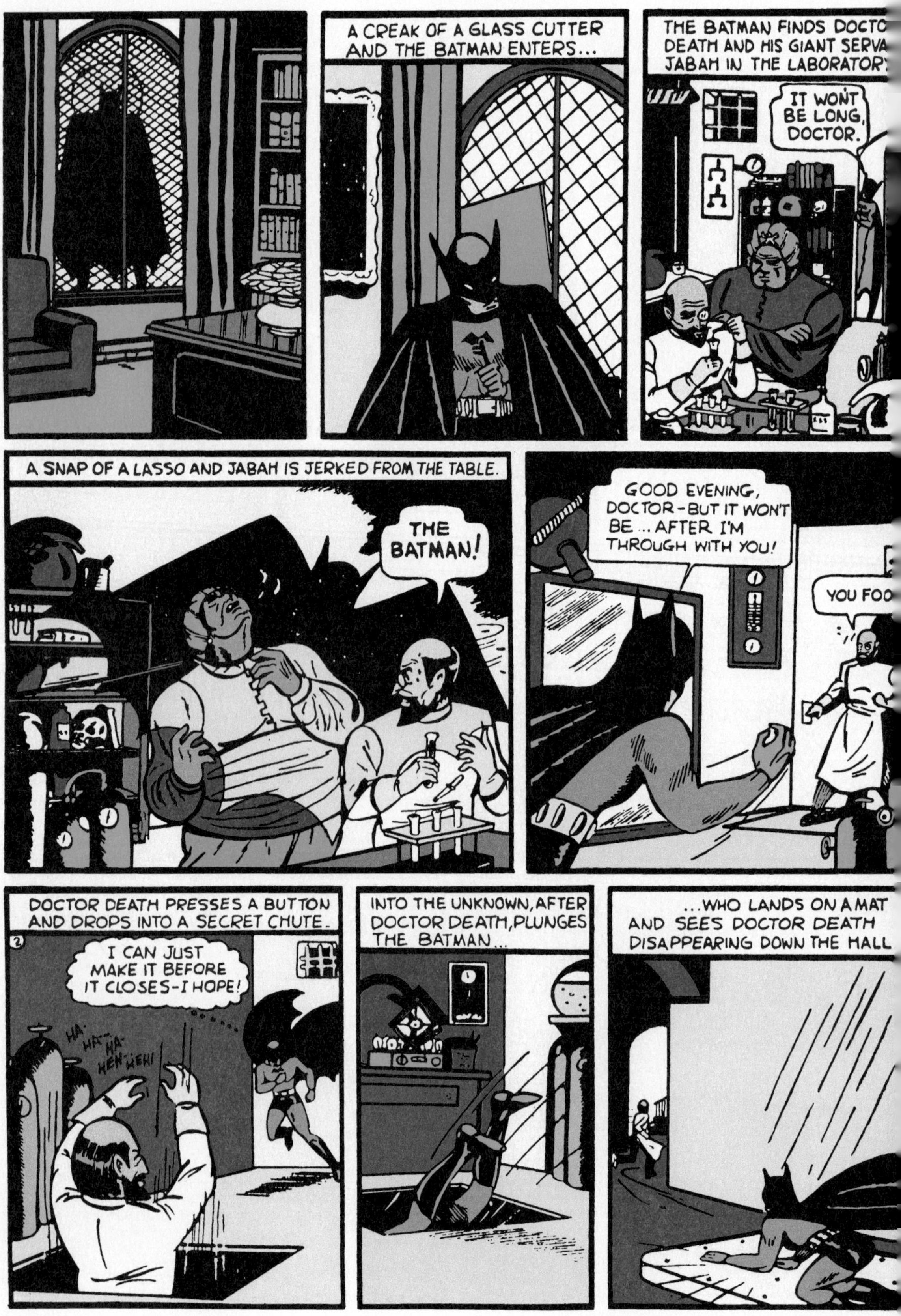
A CREAK OF A GLASS CUTTER AND THE BATMAN ENTERS...
THE BATMAN FINDS DOCTO DEATH AND HIS GIANT SERVA JABAH IN THE LABORATOR
IT WON'T BE LONG, DOCTOR.
A SNAP OF A LASSO AND JABAH IS JERKED FROM THE TABLE.
THE BATMAN!
GOOD EVENING, DOCTOR - BUT IT WON'T BE ... AFTER I'M THROUGH WITH YOU!
YOU FOO
DOCTOR DEATH PRESSES A BUTTON AND DROPS INTO A SECRET CHUTE.
I CAN JUST MAKE IT BEFORE IT CLOSES - I HOPE!
HA-HA-HA-HEH-HEH!
INTO THE UNKNOWN, AFTER DOCTOR DEATH, PLUNGES THE BATMAN...
...WHO LANDS ON A MAT AND SEES DOCTOR DEATH DISAPPEARING DOWN THE HALL

THE BATMAN PURSUES DOCTOR DEATH RELENTLESSLY.

DOCTOR DEATH RETURNS TO THE LABORATORY IN A LAST DESPERATE ATTEMPT TO ELUDE THE BATMAN.

THERE IS YET TIME.

THE BATMAN SEIZES A FIRE EXTINGUISHER ON THE WALL AND..

YOU ARE JUST TOO LATE, MY FOE. WATCH! THE FIERY DEATH_

LINGS IT AT DOCTOR DEATH, KNOCKING THE DEADLY UBE TO THE FLOOR WHERE IT SWIFTLY IGNITES NTO A BLAZING INFERNO!!!

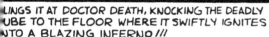

HA! HA! OH-- HA-HA-HA-- YOU.. YOU FOOL!

YOU ARE THE POOR FOOL! HE HAS GONE MAD.

DEATH...TO DOCTOR DEATH!

...BUT IS IT DEATH TO THIS ARCH CRIMINAL? FOLLOW THE FURTHER AMAZING AND UNIQUE ADVENTURES OF THE

BAT-MAN

IN Next Month's DETECTIVE COMICS

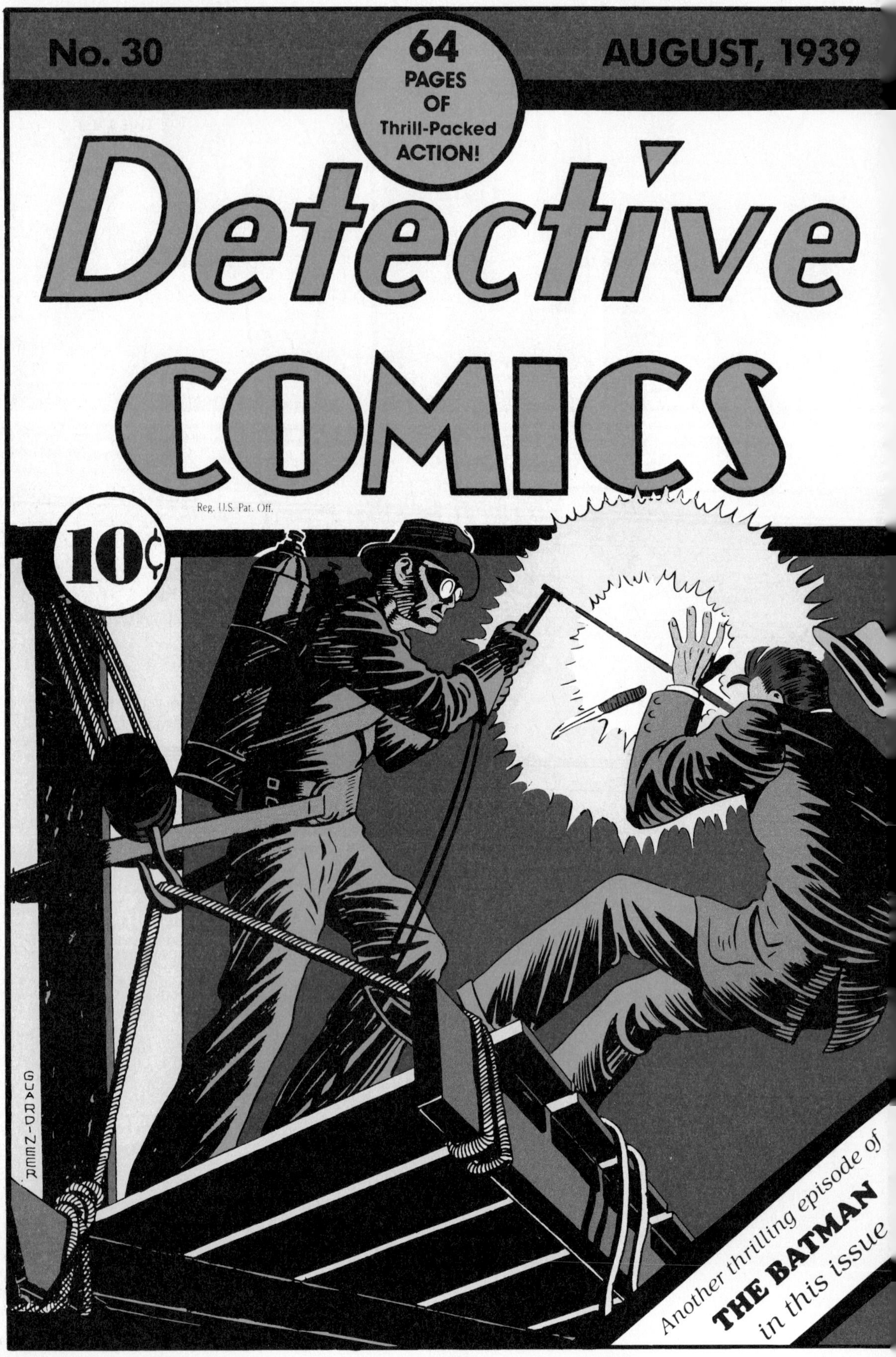
No. 30
64 PAGES OF Thrill-Packed ACTION!
AUGUST, 1939
Detective COMICS
Reg. U.S. Pat. Off.
10¢
GUARDINEER
Another thrilling episode of THE BATMAN in this issue

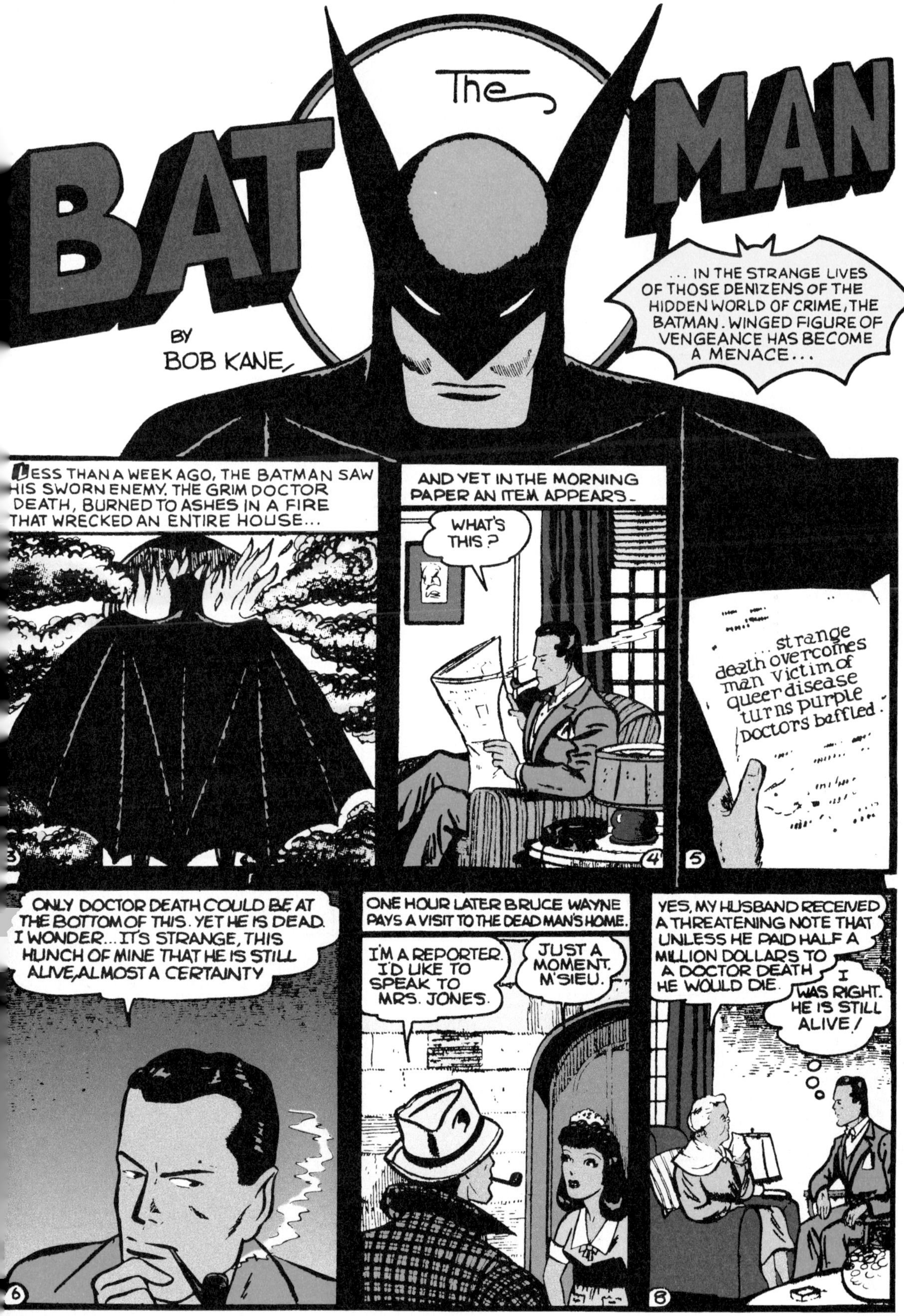

The BATMAN
BY BOB KANE
. . . IN THE STRANGE LIVES OF THOSE DENIZENS OF THE HIDDEN WORLD OF CRIME, THE BATMAN. WINGED FIGURE OF VENGEANCE HAS BECOME A MENACE . . .
LESS THAN A WEEK AGO, THE BATMAN SAW HIS SWORN ENEMY. THE GRIM DOCTOR DEATH, BURNED TO ASHES IN A FIRE THAT WRECKED AN ENTIRE HOUSE...
AND YET IN THE MORNING PAPER AN ITEM APPEARS_
WHAT'S THIS?
. . . strange death overcomes man victim of queer disease turns purple Doctors baffled
ONLY DOCTOR DEATH COULD BE AT THE BOTTOM OF THIS. YET HE IS DEAD. I WONDER... IT'S STRANGE, THIS HUNCH OF MINE THAT HE IS STILL ALIVE, ALMOST A CERTAINTY
ONE HOUR LATER BRUCE WAYNE PAYS A VISIT TO THE DEAD MAN'S HOME.
I'M A REPORTER. I'D LIKE TO SPEAK TO MRS. JONES.
JUST A MOMENT. M'SIEU.
YES, MY HUSBAND RECEIVED A THREATENING NOTE THAT UNLESS HE PAID HALF A MILLION DOLLARS TO A DOCTOR DEATH HE WOULD DIE.
I WAS RIGHT. HE IS STILL ALIVE!

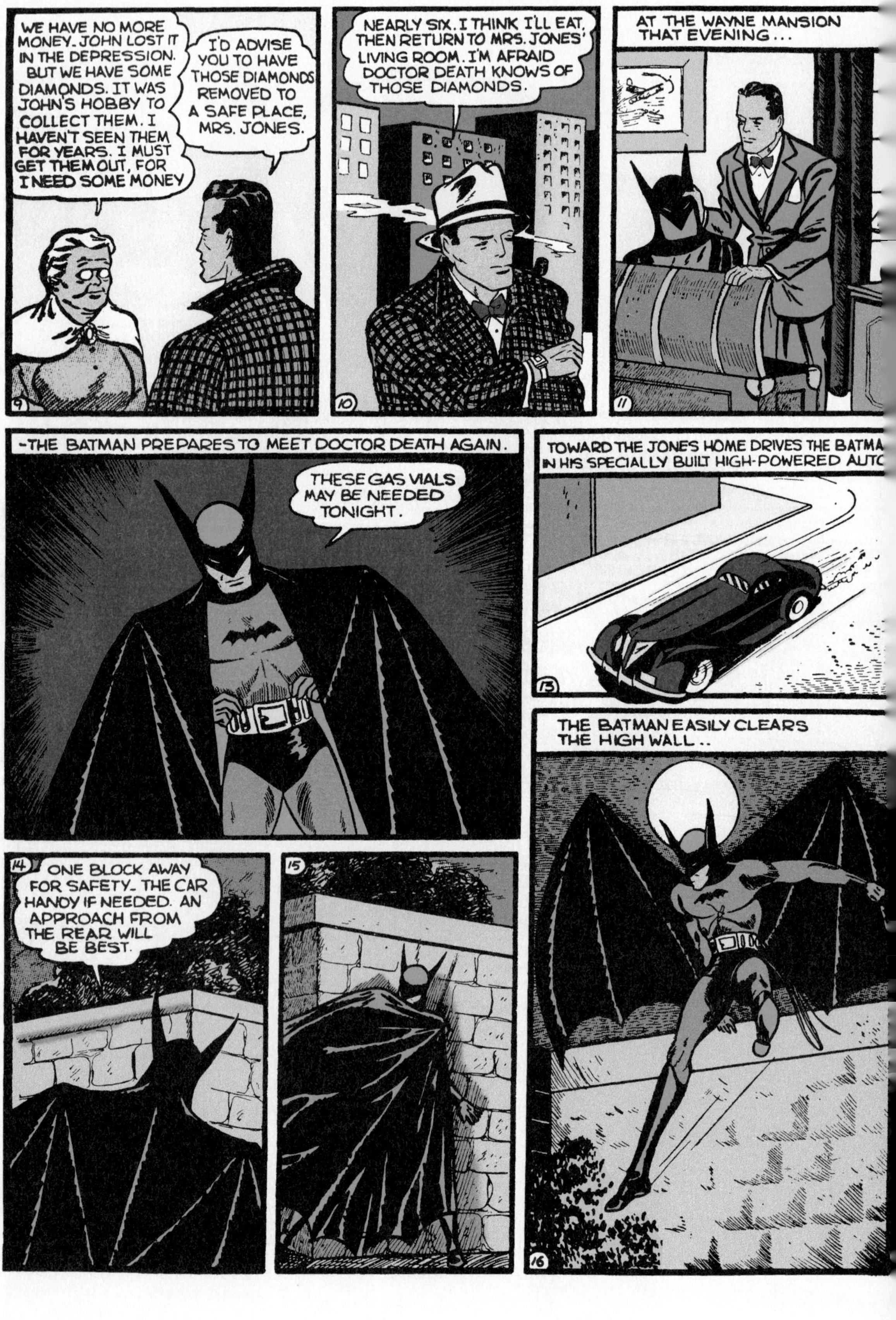

WE HAVE NO MORE MONEY. JOHN LOST IT IN THE DEPRESSION. BUT WE HAVE SOME DIAMONDS. IT WAS JOHN'S HOBBY TO COLLECT THEM. I HAVEN'T SEEN THEM FOR YEARS. I MUST GET THEM OUT, FOR I NEED SOME MONEY
I'D ADVISE YOU TO HAVE THOSE DIAMONDS REMOVED TO A SAFE PLACE, MRS. JONES.
NEARLY SIX. I THINK I'LL EAT, THEN RETURN TO MRS. JONES' LIVING ROOM. I'M AFRAID DOCTOR DEATH KNOWS OF THOSE DIAMONDS.
AT THE WAYNE MANSION THAT EVENING ...
-THE BATMAN PREPARES TO MEET DOCTOR DEATH AGAIN.
THESE GAS VIALS MAY BE NEEDED TONIGHT.
TOWARD THE JONES HOME DRIVES THE BATMA
IN HIS SPECIALLY BUILT HIGH-POWERED AUTO
ONE BLOCK AWAY FOR SAFETY. THE CAR HANDY IF NEEDED. AN APPROACH FROM THE REAR WILL BE BEST.
THE BATMAN EASILY CLEARS THE HIGH WALL ..

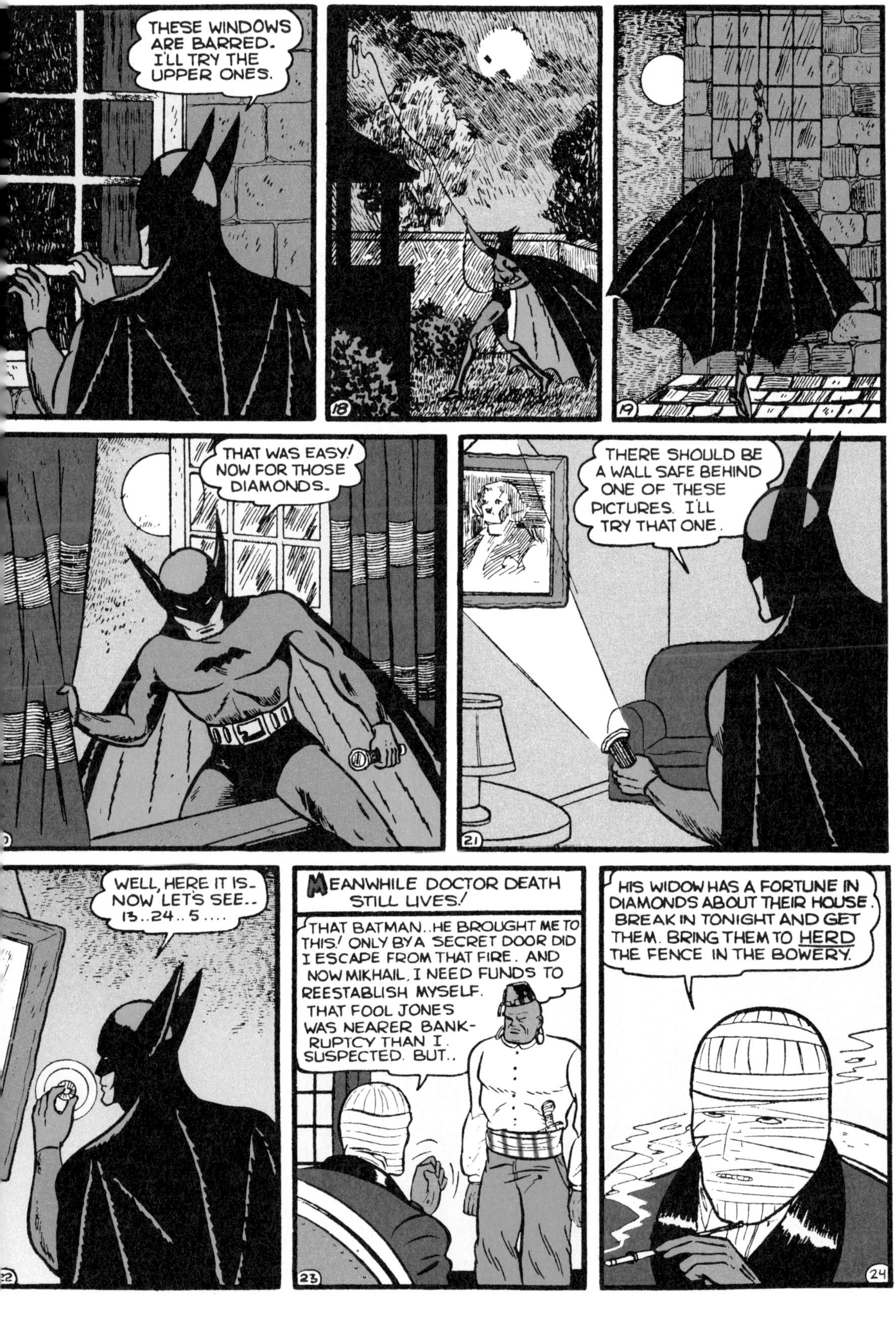
THESE WINDOWS ARE BARRED. I'LL TRY THE UPPER ONES.
THAT WAS EASY! NOW FOR THOSE DIAMONDS.
THERE SHOULD BE A WALL SAFE BEHIND ONE OF THESE PICTURES. I'LL TRY THAT ONE.
WELL, HERE IT IS. NOW LET'S SEE.. 13..24..5....
MEANWHILE DOCTOR DEATH STILL LIVES!
THAT BATMAN..HE BROUGHT ME TO THIS! ONLY BY A SECRET DOOR DID I ESCAPE FROM THAT FIRE. AND NOW MIKHAIL, I NEED FUNDS TO REESTABLISH MYSELF. THAT FOOL JONES WAS NEARER BANKRUPTCY THAN I SUSPECTED. BUT..
HIS WIDOW HAS A FORTUNE IN DIAMONDS ABOUT THEIR HOUSE. BREAK IN TONIGHT AND GET THEM. BRING THEM TO HERD THE FENCE IN THE BOWERY.

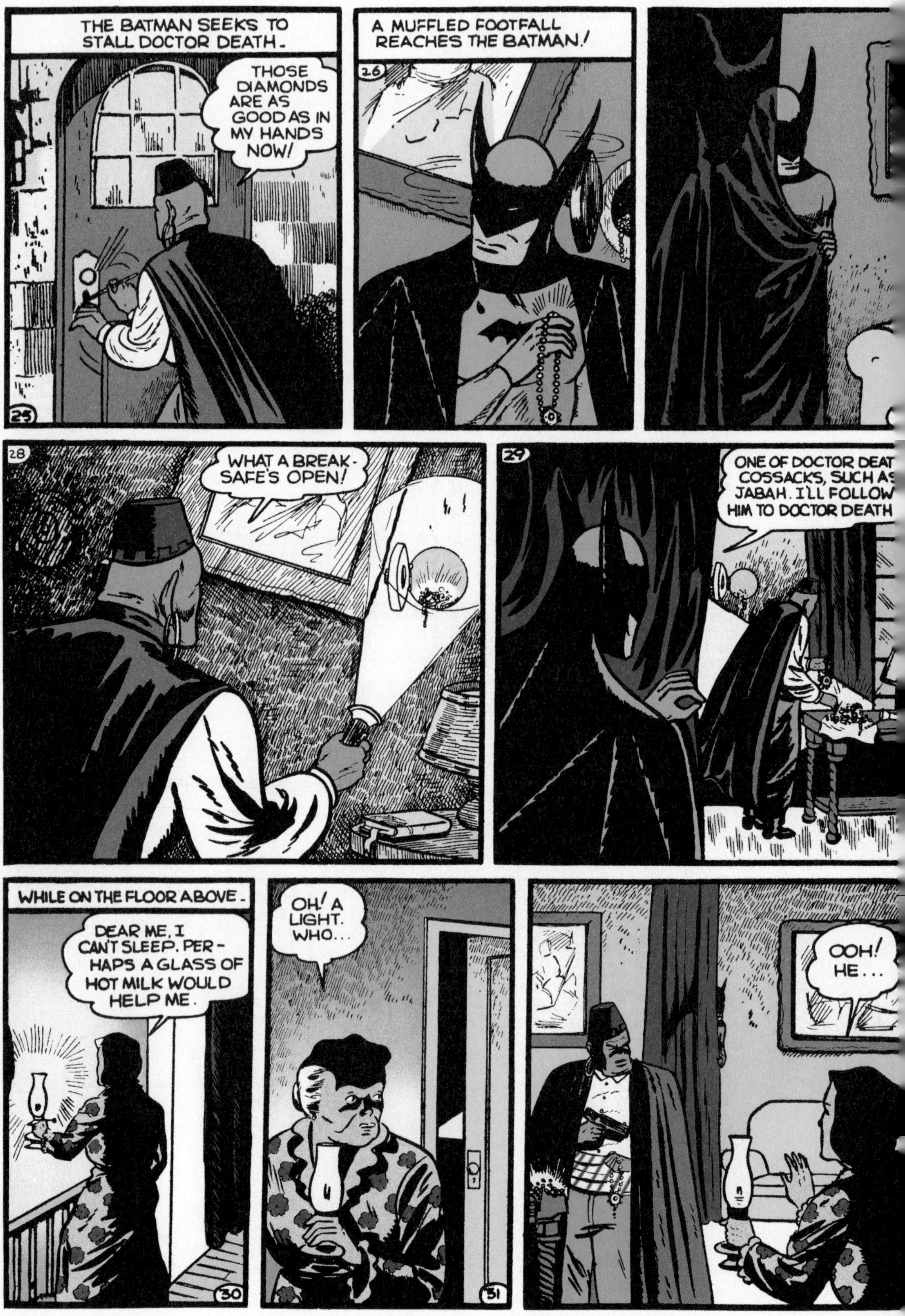
THE BATMAN SEEKS TO STALL DOCTOR DEATH.
THOSE DIAMONDS ARE AS GOOD AS IN MY HANDS NOW!
A MUFFLED FOOTFALL REACHES THE BATMAN!
WHAT A BREAK-SAFE'S OPEN!
ONE OF DOCTOR DEAT COSSACKS, SUCH AS JABAH. I'LL FOLLOW HIM TO DOCTOR DEATH
WHILE ON THE FLOOR ABOVE.
DEAR ME, I CAN'T SLEEP. PER-HAPS A GLASS OF HOT MILK WOULD HELP ME.
OH! A LIGHT. WHO...
OOH! HE...

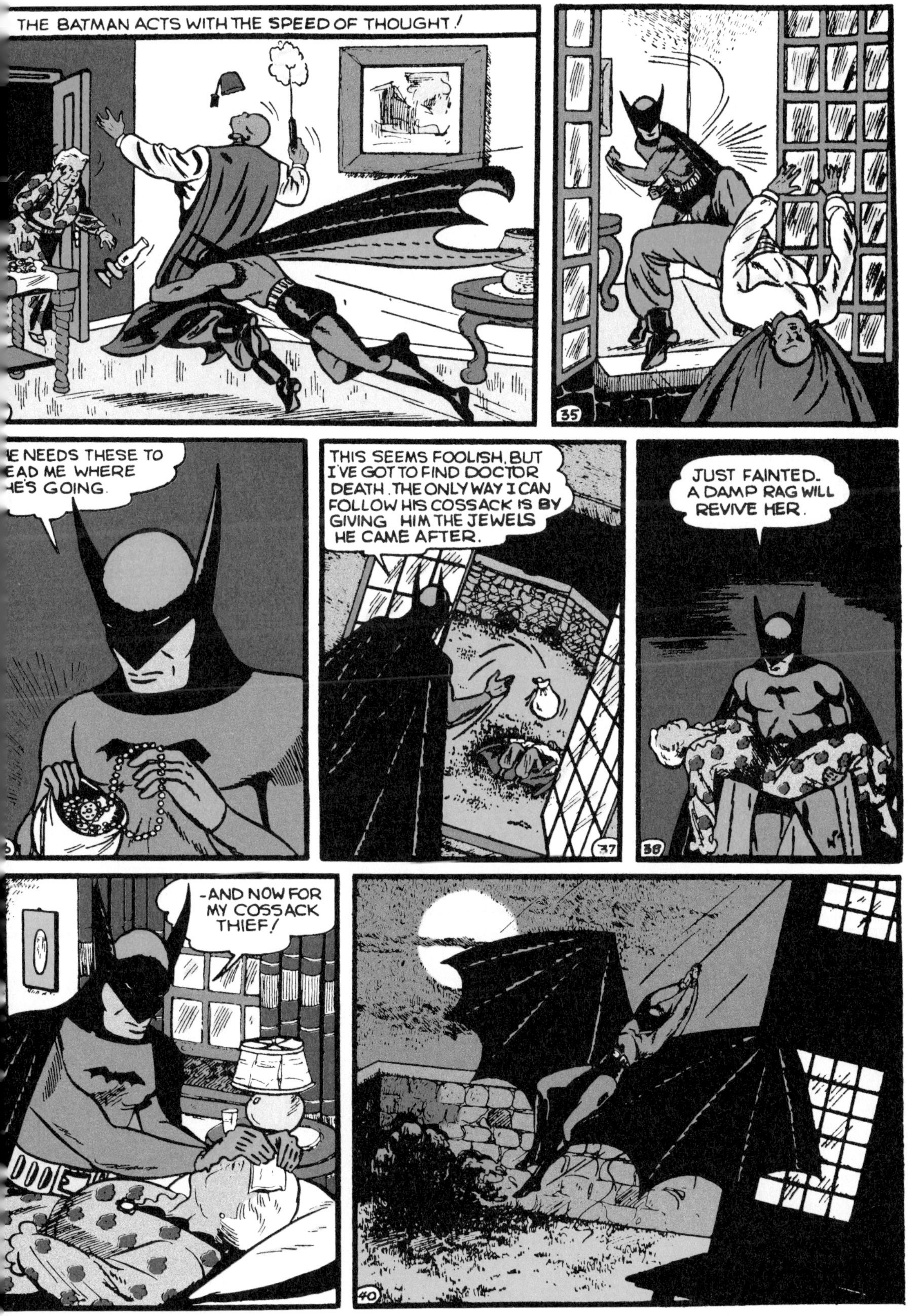
THE BATMAN ACTS WITH THE SPEED OF THOUGHT!
35
E NEEDS THESE TO
EAD ME WHERE
HE'S GOING.
THIS SEEMS FOOLISH, BUT I'VE GOT TO FIND DOCTOR DEATH. THE ONLY WAY I CAN FOLLOW HIS COSSACK IS BY GIVING HIM THE JEWELS HE CAME AFTER.
37
JUST FAINTED. A DAMP RAG WILL REVIVE HER.
38
-AND NOW FOR MY COSSACK THIEF!
40

HE'LL COME TO IN A MOMENT.

WHATEVER HAPPENED UP THERE, I'M GLAD I CLUNG ONTO THIS BAG!

THE BATMAN TRAILS HIS QUAR—

IVAN HERD'S, EH? SO HE'S THE 'FENCE' FOR DEATH'S DIAMONDS.

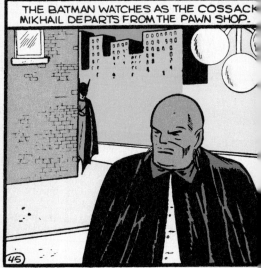

THE BATMAN WATCHES AS THE COSSACK MIKHAIL DEPARTS FROM THE PAWN SHOP.

ONCE MORE THE CHASE IS RESUMED...

QUEER THAT DOCTOR DEATH SHOULD LIVE HERE. BUT THAT FIRE MAY HAVE TAKEN AWAY ALL HIS MONEY. ANYHOW I'LL GIVE IT A TRY.

THEY MIGHT EXPECT A VISITOR FROM THE FRONT DOOR, BUT NOT FROM THE ROOF!

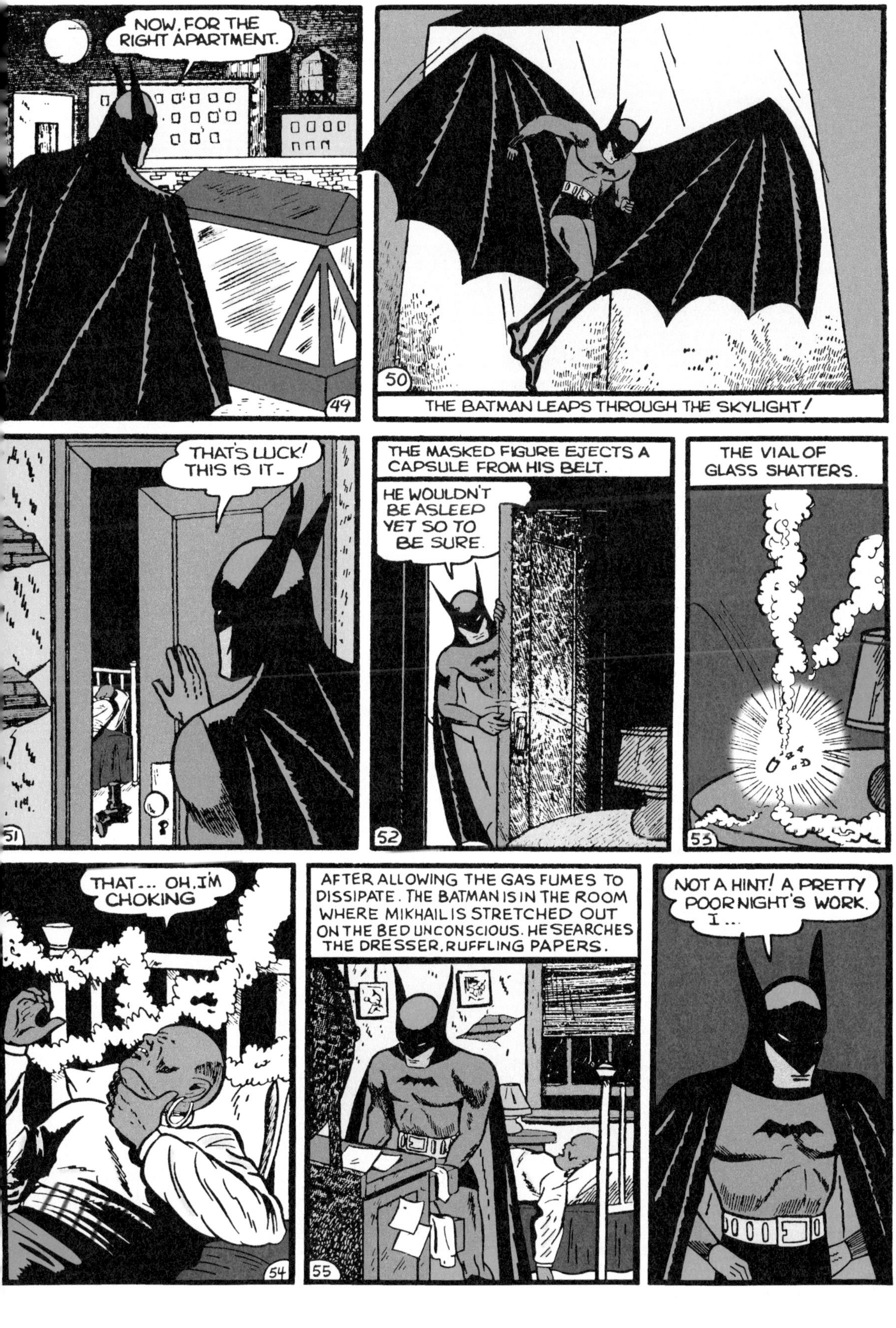
NOW, FOR THE RIGHT APARTMENT.
49
50
THE BATMAN LEAPS THROUGH THE SKYLIGHT!
THAT'S LUCK! THIS IS IT_
51
THE MASKED FIGURE EJECTS A CAPSULE FROM HIS BELT.
HE WOULDN'T BE ASLEEP YET SO TO BE SURE.
52
THE VIAL OF GLASS SHATTERS.
53
THAT... OH, I'M CHOKING
54
AFTER ALLOWING THE GAS FUMES TO DISSIPATE. THE BATMAN IS IN THE ROOM WHERE MIKHAIL IS STRETCHED OUT ON THE BED UNCONSCIOUS. HE SEARCHES THE DRESSER, RUFFLING PAPERS.
55
NOT A HINT! A PRETTY POOR NIGHT'S WORK. I...

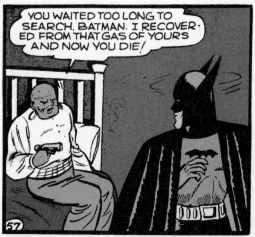

YOU WAITED TOO LONG TO SEARCH, BATMAN. I RECOVERED FROM THAT GAS OF YOURS AND NOW YOU DIE!

57

BUT THE BATMAN WHEELS AND...

58

CATCHES HIS SILKEN ROPE!

59

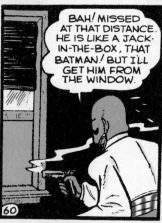

BAH! MISSED AT THAT DISTANCE. HE IS LIKE A JACK-IN-THE-BOX, THAT BATMAN! BUT I'LL GET HIM FROM THE WINDOW.

60

BUT AS MIKHAIL PUTS HIS HEAD THROUGH THE WINDOW..

61

THERE IS A SICKENING SNAP AS THE COSSACK'S NECK BREAKS UNDER THE MIGHTY PRESSURE OF THE BATMAN'S FOOT.

SNAP!

FIRST JABAH, NOW YOU.. AND YET DOCTOR DEATH LIVES ON!

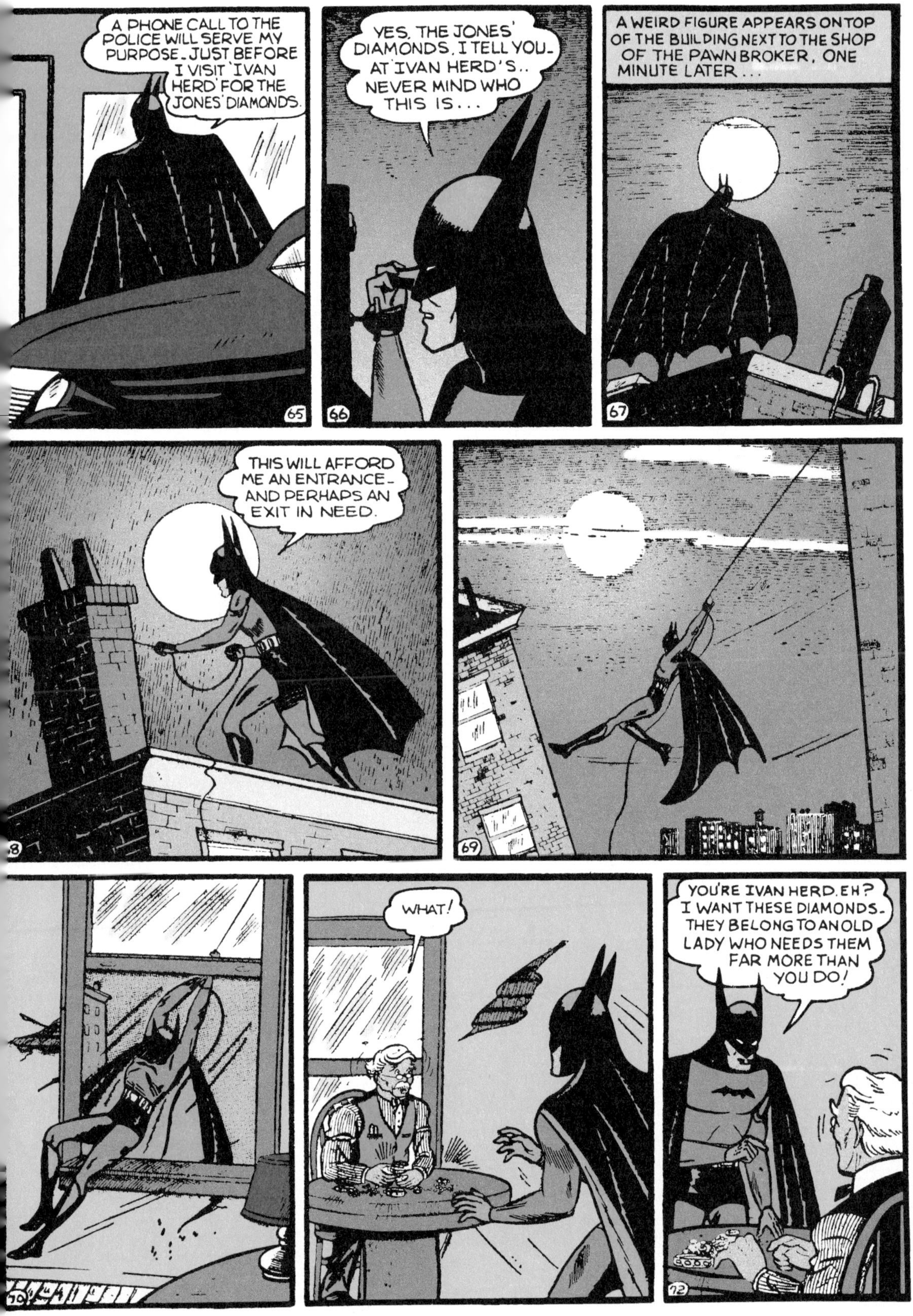
A PHONE CALL TO THE POLICE WILL SERVE MY PURPOSE - JUST BEFORE I VISIT 'IVAN HERD' FOR THE JONES' DIAMONDS.
65
YES, THE JONES' DIAMONDS, I TELL YOU - AT 'IVAN HERD'S.. NEVER MIND WHO THIS IS...
66
A WEIRD FIGURE APPEARS ON TOP OF THE BUILDING NEXT TO THE SHOP OF THE PAWN BROKER, ONE MINUTE LATER...
67
THIS WILL AFFORD ME AN ENTRANCE - AND PERHAPS AN EXIT IN NEED.
69
WHAT!
YOU'RE IVAN HERD, EH? I WANT THESE DIAMONDS - THEY BELONG TO AN OLD LADY WHO NEEDS THEM FAR MORE THAN YOU DO!
72

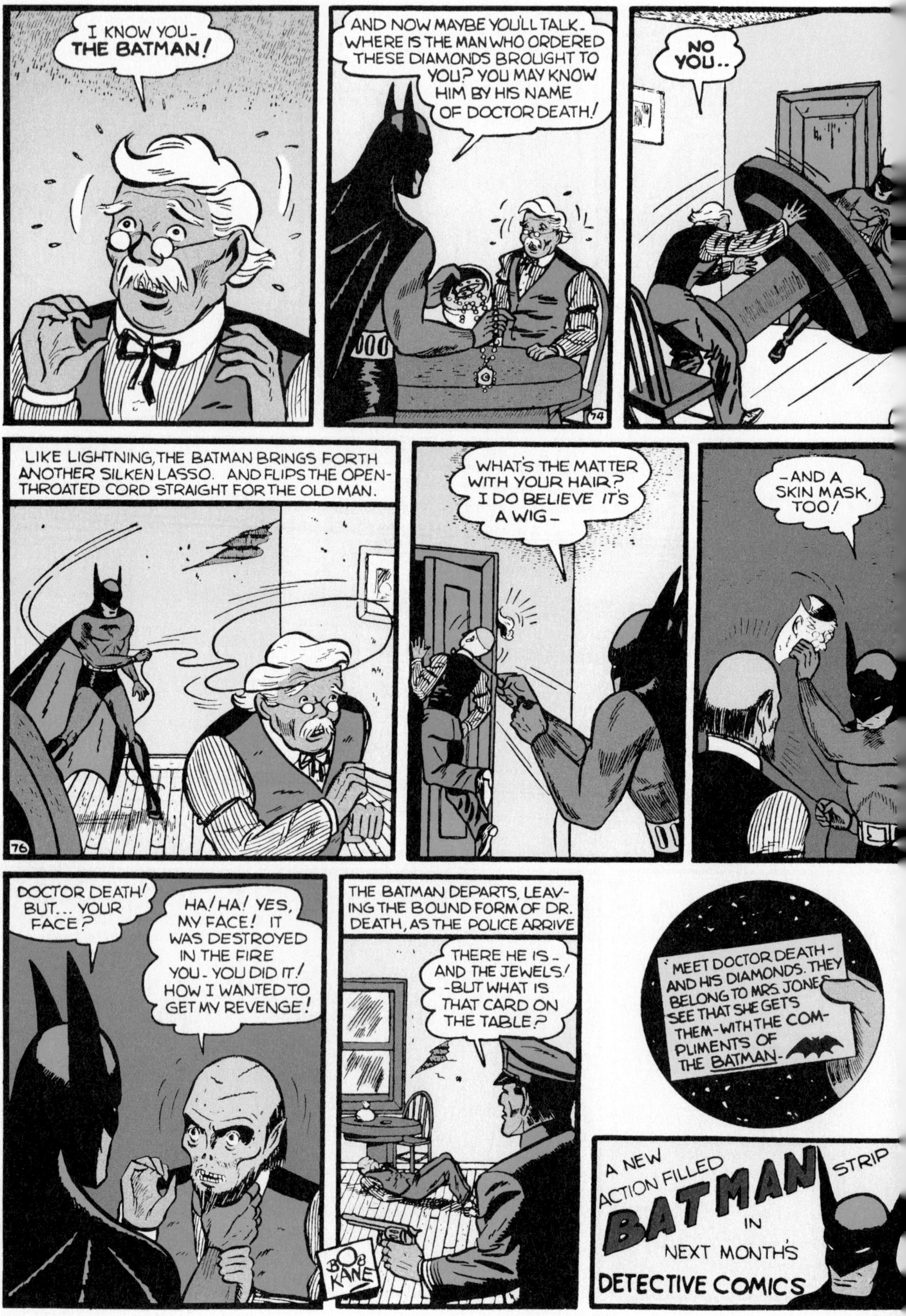
I KNOW YOU- THE BATMAN!
AND NOW MAYBE YOU'LL TALK- WHERE IS THE MAN WHO ORDERED THESE DIAMONDS BROUGHT TO YOU? YOU MAY KNOW HIM BY HIS NAME OF DOCTOR DEATH!
74
NO YOU..
LIKE LIGHTNING, THE BATMAN BRINGS FORTH ANOTHER SILKEN LASSO. AND FLIPS THE OPEN-THROATED CORD STRAIGHT FOR THE OLD MAN.
76
WHAT'S THE MATTER WITH YOUR HAIR? I DO BELIEVE IT'S A WIG-
-AND A SKIN MASK, TOO!
DOCTOR DEATH! BUT... YOUR FACE?
HA! HA! YES, MY FACE! IT WAS DESTROYED IN THE FIRE YOU- YOU DID IT! HOW I WANTED TO GET MY REVENGE!
THE BATMAN DEPARTS, LEAVING THE BOUND FORM OF DR. DEATH, AS THE POLICE ARRIVE
THERE HE IS- AND THE JEWELS! -BUT WHAT IS THAT CARD ON THE TABLE?
BOB KANE
MEET DOCTOR DEATH- AND HIS DIAMONDS. THEY BELONG TO MRS. JONES SEE THAT SHE GETS THEM-WITH THE COMPLIMENTS OF THE BATMAN-
A NEW ACTION FILLED BATMAN STRIP IN NEXT MONTH'S DETECTIVE COMICS

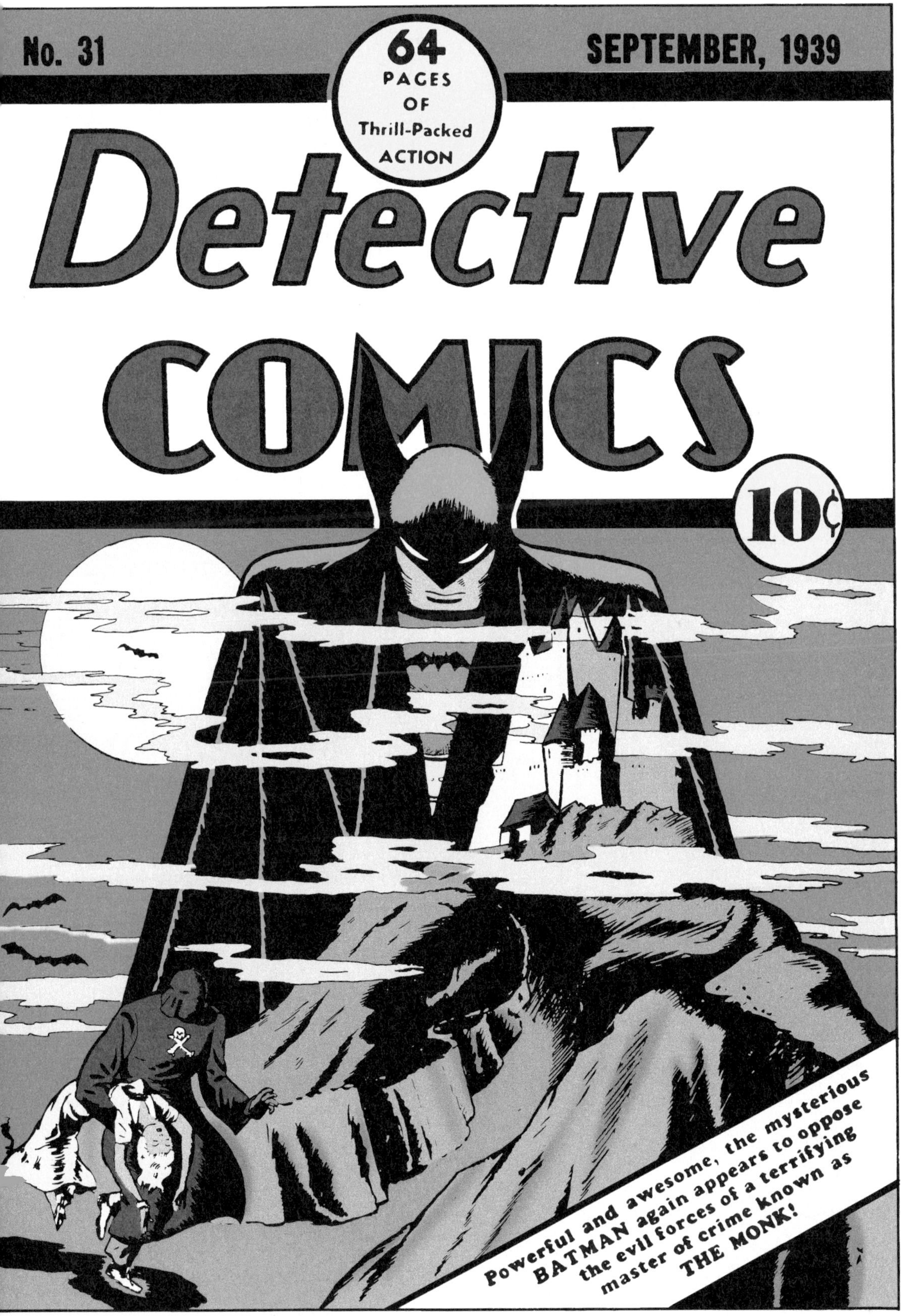
No. 31
64 PAGES OF Thrill-Packed ACTION
SEPTEMBER, 1939
Detective
COMICS
10¢
Powerful and awesome, the mysterious
BATMAN again appears to oppose
the evil forces of a terrifying
master of crime known as
THE MONK!

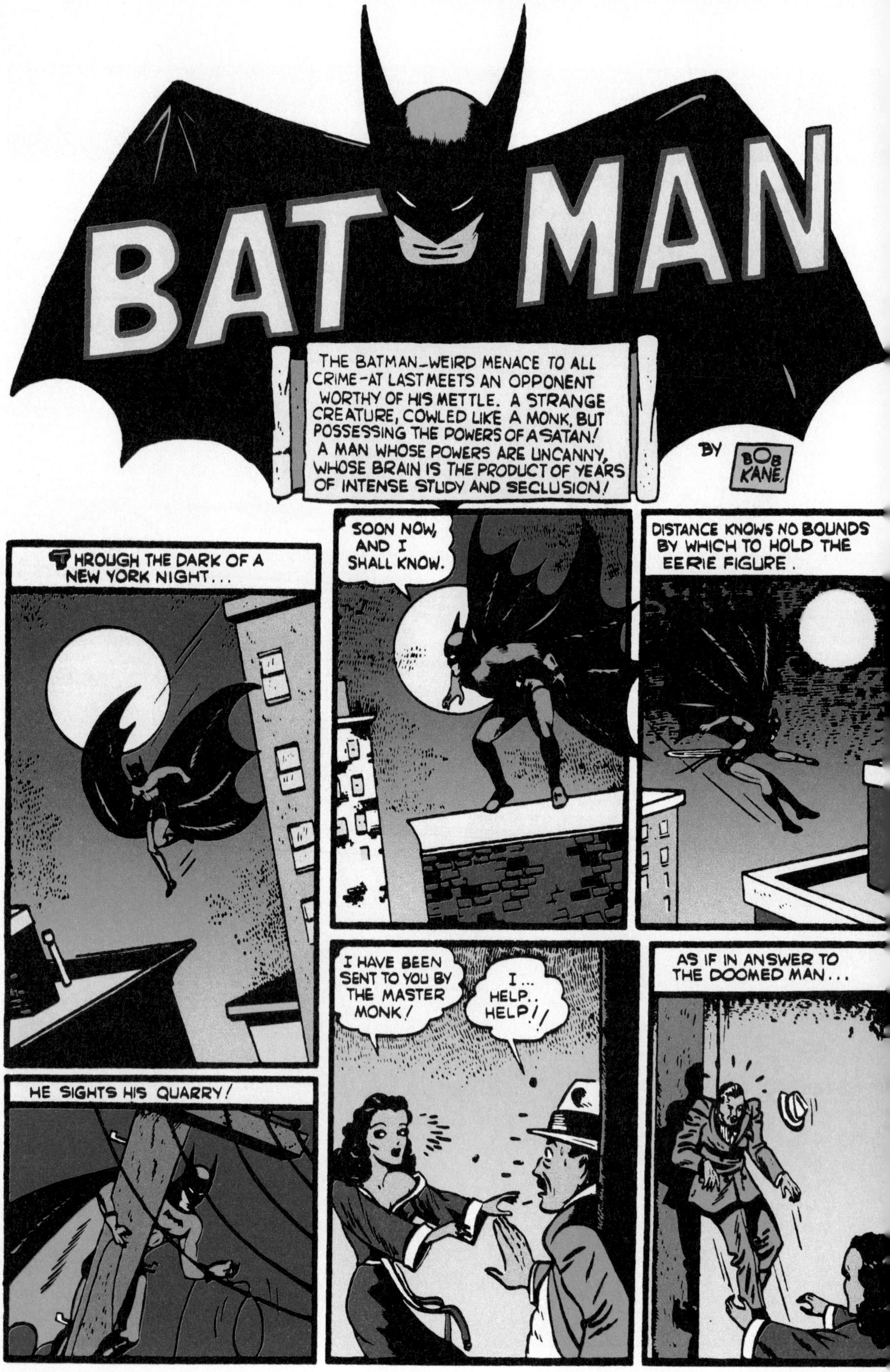
BATMAN
THE BATMAN-WEIRD MENACE TO ALL CRIME-AT LAST MEETS AN OPPONENT WORTHY OF HIS METTLE. A STRANGE CREATURE, COWLED LIKE A MONK, BUT POSSESSING THE POWERS OF A SATAN! A MAN WHOSE POWERS ARE UNCANNY, WHOSE BRAIN IS THE PRODUCT OF YEARS OF INTENSE STUDY AND SECLUSION!
BY BOB KANE
THROUGH THE DARK OF A NEW YORK NIGHT...
SOON NOW, AND I SHALL KNOW.
DISTANCE KNOWS NO BOUNDS BY WHICH TO HOLD THE EERIE FIGURE.
HE SIGHTS HIS QUARRY!
I HAVE BEEN SENT TO YOU BY THE MASTER MONK!
I... HELP.. HELP!!
AS IF IN ANSWER TO THE DOOMED MAN...

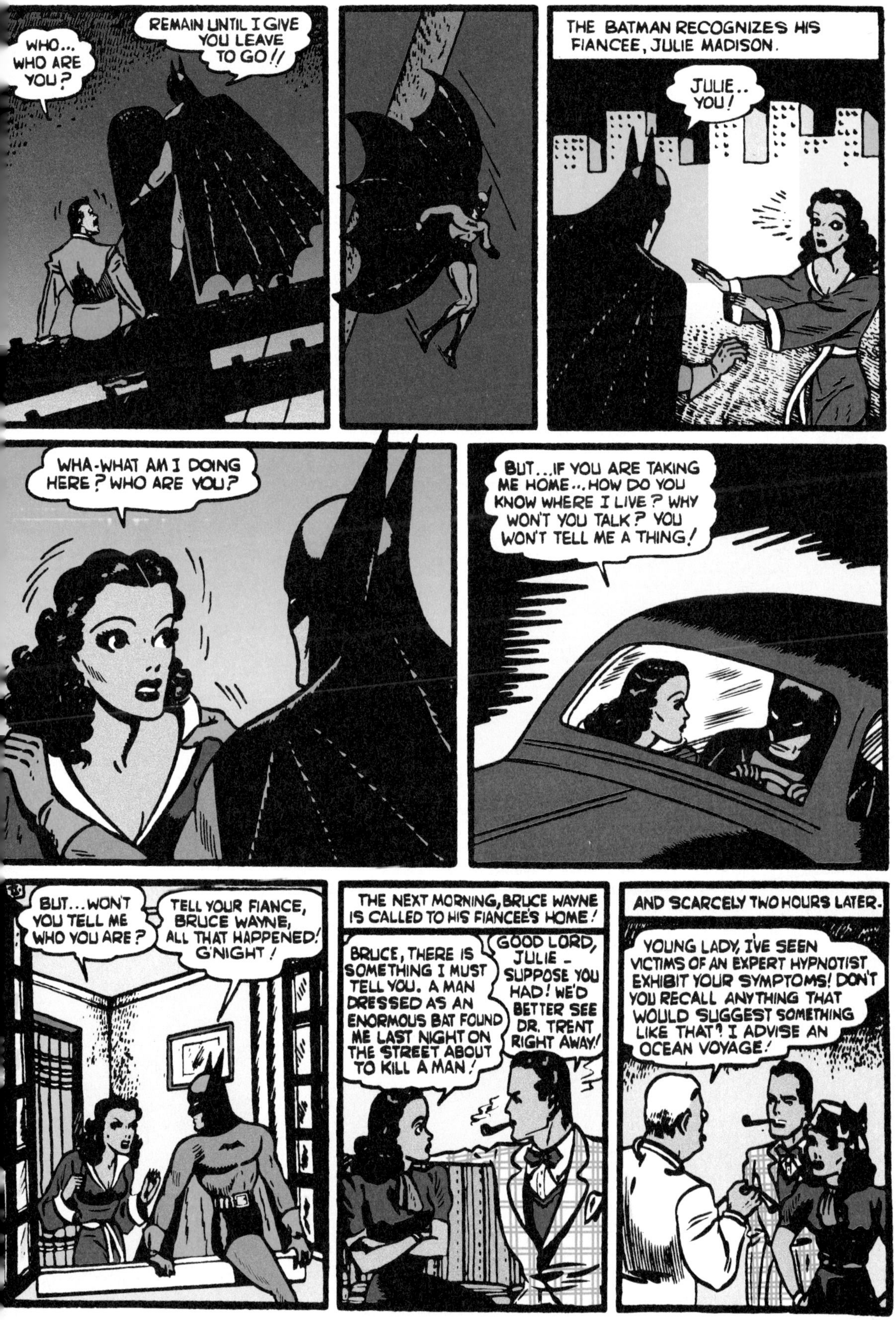
WHO... WHO ARE YOU?
REMAIN UNTIL I GIVE YOU LEAVE TO GO!!
THE BATMAN RECOGNIZES HIS FIANCEE, JULIE MADISON.
JULIE.. YOU!
WHA-WHAT AM I DOING HERE? WHO ARE YOU?
BUT...IF YOU ARE TAKING ME HOME...HOW DO YOU KNOW WHERE I LIVE? WHY WON'T YOU TALK? YOU WON'T TELL ME A THING!
BUT...WON'T YOU TELL ME WHO YOU ARE?
TELL YOUR FIANCE, BRUCE WAYNE, ALL THAT HAPPENED! G'NIGHT!
THE NEXT MORNING, BRUCE WAYNE IS CALLED TO HIS FIANCEE'S HOME!
BRUCE, THERE IS SOMETHING I MUST TELL YOU. A MAN DRESSED AS AN ENORMOUS BAT FOUND ME LAST NIGHT ON THE STREET ABOUT TO KILL A MAN!
GOOD LORD, JULIE - SUPPOSE YOU HAD! WE'D BETTER SEE DR. TRENT RIGHT AWAY!
AND SCARCELY TWO HOURS LATER.
YOUNG LADY, I'VE SEEN VICTIMS OF AN EXPERT HYPNOTIST EXHIBIT YOUR SYMPTOMS! DON'T YOU RECALL ANYTHING THAT WOULD SUGGEST SOMETHING LIKE THAT? I ADVISE AN OCEAN VOYAGE!

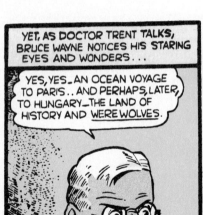

YET, AS DOCTOR TRENT TALKS, BRUCE WAYNE NOTICES HIS STARING EYES AND WONDERS...

YES, YES... AN OCEAN VOYAGE TO PARIS... AND PERHAPS, LATER, TO HUNGARY... THE LAND OF HISTORY AND WEREWOLVES.

ONE TICKET TO PARIS, PLEASE. PORT CABIN.

LUNAR LINES

I DON'T LIKE THE CRACK THE DOCTOR MADE ABOUT WEREWOLVES, JULIE. AND HE SEEMED HYPNOTIZED HIMSELF, WHEN HE GAVE YOU THAT ADVICE. BUT MAYBE I'M IMAGINING THINGS.

OF COURSE YOU ARE! I'VE WORRIED YOU. BUT I'LL BE GOOD, I PROMISE.

BUT BACK AT THE WAYNE MANSION...

JULIE WOULD BE SURPRISED TO KNOW HER BATMAN IS HER FUTURE HUSBAND.

AND IN A SECRET HANGAR KNOWN ONLY TO HIMSELF...

TWO NEW WEAPONS. MY BATGYRO, IN WHICH TO FOLLOW JULIE, AND...

THE FLYING BATERANG - MODELED AFTER THE AUSTRALIAN BUSHMAN'S BOOMERANG!

46

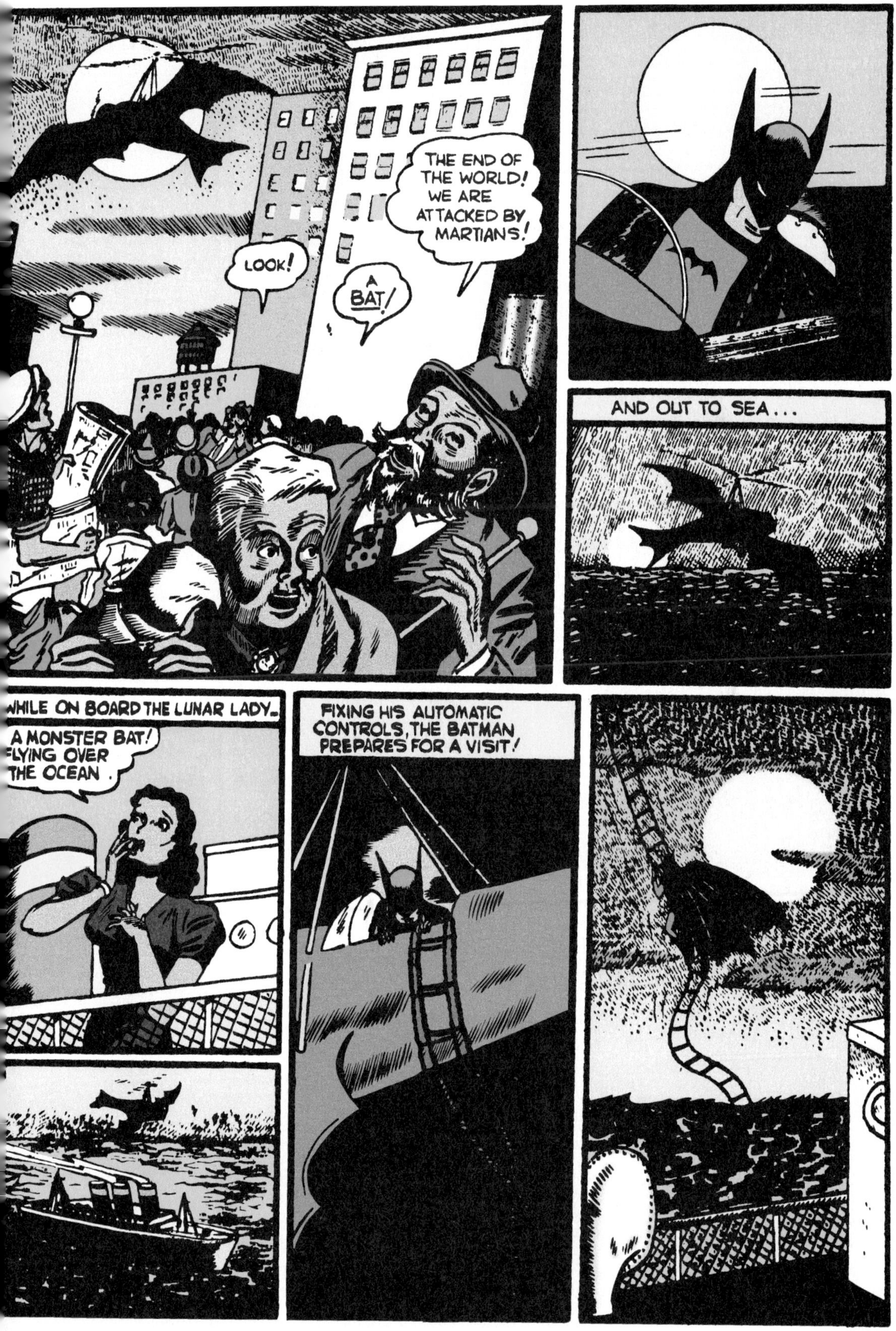
THE END OF THE WORLD! WE ARE ATTACKED BY MARTIANS!
LOOK!
A BAT!
AND OUT TO SEA...
WHILE ON BOARD THE LUNAR LADY..
A MONSTER BAT! FLYING OVER THE OCEAN.
FIXING HIS AUTOMATIC CONTROLS, THE BATMAN PREPARES FOR A VISIT!

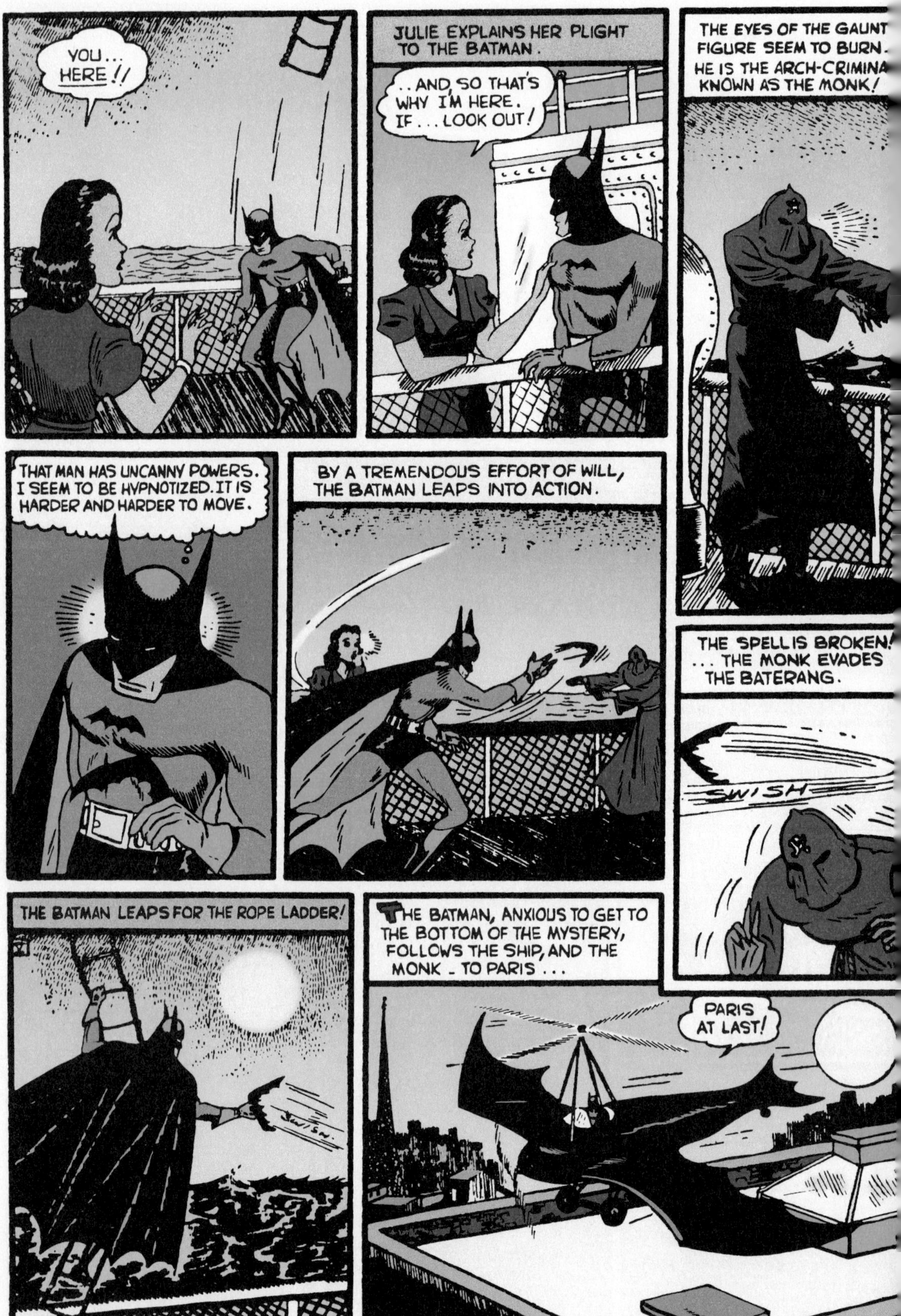
YOU... HERE!!
JULIE EXPLAINS HER PLIGHT TO THE BATMAN.
..AND, SO THAT'S WHY I'M HERE. IF...LOOK OUT!
THE EYES OF THE GAUNT FIGURE SEEM TO BURN. HE IS THE ARCH-CRIMINA KNOWN AS THE MONK!
THAT MAN HAS UNCANNY POWERS. I SEEM TO BE HYPNOTIZED. IT IS HARDER AND HARDER TO MOVE.
BY A TREMENDOUS EFFORT OF WILL, THE BATMAN LEAPS INTO ACTION.
THE SPELL IS BROKEN! ... THE MONK EVADES THE BATERANG.
SWISH
THE BATMAN LEAPS FOR THE ROPE LADDER!
SWISH
THE BATMAN, ANXIOUS TO GET TO THE BOTTOM OF THE MYSTERY, FOLLOWS THE SHIP, AND THE MONK - TO PARIS...
PARIS AT LAST!

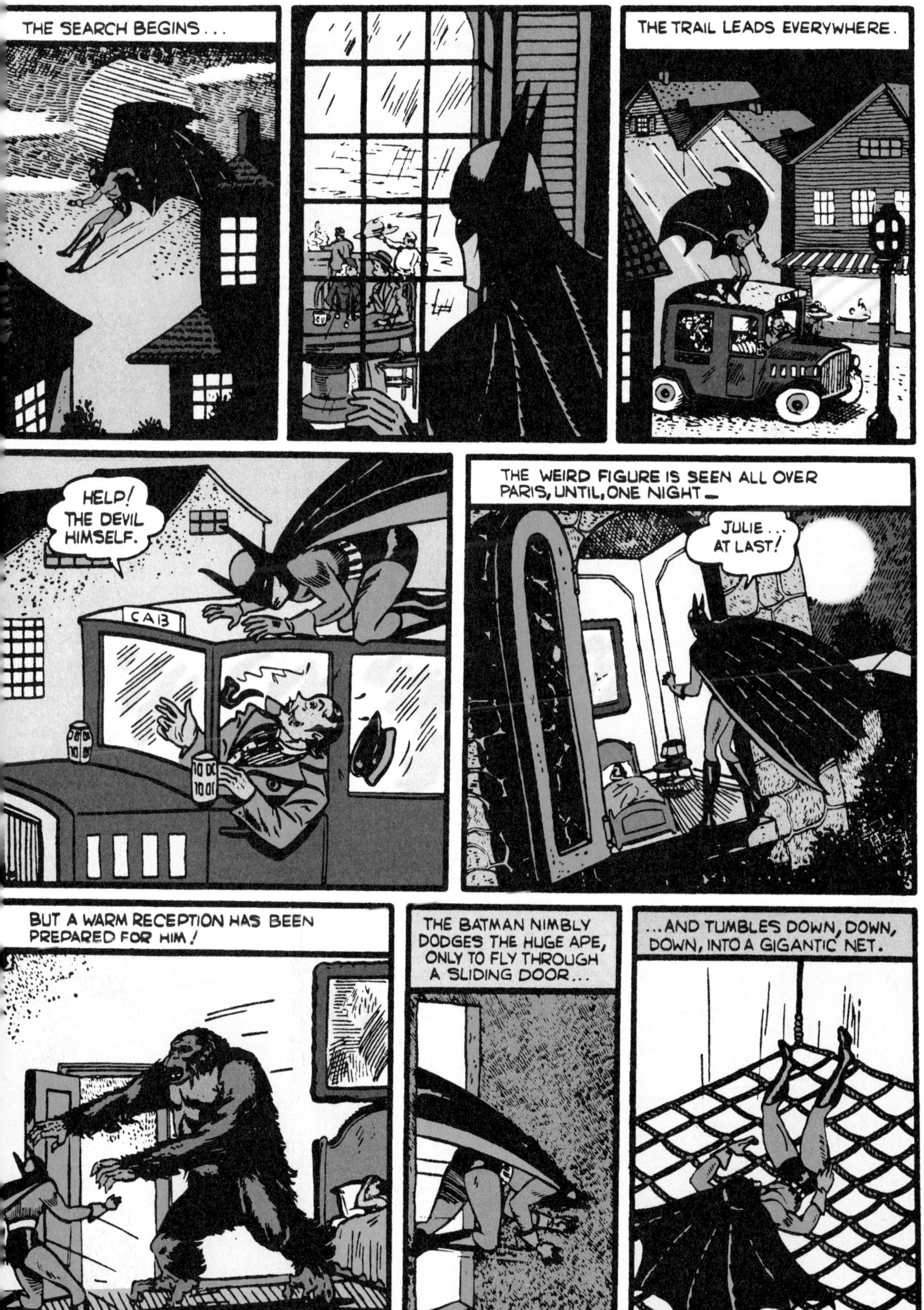

THE SEARCH BEGINS...
THE TRAIL LEADS EVERYWHERE.
CAB
HELP! THE DEVIL HIMSELF.
THE WEIRD FIGURE IS SEEN ALL OVER PARIS, UNTIL, ONE NIGHT—
JULIE... AT LAST!
BUT A WARM RECEPTION HAS BEEN PREPARED FOR HIM!
THE BATMAN NIMBLY DODGES THE HUGE APE, ONLY TO FLY THROUGH A SLIDING DOOR...
...AND TUMBLES DOWN, DOWN, DOWN, INTO A GIGANTIC NET.

CAUGHT LIKE A RAT IN A TRAP, AS THE NET CLOSES ABOUT HIM...

THE BATMAN ONCE AGAIN FACES THE DIABOLICAL MASTER MONK!

RASH MORTAL... TO DARE FACE THE POWER OF THE MONK. LOOK BELOW YOU AT YOUR FATE! WHEN I PULL TH' LEVER—HEH! HEH

THE NET BEGINS TO DROP SLOWLY INTO THE DEN OF SNAKES.

IN A FLASH, THE BATMAN FLIPS HIS BATERANG.

THE NET STOPS IN ITS DOWNWARD FLIGHT AS THE BATERANG KNOCKS OVER THE LEVER.

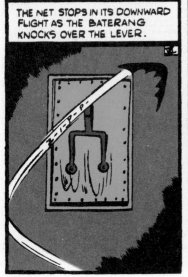

CONTINUING ON ITS UPWARD SWEEP, IT CRASHES INTO A GLASS CHANDELIER.

THE BATMAN GRASPS THE BATERANG AND THE BROKEN GLASS!

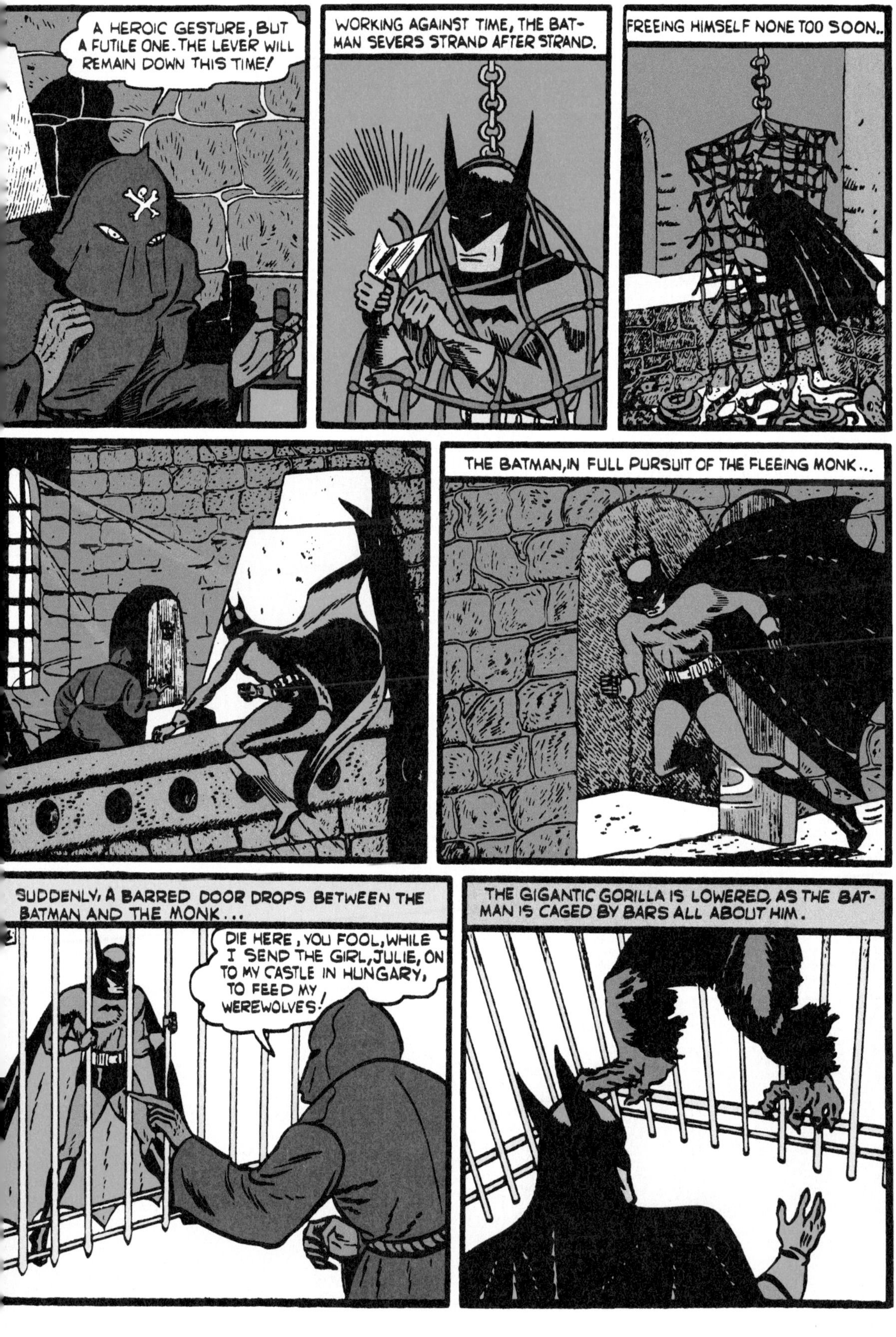
A HEROIC GESTURE, BUT A FUTILE ONE. THE LEVER WILL REMAIN DOWN THIS TIME!
WORKING AGAINST TIME, THE BATMAN SEVERS STRAND AFTER STRAND.
FREEING HIMSELF NONE TOO SOON..
THE BATMAN, IN FULL PURSUIT OF THE FLEEING MONK...
SUDDENLY, A BARRED DOOR DROPS BETWEEN THE BATMAN AND THE MONK...
DIE HERE, YOU FOOL, WHILE I SEND THE GIRL, JULIE, ON TO MY CASTLE IN HUNGARY, TO FEED MY WEREWOLVES!
THE GIGANTIC GORILLA IS LOWERED, AS THE BATMAN IS CAGED BY BARS ALL ABOUT HIM.

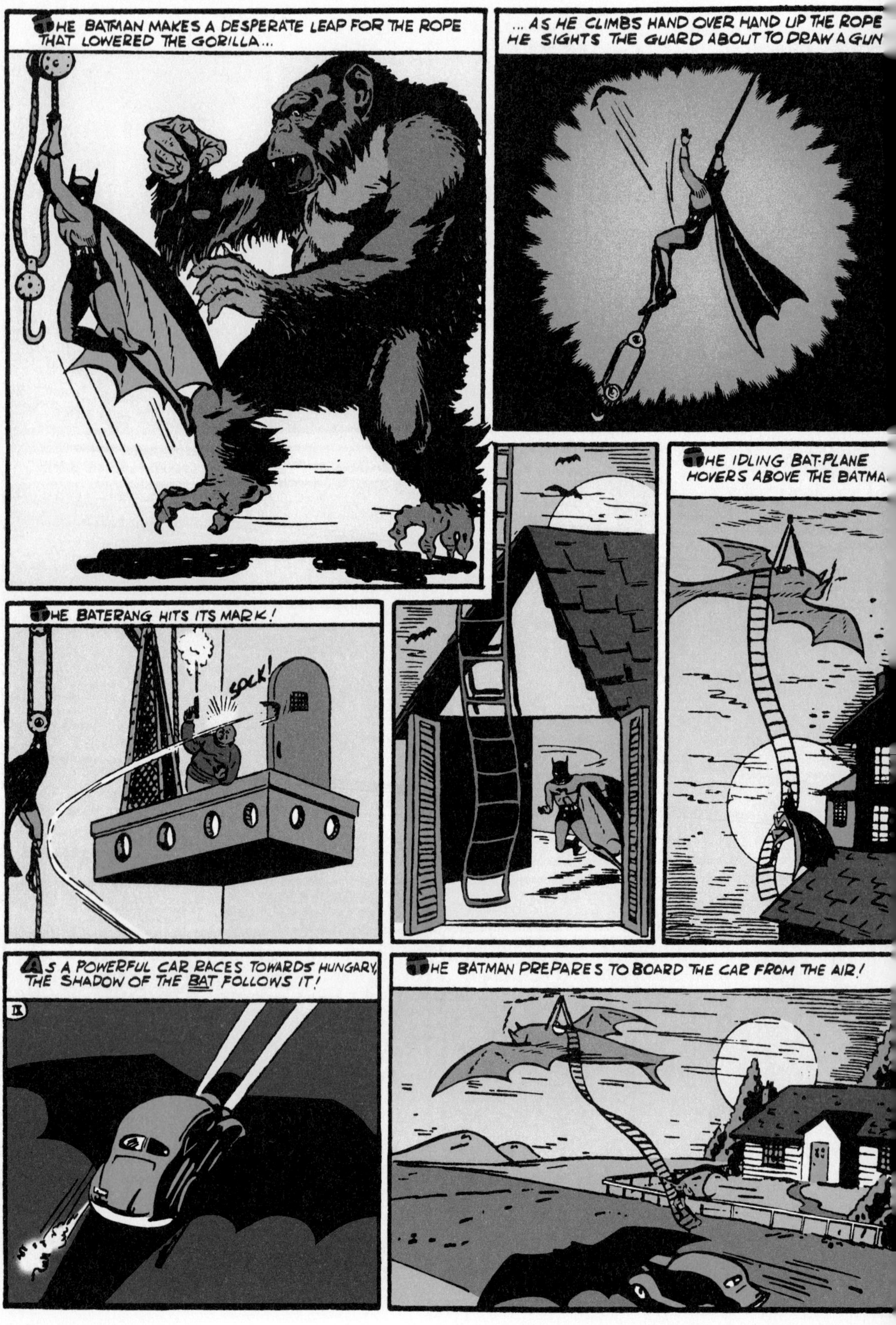
THE BATMAN MAKES A DESPERATE LEAP FOR THE ROPE THAT LOWERED THE GORILLA...
... AS HE CLIMBS HAND OVER HAND UP THE ROPE HE SIGHTS THE GUARD ABOUT TO DRAW A GUN
THE BATERANG HITS ITS MARK!
SOCK!
THE IDLING BAT-PLANE HOVERS ABOVE THE BATMA
AS A POWERFUL CAR RACES TOWARDS HUNGARY, THE SHADOW OF THE BAT FOLLOWS IT!
IX
THE BATMAN PREPARES TO BOARD THE CAR FROM THE AIR!

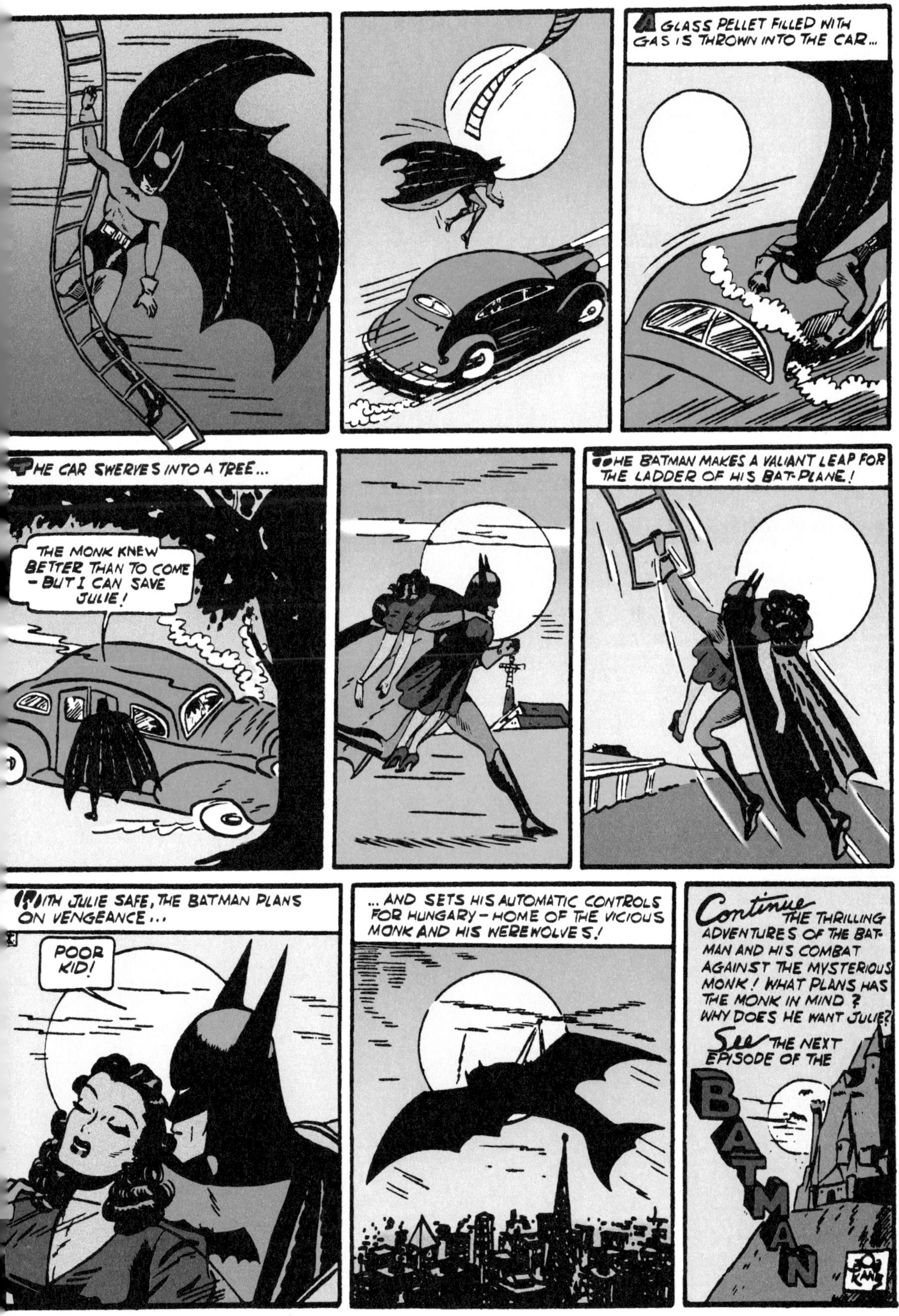
A GLASS PELLET FILLED WITH GAS IS THROWN INTO THE CAR...
THE CAR SWERVES INTO A TREE...
THE MONK KNEW BETTER THAN TO COME - BUT I CAN SAVE JULIE!
THE BATMAN MAKES A VALIANT LEAP FOR THE LADDER OF HIS BAT-PLANE!
WITH JULIE SAFE, THE BATMAN PLANS ON VENGEANCE...
POOR KID!
...AND SETS HIS AUTOMATIC CONTROLS FOR HUNGARY - HOME OF THE VICIOUS MONK AND HIS WEREWOLVES!
Continue THE THRILLING ADVENTURES OF THE BAT-MAN AND HIS COMBAT AGAINST THE MYSTERIOUS MONK! WHAT PLANS HAS THE MONK IN MIND? WHY DOES HE WANT JULIE?
See THE NEXT EPISODE OF THE
BATMAN

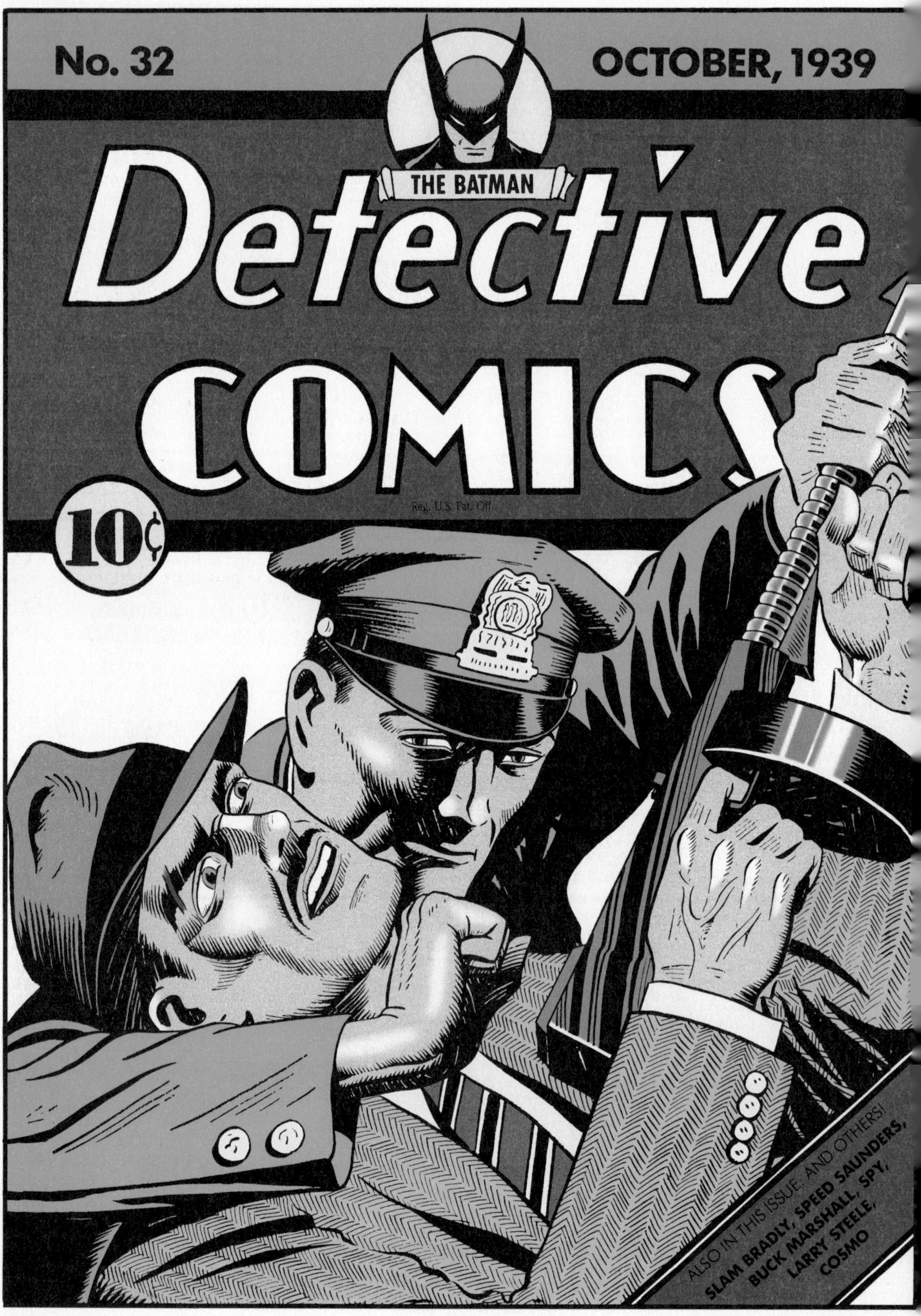
No. 32
OCTOBER, 1939
THE BATMAN
Detective
COMICS
10¢
Reg. U.S. Pat. Off.
ALSO IN THIS ISSUE: AND OTHERS!
SLAM BRADLY, SPEED SAUNDERS,
BUCK MARSHALL, SPY,
LARRY STEELE,
COSMO

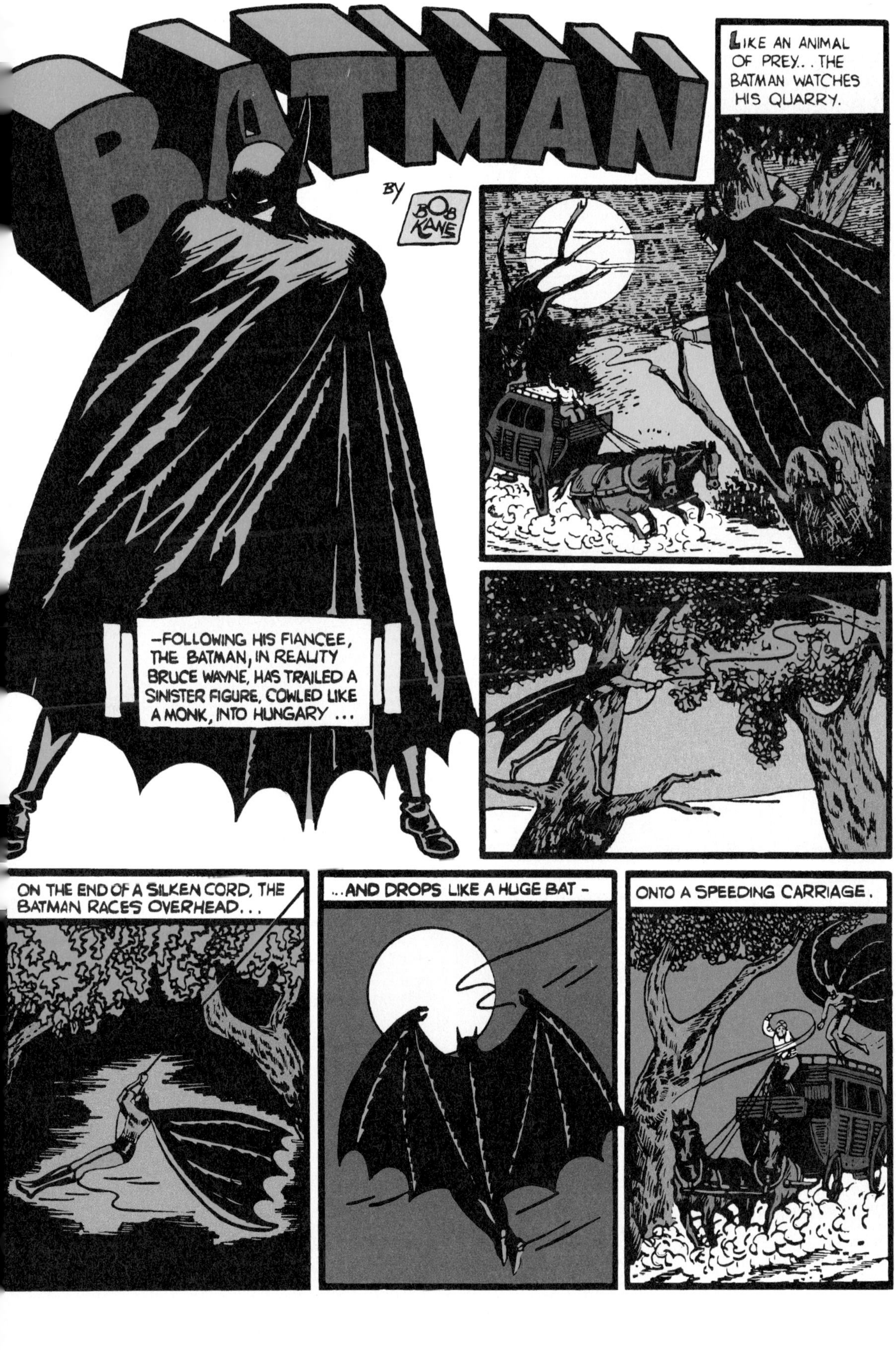
BATMAN
BY BOB KANE
LIKE AN ANIMAL OF PREY.. THE BATMAN WATCHES HIS QUARRY.
–FOLLOWING HIS FIANCEE, THE BATMAN, IN REALITY BRUCE WAYNE, HAS TRAILED A SINISTER FIGURE, COWLED LIKE A MONK, INTO HUNGARY ...
ON THE END OF A SILKEN CORD, THE BATMAN RACES OVERHEAD...
...AND DROPS LIKE A HUGE BAT –
ONTO A SPEEDING CARRIAGE.

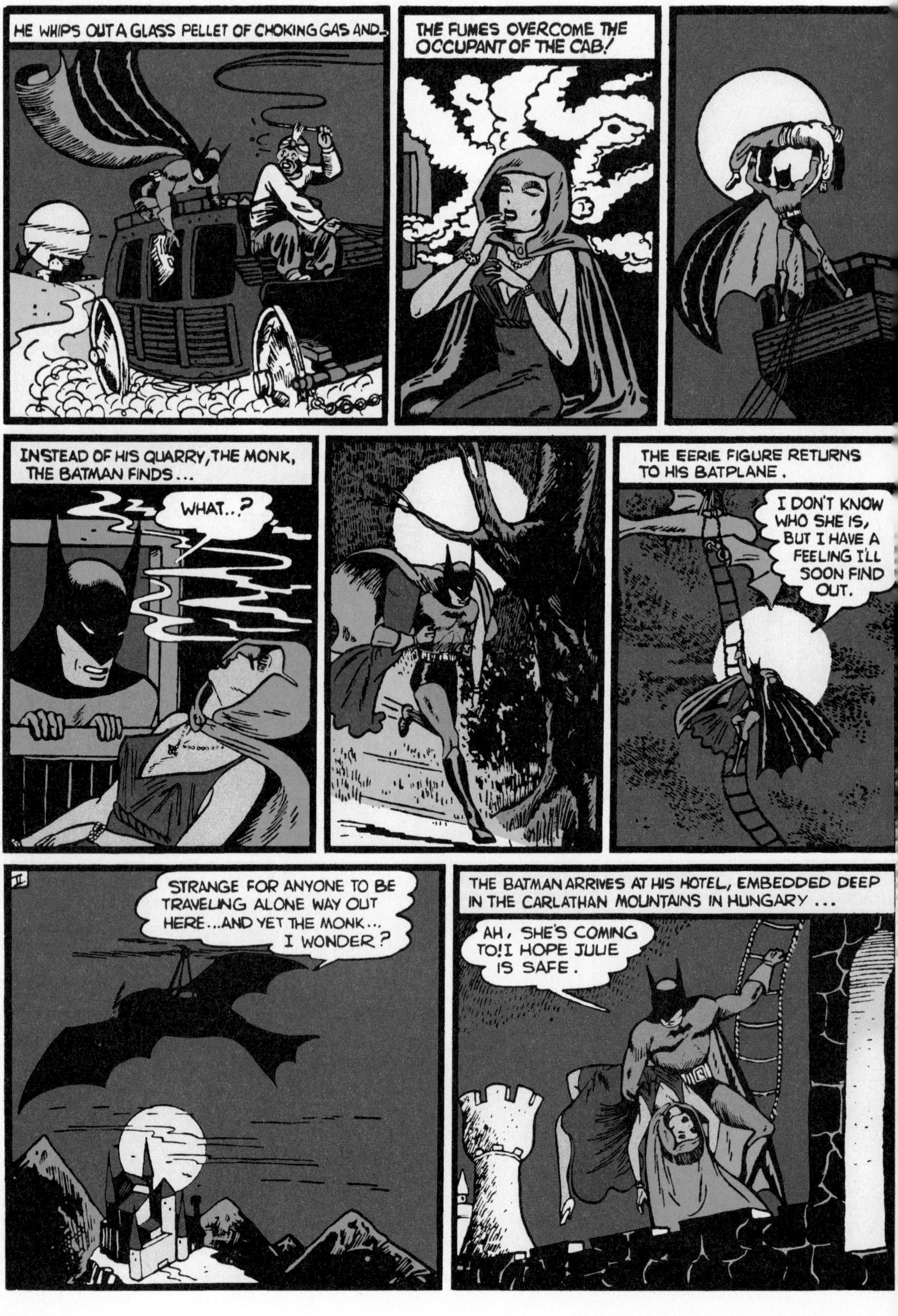
HE WHIPS OUT A GLASS PELLET OF CHOKING GAS AND...
THE FUMES OVERCOME THE OCCUPANT OF THE CAB!
INSTEAD OF HIS QUARRY, THE MONK, THE BATMAN FINDS...
WHAT...?
THE EERIE FIGURE RETURNS TO HIS BATPLANE.
I DON'T KNOW WHO SHE IS, BUT I HAVE A FEELING I'LL SOON FIND OUT.
STRANGE FOR ANYONE TO BE TRAVELING ALONE WAY OUT HERE...AND YET THE MONK... I WONDER?
THE BATMAN ARRIVES AT HIS HOTEL, EMBEDDED DEEP IN THE CARLATHAN MOUNTAINS IN HUNGARY...
AH, SHE'S COMING TO! I HOPE JULIE IS SAFE.

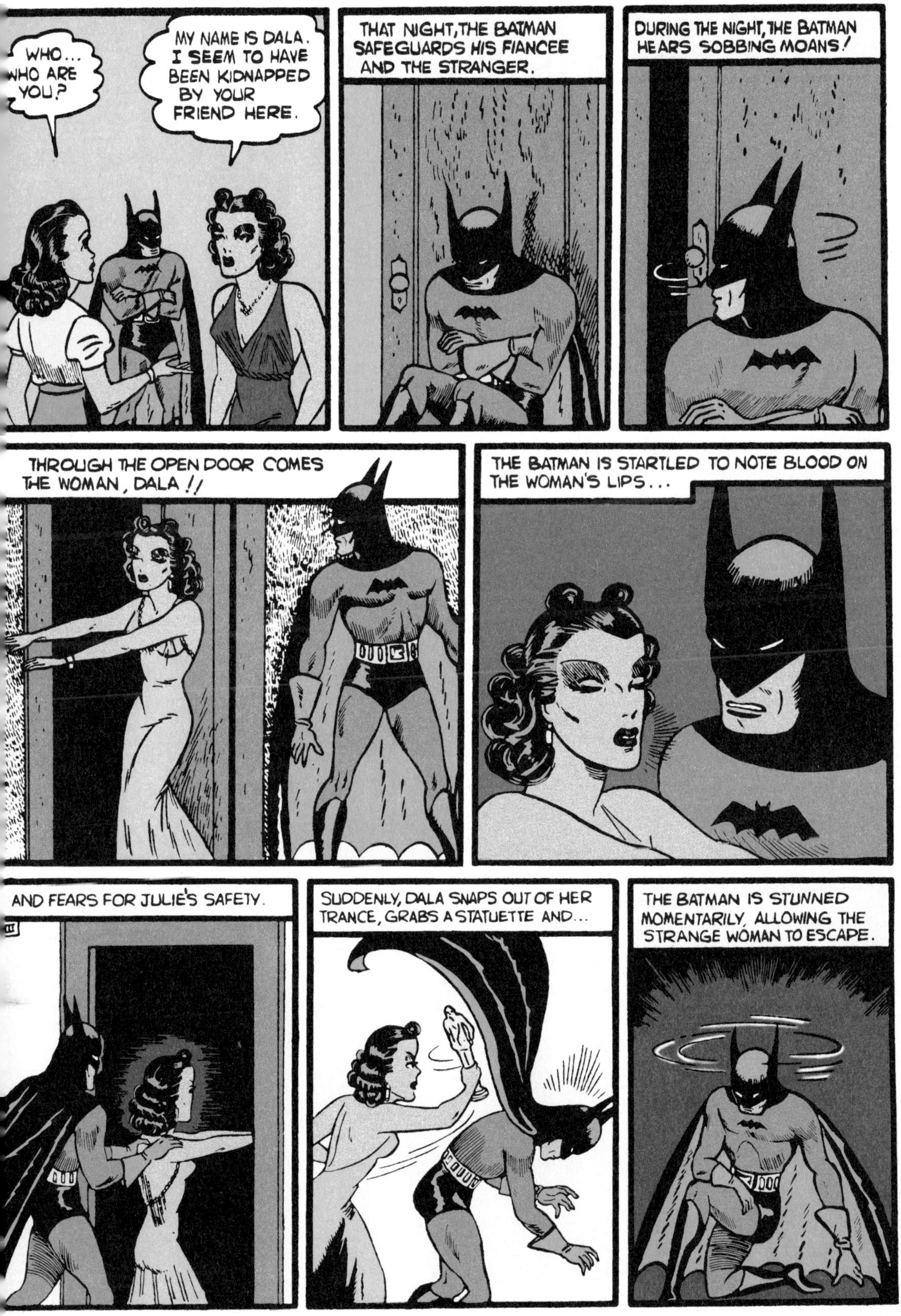
WHO... WHO ARE YOU?
MY NAME IS DALA. I SEEM TO HAVE BEEN KIDNAPPED BY YOUR FRIEND HERE.
THAT NIGHT, THE BATMAN SAFEGUARDS HIS FIANCEE AND THE STRANGER.
DURING THE NIGHT, THE BATMAN HEARS SOBBING MOANS!
THROUGH THE OPEN DOOR COMES THE WOMAN, DALA!!
THE BATMAN IS STARTLED TO NOTE BLOOD ON THE WOMAN'S LIPS...
AND FEARS FOR JULIE'S SAFETY.
SUDDENLY, DALA SNAPS OUT OF HER TRANCE, GRABS A STATUETTE AND...
THE BATMAN IS STUNNED MOMENTARILY, ALLOWING THE STRANGE WOMAN TO ESCAPE.

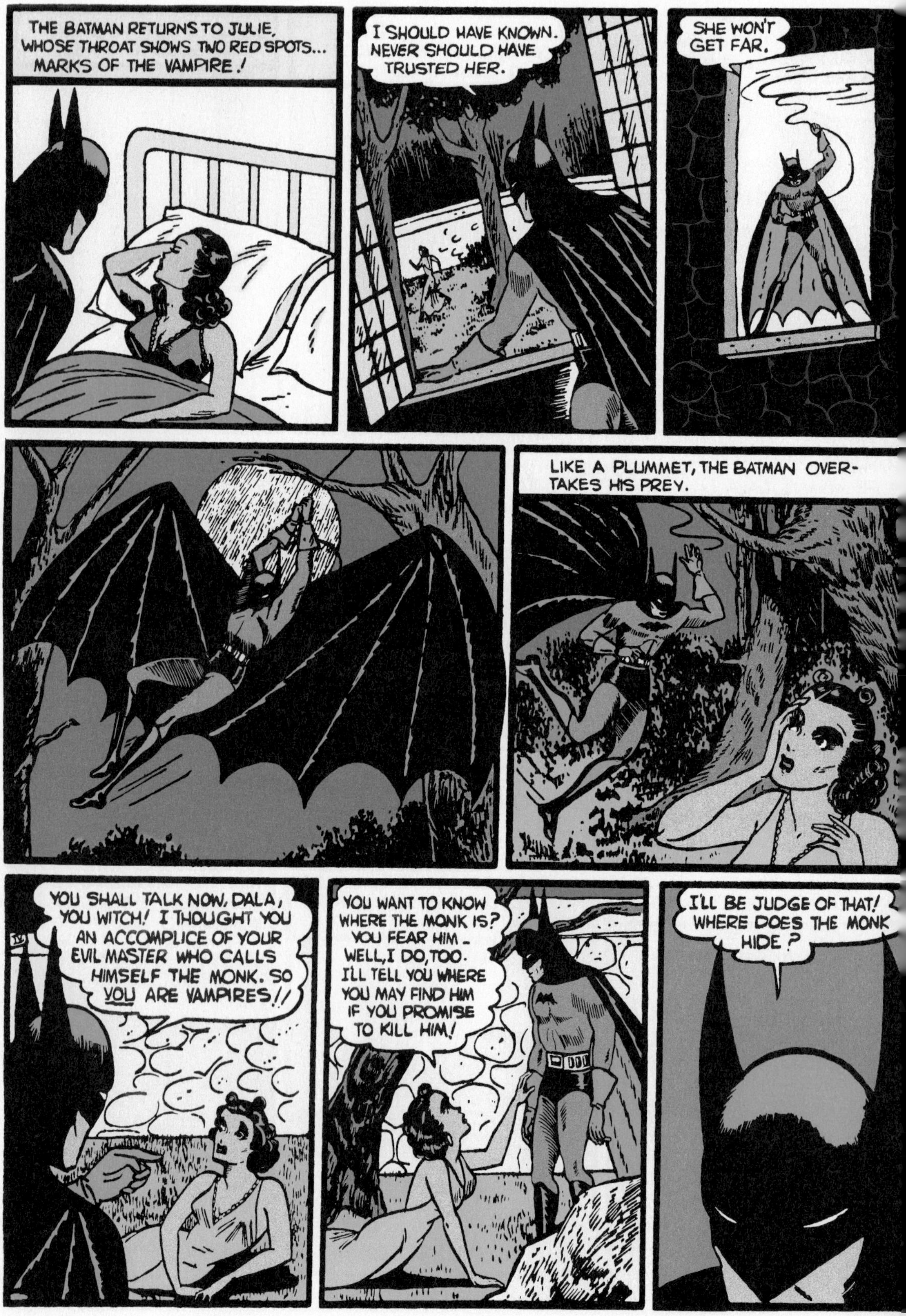
THE BATMAN RETURNS TO JULIE, WHOSE THROAT SHOWS TWO RED SPOTS... MARKS OF THE VAMPIRE!
I SHOULD HAVE KNOWN. NEVER SHOULD HAVE TRUSTED HER.
SHE WON'T GET FAR.
LIKE A PLUMMET, THE BATMAN OVER-TAKES HIS PREY.
YOU SHALL TALK NOW, DALA, YOU WITCH! I THOUGHT YOU AN ACCOMPLICE OF YOUR EVIL MASTER WHO CALLS HIMSELF THE MONK. SO YOU ARE VAMPIRES!!
YOU WANT TO KNOW WHERE THE MONK IS? YOU FEAR HIM - WELL, I DO, TOO. I'LL TELL YOU WHERE YOU MAY FIND HIM IF YOU PROMISE TO KILL HIM!
I'LL BE JUDGE OF THAT! WHERE DOES THE MONK HIDE?

IN THE LOST MOUNTAINS OF CATHALA BY THE TURBULENT RIVER DESS, I SHALL GUIDE YOU.

THIS MONEY WILL SAFE GUARD YOU. I AM GOING. YOU MUST FIGHT AGAINST THE POWER THAT CALLS YOU TO THIS MONK!

OH — I WILL FIGHT. I WILL..., BUT I AM SO AFRAID WITHOUT YOU!!

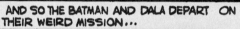

AND SO THE BATMAN AND DALA DEPART ON THEIR WEIRD MISSION...

TOWARD THE STRONGHOLD OF THE 'MONK' WINGS THE EERIE BATPLANE...

SUDDENLY, THE BATMAN SEES...

A GREAT SILVER NET THAT SEEMS TO OPERATE BY MAGIC, WHICH DRAGS THE BATPLANE EARTHWARD

YOU FOOL! PITTING YOUR PUNY BODY AGAINST THE MIGHTY MONK.

MY FRIEND, THE BATMAN! SO YOU ARE STILL ALIVE! AH...DALA..WELCOME.

BY HIS MARVELOUS HYPNOTIC POWERS, THE MONK SLOWLY OVERPOWERS THE BATMAN –

YOU MUST GET RID OF THIS BATMAN.

I THINK A TASTE OF THE WERE WOLF DEN WOULD HELP.

WAIT...YOUR VENGEANCE MUST BE PERFECT.

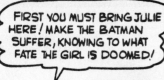

FIRST YOU MUST BRING JULIE HERE! MAKE THE BATMAN SUFFER, KNOWING TO WHAT FATE THE GIRL IS DOOMED!

BY A TREMENDOUS CONCENTRATION OF WILL, THE MONK FORCES HIS POWER THROUGH SPACE.

THE 'MONK'S' MIND FASTENS ON JULIE'S WILL, COMPELLING HER TO COME TO HIM!

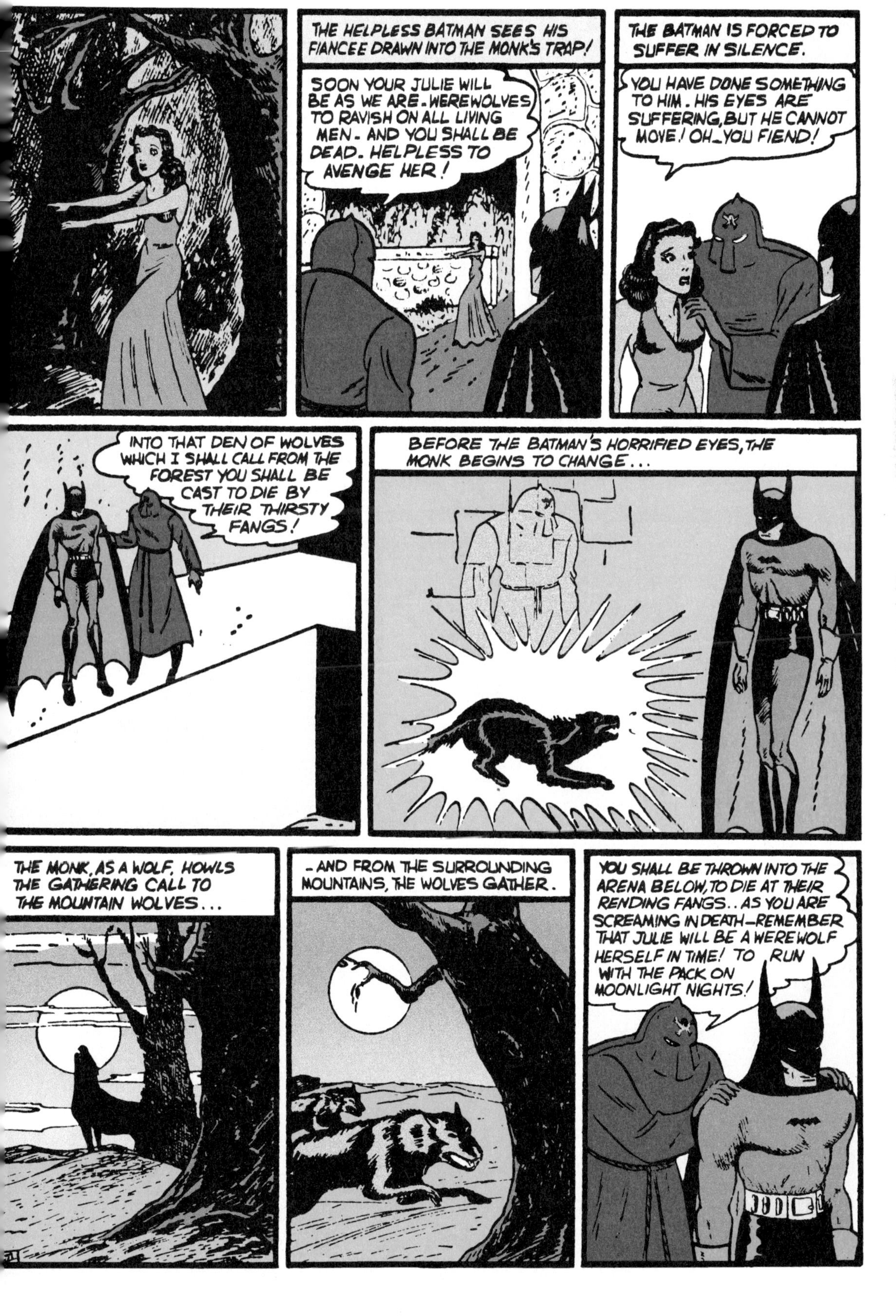
THE HELPLESS BATMAN SEES HIS FIANCEE DRAWN INTO THE MONK'S TRAP!
SOON YOUR JULIE WILL BE AS WE ARE - WEREWOLVES TO RAVISH ON ALL LIVING MEN - AND YOU SHALL BE DEAD - HELPLESS TO AVENGE HER!
THE BATMAN IS FORCED TO SUFFER IN SILENCE.
YOU HAVE DONE SOMETHING TO HIM. HIS EYES ARE SUFFERING, BUT HE CANNOT MOVE! OH-YOU FIEND!
INTO THAT DEN OF WOLVES WHICH I SHALL CALL FROM THE FOREST YOU SHALL BE CAST TO DIE BY THEIR THIRSTY FANGS!
BEFORE THE BATMAN'S HORRIFIED EYES, THE MONK BEGINS TO CHANGE...
THE MONK, AS A WOLF, HOWLS THE GATHERING CALL TO THE MOUNTAIN WOLVES...
- AND FROM THE SURROUNDING MOUNTAINS, THE WOLVES GATHER.
YOU SHALL BE THROWN INTO THE ARENA BELOW, TO DIE AT THEIR RENDING FANGS.. AS YOU ARE SCREAMING IN DEATH - REMEMBER THAT JULIE WILL BE A WEREWOLF HERSELF IN TIME! TO RUN WITH THE PACK ON MOONLIGHT NIGHTS!

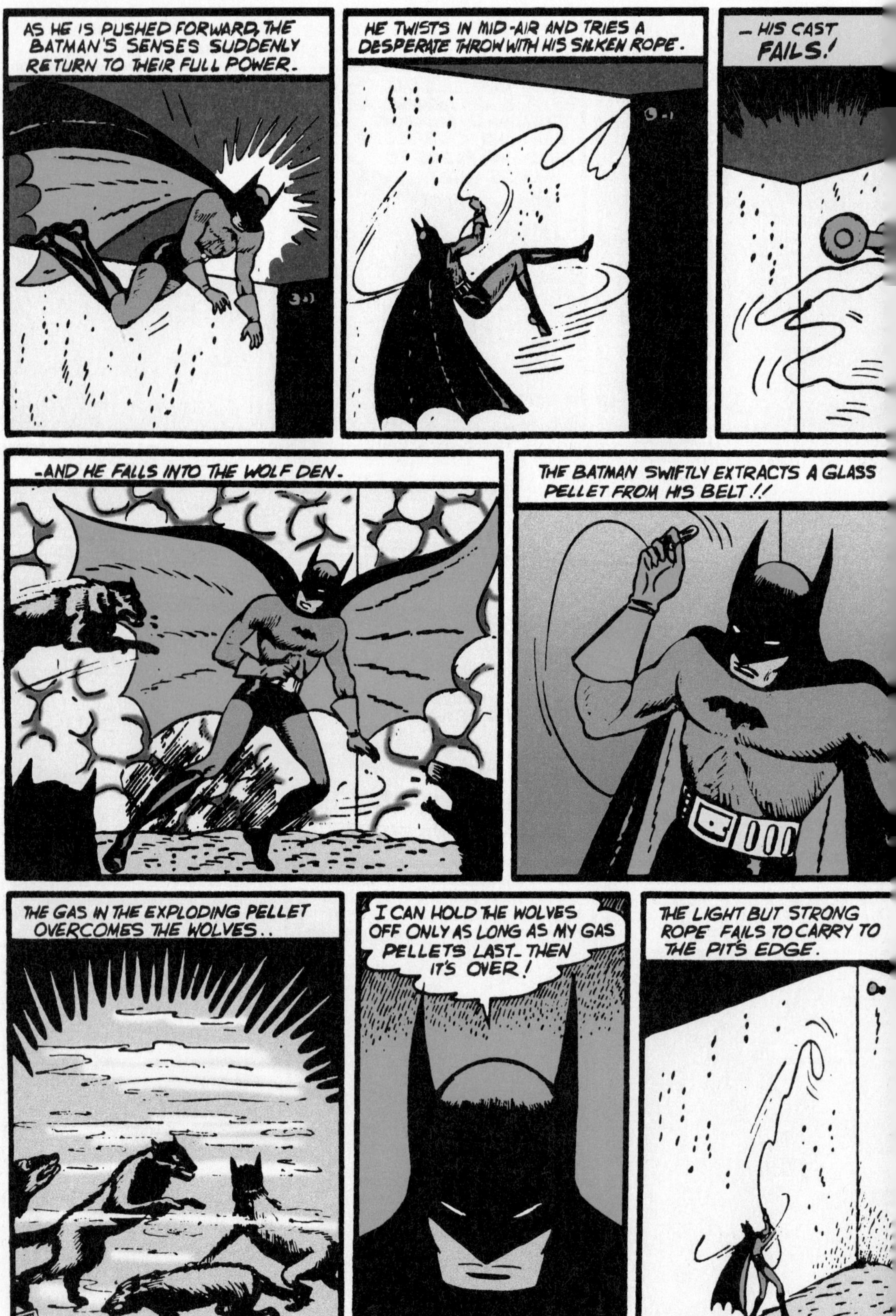
AS HE IS PUSHED FORWARD, THE BATMAN'S SENSES SUDDENLY RETURN TO THEIR FULL POWER.
HE TWISTS IN MID-AIR AND TRIES A DESPERATE THROW WITH HIS SILKEN ROPE.
— HIS CAST FAILS!
-AND HE FALLS INTO THE WOLF DEN.
THE BATMAN SWIFTLY EXTRACTS A GLASS PELLET FROM HIS BELT!!
THE GAS IN THE EXPLODING PELLET OVERCOMES THE WOLVES..
I CAN HOLD THE WOLVES OFF ONLY AS LONG AS MY GAS PELLETS LAST_ THEN IT'S OVER!
THE LIGHT BUT STRONG ROPE FAILS TO CARRY TO THE PIT'S EDGE.

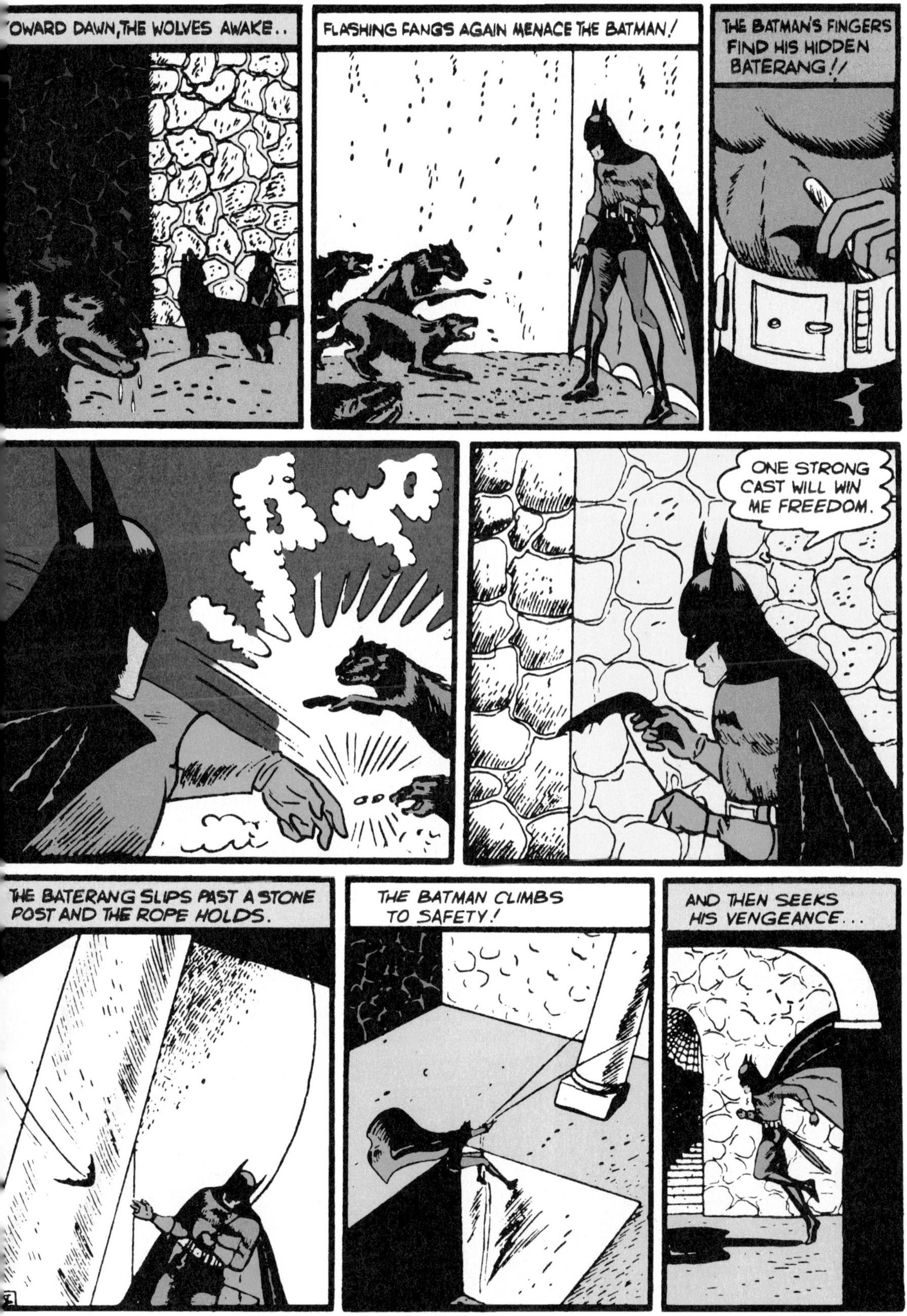

TOWARD DAWN, THE WOLVES AWAKE..
FLASHING FANGS AGAIN MENACE THE BATMAN!
THE BATMAN'S FINGERS FIND HIS HIDDEN BATERANG!!
ONE STRONG CAST WILL WIN ME FREEDOM.
THE BATERANG SLIPS PAST A STONE POST AND THE ROPE HOLDS.
THE BATMAN CLIMBS TO SAFETY!
AND THEN SEEKS HIS VENGEANCE...

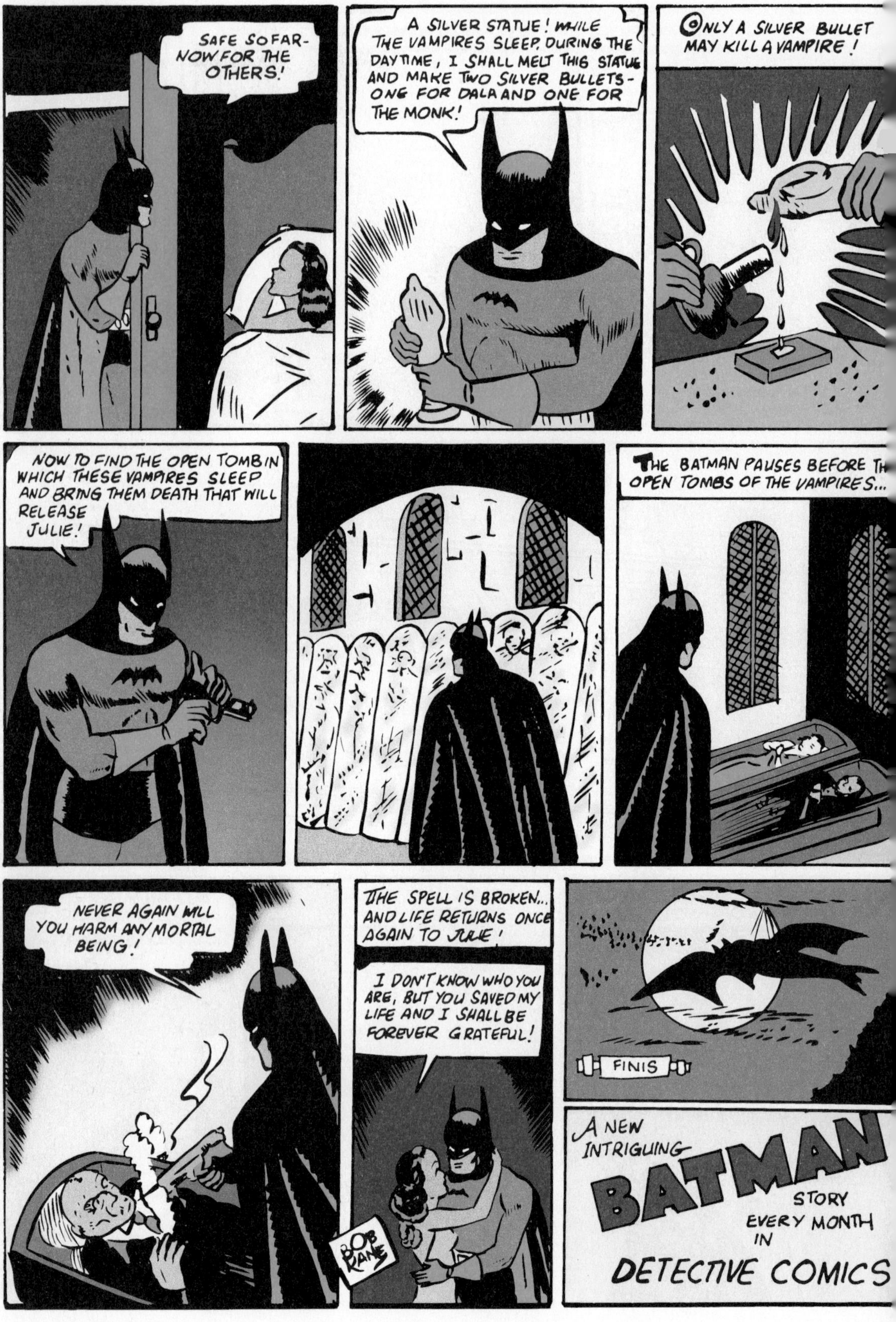
SAFE SO FAR-
NOW FOR THE OTHERS!
A SILVER STATUE! WHILE THE VAMPIRES SLEEP, DURING THE DAYTIME, I SHALL MELT THIS STATUE AND MAKE TWO SILVER BULLETS - ONE FOR DALA AND ONE FOR THE MONK!
ONLY A SILVER BULLET MAY KILL A VAMPIRE!
NOW TO FIND THE OPEN TOMB IN WHICH THESE VAMPIRES SLEEP AND BRING THEM DEATH THAT WILL RELEASE JULIE!
THE BATMAN PAUSES BEFORE TH
OPEN TOMBS OF THE VAMPIRES...
NEVER AGAIN WILL YOU HARM ANY MORTAL BEING!
THE SPELL IS BROKEN... AND LIFE RETURNS ONCE AGAIN TO JULIE!
I DON'T KNOW WHO YOU ARE, BUT YOU SAVED MY LIFE AND I SHALL BE FOREVER GRATEFUL!
BOB KANE
FINIS
A NEW INTRIGUING
BATMAN
STORY
EVERY MONTH
IN
DETECTIVE COMICS

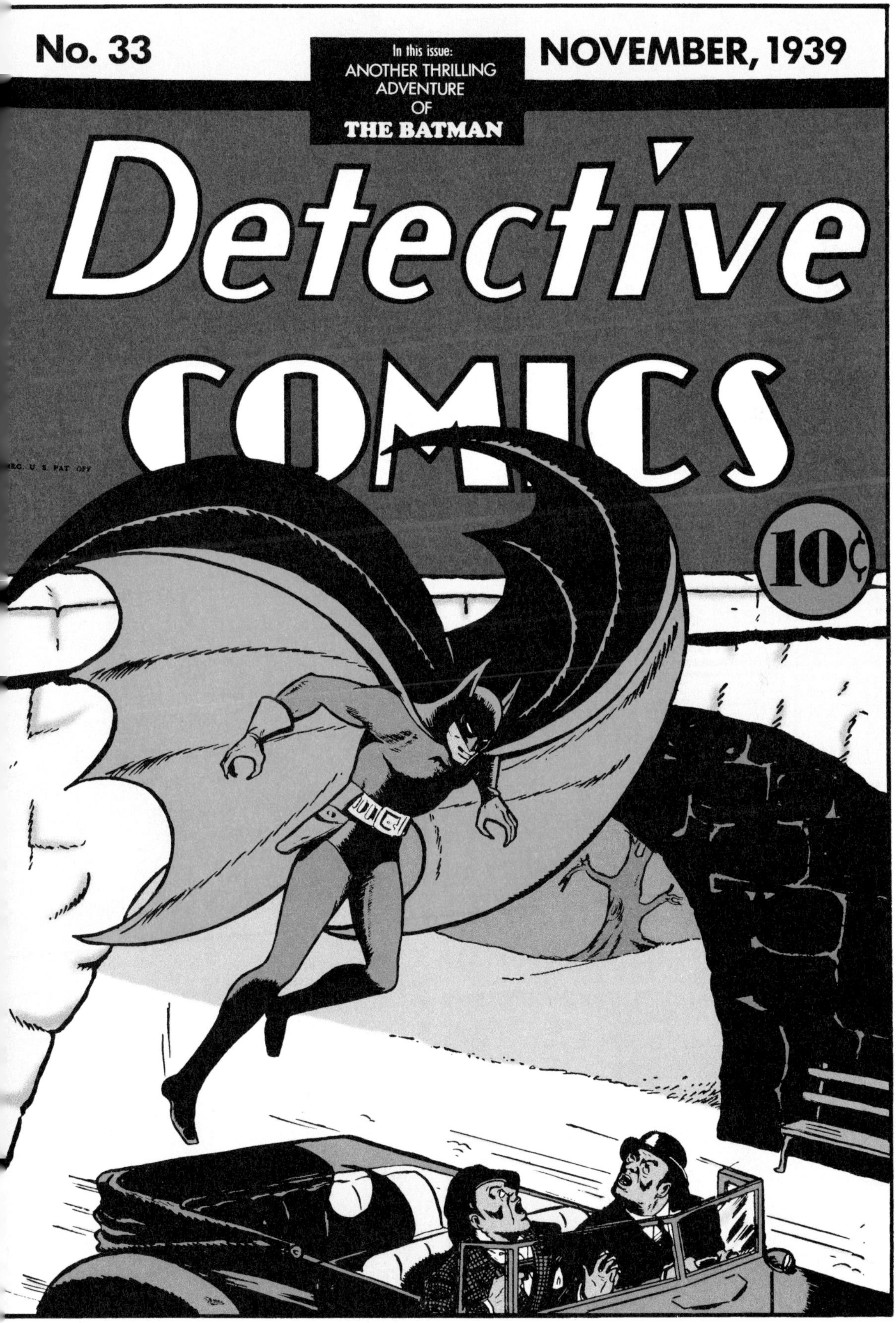
No. 33
In this issue:
ANOTHER THRILLING
ADVENTURE
OF
THE BATMAN
NOVEMBER, 1939
Detective
COMICS
10¢

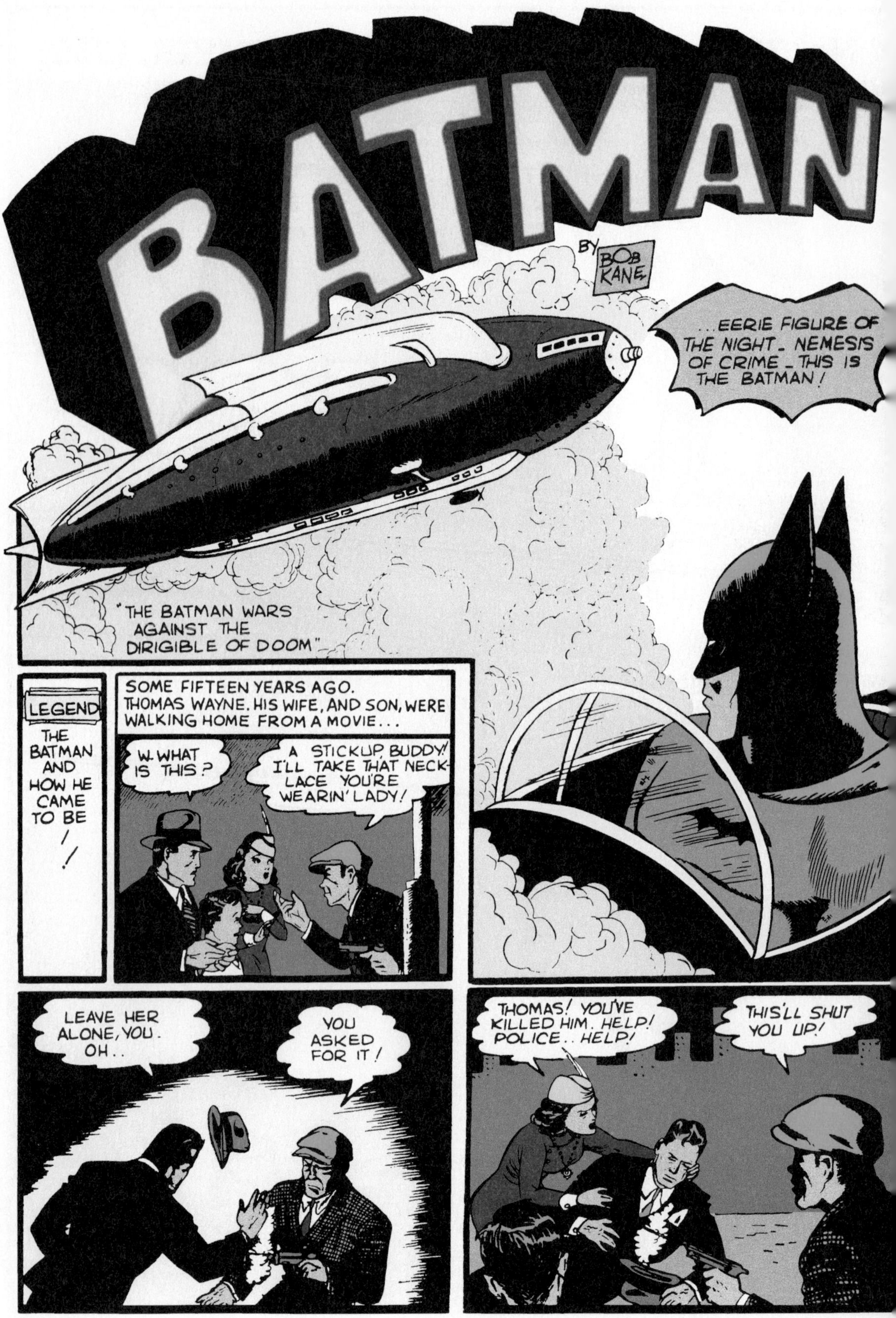
BATMAN
BY BOB KANE
...EERIE FIGURE OF THE NIGHT_ NEMESIS OF CRIME_ THIS IS THE BATMAN!
"THE BATMAN WARS AGAINST THE DIRIGIBLE OF DOOM"
LEGEND THE BATMAN AND HOW HE CAME TO BE !
SOME FIFTEEN YEARS AGO. THOMAS WAYNE. HIS WIFE, AND SON, WERE WALKING HOME FROM A MOVIE...
W. WHAT IS THIS?
A STICKUP, BUDDY! I'LL TAKE THAT NECK-LACE YOU'RE WEARIN' LADY!
LEAVE HER ALONE, YOU. OH..
YOU ASKED FOR IT!
THOMAS! YOU'VE KILLED HIM. HELP! POLICE.. HELP!
THIS'LL SHUT YOU UP!

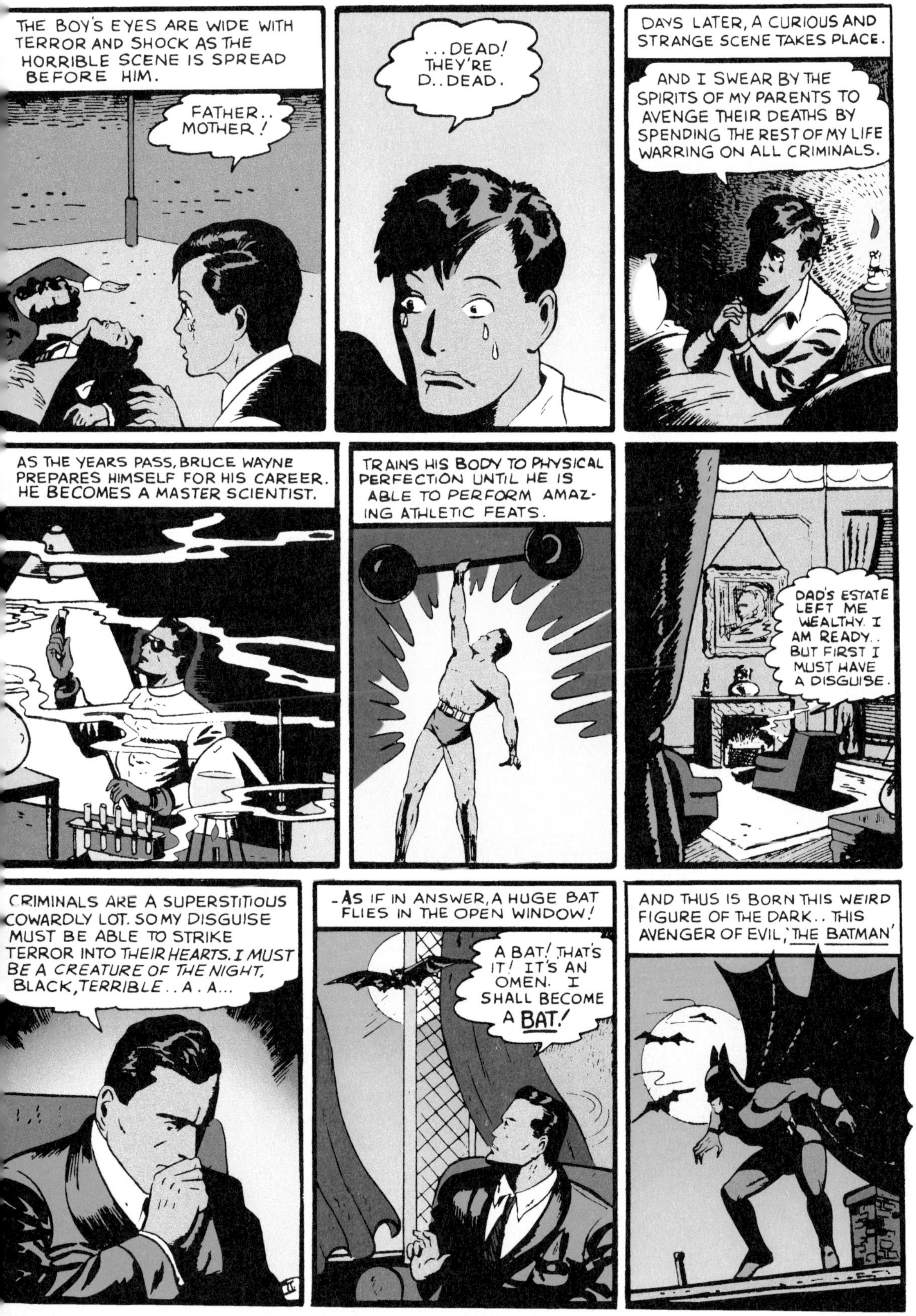
THE BOY'S EYES ARE WIDE WITH TERROR AND SHOCK AS THE HORRIBLE SCENE IS SPREAD BEFORE HIM.
FATHER.. MOTHER!
...DEAD! THEY'RE D..DEAD.
DAYS LATER, A CURIOUS AND STRANGE SCENE TAKES PLACE.
AND I SWEAR BY THE SPIRITS OF MY PARENTS TO AVENGE THEIR DEATHS BY SPENDING THE REST OF MY LIFE WARRING ON ALL CRIMINALS.
AS THE YEARS PASS, BRUCE WAYNE PREPARES HIMSELF FOR HIS CAREER. HE BECOMES A MASTER SCIENTIST.
TRAINS HIS BODY TO PHYSICAL PERFECTION UNTIL HE IS ABLE TO PERFORM AMAZ-ING ATHLETIC FEATS.
DAD'S ESTATE LEFT ME WEALTHY. I AM READY.. BUT FIRST I MUST HAVE A DISGUISE.
CRIMINALS ARE A SUPERSTITIOUS COWARDLY LOT. SO MY DISGUISE MUST BE ABLE TO STRIKE TERROR INTO THEIR HEARTS. I MUST BE A CREATURE OF THE NIGHT, BLACK, TERRIBLE..A.A...
-AS IF IN ANSWER, A HUGE BAT FLIES IN THE OPEN WINDOW!
A BAT! THAT'S IT! IT'S AN OMEN. I SHALL BECOME A BAT!
AND THUS IS BORN THIS WEIRD FIGURE OF THE DARK.. THIS AVENGER OF EVIL, 'THE BATMAN'

NIGHTFALL. BRUCE WAYNE WALKS THE CROWDED STREETS OF DOWNTOWN MANHATTAN.

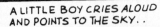

A LITTLE BOY CRIES ALOUD AND POINTS TO THE SKY..

LOOK, MOM! A DIRIGIBLE.

STRANGE-LOOKING SHIP. HMM.. MORE LIKE A ROCKET SHIP.

SUDDENLY RED BEAMS OF LIGHT SHOOT FROM THE SHIP.

RED LIGHTS! WHAT IS IT? HELP! I'M GOING BLIND!

AS THE RAYS STRIKE, THE BUILDINGS EXPLODE. HURLING THEIR WRECKAGE UPON THE CROWDED STREETS BELOW.

HELP!

HELP! THE END OF THE WORLD! HELP!

HELP!

HELP!

HELP! MAMMA, SAVE ME! HELP!!

SUDDENLY FROM THE CRAFT..

WE COME TO RULE THE WORLD. DO NOT RESIST US. OR THE RAYS STRIKE AGAIN.. WE THE 'SCARLET HORDE' WARN YOU..

THE DIRIGIBLE GONE. RESCUE WORK BEGINS. BRUCE WAYNE HELPS.

EASY, OLD MAN.

THE HOME OF BRUCE WAYNE.

-AND THE RESCUE WORK IS STILL GOING ON. THOUSANDS ARE DEAD.. ETC..ETC..

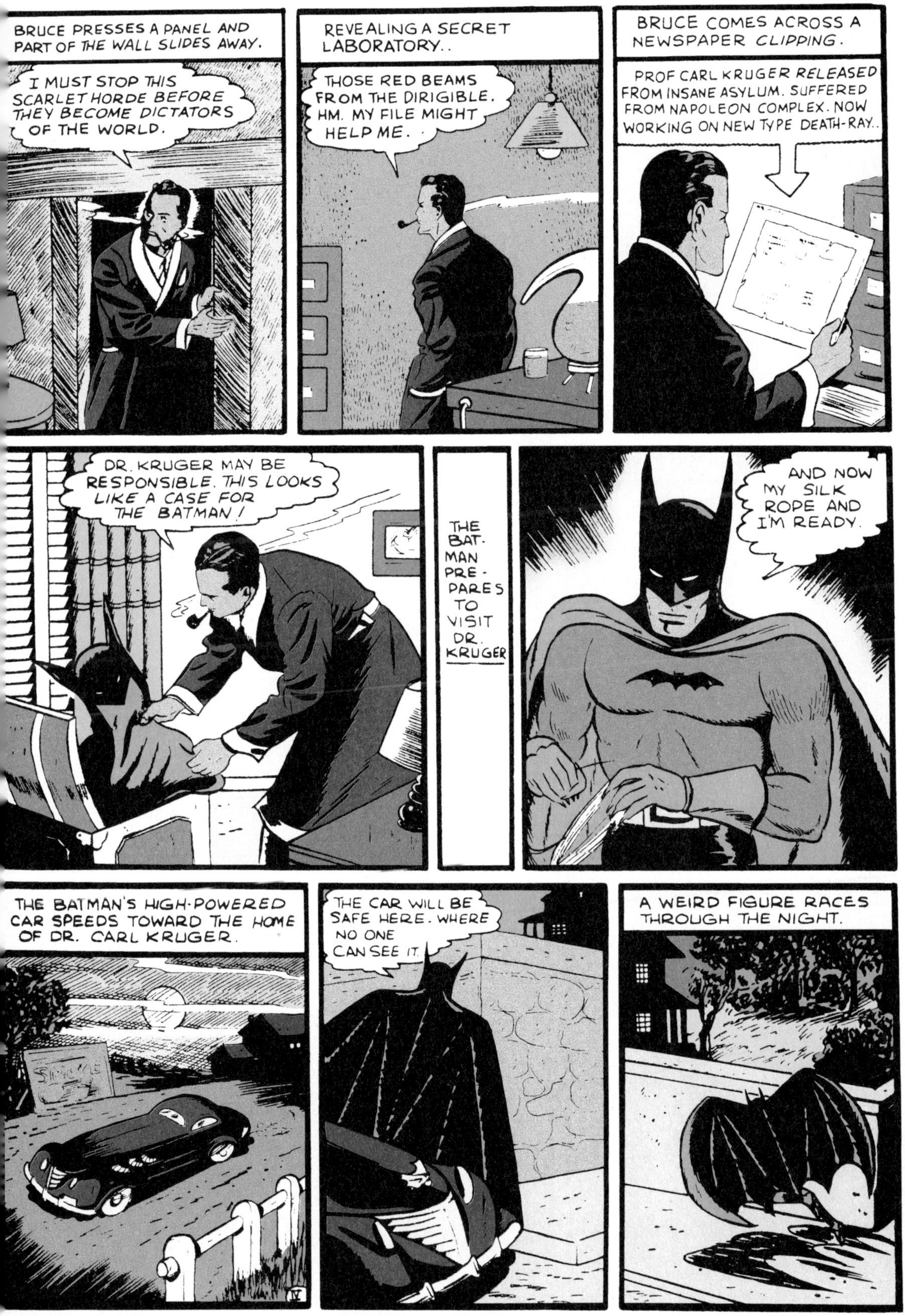

BRUCE PRESSES A PANEL AND PART OF THE WALL SLIDES AWAY.
I MUST STOP THIS SCARLET HORDE BEFORE THEY BECOME DICTATORS OF THE WORLD.
REVEALING A SECRET LABORATORY..
THOSE RED BEAMS FROM THE DIRIGIBLE. HM. MY FILE MIGHT HELP ME.
BRUCE COMES ACROSS A NEWSPAPER CLIPPING.
PROF CARL KRUGER RELEASED FROM INSANE ASYLUM. SUFFERED FROM NAPOLEON COMPLEX. NOW WORKING ON NEW TYPE DEATH-RAY..
DR. KRUGER MAY BE RESPONSIBLE. THIS LOOKS LIKE A CASE FOR THE BATMAN!
THE BATMAN PREPARES TO VISIT DR. KRUGER
AND NOW MY SILK ROPE AND I'M READY.
THE BATMAN'S HIGH-POWERED CAR SPEEDS TOWARD THE HOME OF DR. CARL KRUGER.
THE CAR WILL BE SAFE HERE. WHERE NO ONE CAN SEE IT.
A WEIRD FIGURE RACES THROUGH THE NIGHT.

A LIGHT! I'LL TRY THAT ROOM!

THINKS HE'S NAPOLEON. HMMM..

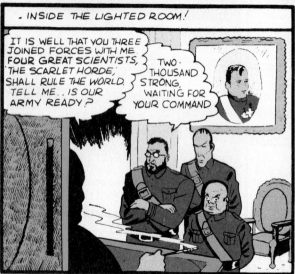

. INSIDE THE LIGHTED ROOM!

IT IS WELL THAT YOU THREE JOINED FORCES WITH ME. FOUR GREAT SCIENTISTS, THE SCARLET HORDE, SHALL RULE THE WORLD. TELL ME.. IS OUR ARMY READY?

TWO THOUSAND STRONG, WAITING FOR YOUR COMMAND

WHEN DO WE STRIKE?

IN TWO DAYS THE DEATH RAY STRIKES AGAIN. DURING THE PANIC OUR MEN WILL LOOT THE BANKS. AND WE WILL HAVE MONEY TO BUILD MORE DIRIGIBLES. YOU TRAVIS, BIXLEY, RYDER, WILL BE MY LIEUTENANTS..

NAPOLEON

AND I, CARL KRUGER, WILL BE DICTATOR OF THE WORLD!

THE THREE MEN LEAVE THE HOUSE OF DR. KRUGER.

MASTER OF THE WORLD. ANOTHER NAPOLEON— AND NO ONE CAN STOP ME!

PERHAPS, I CAN STOP YOU!

THE BATMAN!

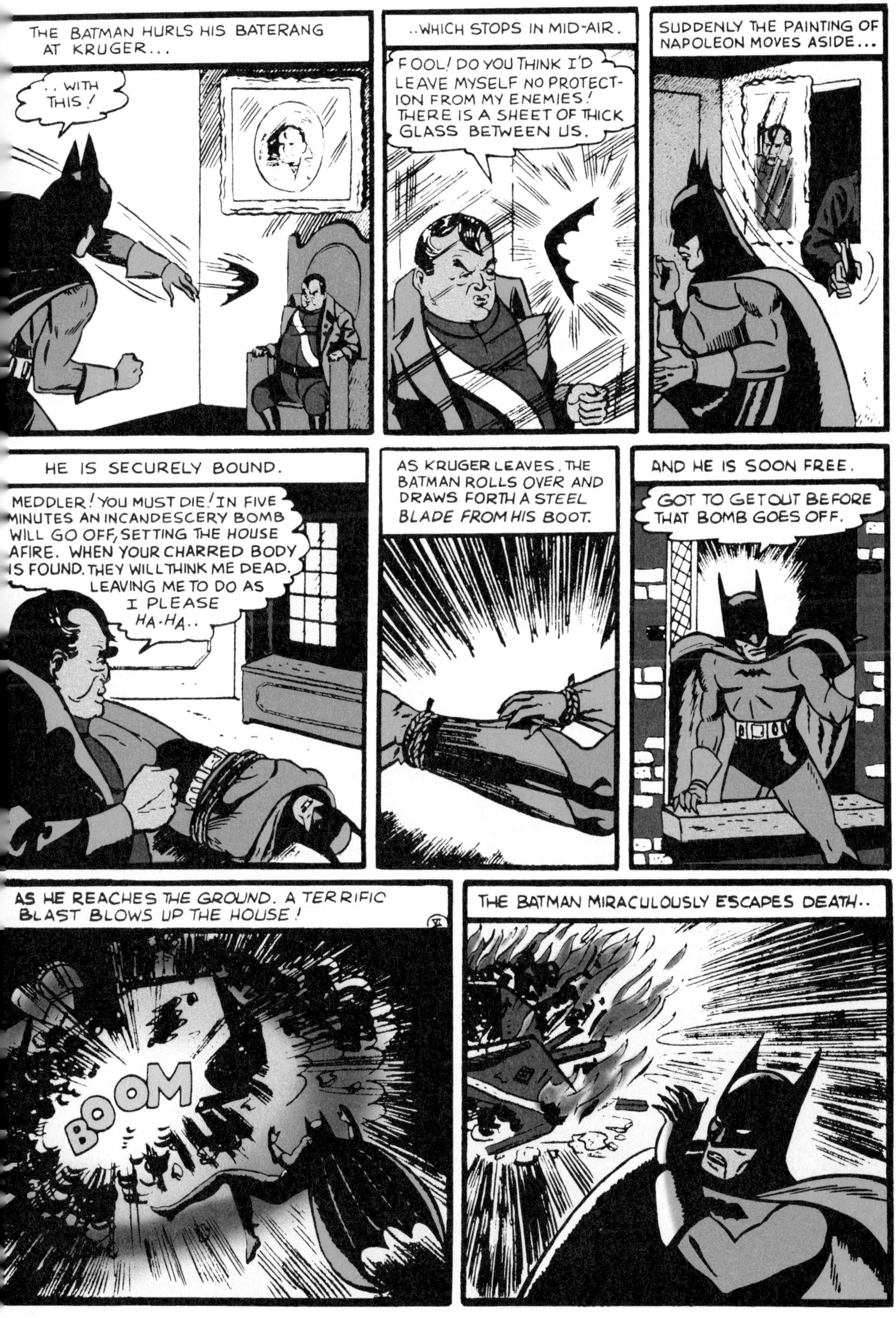
THE BATMAN HURLS HIS BATERANG AT KRUGER...
..WITH THIS!
..WHICH STOPS IN MID-AIR.
FOOL! DO YOU THINK I'D LEAVE MYSELF NO PROTECTION FROM MY ENEMIES! THERE IS A SHEET OF THICK GLASS BETWEEN US.
SUDDENLY THE PAINTING OF NAPOLEON MOVES ASIDE...
HE IS SECURELY BOUND.
MEDDLER! YOU MUST DIE! IN FIVE MINUTES AN INCANDESCERY BOMB WILL GO OFF, SETTING THE HOUSE AFIRE. WHEN YOUR CHARRED BODY IS FOUND. THEY WILL THINK ME DEAD. LEAVING ME TO DO AS I PLEASE HA-HA..
AS KRUGER LEAVES. THE BATMAN ROLLS OVER AND DRAWS FORTH A STEEL BLADE FROM HIS BOOT.
AND HE IS SOON FREE.
GOT TO GET OUT BEFORE THAT BOMB GOES OFF.
AS HE REACHES THE GROUND. A TERRIFIC BLAST BLOWS UP THE HOUSE!
BOOM
THE BATMAN MIRACULOUSLY ESCAPES DEATH..

WHEW! THAT WAS CLOSE. NOW HOME TO REST AND THINK.

THE FOLLOWING NIGHT... THE HOME OF RYDER, ONE OF KRUGER'S LIEUTENANTS.

WHAT IS IT? WHO.?

THE BATMAN.

YES.. AND VERY MUCH ALIVE. TELL THAT TO KRUGER. I SHALL BE BACK FOR YOU LATER. GOOD NIGHT.. AND PLEASANT DREAMS.

H. HE'S GONE. BUT HE SAID HE'D BE BACK FOR ME! I'VE GOT TO GET AWAY FROM HERE.

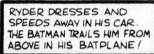

RYDER DRESSES AND SPEEDS AWAY IN HIS CAR. THE BATMAN TRAILS HIM FROM ABOVE IN HIS BATPLANE!

TO THE SECRET HANGAR OF THE DIRIGIBLE.

IT WORKED. HE'S LED ME STRAIGHT TO THE HIDEOUT OF KRUGER.

THE BATMAN BREAKS A GLASS VIAL. A THICK, BLACK, SMOKE POURS FORTH..

. WHICH SOON BLANKETS THE WHOLE PLANE!

THIS WILL PREVENT THE GUARDS FROM SEEING THE PLANE

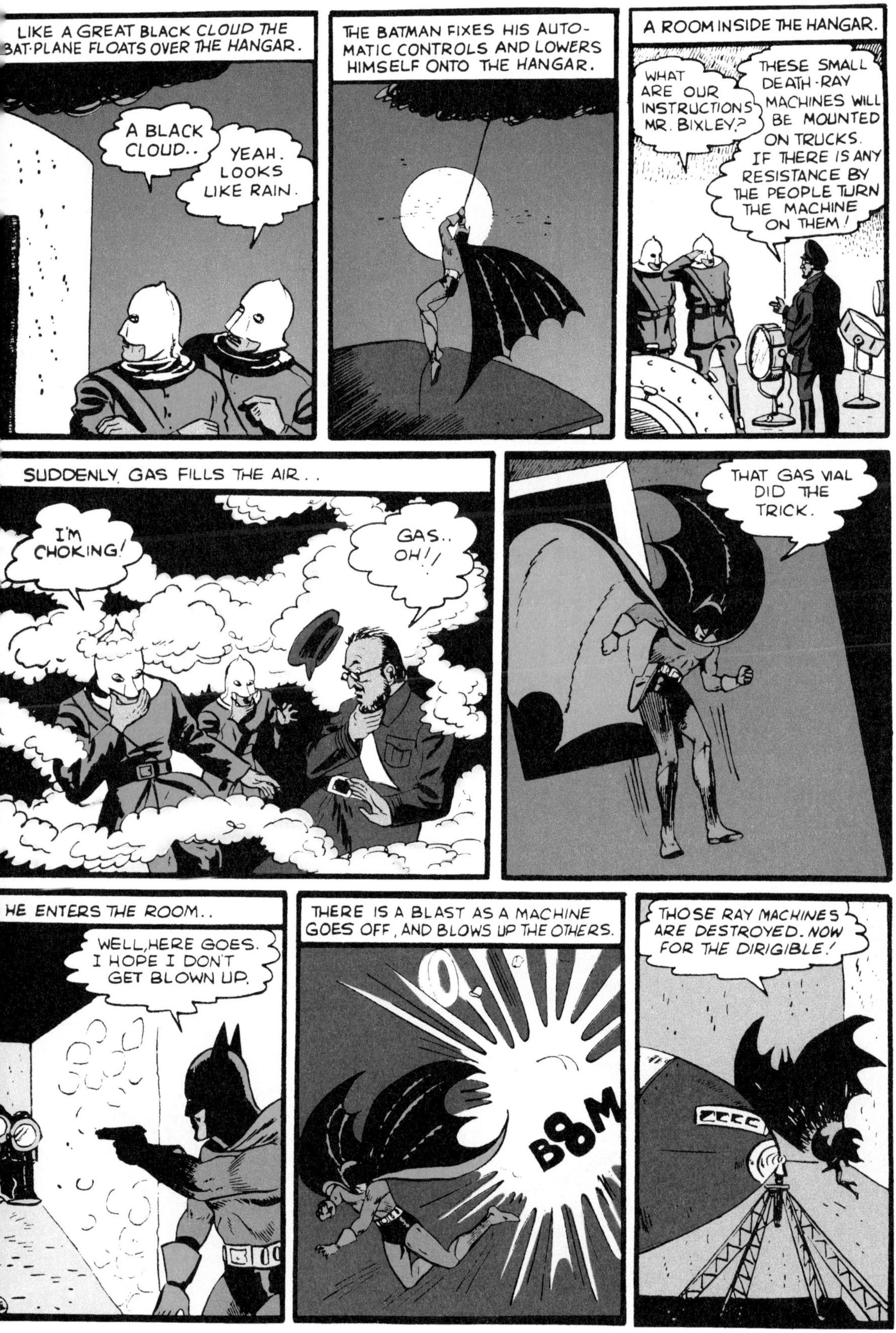

LIKE A GREAT BLACK CLOUD THE BAT-PLANE FLOATS OVER THE HANGAR.
A BLACK CLOUD..
YEAH. LOOKS LIKE RAIN.
THE BATMAN FIXES HIS AUTOMATIC CONTROLS AND LOWERS HIMSELF ONTO THE HANGAR.
A ROOM INSIDE THE HANGAR.
WHAT ARE OUR INSTRUCTIONS MR. BIXLEY?
THESE SMALL DEATH-RAY MACHINES WILL BE MOUNTED ON TRUCKS. IF THERE IS ANY RESISTANCE BY THE PEOPLE TURN THE MACHINE ON THEM!
SUDDENLY GAS FILLS THE AIR..
I'M CHOKING!
GAS.. OH!!
THAT GAS VIAL DID THE TRICK.
HE ENTERS THE ROOM..
WELL, HERE GOES. I HOPE I DON'T GET BLOWN UP.
THERE IS A BLAST AS A MACHINE GOES OFF, AND BLOWS UP THE OTHERS.
BOOM
THOSE RAY MACHINES ARE DESTROYED. NOW FOR THE DIRIGIBLE!

THE BATMAN PICKS UP AN AXE..

SUDDENLY, A SECRET DOOR OPENS. KRUGER POINTS HIS GUN.. FIRES !!

YOU ARE TOO LATE MY FRIEND-- TOO LATE !

THE BATMAN IS HIT--

HE IS FINISHED! --ANOTHER CONQUEST FOR NAPOLEON! HA-HA-HA!!

I WILL DESTROY HIS BODY WITH A DEATH-RAY MACHINE. GUARD! WATCH THIS BODY. I AM GOING TO GET THE ONE THAT IS LEFT !

KRUGER SOON RETURNS.

IT IS IRONICAL THAT HIS BODY SHALL BE DISPOSED OF WITH THE VERY MACHINE HE TRIED TO DESTROY!

THE DEATH RAY STRIKES THE BATMAN--

THERE IS A BLAST. AND WHERE ONCE HAD BEEN THE BODY OF THE BATMAN-- A HEAP OF ASHES.

MY FUSION OF OZONE GAS AND THE GAMMA RAY HAS AT LAST ELIMINATED THE ONE MAN WHO STOOD IN MY PATH.

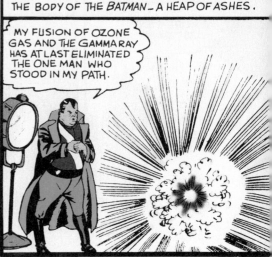

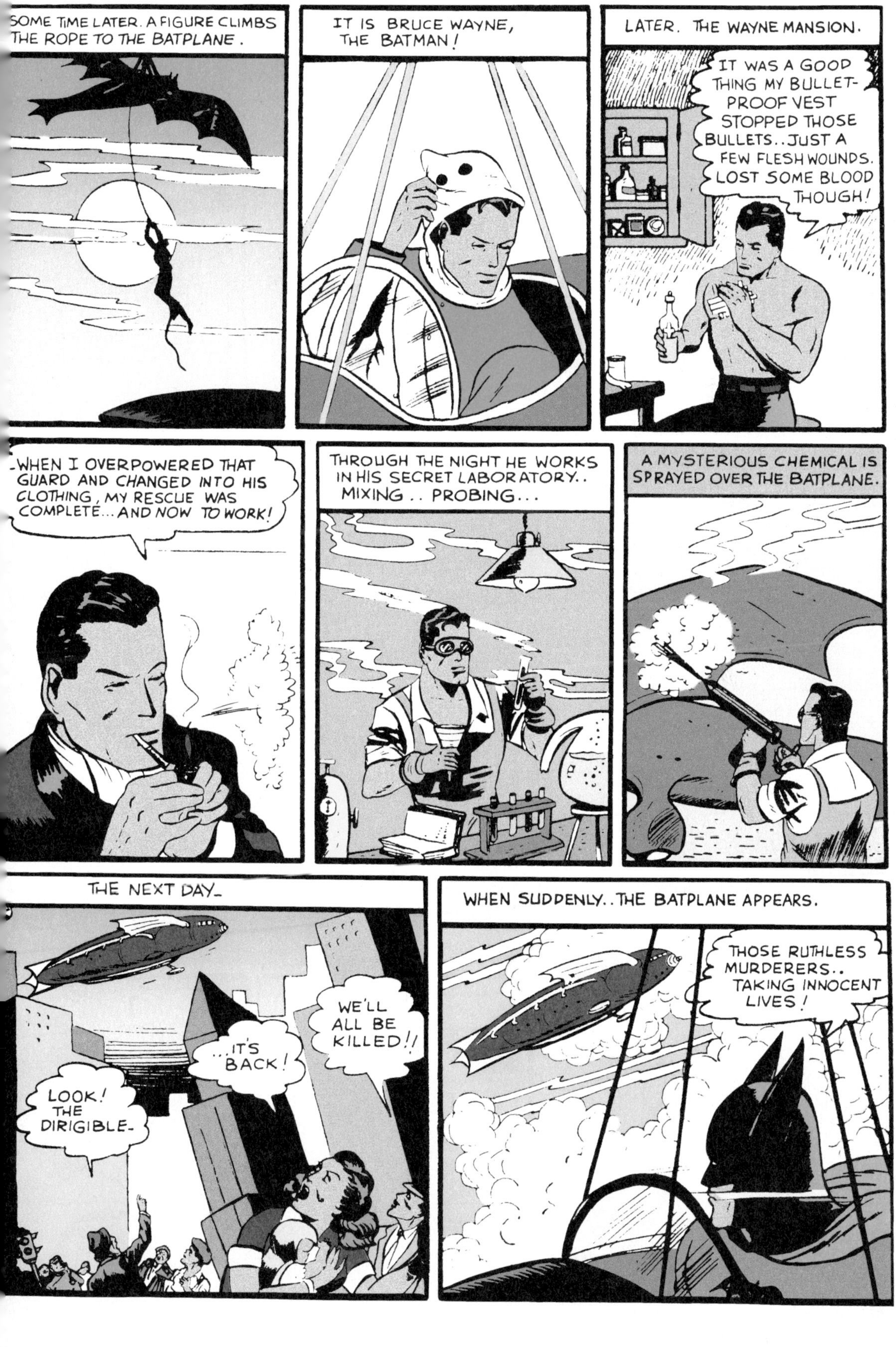
SOME TIME LATER. A FIGURE CLIMBS THE ROPE TO THE BATPLANE.
IT IS BRUCE WAYNE, THE BATMAN!
LATER. THE WAYNE MANSION.
IT WAS A GOOD THING MY BULLET-PROOF VEST STOPPED THOSE BULLETS..JUST A FEW FLESH WOUNDS. LOST SOME BLOOD THOUGH!
-WHEN I OVERPOWERED THAT GUARD AND CHANGED INTO HIS CLOTHING, MY RESCUE WAS COMPLETE...AND NOW TO WORK!
THROUGH THE NIGHT HE WORKS IN HIS SECRET LABORATORY.. MIXING .. PROBING...
A MYSTERIOUS CHEMICAL IS SPRAYED OVER THE BATPLANE.
THE NEXT DAY-
LOOK! THE DIRIGIBLE-
..IT'S BACK!
WE'LL ALL BE KILLED!!
WHEN SUDDENLY..THE BATPLANE APPEARS.
THOSE RUTHLESS MURDERERS.. TAKING INNOCENT LIVES!

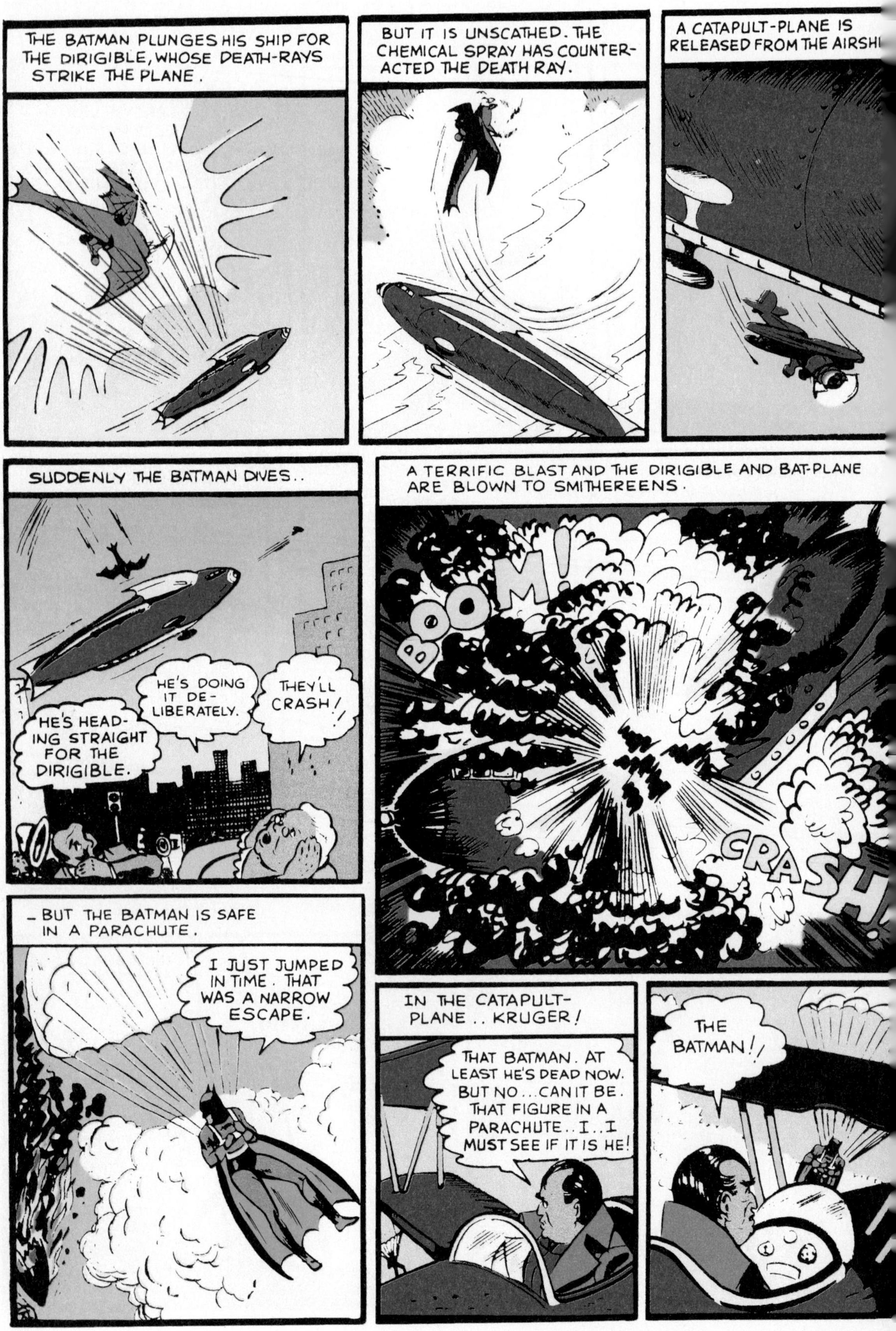
THE BATMAN PLUNGES HIS SHIP FOR THE DIRIGIBLE, WHOSE DEATH-RAYS STRIKE THE PLANE.
BUT IT IS UNSCATHED. THE CHEMICAL SPRAY HAS COUNTER-ACTED THE DEATH RAY.
A CATAPULT-PLANE IS RELEASED FROM THE AIRSHI
SUDDENLY THE BATMAN DIVES..
HE'S HEADING STRAIGHT FOR THE DIRIGIBLE.
HE'S DOING IT DE-LIBERATELY.
THEY'LL CRASH!
A TERRIFIC BLAST AND THE DIRIGIBLE AND BAT-PLANE ARE BLOWN TO SMITHEREENS.
BOOM!
CRASH!
-BUT THE BATMAN IS SAFE IN A PARACHUTE.
I JUST JUMPED IN TIME. THAT WAS A NARROW ESCAPE.
IN THE CATAPULT-PLANE.. KRUGER!
THAT BATMAN. AT LEAST HE'S DEAD NOW. BUT NO...CAN IT BE. THAT FIGURE IN A PARACHUTE..I..I MUST SEE IF IT IS HE!
THE BATMAN!!

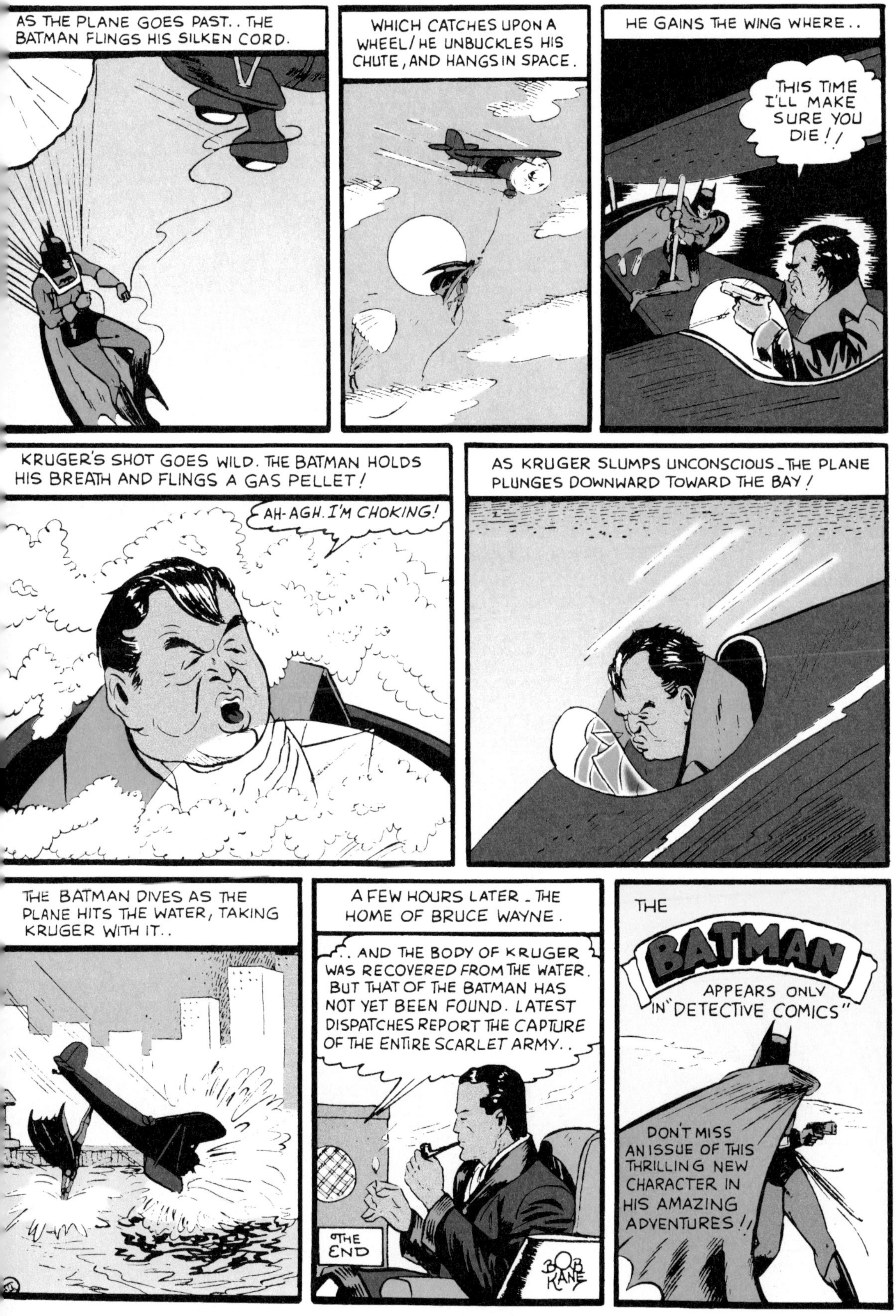
AS THE PLANE GOES PAST.. THE BATMAN FLINGS HIS SILKEN CORD.
WHICH CATCHES UPON A WHEEL/ HE UNBUCKLES HIS CHUTE, AND HANGS IN SPACE.
HE GAINS THE WING WHERE..
THIS TIME I'LL MAKE SURE YOU DIE!!
KRUGER'S SHOT GOES WILD. THE BATMAN HOLDS HIS BREATH AND FLINGS A GAS PELLET!
AH-AGH. I'M CHOKING!
AS KRUGER SLUMPS UNCONSCIOUS_THE PLANE PLUNGES DOWNWARD TOWARD THE BAY!
THE BATMAN DIVES AS THE PLANE HITS THE WATER, TAKING KRUGER WITH IT..
A FEW HOURS LATER_THE HOME OF BRUCE WAYNE.
.. AND THE BODY OF KRUGER WAS RECOVERED FROM THE WATER. BUT THAT OF THE BATMAN HAS NOT YET BEEN FOUND. LATEST DISPATCHES REPORT THE CAPTURE OF THE ENTIRE SCARLET ARMY..
THE END
BOB KANE
THE BATMAN APPEARS ONLY IN "DETECTIVE COMICS"
DON'T MISS AN ISSUE OF THIS THRILLING NEW CHARACTER IN HIS AMAZING ADVENTURES!!

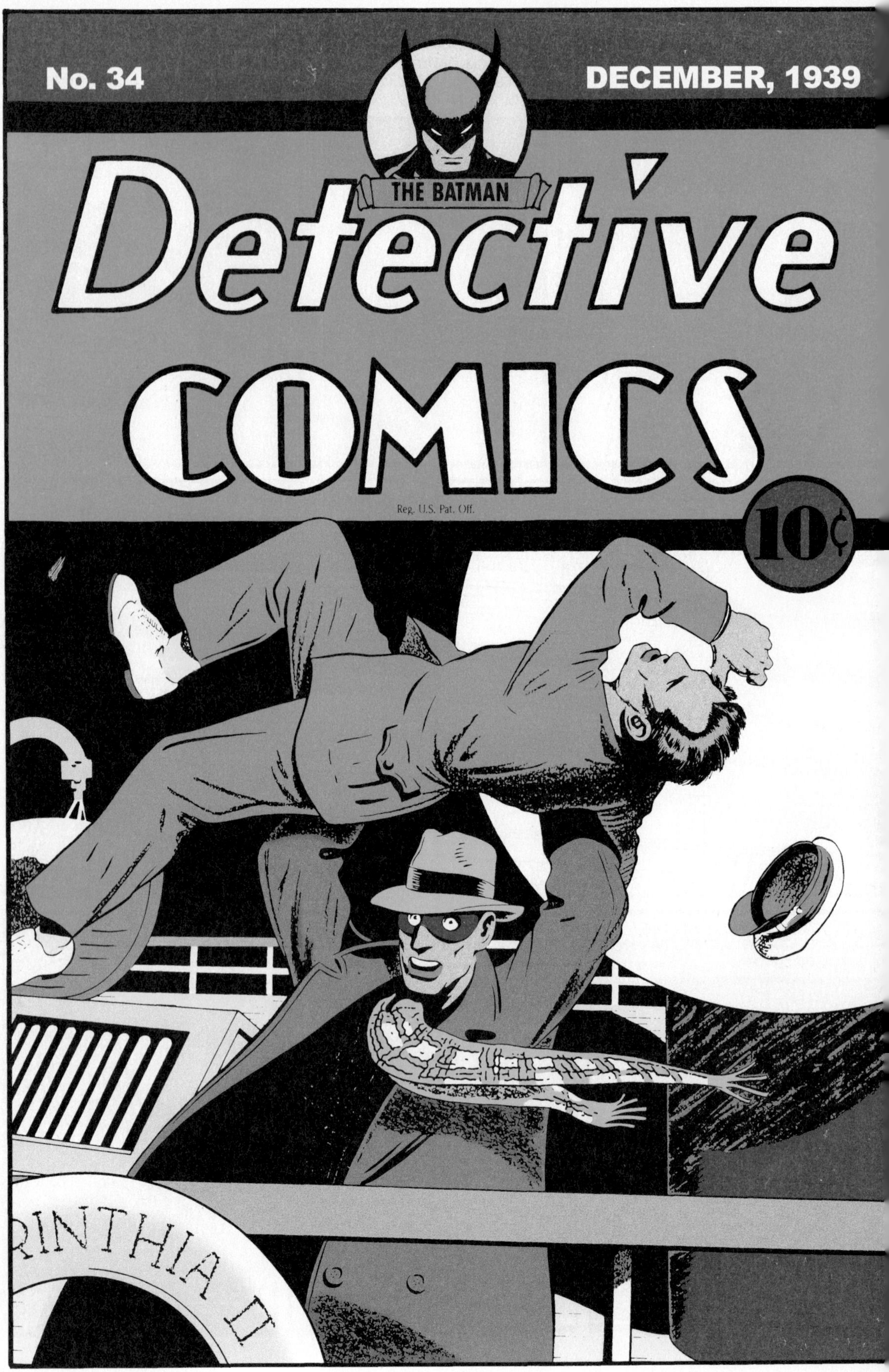
No. 34
DECEMBER, 1939
THE BATMAN
Detective
COMICS
Reg. U.S. Pat. Off.
10¢
RINTHIA II

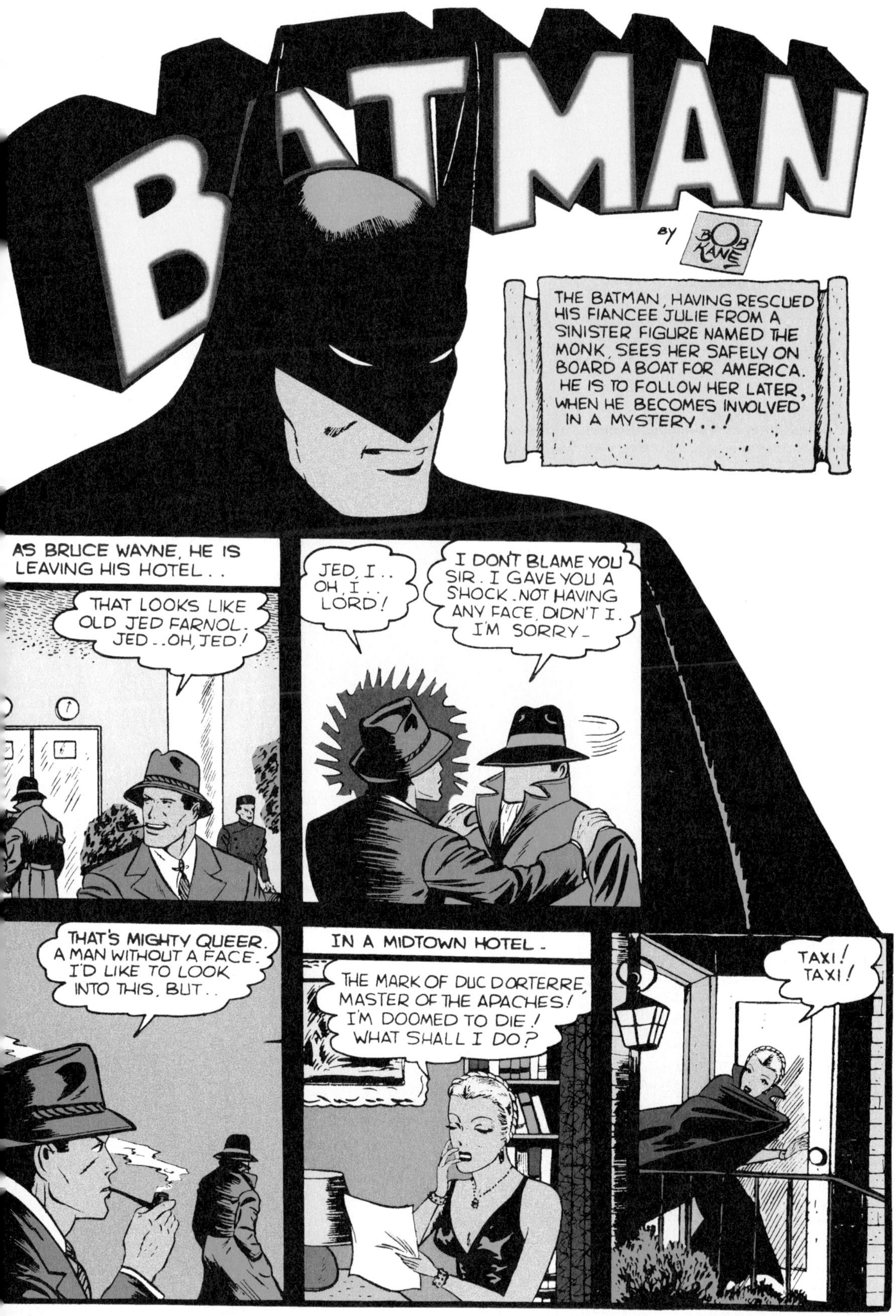
BATMAN
BY BOB KANE
THE BATMAN, HAVING RESCUED HIS FIANCEE JULIE FROM A SINISTER FIGURE NAMED THE MONK, SEES HER SAFELY ON BOARD A BOAT FOR AMERICA. HE IS TO FOLLOW HER LATER, WHEN HE BECOMES INVOLVED IN A MYSTERY..!
AS BRUCE WAYNE, HE IS LEAVING HIS HOTEL..
THAT LOOKS LIKE OLD JED FARNOL. JED..OH, JED!
JED, I.. OH, I.. LORD!
I DON'T BLAME YOU SIR. I GAVE YOU A SHOCK. NOT HAVING ANY FACE, DIDN'T I. I'M SORRY.
THAT'S MIGHTY QUEER. A MAN WITHOUT A FACE. I'D LIKE TO LOOK INTO THIS, BUT..
IN A MIDTOWN HOTEL.
THE MARK OF DUC D'ORTERRE, MASTER OF THE APACHES! I'M DOOMED TO DIE! WHAT SHALL I DO?
TAXI! TAXI!

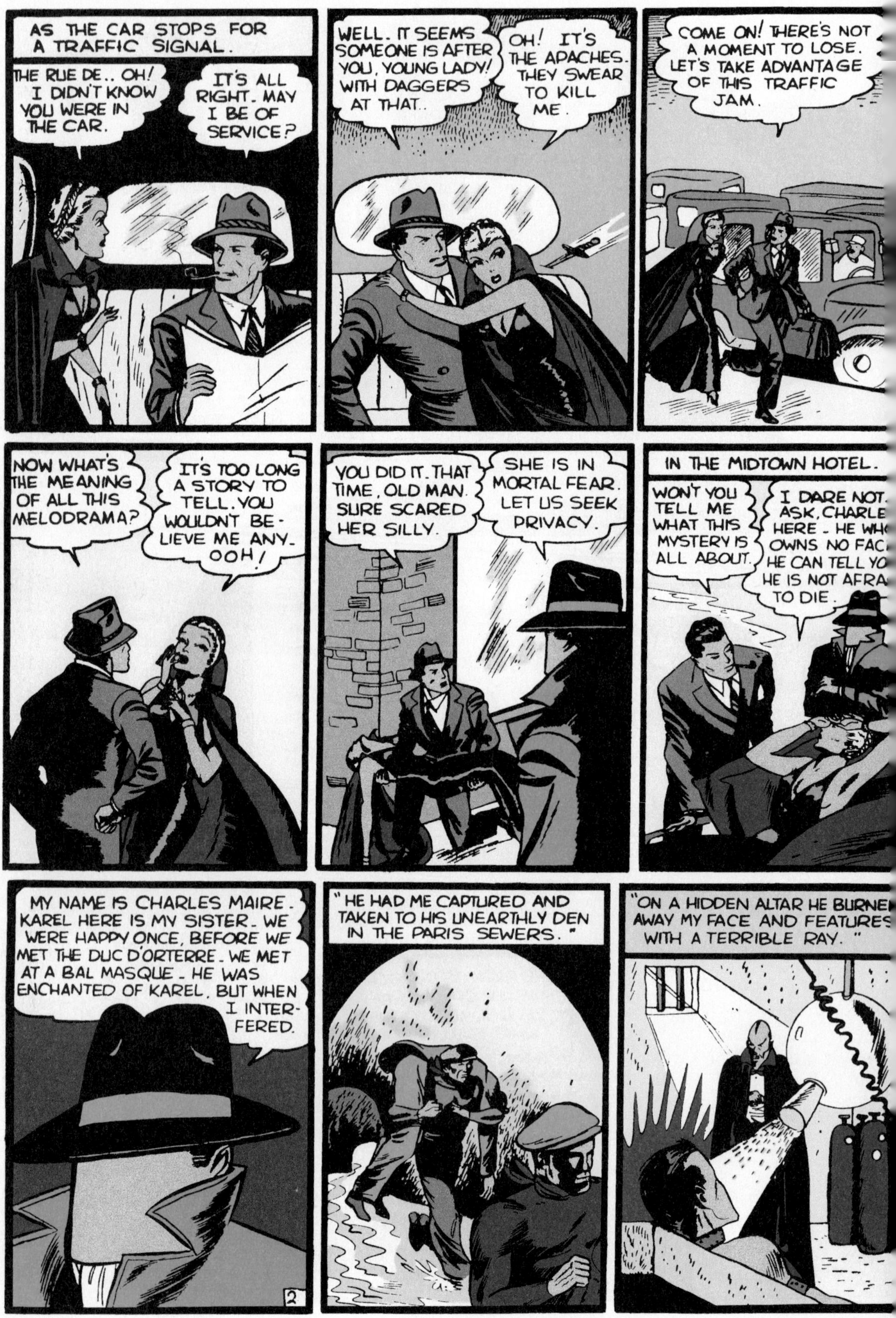
AS THE CAR STOPS FOR A TRAFFIC SIGNAL.
THE RUE DE.. OH! I DIDN'T KNOW YOU WERE IN THE CAR.
IT'S ALL RIGHT. MAY I BE OF SERVICE?
WELL. IT SEEMS SOMEONE IS AFTER YOU, YOUNG LADY! WITH DAGGERS AT THAT..
OH! IT'S THE APACHES. THEY SWEAR TO KILL ME.
COME ON! THERE'S NOT A MOMENT TO LOSE. LET'S TAKE ADVANTAGE OF THIS TRAFFIC JAM.
NOW WHAT'S THE MEANING OF ALL THIS MELODRAMA?
IT'S TOO LONG A STORY TO TELL. YOU WOULDN'T BE-LIEVE ME ANY. OOH!
YOU DID IT. THAT TIME, OLD MAN. SURE SCARED HER SILLY.
SHE IS IN MORTAL FEAR. LET US SEEK PRIVACY.
IN THE MIDTOWN HOTEL.
WON'T YOU TELL ME WHAT THIS MYSTERY IS ALL ABOUT.
I DARE NOT. ASK, CHARLE HERE - HE WHO OWNS NO FAC HE CAN TELL YO HE IS NOT AFRA TO DIE.
MY NAME IS CHARLES MAIRE. KAREL HERE IS MY SISTER. WE WERE HAPPY ONCE, BEFORE WE MET THE DUC D'ORTERRE. WE MET AT A BAL MASQUE. HE WAS ENCHANTED OF KAREL, BUT WHEN I INTER-FERED.
2
"HE HAD ME CAPTURED AND TAKEN TO HIS UNEARTHLY DEN IN THE PARIS SEWERS."
"ON A HIDDEN ALTAR HE BURNE AWAY MY FACE AND FEATURES WITH A TERRIBLE RAY."

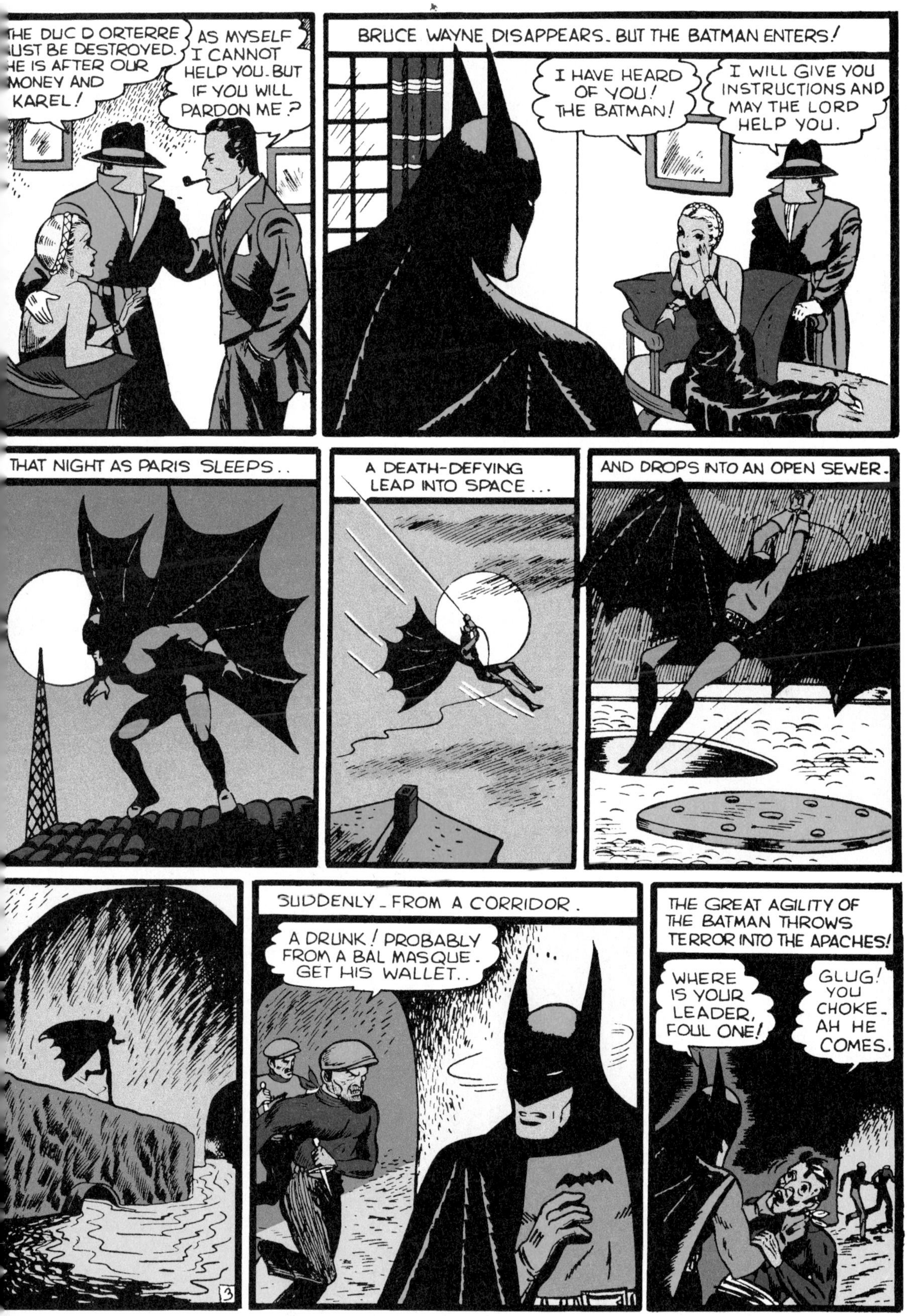
THE DUC D ORTERRE UST BE DESTROYED. HE IS AFTER OUR MONEY AND KAREL!
AS MYSELF I CANNOT HELP YOU. BUT IF YOU WILL PARDON ME?
BRUCE WAYNE DISAPPEARS. BUT THE BATMAN ENTERS!
I HAVE HEARD OF YOU! THE BATMAN!
I WILL GIVE YOU INSTRUCTIONS AND MAY THE LORD HELP YOU.
THAT NIGHT AS PARIS SLEEPS..
A DEATH-DEFYING LEAP INTO SPACE...
AND DROPS INTO AN OPEN SEWER.
SUDDENLY. FROM A CORRIDOR.
A DRUNK! PROBABLY FROM A BAL MASQUE. GET HIS WALLET..
THE GREAT AGILITY OF THE BATMAN THROWS TERROR INTO THE APACHES!
WHERE IS YOUR LEADER, FOUL ONE!
GLUG! YOU CHOKE. AH HE COMES.

AHA! A VISITOR.

THE BATMAN MAKES A FLYING LEAP TOWARD THE DUC. BUT IS STOPPED BY A BLINDING LIGHT WHICH SHOOTS FORTH FROM THE END OF THE DUC'S CANE.

TOO BAD M'SIEU! YOU ARE TOO IMPETUOUS!

EH, MES AMIS! BRING THIS THING TO MY TEMPLE. I SHALL BE AMUSED FOR A LITTLE WHILE.

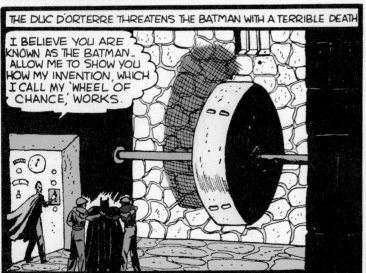

THE DUC D'ORTERRE THREATENS THE BATMAN WITH A TERRIBLE DEATH.

I BELIEVE YOU ARE KNOWN AS THE BATMAN. ALLOW ME TO SHOW YOU HOW MY INVENTION, WHICH I CALL MY 'WHEEL OF CHANCE,' WORKS.

OBSERVE THE WHEEL CLOSELY. IT BEGINS TO WHIRL SLOWLY, THEN FASTER AND FASTER. WATCH!

THE WHEEL OF CHANCE BEGINS TO WHIRL.

WHEN THE WHEEL REVOLVES ITS FASTEST YOU WILL EITHER BE THROWN AGAINST THE CONCRETE WALLS TO BE CRUSHED..OR BE MADDENED BY THE NEVER-CEASING WHIRLING OF THE GREAT WHEEL. MEANWHILE.. I SHALL WATCH FROM BEHIND A GLASS DOOR!

THE BATMAN IS HELPLESS ON THE MIGHTY WHEEL..

ALL READY? GO!

THE WHEEL BEGINS TO TURN..

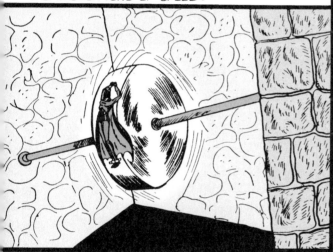

THE WHEEL PICKS UP SPEED.

THE BATMAN TRIES HIS BONDS. BY TENSING HIS STEEL-LIKE MUSCLES, HE BREAKS THE LEATHER THONGS!

HIS HANDS FREE. THE BATMAN TUGS DESPERATELY AT THE REMAINING BONDS AT HIS FEET.

HE IS WORKING HIMSELF FREE - TURN THE WHEEL FASTER! FASTER.

THE BATMAN IS FREE - BUT THE WHEEL IS SPINNING INCREDIBLY FAST!

I'VE GOT TO CHANCE A JUMP.

5

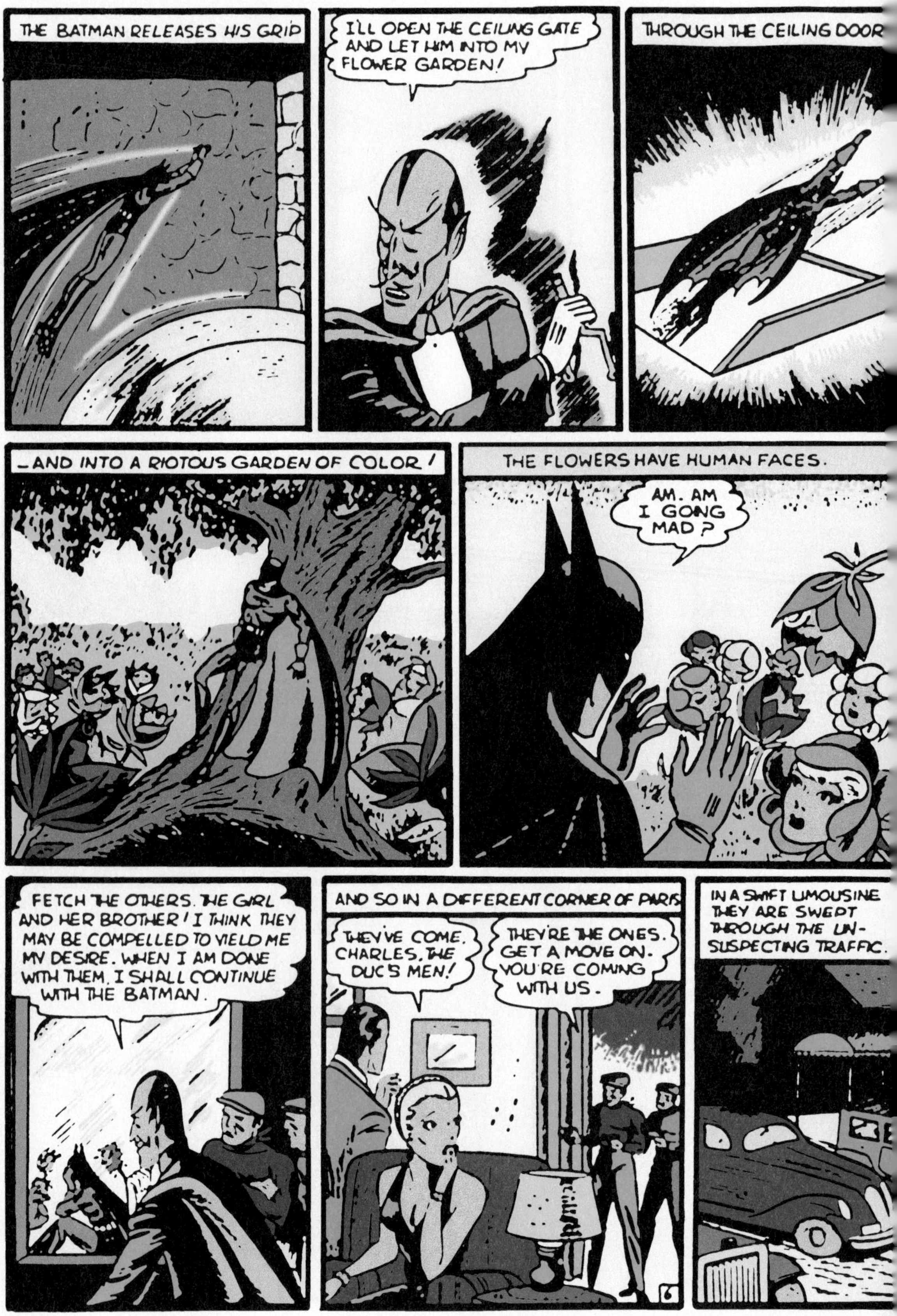
THE BATMAN RELEASES HIS GRIP
I'LL OPEN THE CEILING GATE AND LET HIM INTO MY FLOWER GARDEN!
THROUGH THE CEILING DOOR
—AND INTO A RIOTOUS GARDEN OF COLOR!
THE FLOWERS HAVE HUMAN FACES.
AM. AM I GOING MAD?
FETCH THE OTHERS. THE GIRL AND HER BROTHER! I THINK THEY MAY BE COMPELLED TO YIELD ME MY DESIRE. WHEN I AM DONE WITH THEM, I SHALL CONTINUE WITH THE BATMAN.
AND SO IN A DIFFERENT CORNER OF PARIS
THEY'VE COME, CHARLES, THE DUC'S MEN!
THEY'RE THE ONES. GET A MOVE ON. YOU'RE COMING WITH US.
IN A SWIFT LIMOUSINE THEY ARE SWEPT THROUGH THE UN-SUSPECTING TRAFFIC.

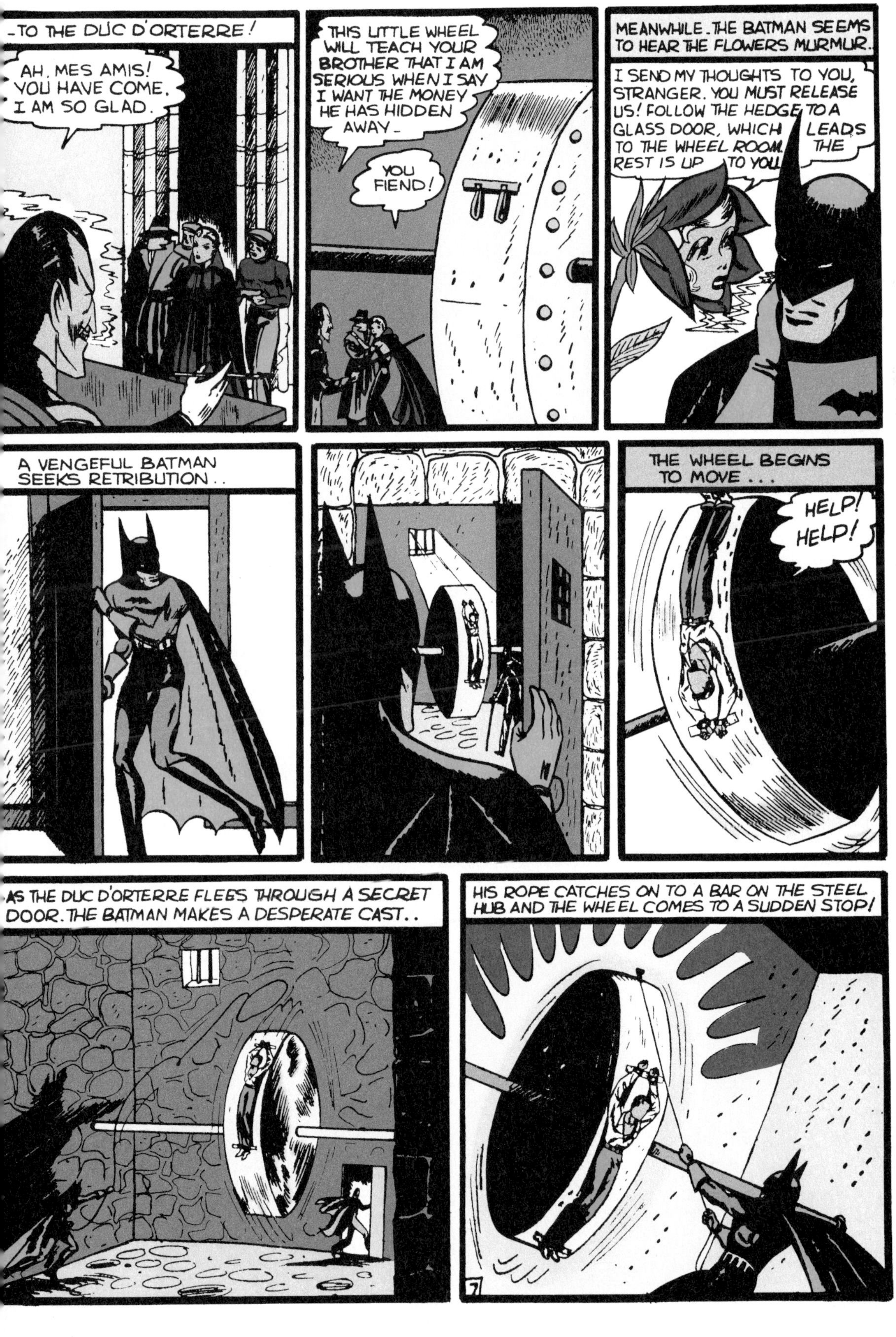
-TO THE DUC D'ORTERRE!
AH, MES AMIS! YOU HAVE COME. I AM SO GLAD.
THIS LITTLE WHEEL WILL TEACH YOUR BROTHER THAT I AM SERIOUS WHEN I SAY I WANT THE MONEY HE HAS HIDDEN AWAY-
YOU FIEND!
MEANWHILE-THE BATMAN SEEMS TO HEAR THE FLOWERS MURMUR.
I SEND MY THOUGHTS TO YOU, STRANGER. YOU MUST RELEASE US! FOLLOW THE HEDGE TO A GLASS DOOR, WHICH LEADS TO THE WHEEL ROOM. THE REST IS UP TO YOU!
A VENGEFUL BATMAN SEEKS RETRIBUTION..
THE WHEEL BEGINS TO MOVE...
HELP! HELP!
AS THE DUC D'ORTERRE FLEES THROUGH A SECRET DOOR. THE BATMAN MAKES A DESPERATE CAST..
HIS ROPE CATCHES ON TO A BAR ON THE STEEL HUB AND THE WHEEL COMES TO A SUDDEN STOP!
7

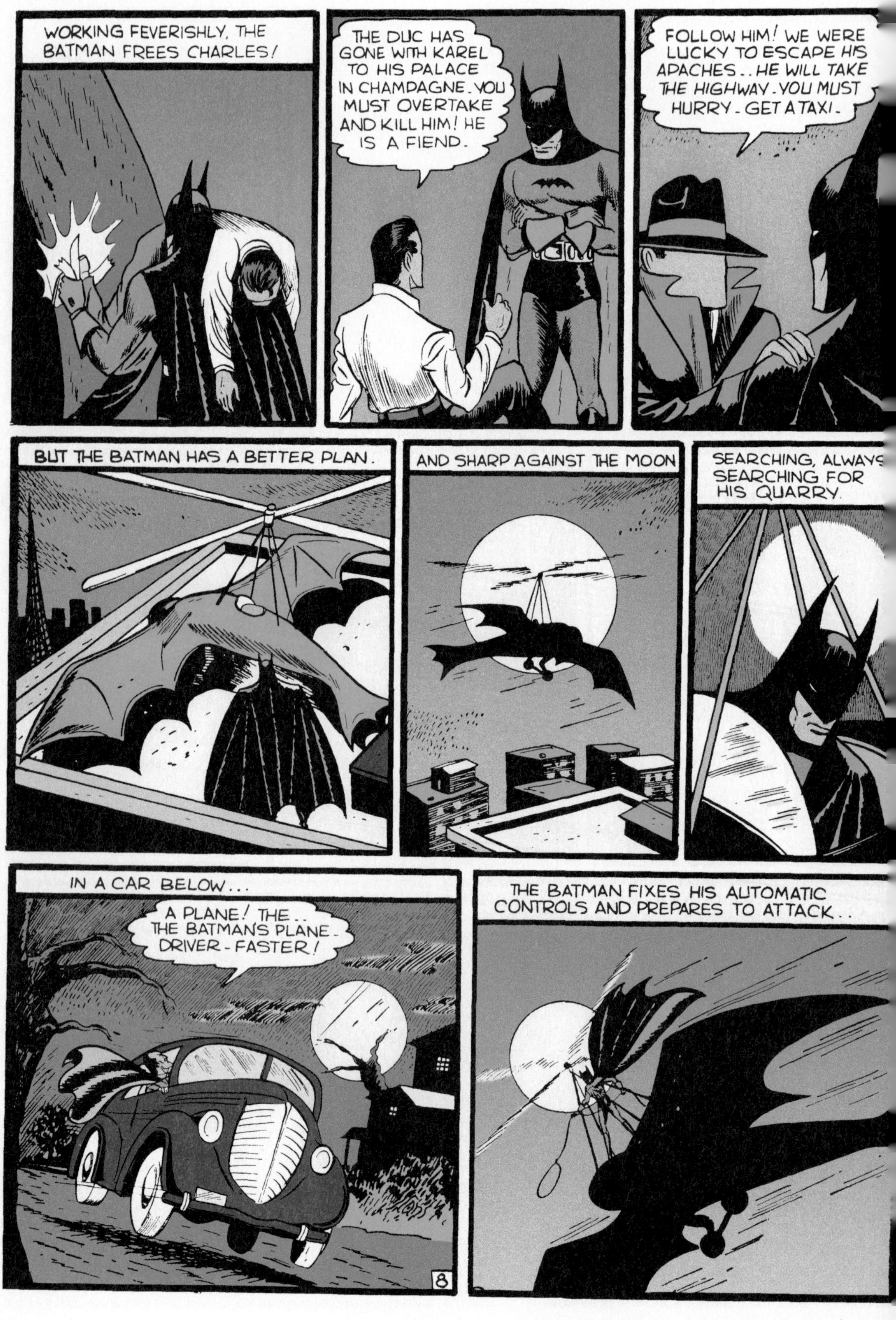
WORKING FEVERISHLY, THE BATMAN FREES CHARLES!
THE DUC HAS GONE WITH KAREL TO HIS PALACE IN CHAMPAGNE. YOU MUST OVERTAKE AND KILL HIM! HE IS A FIEND.
FOLLOW HIM! WE WERE LUCKY TO ESCAPE HIS APACHES.. HE WILL TAKE THE HIGHWAY. YOU MUST HURRY. GET A TAXI.
BUT THE BATMAN HAS A BETTER PLAN.
AND SHARP AGAINST THE MOON
SEARCHING, ALWAYS SEARCHING FOR HIS QUARRY.
IN A CAR BELOW...
A PLANE! THE.. THE BATMAN'S PLANE. DRIVER. FASTER!
8
THE BATMAN FIXES HIS AUTOMATIC CONTROLS AND PREPARES TO ATTACK..

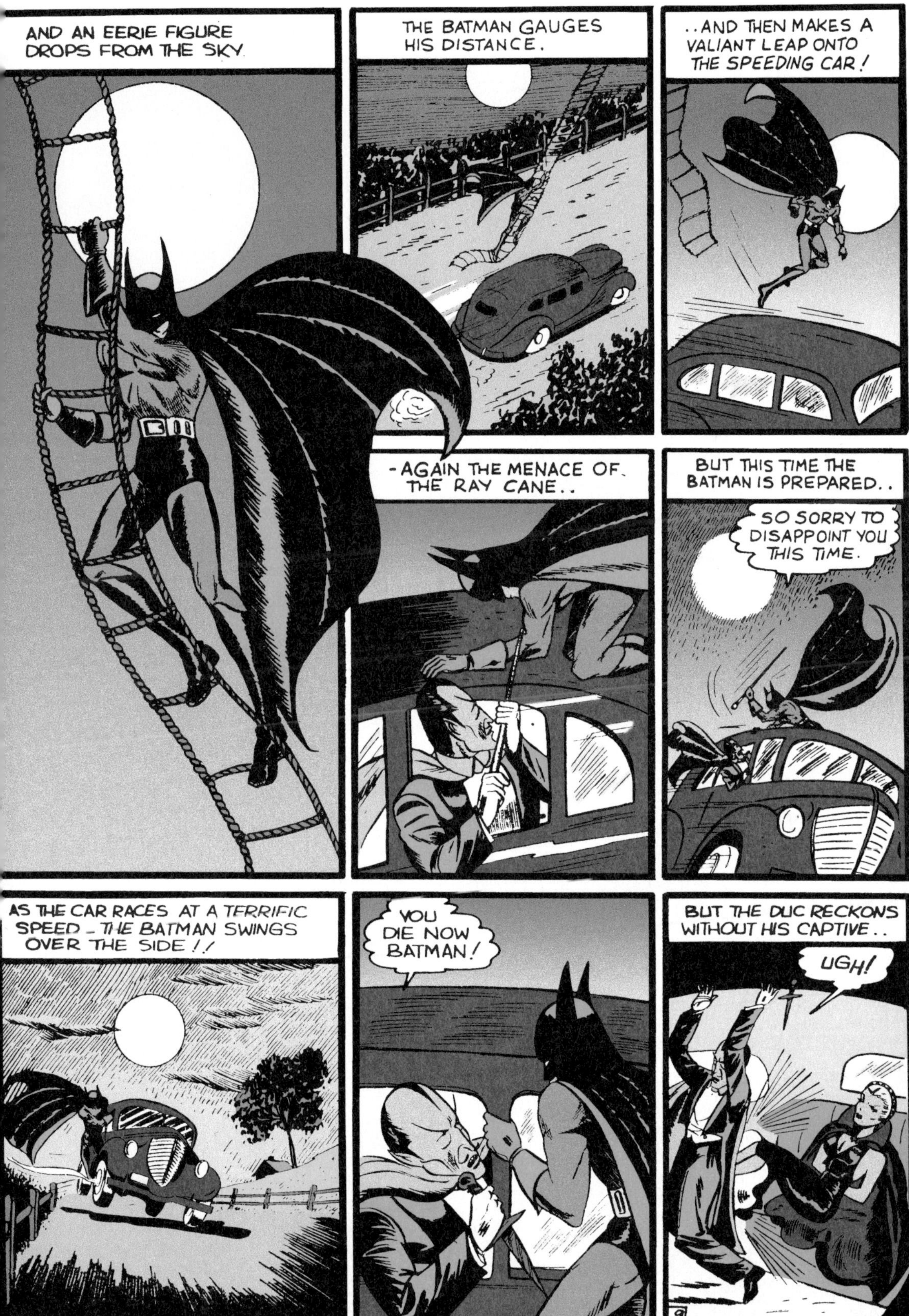

AND AN EERIE FIGURE DROPS FROM THE SKY.
THE BATMAN GAUGES HIS DISTANCE.
..AND THEN MAKES A VALIANT LEAP ONTO THE SPEEDING CAR!
-AGAIN THE MENACE OF THE RAY CANE..
BUT THIS TIME THE BATMAN IS PREPARED..
SO SORRY TO DISAPPOINT YOU THIS TIME.
AS THE CAR RACES AT A TERRIFIC SPEED - THE BATMAN SWINGS OVER THE SIDE!!
YOU DIE NOW BATMAN!
BUT THE DUC RECKONS WITHOUT HIS CAPTIVE..
UGH!

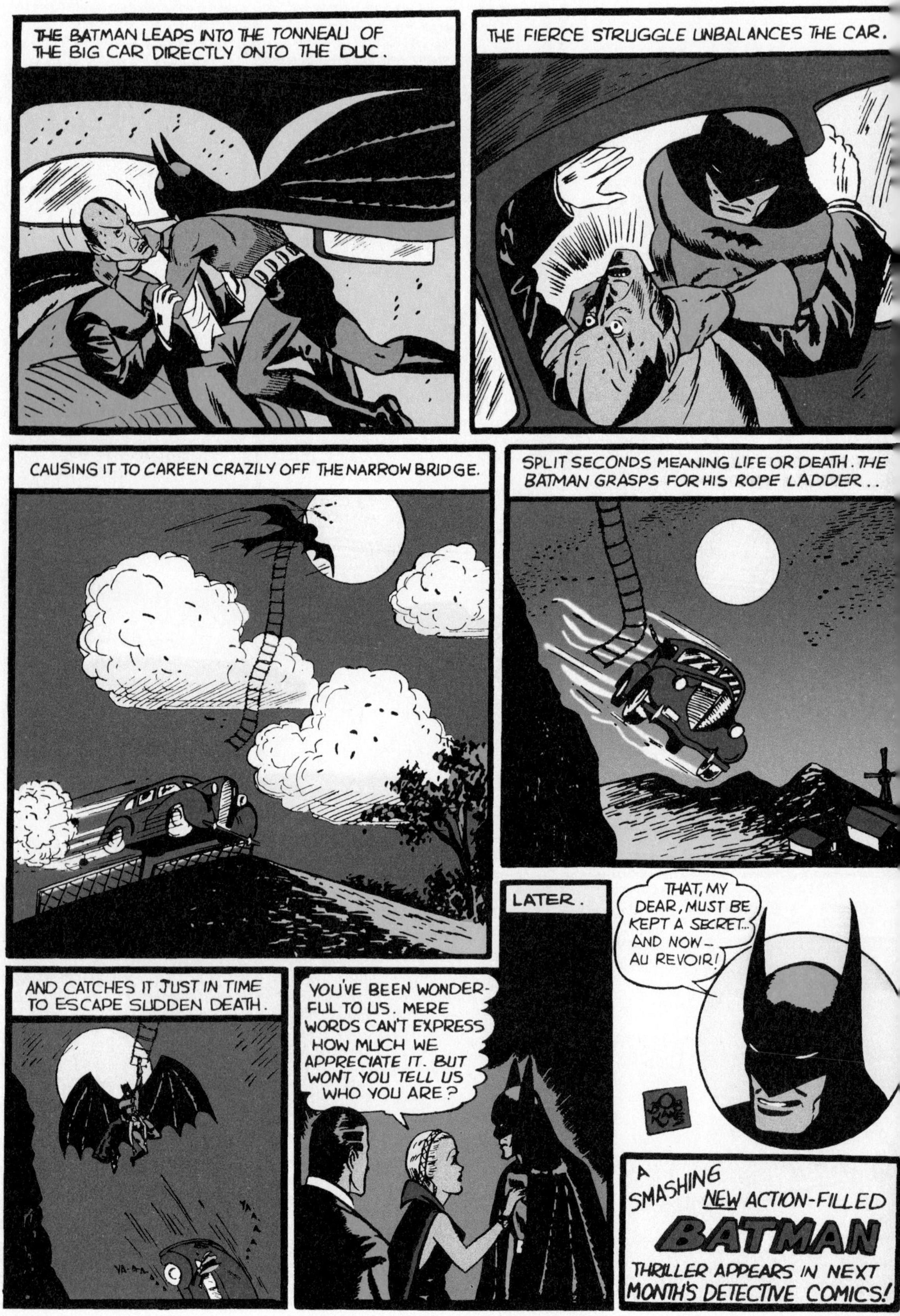
THE BATMAN LEAPS INTO THE TONNEAU OF THE BIG CAR DIRECTLY ONTO THE DUC.
THE FIERCE STRUGGLE UNBALANCES THE CAR.
CAUSING IT TO CAREEN CRAZILY OFF THE NARROW BRIDGE.
SPLIT SECONDS MEANING LIFE OR DEATH. THE BATMAN GRASPS FOR HIS ROPE LADDER..
AND CATCHES IT JUST IN TIME TO ESCAPE SUDDEN DEATH.
YA-A-A-
LATER.
YOU'VE BEEN WONDERFUL TO US. MERE WORDS CAN'T EXPRESS HOW MUCH WE APPRECIATE IT. BUT WON'T YOU TELL US WHO YOU ARE?
THAT, MY DEAR, MUST BE KEPT A SECRET... AND NOW-- AU REVOIR!
A SMASHING NEW ACTION-FILLED
BATMAN
THRILLER APPEARS IN NEXT MONTH'S DETECTIVE COMICS!

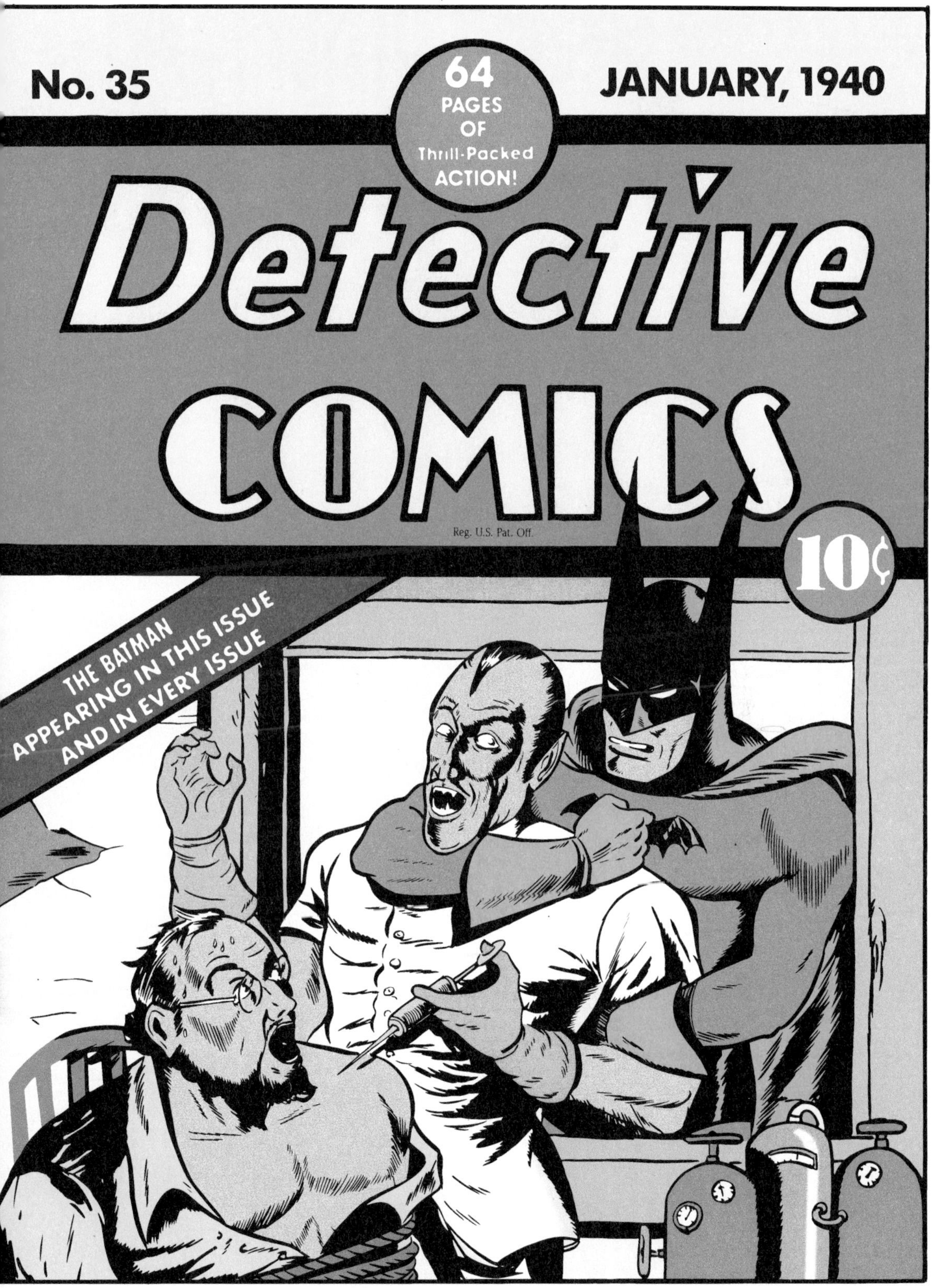
No. 35
64 PAGES OF Thrill-Packed ACTION!
JANUARY, 1940
Detective COMICS
Reg. U.S. Pat. Off.
10¢
THE BATMAN APPEARING IN THIS ISSUE AND IN EVERY ISSUE

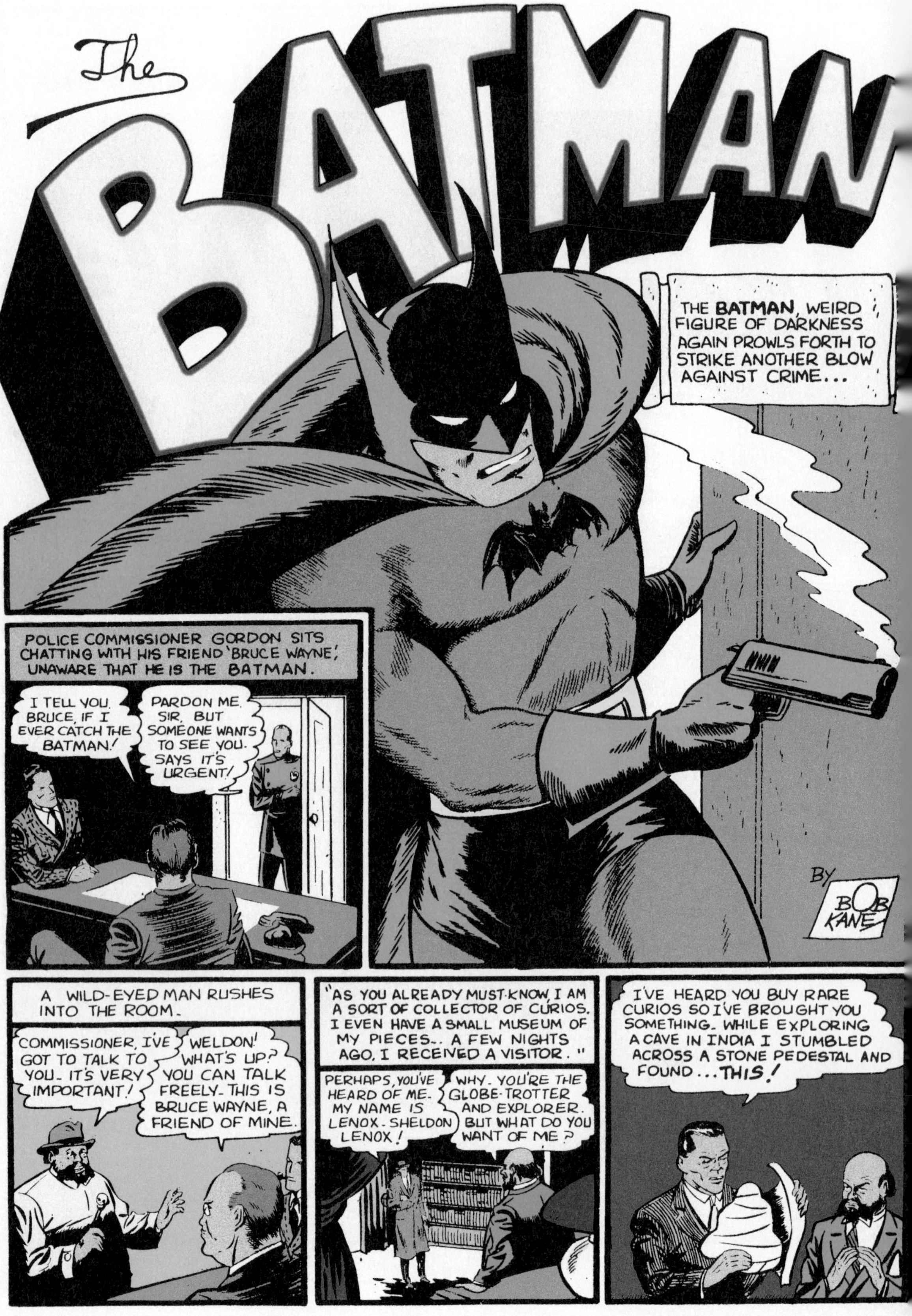
The BATMAN
THE BATMAN, WEIRD FIGURE OF DARKNESS AGAIN PROWLS FORTH TO STRIKE ANOTHER BLOW AGAINST CRIME...
BY BOB KANE
POLICE COMMISSIONER GORDON SITS CHATTING WITH HIS FRIEND 'BRUCE WAYNE', UNAWARE THAT HE IS THE BATMAN.
I TELL YOU. BRUCE, IF I EVER CATCH THE BATMAN!
PARDON ME. SIR, BUT SOMEONE WANTS TO SEE YOU. SAYS IT'S URGENT!
A WILD-EYED MAN RUSHES INTO THE ROOM.
COMMISSIONER, I'VE GOT TO TALK TO YOU. IT'S VERY IMPORTANT!
WELDON! WHAT'S UP? YOU CAN TALK FREELY. THIS IS BRUCE WAYNE, A FRIEND OF MINE.
"AS YOU ALREADY MUST KNOW, I AM A SORT OF COLLECTOR OF CURIOS. I EVEN HAVE A SMALL MUSEUM OF MY PIECES.. A FEW NIGHTS AGO, I RECEIVED A VISITOR."
PERHAPS, YOU'VE HEARD OF ME. MY NAME IS LENOX-SHELDON LENOX!
WHY. YOU'RE THE GLOBE-TROTTER AND EXPLORER. BUT WHAT DO YOU WANT OF ME?
I'VE HEARD YOU BUY RARE CURIOS SO I'VE BROUGHT YOU SOMETHING. WHILE EXPLORING A CAVE IN INDIA I STUMBLED ACROSS A STONE PEDESTAL AND FOUND... THIS!

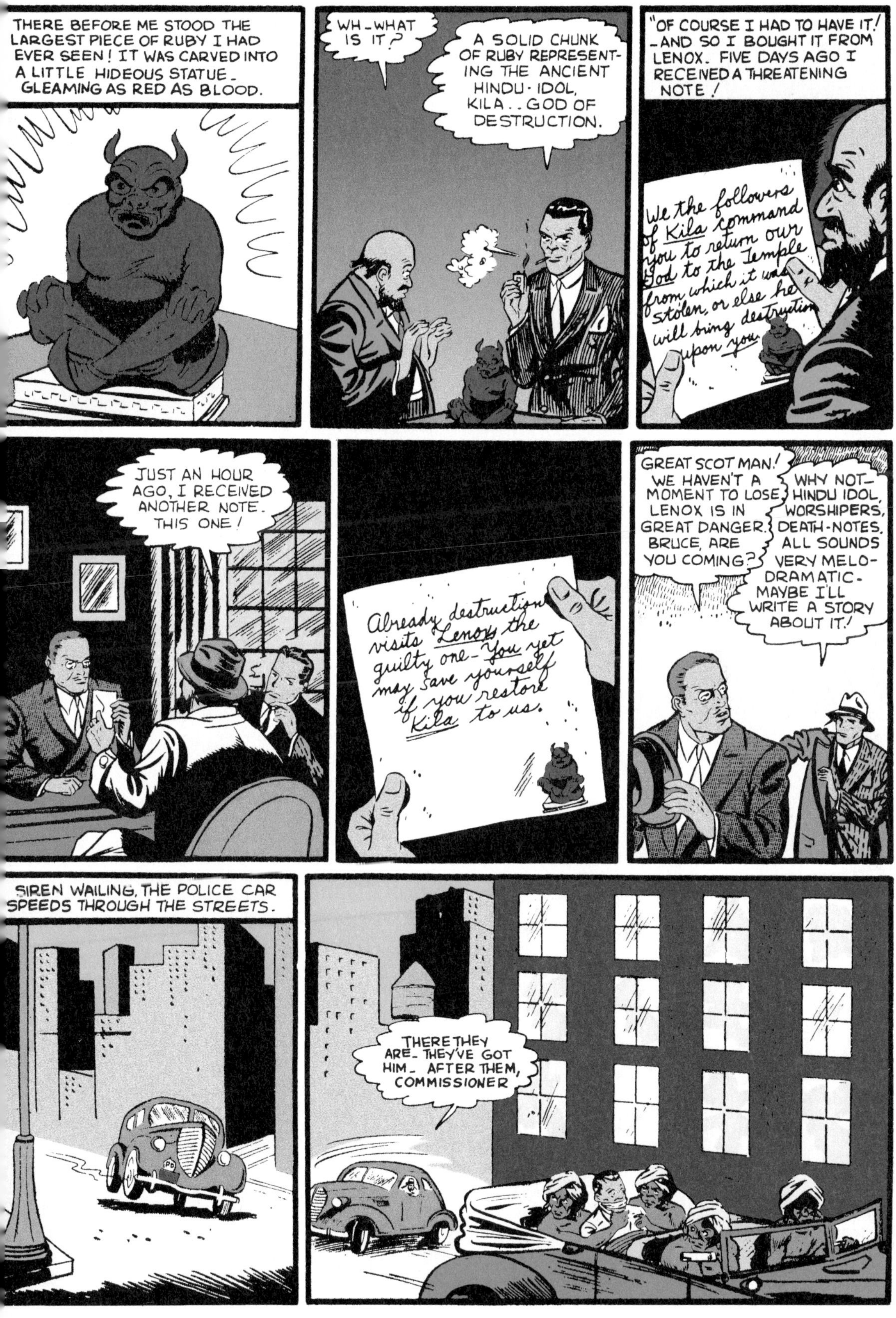
THERE BEFORE ME STOOD THE LARGEST PIECE OF RUBY I HAD EVER SEEN! IT WAS CARVED INTO A LITTLE HIDEOUS STATUE - GLEAMING AS RED AS BLOOD.
WH-WHAT IS IT?
A SOLID CHUNK OF RUBY REPRESENTING THE ANCIENT HINDU-IDOL, KILA.. GOD OF DESTRUCTION.
"OF COURSE I HAD TO HAVE IT! - AND SO I BOUGHT IT FROM LENOX. FIVE DAYS AGO I RECEIVED A THREATENING NOTE!
We the followers of Kila command you to return our God to the Temple from which it was stolen, or else he will bring destruction upon you.
JUST AN HOUR AGO, I RECEIVED ANOTHER NOTE. THIS ONE!
Already destruction visits Lenox the guilty one - You yet may save yourself if you restore Kila to us.
GREAT SCOT MAN! WE HAVEN'T A MOMENT TO LOSE. LENOX IS IN GREAT DANGER. BRUCE, ARE YOU COMING?
WHY NOT - HINDU IDOL, WORSHIPERS, DEATH-NOTES. ALL SOUNDS VERY MELO-DRAMATIC - MAYBE I'LL WRITE A STORY ABOUT IT!
SIREN WAILING, THE POLICE CAR SPEEDS THROUGH THE STREETS.
PD
THERE THEY ARE - THEY'VE GOT HIM - AFTER THEM, COMMISSIONER

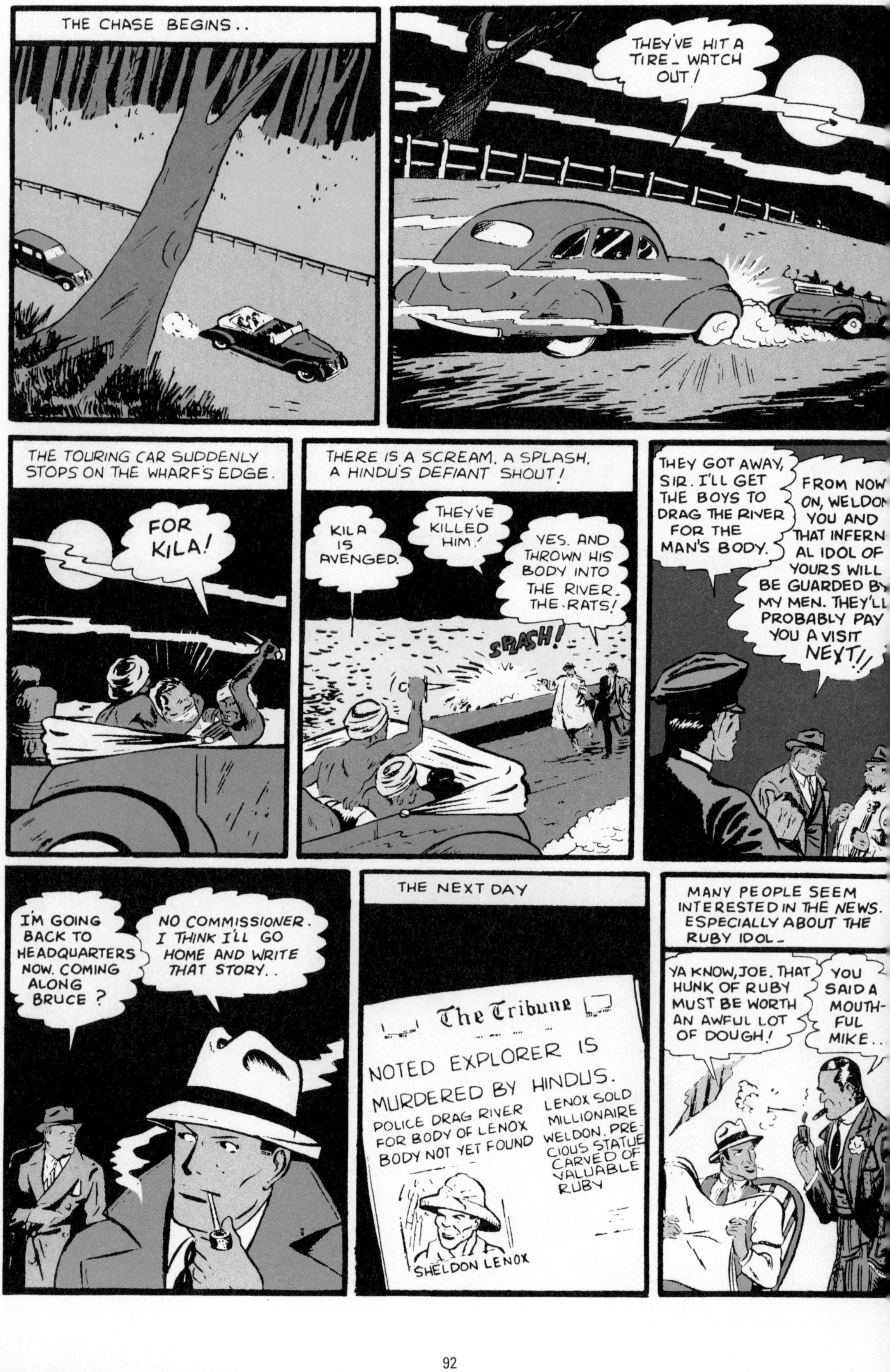
THE CHASE BEGINS..
THEY'VE HIT A TIRE - WATCH OUT!
THE TOURING CAR SUDDENLY STOPS ON THE WHARF'S EDGE.
FOR KILA!
THERE IS A SCREAM, A SPLASH, A HINDU'S DEFIANT SHOUT!
KILA IS AVENGED.
THEY'VE KILLED HIM!
YES. AND THROWN HIS BODY INTO THE RIVER - THE RATS!
SPLASH!
THEY GOT AWAY, SIR. I'LL GET THE BOYS TO DRAG THE RIVER FOR THE MAN'S BODY.
FROM NOW ON, WELDON YOU AND THAT INFERNAL IDOL OF YOURS WILL BE GUARDED BY MY MEN. THEY'LL PROBABLY PAY YOU A VISIT NEXT!!
I'M GOING BACK TO HEADQUARTERS NOW. COMING ALONG BRUCE?
NO COMMISSIONER. I THINK I'LL GO HOME AND WRITE THAT STORY..
THE NEXT DAY
The Tribune
NOTED EXPLORER IS MURDERED BY HINDUS.
POLICE DRAG RIVER FOR BODY OF LENOX BODY NOT YET FOUND
LENOX SOLD MILLIONAIRE WELDON. PRECIOUS STATUE CARVED OF VALUABLE RUBY
SHELDON LENOX
MANY PEOPLE SEEM INTERESTED IN THE NEWS. ESPECIALLY ABOUT THE RUBY IDOL -
YA KNOW, JOE. THAT HUNK OF RUBY MUST BE WORTH AN AWFUL LOT OF DOUGH!
YOU SAID A MOUTHFUL MIKE...

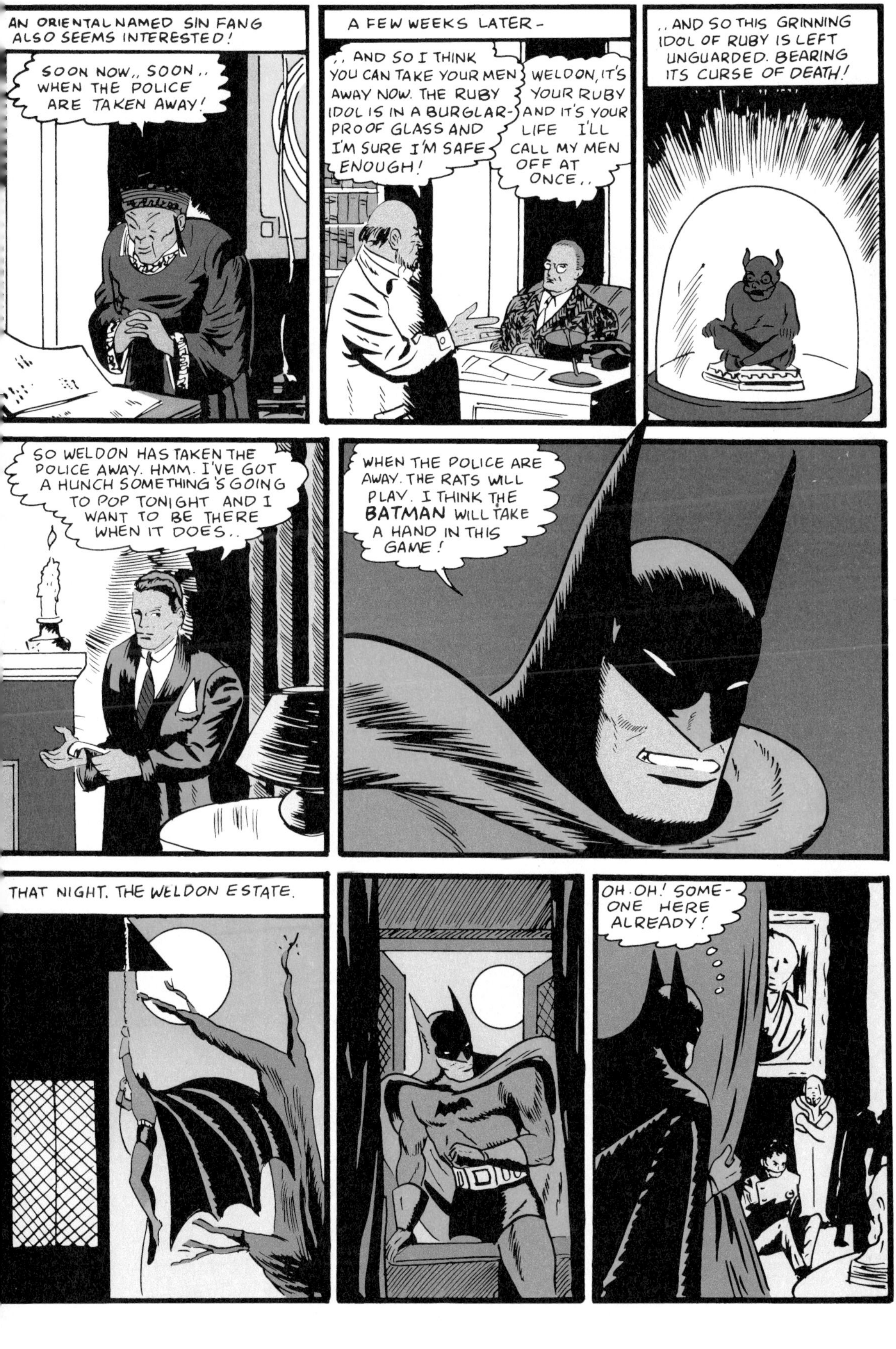
AN ORIENTAL NAMED SIN FANG ALSO SEEMS INTERESTED!
SOON NOW.. SOON.. WHEN THE POLICE ARE TAKEN AWAY!
A FEW WEEKS LATER-
.. AND SO I THINK YOU CAN TAKE YOUR MEN AWAY NOW. THE RUBY IDOL IS IN A BURGLAR-PROOF GLASS AND I'M SURE I'M SAFE ENOUGH!
WELDON, IT'S YOUR RUBY AND IT'S YOUR LIFE I'LL CALL MY MEN OFF AT ONCE..
.. AND SO THIS GRINNING IDOL OF RUBY IS LEFT UNGUARDED. BEARING ITS CURSE OF DEATH!
SO WELDON HAS TAKEN THE POLICE AWAY. HMM. I'VE GOT A HUNCH SOMETHING'S GOING TO POP TONIGHT AND I WANT TO BE THERE WHEN IT DOES..
WHEN THE POLICE ARE AWAY. THE RATS WILL PLAY. I THINK THE BATMAN WILL TAKE A HAND IN THIS GAME!
THAT NIGHT. THE WELDON ESTATE.
OH-OH! SOME-ONE HERE ALREADY!

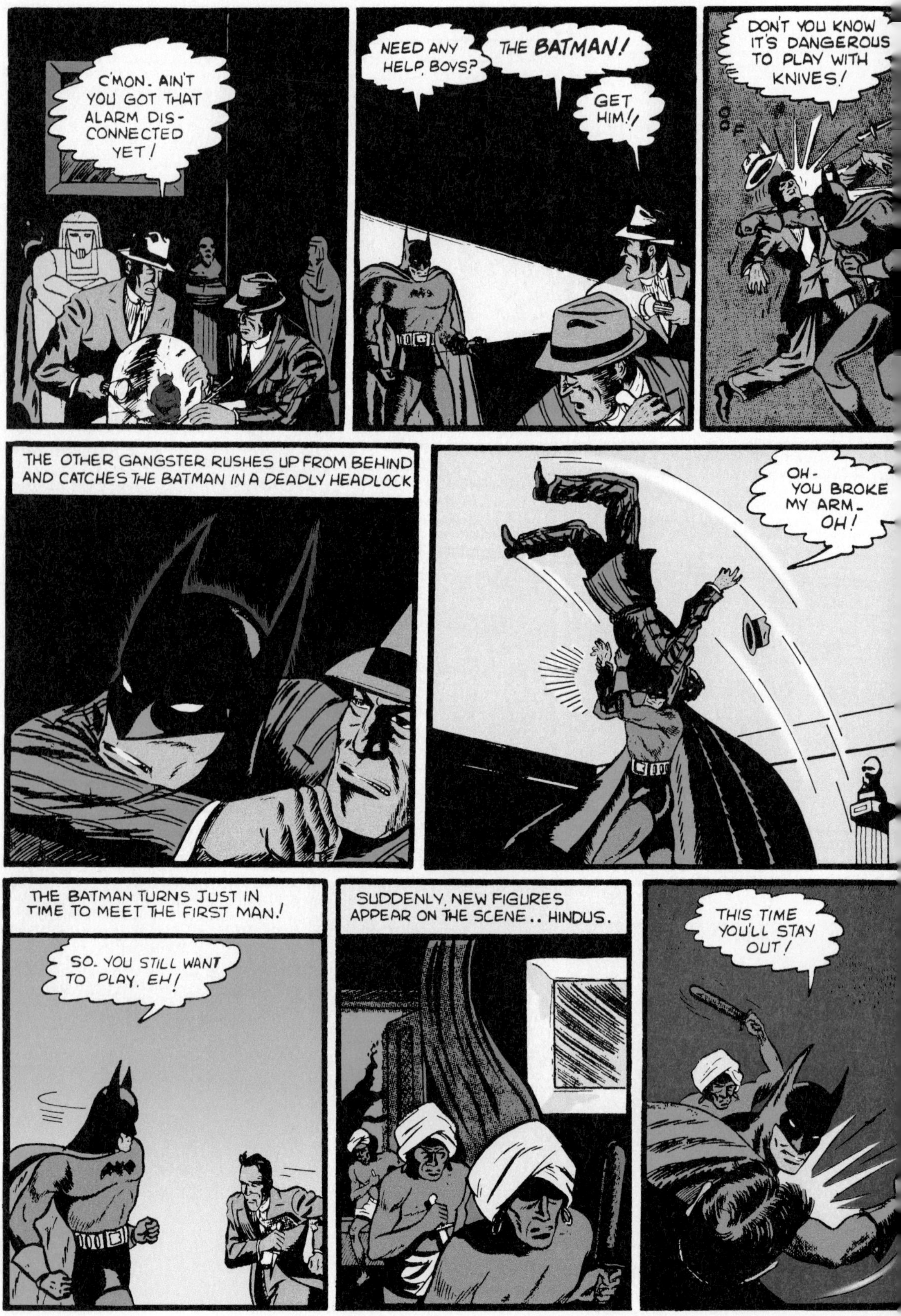

C'MON. AIN'T YOU GOT THAT ALARM DIS- CONNECTED YET!
NEED ANY HELP, BOYS?
THE BATMAN!
GET HIM!!
DON'T YOU KNOW IT'S DANGEROUS TO PLAY WITH KNIVES!
THE OTHER GANGSTER RUSHES UP FROM BEHIND AND CATCHES THE BATMAN IN A DEADLY HEADLOCK
OH- YOU BROKE MY ARM- OH!
THE BATMAN TURNS JUST IN TIME TO MEET THE FIRST MAN!
SO. YOU STILL WANT TO PLAY, EH!
SUDDENLY, NEW FIGURES APPEAR ON THE SCENE.. HINDUS.
THIS TIME YOU'LL STAY OUT!

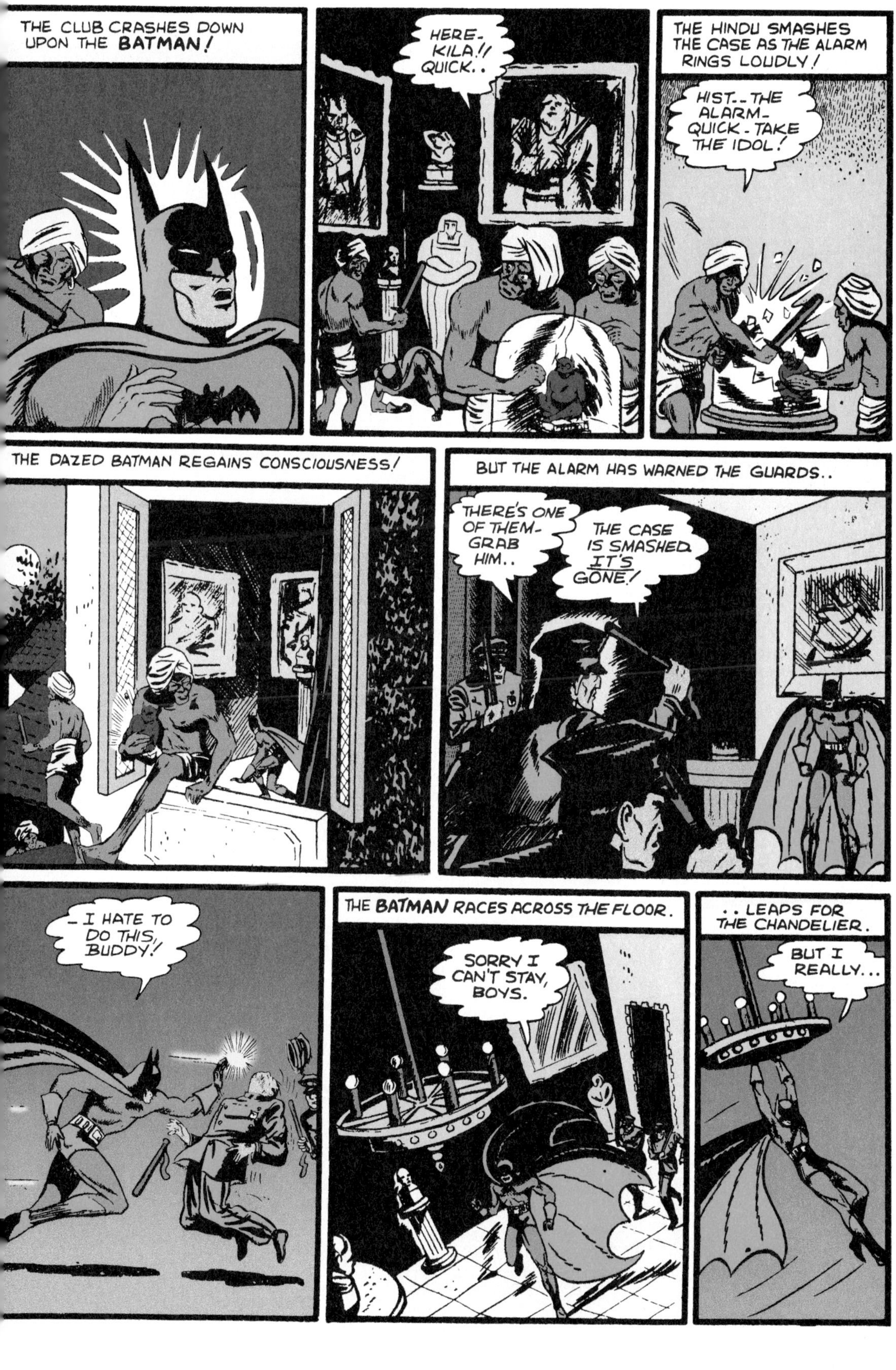
THE CLUB CRASHES DOWN UPON THE BATMAN!
HERE-KILA!! QUICK..
THE HINDU SMASHES THE CASE AS THE ALARM RINGS LOUDLY!
HIST--THE ALARM-QUICK-TAKE THE IDOL!
THE DAZED BATMAN REGAINS CONSCIOUSNESS!
BUT THE ALARM HAS WARNED THE GUARDS..
THERE'S ONE OF THEM-GRAB HIM..
THE CASE IS SMASHED IT'S GONE!
-I HATE TO DO THIS, BUDDY!
THE BATMAN RACES ACROSS THE FLOOR.
SORRY I CAN'T STAY, BOYS.
..LEAPS FOR THE CHANDELIER.
BUT I REALLY...

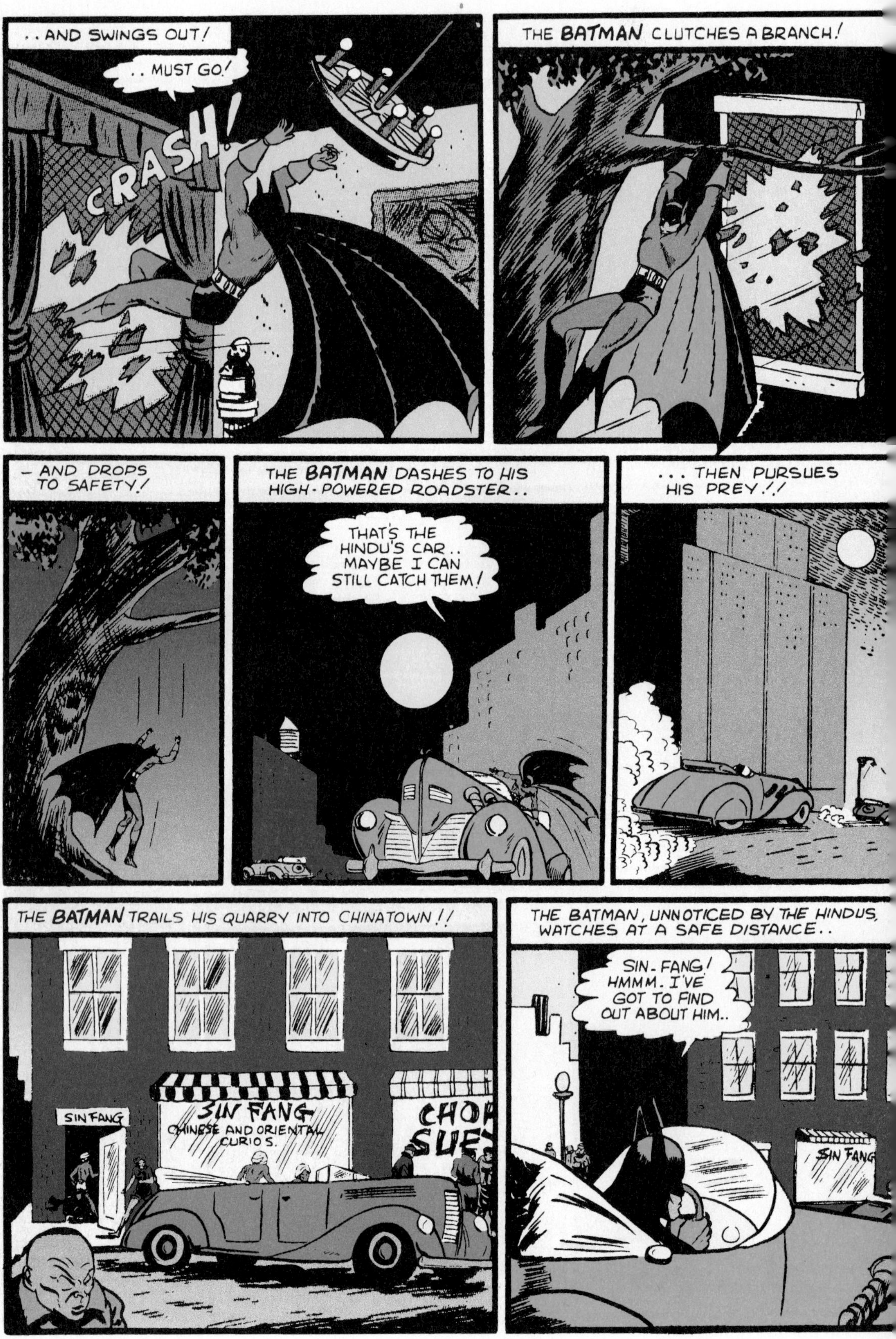

..AND SWINGS OUT!
..MUST GO!
CRASH!
THE BATMAN CLUTCHES A BRANCH!
– AND DROPS TO SAFETY!
THE BATMAN DASHES TO HIS HIGH-POWERED ROADSTER..
THAT'S THE HINDU'S CAR.. MAYBE I CAN STILL CATCH THEM!
... THEN PURSUES HIS PREY!!
THE BATMAN TRAILS HIS QUARRY INTO CHINATOWN!!
SIN FANG
SIN FANG CHINESE AND ORIENTAL CURIOS.
THE BATMAN, UNNOTICED BY THE HINDUS, WATCHES AT A SAFE DISTANCE..
SIN-FANG! HMMM. I'VE GOT TO FIND OUT ABOUT HIM..
SIN FANG

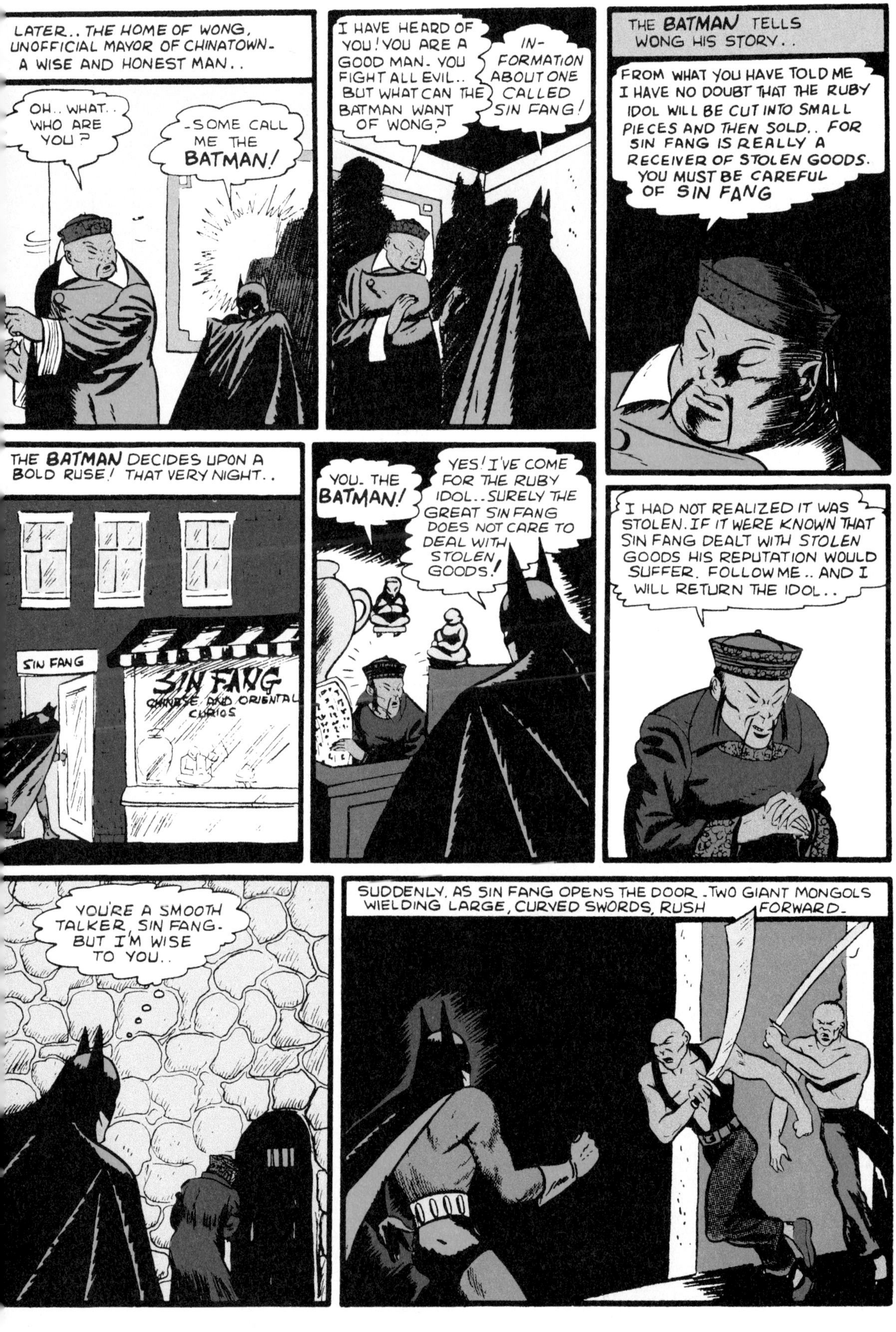
LATER.. THE HOME OF WONG, UNOFFICIAL MAYOR OF CHINATOWN - A WISE AND HONEST MAN..
OH.. WHAT.. WHO ARE YOU?
-SOME CALL ME THE BATMAN!
I HAVE HEARD OF YOU! YOU ARE A GOOD MAN. YOU FIGHT ALL EVIL.. BUT WHAT CAN THE BATMAN WANT OF WONG?
IN-FORMATION ABOUT ONE CALLED SIN FANG!
THE BATMAN TELLS WONG HIS STORY..
FROM WHAT YOU HAVE TOLD ME I HAVE NO DOUBT THAT THE RUBY IDOL WILL BE CUT INTO SMALL PIECES AND THEN SOLD.. FOR SIN FANG IS REALLY A RECEIVER OF STOLEN GOODS. YOU MUST BE CAREFUL OF SIN FANG
THE BATMAN DECIDES UPON A BOLD RUSE! THAT VERY NIGHT..
SIN FANG
SIN FANG
CHINESE AND ORIENTAL CURIOS
YOU. THE BATMAN!
YES! I'VE COME FOR THE RUBY IDOL.. SURELY THE GREAT SIN FANG DOES NOT CARE TO DEAL WITH STOLEN GOODS!
I HAD NOT REALIZED IT WAS STOLEN. IF IT WERE KNOWN THAT SIN FANG DEALT WITH STOLEN GOODS HIS REPUTATION WOULD SUFFER. FOLLOW ME.. AND I WILL RETURN THE IDOL..
YOU'RE A SMOOTH TALKER, SIN FANG. BUT I'M WISE TO YOU..
SUDDENLY, AS SIN FANG OPENS THE DOOR - TWO GIANT MONGOLS WIELDING LARGE, CURVED SWORDS, RUSH FORWARD.

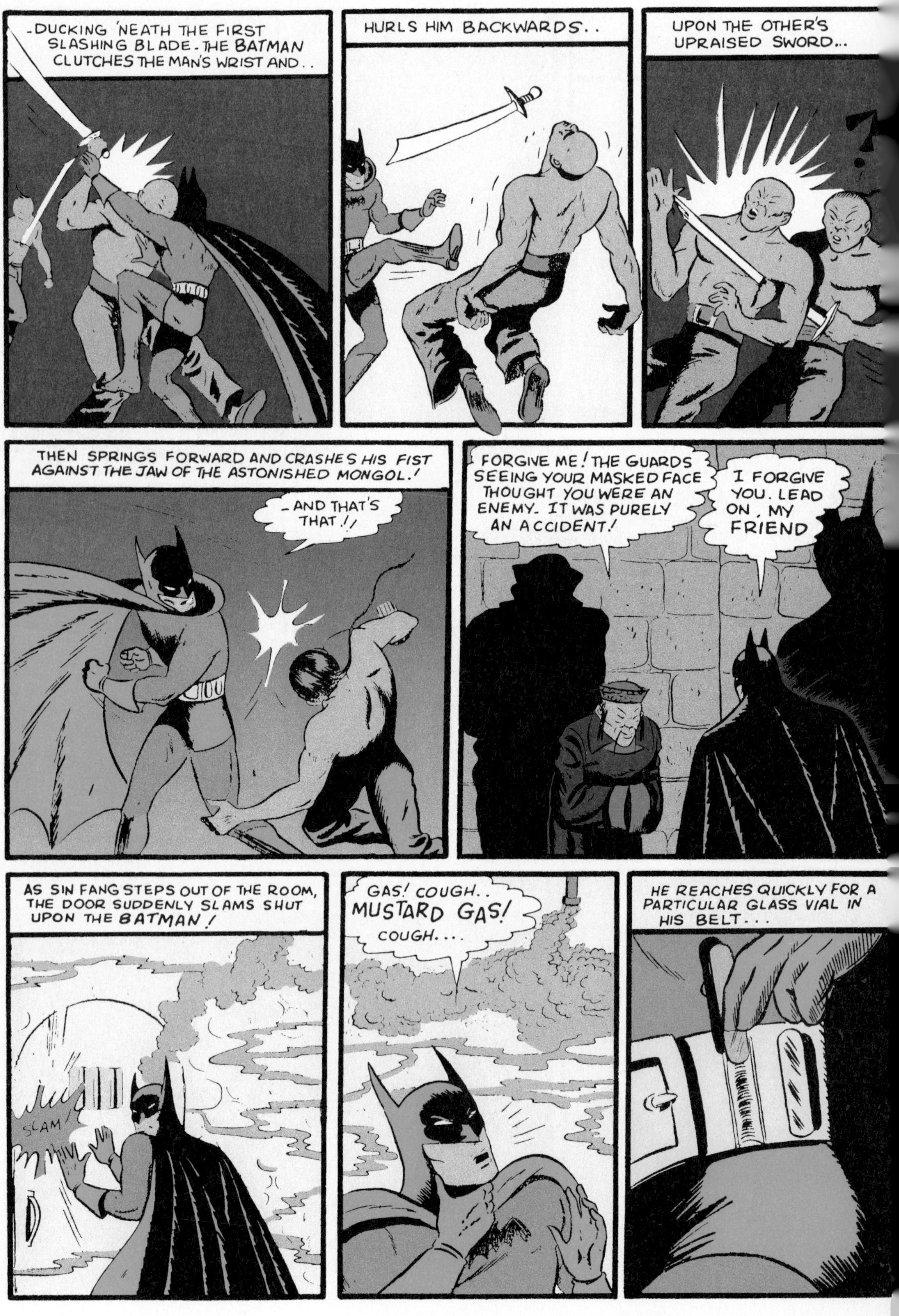
-DUCKING 'NEATH THE FIRST SLASHING BLADE - THE BATMAN CLUTCHES THE MAN'S WRIST AND . .
HURLS HIM BACKWARDS . .
UPON THE OTHER'S UPRAISED SWORD...
THEN SPRINGS FORWARD AND CRASHES HIS FIST AGAINST THE JAW OF THE ASTONISHED MONGOL.!
- AND THAT'S THAT.!!
FORGIVE ME! THE GUARDS SEEING YOUR MASKED FACE THOUGHT YOU WERE AN ENEMY. IT WAS PURELY AN ACCIDENT!
I FORGIVE YOU. LEAD ON, MY FRIEND
AS SIN FANG STEPS OUT OF THE ROOM, THE DOOR SUDDENLY SLAMS SHUT UPON THE BATMAN!
SLAM!
GAS! COUGH.. MUSTARD GAS! COUGH....
HE REACHES QUICKLY FOR A PARTICULAR GLASS VIAL IN HIS BELT...

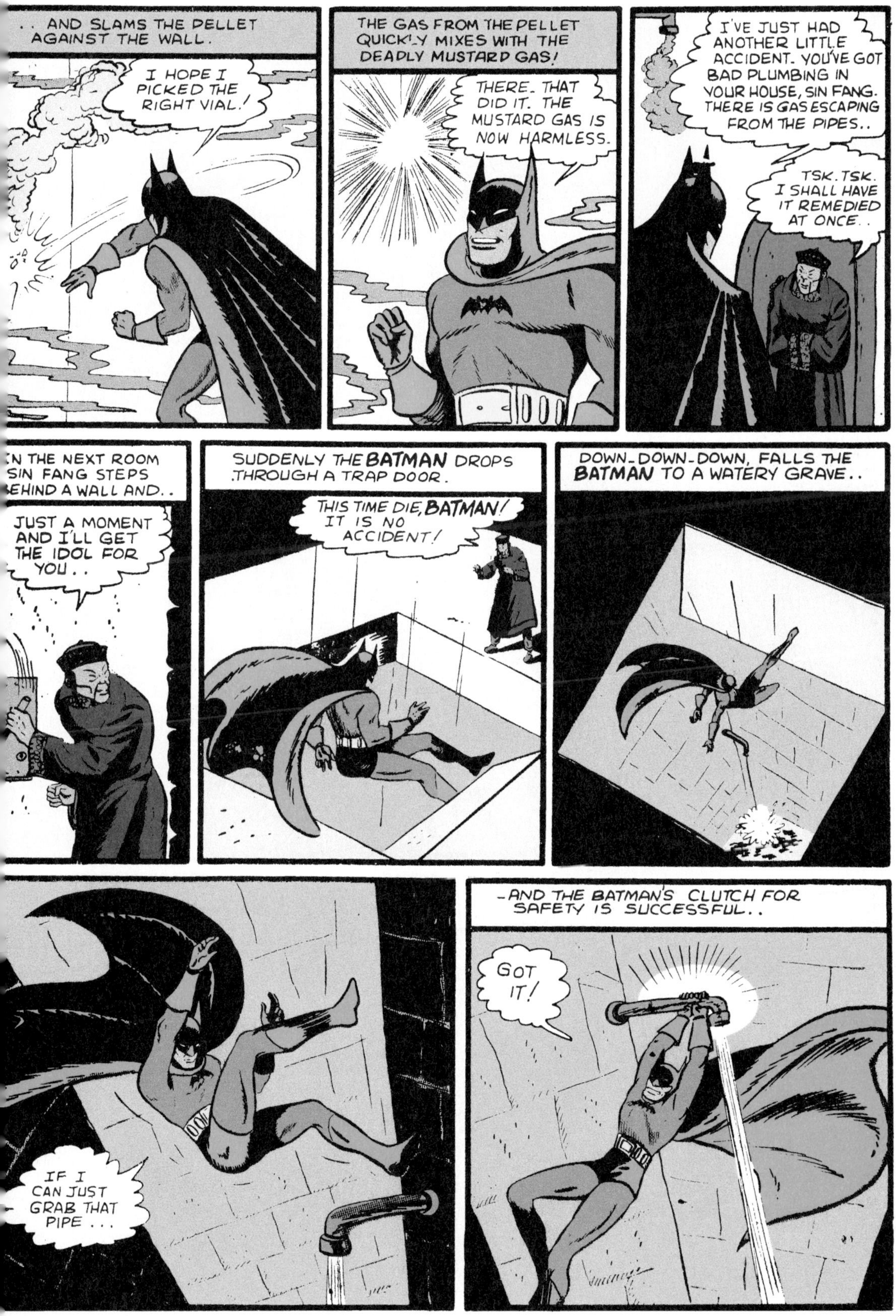
. . AND SLAMS THE PELLET AGAINST THE WALL.
I HOPE I PICKED THE RIGHT VIAL!
THE GAS FROM THE PELLET QUICKLY MIXES WITH THE DEADLY MUSTARD GAS!
THERE. THAT DID IT. THE MUSTARD GAS IS NOW HARMLESS.
I'VE JUST HAD ANOTHER LITTLE ACCIDENT. YOU'VE GOT BAD PLUMBING IN YOUR HOUSE, SIN FANG. THERE IS GAS ESCAPING FROM THE PIPES . .
TSK. TSK. I SHALL HAVE IT REMEDIED AT ONCE . .
IN THE NEXT ROOM SIN FANG STEPS BEHIND A WALL AND . .
JUST A MOMENT AND I'LL GET THE IDOL FOR YOU . .
SUDDENLY THE BATMAN DROPS THROUGH A TRAP DOOR.
THIS TIME DIE, BATMAN! IT IS NO ACCIDENT!
DOWN-DOWN-DOWN, FALLS THE BATMAN TO A WATERY GRAVE . .
IF I CAN JUST GRAB THAT PIPE . . .
-AND THE BATMAN'S CLUTCH FOR SAFETY IS SUCCESSFUL . .
GOT IT!

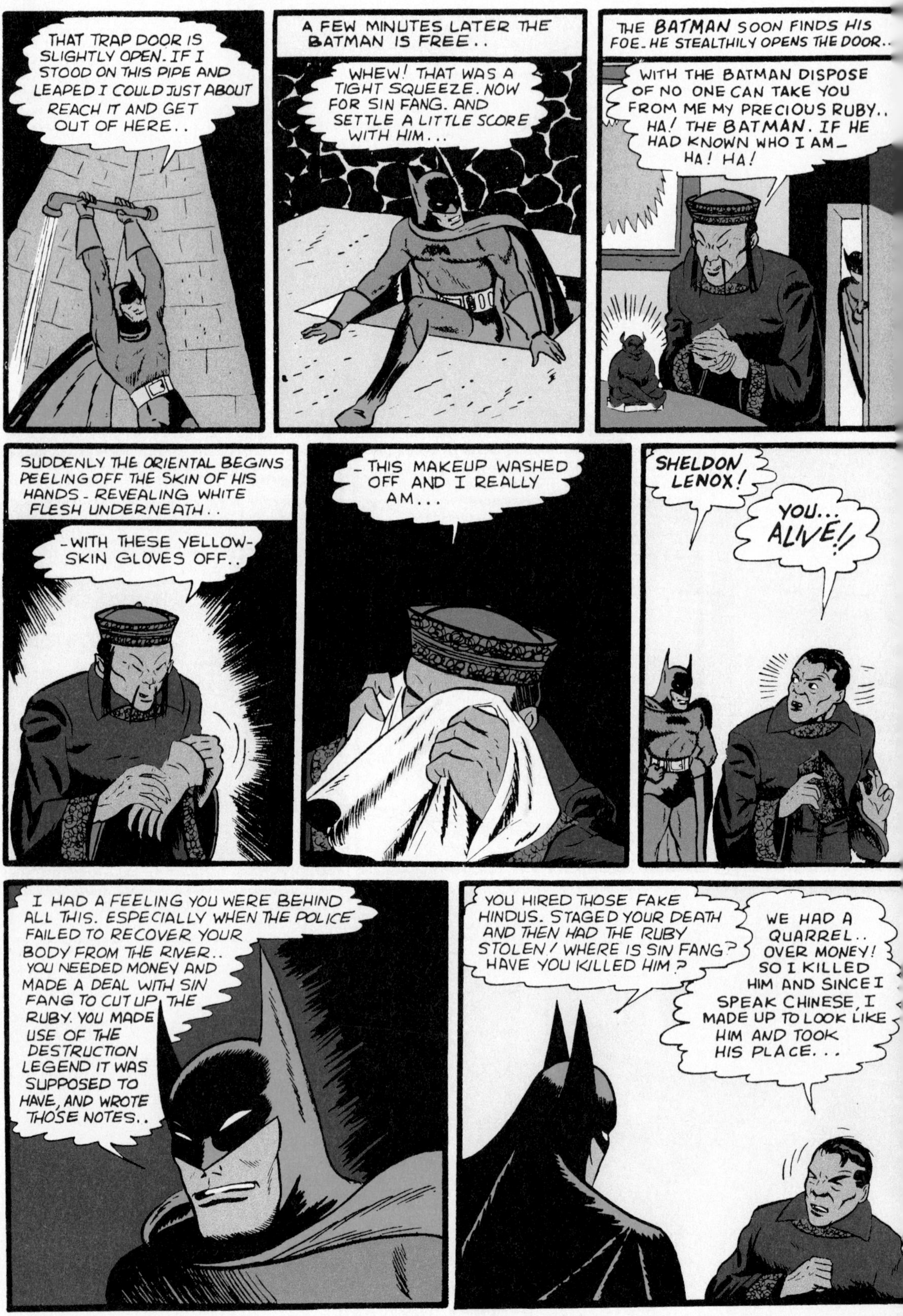
THAT TRAP DOOR IS SLIGHTLY OPEN. IF I STOOD ON THIS PIPE AND LEAPED I COULD JUST ABOUT REACH IT AND GET OUT OF HERE..
A FEW MINUTES LATER THE BATMAN IS FREE..
WHEW! THAT WAS A TIGHT SQUEEZE. NOW FOR SIN FANG. AND SETTLE A LITTLE SCORE WITH HIM...
THE BATMAN SOON FINDS HIS FOE - HE STEALTHILY OPENS THE DOOR..
WITH THE BATMAN DISPOSE OF NO ONE CAN TAKE YOU FROM ME MY PRECIOUS RUBY.. HA! THE BATMAN. IF HE HAD KNOWN WHO I AM— HA! HA!
SUDDENLY THE ORIENTAL BEGINS PEELING OFF THE SKIN OF HIS HANDS - REVEALING WHITE FLESH UNDERNEATH..
-WITH THESE YELLOW-SKIN GLOVES OFF..
-THIS MAKEUP WASHED OFF AND I REALLY AM...
SHELDON LENOX!
YOU... ALIVE!!
I HAD A FEELING YOU WERE BEHIND ALL THIS. ESPECIALLY WHEN THE POLICE FAILED TO RECOVER YOUR BODY FROM THE RIVER.. YOU NEEDED MONEY AND MADE A DEAL WITH SIN FANG TO CUT UP THE RUBY. YOU MADE USE OF THE DESTRUCTION LEGEND IT WAS SUPPOSED TO HAVE, AND WROTE THOSE NOTES..
YOU HIRED THOSE FAKE HINDUS. STAGED YOUR DEATH AND THEN HAD THE RUBY STOLEN! WHERE IS SIN FANG? HAVE YOU KILLED HIM?
WE HAD A QUARREL.. OVER MONEY! SO I KILLED HIM AND SINCE I SPEAK CHINESE, I MADE UP TO LOOK LIKE HIM AND TOOK HIS PLACE...

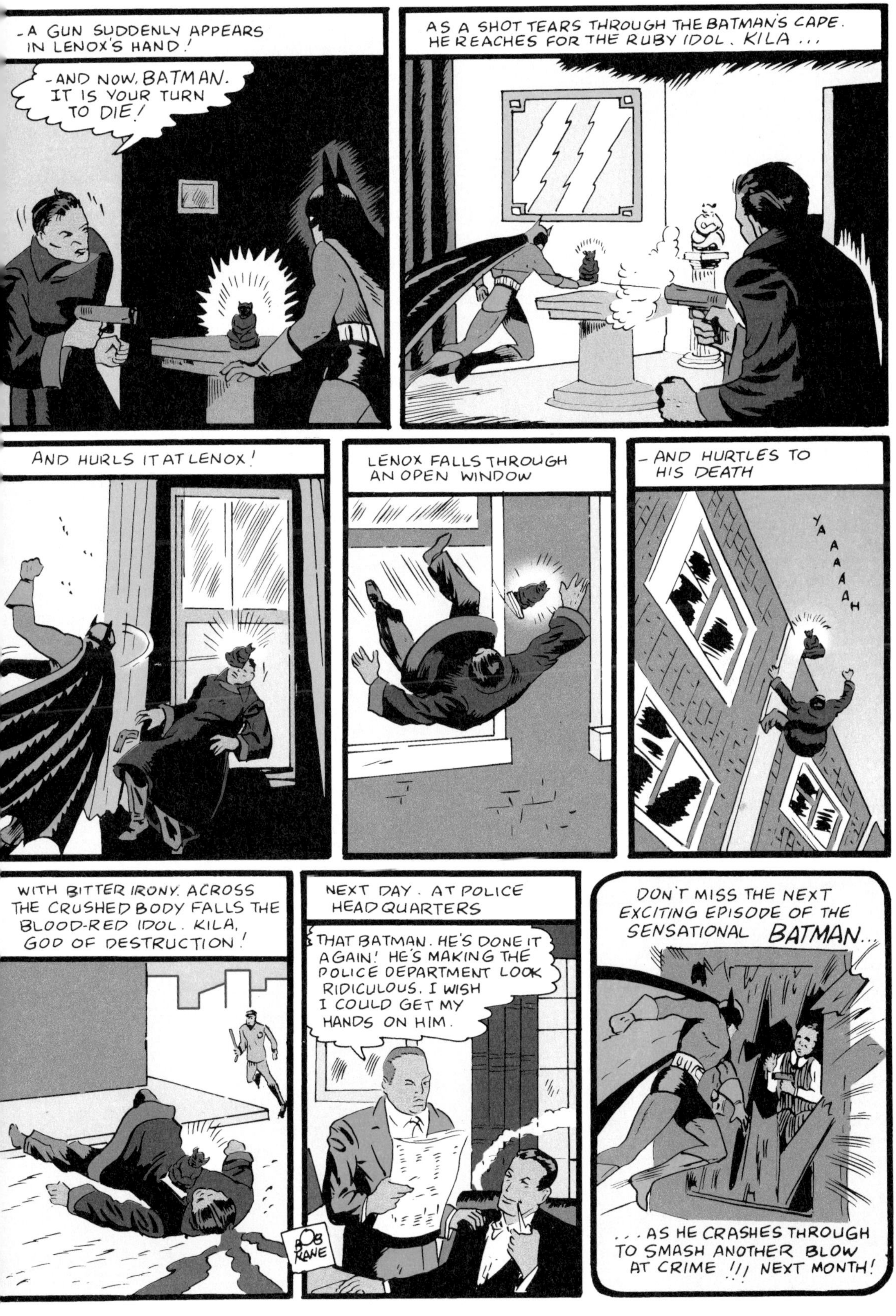
-A GUN SUDDENLY APPEARS IN LENOX'S HAND!
-AND NOW, BATMAN. IT IS YOUR TURN TO DIE!
AS A SHOT TEARS THROUGH THE BATMAN'S CAPE. HE REACHES FOR THE RUBY IDOL. KILA ...
AND HURLS IT AT LENOX!
LENOX FALLS THROUGH AN OPEN WINDOW
-AND HURTLES TO HIS DEATH
YAAAAAH
WITH BITTER IRONY, ACROSS THE CRUSHED BODY FALLS THE BLOOD-RED IDOL. KILA, GOD OF DESTRUCTION!
NEXT DAY. AT POLICE HEADQUARTERS
THAT BATMAN. HE'S DONE IT AGAIN! HE'S MAKING THE POLICE DEPARTMENT LOOK RIDICULOUS. I WISH I COULD GET MY HANDS ON HIM.
BOB KANE
DON'T MISS THE NEXT EXCITING EPISODE OF THE SENSATIONAL BATMAN...
...AS HE CRASHES THROUGH TO SMASH ANOTHER BLOW AT CRIME !!! NEXT MONTH!

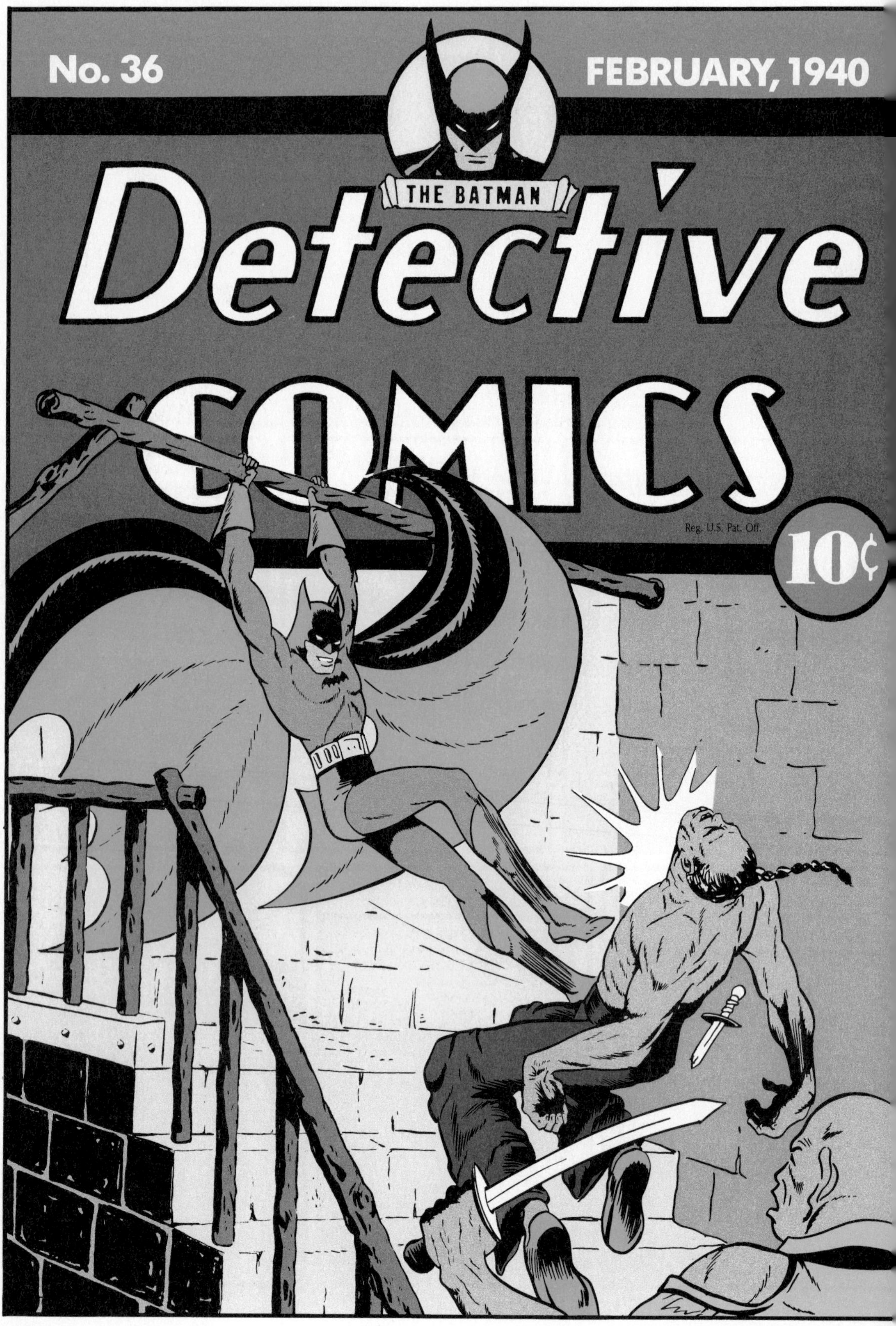
No. 36
FEBRUARY, 1940
THE BATMAN
Detective
COMICS
Reg. U.S. Pat. Off.
10¢

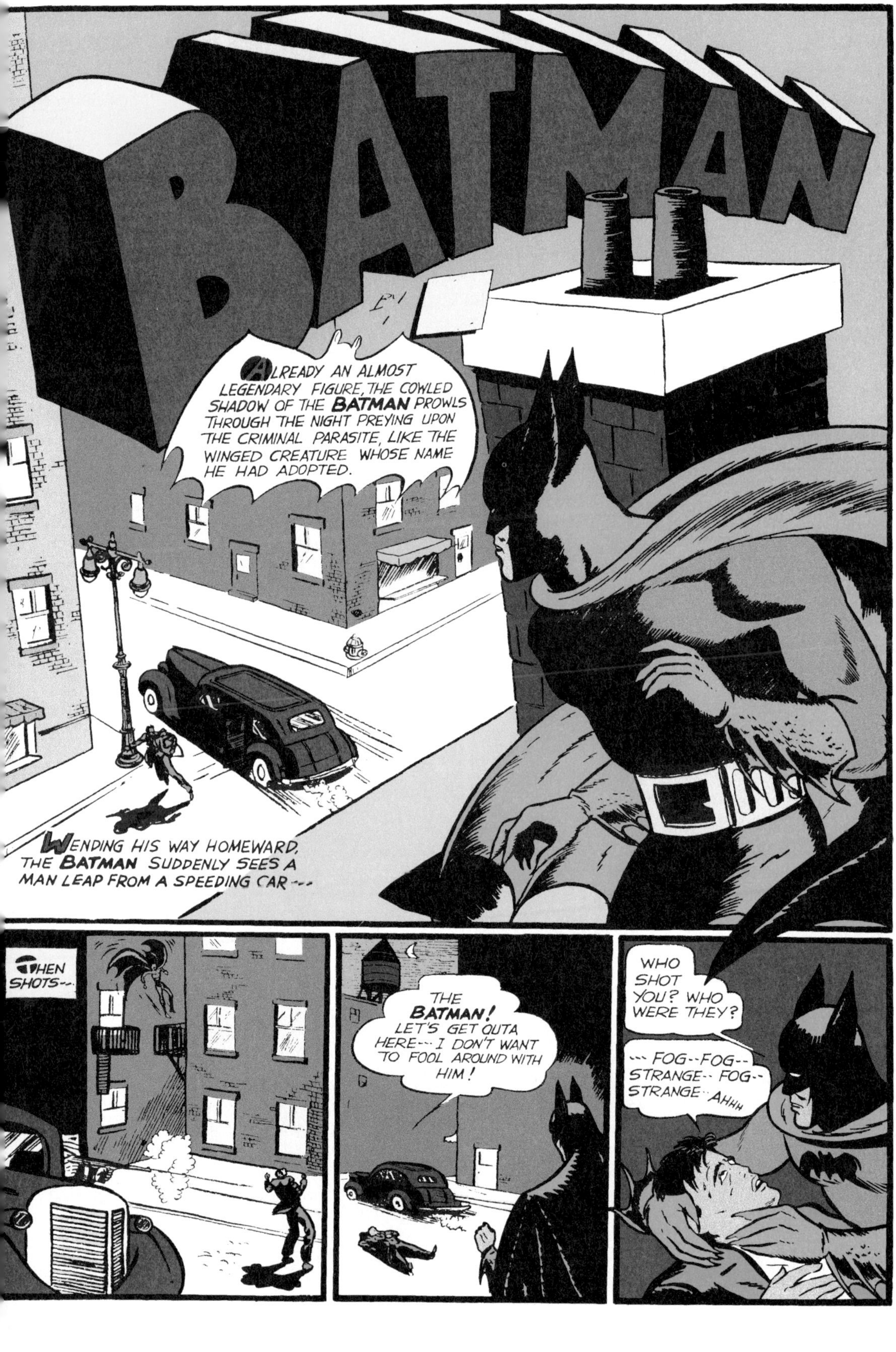
BATMAN
ALREADY AN ALMOST LEGENDARY FIGURE, THE COWLED SHADOW OF THE BATMAN PROWLS THROUGH THE NIGHT PREYING UPON THE CRIMINAL PARASITE, LIKE THE WINGED CREATURE WHOSE NAME HE HAD ADOPTED.
WENDING HIS WAY HOMEWARD, THE BATMAN SUDDENLY SEES A MAN LEAP FROM A SPEEDING CAR---
THEN SHOTS--.
THE BATMAN! LET'S GET OUTA HERE--- I DON'T WANT TO FOOL AROUND WITH HIM!
WHO SHOT YOU? WHO WERE THEY?
--- FOG--FOG-- STRANGE-- FOG-- STRANGE-- AHHH

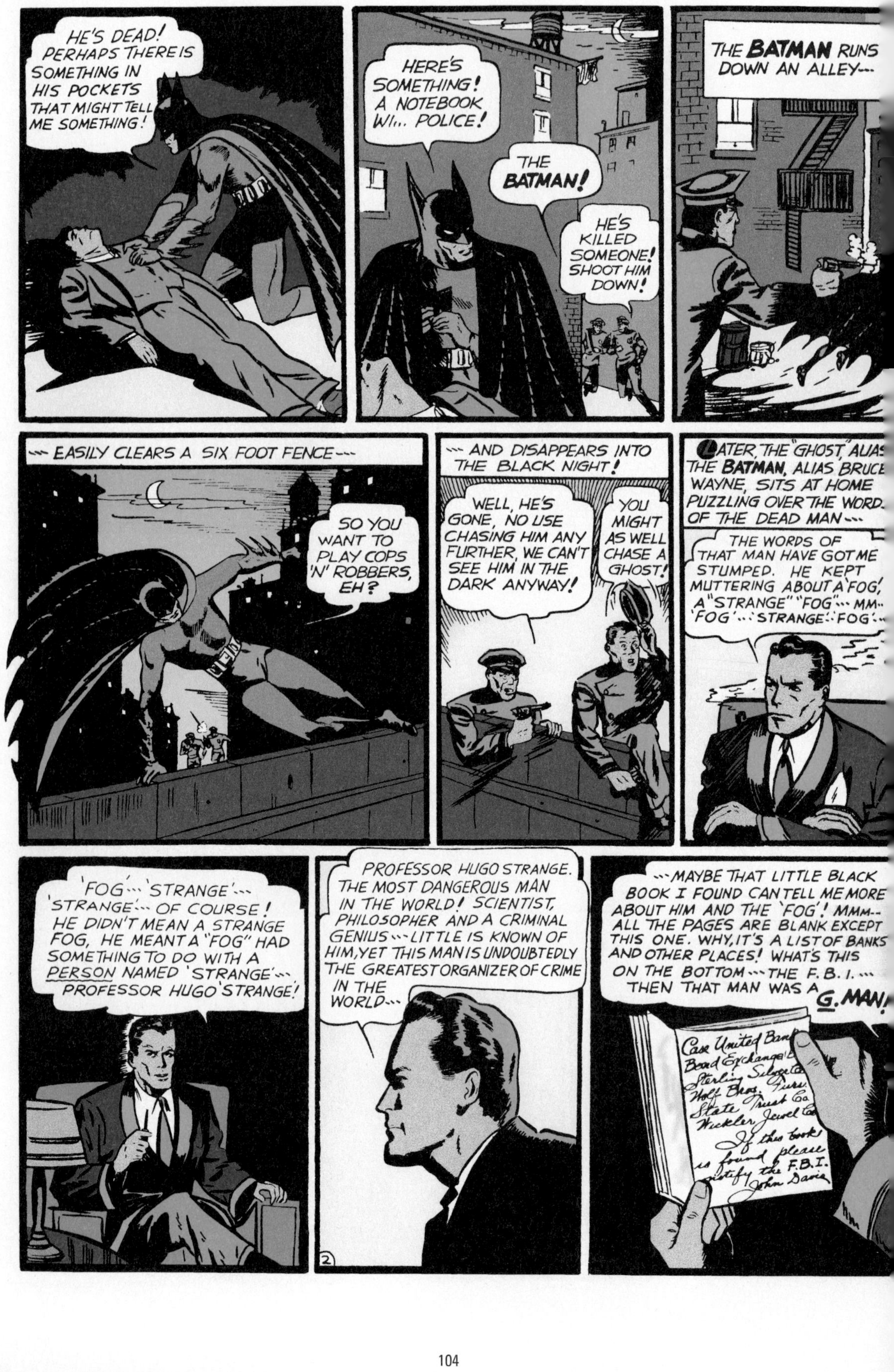

HE'S DEAD! PERHAPS THERE IS SOMETHING IN HIS POCKETS THAT MIGHT TELL ME SOMETHING!
HERE'S SOMETHING! A NOTEBOOK WI... POLICE!
THE BATMAN!
HE'S KILLED SOMEONE! SHOOT HIM DOWN!
THE BATMAN RUNS DOWN AN ALLEY---
--- EASILY CLEARS A SIX FOOT FENCE---
SO YOU WANT TO PLAY COPS 'N' ROBBERS, EH?
--- AND DISAPPEARS INTO THE BLACK NIGHT!
WELL, HE'S GONE, NO USE CHASING HIM ANY FURTHER, WE CAN'T SEE HIM IN THE DARK ANYWAY!
YOU MIGHT AS WELL CHASE A GHOST!
LATER, THE "GHOST," ALIAS THE BATMAN, ALIAS BRUCE WAYNE, SITS AT HOME PUZZLING OVER THE WORDS OF THE DEAD MAN---
THE WORDS OF THAT MAN HAVE GOT ME STUMPED. HE KEPT MUTTERING ABOUT A 'FOG', A "STRANGE" "FOG"--- MM-- 'FOG'--- STRANGE--- FOG'---
'FOG'--- 'STRANGE'--- 'STRANGE'--- OF COURSE! HE DIDN'T MEAN A STRANGE FOG, HE MEANT A "FOG" HAD SOMETHING TO DO WITH A PERSON NAMED 'STRANGE'--- PROFESSOR HUGO 'STRANGE'!
PROFESSOR HUGO STRANGE. THE MOST DANGEROUS MAN IN THE WORLD! SCIENTIST, PHILOSOPHER AND A CRIMINAL GENIUS--- LITTLE IS KNOWN OF HIM, YET THIS MAN IS UNDOUBTEDLY THE GREATEST ORGANIZER OF CRIME IN THE WORLD---
---MAYBE THAT LITTLE BLACK BOOK I FOUND CAN TELL ME MORE ABOUT HIM AND THE 'FOG'! MMM-- ALL THE PAGES ARE BLANK EXCEPT THIS ONE. WHY, IT'S A LIST OF BANKS AND OTHER PLACES! WHAT'S THIS ON THE BOTTOM--- THE F. B. I.--- THEN THAT MAN WAS A G. MAN!
Case United Bank
Wolf Bros. Furs
State Trust Co.
If this book is found please notify the F.B.I.
2

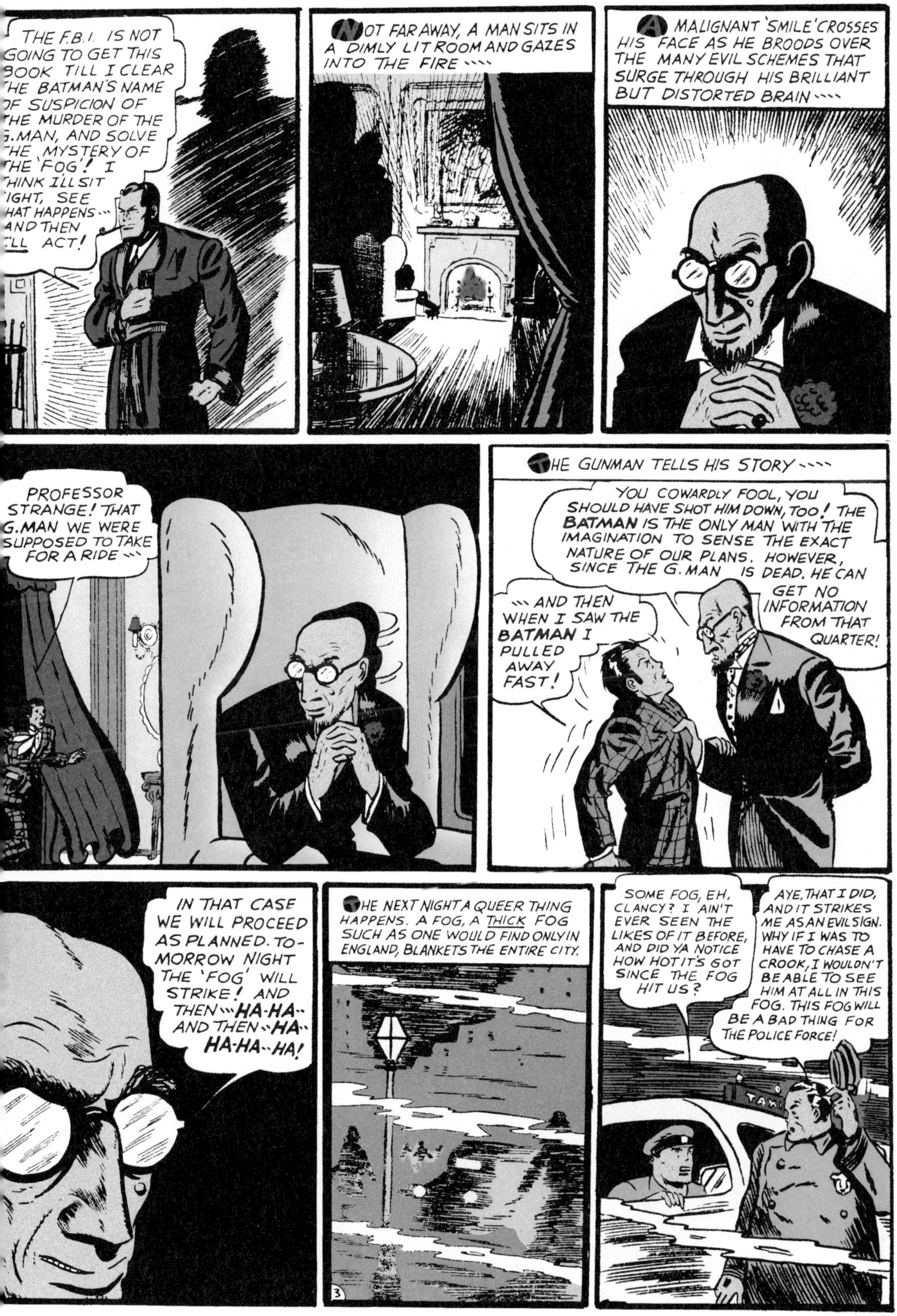
THE F.B.I. IS NOT GOING TO GET THIS BOOK TILL I CLEAR THE BATMAN'S NAME OF SUSPICION OF THE MURDER OF THE G.MAN, AND SOLVE THE MYSTERY OF THE 'FOG'! I THINK I'LL SIT IGHT, SEE HAT HAPPENS... AND THEN 'LL ACT!
NOT FAR AWAY, A MAN SITS IN A DIMLY LIT ROOM AND GAZES INTO THE FIRE....
A MALIGNANT 'SMILE' CROSSES HIS FACE AS HE BROODS OVER THE MANY EVIL SCHEMES THAT SURGE THROUGH HIS BRILLIANT BUT DISTORTED BRAIN....
PROFESSOR STRANGE! THAT G.MAN WE WERE SUPPOSED TO TAKE FOR A RIDE...
THE GUNMAN TELLS HIS STORY....
...AND THEN WHEN I SAW THE BATMAN I PULLED AWAY FAST!
YOU COWARDLY FOOL, YOU SHOULD HAVE SHOT HIM DOWN, TOO! THE BATMAN IS THE ONLY MAN WITH THE IMAGINATION TO SENSE THE EXACT NATURE OF OUR PLANS. HOWEVER, SINCE THE G. MAN IS DEAD, HE CAN GET NO INFORMATION FROM THAT QUARTER!
IN THAT CASE WE WILL PROCEED AS PLANNED. TOMORROW NIGHT THE 'FOG' WILL STRIKE! AND THEN...HA-HA... AND THEN..HA... HA-HA..HA!
THE NEXT NIGHT A QUEER THING HAPPENS. A FOG, A THICK FOG SUCH AS ONE WOULD FIND ONLY IN ENGLAND, BLANKETS THE ENTIRE CITY.
3
SOME FOG, EH, CLANCY? I AIN'T EVER SEEN THE LIKES OF IT BEFORE, AND DID YA NOTICE HOW HOT IT'S GOT SINCE THE FOG HIT US?
AYE, THAT I DID, AND IT STRIKES ME AS AN EVIL SIGN. WHY IF I WAS TO HAVE TO CHASE A CROOK, I WOULDN'T BE ABLE TO SEE HIM AT ALL IN THIS FOG. THIS FOG WILL BE A BAD THING FOR THE POLICE FORCE!
TAXI

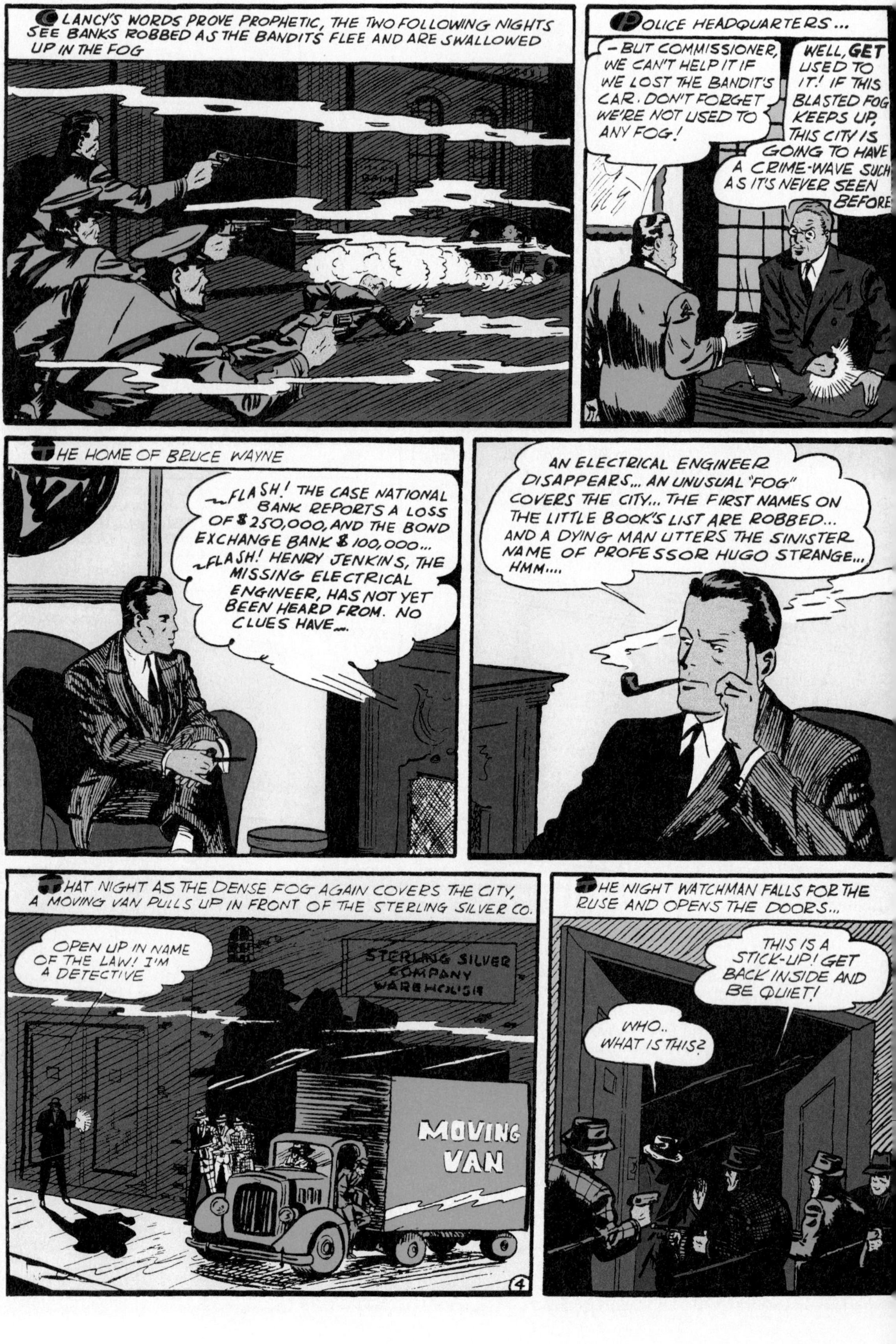
CLANCY'S WORDS PROVE PROPHETIC, THE TWO FOLLOWING NIGHTS SEE BANKS ROBBED AS THE BANDITS FLEE AND ARE SWALLOWED UP IN THE FOG
POLICE HEADQUARTERS...
- BUT COMMISSIONER, WE CAN'T HELP IT IF WE LOST THE BANDIT'S CAR. DON'T FORGET WE'RE NOT USED TO ANY FOG!
WELL, GET USED TO IT! IF THIS BLASTED FOG KEEPS UP, THIS CITY IS GOING TO HAVE A CRIME-WAVE SUCH AS IT'S NEVER SEEN BEFORE
THE HOME OF BRUCE WAYNE
-FLASH! THE CASE NATIONAL BANK REPORTS A LOSS OF $250,000, AND THE BOND EXCHANGE BANK $100,000... -FLASH! HENRY JENKINS, THE MISSING ELECTRICAL ENGINEER, HAS NOT YET BEEN HEARD FROM. NO CLUES HAVE-
AN ELECTRICAL ENGINEER DISAPPEARS... AN UNUSUAL "FOG" COVERS THE CITY... THE FIRST NAMES ON THE LITTLE BOOK'S LIST ARE ROBBED... AND A DYING MAN UTTERS THE SINISTER NAME OF PROFESSOR HUGO STRANGE... HMM....
THAT NIGHT AS THE DENSE FOG AGAIN COVERS THE CITY, A MOVING VAN PULLS UP IN FRONT OF THE STERLING SILVER CO.
OPEN UP IN NAME OF THE LAW! I'M A DETECTIVE
STERLING SILVER COMPANY WAREHOUSE
MOVING VAN
4
THE NIGHT WATCHMAN FALLS FOR THE RUSE AND OPENS THE DOORS...
THIS IS A STICK-UP! GET BACK INSIDE AND BE QUIET!
WHO.. WHAT IS THIS?

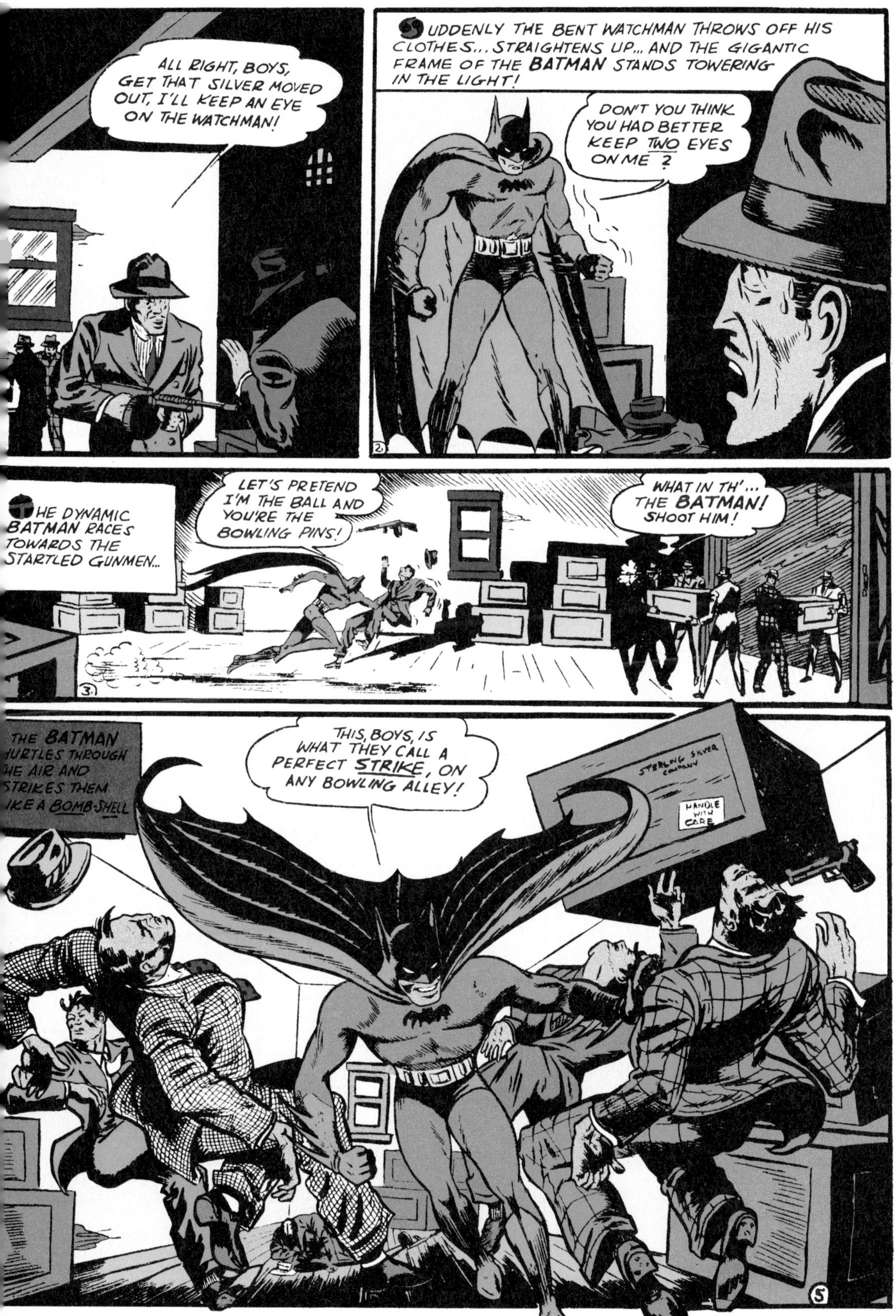
ALL RIGHT, BOYS, GET THAT SILVER MOVED OUT, I'LL KEEP AN EYE ON THE WATCHMAN!
SUDDENLY THE BENT WATCHMAN THROWS OFF HIS CLOTHES... STRAIGHTENS UP... AND THE GIGANTIC FRAME OF THE BATMAN STANDS TOWERING IN THE LIGHT!
DON'T YOU THINK YOU HAD BETTER KEEP TWO EYES ON ME ?
THE DYNAMIC BATMAN RACES TOWARDS THE STARTLED GUNMEN...
LET'S PRETEND I'M THE BALL AND YOU'RE THE BOWLING PINS!
WHAT IN TH'... THE BATMAN! SHOOT HIM!
THE BATMAN HURTLES THROUGH HE AIR AND STRIKES THEM IKE A BOMB-SHELL
THIS, BOYS, IS WHAT THEY CALL A PERFECT STRIKE, ON ANY BOWLING ALLEY!
STERLING SILVER COMPANY
HANDLE WITH CARE

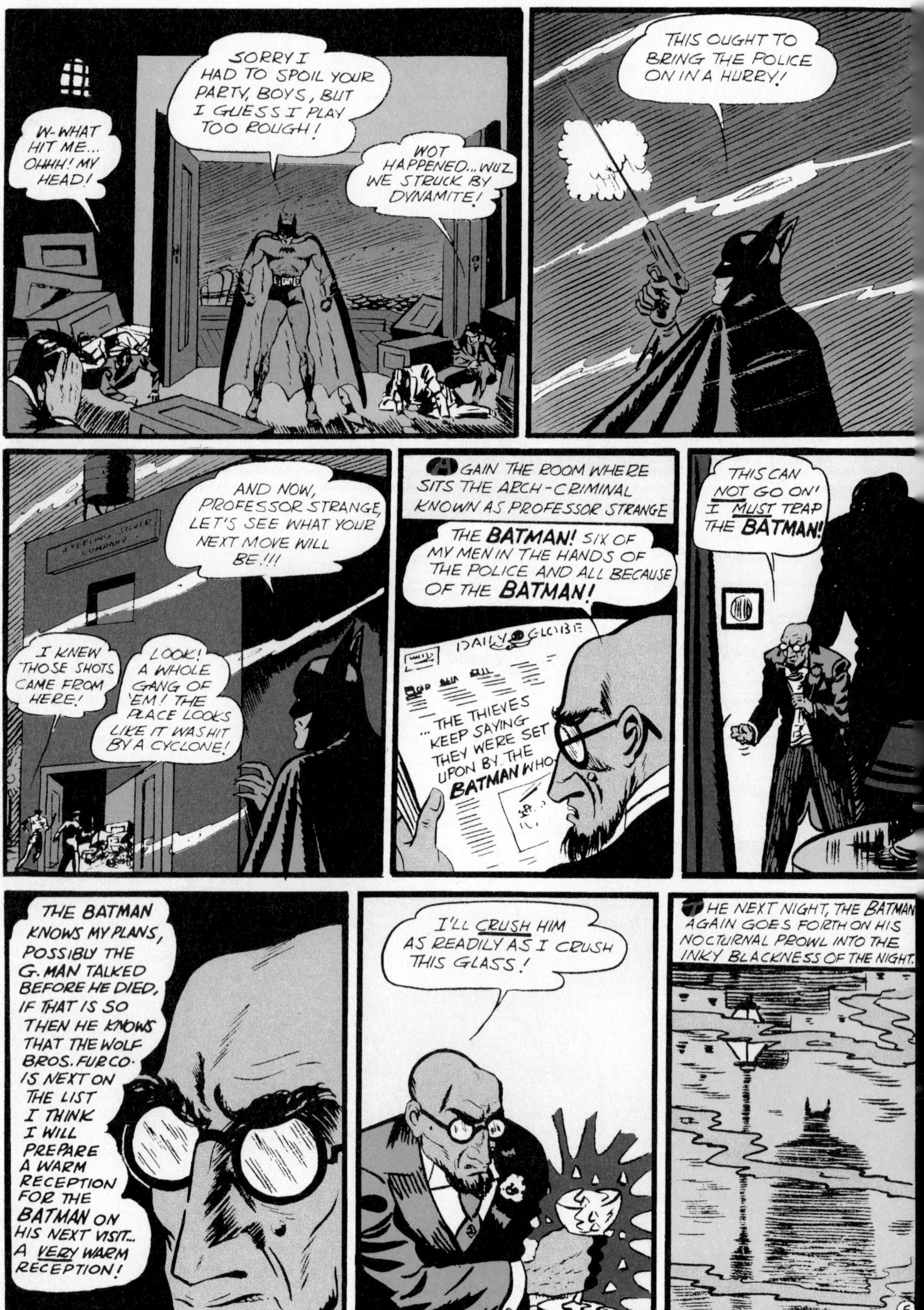
W-WHAT HIT ME... OHHH! MY HEAD!
SORRY I HAD TO SPOIL YOUR PARTY, BOYS, BUT I GUESS I PLAY TOO ROUGH!
WOT HAPPENED... WUZ WE STRUCK BY DYNAMITE!
THIS OUGHT TO BRING THE POLICE ON IN A HURRY!
AND NOW, PROFESSOR STRANGE, LET'S SEE WHAT YOUR NEXT MOVE WILL BE!!!
I KNEW THOSE SHOTS CAME FROM HERE!
LOOK! A WHOLE GANG OF 'EM! THE PLACE LOOKS LIKE IT WAS HIT BY A CYCLONE!
AGAIN THE ROOM WHERE SITS THE ARCH-CRIMINAL KNOWN AS PROFESSOR STRANGE
THE BATMAN! SIX OF MY MEN IN THE HANDS OF THE POLICE AND ALL BECAUSE OF THE BATMAN!
DAILY GLOBE
... THE THIEVES KEEP SAYING THEY WERE SET UPON BY THE BATMAN WHO
THIS CAN NOT GO ON! I MUST TRAP THE BATMAN!
THE BATMAN KNOWS MY PLANS, POSSIBLY THE G. MAN TALKED BEFORE HE DIED, IF THAT IS SO THEN HE KNOWS THAT THE WOLF BROS. FUR CO. IS NEXT ON THE LIST I THINK I WILL PREPARE A WARM RECEPTION FOR THE BATMAN ON HIS NEXT VISIT... A VERY WARM RECEPTION!
I'LL CRUSH HIM AS READILY AS I CRUSH THIS GLASS!
THE NEXT NIGHT, THE BATMAN AGAIN GOES FORTH ON HIS NOCTURNAL PROWL INTO THE INKY BLACKNESS OF THE NIGHT.
6

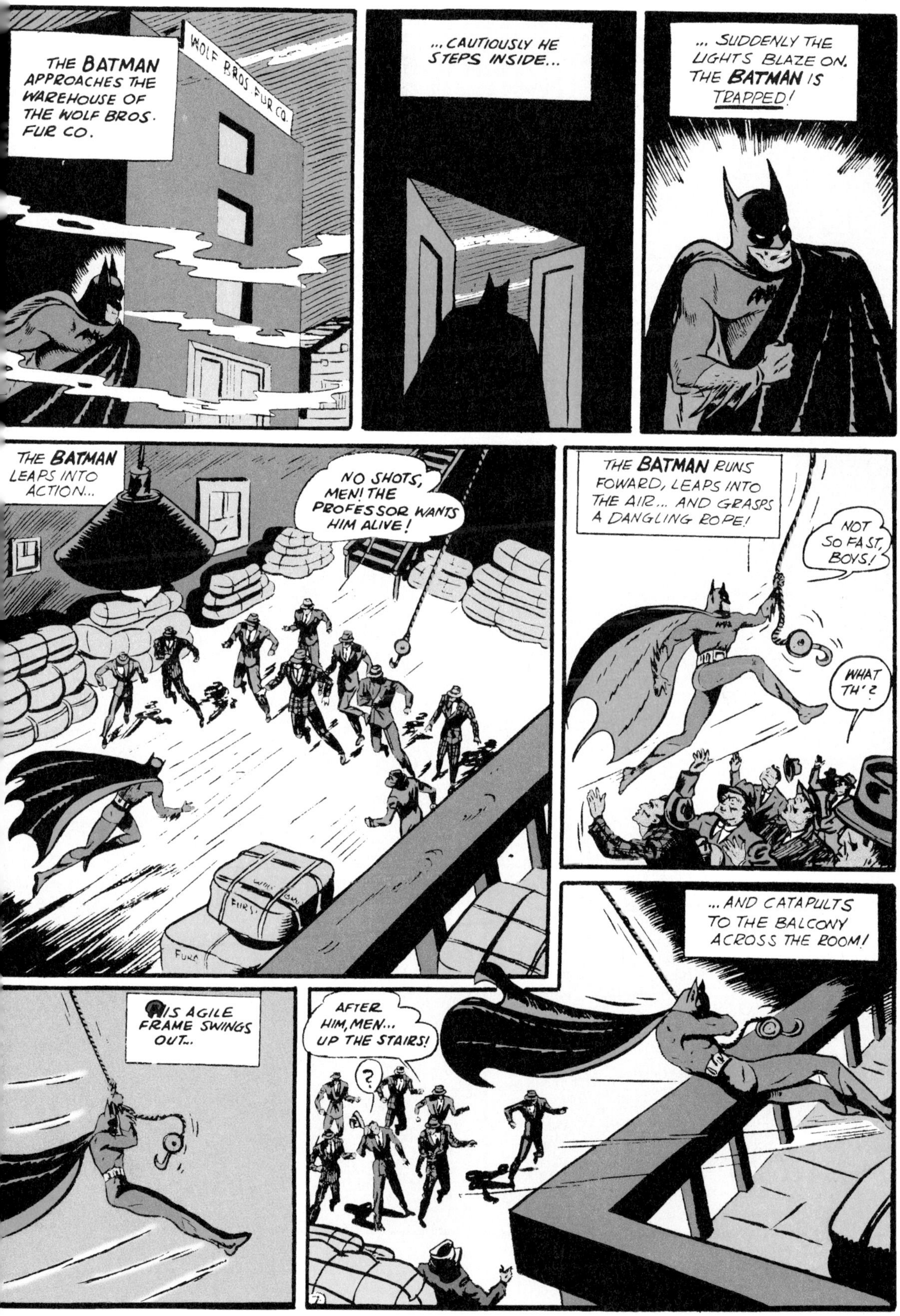
THE BATMAN APPROACHES THE WAREHOUSE OF THE WOLF BROS. FUR CO.
WOLF BROS. FUR CO.
... CAUTIOUSLY HE STEPS INSIDE...
... SUDDENLY THE LIGHTS BLAZE ON. THE BATMAN IS TRAPPED!
THE BATMAN LEAPS INTO ACTION...
NO SHOTS, MEN! THE PROFESSOR WANTS HIM ALIVE!
FURS
FURS
THE BATMAN RUNS FOWARD, LEAPS INTO THE AIR... AND GRASPS A DANGLING ROPE!
NOT SO FAST, BOYS!
WHAT TH'?
HIS AGILE FRAME SWINGS OUT...
AFTER HIM, MEN... UP THE STAIRS!
?
... AND CATAPULTS TO THE BALCONY ACROSS THE ROOM!

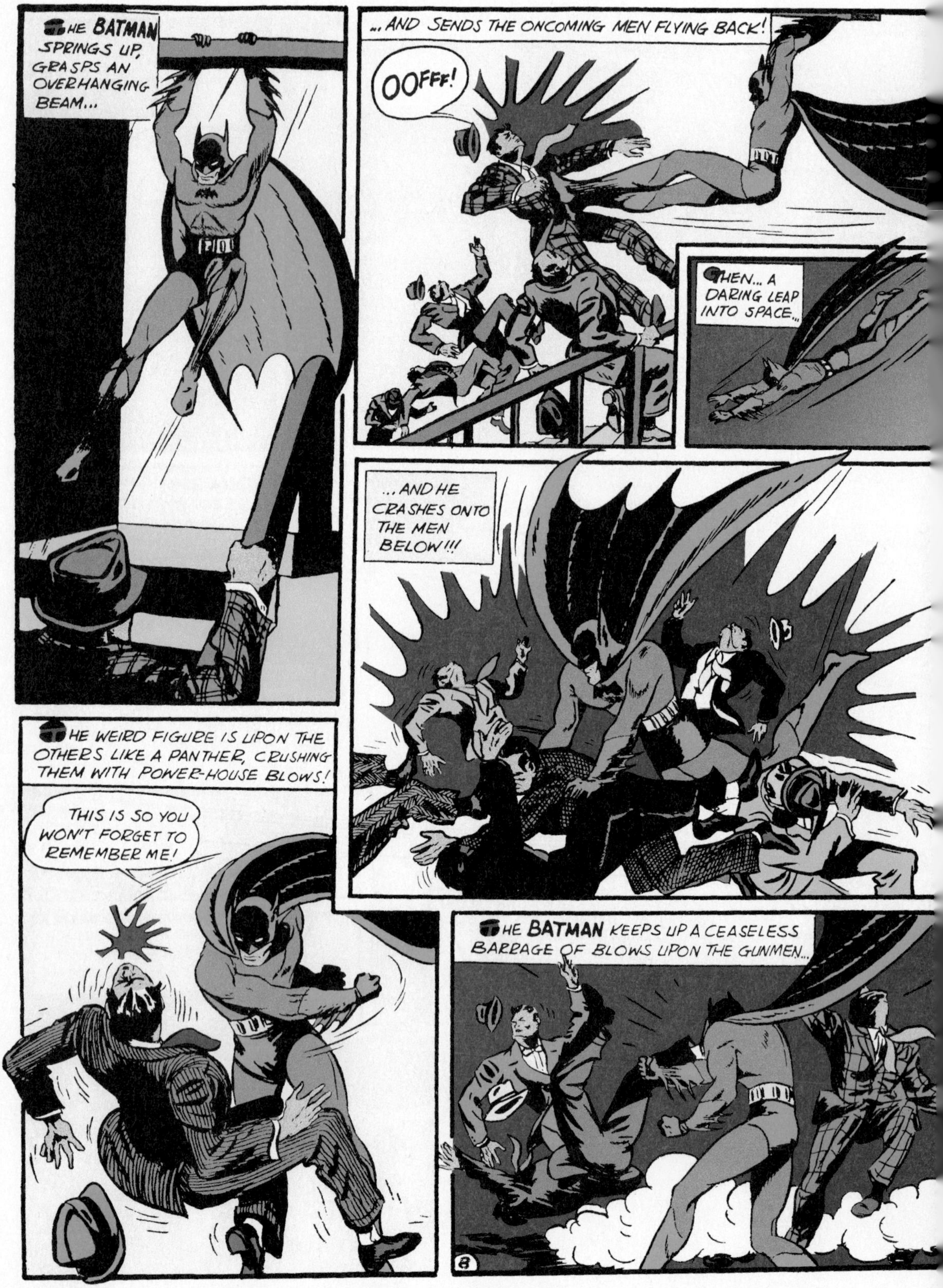
THE BATMAN SPRINGS UP, GRASPS AN OVERHANGING BEAM...
...AND SENDS THE ONCOMING MEN FLYING BACK!
OOFFF!
THEN... A DARING LEAP INTO SPACE...
...AND HE CRASHES ONTO THE MEN BELOW!!!
THE WEIRD FIGURE IS UPON THE OTHERS LIKE A PANTHER, CRUSHING THEM WITH POWER-HOUSE BLOWS!
THIS IS SO YOU WON'T FORGET TO REMEMBER ME!
THE BATMAN KEEPS UP A CEASELESS BARRAGE OF BLOWS UPON THE GUNMEN...
8

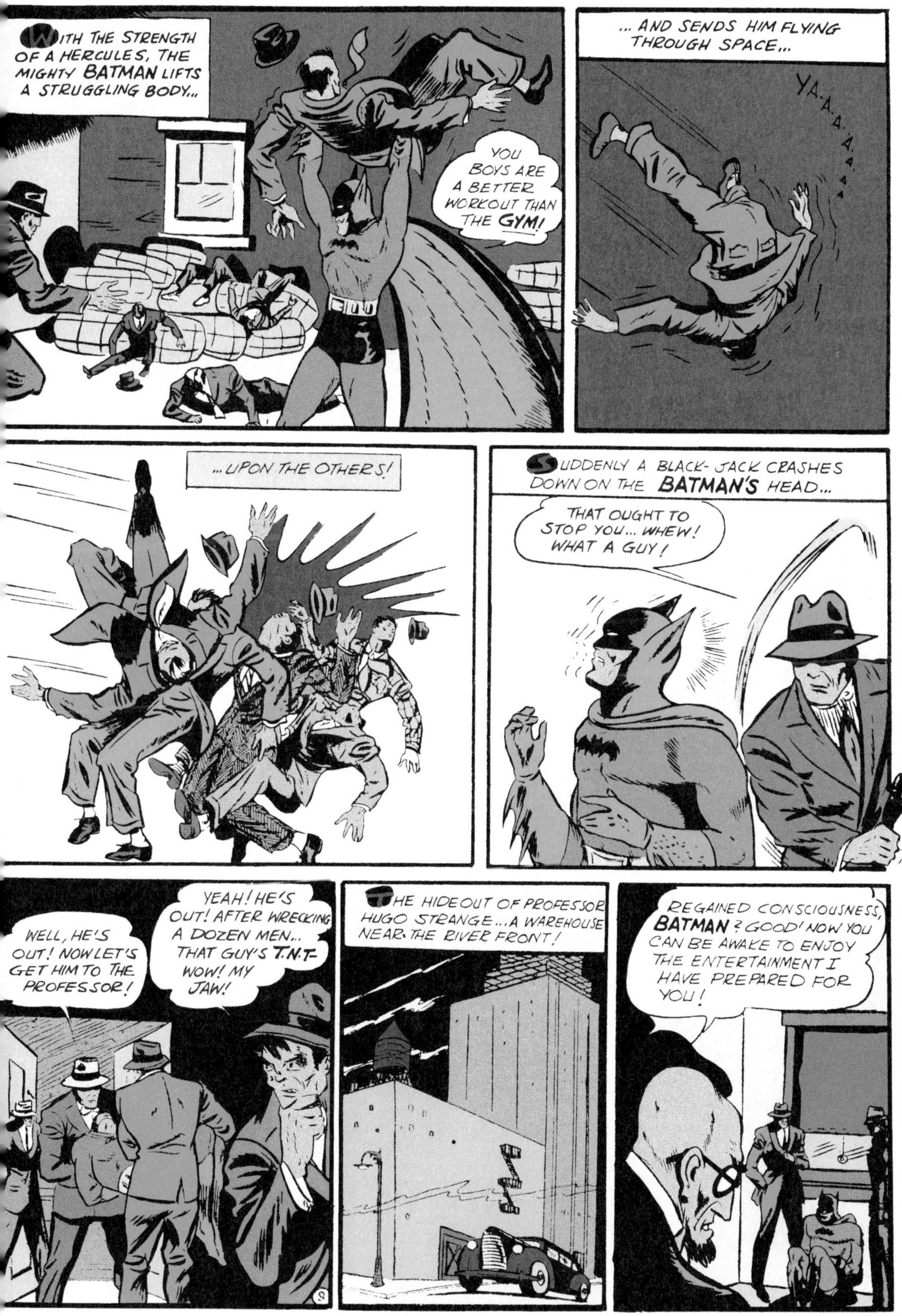
WITH THE STRENGTH OF A HERCULES, THE MIGHTY BATMAN LIFTS A STRUGGLING BODY...
YOU BOYS ARE A BETTER WORKOUT THAN THE GYM!
... AND SENDS HIM FLYING THROUGH SPACE...
YA-A-A-A-A-A-A
...UPON THE OTHERS!
SUDDENLY A BLACK-JACK CRASHES DOWN ON THE BATMAN'S HEAD...
THAT OUGHT TO STOP YOU... WHEW! WHAT A GUY!
WELL, HE'S OUT! NOW LET'S GET HIM TO THE PROFESSOR!
YEAH! HE'S OUT! AFTER WRECKING A DOZEN MEN... THAT GUY'S T.N.T.- WOW! MY JAW!
THE HIDEOUT OF PROFESSOR HUGO STRANGE... A WAREHOUSE NEAR THE RIVER FRONT!
REGAINED CONSCIOUSNESS, BATMAN? GOOD! NOW YOU CAN BE AWAKE TO ENJOY THE ENTERTAINMENT I HAVE PREPARED FOR YOU!

I HAVE BROUGHT YOU HERE ALIVE, SO THAT YOU MAY KNOW WHAT IT MEANS TO INTERFERE WITH PROFESSOR STRANGE!

●HE BATMAN IS MADE READY FOR THE LASH!

I'LL TEACH YOU... WITH A TASTE OF THE LASH!

●HE WHIP CRACKS DOWN ON THE MASSIVE FIGURE...

WHOSE STEEL MUSCLES SUDDENLY SURGE WITH STRENGTH AND SNAP HIS BONDS!

●UICKLY, HE DRAWS FORTH A GLASS PELLET...

...AS HE SLAMS IT TO THE FLOOR, A GAS EMANATES OVERCOMING THE MEN!

SLEEPING GAS (COUGH) WELL, THAT WON'T GET ME!

GAS!

MAYBE THE GAS WON'T, BUT I WILL!

⑩

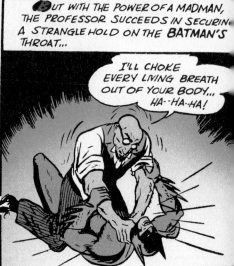

●UT WITH THE POWER OF A MADMAN, THE PROFESSOR SUCCEEDS IN SECURING A STRANGLE HOLD ON THE BATMAN'S THROAT...

I'LL CHOKE EVERY LIVING BREATH OUT OF YOUR BODY... HA--HA--HA!

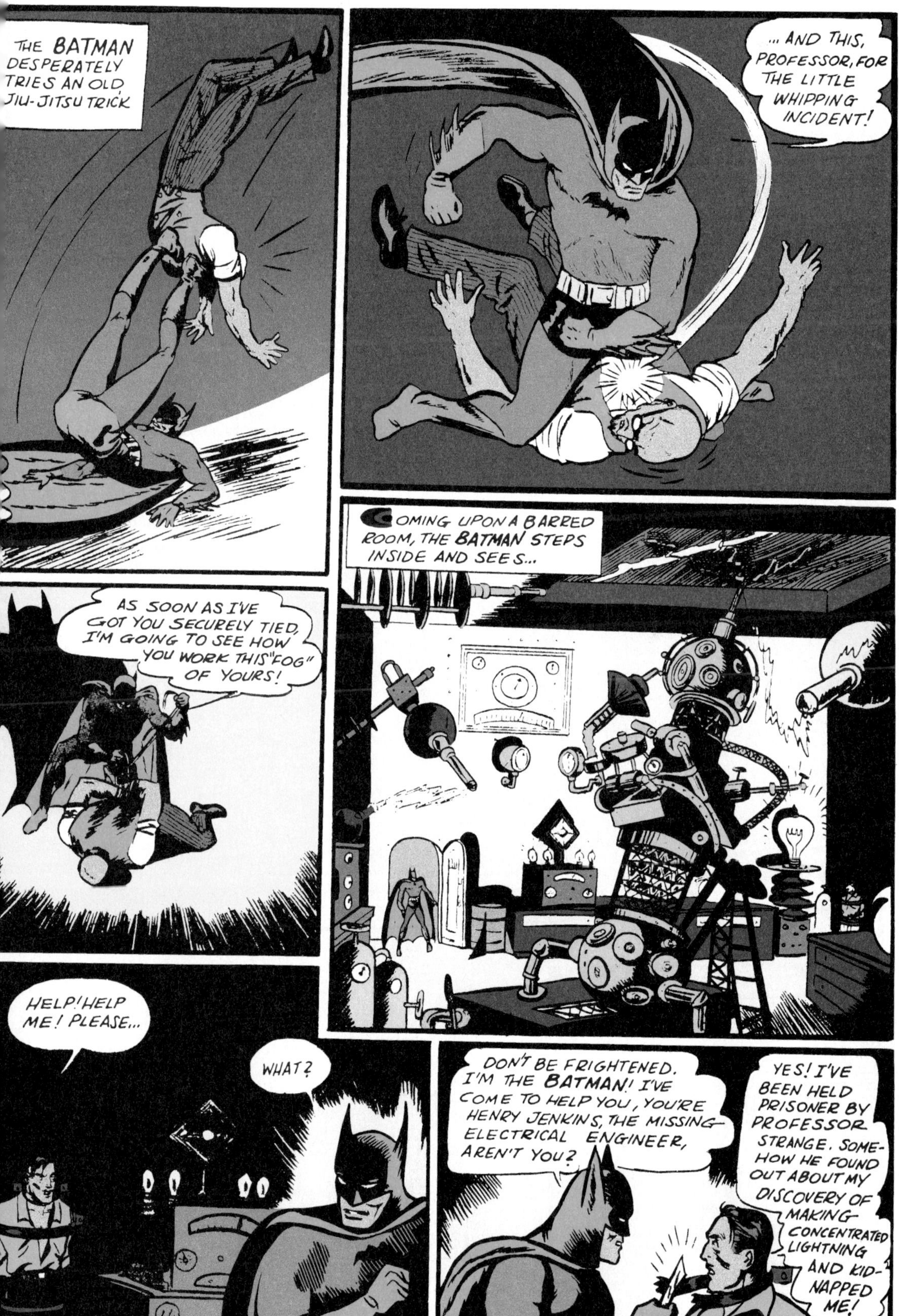
THE BATMAN DESPERATELY TRIES AN OLD JIU-JITSU TRICK
... AND THIS, PROFESSOR, FOR THE LITTLE WHIPPING INCIDENT!
AS SOON AS I'VE GOT YOU SECURELY TIED, I'M GOING TO SEE HOW YOU WORK THIS "FOG" OF YOURS!
COMING UPON A BARRED ROOM, THE BATMAN STEPS INSIDE AND SEES...
HELP! HELP ME! PLEASE...
WHAT?
DON'T BE FRIGHTENED. I'M THE BATMAN! I'VE COME TO HELP YOU, YOU'RE HENRY JENKINS, THE MISSING ELECTRICAL ENGINEER, AREN'T YOU?
YES! I'VE BEEN HELD PRISONER BY PROFESSOR STRANGE. SOMEHOW HE FOUND OUT ABOUT MY DISCOVERY OF MAKING CONCENTRATED LIGHTNING AND KIDNAPPED ME!

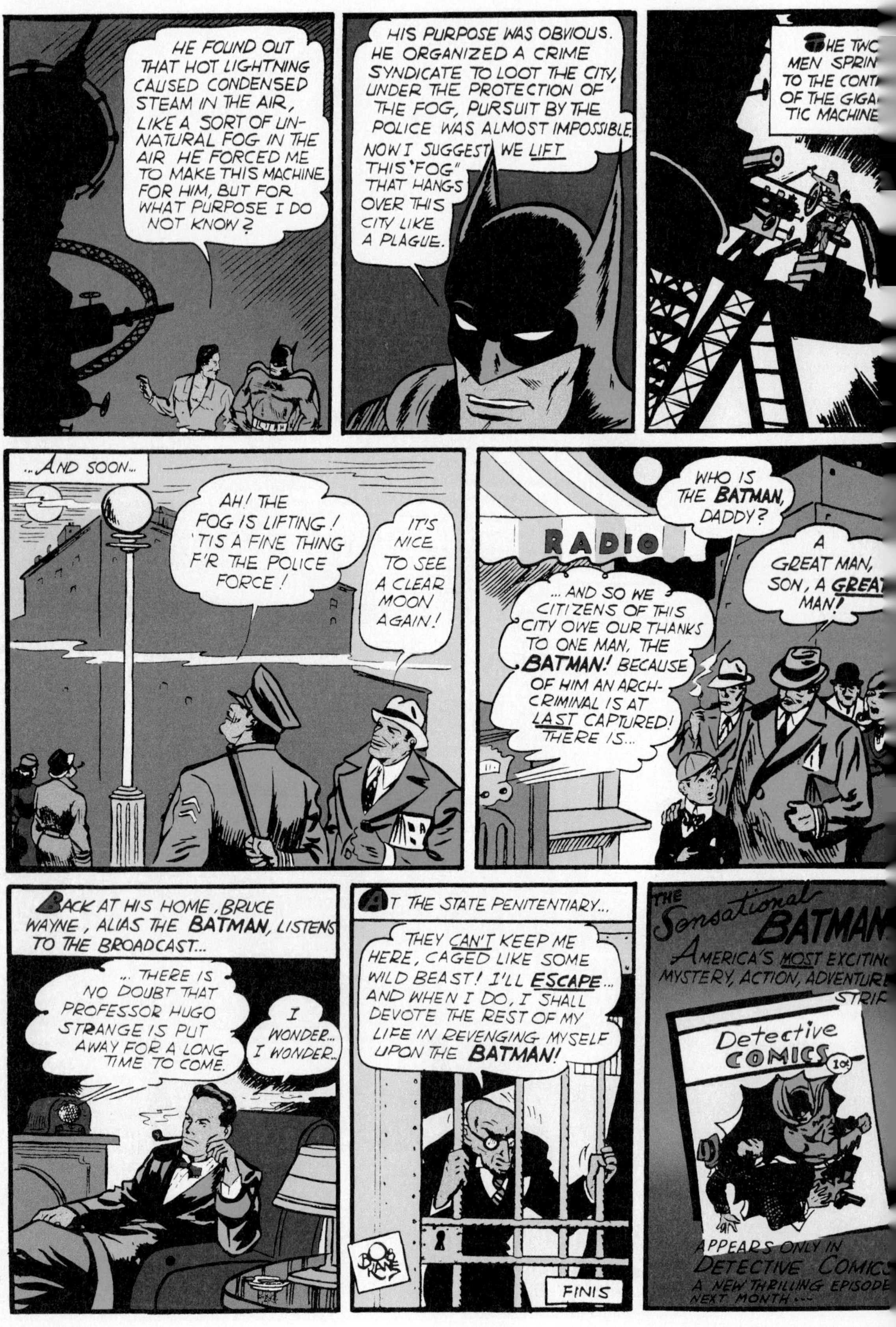
HE FOUND OUT THAT HOT LIGHTNING CAUSED CONDENSED STEAM IN THE AIR, LIKE A SORT OF UN-NATURAL FOG IN THE AIR HE FORCED ME TO MAKE THIS MACHINE FOR HIM, BUT FOR WHAT PURPOSE I DO NOT KNOW?
HIS PURPOSE WAS OBVIOUS. HE ORGANIZED A CRIME SYNDICATE TO LOOT THE CITY, UNDER THE PROTECTION OF THE FOG, PURSUIT BY THE POLICE WAS ALMOST IMPOSSIBLE. NOW I SUGGEST WE LIFT THIS "FOG" THAT HANGS OVER THIS CITY LIKE A PLAGUE.
THE TWO MEN SPRIN TO THE CONT OF THE GIGA TIC MACHINE
...AND SOON...
AH! THE FOG IS LIFTING! 'TIS A FINE THING F'R THE POLICE FORCE!
IT'S NICE TO SEE A CLEAR MOON AGAIN!
RADIO
...AND SO WE CITIZENS OF THIS CITY OWE OUR THANKS TO ONE MAN, THE BATMAN! BECAUSE OF HIM AN ARCH-CRIMINAL IS AT LAST CAPTURED! THERE IS...
WHO IS THE BATMAN, DADDY?
A GREAT MAN, SON, A GREAT MAN!
BACK AT HIS HOME, BRUCE WAYNE, ALIAS THE BATMAN, LISTENS TO THE BROADCAST...
... THERE IS NO DOUBT THAT PROFESSOR HUGO STRANGE IS PUT AWAY FOR A LONG TIME TO COME.
I WONDER... I WONDER...
AT THE STATE PENITENTIARY...
THEY CAN'T KEEP ME HERE, CAGED LIKE SOME WILD BEAST! I'LL ESCAPE... AND WHEN I DO, I SHALL DEVOTE THE REST OF MY LIFE IN REVENGING MYSELF UPON THE BATMAN!
BOB KANE
FINIS
THE Sensational BATMAN
AMERICA'S MOST EXCITING MYSTERY, ACTION, ADVENTURE STRIP
Detective COMICS 10¢
APPEARS ONLY IN DETECTIVE COMICS A NEW THRILLING EPISODE NEXT MONTH...

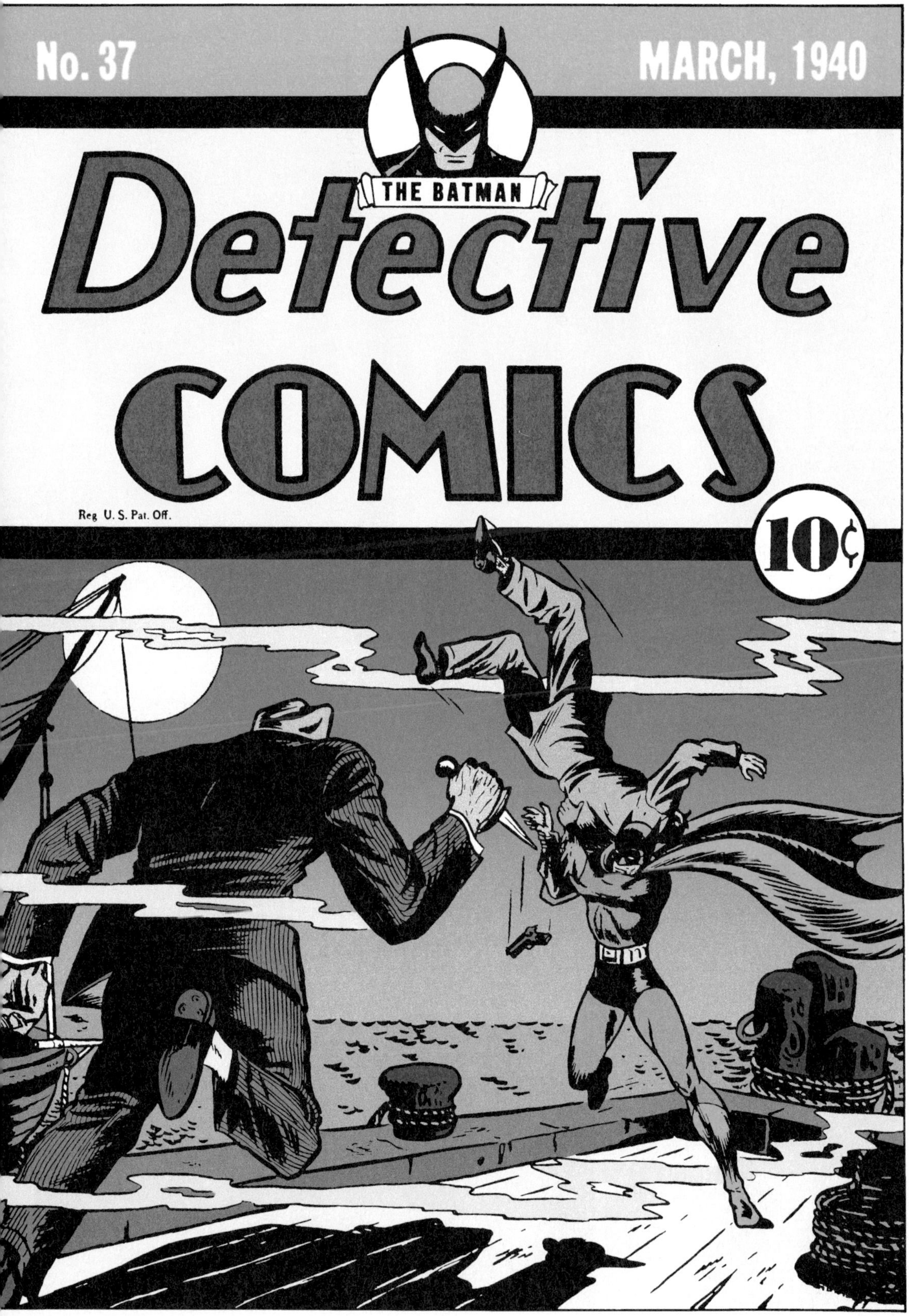
No. 37
MARCH, 1940
THE BATMAN
Detective
COMICS
Reg. U.S. Pat. Off.
10¢

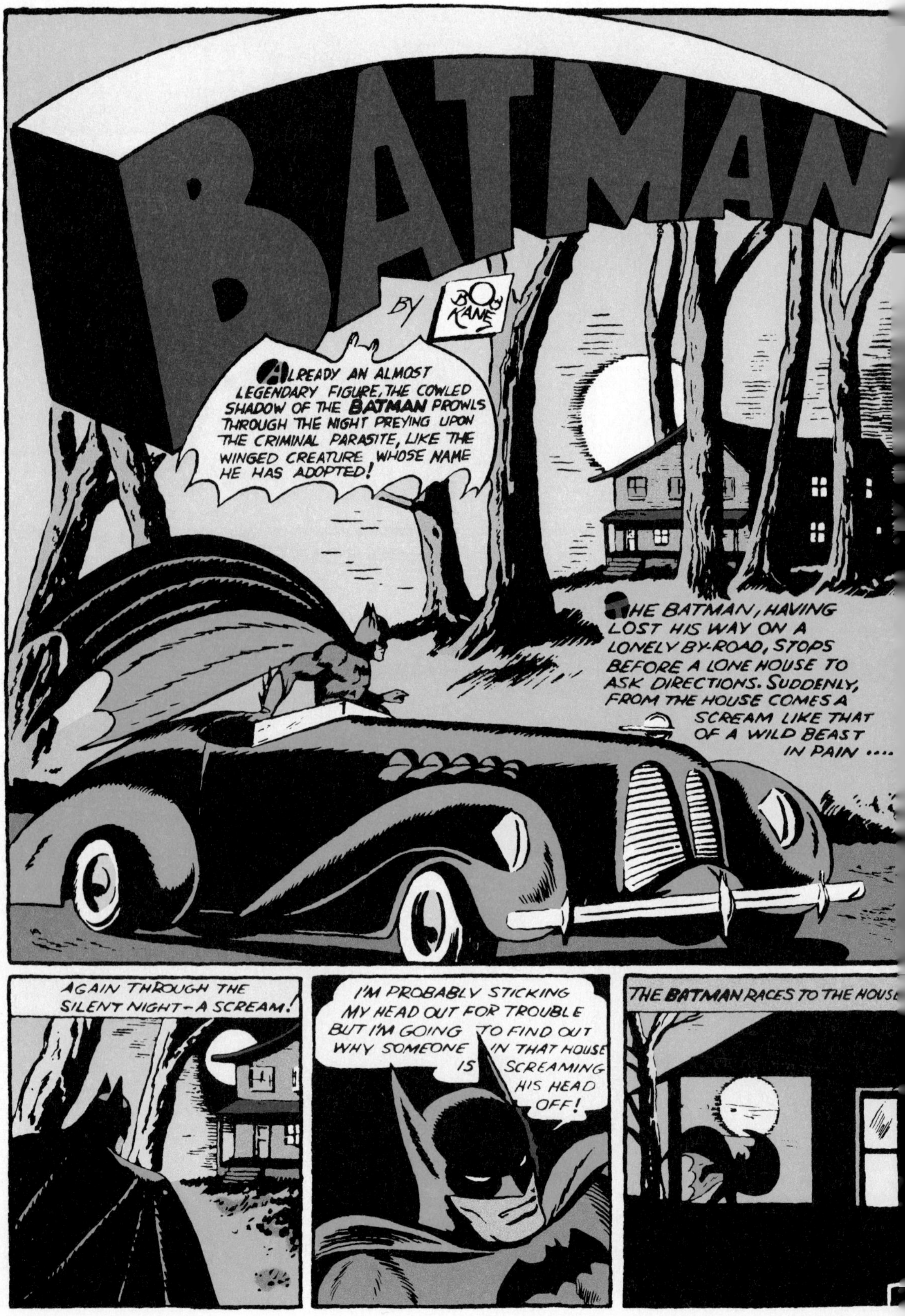
BATMAN
BY BOB KANE
ALREADY AN ALMOST LEGENDARY FIGURE, THE COWLED SHADOW OF THE BATMAN PROWLS THROUGH THE NIGHT PREYING UPON THE CRIMINAL PARASITE, LIKE THE WINGED CREATURE WHOSE NAME HE HAS ADOPTED!
THE BATMAN, HAVING LOST HIS WAY ON A LONELY BY-ROAD, STOPS BEFORE A LONE HOUSE TO ASK DIRECTIONS. SUDDENLY, FROM THE HOUSE COMES A SCREAM LIKE THAT OF A WILD BEAST IN PAIN ....
AGAIN THROUGH THE SILENT NIGHT—A SCREAM!
I'M PROBABLY STICKING MY HEAD OUT FOR TROUBLE BUT I'M GOING TO FIND OUT WHY SOMEONE IN THAT HOUSE IS SCREAMING HIS HEAD OFF!
THE BATMAN RACES TO THE HOUSE

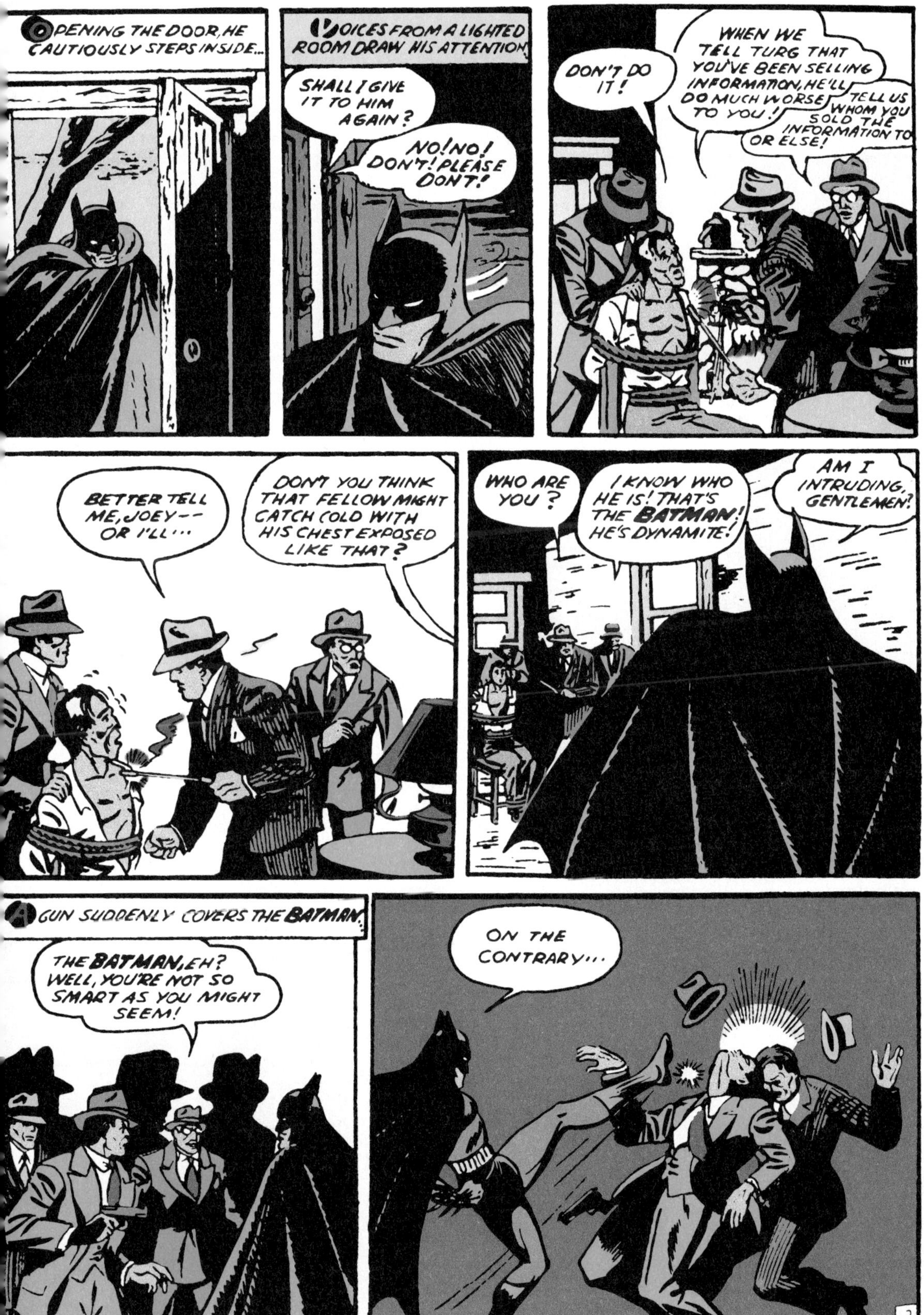
OPENING THE DOOR, HE CAUTIOUSLY STEPS INSIDE...
VOICES FROM A LIGHTED ROOM DRAW HIS ATTENTION
SHALL I GIVE IT TO HIM AGAIN?
NO! NO! DON'T! PLEASE DON'T!
DON'T DO IT!
WHEN WE TELL TURG THAT YOU'VE BEEN SELLING INFORMATION, HE'LL DO MUCH WORSE TO YOU!
TELL US WHOM YOU SOLD THE INFORMATION TO OR ELSE!
BETTER TELL ME, JOEY-- OR I'LL...
DON'T YOU THINK THAT FELLOW MIGHT CATCH COLD WITH HIS CHEST EXPOSED LIKE THAT?
WHO ARE YOU?
I KNOW WHO HE IS! THAT'S THE BATMAN! HE'S DYNAMITE!
AM I INTRUDING, GENTLEMEN?
A GUN SUDDENLY COVERS THE BATMAN
THE BATMAN, EH? WELL, YOU'RE NOT SO SMART AS YOU MIGHT SEEM!
ON THE CONTRARY...
2

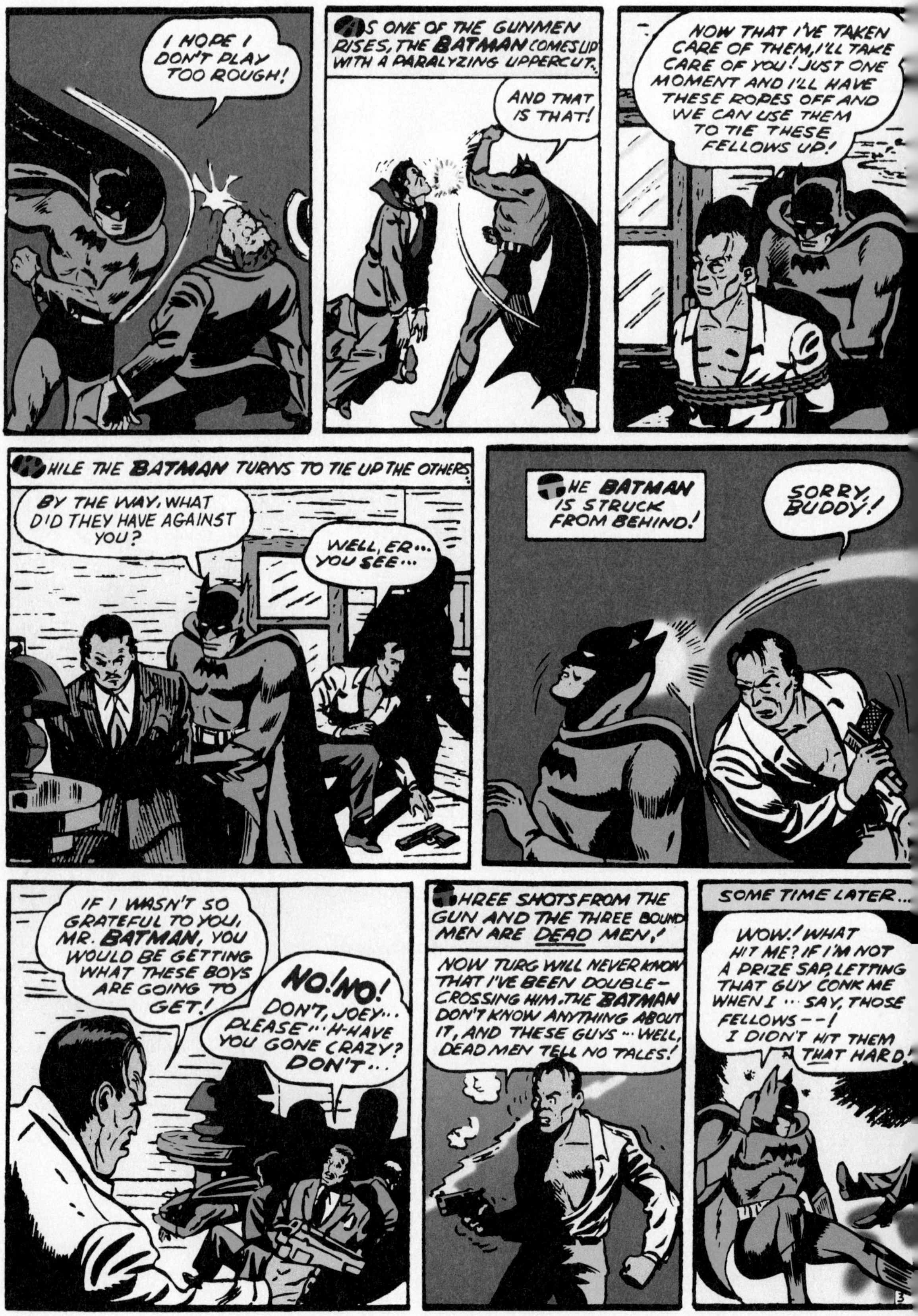
I HOPE I DON'T PLAY TOO ROUGH!
AS ONE OF THE GUNMEN RISES, THE BATMAN COMES UP WITH A PARALYZING UPPERCUT.
AND THAT IS THAT!
NOW THAT I'VE TAKEN CARE OF THEM, I'LL TAKE CARE OF YOU! JUST ONE MOMENT AND I'LL HAVE THESE ROPES OFF AND WE CAN USE THEM TO TIE THESE FELLOWS UP!
WHILE THE BATMAN TURNS TO TIE UP THE OTHERS
BY THE WAY, WHAT DID THEY HAVE AGAINST YOU?
WELL, ER... YOU SEE...
THE BATMAN IS STRUCK FROM BEHIND!
SORRY, BUDDY!
IF I WASN'T SO GRATEFUL TO YOU, MR. BATMAN, YOU WOULD BE GETTING WHAT THESE BOYS ARE GOING TO GET!
NO! NO! DON'T, JOEY... PLEASE... H-HAVE YOU GONE CRAZY? DON'T...
THREE SHOTS FROM THE GUN AND THE THREE BOUND MEN ARE DEAD MEN!
NOW TURG WILL NEVER KNOW THAT I'VE BEEN DOUBLE-CROSSING HIM. THE BATMAN DON'T KNOW ANYTHING ABOUT IT, AND THESE GUYS... WELL, DEAD MEN TELL NO TALES!
SOME TIME LATER...
WOW! WHAT HIT ME? IF I'M NOT A PRIZE SAP, LETTING THAT GUY CONK ME WHEN I ... SAY, THOSE FELLOWS--! I DIDN'T HIT THEM THAT HARD!

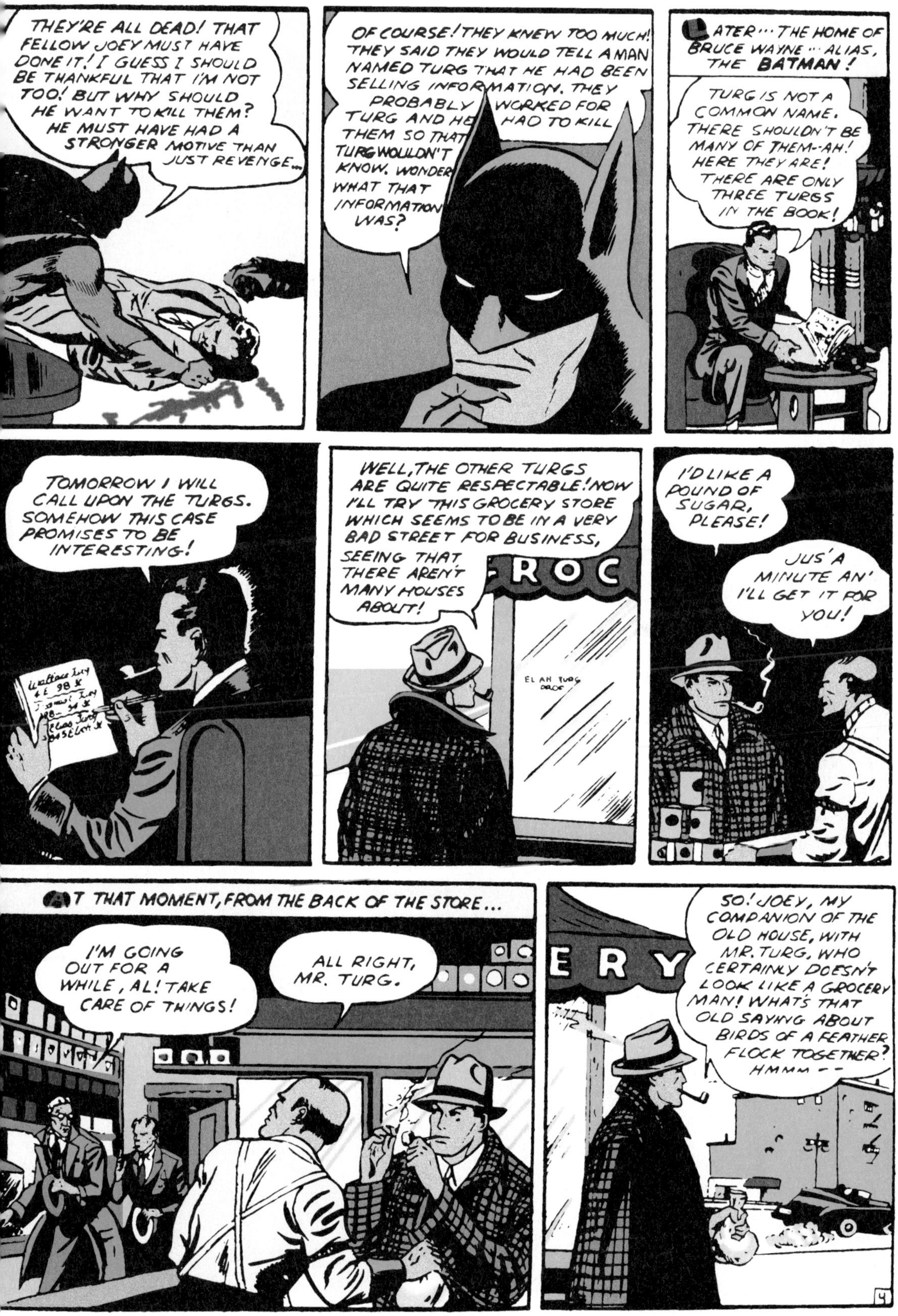
THEY'RE ALL DEAD! THAT FELLOW JOEY MUST HAVE DONE IT! I GUESS I SHOULD BE THANKFUL THAT I'M NOT TOO! BUT WHY SHOULD HE WANT TO KILL THEM? HE MUST HAVE HAD A STRONGER MOTIVE THAN JUST REVENGE...
OF COURSE! THEY KNEW TOO MUCH! THEY SAID THEY WOULD TELL A MAN NAMED TURG THAT HE HAD BEEN SELLING INFORMATION. THEY PROBABLY WORKED FOR TURG AND HE HAD TO KILL THEM SO THAT TURG WOULDN'T KNOW. WONDER WHAT THAT INFORMATION WAS?
LATER... THE HOME OF BRUCE WAYNE... ALIAS, THE BATMAN!
TURG IS NOT A COMMON NAME. THERE SHOULDN'T BE MANY OF THEM--AH! HERE THEY ARE! THERE ARE ONLY THREE TURGS IN THE BOOK!
TOMORROW I WILL CALL UPON THE TURGS. SOMEHOW THIS CASE PROMISES TO BE INTERESTING!
WELL, THE OTHER TURGS ARE QUITE RESPECTABLE! NOW I'LL TRY THIS GROCERY STORE WHICH SEEMS TO BE IN A VERY BAD STREET FOR BUSINESS, SEEING THAT THERE AREN'T MANY HOUSES ABOUT!
ROC
I'D LIKE A POUND OF SUGAR, PLEASE!
JUS' A MINUTE AN' I'LL GET IT FOR YOU!
AT THAT MOMENT, FROM THE BACK OF THE STORE...
I'M GOING OUT FOR A WHILE, AL! TAKE CARE OF THINGS!
ALL RIGHT, MR. TURG.
ERY
SO! JOEY, MY COMPANION OF THE OLD HOUSE, WITH MR. TURG, WHO CERTAINLY DOESN'T LOOK LIKE A GROCERY MAN! WHAT'S THAT OLD SAYING ABOUT BIRDS OF A FEATHER FLOCK TOGETHER? HMMM --
4

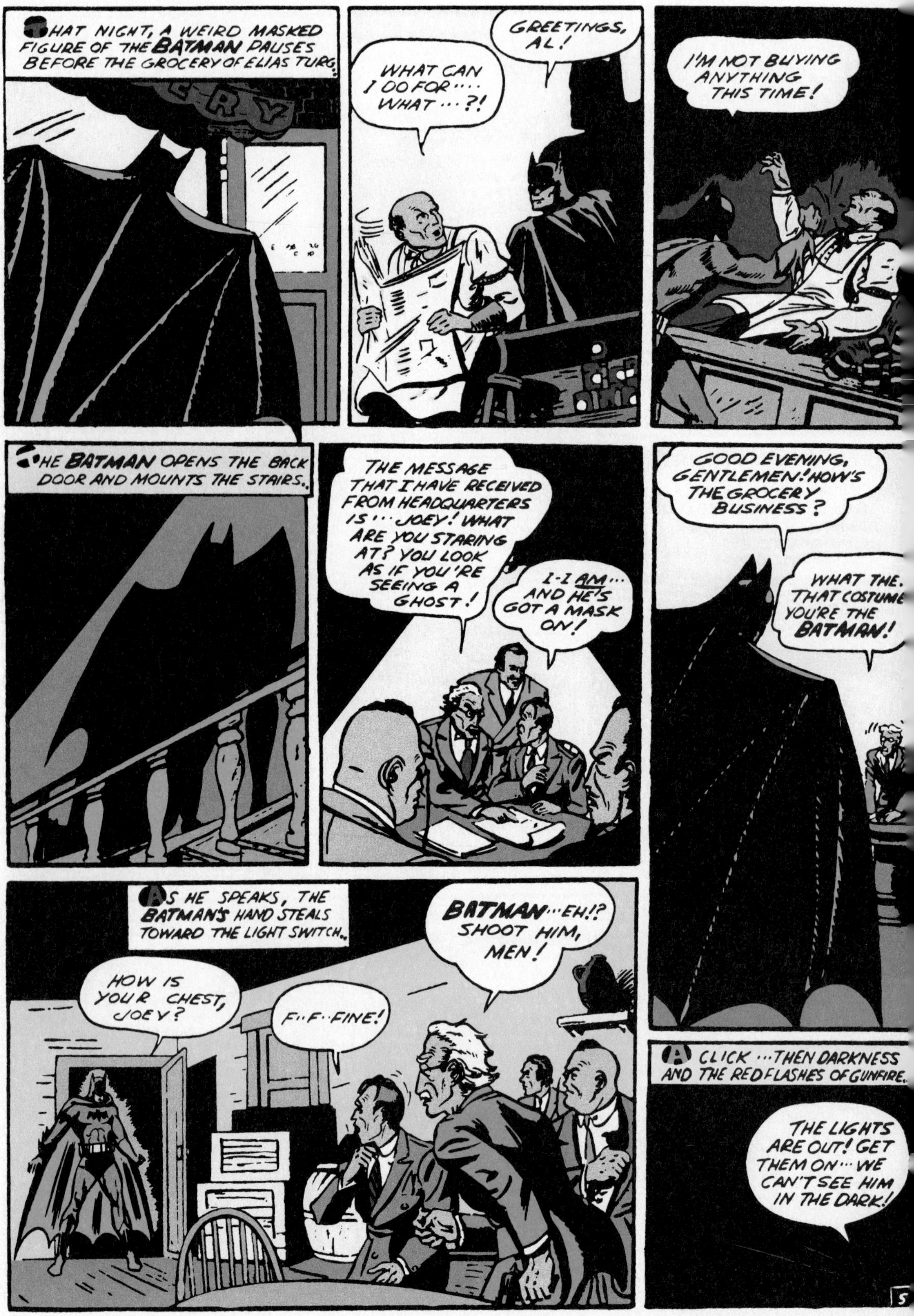
THAT NIGHT, A WEIRD MASKED FIGURE OF THE BATMAN PAUSES BEFORE THE GROCERY OF ELIAS TURG.
GREETINGS, AL!
WHAT CAN I DO FOR.... WHAT...?!
I'M NOT BUYING ANYTHING THIS TIME!
THE BATMAN OPENS THE BACK DOOR AND MOUNTS THE STAIRS..
THE MESSAGE THAT I HAVE RECEIVED FROM HEADQUARTERS IS... JOEY! WHAT ARE YOU STARING AT? YOU LOOK AS IF YOU'RE SEEING A GHOST!
I-I AM... AND HE'S GOT A MASK ON!
GOOD EVENING, GENTLEMEN! HOW'S THE GROCERY BUSINESS?
WHAT THE. THAT COSTUME YOU'RE THE BATMAN!
AS HE SPEAKS, THE BATMAN'S HAND STEALS TOWARD THE LIGHT SWITCH..
HOW IS YOUR CHEST, JOEY?
F..F..FINE!
BATMAN...EH!? SHOOT HIM, MEN!
A CLICK ...THEN DARKNESS AND THE RED FLASHES OF GUNFIRE..
THE LIGHTS ARE OUT! GET THEM ON... WE CAN'T SEE HIM IN THE DARK!
5

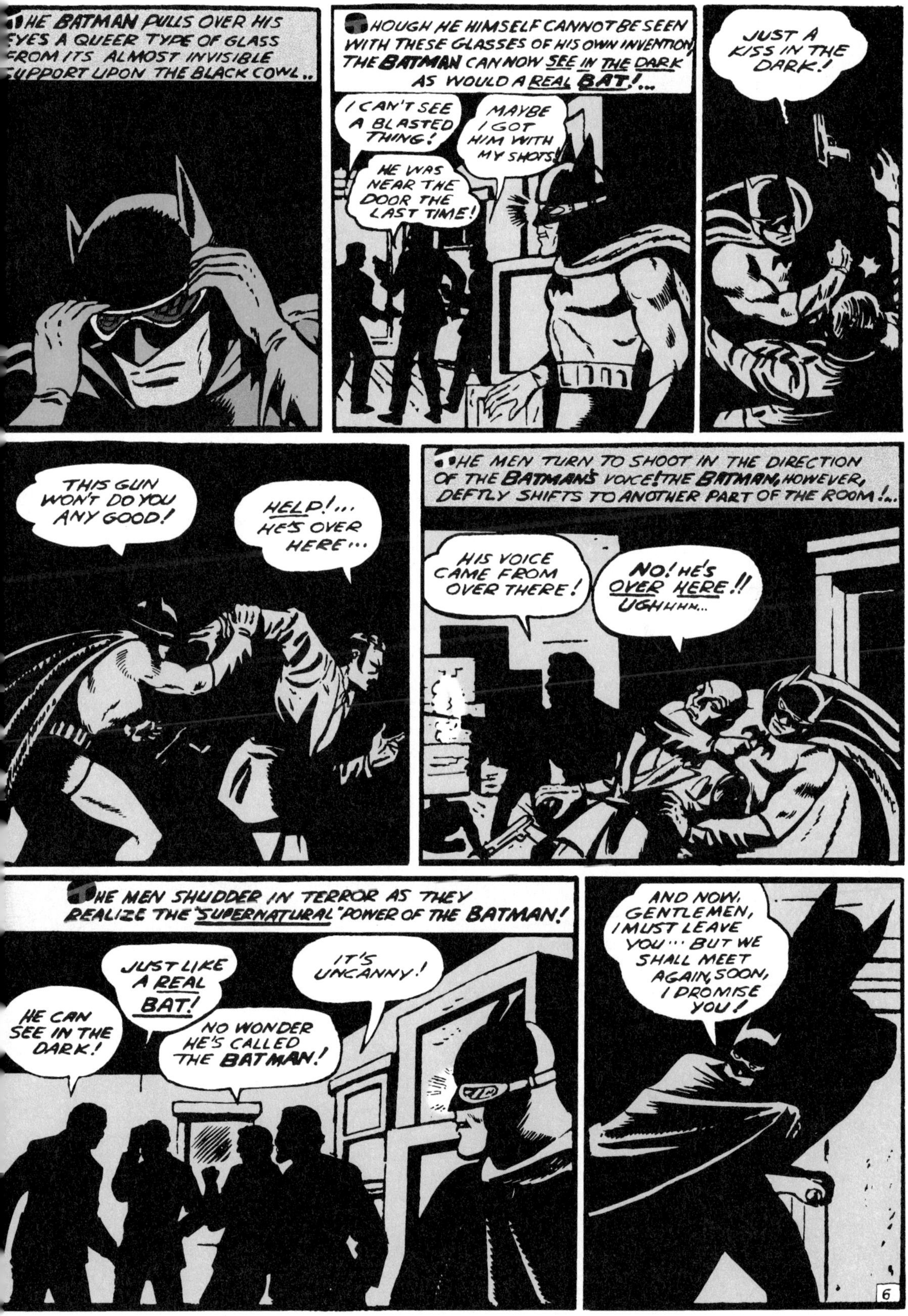
THE BATMAN PULLS OVER HIS EYES A QUEER TYPE OF GLASS FROM ITS ALMOST INVISIBLE SUPPORT UPON THE BLACK COWL..
THOUGH HE HIMSELF CANNOT BE SEEN WITH THESE GLASSES OF HIS OWN INVENTION, THE BATMAN CAN NOW SEE IN THE DARK AS WOULD A REAL BAT!...
I CAN'T SEE A BLASTED THING!
MAYBE I GOT HIM WITH MY SHOTS!
HE WAS NEAR THE DOOR THE LAST TIME!
JUST A KISS IN THE DARK!
THIS GUN WON'T DO YOU ANY GOOD!
HELP!... HE'S OVER HERE...
THE MEN TURN TO SHOOT IN THE DIRECTION OF THE BATMAN'S VOICE! THE BATMAN, HOWEVER, DEFTLY SHIFTS TO ANOTHER PART OF THE ROOM!..
HIS VOICE CAME FROM OVER THERE!
NO! HE'S OVER HERE!! UGHHHH...
THE MEN SHUDDER IN TERROR AS THEY REALIZE THE "SUPERNATURAL" POWER OF THE BATMAN!
HE CAN SEE IN THE DARK!
JUST LIKE A REAL BAT!
NO WONDER HE'S CALLED THE BATMAN!
IT'S UNCANNY!
AND NOW, GENTLEMEN, I MUST LEAVE YOU... BUT WE SHALL MEET AGAIN, SOON, I PROMISE YOU!
6

THE BATMAN GONE, THE LIGHTS ARE SWITCHED ON...

HE'S GONE!

FUNNY HOW HE KNEW ABOUT US USING THE STORE AS OUR HEADQUARTERS!

I THINK JOEY KNOWS, DON'T YOU? HE SPOKE TO YOU -- HE KNEW YOUR NAME! YOU TOLD HIM ABOUT US!

NO! NO! I SWEAR!

YOU LIE! YOU TRAITOR! DIE A TRAITOR'S DEATH!

DO YOU THINK HE TOLD THE BATMAN OF OUR PLANS TO BLOW UP THE SHIP TOMORROW NIGHT!

HE MUST HAVE!

WE CANNOT DELAY. WE MUST SINK THE SHIP TONIGHT! COME, LET US GO TO THE PIER NOW!

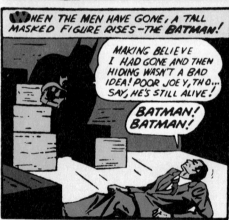

WHEN THE MEN HAVE GONE, A TALL MASKED FIGURE RISES—THE BATMAN!

MAKING BELIEVE I HAD GONE AND THEN HIDING WASN'T A BAD IDEA! POOR JOEY, THO... SAY, HE'S STILL ALIVE!

BATMAN! BATMAN!

JOEY, CAN YOU HEAR ME? WHAT IS THIS ALL ABOUT? WHAT SHIP ARE THEY GOING TO BLOW UP?

THEY'RE SPIES! ..BLOW UP FOREIGN SHIP RONIJ.. MAKE IT LOOK LIKE U.S. DID IT.. START INTERNATIONAL CRISIS... DON'T KNOW WHO HEAD IS...

STOLE PHONE NUMBER FROM TURGAL 5743.. I'M NOT REALLY SPY...NEEDED MONEY...GET THEM FOR GOOD OLE U.S.A... GET--AHHHH...

DON'T WORRY JOEY. I'LL GET THEM!

ON A PIER IN LOWER DOWNTOWN...

WHERE IS TURG? HE HAS NOT YET COME?

HE HAS GONE TO SEE THE HEAD! WE ARE TO GO ON WITH OUR WORK. LISTEN, THE SMALL BOAT BELOW IS LOADED WITH T.N.T. WE LASH THE STEERING WHEEL. HEAD THE BOAT FOR THE RONIJ... AND THEN...

THE EXPLOSION, AND WE ARE FAR AWAY FROM THE SCENE! IT'S PERFECT!

ALMOST A LITTLE TOO PERFECT, I'D SAY!

THE BATMAN!!

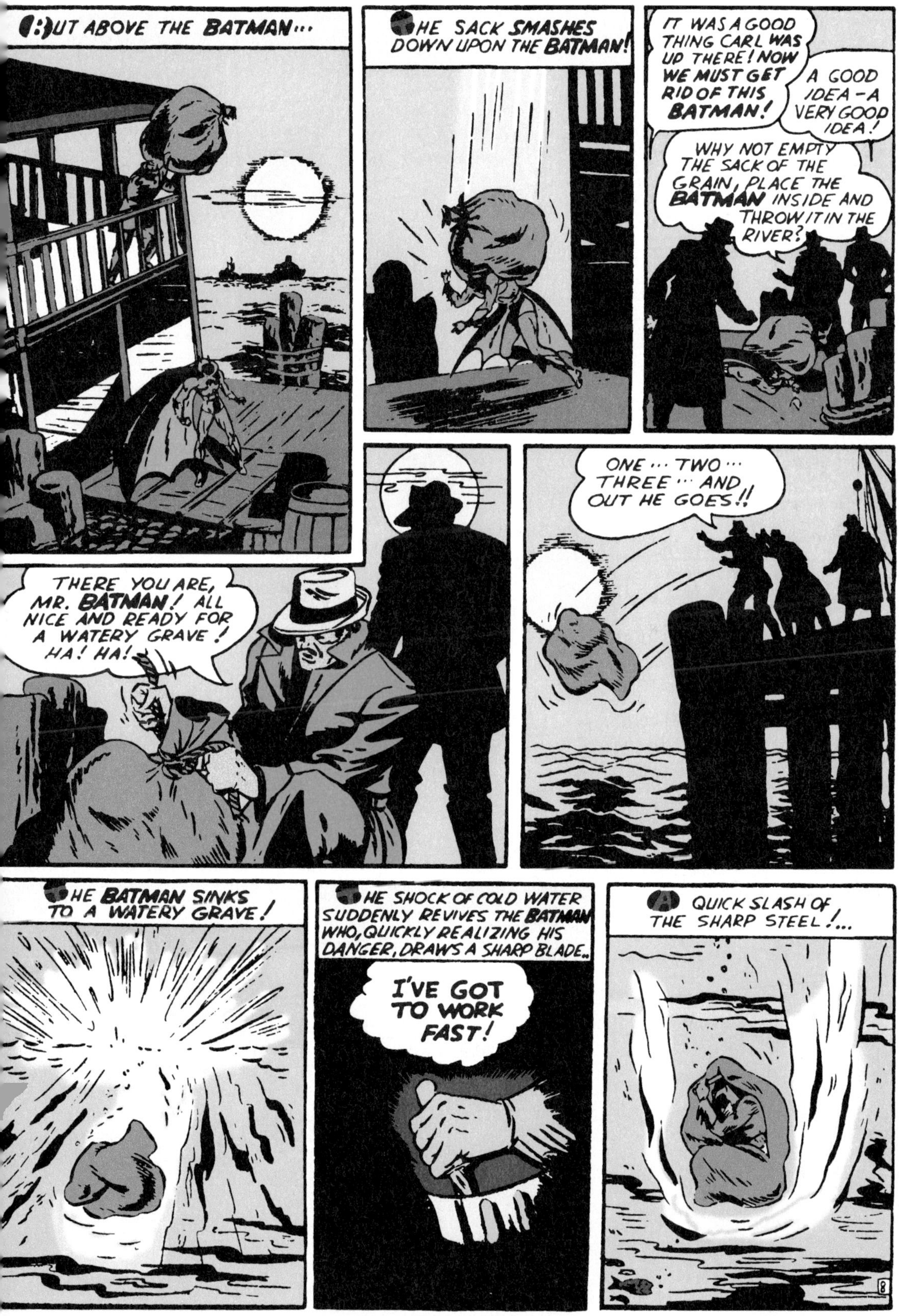
BUT ABOVE THE BATMAN...
THE SACK SMASHES DOWN UPON THE BATMAN!
IT WAS A GOOD THING CARL WAS UP THERE! NOW WE MUST GET RID OF THIS BATMAN!
A GOOD IDEA—A VERY GOOD IDEA!
WHY NOT EMPTY THE SACK OF THE GRAIN, PLACE THE BATMAN INSIDE AND THROW IT IN THE RIVER?
THERE YOU ARE, MR. BATMAN! ALL NICE AND READY FOR A WATERY GRAVE! HA! HA!
ONE ... TWO ... THREE ... AND OUT HE GOES!!
THE BATMAN SINKS TO A WATERY GRAVE!
THE SHOCK OF COLD WATER SUDDENLY REVIVES THE BATMAN WHO, QUICKLY REALIZING HIS DANGER, DRAWS A SHARP BLADE..
I'VE GOT TO WORK FAST!
A QUICK SLASH OF THE SHARP STEEL!...
8

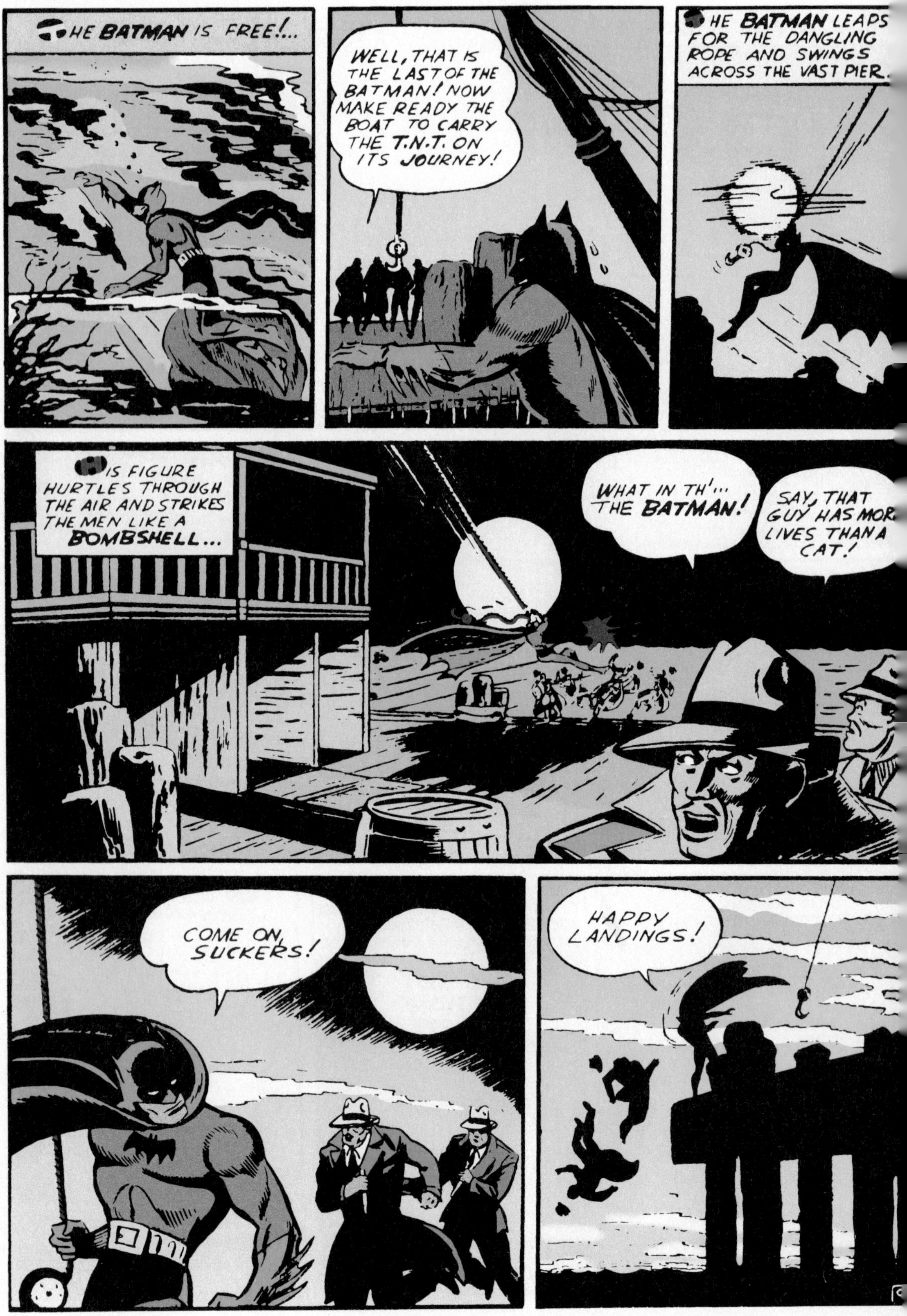
HE BATMAN IS FREE!...
WELL, THAT IS THE LAST OF THE BATMAN! NOW MAKE READY THE BOAT TO CARRY THE T.N.T. ON ITS JOURNEY!
HE BATMAN LEAPS FOR THE DANGLING ROPE AND SWINGS ACROSS THE VAST PIER.
IS FIGURE HURTLES THROUGH THE AIR AND STRIKES THE MEN LIKE A BOMBSHELL...
WHAT IN TH'... THE BATMAN!
SAY, THAT GUY HAS MOR LIVES THAN A CAT!
COME ON, SUCKERS!
HAPPY LANDINGS!

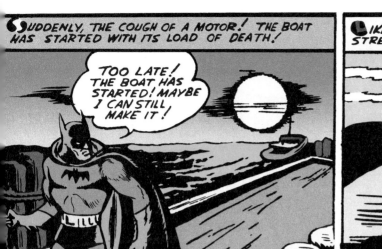

SUDDENLY, THE COUGH OF A MOTOR! THE BOAT HAS STARTED WITH ITS LOAD OF DEATH!

TOO LATE! THE BOAT HAS STARTED! MAYBE I CAN STILL MAKE IT!

LIKE A HUMAN BULLET, THE BATMAN STREAKS ACROSS THE PLATFORM..

FEET, RUN LIKE YOU'VE NEVER RUN BEFORE!

A GREAT LEAP INTO SPACE!

THE LEAP IS SUCCESSFUL!

THE ROPES ARE QUICKLY CUT FROM THE STEERING WHEEL.

IT'S A MATTER OF SECONDS NOW!

TNT

NEARER... NEARER... NEARER- ANOTHER SECOND AND THEN···

THE BATMAN DESPERATELY TAKES THE WHEEL AND TURNS···

IF THIS BOAT DOESN'T TURN IN TIME, I'M A GONER!

THE MOTOR BOAT CARRYING ITS LOAD OF DEATH MISSES THE STEAMSHIP BY INCHES!

10

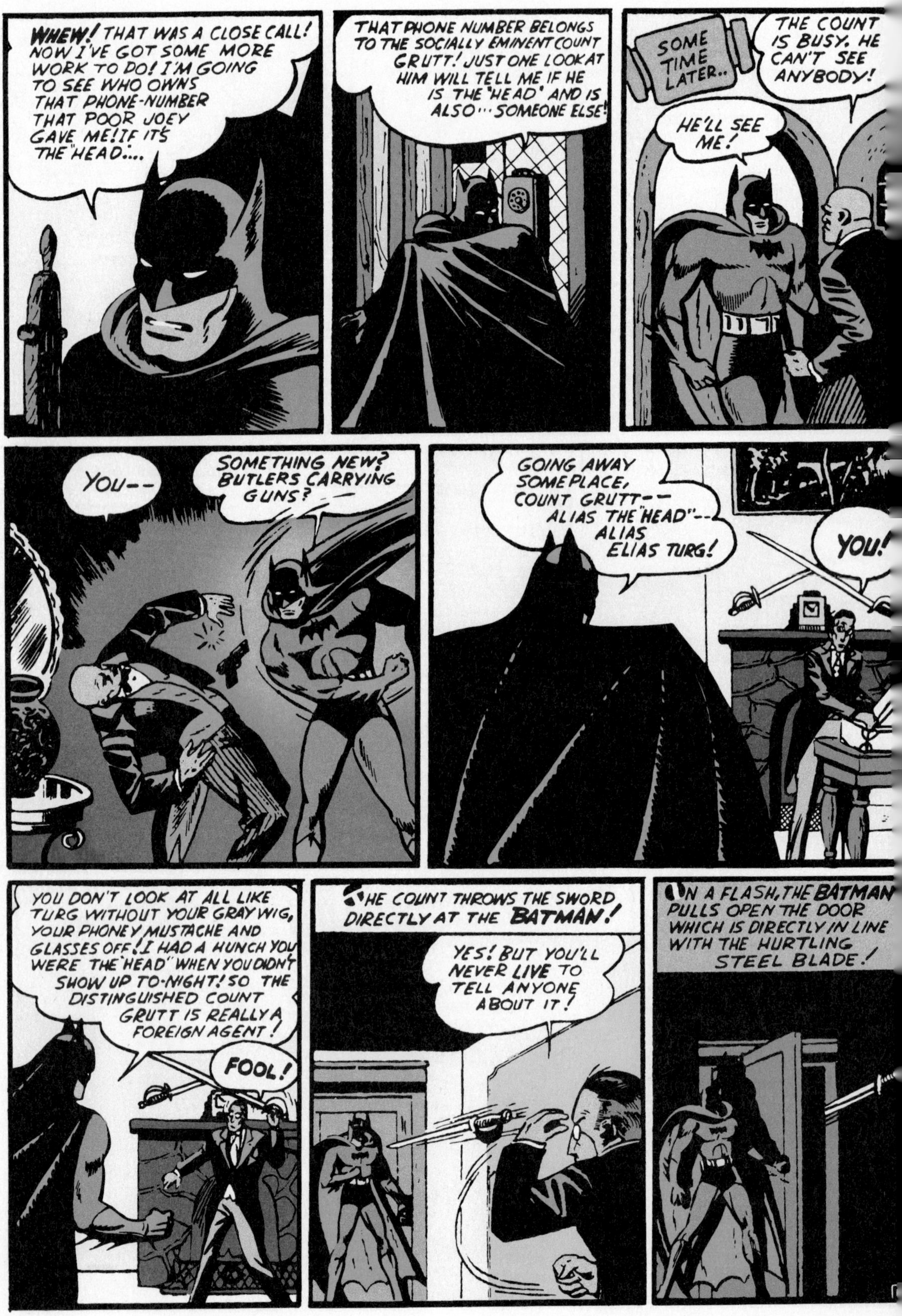
WHEW! THAT WAS A CLOSE CALL! NOW I'VE GOT SOME MORE WORK TO DO! I'M GOING TO SEE WHO OWNS THAT PHONE-NUMBER THAT POOR JOEY GAVE ME! IF IT'S THE "HEAD"....
THAT PHONE NUMBER BELONGS TO THE SOCIALLY EMINENT COUNT GRUTT! JUST ONE LOOK AT HIM WILL TELL ME IF HE IS THE "HEAD" AND IS ALSO... SOMEONE ELSE!
SOME TIME LATER..
THE COUNT IS BUSY. HE CAN'T SEE ANYBODY!
HE'LL SEE ME!
YOU--
SOMETHING NEW? BUTLERS CARRYING GUNS?
GOING AWAY SOMEPLACE, COUNT GRUTT-- ALIAS THE "HEAD"-- ALIAS ELIAS TURG!
YOU!
YOU DON'T LOOK AT ALL LIKE TURG WITHOUT YOUR GRAY WIG, YOUR PHONEY MUSTACHE AND GLASSES OFF! I HAD A HUNCH YOU WERE THE "HEAD" WHEN YOU DIDN'T SHOW UP TO-NIGHT! SO THE DISTINGUISHED COUNT GRUTT IS REALLY A FOREIGN AGENT!
FOOL!
THE COUNT THROWS THE SWORD DIRECTLY AT THE BATMAN!
YES! BUT YOU'LL NEVER LIVE TO TELL ANYONE ABOUT IT!
IN A FLASH, THE BATMAN PULLS OPEN THE DOOR WHICH IS DIRECTLY IN LINE WITH THE HURTLING STEEL BLADE!

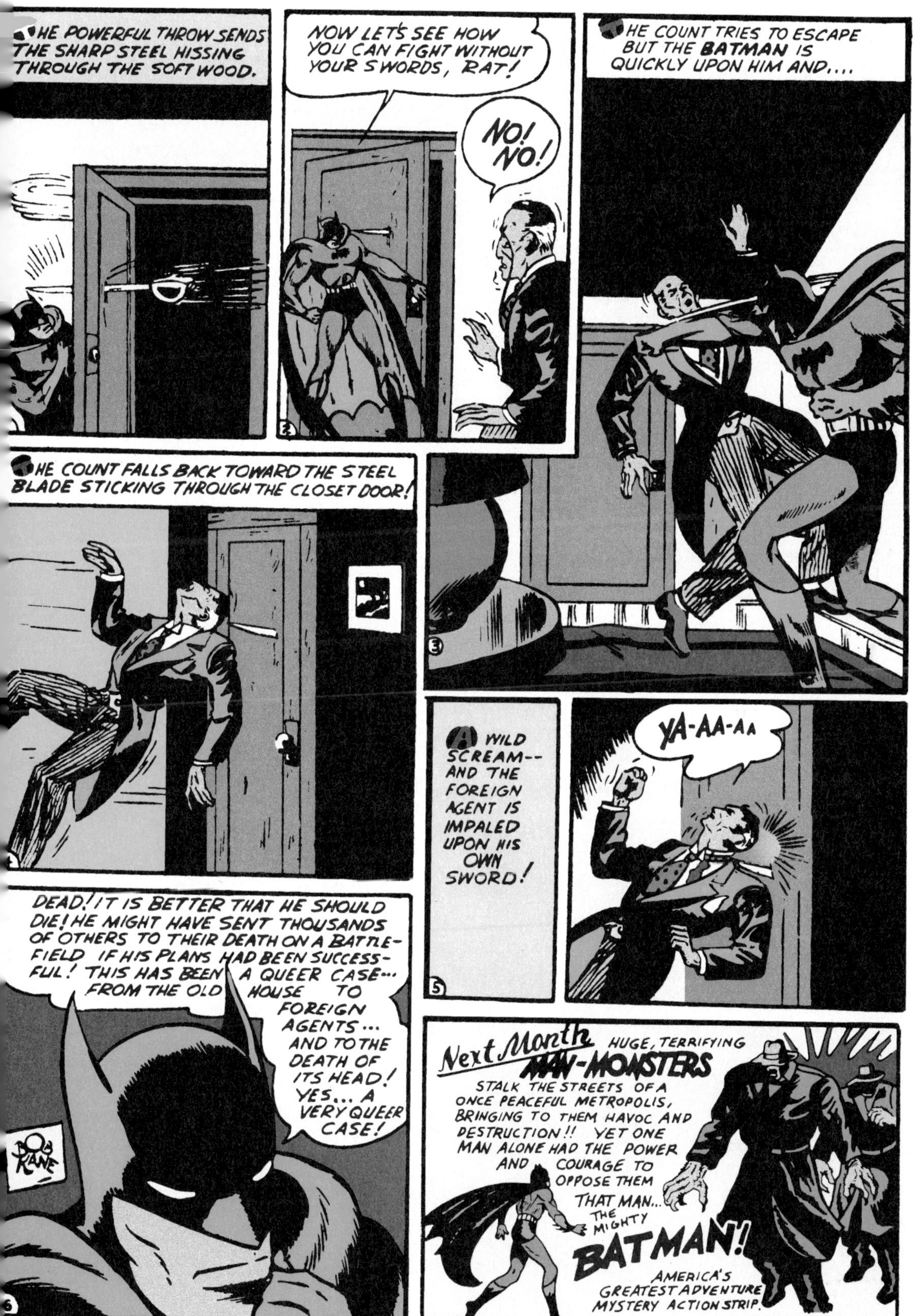
THE POWERFUL THROW SENDS THE SHARP STEEL HISSING THROUGH THE SOFT WOOD.
NOW LET'S SEE HOW YOU CAN FIGHT WITHOUT YOUR SWORDS, RAT!
NO! NO!
THE COUNT TRIES TO ESCAPE BUT THE BATMAN IS QUICKLY UPON HIM AND....
THE COUNT FALLS BACK TOWARD THE STEEL BLADE STICKING THROUGH THE CLOSET DOOR!
A WILD SCREAM-- AND THE FOREIGN AGENT IS IMPALED UPON HIS OWN SWORD!
YA-AA-AA
DEAD! IT IS BETTER THAT HE SHOULD DIE! HE MIGHT HAVE SENT THOUSANDS OF OTHERS TO THEIR DEATH ON A BATTLE-FIELD IF HIS PLANS HAD BEEN SUCCESS-FUL! THIS HAS BEEN A QUEER CASE... FROM THE OLD HOUSE TO FOREIGN AGENTS... AND TO THE DEATH OF ITS HEAD! YES... A VERY QUEER CASE!
BOB KANE
Next Month HUGE, TERRIFYING MAN-MONSTERS STALK THE STREETS OF A ONCE PEACEFUL METROPOLIS, BRINGING TO THEM HAVOC AND DESTRUCTION!! YET ONE MAN ALONE HAD THE POWER AND COURAGE TO OPPOSE THEM
THAT MAN... THE MIGHTY BATMAN!
AMERICA'S GREATEST ADVENTURE MYSTERY ACTION STRIP.

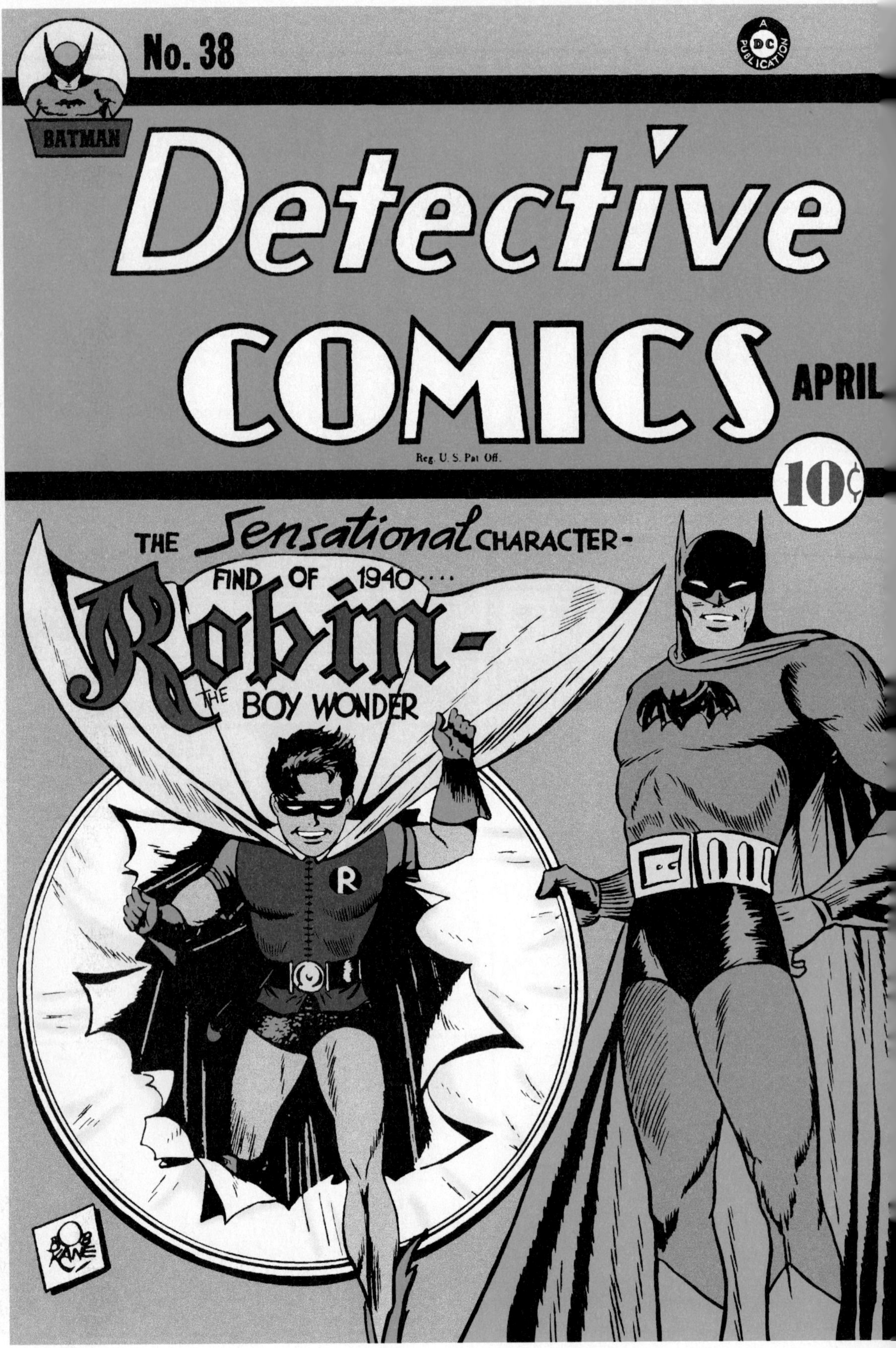
No. 38
A DC PUBLICATION
BATMAN
Detective
COMICS
APRIL
Reg. U. S. Pat Off.
10¢
THE Sensational CHARACTER-
FIND OF 1940....
Robin-
THE BOY WONDER
R
BOB KANE

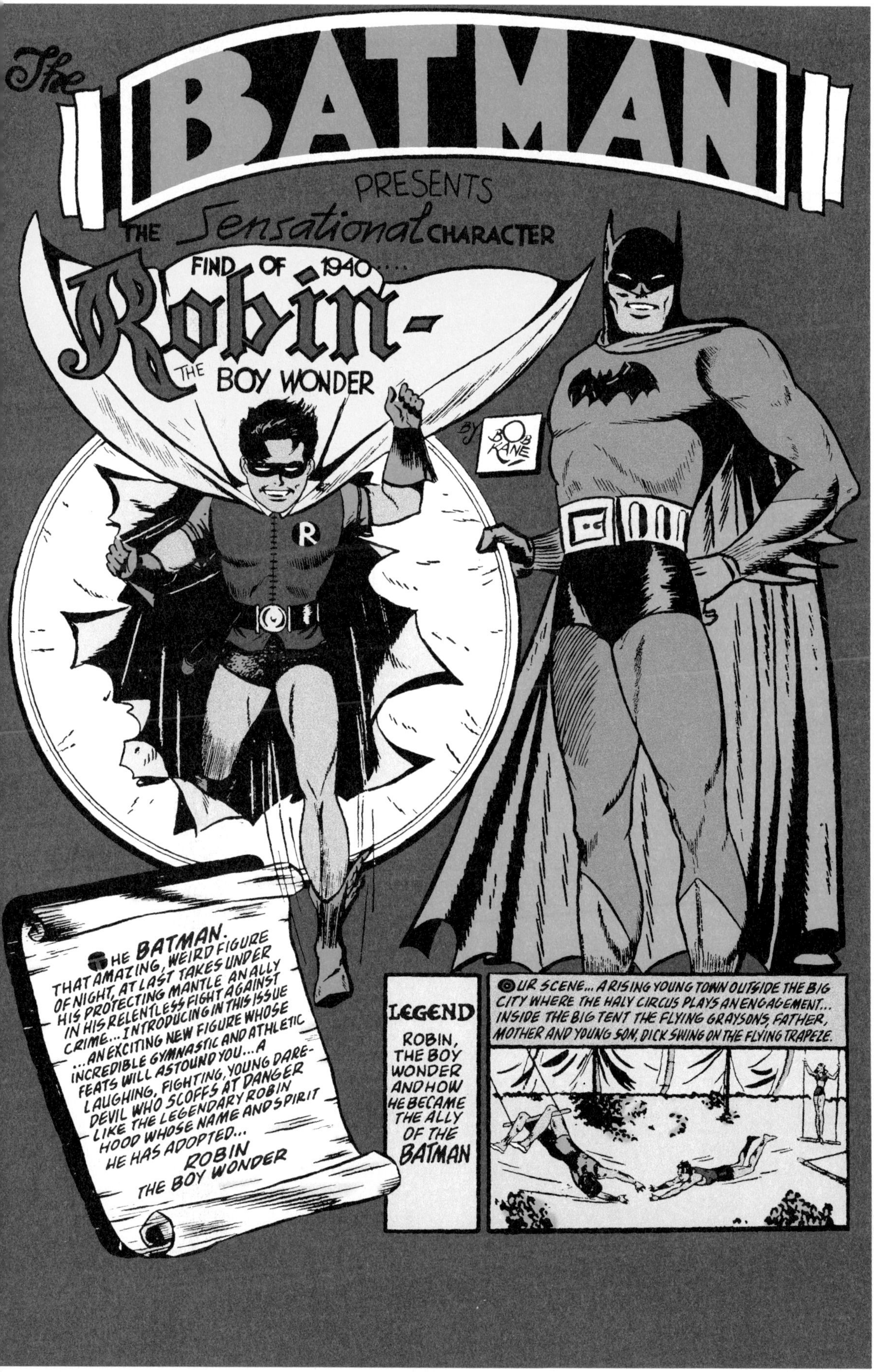
The BATMAN
PRESENTS
THE Sensational CHARACTER
FIND OF 1940....
Robin-
THE BOY WONDER
by BOB KANE
THE BATMAN. THAT AMAZING, WEIRD FIGURE OF NIGHT, AT LAST TAKES UNDER HIS PROTECTING MANTLE AN ALLY IN HIS RELENTLESS FIGHT AGAINST CRIME... INTRODUCING IN THIS ISSUE ...AN EXCITING NEW FIGURE WHOSE INCREDIBLE GYMNASTIC AND ATHLETIC FEATS WILL ASTOUND YOU... A LAUGHING, FIGHTING, YOUNG DARE-DEVIL WHO SCOFFS AT DANGER LIKE THE LEGENDARY ROBIN HOOD WHOSE NAME AND SPIRIT HE HAS ADOPTED...
ROBIN THE BOY WONDER
LEGEND
ROBIN, THE BOY WONDER AND HOW HE BECAME THE ALLY OF THE BATMAN
OUR SCENE... A RISING YOUNG TOWN OUTSIDE THE BIG CITY WHERE THE HALY CIRCUS PLAYS AN ENGAGEMENT... INSIDE THE BIG TENT THE FLYING GRAYSONS, FATHER, MOTHER AND YOUNG SON, DICK SWING ON THE FLYING TRAPEZE.

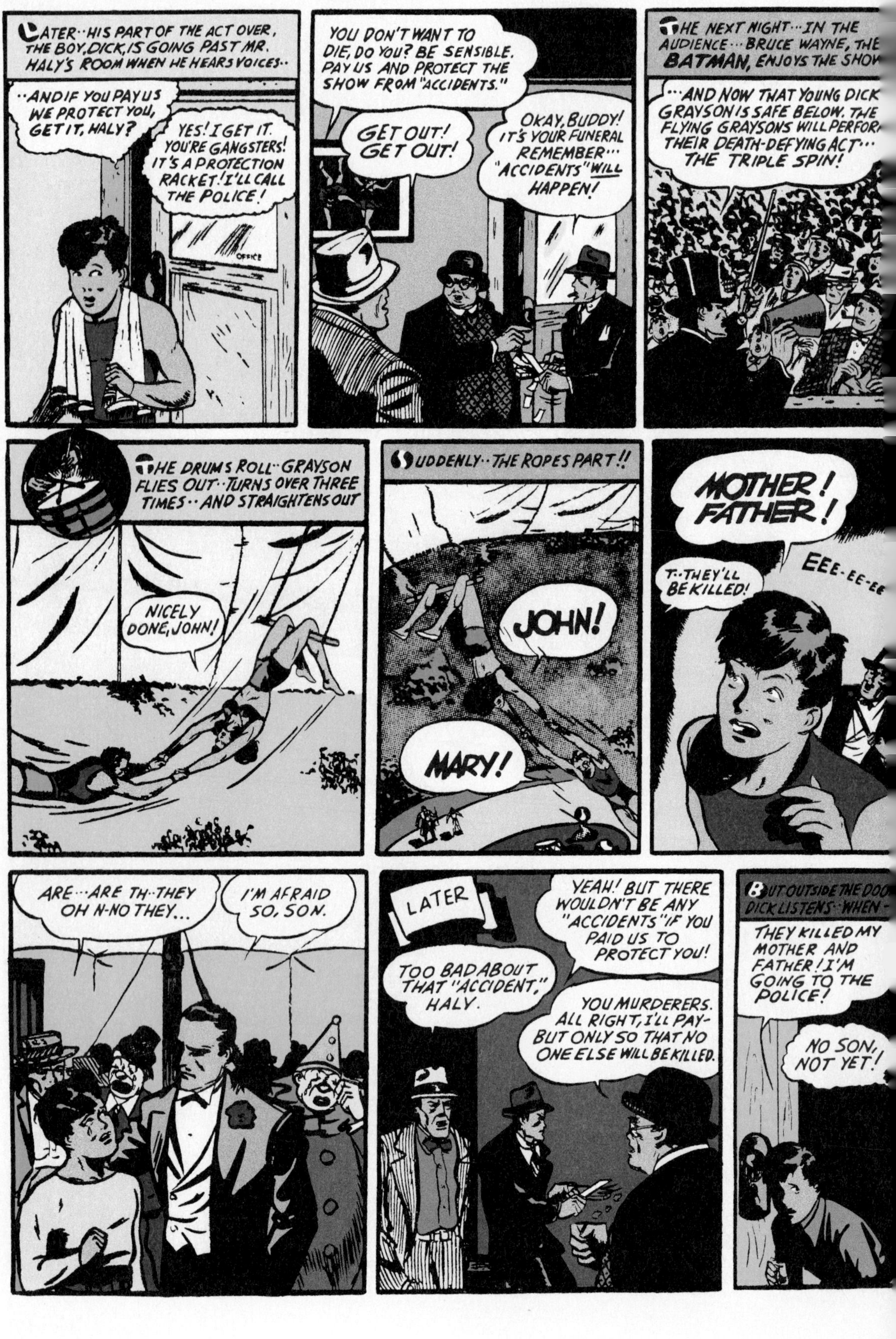
LATER·· HIS PART OF THE ACT OVER, THE BOY, DICK, IS GOING PAST MR. HALY'S ROOM WHEN HE HEARS VOICES··
··AND IF YOU PAY US WE PROTECT YOU, GET IT, HALY?
YES! I GET IT. YOU'RE GANGSTERS! IT'S A PROTECTION RACKET! I'LL CALL THE POLICE!
OFFICE
YOU DON'T WANT TO DIE, DO YOU? BE SENSIBLE. PAY US AND PROTECT THE SHOW FROM "ACCIDENTS."
GET OUT! GET OUT!
OKAY, BUDDY! IT'S YOUR FUNERAL REMEMBER··· "ACCIDENTS" WILL HAPPEN!
THE NEXT NIGHT··· IN THE AUDIENCE··· BRUCE WAYNE, THE BATMAN, ENJOYS THE SHOW
···AND NOW THAT YOUNG DICK GRAYSON IS SAFE BELOW, THE FLYING GRAYSONS WILL PERFORM THEIR DEATH-DEFYING ACT··· THE TRIPLE SPIN!
THE DRUMS ROLL·· GRAYSON FLIES OUT·· TURNS OVER THREE TIMES·· AND STRAIGHTENS OUT
NICELY DONE, JOHN!
SUDDENLY·· THE ROPES PART!!
JOHN!
MARY!
MOTHER! FATHER!
EEE-EE-EE
T··THEY'LL BE KILLED!
ARE···ARE TH··THEY OH N-NO THEY...
I'M AFRAID SO, SON.
LATER
TOO BAD ABOUT THAT "ACCIDENT," HALY.
YEAH! BUT THERE WOULDN'T BE ANY "ACCIDENTS" IF YOU PAID US TO PROTECT YOU!
YOU MURDERERS. ALL RIGHT, I'LL PAY- BUT ONLY SO THAT NO ONE ELSE WILL BE KILLED.
BUT OUTSIDE THE DOOR DICK LISTENS·· WHEN-
THEY KILLED MY MOTHER AND FATHER! I'M GOING TO THE POLICE!
NO SON, NOT YET!

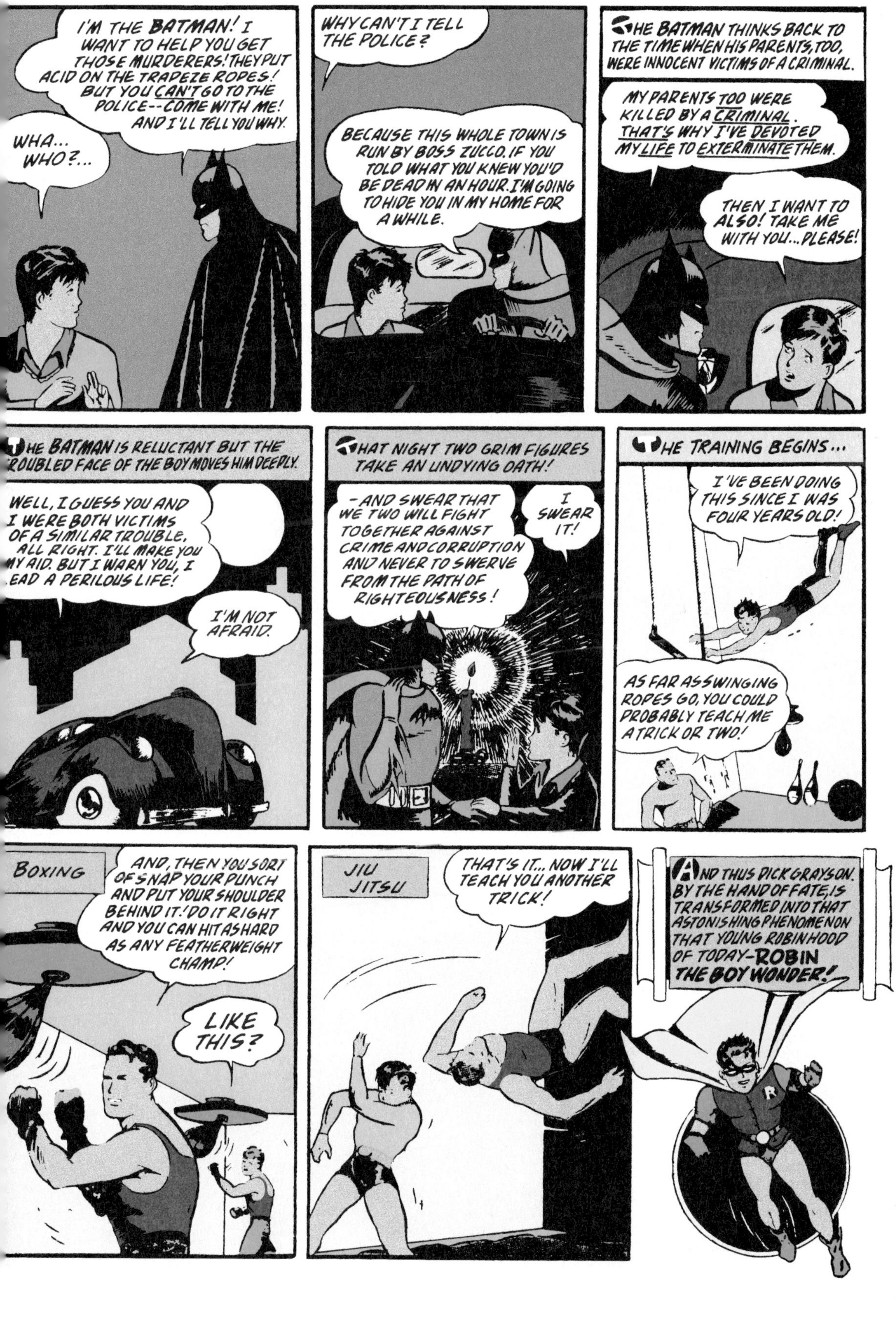

I'M THE BATMAN! I WANT TO HELP YOU GET THOSE MURDERERS! THEY PUT ACID ON THE TRAPEZE ROPES! BUT YOU CAN'T GO TO THE POLICE--COME WITH ME! AND I'LL TELL YOU WHY.
WHA... WHO?...
WHY CAN'T I TELL THE POLICE?
BECAUSE THIS WHOLE TOWN IS RUN BY BOSS ZUCCO. IF YOU TOLD WHAT YOU KNEW YOU'D BE DEAD IN AN HOUR. I'M GOING TO HIDE YOU IN MY HOME FOR A WHILE.
THE BATMAN THINKS BACK TO THE TIME WHEN HIS PARENTS, TOO, WERE INNOCENT VICTIMS OF A CRIMINAL.
MY PARENTS TOO WERE KILLED BY A CRIMINAL. THAT'S WHY I'VE DEVOTED MY LIFE TO EXTERMINATE THEM.
THEN I WANT TO ALSO! TAKE ME WITH YOU... PLEASE!
THE BATMAN IS RELUCTANT BUT THE TROUBLED FACE OF THE BOY MOVES HIM DEEPLY.
WELL, I GUESS YOU AND I WERE BOTH VICTIMS OF A SIMILAR TROUBLE. ALL RIGHT. I'LL MAKE YOU MY AID. BUT I WARN YOU, I LEAD A PERILOUS LIFE!
I'M NOT AFRAID.
THAT NIGHT TWO GRIM FIGURES TAKE AN UNDYING OATH!
-AND SWEAR THAT WE TWO WILL FIGHT TOGETHER AGAINST CRIME AND CORRUPTION AND NEVER TO SWERVE FROM THE PATH OF RIGHTEOUSNESS!
I SWEAR IT!
THE TRAINING BEGINS...
I'VE BEEN DOING THIS SINCE I WAS FOUR YEARS OLD!
AS FAR AS SWINGING ROPES GO, YOU COULD PROBABLY TEACH ME A TRICK OR TWO!
BOXING
AND, THEN YOU SORT OF SNAP YOUR PUNCH AND PUT YOUR SHOULDER BEHIND IT! DO IT RIGHT AND YOU CAN HIT AS HARD AS ANY FEATHERWEIGHT CHAMP!
LIKE THIS?
JIU JITSU
THAT'S IT... NOW I'LL TEACH YOU ANOTHER TRICK!
AND THUS DICK GRAYSON, BY THE HAND OF FATE, IS TRANSFORMED INTO THAT ASTONISHING PHENOMENON THAT YOUNG ROBIN HOOD OF TODAY-ROBIN THE BOY WONDER!

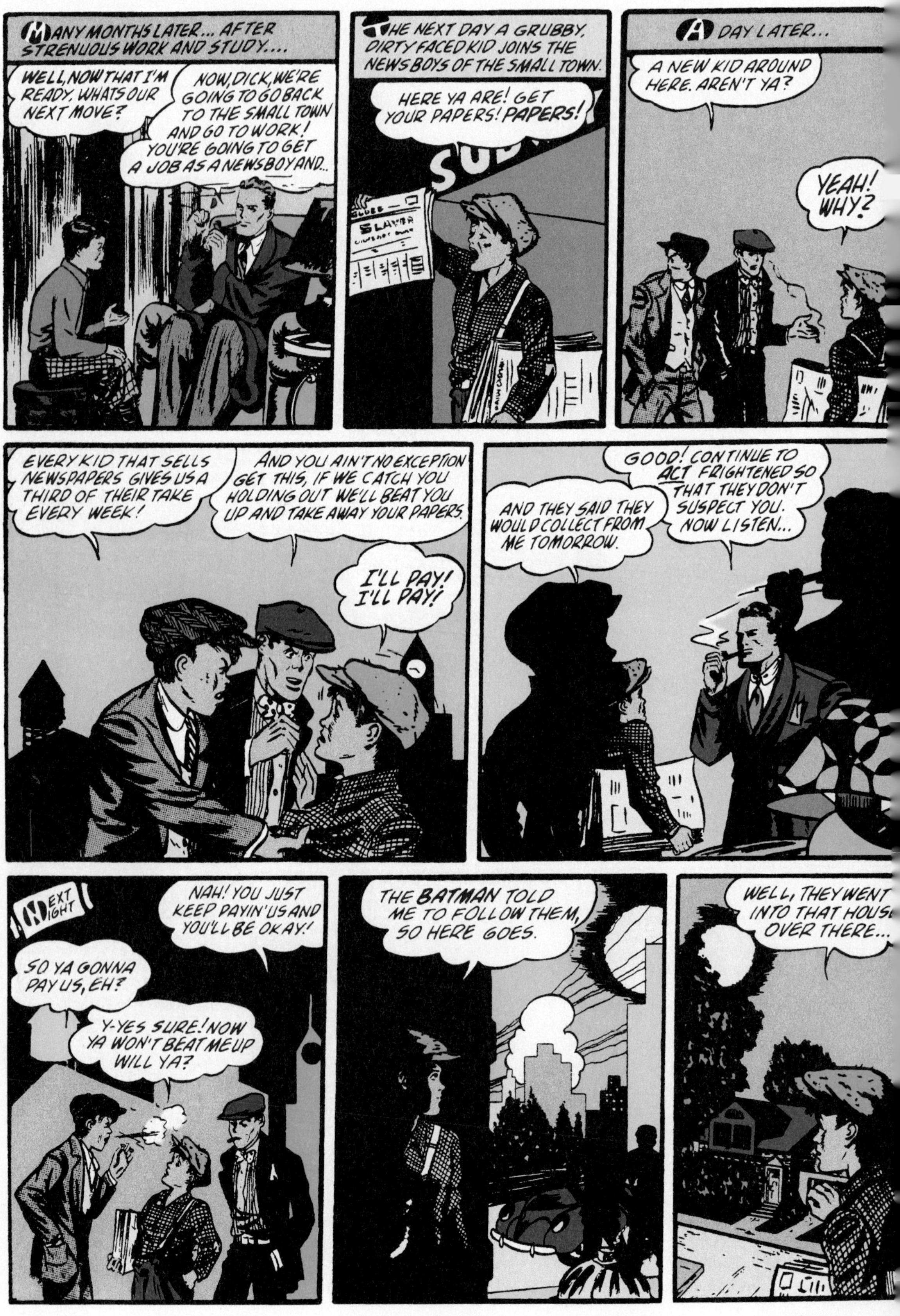
MANY MONTHS LATER... AFTER STRENUOUS WORK AND STUDY....
WELL, NOW THAT I'M READY, WHATS OUR NEXT MOVE?
NOW, DICK, WE'RE GOING TO GO BACK TO THE SMALL TOWN AND GO TO WORK! YOU'RE GOING TO GET A JOB AS A NEWSBOY AND...
THE NEXT DAY A GRUBBY, DIRTY FACED KID JOINS THE NEWSBOYS OF THE SMALL TOWN.
HERE YA ARE! GET YOUR PAPERS! PAPERS!
A DAY LATER...
A NEW KID AROUND HERE. AREN'T YA?
YEAH! WHY?
EVERY KID THAT SELLS NEWSPAPERS GIVES US A THIRD OF THEIR TAKE EVERY WEEK!
AND YOU AIN'T NO EXCEPTION GET THIS, IF WE CATCH YOU HOLDING OUT WE'LL BEAT YOU UP AND TAKE AWAY YOUR PAPERS.
I'LL PAY! I'LL PAY!
AND THEY SAID THEY WOULD COLLECT FROM ME TOMORROW.
GOOD! CONTINUE TO ACT FRIGHTENED SO THAT THEY DON'T SUSPECT YOU. NOW LISTEN...
NEXT NIGHT
SO YA GONNA PAY US, EH?
NAH! YOU JUST KEEP PAYIN' US AND YOU'LL BE OKAY!
Y-YES SURE! NOW YA WON'T BEAT ME UP WILL YA?
THE BATMAN TOLD ME TO FOLLOW THEM, SO HERE GOES.
WELL, THEY WENT INTO THAT HOUSE OVER THERE...

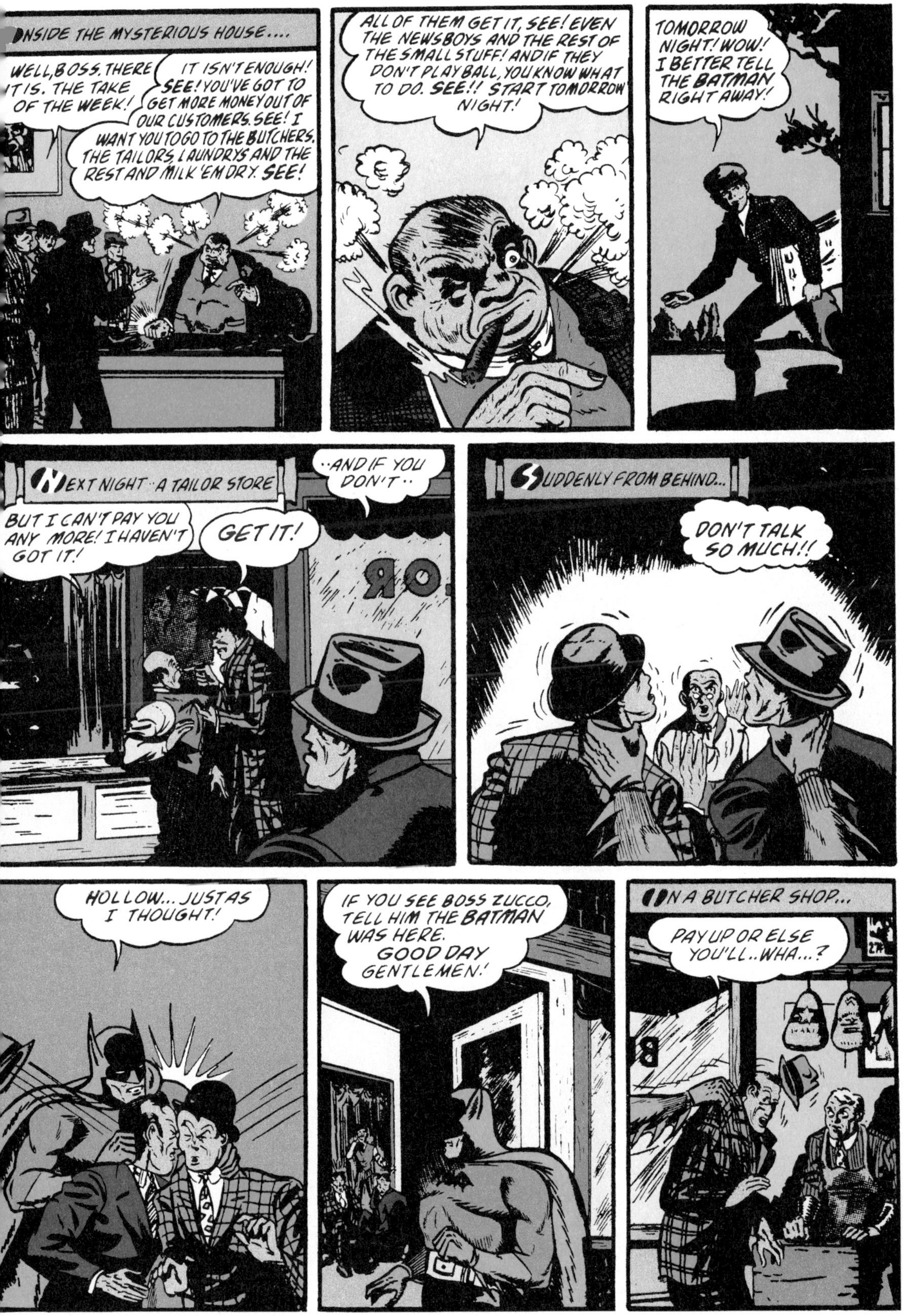
INSIDE THE MYSTERIOUS HOUSE....
WELL, BOSS, THERE IT IS. THE TAKE OF THE WEEK!
IT ISN'T ENOUGH! SEE! YOU'VE GOT TO GET MORE MONEY OUT OF OUR CUSTOMERS. SEE! I WANT YOU TO GO TO THE BUTCHERS, THE TAILORS, LAUNDRYS AND THE REST AND MILK 'EM DRY. SEE!
ALL OF THEM GET IT, SEE! EVEN THE NEWSBOYS AND THE REST OF THE SMALL STUFF! AND IF THEY DON'T PLAY BALL, YOU KNOW WHAT TO DO. SEE!! START TOMORROW NIGHT!
TOMORROW NIGHT! WOW! I BETTER TELL THE BATMAN RIGHT AWAY!
NEXT NIGHT · A TAILOR STORE
BUT I CAN'T PAY YOU ANY MORE! I HAVEN'T GOT IT!
GET IT!
..AND IF YOU DON'T..
SUDDENLY FROM BEHIND...
DON'T TALK SO MUCH!!
HOLLOW... JUST AS I THOUGHT!
IF YOU SEE BOSS ZUCCO, TELL HIM THE BATMAN WAS HERE. GOOD DAY GENTLEMEN!
IN A BUTCHER SHOP...
PAY UP OR ELSE YOU'LL..WHA...?

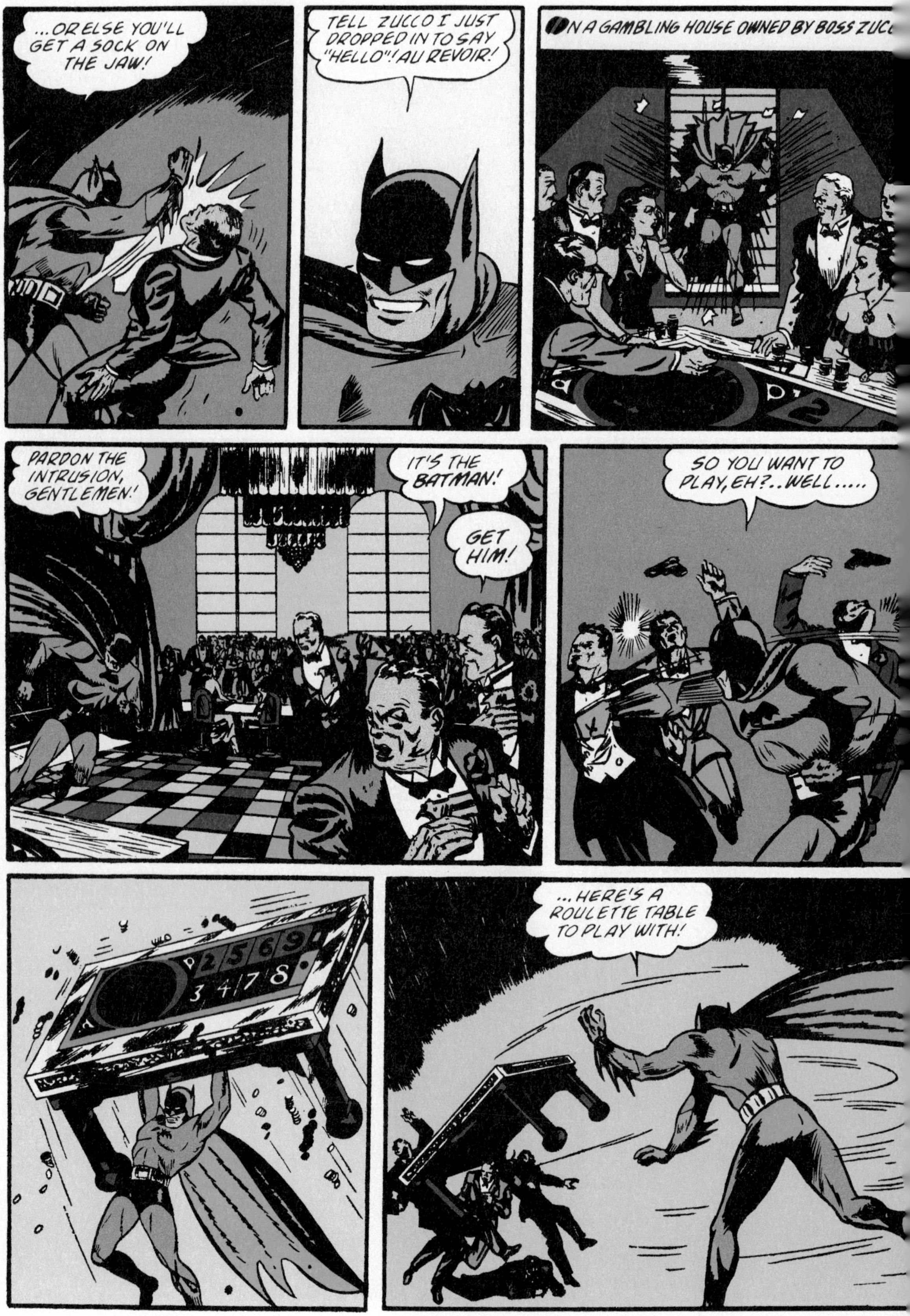

...OR ELSE YOU'LL GET A SOCK ON THE JAW!
TELL ZUCCO I JUST DROPPED IN TO SAY "HELLO"! AU REVOIR!
IN A GAMBLING HOUSE OWNED BY BOSS ZUCC
PARDON THE INTRUSION, GENTLEMEN!
IT'S THE BATMAN!
GET HIM!
SO YOU WANT TO PLAY, EH?..WELL.....
...HERE'S A ROULETTE TABLE TO PLAY WITH!

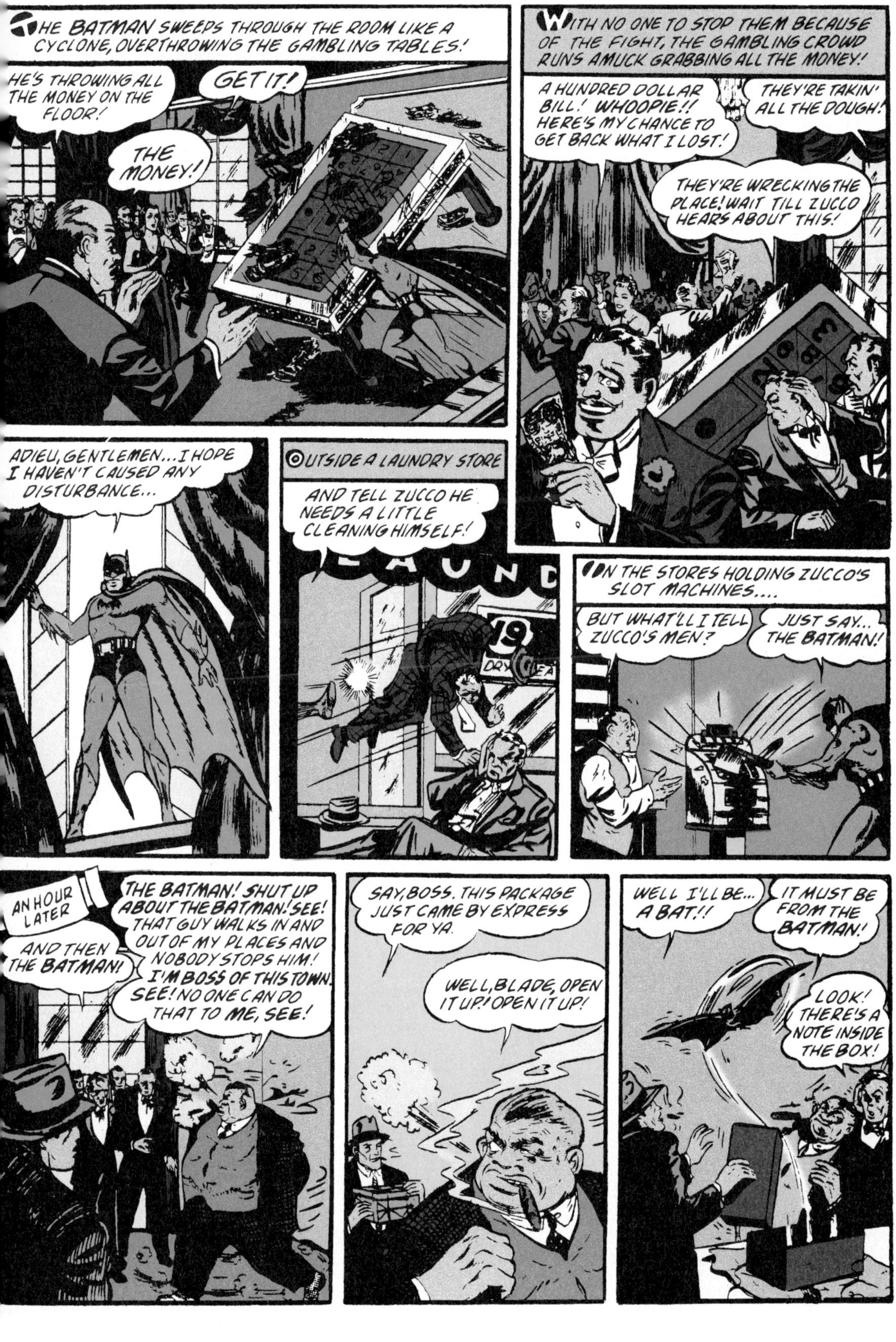
THE BATMAN SWEEPS THROUGH THE ROOM LIKE A CYCLONE, OVERTHROWING THE GAMBLING TABLES!
HE'S THROWING ALL THE MONEY ON THE FLOOR!
GET IT!
THE MONEY!
WITH NO ONE TO STOP THEM BECAUSE OF THE FIGHT, THE GAMBLING CROWD RUNS AMUCK GRABBING ALL THE MONEY!
A HUNDRED DOLLAR BILL! WHOOPIE!! HERE'S MY CHANCE TO GET BACK WHAT I LOST!
THEY'RE TAKIN' ALL THE DOUGH!
THEY'RE WRECKING THE PLACE! WAIT TILL ZUCCO HEARS ABOUT THIS!
ADIEU, GENTLEMEN... I HOPE I HAVEN'T CAUSED ANY DISTURBANCE...
OUTSIDE A LAUNDRY STORE
AND TELL ZUCCO HE NEEDS A LITTLE CLEANING HIMSELF!
LAUND
ON THE STORES HOLDING ZUCCO'S SLOT MACHINES....
BUT WHAT'LL I TELL ZUCCO'S MEN?
JUST SAY... THE BATMAN!
AN HOUR LATER
AND THEN THE BATMAN!
THE BATMAN! SHUT UP ABOUT THE BATMAN! SEE! THAT GUY WALKS IN AND OUT OF MY PLACES AND NOBODY STOPS HIM! I'M BOSS OF THIS TOWN. SEE! NO ONE CAN DO THAT TO ME, SEE!
SAY, BOSS. THIS PACKAGE JUST CAME BY EXPRESS FOR YA.
WELL, BLADE, OPEN IT UP! OPEN IT UP!
WELL I'LL BE... A BAT!!
IT MUST BE FROM THE BATMAN!
LOOK! THERE'S A NOTE INSIDE THE BOX!

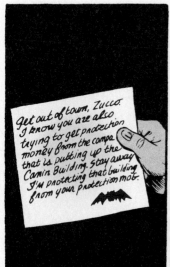

Get out of town, Zucco. I know you are also trying to get protection money from the compa— that is putting up the Canin Building. Stay away. I'm protecting that building from your protection mob.

OH YEAH! I'M BOSS OF THIS TOWN, SEE! NO ONE CAN TALK TO ME LIKE THAT AND GET AWAY WITH IT! C'MON, BOYS, WE'RE GOING TO THE CANIN BUILDING. I'M STILL BOSS ZUCCO, SEE!

I GOTCHA, BOSS!

AS THE CAR LEAVES, THERE RIDING ON THE TIRE RACK...ROBIN, THE BOY WONDER

THE BATMAN'S PLAN WORKED! ZUCCO IS SO MAD HE'S GOING TO DO THE JOB PERSONALLY!

the CANIN BUILDING

OKAY! I TIED UP THE WATCHMAN!

GOOD! YOU STAY DOWN HERE AS GUARD. NOW I'M GOING TO CONVINCE CANIN HE SHOULD PAY UP! BRING THE DYNAMITE BOYS!

AS ZUCCO AND HIS MEN GO UP, SUDDENLY FROM THE SHADOWS THE STREAKING FIGURE OF ROBIN, THE BOY WONDER

HEY...

SORRY, BOY, BUT I'M GOING UP!!

NOW WE'LL JUST BLOW UP THE TOP OF THE BUILDING TO SCARE CANIN INTO PAYING. AND IF HE DON'T, THE NEXT TIME....

BOSS, LOOK! OVER THERE... SOMEONE ON THE GIRDER...

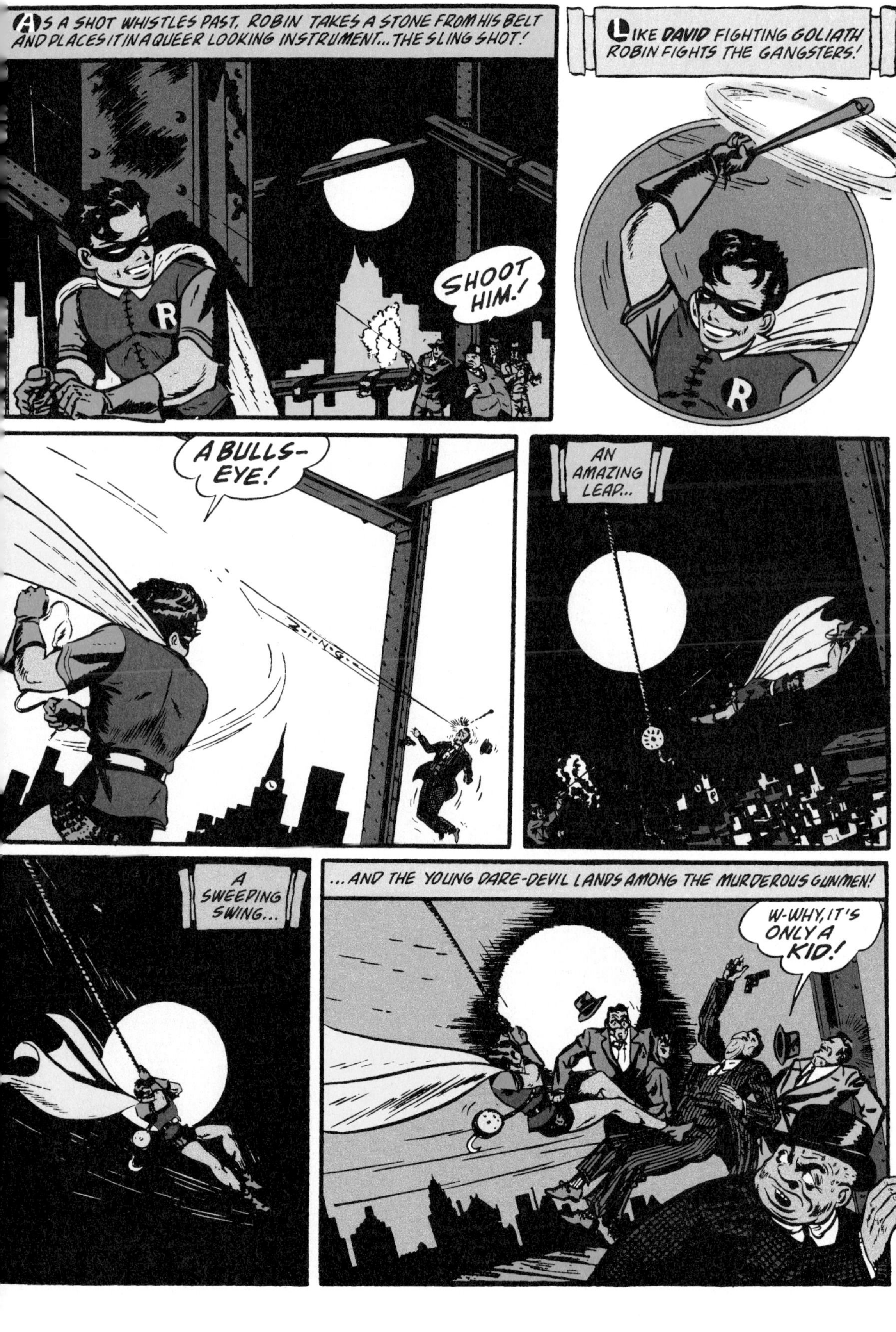
AS A SHOT WHISTLES PAST, ROBIN TAKES A STONE FROM HIS BELT AND PLACES IT IN A QUEER LOOKING INSTRUMENT... THE SLING SHOT!
SHOOT HIM!
LIKE DAVID FIGHTING GOLIATH ROBIN FIGHTS THE GANGSTERS!
A BULLS-EYE!
Z-I-N-G
AN AMAZING LEAP...
A SWEEPING SWING...
...AND THE YOUNG DARE-DEVIL LANDS AMONG THE MURDEROUS GUNMEN!
W-WHY, IT'S ONLY A KID!

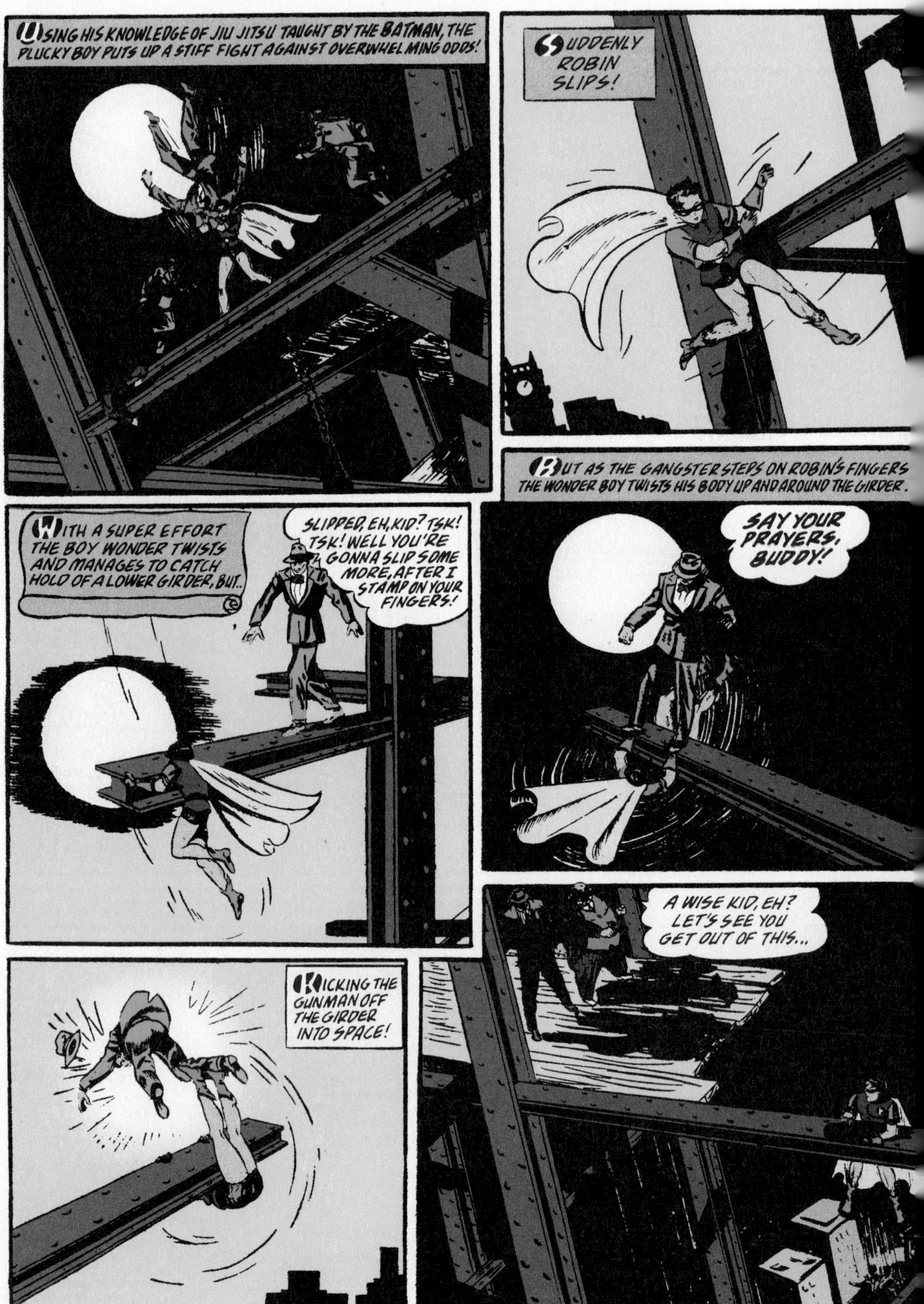
USING HIS KNOWLEDGE OF JIU JITSU TAUGHT BY THE BATMAN, THE PLUCKY BOY PUTS UP A STIFF FIGHT AGAINST OVERWHELMING ODDS!
SUDDENLY ROBIN SLIPS!
WITH A SUPER EFFORT THE BOY WONDER TWISTS AND MANAGES TO CATCH HOLD OF A LOWER GIRDER, BUT..
SLIPPED, EH, KID? TSK! TSK! WELL YOU'RE GONNA SLIP SOME MORE, AFTER I STAMP ON YOUR FINGERS!
BUT AS THE GANGSTER STEPS ON ROBIN'S FINGERS THE WONDER BOY TWISTS HIS BODY UP AND AROUND THE GIRDER.
SAY YOUR PRAYERS, BUDDY!
KICKING THE GUNMAN OFF THE GIRDER INTO SPACE!
A WISE KID, EH? LET'S SEE YOU GET OUT OF THIS...

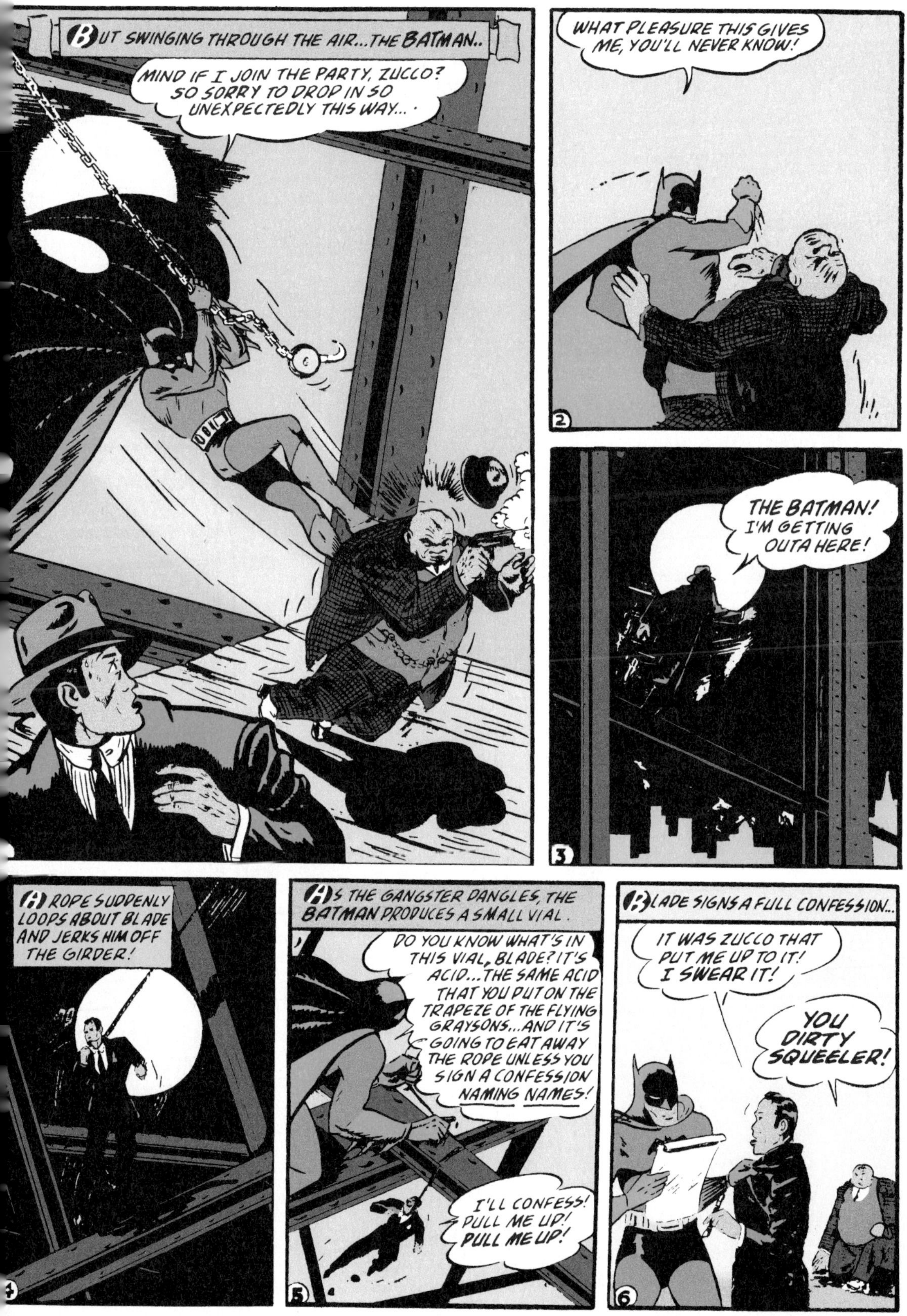
BUT SWINGING THROUGH THE AIR...THE BATMAN..
MIND IF I JOIN THE PARTY, ZUCCO? SO SORRY TO DROP IN SO UNEXPECTEDLY THIS WAY...
WHAT PLEASURE THIS GIVES ME, YOU'LL NEVER KNOW!
THE BATMAN! I'M GETTING OUTA HERE!
A ROPE SUDDENLY LOOPS ABOUT BLADE AND JERKS HIM OFF THE GIRDER!
AS THE GANGSTER DANGLES, THE BATMAN PRODUCES A SMALL VIAL.
DO YOU KNOW WHAT'S IN THIS VIAL, BLADE? IT'S ACID...THE SAME ACID THAT YOU PUT ON THE TRAPEZE OF THE FLYING GRAYSONS...AND IT'S GOING TO EAT AWAY THE ROPE UNLESS YOU SIGN A CONFESSION NAMING NAMES!
I'LL CONFESS! PULL ME UP! PULL ME UP!
BLADE SIGNS A FULL CONFESSION...
IT WAS ZUCCO THAT PUT ME UP TO IT! I SWEAR IT!
YOU DIRTY SQUEELER!

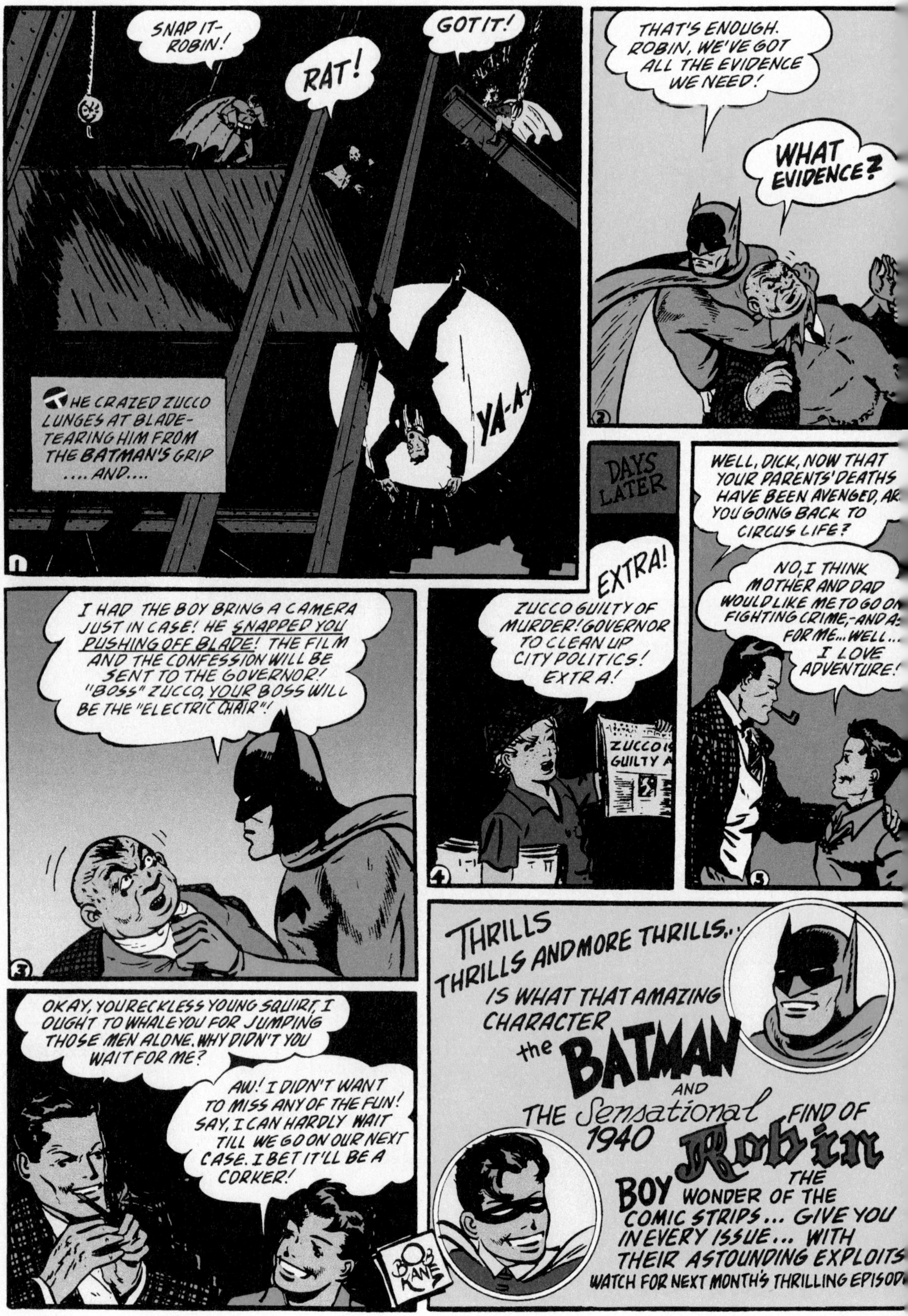
SNAP IT-ROBIN!
RAT!
GOT IT!
THE CRAZED ZUCCO LUNGES AT BLADE-TEARING HIM FROM THE BATMAN'S GRIP ....AND....
YA-A-A
THAT'S ENOUGH. ROBIN, WE'VE GOT ALL THE EVIDENCE WE NEED!
WHAT EVIDENCE?
I HAD THE BOY BRING A CAMERA JUST IN CASE! HE SNAPPED YOU PUSHING OFF BLADE! THE FILM AND THE CONFESSION WILL BE SENT TO THE GOVERNOR! "BOSS" ZUCCO, YOUR BOSS WILL BE THE "ELECTRIC CHAIR"!
DAYS LATER
EXTRA!
ZUCCO GUILTY OF MURDER! GOVERNOR TO CLEAN UP CITY POLITICS! EXTRA!
WELL, DICK, NOW THAT YOUR PARENTS' DEATHS HAVE BEEN AVENGED, AR YOU GOING BACK TO CIRCUS LIFE?
NO, I THINK MOTHER AND DAD WOULD LIKE ME TO GO ON FIGHTING CRIME,-AND AS FOR ME... WELL... I LOVE ADVENTURE!
OKAY, YOU RECKLESS YOUNG SQUIRT, I OUGHT TO WHALE YOU FOR JUMPING THOSE MEN ALONE. WHY DIDN'T YOU WAIT FOR ME?
AW! I DIDN'T WANT TO MISS ANY OF THE FUN! SAY, I CAN HARDLY WAIT TILL WE GO ON OUR NEXT CASE. I BET IT'LL BE A CORKER!
THRILLS THRILLS AND MORE THRILLS... IS WHAT THAT AMAZING CHARACTER the BATMAN AND THE Sensational FIND OF 1940 Robin THE BOY WONDER OF THE COMIC STRIPS... GIVE YOU IN EVERY ISSUE... WITH THEIR ASTOUNDING EXPLOITS
WATCH FOR NEXT MONTH'S THRILLING EPISOD
BOB KANE

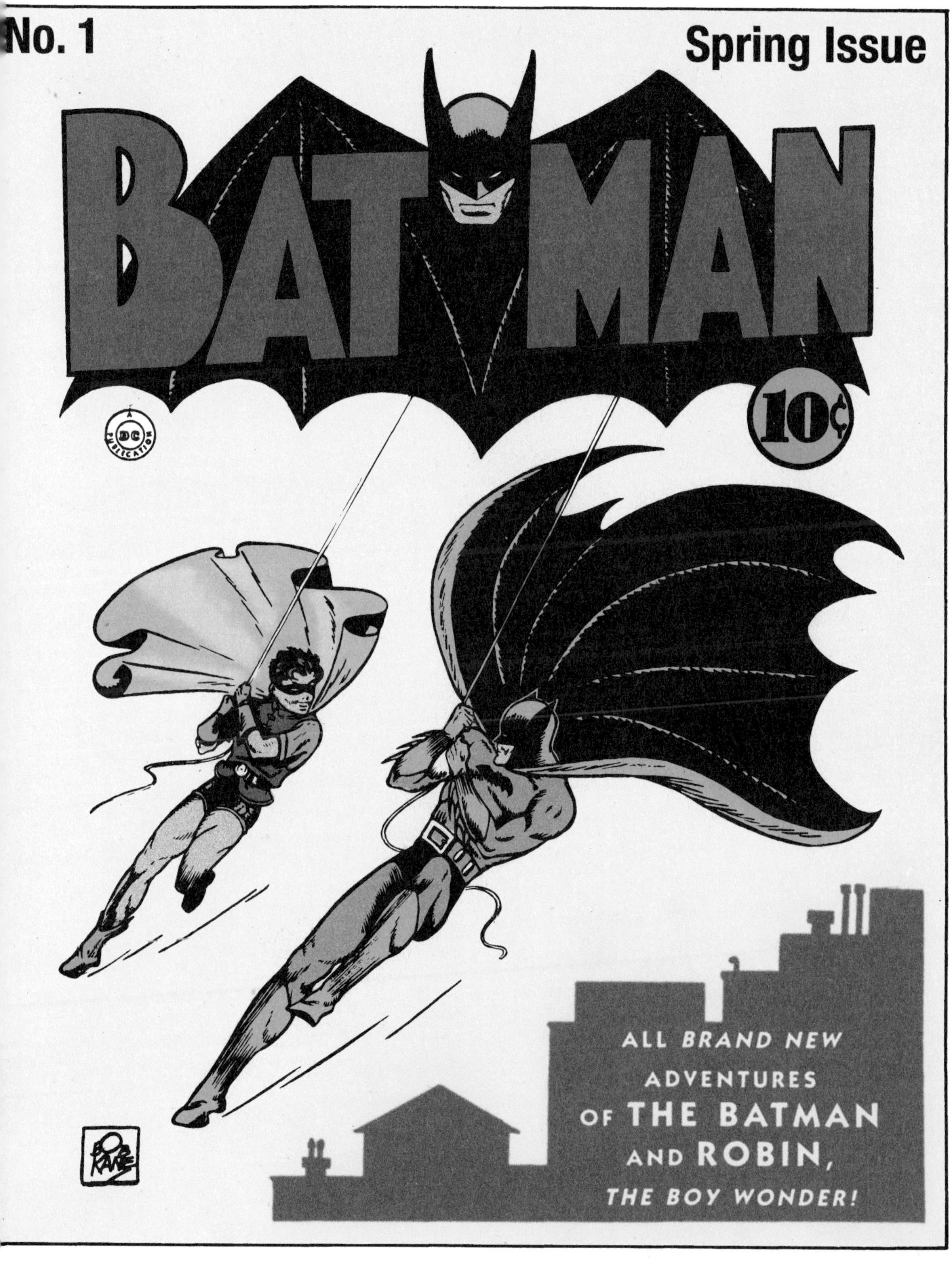
No. 1
Spring Issue
BATMAN
10¢
A DC PUBLICATION
ALL BRAND NEW
ADVENTURES
OF THE BATMAN
AND ROBIN,
THE BOY WONDER!

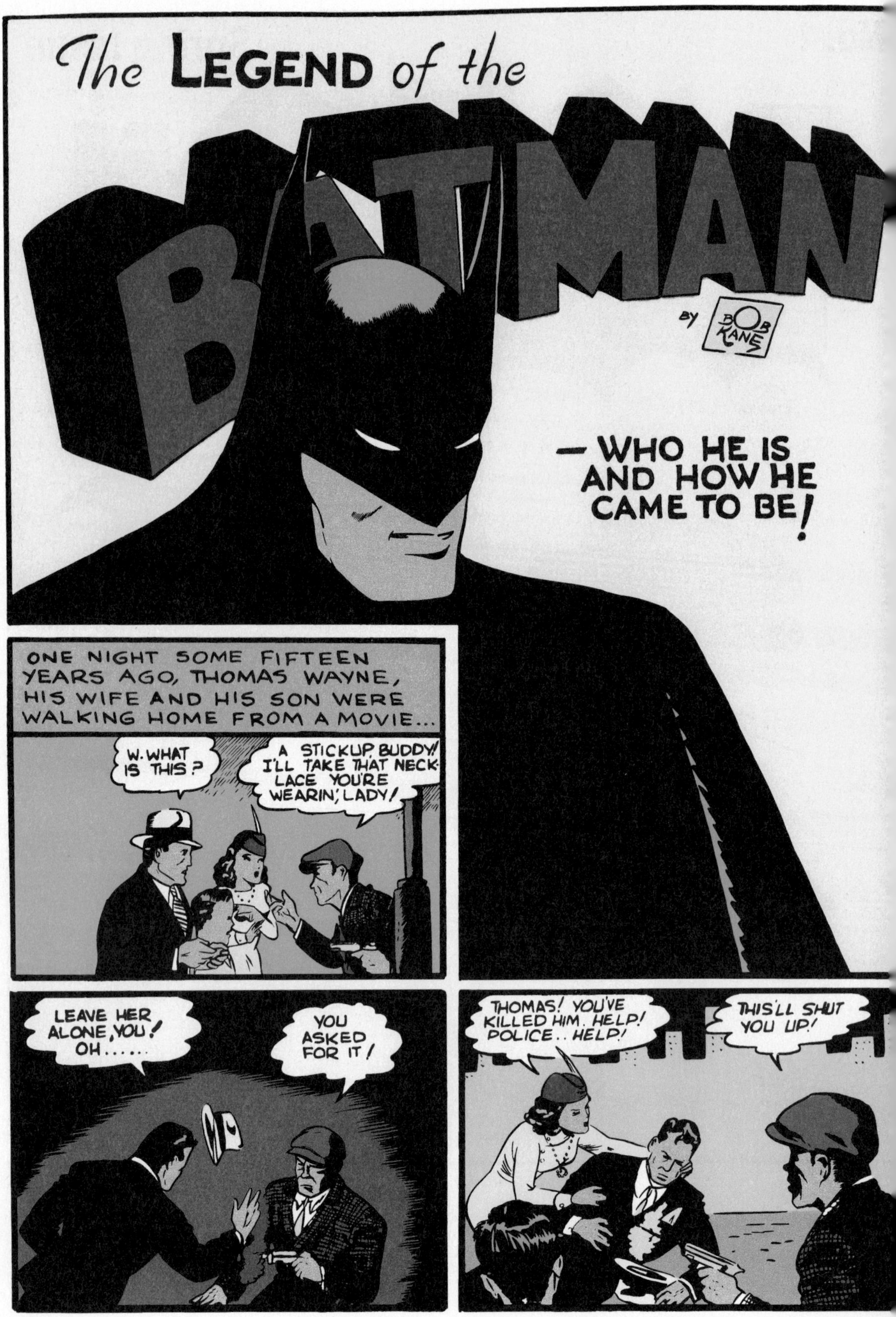
The LEGEND of the
BATMAN
BY BOB KANE
— WHO HE IS AND HOW HE CAME TO BE!
ONE NIGHT SOME FIFTEEN YEARS AGO, THOMAS WAYNE, HIS WIFE AND HIS SON WERE WALKING HOME FROM A MOVIE...
W. WHAT IS THIS?
A STICKUP, BUDDY! I'LL TAKE THAT NECKLACE YOU'RE WEARIN', LADY!
LEAVE HER ALONE, YOU! OH......
YOU ASKED FOR IT!
THOMAS! YOU'VE KILLED HIM. HELP! POLICE.. HELP!
THIS'LL SHUT YOU UP!

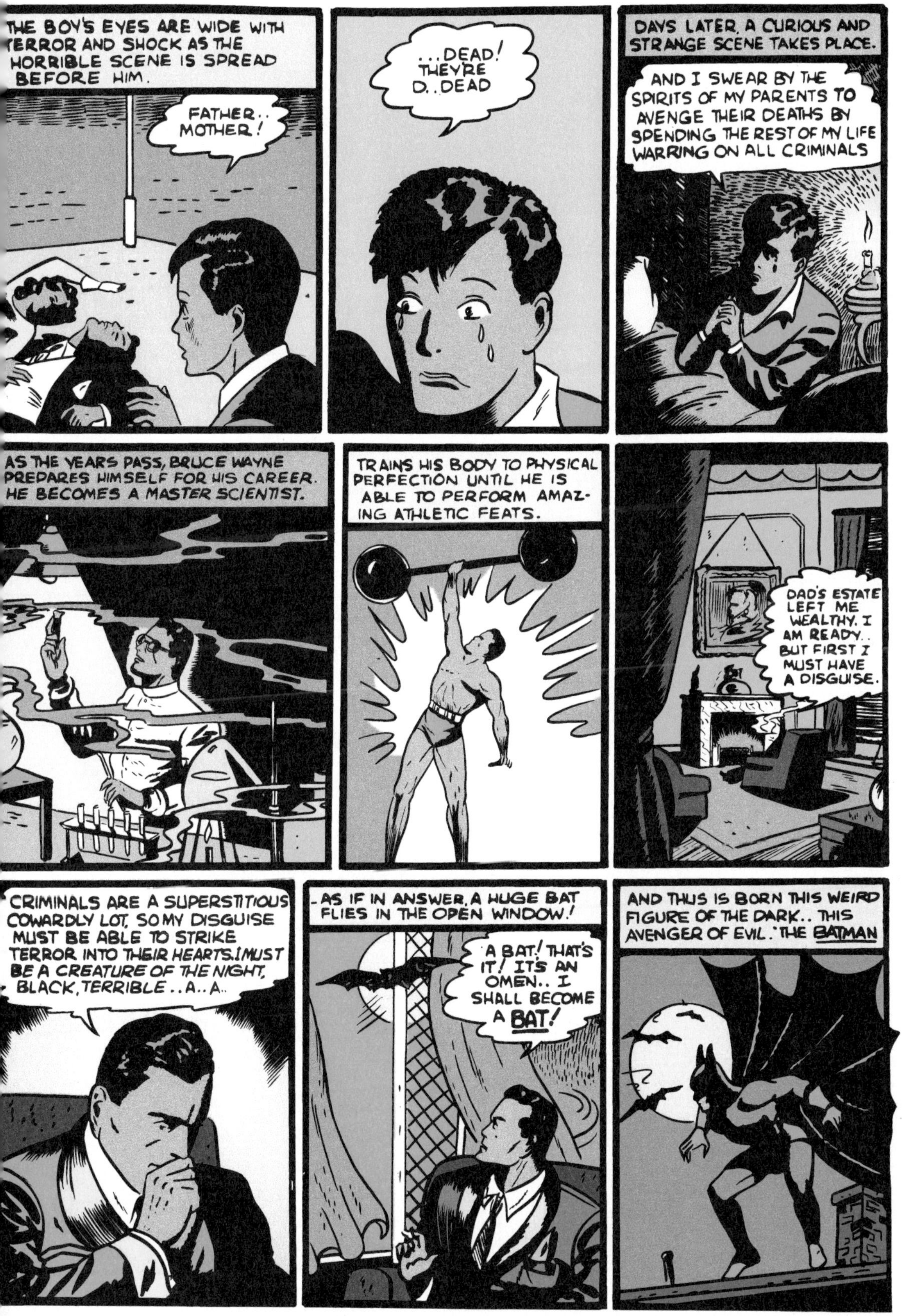
THE BOY'S EYES ARE WIDE WITH TERROR AND SHOCK AS THE HORRIBLE SCENE IS SPREAD BEFORE HIM.
FATHER.. MOTHER!
...DEAD! THEY'RE D..DEAD
DAYS LATER, A CURIOUS AND STRANGE SCENE TAKES PLACE.
AND I SWEAR BY THE SPIRITS OF MY PARENTS TO AVENGE THEIR DEATHS BY SPENDING THE REST OF MY LIFE WARRING ON ALL CRIMINALS
AS THE YEARS PASS, BRUCE WAYNE PREPARES HIMSELF FOR HIS CAREER. HE BECOMES A MASTER SCIENTIST.
TRAINS HIS BODY TO PHYSICAL PERFECTION UNTIL HE IS ABLE TO PERFORM AMAZING ATHLETIC FEATS.
DAD'S ESTATE LEFT ME WEALTHY. I AM READY.. BUT FIRST I MUST HAVE A DISGUISE.
"CRIMINALS ARE A SUPERSTITIOUS COWARDLY LOT, SO MY DISGUISE MUST BE ABLE TO STRIKE TERROR INTO THEIR HEARTS. I MUST BE A CREATURE OF THE NIGHT, BLACK, TERRIBLE..A..A..
-AS IF IN ANSWER, A HUGE BAT FLIES IN THE OPEN WINDOW!
A BAT! THAT'S IT! IT'S AN OMEN.. I SHALL BECOME A BAT!
AND THUS IS BORN THIS WEIRD FIGURE OF THE DARK.. THIS AVENGER OF EVIL. "THE BATMAN"

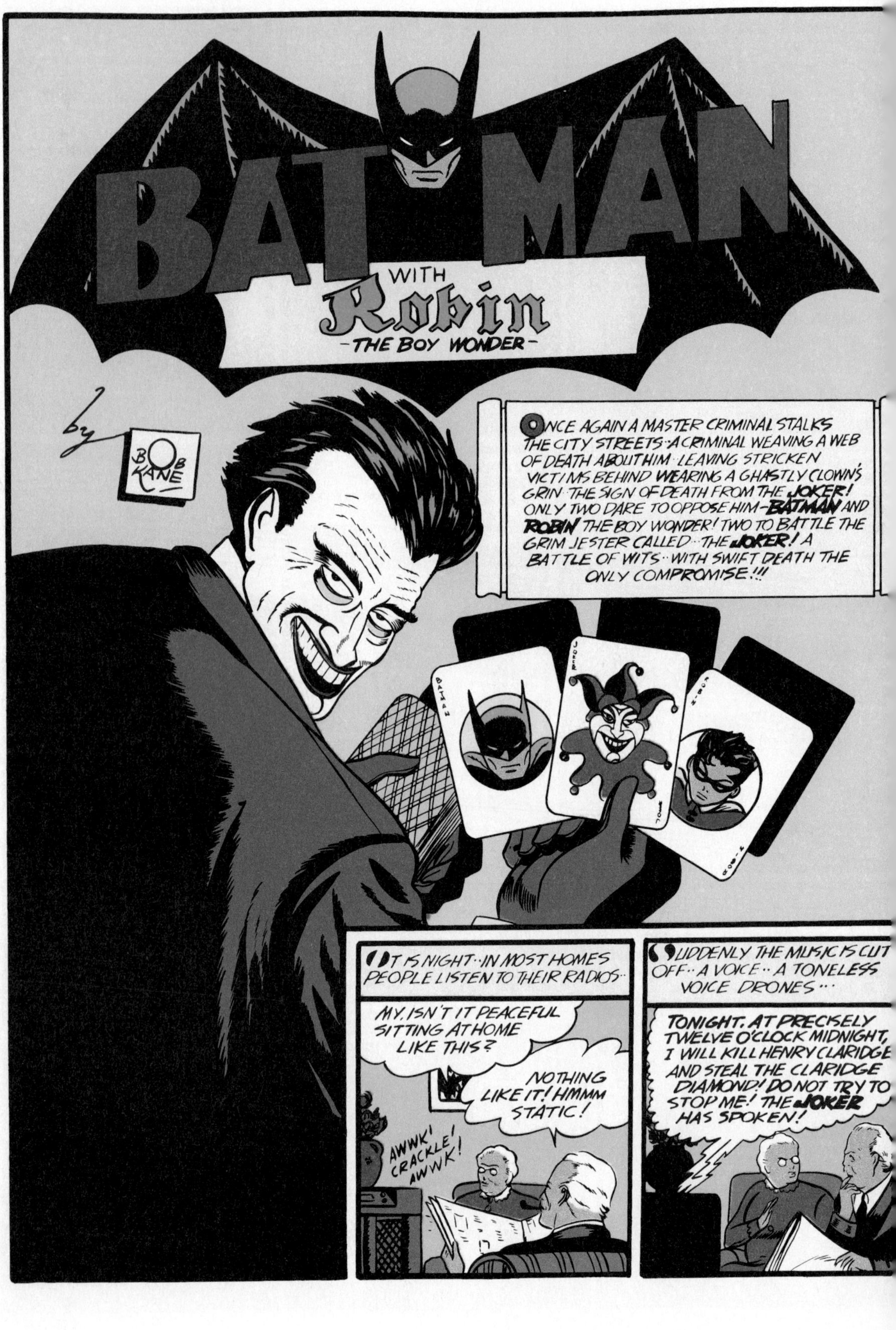

BATMAN
WITH
Robin
-THE BOY WONDER-
by BOB KANE
ONCE AGAIN A MASTER CRIMINAL STALKS THE CITY STREETS··A CRIMINAL WEAVING A WEB OF DEATH ABOUT HIM··LEAVING STRICKEN VICTIMS BEHIND WEARING A GHASTLY CLOWN'S GRIN··THE SIGN OF DEATH FROM THE JOKER! ONLY TWO DARE TO OPPOSE HIM-BATMAN AND ROBIN THE BOY WONDER! TWO TO BATTLE THE GRIM JESTER CALLED··THE JOKER! A BATTLE OF WITS··WITH SWIFT DEATH THE ONLY COMPROMISE!!!
BATMAN
JOKER
ROBIN
IT IS NIGHT··IN MOST HOMES PEOPLE LISTEN TO THEIR RADIOS··
MY, ISN'T IT PEACEFUL SITTING AT HOME LIKE THIS?
NOTHING LIKE IT! HMMM STATIC!
AWWK! CRACKLE! AWWK!
SUDDENLY THE MUSIC IS CUT OFF·· A VOICE·· A TONELESS VOICE DRONES···
TONIGHT, AT PRECISELY TWELVE O'CLOCK MIDNIGHT, I WILL KILL HENRY CLARIDGE AND STEAL THE CLARIDGE DIAMOND! DO NOT TRY TO STOP ME! THE JOKER HAS SPOKEN!

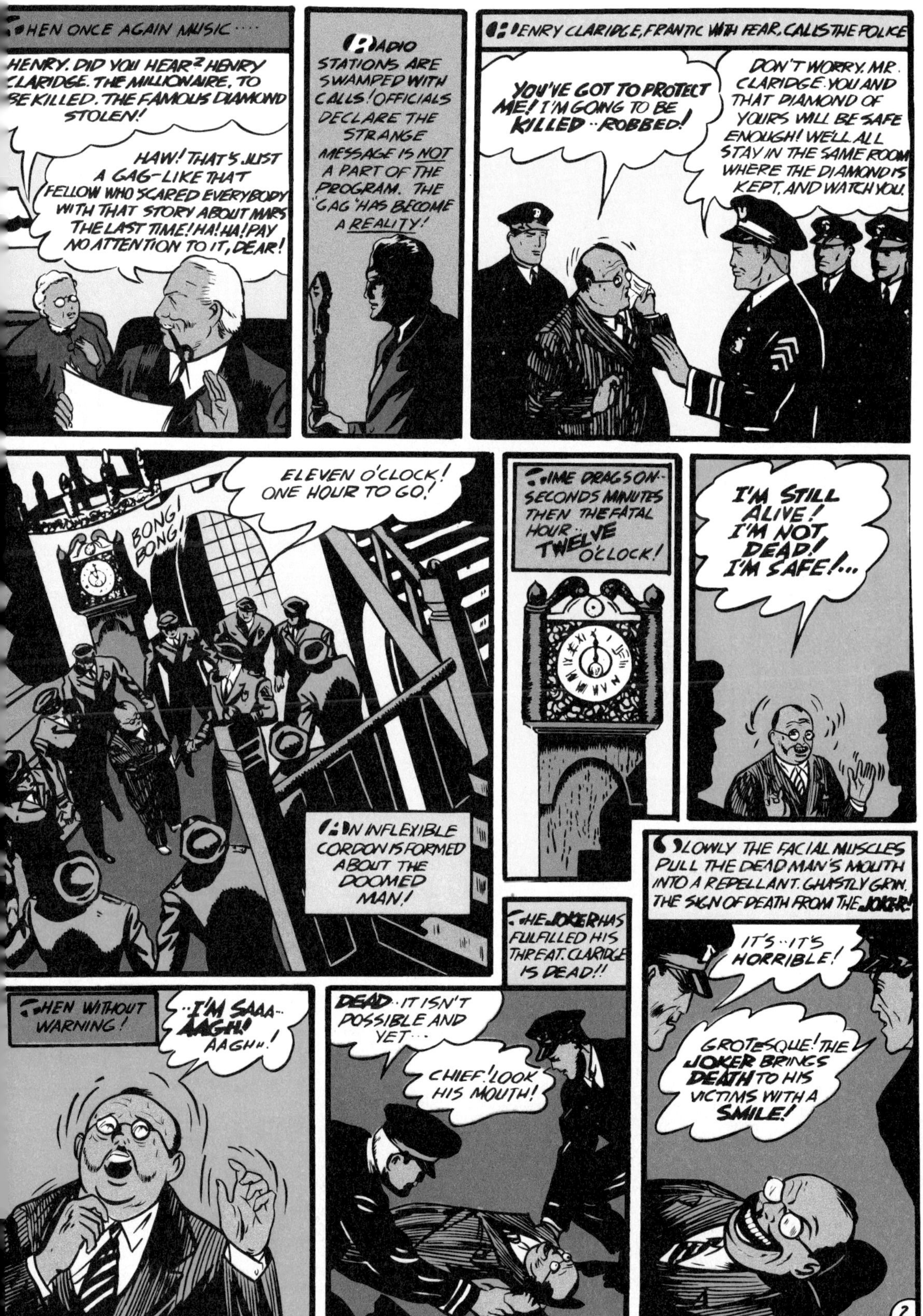
THEN ONCE AGAIN MUSIC....
HENRY. DID YOU HEAR? HENRY CLARIDGE. THE MILLIONAIRE. TO BE KILLED. THE FAMOUS DIAMOND STOLEN!
HAW! THAT'S JUST A GAG-LIKE THAT FELLOW WHO SCARED EVERYBODY WITH THAT STORY ABOUT MARS THE LAST TIME! HA! HA! PAY NO ATTENTION TO IT, DEAR!
RADIO STATIONS ARE SWAMPED WITH CALLS! OFFICIALS DECLARE THE STRANGE MESSAGE IS NOT A PART OF THE PROGRAM. THE "GAG" HAS BECOME A REALITY!
HENRY CLARIDGE, FRANTIC WITH FEAR, CALLS THE POLICE
YOU'VE GOT TO PROTECT ME! I'M GOING TO BE KILLED.. ROBBED!
DON'T WORRY. MR. CLARIDGE. YOU AND THAT DIAMOND OF YOURS WILL BE SAFE ENOUGH! WE'LL ALL STAY IN THE SAME ROOM WHERE THE DIAMOND IS KEPT, AND WATCH YOU.
BONG! BONG!
ELEVEN O'CLOCK! ONE HOUR TO GO!
AN INFLEXIBLE CORDON IS FORMED ABOUT THE DOOMED MAN!
TIME DRAGS ON-- SECONDS MINUTES THEN THE FATAL HOUR.. TWELVE O'CLOCK!
I'M STILL ALIVE! I'M NOT DEAD! I'M SAFE!...
THEN WITHOUT WARNING!
..I'M SAAA.. AAGH! AAGH..!
DEAD.. IT ISN'T POSSIBLE AND YET...
CHIEF! LOOK HIS MOUTH!
THE JOKER HAS FULFILLED HIS THREAT. CLARIDGE IS DEAD!!
SLOWLY THE FACIAL MUSCLES PULL THE DEAD MAN'S MOUTH INTO A REPELLANT, GHASTLY GRIN. THE SIGN OF DEATH FROM THE JOKER!
IT'S.. IT'S HORRIBLE!
GROTESQUE! THE JOKER BRINGS DEATH TO HIS VICTIMS WITH A SMILE!
2

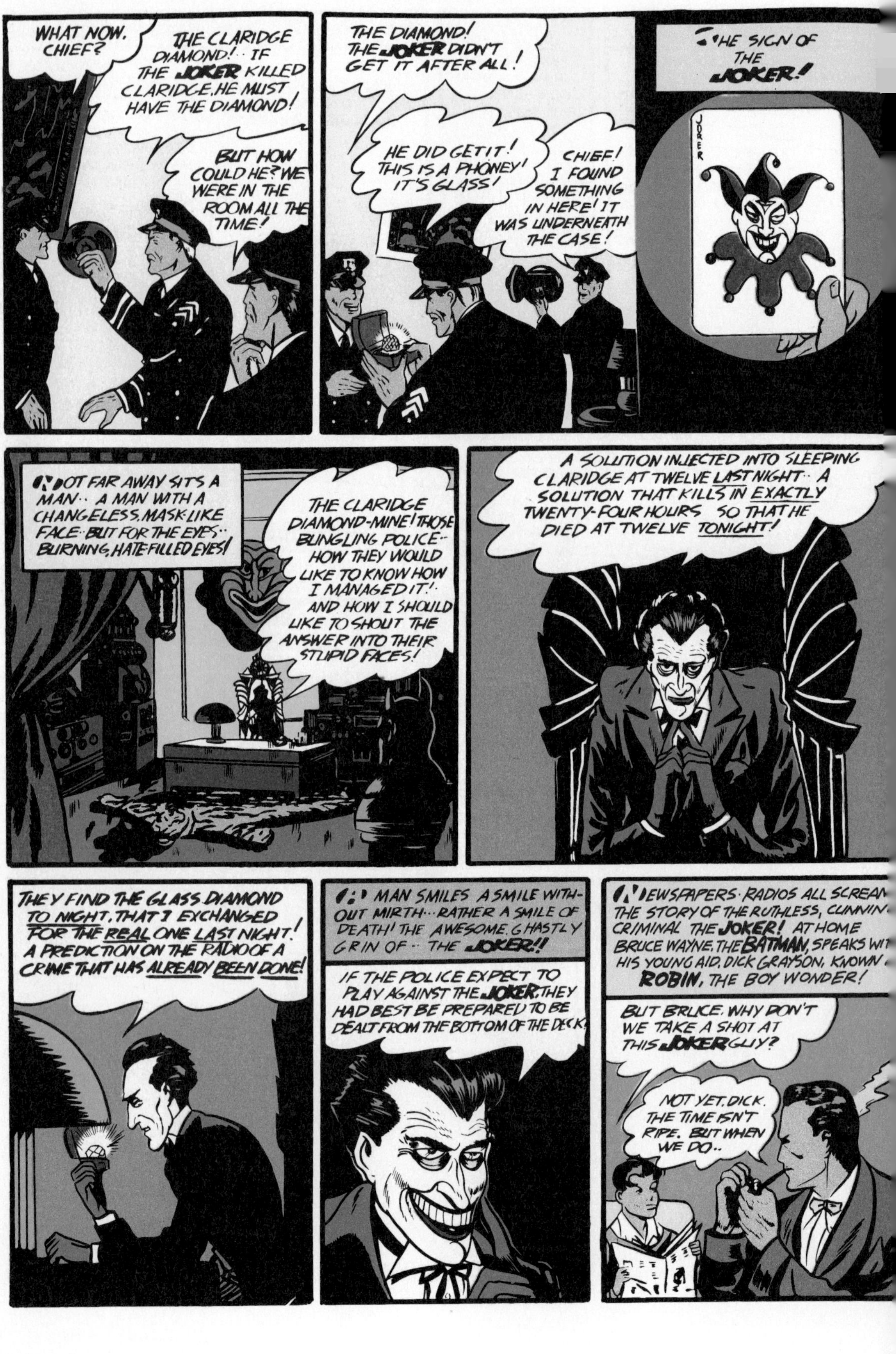

WHAT NOW, CHIEF?
THE CLARIDGE DIAMOND!.. IF THE JOKER KILLED CLARIDGE, HE MUST HAVE THE DIAMOND!
BUT HOW COULD HE? WE WERE IN THE ROOM ALL THE TIME!
THE DIAMOND! THE JOKER DIDN'T GET IT AFTER ALL!
HE DID GET IT! THIS IS A PHONEY! IT'S GLASS!
CHIEF! I FOUND SOMETHING IN HERE! IT WAS UNDERNEATH THE CASE!
THE SIGN OF THE JOKER!
JOKER
NOT FAR AWAY SITS A MAN.. A MAN WITH A CHANGELESS, MASK-LIKE FACE.. BUT FOR THE EYES.. BURNING, HATE-FILLED EYES!
THE CLARIDGE DIAMOND-MINE! THOSE BUNGLING POLICE.. HOW THEY WOULD LIKE TO KNOW HOW I MANAGED IT!.. AND HOW I SHOULD LIKE TO SHOUT THE ANSWER INTO THEIR STUPID FACES!
A SOLUTION INJECTED INTO SLEEPING CLARIDGE AT TWELVE LAST NIGHT.. A SOLUTION THAT KILLS IN EXACTLY TWENTY-FOUR HOURS SO THAT HE DIED AT TWELVE TONIGHT!
THEY FIND THE GLASS DIAMOND TO NIGHT, THAT I EXCHANGED FOR THE REAL ONE LAST NIGHT! A PREDICTION ON THE RADIO OF A CRIME THAT HAS ALREADY BEEN DONE!
THE MAN SMILES A SMILE WITHOUT MIRTH... RATHER A SMILE OF DEATH! THE AWESOME, GHASTLY GRIN OF.. THE JOKER!!
IF THE POLICE EXPECT TO PLAY AGAINST THE JOKER, THEY HAD BEST BE PREPARED TO BE DEALT FROM THE BOTTOM OF THE DECK!
NEWSPAPERS. RADIOS ALL SCREAM THE STORY OF THE RUTHLESS, CUNNIN CRIMINAL THE JOKER! AT HOME BRUCE WAYNE, THE BATMAN, SPEAKS WI HIS YOUNG AID, DICK GRAYSON, KNOWN ROBIN, THE BOY WONDER!
BUT BRUCE, WHY DON'T WE TAKE A SHOT AT THIS JOKER GUY?
NOT YET, DICK. THE TIME ISN'T RIPE. BUT WHEN WE DO..

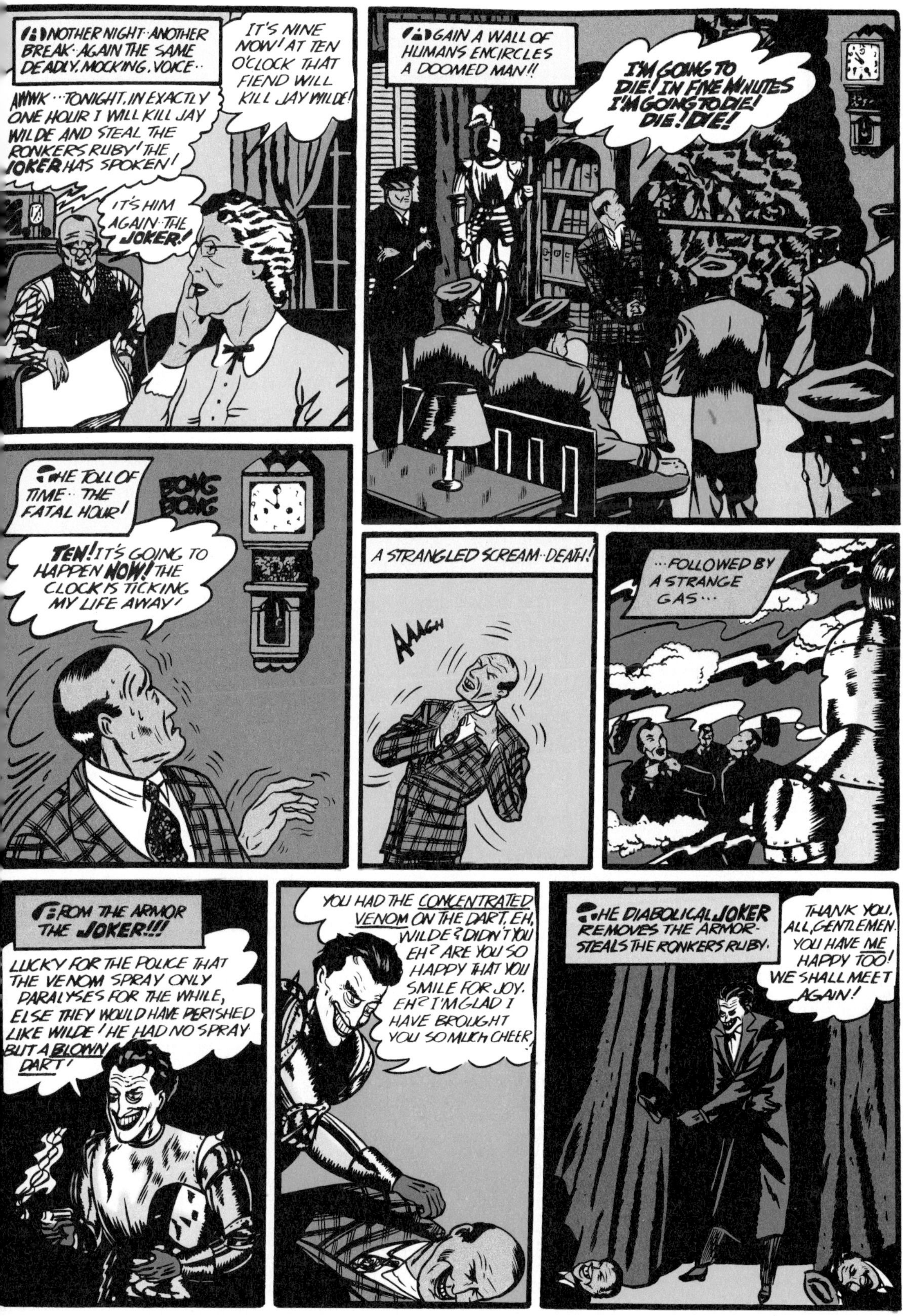
ANOTHER NIGHT· ANOTHER BREAK· AGAIN THE SAME DEADLY, MOCKING, VOICE·
AWWK ···TONIGHT, IN EXACTLY ONE HOUR I WILL KILL JAY WILDE AND STEAL THE RONKERS RUBY! THE JOKER HAS SPOKEN!
IT'S NINE NOW! AT TEN O'CLOCK THAT FIEND WILL KILL JAY WILDE!
IT'S HIM AGAIN·· THE JOKER!
AGAIN A WALL OF HUMANS ENCIRCLES A DOOMED MAN!!
I'M GOING TO DIE! IN FIVE MINUTES I'M GOING TO DIE! DIE! DIE!
THE TOLL OF TIME·· THE FATAL HOUR!
BONG BONG
TEN! IT'S GOING TO HAPPEN NOW! THE CLOCK IS TICKING MY LIFE AWAY!
A STRANGLED SCREAM··DEATH!
AAAGH
···FOLLOWED BY A STRANGE GAS···
FROM THE ARMOR THE JOKER!!!
LUCKY FOR THE POLICE THAT THE VENOM SPRAY ONLY PARALYSES FOR THE WHILE, ELSE THEY WOULD HAVE PERISHED LIKE WILDE! HE HAD NO SPRAY· BUT A BLOWN DART!
YOU HAD THE CONCENTRATED VENOM ON THE DART, EH, WILDE? DIDN'T YOU EH? ARE YOU SO HAPPY THAT YOU SMILE FOR JOY. EH? I'M GLAD I HAVE BROUGHT YOU SO MUCH CHEER!
THE DIABOLICAL JOKER REMOVES THE ARMOR-STEALS THE RONKERS RUBY.
THANK YOU, ALL, GENTLEMEN. YOU HAVE ME HAPPY TOO! WE SHALL MEET AGAIN!

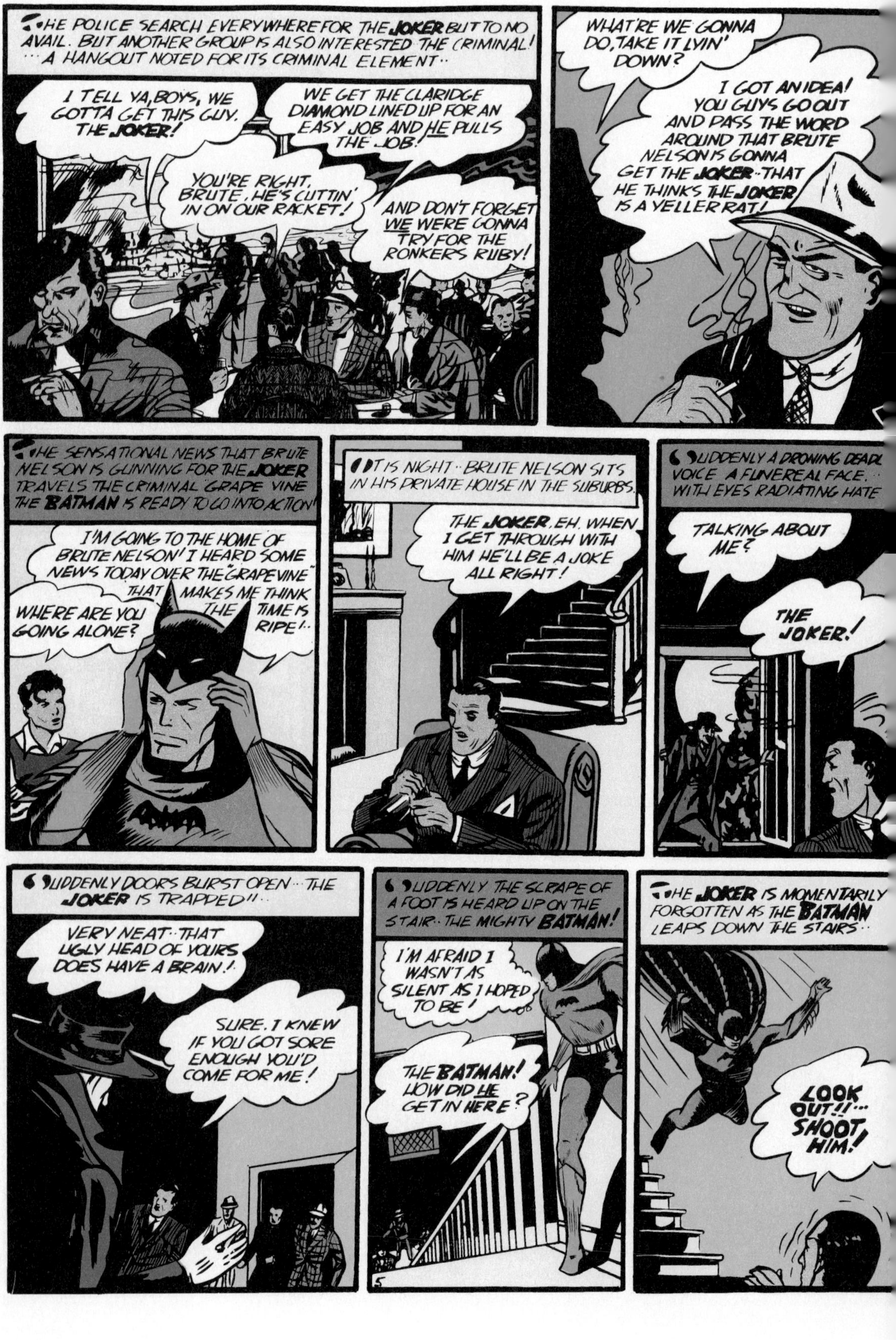
THE POLICE SEARCH EVERYWHERE FOR THE JOKER BUT TO NO AVAIL. BUT ANOTHER GROUP IS ALSO INTERESTED THE CRIMINAL! ... A HANGOUT NOTED FOR ITS CRIMINAL ELEMENT..
I TELL YA, BOYS, WE GOTTA GET THIS GUY. THE JOKER!
WE GET THE CLARIDGE DIAMOND LINED UP FOR AN EASY JOB AND HE PULLS THE JOB!
YOU'RE RIGHT, BRUTE, HE'S CUTTIN' IN ON OUR RACKET!
AND DON'T FORGET WE WERE GONNA TRY FOR THE RONKER'S RUBY!
WHAT'RE WE GONNA DO, TAKE IT LYIN' DOWN?
I GOT AN IDEA! YOU GUYS GO OUT AND PASS THE WORD AROUND THAT BRUTE NELSON IS GONNA GET THE JOKER..THAT HE THINKS THE JOKER IS A YELLER RAT!
THE SENSATIONAL NEWS THAT BRUTE NELSON IS GUNNING FOR THE JOKER TRAVELS THE CRIMINAL GRAPE VINE THE BATMAN IS READY TO GO INTO ACTION!
I'M GOING TO THE HOME OF BRUTE NELSON! I HEARD SOME NEWS TODAY OVER THE "GRAPEVINE" THAT MAKES ME THINK THE TIME IS RIPE!..
WHERE ARE YOU GOING ALONE?
IT IS NIGHT.. BRUTE NELSON SITS IN HIS PRIVATE HOUSE IN THE SUBURBS.
THE JOKER, EH, WHEN I GET THROUGH WITH HIM HE'LL BE A JOKE ALL RIGHT!
SUDDENLY A DRONING DEADL VOICE A FUNEREAL FACE... WITH EYES RADIATING HATE
TALKING ABOUT ME?
THE JOKER!
SUDDENLY DOORS BURST OPEN... THE JOKER IS TRAPPED!!..
VERY NEAT.. THAT UGLY HEAD OF YOURS DOES HAVE A BRAIN!.
SURE. I KNEW IF YOU GOT SORE ENOUGH YOU'D COME FOR ME!
SUDDENLY THE SCRAPE OF A FOOT IS HEARD UP ON THE STAIR.. THE MIGHTY BATMAN!
I'M AFRAID I WASN'T AS SILENT AS I HOPED TO BE!
THE BATMAN! HOW DID HE GET IN HERE?
THE JOKER IS MOMENTARILY FORGOTTEN AS THE BATMAN LEAPS DOWN THE STAIRS..
LOOK OUT!!... SHOOT HIM!

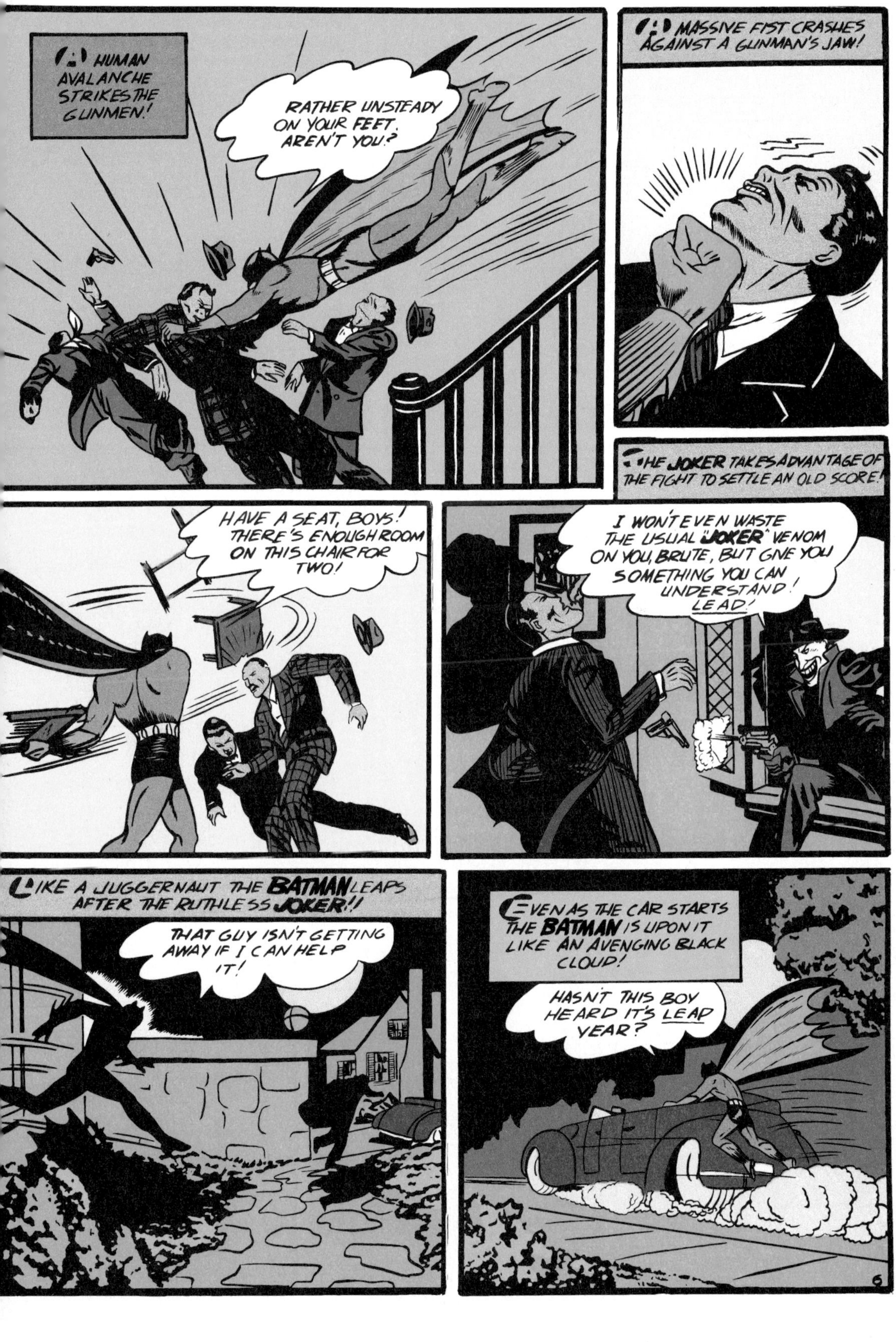
A HUMAN AVALANCHE STRIKES THE GUNMEN!
RATHER UNSTEADY ON YOUR FEET, AREN'T YOU?
A MASSIVE FIST CRASHES AGAINST A GUNMAN'S JAW!
HAVE A SEAT, BOYS! THERE'S ENOUGH ROOM ON THIS CHAIR FOR TWO!
THE JOKER TAKES ADVANTAGE OF THE FIGHT TO SETTLE AN OLD SCORE!
I WON'T EVEN WASTE THE USUAL "JOKER" VENOM ON YOU, BRUTE, BUT GIVE YOU SOMETHING YOU CAN UNDERSTAND! LEAD!
LIKE A JUGGERNAUT THE BATMAN LEAPS AFTER THE RUTHLESS JOKER!!
THAT GUY ISN'T GETTING AWAY IF I CAN HELP IT!
EVEN AS THE CAR STARTS THE BATMAN IS UPON IT LIKE AN AVENGING BLACK CLOUD!
HASN'T THIS BOY HEARD IT'S LEAP YEAR?
6

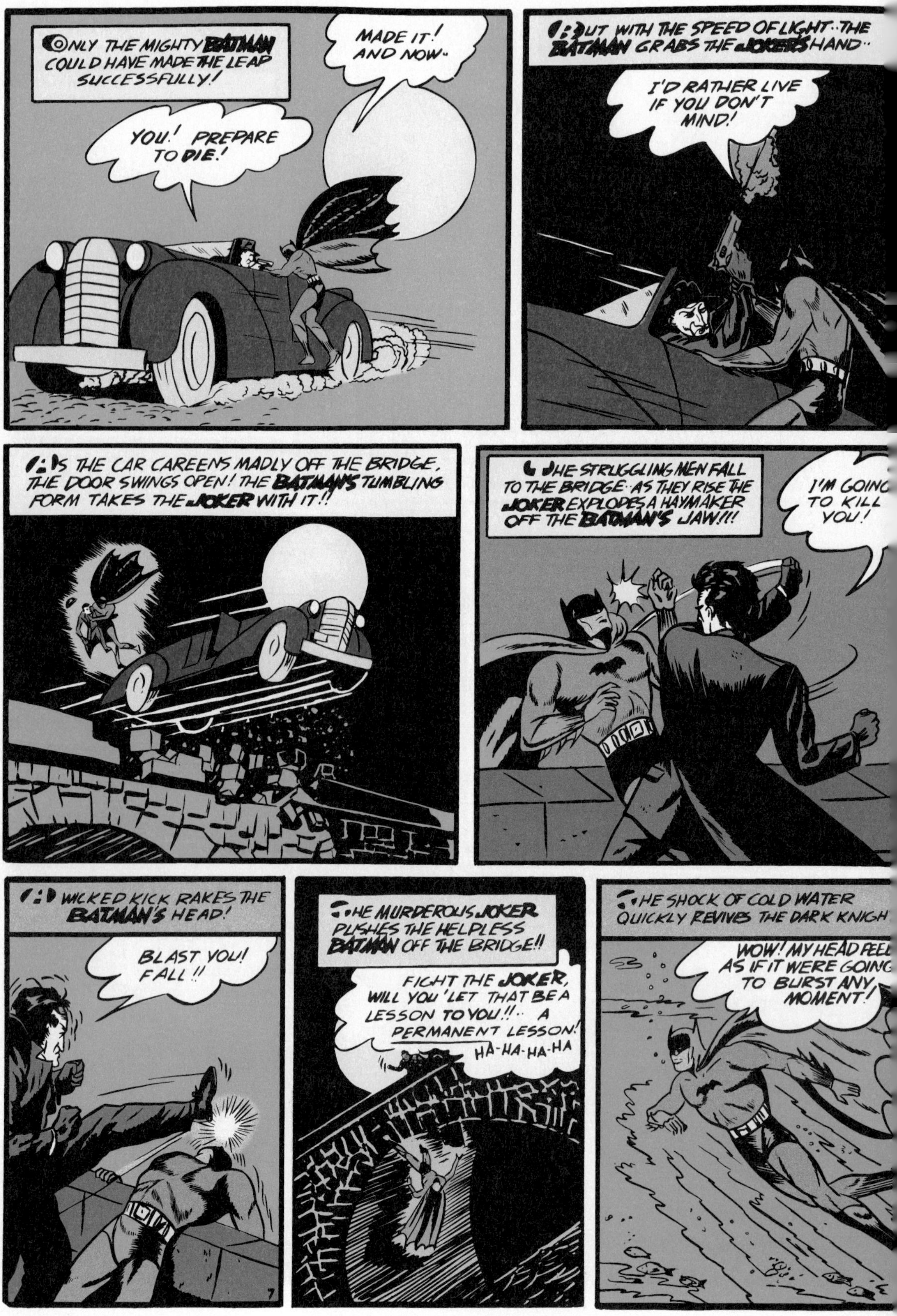

ONLY THE MIGHTY BATMAN COULD HAVE MADE THE LEAP SUCCESSFULLY!
MADE IT! AND NOW..
YOU! PREPARE TO DIE!
BUT WITH THE SPEED OF LIGHT.. THE BATMAN GRABS THE JOKER'S HAND..
I'D RATHER LIVE IF YOU DON'T MIND!
AS THE CAR CAREENS MADLY OFF THE BRIDGE, THE DOOR SWINGS OPEN! THE BATMAN'S TUMBLING FORM TAKES THE JOKER WITH IT!!
THE STRUGGLING MEN FALL TO THE BRIDGE.. AS THEY RISE THE JOKER EXPLODES A HAYMAKER OFF THE BATMAN'S JAW!!!
I'M GOIN TO KILL YOU!
A WICKED KICK RAKES THE BATMAN'S HEAD!
BLAST YOU! FALL!!
7
THE MURDEROUS JOKER PUSHES THE HELPLESS BATMAN OFF THE BRIDGE!!
FIGHT THE JOKER, WILL YOU! LET THAT BE A LESSON TO YOU!!.. A PERMANENT LESSON!
HA-HA-HA-HA
THE SHOCK OF COLD WATER QUICKLY REVIVES THE DARK KNIGH
WOW! MY HEAD FEEL AS IF IT WERE GOING TO BURST ANY MOMENT!

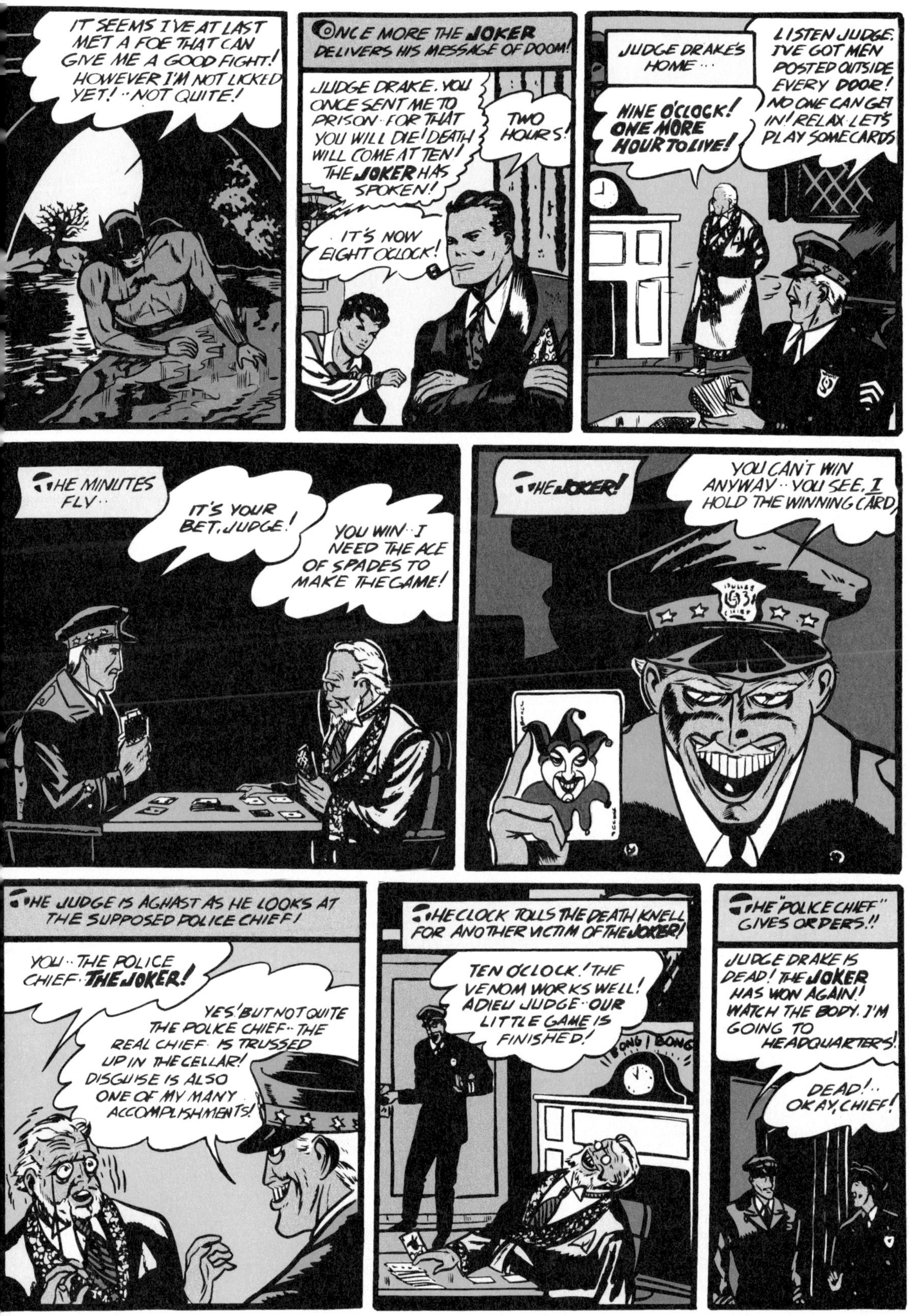
IT SEEMS I'VE AT LAST MET A FOE THAT CAN GIVE ME A GOOD FIGHT! HOWEVER I'M NOT LICKED YET! .. NOT QUITE!
ONCE MORE THE JOKER DELIVERS HIS MESSAGE OF DOOM!
JUDGE DRAKE, YOU ONCE SENT ME TO PRISON .. FOR THAT YOU WILL DIE! DEATH WILL COME AT TEN! THE JOKER HAS SPOKEN!
TWO HOURS!
IT'S NOW EIGHT O'CLOCK!
JUDGE DRAKE'S HOME ...
NINE O'CLOCK! ONE MORE HOUR TO LIVE!
LISTEN JUDGE. I'VE GOT MEN POSTED OUTSIDE EVERY DOOR! NO ONE CAN GET IN! RELAX. LET'S PLAY SOME CARDS
THE MINUTES FLY ..
IT'S YOUR BET, JUDGE!
YOU WIN .. I NEED THE ACE OF SPADES TO MAKE THE GAME!
THE JOKER!
YOU CAN'T WIN ANYWAY .. YOU SEE, I HOLD THE WINNING CARD!
THE JUDGE IS AGHAST AS HE LOOKS AT THE SUPPOSED POLICE CHIEF!
YOU .. THE POLICE CHIEF .. THE JOKER!
YES! BUT NOT QUITE THE POLICE CHIEF .. THE REAL CHIEF IS TRUSSED UP IN THE CELLAR! DISGUISE IS ALSO ONE OF MY MANY ACCOMPLISHMENTS!
THE CLOCK TOLLS THE DEATH KNELL FOR ANOTHER VICTIM OF THE JOKER!
TEN O'CLOCK! THE VENOM WORKS WELL! ADIEU JUDGE .. OUR LITTLE GAME IS FINISHED!
BONG! BONG
THE "POLICE CHIEF" GIVES ORDERS!!
JUDGE DRAKE IS DEAD! THE JOKER HAS WON AGAIN! WATCH THE BODY. I'M GOING TO HEADQUARTERS!
DEAD! .. OKAY, CHIEF!

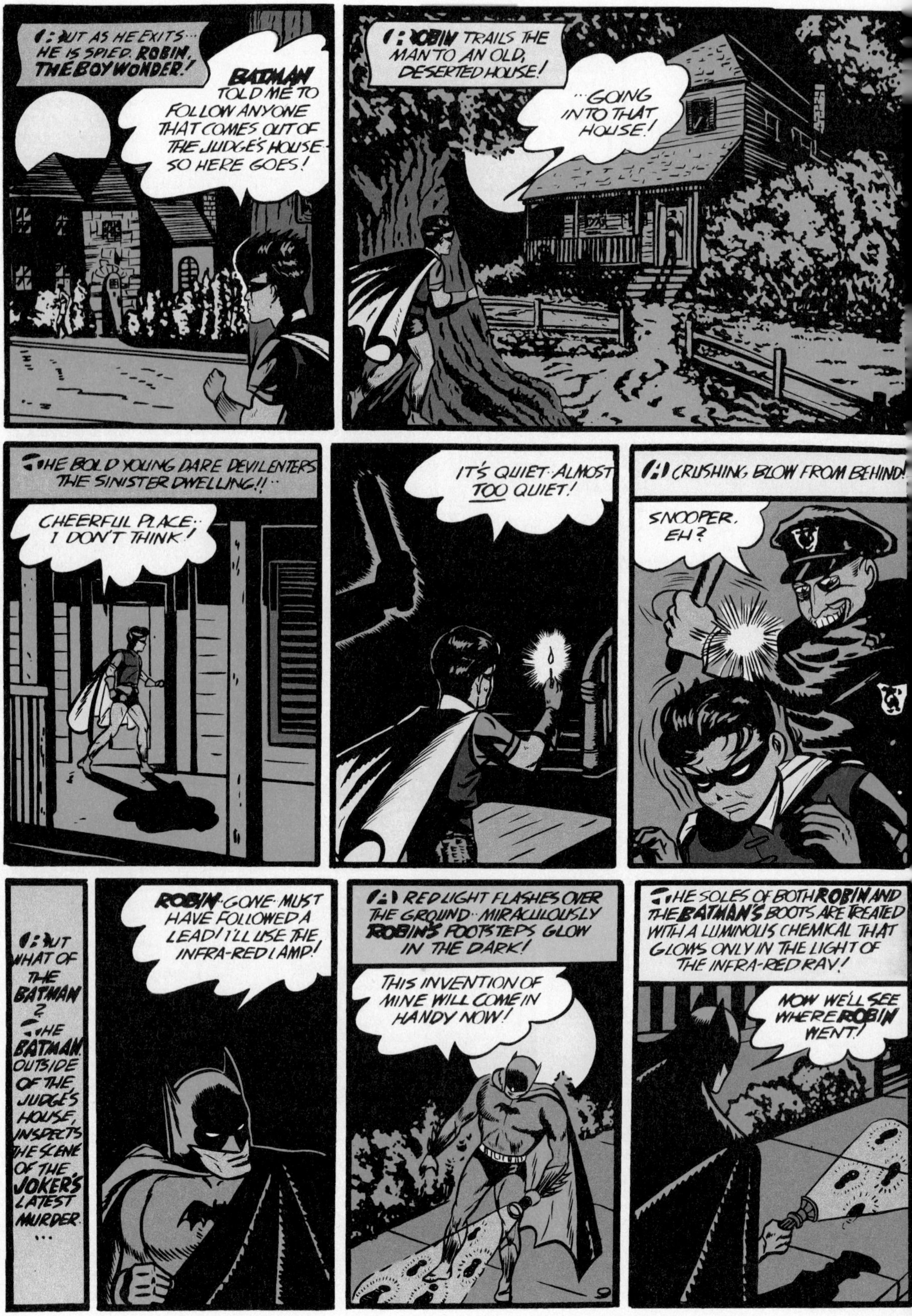
BUT AS HE EXITS... HE IS SPIED. ROBIN, THE BOY WONDER!
BATMAN TOLD ME TO FOLLOW ANYONE THAT COMES OUT OF THE JUDGE'S HOUSE - SO HERE GOES!
ROBIN TRAILS THE MAN TO AN OLD, DESERTED HOUSE!
...GOING INTO THAT HOUSE!
THE BOLD YOUNG DARE DEVIL ENTERS THE SINISTER DWELLING!!..
CHEERFUL PLACE.. I DON'T THINK!
IT'S QUIET.. ALMOST TOO QUIET!
A CRUSHING BLOW FROM BEHIND!
SNOOPER, EH?
BUT WHAT OF THE BATMAN? THE BATMAN, OUTSIDE OF THE JUDGE'S HOUSE, INSPECTS THE SCENE OF THE JOKER'S LATEST MURDER...
ROBIN-GONE-MUST HAVE FOLLOWED A LEAD! I'LL USE THE INFRA-RED LAMP!
A RED LIGHT FLASHES OVER THE GROUND.. MIRACULOUSLY ROBIN'S FOOTSTEPS GLOW IN THE DARK!
THIS INVENTION OF MINE WILL COME IN HANDY NOW!
THE SOLES OF BOTH ROBIN AND THE BATMAN'S BOOTS ARE TREATED WITH A LUMINOUS CHEMICAL THAT GLOWS ONLY IN THE LIGHT OF THE INFRA-RED RAY!
NOW WE'LL SEE WHERE ROBIN WENT!

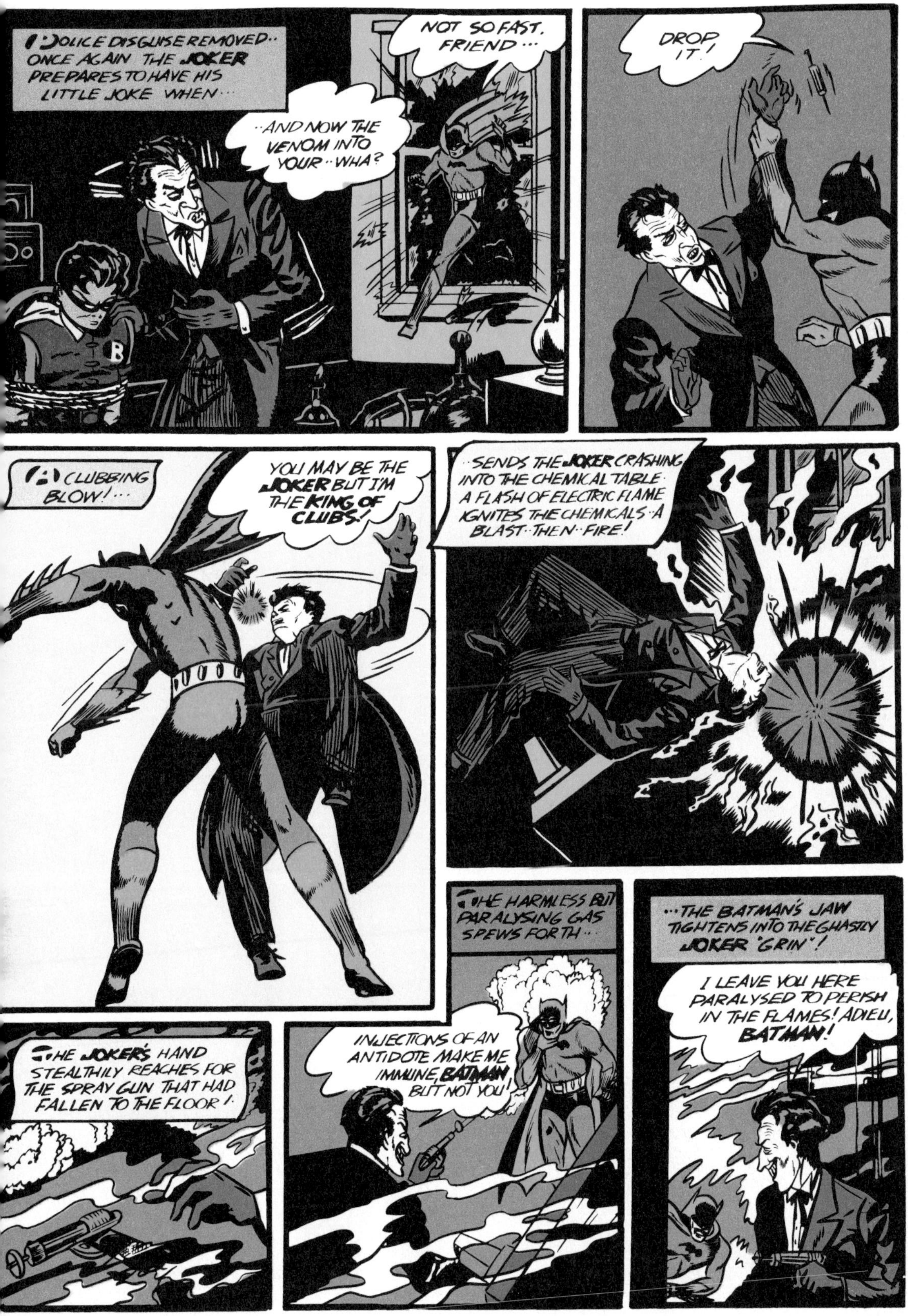
POLICE DISGUISE REMOVED.. ONCE AGAIN THE JOKER PREPARES TO HAVE HIS LITTLE JOKE WHEN...
..AND NOW THE VENOM INTO YOUR..WHA?
NOT SO FAST, FRIEND...
DROP IT!
A CLUBBING BLOW!...
YOU MAY BE THE JOKER BUT I'M THE KING OF CLUBS!
..SENDS THE JOKER CRASHING INTO THE CHEMICAL TABLE. A FLASH OF ELECTRIC FLAME IGNITES THE CHEMICALS..A BLAST..THEN..FIRE!
THE JOKER'S HAND STEALTHILY REACHES FOR THE SPRAY GUN THAT HAD FALLEN TO THE FLOOR!
THE HARMLESS BUT PARALYSING GAS SPEWS FORTH...
INJECTIONS OF AN ANTIDOTE MAKE ME IMMUNE, BATMAN BUT NOT YOU!
...THE BATMAN'S JAW TIGHTENS INTO THE GHASTLY JOKER "GRIN"!
I LEAVE YOU HERE PARALYSED TO PERISH IN THE FLAMES! ADIEU, BATMAN!

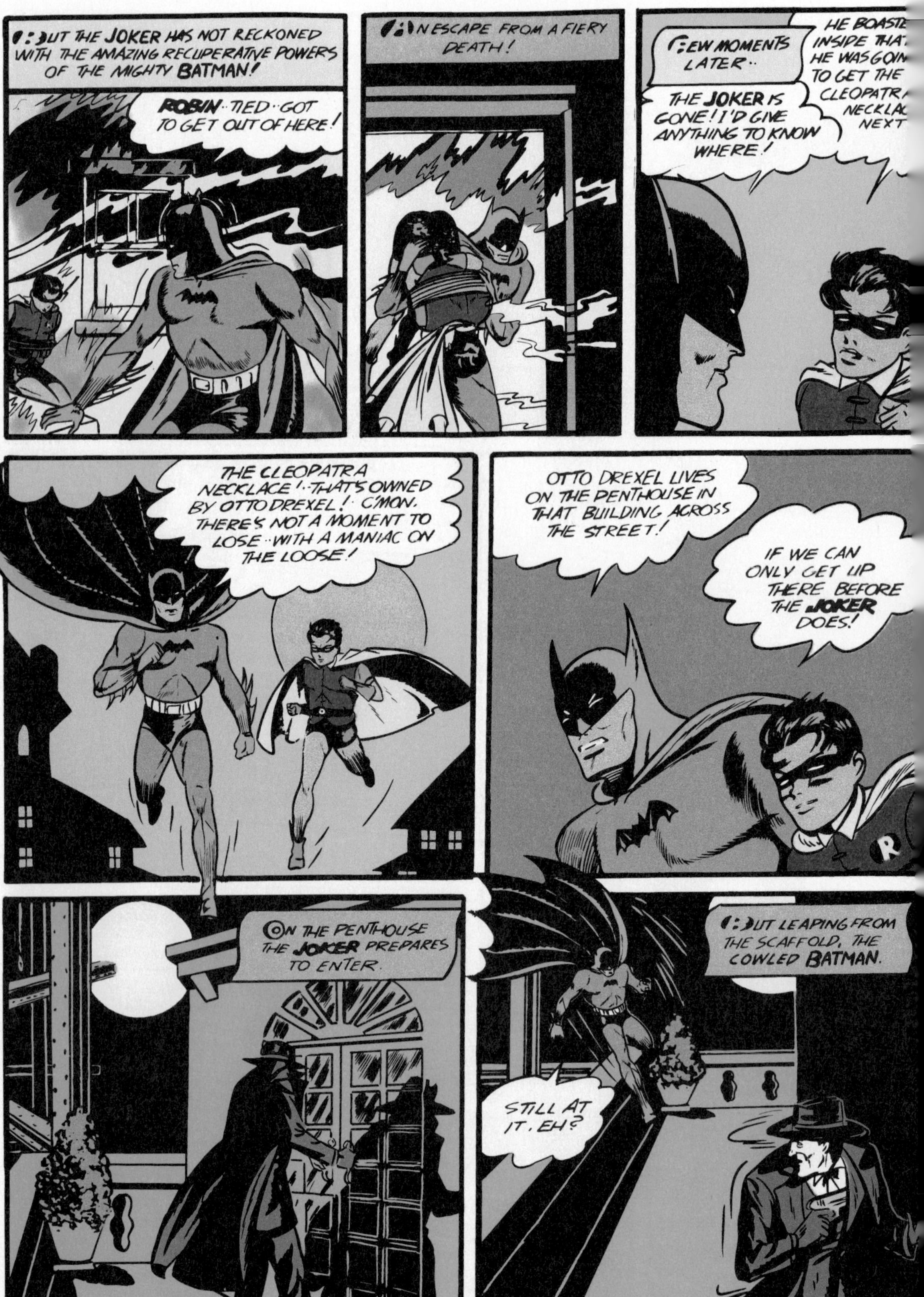
BUT THE JOKER HAS NOT RECKONED WITH THE AMAZING RECUPERATIVE POWERS OF THE MIGHTY BATMAN!
ROBIN.. TIED.. GOT TO GET OUT OF HERE!
AN ESCAPE FROM A FIERY DEATH!
FEW MOMENTS LATER..
THE JOKER IS GONE! I'D GIVE ANYTHING TO KNOW WHERE!
HE BOASTE INSIDE THA HE WAS GOIN TO GET THE CLEOPATR NECKLA NEXT
THE CLEOPATRA NECKLACE!.. THAT'S OWNED BY OTTO DREXEL! C'MON. THERE'S NOT A MOMENT TO LOSE.. WITH A MANIAC ON THE LOOSE!
OTTO DREXEL LIVES ON THE PENTHOUSE IN THAT BUILDING ACROSS THE STREET!
IF WE CAN ONLY GET UP THERE BEFORE THE JOKER DOES!
ON THE PENTHOUSE THE JOKER PREPARES TO ENTER.
BUT LEAPING FROM THE SCAFFOLD, THE COWLED BATMAN.
STILL AT IT, EH?
11

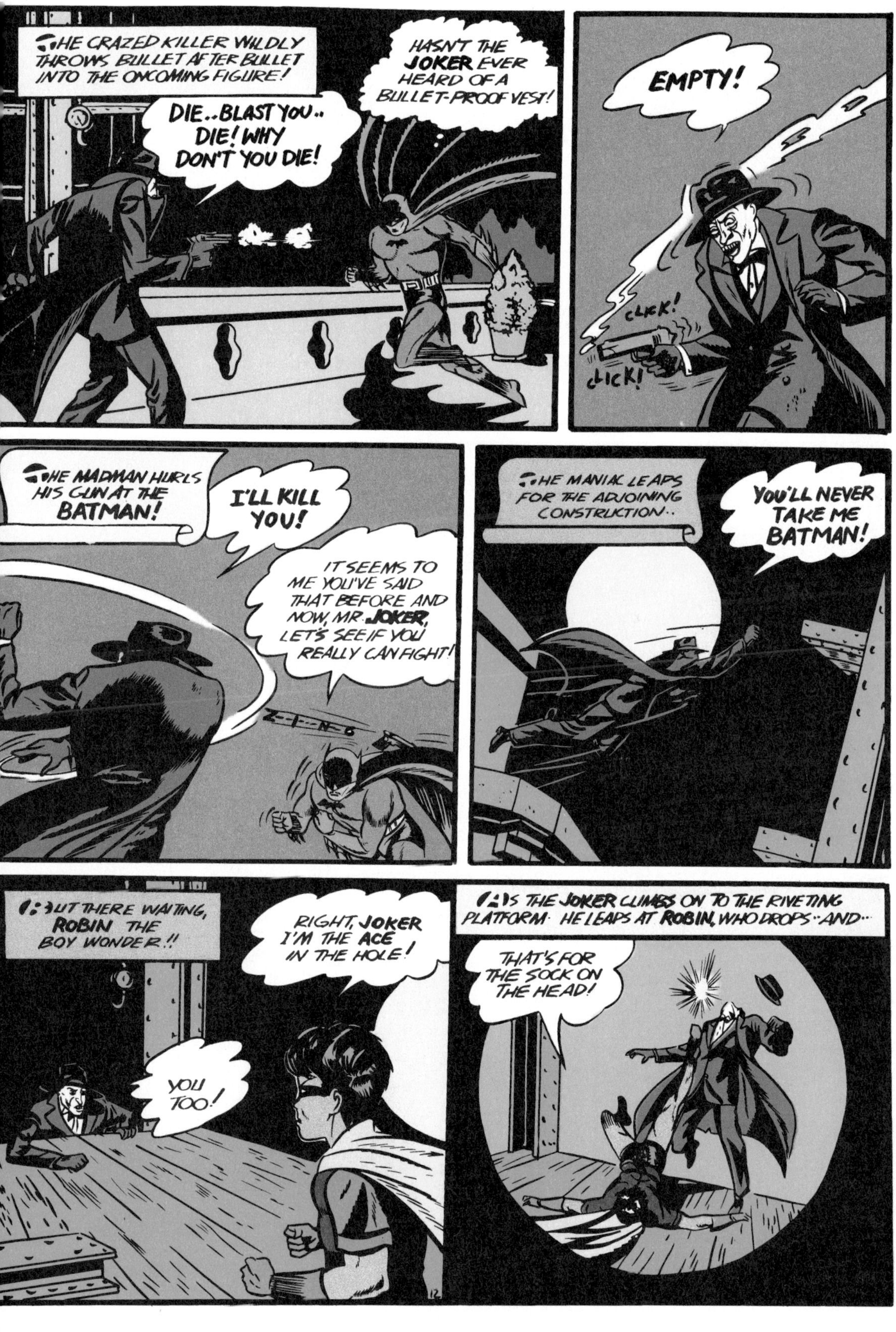
THE CRAZED KILLER WILDLY THROWS BULLET AFTER BULLET INTO THE ONCOMING FIGURE!
DIE..BLAST YOU.. DIE! WHY DON'T YOU DIE!
HASN'T THE JOKER EVER HEARD OF A BULLET-PROOF VEST!
EMPTY!
CLICK!
CLICK!
THE MADMAN HURLS HIS GUN AT THE BATMAN!
I'LL KILL YOU!
IT SEEMS TO ME YOU'VE SAID THAT BEFORE AND NOW, MR. JOKER, LET'S SEE IF YOU REALLY CAN FIGHT!
Z-I-N-G
THE MANIAC LEAPS FOR THE ADJOINING CONSTRUCTION..
YOU'LL NEVER TAKE ME BATMAN!
BUT THERE WAITING, ROBIN THE BOY WONDER!!
RIGHT, JOKER I'M THE ACE IN THE HOLE!
YOU TOO!
AS THE JOKER CLIMBS ON TO THE RIVETING PLATFORM HE LEAPS AT ROBIN, WHO DROPS..AND..
THAT'S FOR THE SOCK ON THE HEAD!
12

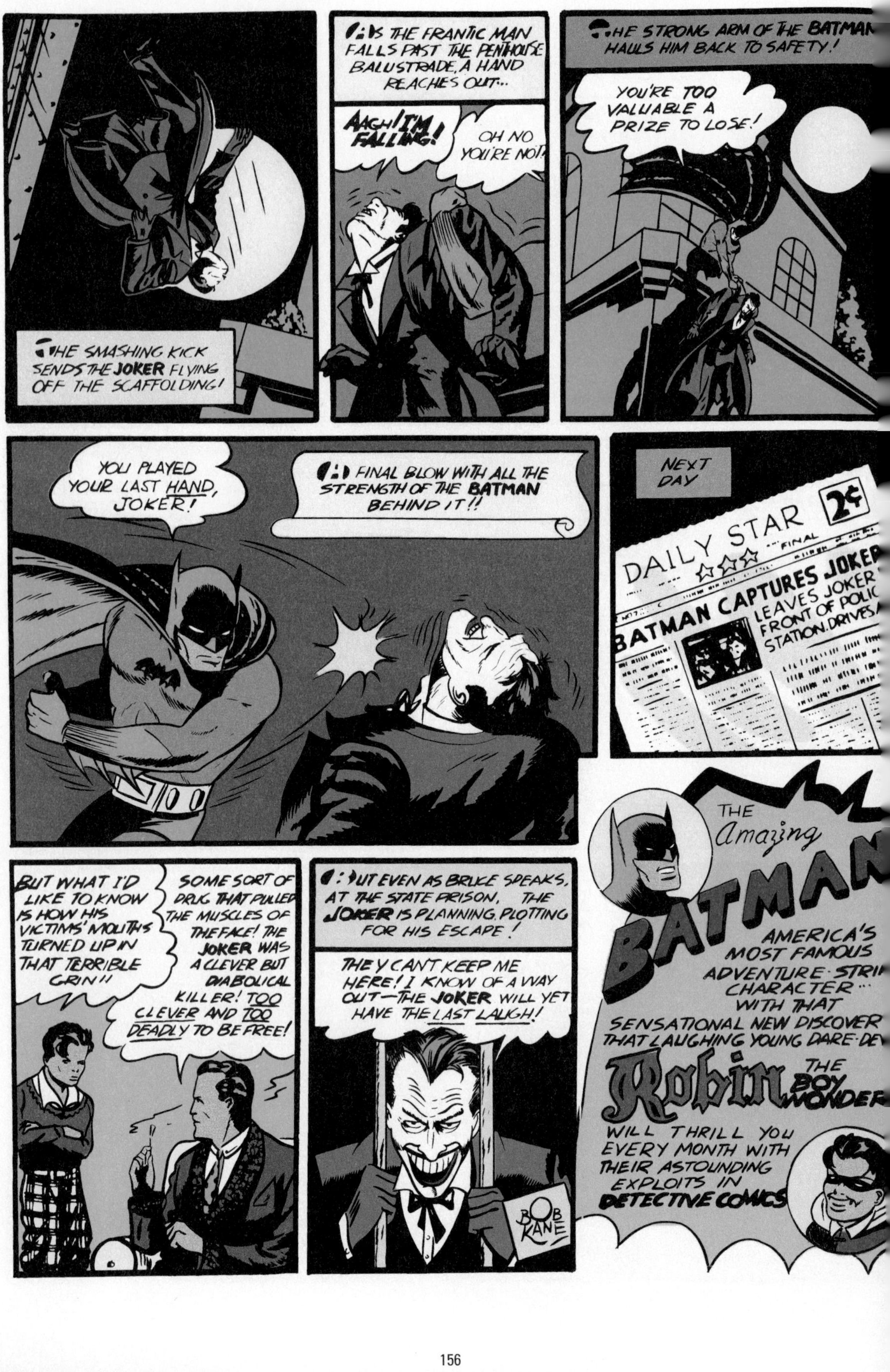
THE SMASHING KICK SENDS THE JOKER FLYING OFF THE SCAFFOLDING!
AS THE FRANTIC MAN FALLS PAST THE PENTHOUSE BALUSTRADE, A HAND REACHES OUT...
AAGH! I'M FALLING!
OH NO YOU'RE NOT!
THE STRONG ARM OF THE BATMAN HAULS HIM BACK TO SAFETY!
YOU'RE TOO VALUABLE A PRIZE TO LOSE!
YOU PLAYED YOUR LAST HAND, JOKER!
A FINAL BLOW WITH ALL THE STRENGTH OF THE BATMAN BEHIND IT!!
NEXT DAY
DAILY STAR
2¢
FINAL
BATMAN CAPTURES JOKER
LEAVES JOKER FRONT OF POLIC STATION. DRIVES
BUT WHAT I'D LIKE TO KNOW IS HOW HIS VICTIMS' MOUTHS TURNED UP IN THAT TERRIBLE GRIN!!
SOME SORT OF DRUG THAT PULLED THE MUSCLES OF THE FACE! THE JOKER WAS A CLEVER BUT DIABOLICAL KILLER! TOO CLEVER AND TOO DEADLY TO BE FREE!
BUT EVEN AS BRUCE SPEAKS, AT THE STATE PRISON, THE JOKER IS PLANNING, PLOTTING FOR HIS ESCAPE!
THEY CAN'T KEEP ME HERE! I KNOW OF A WAY OUT—THE JOKER WILL YET HAVE THE LAST LAUGH!
BOB KANE
THE Amazing
BATMA
AMERICA'S MOST FAMOUS ADVENTURE-STRI CHARACTER... WITH THAT
SENSATIONAL NEW DISCOVER THAT LAUGHING YOUNG DARE-DE
Robin THE BOY WONDER
WILL THRILL YOU EVERY MONTH WITH THEIR ASTOUNDING EXPLOITS IN DETECTIVE COMICS

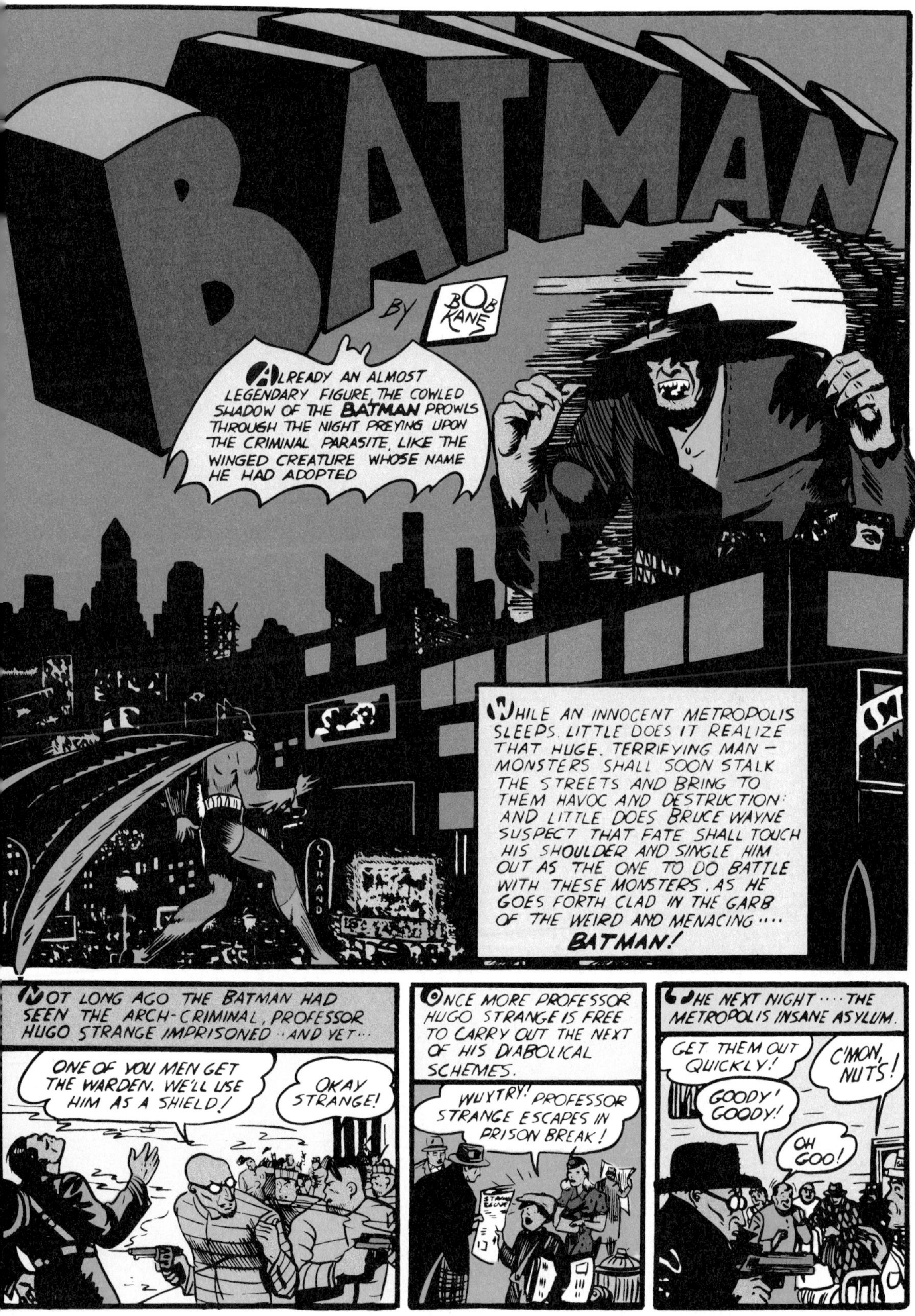
BATMAN
BY BOB KANE
ALREADY AN ALMOST LEGENDARY FIGURE, THE COWLED SHADOW OF THE BATMAN PROWLS THROUGH THE NIGHT PREYING UPON THE CRIMINAL PARASITE, LIKE THE WINGED CREATURE WHOSE NAME HE HAD ADOPTED
WHILE AN INNOCENT METROPOLIS SLEEPS. LITTLE DOES IT REALIZE THAT HUGE, TERRIFYING MAN-MONSTERS SHALL SOON STALK THE STREETS AND BRING TO THEM HAVOC AND DESTRUCTION: AND LITTLE DOES BRUCE WAYNE SUSPECT THAT FATE SHALL TOUCH HIS SHOULDER AND SINGLE HIM OUT AS THE ONE TO DO BATTLE WITH THESE MONSTERS, AS HE GOES FORTH CLAD IN THE GARB OF THE WEIRD AND MENACING.... BATMAN!
STRAND
NOT LONG AGO THE BATMAN HAD SEEN THE ARCH-CRIMINAL, PROFESSOR HUGO STRANGE IMPRISONED .. AND YET...
ONE OF YOU MEN GET THE WARDEN. WE'LL USE HIM AS A SHIELD!
OKAY STRANGE!
ONCE MORE PROFESSOR HUGO STRANGE IS FREE TO CARRY OUT THE NEXT OF HIS DIABOLICAL SCHEMES.
WUXTRY! PROFESSOR STRANGE ESCAPES IN PRISON BREAK!
THE NEXT NIGHT.... THE METROPOLIS INSANE ASYLUM.
GET THEM OUT QUICKLY!
C'MON, NUTS!
GOODY! GOODY!
OH GOO!

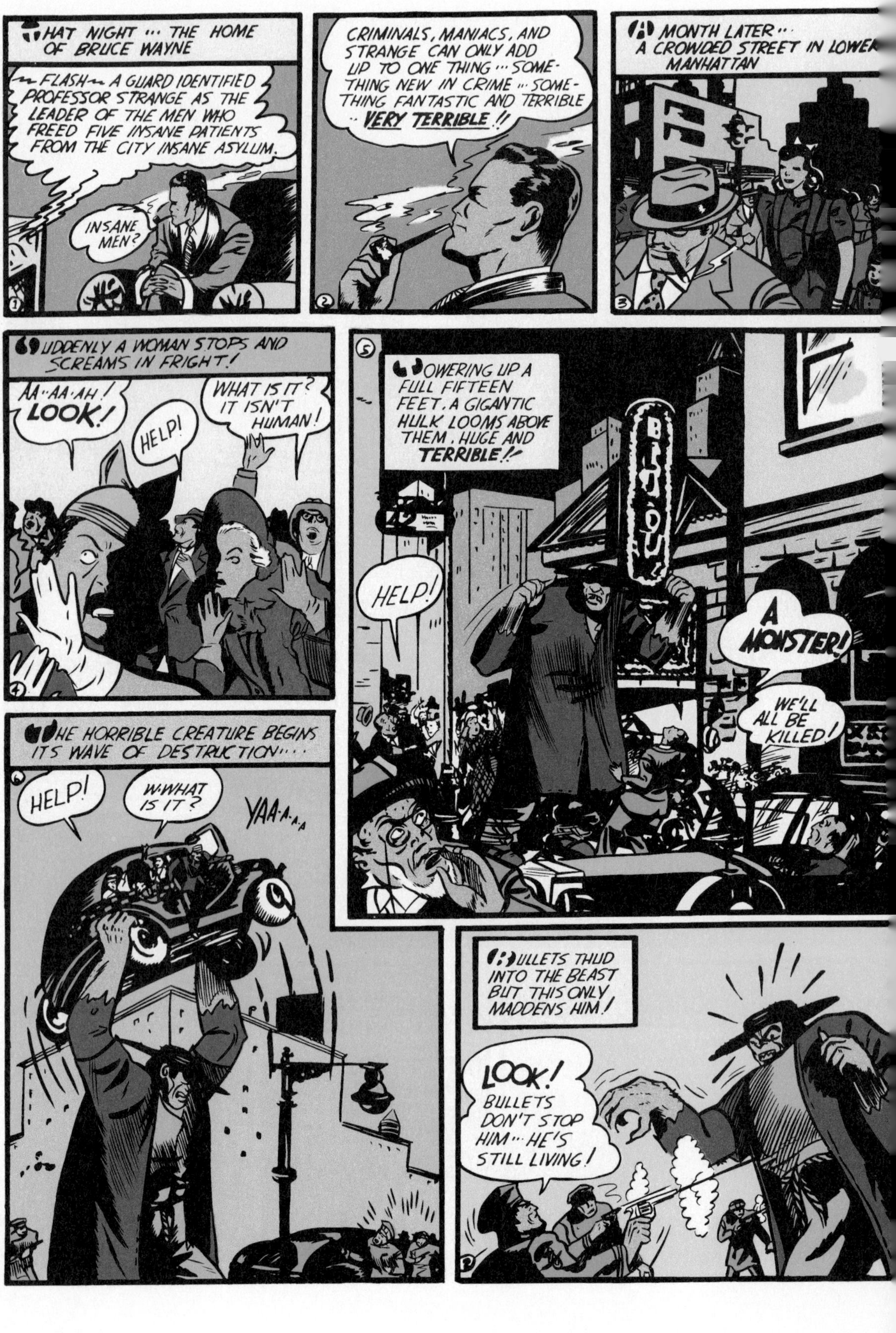
THAT NIGHT ... THE HOME OF BRUCE WAYNE
FLASH — A GUARD IDENTIFIED PROFESSOR STRANGE AS THE LEADER OF THE MEN WHO FREED FIVE INSANE PATIENTS FROM THE CITY INSANE ASYLUM.
INSANE MEN?
CRIMINALS, MANIACS, AND STRANGE CAN ONLY ADD UP TO ONE THING ... SOMETHING NEW IN CRIME ... SOMETHING FANTASTIC AND TERRIBLE .. VERY TERRIBLE!!
A MONTH LATER ... A CROWDED STREET IN LOWER MANHATTAN
SUDDENLY A WOMAN STOPS AND SCREAMS IN FRIGHT!
AA..AA.AH! LOOK!
HELP!
WHAT IS IT? IT ISN'T HUMAN!
TOWERING UP A FULL FIFTEEN FEET, A GIGANTIC HULK LOOMS ABOVE THEM, HUGE AND TERRIBLE!!
HELP!
A MONSTER!
WE'LL ALL BE KILLED!
THE HORRIBLE CREATURE BEGINS ITS WAVE OF DESTRUCTION...
HELP!
W-WHAT IS IT?
YAA-A-A-A
BULLETS THUD INTO THE BEAST BUT THIS ONLY MADDENS HIM!
LOOK! BULLETS DON'T STOP HIM... HE'S STILL LIVING!

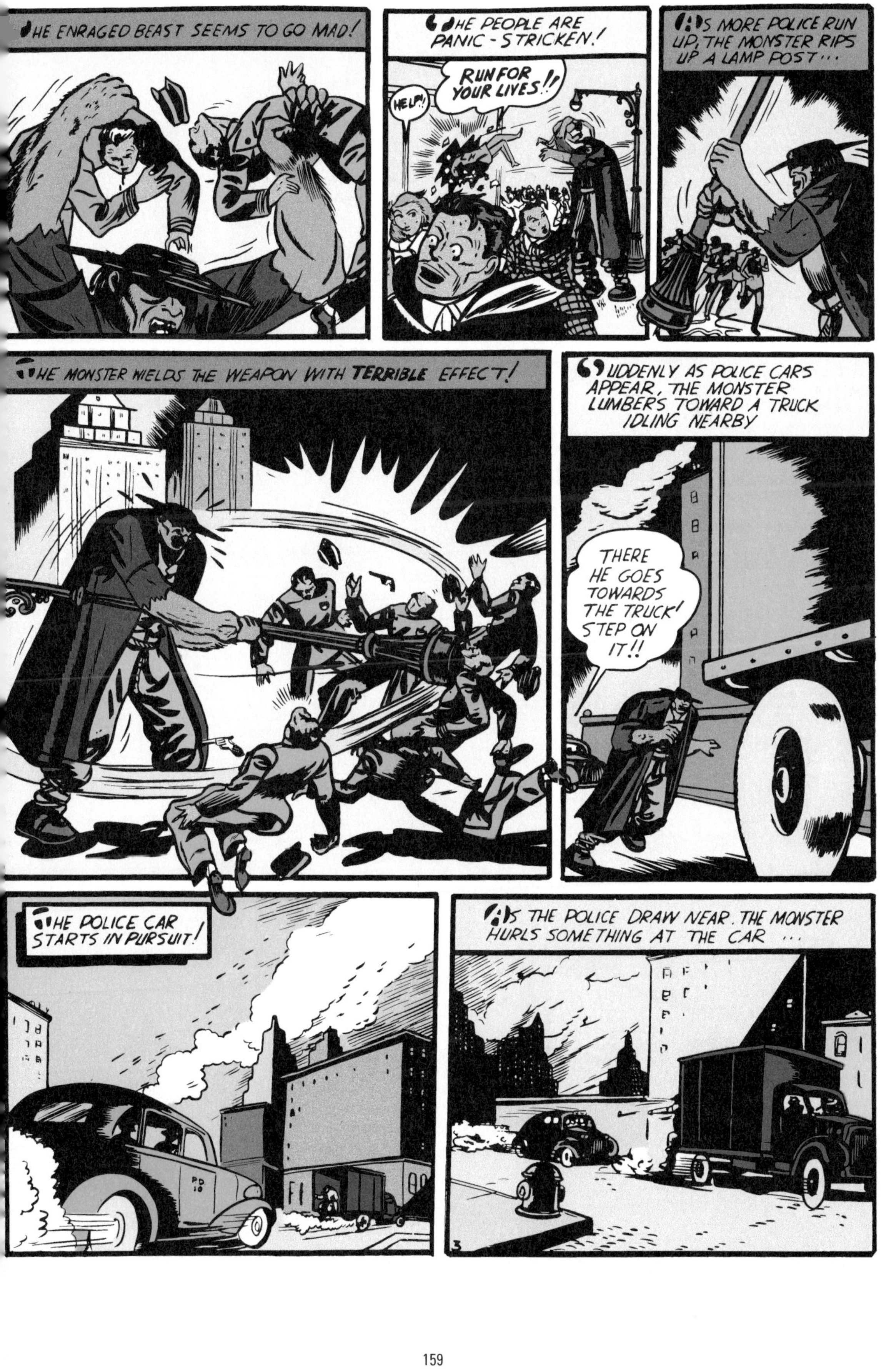
THE ENRAGED BEAST SEEMS TO GO MAD!
THE PEOPLE ARE PANIC-STRICKEN!
HELP!
RUN FOR YOUR LIVES!!
AS MORE POLICE RUN UP, THE MONSTER RIPS UP A LAMP POST...
THE MONSTER WIELDS THE WEAPON WITH TERRIBLE EFFECT!
SUDDENLY AS POLICE CARS APPEAR, THE MONSTER LUMBERS TOWARD A TRUCK IDLING NEARBY
THERE HE GOES TOWARDS THE TRUCK! STEP ON IT!!
THE POLICE CAR STARTS IN PURSUIT!
PD 10
AS THE POLICE DRAW NEAR, THE MONSTER HURLS SOMETHING AT THE CAR ...

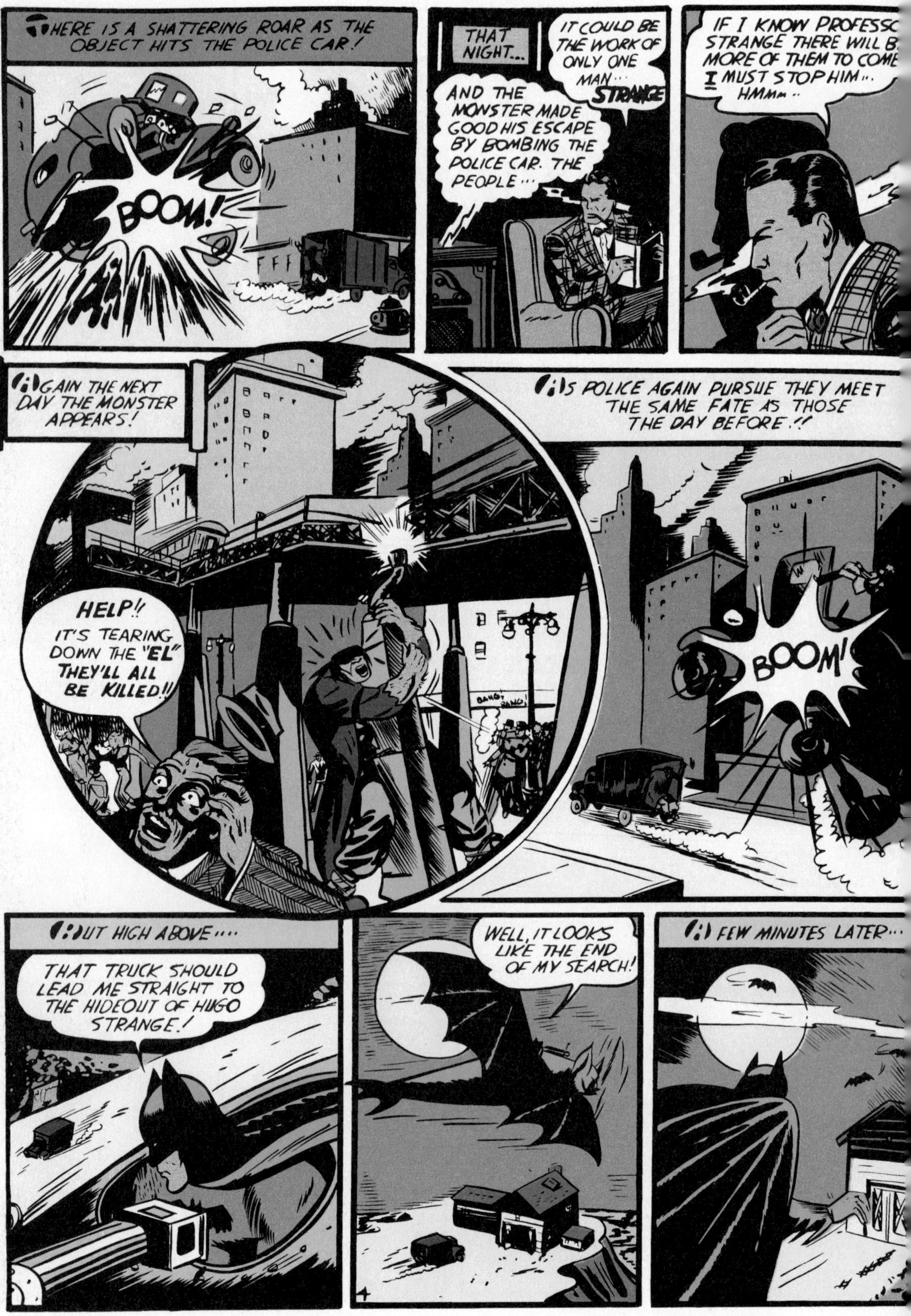
THERE IS A SHATTERING ROAR AS THE OBJECT HITS THE POLICE CAR!
BOOM!
THAT NIGHT...
IT COULD BE THE WORK OF ONLY ONE MAN... STRANGE
AND THE MONSTER MADE GOOD HIS ESCAPE BY BOMBING THE POLICE CAR. THE PEOPLE...
IF I KNOW PROFESSO STRANGE THERE WILL B MORE OF THEM TO COME I MUST STOP HIM... HMMM...
AGAIN THE NEXT DAY THE MONSTER APPEARS!
HELP!! IT'S TEARING DOWN THE "EL" THEY'LL ALL BE KILLED!!
BANG! BANG!
AS POLICE AGAIN PURSUE THEY MEET THE SAME FATE AS THOSE THE DAY BEFORE!!
BOOM!
BUT HIGH ABOVE....
THAT TRUCK SHOULD LEAD ME STRAIGHT TO THE HIDEOUT OF HUGO STRANGE!
WELL, IT LOOKS LIKE THE END OF MY SEARCH!
A FEW MINUTES LATER...

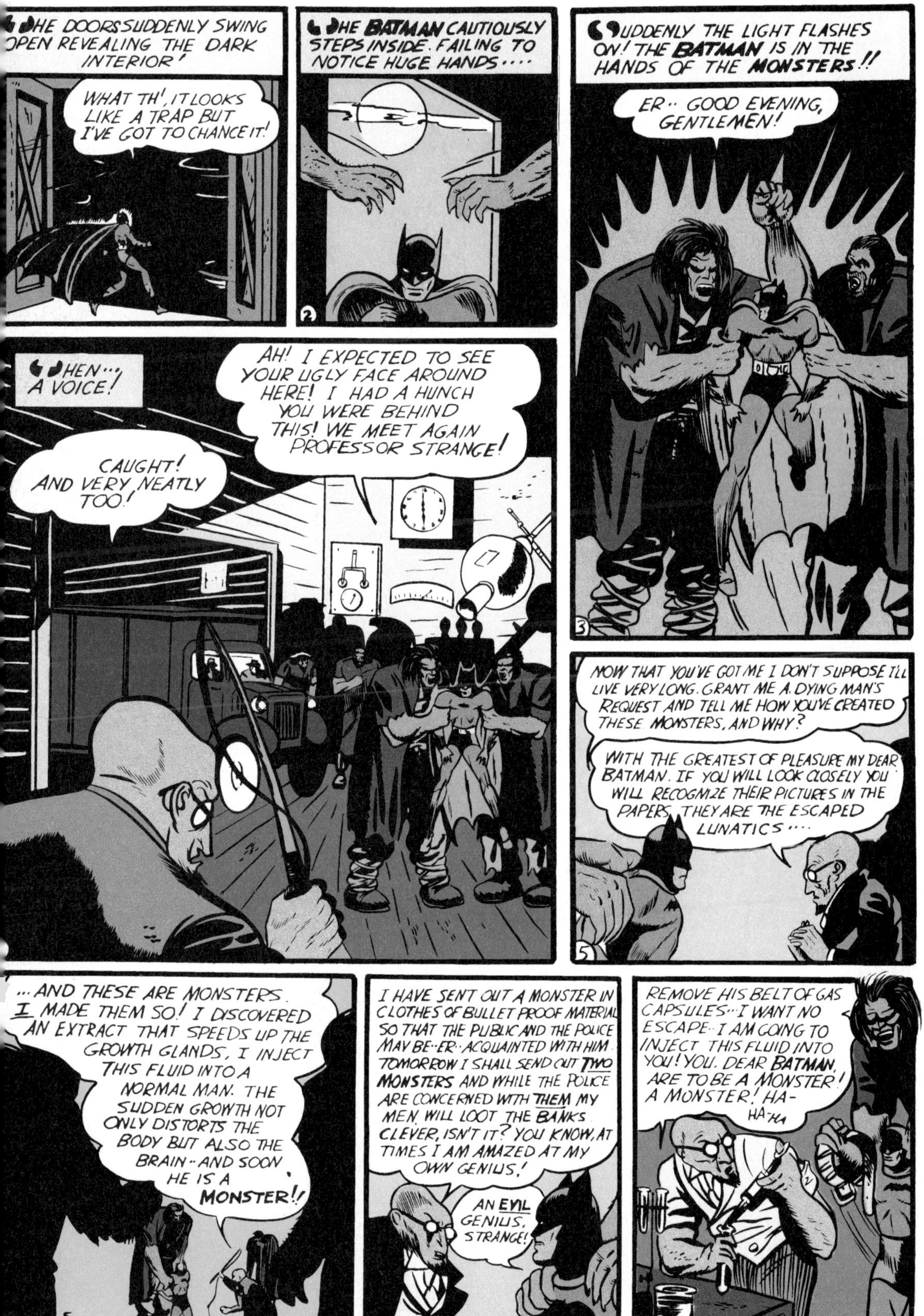
THE DOORSSUDDENLY SWING OPEN REVEALING THE DARK INTERIOR!
WHAT TH', IT LOOKS LIKE A TRAP BUT I'VE GOT TO CHANCE IT!
THE BATMAN CAUTIOUSLY STEPS INSIDE. FAILING TO NOTICE HUGE HANDS....
2
SUDDENLY THE LIGHT FLASHES ON! THE BATMAN IS IN THE HANDS OF THE MONSTERS!!
ER.. GOOD EVENING, GENTLEMEN!
3
THEN... A VOICE!
CAUGHT! AND VERY NEATLY TOO!
AH! I EXPECTED TO SEE YOUR UGLY FACE AROUND HERE! I HAD A HUNCH YOU WERE BEHIND THIS! WE MEET AGAIN PROFESSOR STRANGE!
NOW THAT YOU'VE GOT ME I DON'T SUPPOSE I'LL LIVE VERY LONG. GRANT ME A DYING MAN'S REQUEST AND TELL ME HOW YOU'VE CREATED THESE MONSTERS, AND WHY?
WITH THE GREATEST OF PLEASURE MY DEAR BATMAN. IF YOU WILL LOOK CLOSELY YOU WILL RECOGNIZE THEIR PICTURES IN THE PAPERS. THEY ARE THE ESCAPED LUNATICS....
5
...AND THESE ARE MONSTERS. I MADE THEM SO! I DISCOVERED AN EXTRACT THAT SPEEDS UP THE GROWTH GLANDS, I INJECT THIS FLUID INTO A NORMAL MAN. THE SUDDEN GROWTH NOT ONLY DISTORTS THE BODY BUT ALSO THE BRAIN.. AND SOON HE IS A MONSTER!!
5.
I HAVE SENT OUT A MONSTER IN CLOTHES OF BULLET PROOF MATERIAL SO THAT THE PUBLIC AND THE POLICE MAY BE..ER..ACQUAINTED WITH HIM. TOMORROW I SHALL SEND OUT TWO MONSTERS AND WHILE THE POLICE ARE CONCERNED WITH THEM MY MEN WILL LOOT THE BANKS. CLEVER, ISN'T IT? YOU KNOW, AT TIMES I AM AMAZED AT MY OWN GENIUS!
AN EVIL GENIUS, STRANGE!
REMOVE HIS BELT OF GAS CAPSULES... I WANT NO ESCAPE.. I AM GOING TO INJECT THIS FLUID INTO YOU! YOU, DEAR BATMAN, ARE TO BE A MONSTER! A MONSTER! HA-HA-HA

THE BATMAN STRUGGLES MIGHTILY, BUT THE MONSTERS HOLD HIM FIRM!
YOU FIEND!!
THAT IS NO WAY TO TALK TO YOUR MASTER! SOON YOU WILL BE A MONSTER AND OBEY ME AS THEY DO! PREPARE TO MEET YOUR FATE!
THE DEADLY NEEDLE PLUNGES DEEP INTO THE ARM OF THE BATMAN!
DONE!!
OBSERVE THE CLOCK, BATMAN! IT IS EXACTLY SIX O'CLOCK AT NIGHT. THE SERUM TAKES EIGHTEEN HOURS BEFORE IT WORKS AT PRECISELY NOON. TOMORROW THE SERUM WILL TAKE EFFECT! AH-HA-HA!
A MASSIVE FIST CRASHES AGAINST THE BATMAN'S JAW -- THEN BLACKNESS
HOURS LATER
NOW! WHAT HIT ME! THE CLOCK! IT SAYS ALMOST A QUARTER TO TWELVE I'VE BEEN UNCONSCIOUS ALMOST EIGHTEEN HOURS... AND IT'S ALMOST TIME FOR THE SERUM TO WORK!
THEN THE BATMAN SEES...
NOW REMEMBER! THREE MEN TAKE A MONSTER ONE TRUCK WILL GO BY DALY AVENUE AND THE OTHER BY THE POST ROAD. NOW GET GOING .. AND NO SLIP UPS!
DON'T WORRY STRANGE! THOSE BANKS ARE AS GOOD AS OPENED RIGHT NOW!
I'VE GOT TO GET OUT OF HERE! THEY TOOK MY BELT BUT THEY DIDN'T KNOW ABOUT MY BOOT HEELS. BY MIXING SOME CHEMICALS I HAVE IN THEM I CAN MAKE AN EXPLOSIVE! THE TRUCKS HAVE GONE WITH TWO OF THE MONSTERS, SO THAT AT LEAST GIVES ME A CHANCE!
A MOMENT LATER...
THAT DOES IT!
BOOM!

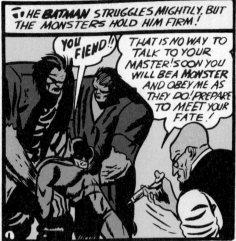

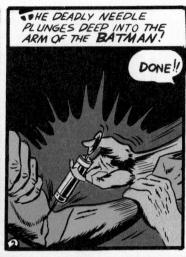

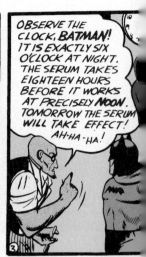

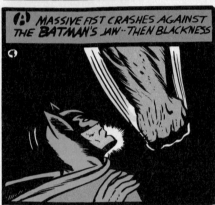

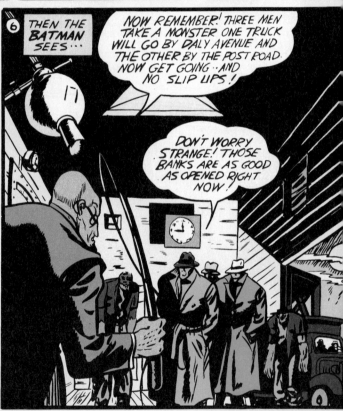

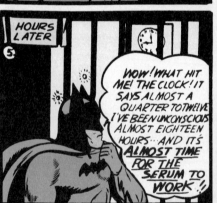

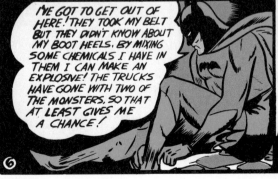

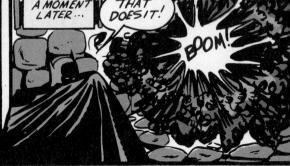

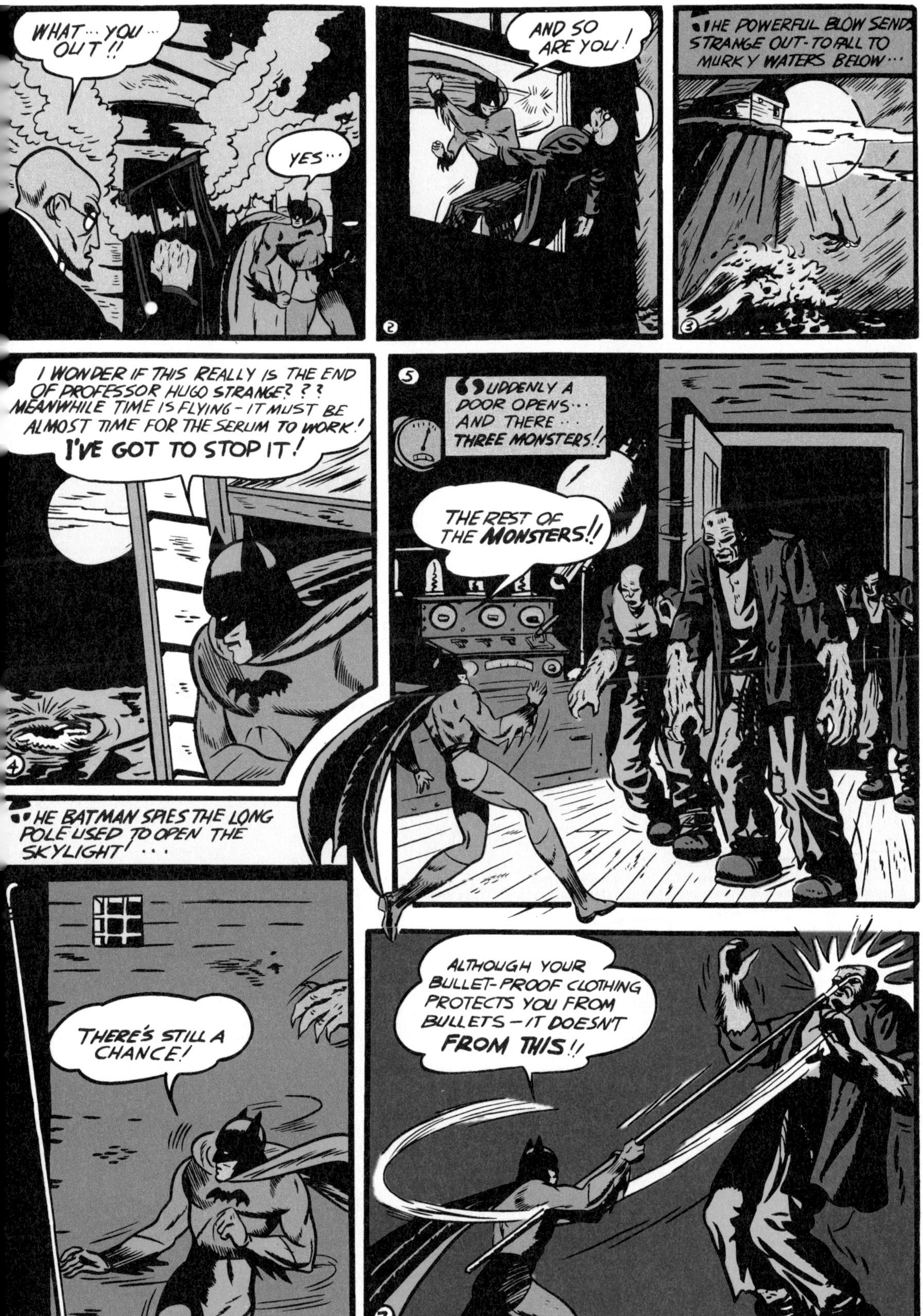

WHAT... YOU... OUT!!
YES...
AND SO ARE YOU!
THE POWERFUL BLOW SENDS STRANGE OUT-TO FALL TO MURKY WATERS BELOW...
I WONDER IF THIS REALLY IS THE END OF PROFESSOR HUGO STRANGE??? MEANWHILE TIME IS FLYING - IT MUST BE ALMOST TIME FOR THE SERUM TO WORK! I'VE GOT TO STOP IT!
SUDDENLY A DOOR OPENS... AND THERE... THREE MONSTERS!!
THE REST OF THE MONSTERS!!
THE BATMAN SPIES THE LONG POLE USED TO OPEN THE SKYLIGHT...
THERE'S STILL A CHANCE!
ALTHOUGH YOUR BULLET-PROOF CLOTHING PROTECTS YOU FROM BULLETS - IT DOESN'T FROM THIS!!

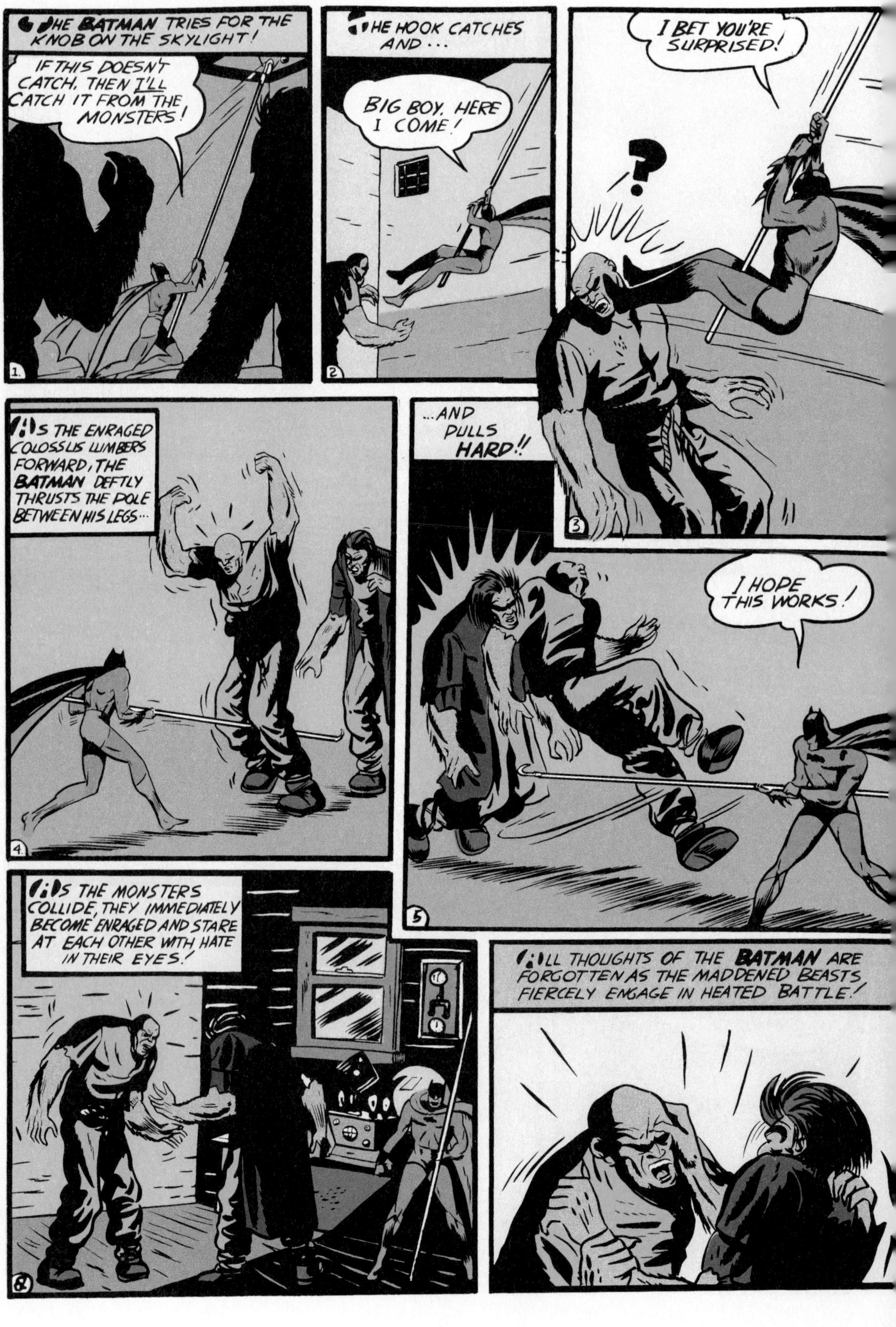
THE BATMAN TRIES FOR THE KNOB ON THE SKYLIGHT!
IF THIS DOESN'T CATCH, THEN I'LL CATCH IT FROM THE MONSTERS!
1.
THE HOOK CATCHES AND...
BIG BOY, HERE I COME!
2
I BET YOU'RE SURPRISED!
?
3
AS THE ENRAGED COLOSSUS LUMBERS FORWARD, THE BATMAN DEFTLY THRUSTS THE POLE BETWEEN HIS LEGS...
4.
...AND PULLS HARD!!
I HOPE THIS WORKS!
5
AS THE MONSTERS COLLIDE, THEY IMMEDIATELY BECOME ENRAGED AND STARE AT EACH OTHER WITH HATE IN THEIR EYES!
6
ALL THOUGHTS OF THE BATMAN ARE FORGOTTEN AS THE MADDENED BEASTS FIERCELY ENGAGE IN HEATED BATTLE!

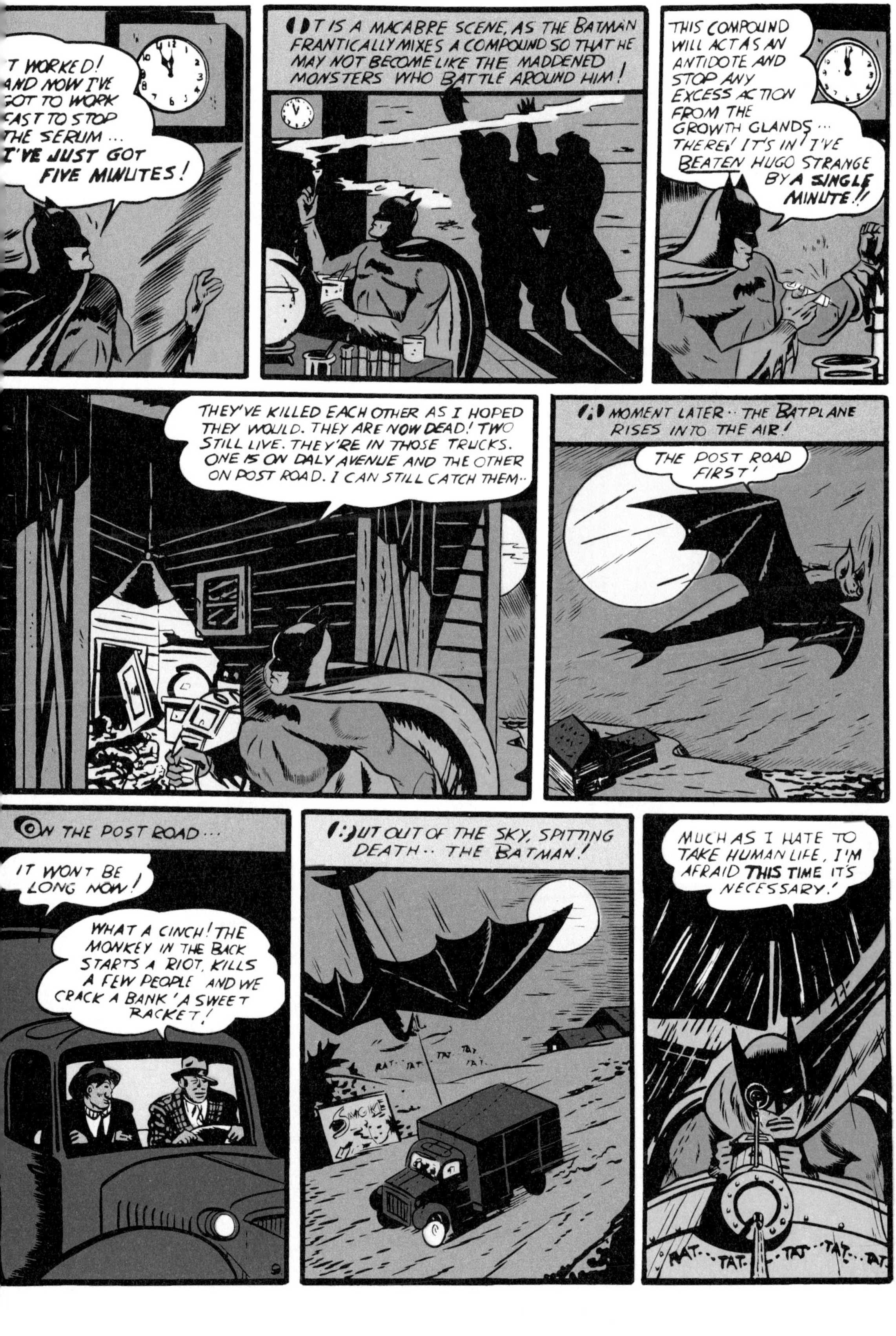
IT WORKED! AND NOW I'VE GOT TO WORK FAST TO STOP THE SERUM ... I'VE JUST GOT FIVE MINUTES!
IT IS A MACABRE SCENE, AS THE BATMAN FRANTICALLY MIXES A COMPOUND SO THAT HE MAY NOT BECOME LIKE THE MADDENED MONSTERS WHO BATTLE AROUND HIM!
THIS COMPOUND WILL ACT AS AN ANTIDOTE AND STOP ANY EXCESS ACTION FROM THE GROWTH GLANDS ... THERE! IT'S IN! I'VE BEATEN HUGO STRANGE BY A SINGLE MINUTE!!
THEY'VE KILLED EACH OTHER AS I HOPED THEY WOULD. THEY ARE NOW DEAD! TWO STILL LIVE. THEY'RE IN THOSE TRUCKS. ONE IS ON DALY AVENUE AND THE OTHER ON POST ROAD. I CAN STILL CATCH THEM..
A MOMENT LATER.. THE BATPLANE RISES INTO THE AIR!
THE POST ROAD FIRST!
ON THE POST ROAD ...
IT WON'T BE LONG NOW!
WHAT A CINCH! THE MONKEY IN THE BACK STARTS A RIOT, KILLS A FEW PEOPLE AND WE CRACK A BANK! A SWEET RACKET!
BUT OUT OF THE SKY, SPITTING DEATH.. THE BATMAN!
RAT-TAT-TAT-TAT
MUCH AS I HATE TO TAKE HUMAN LIFE, I'M AFRAID THIS TIME IT'S NECESSARY!
RAT-TAT-TAT-TAT-TAT

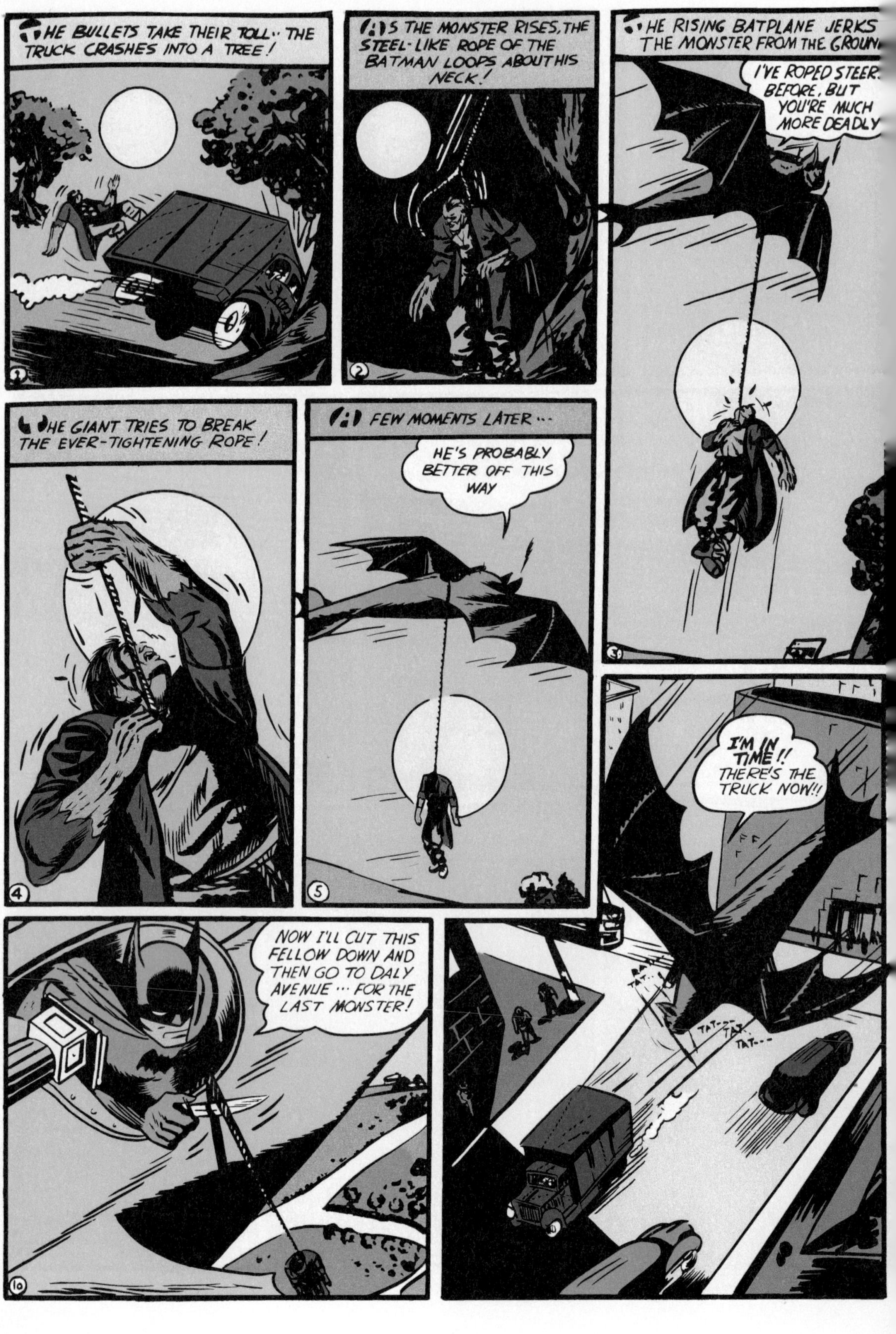
THE BULLETS TAKE THEIR TOLL.. THE TRUCK CRASHES INTO A TREE!
AS THE MONSTER RISES, THE STEEL-LIKE ROPE OF THE BATMAN LOOPS ABOUT HIS NECK!
THE RISING BATPLANE JERKS THE MONSTER FROM THE GROUN
I'VE ROPED STEER BEFORE, BUT YOU'RE MUCH MORE DEADLY
THE GIANT TRIES TO BREAK THE EVER-TIGHTENING ROPE!
A FEW MOMENTS LATER...
HE'S PROBABLY BETTER OFF THIS WAY
I'M IN TIME!! THERE'S THE TRUCK NOW!!
TAT-- TAT-- TAT--
NOW I'LL CUT THIS FELLOW DOWN AND THEN GO TO DALY AVENUE ... FOR THE LAST MONSTER!

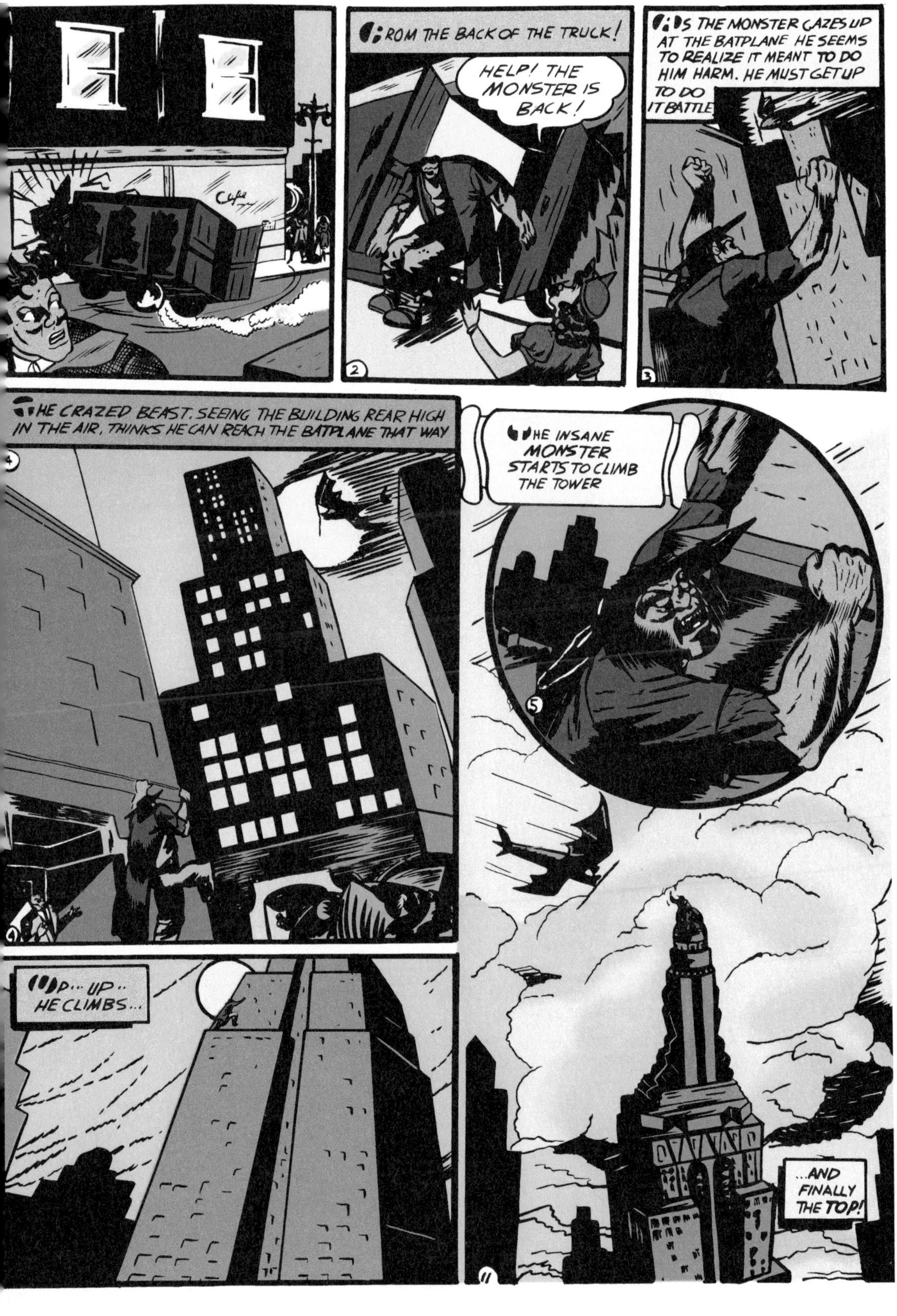
ROM THE BACK OF THE TRUCK!
HELP! THE MONSTER IS BACK!
S THE MONSTER GAZES UP AT THE BATPLANE HE SEEMS TO REALIZE IT MEANT TO DO HIM HARM. HE MUST GET UP TO DO IT BATTLE
HE CRAZED BEAST, SEEING THE BUILDING REAR HIGH IN THE AIR, THINKS HE CAN REACH THE BATPLANE THAT WAY
HE INSANE MONSTER STARTS TO CLIMB THE TOWER
P... UP.. HE CLIMBS...
...AND FINALLY THE TOP!

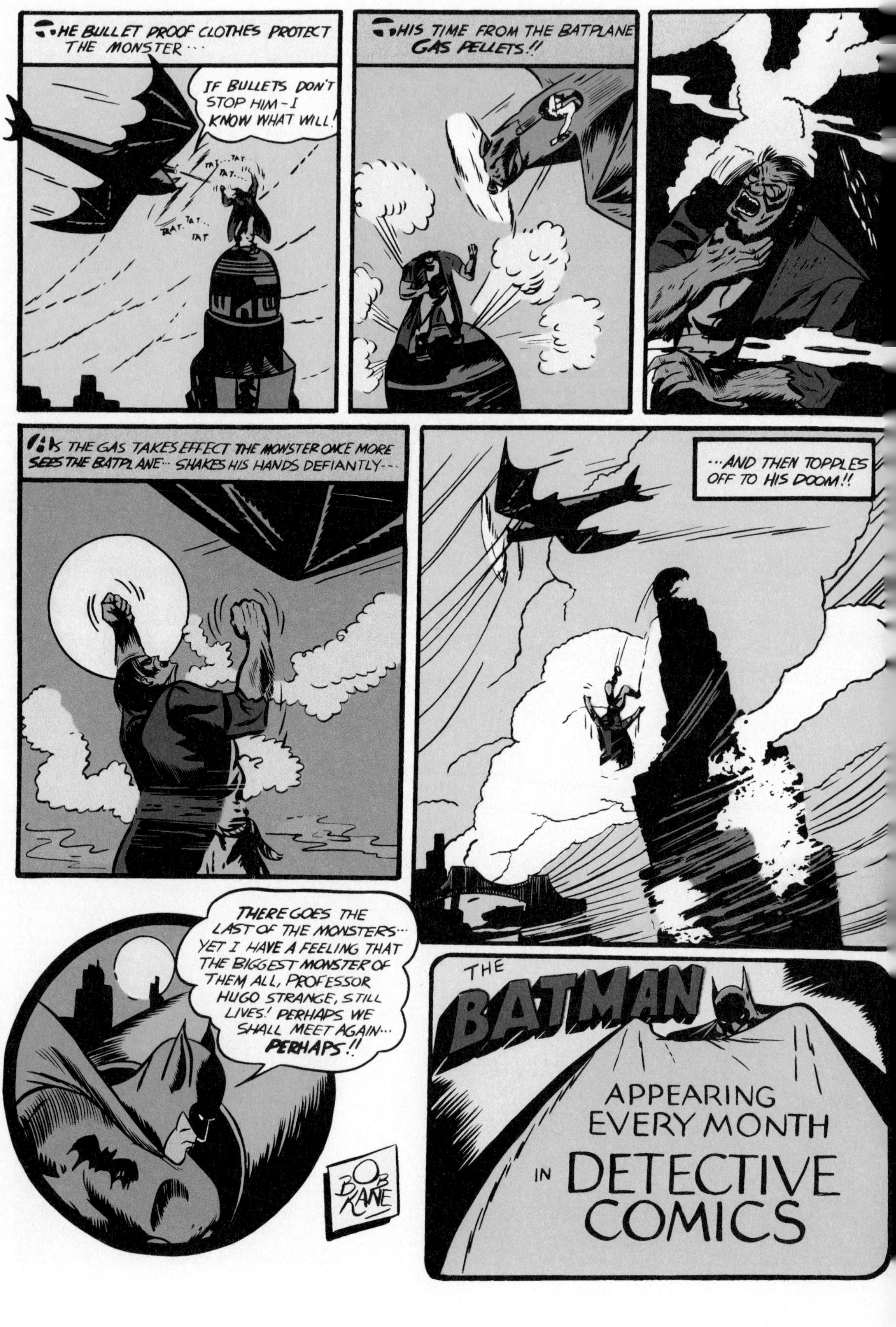
THE BULLET PROOF CLOTHES PROTECT THE MONSTER···
IF BULLETS DON'T STOP HIM - I KNOW WHAT WILL!
TAT...TAT...
TAT...TAT
THIS TIME FROM THE BATPLANE GAS PELLETS!!
AS THE GAS TAKES EFFECT THE MONSTER ONCE MORE SEES THE BATPLANE··· SHAKES HIS HANDS DEFIANTLY···
···AND THEN TOPPLES OFF TO HIS DOOM!!
THERE GOES THE LAST OF THE MONSTERS··· YET I HAVE A FEELING THAT THE BIGGEST MONSTER OF THEM ALL, PROFESSOR HUGO STRANGE, STILL LIVES! PERHAPS WE SHALL MEET AGAIN··· PERHAPS!!
BOB KANE
THE BATMAN
APPEARING EVERY MONTH IN DETECTIVE COMICS

BAT MAN

WITH Robin
—THE BOY WONDER—

BY BOB KANE

ONCE MORE THAT EERIE FIGURE OF THE NIGHT, THE **BATMAN**, AND HIS YOUNG AIDE, THAT LAUGHING DARE-DEVIL, THAT YOUNG ROBIN HOOD OF TODAY, **ROBIN** THE BOY WONDER, FIND THEMSELVES SWIMMING IN TROUBLED WATERS! A YACHT SAILS A SEA OF INTRIGUE WHILE ABOARD HER DECK LURKS AN UNSEEN MENACE·· A FIGURE SHROUDED BY AN AURA OF MYSTERY!

AMONG THE GUESTS WALKS A YOUNG STEWARD·DICK GRAYSON WHO IS IN REALITY··· **ROBIN** THE BOY WONDER!

HOW DOES HE COME HERE?

WHY?

IT HAD COME ABOUT WHEN...

BRUCE WAYNE···THE **BATMAN** HAD READ ALOUD THIS ITEM IN THE NEWSPAPER···

SOCIETY

MRS. JOHN TRAVERS IS TAKING A GROUP OF SELECTED GUESTS ON A TRIP ABOARD HER YACHT. THE DOLPHIN MRS.TRAVERS WILL WEAR HER FAMOUS EMERALD NECKLACE THAT IS VALUED AT HALF A MILLION. A MASQUERADE PARTY AT WHICH TH...

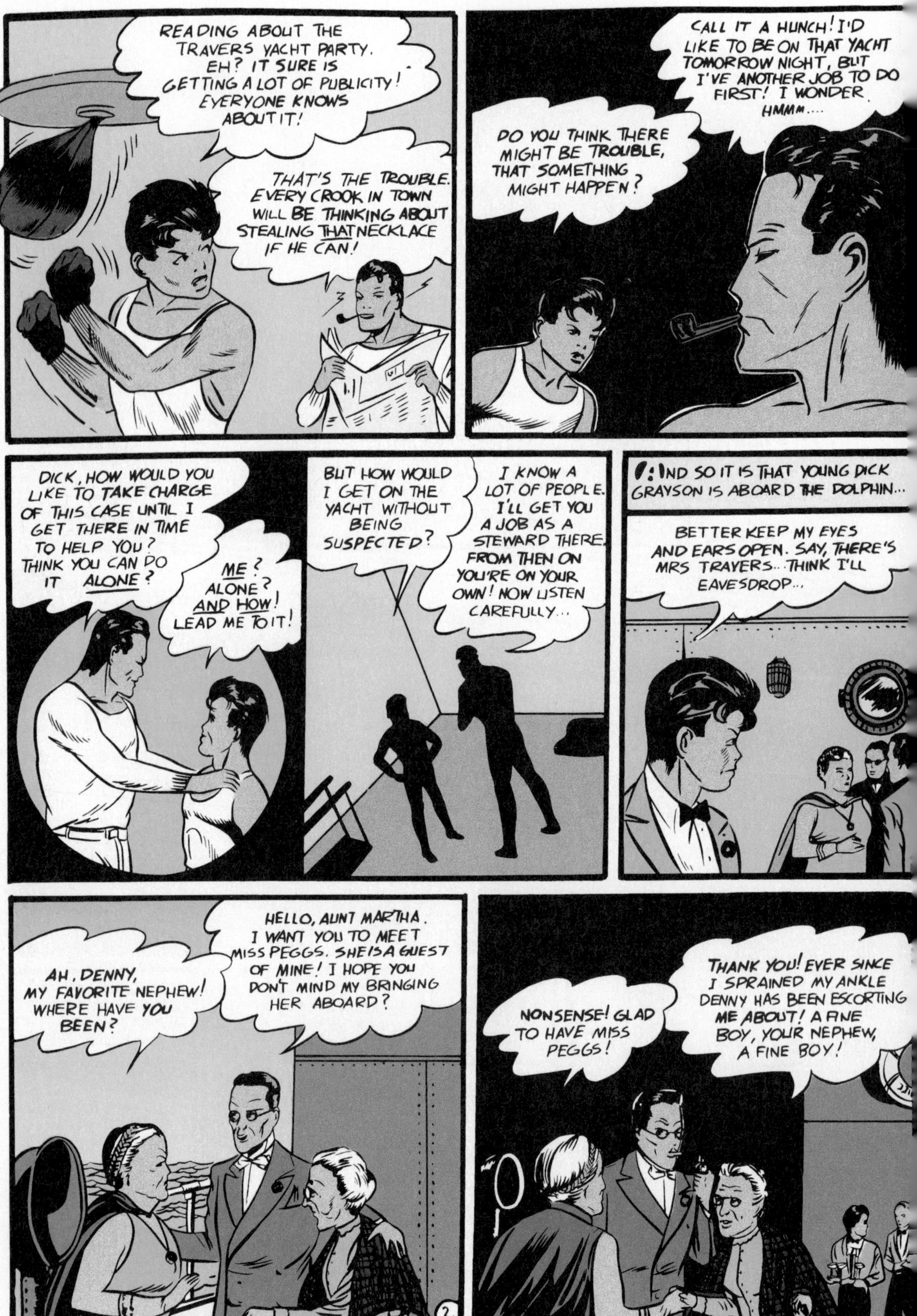
READING ABOUT THE TRAVERS YACHT PARTY. EH? IT SURE IS GETTING A LOT OF PUBLICITY! EVERYONE KNOWS ABOUT IT!
THAT'S THE TROUBLE. EVERY CROOK IN TOWN WILL BE THINKING ABOUT STEALING THAT NECKLACE IF HE CAN!
DO YOU THINK THERE MIGHT BE TROUBLE, THAT SOMETHING MIGHT HAPPEN?
CALL IT A HUNCH! I'D LIKE TO BE ON THAT YACHT TOMORROW NIGHT, BUT I'VE ANOTHER JOB TO DO FIRST! I WONDER. HMMM....
DICK, HOW WOULD YOU LIKE TO TAKE CHARGE OF THIS CASE UNTIL I GET THERE IN TIME TO HELP YOU? THINK YOU CAN DO IT ALONE?
ME? ALONE? AND HOW! LEAD ME TO IT!
BUT HOW WOULD I GET ON THE YACHT WITHOUT BEING SUSPECTED?
I KNOW A LOT OF PEOPLE. I'LL GET YOU A JOB AS A STEWARD THERE. FROM THEN ON YOU'RE ON YOUR OWN! NOW LISTEN CAREFULLY...
AND SO IT IS THAT YOUNG DICK GRAYSON IS ABOARD THE DOLPHIN...
BETTER KEEP MY EYES AND EARS OPEN. SAY, THERE'S MRS TRAVERS... THINK I'LL EAVESDROP...
AH, DENNY, MY FAVORITE NEPHEW! WHERE HAVE YOU BEEN?
HELLO, AUNT MARTHA. I WANT YOU TO MEET MISS PEGGS. SHE IS A GUEST OF MINE! I HOPE YOU DON'T MIND MY BRINGING HER ABOARD?
2.
NONSENSE! GLAD TO HAVE MISS PEGGS!
THANK YOU! EVER SINCE I SPRAINED MY ANKLE DENNY HAS BEEN ESCORTING ME ABOUT! A FINE BOY, YOUR NEPHEW, A FINE BOY!

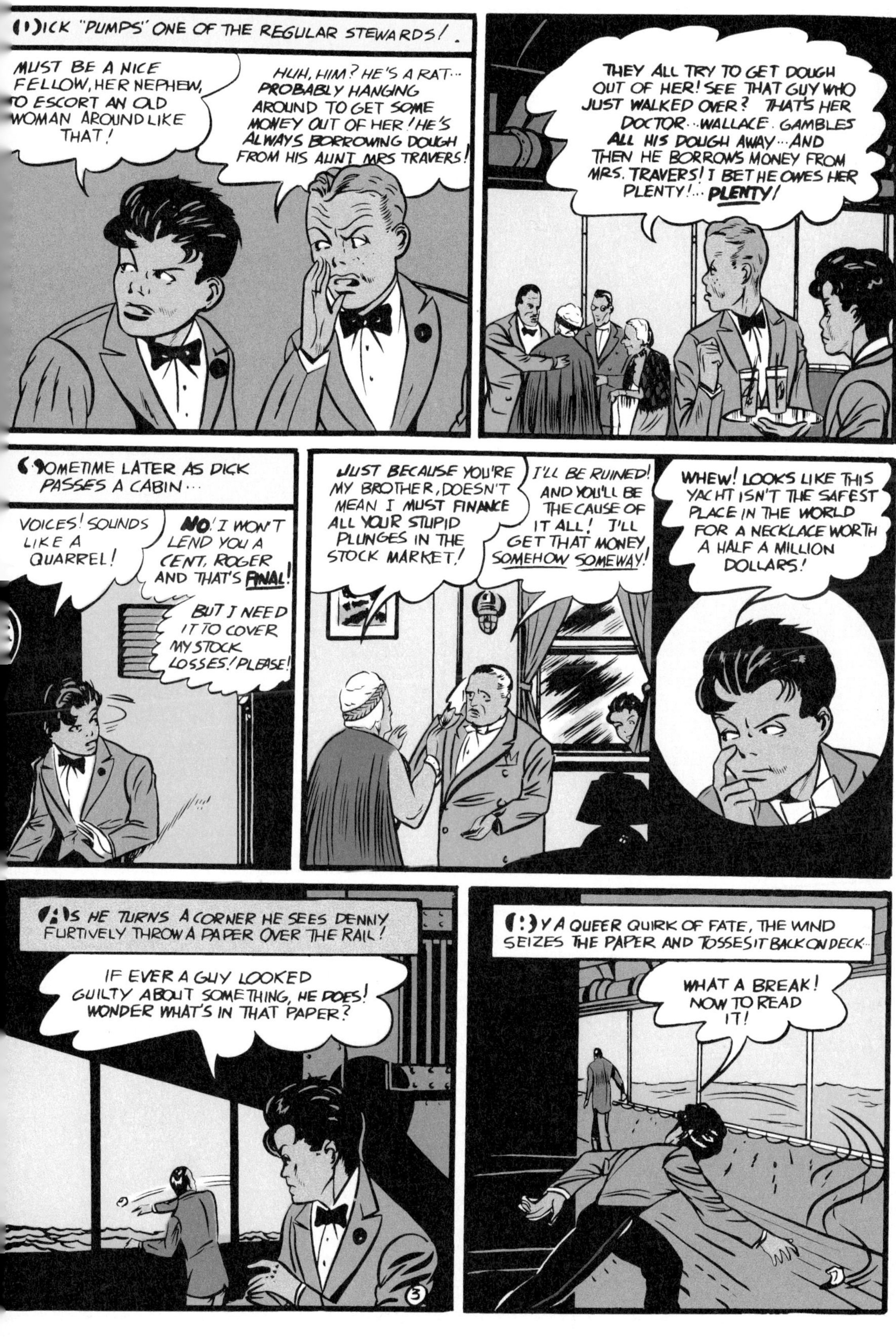
(D)ICK "PUMPS" ONE OF THE REGULAR STEWARDS!
MUST BE A NICE FELLOW, HER NEPHEW, TO ESCORT AN OLD WOMAN AROUND LIKE THAT!
HUH, HIM? HE'S A RAT... PROBABLY HANGING AROUND TO GET SOME MONEY OUT OF HER! HE'S ALWAYS BORROWING DOUGH FROM HIS AUNT MRS TRAVERS!
THEY ALL TRY TO GET DOUGH OUT OF HER! SEE THAT GUY WHO JUST WALKED OVER? THAT'S HER DOCTOR...WALLACE. GAMBLES ALL HIS DOUGH AWAY...AND THEN HE BORROWS MONEY FROM MRS. TRAVERS! I BET HE OWES HER PLENTY!... PLENTY!
(S)OMETIME LATER AS DICK PASSES A CABIN...
VOICES! SOUNDS LIKE A QUARREL!
NO! I WON'T LEND YOU A CENT, ROGER AND THAT'S FINAL!
BUT I NEED IT TO COVER MY STOCK LOSSES! PLEASE!
JUST BECAUSE YOU'RE MY BROTHER, DOESN'T MEAN I MUST FINANCE ALL YOUR STUPID PLUNGES IN THE STOCK MARKET!
I'LL BE RUINED! AND YOU'LL BE THE CAUSE OF IT ALL! I'LL GET THAT MONEY SOMEHOW SOMEWAY!
WHEW! LOOKS LIKE THIS YACHT ISN'T THE SAFEST PLACE IN THE WORLD FOR A NECKLACE WORTH A HALF A MILLION DOLLARS!
(A)S HE TURNS A CORNER HE SEES DENNY FURTIVELY THROW A PAPER OVER THE RAIL!
IF EVER A GUY LOOKED GUILTY ABOUT SOMETHING, HE DOES! WONDER WHAT'S IN THAT PAPER?
3
(B)Y A QUEER QUIRK OF FATE, THE WIND SEIZES THE PAPER AND TOSSES IT BACK ON DECK...
WHAT A BREAK! NOW TO READ IT!

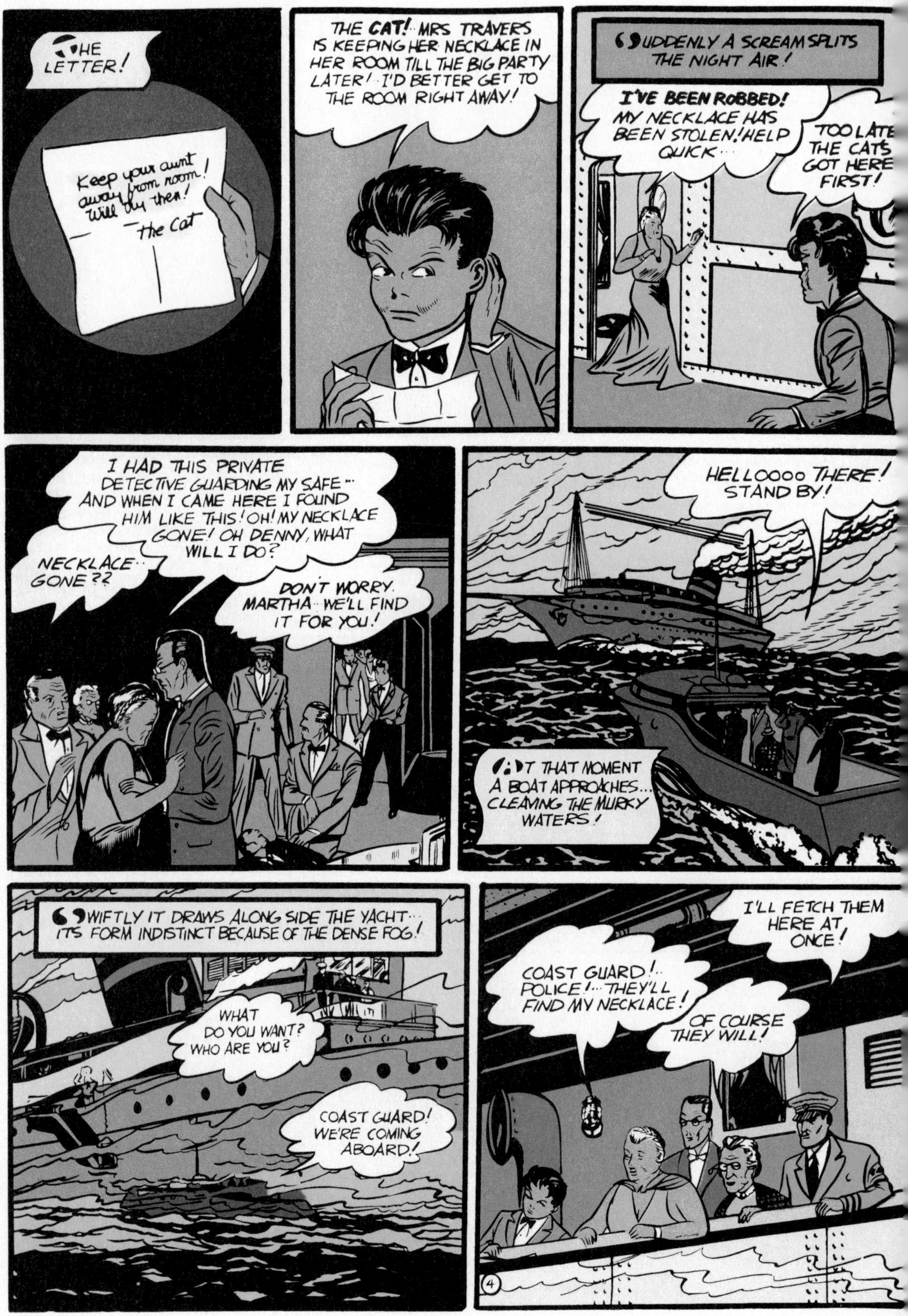
THE LETTER!
Keep your aunt away from room! Will try then! — The Cat
THE CAT! MRS TRAVERS IS KEEPING HER NECKLACE IN HER ROOM TILL THE BIG PARTY LATER! I'D BETTER GET TO THE ROOM RIGHT AWAY!
SUDDENLY A SCREAM SPLITS THE NIGHT AIR!
I'VE BEEN ROBBED! MY NECKLACE HAS BEEN STOLEN! HELP QUICK...
TOO LATE THE CAT'S GOT HERE FIRST!
I HAD THIS PRIVATE DETECTIVE GUARDING MY SAFE... AND WHEN I CAME HERE I FOUND HIM LIKE THIS! OH! MY NECKLACE GONE! OH DENNY, WHAT WILL I DO?
NECKLACE.. GONE??
DON'T WORRY MARTHA.. WE'LL FIND IT FOR YOU!
HELLOOOO THERE! STAND BY!
AT THAT MOMENT A BOAT APPROACHES... CLEAVING THE MURKY WATERS!
SWIFTLY IT DRAWS ALONG SIDE THE YACHT... ITS FORM INDISTINCT BECAUSE OF THE DENSE FOG!
WHAT DO YOU WANT? WHO ARE YOU?
COAST GUARD! WE'RE COMING ABOARD!
I'LL FETCH THEM HERE AT ONCE!
COAST GUARD!.. POLICE!... THEY'LL FIND MY NECKLACE!
OF COURSE THEY WILL!
4

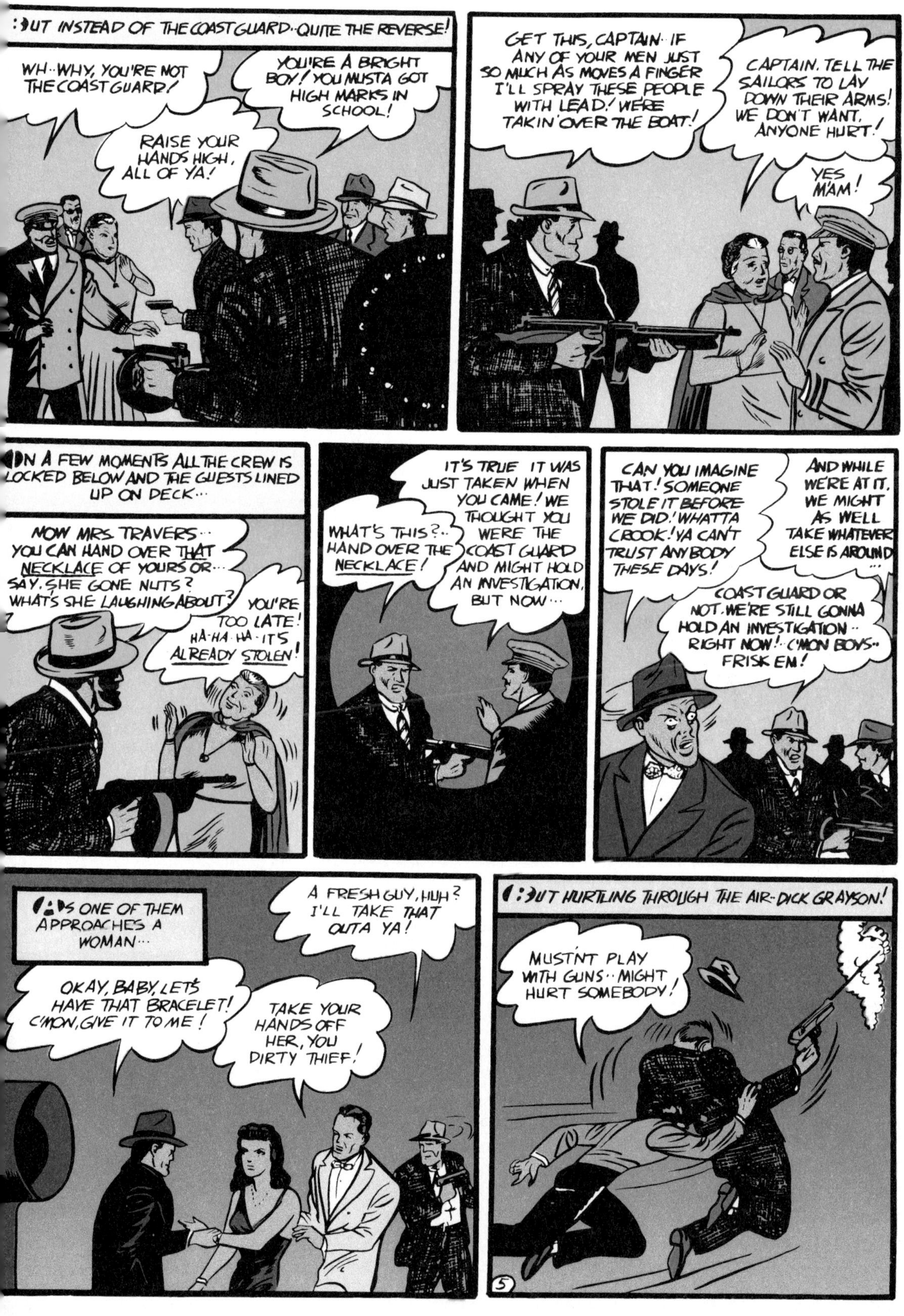
BUT INSTEAD OF THE COAST GUARD.. QUITE THE REVERSE!
WH.. WHY, YOU'RE NOT THE COAST GUARD!
YOU'RE A BRIGHT BOY! YOU MUSTA GOT HIGH MARKS IN SCHOOL!
RAISE YOUR HANDS HIGH, ALL OF YA!
GET THIS, CAPTAIN.. IF ANY OF YOUR MEN JUST SO MUCH AS MOVES A FINGER I'LL SPRAY THESE PEOPLE WITH LEAD! WE'RE TAKIN' OVER THE BOAT!
CAPTAIN. TELL THE SAILORS TO LAY DOWN THEIR ARMS! WE DON'T WANT, ANYONE HURT!
YES M'AM!
IN A FEW MOMENTS ALL THE CREW IS LOCKED BELOW AND THE GUESTS LINED UP ON DECK...
NOW MRS. TRAVERS.. YOU CAN HAND OVER THAT NECKLACE OF YOURS OR... SAY. SHE GONE NUTS? WHAT'S SHE LAUGHING ABOUT?
YOU'RE TOO LATE! HA-HA-HA-IT'S ALREADY STOLEN!
WHAT'S THIS?.. HAND OVER THE NECKLACE!
IT'S TRUE IT WAS JUST TAKEN WHEN YOU CAME! WE THOUGHT YOU WERE THE COAST GUARD AND MIGHT HOLD AN INVESTIGATION, BUT NOW...
CAN YOU IMAGINE THAT! SOMEONE STOLE IT BEFORE WE DID! WHATTA CROOK! YA CAN'T TRUST ANYBODY THESE DAYS!
AND WHILE WE'RE AT IT, WE MIGHT AS WELL TAKE WHATEVER ELSE IS AROUND...
COAST GUARD OR NOT, WE'RE STILL GONNA HOLD AN INVESTIGATION.. RIGHT NOW!.. C'MON BOYS.. FRISK EM!
AS ONE OF THEM APPROACHES A WOMAN...
A FRESH GUY, HUH? I'LL TAKE THAT OUTA YA!
OKAY, BABY, LET'S HAVE THAT BRACELET! C'MON, GIVE IT TO ME!
TAKE YOUR HANDS OFF HER, YOU DIRTY THIEF!
BUT HURTLING THROUGH THE AIR.. DICK GRAYSON!
MUSTN'T PLAY WITH GUNS.. MIGHT HURT SOMEBODY!
5

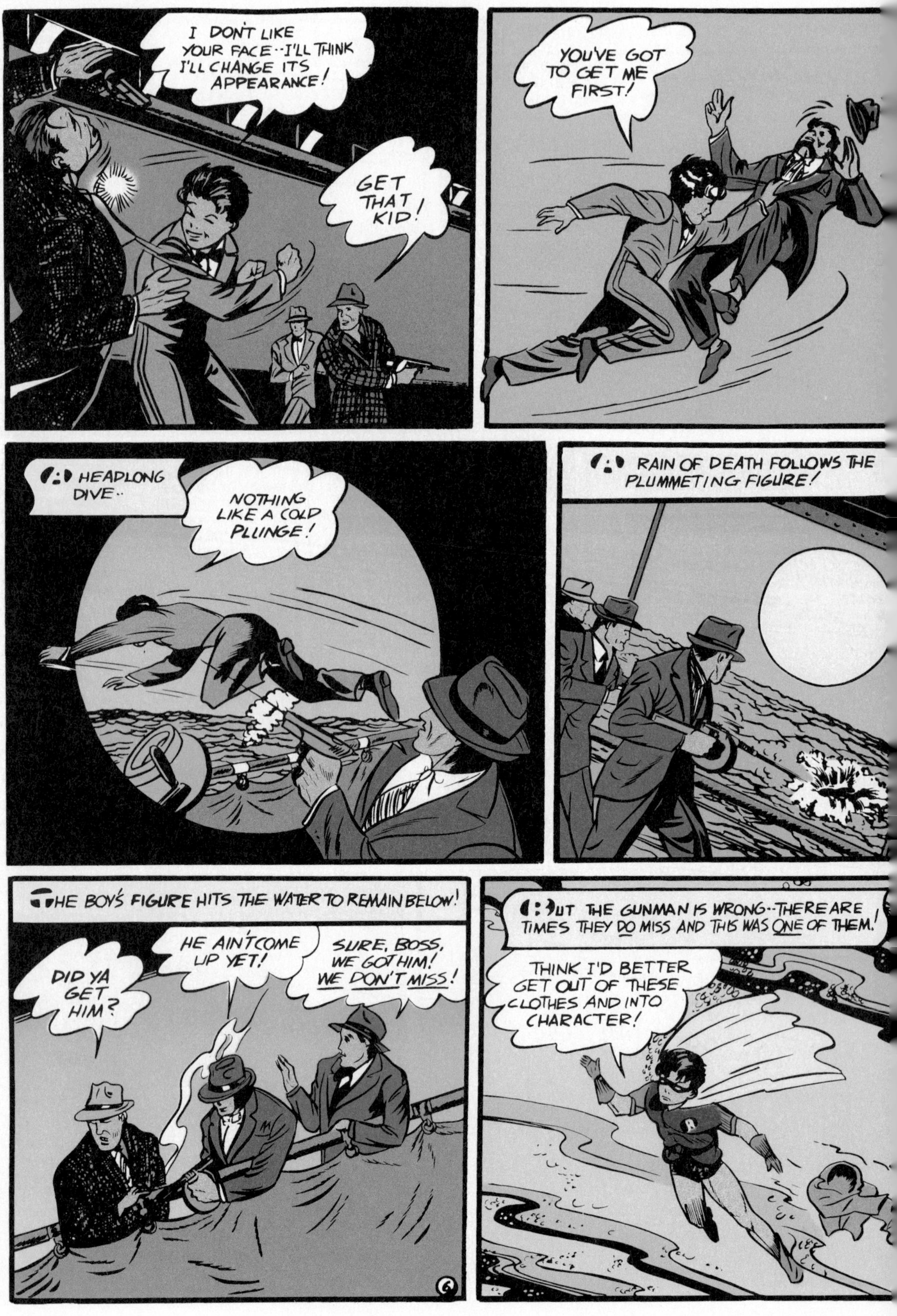

I DON'T LIKE YOUR FACE--I'LL THINK I'LL CHANGE ITS APPEARANCE!
GET THAT KID!
YOU'VE GOT TO GET ME FIRST!
HEADLONG DIVE..
NOTHING LIKE A COLD PLUNGE!
RAIN OF DEATH FOLLOWS THE PLUMMETING FIGURE!
THE BOY'S FIGURE HITS THE WATER TO REMAIN BELOW!
DID YA GET HIM?
HE AIN'T COME UP YET!
SURE, BOSS, WE GOT HIM! WE DON'T MISS!
BUT THE GUNMAN IS WRONG--THERE ARE TIMES THEY DO MISS AND THIS WAS ONE OF THEM!
THINK I'D BETTER GET OUT OF THESE CLOTHES AND INTO CHARACTER!
6

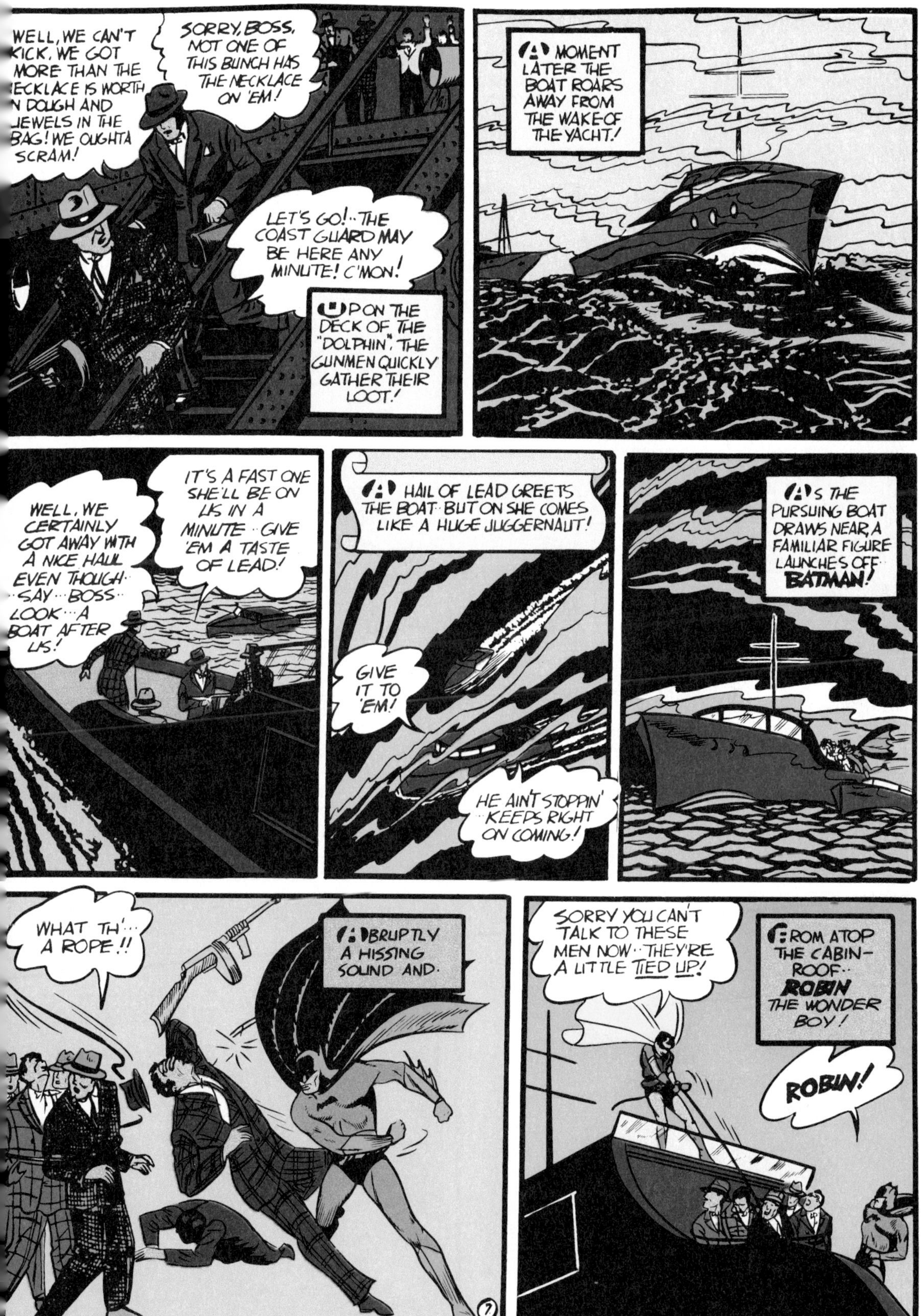
WELL, WE CAN'T KICK. WE GOT MORE THAN THE NECKLACE IS WORTH IN DOUGH AND JEWELS IN THE BAG! WE OUGHTA SCRAM!
SORRY, BOSS, NOT ONE OF THIS BUNCH HAS THE NECKLACE ON 'EM!
LET'S GO!.. THE COAST GUARD MAY BE HERE ANY MINUTE! C'MON!
UPON THE DECK OF THE "DOLPHIN", THE GUNMEN QUICKLY GATHER THEIR LOOT!
A MOMENT LATER THE BOAT ROARS AWAY FROM THE WAKE OF THE YACHT!
WELL, WE CERTAINLY GOT AWAY WITH A NICE HAUL EVEN THOUGH.. ..SAY.. BOSS.. LOOK.. A BOAT AFTER US!
IT'S A FAST ONE SHE'LL BE ON US IN A MINUTE .. GIVE 'EM A TASTE OF LEAD!
A HAIL OF LEAD GREETS THE BOAT. BUT ON SHE COMES LIKE A HUGE JUGGERNAUT!
GIVE IT TO 'EM!
HE AIN'T STOPPIN' ..KEEPS RIGHT ON COMING!
AS THE PURSUING BOAT DRAWS NEAR, A FAMILIAR FIGURE LAUNCHES OFF.. BATMAN!
WHAT TH'... A ROPE!!
ABRUPTLY A HISSING SOUND AND.
7
SORRY YOU CAN'T TALK TO THESE MEN NOW.. THEY'RE A LITTLE TIED UP!
FROM ATOP THE CABIN-ROOF.. ROBIN THE WONDER BOY!
ROBIN!

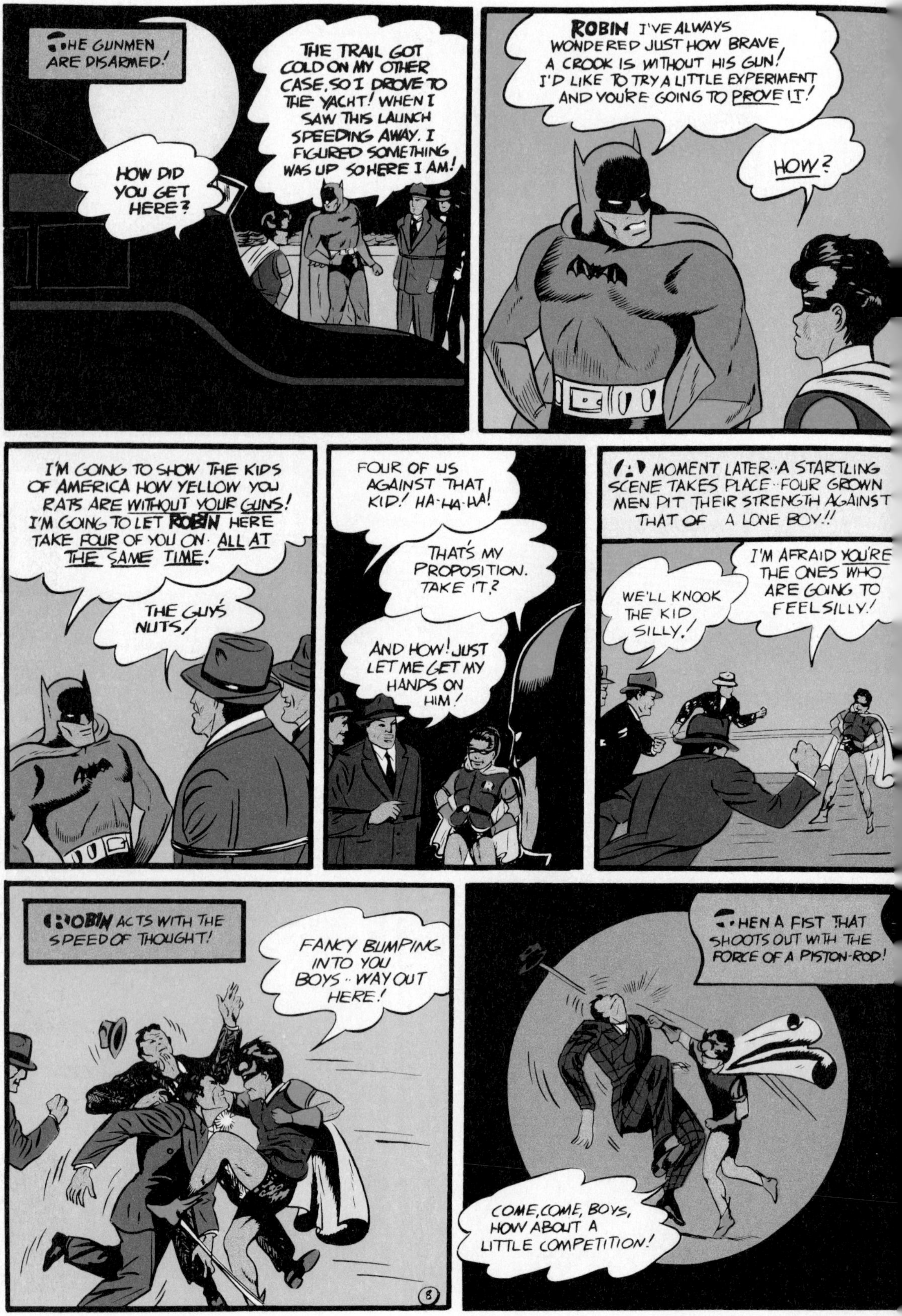
THE GUNMEN ARE DISARMED!
HOW DID YOU GET HERE?
THE TRAIL GOT COLD ON MY OTHER CASE, SO I DROVE TO THE YACHT! WHEN I SAW THIS LAUNCH SPEEDING AWAY, I FIGURED SOMETHING WAS UP SO HERE I AM!
ROBIN I'VE ALWAYS WONDERED JUST HOW BRAVE A CROOK IS WITHOUT HIS GUN! I'D LIKE TO TRY A LITTLE EXPERIMENT AND YOU'RE GOING TO PROVE IT!
HOW?
I'M GOING TO SHOW THE KIDS OF AMERICA HOW YELLOW YOU RATS ARE WITHOUT YOUR GUNS! I'M GOING TO LET ROBIN HERE TAKE FOUR OF YOU ON - ALL AT THE SAME TIME!
THE GUY'S NUTS!
FOUR OF US AGAINST THAT KID! HA-HA-HA!
THAT'S MY PROPOSITION. TAKE IT?
AND HOW! JUST LET ME GET MY HANDS ON HIM!
A MOMENT LATER - A STARTLING SCENE TAKES PLACE - FOUR GROWN MEN PIT THEIR STRENGTH AGAINST THAT OF A LONE BOY!!
WE'LL KNOCK THE KID SILLY!
I'M AFRAID YOU'RE THE ONES WHO ARE GOING TO FEEL SILLY!
ROBIN ACTS WITH THE SPEED OF THOUGHT!
FANCY BUMPING INTO YOU BOYS - WAY OUT HERE!
8
THEN A FIST THAT SHOOTS OUT WITH THE FORCE OF A PISTON-ROD!
COME, COME, BOYS, HOW ABOUT A LITTLE COMPETITION!

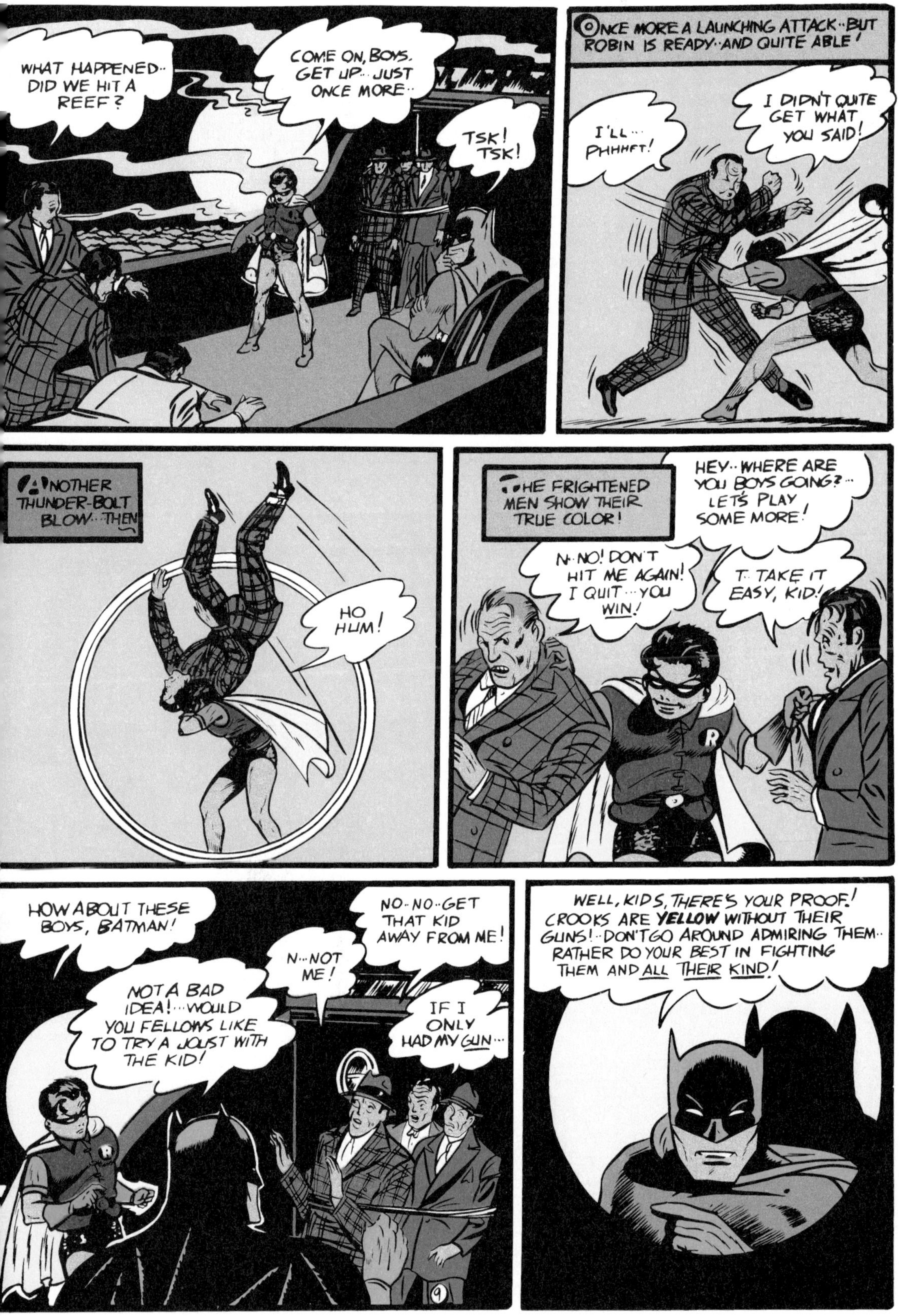
WHAT HAPPENED.. DID WE HIT A REEF?
COME ON, BOYS. GET UP.. JUST ONCE MORE..
TSK! TSK!
ONCE MORE A LAUNCHING ATTACK..BUT ROBIN IS READY..AND QUITE ABLE!
I'LL... PHHHFT!
I DIDN'T QUITE GET WHAT YOU SAID!
ANOTHER THUNDER-BOLT BLOW...THEN
HO HUM!
THE FRIGHTENED MEN SHOW THEIR TRUE COLOR!
HEY..WHERE ARE YOU BOYS GOING?... LET'S PLAY SOME MORE!
N-NO! DON'T HIT ME AGAIN! I QUIT...YOU WIN!
T-TAKE IT EASY, KID!
HOW ABOUT THESE BOYS, BATMAN!
NOT A BAD IDEA!...WOULD YOU FELLOWS LIKE TO TRY A JOUST WITH THE KID!
N...NOT ME!
NO-NO-GET THAT KID AWAY FROM ME!
IF I ONLY HAD MY GUN...
9
WELL, KIDS, THERE'S YOUR PROOF! CROOKS ARE YELLOW WITHOUT THEIR GUNS!..DON'T GO AROUND ADMIRING THEM.. RATHER DO YOUR BEST IN FIGHTING THEM AND ALL THEIR KIND!

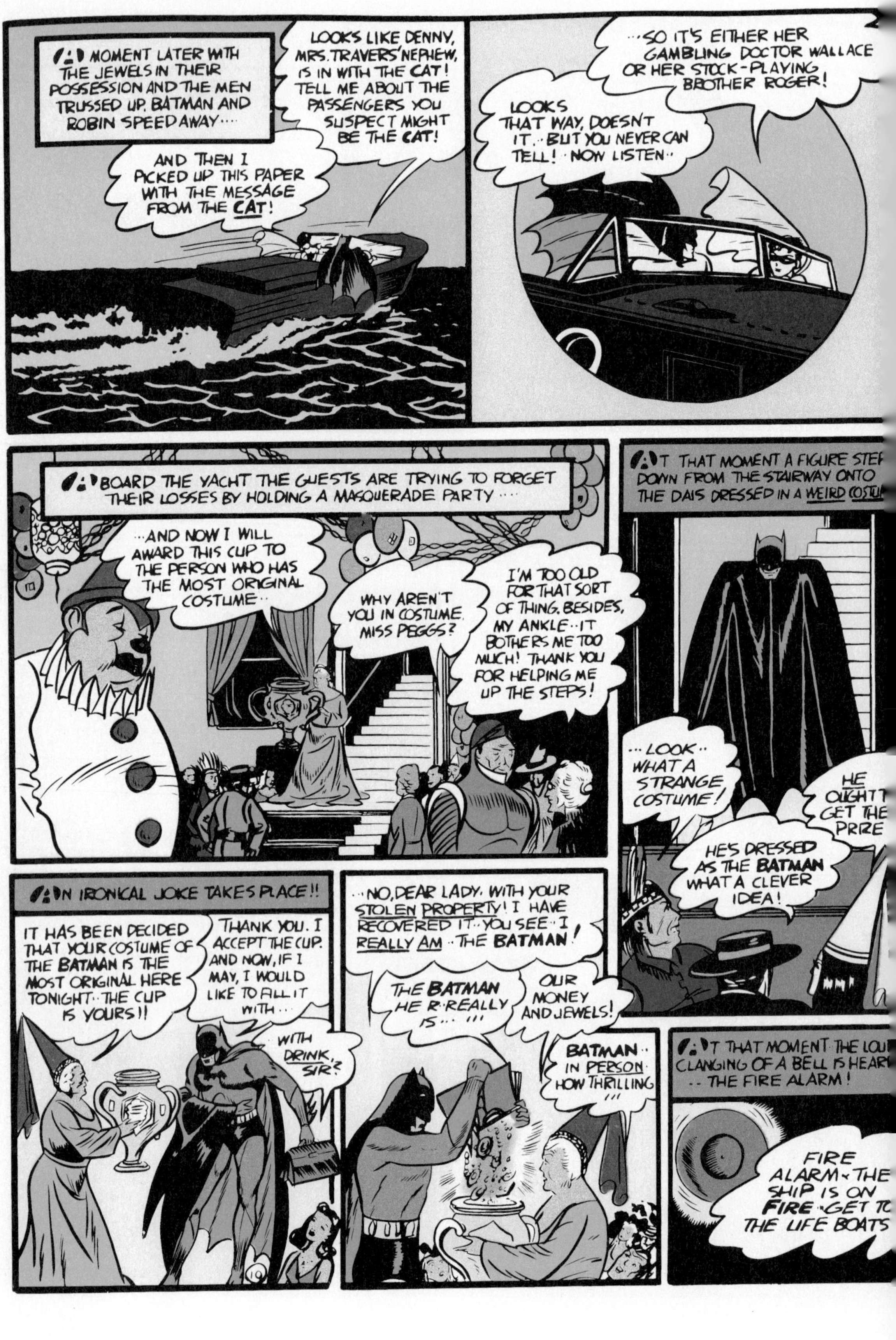

A MOMENT LATER WITH THE JEWELS IN THEIR POSSESSION AND THE MEN TRUSSED UP, BATMAN AND ROBIN SPEED AWAY....
LOOKS LIKE DENNY, MRS. TRAVERS' NEPHEW, IS IN WITH THE CAT! TELL ME ABOUT THE PASSENGERS YOU SUSPECT MIGHT BE THE CAT!
AND THEN I PICKED UP THIS PAPER WITH THE MESSAGE FROM THE CAT!
...SO IT'S EITHER HER GAMBLING DOCTOR WALLACE OR HER STOCK-PLAYING BROTHER ROGER!
LOOKS THAT WAY, DOESN'T IT.. BUT YOU NEVER CAN TELL! NOW LISTEN..
ABOARD THE YACHT THE GUESTS ARE TRYING TO FORGET THEIR LOSSES BY HOLDING A MASQUERADE PARTY....
...AND NOW I WILL AWARD THIS CUP TO THE PERSON WHO HAS THE MOST ORIGINAL COSTUME..
WHY AREN'T YOU IN COSTUME, MISS PEGGS?
I'M TOO OLD FOR THAT SORT OF THING. BESIDES, MY ANKLE.. IT BOTHERS ME TOO MUCH! THANK YOU FOR HELPING ME UP THE STEPS!
AT THAT MOMENT A FIGURE STEF DOWN FROM THE STAIRWAY ONTO THE DAIS DRESSED IN A WEIRD COSTU
...LOOK.. WHAT A STRANGE COSTUME!
HE OUGHT T GET THE PRIZE
HE'S DRESSED AS THE BATMAN WHAT A CLEVER IDEA!
AN IRONICAL JOKE TAKES PLACE!!
IT HAS BEEN DECIDED THAT YOUR COSTUME OF THE BATMAN IS THE MOST ORIGINAL HERE TONIGHT.. THE CUP IS YOURS!!
THANK YOU. I ACCEPT THE CUP. AND NOW, IF I MAY, I WOULD LIKE TO FILL IT WITH...
WITH DRINK, SIR?
...NO, DEAR LADY. WITH YOUR STOLEN PROPERTY! I HAVE RECOVERED IT.. YOU SEE.. I REALLY AM.. THE BATMAN!
THE BATMAN HE R-REALLY IS... !!!
OUR MONEY AND JEWELS!
BATMAN.. IN PERSON HOW THRILLING !!!
AT THAT MOMENT THE LOU CLANGING OF A BELL IS HEAR -- THE FIRE ALARM!
FIRE ALARM - THE SHIP IS ON FIRE - GET TO THE LIFE BOATS

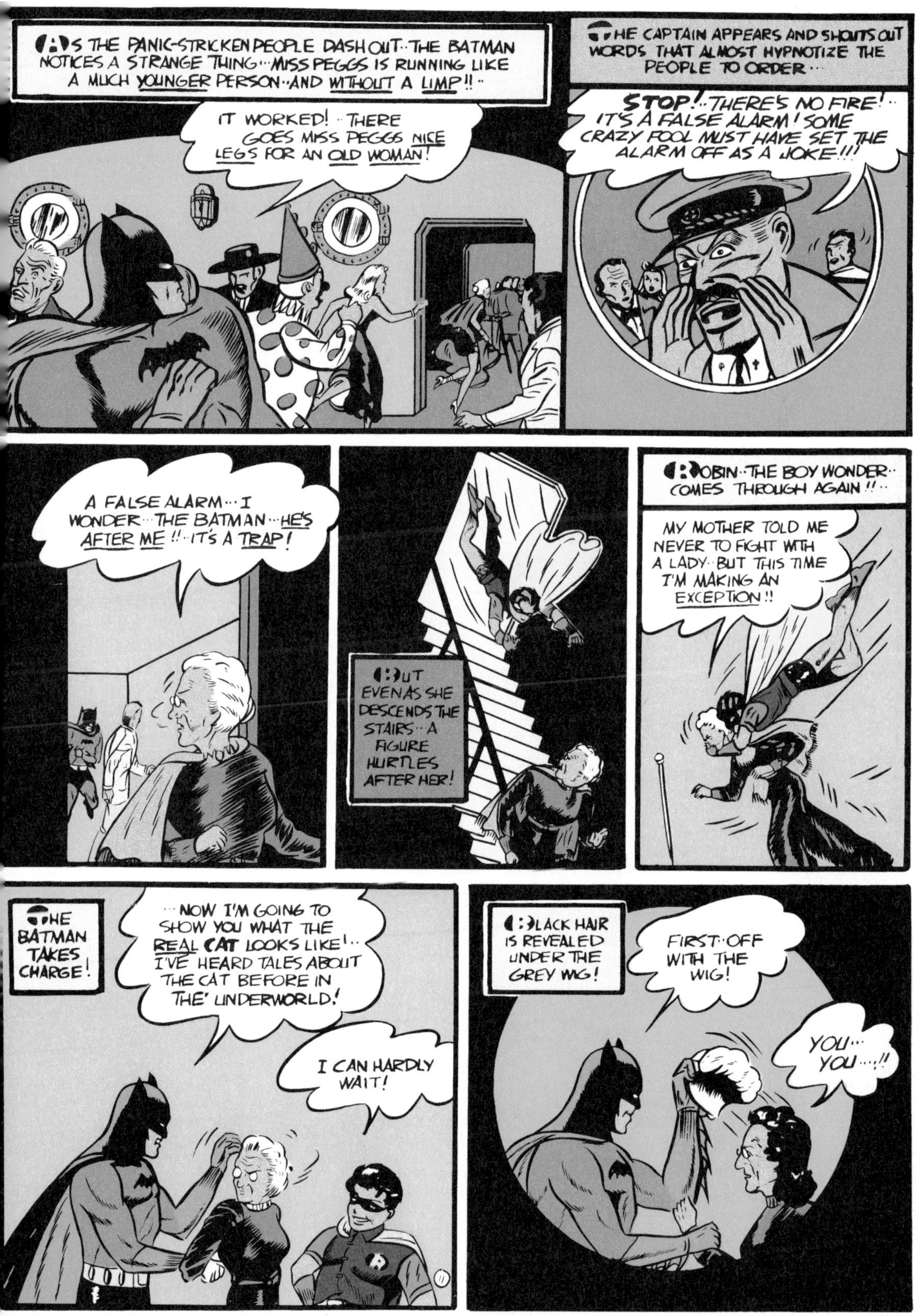
AS THE PANIC-STRICKEN PEOPLE DASH OUT.. THE BATMAN NOTICES A STRANGE THING... MISS PEGGS IS RUNNING LIKE A MUCH YOUNGER PERSON.. AND WITHOUT A LIMP!!..
IT WORKED! .. THERE GOES MISS PEGGS NICE LEGS FOR AN OLD WOMAN!
THE CAPTAIN APPEARS AND SHOUTS OUT WORDS THAT ALMOST HYPNOTIZE THE PEOPLE TO ORDER...
STOP!..THERE'S NO FIRE!.. IT'S A FALSE ALARM! SOME CRAZY FOOL MUST HAVE SET THE ALARM OFF AS A JOKE!!!
A FALSE ALARM... I WONDER.. THE BATMAN.. HE'S AFTER ME!!.. IT'S A TRAP!
BUT EVEN AS SHE DESCENDS THE STAIRS.. A FIGURE HURTLES AFTER HER!
ROBIN.. THE BOY WONDER.. COMES THROUGH AGAIN!!..
MY MOTHER TOLD ME NEVER TO FIGHT WITH A LADY.. BUT THIS TIME I'M MAKING AN EXCEPTION!!
THE BATMAN TAKES CHARGE!
...NOW I'M GOING TO SHOW YOU WHAT THE REAL CAT LOOKS LIKE!.. I'VE HEARD TALES ABOUT THE CAT BEFORE IN THE' UNDERWORLD!
I CAN HARDLY WAIT!
BLACK HAIR IS REVEALED UNDER THE GREY WIG!
FIRST.. OFF WITH THE WIG!
YOU... YOU...!!

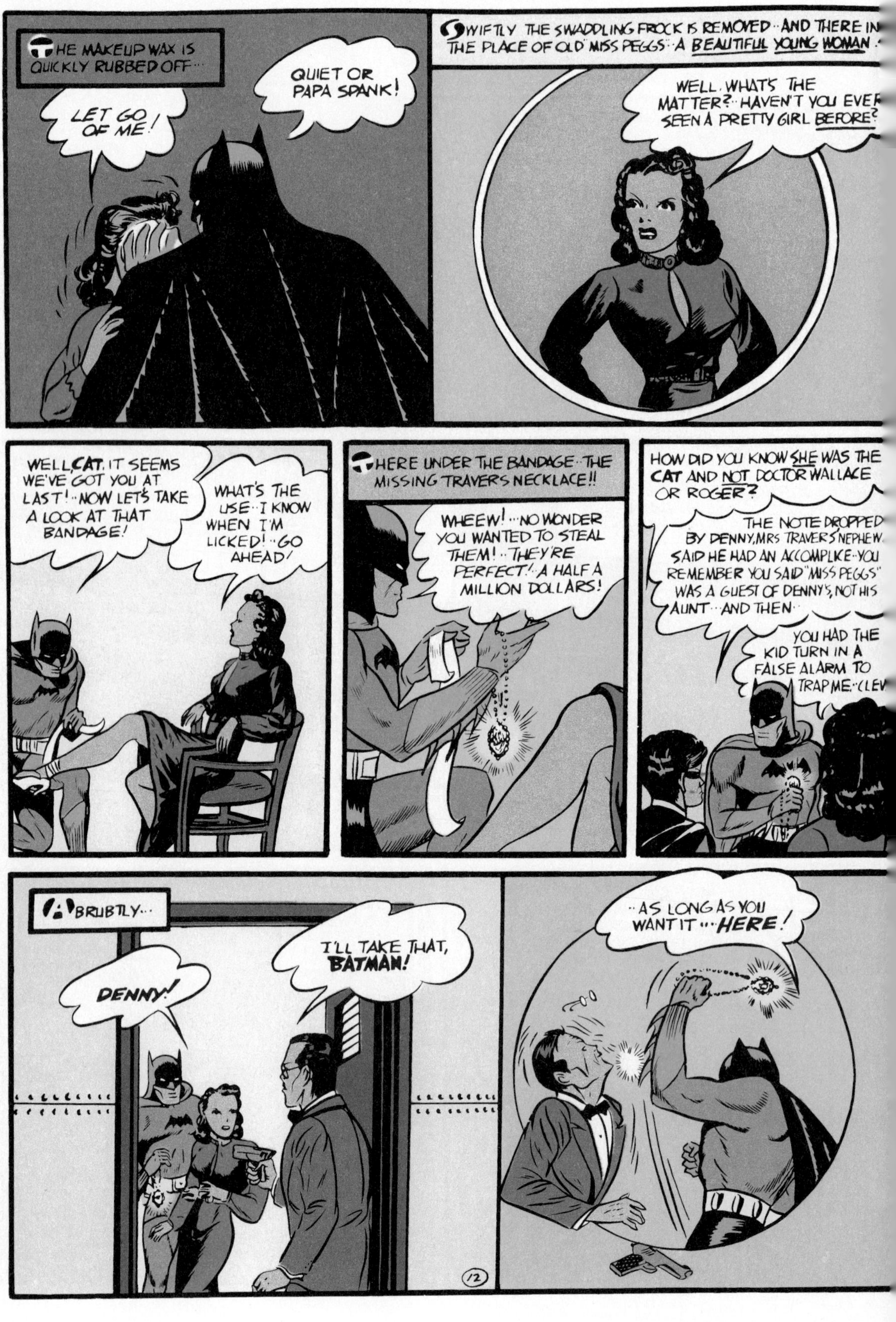
THE MAKEUP WAX IS QUICKLY RUBBED OFF...
LET GO OF ME!
QUIET OR PAPA SPANK!
SWIFTLY THE SWADDLING FROCK IS REMOVED..AND THERE IN THE PLACE OF OLD MISS PEGGS..A BEAUTIFUL YOUNG WOMAN.
WELL..WHAT'S THE MATTER?..HAVEN'T YOU EVER SEEN A PRETTY GIRL BEFORE?
WELL, CAT, IT SEEMS WE'VE GOT YOU AT LAST!..NOW LET'S TAKE A LOOK AT THAT BANDAGE!
WHAT'S THE USE..I KNOW WHEN I'M LICKED!..GO AHEAD!
THERE UNDER THE BANDAGE..THE MISSING TRAVERS NECKLACE!!
WHEEW!...NO WONDER YOU WANTED TO STEAL THEM!..THEY'RE PERFECT!..A HALF A MILLION DOLLARS!
HOW DID YOU KNOW SHE WAS THE CAT AND NOT DOCTOR WALLACE OR ROGER?
THE NOTE DROPPED BY DENNY, MRS TRAVERS'S NEPHEW, SAID HE HAD AN ACCOMPLICE..YOU REMEMBER YOU SAID "MISS PEGGS" WAS A GUEST OF DENNY'S, NOT HIS AUNT...AND THEN..
YOU HAD THE KID TURN IN A FALSE ALARM TO TRAP ME..CLEV
ABRUPTLY...
DENNY!
I'LL TAKE THAT, BATMAN!
..AS LONG AS YOU WANT IT...HERE!
12

BOY, HE'S OUT COLDER THAN A DEAD MACKEREL!

BATMAN... I WAS SUPPOSED TO GIVE DENNY HALF OF THE JEWELS... WHY DON'T YOU COME IN AS A PARTNER WITH ME! YOU AND I TOGETHER!

YOU AND I... KING AND QUEEN OF CRIME!... WE'D MAKE A GREAT TEAM! WITH YOU AS MY PARTNER WE...

SORRY, YOUR PROPOSITION TEMPTS ME BUT WE WORK ON DIFFERENT SIDES OF THE LAW! LET'S GO!

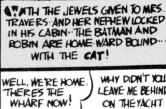

WITH THE JEWELS GIVEN TO MRS. TRAVERS...AND HER NEPHEW LOCKED IN HIS CABIN... THE BATMAN AND ROBIN ARE HOME-WARD BOUND... WITH THE CAT!

WELL, WE'RE HOME. THERE'S THE WHARF NOW!

WHY DIDN'T YOU LEAVE ME BEHIND ON THE YACHT INSTEAD OF TAKING ME TO THE POLICE YOURSELF?

I'VE GOT MY REASONS!

SUDDENLY THE CAT LEAPS TO HER FEET AND...

WATCH HER...SHE'S JUMPED OVERBOARD!

FANCY THAT.

AS ROBIN MAKES READY TO JUMP AFTER THE CAT...THE BATMAN CLUMSILY 'BUMPS' INTO HIM!...

HEY!

OOPS-SORRY, ROBIN!

BY THE TIME THEY RECOVER, THE CAT HAS MADE GOOD HER ESCAPE!

TOO LATE...SHE'S GONE!...AND SAY...I'LL BET YOU BUMPED INTO ME ON PURPOSE!...THAT'S WHY YOU TOOK HER ALONG WITH US...SO SHE MIGHT TRY A BREAK!

WHY, ROBIN, MY BOY, WHATEVER GAVE YOU SUCH AN IDEA!... HMM...NICE NIGHT, ISN'T IT?

...LOVELY GIRL!...WHAT EYES!... SAY...MUSTN'T FORGET I'VE GOT A GIRL NAMED JULIE!... OH WELL...SHE STILL HAD LOVELY EYES! MAYBE I'LL BUMP INTO HER AGAIN SOMETIME...

HMMM...

SO MANY OF OUR READERS HAVE WRITTEN US SUCH NICE LETTERS THAT WE HAVE DECIDED TO SHOW OUR APPRECIATION... THEREFORE ON THE BACK COVER OF THIS MAGAZINE YOU WILL FIND A FULL-PAGE AUTOGRAPHED PICTURE, SUITABLE FOR FRAMING, OF BOTH BATMAN AND ROBIN...THE BOY WONDER....

THIS IS OUR WAY OF SAYING THANKS ....

Bob Kane

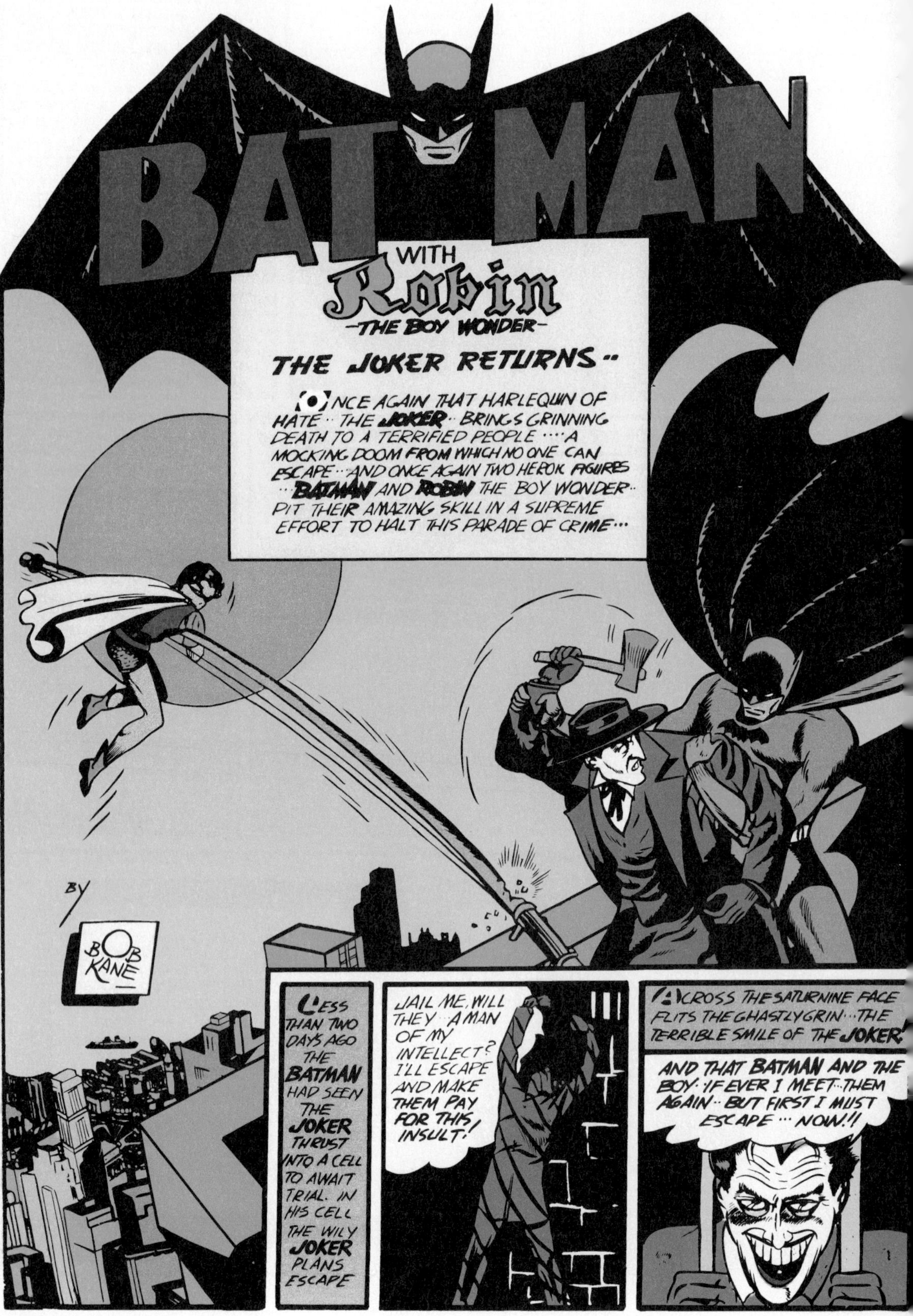
BATMAN
WITH
Robin
-THE BOY WONDER-
THE JOKER RETURNS..
ONCE AGAIN THAT HARLEQUIN OF HATE.. THE JOKER.. BRINGS GRINNING DEATH TO A TERRIFIED PEOPLE .... A MOCKING DOOM FROM WHICH NO ONE CAN ESCAPE... AND ONCE AGAIN TWO HEROIC FIGURES ... BATMAN AND ROBIN THE BOY WONDER.. PIT THEIR AMAZING SKILL IN A SUPREME EFFORT TO HALT THIS PARADE OF CRIME...
BY
BOB KANE
LESS THAN TWO DAYS AGO THE BATMAN HAD SEEN THE JOKER THRUST INTO A CELL TO AWAIT TRIAL. IN HIS CELL THE WILY JOKER PLANS ESCAPE
JAIL ME, WILL THEY.. A MAN OF MY INTELLECT? I'LL ESCAPE AND MAKE THEM PAY FOR THIS INSULT!
ACROSS THE SATURNINE FACE FLITS THE GHASTLY GRIN... THE TERRIBLE SMILE OF THE JOKER!
AND THAT BATMAN AND THE BOY.. IF EVER I MEET.. THEM AGAIN.. BUT FIRST I MUST ESCAPE ... NOW!!

FROM THE BACK OF HIS MOUTH THE JOKER UNSCREWS TWO FALSE TEETH!

INSIDE EACH TOOTH IS A CHEMICAL, WHICH WHEN MIXED TOGETHER, FORMS A POWERFUL EXPLOSIVE··· MY MEANS OF ESCAPE!

MOMENTS LATER A TERRIFIC EXPLOSION BLOWS A GAPING HOLE IN THE CELL WALL!!

FREEDOM! AU REVOIR GENTLEMEN···TILL WE MEET AGAIN-HA-HA-HA

STARTLING NEWS STIRS BRUCE WAYNE AND YOUNG DICK GRAYSON!

FLASH! WE'VE JUST RECEIVED WORD THAT THE JOKER HAS JUST ESCAPED PRISON! AFTER MYSTERIOUSLY BLOWING UP HIS CELL, HE OVERPOWERED TWO GUARDS AND···

WELL I'LL BE···!

THE JOKER FREE! I CAN HARDLY BELIEVE IT!

I CAN! HE'S A VERY UNUSUAL MAN! HE'S SHREWD, SUBTLE AND ABOVE ALL RUTHLESS!! MARK MY WORDS, THE JOKER WILL RETURN WITH A VENGEANCE!

AT THAT MOMENT A FIGURE GHOSTS THROUGH THE GLOOM THAT HANGS OVER THE DECAYING GRAVE-STONES OF A DESERTED CEMETERY!

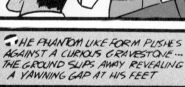

THE PHANTOM LIKE FORM PUSHES AGAINST A CURIOUS GRAVESTONE··· THE GROUND SLIPS AWAY REVEALING A YAWNING GAP AT HIS FEET

THE FIGURE DESCENDS INTO THE CRYPT···A LIGHT SWITCHES ON··· AND REVEALS THE JOKER!!

HERE IN MY LABORATORY I WILL ONCE MORE LET ALL KNOW THAT THE JOKER IS STILL IN THE GAME AND IS STILL HIGH CARD!!

ONCE AGAIN AS PEOPLE LISTEN AT RADIOS COMES THAT BREAK···A DEADLY VOICE A MESSAGE OF DOOM!!

AWWK···HEAR ME NOW! TO CHIEF OF POLICE CHALMERS I BRING DEATH···TONIGHT AT TEN O'CLOCK··· THE JOKER HAS SPOKEN!

THAT NIGHT··A POLICE CORDON PROTECTS THE MAN MARKED FOR DEATH!

HE WOULDN'T DARE··· NOT TO A POLICE CHIEF. **HE WOULDN'T DARE!**··ALMOST TIME··· **ALMOST TIME**···

SUDDENLY THE JINGLE OF THE TELEPHONE BELL··

WHO? YOU **WANT** TO SPEAK TO THE CHIEF? JUST A MINUTE. I'LL PUT HIM ON!!

WHAT! I CAN'T HEAR YOU, SPEAK LOUDER!!

AAAAAAAAAAAG!

JOKER

THE CLOCK TOLLS THE HOUR··TEN O'CLOCK··THE **JOKER** HAS STRUCK AGAIN!

DEAD! HE'S DEAD!

LOOK! ON HIS FACE··· THAT TERRIBLE GRIN···THE SIGN OF DEATH FROM THE **JOKER**

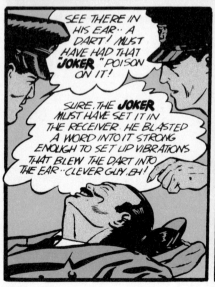

SEE THERE IN HIS EAR··A DART! MUST HAVE HAD THAT "**JOKER**" POISON ON IT!

SURE, THE **JOKER** MUST HAVE SET IT IN THE RECEIVER··HE BLASTED A WORD INTO IT STRONG ENOUGH TO SET UP VIBRATIONS THAT BLEW THE DART INTO THE EAR··CLEVER GUY, EH!

THE FOLLOWING DAY A FAMOUS PAINTING IS STOLEN FROM A GALLERY AND IN ITS PLACE FOR ALL THE WORLD TO SEE···

THE **JOKER** AGAIN!

A RARE GEM IS STOLEN··· THE OWNER, GRINNING IN DEATH··AS IF HE ENJOYED THE VISIT FROM·THE **JOKER**!

3

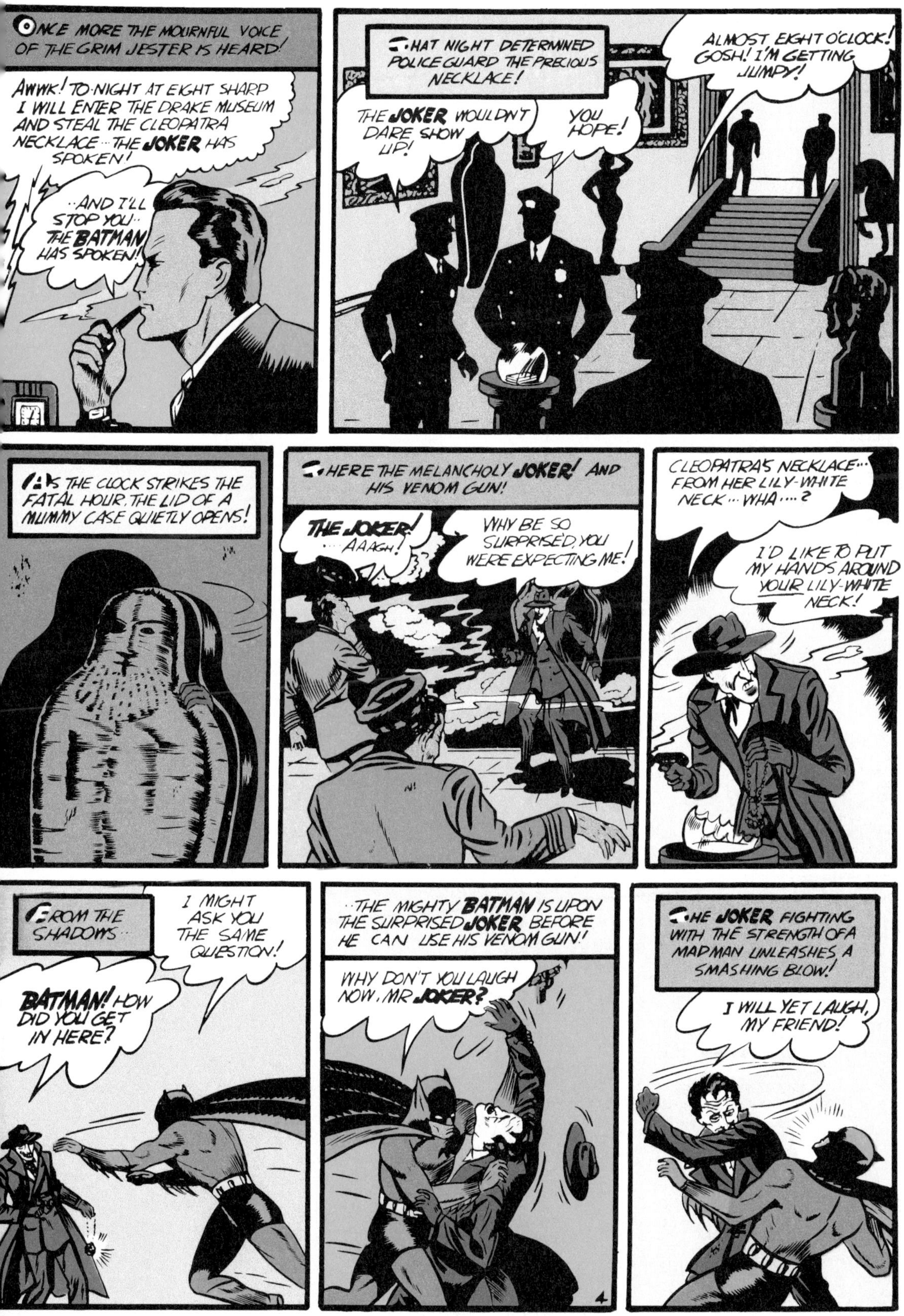
ONCE MORE THE MOURNFUL VOICE OF THE GRIM JESTER IS HEARD!
AWWK! TO-NIGHT AT EIGHT SHARP I WILL ENTER THE DRAKE MUSEUM AND STEAL THE CLEOPATRA NECKLACE... THE JOKER HAS SPOKEN!
...AND I'LL STOP YOU... THE BATMAN HAS SPOKEN!
THAT NIGHT DETERMINED POLICE GUARD THE PRECIOUS NECKLACE!
ALMOST EIGHT O'CLOCK! GOSH! I'M GETTING JUMPY!
THE JOKER WOULDN'T DARE SHOW UP!
YOU HOPE!
AS THE CLOCK STRIKES THE FATAL HOUR, THE LID OF A MUMMY CASE QUIETLY OPENS!
THERE THE MELANCHOLY JOKER! AND HIS VENOM GUN!
THE JOKER! ....AAAGH!
WHY BE SO SURPRISED, YOU WERE EXPECTING ME!
CLEOPATRA'S NECKLACE... FROM HER LILY-WHITE NECK... WHA....?
I'D LIKE TO PUT MY HANDS AROUND YOUR LILY-WHITE NECK!
FROM THE SHADOWS...
I MIGHT ASK YOU THE SAME QUESTION!
BATMAN! HOW DID YOU GET IN HERE?
...THE MIGHTY BATMAN IS UPON THE SURPRISED JOKER BEFORE HE CAN USE HIS VENOM GUN!
WHY DON'T YOU LAUGH NOW, MR. JOKER?
4
THE JOKER FIGHTING WITH THE STRENGTH OF A MADMAN UNLEASHES A SMASHING BLOW!
I WILL YET LAUGH, MY FRIEND!

THE MADMAN REACHES FOR AN ANCIENT MACE!

I'LL FINISH YOU ONCE AND FOR ALL...MR. BATMAN... HA...HA...HA...HA...

(A) SHEER, DESPERATE TWIST OF THE BATMAN'S BODY AND THE MACE GIVES HIM A GLANCING BLOW ON THE SIDE OF THE HEAD

SUDDENLY THE POUNDING OF RUNNING FEET...RAISED VOICES...

THE POLICE FROM DOWNSTAIRS -- THEY MUSN'T FIND ME!

IT'S AFTER EIGHT!...LETS SEE IF THE BOYS ARE ALL RIGHT!

LOOK! THE JOKER'S BEEN HERE! THE NECKLACE IS GONE!

NEVER MIND THE JOKER, LOOK WHAT I FOUND -THE BATMAN

THE BOYS...THEY ALL HAVE THE SIGN OF THE JOKER ON THEIR FACES.

THE BATMAN! WELL. WE HAVE CAUGHT SOMEBODY! NOW I'M GOING TO DO SOMETHING I'VE WANTED TO DO FOR A LONG TIME...TAKE OFF THE BATMAN'S MASK AND SEE WHO HE REALLY IS!

(A) HAND REACHES OUT TO WRENCH OFF BATMAN'S COWL!

5

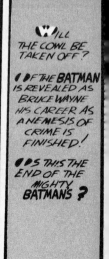

WILL THE COWL BE TAKEN OFF?

IF THE BATMAN IS REVEALED AS BRUCE WAYNE HIS CAREER AS A NEMESIS OF CRIME IS FINISHED!

IS THIS THE END OF THE MIGHTY BATMAN?

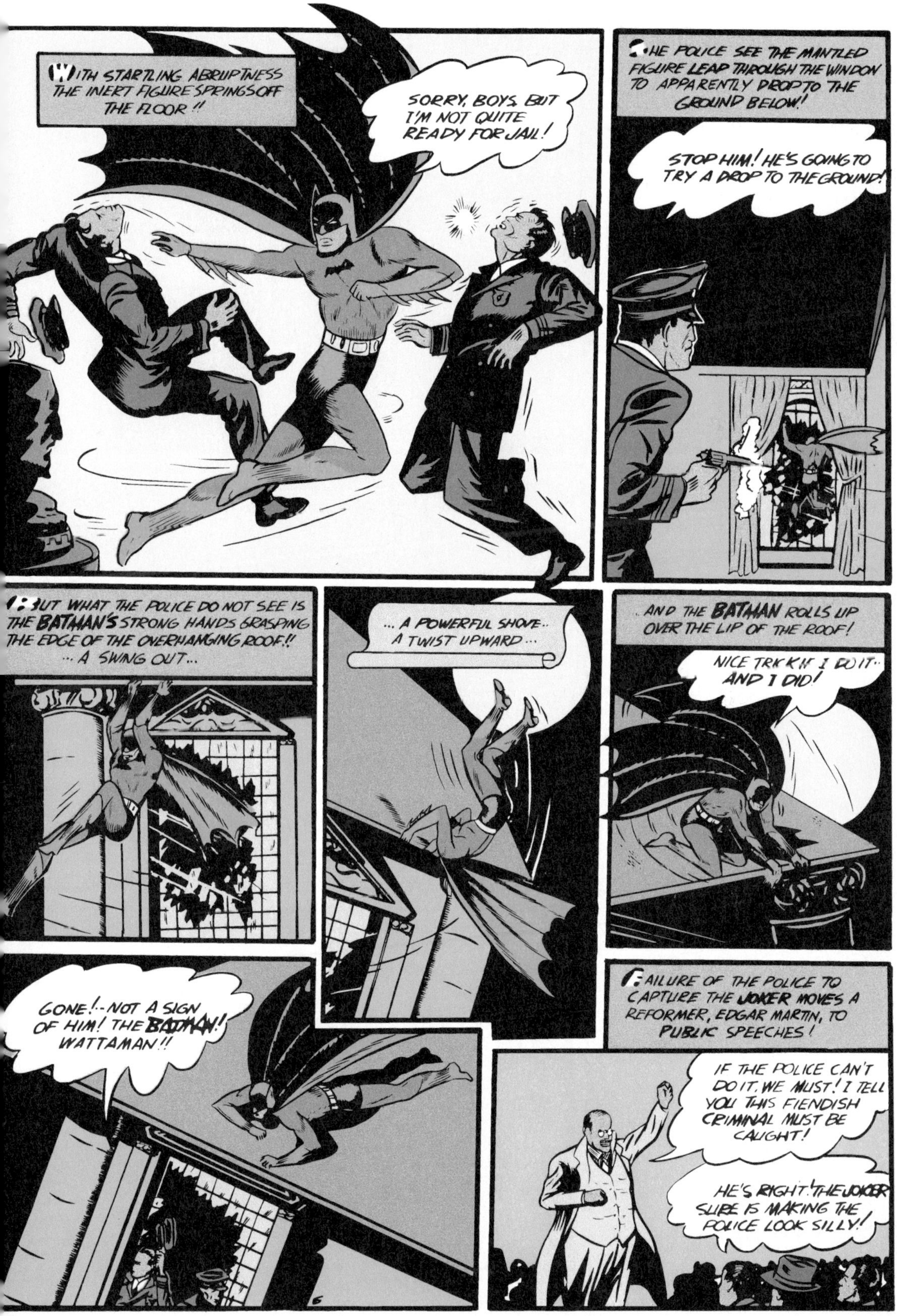
WITH STARTLING ABRUPTNESS THE INERT FIGURE SPRINGS OFF THE FLOOR!!
SORRY, BOYS, BUT I'M NOT QUITE READY FOR JAIL!
THE POLICE SEE THE MANTLED FIGURE LEAP THROUGH THE WINDOW TO APPARENTLY DROP TO THE GROUND BELOW!
STOP HIM! HE'S GOING TO TRY A DROP TO THE GROUND!
BUT WHAT THE POLICE DO NOT SEE IS THE BATMAN'S STRONG HANDS GRASPING THE EDGE OF THE OVERHANGING ROOF!! ... A SWING OUT...
... A POWERFUL SHOVE.. A TWIST UPWARD...
.. AND THE BATMAN ROLLS UP OVER THE LIP OF THE ROOF!
NICE TRICK IF I DO IT.. AND I DID!
GONE!-- NOT A SIGN OF HIM! THE BATMAN! WATTAMAN!!
FAILURE OF THE POLICE TO CAPTURE THE JOKER MOVES A REFORMER, EDGAR MARTIN, TO PUBLIC SPEECHES!
IF THE POLICE CAN'T DO IT, WE MUST! I TELL YOU THIS FIENDISH CRIMINAL MUST BE CAUGHT!
HE'S RIGHT! THE JOKER SURE IS MAKING THE POLICE LOOK SILLY!

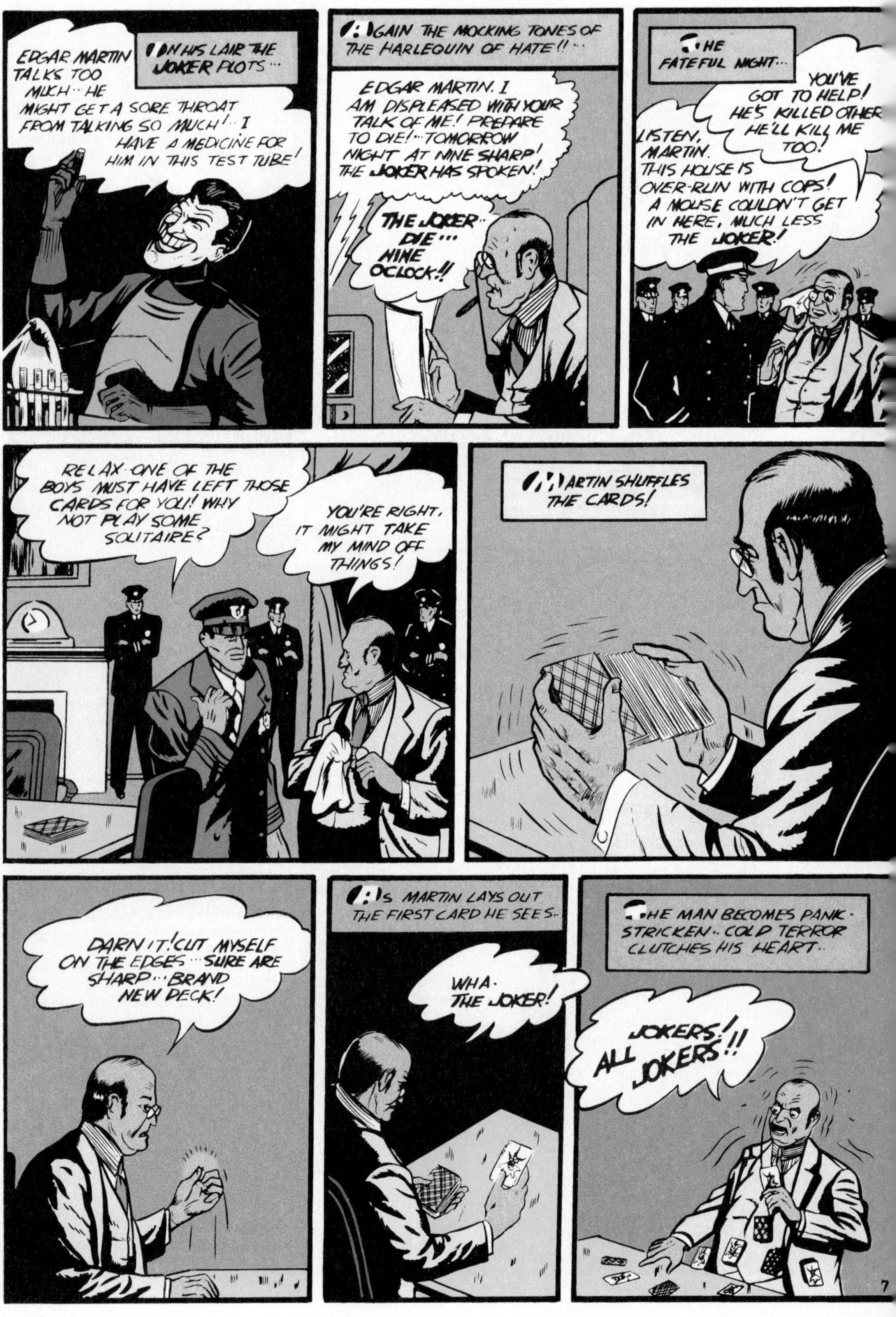
IN HIS LAIR THE JOKER PLOTS...
EDGAR MARTIN TALKS TOO MUCH... HE MIGHT GET A SORE THROAT FROM TALKING SO MUCH!.. I HAVE A MEDICINE FOR HIM IN THIS TEST TUBE!
AGAIN THE MOCKING TONES OF THE HARLEQUIN OF HATE!!...
EDGAR MARTIN, I AM DISPLEASED WITH YOUR TALK OF ME! PREPARE TO DIE!...TOMORROW NIGHT AT NINE SHARP! THE JOKER HAS SPOKEN!
THE JOKER.. DIE... NINE OCLOCK!!
THE FATEFUL NIGHT...
YOU'VE GOT TO HELP! HE'S KILLED OTHER HE'LL KILL ME TOO!
LISTEN, MARTIN. THIS HOUSE IS OVER-RUN WITH COPS! A MOUSE COULDN'T GET IN HERE, MUCH LESS THE JOKER!
RELAX. ONE OF THE BOYS MUST HAVE LEFT THOSE CARDS FOR YOU! WHY NOT PLAY SOME SOLITAIRE?
YOU'RE RIGHT, IT MIGHT TAKE MY MIND OFF THINGS!
MARTIN SHUFFLES THE CARDS!
DARN IT! CUT MYSELF ON THE EDGES... SURE ARE SHARP... BRAND NEW DECK!
AS MARTIN LAYS OUT THE FIRST CARD HE SEES..
WHA. THE JOKER!
THE MAN BECOMES PANIC-STRICKEN.. COLD TERROR CLUTCHES HIS HEART..
JOKERS! ALL JOKERS!!
7

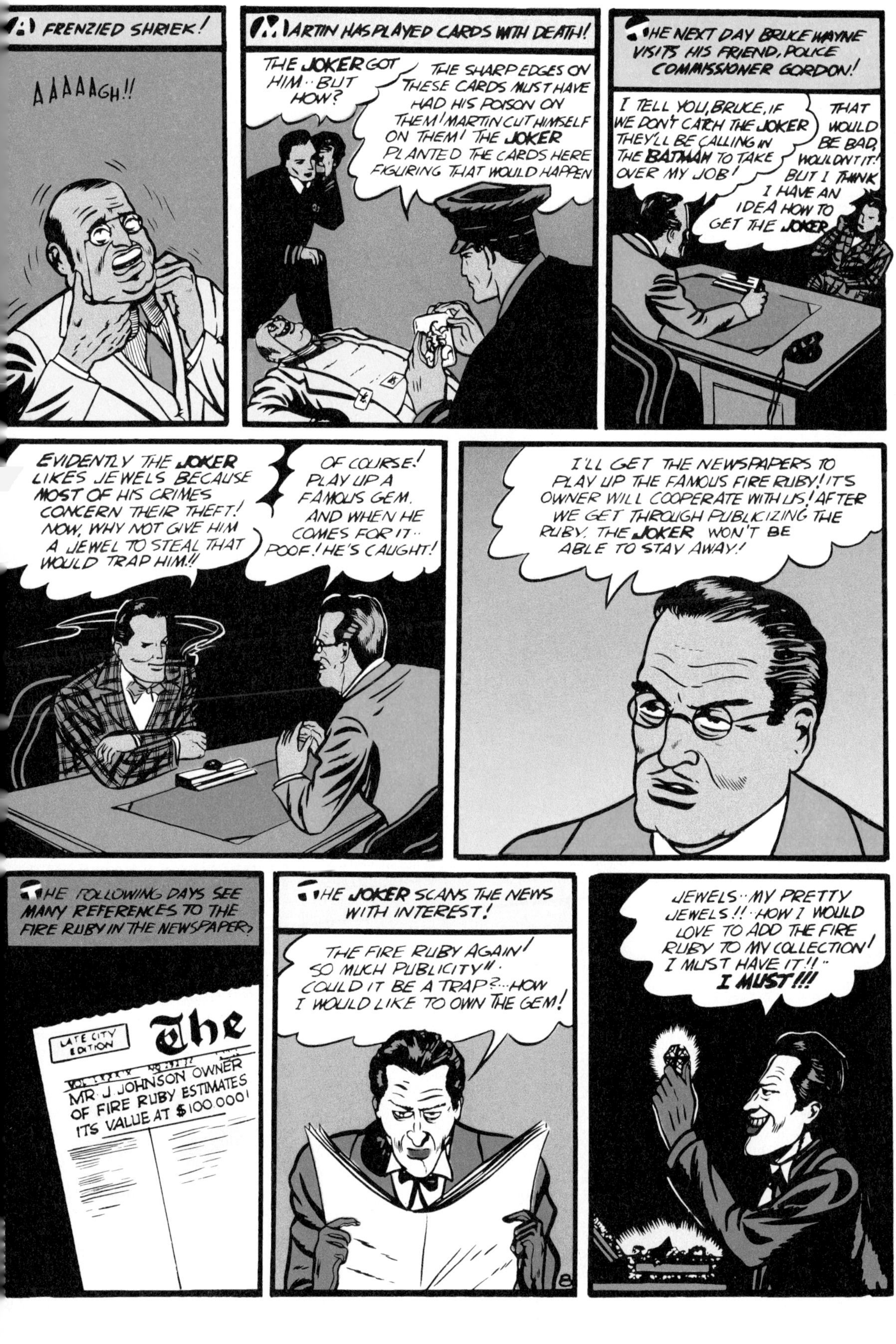
A FRENZIED SHRIEK!
AAAAAGH!!
MARTIN HAS PLAYED CARDS WITH DEATH!
THE JOKER GOT HIM.. BUT HOW?
THE SHARP EDGES ON THESE CARDS MUST HAVE HAD HIS POISON ON THEM! MARTIN CUT HIMSELF ON THEM! THE JOKER PLANTED THE CARDS HERE FIGURING THAT WOULD HAPPEN
THE NEXT DAY BRUCE WAYNE VISITS HIS FRIEND, POLICE COMMISSIONER GORDON!
I TELL YOU, BRUCE, IF WE DON'T CATCH THE JOKER THEY'LL BE CALLING IN THE BATMAN TO TAKE OVER MY JOB!
THAT WOULD BE BAD, WOULDN'T IT! BUT I THINK I HAVE AN IDEA HOW TO GET THE JOKER
EVIDENTLY THE JOKER LIKES JEWELS BECAUSE MOST OF HIS CRIMES CONCERN THEIR THEFT! NOW, WHY NOT GIVE HIM A JEWEL TO STEAL THAT WOULD TRAP HIM!!
OF COURSE! PLAY UP A FAMOUS GEM. AND WHEN HE COMES FOR IT.. POOF! HE'S CAUGHT!
I'LL GET THE NEWSPAPERS TO PLAY UP THE FAMOUS FIRE RUBY! IT'S OWNER WILL COOPERATE WITH US! AFTER WE GET THROUGH PUBLICIZING THE RUBY, THE JOKER WON'T BE ABLE TO STAY AWAY!
THE FOLLOWING DAYS SEE MANY REFERENCES TO THE FIRE RUBY IN THE NEWSPAPERS
LATE CITY EDITION
The
MR. J. JOHNSON OWNER OF FIRE RUBY ESTIMATES ITS VALUE AT $100,000!
THE JOKER SCANS THE NEWS WITH INTEREST!
THE FIRE RUBY AGAIN! SO MUCH PUBLICITY!.. COULD IT BE A TRAP?...HOW I WOULD LIKE TO OWN THE GEM!
JEWELS.. MY PRETTY JEWELS!!.. HOW I WOULD LOVE TO ADD THE FIRE RUBY TO MY COLLECTION! I MUST HAVE IT!!.. I MUST!!!
8

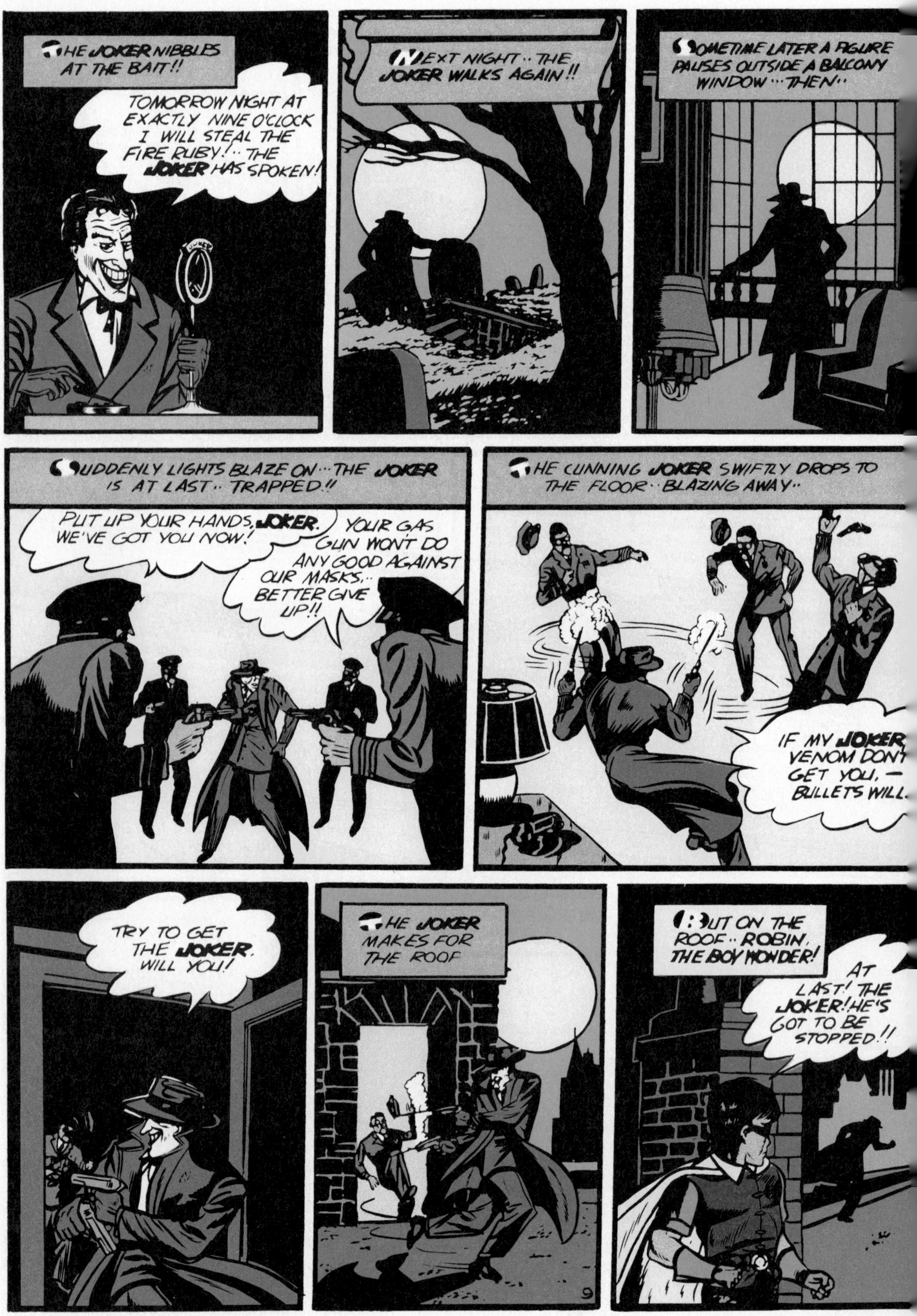
THE JOKER NIBBLES AT THE BAIT!!
TOMORROW NIGHT AT EXACTLY NINE O'CLOCK I WILL STEAL THE FIRE RUBY!.. THE JOKER HAS SPOKEN!
NEXT NIGHT .. THE JOKER WALKS AGAIN!!
SOMETIME LATER A FIGURE PAUSES OUTSIDE A BALCONY WINDOW ... THEN ..
SUDDENLY LIGHTS BLAZE ON .. THE JOKER IS AT LAST .. TRAPPED!!
PUT UP YOUR HANDS, JOKER. WE'VE GOT YOU NOW!
YOUR GAS GUN WON'T DO ANY GOOD AGAINST OUR MASKS.. BETTER GIVE UP!!
THE CUNNING JOKER SWIFTLY DROPS TO THE FLOOR .. BLAZING AWAY ..
IF MY JOKER VENOM DON'T GET YOU, - BULLETS WILL.
TRY TO GET THE JOKER, WILL YOU!
THE JOKER MAKES FOR THE ROOF
BUT ON THE ROOF .. ROBIN, THE BOY WONDER!
AT LAST! THE JOKER! HE'S GOT TO BE STOPPED!!
9

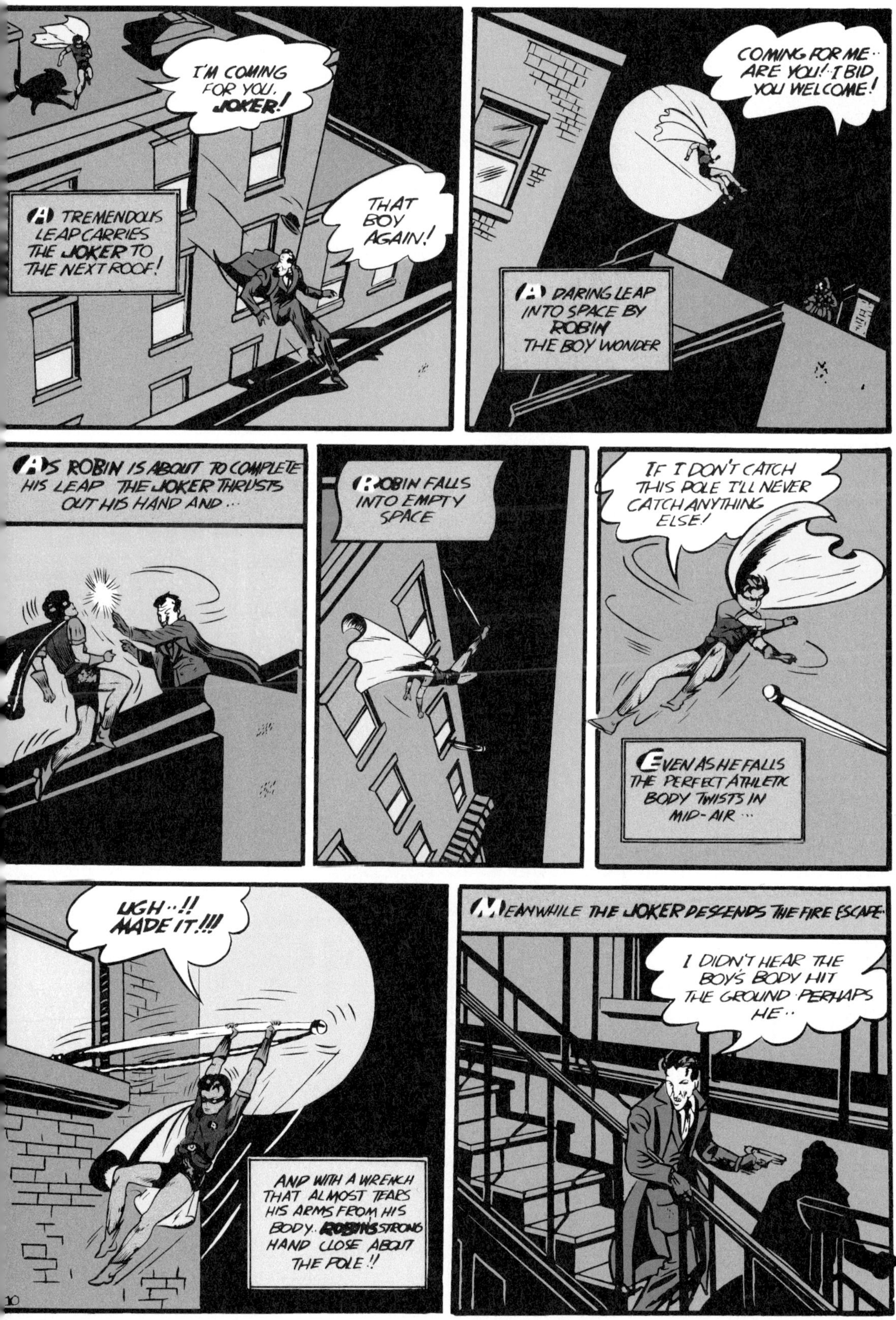
I'M COMING FOR YOU, JOKER!
A TREMENDOUS LEAP CARRIES THE JOKER TO THE NEXT ROOF!
THAT BOY AGAIN!
COMING FOR ME.. ARE YOU!..I BID YOU WELCOME!
A DARING LEAP INTO SPACE BY ROBIN THE BOY WONDER
AS ROBIN IS ABOUT TO COMPLETE HIS LEAP THE JOKER THRUSTS OUT HIS HAND AND...
ROBIN FALLS INTO EMPTY SPACE
IF I DON'T CATCH THIS POLE I'LL NEVER CATCH ANYTHING ELSE!
EVEN AS HE FALLS THE PERFECT ATHLETIC BODY TWISTS IN MID-AIR...
UGH..!! MADE IT!!!
AND WITH A WRENCH THAT ALMOST TEARS HIS ARMS FROM HIS BODY.. ROBIN'S STRONG HAND CLOSE ABOUT THE POLE!!
MEANWHILE THE JOKER DESCENDS THE FIRE ESCAPE..
I DIDN'T HEAR THE BOY'S BODY HIT THE GROUND.PERHAPS HE..

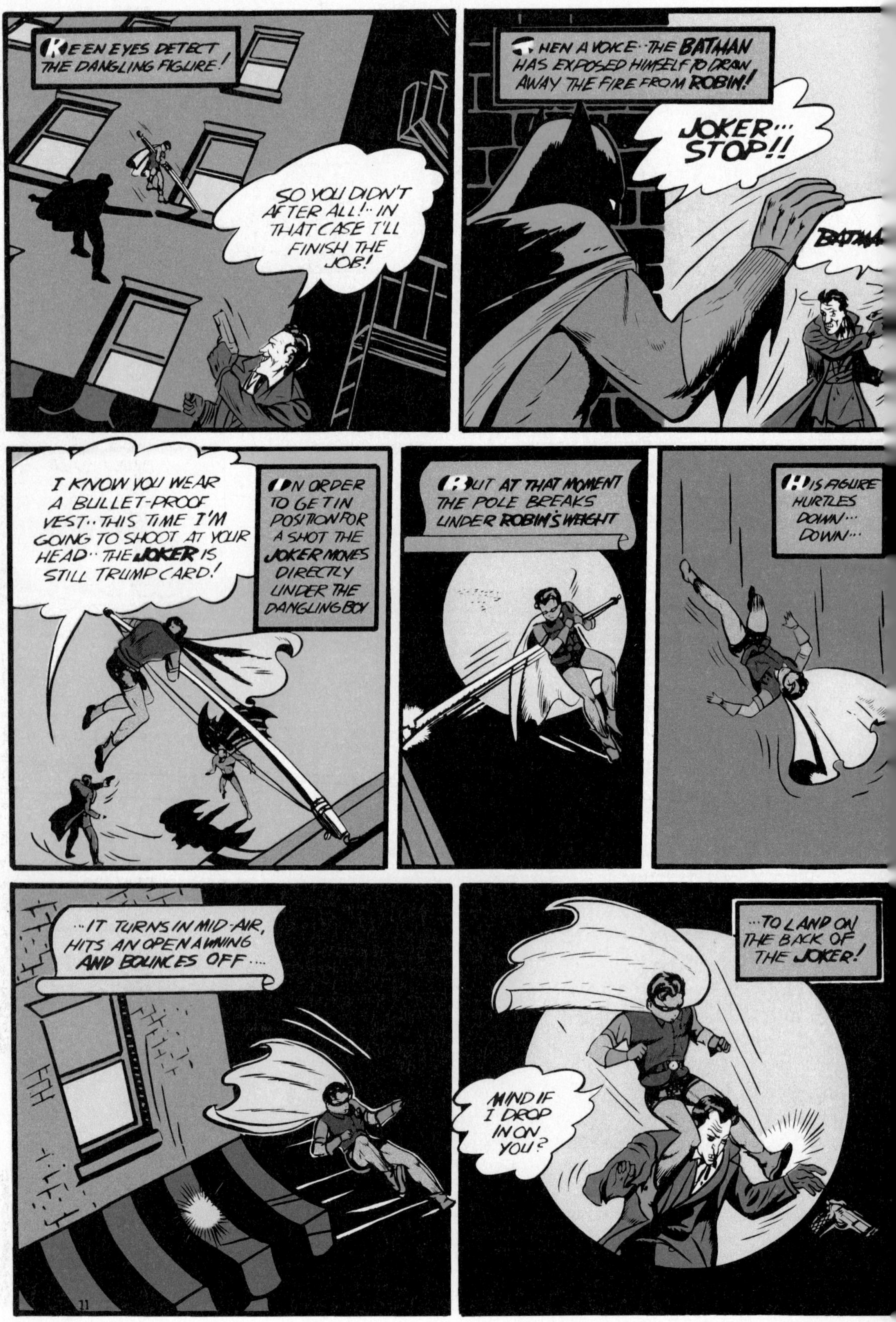
KEEN EYES DETECT THE DANGLING FIGURE!
SO YOU DIDN'T AFTER ALL!.. IN THAT CASE I'LL FINISH THE JOB!
THEN A VOICE.. THE BATMAN HAS EXPOSED HIMSELF TO DRAW AWAY THE FIRE FROM ROBIN!
JOKER... STOP!!
I KNOW YOU WEAR A BULLET-PROOF VEST.. THIS TIME I'M GOING TO SHOOT AT YOUR HEAD.. THE JOKER IS STILL TRUMP CARD!
IN ORDER TO GET IN POSITION FOR A SHOT THE JOKER MOVES DIRECTLY UNDER THE DANGLING BOY
BUT AT THAT MOMENT THE POLE BREAKS UNDER ROBIN'S WEIGHT
HIS FIGURE HURTLES DOWN... DOWN...
...IT TURNS IN MID-AIR, HITS AN OPEN AWNING AND BOUNCES OFF....
...TO LAND ON THE BACK OF THE JOKER!
MIND IF I DROP IN ON YOU?
11

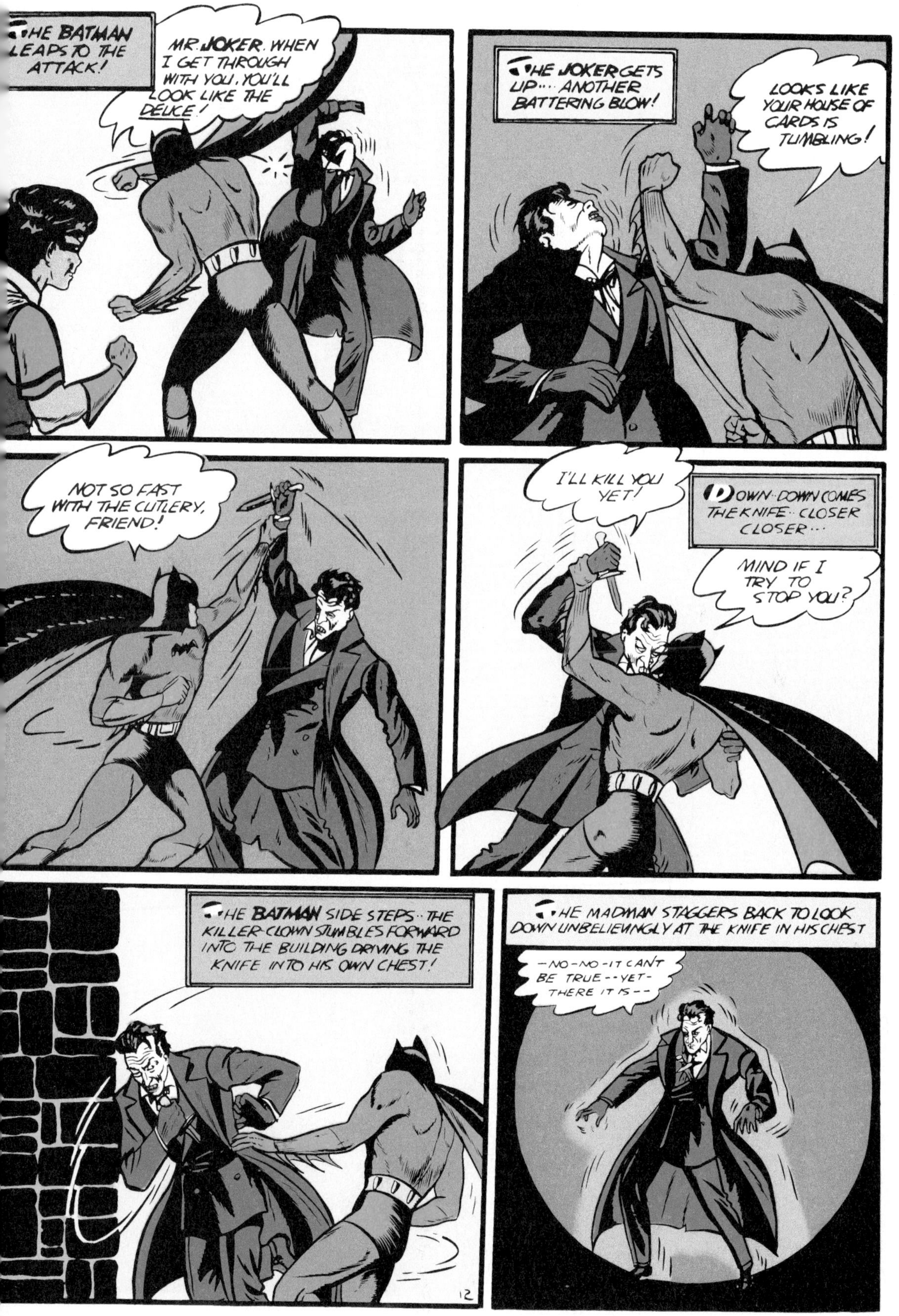
THE BATMAN LEAPS TO THE ATTACK!
MR. JOKER. WHEN I GET THROUGH WITH YOU, YOU'LL LOOK LIKE THE DEUCE!
THE JOKER GETS UP.... ANOTHER BATTERING BLOW!
LOOKS LIKE YOUR HOUSE OF CARDS IS TUMBLING!
NOT SO FAST WITH THE CUTLERY, FRIEND!
I'LL KILL YOU YET!
DOWN.. DOWN COMES THE KNIFE.. CLOSER CLOSER...
MIND IF I TRY TO STOP YOU?
THE BATMAN SIDE STEPS.. THE KILLER-CLOWN STUMBLES FORWARD INTO THE BUILDING DRIVING THE KNIFE INTO HIS OWN CHEST!
12
THE MADMAN STAGGERS BACK TO LOOK DOWN UNBELIEVINGLY AT THE KNIFE IN HIS CHEST
-NO-NO-IT CAN'T BE TRUE--YET-THERE IT IS--

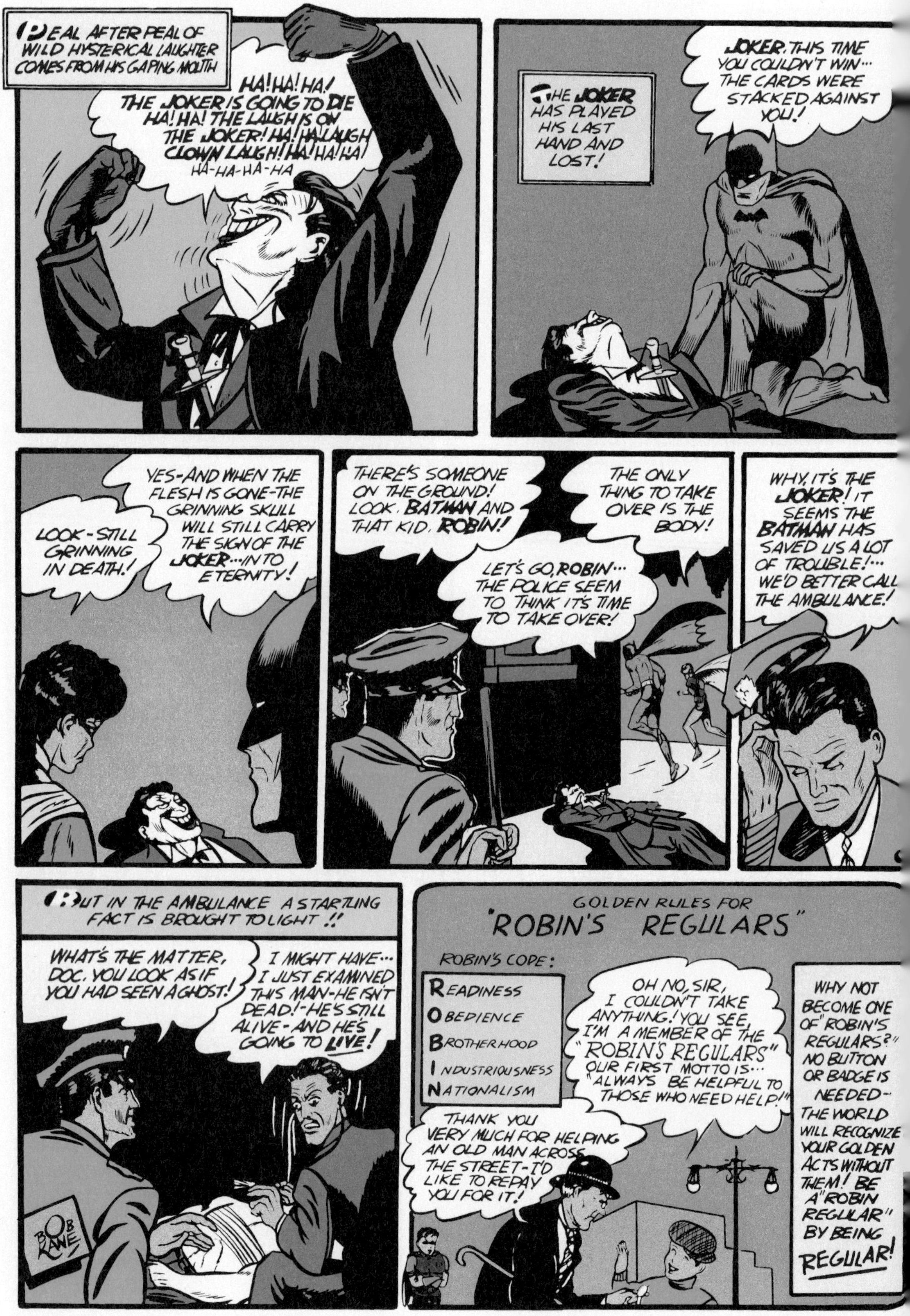
PEAL AFTER PEAL OF WILD HYSTERICAL LAUGHTER COMES FROM HIS GAPING MOUTH
HA! HA! HA! THE JOKER IS GOING TO DIE HA! HA! THE LAUGH IS ON THE JOKER! HA! HA! LAUGH CLOWN LAUGH! HA! HA! HA! HA-HA-HA-HA
THE JOKER HAS PLAYED HIS LAST HAND AND LOST!
JOKER, THIS TIME YOU COULDN'T WIN... THE CARDS WERE STACKED AGAINST YOU!
LOOK - STILL GRINNING IN DEATH!
YES-AND WHEN THE FLESH IS GONE-THE GRINNING SKULL WILL STILL CARRY THE SIGN OF THE JOKER...INTO ETERNITY!
THERE'S SOMEONE ON THE GROUND! LOOK, BATMAN AND THAT KID, ROBIN!
THE ONLY THING TO TAKE OVER IS THE BODY!
LET'S GO, ROBIN... THE POLICE SEEM TO THINK IT'S TIME TO TAKE OVER!
WHY, IT'S THE JOKER! IT SEEMS THE BATMAN HAS SAVED US A LOT OF TROUBLE!... WE'D BETTER CALL THE AMBULANCE!
BUT IN THE AMBULANCE A STARTLING FACT IS BROUGHT TO LIGHT!!
WHAT'S THE MATTER, DOC, YOU LOOK AS IF YOU HAD SEEN A GHOST!
I MIGHT HAVE... I JUST EXAMINED THIS MAN-HE ISN'T DEAD!-HE'S STILL ALIVE-AND HE'S GOING TO LIVE!
BOB KANE
GOLDEN RULES FOR "ROBIN'S REGULARS"
ROBIN'S CODE:
READINESS
OBEDIENCE
BROTHERHOOD
INDUSTRIOUSNESS
NATIONALISM
THANK YOU VERY MUCH FOR HELPING AN OLD MAN ACROSS THE STREET-I'D LIKE TO REPAY YOU FOR IT!
OH NO, SIR, I COULDN'T TAKE ANYTHING! YOU SEE, I'M A MEMBER OF THE "ROBIN'S REGULARS" OUR FIRST MOTTO IS... "ALWAYS BE HELPFUL TO THOSE WHO NEED HELP!"
WHY NOT BECOME ONE OF "ROBIN'S REGULARS?" NO BUTTON OR BADGE IS NEEDED- THE WORLD WILL RECOGNIZE YOUR GOLDEN ACTS WITHOUT THEM! BE A "ROBIN REGULAR" BY BEING REGULAR!

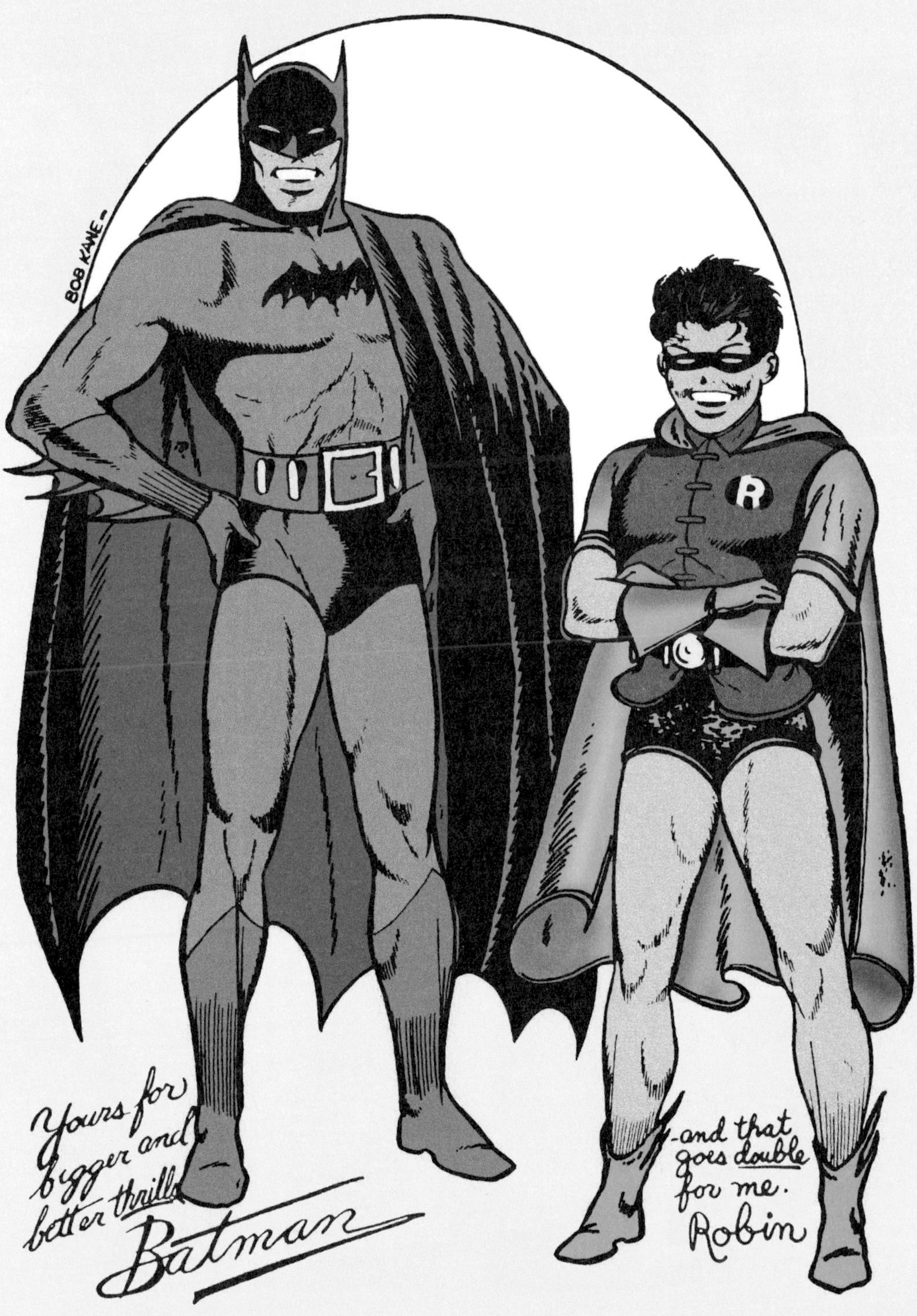
BOB KANE
Yours for bigger and better thrills
Batman
-and that goes double for me.
Robin

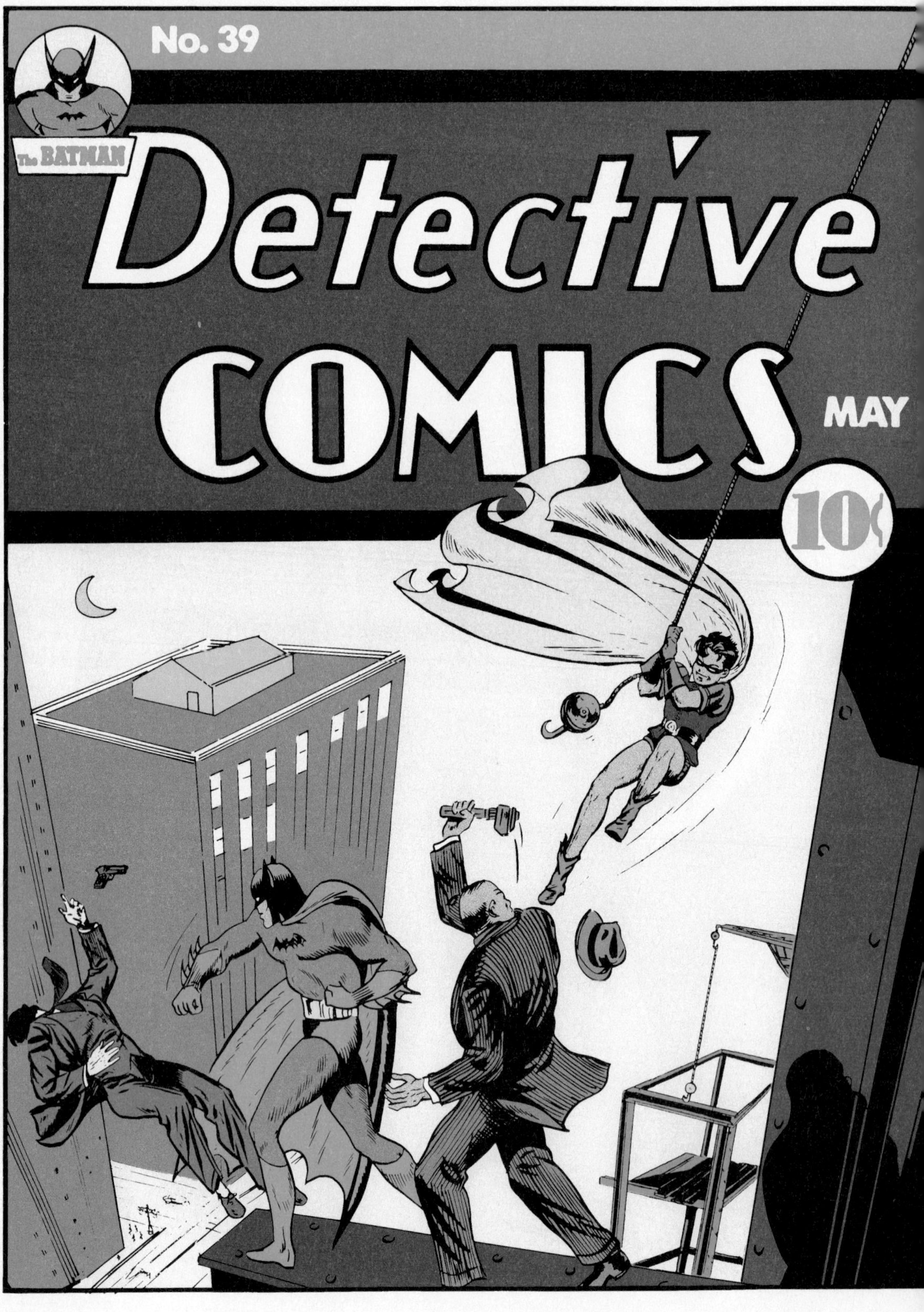
No. 39
The BATMAN
Detective
COMICS
MAY
10¢

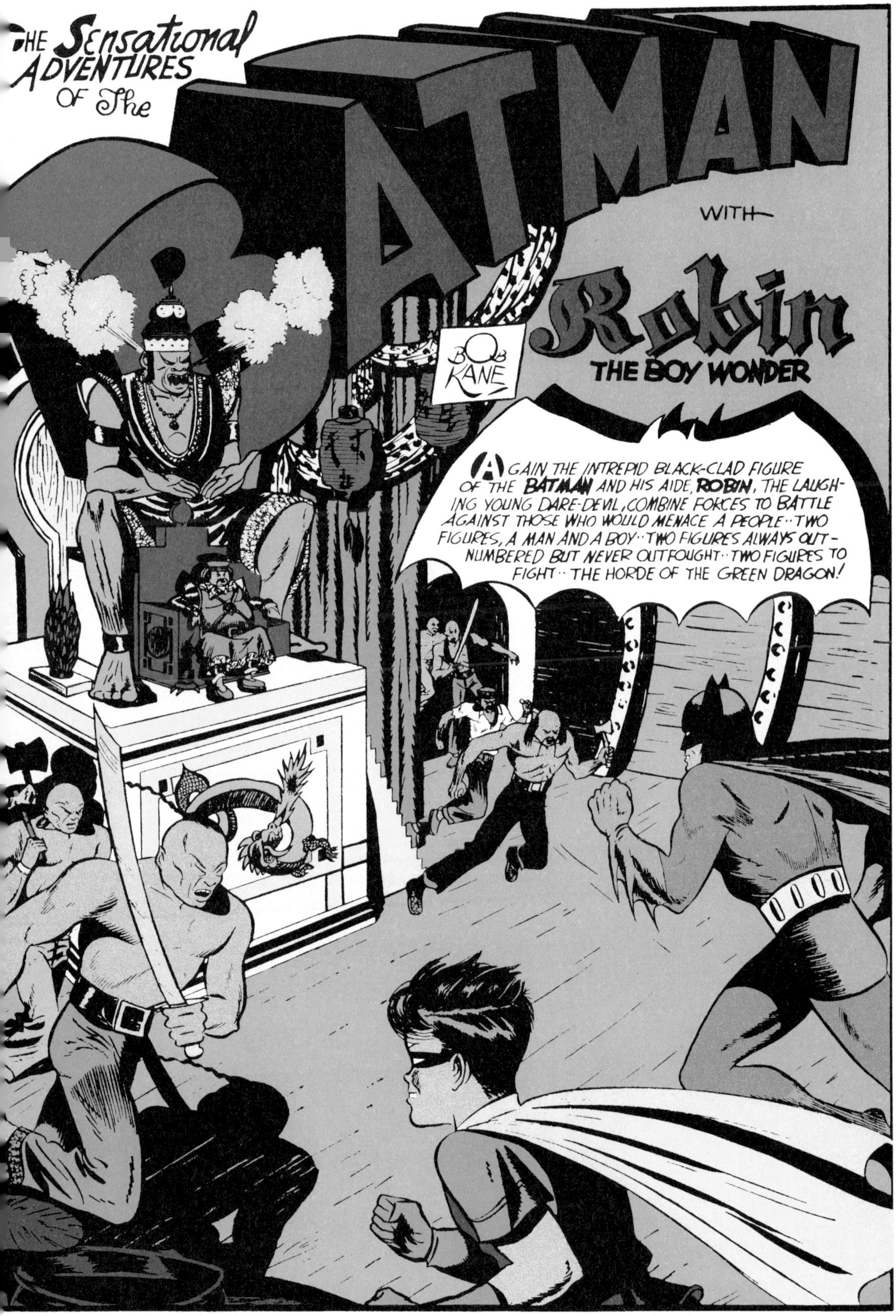
The Sensational Adventures of The
BATMAN
with
Robin
THE BOY WONDER
BOB KANE
AGAIN THE INTREPID BLACK-CLAD FIGURE OF THE BATMAN AND HIS AIDE, ROBIN, THE LAUGHING YOUNG DARE-DEVIL, COMBINE FORCES TO BATTLE AGAINST THOSE WHO WOULD MENACE A PEOPLE.. TWO FIGURES, A MAN AND A BOY.. TWO FIGURES ALWAYS OUT-NUMBERED BUT NEVER OUTFOUGHT.. TWO FIGURES TO FIGHT.. THE HORDE OF THE GREEN DRAGON!

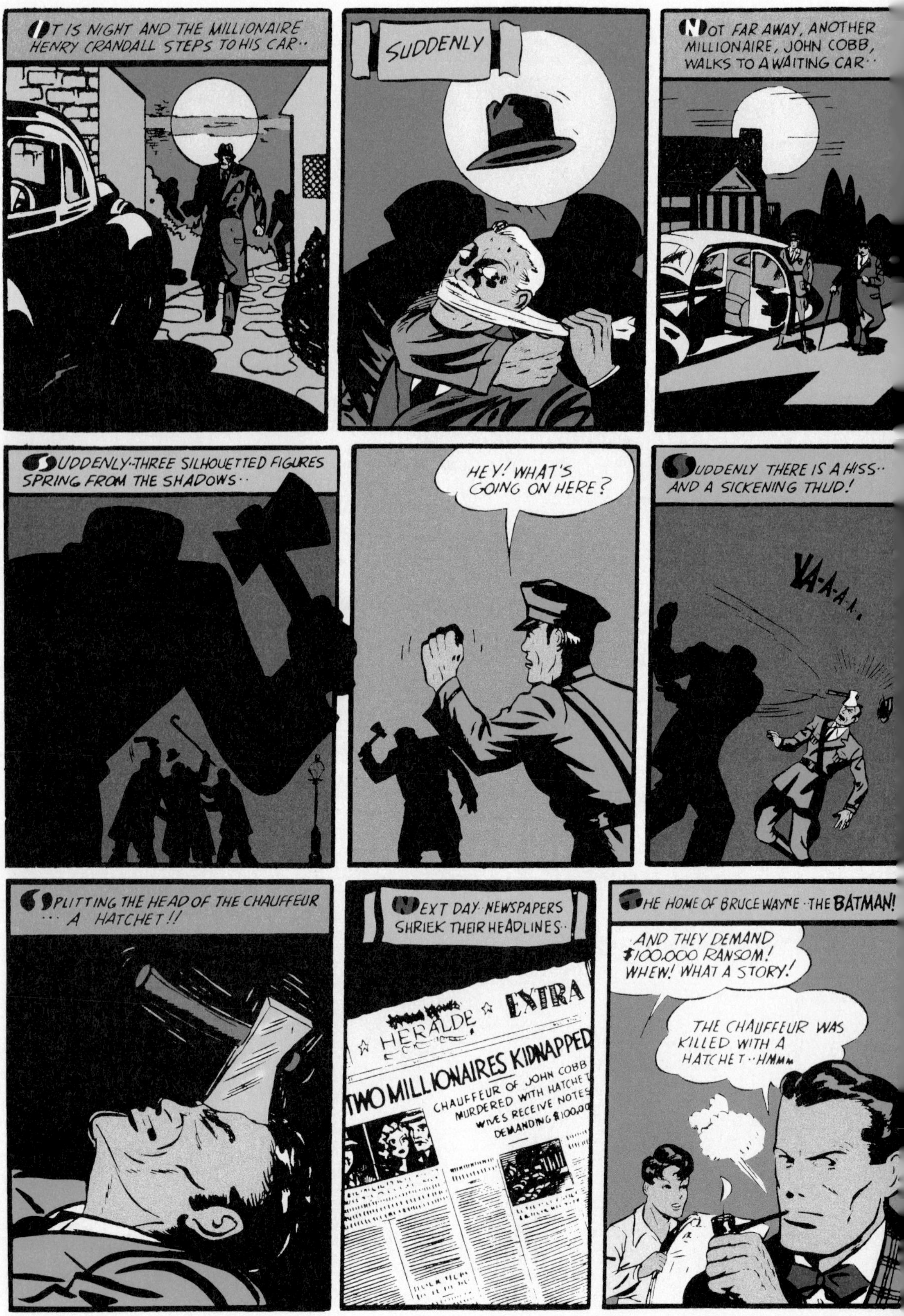
IT IS NIGHT AND THE MILLIONAIRE HENRY CRANDALL STEPS TO HIS CAR··
SUDDENLY
NOT FAR AWAY, ANOTHER MILLIONAIRE, JOHN COBB, WALKS TO A WAITING CAR··
SUDDENLY··THREE SILHOUETTED FIGURES SPRING FROM THE SHADOWS··
HEY! WHAT'S GOING ON HERE?
SUDDENLY THERE IS A HISS·· AND A SICKENING THUD!
YA-A-A-A.
SPLITTING THE HEAD OF THE CHAUFFEUR ··· A HATCHET!!
NEXT DAY NEWSPAPERS SHRIEK THEIR HEADLINES··
HERALDE ☆ EXTRA
TWO MILLIONAIRES KIDNAPPED
CHAUFFEUR OF JOHN COBB MURDERED WITH HATCHET
WIVES RECEIVE NOTES DEMANDING $100,00
THE HOME OF BRUCE WAYNE ·THE BATMAN!
AND THEY DEMAND $100,000 RANSOM! WHEW! WHAT A STORY!
THE CHAUFFEUR WAS KILLED WITH A HATCHET··HMMM

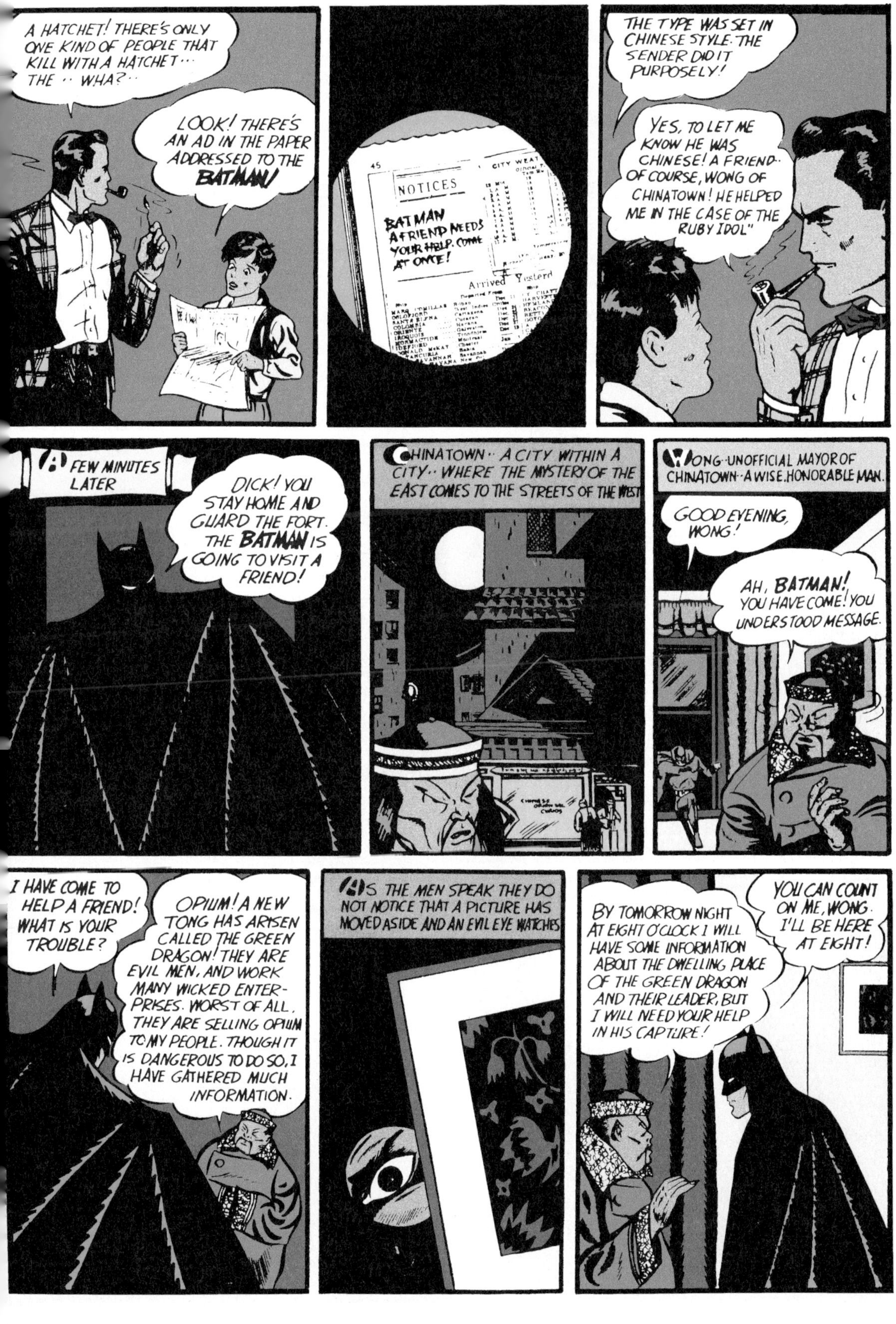

A HATCHET! THERE'S ONLY ONE KIND OF PEOPLE THAT KILL WITH A HATCHET... THE .. WHA?..
LOOK! THERE'S AN AD IN THE PAPER ADDRESSED TO THE BATMAN!
NOTICES
BATMAN A FRIEND NEEDS YOUR HELP. COME AT ONCE!
Arrived Yesterd
THE TYPE WAS SET IN CHINESE STYLE. THE SENDER DID IT PURPOSELY!
YES, TO LET ME KNOW HE WAS CHINESE! A FRIEND.. OF COURSE, WONG OF CHINATOWN! HE HELPED ME IN THE CASE OF THE RUBY IDOL"
A FEW MINUTES LATER
DICK! YOU STAY HOME AND GUARD THE FORT. THE BATMAN IS GOING TO VISIT A FRIEND!
CHINATOWN.. A CITY WITHIN A CITY.. WHERE THE MYSTERY OF THE EAST COMES TO THE STREETS OF THE WEST
WONG.. UNOFFICIAL MAYOR OF CHINATOWN.. A WISE, HONORABLE MAN.
GOOD EVENING, WONG!
AH, BATMAN! YOU HAVE COME! YOU UNDERSTOOD MESSAGE.
I HAVE COME TO HELP A FRIEND! WHAT IS YOUR TROUBLE?
OPIUM! A NEW TONG HAS ARISEN CALLED THE GREEN DRAGON! THEY ARE EVIL MEN, AND WORK MANY WICKED ENTER-PRISES. WORST OF ALL, THEY ARE SELLING OPIUM TO MY PEOPLE. THOUGH IT IS DANGEROUS TO DO SO, I HAVE GATHERED MUCH INFORMATION.
AS THE MEN SPEAK THEY DO NOT NOTICE THAT A PICTURE HAS MOVED ASIDE AND AN EVIL EYE WATCHES
BY TOMORROW NIGHT AT EIGHT O'CLOCK I WILL HAVE SOME INFORMATION ABOUT THE DWELLING PLACE OF THE GREEN DRAGON AND THEIR LEADER, BUT I WILL NEED YOUR HELP IN HIS CAPTURE!
YOU CAN COUNT ON ME, WONG. I'LL BE HERE AT EIGHT!

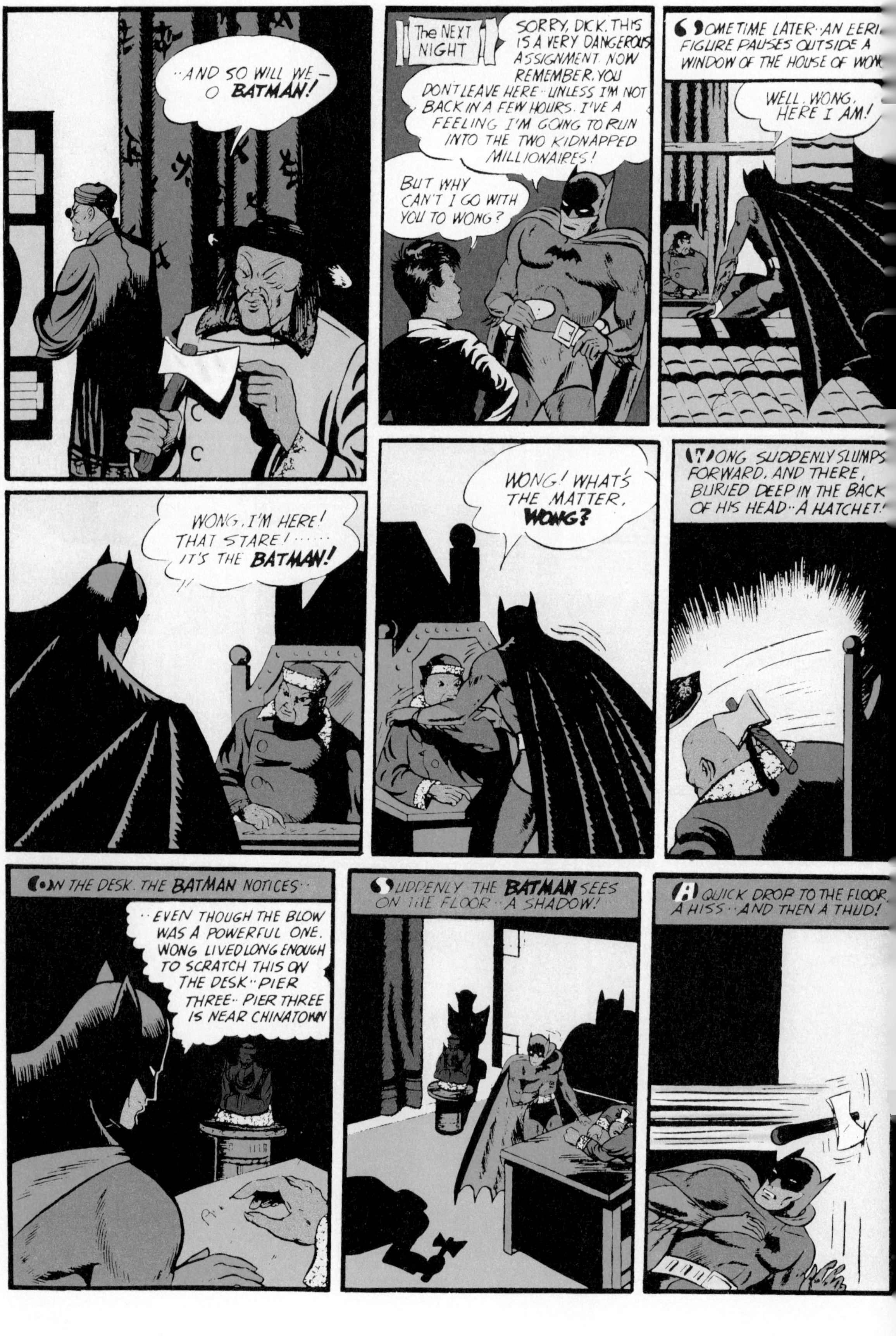
..AND SO WILL WE— O BATMAN!
The NEXT NIGHT
SORRY, DICK. THIS IS A VERY DANGEROUS ASSIGNMENT. NOW REMEMBER, YOU DON'T LEAVE HERE.. UNLESS I'M NOT BACK IN A FEW HOURS. I'VE A FEELING I'M GOING TO RUN INTO THE TWO KIDNAPPED MILLIONAIRES!
BUT WHY CAN'T I GO WITH YOU TO WONG?
SOMETIME LATER..AN EERIE FIGURE PAUSES OUTSIDE A WINDOW OF THE HOUSE OF WONG
WELL, WONG, HERE I AM!
WONG, I'M HERE! THAT STARE!...... IT'S THE BATMAN!
WONG! WHAT'S THE MATTER, WONG?
WONG SUDDENLY SLUMPS FORWARD, AND THERE, BURIED DEEP IN THE BACK OF HIS HEAD..A HATCHET!
ON THE DESK THE BATMAN NOTICES..
..EVEN THOUGH THE BLOW WAS A POWERFUL ONE, WONG LIVED LONG ENOUGH TO SCRATCH THIS ON THE DESK..PIER THREE.. PIER THREE IS NEAR CHINATOWN
SUDDENLY THE BATMAN SEES ON THE FLOOR..A SHADOW!
A QUICK DROP TO THE FLOOR, A HISS..AND THEN A THUD!

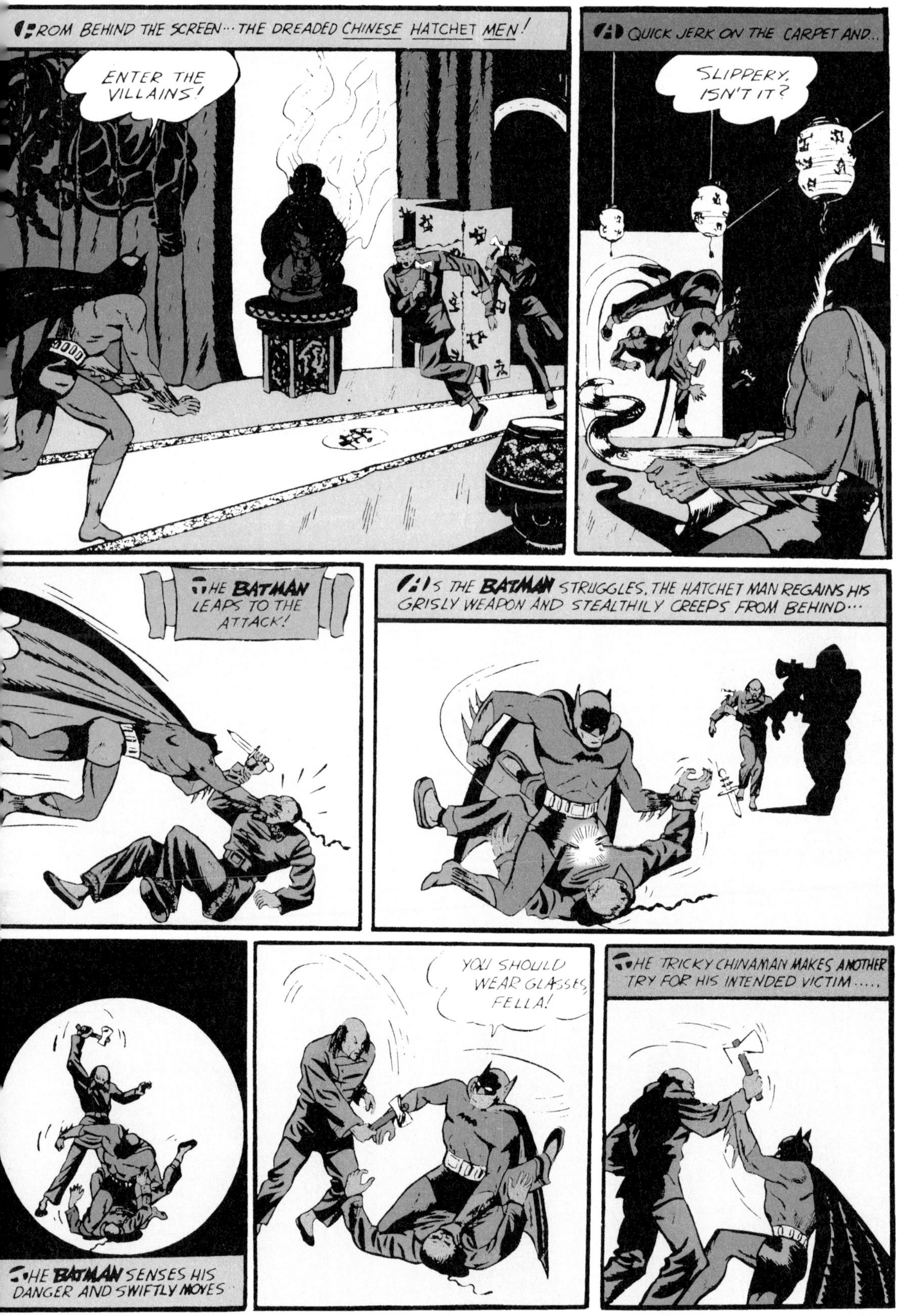
FROM BEHIND THE SCREEN... THE DREADED CHINESE HATCHET MEN!
ENTER THE VILLAINS!
A QUICK JERK ON THE CARPET AND...
SLIPPERY, ISN'T IT?
THE BATMAN LEAPS TO THE ATTACK!
AS THE BATMAN STRUGGLES, THE HATCHET MAN REGAINS HIS GRISLY WEAPON AND STEALTHILY CREEPS FROM BEHIND...
THE BATMAN SENSES HIS DANGER AND SWIFTLY MOVES
YOU SHOULD WEAR GLASSES, FELLA!
THE TRICKY CHINAMAN MAKES ANOTHER TRY FOR HIS INTENDED VICTIM.....

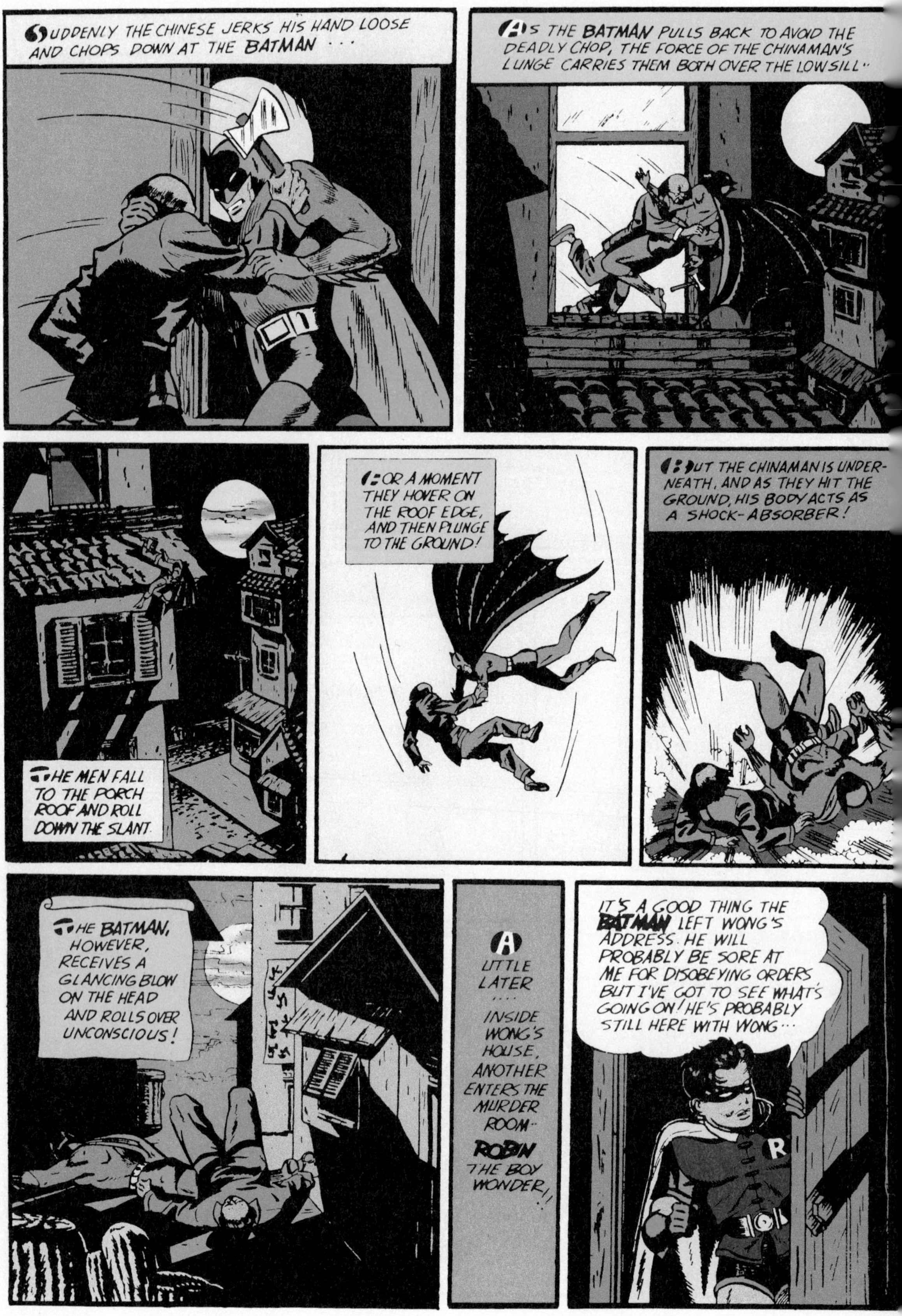
SUDDENLY THE CHINESE JERKS HIS HAND LOOSE AND CHOPS DOWN AT THE BATMAN . . .
AS THE BATMAN PULLS BACK TO AVOID THE DEADLY CHOP, THE FORCE OF THE CHINAMAN'S LUNGE CARRIES THEM BOTH OVER THE LOW SILL ..
THE MEN FALL TO THE PORCH ROOF AND ROLL DOWN THE SLANT.
FOR A MOMENT THEY HOVER ON THE ROOF EDGE, AND THEN PLUNGE TO THE GROUND!
BUT THE CHINAMAN IS UNDERNEATH, AND AS THEY HIT THE GROUND, HIS BODY ACTS AS A SHOCK-ABSORBER!
THE BATMAN, HOWEVER, RECEIVES A GLANCING BLOW ON THE HEAD AND ROLLS OVER UNCONSCIOUS!
A LITTLE LATER .... INSIDE WONG'S HOUSE, ANOTHER ENTERS THE MURDER ROOM-- ROBIN THE BOY WONDER!!
IT'S A GOOD THING THE BATMAN LEFT WONG'S ADDRESS. HE WILL PROBABLY BE SORE AT ME FOR DISOBEYING ORDERS BUT I'VE GOT TO SEE WHAT'S GOING ON! HE'S PROBABLY STILL HERE WITH WONG ...

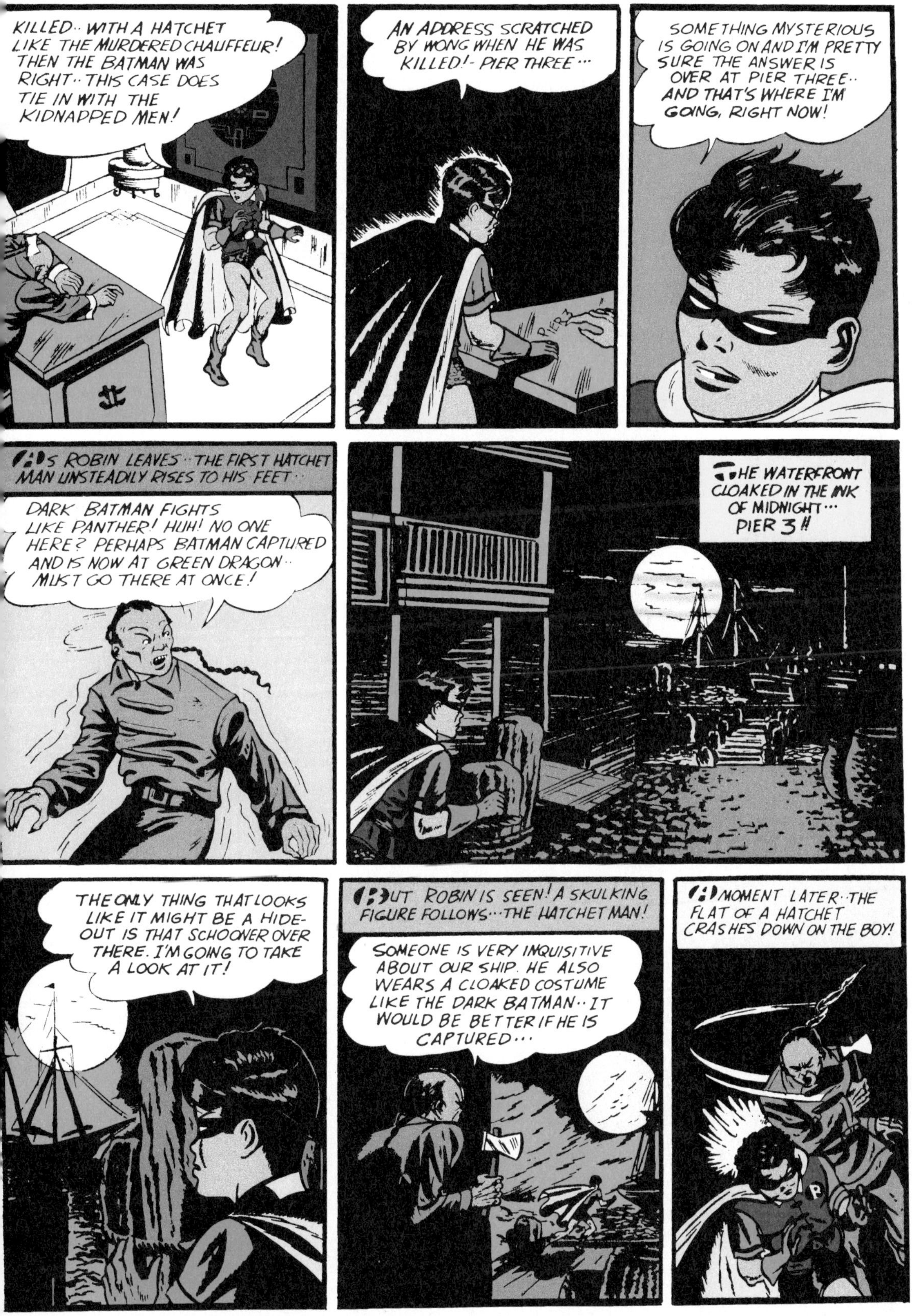
KILLED.. WITH A HATCHET LIKE THE MURDERED CHAUFFEUR! THEN THE BATMAN WAS RIGHT.. THIS CASE DOES TIE IN WITH THE KIDNAPPED MEN!
AN ADDRESS SCRATCHED BY WONG WHEN HE WAS KILLED!- PIER THREE...
PIER 3
SOMETHING MYSTERIOUS IS GOING ON AND I'M PRETTY SURE THE ANSWER IS OVER AT PIER THREE.. AND THAT'S WHERE I'M GOING, RIGHT NOW!
AS ROBIN LEAVES.. THE FIRST HATCHET MAN UNSTEADILY RISES TO HIS FEET..
DARK BATMAN FIGHTS LIKE PANTHER! HUH! NO ONE HERE? PERHAPS BATMAN CAPTURED AND IS NOW AT GREEN DRAGON.. MUST GO THERE AT ONCE!
THE WATERFRONT CLOAKED IN THE INK OF MIDNIGHT... PIER 3!!
THE ONLY THING THAT LOOKS LIKE IT MIGHT BE A HIDE-OUT IS THAT SCHOONER OVER THERE. I'M GOING TO TAKE A LOOK AT IT!
BUT ROBIN IS SEEN! A SKULKING FIGURE FOLLOWS.. THE HATCHET MAN!
SOMEONE IS VERY INQUISITIVE ABOUT OUR SHIP. HE ALSO WEARS A CLOAKED COSTUME LIKE THE DARK BATMAN.. IT WOULD BE BETTER IF HE IS CAPTURED...
A MOMENT LATER.. THE FLAT OF A HATCHET CRASHES DOWN ON THE BOY!

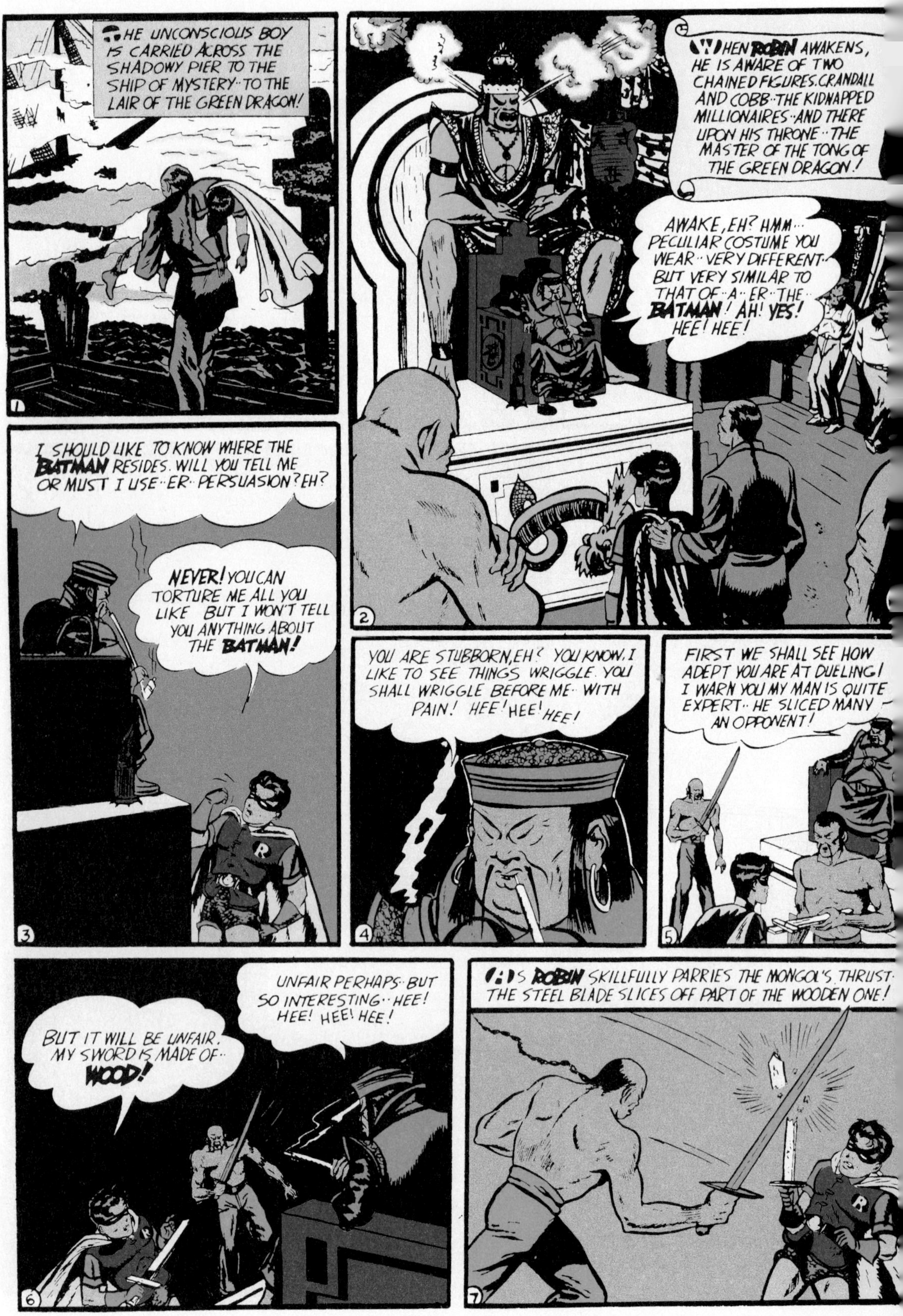
THE UNCONSCIOUS BOY IS CARRIED ACROSS THE SHADOWY PIER TO THE SHIP OF MYSTERY··TO THE LAIR OF THE GREEN DRAGON!
WHEN ROBIN AWAKENS, HE IS AWARE OF TWO CHAINED FIGURES. CRANDALL AND COBB··THE KIDNAPPED MILLIONAIRES··AND THERE UPON HIS THRONE··THE MASTER OF THE TONG OF THE GREEN DRAGON!
AWAKE, EH? HMM... PECULIAR COSTUME YOU WEAR··VERY DIFFERENT·· BUT VERY SIMILAR TO THAT OF··A··ER··THE·· BATMAN! AH! YES! HEE! HEE!
I SHOULD LIKE TO KNOW WHERE THE BATMAN RESIDES. WILL YOU TELL ME OR MUST I USE··ER··PERSUASION? EH?
NEVER! YOU CAN TORTURE ME ALL YOU LIKE BUT I WON'T TELL YOU ANYTHING ABOUT THE BATMAN!
YOU ARE STUBBORN, EH? YOU KNOW, I LIKE TO SEE THINGS WRIGGLE. YOU SHALL WRIGGLE BEFORE ME·· WITH PAIN! HEE! HEE! HEE!
FIRST WE SHALL SEE HOW ADEPT YOU ARE AT DUELING! I WARN YOU MY MAN IS QUITE EXPERT·· HE SLICED MANY AN OPPONENT!
BUT IT WILL BE UNFAIR. MY SWORD IS MADE OF·· WOOD!
UNFAIR PERHAPS··BUT SO INTERESTING··HEE! HEE! HEE! HEE!
AS ROBIN SKILLFULLY PARRIES THE MONGOL'S THRUST· THE STEEL BLADE SLICES OFF PART OF THE WOODEN ONE!

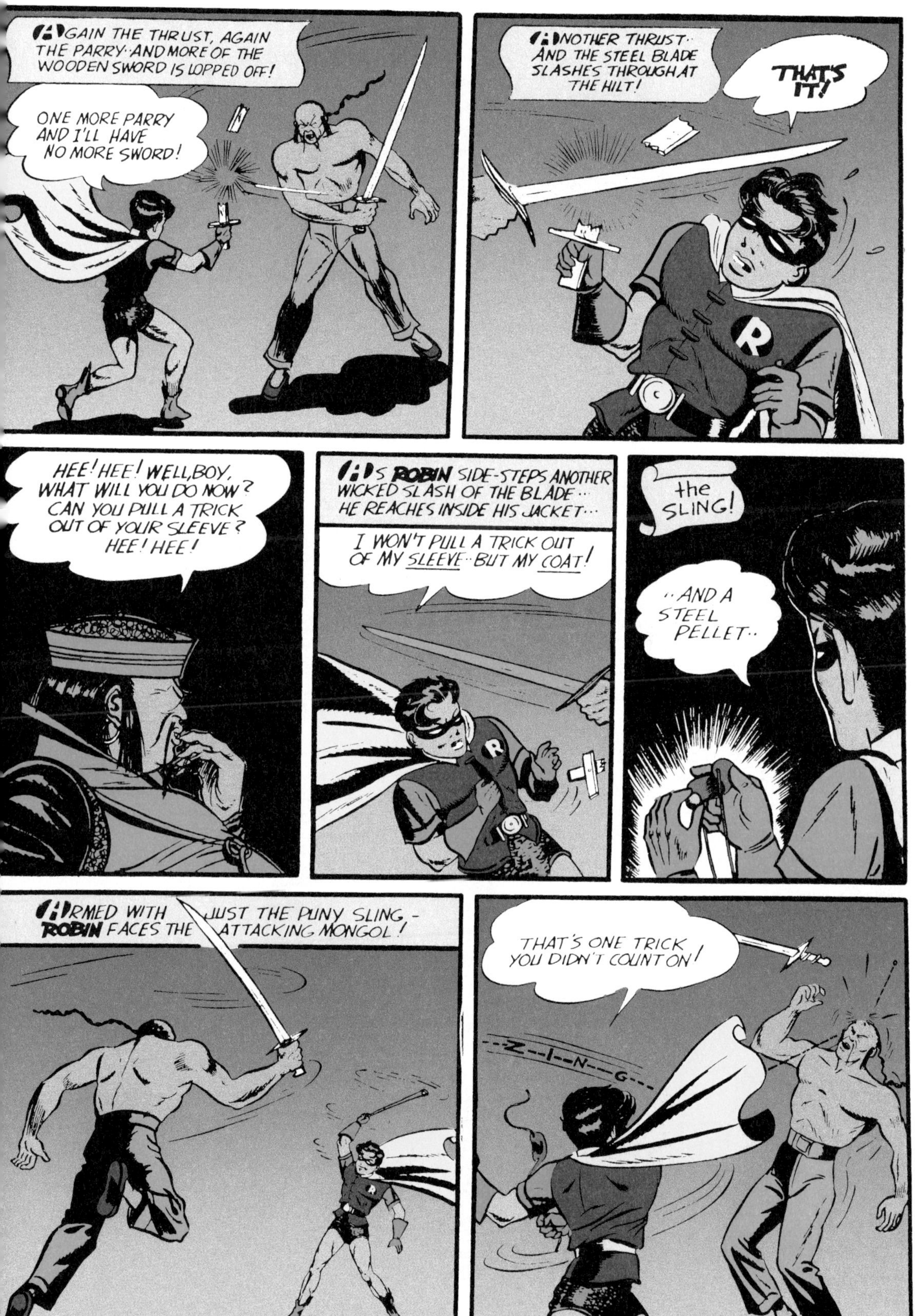
AGAIN THE THRUST, AGAIN THE PARRY· AND MORE OF THE WOODEN SWORD IS LOPPED OFF!
ONE MORE PARRY AND I'LL HAVE NO MORE SWORD!
ANOTHER THRUST·· AND THE STEEL BLADE SLASHES THROUGH AT THE HILT!
THAT'S IT!
HEE! HEE! WELL, BOY, WHAT WILL YOU DO NOW? CAN YOU PULL A TRICK OUT OF YOUR SLEEVE? HEE! HEE!
AS ROBIN SIDE-STEPS ANOTHER WICKED SLASH OF THE BLADE·· HE REACHES INSIDE HIS JACKET··
I WON'T PULL A TRICK OUT OF MY SLEEVE·· BUT MY COAT!
the SLING!
··AND A STEEL PELLET··
ARMED WITH JUST THE PUNY SLING - ROBIN FACES THE ATTACKING MONGOL!
THAT'S ONE TRICK YOU DIDN'T COUNT ON!
--Z--I--N--G--

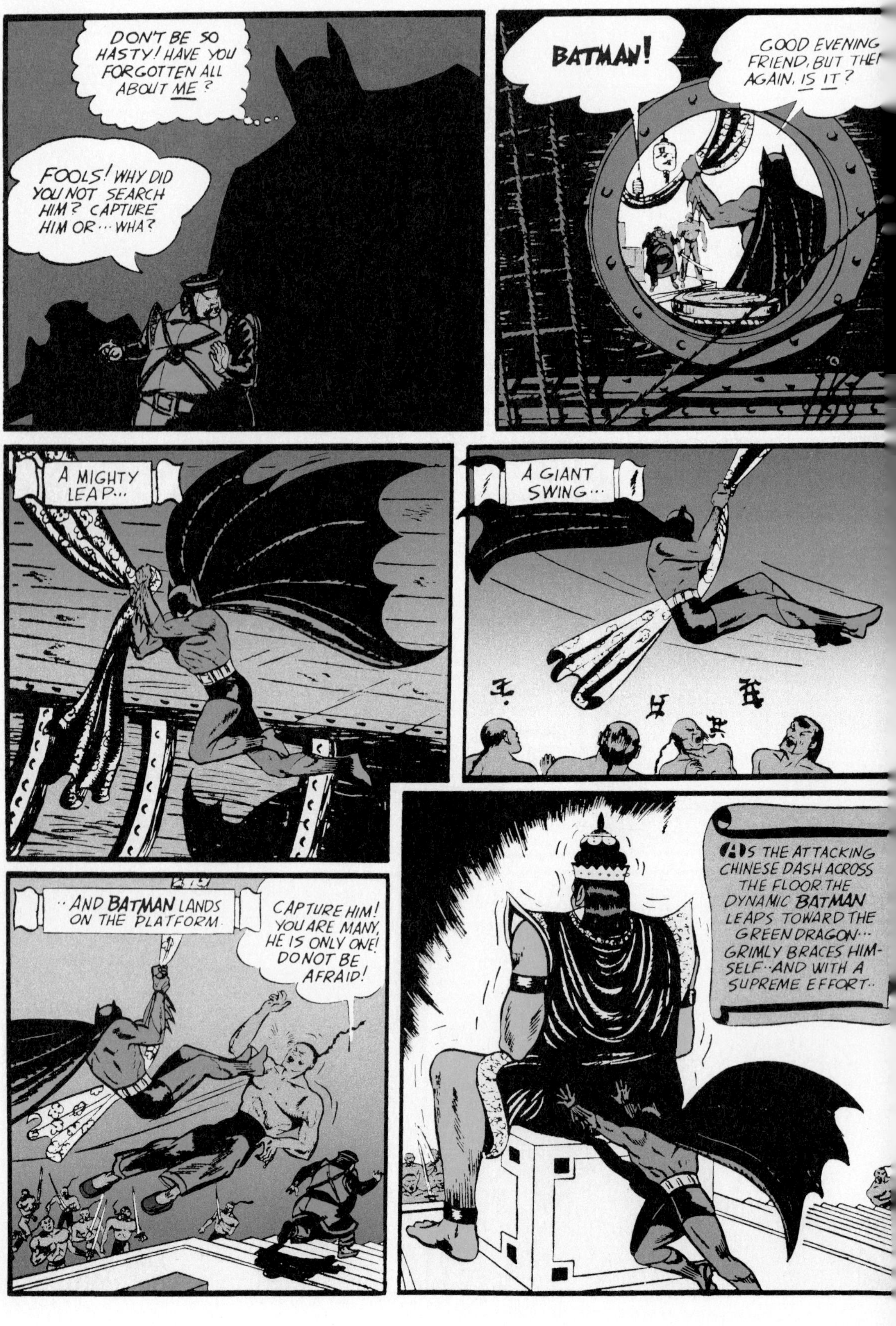
DON'T BE SO HASTY! HAVE YOU FORGOTTEN ALL ABOUT ME?
FOOLS! WHY DID YOU NOT SEARCH HIM? CAPTURE HIM OR ... WHA?
BATMAN!
GOOD EVENING FRIEND, BUT THEN AGAIN, IS IT?
A MIGHTY LEAP...
A GIANT SWING...
.. AND BATMAN LANDS ON THE PLATFORM.
CAPTURE HIM! YOU ARE MANY, HE IS ONLY ONE! DO NOT BE AFRAID!
AS THE ATTACKING CHINESE DASH ACROSS THE FLOOR THE DYNAMIC BATMAN LEAPS TOWARD THE GREEN DRAGON... GRIMLY BRACES HIMSELF.. AND WITH A SUPREME EFFORT..

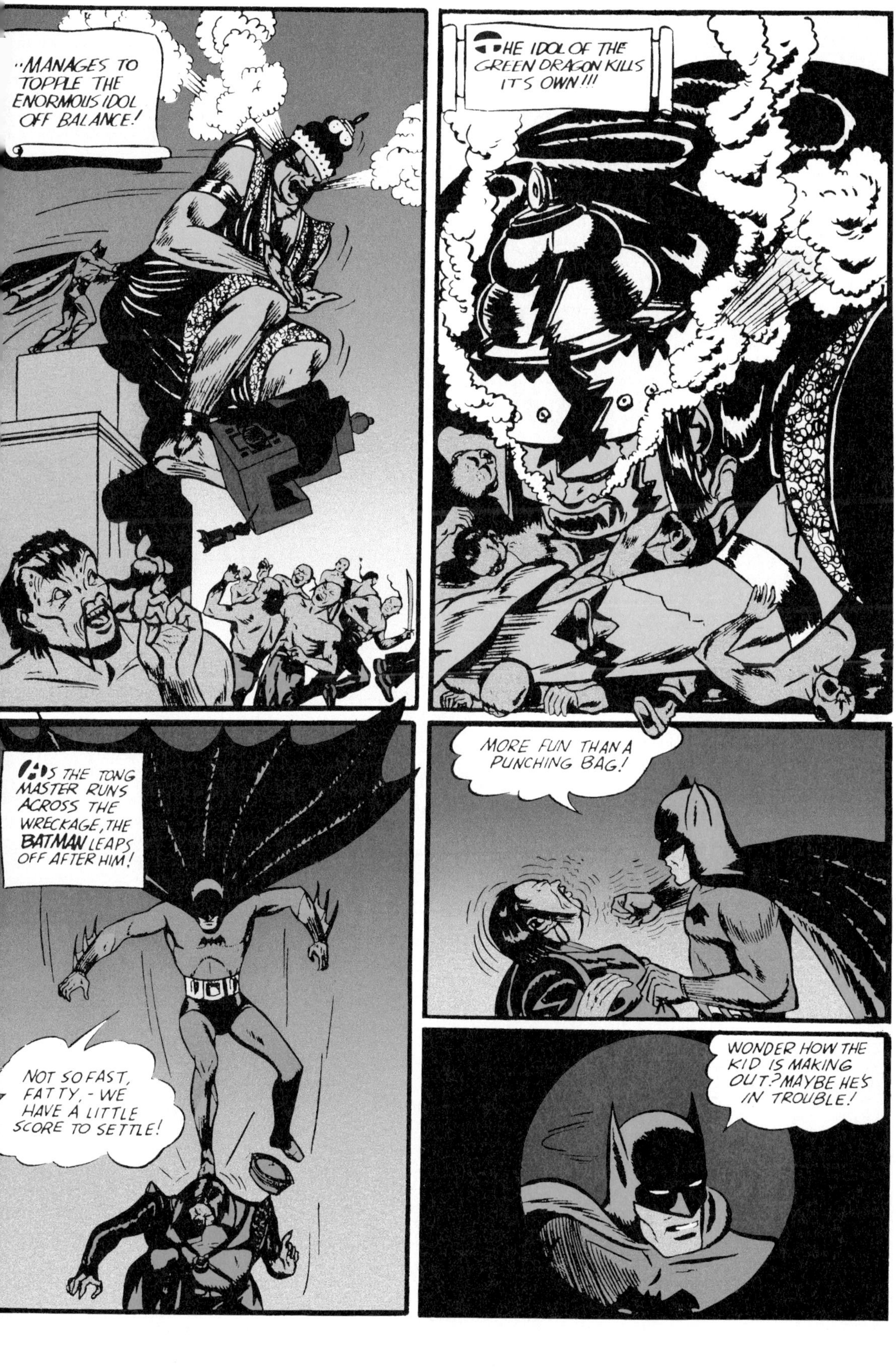
..MANAGES TO TOPPLE THE ENORMOUS IDOL OFF BALANCE!
THE IDOL OF THE GREEN DRAGON KILLS IT'S OWN!!!
AS THE TONG MASTER RUNS ACROSS THE WRECKAGE, THE BATMAN LEAPS OFF AFTER HIM!
NOT SO FAST, FATTY, - WE HAVE A LITTLE SCORE TO SETTLE!
MORE FUN THAN A PUNCHING BAG!
WONDER HOW THE KID IS MAKING OUT? MAYBE HE'S IN TROUBLE!

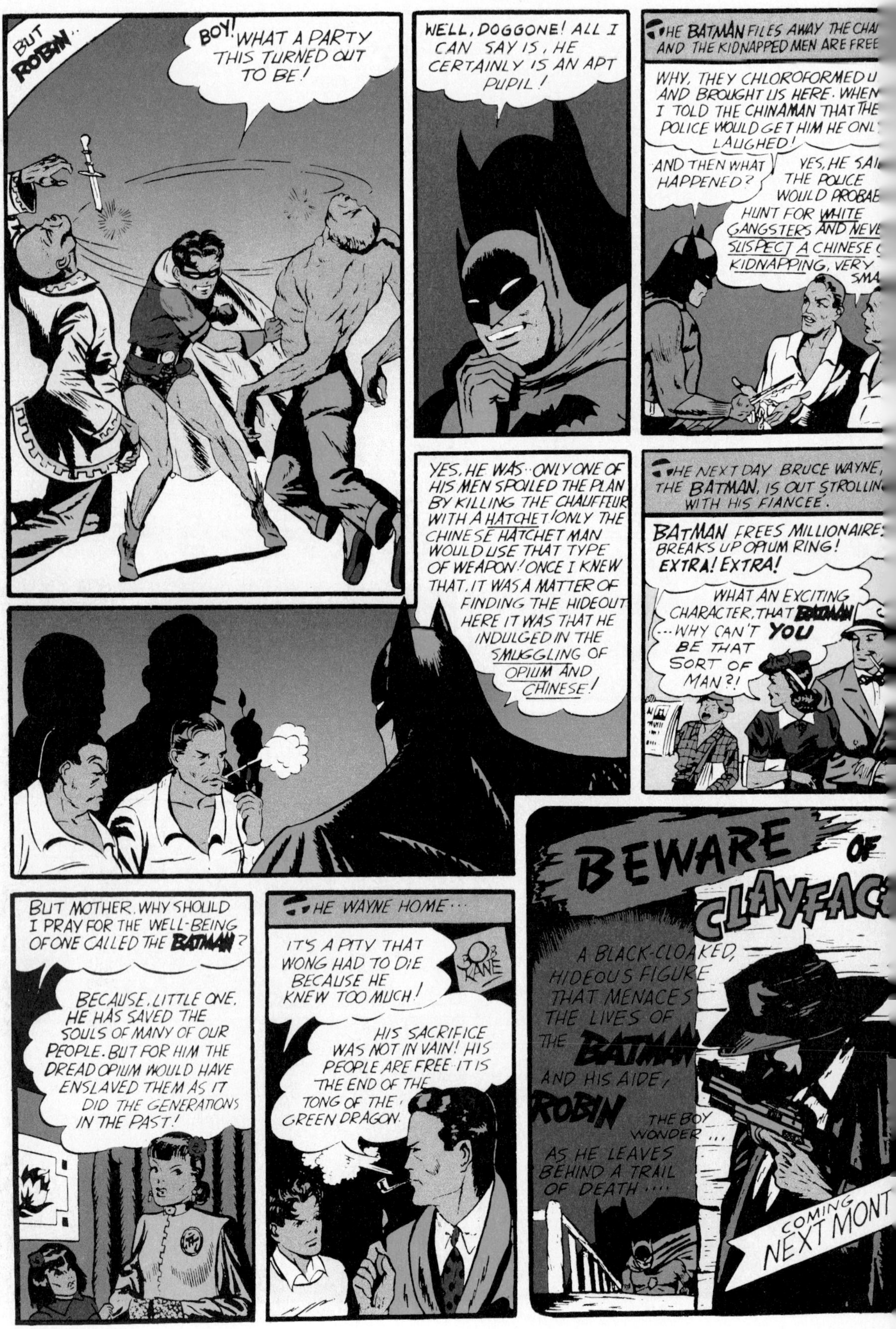

BUT ROBIN..
BOY! WHAT A PARTY THIS TURNED OUT TO BE!
WELL, DOGGONE! ALL I CAN SAY IS, HE CERTAINLY IS AN APT PUPIL!
THE BATMAN FILES AWAY THE CHA AND THE KIDNAPPED MEN ARE FREE
WHY, THEY CHLOROFORMED U AND BROUGHT US HERE. WHEN I TOLD THE CHINAMAN THAT THE POLICE WOULD GET HIM HE ONL LAUGHED!
AND THEN WHAT HAPPENED?
YES, HE SAI THE POLICE WOULD PROBAB HUNT FOR WHITE GANGSTERS AND NEVE SUSPECT A CHINESE KIDNAPPING, VERY SMA
YES, HE WAS.. ONLY ONE OF HIS MEN SPOILED THE PLAN BY KILLING THE CHAUFFEUR WITH A HATCHET! ONLY THE CHINESE HATCHET MAN WOULD USE THAT TYPE OF WEAPON! ONCE I KNEW THAT, IT WAS A MATTER OF FINDING THE HIDEOUT HERE IT WAS THAT HE INDULGED IN THE SMUGGLING OF OPIUM AND CHINESE!
THE NEXT DAY BRUCE WAYNE, THE BATMAN, IS OUT STROLLIN WITH HIS FIANCEE.
BATMAN FREES MILLIONAIRES BREAKS UP OPIUM RING! EXTRA! EXTRA!
WHAT AN EXCITING CHARACTER, THAT BATMAN ... WHY CAN'T YOU BE THAT SORT OF MAN?!
BUT MOTHER, WHY SHOULD I PRAY FOR THE WELL-BEING OF ONE CALLED THE BATMAN?
BECAUSE, LITTLE ONE, HE HAS SAVED THE SOULS OF MANY OF OUR PEOPLE. BUT FOR HIM THE DREAD OPIUM WOULD HAVE ENSLAVED THEM AS IT DID THE GENERATIONS IN THE PAST!
THE WAYNE HOME...
BOB KANE
IT'S A PITY THAT WONG HAD TO DIE BECAUSE HE KNEW TOO MUCH!
HIS SACRIFICE WAS NOT IN VAIN! HIS PEOPLE ARE FREE. IT IS THE END OF THE TONG OF THE GREEN DRAGON.
BEWARE OF
A BLACK-CLOAKED, HIDEOUS FIGURE THAT MENACES THE LIVES OF THE BATMAN AND HIS AIDE, ROBIN THE BOY WONDER... AS HE LEAVES BEHIND A TRAIL OF DEATH....
COMING NEXT MONT

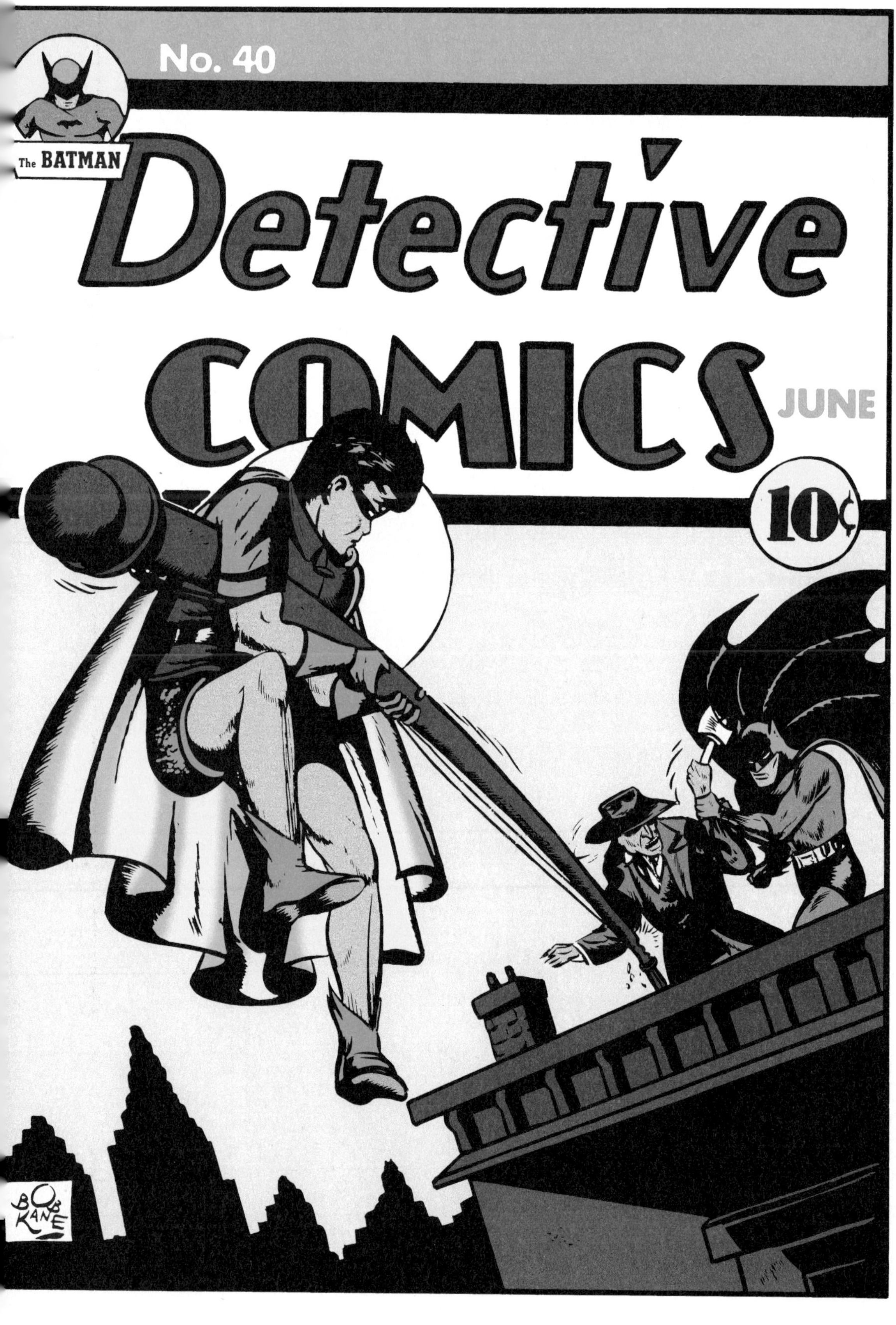
No. 40
The BATMAN
Detective
COMICS
JUNE
10¢
BOB KANE

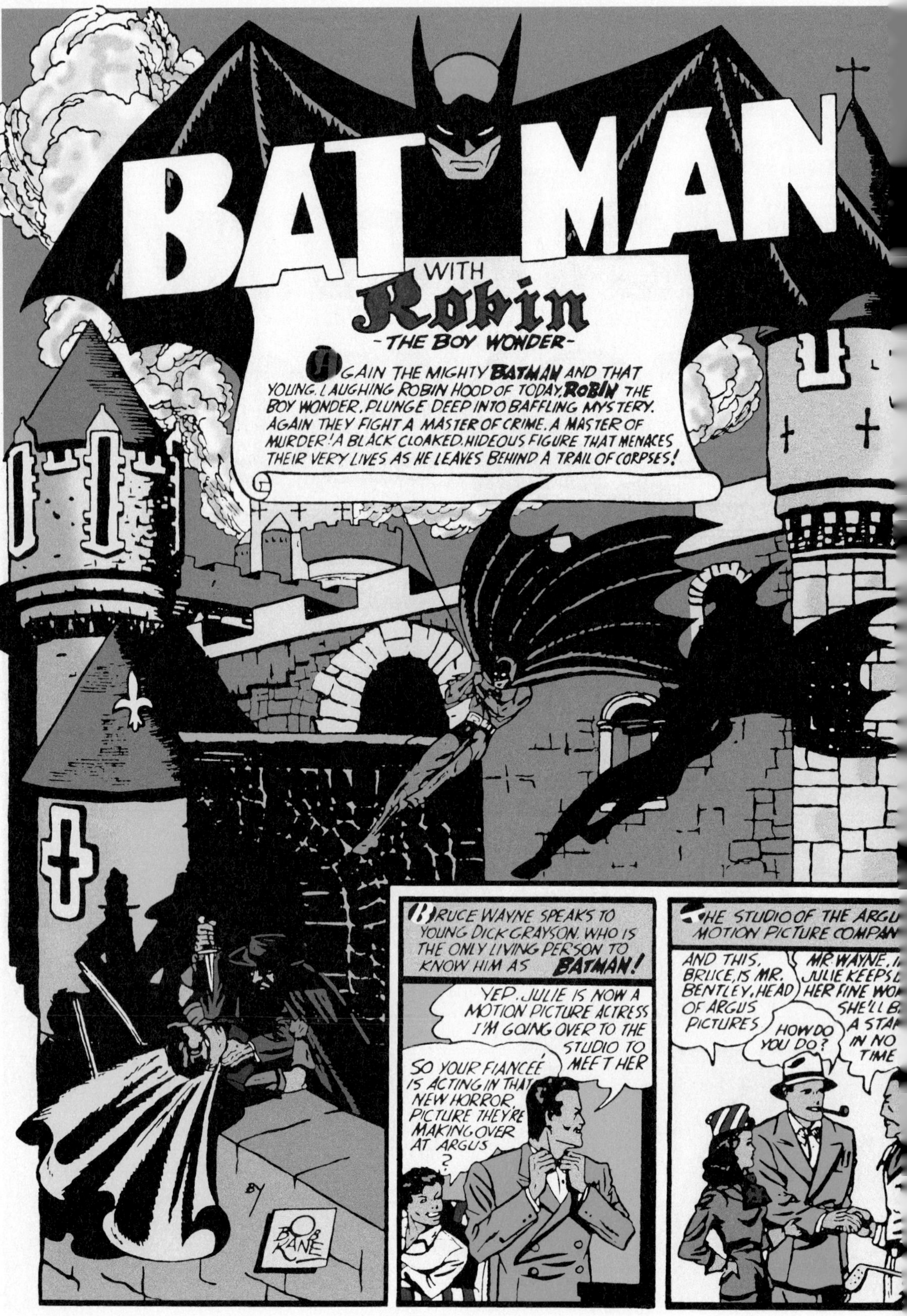
BATMAN
WITH
Robin
-THE BOY WONDER-
AGAIN THE MIGHTY BATMAN AND THAT YOUNG, LAUGHING ROBIN HOOD OF TODAY, ROBIN THE BOY WONDER, PLUNGE DEEP INTO BAFFLING MYSTERY. AGAIN THEY FIGHT A MASTER OF CRIME, A MASTER OF MURDER! A BLACK CLOAKED, HIDEOUS FIGURE THAT MENACES THEIR VERY LIVES AS HE LEAVES BEHIND A TRAIL OF CORPSES!
BY BOB KANE
BRUCE WAYNE SPEAKS TO YOUNG DICK GRAYSON, WHO IS THE ONLY LIVING PERSON TO KNOW HIM AS BATMAN!
SO YOUR FIANCÉE IS ACTING IN THAT NEW HORROR PICTURE THEY'RE MAKING OVER AT ARGUS ?
YEP, JULIE IS NOW A MOTION PICTURE ACTRESS I'M GOING OVER TO THE STUDIO TO MEET HER
THE STUDIO OF THE ARGU MOTION PICTURE COMPAN
AND THIS, BRUCE, IS MR. BENTLEY, HEAD OF ARGUS PICTURES
HOW DO YOU DO?

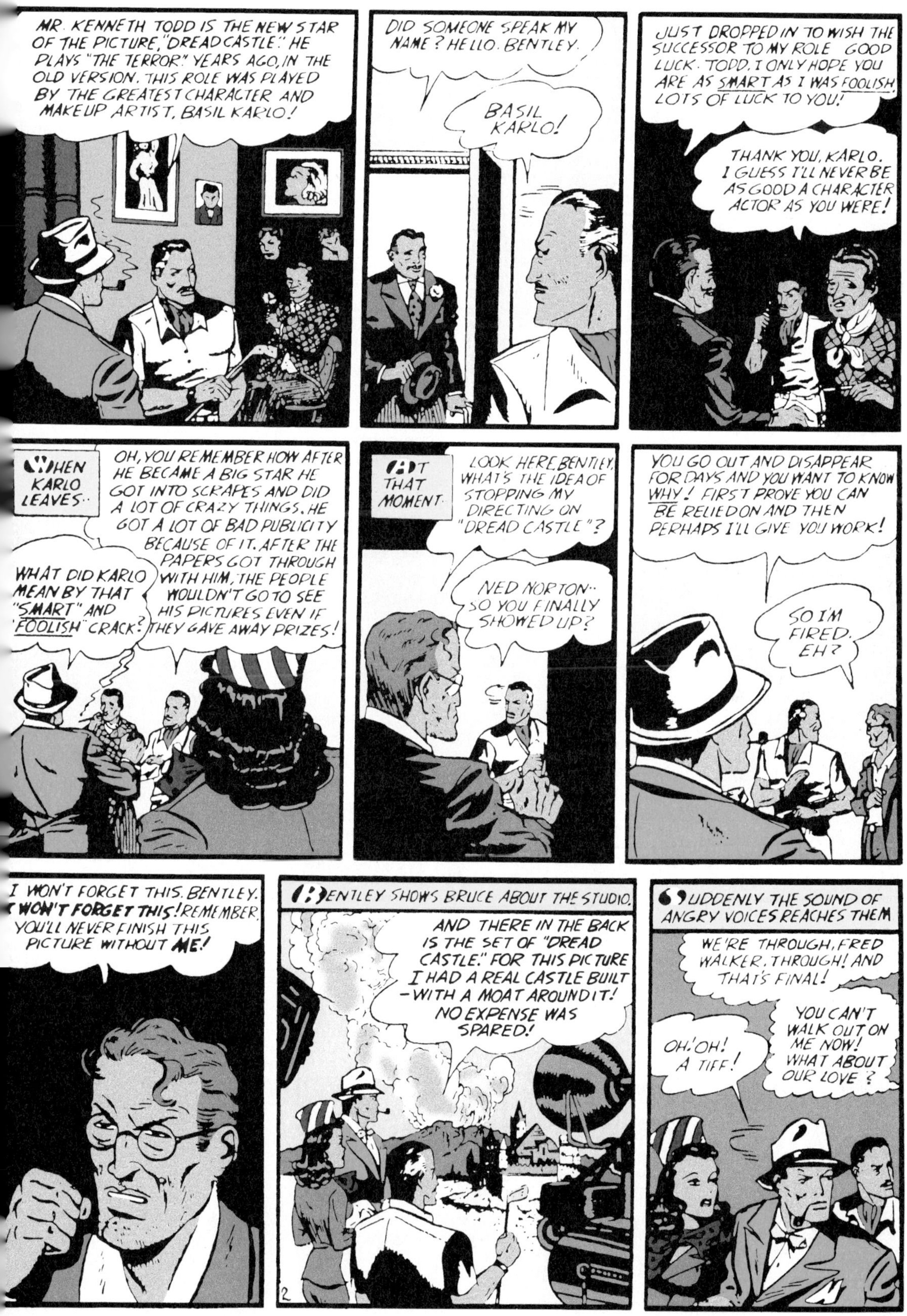
MR. KENNETH TODD IS THE NEW STAR OF THE PICTURE, "DREAD CASTLE." HE PLAYS "THE TERROR." YEARS AGO, IN THE OLD VERSION, THIS ROLE WAS PLAYED BY THE GREATEST CHARACTER AND MAKEUP ARTIST, BASIL KARLO!
DID SOMEONE SPEAK MY NAME? HELLO, BENTLEY.
BASIL KARLO!
JUST DROPPED IN TO WISH THE SUCCESSOR TO MY ROLE GOOD LUCK. TODD, I ONLY HOPE YOU ARE AS SMART AS I WAS FOOLISH. LOTS OF LUCK TO YOU!
THANK YOU, KARLO. I GUESS I'LL NEVER BE AS GOOD A CHARACTER ACTOR AS YOU WERE!
WHEN KARLO LEAVES..
WHAT DID KARLO MEAN BY THAT "SMART" AND "FOOLISH" CRACK?
OH, YOU REMEMBER HOW AFTER HE BECAME A BIG STAR HE GOT INTO SCRAPES AND DID A LOT OF CRAZY THINGS. HE GOT A LOT OF BAD PUBLICITY BECAUSE OF IT. AFTER THE PAPERS GOT THROUGH WITH HIM, THE PEOPLE WOULDN'T GO TO SEE HIS PICTURES EVEN IF THEY GAVE AWAY PRIZES!
AT THAT MOMENT.
LOOK HERE, BENTLEY, WHAT'S THE IDEA OF STOPPING MY DIRECTING ON "DREAD CASTLE"?
NED NORTON.. SO YOU FINALLY SHOWED UP?
YOU GO OUT AND DISAPPEAR FOR DAYS AND YOU WANT TO KNOW WHY! FIRST PROVE YOU CAN BE RELIED ON AND THEN PERHAPS I'LL GIVE YOU WORK!
SO I'M FIRED, EH?
I WON'T FORGET THIS, BENTLEY. I WON'T FORGET THIS! REMEMBER, YOU'LL NEVER FINISH THIS PICTURE WITHOUT ME!
BENTLEY SHOWS BRUCE ABOUT THE STUDIO.
AND THERE IN THE BACK IS THE SET OF "DREAD CASTLE." FOR THIS PICTURE I HAD A REAL CASTLE BUILT -WITH A MOAT AROUND IT! NO EXPENSE WAS SPARED!
SUDDENLY THE SOUND OF ANGRY VOICES REACHES THEM
WE'RE THROUGH, FRED WALKER, THROUGH! AND THAT'S FINAL!
YOU CAN'T WALK OUT ON ME NOW! WHAT ABOUT OUR LOVE?
OH, OH! A TIFF!

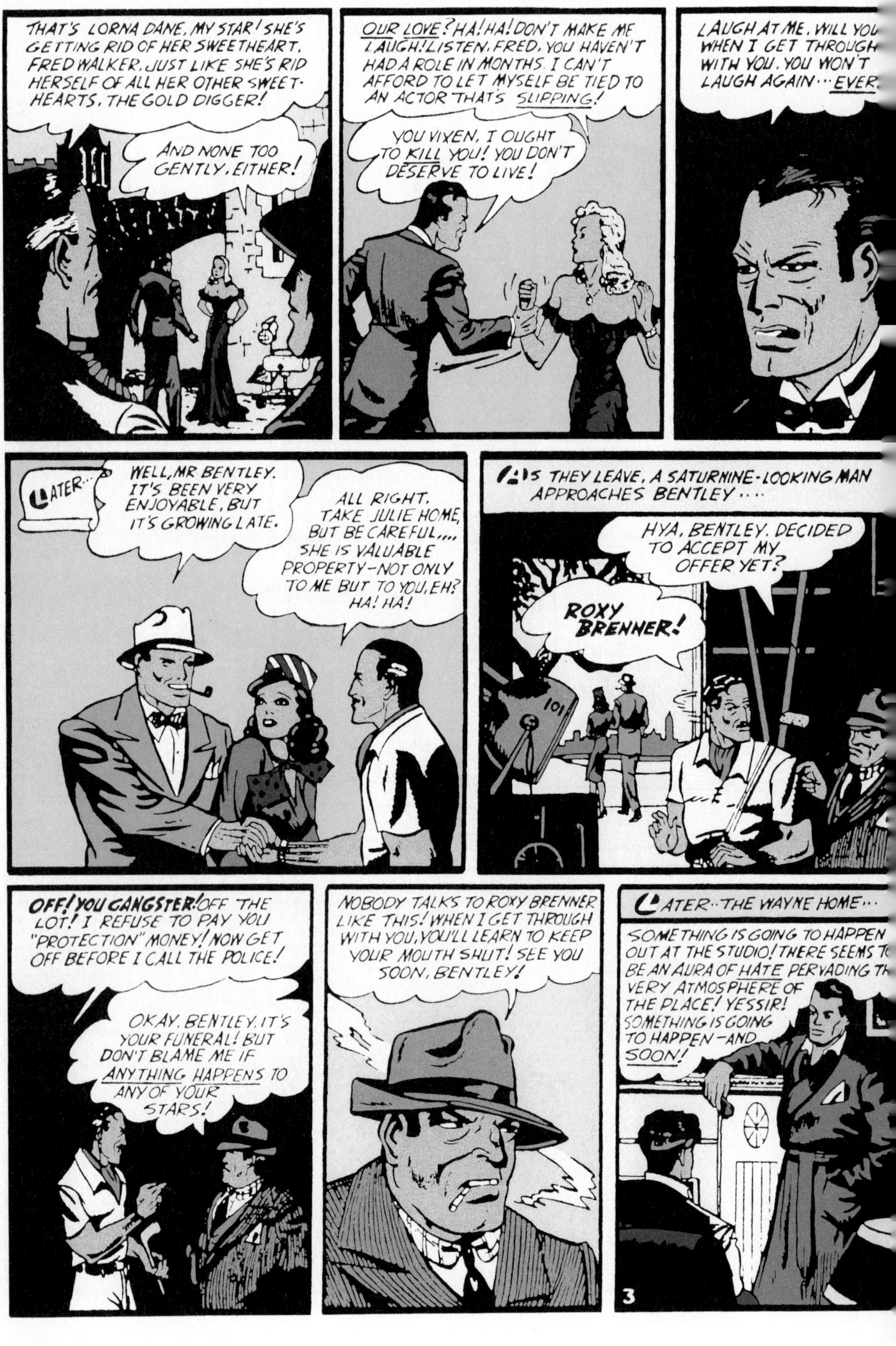
THAT'S LORNA DANE, MY STAR! SHE'S GETTING RID OF HER SWEETHEART, FRED WALKER, JUST LIKE SHE'S RID HERSELF OF ALL HER OTHER SWEET-HEARTS. THE GOLD DIGGER!
AND NONE TOO GENTLY, EITHER!
OUR LOVE? HA! HA! DON'T MAKE ME LAUGH! LISTEN, FRED, YOU HAVEN'T HAD A ROLE IN MONTHS. I CAN'T AFFORD TO LET MYSELF BE TIED TO AN ACTOR THAT'S SLIPPING!
YOU VIXEN, I OUGHT TO KILL YOU! YOU DON'T DESERVE TO LIVE!
LAUGH AT ME, WILL YOU WHEN I GET THROUGH WITH YOU, YOU WON'T LAUGH AGAIN... EVER
LATER...
WELL, MR BENTLEY. IT'S BEEN VERY ENJOYABLE, BUT IT'S GROWING LATE.
ALL RIGHT. TAKE JULIE HOME, BUT BE CAREFUL,... SHE IS VALUABLE PROPERTY—NOT ONLY TO ME BUT TO YOU, EH? HA! HA!
AS THEY LEAVE, A SATURNINE-LOOKING MAN APPROACHES BENTLEY...
HYA, BENTLEY. DECIDED TO ACCEPT MY OFFER YET?
ROXY BRENNER!
OFF! YOU GANGSTER! OFF THE LOT! I REFUSE TO PAY YOU "PROTECTION" MONEY! NOW GET OFF BEFORE I CALL THE POLICE!
OKAY, BENTLEY, IT'S YOUR FUNERAL! BUT DON'T BLAME ME IF ANYTHING HAPPENS TO ANY OF YOUR STARS!
NOBODY TALKS TO ROXY BRENNER LIKE THIS! WHEN I GET THROUGH WITH YOU, YOU'LL LEARN TO KEEP YOUR MOUTH SHUT! SEE YOU SOON, BENTLEY!
LATER.. THE WAYNE HOME...
SOMETHING IS GOING TO HAPPEN OUT AT THE STUDIO! THERE SEEMS TO BE AN AURA OF HATE PERVADING TH VERY ATMOSPHERE OF THE PLACE! YESSIR! SOMETHING IS GOING TO HAPPEN—AND SOON!
3

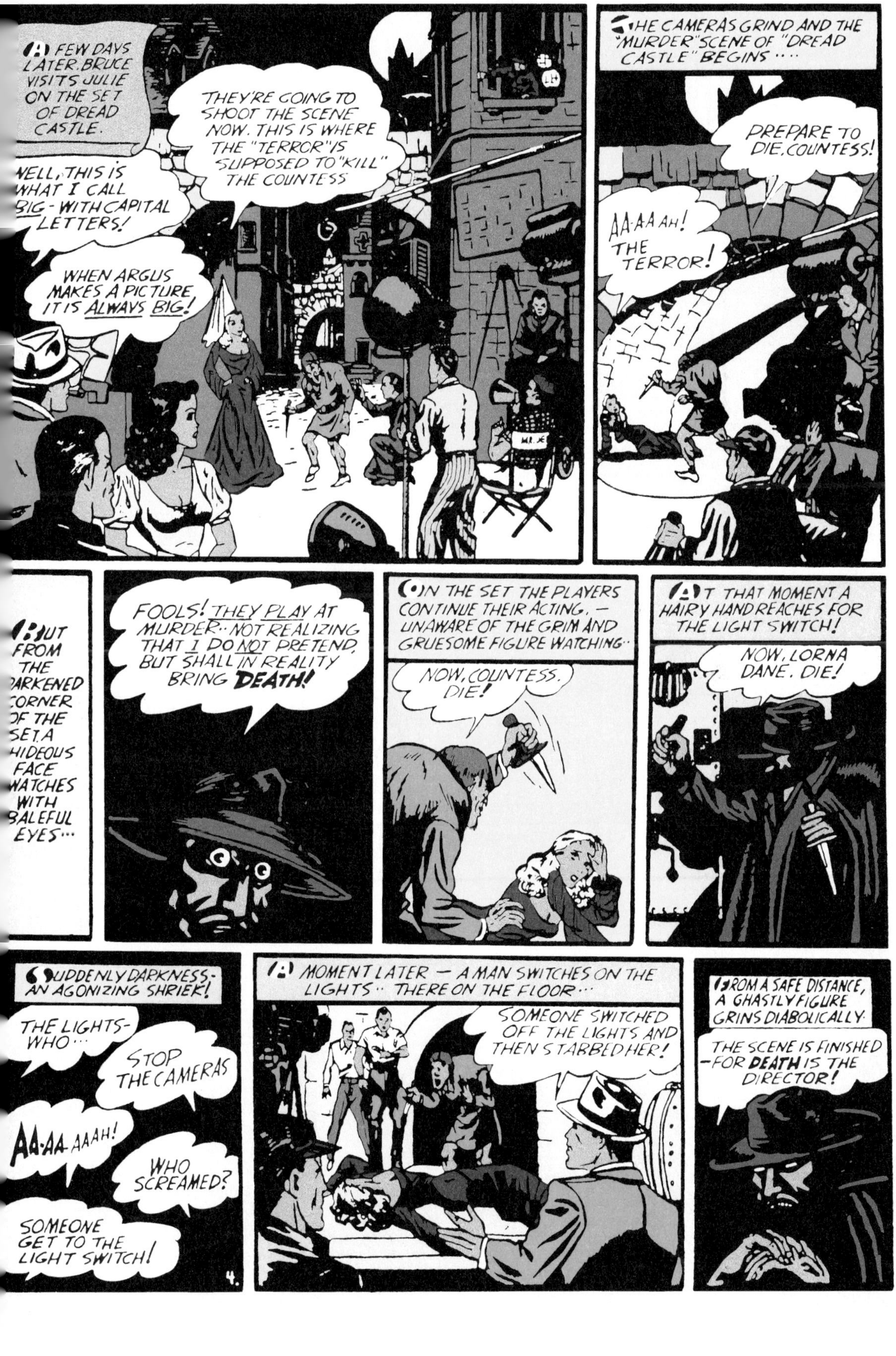
A FEW DAYS LATER, BRUCE VISITS JULIE ON THE SET OF DREAD CASTLE.
THEY'RE GOING TO SHOOT THE SCENE NOW. THIS IS WHERE THE "TERROR" IS SUPPOSED TO "KILL" THE COUNTESS
WELL, THIS IS WHAT I CALL BIG - WITH CAPITAL LETTERS!
WHEN ARGUS MAKES A PICTURE, IT IS ALWAYS BIG!
THE CAMERAS GRIND AND THE "MURDER" SCENE OF "DREAD CASTLE" BEGINS . . .
PREPARE TO DIE, COUNTESS!
AA-AA AH! THE TERROR!
BUT FROM THE DARKENED CORNER OF THE SET, A HIDEOUS FACE WATCHES WITH BALEFUL EYES...
FOOLS! THEY PLAY AT MURDER.. NOT REALIZING THAT I DO NOT PRETEND, BUT SHALL IN REALITY BRING DEATH!
ON THE SET THE PLAYERS CONTINUE THEIR ACTING, — UNAWARE OF THE GRIM AND GRUESOME FIGURE WATCHING..
NOW, COUNTESS. DIE!
AT THAT MOMENT A HAIRY HAND REACHES FOR THE LIGHT SWITCH!
NOW, LORNA DANE. DIE!
SUDDENLY DARKNESS - AN AGONIZING SHRIEK!
THE LIGHTS - WHO ...
STOP THE CAMERAS
AA-AA AAAH!
WHO SCREAMED?
SOMEONE GET TO THE LIGHT SWITCH!
4.
A MOMENT LATER — A MAN SWITCHES ON THE LIGHTS.. THERE ON THE FLOOR...
SOMEONE SWITCHED OFF THE LIGHTS AND THEN STABBED HER!
FROM A SAFE DISTANCE, A GHASTLY FIGURE GRINS DIABOLICALLY.
THE SCENE IS FINISHED - FOR DEATH IS THE DIRECTOR!

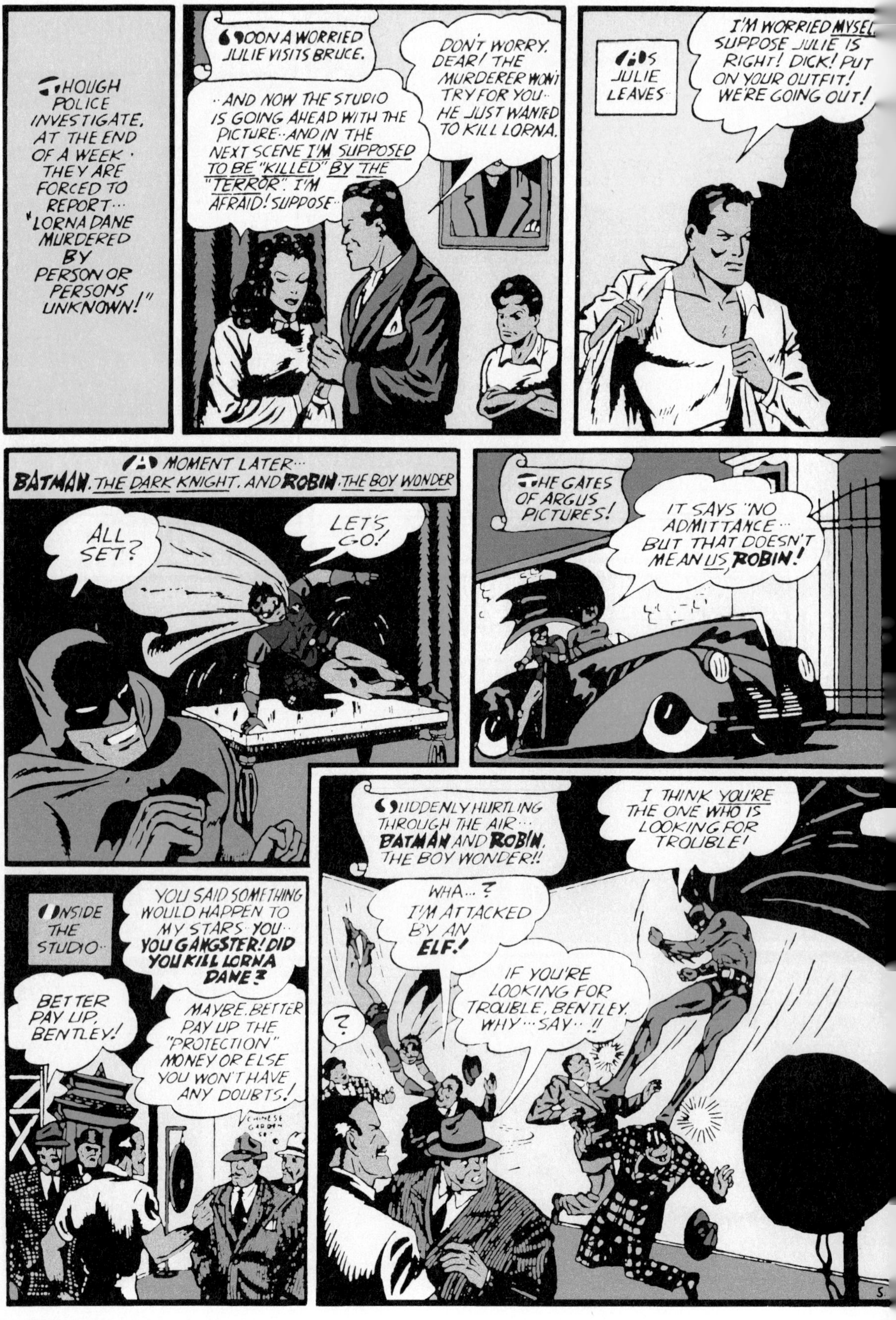
THOUGH POLICE INVESTIGATE, AT THE END OF A WEEK THEY ARE FORCED TO REPORT... "LORNA DANE MURDERED BY PERSON OR PERSONS UNKNOWN!"
SOON A WORRIED JULIE VISITS BRUCE.
..AND NOW THE STUDIO IS GOING AHEAD WITH THE PICTURE..AND IN THE NEXT SCENE I'M SUPPOSED TO BE "KILLED" BY THE "TERROR". I'M AFRAID! SUPPOSE..
DON'T WORRY, DEAR! THE MURDERER WON'T TRY FOR YOU.. HE JUST WANTED TO KILL LORNA.
AS JULIE LEAVES..
I'M WORRIED MYSEL.. SUPPOSE JULIE IS RIGHT! DICK! PUT ON YOUR OUTFIT! WE'RE GOING OUT!
A MOMENT LATER... BATMAN, THE DARK KNIGHT, AND ROBIN, THE BOY WONDER
ALL SET?
LET'S GO!
THE GATES OF ARGUS PICTURES!
IT SAYS "NO ADMITTANCE"... BUT THAT DOESN'T MEAN US, ROBIN!
INSIDE THE STUDIO..
YOU SAID SOMETHING WOULD HAPPEN TO MY STARS. YOU.. YOU GANGSTER! DID YOU KILL LORNA DANE?
BETTER PAY UP, BENTLEY!
MAYBE. BETTER PAY UP THE "PROTECTION" MONEY OR ELSE YOU WON'T HAVE ANY DOUBTS!
SUDDENLY HURTLING THROUGH THE AIR... BATMAN AND ROBIN, THE BOY WONDER!!
I THINK YOU'RE THE ONE WHO IS LOOKING FOR TROUBLE!
WHA...? I'M ATTACKED BY AN ELF!
?
IF YOU'RE LOOKING FOR TROUBLE, BENTLEY, WHY... SAY... !!

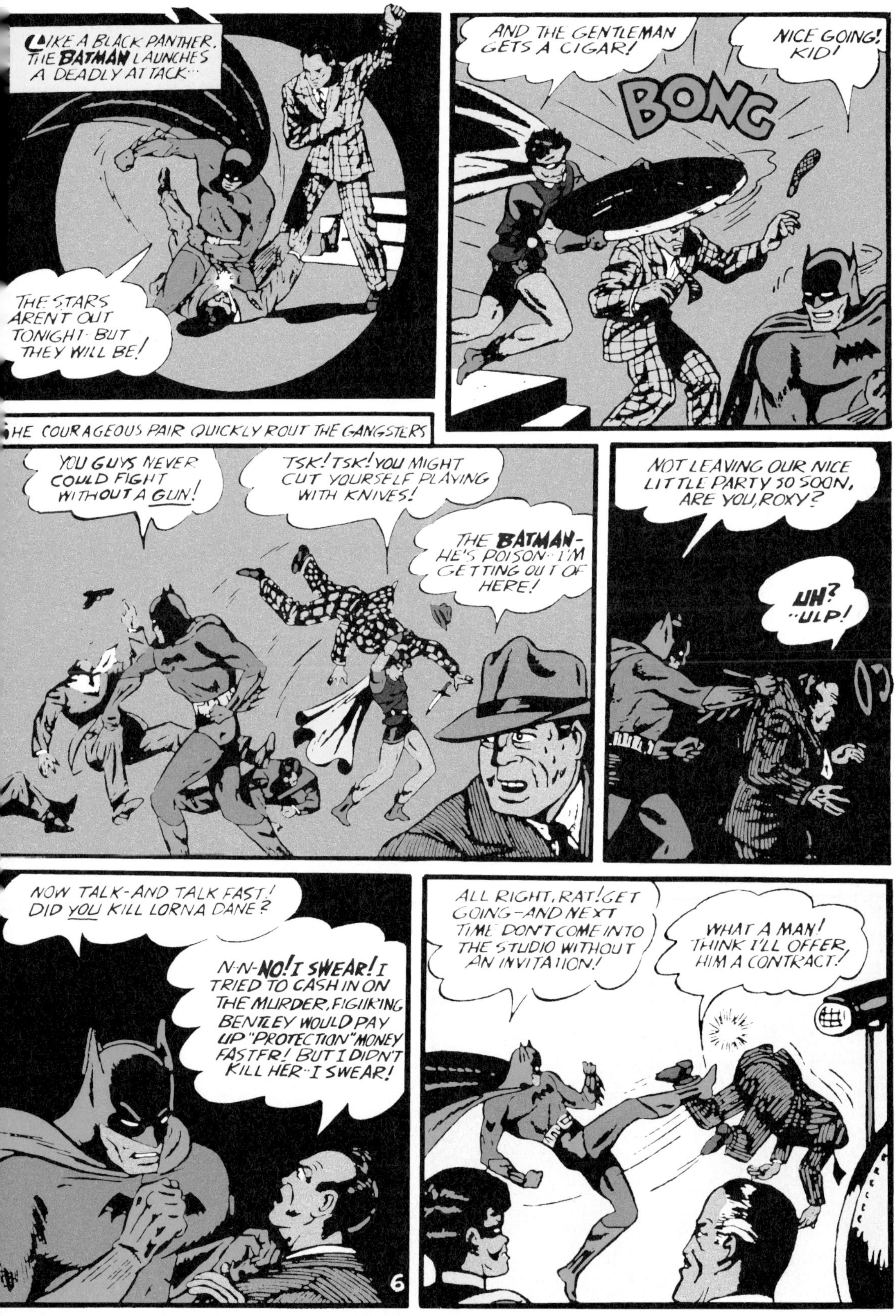
LIKE A BLACK PANTHER, THE BATMAN LAUNCHES A DEADLY ATTACK...
THE STARS AREN'T OUT TONIGHT.. BUT THEY WILL BE!
AND THE GENTLEMAN GETS A CIGAR!
NICE GOING! KID!
BONG
THE COURAGEOUS PAIR QUICKLY ROUT THE GANGSTERS
YOU GUYS NEVER COULD FIGHT WITHOUT A GUN!
TSK! TSK! YOU MIGHT CUT YOURSELF PLAYING WITH KNIVES!
THE BATMAN- HE'S POISON.. I'M GETTING OUT OF HERE!
NOT LEAVING OUR NICE LITTLE PARTY SO SOON, ARE YOU, ROXY?
UH? ..ULP!
NOW TALK-AND TALK FAST! DID YOU KILL LORNA DANE?
N-N-NO! I SWEAR! I TRIED TO CASH IN ON THE MURDER, FIGURING BENTLEY WOULD PAY UP "PROTECTION" MONEY FASTER! BUT I DIDN'T KILL HER.. I SWEAR!
6
ALL RIGHT, RAT! GET GOING-AND NEXT TIME DON'T COME INTO THE STUDIO WITHOUT AN INVITATION!
WHAT A MAN! THINK I'LL OFFER HIM A CONTRACT!

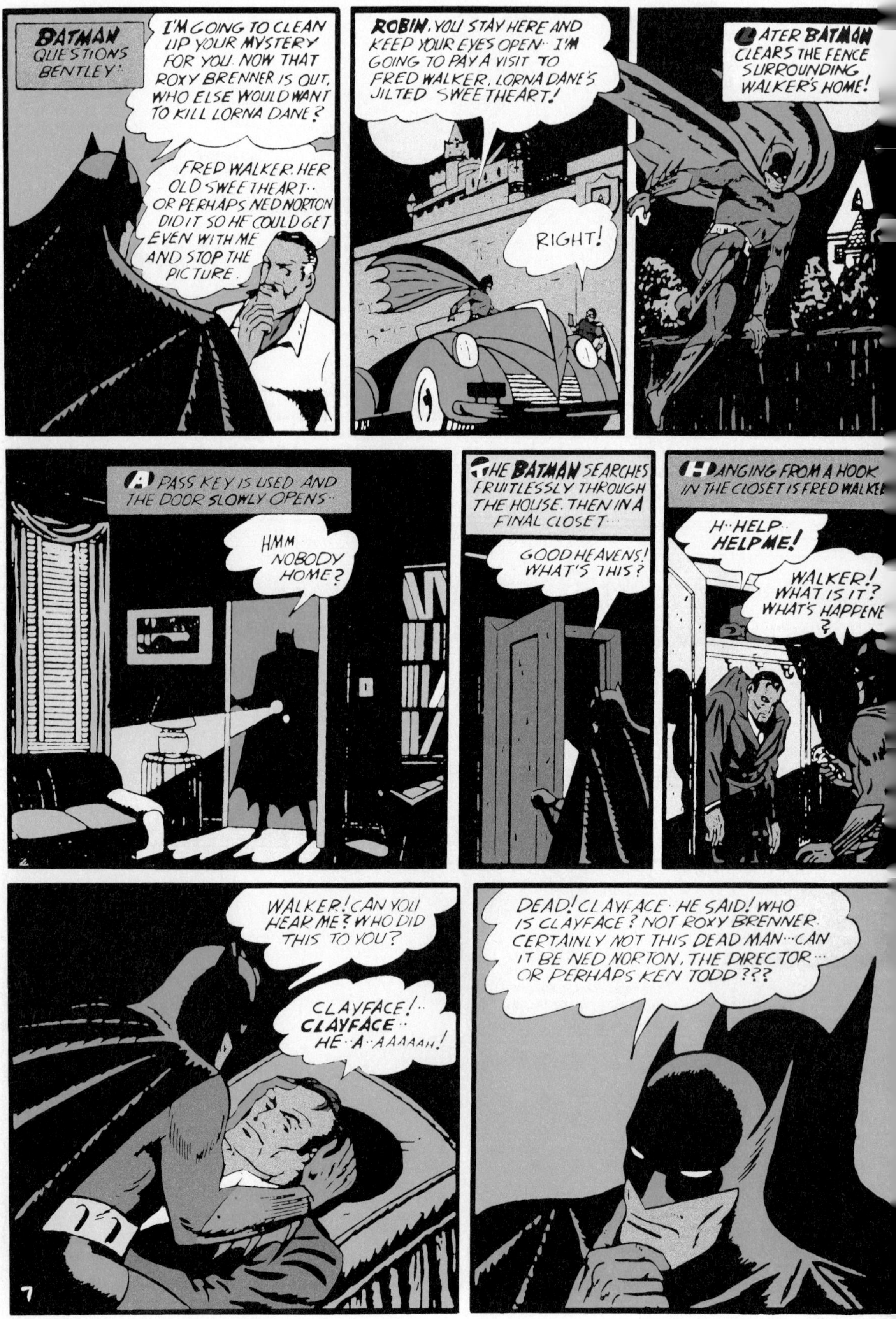
BATMAN QUESTIONS BENTLEY:
I'M GOING TO CLEAN UP YOUR MYSTERY FOR YOU. NOW THAT ROXY BRENNER IS OUT, WHO ELSE WOULD WANT TO KILL LORNA DANE?
FRED WALKER. HER OLD SWEETHEART.. OR PERHAPS NED NORTON DID IT SO HE COULD GET EVEN WITH ME AND STOP THE PICTURE.
ROBIN, YOU STAY HERE AND KEEP YOUR EYES OPEN.. I'M GOING TO PAY A VISIT TO FRED WALKER, LORNA DANE'S JILTED SWEETHEART!
RIGHT!
LATER BATMAN CLEARS THE FENCE SURROUNDING WALKER'S HOME!
A PASS KEY IS USED AND THE DOOR SLOWLY OPENS..
HMM NOBODY HOME?
THE BATMAN SEARCHES FRUITLESSLY THROUGH THE HOUSE. THEN IN A FINAL CLOSET..
GOOD HEAVENS! WHAT'S THIS?
HANGING FROM A HOOK IN THE CLOSET IS FRED WALKER
H..HELP.. HELP ME!
WALKER! WHAT IS IT? WHAT'S HAPPENE ?
WALKER! CAN YOU HEAR ME? WHO DID THIS TO YOU?
CLAYFACE!.. CLAYFACE.. HE..A..AAAAAH!
DEAD! CLAYFACE.. HE SAID! WHO IS CLAYFACE? NOT ROXY BRENNER. CERTAINLY NOT THIS DEAD MAN...CAN IT BE NED NORTON, THE DIRECTOR... OR PERHAPS KEN TODD???

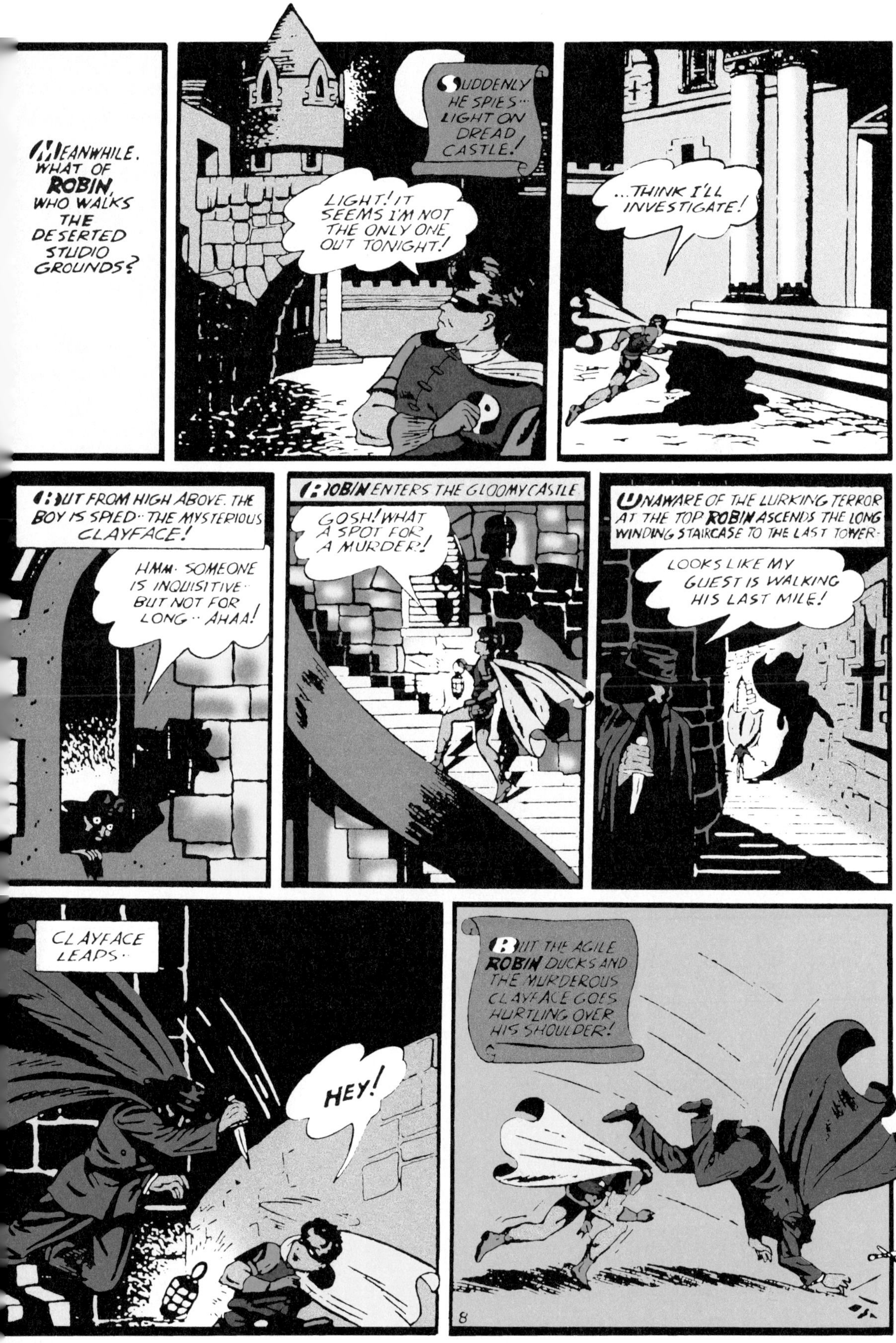
MEANWHILE. WHAT OF ROBIN, WHO WALKS THE DESERTED STUDIO GROUNDS?
SUDDENLY HE SPIES... LIGHT ON DREAD CASTLE!
LIGHT! IT SEEMS I'M NOT THE ONLY ONE OUT TONIGHT!
...THINK I'LL INVESTIGATE!
BUT FROM HIGH ABOVE. THE BOY IS SPIED.. THE MYSTERIOUS CLAYFACE!
HMM. SOMEONE IS INQUISITIVE.. BUT NOT FOR LONG.. AHAA!
ROBIN ENTERS THE GLOOMY CASTLE
GOSH! WHAT A SPOT FOR A MURDER!
UNAWARE OF THE LURKING TERROR AT THE TOP ROBIN ASCENDS THE LONG WINDING STAIRCASE TO THE LAST TOWER-
LOOKS LIKE MY GUEST IS WALKING HIS LAST MILE!
CLAYFACE LEAPS..
HEY!
BUT THE AGILE ROBIN DUCKS AND THE MURDEROUS CLAYFACE GOES HURTLING OVER HIS SHOULDER!
8

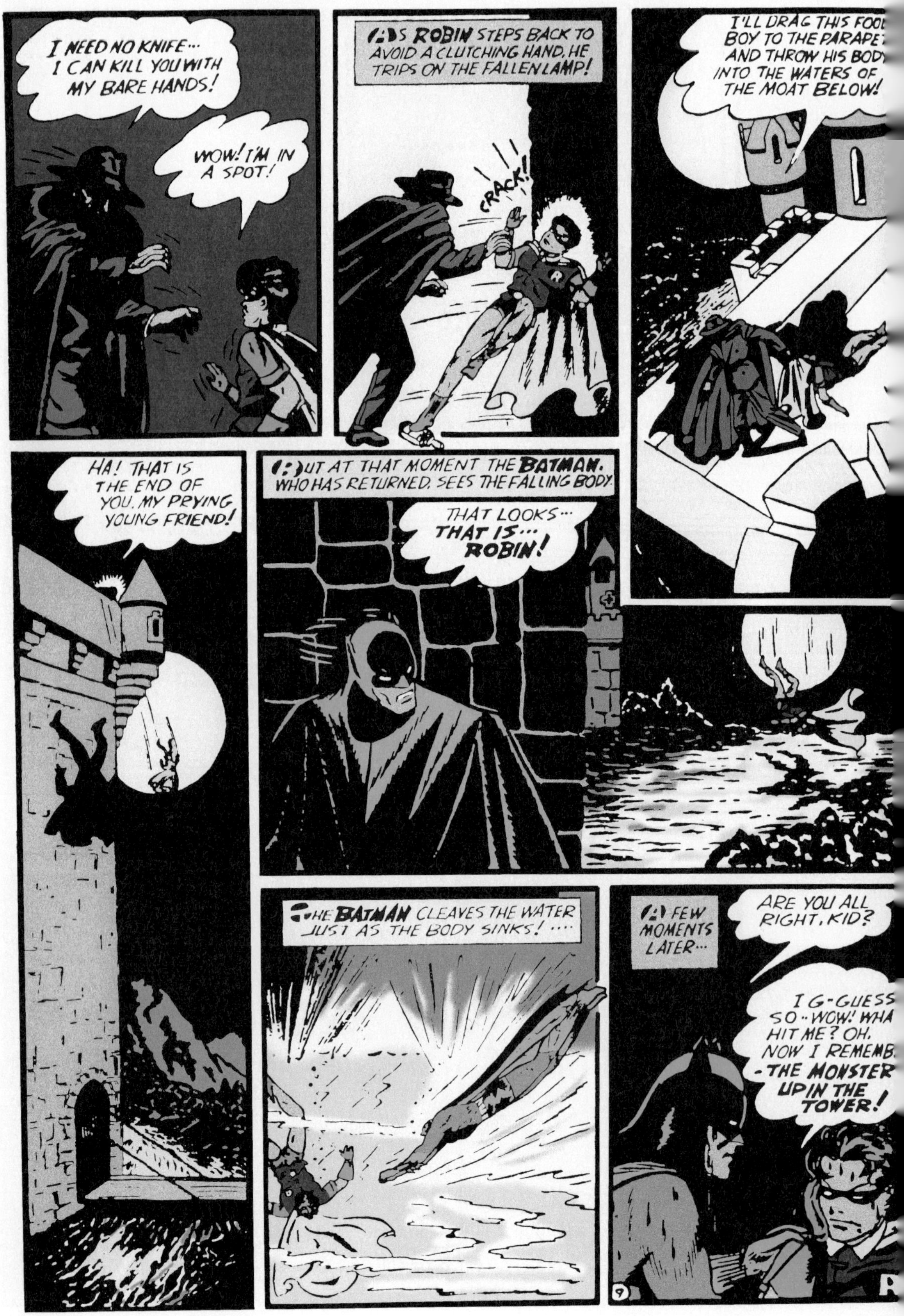
I NEED NO KNIFE... I CAN KILL YOU WITH MY BARE HANDS!
WOW! I'M IN A SPOT!
AS ROBIN STEPS BACK TO AVOID A CLUTCHING HAND, HE TRIPS ON THE FALLEN LAMP!
CRACK!
I'LL DRAG THIS FOOL BOY TO THE PARAPET AND THROW HIS BODY INTO THE WATERS OF THE MOAT BELOW!
HA! THAT IS THE END OF YOU, MY PRYING YOUNG FRIEND!
BUT AT THAT MOMENT THE BATMAN, WHO HAS RETURNED, SEES THE FALLING BODY
THAT LOOKS... THAT IS... ROBIN!
THE BATMAN CLEAVES THE WATER JUST AS THE BODY SINKS! ....
A FEW MOMENTS LATER...
ARE YOU ALL RIGHT, KID?
I G-GUESS SO.. WOW! WHA HIT ME? OH. NOW I REMEMB -THE MONSTER UP IN THE TOWER!
9

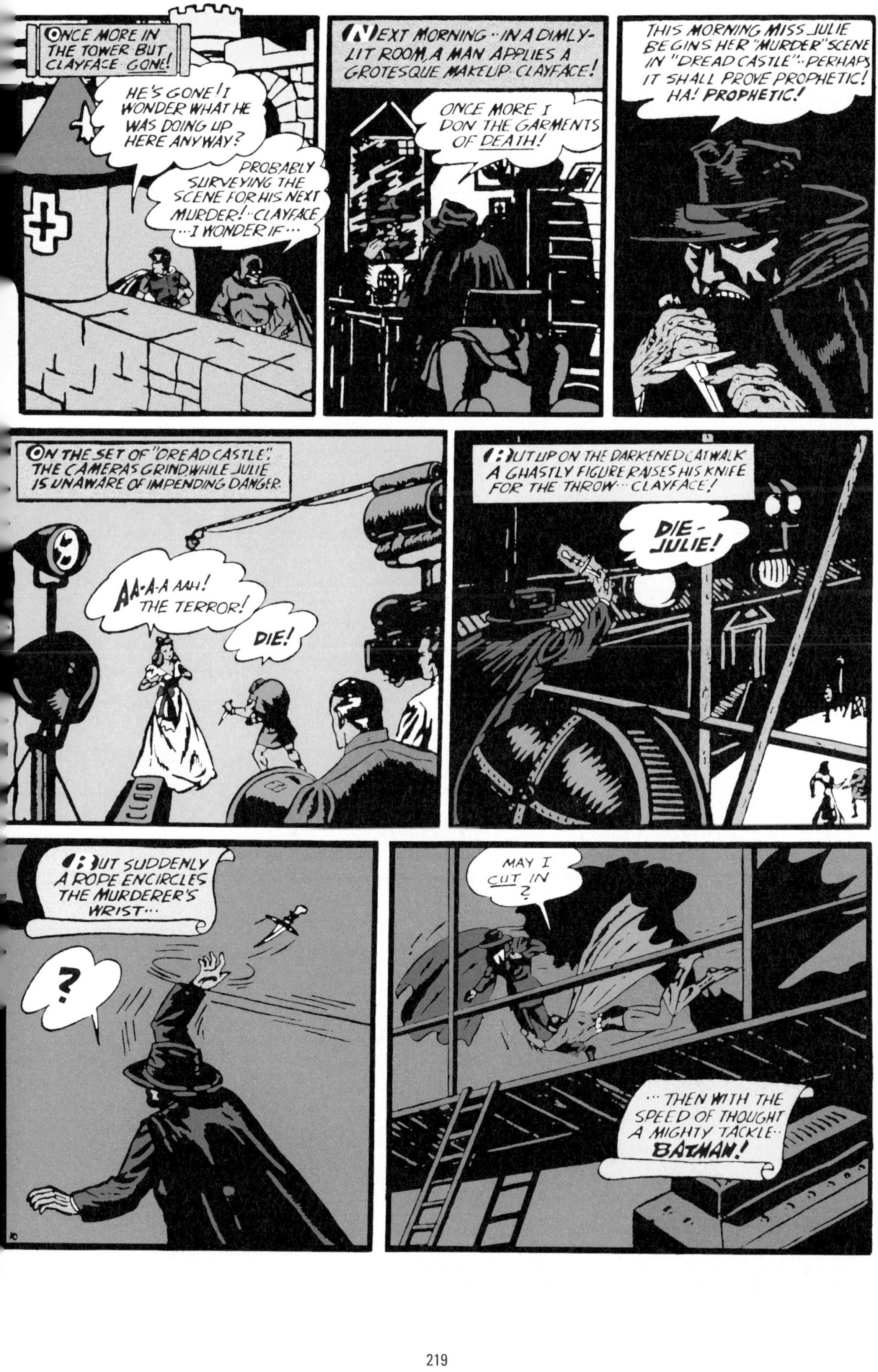
ONCE MORE IN THE TOWER BUT CLAYFACE GONE!
HE'S GONE! I WONDER WHAT HE WAS DOING UP HERE ANYWAY?
PROBABLY SURVEYING THE SCENE FOR HIS NEXT MURDER!··CLAYFACE ···I WONDER IF···
NEXT MORNING··IN A DIMLY-LIT ROOM, A MAN APPLIES A GROTESQUE MAKEUP·CLAYFACE!
ONCE MORE I DON THE GARMENTS OF DEATH!
THIS MORNING MISS JULIE BEGINS HER "MURDER" SCENE IN "DREAD CASTLE"··PERHAPS IT SHALL PROVE PROPHETIC! HA! PROPHETIC!
ON THE SET OF "DREAD CASTLE", THE CAMERAS GRIND WHILE JULIE IS UNAWARE OF IMPENDING DANGER.
AA-A-A AAH! THE TERROR!
DIE!
BUT UP ON THE DARKENED CATWALK A GHASTLY FIGURE RAISES HIS KNIFE FOR THE THROW··· CLAYFACE!
DIE - JULIE!
BUT SUDDENLY A ROPE ENCIRCLES THE MURDERER'S WRIST···
?
MAY I CUT IN ?
··· THEN WITH THE SPEED OF THOUGHT A MIGHTY TACKLE·· BATMAN!

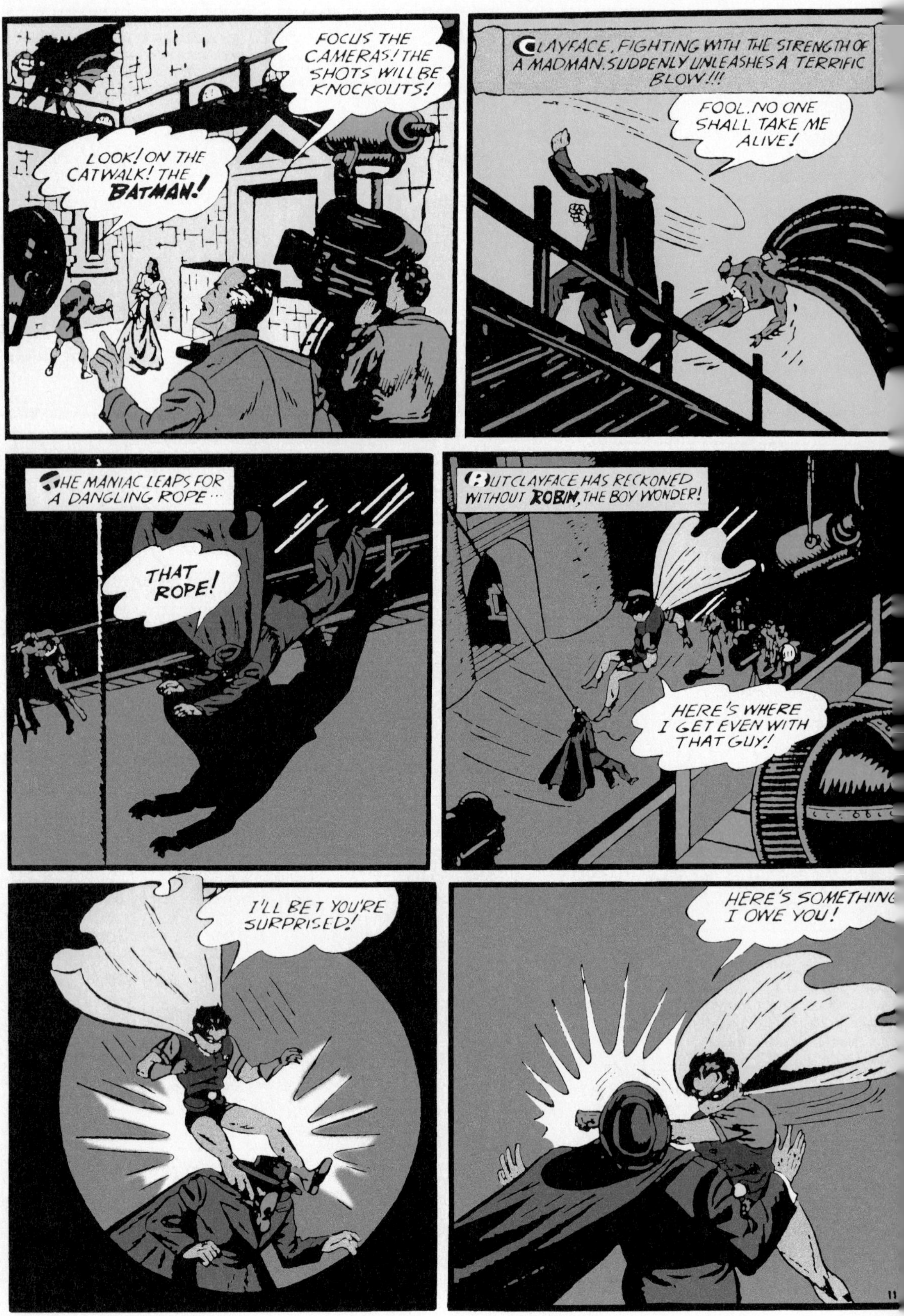
FOCUS THE CAMERAS! THE SHOTS WILL BE KNOCKOUTS!
LOOK! ON THE CATWALK! THE BATMAN!
CLAYFACE, FIGHTING WITH THE STRENGTH OF A MADMAN, SUDDENLY UNLEASHES A TERRIFIC BLOW!!!
FOOL, NO ONE SHALL TAKE ME ALIVE!
THE MANIAC LEAPS FOR A DANGLING ROPE...
THAT ROPE!
BUT CLAYFACE HAS RECKONED WITHOUT ROBIN, THE BOY WONDER!
HERE'S WHERE I GET EVEN WITH THAT GUY!
I'LL BET YOU'RE SURPRISED!
HERE'S SOMETHING I OWE YOU!
11

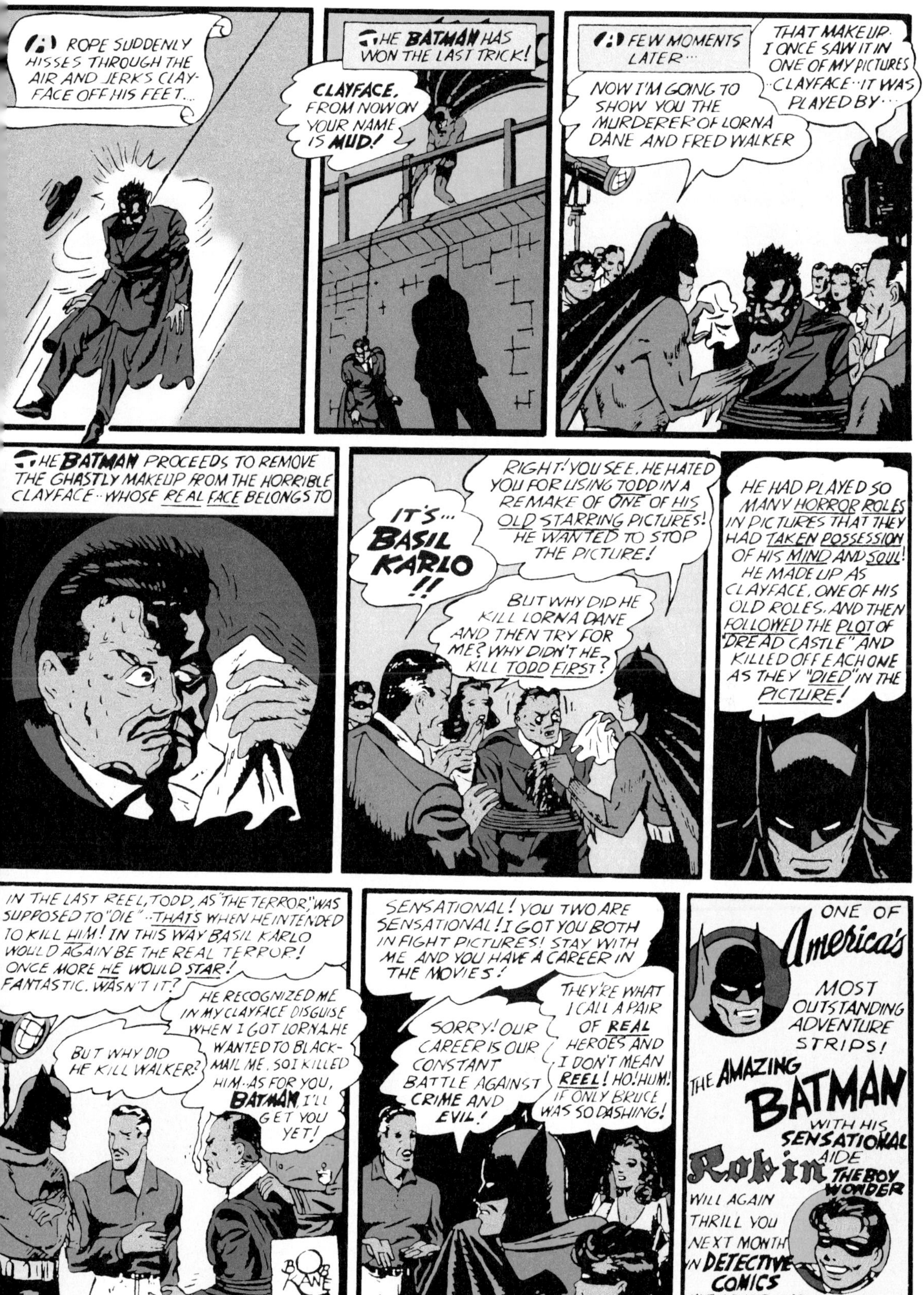
A ROPE SUDDENLY HISSES THROUGH THE AIR AND JERKS CLAYFACE OFF HIS FEET...
THE BATMAN HAS WON THE LAST TRICK!
CLAYFACE, FROM NOW ON YOUR NAME IS MUD!
A FEW MOMENTS LATER...
NOW I'M GOING TO SHOW YOU THE MURDERER OF LORNA DANE AND FRED WALKER
THAT MAKEUP. I ONCE SAW IT IN ONE OF MY PICTURES ..CLAYFACE..IT WAS PLAYED BY...
THE BATMAN PROCEEDS TO REMOVE THE GHASTLY MAKEUP FROM THE HORRIBLE CLAYFACE..WHOSE REAL FACE BELONGS TO
IT'S... BASIL KARLO !!
RIGHT! YOU SEE, HE HATED YOU FOR USING TODD IN A REMAKE OF ONE OF HIS OLD STARRING PICTURES! HE WANTED TO STOP THE PICTURE!
BUT WHY DID HE KILL LORNA DANE AND THEN TRY FOR ME? WHY DIDN'T HE KILL TODD FIRST?
HE HAD PLAYED SO MANY HORROR ROLES IN PICTURES THAT THEY HAD TAKEN POSSESSION OF HIS MIND AND SOUL! HE MADE UP AS CLAYFACE, ONE OF HIS OLD ROLES, AND THEN FOLLOWED THE PLOT OF "DREAD CASTLE" AND KILLED OFF EACH ONE AS THEY "DIED" IN THE PICTURE!
IN THE LAST REEL, TODD, AS "THE TERROR," WAS SUPPOSED TO "DIE"..THAT'S WHEN HE INTENDED TO KILL HIM! IN THIS WAY BASIL KARLO WOULD AGAIN BE THE REAL TERROR! ONCE MORE HE WOULD STAR! FANTASTIC, WASN'T IT?
BUT WHY DID HE KILL WALKER?
HE RECOGNIZED ME IN MY CLAYFACE DISGUISE WHEN I GOT LORNA.HE WANTED TO BLACKMAIL ME, SO I KILLED HIM..AS FOR YOU, BATMAN, I'LL GET YOU YET!
BOB KANE
SENSATIONAL! YOU TWO ARE SENSATIONAL! I GOT YOU BOTH IN FIGHT PICTURES! STAY WITH ME AND YOU HAVE A CAREER IN THE MOVIES!
SORRY! OUR CAREER IS OUR CONSTANT BATTLE AGAINST CRIME AND EVIL!
THEY'RE WHAT I CALL A PAIR OF REAL HEROES AND I DON'T MEAN REEL! HO! HUM! IF ONLY BRUCE WAS SO DASHING!
ONE OF America's MOST OUTSTANDING ADVENTURE STRIPS!
THE AMAZING BATMAN WITH HIS SENSATIONAL AIDE Robin THE BOY WONDER
WILL AGAIN THRILL YOU NEXT MONTH IN DETECTIVE COMICS WITH THEIR DARING EXPLOITS- DON'T MISS THEM!!!

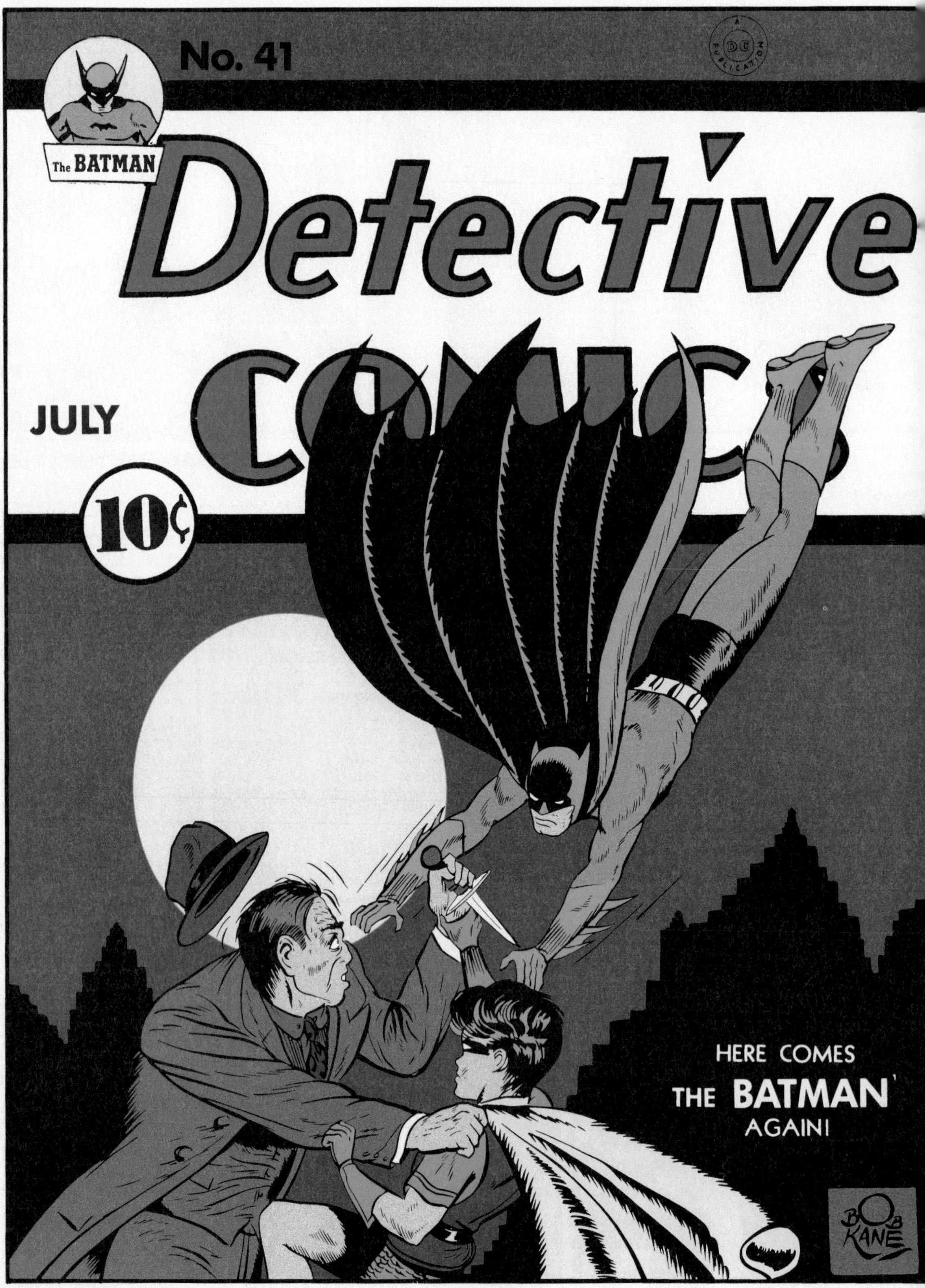
No. 41
The BATMAN
Detective Comics
JULY
10¢
HERE COMES
THE BATMAN
AGAIN!
BOB KANE

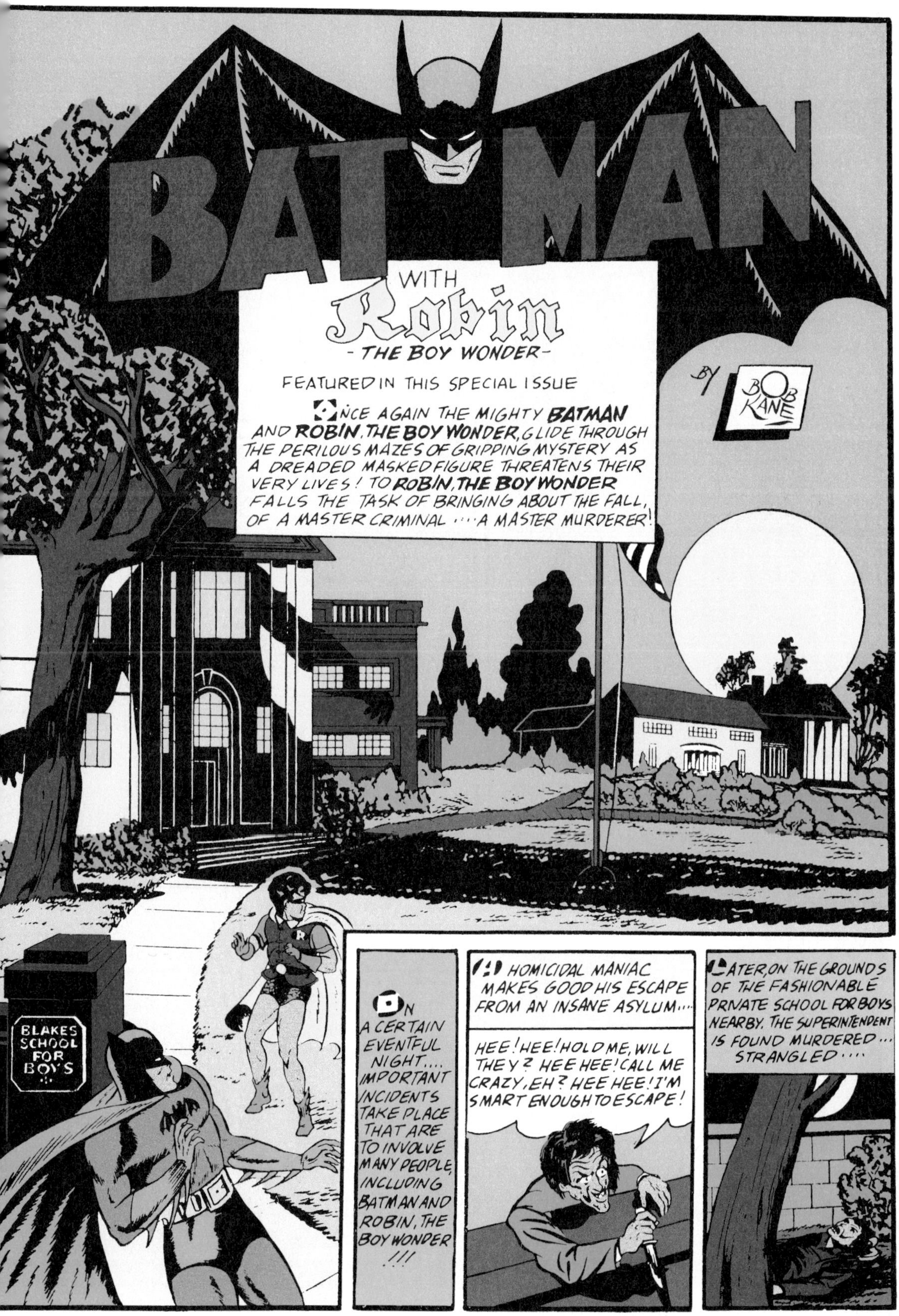
BATMAN
WITH
Robin
-THE BOY WONDER-
FEATURED IN THIS SPECIAL ISSUE
ONCE AGAIN THE MIGHTY BATMAN AND ROBIN, THE BOY WONDER, GLIDE THROUGH THE PERILOUS MAZES OF GRIPPING MYSTERY AS A DREADED MASKED FIGURE THREATENS THEIR VERY LIVES! TO ROBIN, THE BOY WONDER FALLS THE TASK OF BRINGING ABOUT THE FALL, OF A MASTER CRIMINAL .... A MASTER MURDERER!
BY BOB KANE
BLAKES SCHOOL FOR BOYS
ON A CERTAIN EVENTFUL NIGHT.... IMPORTANT INCIDENTS TAKE PLACE THAT ARE TO INVOLVE MANY PEOPLE, INCLUDING BATMAN AND ROBIN, THE BOY WONDER !!!
A HOMICIDAL MANIAC MAKES GOOD HIS ESCAPE FROM AN INSANE ASYLUM....
HEE! HEE! HOLD ME, WILL THEY? HEE HEE! CALL ME CRAZY, EH? HEE HEE! I'M SMART ENOUGH TO ESCAPE!
LATER, ON THE GROUNDS OF THE FASHIONABLE PRIVATE SCHOOL FOR BOYS NEARBY, THE SUPERINTENDENT IS FOUND MURDERED... STRANGLED....

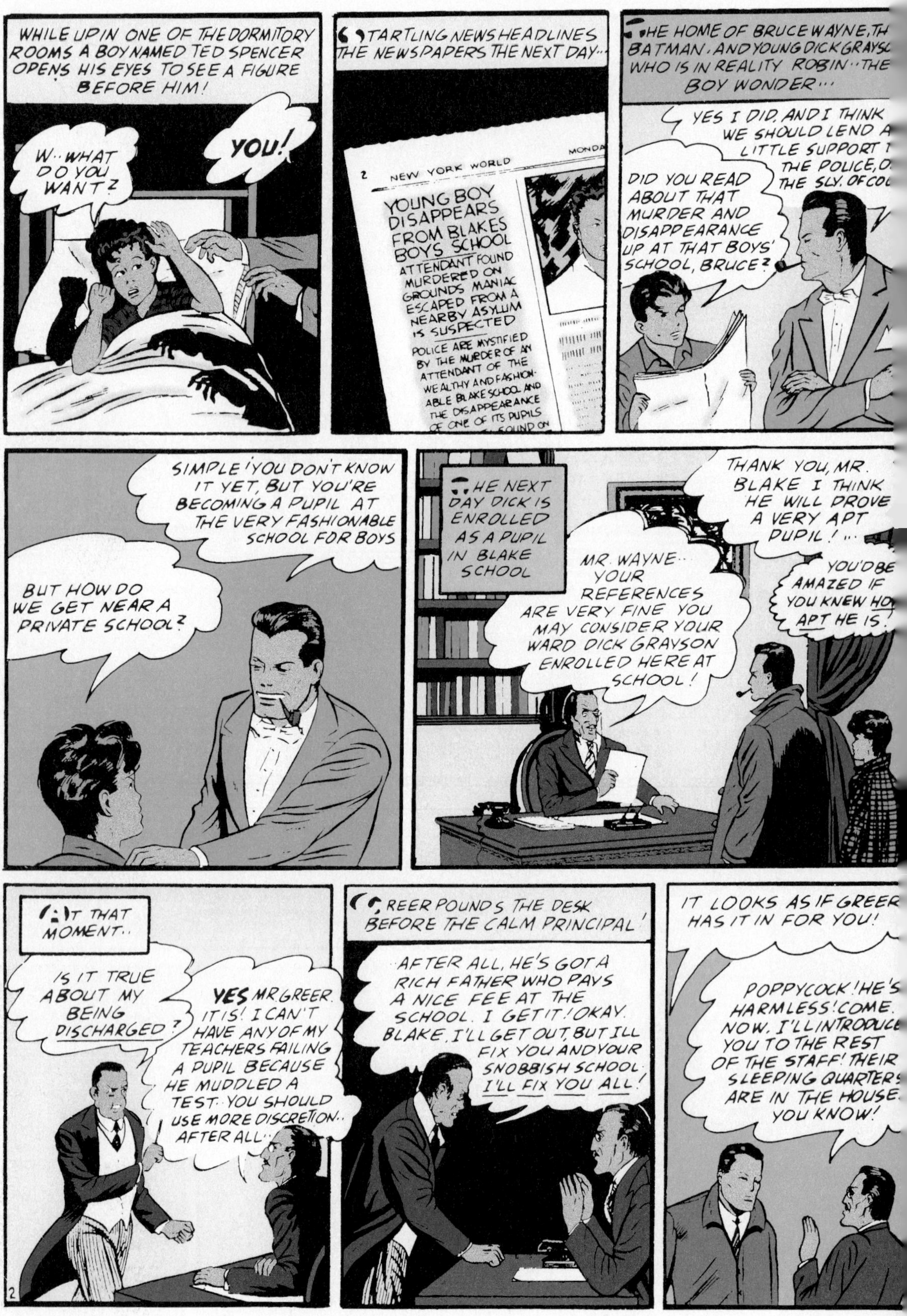

WHILE UP IN ONE OF THE DORMITORY ROOMS A BOY NAMED TED SPENCER OPENS HIS EYES TO SEE A FIGURE BEFORE HIM!
W.. WHAT DO YOU WANT?
YOU!
STARTLING NEWS HEADLINES THE NEWSPAPERS THE NEXT DAY...
2 NEW YORK WORLD MONDA
YOUNG BOY DISAPPEARS FROM BLAKES BOYS SCHOOL
ATTENDANT FOUND MURDERED ON GROUNDS MANIAC ESCAPED FROM A NEARBY ASYLUM IS SUSPECTED
POLICE ARE MYSTIFIED BY THE MURDER OF AN ATTENDANT OF THE WEALTHY AND FASHIONABLE BLAKE SCHOOL AND THE DISAPPEARANCE OF ONE OF ITS PUPILS
THE HOME OF BRUCE WAYNE, TH BATMAN, AND YOUNG DICK GRAYSO WHO IS IN REALITY ROBIN.. THE BOY WONDER...
DID YOU READ ABOUT THAT MURDER AND DISAPPEARANCE UP AT THAT BOYS' SCHOOL, BRUCE?
YES I DID, AND I THINK WE SHOULD LEND A LITTLE SUPPORT T THE POLICE, O THE SLY, OF CO
BUT HOW DO WE GET NEAR A PRIVATE SCHOOL?
SIMPLE! YOU DON'T KNOW IT YET, BUT YOU'RE BECOMING A PUPIL AT THE VERY FASHIONABLE SCHOOL FOR BOYS
THE NEXT DAY DICK IS ENROLLED AS A PUPIL IN BLAKE SCHOOL
MR. WAYNE.. YOUR REFERENCES ARE VERY FINE YOU MAY CONSIDER YOUR WARD DICK GRAYSON ENROLLED HERE AT SCHOOL!
THANK YOU, MR. BLAKE I THINK HE WILL PROVE A VERY APT PUPIL!...
YOU'D BE AMAZED IF YOU KNEW HO APT HE IS!
AT THAT MOMENT..
IS IT TRUE ABOUT MY BEING DISCHARGED?
YES MR. GREER. IT IS! I CAN'T HAVE ANY OF MY TEACHERS FAILING A PUPIL BECAUSE HE MUDDLED A TEST. YOU SHOULD USE MORE DISCRETION.. AFTER ALL..
2
GREER POUNDS THE DESK BEFORE THE CALM PRINCIPAL!
AFTER ALL, HE'S GOT A RICH FATHER WHO PAYS A NICE FEE AT THE SCHOOL. I GET IT! OKAY. BLAKE, I'LL GET OUT, BUT I'LL FIX YOU AND YOUR SNOBBISH SCHOOL. I'LL FIX YOU ALL!
IT LOOKS AS IF GREER HAS IT IN FOR YOU!
POPPYCOCK! HE'S HARMLESS! COME. NOW. I'LL INTRODUCE YOU TO THE REST OF THE STAFF! THEIR SLEEPING QUARTERS ARE IN THE HOUSE. YOU KNOW!

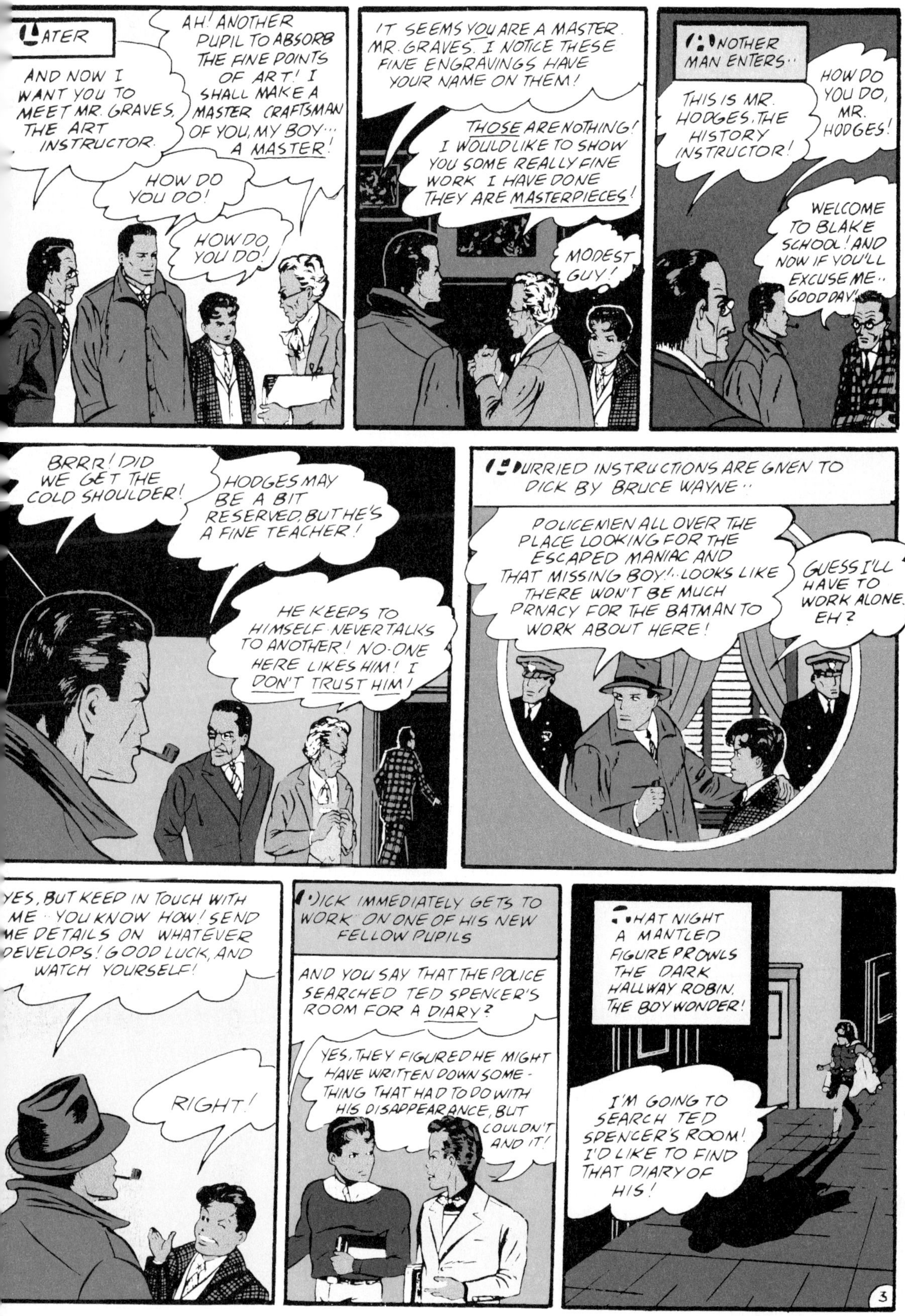
LATER
AND NOW I WANT YOU TO MEET MR. GRAVES, THE ART INSTRUCTOR.
AH! ANOTHER PUPIL TO ABSORB THE FINE POINTS OF ART! I SHALL MAKE A MASTER CRAFTSMAN OF YOU, MY BOY... A MASTER!
HOW DO YOU DO!
HOW DO YOU DO!
IT SEEMS YOU ARE A MASTER, MR. GRAVES. I NOTICE THESE FINE ENGRAVINGS HAVE YOUR NAME ON THEM!
THOSE ARE NOTHING! I WOULD LIKE TO SHOW YOU SOME REALLY FINE WORK I HAVE DONE. THEY ARE MASTERPIECES!
MODEST GUY!
ANOTHER MAN ENTERS..
THIS IS MR. HODGES, THE HISTORY INSTRUCTOR!
HOW DO YOU DO, MR. HODGES!
WELCOME TO BLAKE SCHOOL! AND NOW IF YOU'LL EXCUSE ME.. GOOD DAY!
BRRR! DID WE GET THE COLD SHOULDER!
HODGES MAY BE A BIT RESERVED, BUT HE'S A FINE TEACHER!
HE KEEPS TO HIMSELF. NEVER TALKS TO ANOTHER! NO-ONE HERE LIKES HIM! I DON'T TRUST HIM!
HURRIED INSTRUCTIONS ARE GIVEN TO DICK BY BRUCE WAYNE..
POLICEMEN ALL OVER THE PLACE LOOKING FOR THE ESCAPED MANIAC AND THAT MISSING BOY!..LOOKS LIKE THERE WON'T BE MUCH PRIVACY FOR THE BATMAN TO WORK ABOUT HERE!
GUESS I'LL HAVE TO WORK ALONE, EH?
YES, BUT KEEP IN TOUCH WITH ME.. YOU KNOW HOW! SEND ME DETAILS ON WHATEVER DEVELOPS! GOOD LUCK, AND WATCH YOURSELF!
RIGHT!
DICK IMMEDIATELY GETS TO WORK ON ONE OF HIS NEW FELLOW PUPILS
AND YOU SAY THAT THE POLICE SEARCHED TED SPENCER'S ROOM FOR A DIARY?
YES, THEY FIGURED HE MIGHT HAVE WRITTEN DOWN SOME-THING THAT HAD TO DO WITH HIS DISAPPEARANCE, BUT COULDN'T FIND IT!
THAT NIGHT A MANTLED FIGURE PROWLS THE DARK HALLWAY. ROBIN, THE BOY WONDER!
I'M GOING TO SEARCH TED SPENCER'S ROOM! I'D LIKE TO FIND THAT DIARY OF HIS!
3

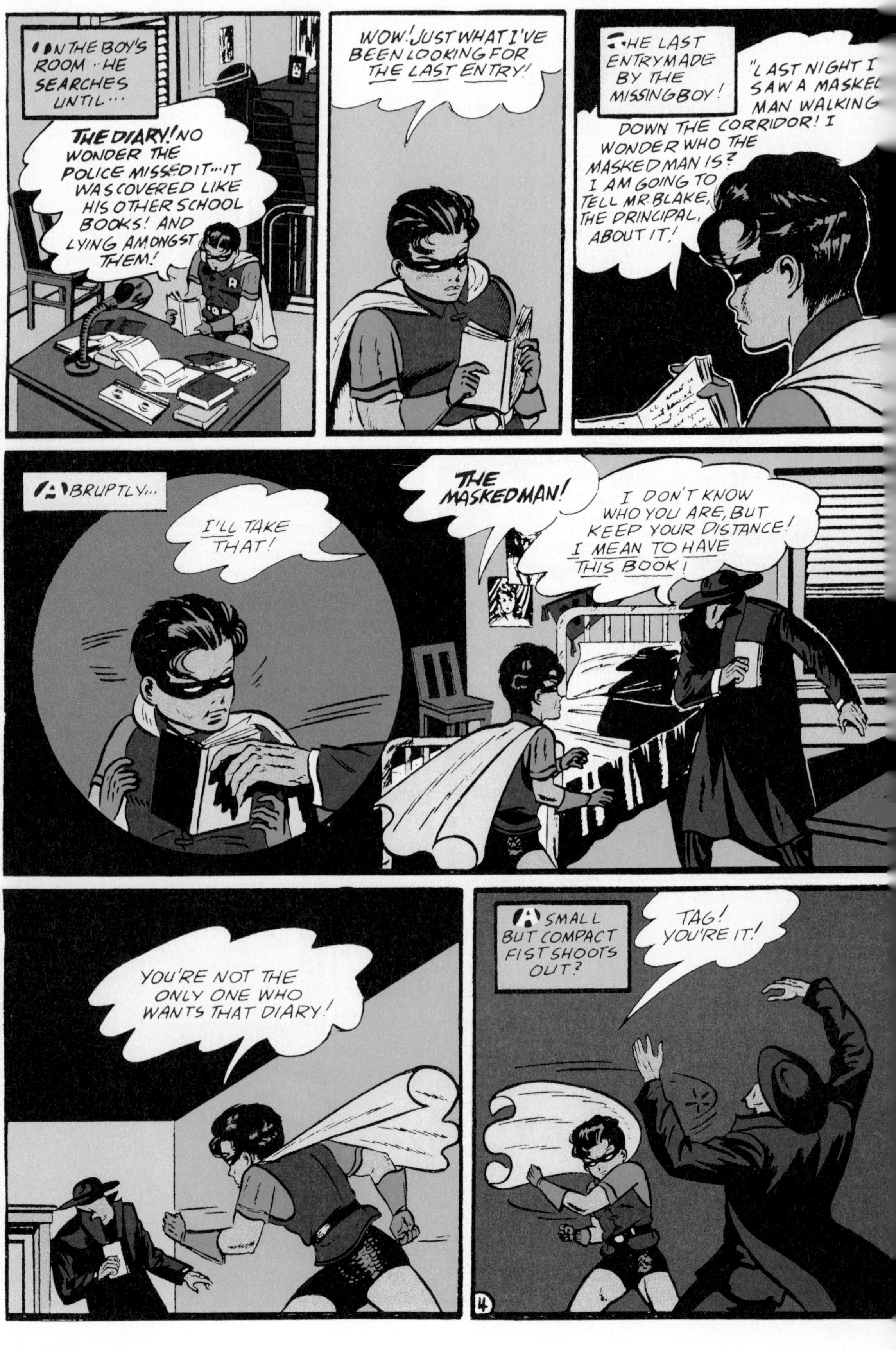
IN THE BOY'S ROOM .. HE SEARCHES UNTIL...
THE DIARY! NO WONDER THE POLICE MISSED IT...IT WAS COVERED LIKE HIS OTHER SCHOOL BOOKS! AND LYING AMONGST THEM!
WOW! JUST WHAT I'VE BEEN LOOKING FOR THE LAST ENTRY!
THE LAST ENTRY MADE BY THE MISSING BOY!
"LAST NIGHT I SAW A MASKED MAN WALKING DOWN THE CORRIDOR! I WONDER WHO THE MASKED MAN IS? I AM GOING TO TELL MR. BLAKE, THE PRINCIPAL, ABOUT IT!
ABRUPTLY...
I'LL TAKE THAT!
THE MASKED MAN!
I DON'T KNOW WHO YOU ARE, BUT KEEP YOUR DISTANCE! I MEAN TO HAVE THIS BOOK!
YOU'RE NOT THE ONLY ONE WHO WANTS THAT DIARY!
A SMALL BUT COMPACT FIST SHOOTS OUT?
TAG! YOU'RE IT!
4

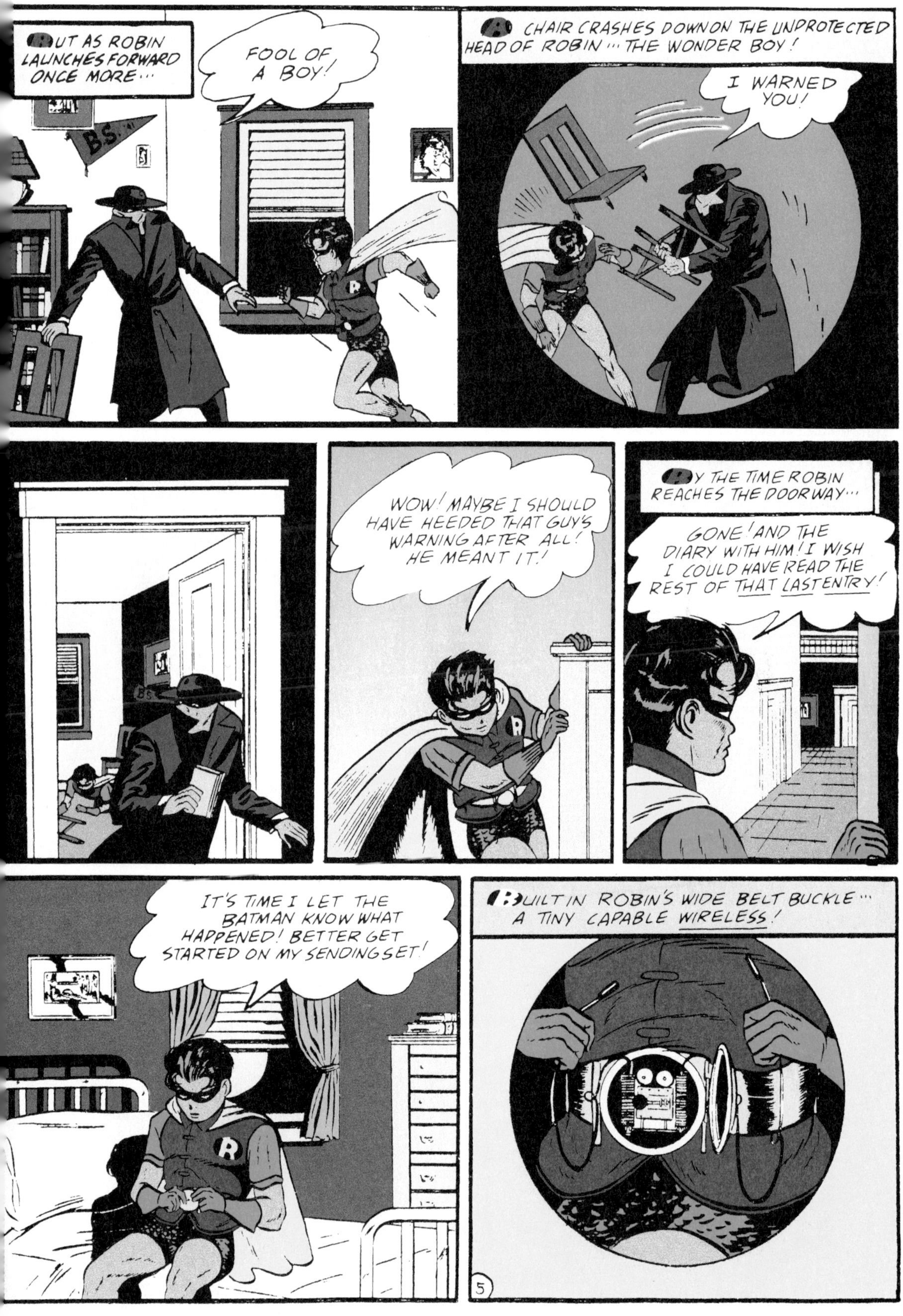
BUT AS ROBIN LAUNCHES FORWARD ONCE MORE...
FOOL OF A BOY!
CHAIR CRASHES DOWN ON THE UNPROTECTED HEAD OF ROBIN ... THE WONDER BOY!
I WARNED YOU!
WOW! MAYBE I SHOULD HAVE HEEDED THAT GUY'S WARNING AFTER ALL! HE MEANT IT!
BY THE TIME ROBIN REACHES THE DOORWAY...
GONE! AND THE DIARY WITH HIM! I WISH I COULD HAVE READ THE REST OF THAT LAST ENTRY!
IT'S TIME I LET THE BATMAN KNOW WHAT HAPPENED! BETTER GET STARTED ON MY SENDING SET!
BUILT IN ROBIN'S WIDE BELT BUCKLE... A TINY CAPABLE WIRELESS!
5

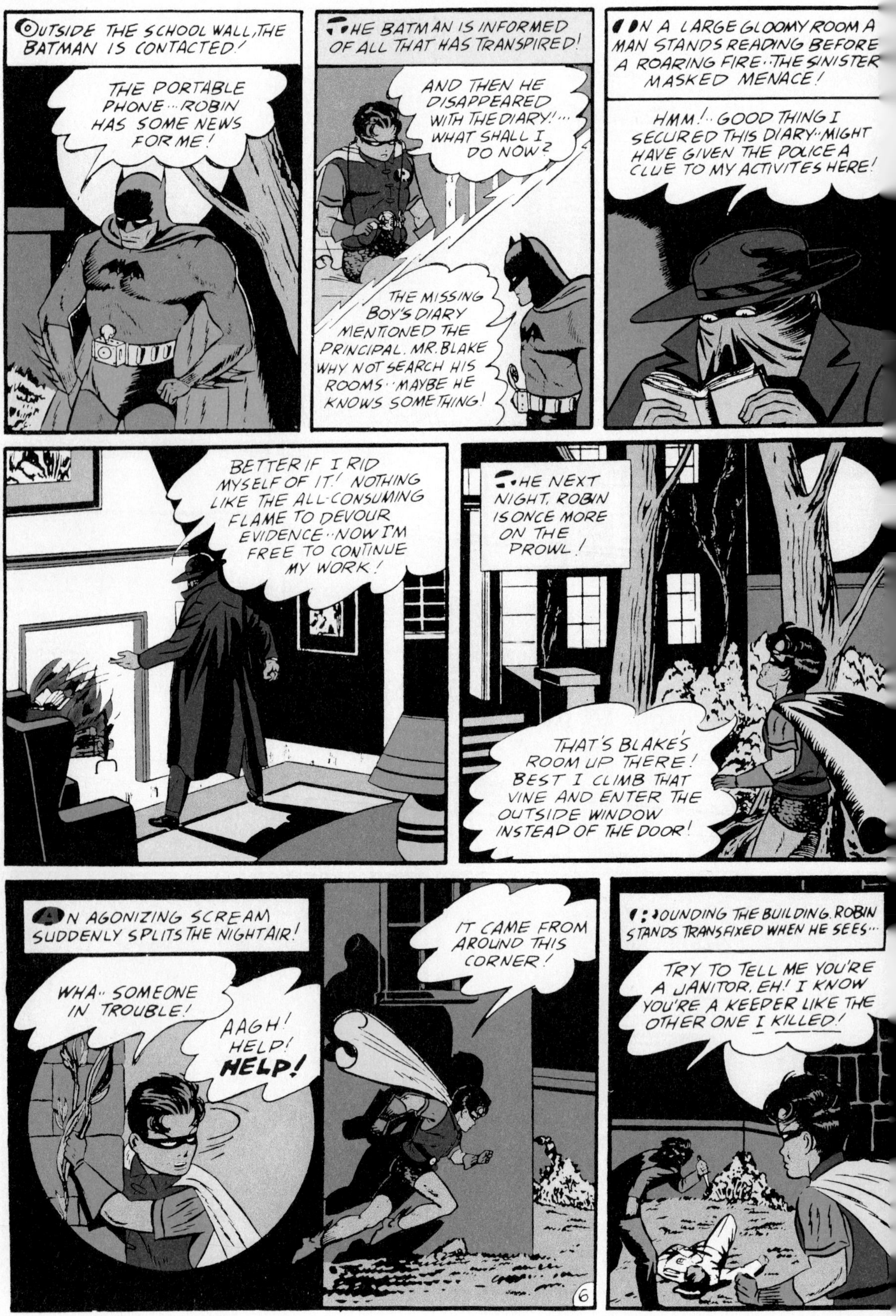
OUTSIDE THE SCHOOL WALL, THE BATMAN IS CONTACTED!
THE PORTABLE PHONE.. ROBIN HAS SOME NEWS FOR ME!
THE BATMAN IS INFORMED OF ALL THAT HAS TRANSPIRED!
AND THEN HE DISAPPEARED WITH THE DIARY!... WHAT SHALL I DO NOW?
THE MISSING BOY'S DIARY MENTIONED THE PRINCIPAL, MR. BLAKE WHY NOT SEARCH HIS ROOMS.. MAYBE HE KNOWS SOMETHING!
IN A LARGE GLOOMY ROOM A MAN STANDS READING BEFORE A ROARING FIRE.. THE SINISTER MASKED MENACE!
HMM!.. GOOD THING I SECURED THIS DIARY.. MIGHT HAVE GIVEN THE POLICE A CLUE TO MY ACTIVITES HERE!
BETTER IF I RID MYSELF OF IT! NOTHING LIKE THE ALL-CONSUMING FLAME TO DEVOUR EVIDENCE.. NOW I'M FREE TO CONTINUE MY WORK!
THE NEXT NIGHT, ROBIN IS ONCE MORE ON THE PROWL!
THAT'S BLAKE'S ROOM UP THERE! BEST I CLIMB THAT VINE AND ENTER THE OUTSIDE WINDOW INSTEAD OF THE DOOR!
AN AGONIZING SCREAM SUDDENLY SPLITS THE NIGHT AIR!
WHA.. SOMEONE IN TROUBLE!
AAGH! HELP! HELP!
IT CAME FROM AROUND THIS CORNER!
ROUNDING THE BUILDING, ROBIN STANDS TRANSFIXED WHEN HE SEES...
TRY TO TELL ME YOU'RE A JANITOR, EH! I KNOW YOU'RE A KEEPER LIKE THE OTHER ONE I KILLED!
6

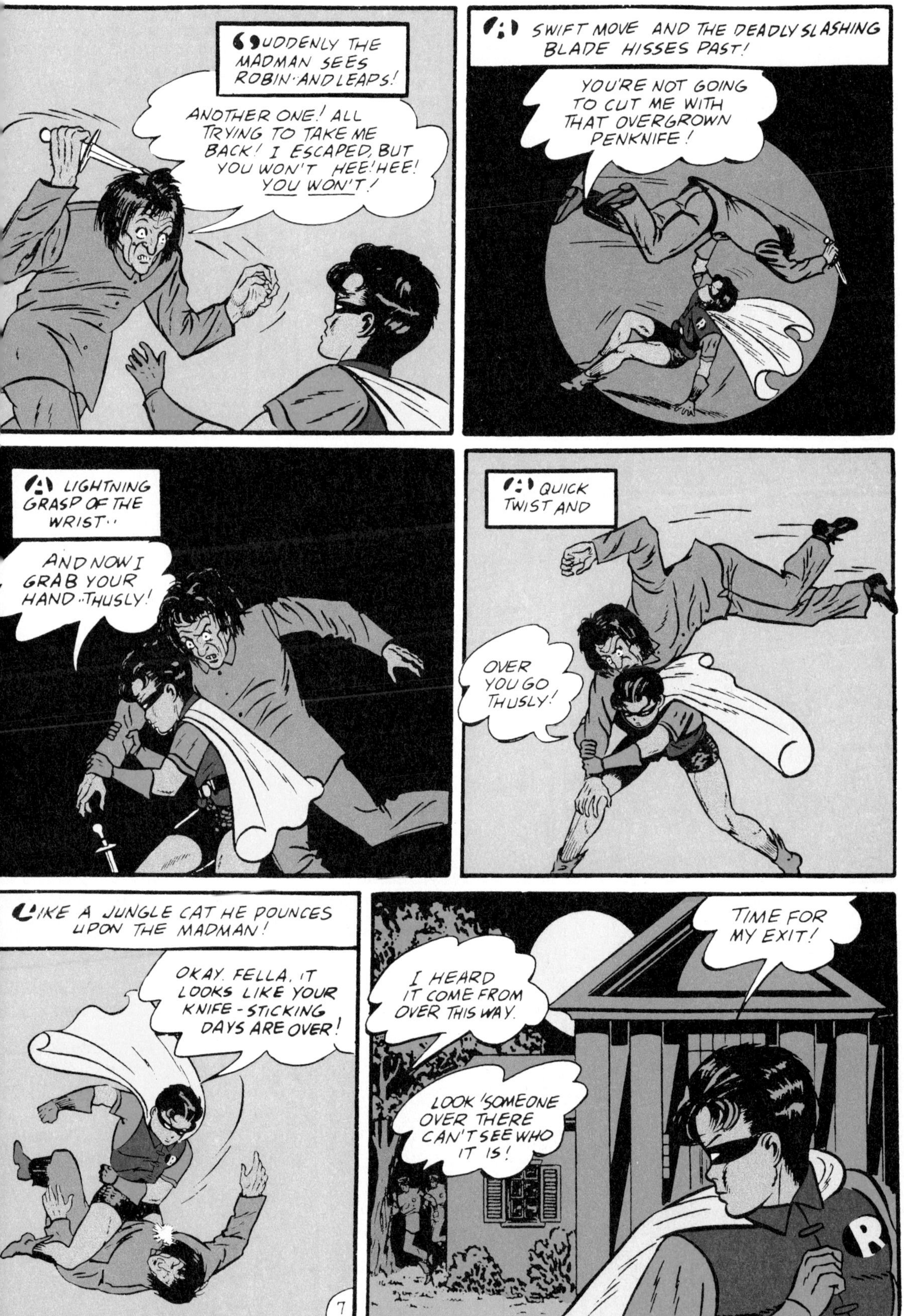
SUDDENLY THE MADMAN SEES ROBIN·AND LEAPS!
ANOTHER ONE! ALL TRYING TO TAKE ME BACK! I ESCAPED, BUT YOU WON'T HEE! HEE! YOU WON'T!
A SWIFT MOVE AND THE DEADLY SLASHING BLADE HISSES PAST!
YOU'RE NOT GOING TO CUT ME WITH THAT OVERGROWN PENKNIFE!
A LIGHTNING GRASP OF THE WRIST··
AND NOW I GRAB YOUR HAND··THUSLY!
A QUICK TWIST AND
OVER YOU GO THUSLY!
LIKE A JUNGLE CAT HE POUNCES UPON THE MADMAN!
OKAY, FELLA, IT LOOKS LIKE YOUR KNIFE-STICKING DAYS ARE OVER!
7
TIME FOR MY EXIT!
I HEARD IT COME FROM OVER THIS WAY.
LOOK! SOMEONE OVER THERE CAN'T SEE WHO IT IS!

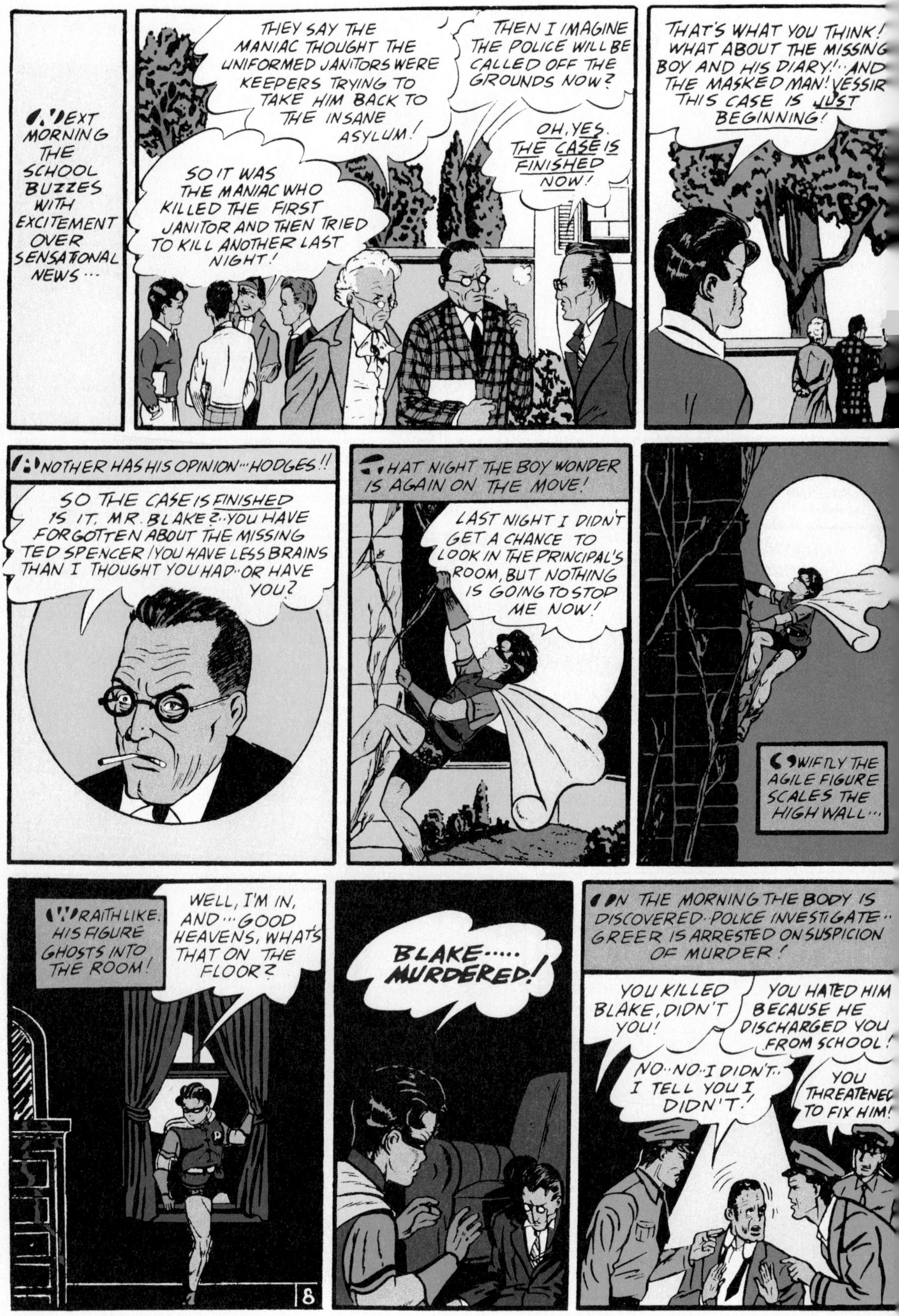
NEXT MORNING THE SCHOOL BUZZES WITH EXCITEMENT OVER SENSATIONAL NEWS...
THEY SAY THE MANIAC THOUGHT THE UNIFORMED JANITORS WERE KEEPERS TRYING TO TAKE HIM BACK TO THE INSANE ASYLUM!
THEN I IMAGINE THE POLICE WILL BE CALLED OFF THE GROUNDS NOW?
SO IT WAS THE MANIAC WHO KILLED THE FIRST JANITOR AND THEN TRIED TO KILL ANOTHER LAST NIGHT!
OH, YES. THE CASE IS FINISHED NOW!
THAT'S WHAT YOU THINK! WHAT ABOUT THE MISSING BOY AND HIS DIARY!.. AND THE MASKED MAN! YESSIR THIS CASE IS JUST BEGINNING!
ANOTHER HAS HIS OPINION... HODGES!!
SO THE CASE IS FINISHED IS IT, MR. BLAKE?..YOU HAVE FORGOTTEN ABOUT THE MISSING TED SPENCER! YOU HAVE LESS BRAINS THAN I THOUGHT YOU HAD..OR HAVE YOU?
THAT NIGHT THE BOY WONDER IS AGAIN ON THE MOVE!
LAST NIGHT I DIDN'T GET A CHANCE TO LOOK IN THE PRINCIPAL'S ROOM, BUT NOTHING IS GOING TO STOP ME NOW!
SWIFTLY THE AGILE FIGURE SCALES THE HIGH WALL...
WRAITHLIKE, HIS FIGURE GHOSTS INTO THE ROOM!
WELL, I'M IN, AND... GOOD HEAVENS, WHAT'S THAT ON THE FLOOR?
8
BLAKE..... MURDERED!
ON THE MORNING THE BODY IS DISCOVERED. POLICE INVESTIGATE.. GREER IS ARRESTED ON SUSPICION OF MURDER!
YOU KILLED BLAKE, DIDN'T YOU!
YOU HATED HIM BECAUSE HE DISCHARGED YOU FROM SCHOOL!
NO..NO..I DIDN'T.. I TELL YOU I DIDN'T!
YOU THREATENED TO FIX HIM!

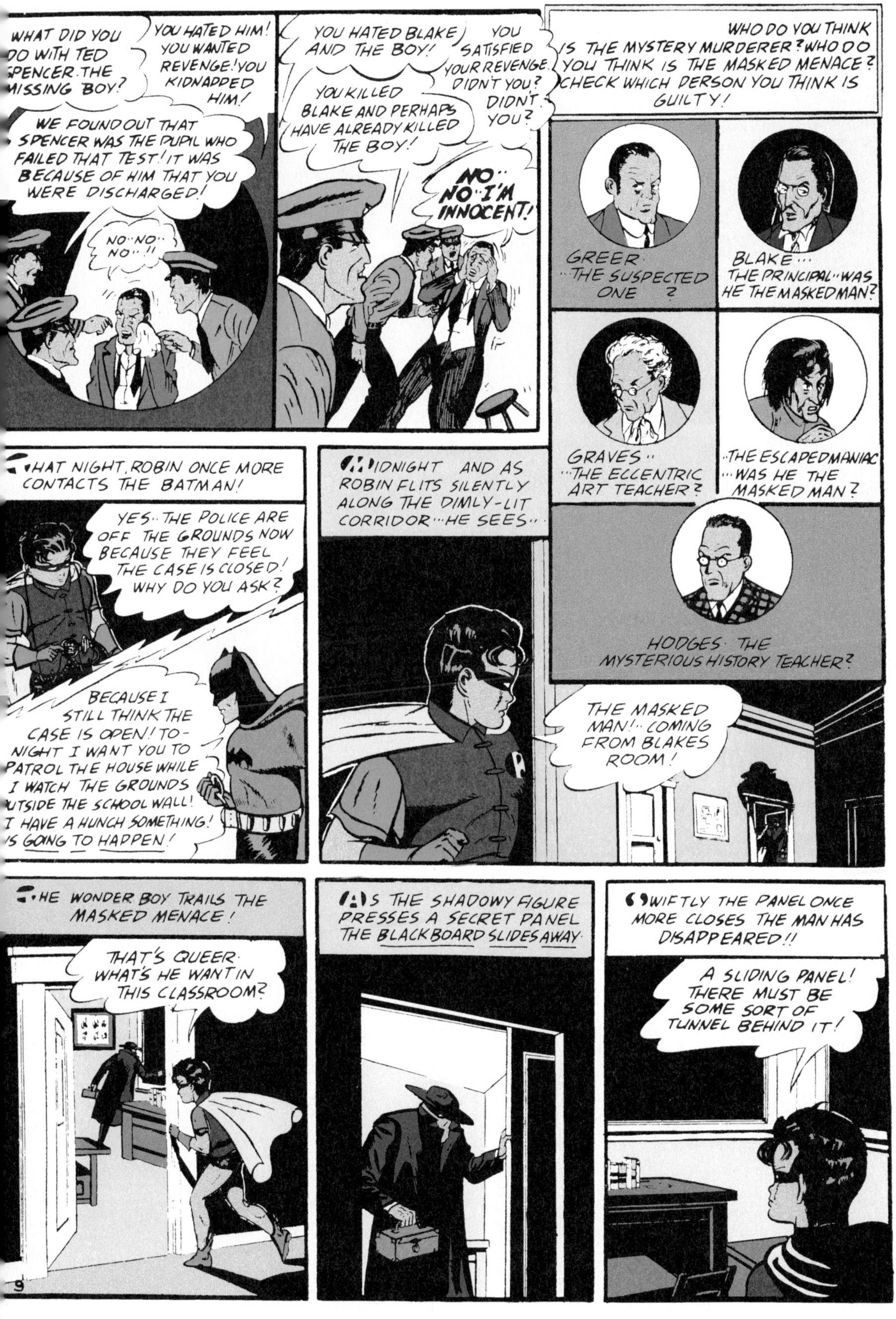
WHAT DID YOU DO WITH TED SPENCER THE MISSING BOY?
YOU HATED HIM! YOU WANTED REVENGE! YOU KIDNAPPED HIM!
WE FOUND OUT THAT SPENCER WAS THE PUPIL WHO FAILED THAT TEST! IT WAS BECAUSE OF HIM THAT YOU WERE DISCHARGED!
NO.. NO.. NO..!!
YOU HATED BLAKE AND THE BOY!
YOU SATISFIED YOUR REVENGE. DIDN'T YOU? DIDN'T YOU?
YOU KILLED BLAKE AND PERHAPS HAVE ALREADY KILLED THE BOY!
NO.. NO.. I'M INNOCENT!
WHO DO YOU THINK IS THE MYSTERY MURDERER? WHO DO YOU THINK IS THE MASKED MENACE? CHECK WHICH PERSON YOU THINK IS GUILTY!
GREER ..THE SUSPECTED ONE ?
BLAKE... THE PRINCIPAL..WAS HE THE MASKED MAN?
GRAVES.. ..THE ECCENTRIC ART TEACHER?
..THE ESCAPED MANIAC ..WAS HE THE MASKED MAN?
HODGES THE MYSTERIOUS HISTORY TEACHER?
THAT NIGHT, ROBIN ONCE MORE CONTACTS THE BATMAN!
YES.. THE POLICE ARE OFF THE GROUNDS NOW BECAUSE THEY FEEL THE CASE IS CLOSED! WHY DO YOU ASK?
BECAUSE I STILL THINK THE CASE IS OPEN! TO-NIGHT I WANT YOU TO PATROL THE HOUSE WHILE I WATCH THE GROUNDS OUTSIDE THE SCHOOL WALL! I HAVE A HUNCH SOMETHING IS GOING TO HAPPEN!
MIDNIGHT AND AS ROBIN FLITS SILENTLY ALONG THE DIMLY-LIT CORRIDOR... HE SEES..
THE MASKED MAN!.. COMING FROM BLAKES ROOM!
THE WONDER BOY TRAILS THE MASKED MENACE!
THAT'S QUEER WHAT'S HE WANT IN THIS CLASSROOM?
AS THE SHADOWY FIGURE PRESSES A SECRET PANEL THE BLACKBOARD SLIDES AWAY.
SWIFTLY THE PANEL ONCE MORE CLOSES THE MAN HAS DISAPPEARED!!
A SLIDING PANEL! THERE MUST BE SOME SORT OF TUNNEL BEHIND IT!
9

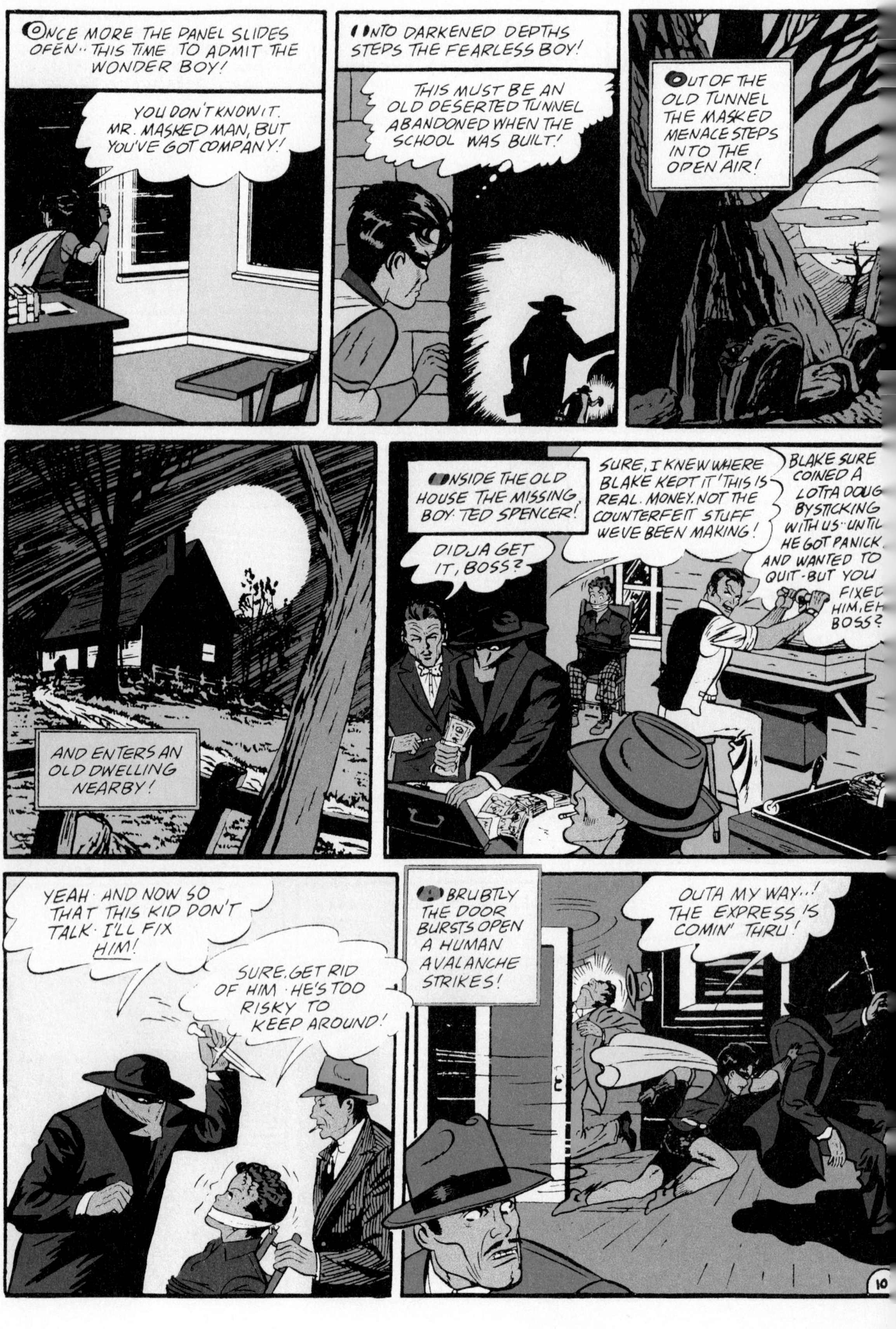
ONCE MORE THE PANEL SLIDES OPEN.. THIS TIME TO ADMIT THE WONDER BOY!
YOU DON'T KNOW IT, MR. MASKED MAN, BUT YOU'VE GOT COMPANY!
INTO DARKENED DEPTHS STEPS THE FEARLESS BOY!
THIS MUST BE AN OLD DESERTED TUNNEL ABANDONED WHEN THE SCHOOL WAS BUILT!
OUT OF THE OLD TUNNEL THE MASKED MENACE STEPS INTO THE OPEN AIR!
AND ENTERS AN OLD DWELLING NEARBY!
INSIDE THE OLD HOUSE THE MISSING BOY: TED SPENCER!
DIDJA GET IT, BOSS?
SURE, I KNEW WHERE BLAKE KEPT IT 'THIS IS REAL MONEY. NOT THE COUNTERFEIT STUFF WE'VE BEEN MAKING!
BLAKE SURE COINED A LOTTA DOUG BY STICKING WITH US.. UNTIL HE GOT PANICK AND WANTED TO QUIT-BUT YOU FIXED HIM, EH BOSS?
YEAH. AND NOW SO THAT THIS KID DON'T TALK. I'LL FIX HIM!
SURE, GET RID OF HIM. HE'S TOO RISKY TO KEEP AROUND!
ABRUBTLY THE DOOR BURSTS OPEN A HUMAN AVALANCHE STRIKES!
OUTA MY WAY..! THE EXPRESS IS COMIN' THRU!
10

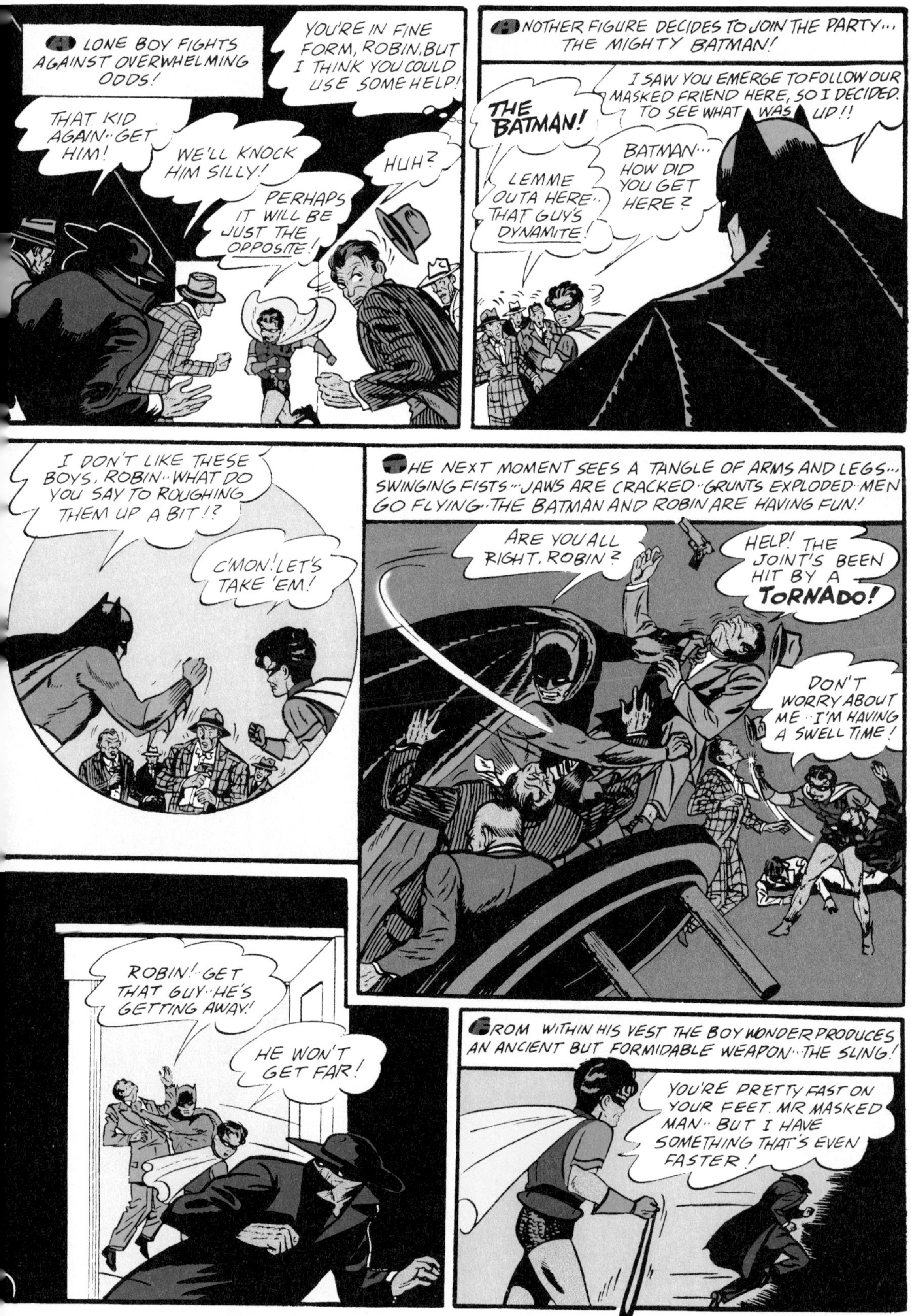
A LONE BOY FIGHTS AGAINST OVERWHELMING ODDS!
THAT KID AGAIN.. GET HIM!
YOU'RE IN FINE FORM, ROBIN, BUT I THINK YOU COULD USE SOME HELP!
WE'LL KNOCK HIM SILLY!
HUH?
PERHAPS IT WILL BE JUST THE OPPOSITE!
ANOTHER FIGURE DECIDES TO JOIN THE PARTY... THE MIGHTY BATMAN!
THE BATMAN!
I SAW YOU EMERGE TO FOLLOW OUR MASKED FRIEND HERE, SO I DECIDED TO SEE WHAT WAS UP!!
LEMME OUTA HERE.. THAT GUY'S DYNAMITE!
BATMAN... HOW DID YOU GET HERE?
I DON'T LIKE THESE BOYS, ROBIN.. WHAT DO YOU SAY TO ROUGHING THEM UP A BIT!?
C'MON! LET'S TAKE 'EM!
THE NEXT MOMENT SEES A TANGLE OF ARMS AND LEGS... SWINGING FISTS.. JAWS ARE CRACKED.. GRUNTS EXPLODED.. MEN GO FLYING.. THE BATMAN AND ROBIN ARE HAVING FUN!
ARE YOU ALL RIGHT, ROBIN?
HELP! THE JOINT'S BEEN HIT BY A TORNADO!
DON'T WORRY ABOUT ME.. I'M HAVING A SWELL TIME!
ROBIN!.. GET THAT GUY.. HE'S GETTING AWAY!
HE WON'T GET FAR!
FROM WITHIN HIS VEST THE BOY WONDER PRODUCES AN ANCIENT BUT FORMIDABLE WEAPON.. THE SLING!
YOU'RE PRETTY FAST ON YOUR FEET, MR MASKED MAN.. BUT I HAVE SOMETHING THAT'S EVEN FASTER!

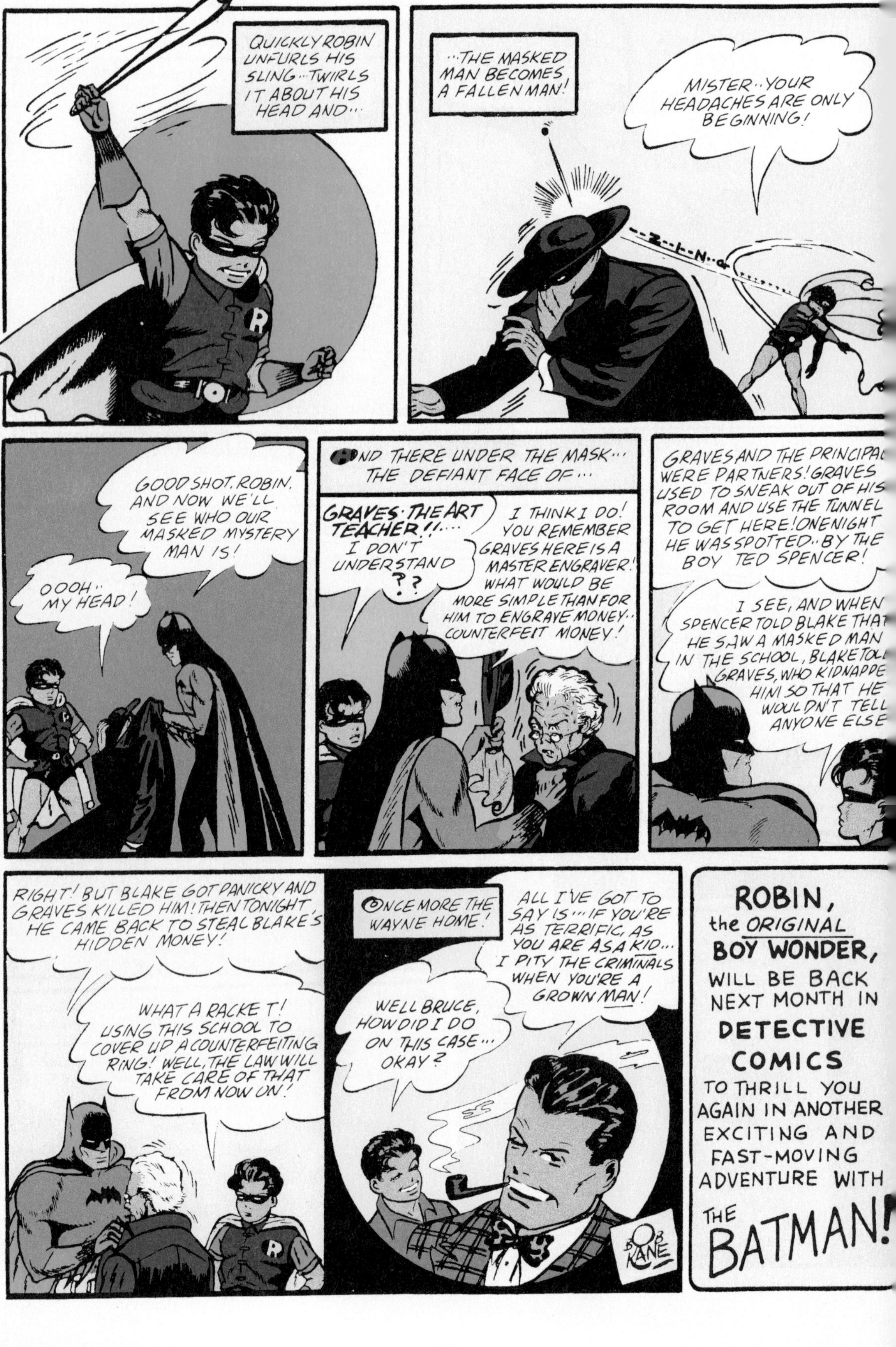
QUICKLY ROBIN UNFURLS HIS SLING...TWIRLS IT ABOUT HIS HEAD AND...
...THE MASKED MAN BECOMES A FALLEN MAN!
MISTER..YOUR HEADACHES ARE ONLY BEGINNING!
Z-I-N-G
GOOD SHOT, ROBIN, AND NOW WE'LL SEE WHO OUR MASKED MYSTERY MAN IS!
OOOH.. MY HEAD!
AND THERE UNDER THE MASK... THE DEFIANT FACE OF...
GRAVES-THE ART TEACHER!!... I DON'T UNDERSTAND ??
I THINK I DO! YOU REMEMBER GRAVES HERE IS A MASTER ENGRAVER! WHAT WOULD BE MORE SIMPLE THAN FOR HIM TO ENGRAVE MONEY.. COUNTERFEIT MONEY!
GRAVES AND THE PRINCIPAL WERE PARTNERS! GRAVES USED TO SNEAK OUT OF HIS ROOM AND USE THE TUNNEL TO GET HERE! ONE NIGHT HE WAS SPOTTED.. BY THE BOY TED SPENCER!
I SEE, AND WHEN SPENCER TOLD BLAKE THAT HE SAW A MASKED MAN IN THE SCHOOL, BLAKE TOLD GRAVES, WHO KIDNAPPED HIM SO THAT HE WOULDN'T TELL ANYONE ELSE
RIGHT! BUT BLAKE GOT PANICKY AND GRAVES KILLED HIM! THEN TONIGHT, HE CAME BACK TO STEAL BLAKE'S HIDDEN MONEY!
WHAT A RACKET! USING THIS SCHOOL TO COVER UP A COUNTERFEITING RING! WELL, THE LAW WILL TAKE CARE OF THAT FROM NOW ON!
ONCE MORE THE WAYNE HOME!
ALL I'VE GOT TO SAY IS... IF YOU'RE AS TERRIFIC, AS YOU ARE AS A KID... I PITY THE CRIMINALS WHEN YOU'RE A GROWN MAN!
WELL BRUCE, HOW DID I DO ON THIS CASE... OKAY?
BOB KANE
ROBIN, the ORIGINAL BOY WONDER, WILL BE BACK NEXT MONTH IN DETECTIVE COMICS TO THRILL YOU AGAIN IN ANOTHER EXCITING AND FAST-MOVING ADVENTURE WITH THE BATMAN!

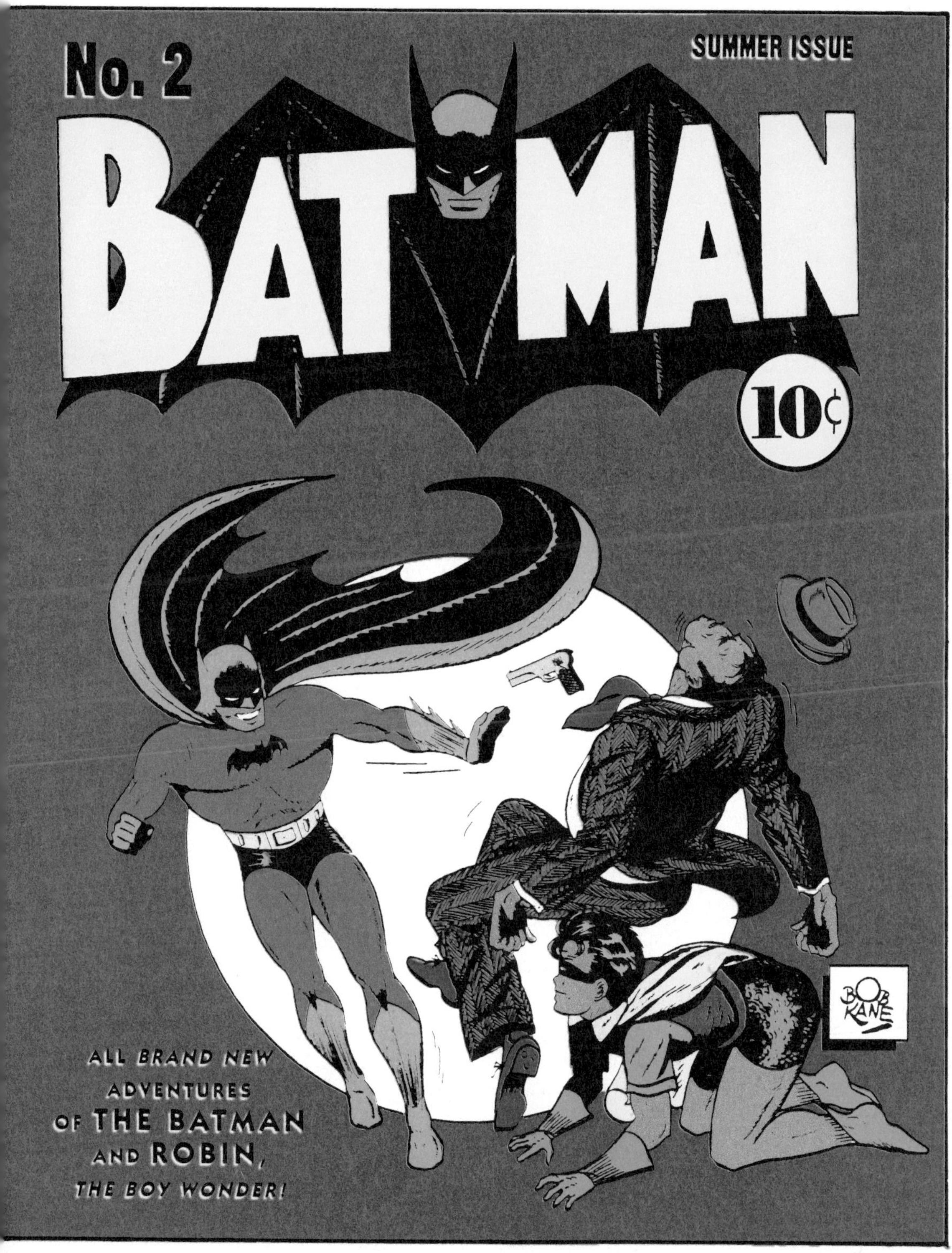
No. 2
SUMMER ISSUE
BATMAN
10¢
ALL BRAND NEW
ADVENTURES
OF THE BATMAN
AND ROBIN,
THE BOY WONDER!
BOB KANE

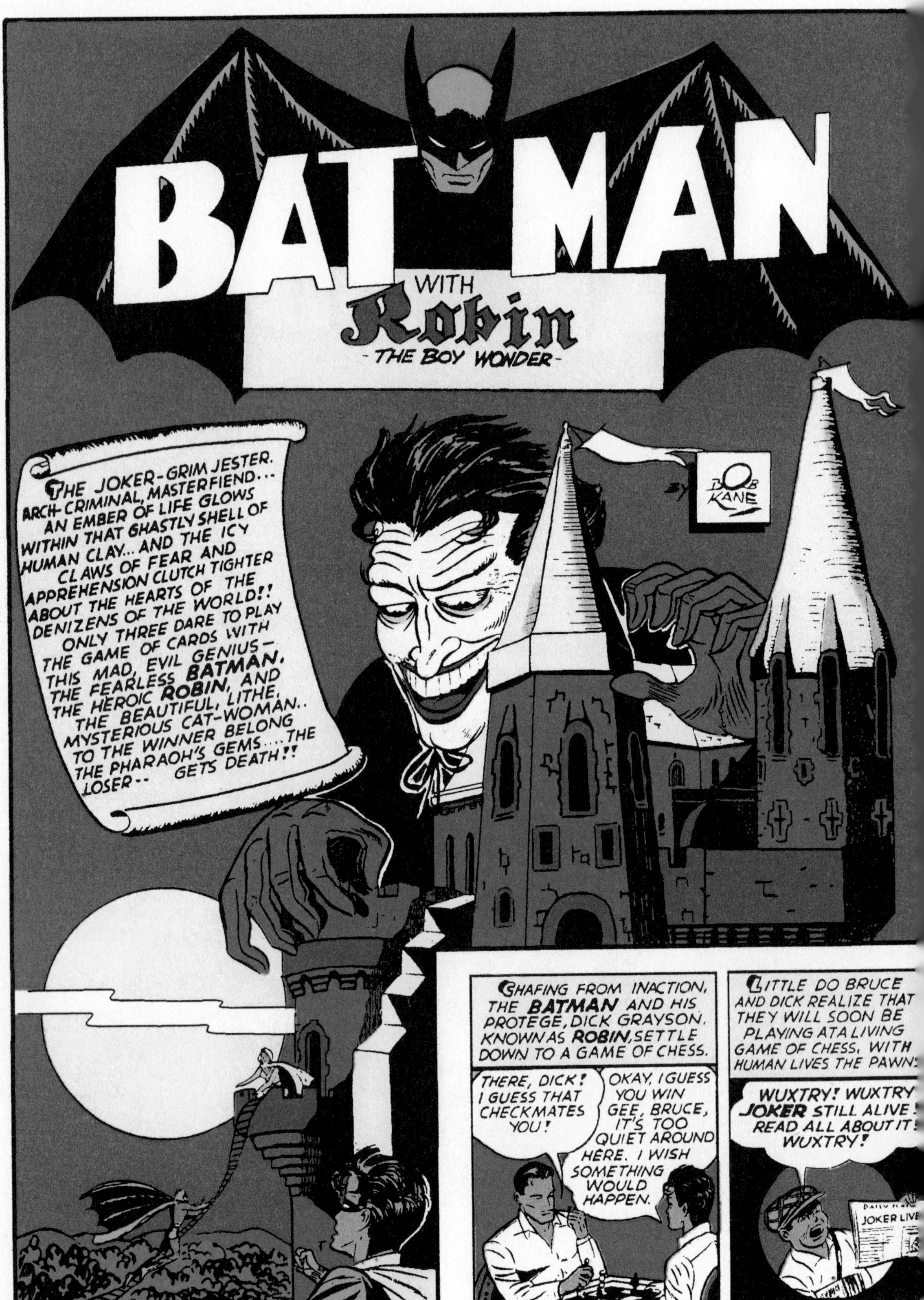
BATMAN
WITH
Robin
-THE BOY WONDER-
BY BOB KANE
THE JOKER-GRIM JESTER. ARCH-CRIMINAL, MASTERFIEND... AN EMBER OF LIFE GLOWS WITHIN THAT GHASTLY SHELL OF HUMAN CLAY... AND THE ICY CLAWS OF FEAR AND APPREHENSION CLUTCH TIGHTER ABOUT THE HEARTS OF THE DENIZENS OF THE WORLD!! ONLY THREE DARE TO PLAY THE GAME OF CARDS WITH THIS MAD, EVIL GENIUS- THE FEARLESS BATMAN, THE HEROIC ROBIN, AND THE BEAUTIFUL, LITHE, MYSTERIOUS CAT-WOMAN.. TO THE WINNER BELONG THE PHARAOH'S GEMS.... THE LOSER-- GETS DEATH!!
CHAFING FROM INACTION, THE BATMAN AND HIS PROTEGE, DICK GRAYSON, KNOWN AS ROBIN, SETTLE DOWN TO A GAME OF CHESS.
THERE, DICK! I GUESS THAT CHECKMATES YOU!
OKAY, I GUESS YOU WIN GEE, BRUCE, IT'S TOO QUIET AROUND HERE. I WISH SOMETHING WOULD HAPPEN.
LITTLE DO BRUCE AND DICK REALIZE THAT THEY WILL SOON BE PLAYING AT A LIVING GAME OF CHESS, WITH HUMAN LIVES THE PAWNS
WUXTRY! WUXTRY JOKER STILL ALIVE! READ ALL ABOUT IT! WUXTRY!
JOKER LIVE

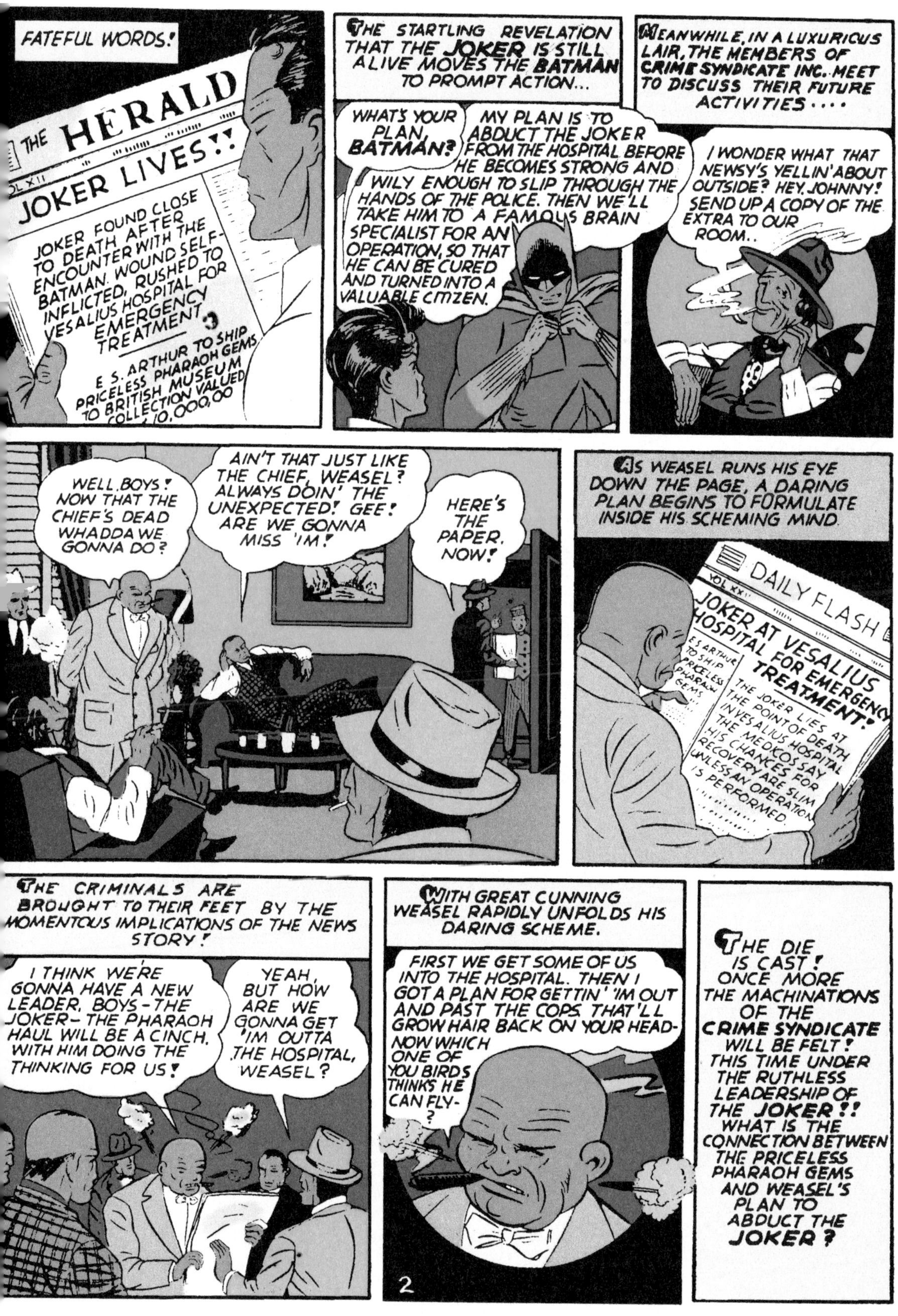
FATEFUL WORDS!
THE HERALD
JOKER LIVES!!
JOKER FOUND CLOSE TO DEATH AFTER ENCOUNTER WITH THE BATMAN. WOUND SELF-INFLICTED, RUSHED TO VESALIUS HOSPITAL FOR EMERGENCY TREATMENT
E. S. ARTHUR TO SHIP PRICELESS PHARAOH GEMS TO BRITISH MUSEUM COLLECTION VALUED
THE STARTLING REVELATION THAT THE JOKER IS STILL ALIVE MOVES THE BATMAN TO PROMPT ACTION...
WHAT'S YOUR PLAN, BATMAN?
MY PLAN IS TO ABDUCT THE JOKER FROM THE HOSPITAL BEFORE HE BECOMES STRONG AND WILY ENOUGH TO SLIP THROUGH THE HANDS OF THE POLICE. THEN WE'LL TAKE HIM TO A FAMOUS BRAIN SPECIALIST FOR AN OPERATION, SO THAT HE CAN BE CURED AND TURNED INTO A VALUABLE CITIZEN.
MEANWHILE, IN A LUXURIOUS LAIR, THE MEMBERS OF CRIME SYNDICATE INC. MEET TO DISCUSS THEIR FUTURE ACTIVITIES....
I WONDER WHAT THAT NEWSY'S YELLIN' ABOUT OUTSIDE? HEY, JOHNNY! SEND UP A COPY OF THE EXTRA TO OUR ROOM..
WELL, BOYS! NOW THAT THE CHIEF'S DEAD WHADDA WE GONNA DO?
AIN'T THAT JUST LIKE THE CHIEF, WEASEL? ALWAYS DOIN' THE UNEXPECTED! GEE! ARE WE GONNA MISS 'IM!
HERE'S THE PAPER, NOW!
AS WEASEL RUNS HIS EYE DOWN THE PAGE, A DARING PLAN BEGINS TO FORMULATE INSIDE HIS SCHEMING MIND.
DAILY FLASH
JOKER AT VESALIUS HOSPITAL FOR EMERGENCY TREATMENT!
THE JOKER LIES AT THE POINT OF DEATH IN VESALIUS HOSPITAL. THE MEDICOS SAY HIS CHANCES FOR RECOVERY ARE SLIM UNLESS AN OPERATION IS PERFORMED.
E.S. ARTHUR TO SHIP PRICELESS PHARAOH GEMS
THE CRIMINALS ARE BROUGHT TO THEIR FEET BY THE MOMENTOUS IMPLICATIONS OF THE NEWS STORY!
I THINK WE'RE GONNA HAVE A NEW LEADER, BOYS - THE JOKER - THE PHARAOH HAUL WILL BE A CINCH, WITH HIM DOING THE THINKING FOR US!
YEAH, BUT HOW ARE WE GONNA GET 'IM OUTTA THE HOSPITAL, WEASEL?
WITH GREAT CUNNING WEASEL RAPIDLY UNFOLDS HIS DARING SCHEME.
FIRST WE GET SOME OF US INTO THE HOSPITAL. THEN I GOT A PLAN FOR GETTIN' 'IM OUT AND PAST THE COPS THAT'LL GROW HAIR BACK ON YOUR HEAD - NOW WHICH ONE OF YOU BIRDS THINKS HE CAN FLY-?
2
THE DIE IS CAST! ONCE MORE THE MACHINATIONS OF THE CRIME SYNDICATE WILL BE FELT! THIS TIME UNDER THE RUTHLESS LEADERSHIP OF THE JOKER!! WHAT IS THE CONNECTION BETWEEN THE PRICELESS PHARAOH GEMS AND WEASEL'S PLAN TO ABDUCT THE JOKER?

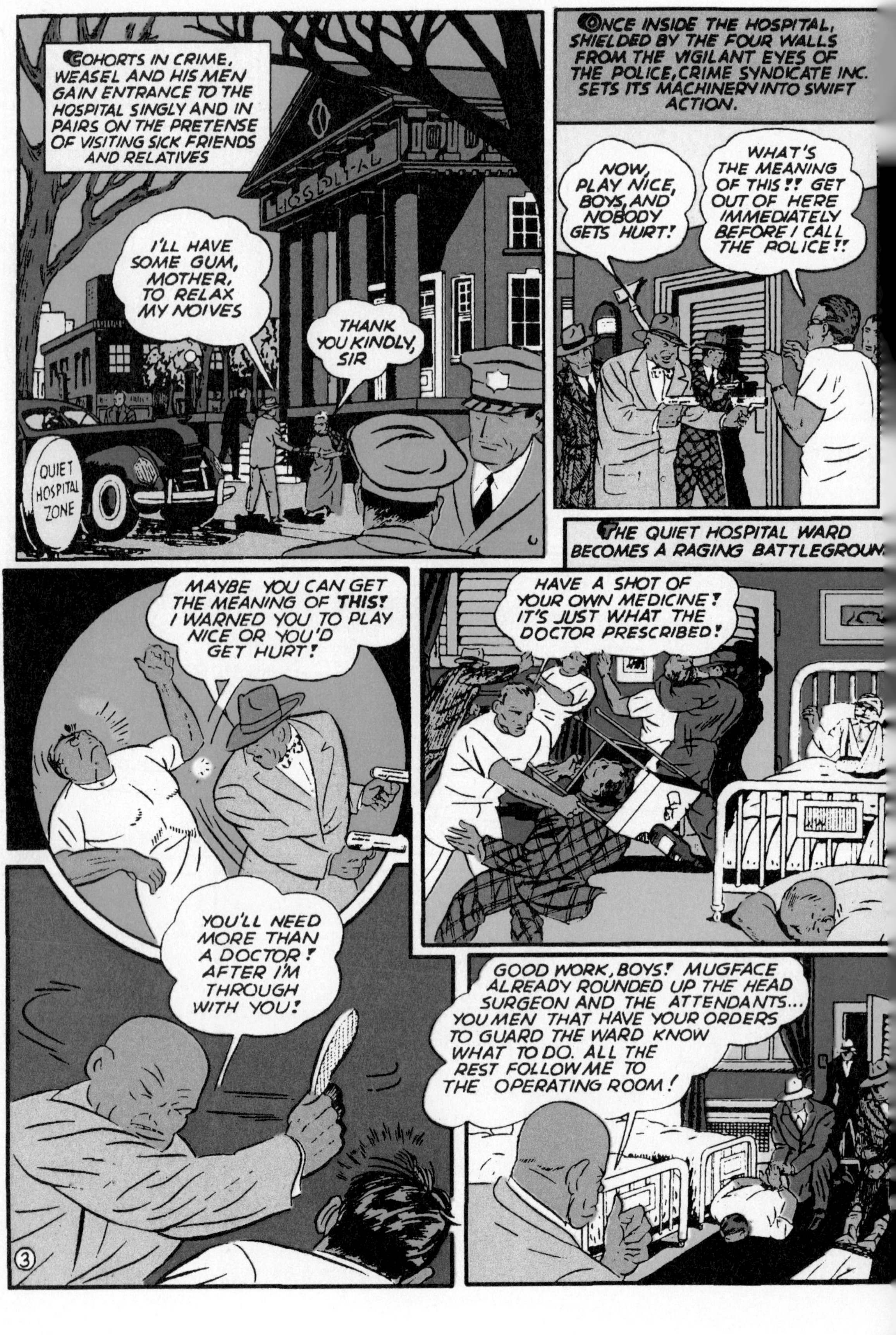
COHORTS IN CRIME, WEASEL AND HIS MEN GAIN ENTRANCE TO THE HOSPITAL SINGLY AND IN PAIRS ON THE PRETENSE OF VISITING SICK FRIENDS AND RELATIVES
HOSPITAL
I'LL HAVE SOME GUM, MOTHER, TO RELAX MY NOIVES
THANK YOU KINDLY, SIR
QUIET HOSPITAL ZONE
ONCE INSIDE THE HOSPITAL, SHIELDED BY THE FOUR WALLS FROM THE VIGILANT EYES OF THE POLICE, CRIME SYNDICATE INC. SETS ITS MACHINERY INTO SWIFT ACTION.
NOW, PLAY NICE, BOYS, AND NOBODY GETS HURT!
WHAT'S THE MEANING OF THIS!! GET OUT OF HERE IMMEDIATELY BEFORE I CALL THE POLICE!!
THE QUIET HOSPITAL WARD BECOMES A RAGING BATTLEGROUN
MAYBE YOU CAN GET THE MEANING OF THIS! I WARNED YOU TO PLAY NICE OR YOU'D GET HURT!
HAVE A SHOT OF YOUR OWN MEDICINE! IT'S JUST WHAT THE DOCTOR PRESCRIBED!
YOU'LL NEED MORE THAN A DOCTOR! AFTER I'M THROUGH WITH YOU!
GOOD WORK, BOYS! MUGFACE ALREADY ROUNDED UP THE HEAD SURGEON AND THE ATTENDANTS... YOU MEN THAT HAVE YOUR ORDERS TO GUARD THE WARD KNOW WHAT TO DO. ALL THE REST FOLLOW ME TO THE OPERATING ROOM!
3

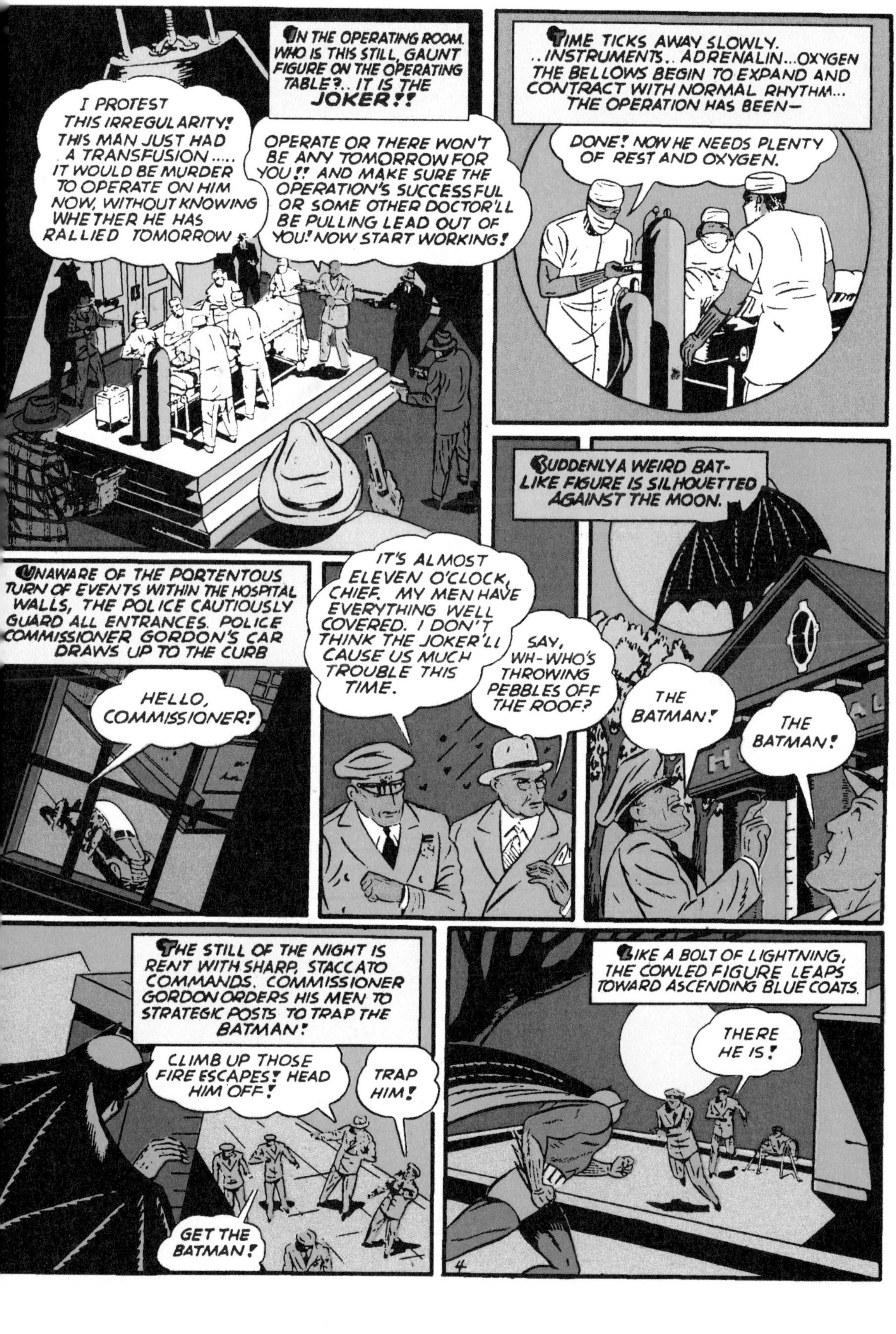
IN THE OPERATING ROOM. WHO IS THIS STILL, GAUNT FIGURE ON THE OPERATING TABLE?.. IT IS THE JOKER!!
I PROTEST THIS IRREGULARITY! THIS MAN JUST HAD A TRANSFUSION..... IT WOULD BE MURDER TO OPERATE ON HIM NOW, WITHOUT KNOWING WHETHER HE HAS RALLIED TOMORROW
OPERATE OR THERE WON'T BE ANY TOMORROW FOR YOU!! AND MAKE SURE THE OPERATION'S SUCCESSFUL OR SOME OTHER DOCTOR'LL BE PULLING LEAD OUT OF YOU! NOW START WORKING!
TIME TICKS AWAY SLOWLY. ..INSTRUMENTS.. ADRENALIN...OXYGEN THE BELLOWS BEGIN TO EXPAND AND CONTRACT WITH NORMAL RHYTHM... THE OPERATION HAS BEEN—
DONE! NOW HE NEEDS PLENTY OF REST AND OXYGEN.
UNAWARE OF THE PORTENTOUS TURN OF EVENTS WITHIN THE HOSPITAL WALLS, THE POLICE CAUTIOUSLY GUARD ALL ENTRANCES. POLICE COMMISSIONER GORDON'S CAR DRAWS UP TO THE CURB
HELLO, COMMISSIONER!
IT'S ALMOST ELEVEN O'CLOCK, CHIEF. MY MEN HAVE EVERYTHING WELL COVERED. I DON'T THINK THE JOKER'LL CAUSE US MUCH TROUBLE THIS TIME.
SAY, WH-WHO'S THROWING PEBBLES OFF THE ROOF?
SUDDENLY A WEIRD BAT-LIKE FIGURE IS SILHOUETTED AGAINST THE MOON.
THE BATMAN!
THE BATMAN!
THE STILL OF THE NIGHT IS RENT WITH SHARP, STACCATO COMMANDS. COMMISSIONER GORDON ORDERS HIS MEN TO STRATEGIC POSTS TO TRAP THE BATMAN!
CLIMB UP THOSE FIRE ESCAPES! HEAD HIM OFF!
TRAP HIM!
GET THE BATMAN!
LIKE A BOLT OF LIGHTNING, THE COWLED FIGURE LEAPS TOWARD ASCENDING BLUE COATS.
THERE HE IS!
4

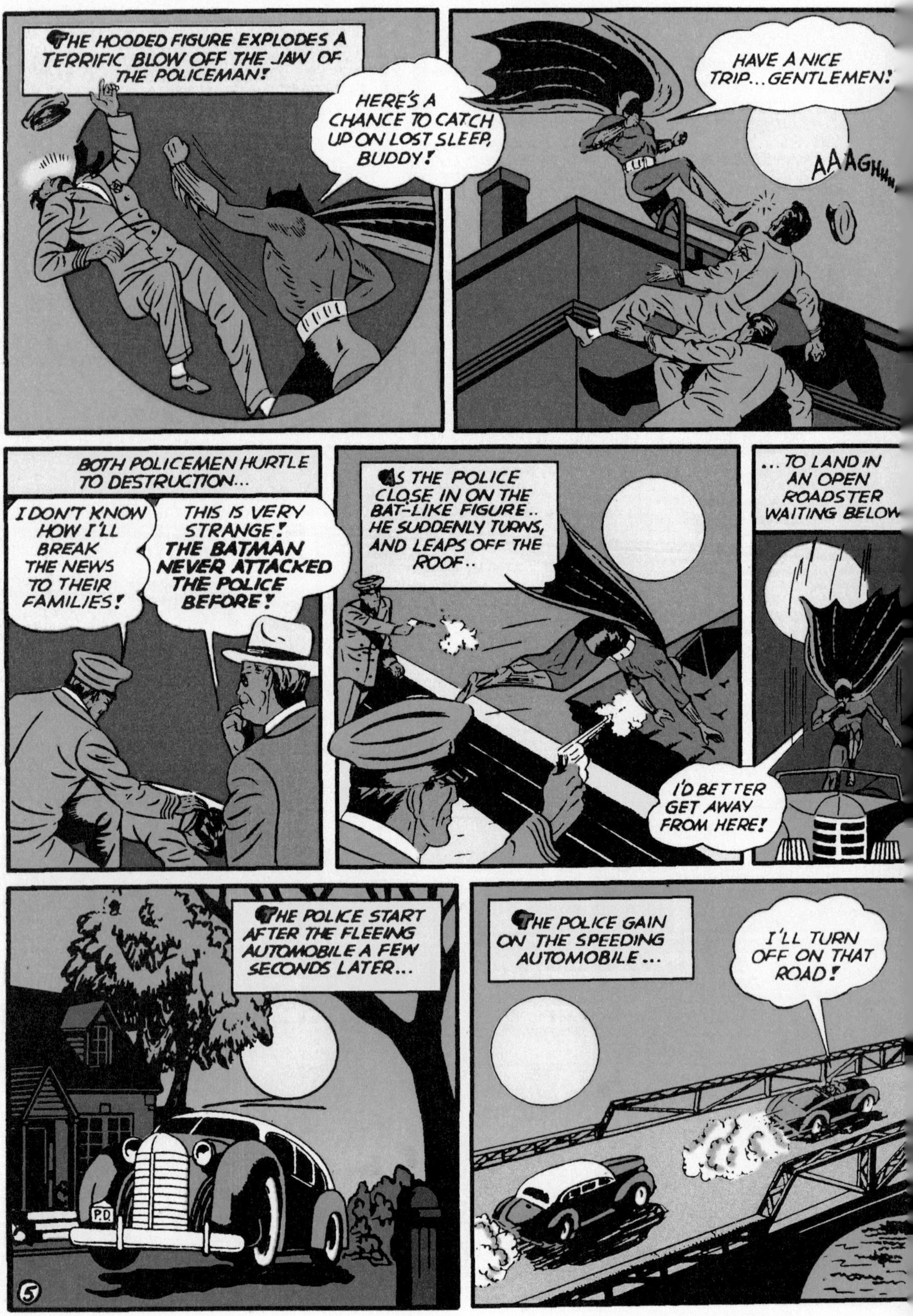
THE HOODED FIGURE EXPLODES A TERRIFIC BLOW OFF THE JAW OF THE POLICEMAN!
HERE'S A CHANCE TO CATCH UP ON LOST SLEEP, BUDDY!
HAVE A NICE TRIP... GENTLEMEN!
AAAGHHH
BOTH POLICEMEN HURTLE TO DESTRUCTION...
I DON'T KNOW HOW I'LL BREAK THE NEWS TO THEIR FAMILIES!
THIS IS VERY STRANGE! THE BATMAN NEVER ATTACKED THE POLICE BEFORE!
AS THE POLICE CLOSE IN ON THE BAT-LIKE FIGURE.. HE SUDDENLY TURNS, AND LEAPS OFF THE ROOF..
...TO LAND IN AN OPEN ROADSTER WAITING BELOW
I'D BETTER GET AWAY FROM HERE!
THE POLICE START AFTER THE FLEEING AUTOMOBILE A FEW SECONDS LATER...
P.D.
5
THE POLICE GAIN ON THE SPEEDING AUTOMOBILE...
I'LL TURN OFF ON THAT ROAD!

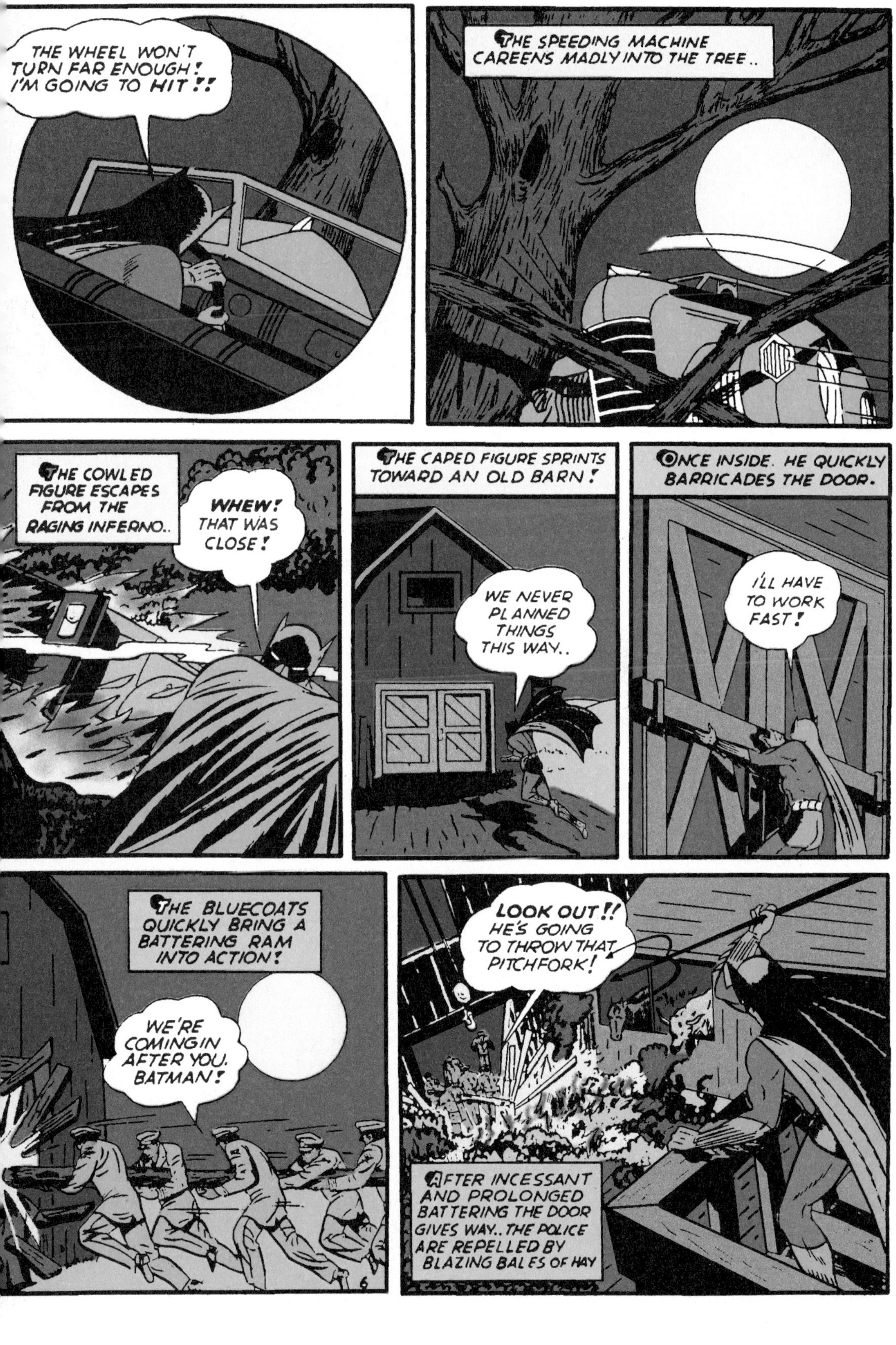
THE WHEEL WON'T TURN FAR ENOUGH! I'M GOING TO HIT!!
THE SPEEDING MACHINE CAREENS MADLY INTO THE TREE..
THE COWLED FIGURE ESCAPES FROM THE RAGING INFERNO..
WHEW! THAT WAS CLOSE!
THE CAPED FIGURE SPRINTS TOWARD AN OLD BARN!
WE NEVER PLANNED THINGS THIS WAY..
ONCE INSIDE. HE QUICKLY BARRICADES THE DOOR.
I'LL HAVE TO WORK FAST!
THE BLUECOATS QUICKLY BRING A BATTERING RAM INTO ACTION!
WE'RE COMINGIN AFTER YOU. BATMAN!
LOOK OUT!! HE'S GOING TO THROW THAT PITCHFORK!
AFTER INCESSANT AND PROLONGED BATTERING THE DOOR GIVES WAY.. THE POLICE ARE REPELLED BY BLAZING BALES OF HAY

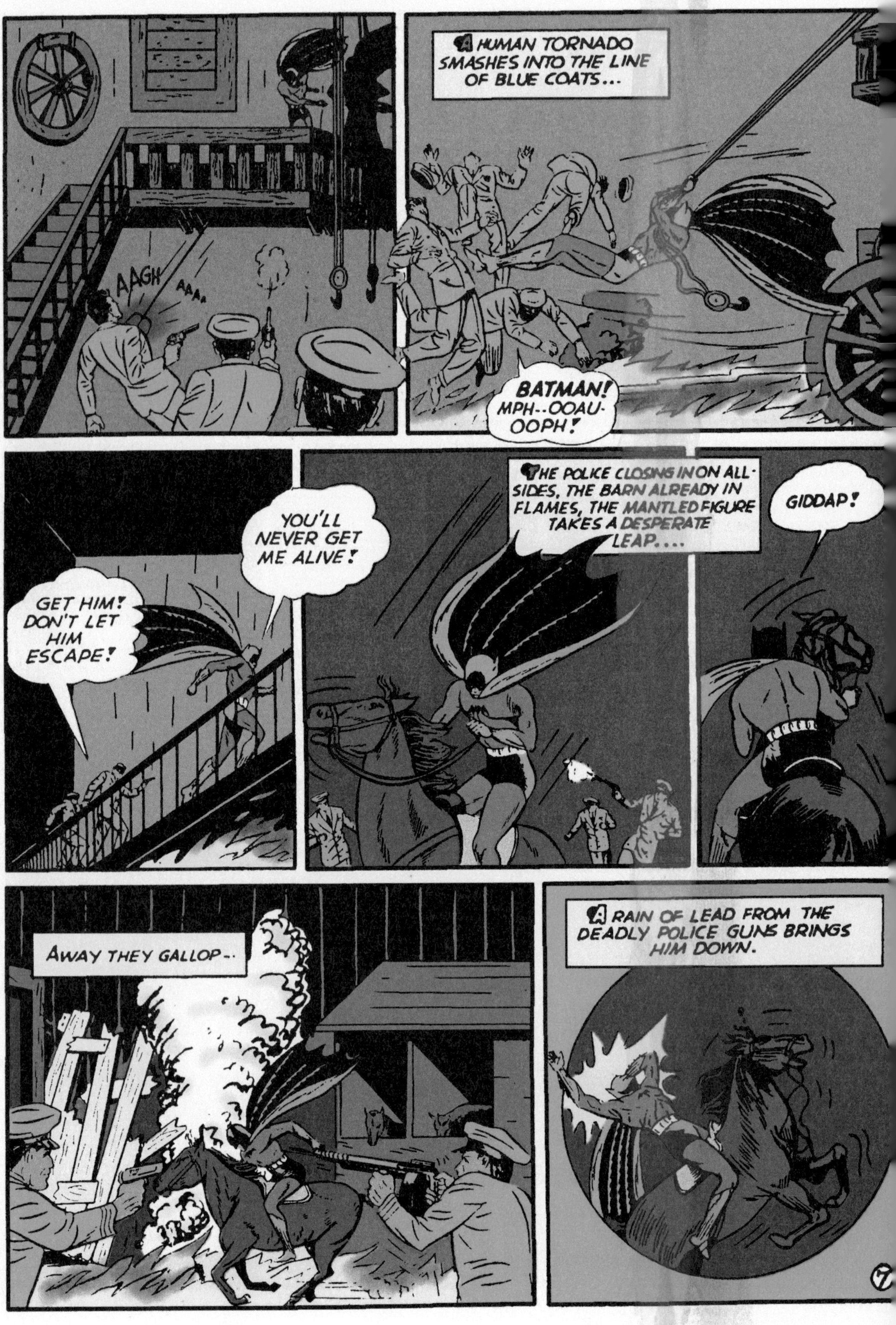
AAGH
AAAA
A HUMAN TORNADO SMASHES INTO THE LINE OF BLUE COATS...
BATMAN! MPH--OOAU-OOPH!
YOU'LL NEVER GET ME ALIVE!
GET HIM! DON'T LET HIM ESCAPE!
THE POLICE CLOSING IN ON ALL SIDES, THE BARN ALREADY IN FLAMES, THE MANTLED FIGURE TAKES A DESPERATE LEAP....
GIDDAP!
AWAY THEY GALLOP--
A RAIN OF LEAD FROM THE DEADLY POLICE GUNS BRINGS HIM DOWN.
7

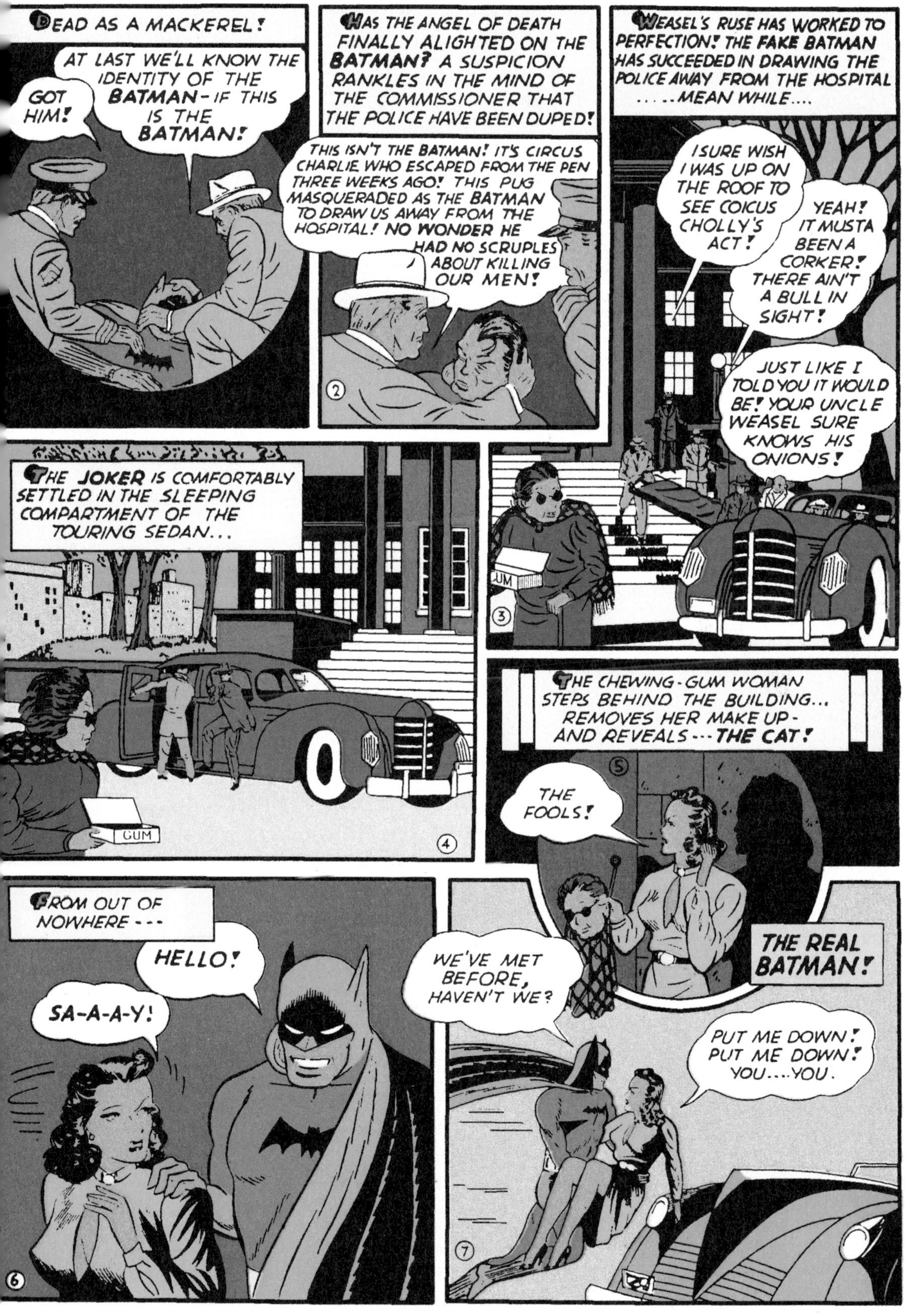
DEAD AS A MACKEREL!
GOT HIM!
AT LAST WE'LL KNOW THE IDENTITY OF THE BATMAN - IF THIS IS THE BATMAN!
HAS THE ANGEL OF DEATH FINALLY ALIGHTED ON THE BATMAN? A SUSPICION RANKLES IN THE MIND OF THE COMMISSIONER THAT THE POLICE HAVE BEEN DUPED!
THIS ISN'T THE BATMAN! IT'S CIRCUS CHARLIE WHO ESCAPED FROM THE PEN THREE WEEKS AGO! THIS PUG MASQUERADED AS THE BATMAN TO DRAW US AWAY FROM THE HOSPITAL! NO WONDER HE HAD NO SCRUPLES ABOUT KILLING OUR MEN!
WEASEL'S RUSE HAS WORKED TO PERFECTION! THE FAKE BATMAN HAS SUCCEEDED IN DRAWING THE POLICE AWAY FROM THE HOSPITAL .....MEAN WHILE....
I SURE WISH I WAS UP ON THE ROOF TO SEE COICUS CHOLLY'S ACT!
YEAH! IT MUSTA BEEN A CORKER! THERE AIN'T A BULL IN SIGHT!
JUST LIKE I TOLD YOU IT WOULD BE! YOUR UNCLE WEASEL SURE KNOWS HIS ONIONS!
GUM
THE JOKER IS COMFORTABLY SETTLED IN THE SLEEPING COMPARTMENT OF THE TOURING SEDAN...
GUM
THE CHEWING-GUM WOMAN STEPS BEHIND THE BUILDING... REMOVES HER MAKE UP-AND REVEALS---THE CAT!
THE FOOLS!
FROM OUT OF NOWHERE---
HELLO!
SA-A-A-Y!
WE'VE MET BEFORE, HAVEN'T WE?
THE REAL BATMAN!
PUT ME DOWN! PUT ME DOWN! YOU....YOU.

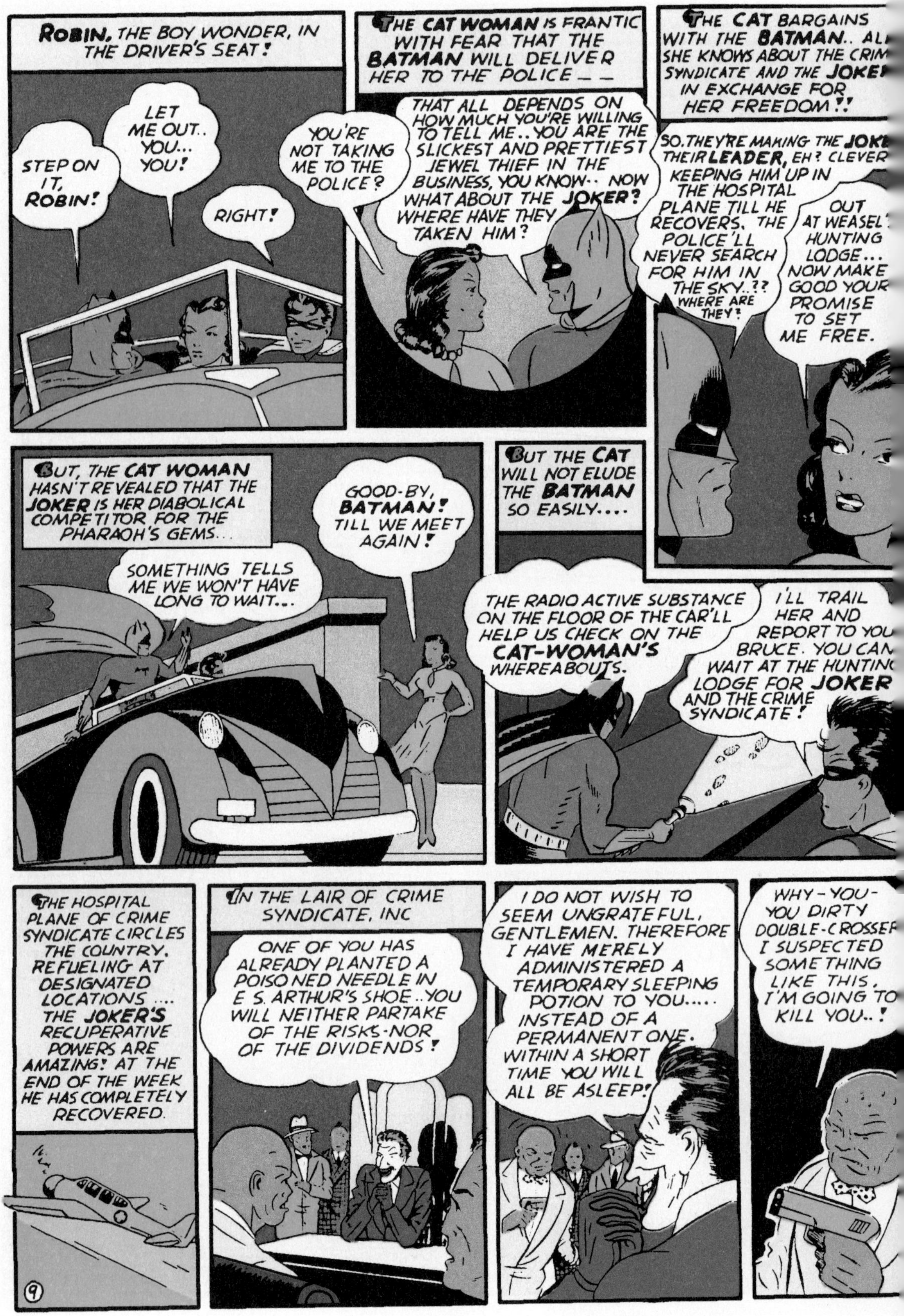
ROBIN, THE BOY WONDER, IN THE DRIVER'S SEAT!
LET ME OUT.. YOU... YOU!
STEP ON IT, ROBIN!
RIGHT!
THE CAT WOMAN IS FRANTIC WITH FEAR THAT THE BATMAN WILL DELIVER HER TO THE POLICE --
YOU'RE NOT TAKING ME TO THE POLICE?
THAT ALL DEPENDS ON HOW MUCH YOU'RE WILLING TO TELL ME.. YOU ARE THE SLICKEST AND PRETTIEST JEWEL THIEF IN THE BUSINESS, YOU KNOW-. NOW WHAT ABOUT THE JOKER? WHERE HAVE THEY TAKEN HIM?
THE CAT BARGAINS WITH THE BATMAN.. ALL SHE KNOWS ABOUT THE CRIME SYNDICATE AND THE JOKER IN EXCHANGE FOR HER FREEDOM!!
SO. THEY'RE MAKING THE JOKER THEIR LEADER, EH? CLEVER KEEPING HIM UP IN THE HOSPITAL PLANE TILL HE RECOVERS. THE POLICE'LL NEVER SEARCH FOR HIM IN THE SKY..?? WHERE ARE THEY?
OUT AT WEASEL'S HUNTING LODGE... NOW MAKE GOOD YOUR PROMISE TO SET ME FREE.
BUT, THE CAT WOMAN HASN'T REVEALED THAT THE JOKER IS HER DIABOLICAL COMPETITOR FOR THE PHARAOH'S GEMS...
GOOD-BY, BATMAN! TILL WE MEET AGAIN!
SOMETHING TELLS ME WE WON'T HAVE LONG TO WAIT...
BUT THE CAT WILL NOT ELUDE THE BATMAN SO EASILY....
THE RADIO ACTIVE SUBSTANCE ON THE FLOOR OF THE CAR'LL HELP US CHECK ON THE CAT-WOMAN'S WHEREABOUTS.
I'LL TRAIL HER AND REPORT TO YOU BRUCE. YOU CAN WAIT AT THE HUNTING LODGE FOR JOKER AND THE CRIME SYNDICATE!
THE HOSPITAL PLANE OF CRIME SYNDICATE CIRCLES THE COUNTRY, REFUELING AT DESIGNATED LOCATIONS .... THE JOKER'S RECUPERATIVE POWERS ARE AMAZING! AT THE END OF THE WEEK HE HAS COMPLETELY RECOVERED.
9
IN THE LAIR OF CRIME SYNDICATE, INC
ONE OF YOU HAS ALREADY PLANTED A POISONED NEEDLE IN E. S. ARTHUR'S SHOE..YOU WILL NEITHER PARTAKE OF THE RISKS-NOR OF THE DIVIDENDS!
I DO NOT WISH TO SEEM UNGRATEFUL, GENTLEMEN. THEREFORE I HAVE MERELY ADMINISTERED A TEMPORARY SLEEPING POTION TO YOU..... INSTEAD OF A PERMANENT ONE. WITHIN A SHORT TIME YOU WILL ALL BE ASLEEP!
WHY-YOU-YOU DIRTY DOUBLE-CROSSER I SUSPECTED SOMETHING LIKE THIS. I'M GOING TO KILL YOU..!

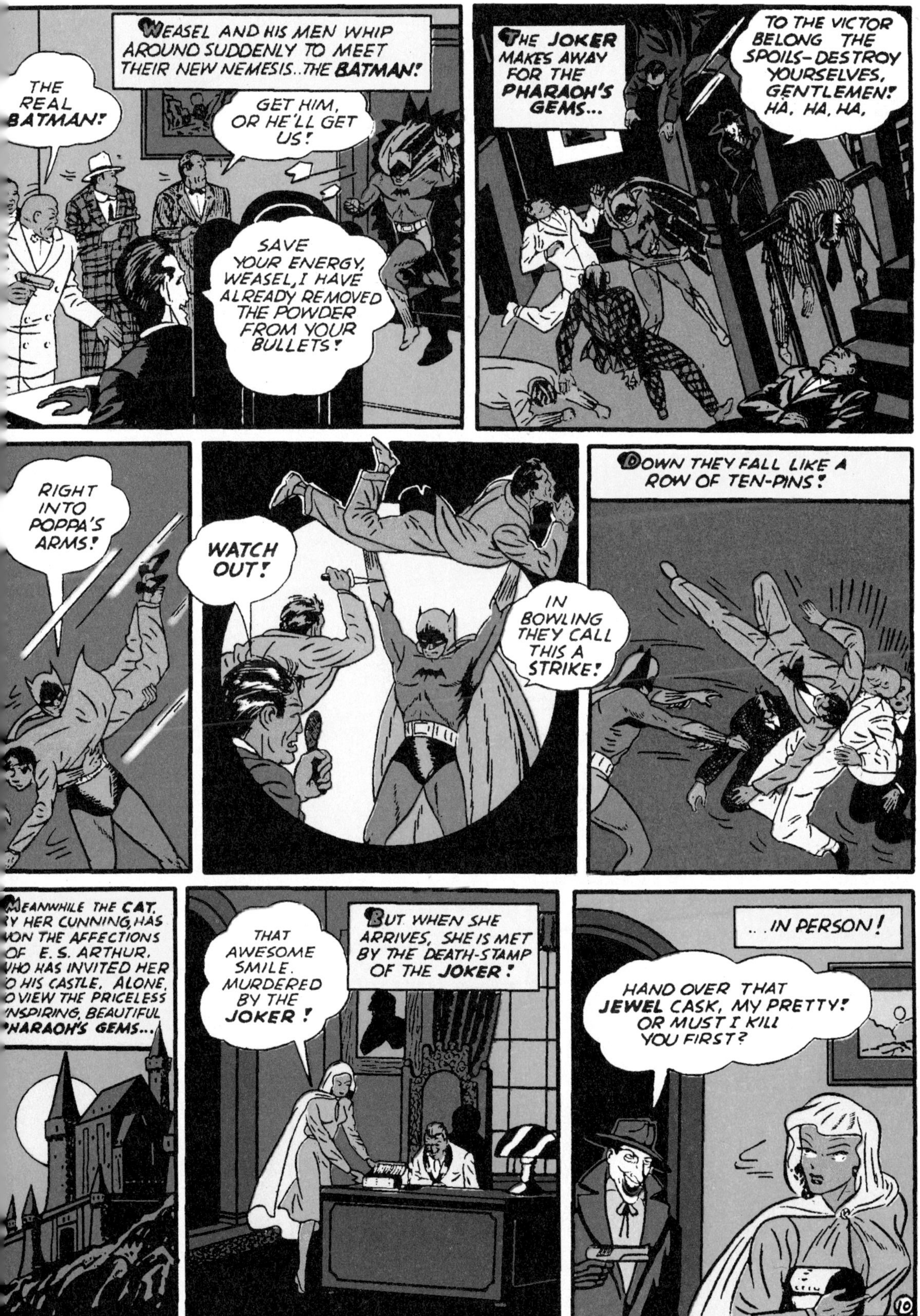
WEASEL AND HIS MEN WHIP AROUND SUDDENLY TO MEET THEIR NEW NEMESIS...THE BATMAN!
THE REAL BATMAN!
GET HIM, OR HE'LL GET US!
SAVE YOUR ENERGY, WEASEL, I HAVE ALREADY REMOVED THE POWDER FROM YOUR BULLETS!
THE JOKER MAKES AWAY FOR THE PHARAOH'S GEMS...
TO THE VICTOR BELONG THE SPOILS-DESTROY YOURSELVES, GENTLEMEN! HA, HA, HA,
RIGHT INTO POPPA'S ARMS!
WATCH OUT!
IN BOWLING THEY CALL THIS A STRIKE!
DOWN THEY FALL LIKE A ROW OF TEN-PINS!
MEANWHILE THE CAT, BY HER CUNNING, HAS WON THE AFFECTIONS OF E. S. ARTHUR, WHO HAS INVITED HER TO HIS CASTLE, ALONE, TO VIEW THE PRICELESS INSPIRING, BEAUTIFUL PHARAOH'S GEMS...
THAT AWESOME SMILE. MURDERED BY THE JOKER!
BUT WHEN SHE ARRIVES, SHE IS MET BY THE DEATH-STAMP OF THE JOKER!
...IN PERSON!
HAND OVER THAT JEWEL CASK, MY PRETTY! OR MUST I KILL YOU FIRST?
10

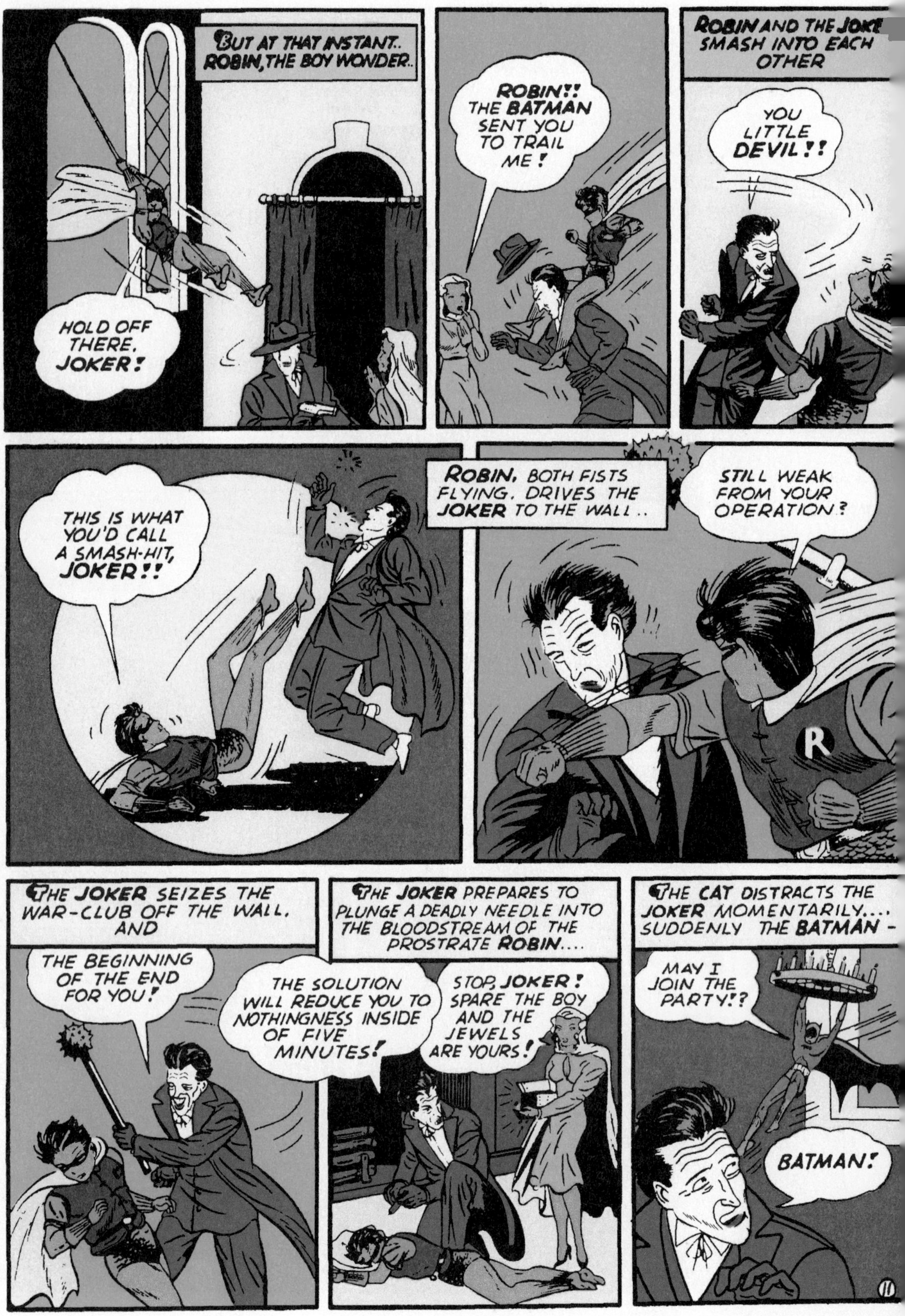
BUT AT THAT INSTANT.. ROBIN, THE BOY WONDER..
HOLD OFF THERE, JOKER!
ROBIN!! THE BATMAN SENT YOU TO TRAIL ME!
ROBIN AND THE JOKE SMASH INTO EACH OTHER
YOU LITTLE DEVIL!!
THIS IS WHAT YOU'D CALL A SMASH-HIT, JOKER!!
ROBIN, BOTH FISTS FLYING, DRIVES THE JOKER TO THE WALL..
STILL WEAK FROM YOUR OPERATION?
THE JOKER SEIZES THE WAR-CLUB OFF THE WALL, AND
THE BEGINNING OF THE END FOR YOU!
THE JOKER PREPARES TO PLUNGE A DEADLY NEEDLE INTO THE BLOODSTREAM OF THE PROSTRATE ROBIN....
THE SOLUTION WILL REDUCE YOU TO NOTHINGNESS INSIDE OF FIVE MINUTES!
STOP, JOKER! SPARE THE BOY AND THE JEWELS ARE YOURS!
THE CAT DISTRACTS THE JOKER MOMENTARILY.... SUDDENLY THE BATMAN -
MAY I JOIN THE PARTY!?
BATMAN!
11

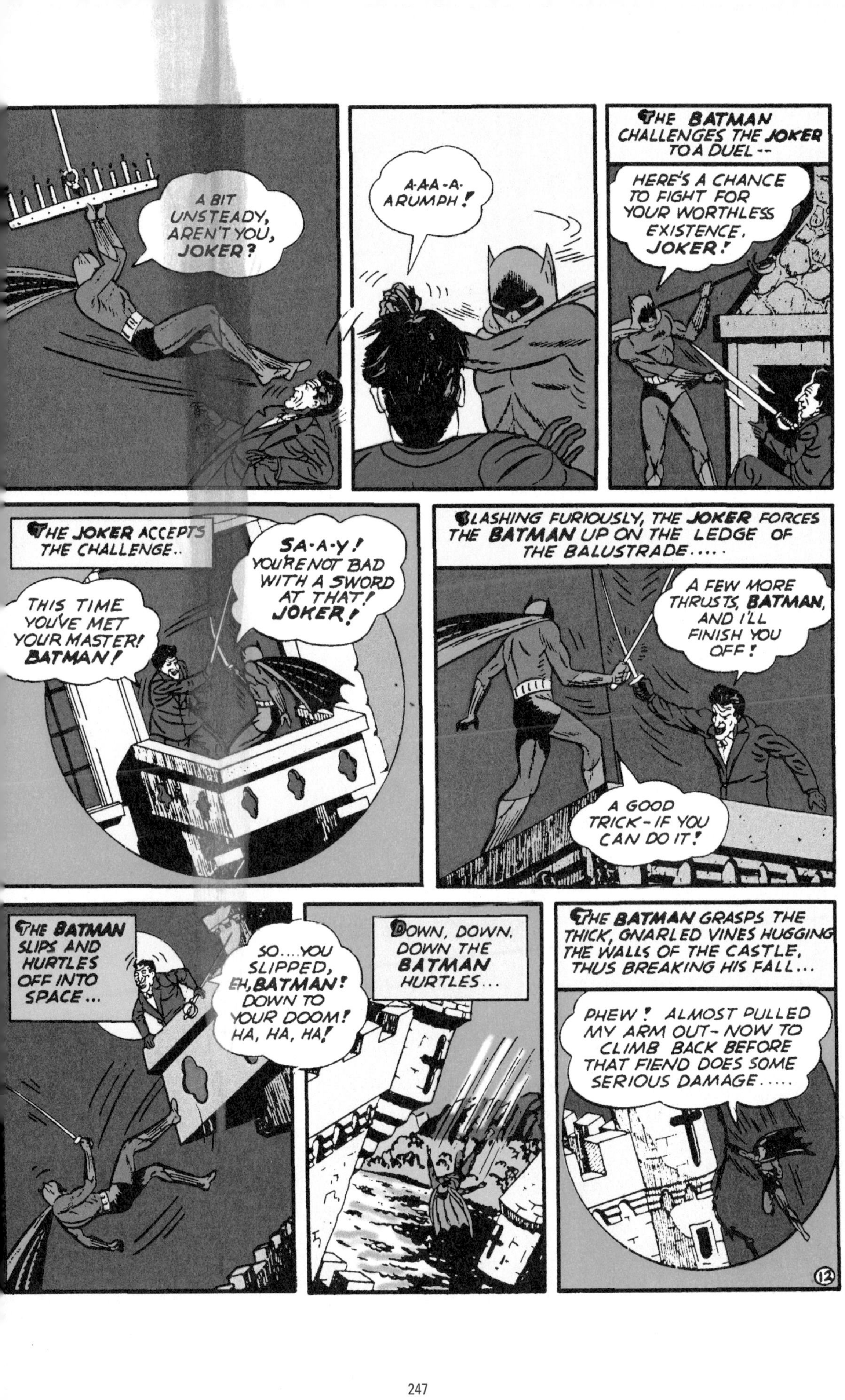
A BIT UNSTEADY, AREN'T YOU, JOKER?
A-AA-A-ARUMPH!
THE BATMAN CHALLENGES THE JOKER TO A DUEL --
HERE'S A CHANCE TO FIGHT FOR YOUR WORTHLESS EXISTENCE, JOKER!
THE JOKER ACCEPTS THE CHALLENGE..
THIS TIME YOU'VE MET YOUR MASTER! BATMAN!
SA-A-Y! YOU'RE NOT BAD WITH A SWORD AT THAT! JOKER!
SLASHING FURIOUSLY, THE JOKER FORCES THE BATMAN UP ON THE LEDGE OF THE BALUSTRADE....
A FEW MORE THRUSTS, BATMAN, AND I'LL FINISH YOU OFF!
A GOOD TRICK - IF YOU CAN DO IT!
THE BATMAN SLIPS AND HURTLES OFF INTO SPACE...
SO....YOU SLIPPED, EH, BATMAN! DOWN TO YOUR DOOM! HA, HA, HA!
DOWN, DOWN, DOWN THE BATMAN HURTLES...
THE BATMAN GRASPS THE THICK, GNARLED VINES HUGGING THE WALLS OF THE CASTLE, THUS BREAKING HIS FALL...
PHEW! ALMOST PULLED MY ARM OUT - NOW TO CLIMB BACK BEFORE THAT FIEND DOES SOME SERIOUS DAMAGE.....
12

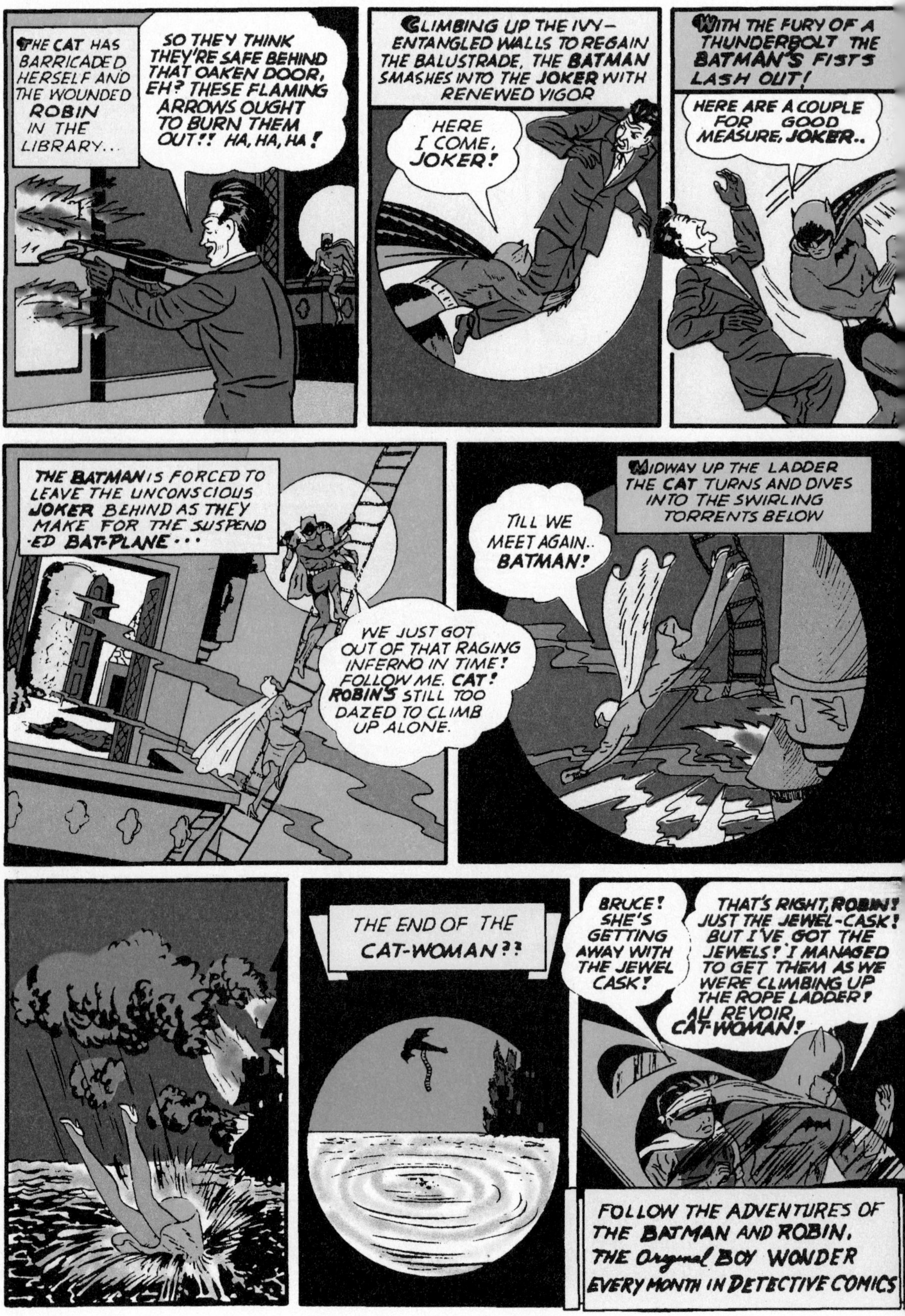
THE CAT HAS BARRICADED HERSELF AND THE WOUNDED ROBIN IN THE LIBRARY...
SO THEY THINK THEY'RE SAFE BEHIND THAT OAKEN DOOR, EH? THESE FLAMING ARROWS OUGHT TO BURN THEM OUT!! HA, HA, HA!
CLIMBING UP THE IVY-ENTANGLED WALLS TO REGAIN THE BALUSTRADE, THE BATMAN SMASHES INTO THE JOKER WITH RENEWED VIGOR
HERE I COME, JOKER!
WITH THE FURY OF A THUNDERBOLT THE BATMAN'S FISTS LASH OUT!
HERE ARE A COUPLE FOR GOOD MEASURE, JOKER..
THE BATMAN IS FORCED TO LEAVE THE UNCONSCIOUS JOKER BEHIND AS THEY MAKE FOR THE SUSPEND-ED BAT-PLANE...
WE JUST GOT OUT OF THAT RAGING INFERNO IN TIME! FOLLOW ME, CAT! ROBIN'S STILL TOO DAZED TO CLIMB UP ALONE.
MIDWAY UP THE LADDER THE CAT TURNS AND DIVES INTO THE SWIRLING TORRENTS BELOW
TILL WE MEET AGAIN.. BATMAN!
THE END OF THE CAT-WOMAN?!
BRUCE! SHE'S GETTING AWAY WITH THE JEWEL CASK!
THAT'S RIGHT, ROBIN! JUST THE JEWEL-CASK! BUT I'VE GOT THE JEWELS! I MANAGED TO GET THEM AS WE WERE CLIMBING UP THE ROPE LADDER! AU REVOIR, CAT-WOMAN!
FOLLOW THE ADVENTURES OF THE BATMAN AND ROBIN, THE Original BOY WONDER EVERY MONTH IN DETECTIVE COMICS

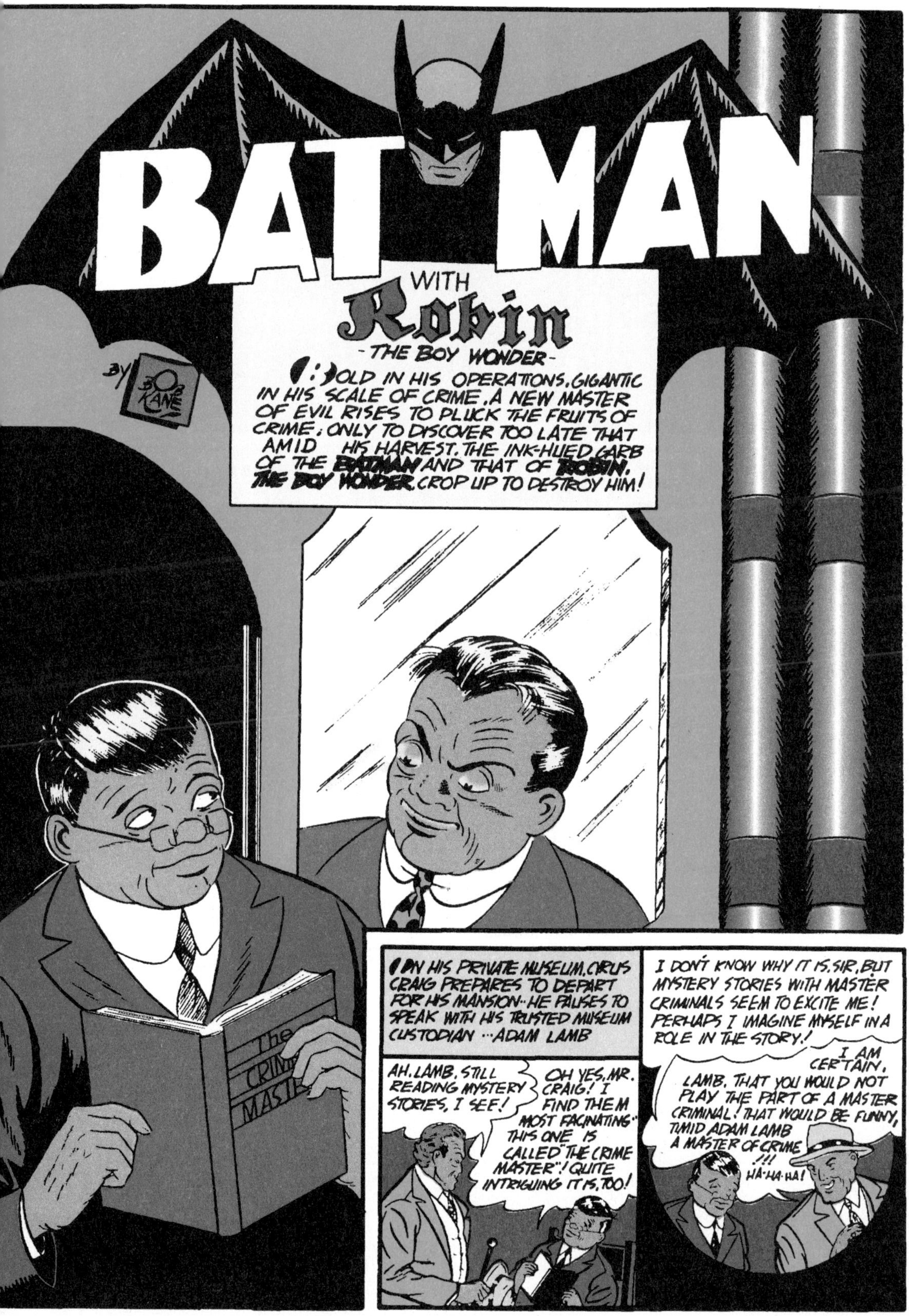
BAT MAN
WITH Robin
-THE BOY WONDER-
BY BOB KANE
BOLD IN HIS OPERATIONS, GIGANTIC IN HIS SCALE OF CRIME, A NEW MASTER OF EVIL RISES TO PLUCK THE FRUITS OF CRIME; ONLY TO DISCOVER TOO LATE THAT AMID HIS HARVEST, THE INK-HUED GARB OF THE BATMAN AND THAT OF ROBIN, THE BOY WONDER CROP UP TO DESTROY HIM!
IN HIS PRIVATE MUSEUM, CYRUS CRAIG PREPARES TO DEPART FOR HIS MANSION.. HE PAUSES TO SPEAK WITH HIS TRUSTED MUSEUM CUSTODIAN ...ADAM LAMB
AH, LAMB, STILL READING MYSTERY STORIES, I SEE!
OH YES, MR. CRAIG! I FIND THEM MOST FACINATING.. THIS ONE IS CALLED "THE CRIME MASTER"! QUITE INTRIGUING IT IS, TOO!
I DON'T KNOW WHY IT IS, SIR, BUT MYSTERY STORIES WITH MASTER CRIMINALS SEEM TO EXCITE ME! PERHAPS I IMAGINE MYSELF IN A ROLE IN THE STORY!
I AM CERTAIN, LAMB, THAT YOU WOULD NOT PLAY THE PART OF A MASTER CRIMINAL! THAT WOULD BE FUNNY, TIMID ADAM LAMB A MASTER OF CRIME !!! HA-HA-HA!

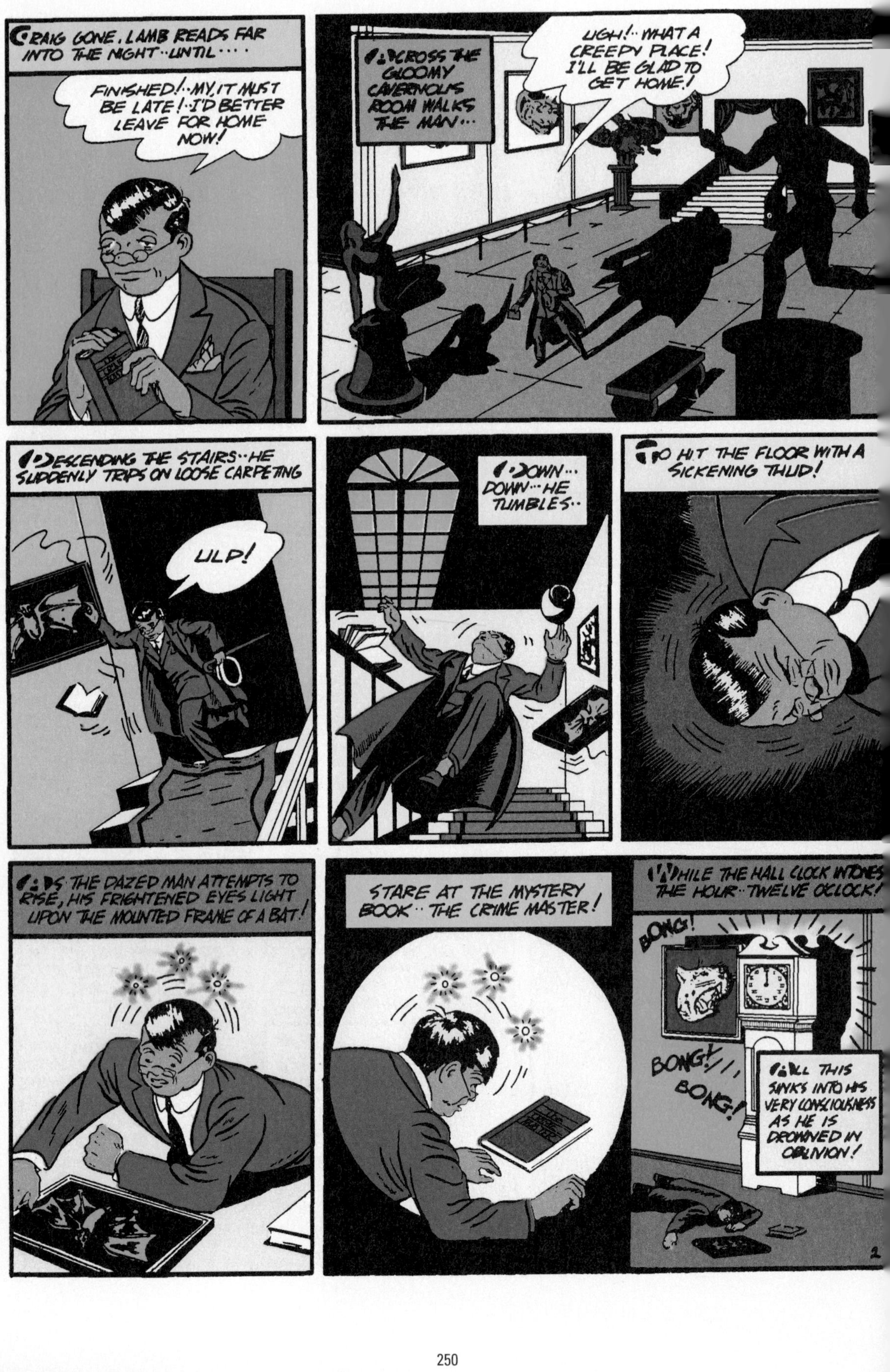
CRAIG GONE. LAMB READS FAR INTO THE NIGHT..UNTIL....
FINISHED!..MY, IT MUST BE LATE!..I'D BETTER LEAVE FOR HOME NOW!
ACROSS THE GLOOMY CAVERNOUS ROOM WALKS THE MAN...
UGH!..WHAT A CREEPY PLACE! I'LL BE GLAD TO GET HOME!
DESCENDING THE STAIRS..HE SUDDENLY TRIPS ON LOOSE CARPETING
ULP!
DOWN... DOWN...HE TUMBLES..
TO HIT THE FLOOR WITH A SICKENING THUD!
AS THE DAZED MAN ATTEMPTS TO RISE, HIS FRIGHTENED EYES LIGHT UPON THE MOUNTED FRAME OF A BAT!
STARE AT THE MYSTERY BOOK.. THE CRIME MASTER!
WHILE THE HALL CLOCK INTONES THE HOUR..TWELVE O'CLOCK!
BONG!
BONG!
BONG!
ALL THIS SINKS INTO HIS VERY CONSCIOUSNESS AS HE IS DROWNED IN OBLIVION!
2

HOURS LATER, LAMB RISES UNSTEADILY, SHAKILY...

WHA··WHAT HAPPENED? OH. NOW I REMEMBER··· I TRIPPED··FELL DOWN THE STAIRS! I SEEM TO BE ALL RIGHT! NOTHING SERIOUS!

BUT LITTLE DOES TIMID ADAM LAMB REALIZE HOW SERIOUS IS HIS PLIGHT··· HOW HIS VERY BEING HAS ALTERED AS A RESULT OF THAT FALL!

NEXT NIGHT ADAM LAMB ONCE MORE LEAVES FOR HOME!

AS HIS HEELS AND· CANE TAP ON THE SIDEWALK··A THIRD SOUND FILLS THE AIR··· THE BONG OF THE CLOCK··· MIDNIGHT··· TWELVE O'CLOCK!

AS THE CLOCK TOLLS THE HOUR, LAMB STOPS. FROZEN, AS IF HYPNOTIZED

THEN A STARTLING, DREADFUL CHANGE COMES OVER HIS CHERUBIC FEATURES··· HIS MOUTH TWISTS INTO A VICIOUS, SLITTED LEER

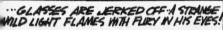

···GLASSES ARE JERKED OFF··A STRANGE WILD LIGHT FLAMES WITH FURY IN HIS EYES!

AS FORM STRAIGHTENS, BECOMES LIKE THAT OF A WILD CAGED AND RESTLESS ANIMAL!

···LAMB HAS BECOME A WOLF··· A BEAST··· A SNARLING, CUNNING BEAST!

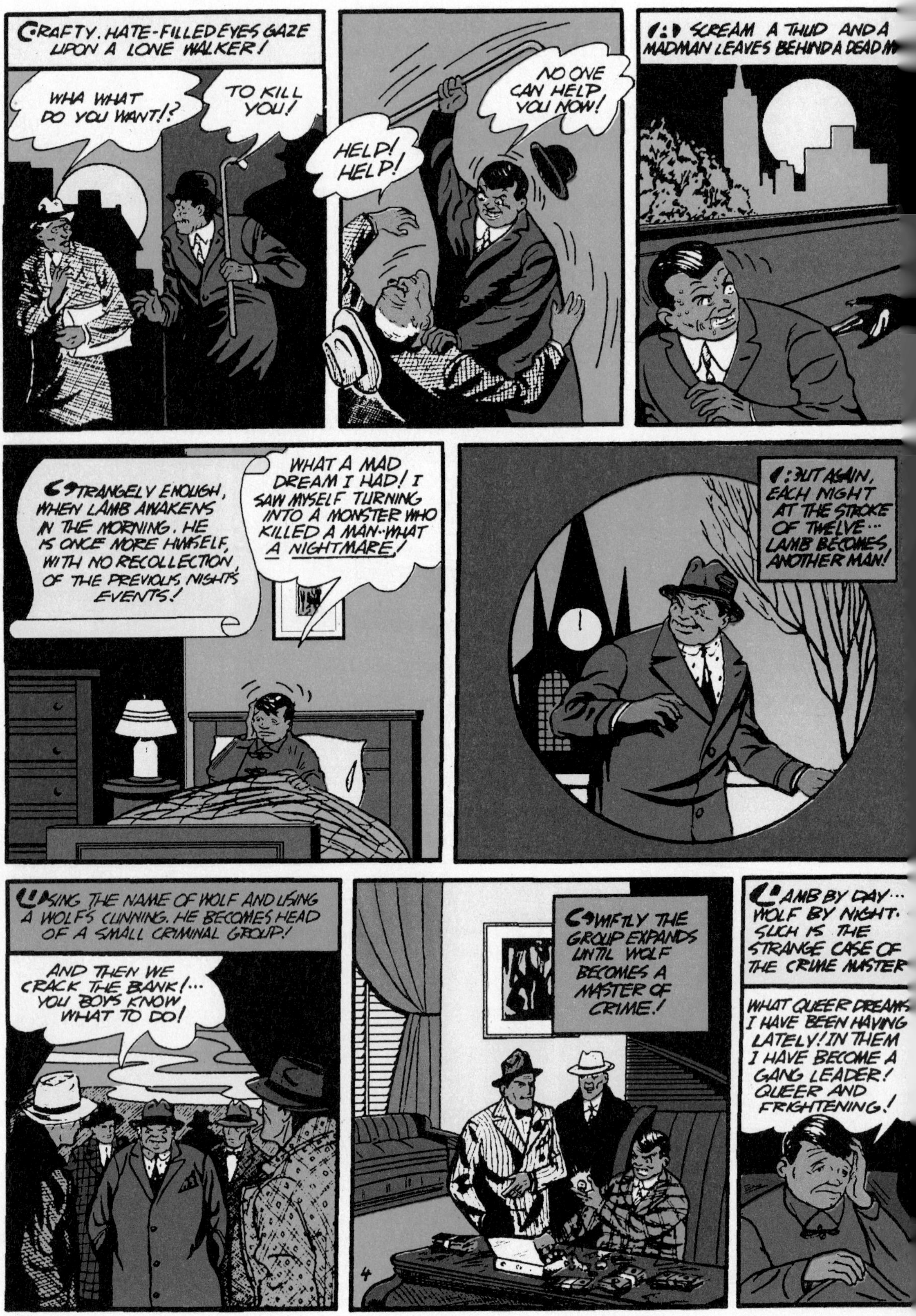
CRAFTY, HATE-FILLED EYES GAZE UPON A LONE WALKER!
WHA WHAT DO YOU WANT!?
TO KILL YOU!
HELP! HELP!
NO ONE CAN HELP YOU NOW!
A SCREAM A THUD AND A MADMAN LEAVES BEHIND A DEAD M
STRANGELY ENOUGH, WHEN LAMB AWAKENS IN THE MORNING, HE IS ONCE MORE HIMSELF, WITH NO RECOLLECTION OF THE PREVIOUS NIGHT'S EVENTS!
WHAT A MAD DREAM I HAD! I SAW MYSELF TURNING INTO A MONSTER WHO KILLED A MAN--WHAT A NIGHTMARE!
BUT AGAIN, EACH NIGHT AT THE STROKE OF TWELVE... LAMB BECOMES ANOTHER MAN!
USING THE NAME OF WOLF AND USING A WOLF'S CUNNING, HE BECOMES HEAD OF A SMALL CRIMINAL GROUP!
AND THEN WE CRACK THE BANK!... YOU BOYS KNOW WHAT TO DO!
SWIFTLY THE GROUP EXPANDS UNTIL WOLF BECOMES A MASTER OF CRIME!
4
LAMB BY DAY... WOLF BY NIGHT. SUCH IS THE STRANGE CASE OF THE CRIME MASTER
WHAT QUEER DREAMS I HAVE BEEN HAVING LATELY! IN THEM I HAVE BECOME A GANG LEADER! QUEER AND FRIGHTENING!

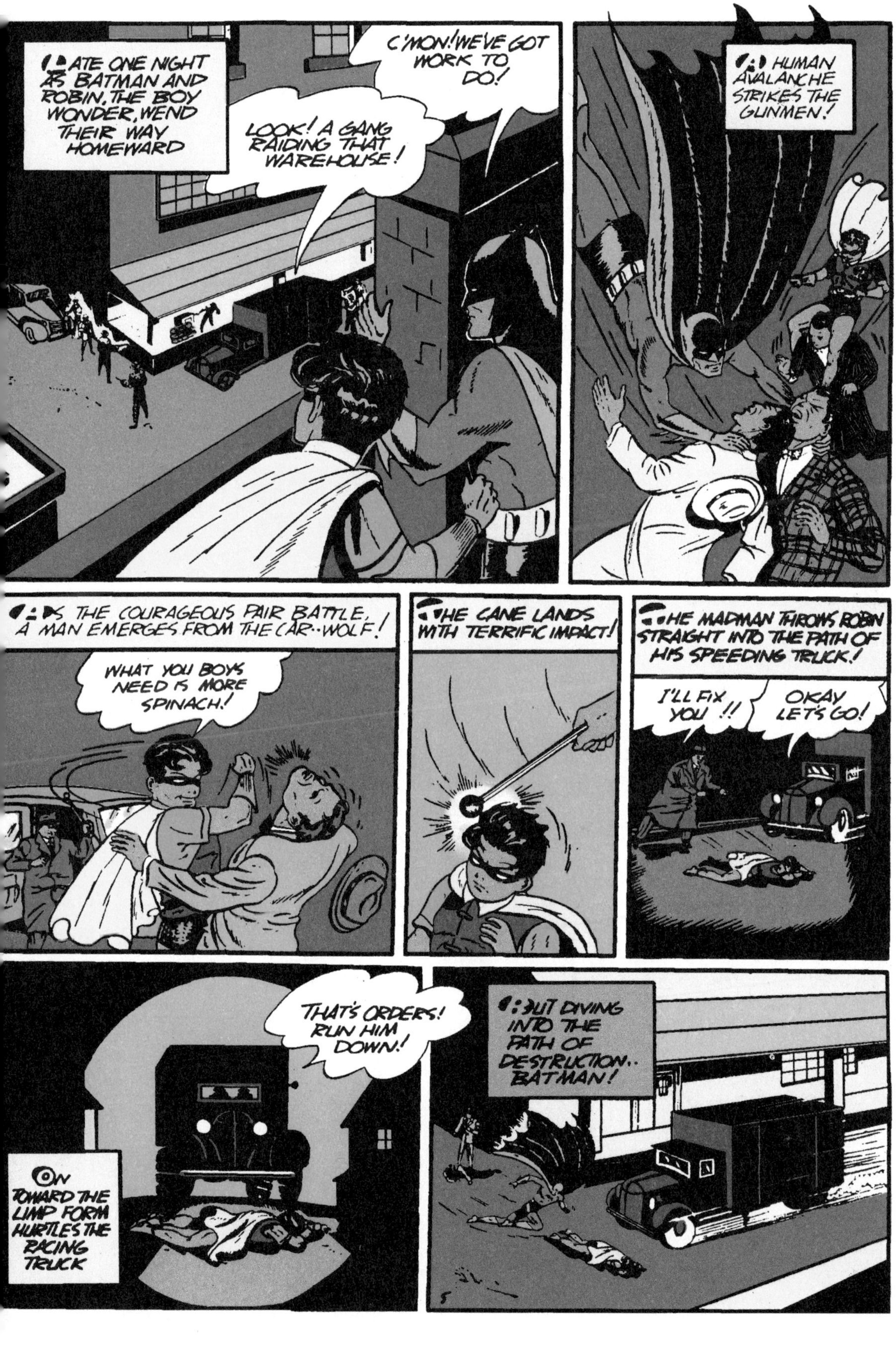
LATE ONE NIGHT AS BATMAN AND ROBIN, THE BOY WONDER, WEND THEIR WAY HOMEWARD
LOOK! A GANG RAIDING THAT WAREHOUSE!
C'MON! WE'VE GOT WORK TO DO!
A HUMAN AVALANCHE STRIKES THE GUNMEN!
AS THE COURAGEOUS PAIR BATTLE, A MAN EMERGES FROM THE CAR..WOLF!
WHAT YOU BOYS NEED IS MORE SPINACH!
THE CANE LANDS WITH TERRIFIC IMPACT!
THE MADMAN THROWS ROBIN STRAIGHT INTO THE PATH OF HIS SPEEDING TRUCK!
I'LL FIX YOU!!
OKAY LET'S GO!
THAT'S ORDERS! RUN HIM DOWN!
ON TOWARD THE LIMP FORM HURTLES THE RACING TRUCK
BUT DIVING INTO THE PATH OF DESTRUCTION.. BATMAN!

"IS SHOULDER PLOWS INTO ROBIN, ROLLING HIM TOWARD THE CURB!

..A QUICK SWERVE AND THE BATMAN ESCAPES THE CRUSHING, LOOMING DEATH

OTHERS WERE ALSO MAKING GOOD THEIR ESCAPE..WOLF AND HIS MEN!

THE MURDERING RATS!..I'D LIKE TO.....

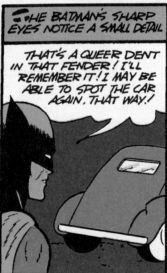

THE BATMAN'S SHARP EYES NOTICE A SMALL DETAIL

THAT'S A QUEER DENT IN THAT FENDER! I'LL REMEMBER IT! I MAY BE ABLE TO SPOT THE CAR AGAIN, THAT WAY!

WOW! WHAT HIT ME! THE EMPIRE STATE BUILDING?

GOOD THING YOU HAVE A THICK HEAD OF HAIR! IT CUSHIONED THE BLOW!

I THINK THAT'S THE NEW MOB THAT'S BEEN TROUBLING THE POLICE LATELY! BUT FROM NOW ON THEY'RE THE ONES WHO'LL HAVE TROUBLE! I'LL SEE TO THAT!

SAY, WHO IS THAT GANG, ANYWAY?

"AYS PASS, AND EACH MORNING LAMB AWAKES A PUZZLED MAN!

I DON'T UNDERSTAND IT THOSE DREAMS OF MINE AND THIS SUIT HANGING HERE!..WHO DOES IT BELONG TO..HOW DID IT GET HERE?

ONE NIGHT HE LIES AWAKE PLANNING TO TRAP THE MYSTICAL OWNER OF THE SUIT!

I MUST SEE WHO IT IS THAT WEARS THE SUIT! I.... TWELVE O'CLOCK

6

ABRUPTLY, HIS FEATURES CHANGE. LAMB HAS ONLY WAITED FOR HIS OTHER SELF.. WOLF THE CRIME MASTER!

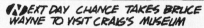

NEXT DAY CHANCE TAKES BRUCE WAYNE TO VISIT CRAIG'S MUSEUM

SO YOU LIKE MY LITTLE COLLECTION, EH BRUCE?

IT'S VERY FINE! BY THE WAY I NOTICE YOUR KEEPER SEEMS QUITE ABSORBED IN HIS BOOK!

BELIEVE IT OR NOT, LAMB HAS READ THAT BOOK OVER AND OVER AGAIN! CRIME-MASTER, IT'S CALLED!

SEEMS RATHER A TIMID SORT OF MAN TO RELISH THAT SORT OF THING, BUT THEN YOU NEVER CAN TELL, CAN YOU!

ON HIS WAY HOME BRUCE SUDDENLY HALTS. STOCK-STILL

THE BANDIT'S CAR OF LAST NIGHT!

QUEER DENT AND EVERYTHING! WELL IT LOOKS AS IF BATMAN AND ROBIN ARE GOING TO DO A LITTLE TRAILING TONIGHT!

NIGHTFALL ON THE WATERFRONT TWO FIGURES SLINK THROUGH THE SHADOWS BATMAN AND THE WONDERBOY

WELL KID, TRAILING THIS CAR HAS CERTAINLY LED US TO THE MEN OF LAST NIGHT! LOOKS LIKE THEY'RE SET TO PULL ANOTHER WAREHOUSE JOB!

I SEE THE SMALL MAN WHO CLUBBED ME!

THEY'LL KILL HIM! WE'VE GOT TO SAVE HIM! LET'S GO, ROBIN!

LOOK! THEY'VE GOT THE WATCHMAN!

ACROSS THE VAST PIER LAUNCH THE TWO FIGURES WITH HURRICANE SPEED!

THEY'RE BACK AGAIN!

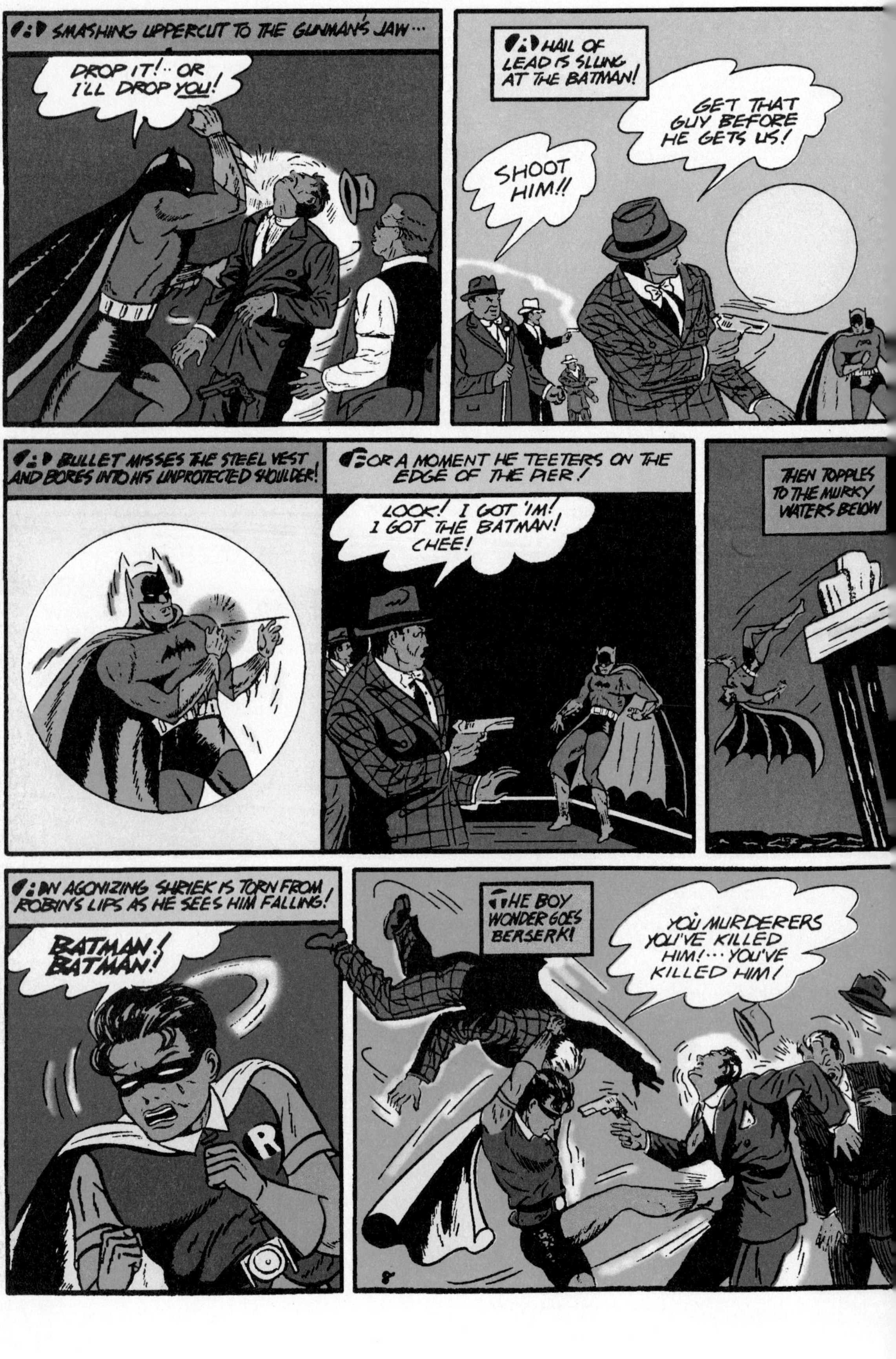
SMASHING UPPERCUT TO THE GUNMAN'S JAW...
DROP IT!.. OR I'LL DROP YOU!
HAIL OF LEAD IS SLUNG AT THE BATMAN!
SHOOT HIM!!
GET THAT GUY BEFORE HE GETS US!
BULLET MISSES THE STEEL VEST AND BORES INTO HIS UNPROTECTED SHOULDER!
OR A MOMENT HE TEETERS ON THE EDGE OF THE PIER!
LOOK! I GOT 'IM! I GOT THE BATMAN! CHEE!
THEN TOPPLES TO THE MURKY WATERS BELOW
AN AGONIZING SHRIEK IS TORN FROM ROBIN'S LIPS AS HE SEES HIM FALLING!
BATMAN! BATMAN!
THE BOY WONDER GOES BERSERK!
YOU MURDERERS YOU'VE KILLED HIM!... YOU'VE KILLED HIM!

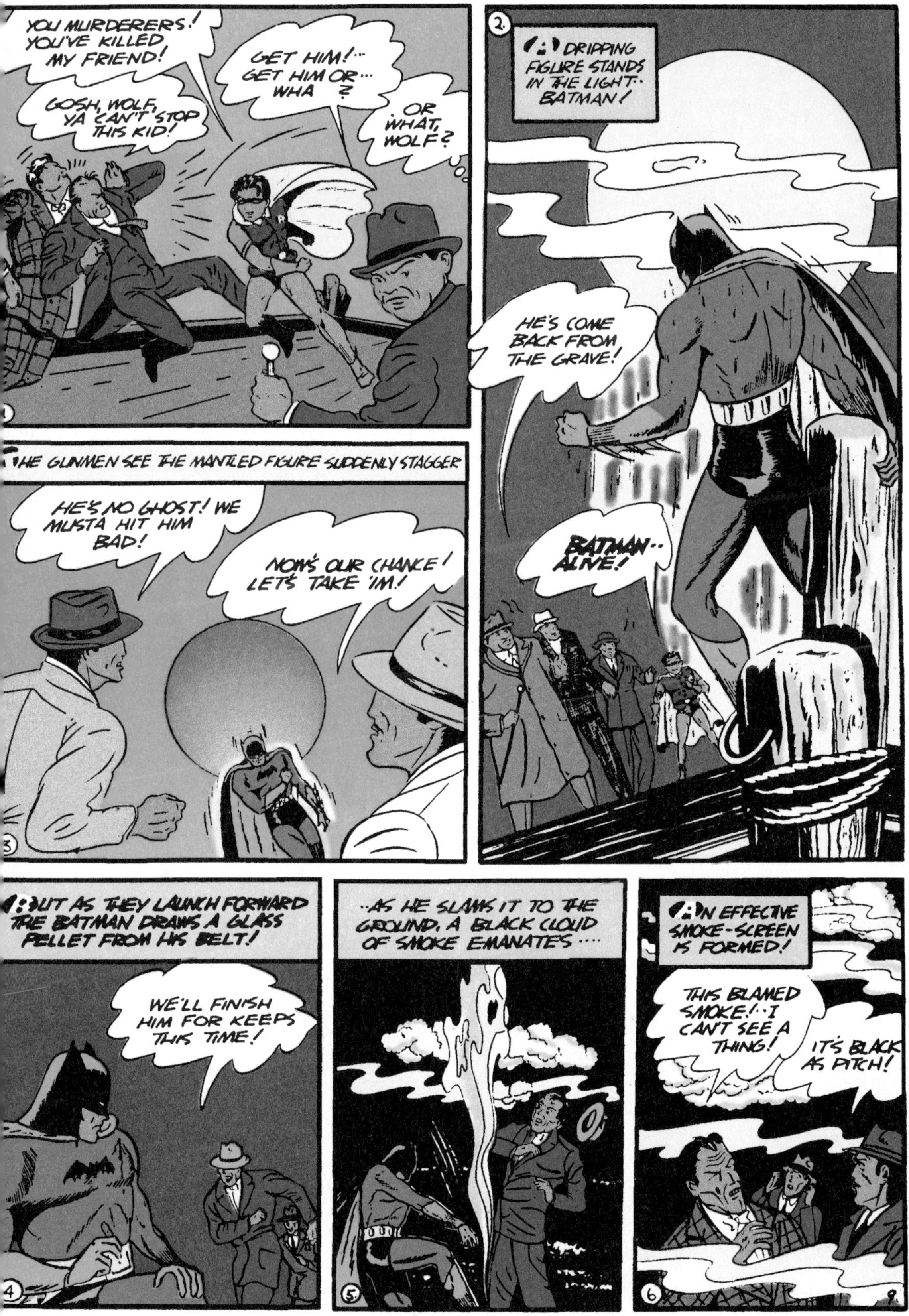
YOU MURDERERS! YOU'VE KILLED MY FRIEND!
GET HIM!... GET HIM OR... WHA ?
GOSH, WOLF, YA CAN'T STOP THIS KID!
OR WHAT, WOLF?
A DRIPPING FIGURE STANDS IN THE LIGHT.. BATMAN!
HE'S COME BACK FROM THE GRAVE!
BATMAN.. ALIVE!
THE GUNMEN SEE THE MANTLED FIGURE SUDDENLY STAGGER
HE'S NO GHOST! WE MUSTA HIT HIM BAD!
NOW'S OUR CHANCE! LET'S TAKE 'IM!
BUT AS THEY LAUNCH FORWARD THE BATMAN DRAWS A GLASS PELLET FROM HIS BELT!
WE'LL FINISH HIM FOR KEEPS THIS TIME!
..AS HE SLAMS IT TO THE GROUND, A BLACK CLOUD OF SMOKE EMANATES....
AN EFFECTIVE SMOKE-SCREEN IS FORMED!
THIS BLAMED SMOKE!..I CAN'T SEE A THING!
IT'S BLACK AS PITCH!

BY AIDING THE WEAKENED BATMAN, ROBIN HELPS TO EFFECT THEIR ESCAPE!

THE DIRTY RATS! THEY TRIED TO KILL YOU!...I'D LIKE TO....

THERE'LL BE PLENTY OF TIME FOR THAT LATER! LET'S GET AWAY FROM HERE, FIRST!

OKAY BRUCE.. READY?

READY!

LATER.. IN BRUCE'S LABORATORY A NERVOUS BOY FACES A GIANT TASK!

BREATHING A SILENT PRAYER, DICK BEGINS TO PROBE FOR THE BULLET LODGED IN BRUCE'S SHOULDER!

I'VE GOT TO FIND IT!... I'VE GOT TO!

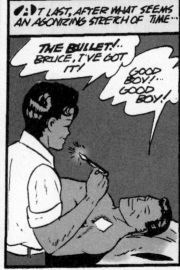

AT LAST, AFTER WHAT SEEMS AN AGONIZING STRETCH OF TIME...

THE BULLET!... BRUCE, I'VE GOT IT!

GOOD BOY!... GOOD BOY!

LATE THE NEXT NIGHT DICK WALKS INTO THE LIBRARY TO SEE BRUCE UP, READING...

BRUCE, IT'S NEAR TWELVE O'CLOCK! YOU SHOULD BE IN BED RESTING YOUR ARM!

DICK!..I'VE JUST FOUND OUT A STARTLING FACT!...IT'S FANTASTIC.. FANTASTIC!

IT ALL TIES UP WITH A MYSTERY BOOK CALLED· THE CRIME MASTER! I'VE MADE A LIST OF CRIMES COMMITTED BY THE WOLF MOB, AND BELIEVE IT OR NOT..IT COINCIDES WITH THE MYTHICAL CRIMES DONE IN THIS BOOK!

BUT I DON'T UNDERSTAND...

FOR SOME REASON, WOLF IS FOLLOWING THE EXACT PLAN OF THE BOOK! THE CRIME MASTER!...IT'S CRAZY..CRAZY!

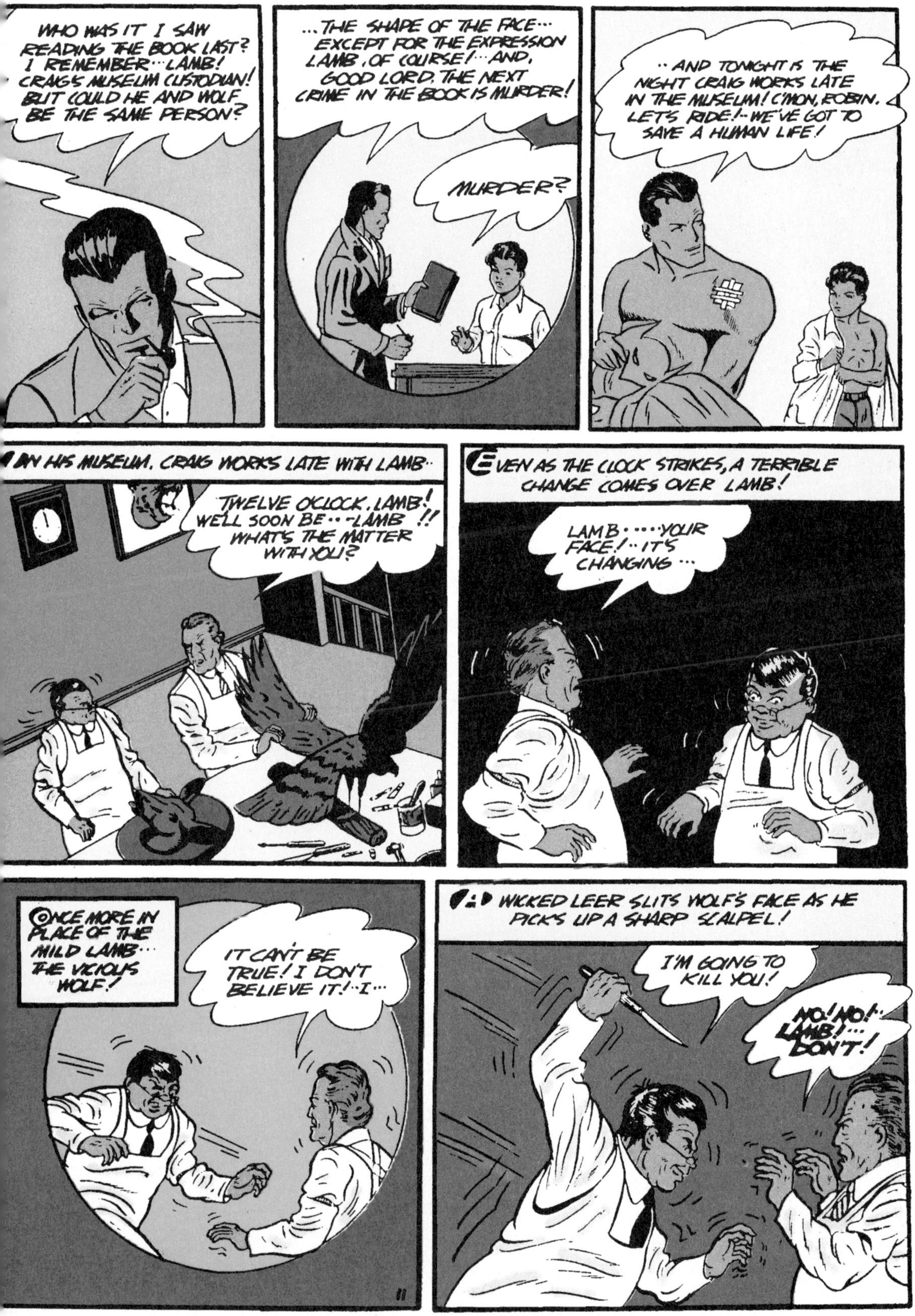
WHO WAS IT I SAW READING THE BOOK LAST? I REMEMBER···LAMB! CRAIG'S MUSEUM CUSTODIAN! BUT COULD HE AND WOLF BE THE SAME PERSON?
...THE SHAPE OF THE FACE··· EXCEPT FOR THE EXPRESSION LAMB, OF COURSE!··· AND, GOOD LORD, THE NEXT CRIME IN THE BOOK IS MURDER!
MURDER?
·· AND TONIGHT IS THE NIGHT CRAIG WORKS LATE IN THE MUSEUM! C'MON, ROBIN. LET'S RIDE!-- WE'VE GOT TO SAVE A HUMAN LIFE!
IN HIS MUSEUM, CRAIG WORKS LATE WITH LAMB··
TWELVE O'CLOCK, LAMB! WE'LL SOON BE···-LAMB!! WHAT'S THE MATTER WITH YOU?
EVEN AS THE CLOCK STRIKES, A TERRIBLE CHANGE COMES OVER LAMB!
LAMB·····YOUR FACE!·· IT'S CHANGING···
ONCE MORE IN PLACE OF THE MILD LAMB··· THE VICIOUS WOLF!
IT CAN'T BE TRUE! I DON'T BELIEVE IT!··I···
A WICKED LEER SLITS WOLF'S FACE AS HE PICKS UP A SHARP SCALPEL!
I'M GOING TO KILL YOU!
NO! NO!·· LAMB!··· DON'T!

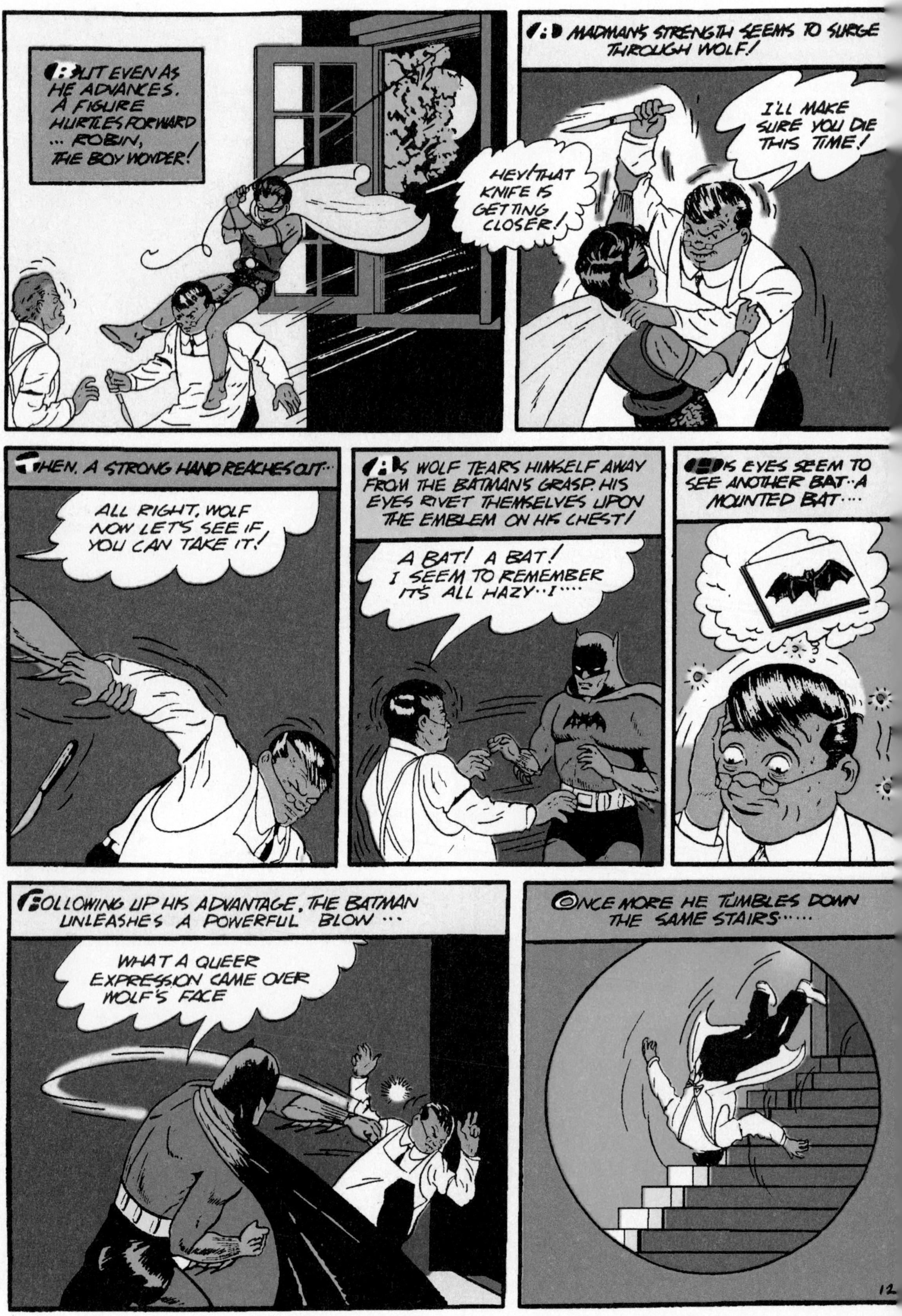
BUT EVEN AS HE ADVANCES, A FIGURE HURTLES FORWARD ... ROBIN, THE BOY WONDER!
A MADMAN'S STRENGTH SEEMS TO SURGE THROUGH WOLF!
HEY! THAT KNIFE IS GETTING CLOSER!
I'LL MAKE SURE YOU DIE THIS TIME!
THEN, A STRONG HAND REACHES OUT...
ALL RIGHT, WOLF NOW LET'S SEE IF YOU CAN TAKE IT!
AS WOLF TEARS HIMSELF AWAY FROM THE BATMAN'S GRASP, HIS EYES RIVET THEMSELVES UPON THE EMBLEM ON HIS CHEST!
A BAT! A BAT! I SEEM TO REMEMBER IT'S ALL HAZY..I....
HIS EYES SEEM TO SEE ANOTHER BAT..A MOUNTED BAT....
FOLLOWING UP HIS ADVANTAGE, THE BATMAN UNLEASHES A POWERFUL BLOW ...
WHAT A QUEER EXPRESSION CAME OVER WOLF'S FACE
ONCE MORE HE TUMBLES DOWN THE SAME STAIRS......
12

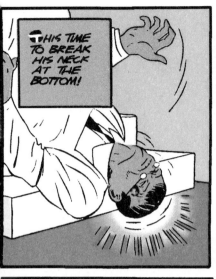

THIS TIME TO BREAK HIS NECK AT THE BOTTOM!

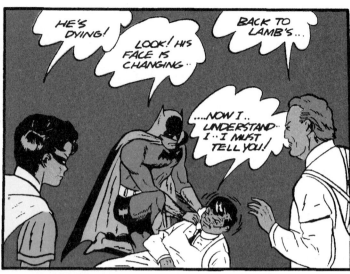

HE'S DYING!

LOOK! HIS FACE IS CHANGING...

BACK TO LAMB'S...

...NOW I.. UNDERSTAND.. I..I MUST TELL YOU!

IN HIS LAST MOMENTS. ALL SUDDENLY SEEMS CLEAR TO LAMB. HE KNOWS HE MUST MAKE THEM UNDERSTAND THAT THEY MUST NOT HATE HIM!

I MUST TELL YOU! IT WAS ONE NIGHT. TWELVE O'CLOCK. I WAS...

AS THEY LISTEN TO THE TALE WITH GROWING AMAZEMENT. LAMB SUDDENLY LOOKS UP WITH TROUBLED EYES...AND EXPIRES!

AND THAT'S HOW I BECAME THE CRIME MASTER! I'M SORRY I CAUSED ANY TROUBLE. I'M SORRY, SORRY. AAAH!

DEAD!

WHAT A STORY! SEEMS IMPOSSIBLE TO BELIEVE!

LAMB! POOR TIMID LAMB. I FORGIVE YOU!

CAN YOU IMAGINE! WHEN HIS HEAD HIT THE FLOOR THE STORY OF THE CRIME-MASTER PENETRATED INTO HIS VERY SOUL!

AND THAT'S WHY HE CHANGED AT TWELVE O'CLOCK. BECAUSE THAT'S WHEN HE HIT HIS HEAD!

THE LAST THING HE SAW WAS THE MOUNTED PELT OF THE BAT, WHICH EXPLAINS WHY HE WAS SO FRIGHTENED WHEN HE SAW MY EMBLEM!

A BUMP ON THE HEAD CAUSED ALL THAT! THE BRAIN IS CERTAINLY A DELICATE THING!

LAMB WAS A PSYCHOLOGICAL JEKYLL AND HYDE! THIS IS THE ONLY TIME I WAS EVER SORRY TO SEE A CRIMINAL DIE! MEDICAL ATTENTION MIGHT HAVE CURED HIM!

Y'KNOW, I FEEL SORT OF SORRY FOR HIM!.. NOT FOR WOLF, BUT FOR LAMB!

IT WAS OUR JOB! WE'VE GOT STEADY EMPLOYMENT ALL THE TIME IN THIS SORT OF THING!

BATMAN.. I DON'T KNOW HOW TO THANK YOU!

AS LONG AS THERE'S A CRIMINAL ABOUT, WE GO TO WORK ON HIM! YES, SIR, WORK. AND HOW!

FOR a thrill a-minute READ THE AMAZING ADVENTURES OF *Batman* WITH *Robin* THE ORIGINAL BOY WONDER

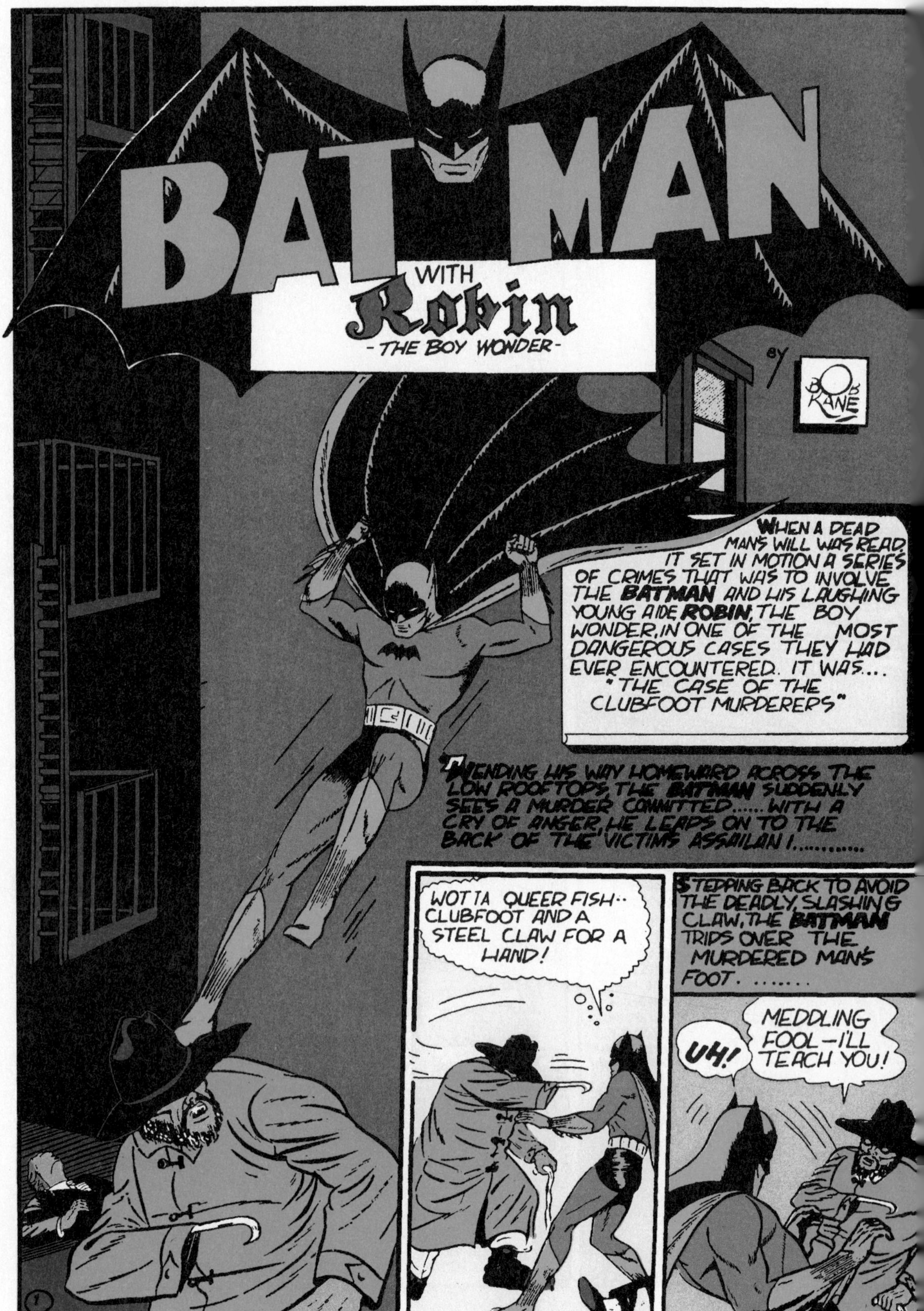
BATMAN
WITH
Robin
-THE BOY WONDER-
BY
BOB KANE
WHEN A DEAD MAN'S WILL WAS READ, IT SET IN MOTION A SERIES OF CRIMES THAT WAS TO INVOLVE THE BATMAN AND HIS LAUGHING YOUNG AIDE, ROBIN, THE BOY WONDER, IN ONE OF THE MOST DANGEROUS CASES THEY HAD EVER ENCOUNTERED. IT WAS... "THE CASE OF THE CLUBFOOT MURDERERS"
WENDING HIS WAY HOMEWARD ACROSS THE LOW ROOFTOPS, THE BATMAN SUDDENLY SEES A MURDER COMMITTED...... WITH A CRY OF ANGER, HE LEAPS ON TO THE BACK OF THE VICTIM'S ASSAILANT.........
WOTTA QUEER FISH.. CLUBFOOT AND A STEEL CLAW FOR A HAND!
STEPPING BACK TO AVOID THE DEADLY, SLASHING CLAW, THE BATMAN TRIPS OVER THE MURDERED MAN'S FOOT. ....
MEDDLING FOOL—I'LL TEACH YOU!
UH!

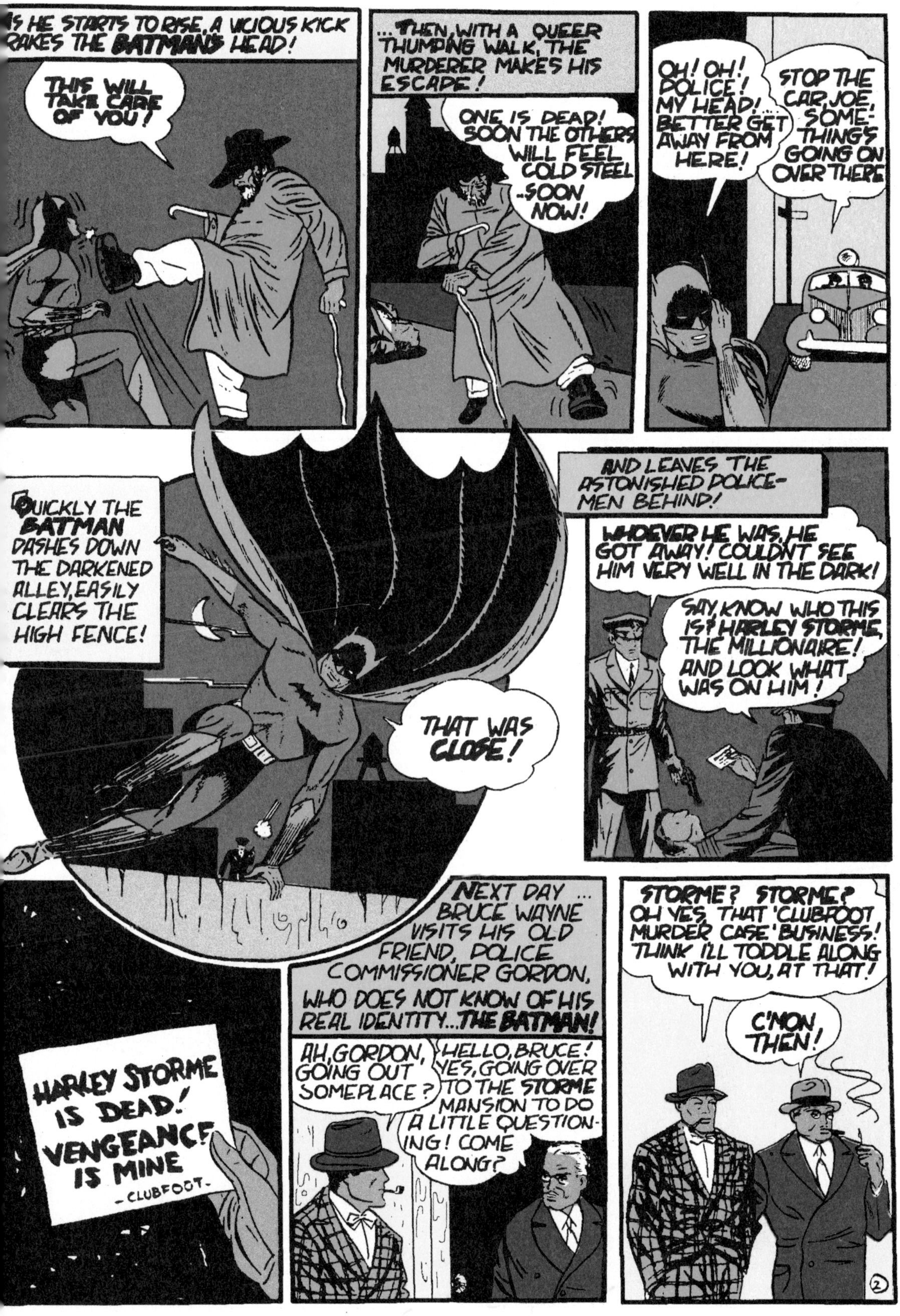

AS HE STARTS TO RISE, A VICIOUS KICK RAKES THE BATMAN'S HEAD!
THIS WILL TAKE CARE OF YOU!
...THEN, WITH A QUEER THUMPING WALK, THE MURDERER MAKES HIS ESCAPE!
ONE IS DEAD! SOON THE OTHERS WILL FEEL COLD STEEL --SOON NOW!
OH! OH! POLICE! MY HEAD!... BETTER GET AWAY FROM HERE!
STOP THE CAR, JOE. SOMETHING'S GOING ON OVER THERE!
QUICKLY THE BATMAN DASHES DOWN THE DARKENED ALLEY, EASILY CLEARS THE HIGH FENCE!
THAT WAS CLOSE!
AND LEAVES THE ASTONISHED POLICEMEN BEHIND!
WHOEVER HE WAS, HE GOT AWAY! COULDN'T SEE HIM VERY WELL IN THE DARK!
SAY, KNOW WHO THIS IS? HARLEY STORME, THE MILLIONAIRE! AND LOOK WHAT WAS ON HIM!
HARLEY STORME IS DEAD! VENGEANCE IS MINE -CLUBFOOT-
NEXT DAY ... BRUCE WAYNE VISITS HIS OLD FRIEND, POLICE COMMISSIONER GORDON, WHO DOES NOT KNOW OF HIS REAL IDENTITY...THE BATMAN!
AH, GORDON, GOING OUT SOMEPLACE?
HELLO, BRUCE! YES, GOING OVER TO THE STORME MANSION TO DO A LITTLE QUESTIONING! COME ALONG?
STORME? STORME? OH YES, THAT 'CLUBFOOT MURDER CASE' BUSINESS! THINK I'LL TODDLE ALONG WITH YOU, AT THAT!
C'MON, THEN!
2

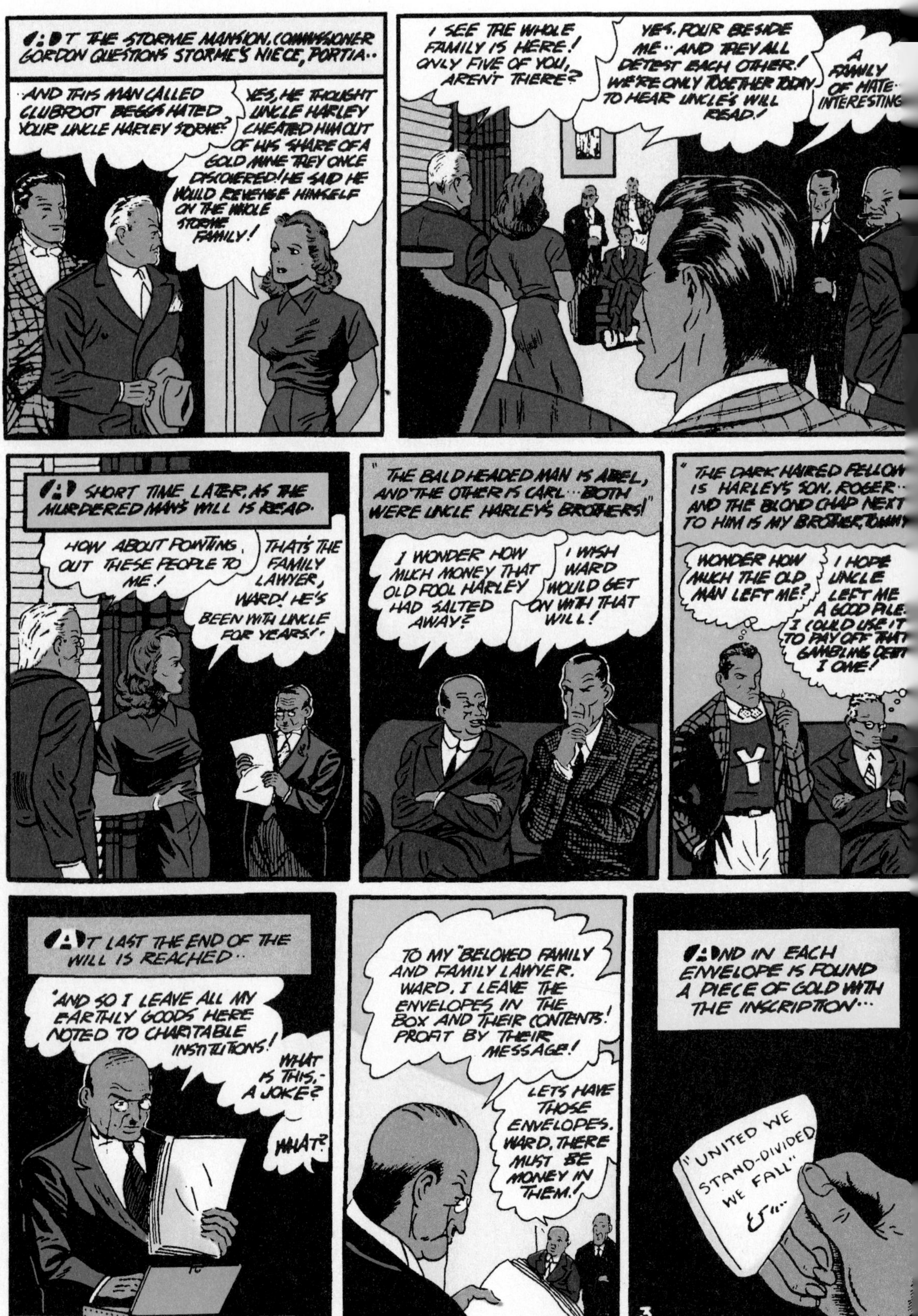
AT THE STORME MANSION, COMMISSIONER GORDON QUESTIONS STORME'S NIECE, PORTIA..
..AND THIS MAN CALLED CLUBFOOT BEGGS HATED YOUR UNCLE HARLEY STORME?
YES, HE THOUGHT UNCLE HARLEY CHEATED HIM OUT OF HIS SHARE OF A GOLD MINE THEY ONCE DISCOVERED! HE SAID HE WOULD REVENGE HIMSELF ON THE WHOLE STORME FAMILY!
I SEE THE WHOLE FAMILY IS HERE! ONLY FIVE OF YOU, AREN'T THERE?
YES, FOUR BESIDE ME.. AND THEY ALL DETEST EACH OTHER! WE'RE ONLY TOGETHER TODAY TO HEAR UNCLE'S WILL READ!
A FAMILY OF HATE- INTERESTING
A SHORT TIME LATER, AS THE MURDERED MAN'S WILL IS READ.
HOW ABOUT POINTING OUT THESE PEOPLE TO ME!
THAT'S THE FAMILY LAWYER, WARD! HE'S BEEN WITH UNCLE FOR YEARS!..
"THE BALD HEADED MAN IS ABEL, AND THE OTHER IS CARL...BOTH WERE UNCLE HARLEY'S BROTHERS!"
I WONDER HOW MUCH MONEY THAT OLD FOOL HARLEY HAD SALTED AWAY?
I WISH WARD WOULD GET ON WITH THAT WILL!
"THE DARK HAIRED FELLOW IS HARLEY'S SON, ROGER.. AND THE BLOND CHAP NEXT TO HIM IS MY BROTHER, TOMMY
WONDER HOW MUCH THE OLD MAN LEFT ME?
I HOPE UNCLE LEFT ME A GOOD PILE. I COULD USE IT TO PAY OFF THAT GAMBLING DEBT I OWE!
AT LAST THE END OF THE WILL IS REACHED..
"AND SO I LEAVE ALL MY EARTHLY GOODS HERE NOTED TO CHARITABLE INSTITUTIONS!
WHAT IS THIS,- A JOKE?
WHAT?
TO MY "BELOVED FAMILY AND FAMILY LAWYER, WARD, I LEAVE THE ENVELOPES IN THE BOX AND THEIR CONTENTS! PROFIT BY THEIR MESSAGE!
LETS HAVE THOSE ENVELOPES, WARD, THERE MUST BE MONEY IN THEM!
AND IN EACH ENVELOPE IS FOUND A PIECE OF GOLD WITH THE INSCRIPTION...
"UNITED WE STAND-DIVIDED WE FALL"
3

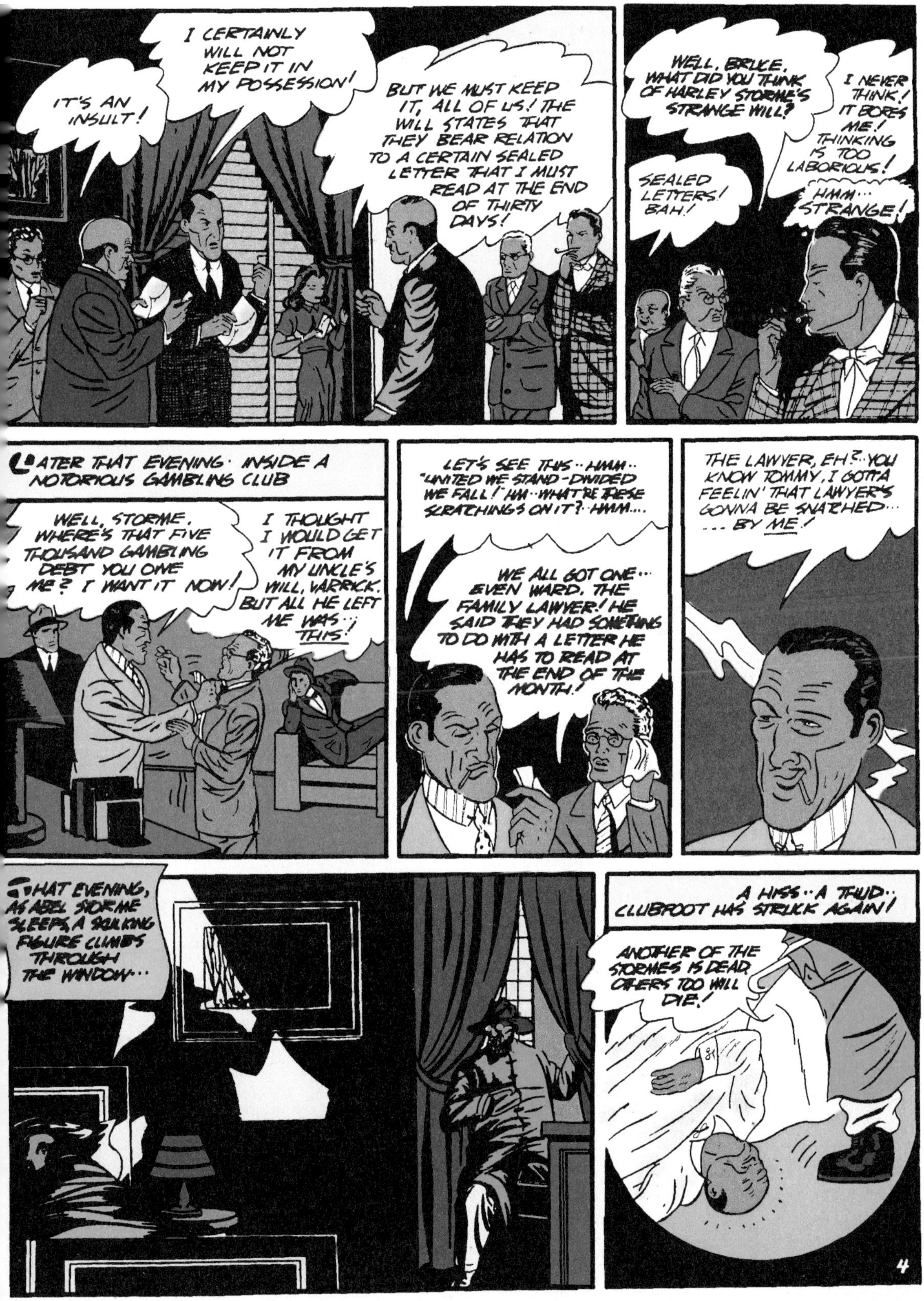
IT'S AN INSULT!
I CERTAINLY WILL NOT KEEP IT IN MY POSSESSION!
BUT WE MUST KEEP IT, ALL OF US! THE WILL STATES THAT THEY BEAR RELATION TO A CERTAIN SEALED LETTER THAT I MUST READ AT THE END OF THIRTY DAYS!
WELL, BRUCE, WHAT DID YOU THINK OF HARLEY STORME'S STRANGE WILL?
I NEVER THINK! IT BORES ME! THINKING IS TOO LABORIOUS!
SEALED LETTERS! BAH!
HMM... STRANGE!
LATER THAT EVENING · INSIDE A NOTORIOUS GAMBLING CLUB
WELL, STORME, WHERE'S THAT FIVE THOUSAND GAMBLING DEBT YOU OWE ME? I WANT IT NOW!
I THOUGHT I WOULD GET IT FROM MY UNCLE'S WILL, VARRICK. BUT ALL HE LEFT ME WAS... THIS!
LET'S SEE THIS... HMM... "UNITED WE STAND - DIVIDED WE FALL!" HM... WHAT'RE THESE SCRATCHINGS ON IT? HMM....
WE ALL GOT ONE... EVEN WARD, THE FAMILY LAWYER! HE SAID THEY HAD SOMETHING TO DO WITH A LETTER HE HAS TO READ AT THE END OF THE MONTH!
THE LAWYER, EH? YOU KNOW TOMMY, I GOTTA FEELIN' THAT LAWYER'S GONNA BE SNATCHED... ... BY ME!
THAT EVENING, AS ABEL STORME SLEEPS, A SKULKING FIGURE CLIMBS THROUGH THE WINDOW...
A HISS.. A THUD.. CLUBFOOT HAS STRUCK AGAIN!
ANOTHER OF THE STORMES IS DEAD. OTHERS TOO WILL DIE!
4

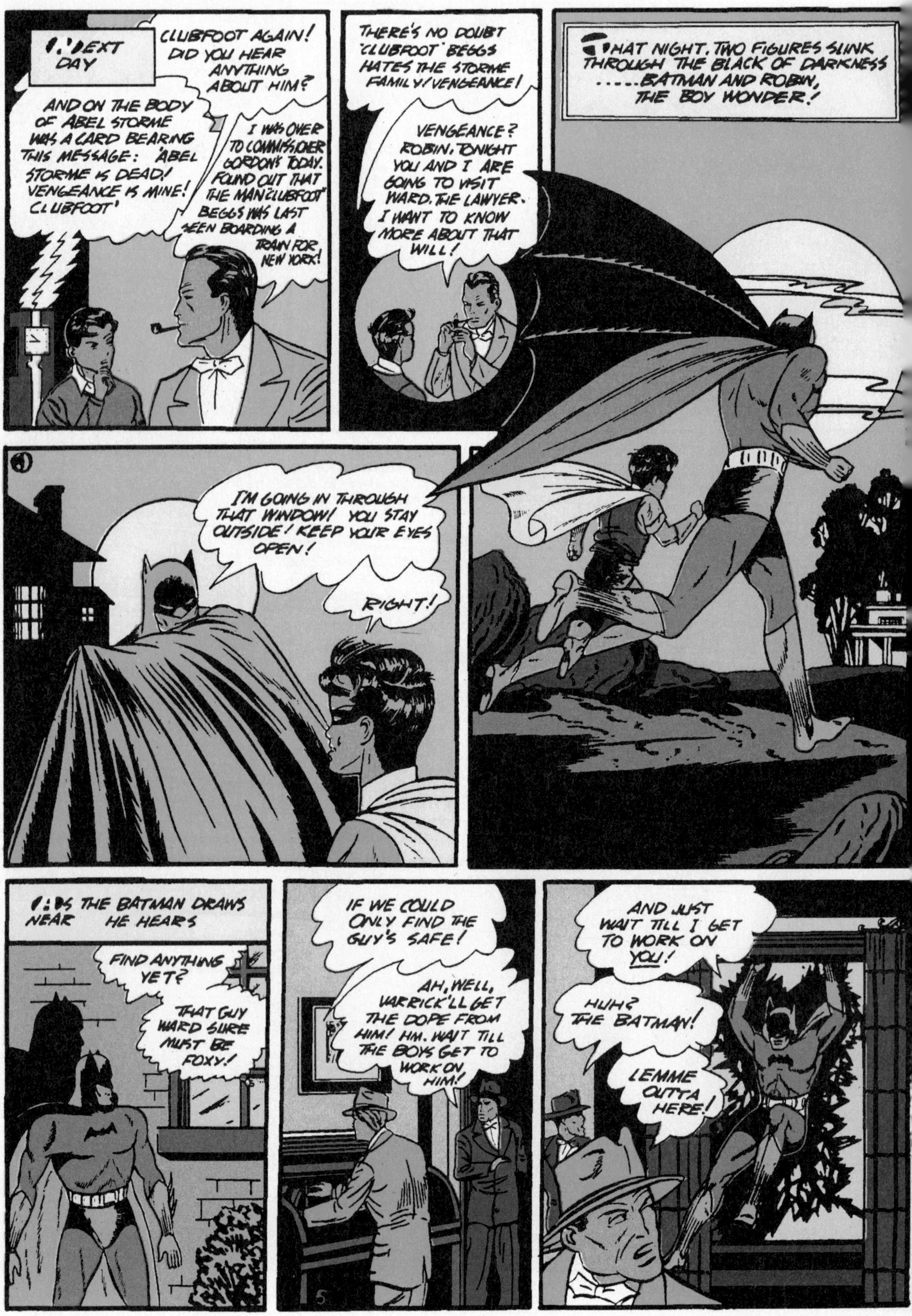

NEXT DAY
CLUBFOOT AGAIN! DID YOU HEAR ANYTHING ABOUT HIM?
AND ON THE BODY OF ABEL STORME WAS A CARD BEARING THIS MESSAGE: 'ABEL STORME IS DEAD! VENGEANCE IS MINE! CLUBFOOT'
I WAS OVER TO COMMISSIONER GORDON'S TODAY. FOUND OUT THAT THE MAN "CLUBFOOT" BEGGS WAS LAST SEEN BOARDING A TRAIN FOR NEW YORK!
THERE'S NO DOUBT "CLUBFOOT" BEGGS HATES THE STORME FAMILY! VENGEANCE!
VENGEANCE? ROBIN, TONIGHT YOU AND I ARE GOING TO VISIT WARD, THE LAWYER. I WANT TO KNOW MORE ABOUT THAT WILL!
THAT NIGHT, TWO FIGURES SLINK THROUGH THE BLACK OF DARKNESS .....BATMAN AND ROBIN, THE BOY WONDER!
I'M GOING IN THROUGH THAT WINDOW! YOU STAY OUTSIDE! KEEP YOUR EYES OPEN!
RIGHT!
AS THE BATMAN DRAWS NEAR HE HEARS
FIND ANYTHING YET?
THAT GUY WARD SURE MUST BE FOXY!
IF WE COULD ONLY FIND THE GUY'S SAFE!
AH, WELL, VARRICK'LL GET THE DOPE FROM HIM! HM. WAIT TILL THE BOYS GET TO WORK ON HIM!
AND JUST WAIT TILL I GET TO WORK ON YOU!
HUH? THE BATMAN!
LEMME OUTTA HERE!

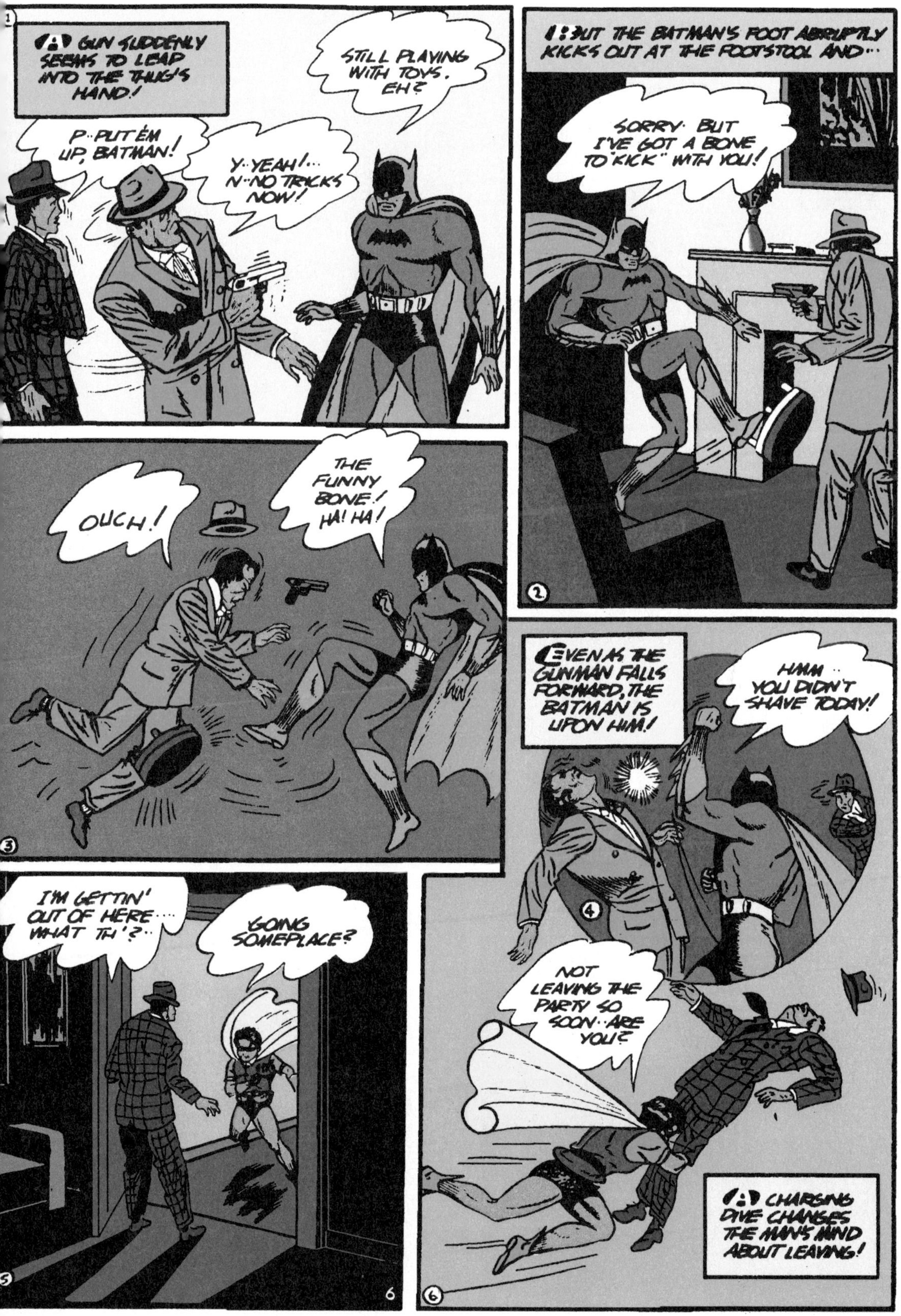
A GUN SUDDENLY SEEMS TO LEAP INTO THE THUG'S HAND!
STILL PLAYING WITH TOYS, EH?
P-PUT'EM UP, BATMAN!
Y-YEAH!... N-NO TRICKS NOW!
BUT THE BATMAN'S FOOT ABRUPTLY KICKS OUT AT THE FOOTSTOOL AND...
SORRY- BUT I'VE GOT A BONE TO "KICK" WITH YOU!
OUCH!
THE FUNNY BONE! HA! HA!
EVEN AS THE GUNMAN FALLS FORWARD, THE BATMAN IS UPON HIM!
HMM.. YOU DIDN'T SHAVE TODAY!
I'M GETTIN' OUT OF HERE.... WHAT TH'?..
GOING SOMEPLACE?
NOT LEAVING THE PARTY SO SOON.. ARE YOU?
A CHARGING DIVE CHANGES THE MAN'S MIND ABOUT LEAVING!

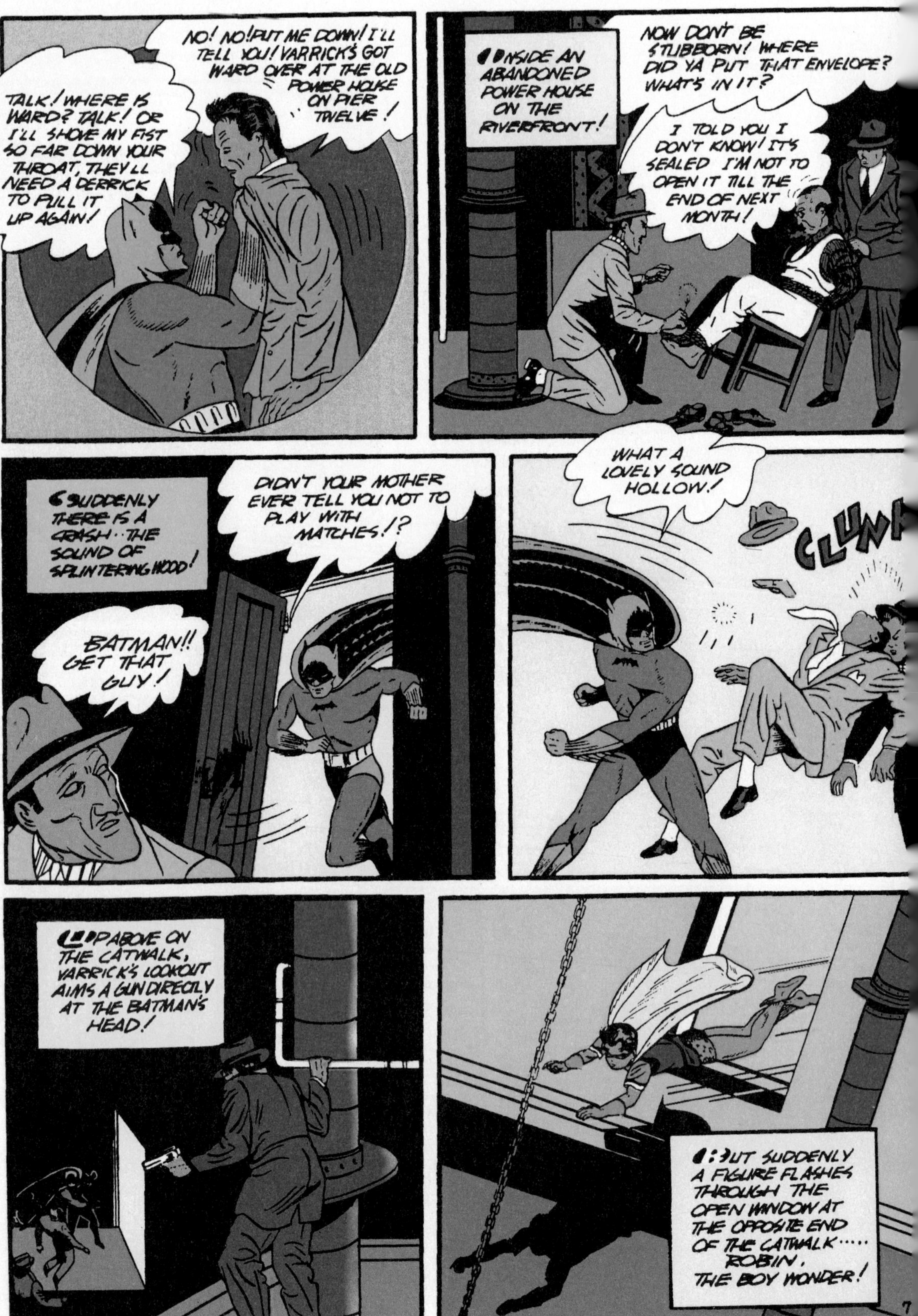

TALK! WHERE IS WARD? TALK! OR I'LL SHOVE MY FIST SO FAR DOWN YOUR THROAT, THEY'LL NEED A DERRICK TO PULL IT UP AGAIN!
NO! NO! PUT ME DOWN! I'LL TELL YOU! VARRICK'S GOT WARD OVER AT THE OLD POWER HOUSE ON PIER TWELVE!
INSIDE AN ABANDONED POWER HOUSE ON THE RIVERFRONT!
NOW DON'T BE STUBBORN! WHERE DID YA PUT THAT ENVELOPE? WHAT'S IN IT?
I TOLD YOU I DON'T KNOW! IT'S SEALED. I'M NOT TO OPEN IT TILL THE END OF NEXT MONTH!
SUDDENLY THERE IS A CRASH..THE SOUND OF SPLINTERING WOOD!
DIDN'T YOUR MOTHER EVER TELL YOU NOT TO PLAY WITH MATCHES!?
BATMAN!! GET THAT GUY!
WHAT A LOVELY SOUND HOLLOW!
CLUN
ABOVE ON THE CATWALK, VARRICK'S LOOKOUT AIMS A GUN DIRECTLY AT THE BATMAN'S HEAD!
BUT SUDDENLY A FIGURE FLASHES THROUGH THE OPEN WINDOW AT THE OPPOSITE END OF THE CATWALK..... ROBIN, THE BOY WONDER!
7

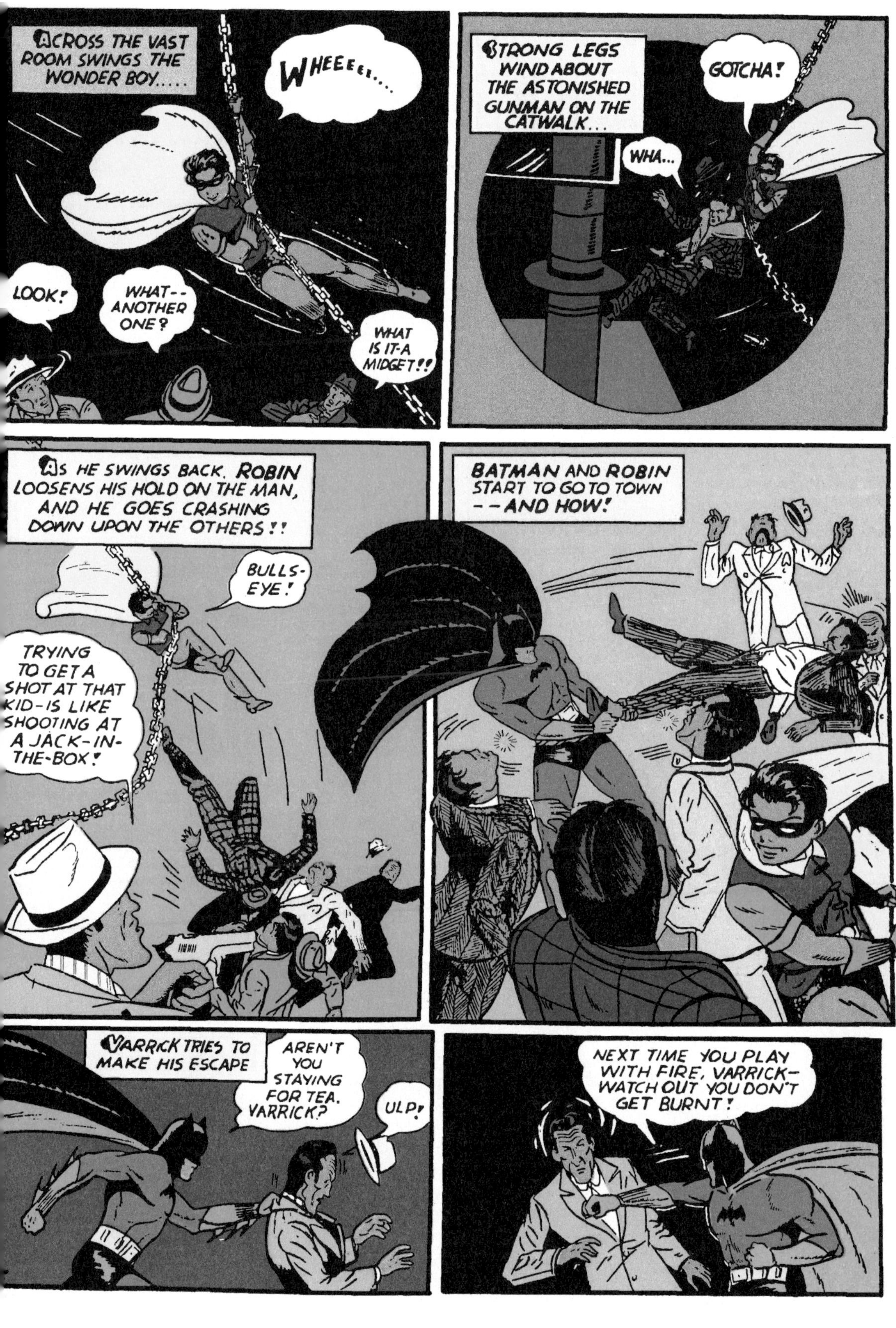
ACROSS THE VAST ROOM SWINGS THE WONDER BOY.....
WHEEEEE.....
LOOK!
WHAT-- ANOTHER ONE?
WHAT IS IT-A MIDGET!!
STRONG LEGS WIND ABOUT THE ASTONISHED GUNMAN ON THE CATWALK...
GOTCHA!
WHA...
AS HE SWINGS BACK, ROBIN LOOSENS HIS HOLD ON THE MAN, AND HE GOES CRASHING DOWN UPON THE OTHERS!!
BULLS-EYE!
TRYING TO GET A SHOT AT THAT KID-IS LIKE SHOOTING AT A JACK-IN-THE-BOX!
BATMAN AND ROBIN START TO GO TO TOWN --AND HOW!
VARRICK TRIES TO MAKE HIS ESCAPE
AREN'T YOU STAYING FOR TEA, VARRICK?
ULP!
NEXT TIME YOU PLAY WITH FIRE, VARRICK-WATCH OUT YOU DON'T GET BURNT!

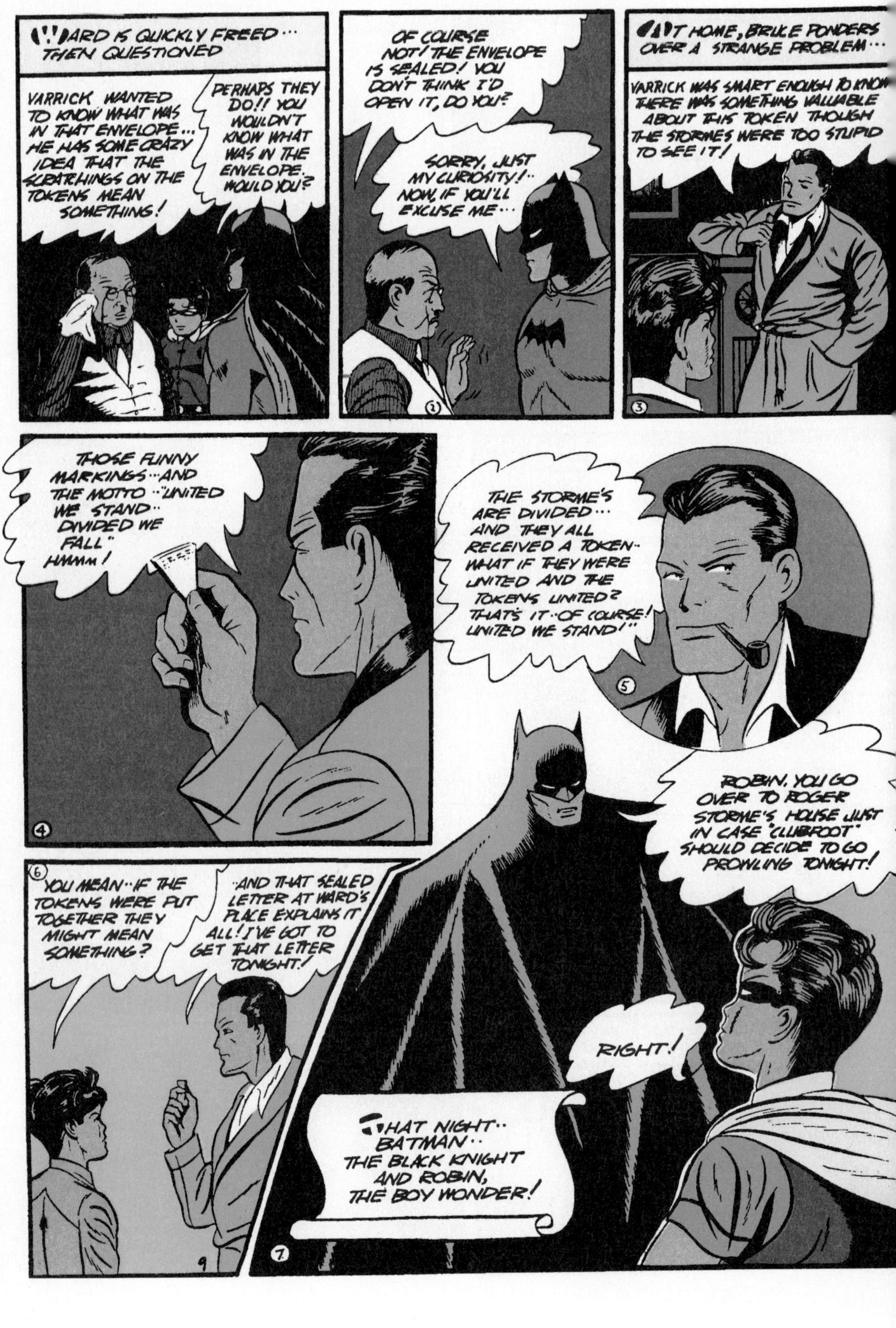
WARD IS QUICKLY FREED... THEN QUESTIONED
VARRICK WANTED TO KNOW WHAT WAS IN THAT ENVELOPE... HE HAS SOME CRAZY IDEA THAT THE SCRATCHINGS ON THE TOKENS MEAN SOMETHING!
PERHAPS THEY DO!! YOU WOULDN'T KNOW WHAT WAS IN THE ENVELOPE.. WOULD YOU?
OF COURSE NOT! THE ENVELOPE IS SEALED! YOU DON'T THINK I'D OPEN IT, DO YOU?
SORRY, JUST MY CURIOSITY!.. NOW, IF YOU'LL EXCUSE ME...
AT HOME, BRUCE PONDERS OVER A STRANGE PROBLEM...
VARRICK WAS SMART ENOUGH TO KNOW THERE WAS SOMETHING VALUABLE ABOUT THIS TOKEN THOUGH THE STORMES WERE TOO STUPID TO SEE IT!
THOSE FUNNY MARKINGS...AND THE MOTTO..."UNITED WE STAND.. DIVIDED WE FALL" HMMM!
THE STORME'S ARE DIVIDED... AND THEY ALL RECEIVED A TOKEN.. WHAT IF THEY WERE UNITED AND THE TOKENS UNITED? THAT'S IT..OF COURSE! UNITED WE STAND!"
YOU MEAN..IF THE TOKENS WERE PUT TOGETHER THEY MIGHT MEAN SOMETHING?
..AND THAT SEALED LETTER AT WARD'S PLACE EXPLAINS IT ALL! I'VE GOT TO GET THAT LETTER TONIGHT!
ROBIN, YOU GO OVER TO ROGER STORME'S HOUSE JUST IN CASE "CLUBFOOT" SHOULD DECIDE TO GO PROWLING TONIGHT!
RIGHT!
THAT NIGHT.. BATMAN.. THE BLACK KNIGHT AND ROBIN, THE BOY WONDER!

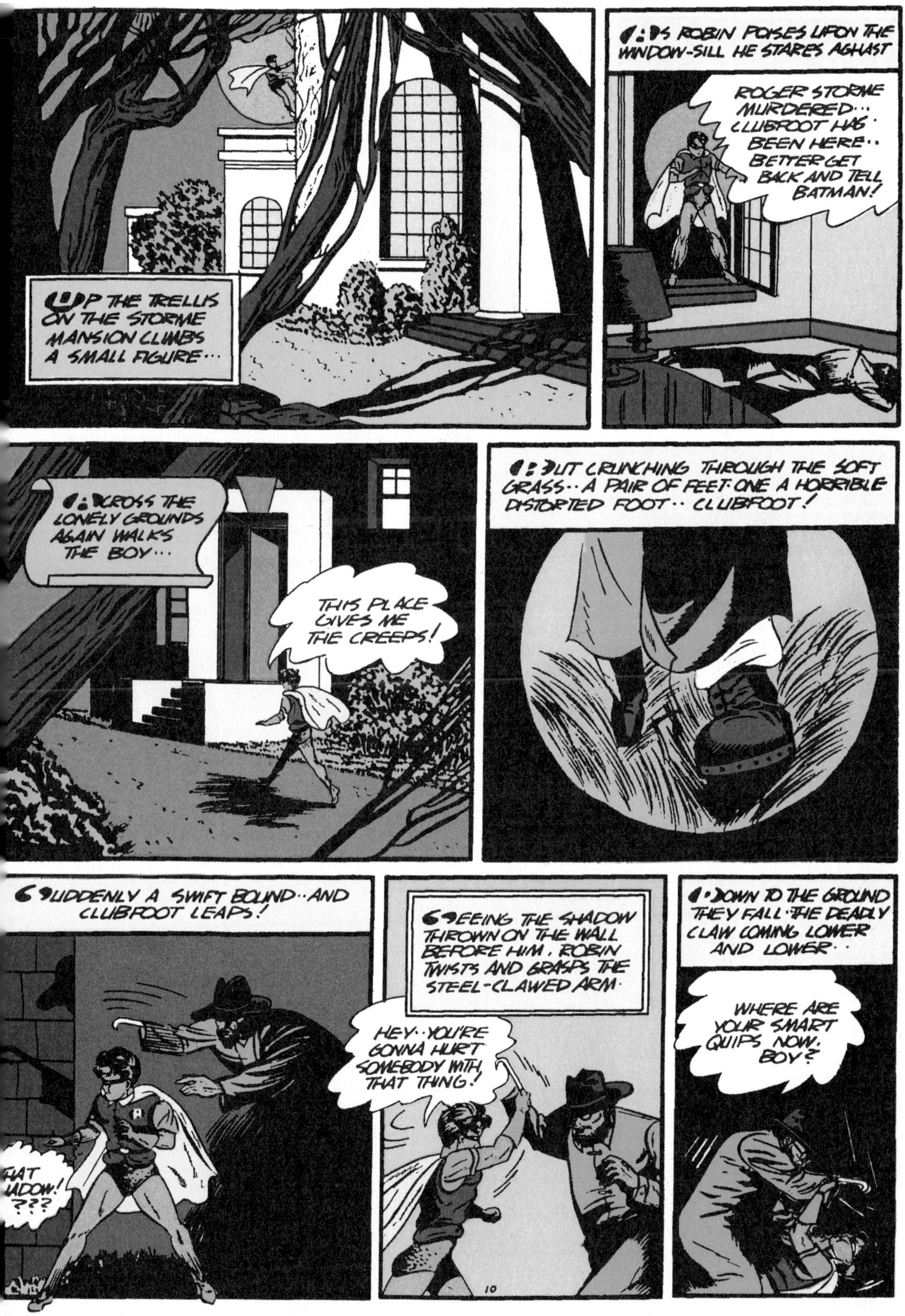
UP THE TRELLIS ON THE STORME MANSION CLIMBS A SMALL FIGURE...
AS ROBIN POISES UPON THE WINDOW-SILL HE STARES AGHAST
ROGER STORME MURDERED... CLUBFOOT HAS BEEN HERE.. BETTER GET BACK AND TELL BATMAN!
ACROSS THE LONELY GROUNDS AGAIN WALKS THE BOY...
THIS PLACE GIVES ME THE CREEPS!
BUT CRUNCHING THROUGH THE SOFT GRASS.. A PAIR OF FEET. ONE A HORRIBLE DISTORTED FOOT.. CLUBFOOT!
SUDDENLY A SWIFT BOUND..AND CLUBFOOT LEAPS!
THAT SHADOW! ???
SEEING THE SHADOW THROWN ON THE WALL BEFORE HIM, ROBIN TWISTS AND GRASPS THE STEEL-CLAWED ARM.
HEY..YOU'RE GONNA HURT SOMEBODY WITH THAT THING!
DOWN TO THE GROUND THEY FALL. THE DEADLY CLAW COMING LOWER AND LOWER..
WHERE ARE YOUR SMART QUIPS NOW, BOY?

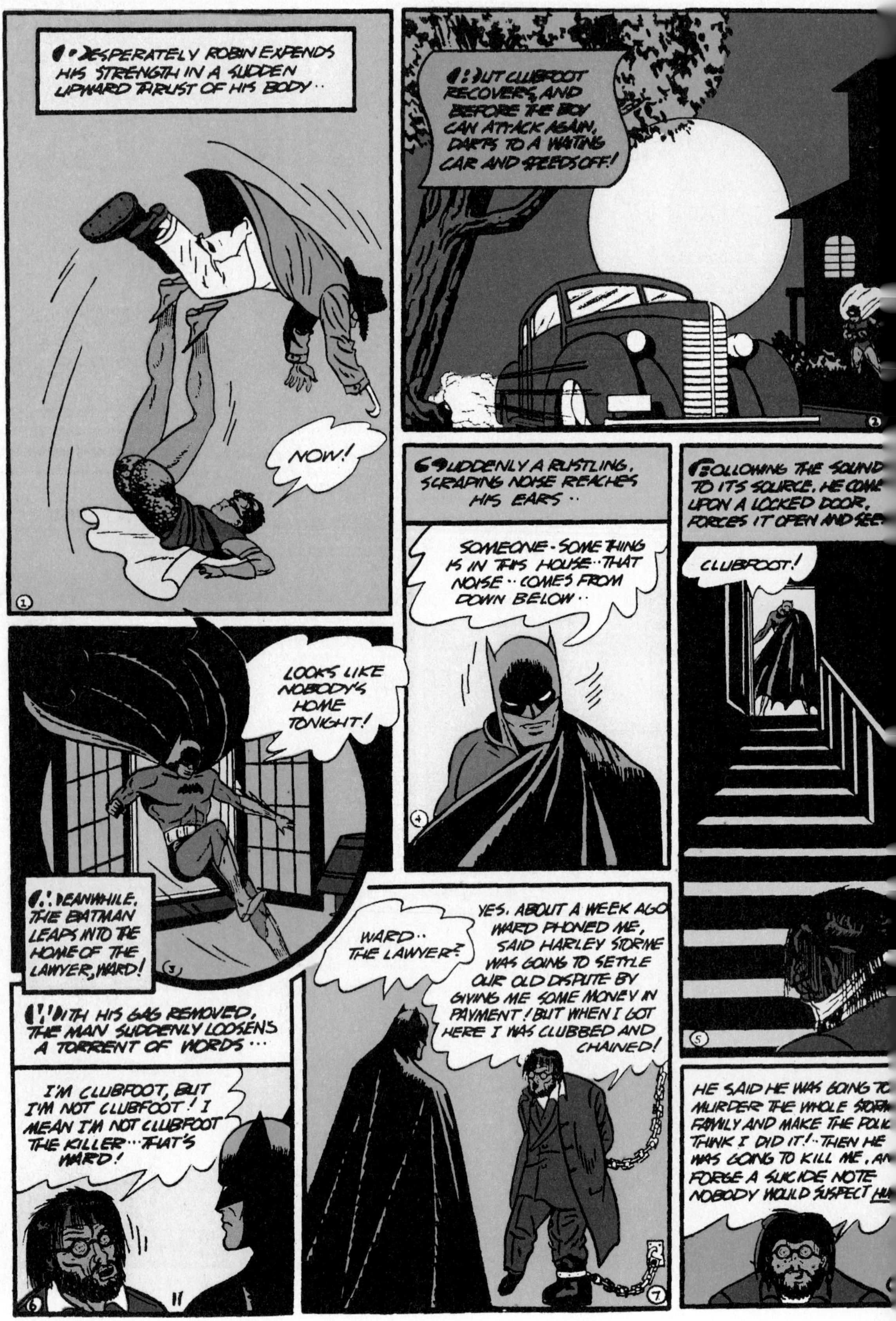
DESPERATELY ROBIN EXPENDS HIS STRENGTH IN A SUDDEN UPWARD THRUST OF HIS BODY..
NOW!
BUT CLUBFOOT RECOVERS, AND BEFORE THE BOY CAN ATTACK AGAIN, DARTS TO A WAITING CAR AND SPEEDS OFF!
MEANWHILE, THE BATMAN LEAPS INTO THE HOME OF THE LAWYER, WARD!
LOOKS LIKE NOBODY'S HOME TONIGHT!
SUDDENLY A RUSTLING, SCRAPING NOISE REACHES HIS EARS..
SOMEONE-SOMETHING IS IN THIS HOUSE..THAT NOISE..COMES FROM DOWN BELOW..
FOLLOWING THE SOUND TO IT'S SOURCE, HE COM UPON A LOCKED DOOR, FORCES IT OPEN AND SEE
CLUBFOOT!
WITH HIS GAG REMOVED, THE MAN SUDDENLY LOOSENS A TORRENT OF WORDS...
I'M CLUBFOOT, BUT I'M NOT CLUBFOOT! I MEAN I'M NOT CLUBFOOT THE KILLER...THAT'S WARD!
WARD.. THE LAWYER?
YES. ABOUT A WEEK AGO WARD PHONED ME, SAID HARLEY STORME WAS GOING TO SETTLE OUR OLD DISPUTE BY GIVING ME SOME MONEY IN PAYMENT! BUT WHEN I GOT HERE I WAS CLUBBED AND CHAINED!
HE SAID HE WAS GOING TO MURDER THE WHOLE STORM FAMILY AND MAKE THE POLIC THINK I DID IT!..THEN HE WAS GOING TO KILL ME, AN FORGE A SUICIDE NOTE NOBODY WOULD SUSPECT HI

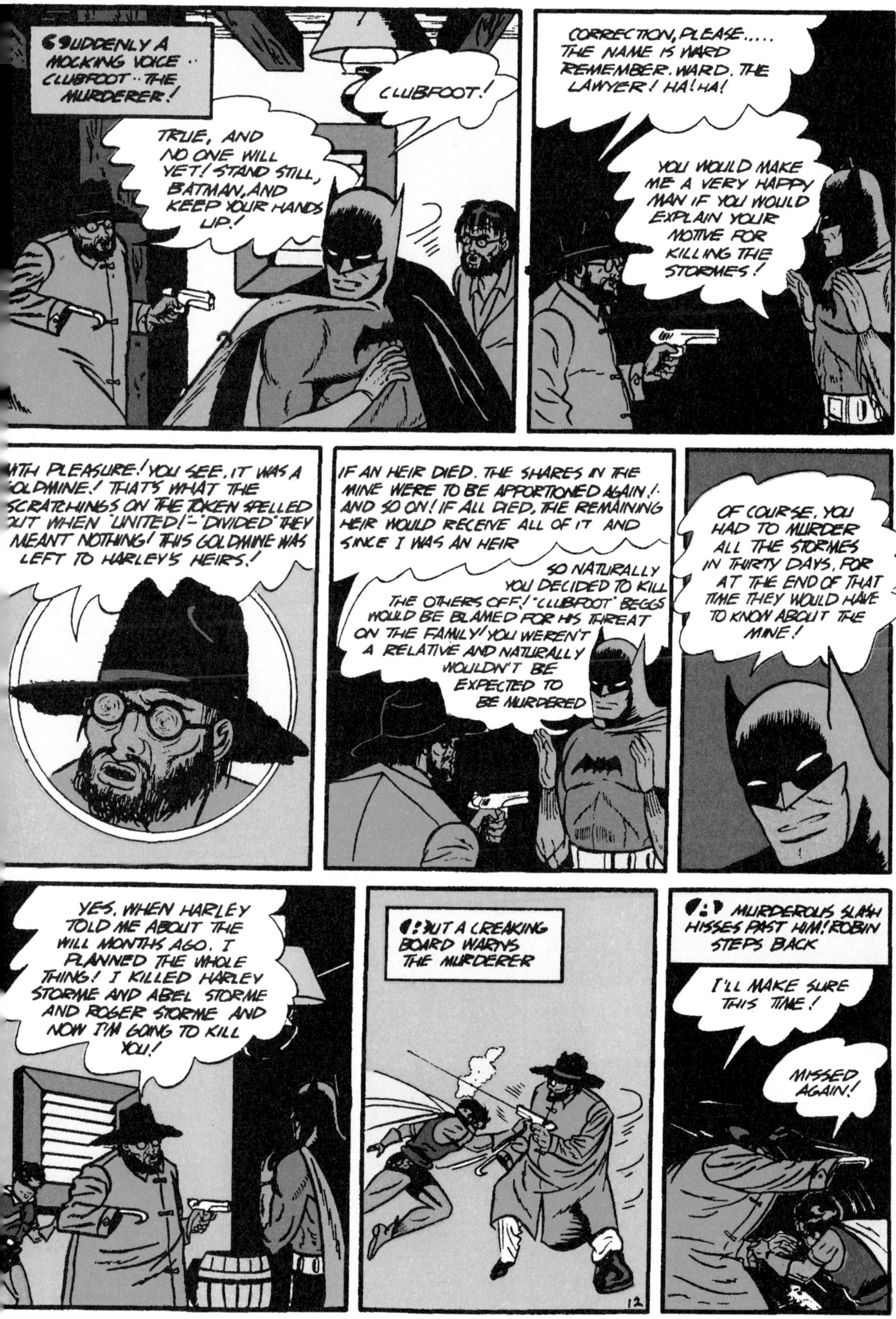
SUDDENLY A MOCKING VOICE .. CLUBFOOT .. THE MURDERER!
CLUBFOOT!
TRUE, AND NO ONE WILL YET! STAND STILL, BATMAN, AND KEEP YOUR HANDS UP!
CORRECTION, PLEASE..... THE NAME IS WARD REMEMBER. WARD. THE LAWYER! HA! HA!
YOU WOULD MAKE ME A VERY HAPPY MAN IF YOU WOULD EXPLAIN YOUR MOTIVE FOR KILLING THE STORMES!
ITH PLEASURE! YOU SEE, IT WAS A OLDMINE! THAT'S WHAT THE SCRATCHINGS ON THE TOKEN SPELLED UT WHEN "UNITED!"-"DIVIDED" THEY MEANT NOTHING! THIS GOLDMINE WAS LEFT TO HARLEY'S HEIRS!
IF AN HEIR DIED, THE SHARES IN THE MINE WERE TO BE APPORTIONED AGAIN!.. AND SO ON! IF ALL DIED, THE REMAINING HEIR WOULD RECEIVE ALL OF IT AND SINCE I WAS AN HEIR
SO NATURALLY YOU DECIDED TO KILL THE OTHERS OFF! "CLUBFOOT" BEGGS WOULD BE BLAMED FOR HIS THREAT ON THE FAMILY! YOU WEREN'T A RELATIVE AND NATURALLY WOULDN'T BE EXPECTED TO BE MURDERED
OF COURSE, YOU HAD TO MURDER ALL THE STORMES IN THIRTY DAYS, FOR AT THE END OF THAT TIME THEY WOULD HAVE TO KNOW ABOUT THE MINE!
YES, WHEN HARLEY TOLD ME ABOUT THE WILL MONTHS AGO, I PLANNED THE WHOLE THING! I KILLED HARLEY STORME AND ABEL STORME AND ROGER STORME AND NOW I'M GOING TO KILL YOU!
BUT A CREAKING BOARD WARNS THE MURDERER
12
A MURDEROUS SLASH HISSES PAST HIM! ROBIN STEPS BACK
I'LL MAKE SURE THIS TIME!
MISSED AGAIN!

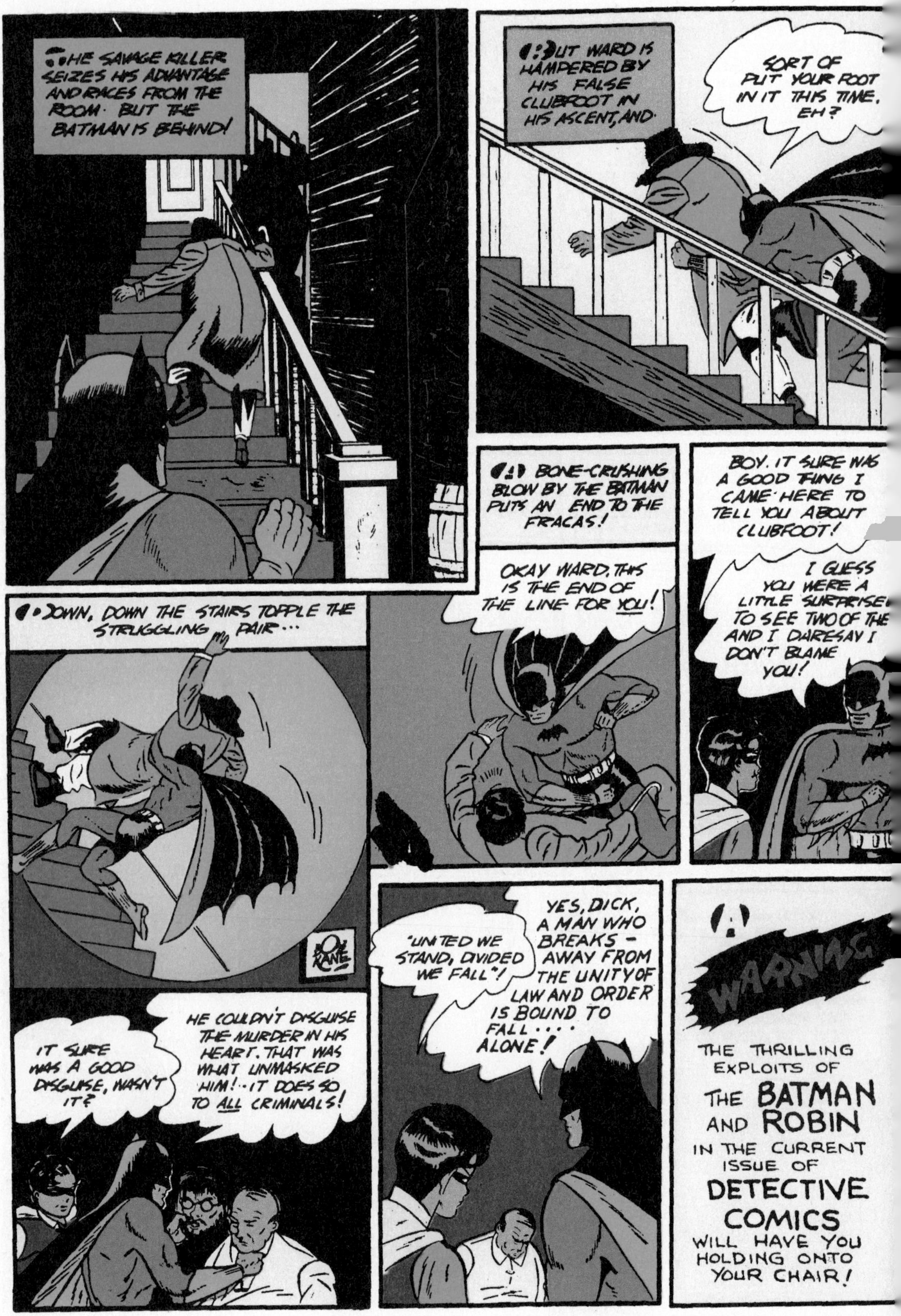
THE SAVAGE KILLER SEIZES HIS ADVANTAGE AND RACES FROM THE ROOM. BUT THE BATMAN IS BEHIND!
BUT WARD IS HAMPERED BY HIS FALSE CLUBFOOT IN HIS ASCENT, AND
SORT OF PUT YOUR FOOT IN IT THIS TIME, EH?
DOWN, DOWN THE STAIRS TOPPLE THE STRUGGLING PAIR...
A BONE-CRUSHING BLOW BY THE BATMAN PUTS AN END TO THE FRACAS!
OKAY WARD, THIS IS THE END OF THE LINE FOR YOU!
BOY, IT SURE WAS A GOOD THING I CAME HERE TO TELL YOU ABOUT CLUBFOOT!
I GUESS YOU WERE A LITTLE SURPRISE TO SEE TWO OF THE AND I DARESAY I DON'T BLAME YOU!
IT SURE WAS A GOOD DISGUISE, WASN'T IT?
HE COULDN'T DISGUISE THE MURDER IN HIS HEART. THAT WAS WHAT UNMASKED HIM!.. IT DOES SO TO ALL CRIMINALS!
YES, DICK, A MAN WHO BREAKS - AWAY FROM THE UNITY OF LAW AND ORDER IS BOUND TO FALL.... ALONE!
"UNITED WE STAND, DIVIDED WE FALL"!
WARNING
THE THRILLING EXPLOITS OF THE BATMAN AND ROBIN IN THE CURRENT ISSUE OF DETECTIVE COMICS WILL HAVE YOU HOLDING ONTO YOUR CHAIR!

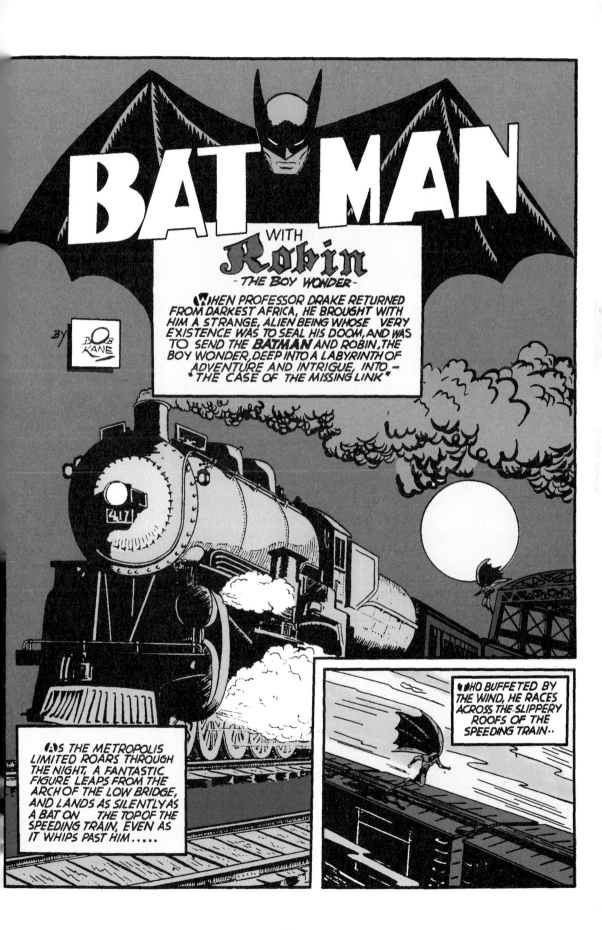

BAT MAN

WITH

Robin
-THE BOY WONDER-

WHEN PROFESSOR DRAKE RETURNED FROM DARKEST AFRICA, HE BROUGHT WITH HIM A STRANGE, ALIEN BEING WHOSE VERY EXISTENCE WAS TO SEAL HIS DOOM, AND WAS TO SEND THE **BATMAN** AND ROBIN, THE BOY WONDER, DEEP INTO A LABYRINTH OF ADVENTURE AND INTRIGUE, INTO "THE CASE OF THE MISSING LINK"

BY BOB KANE

AS THE METROPOLIS LIMITED ROARS THROUGH THE NIGHT, A FANTASTIC FIGURE LEAPS FROM THE ARCH OF THE LOW BRIDGE, AND LANDS AS SILENTLY AS A BAT ON THE TOP OF THE SPEEDING TRAIN, EVEN AS IT WHIPS PAST HIM.....

WHO BUFFETED BY THE WIND, HE RACES ACROSS THE SLIPPERY ROOFS OF THE SPEEDING TRAIN..

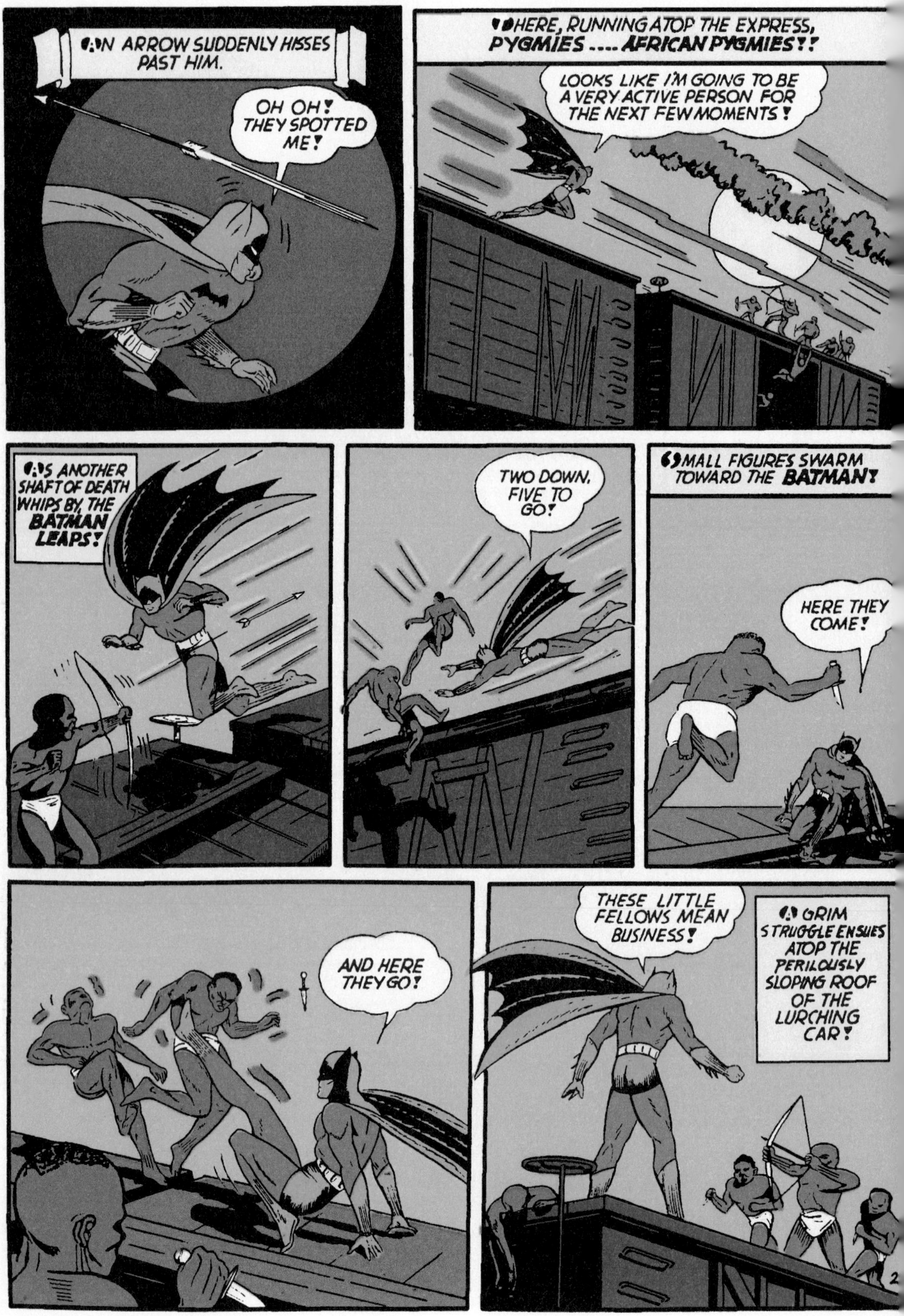
AN ARROW SUDDENLY HISSES PAST HIM.
OH OH! THEY SPOTTED ME!
THERE, RUNNING ATOP THE EXPRESS, PYGMIES .... AFRICAN PYGMIES!!
LOOKS LIKE I'M GOING TO BE A VERY ACTIVE PERSON FOR THE NEXT FEW MOMENTS!
AS ANOTHER SHAFT OF DEATH WHIPS BY, THE BATMAN LEAPS!
TWO DOWN, FIVE TO GO!
SMALL FIGURES SWARM TOWARD THE BATMAN!
HERE THEY COME!
AND HERE THEY GO!
THESE LITTLE FELLOWS MEAN BUSINESS!
A GRIM STRUGGLE ENSUES ATOP THE PERILOUSLY SLOPING ROOF OF THE LURCHING CAR!

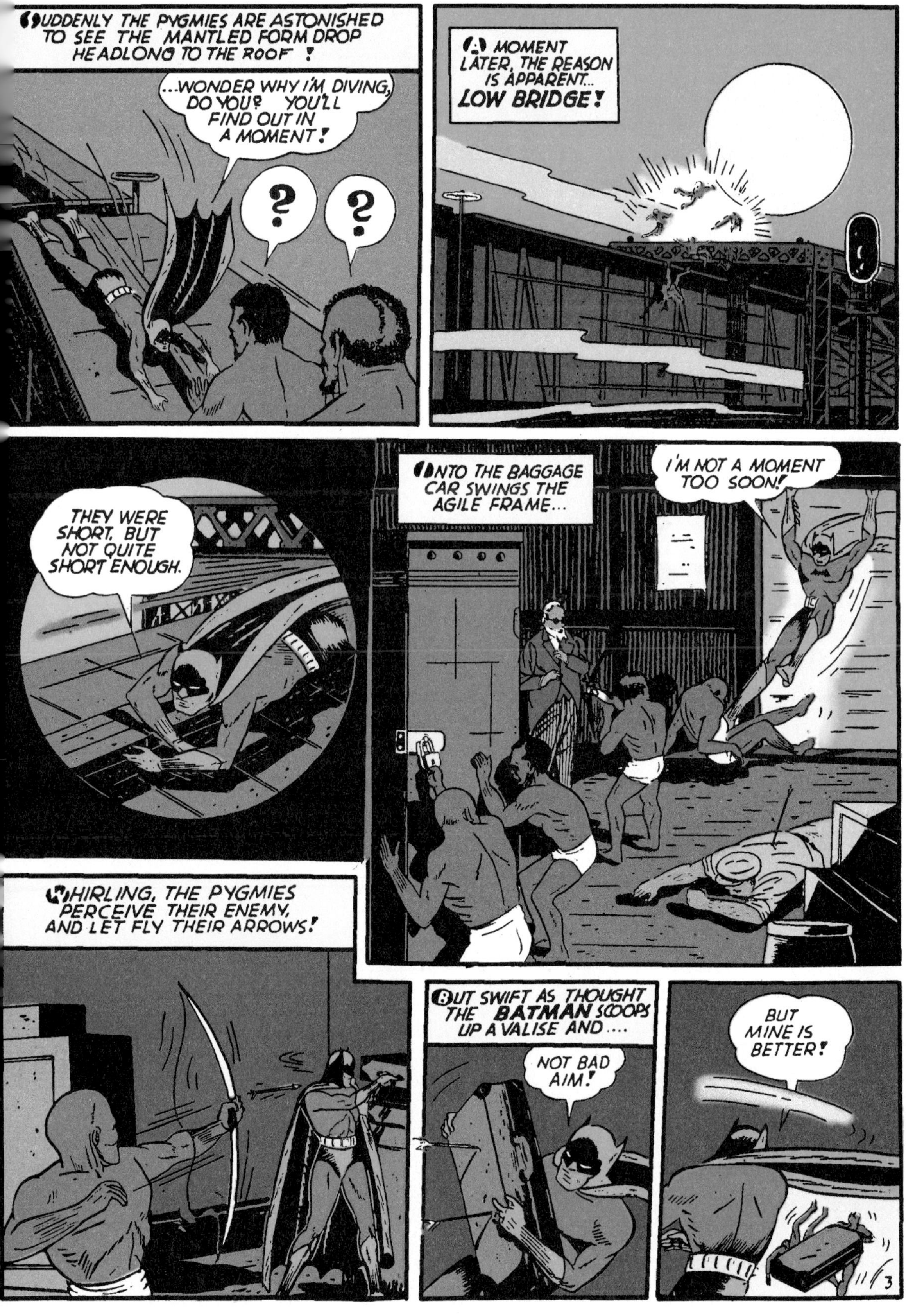
SUDDENLY THE PYGMIES ARE ASTONISHED TO SEE THE MANTLED FORM DROP HEADLONG TO THE ROOF!
...WONDER WHY I'M DIVING, DO YOU? YOU'LL FIND OUT IN A MOMENT!
?
?
A MOMENT LATER, THE REASON IS APPARENT... LOW BRIDGE!
THEY WERE SHORT, BUT NOT QUITE SHORT ENOUGH.
ONTO THE BAGGAGE CAR SWINGS THE AGILE FRAME...
I'M NOT A MOMENT TOO SOON!
WHIRLING, THE PYGMIES PERCEIVE THEIR ENEMY, AND LET FLY THEIR ARROWS!
BUT SWIFT AS THOUGHT THE BATMAN SCOOPS UP A VALISE AND....
NOT BAD AIM!
BUT MINE IS BETTER!
3

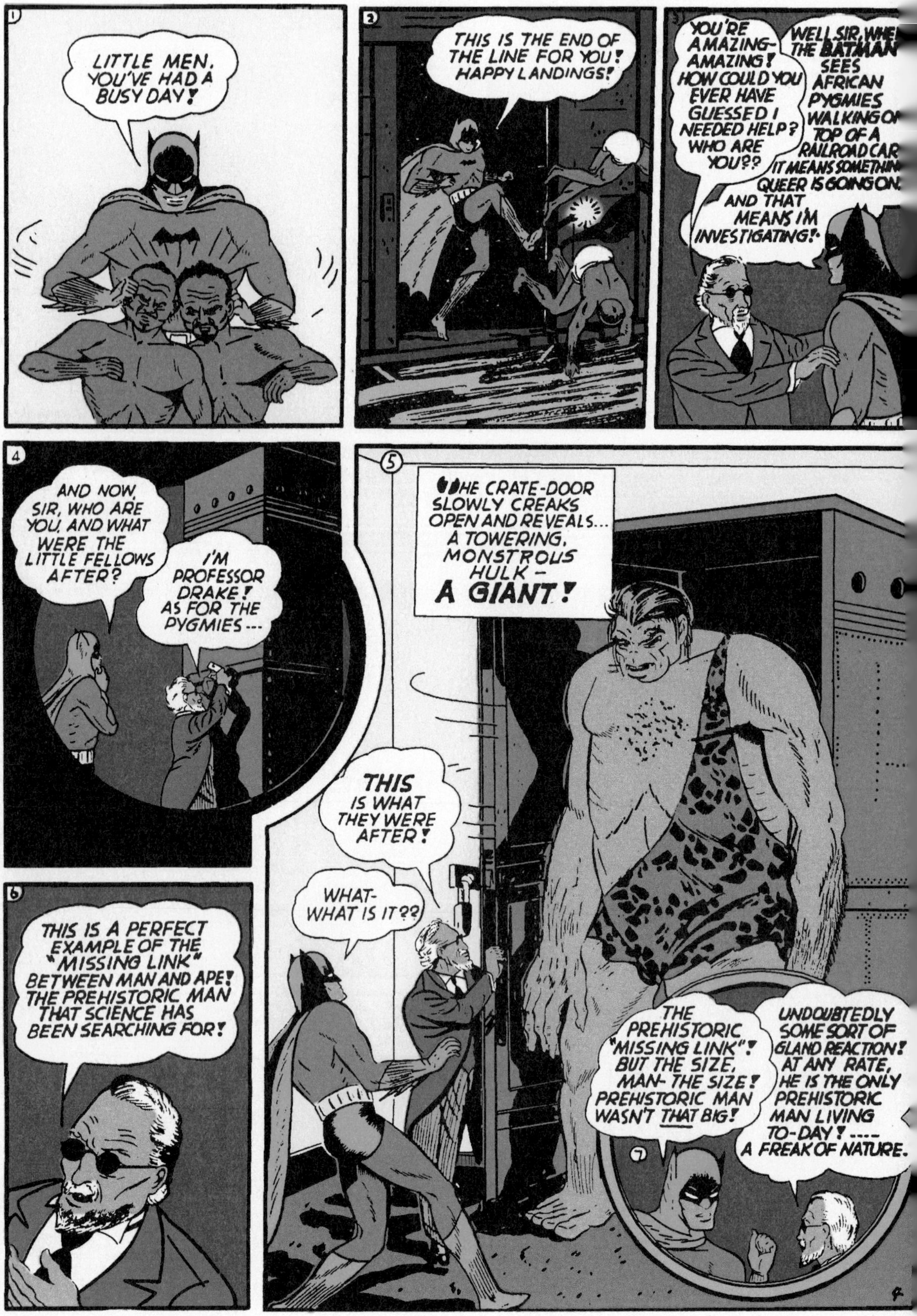

LITTLE MEN, YOU'VE HAD A BUSY DAY!
THIS IS THE END OF THE LINE FOR YOU! HAPPY LANDINGS!
YOU'RE AMAZING— AMAZING! HOW COULD YOU EVER HAVE GUESSED I NEEDED HELP? WHO ARE YOU??
WELL SIR, WHE THE BATMAN SEES AFRICAN PYGMIES WALKING O TOP OF A RAILROAD CAR IT MEANS SOMETHIN QUEER IS GOING ON. AND THAT MEANS I'M INVESTIGATING!
AND NOW, SIR, WHO ARE YOU, AND WHAT WERE THE LITTLE FELLOWS AFTER?
I'M PROFESSOR DRAKE! AS FOR THE PYGMIES ---
THE CRATE-DOOR SLOWLY CREAKS OPEN AND REVEALS... A TOWERING, MONSTROUS HULK — A GIANT!
THIS IS WHAT THEY WERE AFTER!
WHAT- WHAT IS IT??
THIS IS A PERFECT EXAMPLE OF THE "MISSING LINK" BETWEEN MAN AND APE! THE PREHISTORIC MAN THAT SCIENCE HAS BEEN SEARCHING FOR!
THE PREHISTORIC "MISSING LINK"! BUT THE SIZE, MAN- THE SIZE! PREHISTORIC MAN WASN'T THAT BIG!
UNDOUBTEDLY SOME SORT OF GLAND REACTION! AT ANY RATE, HE IS THE ONLY PREHISTORIC MAN LIVING TO-DAY! .... A FREAK OF NATURE.

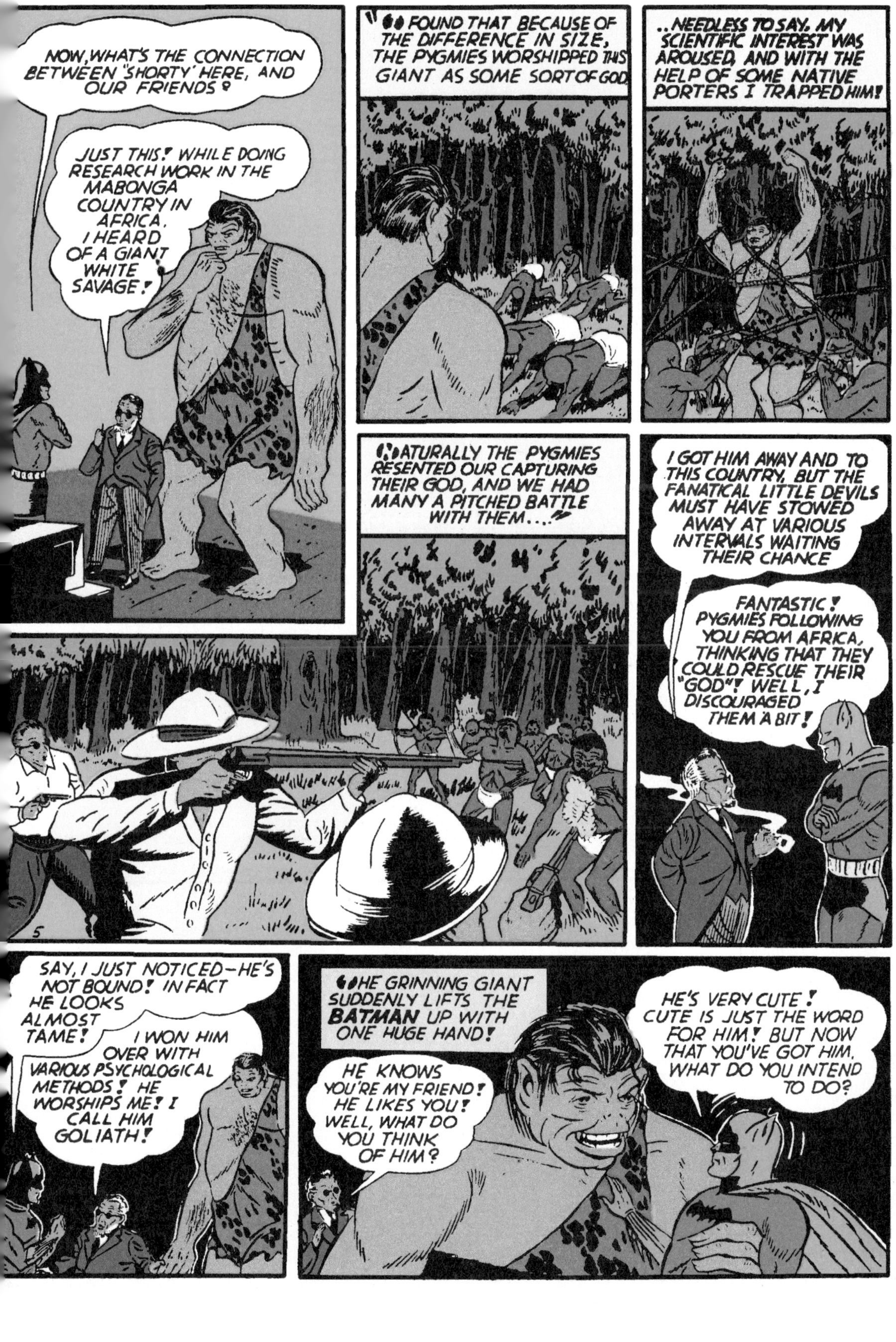
NOW, WHAT'S THE CONNECTION BETWEEN "SHORTY" HERE, AND OUR FRIENDS?
JUST THIS! WHILE DOING RESEARCH WORK IN THE MABONGA COUNTRY IN AFRICA, I HEARD OF A GIANT WHITE SAVAGE!
"I FOUND THAT BECAUSE OF THE DIFFERENCE IN SIZE, THE PYGMIES WORSHIPPED THIS GIANT AS SOME SORT OF GOD
..NEEDLESS TO SAY, MY SCIENTIFIC INTEREST WAS AROUSED, AND WITH THE HELP OF SOME NATIVE PORTERS I TRAPPED HIM!
"NATURALLY THE PYGMIES RESENTED OUR CAPTURING THEIR GOD, AND WE HAD MANY A PITCHED BATTLE WITH THEM...."
5
I GOT HIM AWAY AND TO THIS COUNTRY, BUT THE FANATICAL LITTLE DEVILS MUST HAVE STOWED AWAY AT VARIOUS INTERVALS WAITING THEIR CHANCE
FANTASTIC! PYGMIES FOLLOWING YOU FROM AFRICA, THINKING THAT THEY COULD RESCUE THEIR "GOD"! WELL, I DISCOURAGED THEM A BIT!
SAY, I JUST NOTICED—HE'S NOT BOUND! IN FACT HE LOOKS ALMOST TAME!
I WON HIM OVER WITH VARIOUS PSYCHOLOGICAL METHODS! HE WORSHIPS ME! I CALL HIM GOLIATH!
THE GRINNING GIANT SUDDENLY LIFTS THE BATMAN UP WITH ONE HUGE HAND!
HE KNOWS YOU'RE MY FRIEND! HE LIKES YOU! WELL, WHAT DO YOU THINK OF HIM?
HE'S VERY CUTE! CUTE IS JUST THE WORD FOR HIM! BUT NOW THAT YOU'VE GOT HIM, WHAT DO YOU INTEND TO DO?

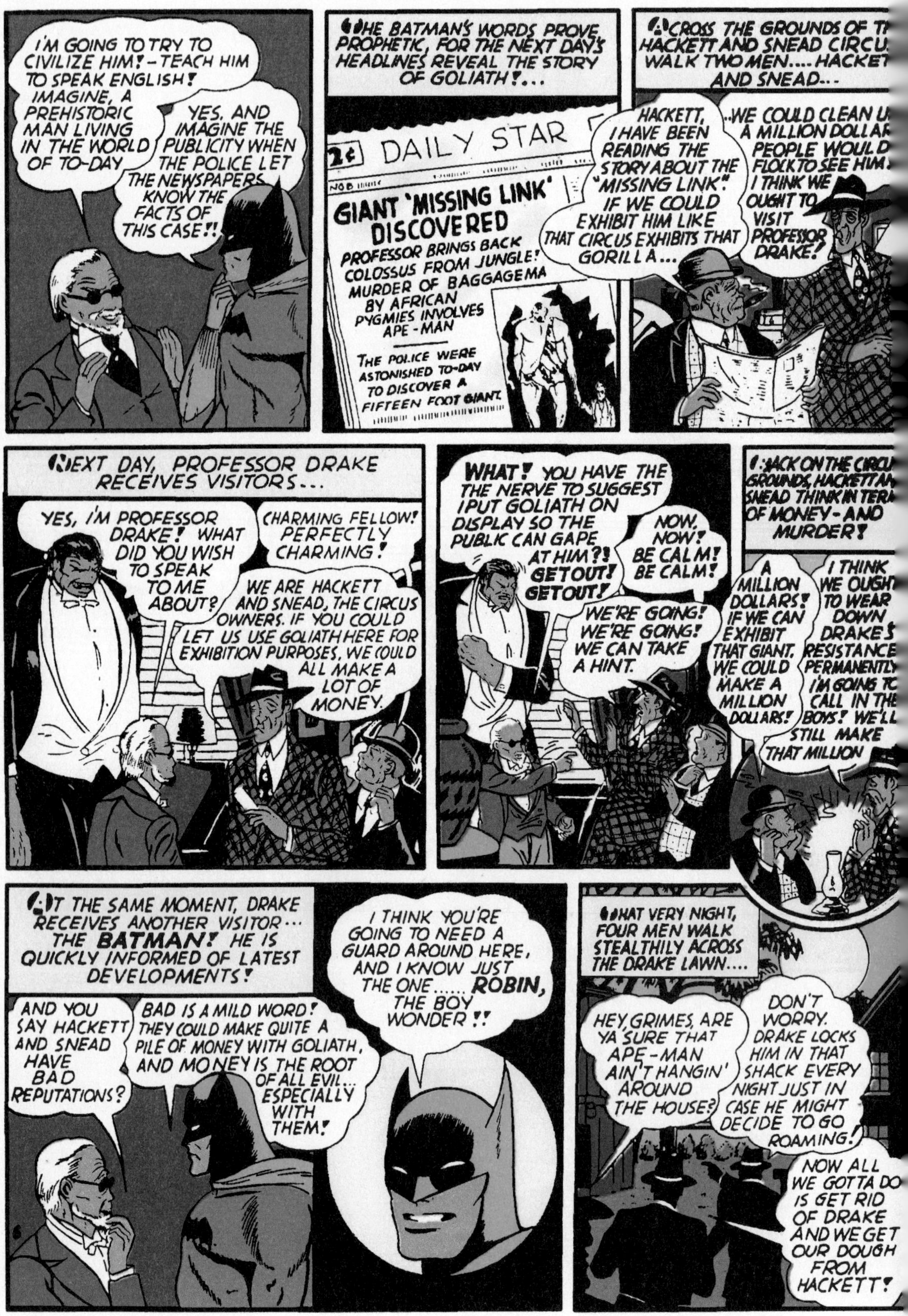

I'M GOING TO TRY TO CIVILIZE HIM! - TEACH HIM TO SPEAK ENGLISH! IMAGINE, A PREHISTORIC MAN LIVING IN THE WORLD OF TO-DAY
YES, AND IMAGINE THE PUBLICITY WHEN THE POLICE LET THE NEWSPAPERS KNOW THE FACTS OF THIS CASE!!
THE BATMAN'S WORDS PROVE PROPHETIC, FOR THE NEXT DAY'S HEADLINES REVEAL THE STORY OF GOLIATH!...
DAILY STAR
2¢
GIANT 'MISSING LINK' DISCOVERED
PROFESSOR BRINGS BACK COLOSSUS FROM JUNGLE! MURDER OF BAGGAGEMA BY AFRICAN PYGMIES INVOLVES APE-MAN
THE POLICE WERE ASTONISHED TO-DAY TO DISCOVER A FIFTEEN FOOT GIANT
ACROSS THE GROUNDS OF TH HACKETT AND SNEAD CIRCU WALK TWO MEN.... HACKET AND SNEAD...
HACKETT, I HAVE BEEN READING THE STORY ABOUT THE "MISSING LINK." IF WE COULD EXHIBIT HIM LIKE THAT CIRCUS EXHIBITS THAT GORILLA...
..WE COULD CLEAN U A MILLION DOLLA PEOPLE WOULD FLOCK TO SEE HIM! I THINK WE OUGHT TO VISIT PROFESSOR DRAKE!
NEXT DAY, PROFESSOR DRAKE RECEIVES VISITORS...
YES, I'M PROFESSOR DRAKE! WHAT DID YOU WISH TO SPEAK TO ME ABOUT?
CHARMING FELLOW! PERFECTLY CHARMING!
WE ARE HACKETT AND SNEAD, THE CIRCUS OWNERS. IF YOU COULD LET US USE GOLIATH HERE FOR EXHIBITION PURPOSES, WE COULD ALL MAKE A LOT OF MONEY.
WHAT! YOU HAVE THE THE NERVE TO SUGGEST I PUT GOLIATH ON DISPLAY SO THE PUBLIC CAN GAPE AT HIM?! GET OUT! GET OUT!
NOW, NOW! BE CALM! BE CALM!
WE'RE GOING! WE'RE GOING! WE CAN TAKE A HINT.
BACK ON THE CIRCU GROUNDS, HACKETT AN SNEAD THINK IN TER OF MONEY - AND MURDER!
A MILLION DOLLARS! IF WE CAN EXHIBIT THAT GIANT, WE COULD MAKE A MILLION DOLLARS!
I THINK WE OUGHT TO WEAR DOWN DRAKE'S RESISTANCE PERMANENTLY I'M GOING TO CALL IN THE BOYS! WE'LL STILL MAKE THAT MILLION
AT THE SAME MOMENT, DRAKE RECEIVES ANOTHER VISITOR... THE BATMAN! HE IS QUICKLY INFORMED OF LATEST DEVELOPMENTS!
AND YOU SAY HACKETT AND SNEAD HAVE BAD REPUTATIONS?
BAD IS A MILD WORD! THEY COULD MAKE QUITE A PILE OF MONEY WITH GOLIATH, AND MONEY IS THE ROOT OF ALL EVIL... ESPECIALLY WITH THEM!
I THINK YOU'RE GOING TO NEED A GUARD AROUND HERE, AND I KNOW JUST THE ONE...... ROBIN, THE BOY WONDER!!
THAT VERY NIGHT, FOUR MEN WALK STEALTHILY ACROSS THE DRAKE LAWN....
HEY, GRIMES, ARE YA SURE THAT APE-MAN AIN'T HANGIN' AROUND THE HOUSE?
DON'T WORRY. DRAKE LOCKS HIM IN THAT SHACK EVERY NIGHT JUST IN CASE HE MIGHT DECIDE TO GO ROAMING!
NOW ALL WE GOTTA DO IS GET RID OF DRAKE AND WE GET OUR DOUGH FROM HACKETT!

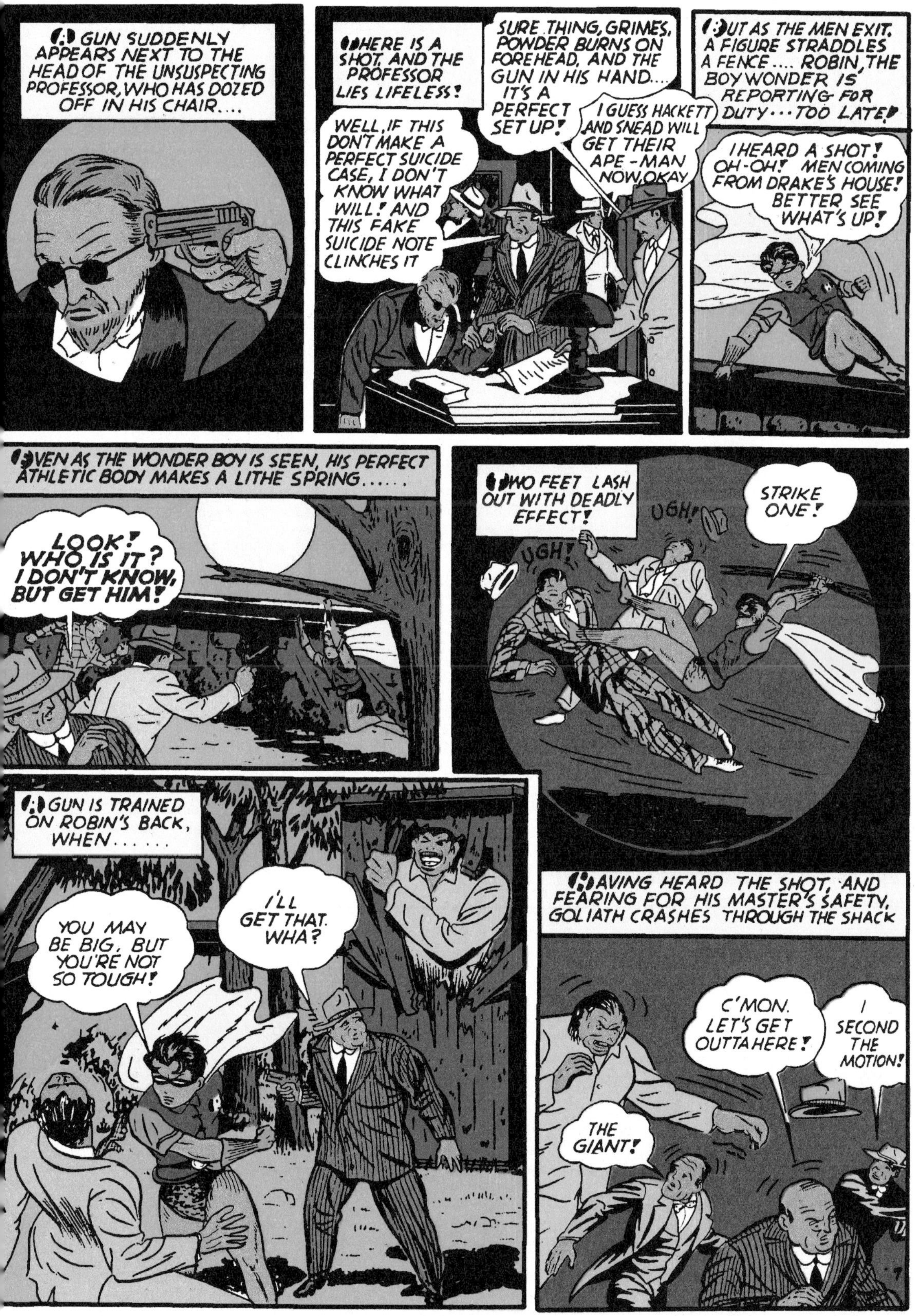
A GUN SUDDENLY APPEARS NEXT TO THE HEAD OF THE UNSUSPECTING PROFESSOR, WHO HAS DOZED OFF IN HIS CHAIR....
WHERE IS A SHOT, AND THE PROFESSOR LIES LIFELESS!
WELL, IF THIS DON'T MAKE A PERFECT SUICIDE CASE, I DON'T KNOW WHAT WILL! AND THIS FAKE SUICIDE NOTE CLINCHES IT
SURE THING, GRIMES, POWDER BURNS ON FOREHEAD, AND THE GUN IN HIS HAND.... IT'S A PERFECT SET UP!
I GUESS HACKETT AND SNEAD WILL GET THEIR APE-MAN NOW, OKAY
BUT AS THE MEN EXIT, A FIGURE STRADDLES A FENCE.... ROBIN, THE BOY WONDER IS REPORTING FOR DUTY...TOO LATE!
I HEARD A SHOT! OH-OH! MEN COMING FROM DRAKE'S HOUSE! BETTER SEE WHAT'S UP!
EVEN AS THE WONDER BOY IS SEEN, HIS PERFECT ATHLETIC BODY MAKES A LITHE SPRING......
LOOK! WHO IS IT? I DON'T KNOW, BUT GET HIM!
TWO FEET LASH OUT WITH DEADLY EFFECT!
UGH!
UGH!
STRIKE ONE!
A GUN IS TRAINED ON ROBIN'S BACK, WHEN......
YOU MAY BE BIG, BUT YOU'RE NOT SO TOUGH!
I'LL GET THAT. WHA?
HAVING HEARD THE SHOT, AND FEARING FOR HIS MASTER'S SAFETY, GOLIATH CRASHES THROUGH THE SHACK
C'MON. LET'S GET OUTTA HERE!
I SECOND THE MOTION!
THE GIANT!

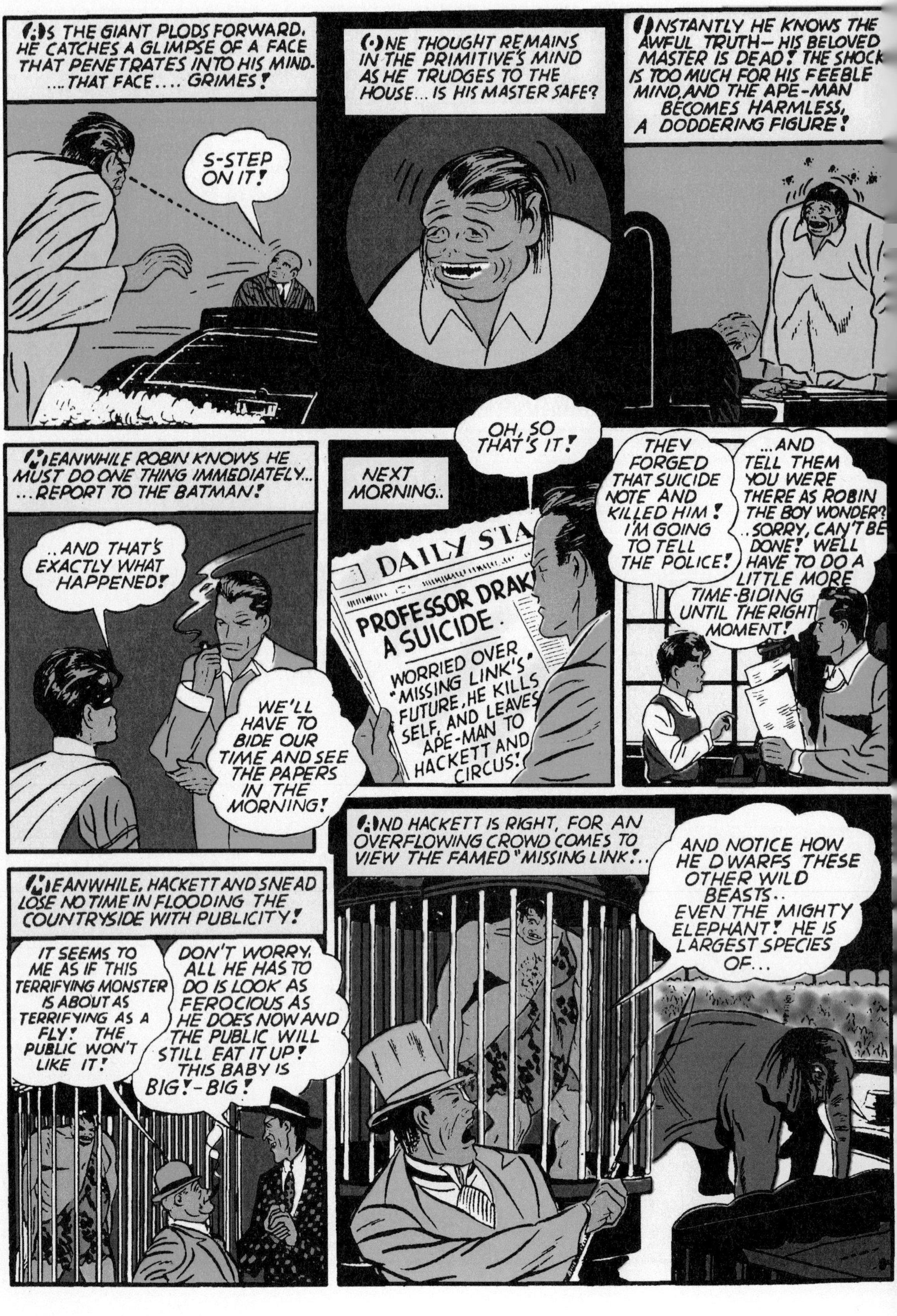
AS THE GIANT PLODS FORWARD, HE CATCHES A GLIMPSE OF A FACE THAT PENETRATES INTO HIS MIND. ....THAT FACE.... GRIMES!
S-STEP ON IT!
ONE THOUGHT REMAINS IN THE PRIMITIVE'S MIND AS HE TRUDGES TO THE HOUSE... IS HIS MASTER SAFE?
INSTANTLY HE KNOWS THE AWFUL TRUTH-- HIS BELOVED MASTER IS DEAD! THE SHOCK IS TOO MUCH FOR HIS FEEBLE MIND, AND THE APE-MAN BECOMES HARMLESS, A DODDERING FIGURE!
MEANWHILE ROBIN KNOWS HE MUST DO ONE THING IMMEDIATELY... ...REPORT TO THE BATMAN!
..AND THAT'S EXACTLY WHAT HAPPENED!
WE'LL HAVE TO BIDE OUR TIME AND SEE THE PAPERS IN THE MORNING!
NEXT MORNING..
OH, SO THAT'S IT!
DAILY STA
PROFESSOR DRAK
A SUICIDE
WORRIED OVER "MISSING LINK'S" FUTURE, HE KILLS SELF, AND LEAVES APE-MAN TO HACKETT AND CIRCUS!
THEY FORGED THAT SUICIDE NOTE AND KILLED HIM! I'M GOING TO TELL THE POLICE!
...AND TELL THEM YOU WERE THERE AS ROBIN THE BOY WONDER? ..SORRY, CAN'T BE DONE! WELL HAVE TO DO A LITTLE MORE TIME-BIDING UNTIL THE RIGHT MOMENT!
MEANWHILE, HACKETT AND SNEAD LOSE NO TIME IN FLOODING THE COUNTRYSIDE WITH PUBLICITY!
IT SEEMS TO ME AS IF THIS TERRIFYING MONSTER IS ABOUT AS TERRIFYING AS A FLY! THE PUBLIC WON'T LIKE IT!
DON'T WORRY, ALL HE HAS TO DO IS LOOK AS FEROCIOUS AS HE DOES NOW AND THE PUBLIC WILL STILL EAT IT UP! THIS BABY IS BIG!-BIG!
AND HACKETT IS RIGHT, FOR AN OVERFLOWING CROWD COMES TO VIEW THE FAMED "MISSING LINK"!..
AND NOTICE HOW HE DWARFS THESE OTHER WILD BEASTS.. EVEN THE MIGHTY ELEPHANT! HE IS LARGEST SPECIES OF...

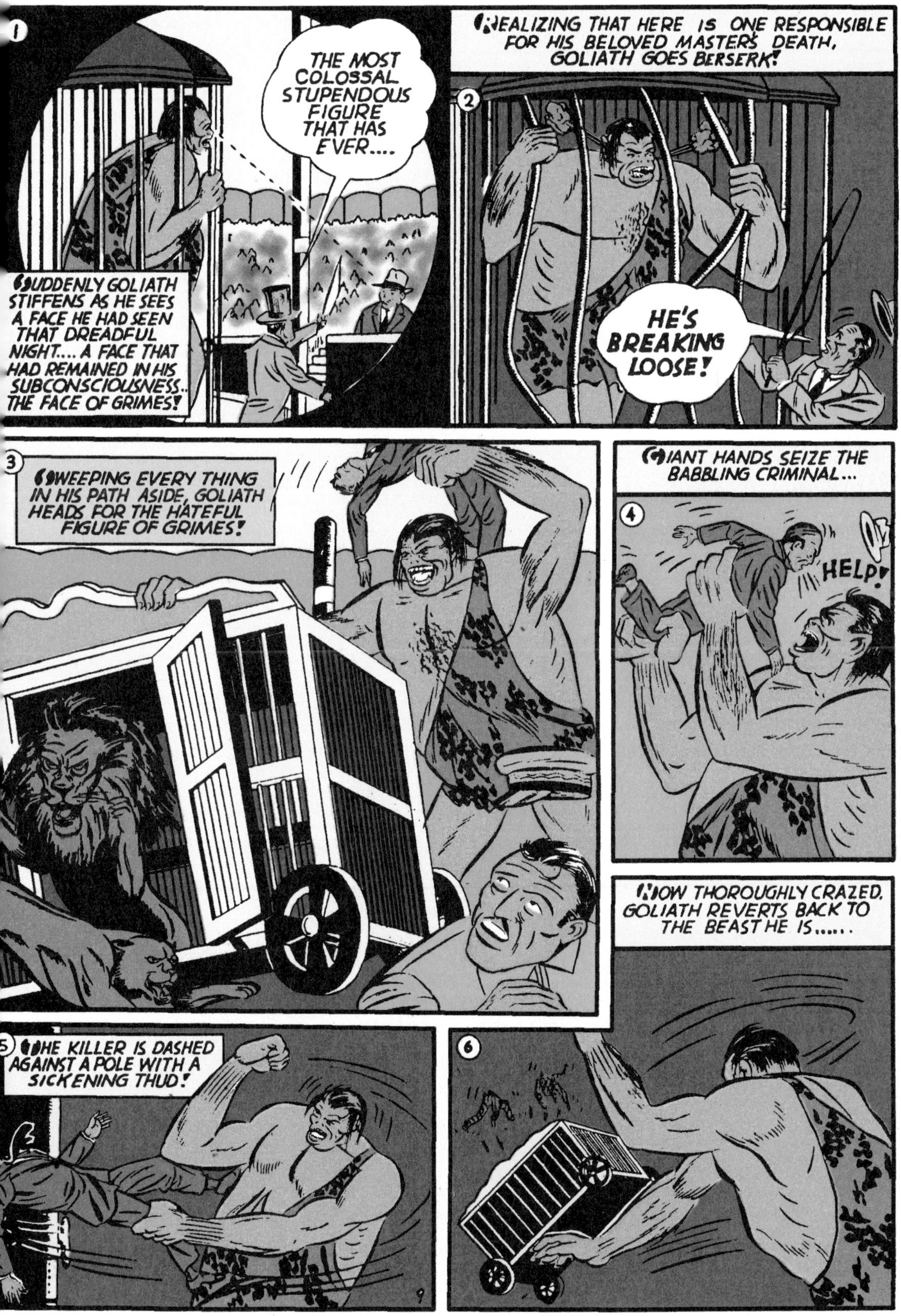
THE MOST COLOSSAL STUPENDOUS FIGURE THAT HAS EVER....
SUDDENLY GOLIATH STIFFENS AS HE SEES A FACE HE HAD SEEN THAT DREADFUL NIGHT.... A FACE THAT HAD REMAINED IN HIS SUBCONSCIOUSNESS.. THE FACE OF GRIMES!
REALIZING THAT HERE IS ONE RESPONSIBLE FOR HIS BELOVED MASTER'S DEATH, GOLIATH GOES BERSERK!
HE'S BREAKING LOOSE!
SWEEPING EVERY THING IN HIS PATH ASIDE, GOLIATH HEADS FOR THE HATEFUL FIGURE OF GRIMES!
GIANT HANDS SEIZE THE BABBLING CRIMINAL...
HELP!
NOW THOROUGHLY CRAZED, GOLIATH REVERTS BACK TO THE BEAST HE IS......
THE KILLER IS DASHED AGAINST A POLE WITH A SICKENING THUD!

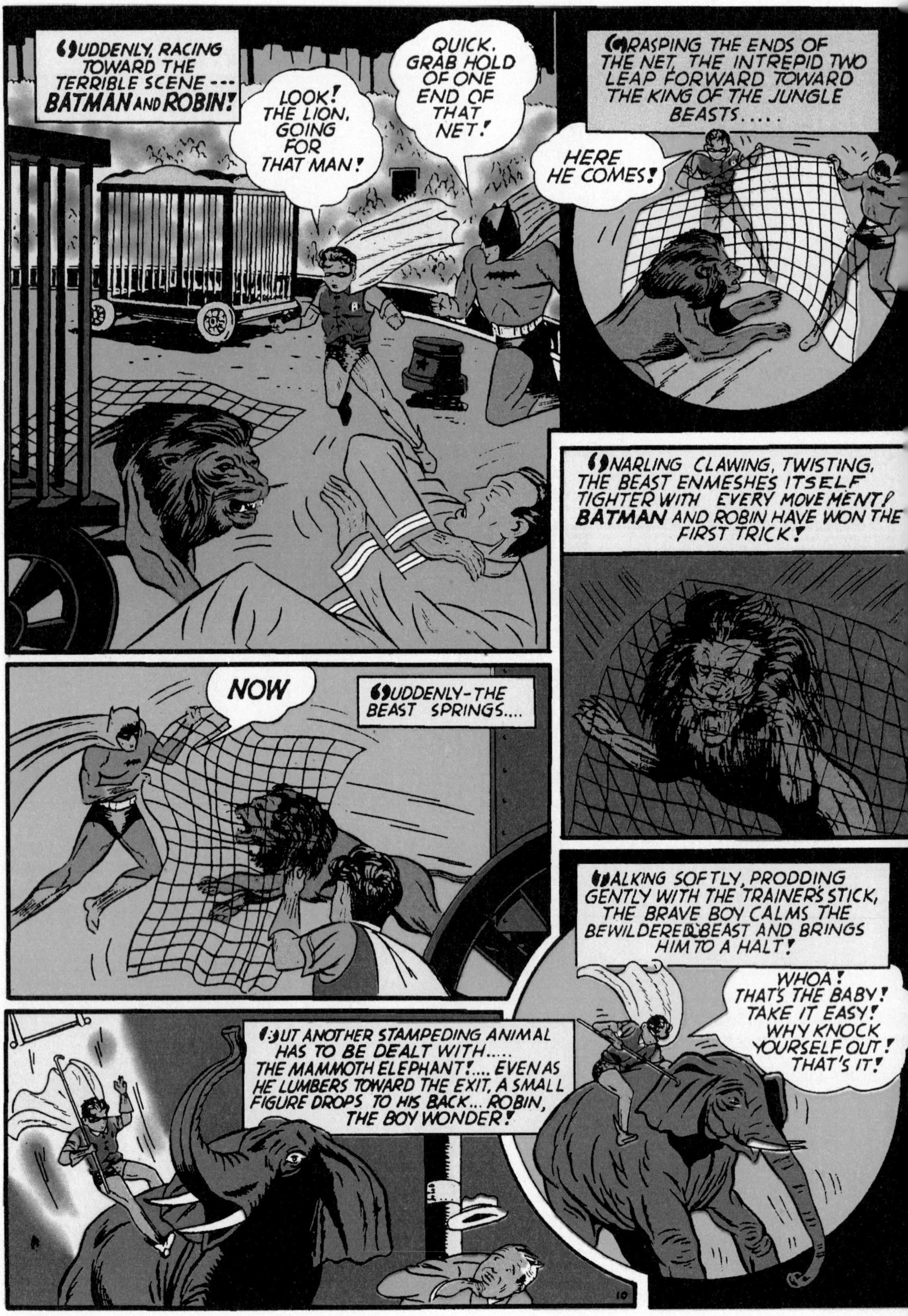
SUDDENLY, RACING TOWARD THE TERRIBLE SCENE --- BATMAN AND ROBIN!
LOOK! THE LION, GOING FOR THAT MAN!
QUICK, GRAB HOLD OF ONE END OF THAT NET!
GRASPING THE ENDS OF THE NET, THE INTREPID TWO LEAP FORWARD TOWARD THE KING OF THE JUNGLE BEASTS.....
HERE HE COMES!
NOW
SUDDENLY-THE BEAST SPRINGS....
SNARLING CLAWING, TWISTING, THE BEAST ENMESHES ITSELF TIGHTER WITH EVERY MOVEMENT! BATMAN AND ROBIN HAVE WON THE FIRST TRICK!
BUT ANOTHER STAMPEDING ANIMAL HAS TO BE DEALT WITH..... THE MAMMOTH ELEPHANT!.... EVEN AS HE LUMBERS TOWARD THE EXIT, A SMALL FIGURE DROPS TO HIS BACK... ROBIN, THE BOY WONDER!
10
WALKING SOFTLY, PRODDING GENTLY WITH THE TRAINER'S STICK, THE BRAVE BOY CALMS THE BEWILDERED BEAST AND BRINGS HIM TO A HALT!
WHOA! THAT'S THE BABY! TAKE IT EASY! WHY KNOCK YOURSELF OUT! THAT'S IT!

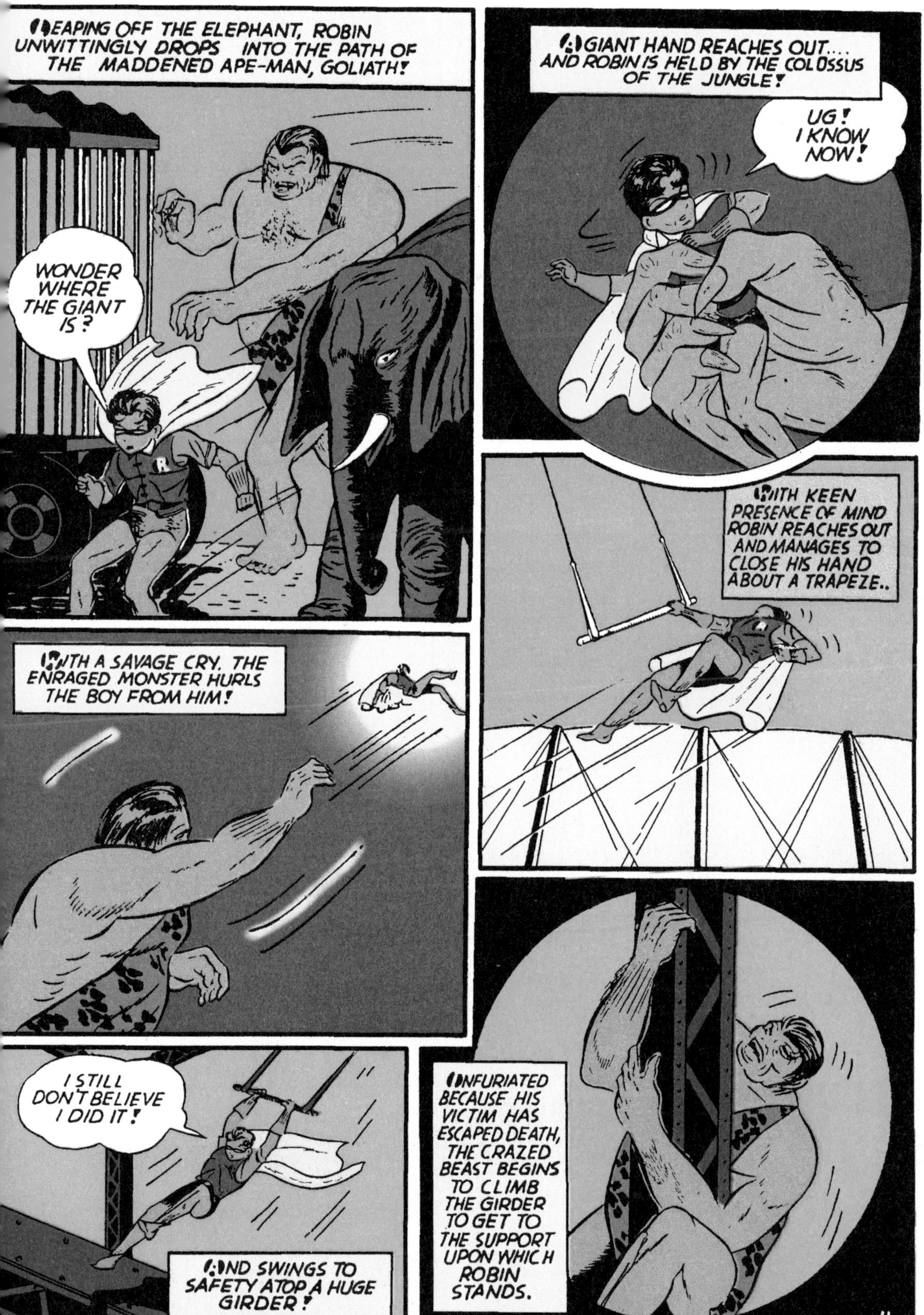
LEAPING OFF THE ELEPHANT, ROBIN UNWITTINGLY DROPS INTO THE PATH OF THE MADDENED APE-MAN, GOLIATH!
WONDER WHERE THE GIANT IS?
A GIANT HAND REACHES OUT.... AND ROBIN IS HELD BY THE COLOSSUS OF THE JUNGLE!
UG! I KNOW NOW!
WITH A SAVAGE CRY, THE ENRAGED MONSTER HURLS THE BOY FROM HIM!
WITH KEEN PRESENCE OF MIND ROBIN REACHES OUT AND MANAGES TO CLOSE HIS HAND ABOUT A TRAPEZE..
I STILL DON'T BELIEVE I DID IT!
AND SWINGS TO SAFETY ATOP A HUGE GIRDER!
INFURIATED BECAUSE HIS VICTIM HAS ESCAPED DEATH, THE CRAZED BEAST BEGINS TO CLIMB THE GIRDER TO GET TO THE SUPPORT UPON WHICH ROBIN STANDS.
11

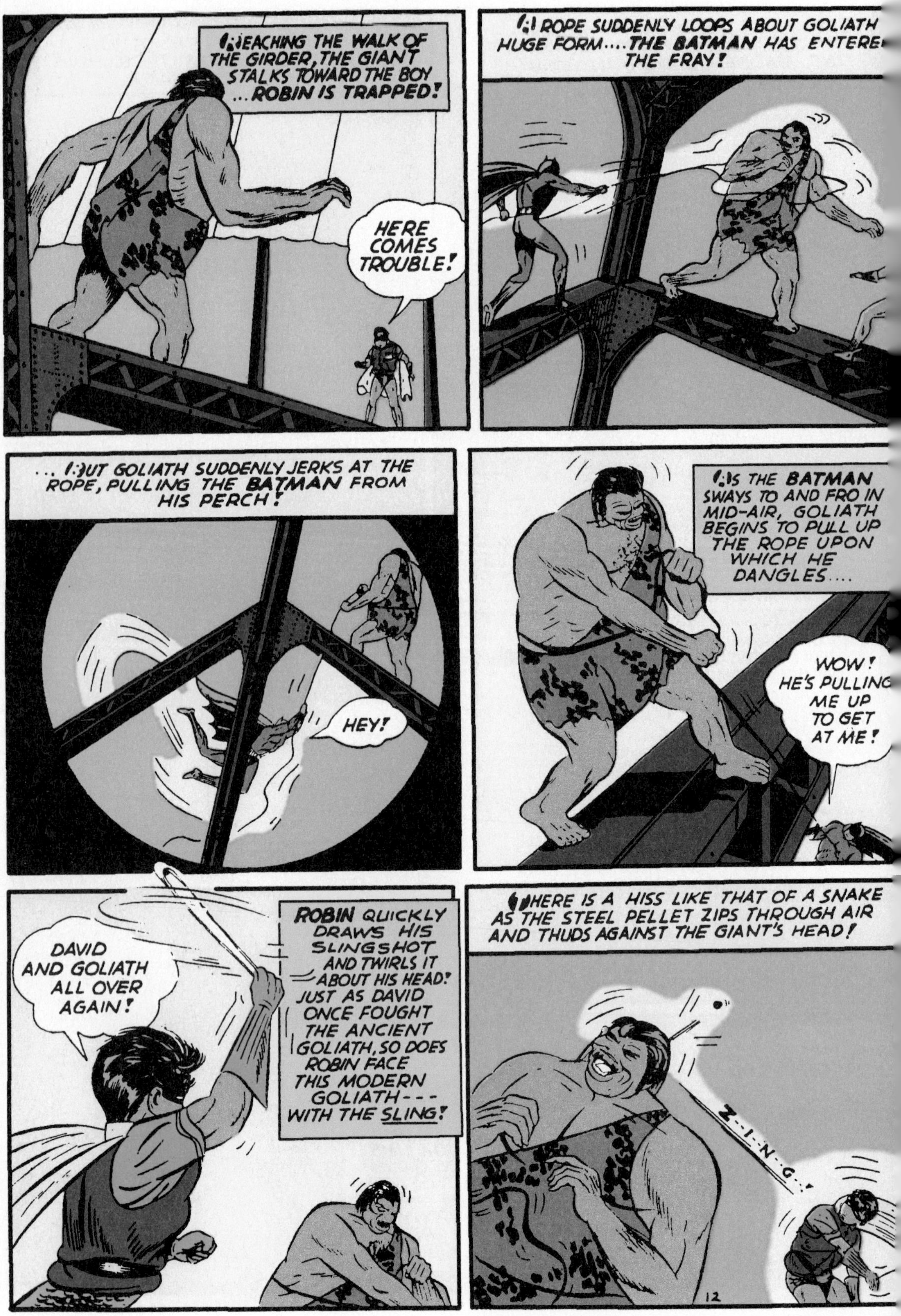
REACHING THE WALK OF THE GIRDER, THE GIANT STALKS TOWARD THE BOY ...ROBIN IS TRAPPED!
HERE COMES TROUBLE!
A ROPE SUDDENLY LOOPS ABOUT GOLIATH HUGE FORM.... THE BATMAN HAS ENTERED THE FRAY!
... BUT GOLIATH SUDDENLY JERKS AT THE ROPE, PULLING THE BATMAN FROM HIS PERCH!
HEY!
AS THE BATMAN SWAYS TO AND FRO IN MID-AIR, GOLIATH BEGINS TO PULL UP THE ROPE UPON WHICH HE DANGLES....
WOW! HE'S PULLING ME UP TO GET AT ME!
DAVID AND GOLIATH ALL OVER AGAIN!
ROBIN QUICKLY DRAWS HIS SLINGSHOT AND TWIRLS IT ABOUT HIS HEAD! JUST AS DAVID ONCE FOUGHT THE ANCIENT GOLIATH, SO DOES ROBIN FACE THIS MODERN GOLIATH--- WITH THE SLING!
THERE IS A HISS LIKE THAT OF A SNAKE AS THE STEEL PELLET ZIPS THROUGH AIR AND THUDS AGAINST THE GIANT'S HEAD!
Z-I-N-G-!
12

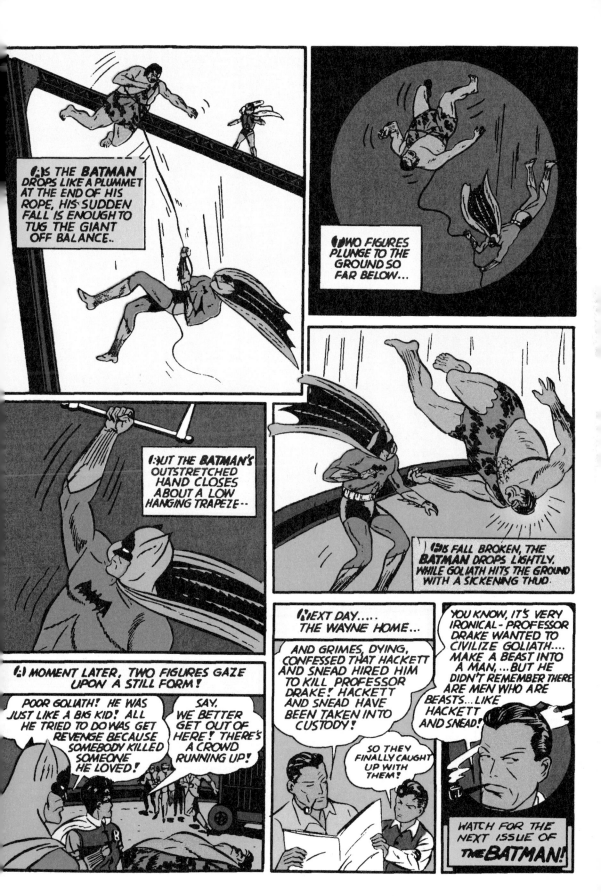

AS THE BATMAN DROPS LIKE A PLUMMET AT THE END OF HIS ROPE, HIS SUDDEN FALL IS ENOUGH TO TUG THE GIANT OFF BALANCE..

TWO FIGURES PLUNGE TO THE GROUND SO FAR BELOW...

BUT THE BATMAN'S OUTSTRETCHED HAND CLOSES ABOUT A LOW HANGING TRAPEZE--

HIS FALL BROKEN, THE BATMAN DROPS LIGHTLY, WHILE GOLIATH HITS THE GROUND WITH A SICKENING THUD.

A MOMENT LATER, TWO FIGURES GAZE UPON A STILL FORM!

POOR GOLIATH! HE WAS JUST LIKE A BIG KID! ALL HE TRIED TO DO WAS GET REVENGE BECAUSE SOMEBODY KILLED SOMEONE HE LOVED!

SAY, WE BETTER GET OUT OF HERE! THERE'S A CROWD RUNNING UP!

NEXT DAY..... THE WAYNE HOME...

AND GRIMES, DYING, CONFESSED THAT HACKETT AND SNEAD HIRED HIM TO KILL PROFESSOR DRAKE! HACKETT AND SNEAD HAVE BEEN TAKEN INTO CUSTODY!

SO THEY FINALLY CAUGHT UP WITH THEM!

YOU KNOW, IT'S VERY IRONICAL - PROFESSOR DRAKE WANTED TO CIVILIZE GOLIATH..... MAKE A BEAST INTO A MAN, ...BUT HE DIDN'T REMEMBER THERE ARE MEN WHO ARE BEASTS...LIKE HACKETT AND SNEAD!

WATCH FOR THE NEXT ISSUE OF THE BATMAN!

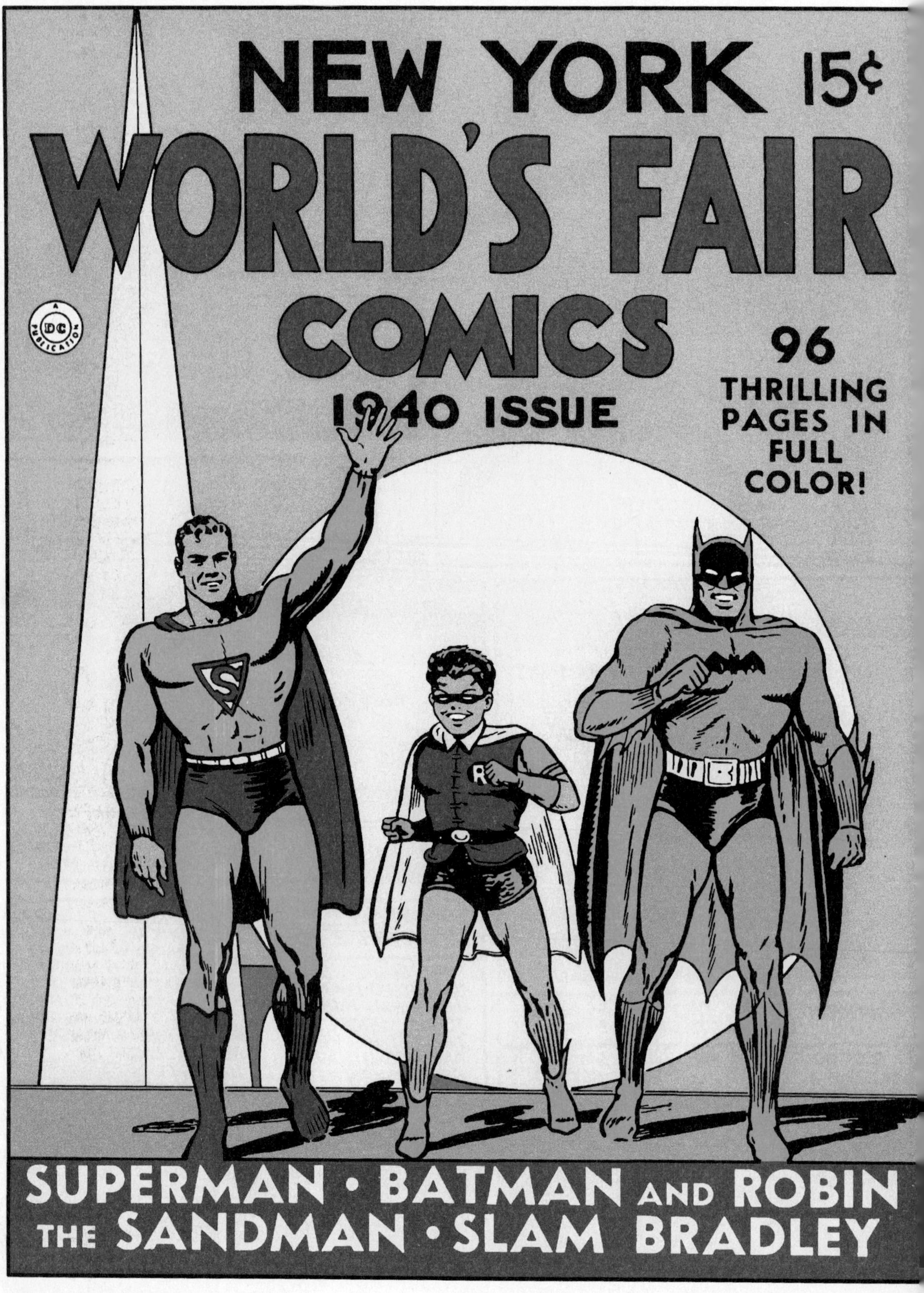
NEW YORK
15¢
WORLD'S FAIR
COMICS
1940 ISSUE
96 THRILLING PAGES IN FULL COLOR!
SUPERMAN • BATMAN AND ROBIN
THE SANDMAN • SLAM BRADLEY

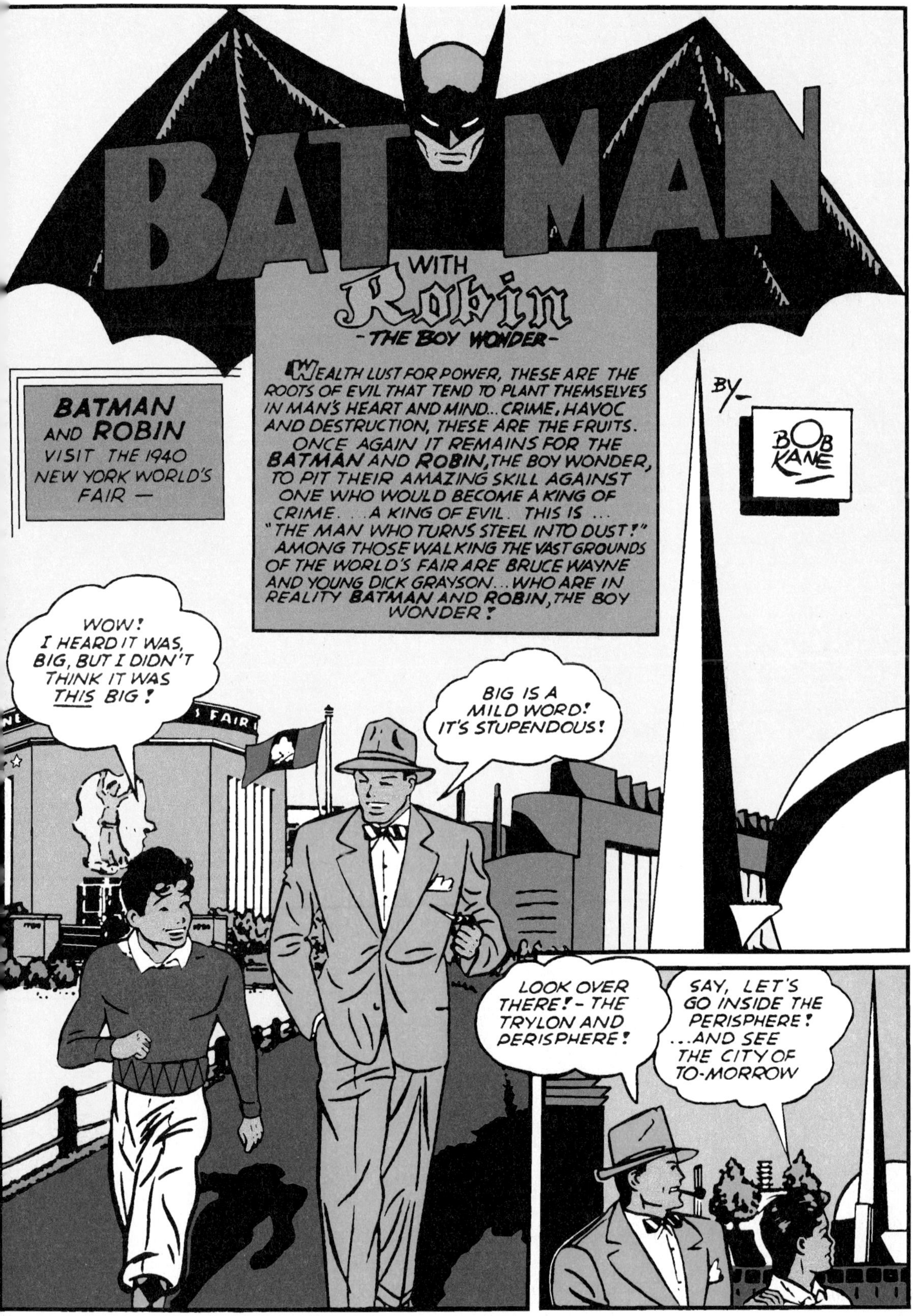
BATMAN
WITH
Robin
-THE BOY WONDER-
WEALTH LUST FOR POWER, THESE ARE THE ROOTS OF EVIL THAT TEND TO PLANT THEMSELVES IN MAN'S HEART AND MIND... CRIME, HAVOC AND DESTRUCTION, THESE ARE THE FRUITS. ONCE AGAIN IT REMAINS FOR THE BATMAN AND ROBIN, THE BOY WONDER, TO PIT THEIR AMAZING SKILL AGAINST ONE WHO WOULD BECOME A KING OF CRIME.... A KING OF EVIL. THIS IS ... "THE MAN WHO TURNS STEEL INTO DUST!" AMONG THOSE WALKING THE VAST GROUNDS OF THE WORLD'S FAIR ARE BRUCE WAYNE AND YOUNG DICK GRAYSON... WHO ARE IN REALITY BATMAN AND ROBIN, THE BOY WONDER!
BATMAN AND ROBIN VISIT THE 1940 NEW YORK WORLD'S FAIR —
BY— BOB KANE
WOW! I HEARD IT WAS, BIG, BUT I DIDN'T THINK IT WAS THIS BIG!
BIG IS A MILD WORD! IT'S STUPENDOUS!
LOOK OVER THERE! - THE TRYLON AND PERISPHERE!
SAY, LET'S GO INSIDE THE PERISPHERE! ...AND SEE THE CITY OF TO-MORROW

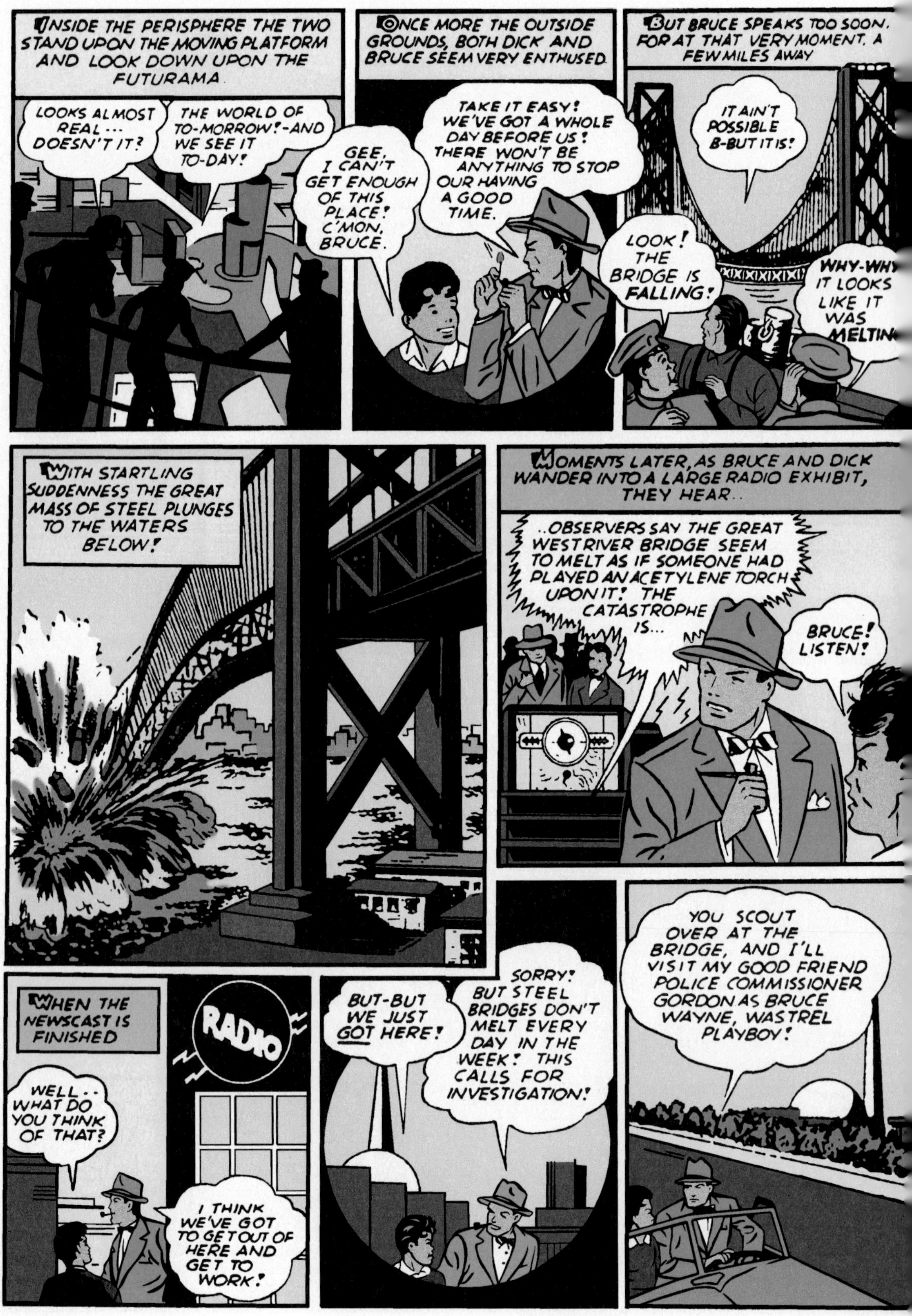
INSIDE THE PERISPHERE THE TWO STAND UPON THE MOVING PLATFORM AND LOOK DOWN UPON THE FUTURAMA.
LOOKS ALMOST REAL... DOESN'T IT?
THE WORLD OF TO-MORROW!-AND WE SEE IT TO-DAY!
ONCE MORE THE OUTSIDE GROUNDS, BOTH DICK AND BRUCE SEEM VERY ENTHUSED.
GEE, I CAN'T GET ENOUGH OF THIS PLACE! C'MON, BRUCE.
TAKE IT EASY! WE'VE GOT A WHOLE DAY BEFORE US! THERE WON'T BE ANYTHING TO STOP OUR HAVING A GOOD TIME.
BUT BRUCE SPEAKS TOO SOON, FOR AT THAT VERY MOMENT, A FEW MILES AWAY
IT AIN'T POSSIBLE B-BUT IT IS!
LOOK! THE BRIDGE IS FALLING!
WHY-WHY IT LOOKS LIKE IT WAS MELTIN
WITH STARTLING SUDDENNESS THE GREAT MASS OF STEEL PLUNGES TO THE WATERS BELOW!
MOMENTS LATER, AS BRUCE AND DICK WANDER INTO A LARGE RADIO EXHIBIT, THEY HEAR..
..OBSERVERS SAY THE GREAT WEST RIVER BRIDGE SEEM TO MELT AS IF SOMEONE HAD PLAYED AN ACETYLENE TORCH UPON IT! THE CATASTROPHE IS...
BRUCE! LISTEN!
WHEN THE NEWSCAST IS FINISHED
RADIO
WELL.. WHAT DO YOU THINK OF THAT?
I THINK WE'VE GOT TO GET OUT OF HERE AND GET TO WORK!
BUT-BUT WE JUST GOT HERE!
SORRY! BUT STEEL BRIDGES DON'T MELT EVERY DAY IN THE WEEK! THIS CALLS FOR INVESTIGATION!
YOU SCOUT OVER AT THE BRIDGE, AND I'LL VISIT MY GOOD FRIEND POLICE COMMISSIONER GORDON AS BRUCE WAYNE, WASTREL PLAYBOY!

BRUCE WAYNE! FINALLY ROUSED YOURSELF ENOUGH TO TO PAY ME A VISIT, EH?

HELLO, GORDON!

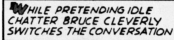

WHILE PRETENDING IDLE CHATTER BRUCE CLEVERLY SWITCHES THE CONVERSATION

AND YOU MEAN TO SAY THE BRIDGE ACTUALLY MELTED AWAY?

ABSOLUTELY! JUST SEEMED TO CRUMPLE INTO DUST!

THE DOOR SUDDENLY BURSTS OPEN AND

MY NAME IS TRAVERS OF TRAVERS ENGINEERS! JUST READ THIS LETTER I RECEIVED!

WHO?

The destruction of the West Bridge is a warning and proof of what I can do. Either pay me $300,000 or your new bridge under construction will meet the same fate. Instructions will follow!

WE HAVE A NEW BRIDGE UNDER CONSTRUCTION! IF IT IS DESTROYED WE'LL LOSE HUNDREDS OF THOUSANDS OF DOLLARS! WHAT SHALL I DO?

IGNORE IT! PROBABLY A CRACKPOT TRYING TO CASH IN ON EASY MONEY! NOBODY CAN DESTROY A BRIDGE! THE STEEL WAS PROBABLY FAULTY, THAT'S ALL!

I WONDER GORDON, WHETHER YOU'RE WONDERING IF THE BRIDGE WAS REALLY DESTROYED BY THE WRITER OF THAT LETTER....

MEANWHILE, WHAT OF YOUNG DICK GRAYSON WHO IS INSPECTING THE SITE OF THE CATASTROPHE?

WELL, NOW I'LL SEE IF I CAN DIG UP ANYTHING IMPORTANT!

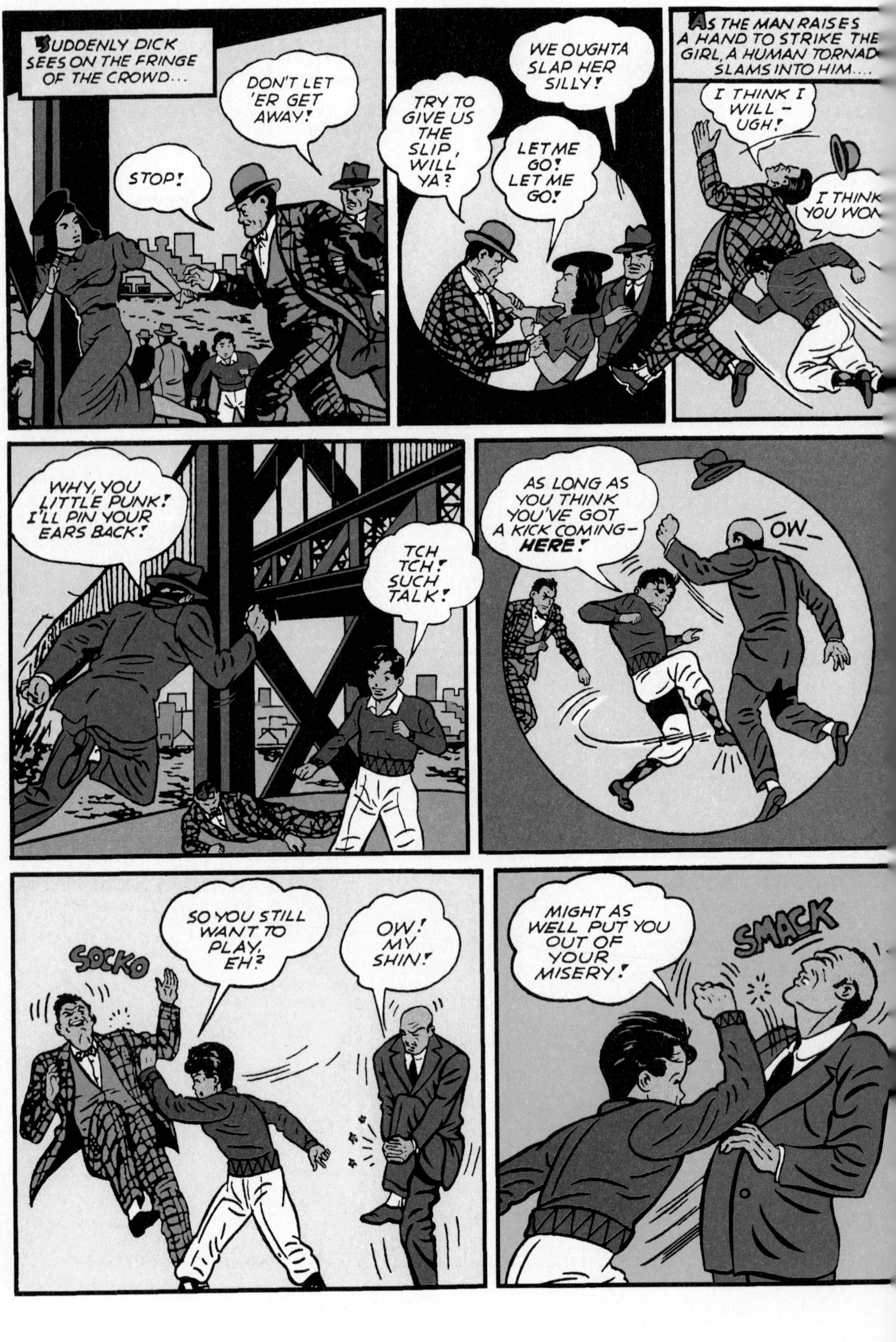
SUDDENLY DICK SEES ON THE FRINGE OF THE CROWD...
DON'T LET 'ER GET AWAY!
STOP!
TRY TO GIVE US THE SLIP, WILL YA?
WE OUGHTA SLAP HER SILLY!
LET ME GO! LET ME GO!
AS THE MAN RAISES A HAND TO STRIKE THE GIRL, A HUMAN TORNAD SLAMS INTO HIM....
I THINK I WILL - UGH!
I THINK YOU WON
WHY, YOU LITTLE PUNK! I'LL PIN YOUR EARS BACK!
TCH TCH! SUCH TALK!
AS LONG AS YOU THINK YOU'VE GOT A KICK COMING - HERE!
OW-
SO YOU STILL WANT TO PLAY, EH?
SOCKO
OW! MY SHIN!
MIGHT AS WELL PUT YOU OUT OF YOUR MISERY!
SMACK

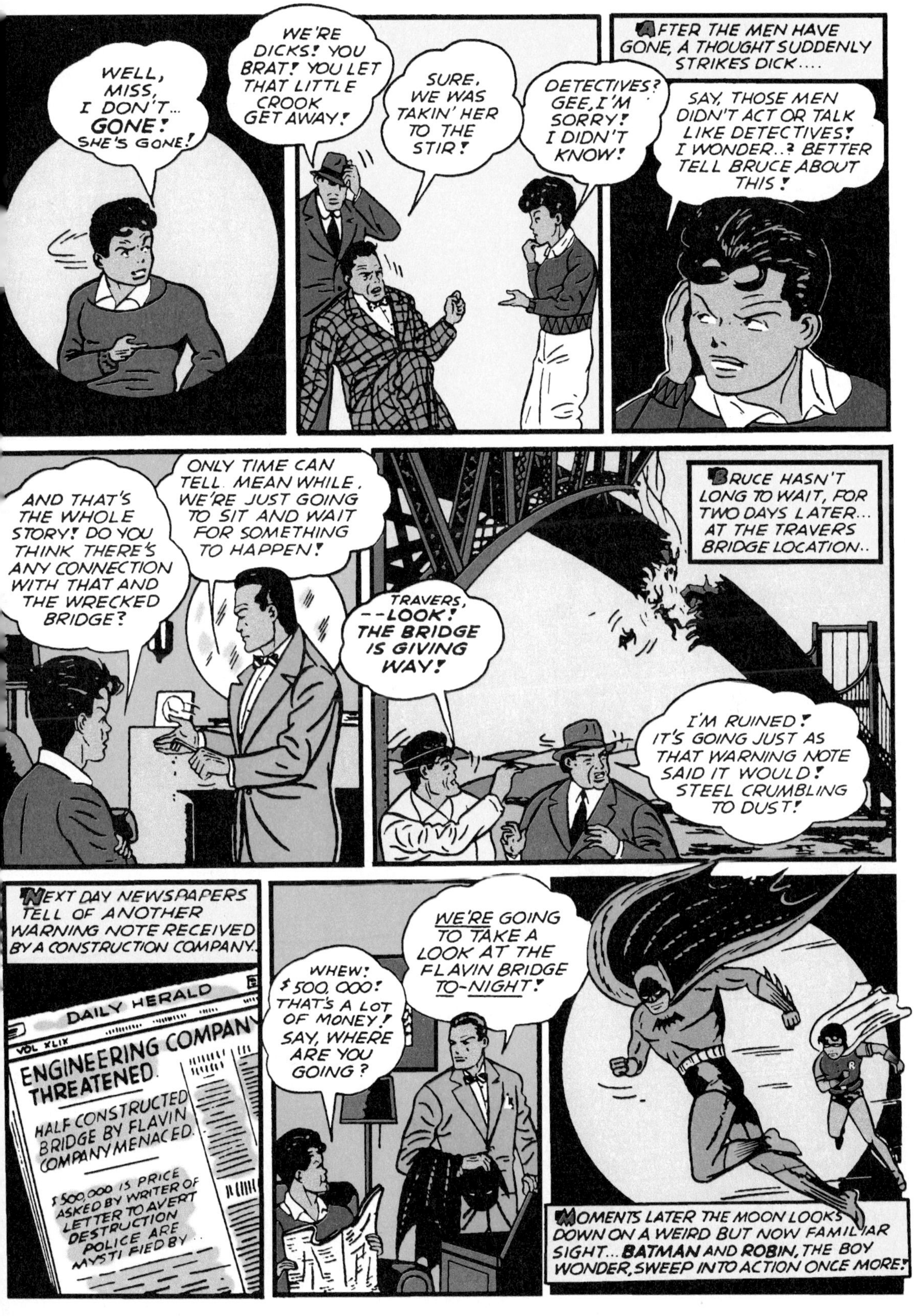
WELL, MISS, I DON'T... GONE! SHE'S GONE!
WE'RE DICKS! YOU BRAT! YOU LET THAT LITTLE CROOK GET AWAY!
SURE. WE WAS TAKIN' HER TO THE STIR!
DETECTIVES? GEE, I'M SORRY! I DIDN'T KNOW!
AFTER THE MEN HAVE GONE, A THOUGHT SUDDENLY STRIKES DICK....
SAY, THOSE MEN DIDN'T ACT OR TALK LIKE DETECTIVES! I WONDER..? BETTER TELL BRUCE ABOUT THIS!
AND THAT'S THE WHOLE STORY! DO YOU THINK THERE'S ANY CONNECTION WITH THAT AND THE WRECKED BRIDGE?
ONLY TIME CAN TELL. MEANWHILE, WE'RE JUST GOING TO SIT AND WAIT FOR SOMETHING TO HAPPEN!
BRUCE HASN'T LONG TO WAIT, FOR TWO DAYS LATER... AT THE TRAVERS BRIDGE LOCATION..
TRAVERS, --LOOK! THE BRIDGE IS GIVING WAY!
I'M RUINED! IT'S GOING JUST AS THAT WARNING NOTE SAID IT WOULD! STEEL CRUMBLING TO DUST!
NEXT DAY NEWSPAPERS TELL OF ANOTHER WARNING NOTE RECEIVED BY A CONSTRUCTION COMPANY.
DAILY HERALD
VOL XLIX
ENGINEERING COMPANY THREATENED
HALF CONSTRUCTED BRIDGE BY FLAVIN COMPANY MENACED.
$500,000 IS PRICE ASKED BY WRITER OF LETTER TO AVERT DESTRUCTION POLICE ARE MYSTIFIED BY..
WHEW! $500,000! THAT'S A LOT OF MONEY! SAY, WHERE ARE YOU GOING?
WE'RE GOING TO TAKE A LOOK AT THE FLAVIN BRIDGE TO-NIGHT!
MOMENTS LATER THE MOON LOOKS DOWN ON A WEIRD BUT NOW FAMILIAR SIGHT... BATMAN AND ROBIN, THE BOY WONDER, SWEEP INTO ACTION ONCE MORE!

LOOK—MEN!

GOOD THING WE ARRIVED A NIGHT EARLIER!

SHORTLY AFTER...

CONSTR'N

SECONDS LATER A FLINGING FORM DIVES INTO THE DARKNESS

HUH?!

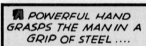

A POWERFUL HAND GRASPS THE MAN IN A GRIP OF STEEL....

LET'S PLAY SOME BASEBALL!

THE STRUGGLING FORM IS EASILY HELD ALOFT....

LOOK! WHO—?

THAT'S— THAT'S THE BATMAN!

I'LL PITCH!....

A POWERFUL THROW, AND THE MEN GO TOPPLING LIKE TEN-PINS!

...STRIKE THREE AND YOU'RE OUT!!

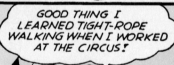

GOOD THING I LEARNED TIGHT-ROPE WALKING WHEN I WORKED AT THE CIRCUS!

AT THAT VERY MOMENT ROBIN IS ALSO ABOUT TO ENTER THE FRAY—BY WALKING ATOP THE TOPMOST CABLE OF THE BRIDGE.

GOT THAT THING SET UP YET, JOEY?

YEAH... IN ANOTHER MINUTE...

CAREFULLY, HE PICKS HIS PERILOUS WAY ACROSS THE SLIM STRIP OF STEEL.. UNNOTICED BY THE TWO GUNMEN BUSILY ENGAGED ON A LOWER GIRDER

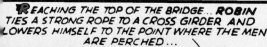

REACHING THE TOP OF THE BRIDGE... ROBIN TIES A STRONG ROPE TO A CROSS GIRDER AND LOWERS HIMSELF TO THE POINT WHERE THE MEN ARE PERCHED...

PEEK-A-BOO!

CATCH!

PICKING UP THE MAN, THE BOY WONDER DROPS HIM TOWARD THE BATMAN!

CAUGHT HIM...ON THE JAW!

AFTER DISPOSING OF THE OTHER GUNMAN, THE WONDERBOY SUDDENLY SEES DANGER MENACE THE BATMAN! --WITH A SWEEPING SWING.....

NOT NICE, TRYING TO SHOOT PEOPLE IN THE BACK!

THE WONDER BOY LANDS A WONDER PUNCH!

YOU MUST BE TIRED-LIE DOWN!

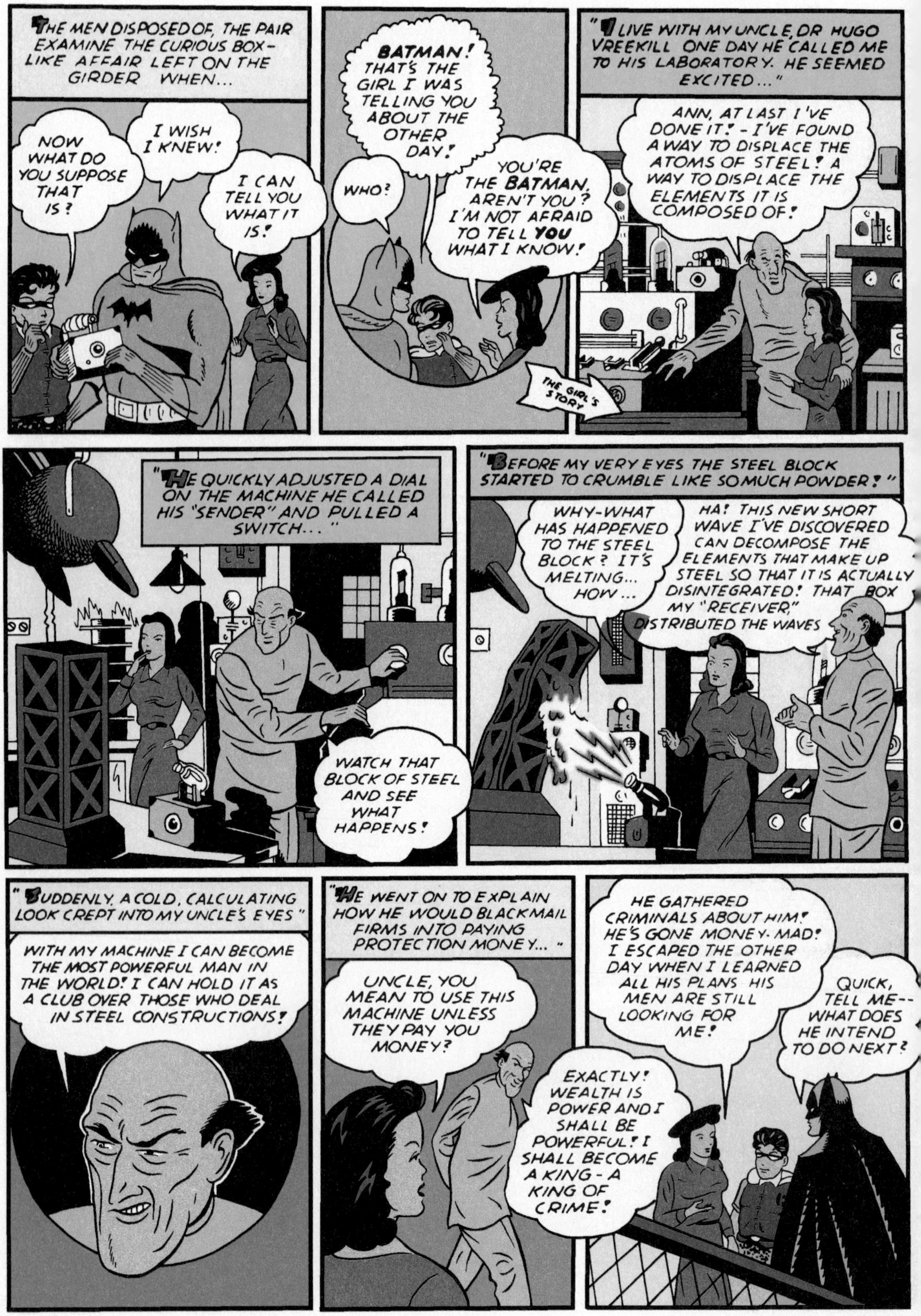
THE MEN DISPOSED OF, THE PAIR EXAMINE THE CURIOUS BOX-LIKE AFFAIR LEFT ON THE GIRDER WHEN...
NOW WHAT DO YOU SUPPOSE THAT IS?
I WISH I KNEW!
I CAN TELL YOU WHAT IT IS!
BATMAN! THAT'S THE GIRL I WAS TELLING YOU ABOUT THE OTHER DAY!
WHO?
YOU'RE THE BATMAN, AREN'T YOU? I'M NOT AFRAID TO TELL YOU WHAT I KNOW!
THE GIRL'S STORY
"I LIVE WITH MY UNCLE, DR HUGO VREEKILL ONE DAY HE CALLED ME TO HIS LABORATORY. HE SEEMED EXCITED..."
ANN, AT LAST I'VE DONE IT! - I'VE FOUND A WAY TO DISPLACE THE ATOMS OF STEEL! A WAY TO DISPLACE THE ELEMENTS IT IS COMPOSED OF!
"HE QUICKLY ADJUSTED A DIAL ON THE MACHINE HE CALLED HIS "SENDER" AND PULLED A SWITCH..."
WATCH THAT BLOCK OF STEEL AND SEE WHAT HAPPENS!
"BEFORE MY VERY EYES THE STEEL BLOCK STARTED TO CRUMBLE LIKE SO MUCH POWDER!"
WHY-WHAT HAS HAPPENED TO THE STEEL BLOCK? IT'S MELTING... HOW...
HA! THIS NEW SHORT WAVE I'VE DISCOVERED CAN DECOMPOSE THE ELEMENTS THAT MAKE UP STEEL SO THAT IT IS ACTUALLY DISINTEGRATED! THAT BOX MY "RECEIVER," DISTRIBUTED THE WAVES
"SUDDENLY, A COLD, CALCULATING LOOK CREPT INTO MY UNCLE'S EYES"
WITH MY MACHINE I CAN BECOME THE MOST POWERFUL MAN IN THE WORLD! I CAN HOLD IT AS A CLUB OVER THOSE WHO DEAL IN STEEL CONSTRUCTIONS!
"HE WENT ON TO EXPLAIN HOW HE WOULD BLACKMAIL FIRMS INTO PAYING PROTECTION MONEY..."
UNCLE, YOU MEAN TO USE THIS MACHINE UNLESS THEY PAY YOU MONEY?
EXACTLY! WEALTH IS POWER AND I SHALL BE POWERFUL! I SHALL BECOME A KING - A KING OF CRIME!
HE GATHERED CRIMINALS ABOUT HIM! HE'S GONE MONEY-MAD! I ESCAPED THE OTHER DAY WHEN I LEARNED ALL HIS PLANS HIS MEN ARE STILL LOOKING FOR ME!
QUICK, TELL ME-- WHAT DOES HE INTEND TO DO NEXT?

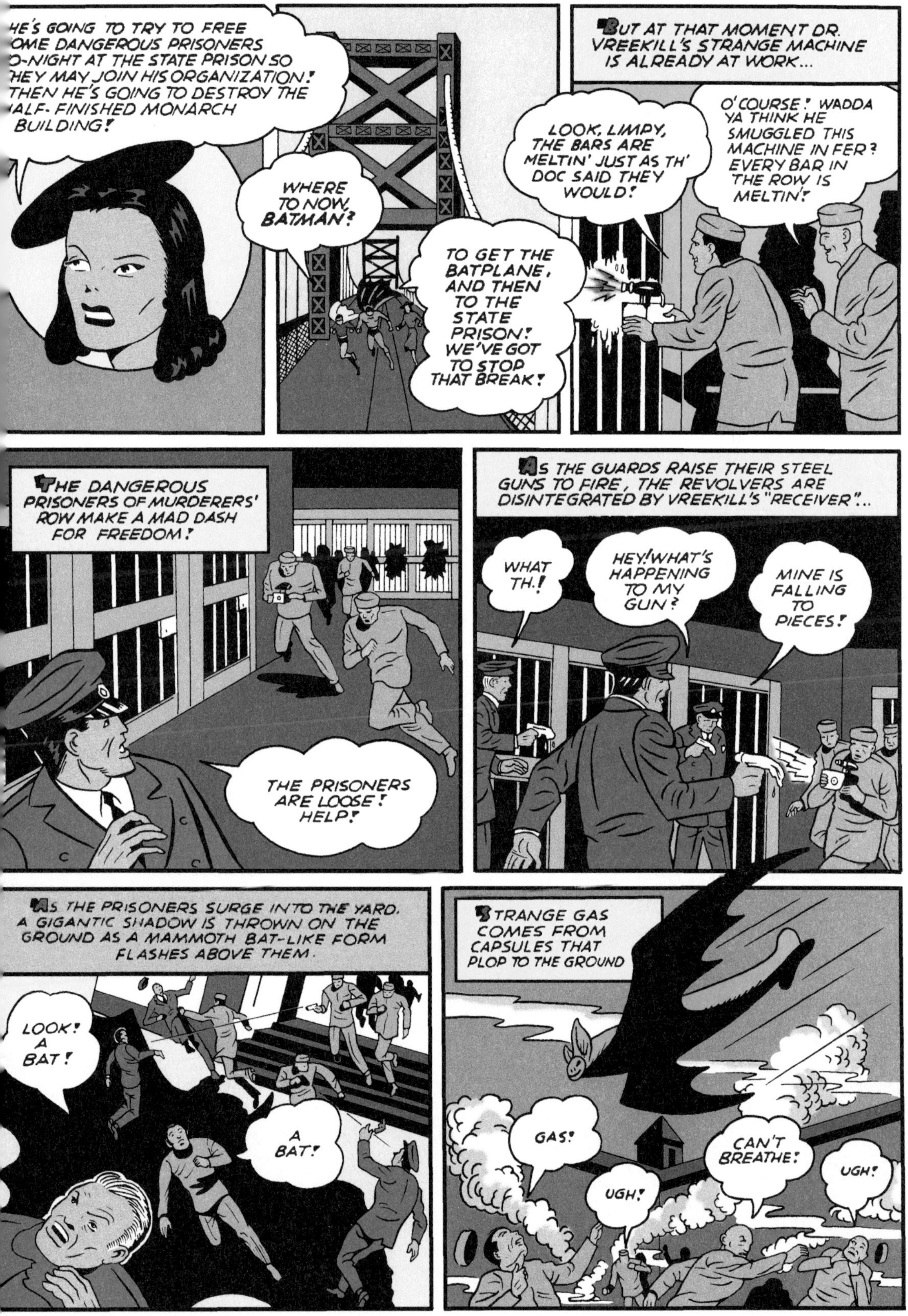
HE'S GOING TO TRY TO FREE
OME DANGEROUS PRISONERS
O-NIGHT AT THE STATE PRISON SO
HEY MAY JOIN HIS ORGANIZATION!
THEN HE'S GOING TO DESTROY THE
ALF-FINISHED MONARCH
BUILDING!
WHERE TO NOW, BATMAN?
TO GET THE BATPLANE, AND THEN TO THE STATE PRISON! WE'VE GOT TO STOP THAT BREAK!
BUT AT THAT MOMENT DR. VREEKILL'S STRANGE MACHINE IS ALREADY AT WORK...
LOOK, LIMPY, THE BARS ARE MELTIN' JUST AS TH' DOC SAID THEY WOULD!
O'COURSE! WADDA YA THINK HE SMUGGLED THIS MACHINE IN FER? EVERY BAR IN THE ROW IS MELTIN'!
THE DANGEROUS PRISONERS OF MURDERERS' ROW MAKE A MAD DASH FOR FREEDOM!
THE PRISONERS ARE LOOSE! HELP!
AS THE GUARDS RAISE THEIR STEEL GUNS TO FIRE, THE REVOLVERS ARE DISINTEGRATED BY VREEKILL'S "RECEIVER"...
WHAT TH.!
HEY! WHAT'S HAPPENING TO MY GUN?
MINE IS FALLING TO PIECES!
AS THE PRISONERS SURGE INTO THE YARD, A GIGANTIC SHADOW IS THROWN ON THE GROUND AS A MAMMOTH BAT-LIKE FORM FLASHES ABOVE THEM.
LOOK! A BAT!
A BAT!
STRANGE GAS COMES FROM CAPSULES THAT PLOP TO THE GROUND
GAS!
UGH!
CAN'T BREATHE!
UGH!

THE WEIRD CRAFT GLIDES TO A LANDING, AND LEAPING FROM IT... *BATMAN* AND *ROBIN, THE BOY WONDER!*

ROBIN, THAT FLAGPOLE-GRAB ONE END OF IT!

BEARING THE BATTERING RAM BETWEEN THEM, THE TWO MANTLED FIGURES BEAR DOWN UPON THE HORDE OF PRISONERS!

IT'S-IT'S THE BATMAN!

BATMAN!

LOOKS LIKE THEY'RE OVERWHELMED AT SEEING US, EH, ROBIN?

BEFORE THE ASTONISHED PRISONERS CAN RECOVER, THE LONG POLE SMASHES INTO THEM!

I SHOULD SAY THEY WERE BOWLED OVER!

C'MON, ROBIN—LET'S TIE THEM UP AND GET GOING... I AM SURE THE POLICE WOULD "INDUCE" ME TO STAY *HERE* IF THEY CAUGHT ME!

DRAGGING THEIR PRISONERS TO A PIPE -- ROBIN RACES 'ROUND AND ROUND THEM, MAKING THEIR CAPTIVES FAST!

JUST LIKE "RING AROUND THE ROSY!"

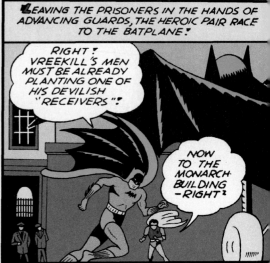

LEAVING THE PRISONERS IN THE HANDS OF ADVANCING GUARDS, THE HEROIC PAIR RACE TO THE BATPLANE!

RIGHT! VREEKILL'S MEN MUST BE ALREADY PLANTING ONE OF HIS DEVILISH "RECEIVERS"!

NOW TO THE MONARCH-BUILDING -RIGHT?

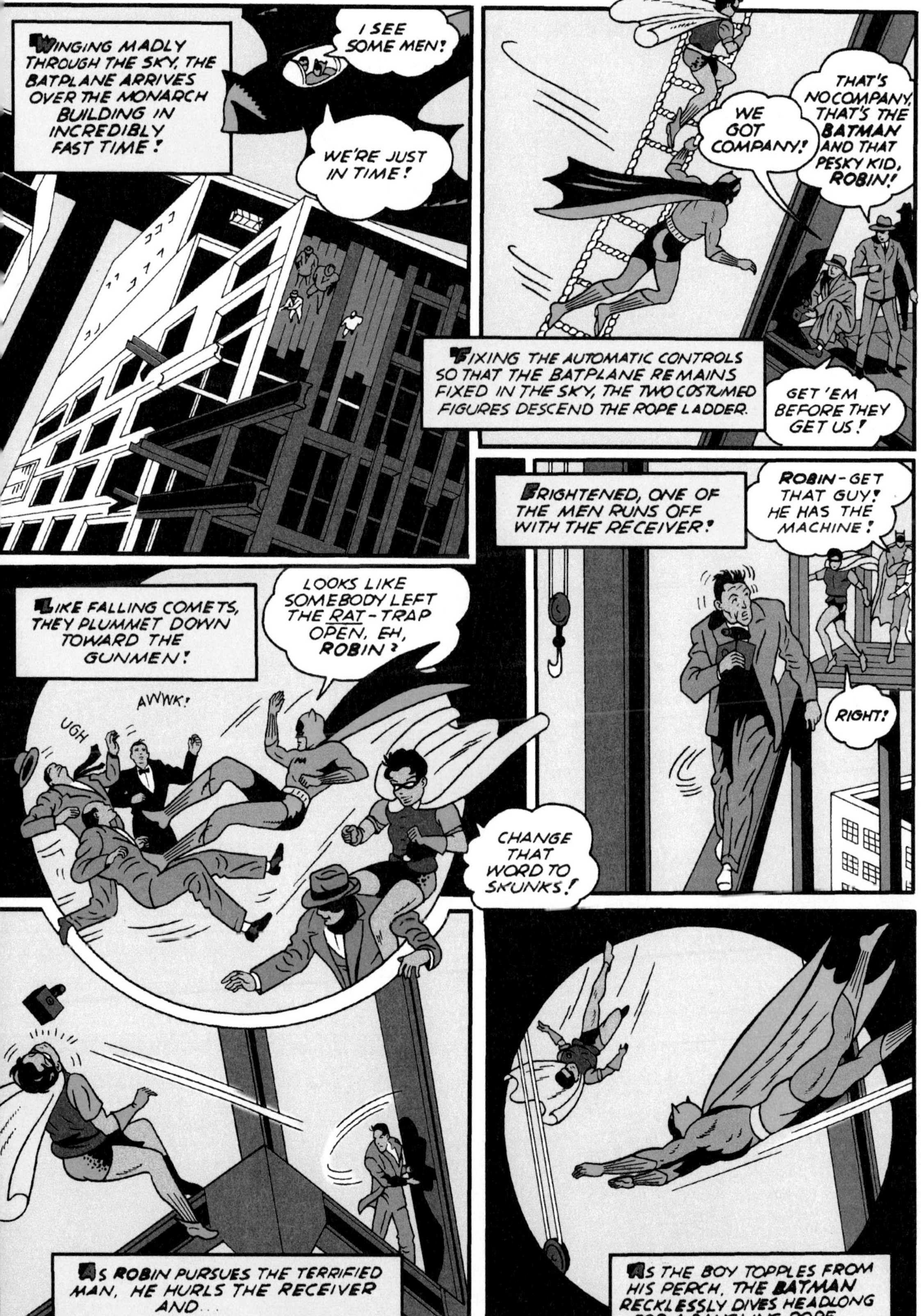
WINGING MADLY THROUGH THE SKY, THE BATPLANE ARRIVES OVER THE MONARCH BUILDING IN INCREDIBLY FAST TIME!
I SEE SOME MEN!
WE'RE JUST IN TIME!
FIXING THE AUTOMATIC CONTROLS SO THAT THE BATPLANE REMAINS FIXED IN THE SKY, THE TWO COSTUMED FIGURES DESCEND THE ROPE LADDER.
WE GOT COMPANY!
THAT'S NO COMPANY, THAT'S THE BATMAN AND THAT PESKY KID, ROBIN!
GET 'EM BEFORE THEY GET US!
FRIGHTENED, ONE OF THE MEN RUNS OFF WITH THE RECEIVER!
ROBIN - GET THAT GUY! HE HAS THE MACHINE!
RIGHT!
LIKE FALLING COMETS, THEY PLUMMET DOWN TOWARD THE GUNMEN!
LOOKS LIKE SOMEBODY LEFT THE RAT-TRAP OPEN, EH, ROBIN?
AWWK!
UGH
CHANGE THAT WORD TO SKUNKS!
AS ROBIN PURSUES THE TERRIFIED MAN, HE HURLS THE RECEIVER AND...
AS THE BOY TOPPLES FROM HIS PERCH, THE BATMAN RECKLESSLY DIVES HEADLONG FOR A DANGLING ROPE.

...GRASPING THE ROPE, THE **BATMAN** SWINGS FORWARD!

UGH!

WITH A WRENCH THAT ALMOST TEARS IT FROM IT'S SOCKET, HIS STRONG ARM CLOSES ABOUT THE FALLING BOY

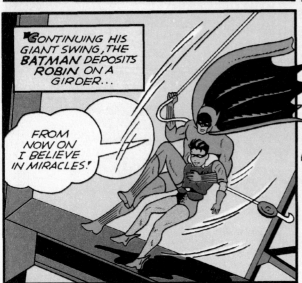

CONTINUING HIS GIANT SWING, THE **BATMAN** DEPOSITS **ROBIN** ON A GIRDER...

FROM NOW ON I BELIEVE IN MIRACLES!

CONTINUING HIS SPECTACULAR SWING, THE COWLED FIGURE ARCS BACK TO LAND AMIDST THE ASTOUNDED THUGS!

NOW-NOW! YOU DIDN'T REALLY THINK I'D GO AND LEAVE YOU!

AS THE **BATMAN** DISPOSES OF A THUG, ANOTHER RISES AND AIMS HIS GUN DIRECTLY AT THE **BATMAN'S** HEAD.

OKAY, WISEGUY! HERE'S WHERE YOU GET YOURS!

BUT BEFORE THE MAN CAN SQUEEZE THE TRIGGER, HE UTTERS A SOFT MOAN AND COLLAPSES! **ROBIN'S** SKILL WITH THE SLING HAS BEEN PROVEN ONCE MORE...

OOOH!

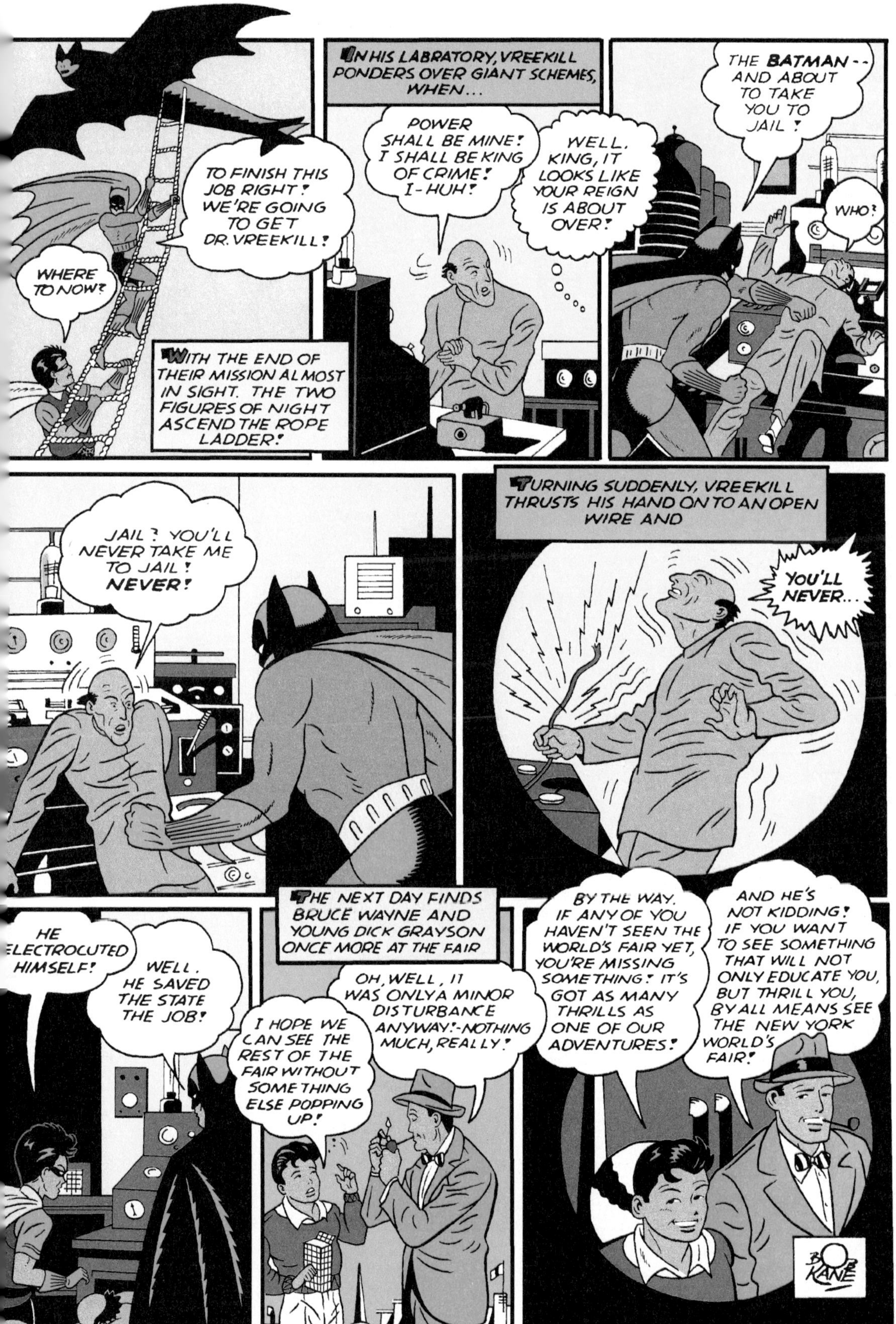
WHERE TO NOW?
TO FINISH THIS JOB RIGHT! WE'RE GOING TO GET DR. VREEKILL!
WITH THE END OF THEIR MISSION ALMOST IN SIGHT. THE TWO FIGURES OF NIGHT ASCEND THE ROPE LADDER!
IN HIS LABRATORY, VREEKILL PONDERS OVER GIANT SCHEMES, WHEN...
POWER SHALL BE MINE! I SHALL BE KING OF CRIME! I-HUH!
WELL, KING, IT LOOKS LIKE YOUR REIGN IS ABOUT OVER!
WHO?
THE BATMAN -- AND ABOUT TO TAKE YOU TO JAIL!
JAIL? YOU'LL NEVER TAKE ME TO JAIL! NEVER!
TURNING SUDDENLY, VREEKILL THRUSTS HIS HAND ON TO AN OPEN WIRE AND
YOU'LL NEVER...
HE ELECTROCUTED HIMSELF!
WELL. HE SAVED THE STATE THE JOB!
THE NEXT DAY FINDS BRUCE WAYNE AND YOUNG DICK GRAYSON ONCE MORE AT THE FAIR
I HOPE WE CAN SEE THE REST OF THE FAIR WITHOUT SOME THING ELSE POPPING UP!
OH, WELL, IT WAS ONLY A MINOR DISTURBANCE ANYWAY!-NOTHING MUCH, REALLY!
BY THE WAY. IF ANY OF YOU HAVEN'T SEEN THE WORLD'S FAIR YET, YOU'RE MISSING SOMETHING! IT'S GOT AS MANY THRILLS AS ONE OF OUR ADVENTURES!
AND HE'S NOT KIDDING! IF YOU WANT TO SEE SOMETHING THAT WILL NOT ONLY EDUCATE YOU, BUT THRILL YOU, BY ALL MEANS SEE THE NEW YORK WORLD'S FAIR!
BOB KANE

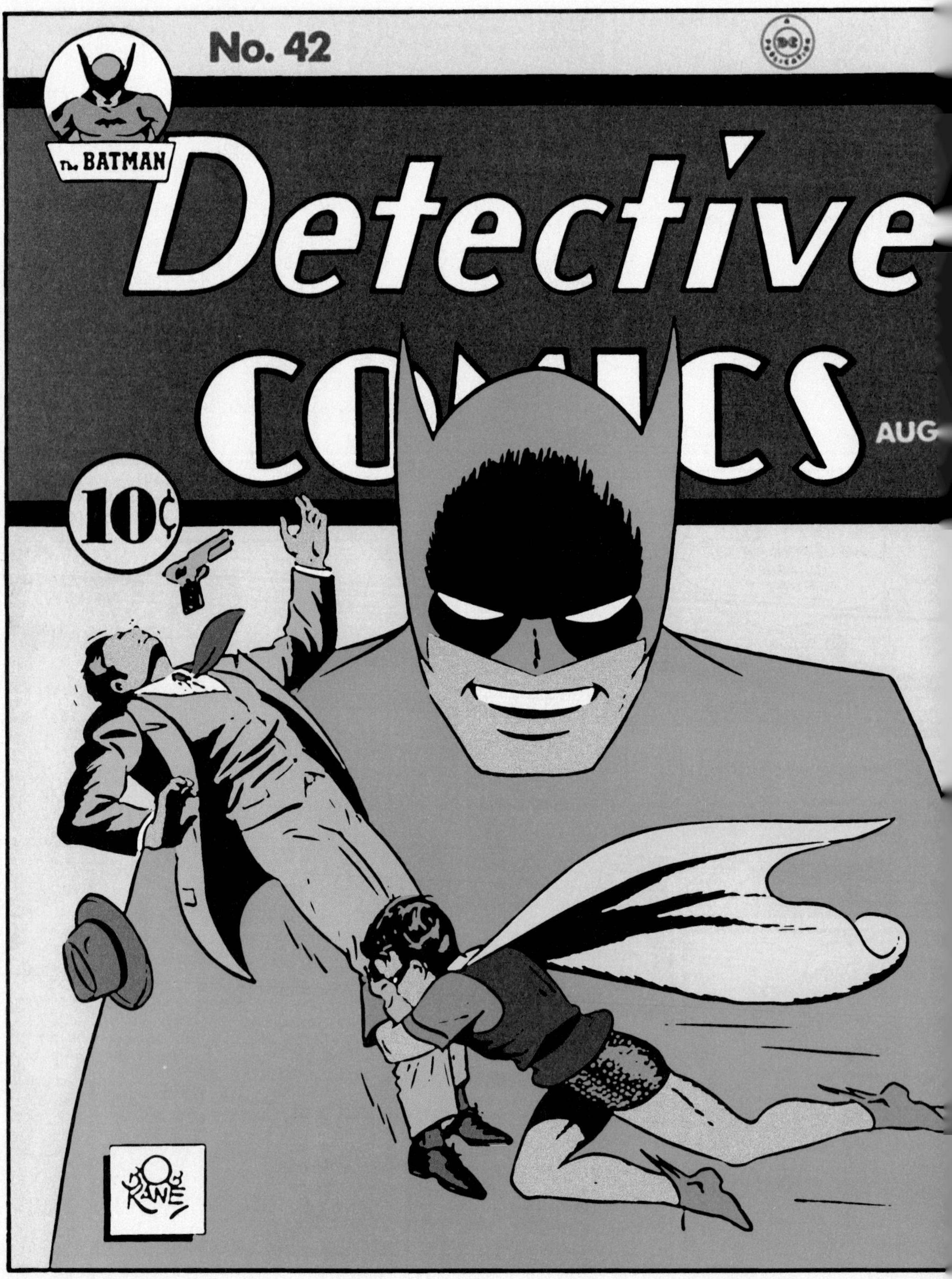
No. 42
The BATMAN
Detective
COMICS
AUG
10¢
KANE

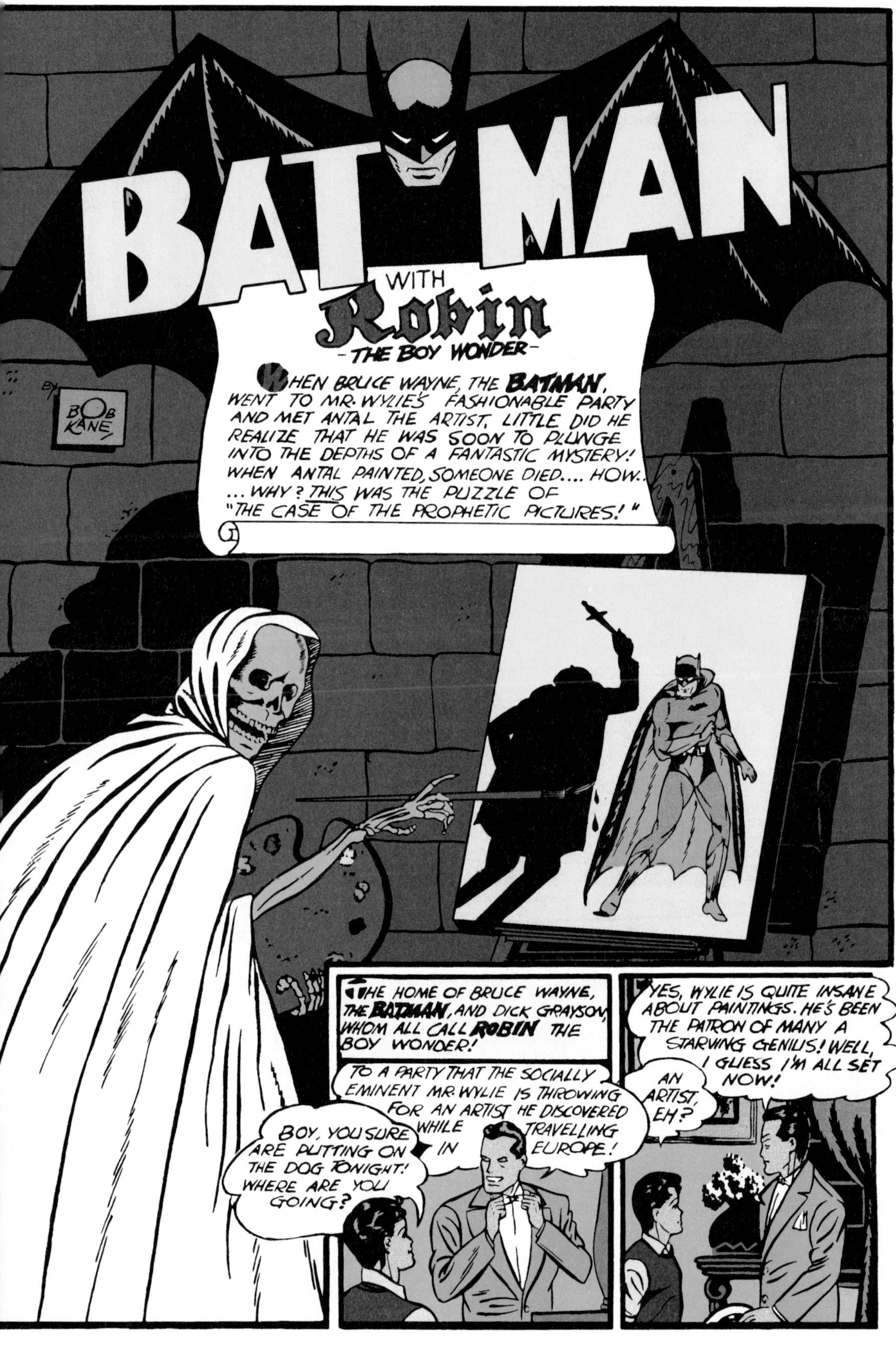

BATMAN
WITH Robin -THE BOY WONDER-
BY BOB KANE
WHEN BRUCE WAYNE, THE BATMAN, WENT TO MR. WYLIE'S FASHIONABLE PARTY AND MET ANTAL THE ARTIST, LITTLE DID HE REALIZE THAT HE WAS SOON TO PLUNGE INTO THE DEPTHS OF A FANTASTIC MYSTERY! WHEN ANTAL PAINTED, SOMEONE DIED.... HOW.. ... WHY? THIS WAS THE PUZZLE OF "THE CASE OF THE PROPHETIC PICTURES!"
THE HOME OF BRUCE WAYNE, THE BATMAN, AND DICK GRAYSON, WHOM ALL CALL ROBIN THE BOY WONDER!
BOY, YOU SURE ARE PUTTING ON THE DOG TONIGHT! WHERE ARE YOU GOING?
TO A PARTY THAT THE SOCIALLY EMINENT MR. WYLIE IS THROWING FOR AN ARTIST HE DISCOVERED WHILE TRAVELLING IN EUROPE!
AN ARTIST, EH?
YES, WYLIE IS QUITE INSANE ABOUT PAINTINGS. HE'S BEEN THE PATRON OF MANY A STARVING GENIUS! WELL, I GUESS I'M ALL SET NOW!

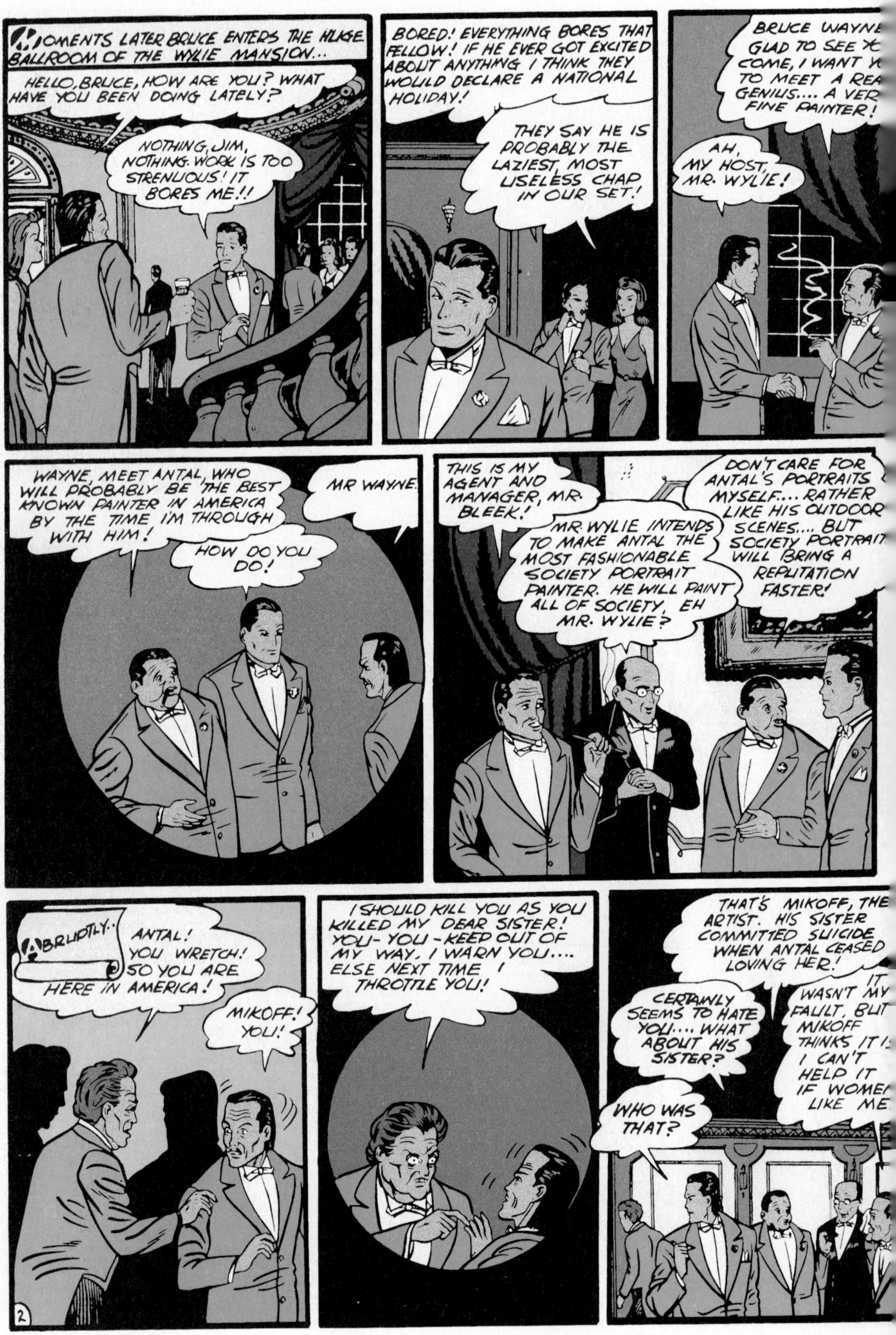
MOMENTS LATER BRUCE ENTERS THE HUGE BALLROOM OF THE WYLIE MANSION...
HELLO, BRUCE, HOW ARE YOU? WHAT HAVE YOU BEEN DOING LATELY?
NOTHING, JIM, NOTHING. WORK IS TOO STRENUOUS! IT BORES ME!!
BORED! EVERYTHING BORES THAT FELLOW! IF HE EVER GOT EXCITED ABOUT ANYTHING I THINK THEY WOULD DECLARE A NATIONAL HOLIDAY!
THEY SAY HE IS PROBABLY THE LAZIEST, MOST USELESS CHAP IN OUR SET!
BRUCE WAYNE GLAD TO SEE YO COME, I WANT YO TO MEET A REA GENIUS.... A VER FINE PAINTER!
AH, MY HOST, MR. WYLIE!
WAYNE, MEET ANTAL, WHO WILL PROBABLY BE THE BEST KNOWN PAINTER IN AMERICA BY THE TIME I'M THROUGH WITH HIM!
MR WAYNE.
HOW DO YOU DO!
THIS IS MY AGENT AND MANAGER, MR. BLEEK!
MR. WYLIE INTENDS TO MAKE ANTAL THE MOST FASHIONABLE SOCIETY PORTRAIT PAINTER. HE WILL PAINT ALL OF SOCIETY, EH MR. WYLIE?
DON'T CARE FOR ANTAL'S PORTRAITS MYSELF.... RATHER LIKE HIS OUTDOOR SCENES.... BUT SOCIETY PORTRAIT WILL BRING A REPUTATION FASTER!
ABRUPTLY..
ANTAL! YOU WRETCH! SO YOU ARE HERE IN AMERICA!
MIKOFF! YOU!
2
I SHOULD KILL YOU AS YOU KILLED MY DEAR SISTER! YOU- YOU- KEEP OUT OF MY WAY. I WARN YOU.... ELSE NEXT TIME I THROTTLE YOU!
WHO WAS THAT?
THAT'S MIKOFF, THE ARTIST. HIS SISTER COMMITTED SUICIDE WHEN ANTAL CEASED LOVING HER!
CERTAINLY SEEMS TO HATE YOU.... WHAT ABOUT HIS SISTER?
IT WASN'T MY FAULT, BUT MIKOFF THINKS IT IS I CAN'T HELP IT IF WOMEN LIKE ME

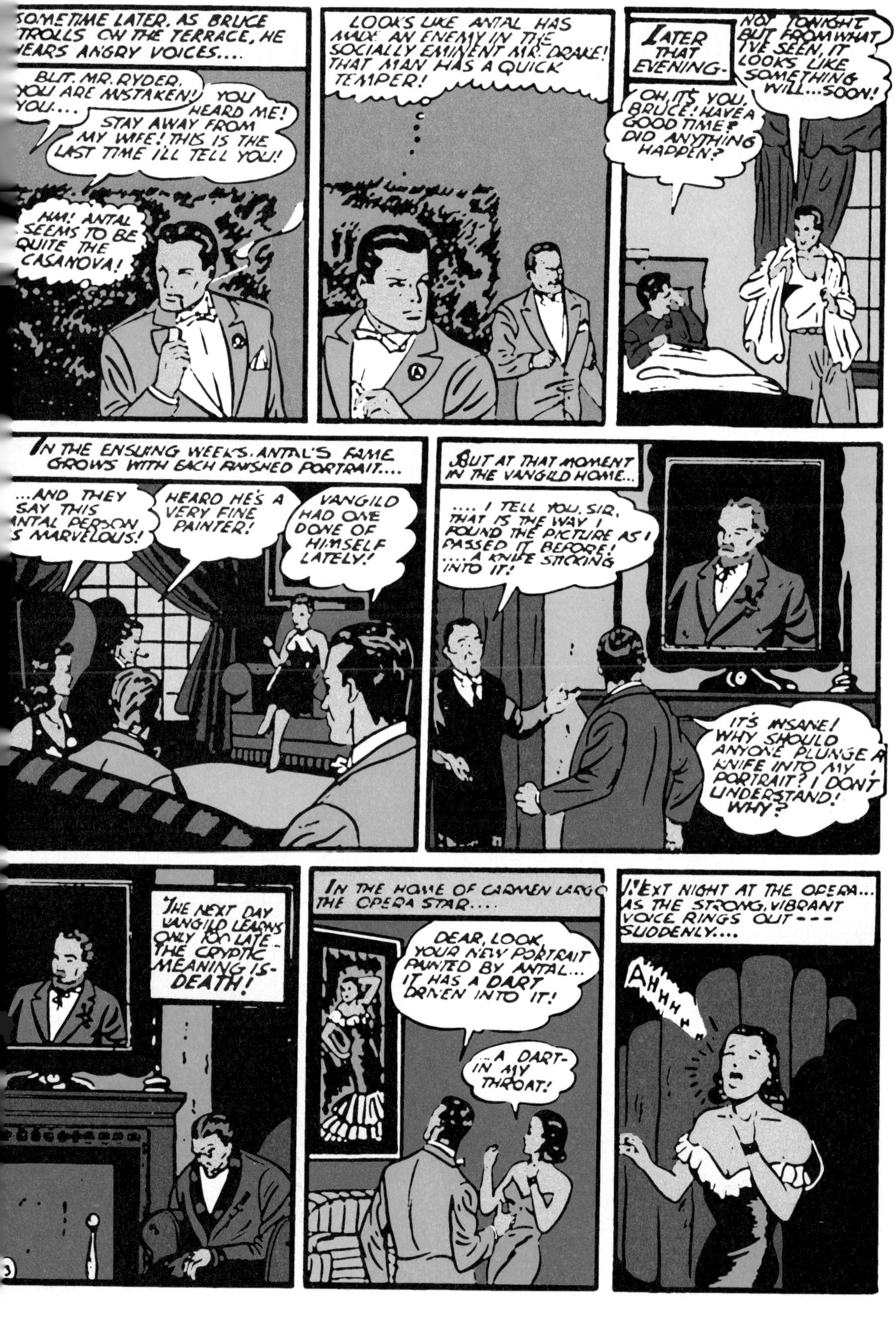
SOMETIME LATER, AS BRUCE TROLLS ON THE TERRACE, HE HEARS ANGRY VOICES....
BUT, MR. RYDER, YOU ARE MISTAKEN! YOU....
YOU HEARD ME! STAY AWAY FROM MY WIFE! THIS IS THE LAST TIME I'LL TELL YOU!
HM! ANTAL SEEMS TO BE QUITE THE CASANOVA!
LOOKS LIKE ANTAL HAS MADE AN ENEMY IN THE SOCIALLY EMINENT MR. DRAKE! THAT MAN HAS A QUICK TEMPER!
LATER THAT EVENING-
OH, IT'S YOU, BRUCE! HAVE A GOOD TIME? DID ANYTHING HAPPEN?
NOT TONIGHT BUT FROM WHAT I'VE SEEN, IT LOOKS LIKE SOMETHING WILL...SOON!
IN THE ENSUING WEEKS, ANTAL'S FAME GROWS WITH EACH FINISHED PORTRAIT....
...AND THEY SAY THIS ANTAL PERSON IS MARVELOUS!
HEARD HE'S A VERY FINE PAINTER!
VANGILD HAD ONE DONE OF HIMSELF LATELY!
BUT AT THAT MOMENT IN THE VANGILD HOME...
.... I TELL YOU, SIR, THAT IS THE WAY I FOUND THE PICTURE AS I PASSED IT BEFORE! ....A KNIFE STICKING INTO IT!
IT'S INSANE! WHY SHOULD ANYONE PLUNGE A KNIFE INTO MY PORTRAIT? I DON'T UNDERSTAND! WHY?
THE NEXT DAY VANGILD LEARNS ONLY TOO LATE THE CRYPTIC MEANING IS- DEATH!
IN THE HOME OF CARMEN LARGO THE OPERA STAR....
DEAR, LOOK, YOUR NEW PORTRAIT PAINTED BY ANTAL... IT HAS A DART DRIVEN INTO IT!
...A DART- IN MY THROAT!
NEXT NIGHT AT THE OPERA... AS THE STRONG, VIBRANT VOICE RINGS OUT--- SUDDENLY....
AHHHH

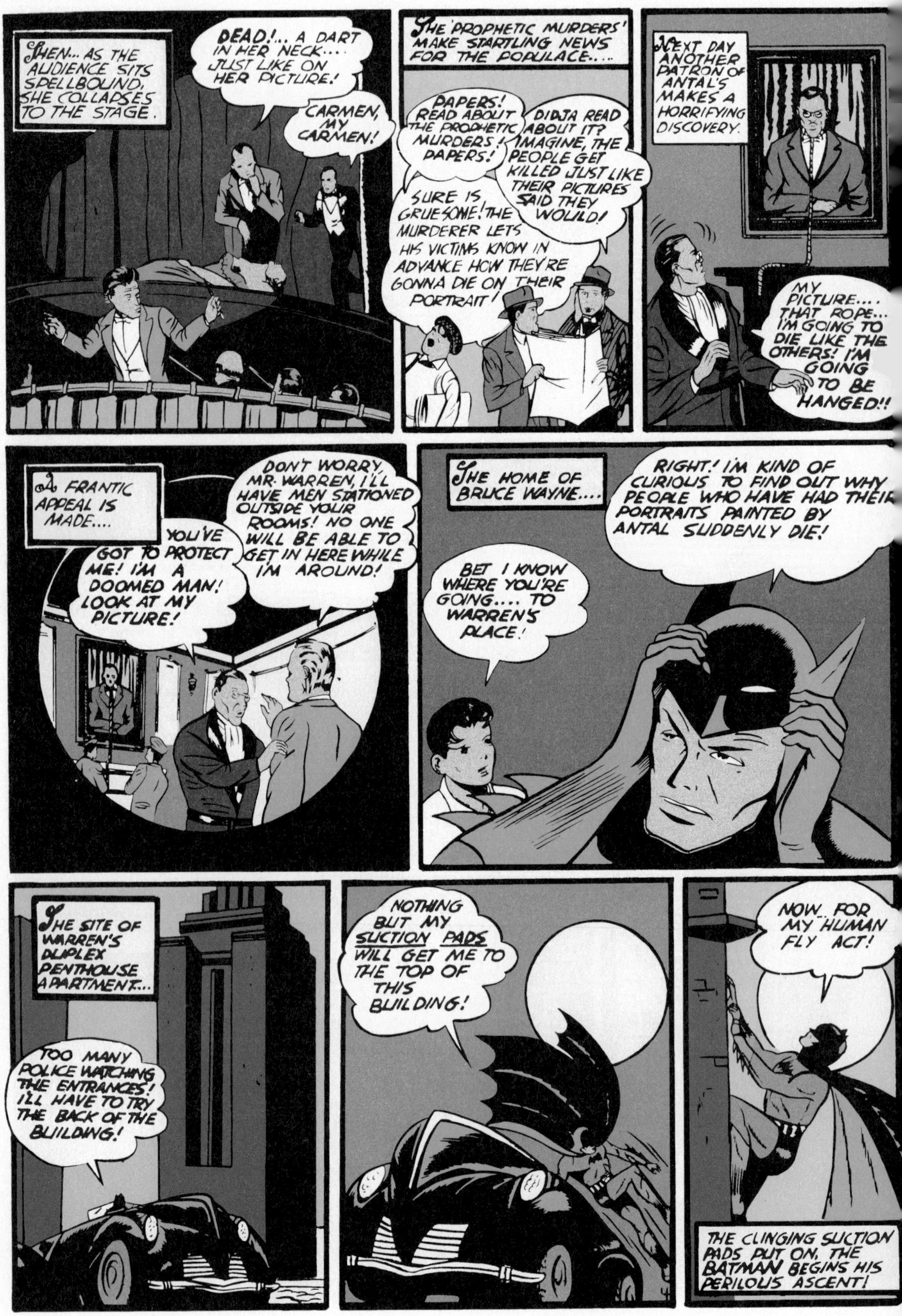
THEN... AS THE AUDIENCE SITS SPELLBOUND, SHE COLLAPSES TO THE STAGE.
DEAD!... A DART IN HER NECK... JUST LIKE ON HER PICTURE!
CARMEN, MY CARMEN!
THE 'PROPHETIC MURDERS' MAKE STARTLING NEWS FOR THE POPULACE....
PAPERS! READ ABOUT THE PROPHETIC MURDERS! PAPERS!
DIDJA READ ABOUT IT? IMAGINE, THE PEOPLE GET KILLED JUST LIKE THEIR PICTURES SAID THEY WOULD!
SURE IS GRUESOME! THE MURDERER LETS HIS VICTIMS KNOW IN ADVANCE HOW THEY'RE GONNA DIE ON THEIR PORTRAIT!
NEXT DAY ANOTHER PATRON OF ANTAL'S MAKES A HORRIFYING DISCOVERY.
MY PICTURE.... THAT ROPE... I'M GOING TO DIE LIKE THE OTHERS! I'M GOING TO BE HANGED!!
A FRANTIC APPEAL IS MADE....
YOU'VE GOT TO PROTECT ME! I'M A DOOMED MAN! LOOK AT MY PICTURE!
DON'T WORRY, MR. WARREN, I'LL HAVE MEN STATIONED OUTSIDE YOUR ROOMS! NO ONE WILL BE ABLE TO GET IN HERE WHILE I'M AROUND!
THE HOME OF BRUCE WAYNE....
BET I KNOW WHERE YOU'RE GOING.... TO WARREN'S PLACE!
RIGHT! I'M KIND OF CURIOUS TO FIND OUT WHY PEOPLE WHO HAVE HAD THEIR PORTRAITS PAINTED BY ANTAL SUDDENLY DIE!
THE SITE OF WARREN'S DUPLEX PENTHOUSE APARTMENT...
TOO MANY POLICE WATCHING THE ENTRANCES! I'LL HAVE TO TRY THE BACK OF THE BUILDING!
NOTHING BUT MY SUCTION PADS WILL GET ME TO THE TOP OF THIS BUILDING!
NOW.. FOR MY HUMAN FLY ACT!
THE CLINGING SUCTION PADS PUT ON, THE BATMAN BEGINS HIS PERILOUS ASCENT!

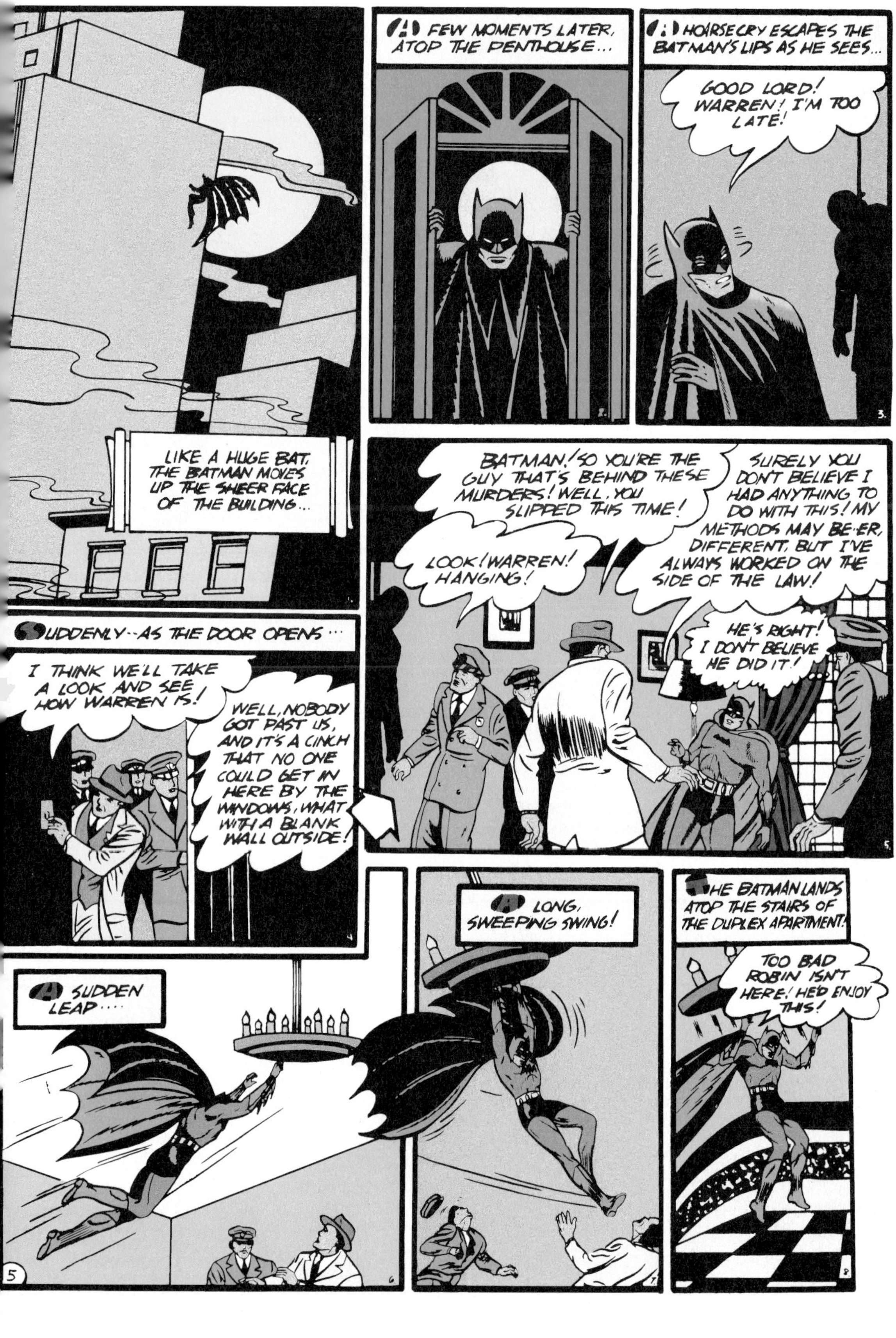
LIKE A HUGE BAT, THE BATMAN MOVES UP THE SHEER FACE OF THE BUILDING...
A FEW MOMENTS LATER, ATOP THE PENTHOUSE...
A HOARSE CRY ESCAPES THE BATMAN'S LIPS AS HE SEES...
GOOD LORD! WARREN! I'M TOO LATE!
SUDDENLY--AS THE DOOR OPENS...
I THINK WE'LL TAKE A LOOK AND SEE HOW WARREN IS!
WELL, NOBODY GOT PAST US, AND IT'S A CINCH THAT NO ONE COULD GET IN HERE BY THE WINDOWS, WHAT WITH A BLANK WALL OUTSIDE!
LOOK! WARREN! HANGING!
BATMAN! SO YOU'RE THE GUY THAT'S BEHIND THESE MURDERS! WELL, YOU SLIPPED THIS TIME!
SURELY YOU DON'T BELIEVE I HAD ANYTHING TO DO WITH THIS! MY METHODS MAY BE-ER, DIFFERENT, BUT I'VE ALWAYS WORKED ON THE SIDE OF THE LAW!
HE'S RIGHT! I DON'T BELIEVE HE DID IT!
A SUDDEN LEAP....
A LONG, SWEEPING SWING!
THE BATMAN LANDS ATOP THE STAIRS OF THE DUPLEX APARTMENT!
TOO BAD ROBIN ISN'T HERE! HE'D ENJOY THIS!
5

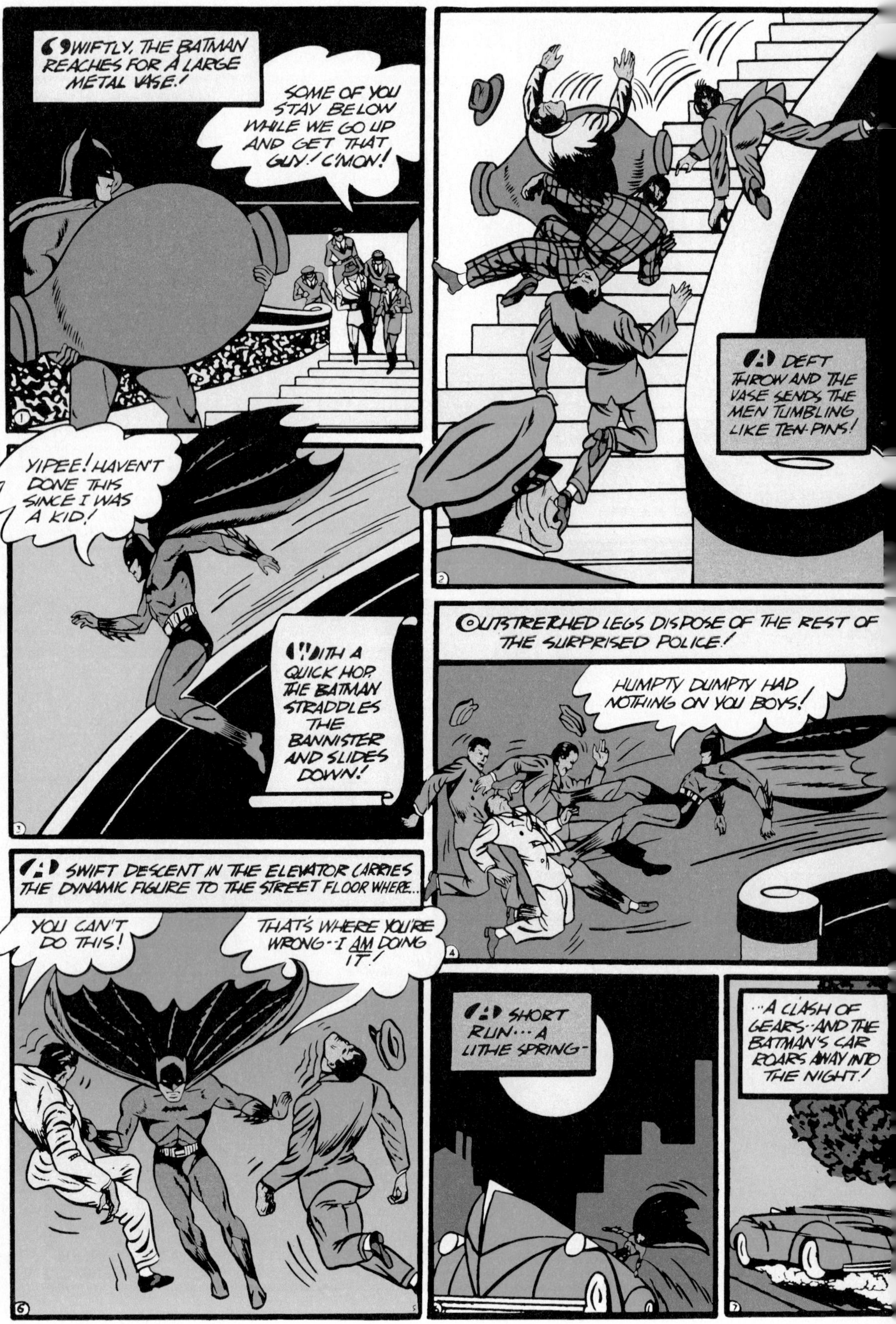
SWIFTLY, THE BATMAN REACHES FOR A LARGE METAL VASE!
SOME OF YOU STAY BELOW WHILE WE GO UP AND GET THAT GUY! C'MON!
A DEFT THROW AND THE VASE SENDS THE MEN TUMBLING LIKE TEN-PINS!
YIPEE! HAVEN'T DONE THIS SINCE I WAS A KID!
WITH A QUICK HOP, THE BATMAN STRADDLES THE BANNISTER AND SLIDES DOWN!
OUTSTRETCHED LEGS DISPOSE OF THE REST OF THE SURPRISED POLICE!
HUMPTY DUMPTY HAD NOTHING ON YOU BOYS!
A SWIFT DESCENT IN THE ELEVATOR CARRIES THE DYNAMIC FIGURE TO THE STREET FLOOR WHERE...
YOU CAN'T DO THIS!
THAT'S WHERE YOU'RE WRONG--I AM DOING IT!
A SHORT RUN... A LITHE SPRING-
...A CLASH OF GEARS--AND THE BATMAN'S CAR ROARS AWAY INTO THE NIGHT!

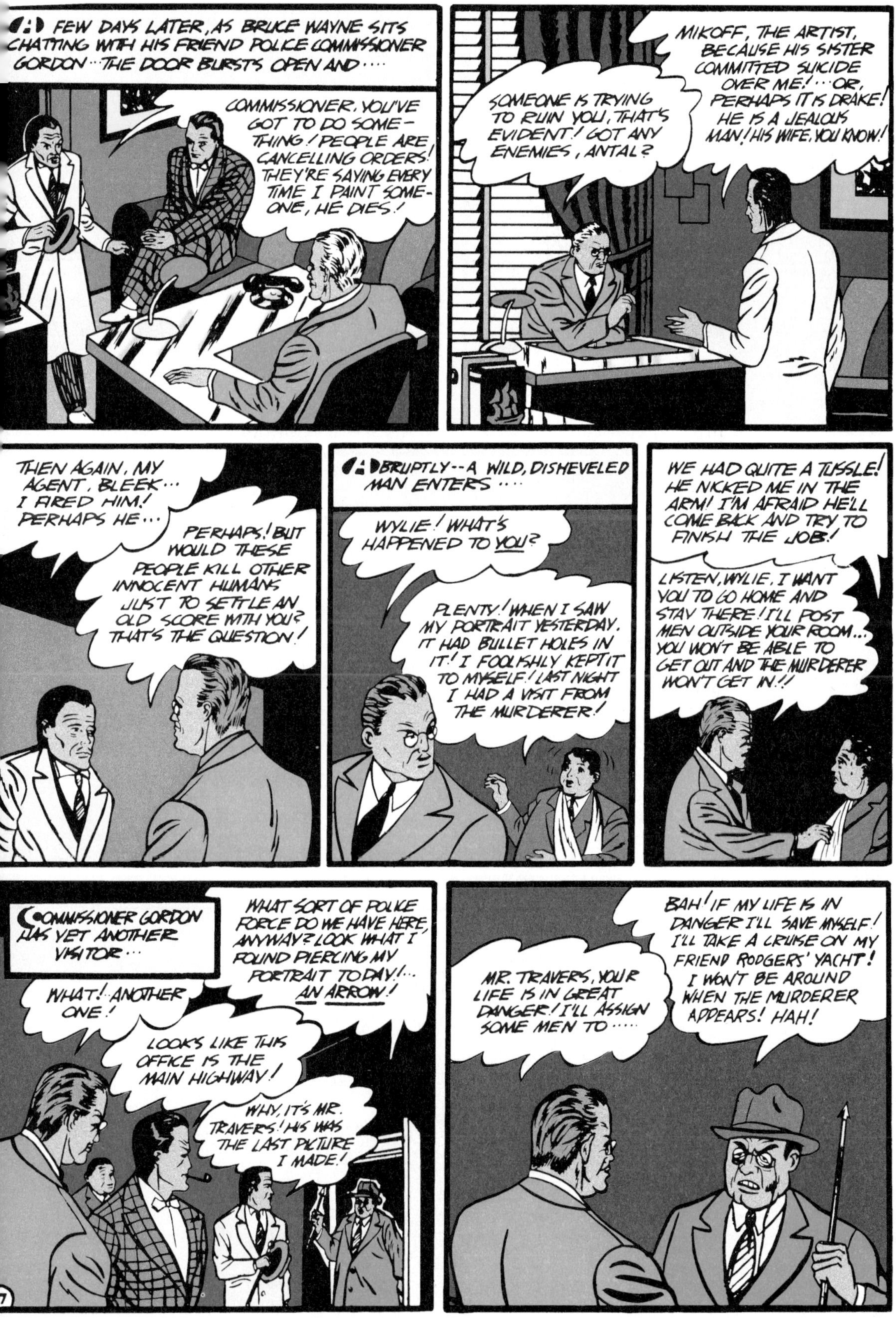
A FEW DAYS LATER, AS BRUCE WAYNE SITS CHATTING WITH HIS FRIEND POLICE COMMISSIONER GORDON ··· THE DOOR BURSTS OPEN AND ····
COMMISSIONER, YOU'VE GOT TO DO SOMETHING! PEOPLE ARE CANCELLING ORDERS! THEY'RE SAYING EVERY TIME I PAINT SOMEONE, HE DIES!
SOMEONE IS TRYING TO RUIN YOU, THAT'S EVIDENT! GOT ANY ENEMIES, ANTAL?
MIKOFF, THE ARTIST, BECAUSE HIS SISTER COMMITTED SUICIDE OVER ME! ··· OR, PERHAPS IT IS DRAKE! HE IS A JEALOUS MAN! HIS WIFE, YOU KNOW!
THEN AGAIN, MY AGENT, BLEEK ··· I FIRED HIM! PERHAPS HE ···
PERHAPS! BUT WOULD THESE PEOPLE KILL OTHER INNOCENT HUMANS JUST TO SETTLE AN OLD SCORE WITH YOU? THAT'S THE QUESTION!
ABRUPTLY -- A WILD, DISHEVELED MAN ENTERS ····
WYLIE! WHAT'S HAPPENED TO YOU?
PLENTY! WHEN I SAW MY PORTRAIT YESTERDAY, IT HAD BULLET HOLES IN IT! I FOOLISHLY KEPT IT TO MYSELF! LAST NIGHT I HAD A VISIT FROM THE MURDERER!
WE HAD QUITE A TUSSLE! HE NICKED ME IN THE ARM! I'M AFRAID HE'LL COME BACK AND TRY TO FINISH THE JOB!
LISTEN, WYLIE, I WANT YOU TO GO HOME AND STAY THERE! I'LL POST MEN OUTSIDE YOUR ROOM ... YOU WON'T BE ABLE TO GET OUT AND THE MURDERER WON'T GET IN!!
COMMISSIONER GORDON HAS YET ANOTHER VISITOR ···
WHAT SORT OF POLICE FORCE DO WE HAVE HERE, ANYWAY? LOOK WHAT I FOUND PIERCING MY PORTRAIT TODAY! ... AN ARROW!
WHAT! ANOTHER ONE!
LOOKS LIKE THIS OFFICE IS THE MAIN HIGHWAY!
WHY, IT'S MR. TRAVERS! HIS WAS THE LAST PICTURE I MADE!
7
MR. TRAVERS, YOUR LIFE IS IN GREAT DANGER! I'LL ASSIGN SOME MEN TO ····
BAH! IF MY LIFE IS IN DANGER I'LL SAVE MYSELF! I'LL TAKE A CRUISE ON MY FRIEND RODGERS' YACHT! I WON'T BE AROUND WHEN THE MURDERER APPEARS! HAH!

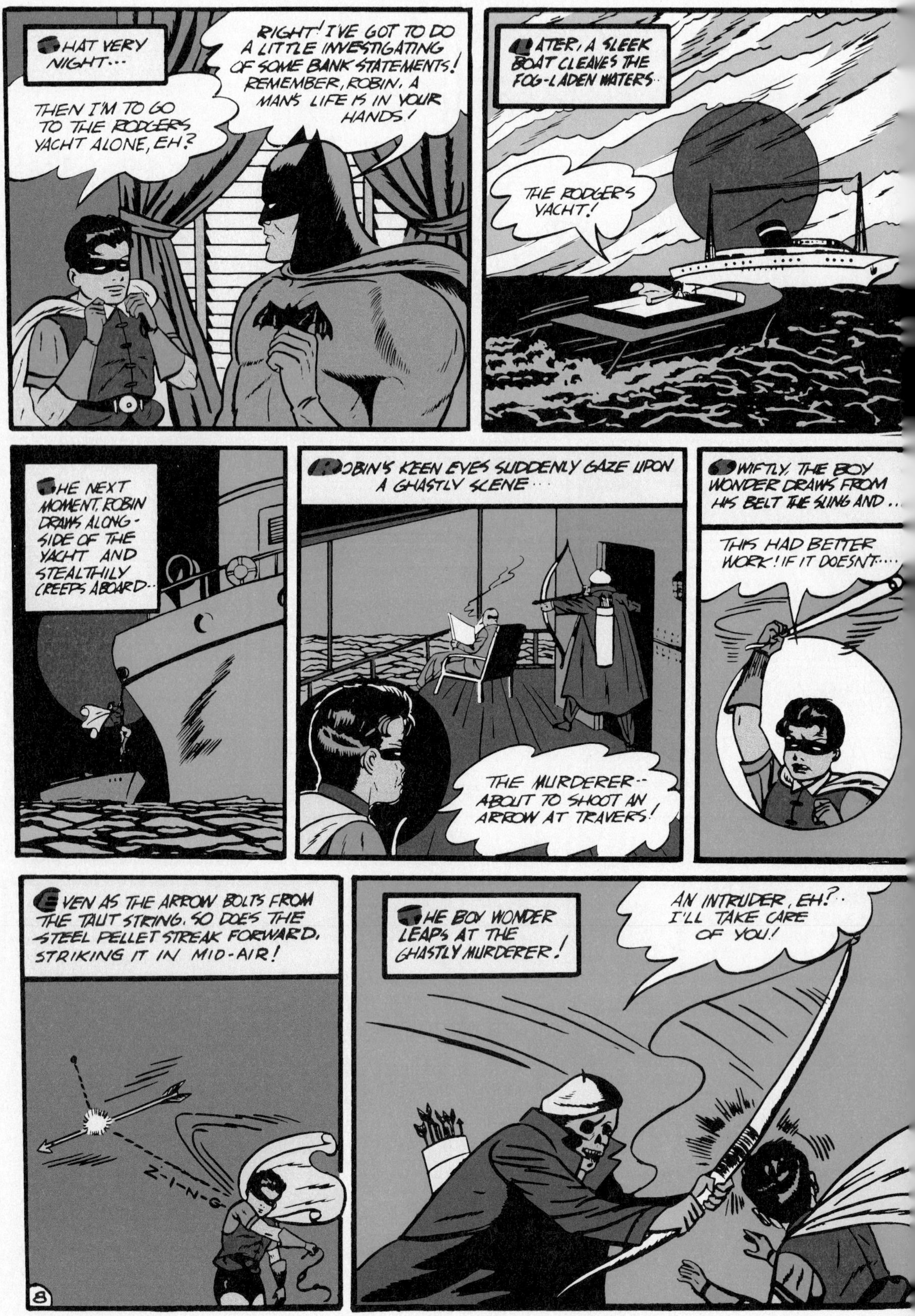
THAT VERY NIGHT...
THEN I'M TO GO TO THE RODGERS YACHT ALONE, EH?
RIGHT! I'VE GOT TO DO A LITTLE INVESTIGATING OF SOME BANK STATEMENTS! REMEMBER, ROBIN, A MAN'S LIFE IS IN YOUR HANDS!
LATER, A SLEEK BOAT CLEAVES THE FOG-LADEN WATERS...
THE RODGERS YACHT!
THE NEXT MOMENT, ROBIN DRAWS ALONG-SIDE OF THE YACHT AND STEALTHILY CREEPS ABOARD...
ROBIN'S KEEN EYES SUDDENLY GAZE UPON A GHASTLY SCENE...
THE MURDERER-- ABOUT TO SHOOT AN ARROW AT TRAVERS!
SWIFTLY, THE BOY WONDER DRAWS FROM HIS BELT THE SLING AND...
THIS HAD BETTER WORK! IF IT DOESN'T.....
EVEN AS THE ARROW BOLTS FROM THE TAUT STRING, SO DOES THE STEEL PELLET STREAK FORWARD, STRIKING IT IN MID-AIR!
Z-I-N-G
8
THE BOY WONDER LEAPS AT THE GHASTLY MURDERER!
AN INTRUDER, EH?.. I'LL TAKE CARE OF YOU!

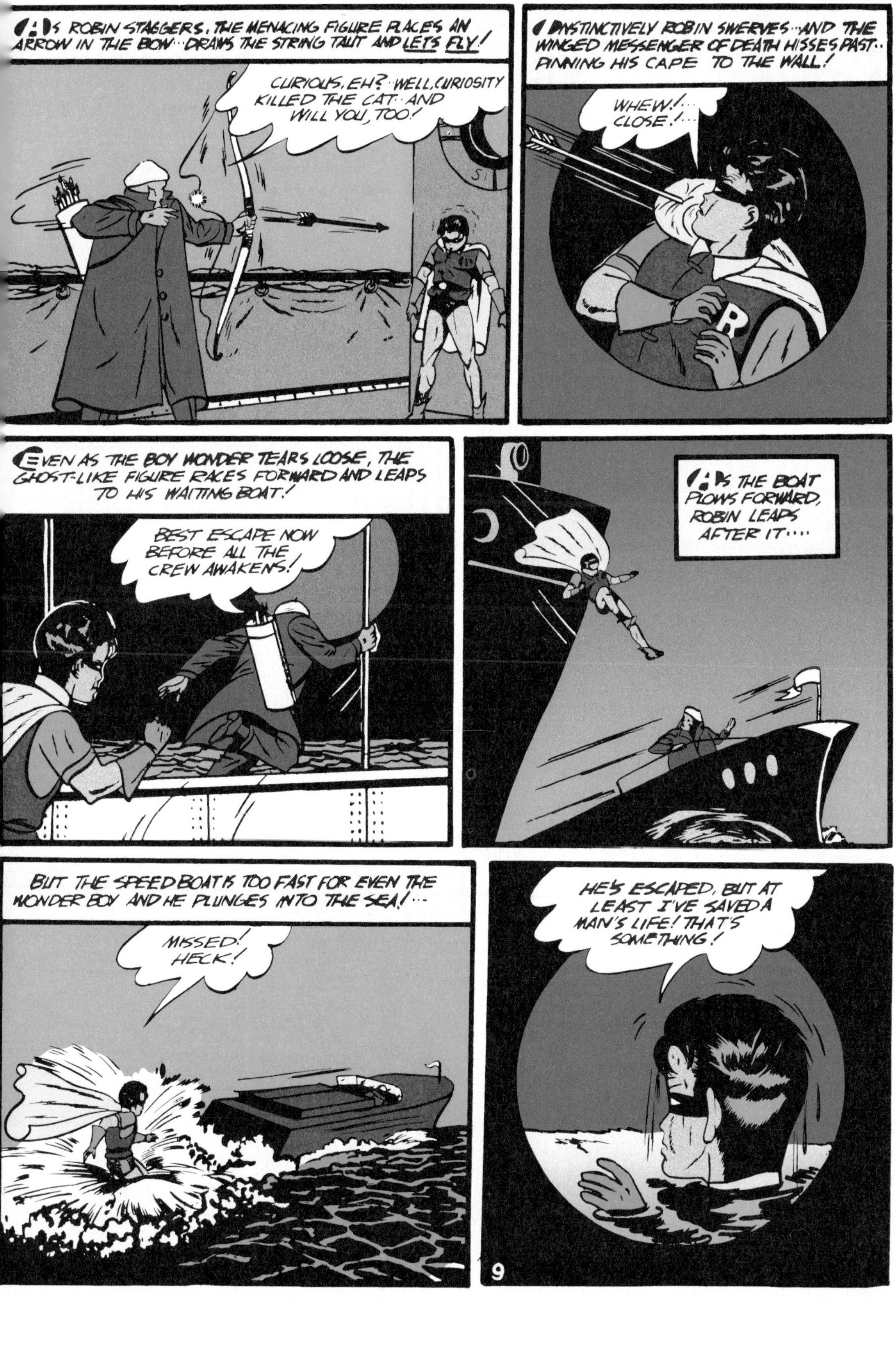
AS ROBIN STAGGERS, THE MENACING FIGURE PLACES AN ARROW IN THE BOW...DRAWS THE STRING TAUT AND LETS FLY!
CURIOUS, EH? WELL, CURIOSITY KILLED THE CAT...AND WILL YOU, TOO!
INSTINCTIVELY ROBIN SWERVES...AND THE WINGED MESSENGER OF DEATH HISSES PAST... PINNING HIS CAPE TO THE WALL!
WHEW!... CLOSE!...
EVEN AS THE BOY WONDER TEARS LOOSE, THE GHOST-LIKE FIGURE RACES FORWARD AND LEAPS TO HIS WAITING BOAT!
BEST ESCAPE NOW BEFORE ALL THE CREW AWAKENS!
AS THE BOAT PLOWS FORWARD, ROBIN LEAPS AFTER IT....
BUT THE SPEED BOAT IS TOO FAST FOR EVEN THE WONDER BOY AND HE PLUNGES INTO THE SEA!...
MISSED! HECK!
HE'S ESCAPED, BUT AT LEAST I'VE SAVED A MAN'S LIFE! THAT'S SOMETHING!
9

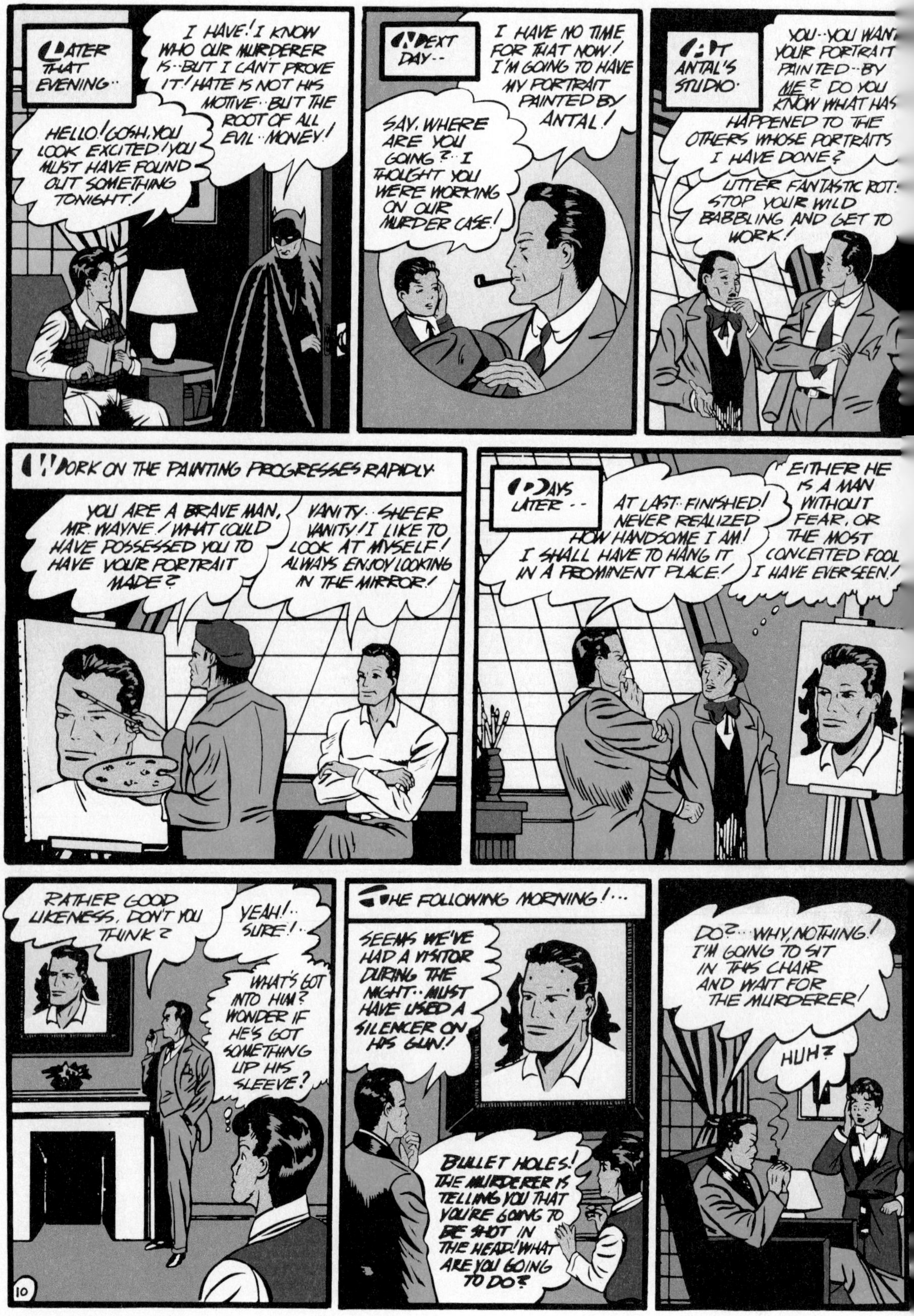
LATER THAT EVENING..
HELLO! GOSH, YOU LOOK EXCITED! YOU MUST HAVE FOUND OUT SOMETHING TONIGHT!
I HAVE! I KNOW WHO OUR MURDERER IS..BUT I CAN'T PROVE IT! HATE IS NOT HIS MOTIVE..BUT THE ROOT OF ALL EVIL..MONEY!
NEXT DAY--
SAY, WHERE ARE YOU GOING?..I THOUGHT YOU WERE WORKING ON OUR MURDER CASE!
I HAVE NO TIME FOR THAT NOW! I'M GOING TO HAVE MY PORTRAIT PAINTED BY ANTAL!
AT ANTAL'S STUDIO.
YOU--YOU WANT YOUR PORTRAIT PAINTED--BY ME? DO YOU KNOW WHAT HAS HAPPENED TO THE OTHERS WHOSE PORTRAITS I HAVE DONE?
UTTER FANTASTIC ROT! STOP YOUR WILD BABBLING AND GET TO WORK!
WORK ON THE PAINTING PROGRESSES RAPIDLY.
YOU ARE A BRAVE MAN, MR. WAYNE! WHAT COULD HAVE POSSESSED YOU TO HAVE YOUR PORTRAIT MADE?
VANITY..SHEER VANITY! I LIKE TO LOOK AT MYSELF! ALWAYS ENJOY LOOKING IN THE MIRROR!
DAYS LATER --
AT LAST..FINISHED! NEVER REALIZED HOW HANDSOME I AM! I SHALL HAVE TO HANG IT IN A PROMINENT PLACE!
EITHER HE IS A MAN WITHOUT FEAR, OR THE MOST CONCEITED FOOL I HAVE EVER SEEN!
RATHER GOOD LIKENESS, DON'T YOU THINK?
YEAH!.. SURE!..
WHAT'S GOT INTO HIM? WONDER IF HE'S GOT SOMETHING UP HIS SLEEVE?
10
THE FOLLOWING MORNING!...
SEEMS WE'VE HAD A VISITOR DURING THE NIGHT..MUST HAVE USED A SILENCER ON HIS GUN!
BULLET HOLES! THE MURDERER IS TELLING YOU THAT YOU'RE GOING TO BE SHOT IN THE HEAD! WHAT ARE YOU GOING TO DO?
DO?...WHY, NOTHING! I'M GOING TO SIT IN THIS CHAIR AND WAIT FOR THE MURDERER!
HUH?

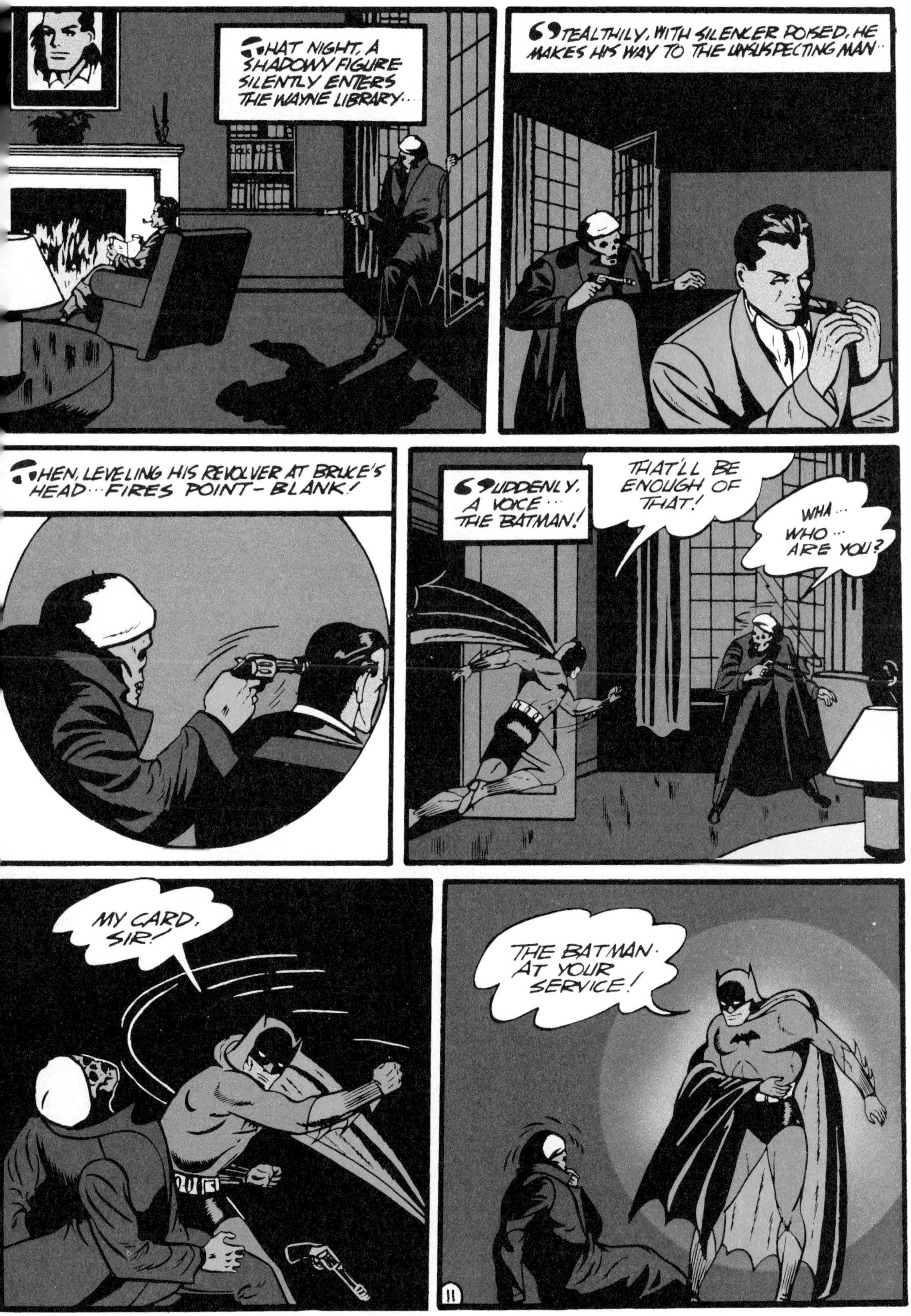
THAT NIGHT, A SHADOWY FIGURE SILENTLY ENTERS THE WAYNE LIBRARY...
STEALTHILY, WITH SILENCER POISED, HE MAKES HIS WAY TO THE UNSUSPECTING MAN...
THEN, LEVELING HIS REVOLVER AT BRUCE'S HEAD... FIRES POINT-BLANK!
SUDDENLY, A VOICE... THE BATMAN!
THAT'LL BE ENOUGH OF THAT!
WHA... WHO... ARE YOU?
MY CARD, SIR!
THE BATMAN AT YOUR SERVICE!
11

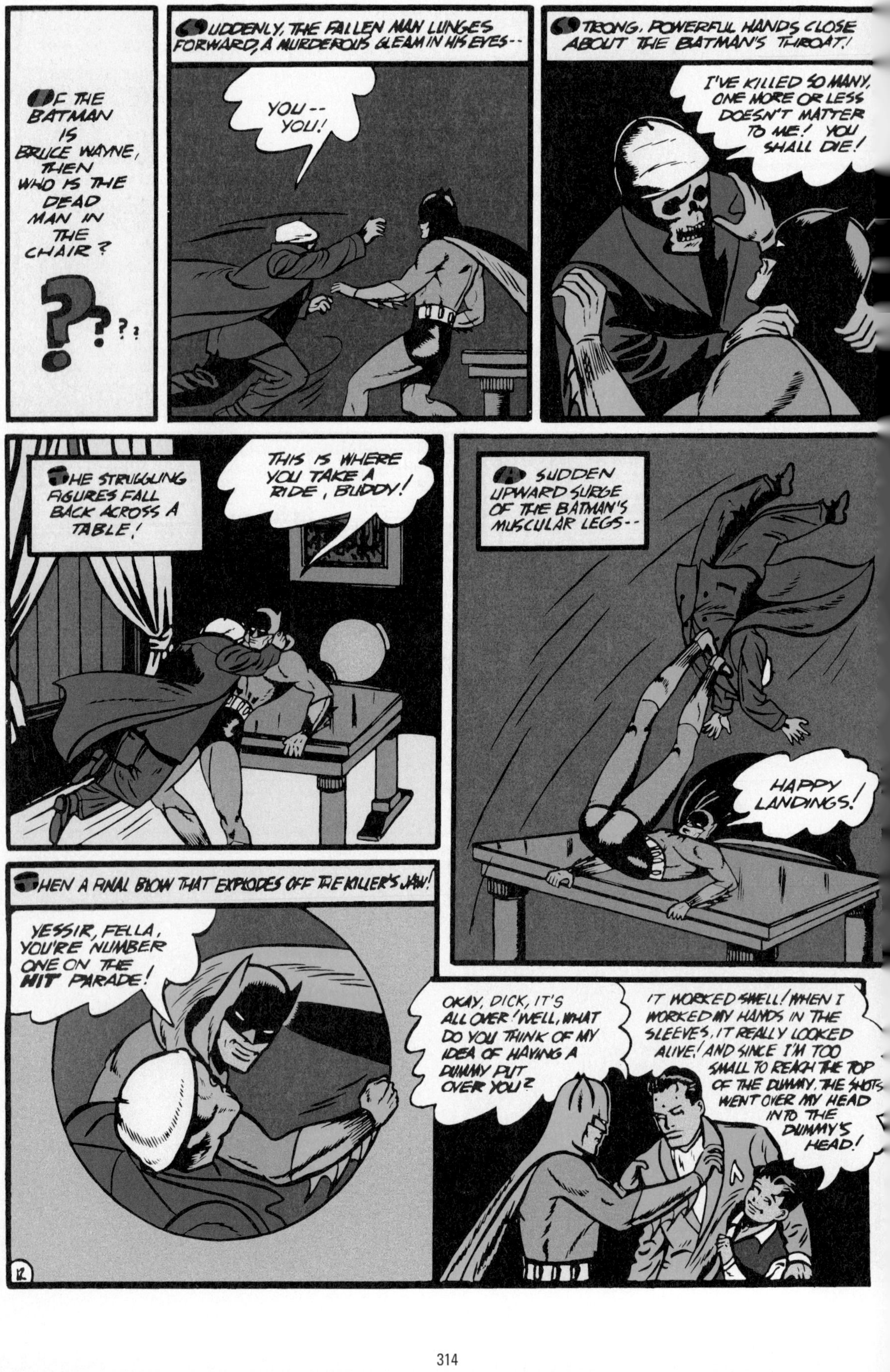
OF THE BATMAN IS BRUCE WAYNE, THEN WHO IS THE DEAD MAN IN THE CHAIR?
???
SUDDENLY, THE FALLEN MAN LUNGES FORWARD, A MURDEROUS GLEAM IN HIS EYES--
YOU-- YOU!
STRONG, POWERFUL HANDS CLOSE ABOUT THE BATMAN'S THROAT!
I'VE KILLED SO MANY, ONE MORE OR LESS DOESN'T MATTER TO ME! YOU SHALL DIE!
THE STRUGGLING FIGURES FALL BACK ACROSS A TABLE!
THIS IS WHERE YOU TAKE A RIDE, BUDDY!
A SUDDEN UPWARD SURGE OF THE BATMAN'S MUSCULAR LEGS--
HAPPY LANDINGS!
THEN A FINAL BLOW THAT EXPLODES OFF THE KILLER'S JAW!
YESSIR, FELLA, YOU'RE NUMBER ONE ON THE HIT PARADE!
12
OKAY, DICK, IT'S ALL OVER! WELL, WHAT DO YOU THINK OF MY IDEA OF HAVING A DUMMY PUT OVER YOU?
IT WORKED SWELL! WHEN I WORKED MY HANDS IN THE SLEEVES, IT REALLY LOOKED ALIVE! AND SINCE I'M TOO SMALL TO REACH THE TOP OF THE DUMMY, THE SHOTS WENT OVER MY HEAD INTO THE DUMMY'S HEAD!

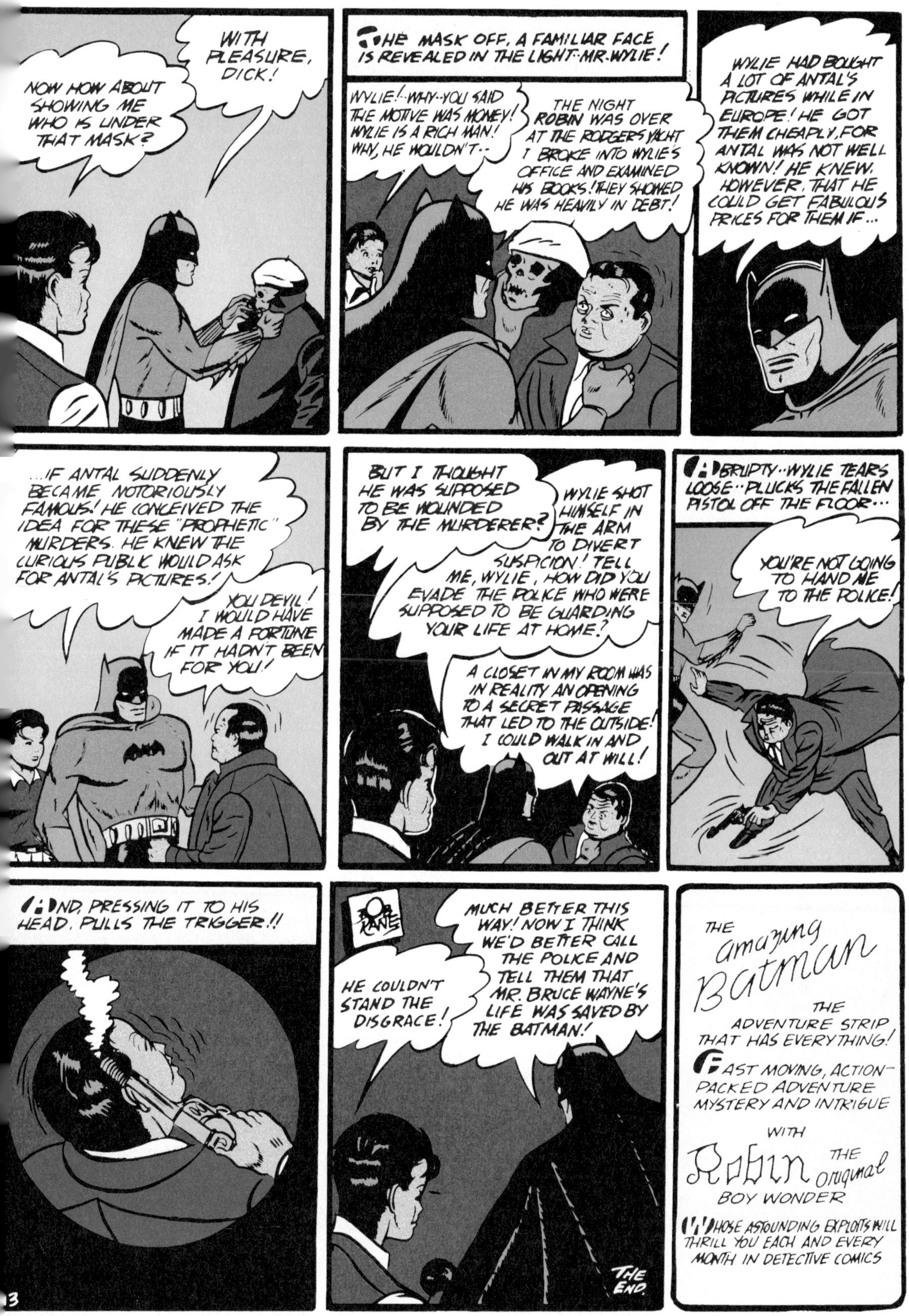
NOW HOW ABOUT SHOWING ME WHO IS UNDER THAT MASK?
WITH PLEASURE, DICK!
THE MASK OFF, A FAMILIAR FACE IS REVEALED IN THE LIGHT-MR. WYLIE!
WYLIE!--WHY--YOU SAID THE MOTIVE WAS MONEY! WYLIE IS A RICH MAN! WHY, HE WOULDN'T--
THE NIGHT ROBIN WAS OVER AT THE RODGERS YACHT I BROKE INTO WYLIE'S OFFICE AND EXAMINED HIS BOOKS! THEY SHOWED HE WAS HEAVILY IN DEBT!
WYLIE HAD BOUGHT A LOT OF ANTAL'S PICTURES WHILE IN EUROPE! HE GOT THEM CHEAPLY, FOR ANTAL WAS NOT WELL KNOWN! HE KNEW, HOWEVER, THAT HE COULD GET FABULOUS PRICES FOR THEM IF...
...IF ANTAL SUDDENLY BECAME NOTORIOUSLY FAMOUS! HE CONCEIVED THE IDEA FOR THESE "PROPHETIC" MURDERS. HE KNEW THE CURIOUS PUBLIC WOULD ASK FOR ANTAL'S PICTURES!
YOU DEVIL! I WOULD HAVE MADE A FORTUNE IF IT HADN'T BEEN FOR YOU!
BUT I THOUGHT HE WAS SUPPOSED TO BE WOUNDED BY THE MURDERER?
WYLIE SHOT HIMSELF IN THE ARM TO DIVERT SUSPICION! TELL ME, WYLIE, HOW DID YOU EVADE THE POLICE WHO WERE SUPPOSED TO BE GUARDING YOUR LIFE AT HOME?
A CLOSET IN MY ROOM WAS IN REALITY AN OPENING TO A SECRET PASSAGE THAT LED TO THE OUTSIDE! I COULD WALK IN AND OUT AT WILL!
ABRUPTLY--WYLIE TEARS LOOSE--PLUCKS THE FALLEN PISTOL OFF THE FLOOR...
YOU'RE NOT GOING TO HAND ME TO THE POLICE!
AND, PRESSING IT TO HIS HEAD, PULLS THE TRIGGER!!
3
BOB KANE
HE COULDN'T STAND THE DISGRACE!
MUCH BETTER THIS WAY! NOW I THINK WE'D BETTER CALL THE POLICE AND TELL THEM THAT MR. BRUCE WAYNE'S LIFE WAS SAVED BY THE BATMAN!
THE END.
THE amazing Batman THE ADVENTURE STRIP THAT HAS EVERYTHING!
FAST MOVING, ACTION-PACKED ADVENTURE MYSTERY AND INTRIGUE
WITH Robin THE original BOY WONDER
WHOSE ASTOUNDING EXPLOITS WILL THRILL YOU EACH AND EVERY MONTH IN DETECTIVE COMICS

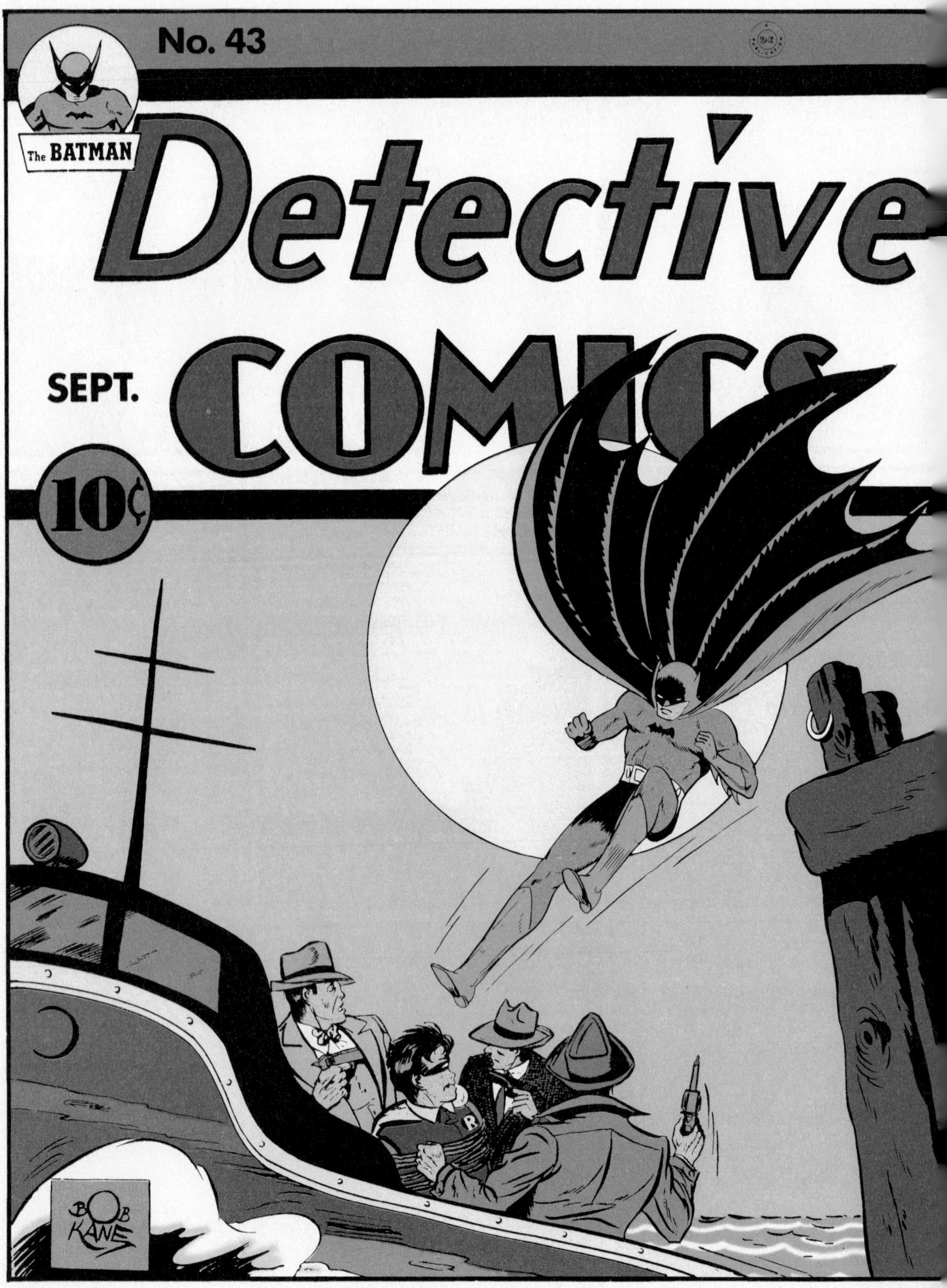
No. 43
The BATMAN
Detective
SEPT.
COMICS
10¢
BOB KANE

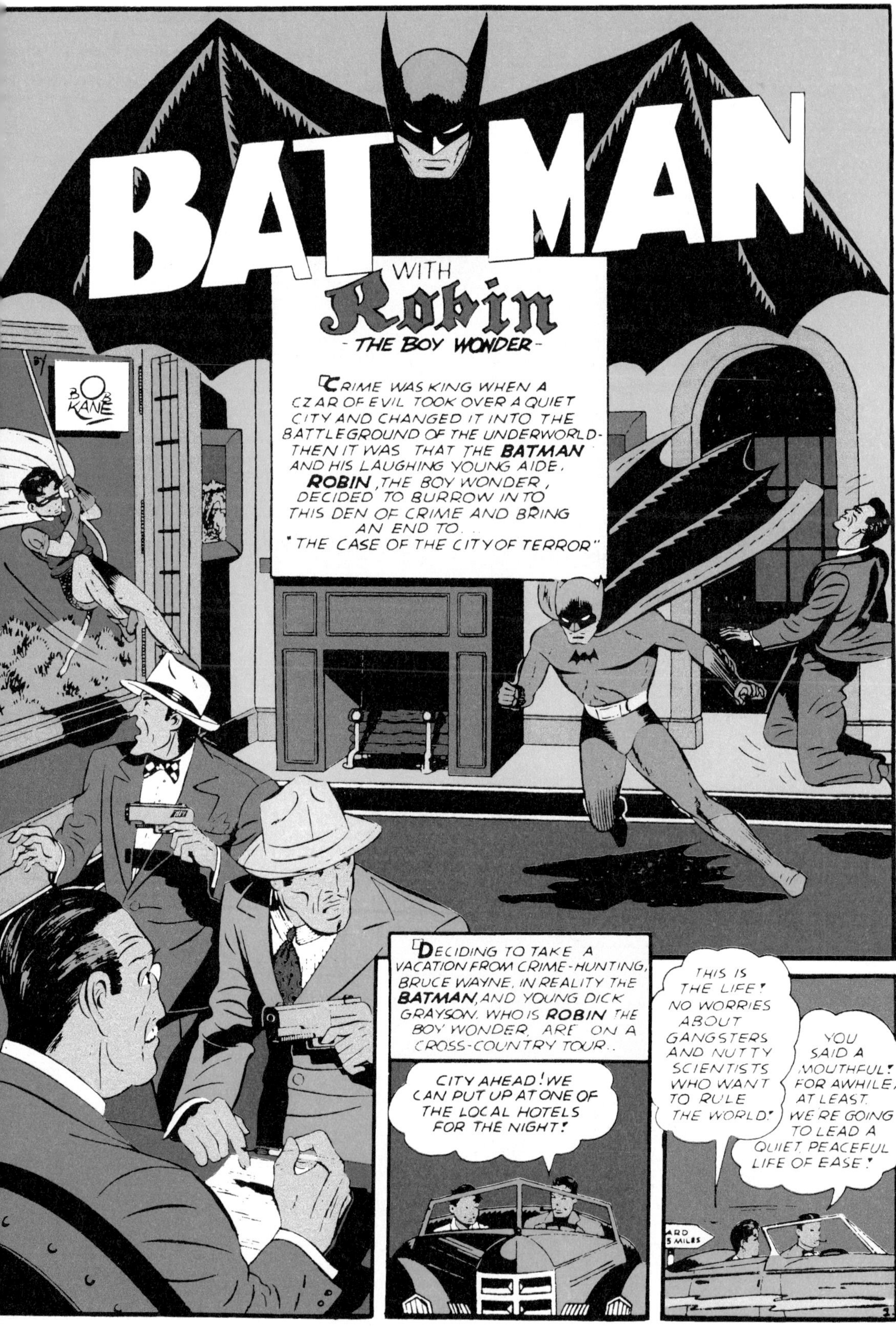
BATMAN
WITH
Robin
-THE BOY WONDER-
BOB KANE
CRIME WAS KING WHEN A CZAR OF EVIL TOOK OVER A QUIET CITY AND CHANGED IT INTO THE BATTLEGROUND OF THE UNDERWORLD- THEN IT WAS THAT THE BATMAN AND HIS LAUGHING YOUNG AIDE, ROBIN, THE BOY WONDER, DECIDED TO BURROW INTO THIS DEN OF CRIME AND BRING AN END TO... "THE CASE OF THE CITY OF TERROR"
DECIDING TO TAKE A VACATION FROM CRIME-HUNTING, BRUCE WAYNE, IN REALITY THE BATMAN, AND YOUNG DICK GRAYSON, WHO IS ROBIN THE BOY WONDER, ARE ON A CROSS-COUNTRY TOUR..
CITY AHEAD! WE CAN PUT UP AT ONE OF THE LOCAL HOTELS FOR THE NIGHT!
THIS IS THE LIFE! NO WORRIES ABOUT GANGSTERS AND NUTTY SCIENTISTS WHO WANT TO RULE THE WORLD!
YOU SAID A MOUTHFUL! FOR AWHILE, AT LEAST. WE'RE GOING TO LEAD A QUIET, PEACEFUL LIFE OF EASE!

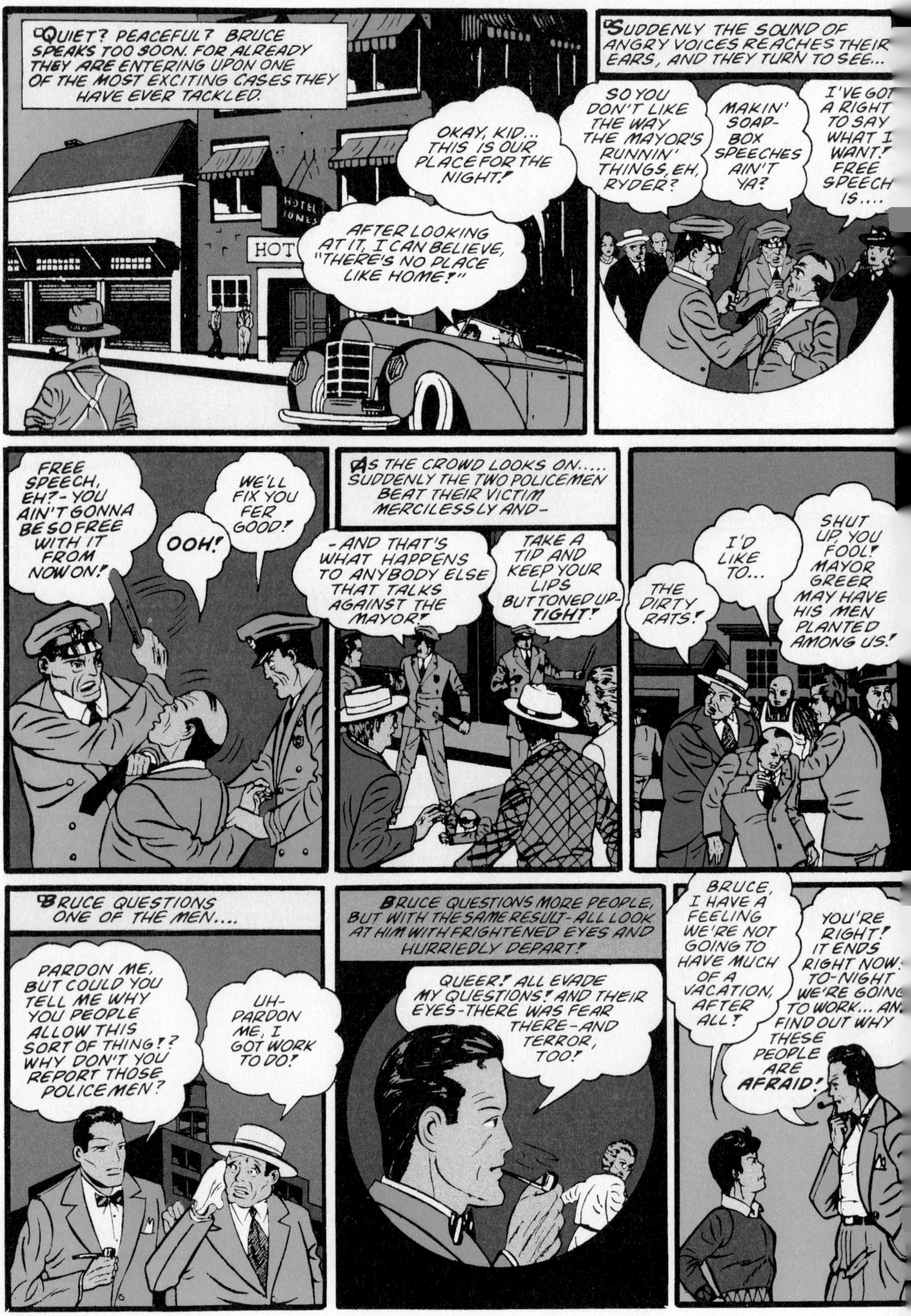
QUIET? PEACEFUL? BRUCE SPEAKS TOO SOON. FOR ALREADY THEY ARE ENTERING UPON ONE OF THE MOST EXCITING CASES THEY HAVE EVER TACKLED.
OKAY, KID... THIS IS OUR PLACE FOR THE NIGHT!
AFTER LOOKING AT IT, I CAN BELIEVE, "THERE'S NO PLACE LIKE HOME!"
HOTEL JONES
SUDDENLY THE SOUND OF ANGRY VOICES REACHES THEIR EARS, AND THEY TURN TO SEE...
SO YOU DON'T LIKE THE WAY THE MAYOR'S RUNNIN' THINGS, EH, RYDER?
MAKIN' SOAP-BOX SPEECHES AIN'T YA?
I'VE GOT A RIGHT TO SAY WHAT I WANT! FREE SPEECH IS....
FREE SPEECH, EH?- YOU AIN'T GONNA BE SO FREE WITH IT FROM NOW ON!
OOH!
WE'LL FIX YOU FER GOOD!
AS THE CROWD LOOKS ON..... SUDDENLY THE TWO POLICEMEN BEAT THEIR VICTIM MERCILESSLY AND-
-AND THAT'S WHAT HAPPENS TO ANYBODY ELSE THAT TALKS AGAINST THE MAYOR!
TAKE A TIP AND KEEP YOUR LIPS BUTTONED UP-TIGHT!
THE DIRTY RATS!
I'D LIKE TO...
SHUT UP, YOU FOOL! MAYOR GREER MAY HAVE HIS MEN PLANTED AMONG US!
BRUCE QUESTIONS ONE OF THE MEN....
PARDON ME, BUT COULD YOU TELL ME WHY YOU PEOPLE ALLOW THIS SORT OF THING!? WHY DON'T YOU REPORT THOSE POLICEMEN?
UH-PARDON ME, I GOT WORK TO DO!
BRUCE QUESTIONS MORE PEOPLE, BUT WITH THE SAME RESULT-ALL LOOK AT HIM WITH FRIGHTENED EYES AND HURRIEDLY DEPART!
QUEER! ALL EVADE MY QUESTIONS! AND THEIR EYES-THERE WAS FEAR THERE-AND TERROR, TOO!
BRUCE, I HAVE A FEELING WE'RE NOT GOING TO HAVE MUCH OF A VACATION, AFTER ALL!
YOU'RE RIGHT! IT ENDS RIGHT NOW. TO-NIGHT WE'RE GOING TO WORK... AND FIND OUT WHY THESE PEOPLE ARE AFRAID!

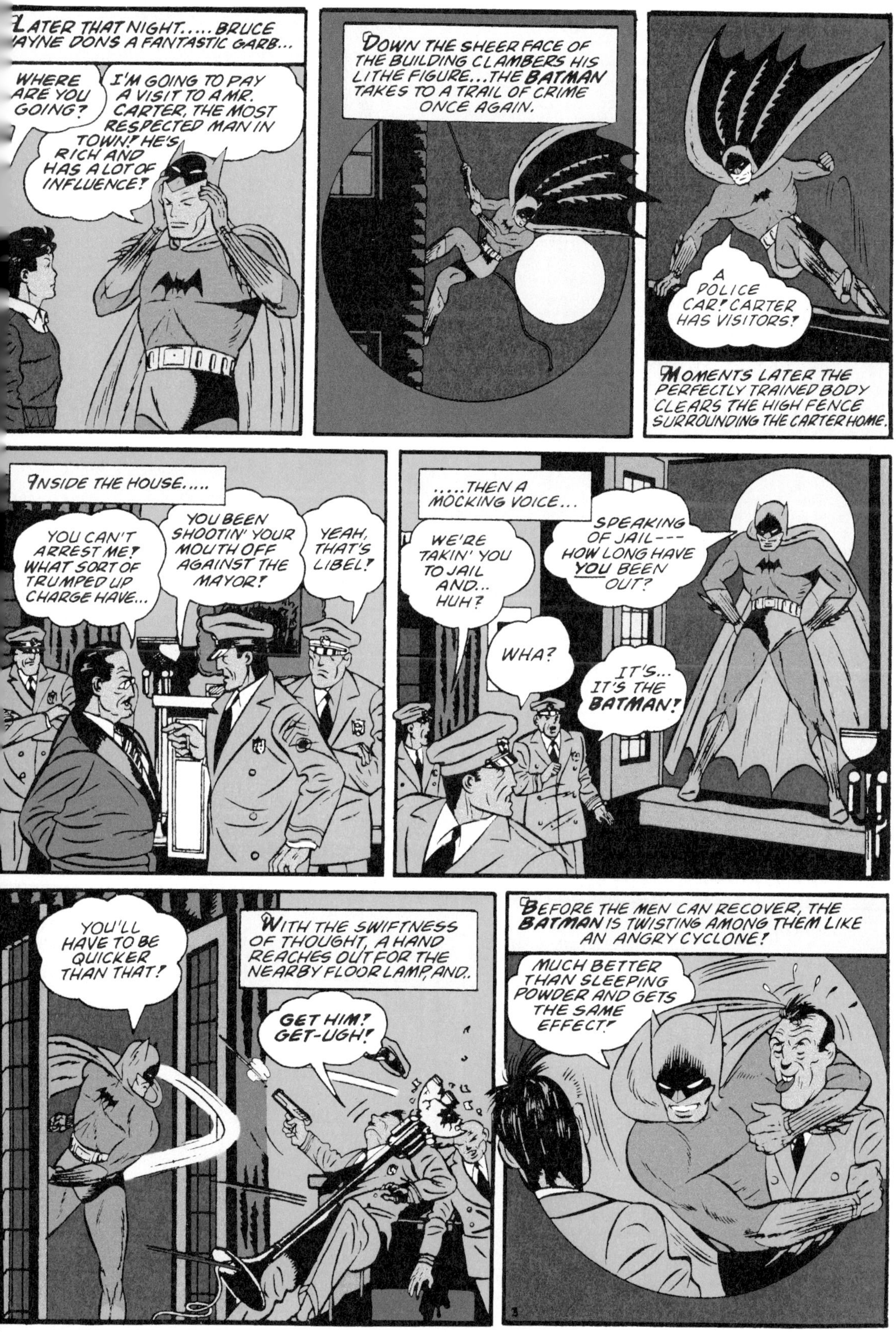
LATER THAT NIGHT..... BRUCE WAYNE DONS A FANTASTIC GARB...
WHERE ARE YOU GOING?
I'M GOING TO PAY A VISIT TO A MR. CARTER, THE MOST RESPECTED MAN IN TOWN! HE'S RICH AND HAS A LOT OF INFLUENCE!
DOWN THE SHEER FACE OF THE BUILDING CLAMBERS HIS LITHE FIGURE...THE BATMAN TAKES TO A TRAIL OF CRIME ONCE AGAIN.
A POLICE CAR! CARTER HAS VISITORS!
MOMENTS LATER THE PERFECTLY TRAINED BODY CLEARS THE HIGH FENCE SURROUNDING THE CARTER HOME.
INSIDE THE HOUSE.....
YOU CAN'T ARREST ME! WHAT SORT OF TRUMPED UP CHARGE HAVE...
YOU BEEN SHOOTIN' YOUR MOUTH OFF AGAINST THE MAYOR!
YEAH, THAT'S LIBEL!
.....THEN A MOCKING VOICE...
WE'RE TAKIN' YOU TO JAIL AND... HUH?
SPEAKING OF JAIL--- HOW LONG HAVE YOU BEEN OUT?
WHA?
IT'S... IT'S THE BATMAN!
YOU'LL HAVE TO BE QUICKER THAN THAT!
WITH THE SWIFTNESS OF THOUGHT, A HAND REACHES OUT FOR THE NEARBY FLOOR LAMP, AND..
GET HIM! GET-UGH!
BEFORE THE MEN CAN RECOVER, THE BATMAN IS TWISTING AMONG THEM LIKE AN ANGRY CYCLONE!
MUCH BETTER THAN SLEEPING POWDER AND GETS THE SAME EFFECT!
3

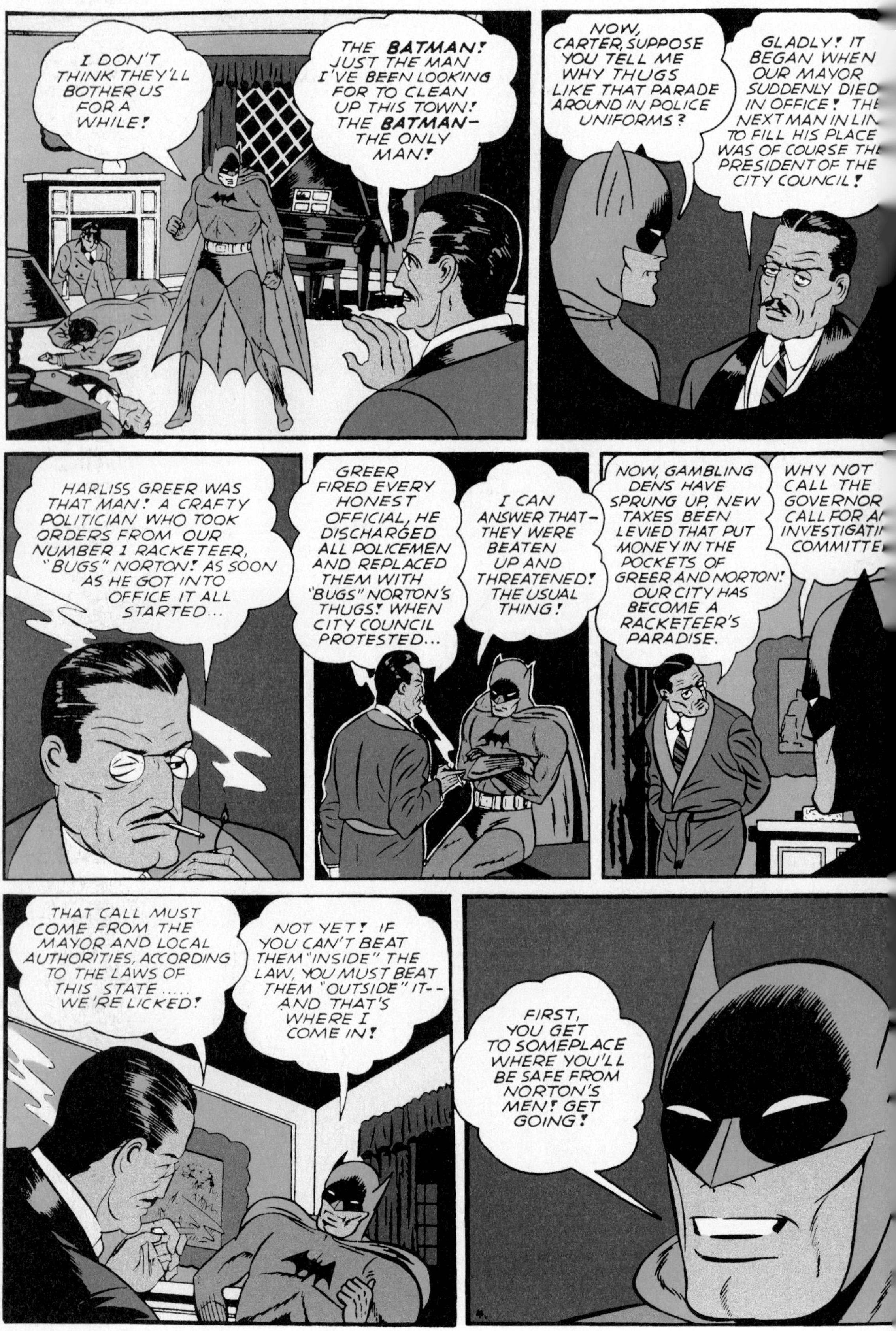

I DON'T THINK THEY'LL BOTHER US FOR A WHILE!
THE BATMAN! JUST THE MAN I'VE BEEN LOOKING FOR TO CLEAN UP THIS TOWN! THE BATMAN— THE ONLY MAN!
NOW, CARTER, SUPPOSE YOU TELL ME WHY THUGS LIKE THAT PARADE AROUND IN POLICE UNIFORMS?
GLADLY! IT BEGAN WHEN OUR MAYOR SUDDENLY DIED IN OFFICE! THE NEXT MAN IN LIN TO FILL HIS PLACE WAS OF COURSE THE PRESIDENT OF THE CITY COUNCIL!
HARLISS GREER WAS THAT MAN! A CRAFTY POLITICIAN WHO TOOK ORDERS FROM OUR NUMBER 1 RACKETEER, "BUGS" NORTON! AS SOON AS HE GOT INTO OFFICE IT ALL STARTED...
GREER FIRED EVERY HONEST OFFICIAL, HE DISCHARGED ALL POLICEMEN AND REPLACED THEM WITH "BUGS" NORTON'S THUGS! WHEN CITY COUNCIL PROTESTED...
I CAN ANSWER THAT— THEY WERE BEATEN UP AND THREATENED! THE USUAL THING!
NOW, GAMBLING DENS HAVE SPRUNG UP, NEW TAXES BEEN LEVIED THAT PUT MONEY IN THE POCKETS OF GREER AND NORTON! OUR CITY HAS BECOME A RACKETEER'S PARADISE.
WHY NOT CALL THE GOVERNOR CALL FOR A INVESTIGATI COMMITTE
THAT CALL MUST COME FROM THE MAYOR AND LOCAL AUTHORITIES, ACCORDING TO THE LAWS OF THIS STATE..... WE'RE LICKED!
NOT YET! IF YOU CAN'T BEAT THEM "INSIDE" THE LAW, YOU MUST BEAT THEM "OUTSIDE" IT-- AND THAT'S WHERE I COME IN!
FIRST, YOU GET TO SOMEPLACE WHERE YOU'LL BE SAFE FROM NORTON'S MEN! GET GOING!

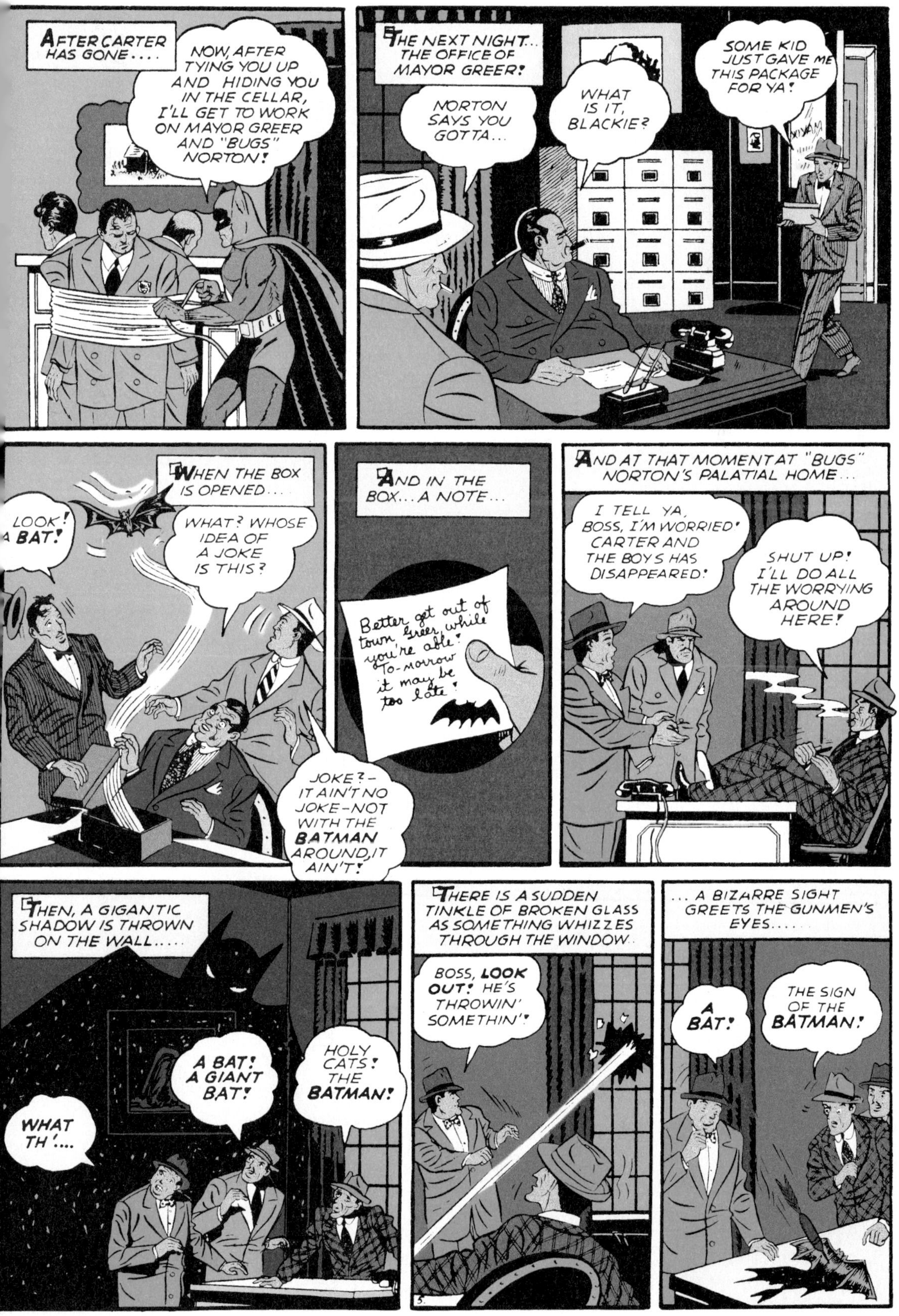
AFTER CARTER HAS GONE....
NOW, AFTER TYING YOU UP AND HIDING YOU IN THE CELLAR, I'LL GET TO WORK ON MAYOR GREER AND "BUGS" NORTON!
THE NEXT NIGHT... THE OFFICE OF MAYOR GREER!
NORTON SAYS YOU GOTTA...
WHAT IS IT, BLACKIE?
SOME KID JUST GAVE ME THIS PACKAGE FOR YA!
WHEN THE BOX IS OPENED...
LOOK! A BAT!
WHAT? WHOSE IDEA OF A JOKE IS THIS?
JOKE?- IT AIN'T NO JOKE-NOT WITH THE BATMAN AROUND, IT AIN'T!
AND IN THE BOX... A NOTE...
Better get out of town Greer while you're able! To-morrow it may be too late!
AND AT THAT MOMENT AT "BUGS" NORTON'S PALATIAL HOME...
I TELL YA, BOSS, I'M WORRIED! CARTER AND THE BOYS HAS DISAPPEARED!
SHUT UP! I'LL DO ALL THE WORRYING AROUND HERE!
THEN, A GIGANTIC SHADOW IS THROWN ON THE WALL.....
WHAT TH'....
A BAT! A GIANT BAT!
HOLY CATS! THE BATMAN!
THERE IS A SUDDEN TINKLE OF BROKEN GLASS AS SOMETHING WHIZZES THROUGH THE WINDOW.
BOSS, LOOK OUT! HE'S THROWIN' SOMETHIN'!
... A BIZARRE SIGHT GREETS THE GUNMEN'S EYES......
A BAT!
THE SIGN OF THE BATMAN!

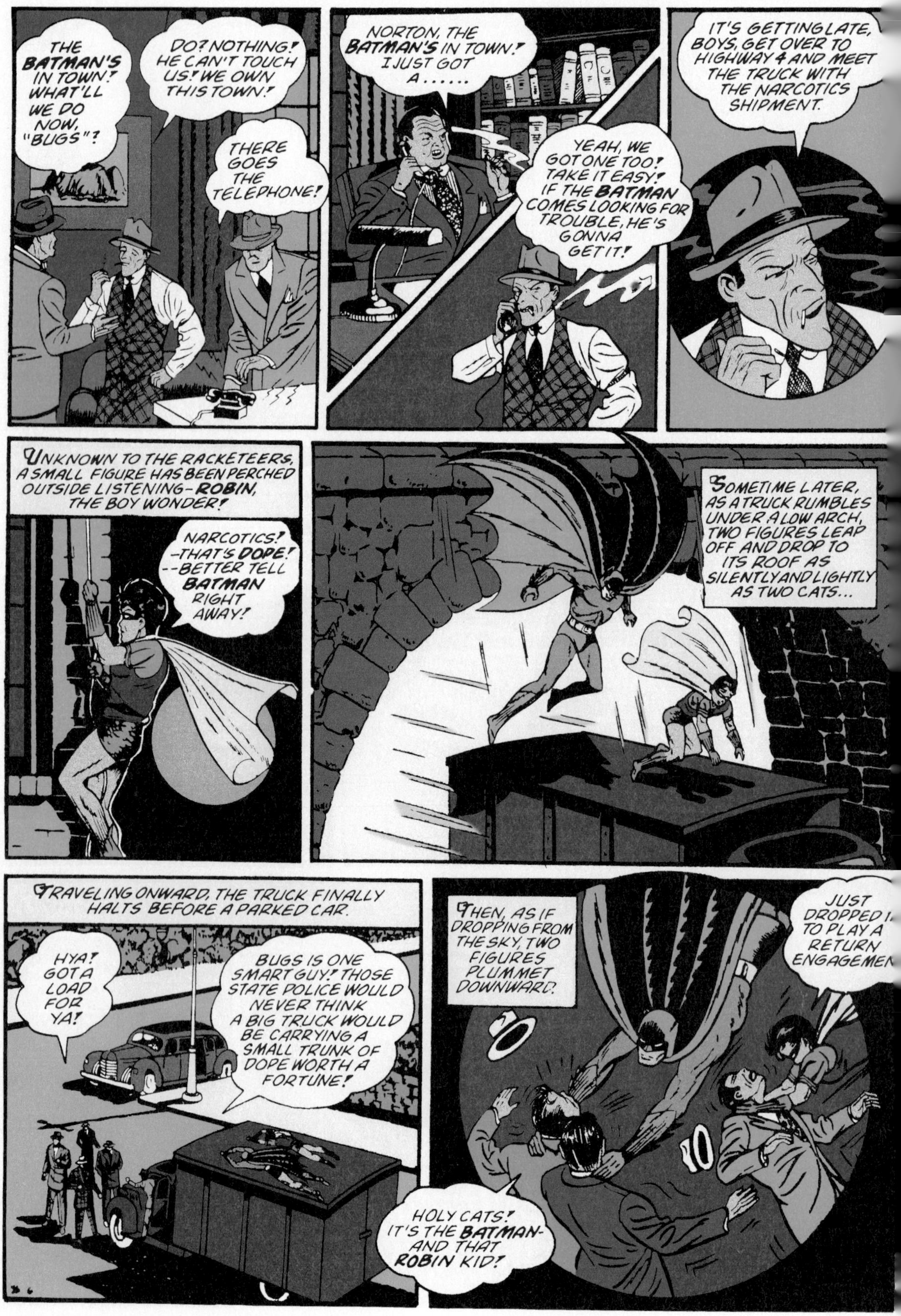
THE BATMAN'S IN TOWN! WHAT'LL WE DO NOW, "BUGS"?
DO? NOTHING! HE CAN'T TOUCH US! WE OWN THIS TOWN!
THERE GOES THE TELEPHONE!
NORTON, THE BATMAN'S IN TOWN! I JUST GOT A......
YEAH, WE GOT ONE TOO! TAKE IT EASY! IF THE BATMAN COMES LOOKING FOR TROUBLE, HE'S GONNA GET IT!
IT'S GETTING LATE, BOYS, GET OVER TO HIGHWAY 4 AND MEET THE TRUCK WITH THE NARCOTICS SHIPMENT.
UNKNOWN TO THE RACKETEERS, A SMALL FIGURE HAS BEEN PERCHED OUTSIDE LISTENING-ROBIN, THE BOY WONDER!
NARCOTICS! -THAT'S DOPE! --BETTER TELL BATMAN RIGHT AWAY!
SOMETIME LATER, AS A TRUCK RUMBLES UNDER A LOW ARCH, TWO FIGURES LEAP OFF AND DROP TO ITS ROOF AS SILENTLY AND LIGHTLY AS TWO CATS...
TRAVELING ONWARD, THE TRUCK FINALLY HALTS BEFORE A PARKED CAR.
HYA! GOT A LOAD FOR YA!
BUGS IS ONE SMART GUY! THOSE STATE POLICE WOULD NEVER THINK A BIG TRUCK WOULD BE CARRYING A SMALL TRUNK OF DOPE WORTH A FORTUNE!
THEN, AS IF DROPPING FROM THE SKY, TWO FIGURES PLUMMET DOWNWARD.
JUST DROPPED I TO PLAY A RETURN ENGAGEMEN
HOLY CATS! IT'S THE BATMAN- AND THAT ROBIN KID!

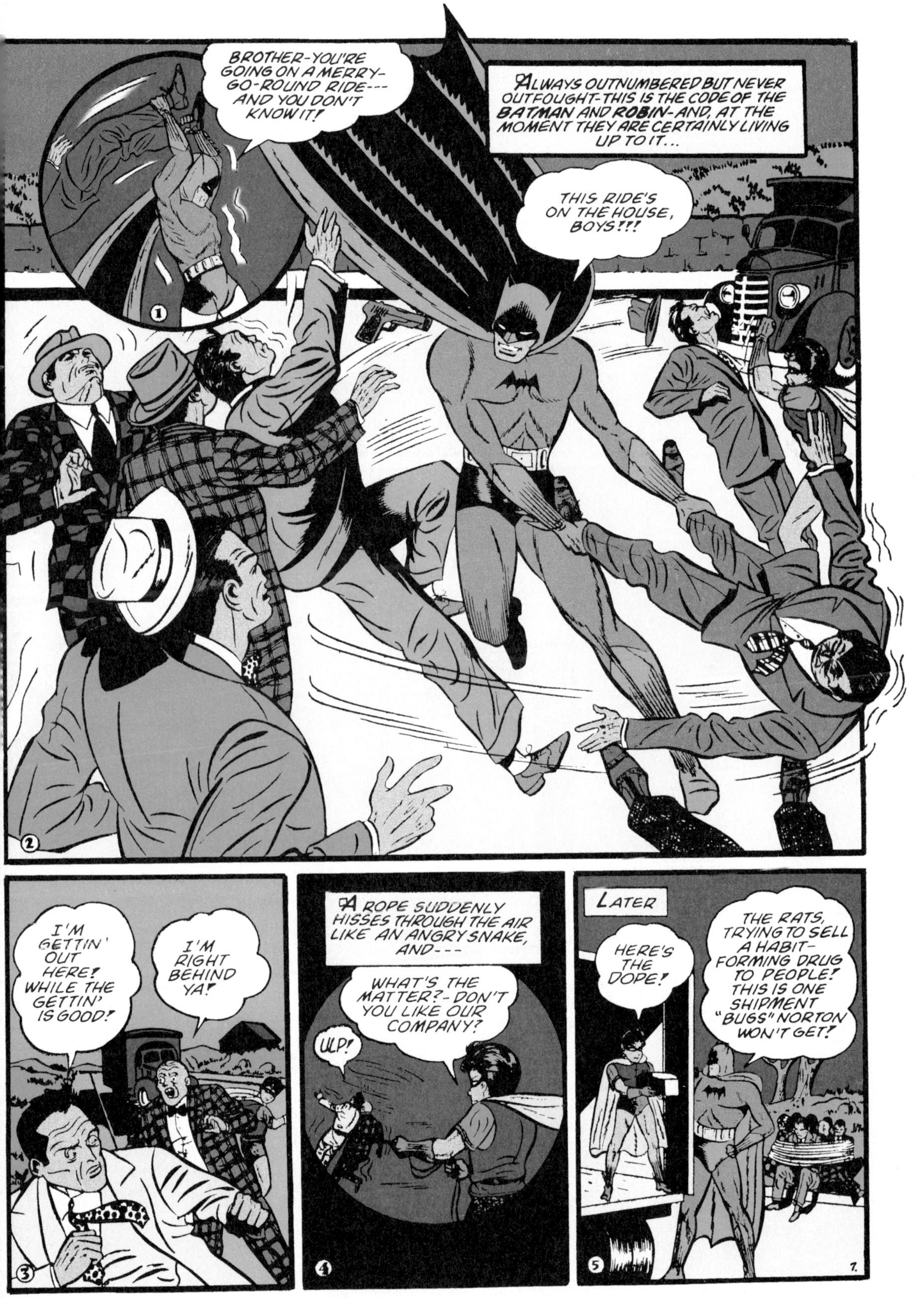
ALWAYS OUTNUMBERED BUT NEVER OUTFOUGHT-THIS IS THE CODE OF THE BATMAN AND ROBIN-AND, AT THE MOMENT THEY ARE CERTAINLY LIVING UP TO IT...
BROTHER-YOU'RE GOING ON A MERRY-GO-ROUND RIDE---AND YOU DON'T KNOW IT!
THIS RIDE'S ON THE HOUSE, BOYS?!!
I'M GETTIN' OUT HERE! WHILE THE GETTIN' IS GOOD!
I'M RIGHT BEHIND YA!
A ROPE SUDDENLY HISSES THROUGH THE AIR LIKE AN ANGRY SNAKE, AND---
WHAT'S THE MATTER?-DON'T YOU LIKE OUR COMPANY?
ULP!
LATER
HERE'S THE DOPE!
THE RATS, TRYING TO SELL A HABIT-FORMING DRUG TO PEOPLE! THIS IS ONE SHIPMENT "BUGS" NORTON WON'T GET!
7.

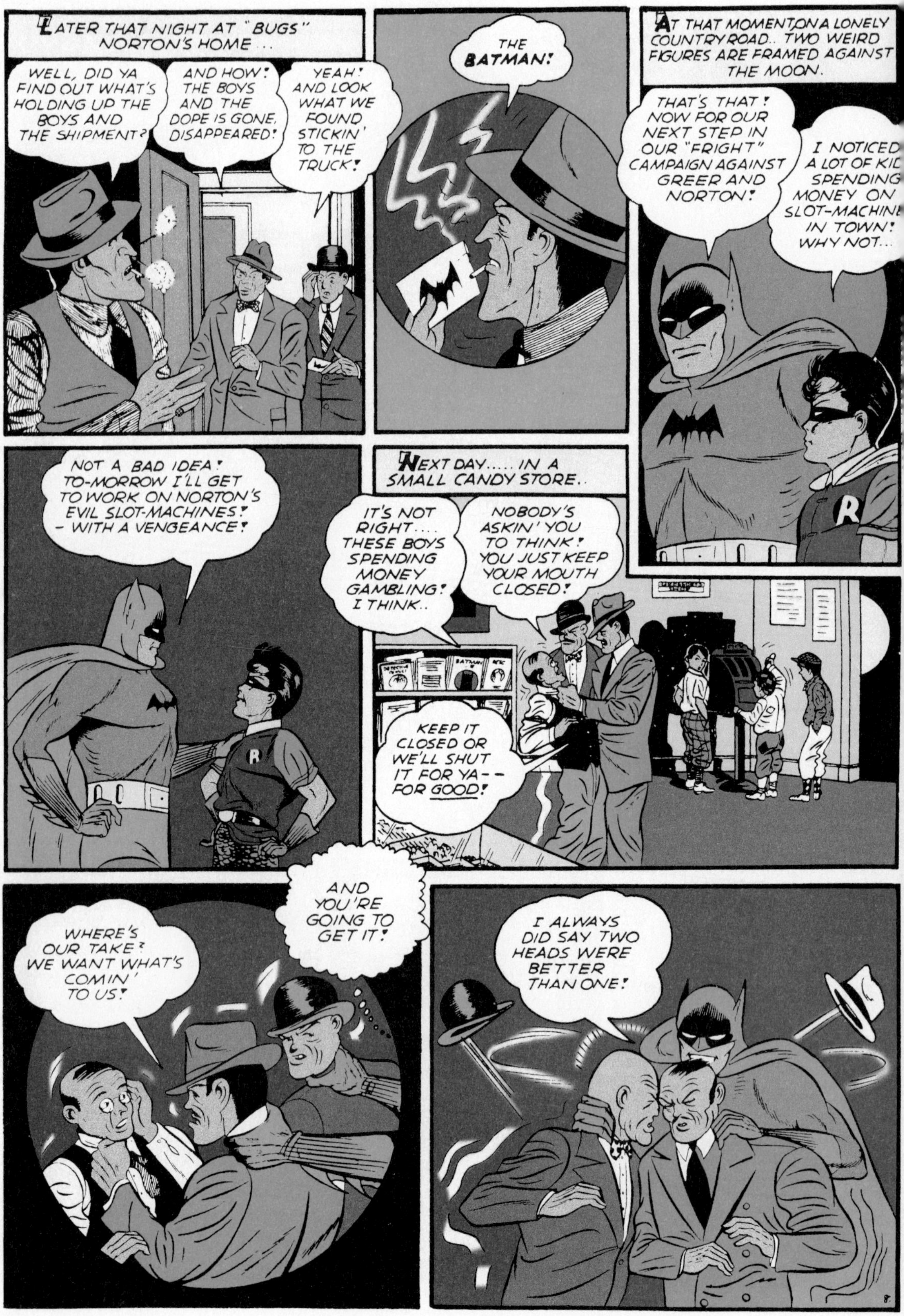
LATER THAT NIGHT AT "BUGS" NORTON'S HOME . . .
WELL, DID YA FIND OUT WHAT'S HOLDING UP THE BOYS AND THE SHIPMENT?
AND HOW! THE BOYS AND THE DOPE IS GONE. DISAPPEARED!
YEAH! AND LOOK WHAT WE FOUND STICKIN' TO THE TRUCK!
THE BATMAN!
AT THAT MOMENT, ON A LONELY COUNTRY ROAD.. TWO WEIRD FIGURES ARE FRAMED AGAINST THE MOON.
THAT'S THAT! NOW FOR OUR NEXT STEP IN OUR "FRIGHT" CAMPAIGN AGAINST GREER AND NORTON!
I NOTICED A LOT OF KID SPENDING MONEY ON SLOT-MACHINE IN TOWN! WHY NOT...
NOT A BAD IDEA! TO-MORROW I'LL GET TO WORK ON NORTON'S EVIL SLOT-MACHINES! - WITH A VENGEANCE!
NEXT DAY..... IN A SMALL CANDY STORE..
IT'S NOT RIGHT.... THESE BOYS SPENDING MONEY GAMBLING! I THINK..
NOBODY'S ASKIN' YOU TO THINK! YOU JUST KEEP YOUR MOUTH CLOSED!
KEEP IT CLOSED OR WE'LL SHUT IT FOR YA-- FOR GOOD!
WHERE'S OUR TAKE? WE WANT WHAT'S COMIN' TO US!
AND YOU'RE GOING TO GET IT!
I ALWAYS DID SAY TWO HEADS WERE BETTER THAN ONE!

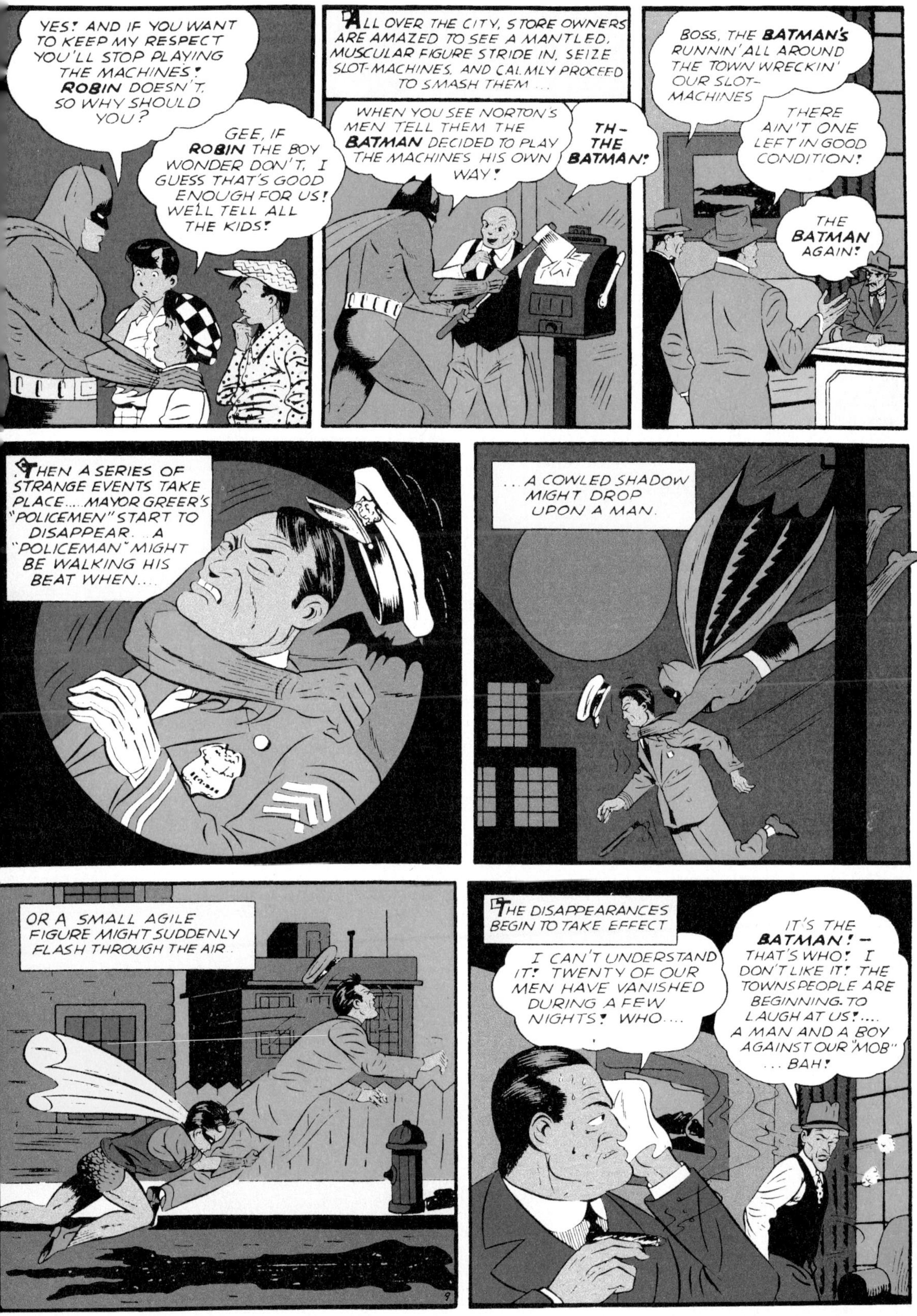
YES! AND IF YOU WANT TO KEEP MY RESPECT YOU'LL STOP PLAYING THE MACHINES! ROBIN DOESN'T, SO WHY SHOULD YOU?
GEE, IF ROBIN THE BOY WONDER DON'T, I GUESS THAT'S GOOD ENOUGH FOR US! WE'LL TELL ALL THE KIDS!
ALL OVER THE CITY, STORE OWNERS ARE AMAZED TO SEE A MANTLED, MUSCULAR FIGURE STRIDE IN, SEIZE SLOT-MACHINES, AND CALMLY PROCEED TO SMASH THEM ...
WHEN YOU SEE NORTON'S MEN TELL THEM THE BATMAN DECIDED TO PLAY THE MACHINES HIS OWN WAY!
TH-THE BATMAN!
BOSS, THE BATMAN'S RUNNIN' ALL AROUND THE TOWN WRECKIN' OUR SLOT-MACHINES
THERE AIN'T ONE LEFT IN GOOD CONDITION!
THE BATMAN AGAIN!
THEN A SERIES OF STRANGE EVENTS TAKE PLACE.... MAYOR GREER'S "POLICEMEN" START TO DISAPPEAR... A "POLICEMAN" MIGHT BE WALKING HIS BEAT WHEN....
... A COWLED SHADOW MIGHT DROP UPON A MAN.
OR A SMALL AGILE FIGURE MIGHT SUDDENLY FLASH THROUGH THE AIR..
THE DISAPPEARANCES BEGIN TO TAKE EFFECT
I CAN'T UNDERSTAND IT! TWENTY OF OUR MEN HAVE VANISHED DURING A FEW NIGHTS! WHO....
IT'S THE BATMAN! — THAT'S WHO! I DON'T LIKE IT! THE TOWNSPEOPLE ARE BEGINNING TO LAUGH AT US!.... A MAN AND A BOY AGAINST OUR "MOB" ... BAH!

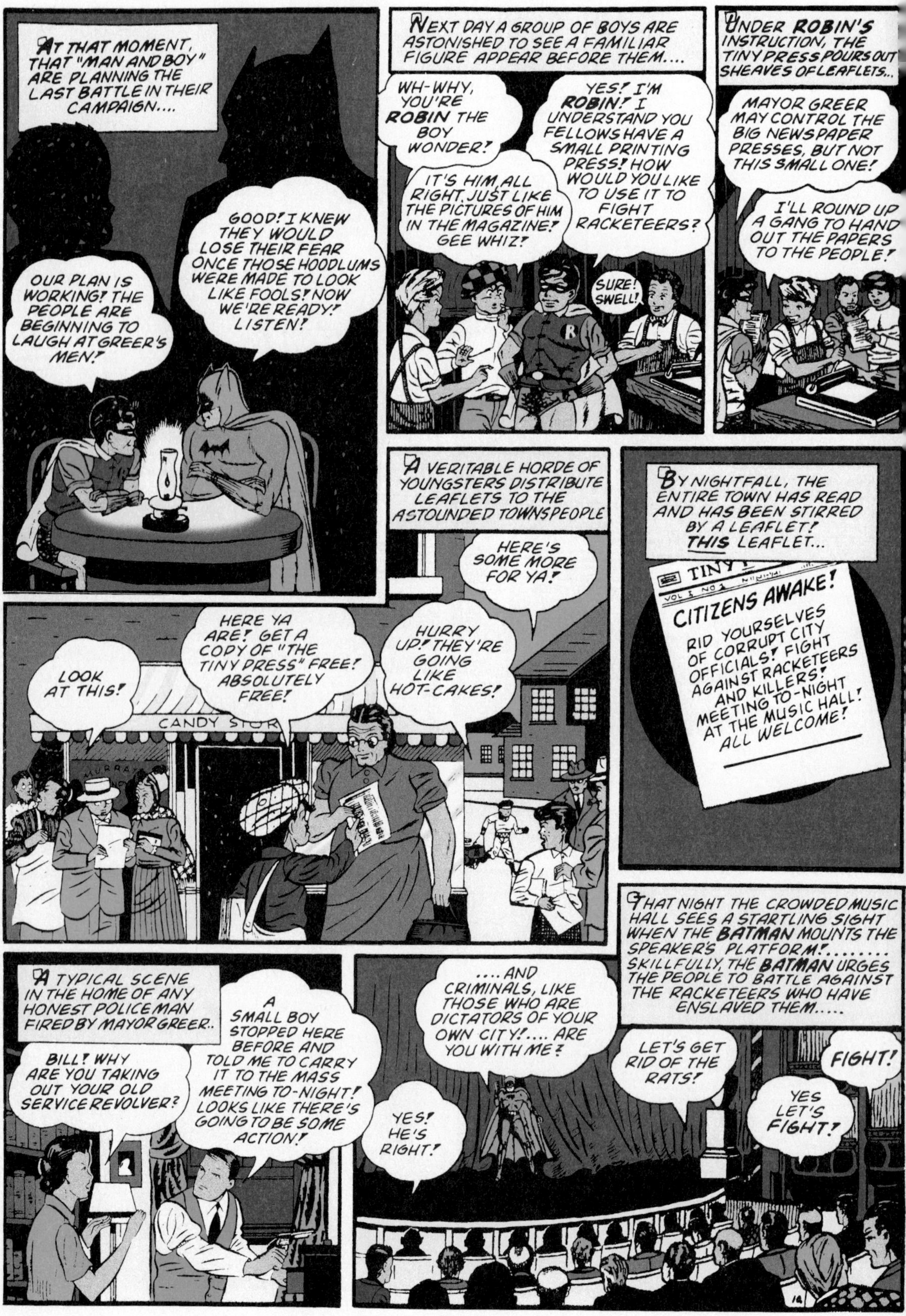
AT THAT MOMENT, THAT "MAN AND BOY" ARE PLANNING THE LAST BATTLE IN THEIR CAMPAIGN....
OUR PLAN IS WORKING! THE PEOPLE ARE BEGINNING TO LAUGH AT GREER'S MEN!
GOOD! I KNEW THEY WOULD LOSE THEIR FEAR ONCE THOSE HOODLUMS WERE MADE TO LOOK LIKE FOOLS! NOW WE'RE READY! LISTEN!
NEXT DAY A GROUP OF BOYS ARE ASTONISHED TO SEE A FAMILIAR FIGURE APPEAR BEFORE THEM....
WH-WHY, YOU'RE ROBIN THE BOY WONDER!
IT'S HIM, ALL RIGHT, JUST LIKE THE PICTURES OF HIM IN THE MAGAZINE! GEE WHIZ!
YES! I'M ROBIN! I UNDERSTAND YOU FELLOWS HAVE A SMALL PRINTING PRESS! HOW WOULD YOU LIKE TO USE IT TO FIGHT RACKETEERS?
SURE! SWELL!
UNDER ROBIN'S INSTRUCTION, THE TINY PRESS POURS OUT SHEAVES OF LEAFLETS...
MAYOR GREER MAY CONTROL THE BIG NEWSPAPER PRESSES, BUT NOT THIS SMALL ONE!
I'LL ROUND UP A GANG TO HAND OUT THE PAPERS TO THE PEOPLE!
A VERITABLE HORDE OF YOUNGSTERS DISTRIBUTE LEAFLETS TO THE ASTOUNDED TOWNSPEOPLE
LOOK AT THIS!
HERE YA ARE! GET A COPY OF "THE TINY PRESS" FREE! ABSOLUTELY FREE!
HURRY UP! THEY'RE GOING LIKE HOT-CAKES!
HERE'S SOME MORE FOR YA!
CANDY STOR
BY NIGHTFALL, THE ENTIRE TOWN HAS READ AND HAS BEEN STIRRED BY A LEAFLET! THIS LEAFLET...
TINY
VOL 1 NO 1
CITIZENS AWAKE!
RID YOURSELVES OF CORRUPT CITY OFFICIALS! FIGHT AGAINST RACKETEERS AND KILLERS! MEETING TO-NIGHT AT THE MUSIC HALL! ALL WELCOME!
A TYPICAL SCENE IN THE HOME OF ANY HONEST POLICEMAN FIRED BY MAYOR GREER..
BILL! WHY ARE YOU TAKING OUT YOUR OLD SERVICE REVOLVER?
A SMALL BOY STOPPED HERE BEFORE AND TOLD ME TO CARRY IT TO THE MASS MEETING TO-NIGHT! LOOKS LIKE THERE'S GOING TO BE SOME ACTION!
THAT NIGHT THE CROWDED MUSIC HALL SEES A STARTLING SIGHT WHEN THE BATMAN MOUNTS THE SPEAKER'S PLATFORM!........ SKILLFULLY, THE BATMAN URGES THE PEOPLE TO BATTLE AGAINST THE RACKETEERS WHO HAVE ENSLAVED THEM.....
....AND CRIMINALS, LIKE THOSE WHO ARE DICTATORS OF YOUR OWN CITY!.... ARE YOU WITH ME?
YES! HE'S RIGHT!
LET'S GET RID OF THE RATS!
FIGHT!
YES LET'S FIGHT!

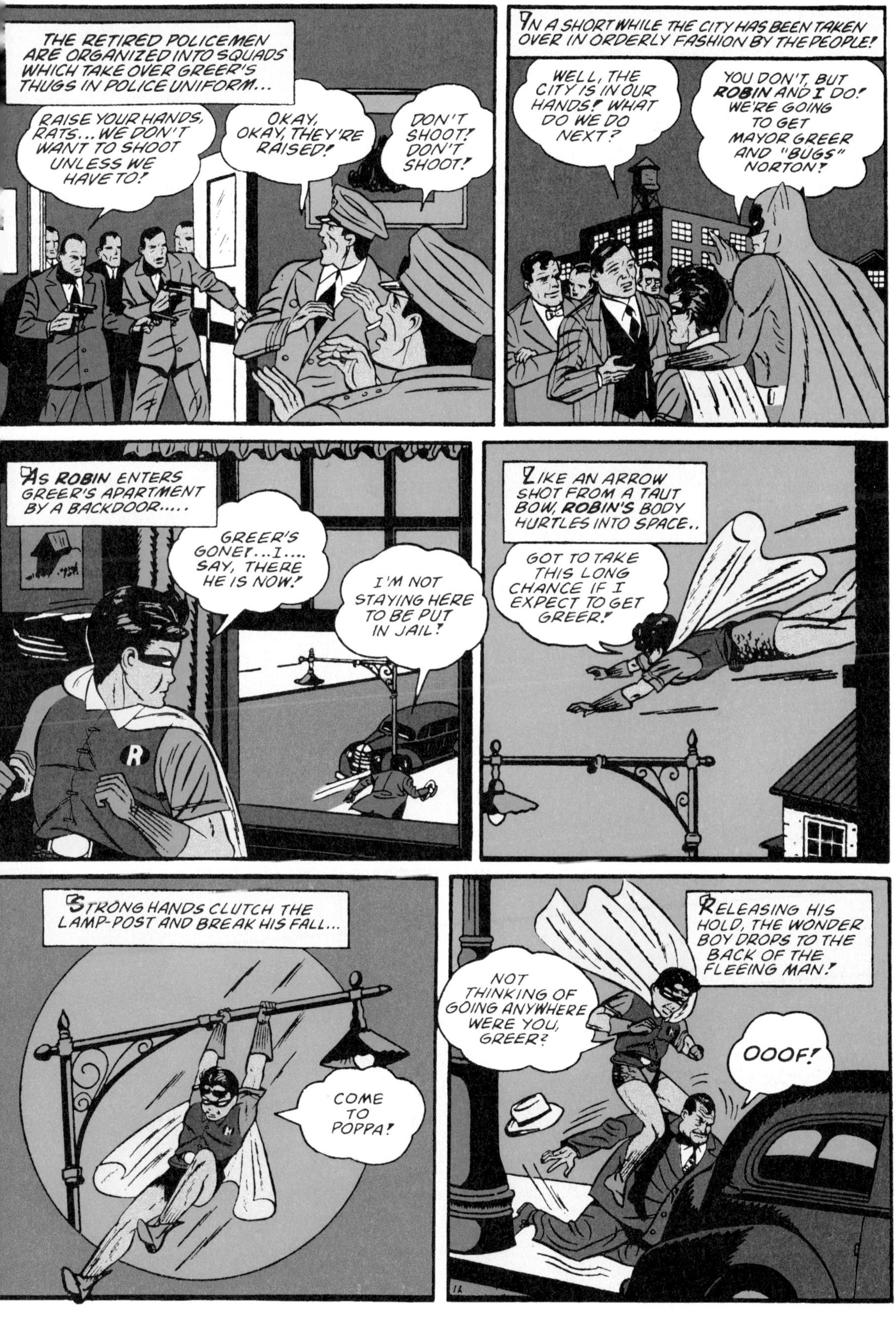
THE RETIRED POLICEMEN ARE ORGANIZED INTO SQUADS WHICH TAKE OVER GREER'S THUGS IN POLICE UNIFORM...
RAISE YOUR HANDS, RATS... WE DON'T WANT TO SHOOT UNLESS WE HAVE TO!
OKAY, OKAY, THEY'RE RAISED!
DON'T SHOOT! DON'T SHOOT!
IN A SHORT WHILE THE CITY HAS BEEN TAKEN OVER IN ORDERLY FASHION BY THE PEOPLE!
WELL, THE CITY IS IN OUR HANDS! WHAT DO WE DO NEXT?
YOU DON'T, BUT ROBIN AND I DO! WE'RE GOING TO GET MAYOR GREER AND "BUGS" NORTON!
AS ROBIN ENTERS GREER'S APARTMENT BY A BACKDOOR.....
GREER'S GONE!...I.... SAY, THERE HE IS NOW!
I'M NOT STAYING HERE TO BE PUT IN JAIL!
LIKE AN ARROW SHOT FROM A TAUT BOW, ROBIN'S BODY HURTLES INTO SPACE..
GOT TO TAKE THIS LONG CHANCE IF I EXPECT TO GET GREER!
STRONG HANDS CLUTCH THE LAMP-POST AND BREAK HIS FALL...
COME TO POPPA!
RELEASING HIS HOLD, THE WONDER BOY DROPS TO THE BACK OF THE FLEEING MAN!
NOT THINKING OF GOING ANYWHERE WERE YOU, GREER?
OOOF!

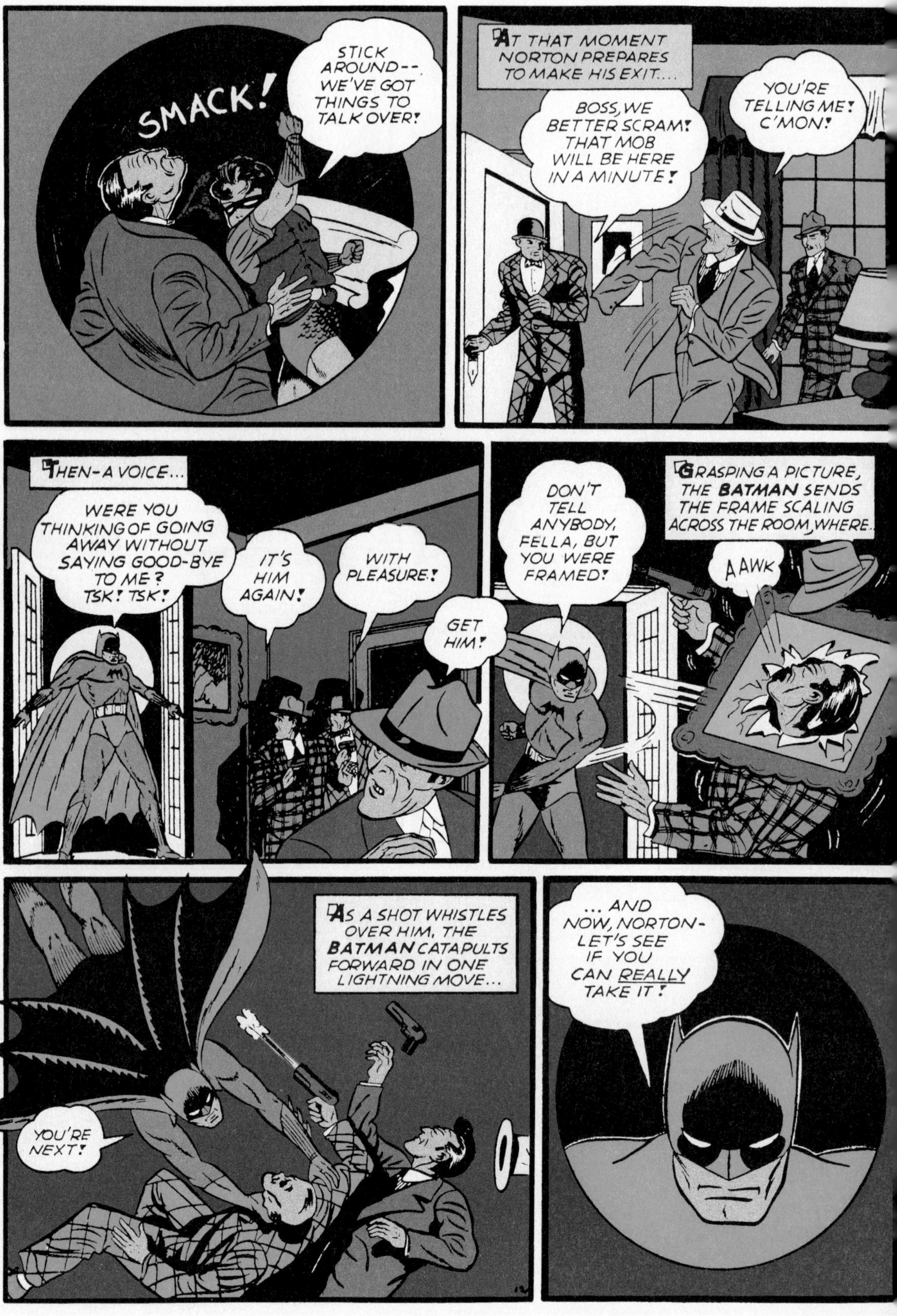
SMACK!
STICK AROUND-- WE'VE GOT THINGS TO TALK OVER!
AT THAT MOMENT NORTON PREPARES TO MAKE HIS EXIT....
BOSS, WE BETTER SCRAM! THAT MOB WILL BE HERE IN A MINUTE!
YOU'RE TELLING ME! C'MON!
THEN-A VOICE...
WERE YOU THINKING OF GOING AWAY WITHOUT SAYING GOOD-BYE TO ME? TSK! TSK!
IT'S HIM AGAIN!
WITH PLEASURE!
GET HIM!
DON'T TELL ANYBODY, FELLA, BUT YOU WERE FRAMED!
GRASPING A PICTURE, THE BATMAN SENDS THE FRAME SCALING ACROSS THE ROOM, WHERE...
AAWK
AS A SHOT WHISTLES OVER HIM, THE BATMAN CATAPULTS FORWARD IN ONE LIGHTNING MOVE...
YOU'RE NEXT!
... AND NOW, NORTON- LET'S SEE IF YOU CAN REALLY TAKE IT!

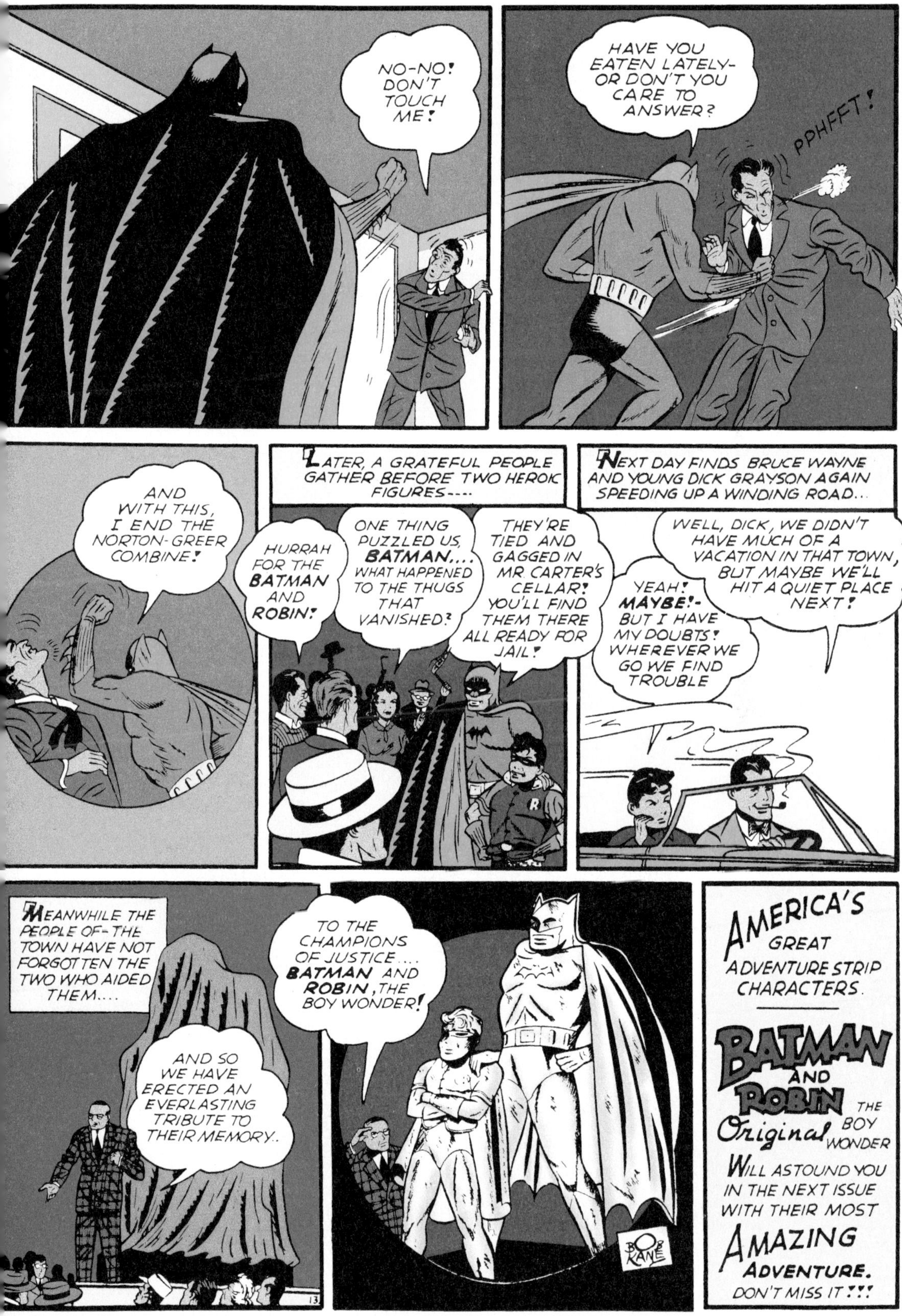
NO-NO! DON'T TOUCH ME!
HAVE YOU EATEN LATELY- OR DON'T YOU CARE TO ANSWER?
PPHFFT!
AND WITH THIS, I END THE NORTON-GREER COMBINE!
LATER, A GRATEFUL PEOPLE GATHER BEFORE TWO HEROIC FIGURES----
HURRAH FOR THE BATMAN AND ROBIN!
ONE THING PUZZLED US, BATMAN,... WHAT HAPPENED TO THE THUGS THAT VANISHED?
THEY'RE TIED AND GAGGED IN MR. CARTER'S CELLAR! YOU'LL FIND THEM THERE ALL READY FOR JAIL!
NEXT DAY FINDS BRUCE WAYNE AND YOUNG DICK GRAYSON AGAIN SPEEDING UP A WINDING ROAD...
WELL, DICK, WE DIDN'T HAVE MUCH OF A VACATION IN THAT TOWN, BUT MAYBE WE'LL HIT A QUIET PLACE NEXT!
YEAH! MAYBE!- BUT I HAVE MY DOUBTS! WHEREVER WE GO WE FIND TROUBLE
MEANWHILE THE PEOPLE OF THE TOWN HAVE NOT FORGOTTEN THE TWO WHO AIDED THEM....
AND SO WE HAVE ERECTED AN EVERLASTING TRIBUTE TO THEIR MEMORY..
13
TO THE CHAMPIONS OF JUSTICE.... BATMAN AND ROBIN, THE BOY WONDER!
BOB KANE
AMERICA'S GREAT ADVENTURE STRIP CHARACTERS.
BATMAN AND ROBIN THE BOY WONDER
Original
WILL ASTOUND YOU IN THE NEXT ISSUE WITH THEIR MOST AMAZING ADVENTURE.
DON'T MISS IT!!!

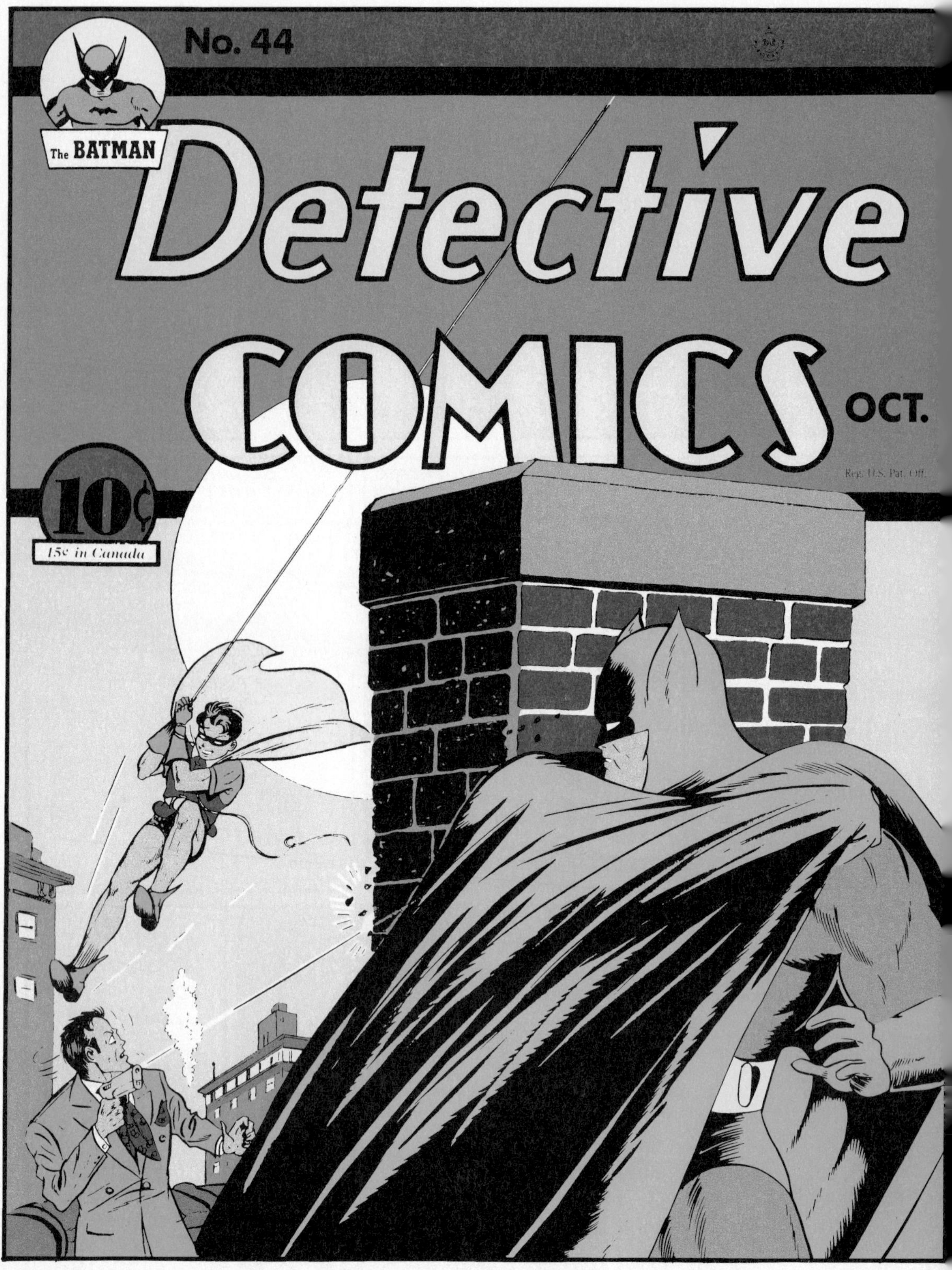
No. 44
The BATMAN
Detective Comics
OCT.
Reg. U.S. Pat. Off.
10¢
15¢ in Canada

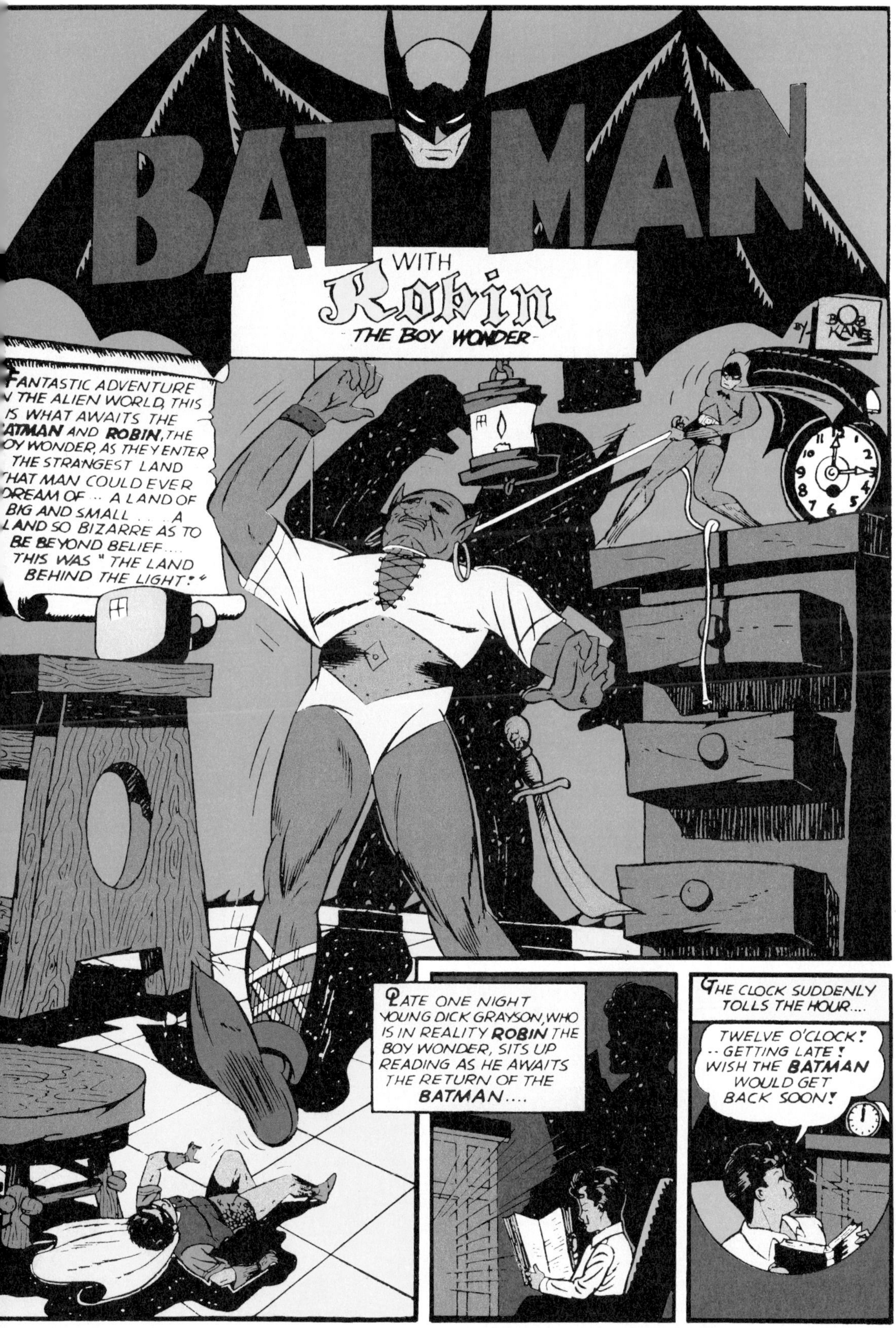
BATMAN
WITH
Robin
-THE BOY WONDER-
BY BOB KANE
FANTASTIC ADVENTURE
N THE ALIEN WORLD, THIS
IS WHAT AWAITS THE
ATMAN AND ROBIN, THE
OY WONDER, AS THEY ENTER
THE STRANGEST LAND
THAT MAN COULD EVER
DREAM OF ... A LAND OF
BIG AND SMALL ... A
LAND SO BIZARRE AS TO
BE BEYOND BELIEF....
THIS WAS "THE LAND
BEHIND THE LIGHT!"
LATE ONE NIGHT YOUNG DICK GRAYSON, WHO IS IN REALITY ROBIN THE BOY WONDER, SITS UP READING AS HE AWAITS THE RETURN OF THE BATMAN....
THE CLOCK SUDDENLY TOLLS THE HOUR....
TWELVE O'CLOCK! -- GETTING LATE! WISH THE BATMAN WOULD GET BACK SOON!

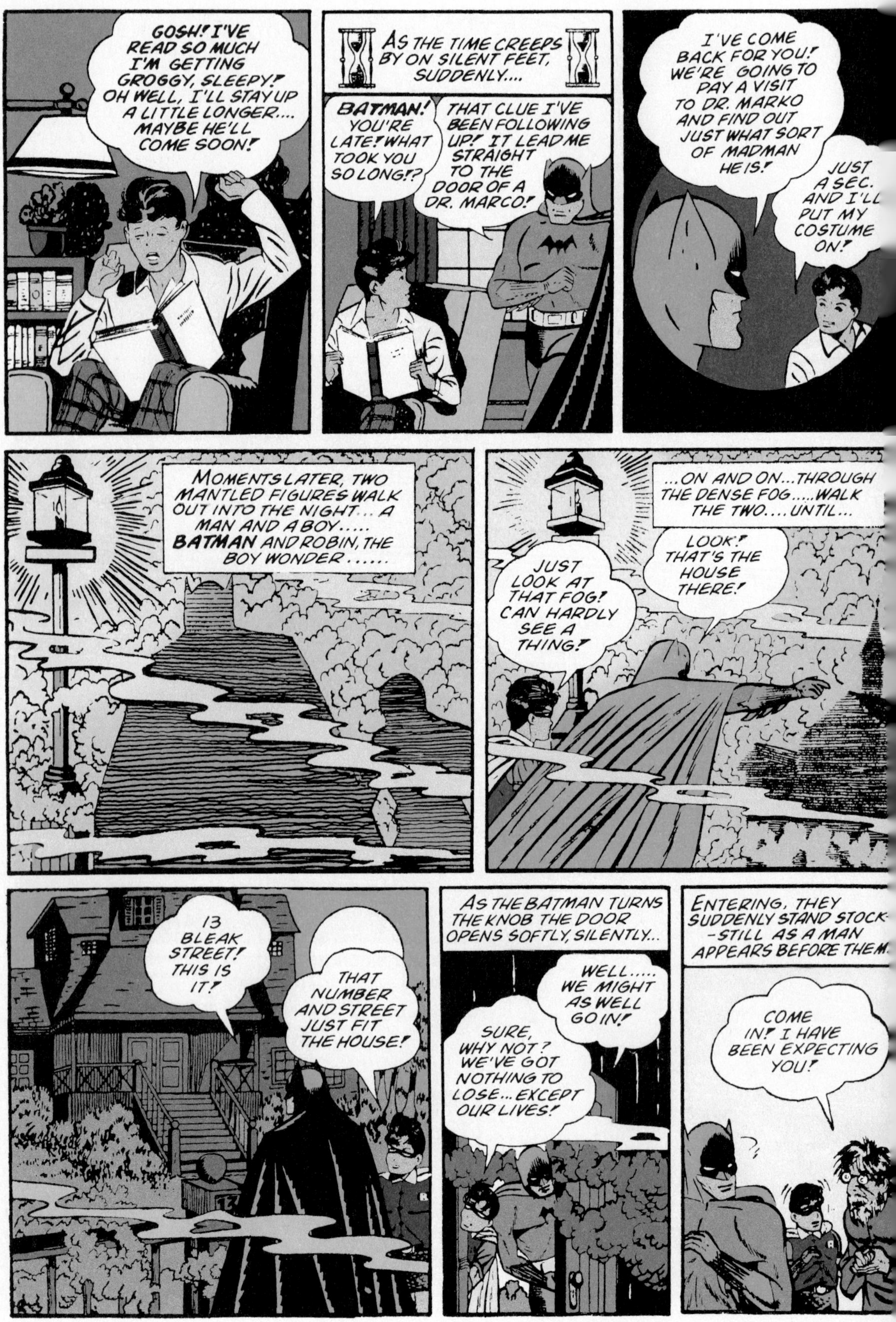
GOSH! I'VE READ SO MUCH I'M GETTING GROGGY, SLEEPY! OH WELL, I'LL STAY UP A LITTLE LONGER.... MAYBE HE'LL COME SOON!
AS THE TIME CREEPS BY ON SILENT FEET, SUDDENLY....
BATMAN! YOU'RE LATE! WHAT TOOK YOU SO LONG!?
THAT CLUE I'VE BEEN FOLLOWING UP! IT LEAD ME STRAIGHT TO THE DOOR OF A DR. MARCO!
I'VE COME BACK FOR YOU! WE'RE GOING TO PAY A VISIT TO DR. MARKO AND FIND OUT JUST WHAT SORT OF MADMAN HE IS!
JUST A SEC. AND I'LL PUT MY COSTUME ON!
MOMENTS LATER, TWO MANTLED FIGURES WALK OUT INTO THE NIGHT... A MAN AND A BOY..... BATMAN AND ROBIN, THE BOY WONDER......
...ON AND ON...THROUGH THE DENSE FOG.....WALK THE TWO....UNTIL...
JUST LOOK AT THAT FOG! CAN HARDLY SEE A THING!
LOOK! THAT'S THE HOUSE THERE!
13 BLEAK STREET! THIS IS IT!
THAT NUMBER AND STREET JUST FIT THE HOUSE!
AS THE BATMAN TURNS THE KNOB THE DOOR OPENS SOFTLY, SILENTLY...
WELL..... WE MIGHT AS WELL GO IN!
SURE, WHY NOT? WE'VE GOT NOTHING TO LOSE... EXCEPT OUR LIVES!
ENTERING, THEY SUDDENLY STAND STOCK-STILL AS A MAN APPEARS BEFORE THEM.
COME IN! I HAVE BEEN EXPECTING YOU!

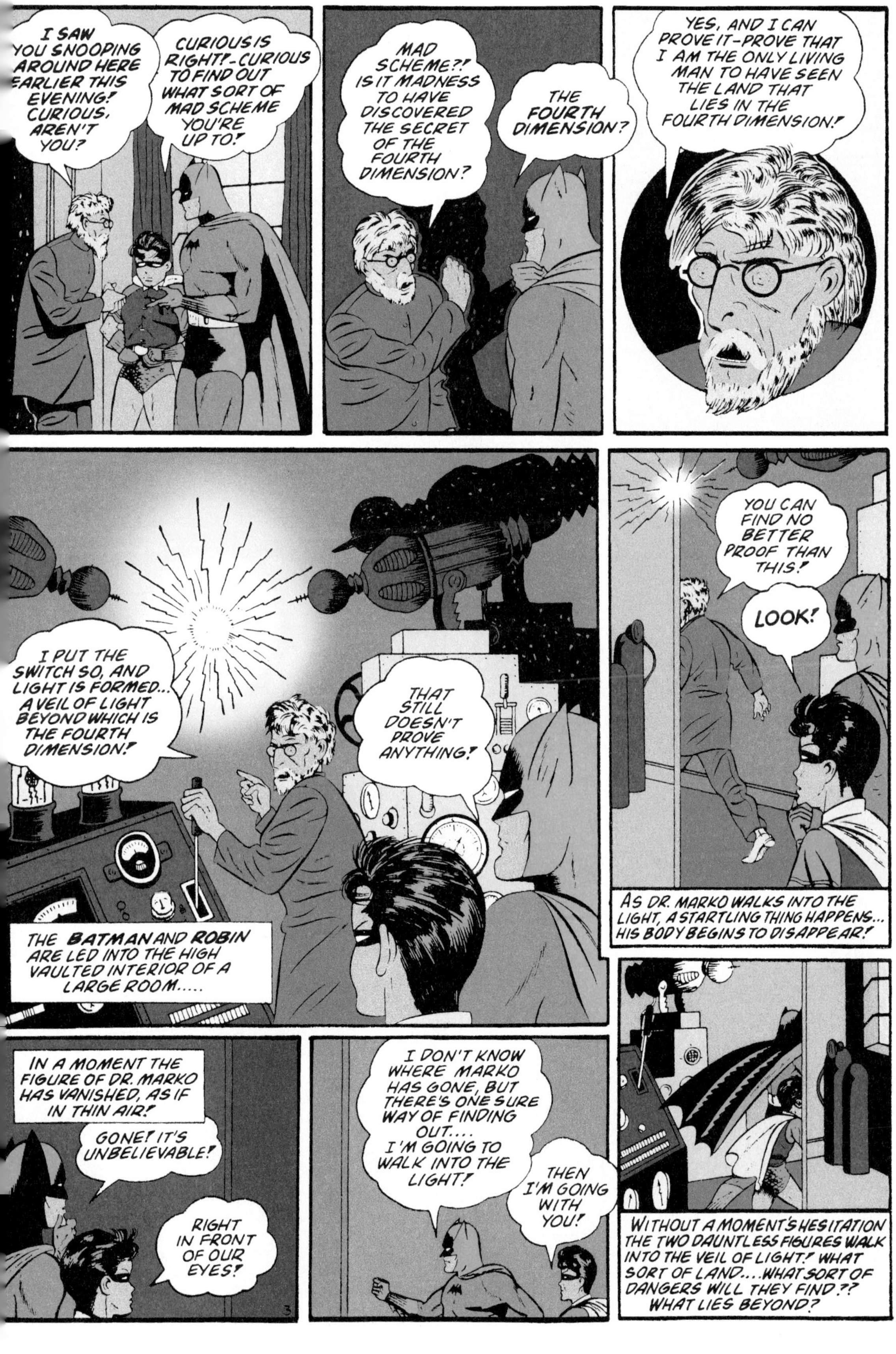
I SAW YOU SNOOPING AROUND HERE EARLIER THIS EVENING! CURIOUS, AREN'T YOU?
CURIOUS IS RIGHT! - CURIOUS TO FIND OUT WHAT SORT OF MAD SCHEME YOU'RE UP TO!
MAD SCHEME?! IS IT MADNESS TO HAVE DISCOVERED THE SECRET OF THE FOURTH DIMENSION?
THE FOURTH DIMENSION?
YES, AND I CAN PROVE IT - PROVE THAT I AM THE ONLY LIVING MAN TO HAVE SEEN THE LAND THAT LIES IN THE FOURTH DIMENSION!
THE BATMAN AND ROBIN ARE LED INTO THE HIGH VAULTED INTERIOR OF A LARGE ROOM.....
I PUT THE SWITCH SO, AND LIGHT IS FORMED... A VEIL OF LIGHT BEYOND WHICH IS THE FOURTH DIMENSION!
THAT STILL DOESN'T PROVE ANYTHING!
YOU CAN FIND NO BETTER PROOF THAN THIS!
LOOK!
AS DR. MARKO WALKS INTO THE LIGHT, A STARTLING THING HAPPENS... HIS BODY BEGINS TO DISAPPEAR!
IN A MOMENT THE FIGURE OF DR. MARKO HAS VANISHED, AS IF IN THIN AIR!
GONE! IT'S UNBELIEVABLE!
RIGHT IN FRONT OF OUR EYES!
3
I DON'T KNOW WHERE MARKO HAS GONE, BUT THERE'S ONE SURE WAY OF FINDING OUT.... I'M GOING TO WALK INTO THE LIGHT!
THEN I'M GOING WITH YOU!
WITHOUT A MOMENT'S HESITATION THE TWO DAUNTLESS FIGURES WALK INTO THE VEIL OF LIGHT! WHAT SORT OF LAND... WHAT SORT OF DANGERS WILL THEY FIND?? WHAT LIES BEYOND?

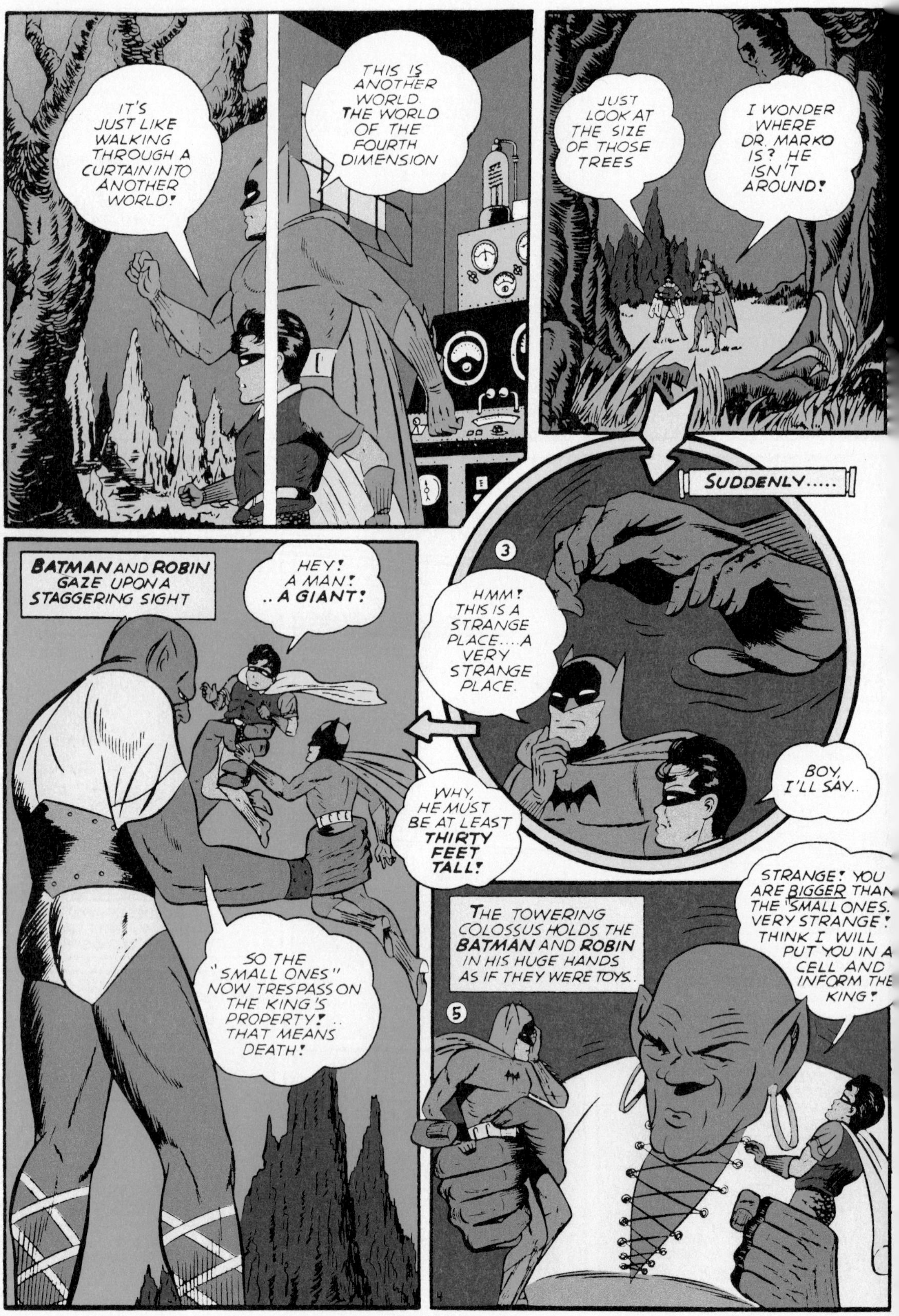
IT'S JUST LIKE WALKING THROUGH A CURTAIN INTO ANOTHER WORLD!
THIS IS ANOTHER WORLD. THE WORLD OF THE FOURTH DIMENSION
JUST LOOK AT THE SIZE OF THOSE TREES
I WONDER WHERE DR. MARKO IS? HE ISN'T AROUND!
SUDDENLY.....
3
HMM! THIS IS A STRANGE PLACE....A VERY STRANGE PLACE.
BOY, I'LL SAY..
BATMAN AND ROBIN GAZE UPON A STAGGERING SIGHT
HEY! A MAN! ..A GIANT!
WHY, HE MUST BE AT LEAST THIRTY FEET TALL!
SO THE "SMALL ONES" NOW TRESPASS ON THE KING'S PROPERTY! .. THAT MEANS DEATH!
THE TOWERING COLOSSUS HOLDS THE BATMAN AND ROBIN IN HIS HUGE HANDS AS IF THEY WERE TOYS.
5
STRANGE! YOU ARE BIGGER THAN THE "SMALL ONES. VERY STRANGE! THINK I WILL PUT YOU IN A CELL AND INFORM THE KING!

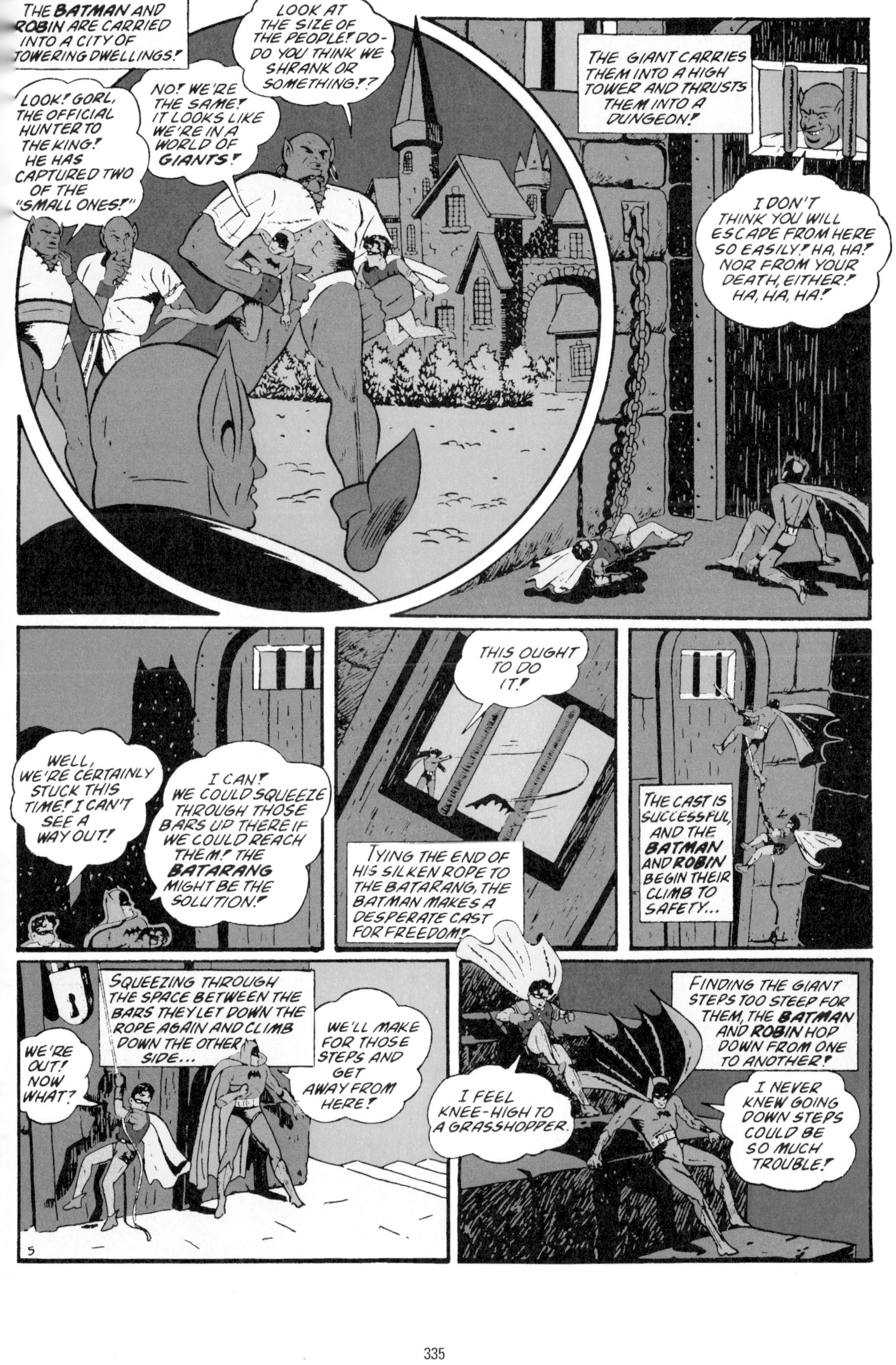
THE BATMAN AND ROBIN ARE CARRIED INTO A CITY OF TOWERING DWELLINGS!
LOOK! GORL, THE OFFICIAL HUNTER TO THE KING! HE HAS CAPTURED TWO OF THE "SMALL ONES!"
NO! WE'RE THE SAME! IT LOOKS LIKE WE'RE IN A WORLD OF GIANTS!
LOOK AT THE SIZE OF THE PEOPLE! DO-DO YOU THINK WE SHRANK OR SOMETHING!?
THE GIANT CARRIES THEM INTO A HIGH TOWER AND THRUSTS THEM INTO A DUNGEON!
I DON'T THINK YOU WILL ESCAPE FROM HERE SO EASILY! HA, HA! NOR FROM YOUR DEATH, EITHER! HA, HA, HA!
WELL, WE'RE CERTAINLY STUCK THIS TIME! I CAN'T SEE A WAY OUT!
I CAN! WE COULD SQUEEZE THROUGH THOSE BARS UP THERE IF WE COULD REACH THEM! THE BATARANG MIGHT BE THE SOLUTION!
THIS OUGHT TO DO IT!
TYING THE END OF HIS SILKEN ROPE TO THE BATARANG, THE BATMAN MAKES A DESPERATE CAST FOR FREEDOM!
THE CAST IS SUCCESSFUL, AND THE BATMAN AND ROBIN BEGIN THEIR CLIMB TO SAFETY...
SQUEEZING THROUGH THE SPACE BETWEEN THE BARS THEY LET DOWN THE ROPE AGAIN AND CLIMB DOWN THE OTHER SIDE...
WE'RE OUT! NOW WHAT?
WE'LL MAKE FOR THOSE STEPS AND GET AWAY FROM HERE!
5
FINDING THE GIANT STEPS TOO STEEP FOR THEM, THE BATMAN AND ROBIN HOP DOWN FROM ONE TO ANOTHER!
I FEEL KNEE-HIGH TO A GRASSHOPPER.
I NEVER KNEW GOING DOWN STEPS COULD BE SO MUCH TROUBLE!

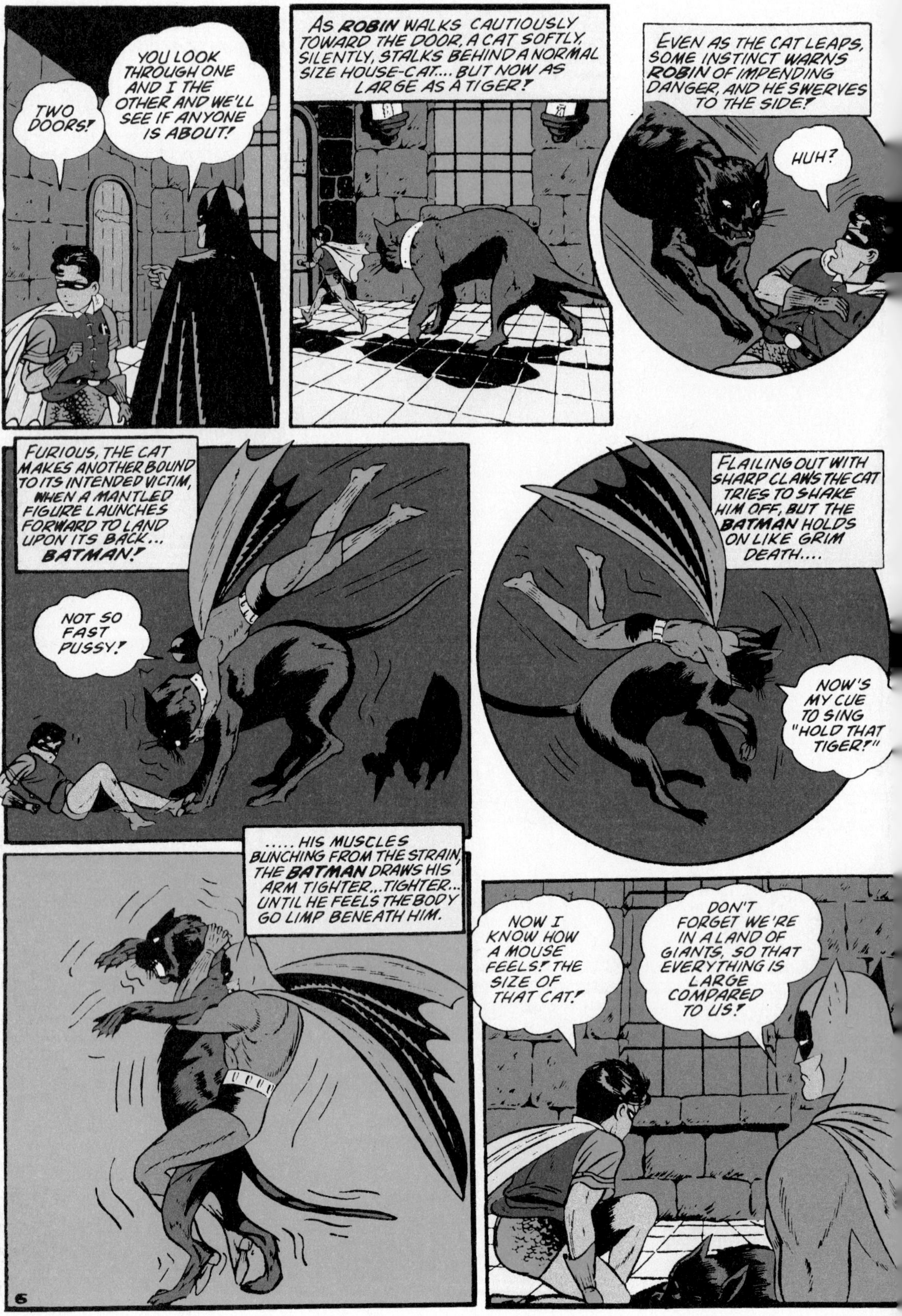

TWO DOORS!
YOU LOOK THROUGH ONE AND I THE OTHER AND WE'LL SEE IF ANYONE IS ABOUT!
AS ROBIN WALKS CAUTIOUSLY TOWARD THE DOOR, A CAT SOFTLY, SILENTLY, STALKS BEHIND A NORMAL SIZE HOUSE-CAT... BUT NOW AS LARGE AS A TIGER!
EVEN AS THE CAT LEAPS, SOME INSTINCT WARNS ROBIN OF IMPENDING DANGER, AND HE SWERVES TO THE SIDE!
HUH?
FURIOUS, THE CAT MAKES ANOTHER BOUND TO ITS INTENDED VICTIM, WHEN A MANTLED FIGURE LAUNCHES FORWARD TO LAND UPON ITS BACK... BATMAN!
NOT SO FAST PUSSY!
FLAILING OUT WITH SHARP CLAWS THE CAT TRIES TO SHAKE HIM OFF, BUT THE BATMAN HOLDS ON LIKE GRIM DEATH....
NOW'S MY CUE TO SING "HOLD THAT TIGER!"
..... HIS MUSCLES BUNCHING FROM THE STRAIN, THE BATMAN DRAWS HIS ARM TIGHTER... TIGHTER... UNTIL HE FEELS THE BODY GO LIMP BENEATH HIM.
6
NOW I KNOW HOW A MOUSE FEELS! THE SIZE OF THAT CAT!
DON'T FORGET WE'RE IN A LAND OF GIANTS, SO THAT EVERYTHING IS LARGE COMPARED TO US!

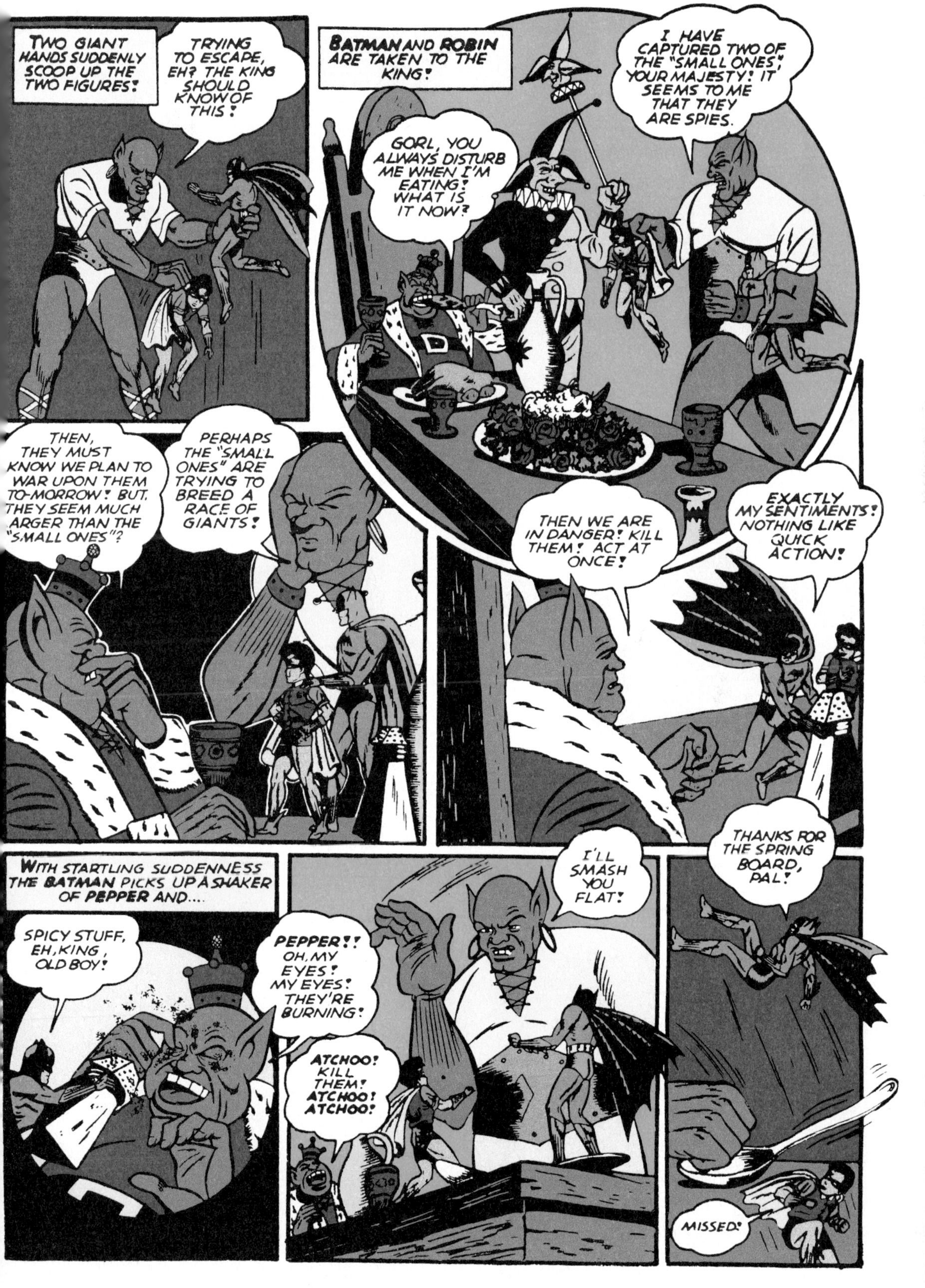
TWO GIANT HANDS SUDDENLY SCOOP UP THE TWO FIGURES!
TRYING TO ESCAPE, EH? THE KING SHOULD KNOW OF THIS!
BATMAN AND ROBIN ARE TAKEN TO THE KING!
I HAVE CAPTURED TWO OF THE "SMALL ONES," YOUR MAJESTY! IT SEEMS TO ME THAT THEY ARE SPIES.
GORL, YOU ALWAYS DISTURB ME WHEN I'M EATING! WHAT IS IT NOW?
THEN, THEY MUST KNOW WE PLAN TO WAR UPON THEM TO-MORROW! BUT, THEY SEEM MUCH ARGER THAN THE "SMALL ONES"?
PERHAPS THE "SMALL ONES" ARE TRYING TO BREED A RACE OF GIANTS!
THEN WE ARE IN DANGER! KILL THEM! ACT AT ONCE!
EXACTLY MY SENTIMENTS! NOTHING LIKE QUICK ACTION!
WITH STARTLING SUDDENNESS THE BATMAN PICKS UP A SHAKER OF PEPPER AND....
SPICY STUFF, EH, KING, OLD BOY!
PEPPER!! OH, MY EYES! MY EYES! THEY'RE BURNING!
ATCHOO! KILL THEM! ATCHOO! ATCHOO!
I'LL SMASH YOU FLAT!
THANKS FOR THE SPRING BOARD, PAL!
MISSED!

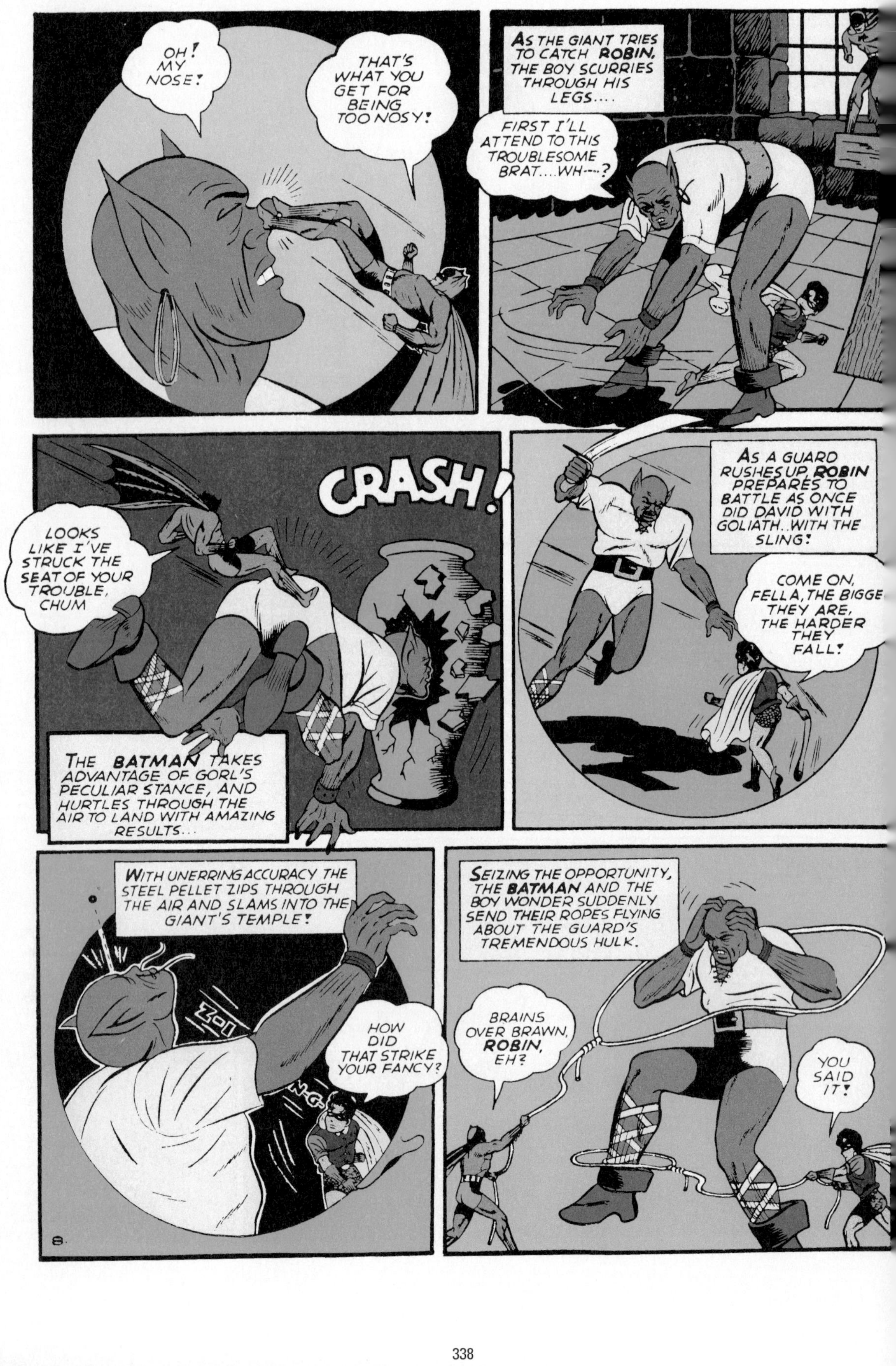
OH! MY NOSE!
THAT'S WHAT YOU GET FOR BEING TOO NOSY!
AS THE GIANT TRIES TO CATCH ROBIN, THE BOY SCURRIES THROUGH HIS LEGS....
FIRST I'LL ATTEND TO THIS TROUBLESOME BRAT....WH---?
CRASH!
LOOKS LIKE I'VE STRUCK THE SEAT OF YOUR TROUBLE, CHUM
THE BATMAN TAKES ADVANTAGE OF GORL'S PECULIAR STANCE, AND HURTLES THROUGH THE AIR TO LAND WITH AMAZING RESULTS...
AS A GUARD RUSHES UP, ROBIN PREPARES TO BATTLE AS ONCE DID DAVID WITH GOLIATH...WITH THE SLING!
COME ON, FELLA, THE BIGGE THEY ARE, THE HARDER THEY FALL!
WITH UNERRING ACCURACY THE STEEL PELLET ZIPS THROUGH THE AIR AND SLAMS INTO THE GIANT'S TEMPLE!
HOW DID THAT STRIKE YOUR FANCY?
SEIZING THE OPPORTUNITY, THE BATMAN AND THE BOY WONDER SUDDENLY SEND THEIR ROPES FLYING ABOUT THE GUARD'S TREMENDOUS HULK.
BRAINS OVER BRAWN, ROBIN, EH?
YOU SAID IT!
8

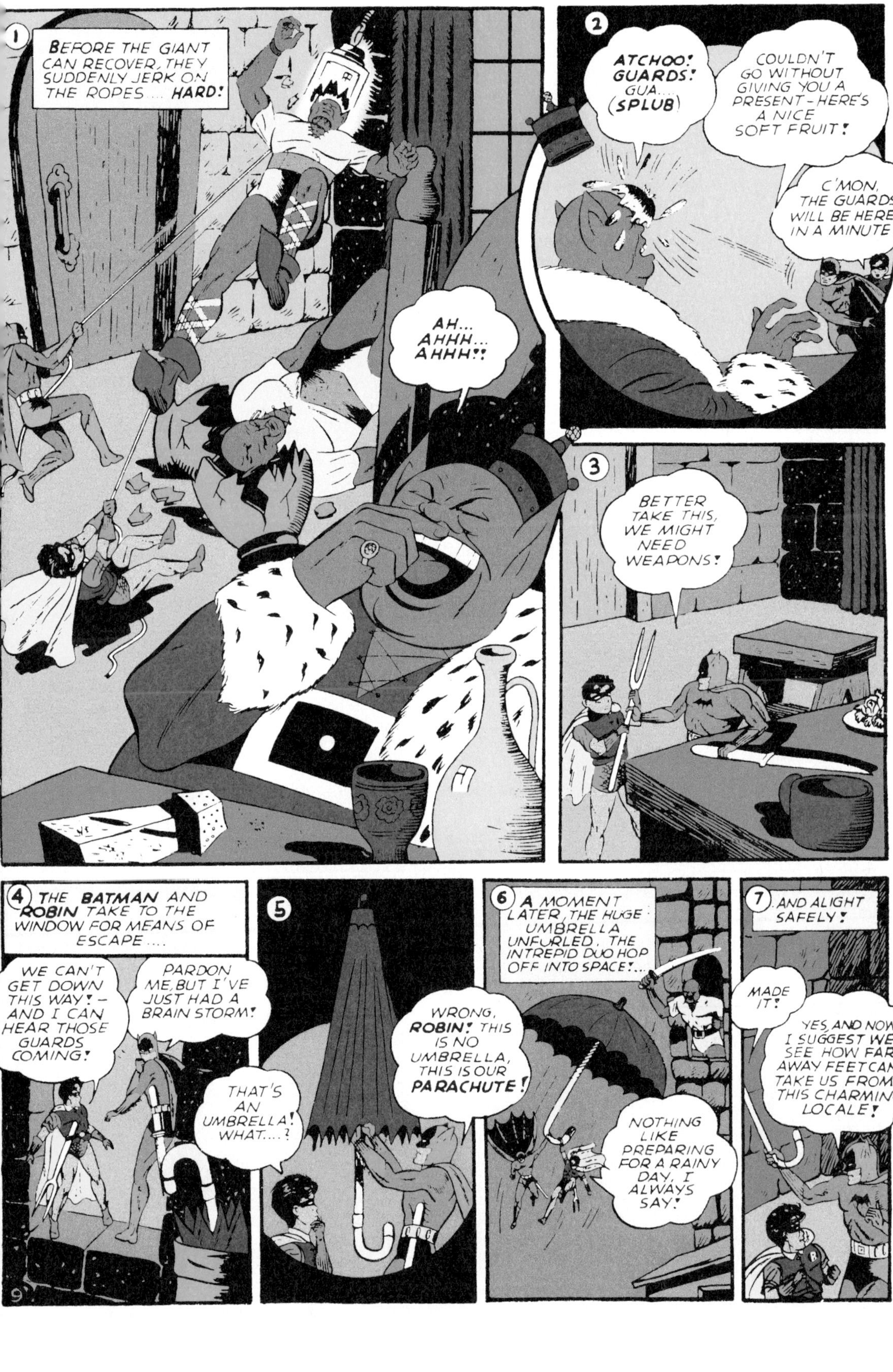
1
BEFORE THE GIANT CAN RECOVER, THEY SUDDENLY JERK ON THE ROPES.... HARD!
AH... AHHH... AHHH!!
2
ATCHOO! GUARDS! GUA.... (SPLUB)
COULDN'T GO WITHOUT GIVING YOU A PRESENT - HERE'S A NICE SOFT FRUIT!
C'MON, THE GUARDS WILL BE HERE IN A MINUTE!
3
BETTER TAKE THIS, WE MIGHT NEED WEAPONS!
4
THE BATMAN AND ROBIN TAKE TO THE WINDOW FOR MEANS OF ESCAPE....
WE CAN'T GET DOWN THIS WAY! - AND I CAN HEAR THOSE GUARDS COMING!
PARDON ME, BUT I'VE JUST HAD A BRAIN STORM!
5
THAT'S AN UMBRELLA! WHAT....?
WRONG, ROBIN! THIS IS NO UMBRELLA, THIS IS OUR PARACHUTE!
6
A MOMENT LATER, THE HUGE UMBRELLA UNFURLED, THE INTREPID DUO HOP OFF INTO SPACE!...
NOTHING LIKE PREPARING FOR A RAINY DAY, I ALWAYS SAY!
7
..AND ALIGHT SAFELY!
MADE IT!
YES, AND NOW I SUGGEST WE SEE HOW FAR AWAY FEET CAN TAKE US FROM THIS CHARMING LOCALE!
9

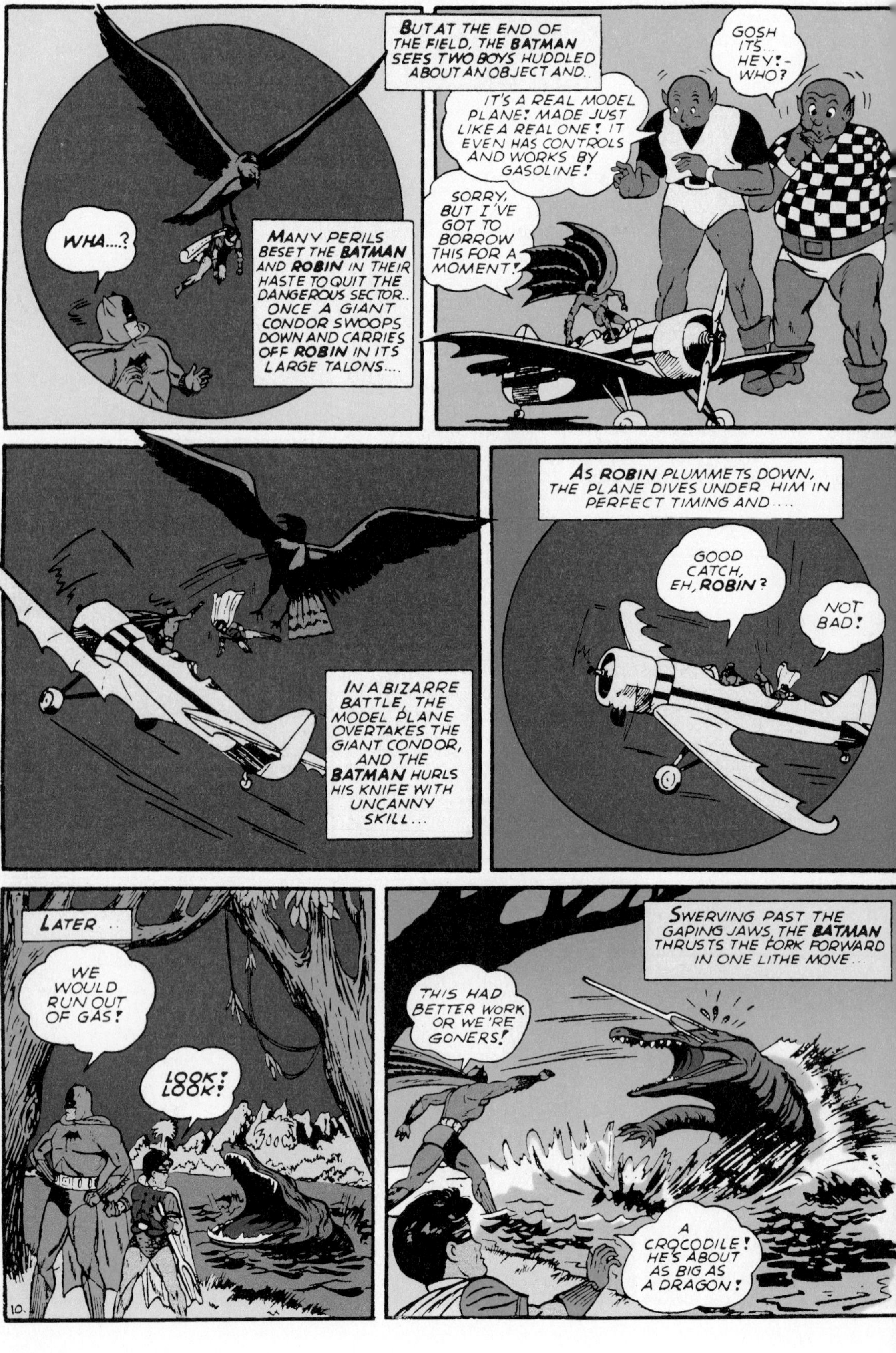
WHA....?
MANY PERILS BESET THE BATMAN AND ROBIN IN THEIR HASTE TO QUIT THE DANGEROUS SECTOR.. ONCE A GIANT CONDOR SWOOPS DOWN AND CARRIES OFF ROBIN IN ITS LARGE TALONS....
BUT AT THE END OF THE FIELD, THE BATMAN SEES TWO BOYS HUDDLED ABOUT AN OBJECT AND..
GOSH ITS... HEY!- WHO?
IT'S A REAL MODEL PLANE! MADE JUST LIKE A REAL ONE! IT EVEN HAS CONTROLS AND WORKS BY GASOLINE!
SORRY, BUT I'VE GOT TO BORROW THIS FOR A MOMENT!
IN A BIZARRE BATTLE, THE MODEL PLANE OVERTAKES THE GIANT CONDOR, AND THE BATMAN HURLS HIS KNIFE WITH UNCANNY SKILL...
AS ROBIN PLUMMETS DOWN, THE PLANE DIVES UNDER HIM IN PERFECT TIMING AND....
GOOD CATCH, EH, ROBIN?
NOT BAD!
LATER ..
WE WOULD RUN OUT OF GAS!
LOOK! LOOK!
10.
SWERVING PAST THE GAPING JAWS, THE BATMAN THRUSTS THE FORK FORWARD IN ONE LITHE MOVE...
THIS HAD BETTER WORK OR WE'RE GONERS!
A CROCODILE! HE'S ABOUT AS BIG AS A DRAGON!

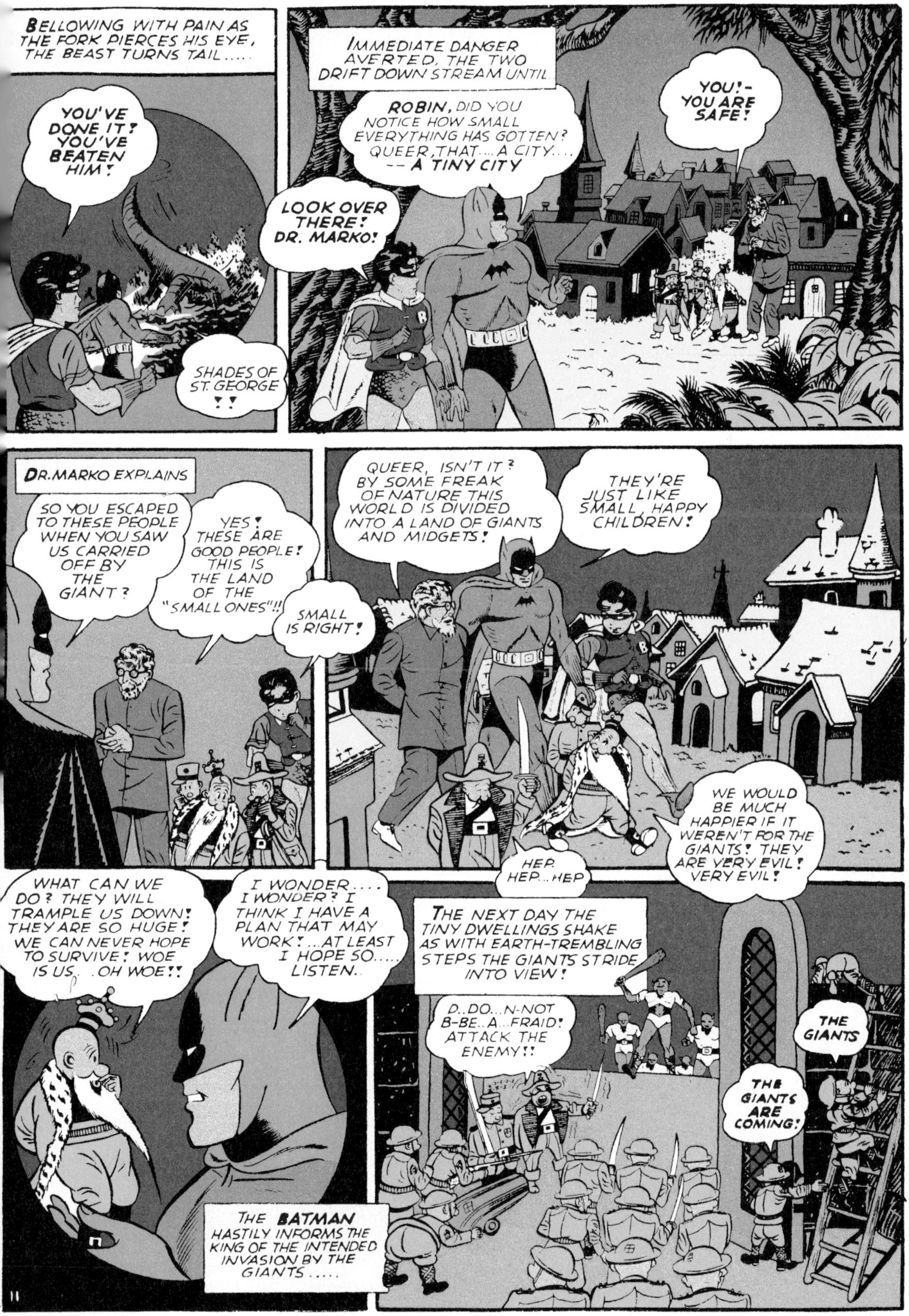
BELLOWING WITH PAIN AS THE FORK PIERCES HIS EYE, THE BEAST TURNS TAIL.....
YOU'VE DONE IT! YOU'VE BEATEN HIM!
SHADES OF ST. GEORGE !!
IMMEDIATE DANGER AVERTED, THE TWO DRIFT DOWN STREAM UNTIL
ROBIN, DID YOU NOTICE HOW SMALL EVERYTHING HAS GOTTEN? QUEER, THAT.... A CITY.... -- A TINY CITY
LOOK OVER THERE! DR. MARKO!
YOU!- YOU ARE SAFE!
DR. MARKO EXPLAINS
SO YOU ESCAPED TO THESE PEOPLE WHEN YOU SAW US CARRIED OFF BY THE GIANT?
YES! THESE ARE GOOD PEOPLE! THIS IS THE LAND OF THE "SMALL ONES"!!
SMALL IS RIGHT!
QUEER, ISN'T IT? BY SOME FREAK OF NATURE THIS WORLD IS DIVIDED INTO A LAND OF GIANTS AND MIDGETS!
THEY'RE JUST LIKE SMALL, HAPPY CHILDREN!
WE WOULD BE MUCH HAPPIER IF IT WEREN'T FOR THE GIANTS! THEY ARE VERY EVIL! VERY EVIL!
HEP. HEP...HEP
WHAT CAN WE DO? THEY WILL TRAMPLE US DOWN! THEY ARE SO HUGE! WE CAN NEVER HOPE TO SURVIVE! WOE IS US.. OH WOE!!
I WONDER.... I WONDER? I THINK I HAVE A PLAN THAT MAY WORK!...AT LEAST I HOPE SO..... LISTEN..
THE BATMAN HASTILY INFORMS THE KING OF THE INTENDED INVASION BY THE GIANTS.....
THE NEXT DAY THE TINY DWELLINGS SHAKE AS WITH EARTH-TREMBLING STEPS THE GIANTS STRIDE INTO VIEW!
D..DO...N-NOT B-BE..A...FRAID! ATTACK THE ENEMY!!
THE GIANTS
THE GIANTS ARE COMING!
11

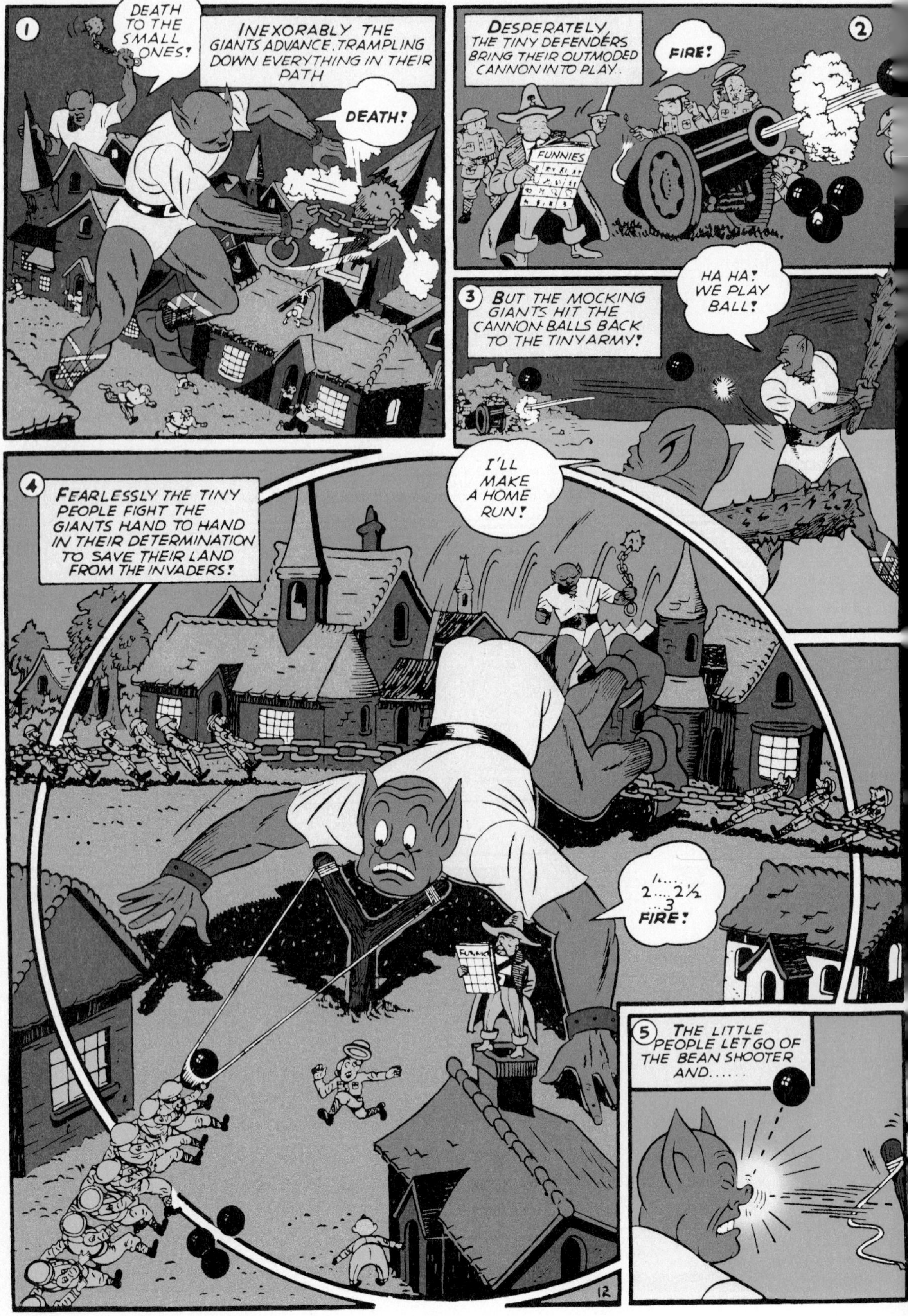
1
DEATH TO THE SMALL ONES!
INEXORABLY THE GIANTS ADVANCE, TRAMPLING DOWN EVERYTHING IN THEIR PATH
DEATH!
DESPERATELY, THE TINY DEFENDERS BRING THEIR OUTMODED CANNON INTO PLAY.
2
FIRE!
FUNNIES
3
BUT THE MOCKING GIANTS HIT THE CANNON-BALLS BACK TO THE TINY ARMY!
HA HA! WE PLAY BALL!
4
FEARLESSLY THE TINY PEOPLE FIGHT THE GIANTS HAND TO HAND IN THEIR DETERMINATION TO SAVE THEIR LAND FROM THE INVADERS!
I'LL MAKE A HOME RUN!
1.... 2.... 2½ ...3 FIRE!
5
THE LITTLE PEOPLE LET GO OF THE BEAN SHOOTER AND......
12

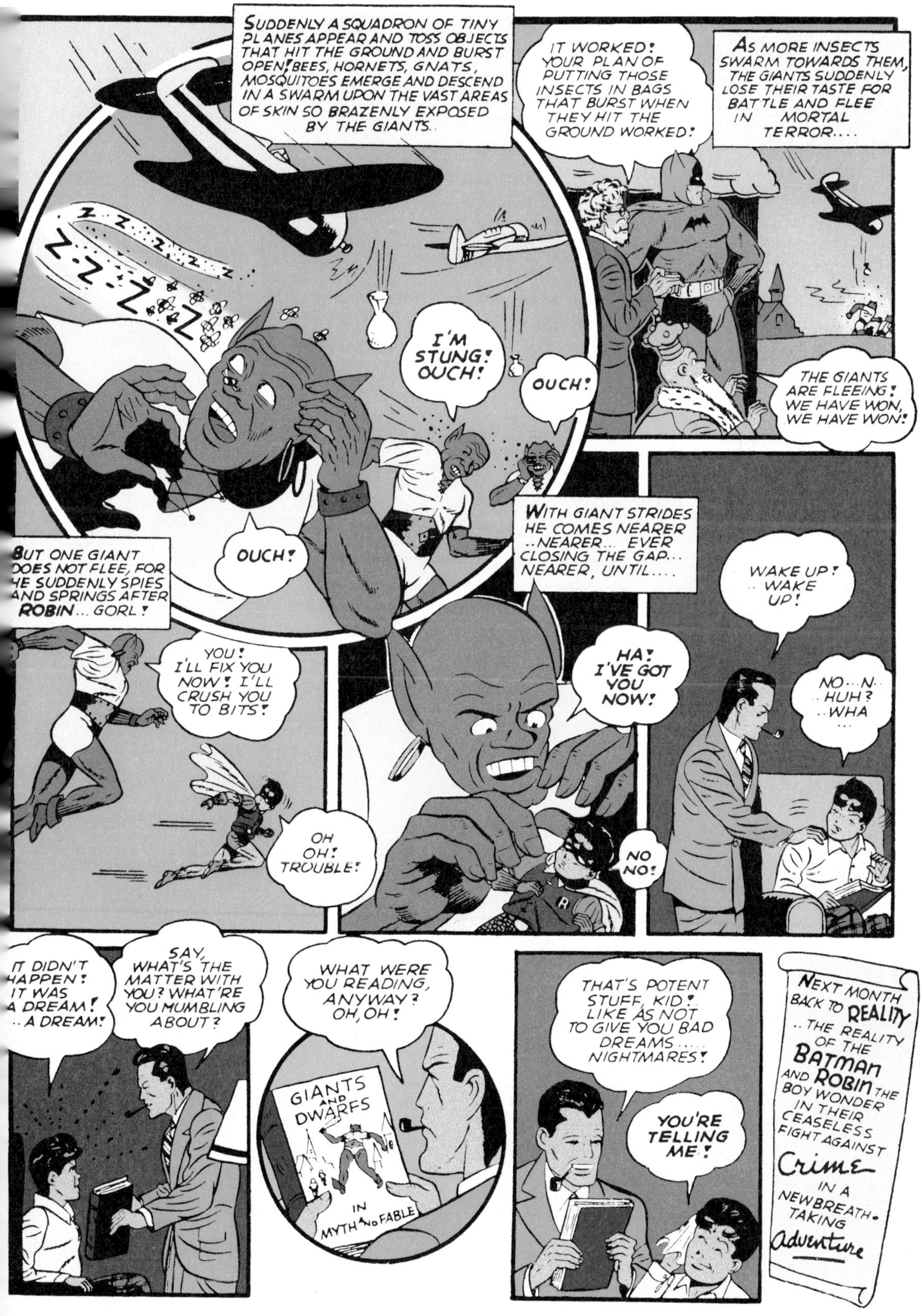
SUDDENLY A SQUADRON OF TINY PLANES APPEAR AND TOSS OBJECTS THAT HIT THE GROUND AND BURST OPEN! BEES, HORNETS, GNATS, MOSQUITOES EMERGE AND DESCEND IN A SWARM UPON THE VAST AREAS OF SKIN SO BRAZENLY EXPOSED BY THE GIANTS..
I'M STUNG! OUCH!
OUCH!
OUCH!
IT WORKED! YOUR PLAN OF PUTTING THOSE INSECTS IN BAGS THAT BURST WHEN THEY HIT THE GROUND WORKED!
AS MORE INSECTS SWARM TOWARDS THEM, THE GIANTS SUDDENLY LOSE THEIR TASTE FOR BATTLE AND FLEE IN MORTAL TERROR....
THE GIANTS ARE FLEEING! WE HAVE WON, WE HAVE WON!
BUT ONE GIANT DOES NOT FLEE, FOR HE SUDDENLY SPIES AND SPRINGS AFTER ROBIN... GORL!
YOU! I'LL FIX YOU NOW! I'LL CRUSH YOU TO BITS!
OH OH! TROUBLE!
WITH GIANT STRIDES HE COMES NEARER ..NEARER... EVER CLOSING THE GAP... NEARER, UNTIL....
HA! I'VE GOT YOU NOW!
NO NO!
WAKE UP! ..WAKE UP!
NO...N.. ..HUH? ..WHA ...
IT DIDN'T HAPPEN! IT WAS A DREAM! ...A DREAM!
SAY, WHAT'S THE MATTER WITH YOU? WHAT'RE YOU MUMBLING ABOUT?
WHAT WERE YOU READING, ANYWAY? OH, OH!
GIANTS AND DWARFS IN MYTH AND FABLE
THAT'S POTENT STUFF, KID! LIKE AS NOT TO GIVE YOU BAD DREAMS..... NIGHTMARES!
YOU'RE TELLING ME!
NEXT MONTH BACK TO REALITY ..THE REALITY OF THE BATMAN AND ROBIN THE BOY WONDER IN THEIR CEASELESS FIGHT AGAINST Crime IN A NEW BREATH-TAKING Adventure

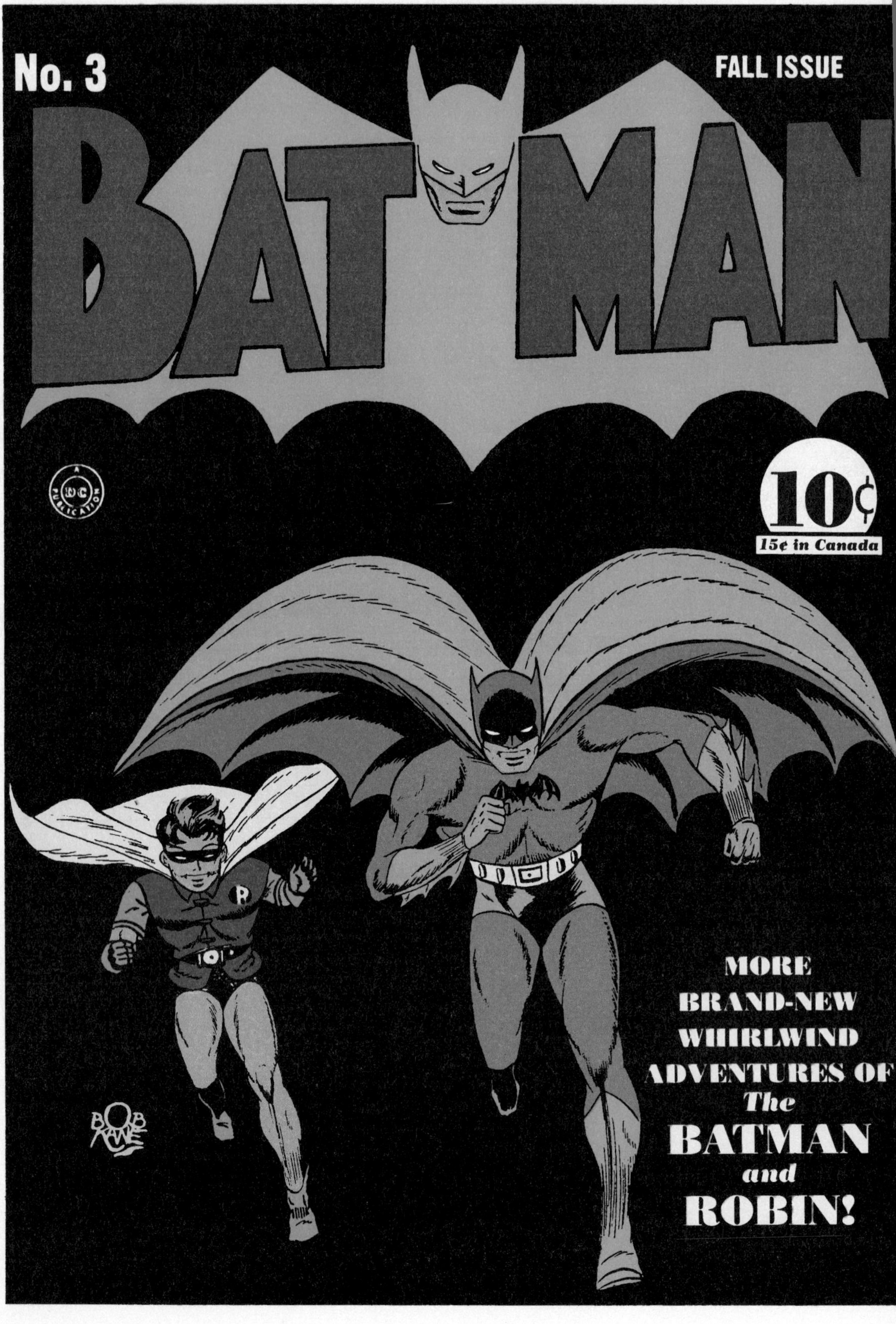
No. 3
FALL ISSUE
BATMAN
A DC PUBLICATION
10¢
15¢ in Canada
BOB KANE
MORE BRAND-NEW WHIRLWIND ADVENTURES OF The BATMAN and ROBIN!

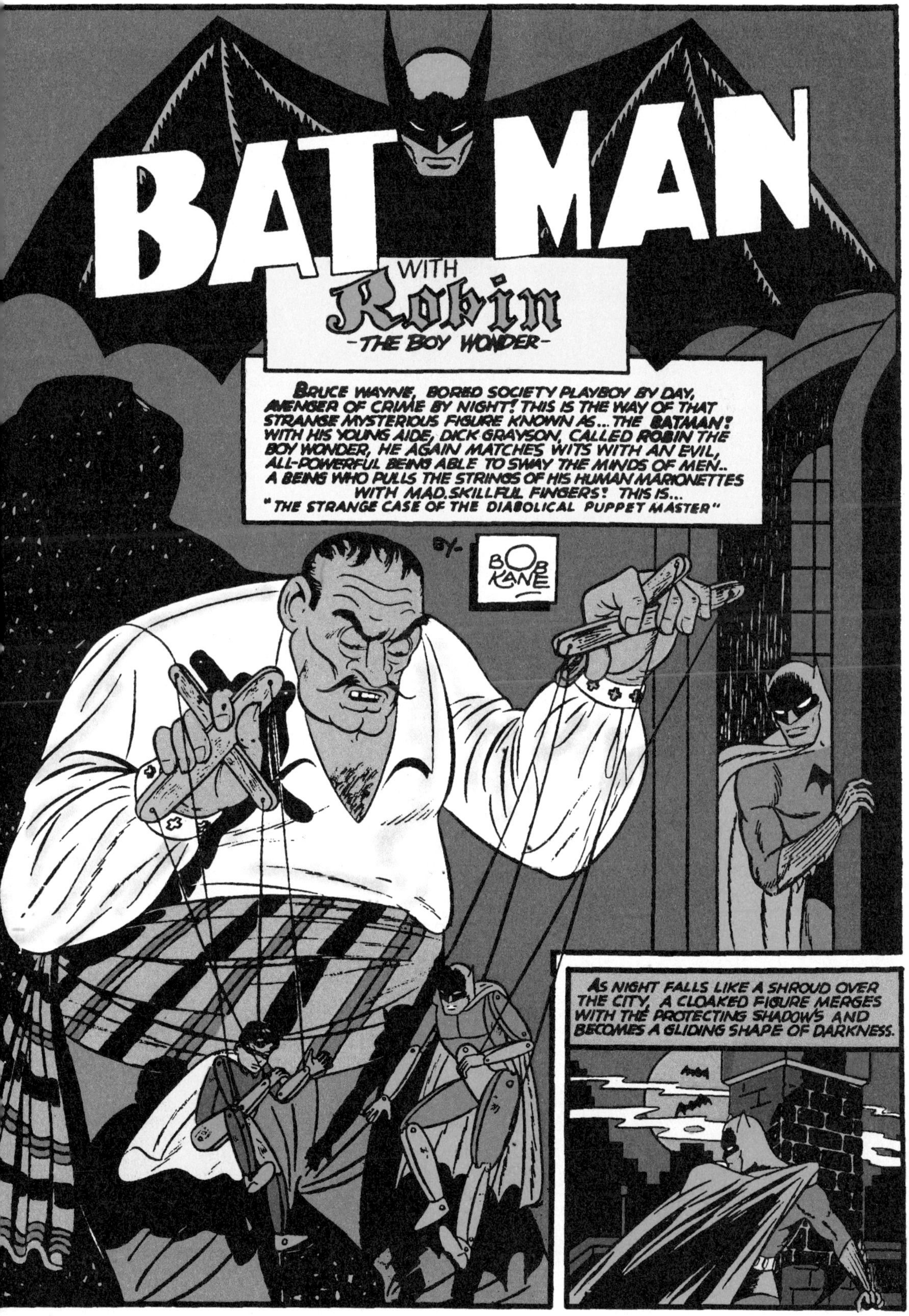
BATMAN
WITH
Robin
-THE BOY WONDER-
BRUCE WAYNE, BORED SOCIETY PLAYBOY BY DAY, AVENGER OF CRIME BY NIGHT! THIS IS THE WAY OF THAT STRANGE MYSTERIOUS FIGURE KNOWN AS... THE BATMAN! WITH HIS YOUNG AIDE, DICK GRAYSON, CALLED ROBIN THE BOY WONDER, HE AGAIN MATCHES WITS WITH AN EVIL, ALL-POWERFUL BEING ABLE TO SWAY THE MINDS OF MEN.. A BEING WHO PULLS THE STRINGS OF HIS HUMAN MARIONETTES WITH MAD, SKILLFUL FINGERS! THIS IS...
"THE STRANGE CASE OF THE DIABOLICAL PUPPET MASTER"
BY- BOB KANE
AS NIGHT FALLS LIKE A SHROUD OVER THE CITY, A CLOAKED FIGURE MERGES WITH THE PROTECTING SHADOWS AND BECOMES A GLIDING SHAPE OF DARKNESS.

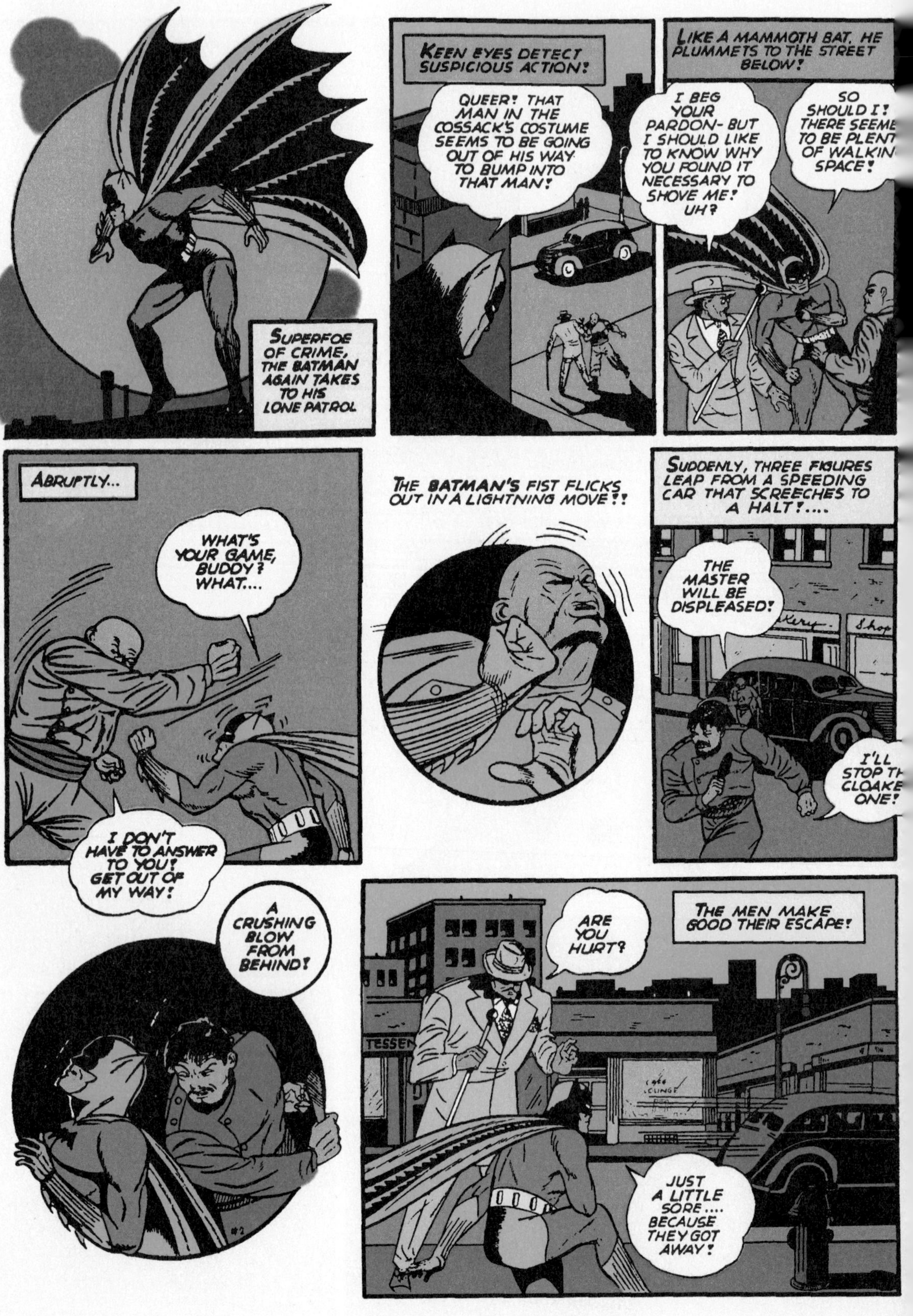
SUPERFOE OF CRIME, THE BATMAN AGAIN TAKES TO HIS LONE PATROL
KEEN EYES DETECT SUSPICIOUS ACTION!
QUEER! THAT MAN IN THE COSSACK'S COSTUME SEEMS TO BE GOING OUT OF HIS WAY TO BUMP INTO THAT MAN!
LIKE A MAMMOTH BAT, HE PLUMMETS TO THE STREET BELOW!
I BEG YOUR PARDON- BUT I SHOULD LIKE TO KNOW WHY YOU FOUND IT NECESSARY TO SHOVE ME! UH?
SO SHOULD I! THERE SEEME TO BE PLENT OF WALKIN SPACE!
ABRUPTLY...
WHAT'S YOUR GAME, BUDDY? WHAT....
I DON'T HAVE TO ANSWER TO YOU! GET OUT OF MY WAY!
THE BATMAN'S FIST FLICKS OUT IN A LIGHTNING MOVE!!
SUDDENLY, THREE FIGURES LEAP FROM A SPEEDING CAR THAT SCREECHES TO A HALT!....
THE MASTER WILL BE DISPLEASED!
I'LL STOP TH CLOAKE ONE!
A CRUSHING BLOW FROM BEHIND!
ARE YOU HURT?
THE MEN MAKE GOOD THEIR ESCAPE!
JUST A LITTLE SORE.... BECAUSE THEY GOT AWAY!

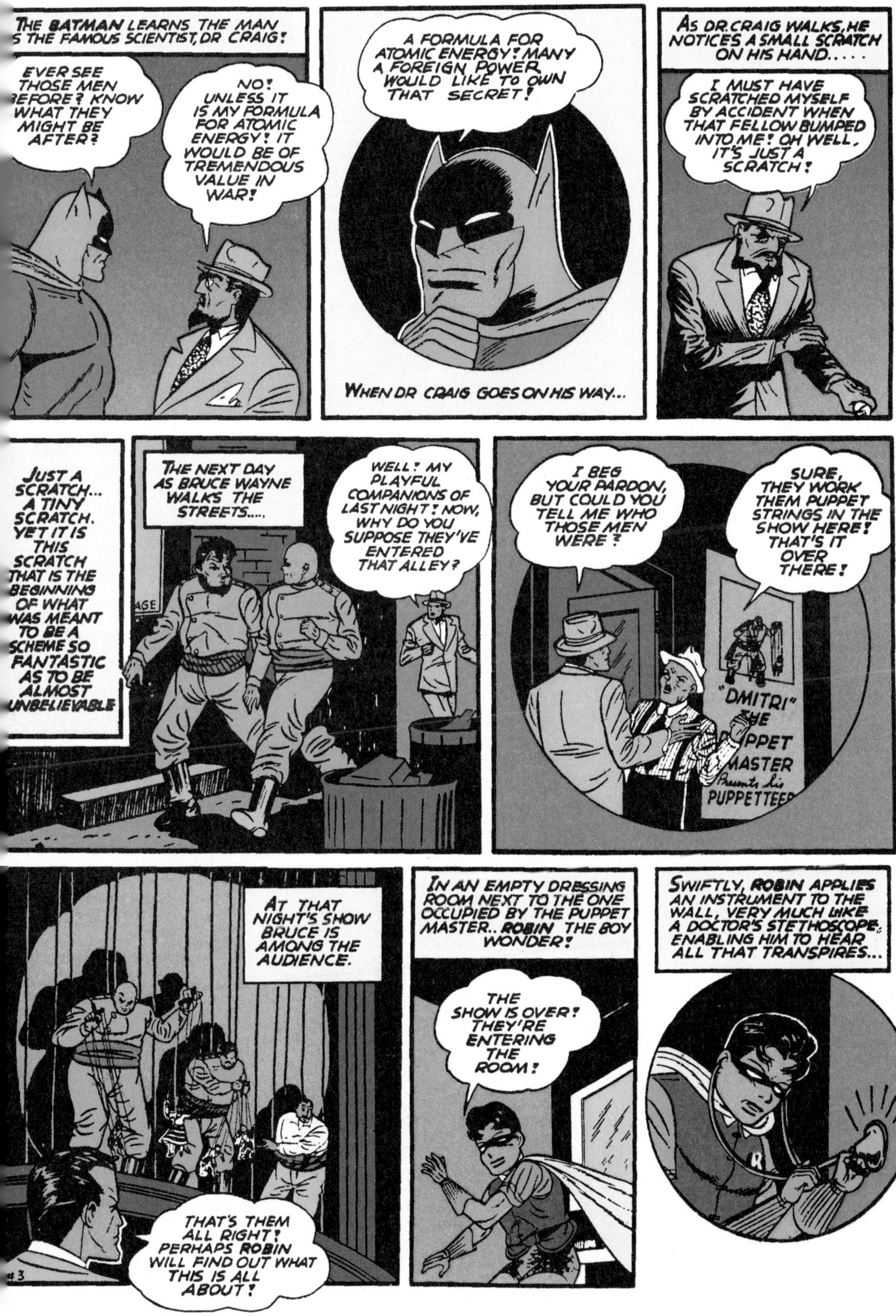
THE BATMAN LEARNS THE MAN IS THE FAMOUS SCIENTIST, DR CRAIG!
EVER SEE THOSE MEN BEFORE? KNOW WHAT THEY MIGHT BE AFTER?
NO! UNLESS IT IS MY FORMULA FOR ATOMIC ENERGY! IT WOULD BE OF TREMENDOUS VALUE IN WAR!
A FORMULA FOR ATOMIC ENERGY! MANY A FOREIGN POWER WOULD LIKE TO OWN THAT SECRET!
WHEN DR CRAIG GOES ON HIS WAY...
AS DR. CRAIG WALKS, HE NOTICES A SMALL SCRATCH ON HIS HAND.....
I MUST HAVE SCRATCHED MYSELF BY ACCIDENT WHEN THAT FELLOW BUMPED INTO ME! OH WELL, IT'S JUST A SCRATCH!
JUST A SCRATCH... A TINY SCRATCH. YET IT IS THIS SCRATCH THAT IS THE BEGINNING OF WHAT WAS MEANT TO BE A SCHEME SO FANTASTIC AS TO BE ALMOST UNBELIEVABLE
THE NEXT DAY AS BRUCE WAYNE WALKS THE STREETS.....
WELL! MY PLAYFUL COMPANIONS OF LAST NIGHT! NOW, WHY DO YOU SUPPOSE THEY'VE ENTERED THAT ALLEY?
I BEG YOUR PARDON, BUT COULD YOU TELL ME WHO THOSE MEN WERE?
SURE, THEY WORK THEM PUPPET STRINGS IN THE SHOW HERE! THAT'S IT OVER THERE!
"DMITRI" THE PUPPET MASTER
PUPPETTEER
AT THAT NIGHT'S SHOW BRUCE IS AMONG THE AUDIENCE.
THAT'S THEM ALL RIGHT! PERHAPS ROBIN WILL FIND OUT WHAT THIS IS ALL ABOUT!
IN AN EMPTY DRESSING ROOM NEXT TO THE ONE OCCUPIED BY THE PUPPET MASTER.. ROBIN THE BOY WONDER!
THE SHOW IS OVER! THEY'RE ENTERING THE ROOM!
SWIFTLY, ROBIN APPLIES AN INSTRUMENT TO THE WALL, VERY MUCH LIKE A DOCTOR'S STETHOSCOPE, ENABLING HIM TO HEAR ALL THAT TRANSPIRES...

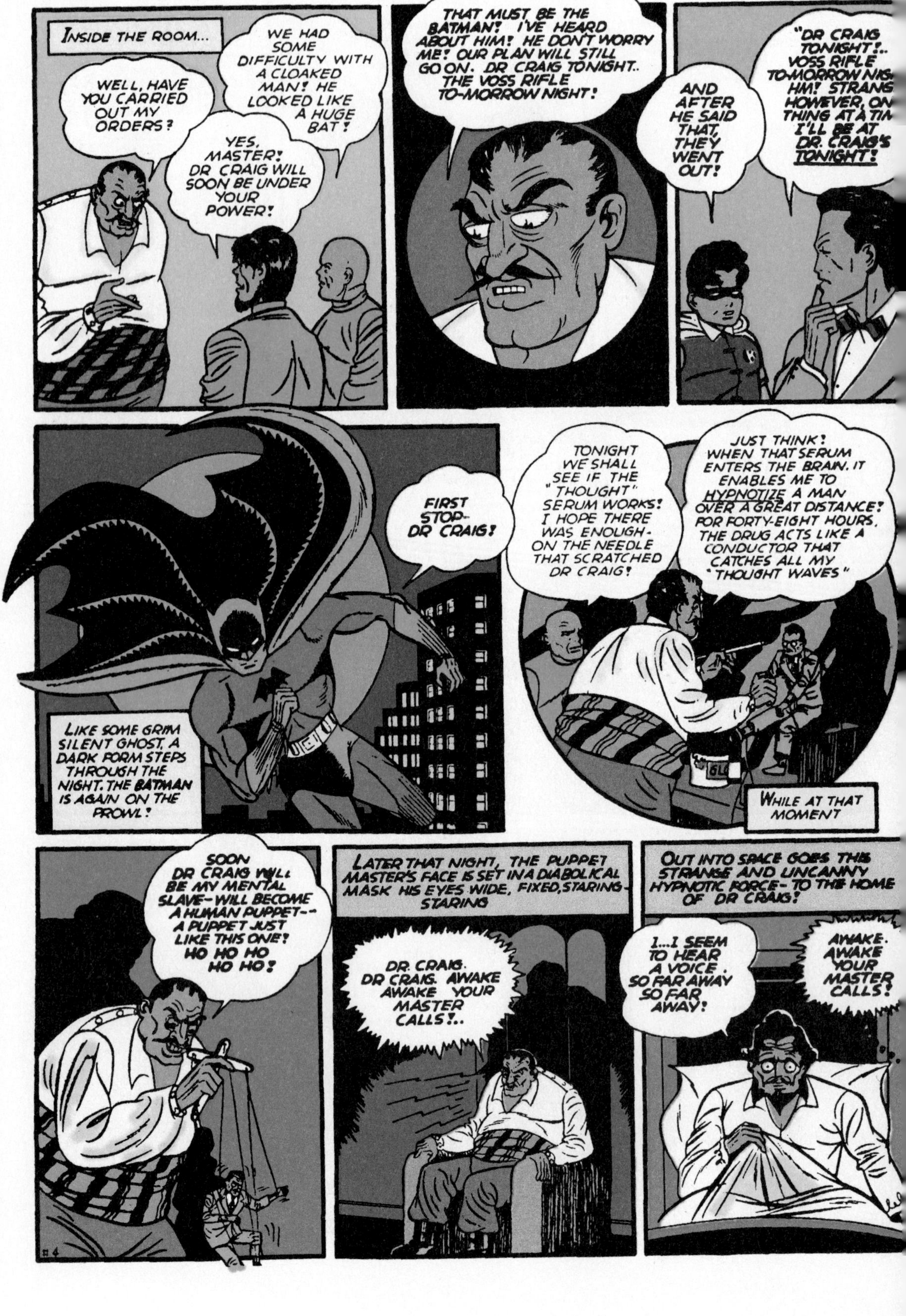
INSIDE THE ROOM...
WELL, HAVE YOU CARRIED OUT MY ORDERS?
WE HAD SOME DIFFICULTY WITH A CLOAKED MAN! HE LOOKED LIKE A HUGE BAT!
YES, MASTER! DR CRAIG WILL SOON BE UNDER YOUR POWER!
THAT MUST BE THE BATMAN! I'VE HEARD ABOUT HIM! HE DON'T WORRY ME! OUR PLAN WILL STILL GO ON. DR CRAIG TONIGHT.. THE VOSS RIFLE TO-MORROW NIGHT!
AND AFTER HE SAID THAT, THEY WENT OUT!
"DR CRAIG TONIGHT!.. VOSS RIFLE TO-MORROW NIG
HM! STRANG HOWEVER, ON THING AT A TIM I'LL BE AT DR. CRAIG'S TONIGHT!
FIRST STOP- DR CRAIG!
LIKE SOME GRIM SILENT GHOST, A DARK FORM STEPS THROUGH THE NIGHT. THE BATMAN IS AGAIN ON THE PROWL!
TONIGHT WE SHALL SEE IF THE "THOUGHT" SERUM WORKS! I HOPE THERE WAS ENOUGH-ON THE NEEDLE THAT SCRATCHED DR CRAIG!
JUST THINK! WHEN THAT SERUM ENTERS THE BRAIN, IT ENABLES ME TO HYPNOTIZE A MAN OVER A GREAT DISTANCE! FOR FORTY-EIGHT HOURS, THE DRUG ACTS LIKE A CONDUCTOR THAT CATCHES ALL MY "THOUGHT WAVES"
WHILE AT THAT MOMENT
SOON DR CRAIG WILL BE MY MENTAL SLAVE-WILL BECOME A HUMAN PUPPET-- A PUPPET JUST LIKE THIS ONE! HO HO HO HO HO!
LATER THAT NIGHT, THE PUPPET MASTER'S FACE IS SET IN A DIABOLICAL MASK HIS EYES WIDE, FIXED, STARING- STARING
DR. CRAIG. DR CRAIG. AWAKE AWAKE YOUR MASTER CALLS!..
OUT INTO SPACE GOES THIS STRANGE AND UNCANNY HYPNOTIC FORCE- TO THE HOME OF DR CRAIG!
I...I SEEM TO HEAR A VOICE. SO FAR AWAY SO FAR AWAY!
AWAKE. AWAKE YOUR MASTER CALLS!

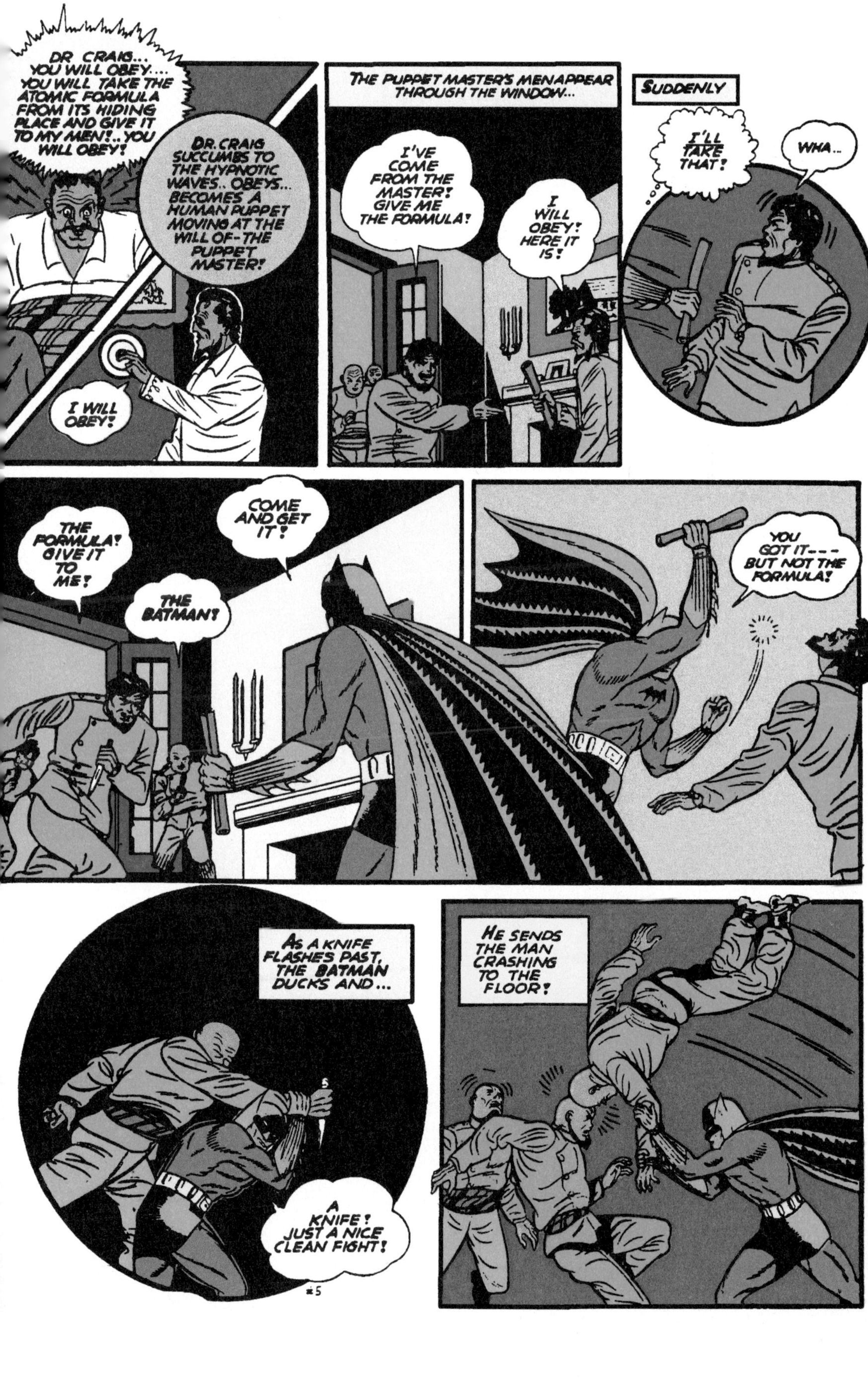
DR. CRAIG... YOU WILL OBEY.... YOU WILL TAKE THE ATOMIC FORMULA FROM ITS HIDING PLACE AND GIVE IT TO MY MEN!.. YOU WILL OBEY!
DR. CRAIG SUCCUMBS TO THE HYPNOTIC WAVES.. OBEYS... BECOMES A HUMAN PUPPET MOVING AT THE WILL OF-THE PUPPET MASTER!
I WILL OBEY!
THE PUPPET MASTER'S MEN APPEAR THROUGH THE WINDOW...
I'VE COME FROM THE MASTER! GIVE ME THE FORMULA!
I WILL OBEY! HERE IT IS!
SUDDENLY
I'LL TAKE THAT!
WHA...
THE FORMULA! GIVE IT TO ME!
COME AND GET IT!
THE BATMAN!
YOU GOT IT--- BUT NOT THE FORMULA!
AS A KNIFE FLASHES PAST, THE BATMAN DUCKS AND...
A KNIFE! JUST A NICE CLEAN FIGHT!
HE SENDS THE MAN CRASHING TO THE FLOOR!

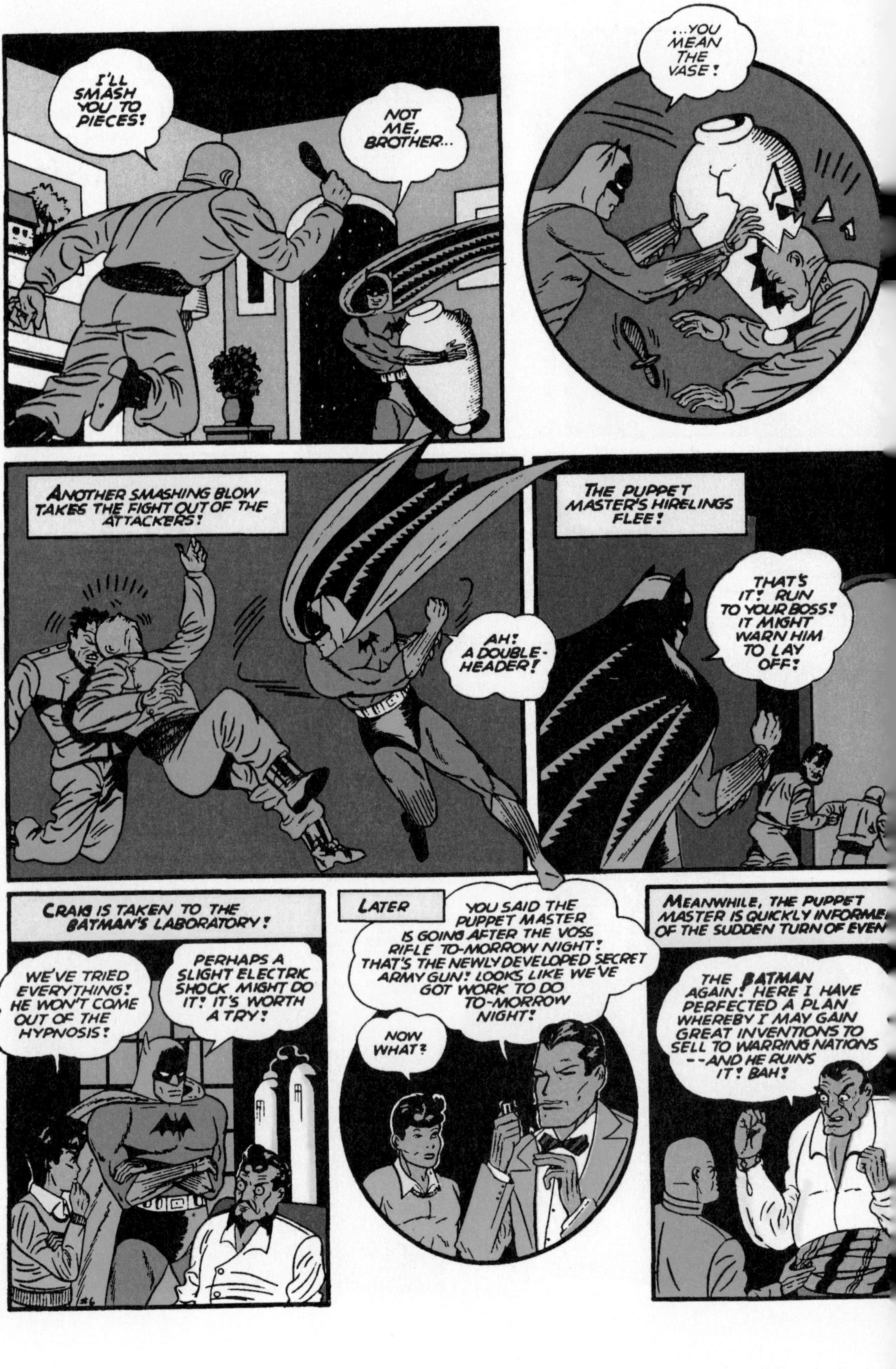
I'LL SMASH YOU TO PIECES!
NOT ME, BROTHER...
...YOU MEAN THE VASE!
ANOTHER SMASHING BLOW TAKES THE FIGHT OUT OF THE ATTACKERS!
AH! A DOUBLE-HEADER!
THE PUPPET MASTER'S HIRELINGS FLEE!
THAT'S IT! RUN TO YOUR BOSS! IT MIGHT WARN HIM TO LAY OFF!
CRAIG IS TAKEN TO THE BATMAN'S LABORATORY!
WE'VE TRIED EVERYTHING! HE WON'T COME OUT OF THE HYPNOSIS!
PERHAPS A SLIGHT ELECTRIC SHOCK MIGHT DO IT! IT'S WORTH A TRY!
LATER
YOU SAID THE PUPPET MASTER IS GOING AFTER THE VOSS RIFLE TO-MORROW NIGHT! THAT'S THE NEWLY DEVELOPED SECRET ARMY GUN! LOOKS LIKE WE'VE GOT WORK TO DO TO-MORROW NIGHT!
NOW WHAT?
MEANWHILE, THE PUPPET MASTER IS QUICKLY INFORME
OF THE SUDDEN TURN OF EVEN
THE BATMAN AGAIN! HERE I HAVE PERFECTED A PLAN WHEREBY I MAY GAIN GREAT INVENTIONS TO SELL TO WARRING NATIONS --AND HE RUINS IT! BAH!

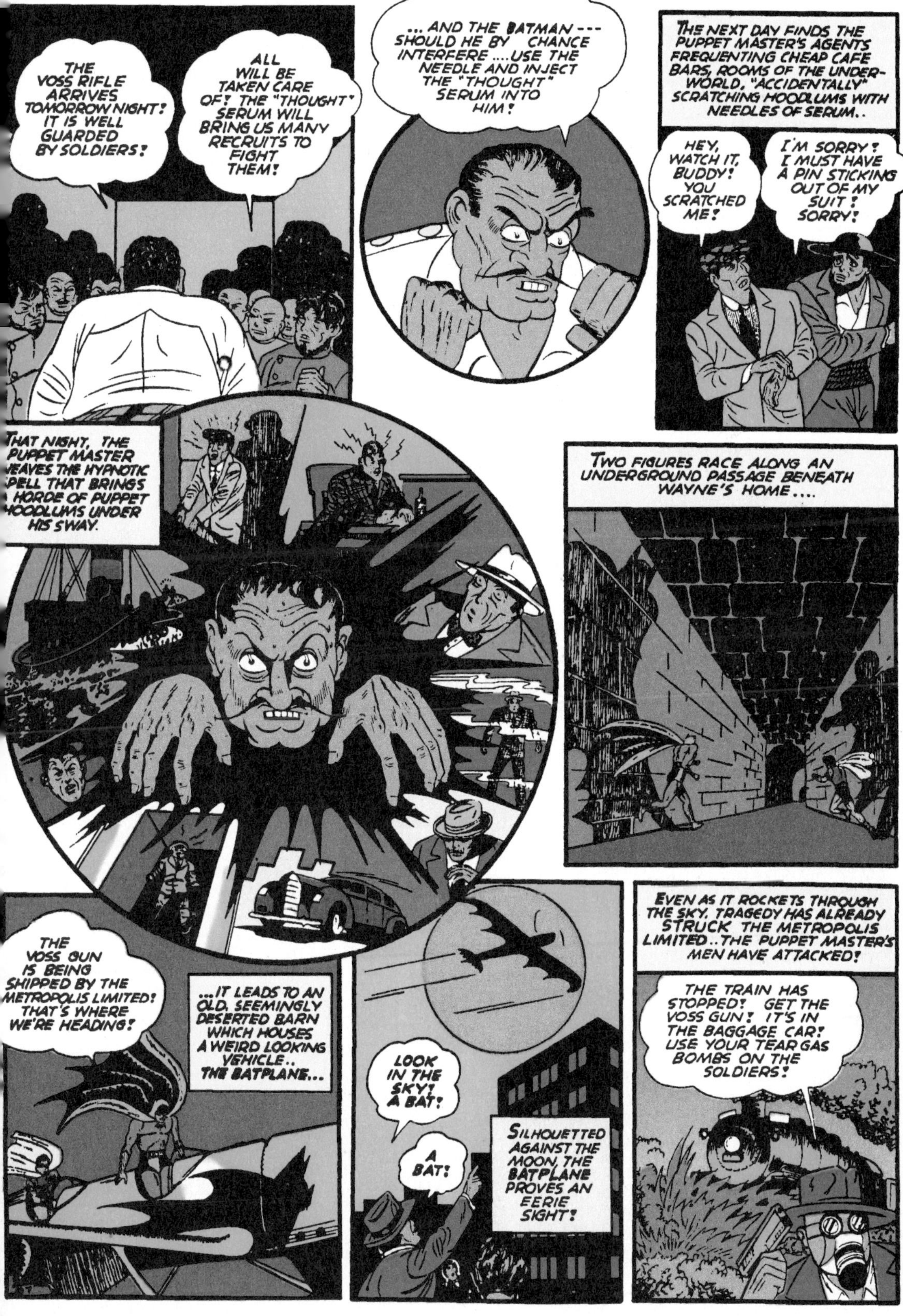
THE VOSS RIFLE ARRIVES TOMORROW NIGHT! IT IS WELL GUARDED BY SOLDIERS!
ALL WILL BE TAKEN CARE OF! THE "THOUGHT" SERUM WILL BRING US MANY RECRUITS TO FIGHT THEM!
... AND THE BATMAN --- SHOULD HE BY CHANCE INTERFERE .... USE THE NEEDLE AND INJECT THE "THOUGHT" SERUM INTO HIM!
THE NEXT DAY FINDS THE PUPPET MASTER'S AGENTS FREQUENTING CHEAP CAFE BARS, ROOMS OF THE UNDER-WORLD, "ACCIDENTALLY" SCRATCHING HOODLUMS WITH NEEDLES OF SERUM..
HEY, WATCH IT, BUDDY! YOU SCRATCHED ME!
I'M SORRY! I MUST HAVE A PIN STICKING OUT OF MY SUIT! SORRY!
THAT NIGHT, THE PUPPET MASTER WEAVES THE HYPNOTIC SPELL THAT BRINGS A HORDE OF PUPPET HOODLUMS UNDER HIS SWAY.
TWO FIGURES RACE ALONG AN UNDERGROUND PASSAGE BENEATH WAYNE'S HOME....
THE VOSS GUN IS BEING SHIPPED BY THE METROPOLIS LIMITED! THAT'S WHERE WE'RE HEADING!
...IT LEADS TO AN OLD, SEEMINGLY DESERTED BARN WHICH HOUSES A WEIRD LOOKING VEHICLE.. THE BATPLANE...
LOOK IN THE SKY! A BAT!
A BAT!
SILHOUETTED AGAINST THE MOON, THE BATPLANE PROVES AN EERIE SIGHT!
EVEN AS IT ROCKETS THROUGH THE SKY, TRAGEDY HAS ALREADY STRUCK THE METROPOLIS LIMITED.. THE PUPPET MASTER'S MEN HAVE ATTACKED!
THE TRAIN HAS STOPPED! GET THE VOSS GUN! IT'S IN THE BAGGAGE CAR! USE YOUR TEAR GAS BOMBS ON THE SOLDIERS!

SUDDENLY THE BATPLANE IS SIGHTED SWOOPING DOWN.

THE BATMAN!

A BAT!

LOOK!

AS THE PLANE WINGS LOW OVER THE TRAIN, ROBIN'S DANGLING FORM TAKES ITS TOLL OF MEN!

OFF YOU GO!

COMING TO GREET ME? HOW TOUCHING!

SETTING THE CONTROLS WHICH ENABLE THE BATPLANE TO REMAIN STATIONARY, THE BATMAN LOWERS HIMSELF INTO THE BAGGAGE CAR.

WHIRLING SWIFTLY, THE CLOAKED FIGHTER'S FIST LASHES OUT!

YOU SHOULDN'T SURPRISE ME LIKE THAT! MY HEART, YOU KNOW!

SORRY! I'M NOT AT HOME TO VISITORS!

...T-THAT (COUGH) TEAR G-GAS (COUGH) (COUGH)

COUGH COUGH

COUGH COUGH

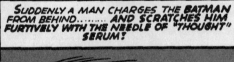

SUDDENLY A MAN CHARGES THE BATMAN FROM BEHIND......... AND SCRATCHES HIM FURTIVELY WITH THE NEEDLE OF "THOUGHT" SERUM!

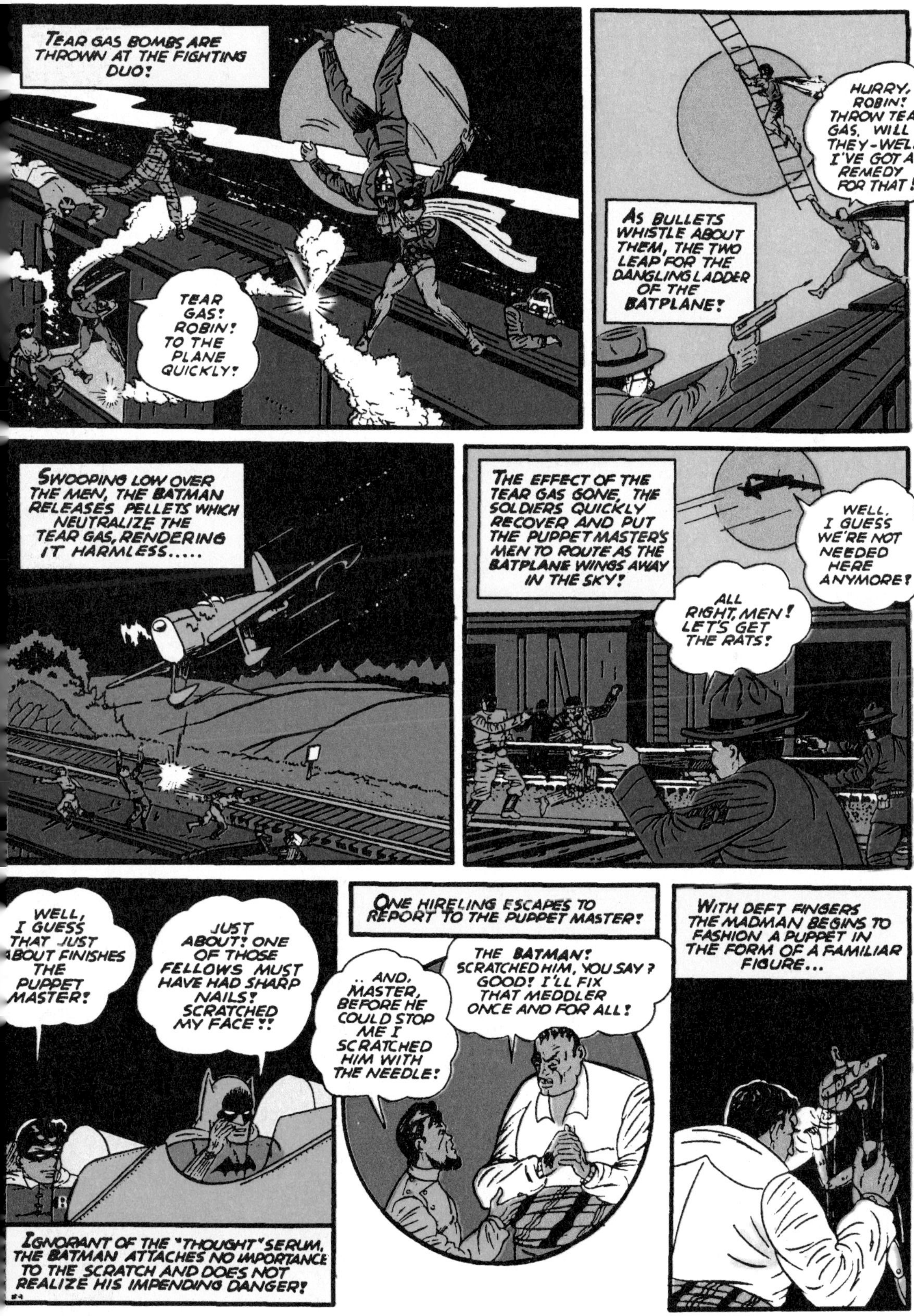

TEAR GAS BOMBS ARE THROWN AT THE FIGHTING DUO!
TEAR GAS! ROBIN! TO THE PLANE QUICKLY!
HURRY, ROBIN! THROW TEAR GAS, WILL THEY-WELL, I'VE GOT A REMEDY FOR THAT!
AS BULLETS WHISTLE ABOUT THEM, THE TWO LEAP FOR THE DANGLING LADDER OF THE BATPLANE!
SWOOPING LOW OVER THE MEN, THE BATMAN RELEASES PELLETS WHICH NEUTRALIZE THE TEAR GAS, RENDERING IT HARMLESS.....
THE EFFECT OF THE TEAR GAS GONE, THE SOLDIERS QUICKLY RECOVER AND PUT THE PUPPET MASTER'S MEN TO ROUTE AS THE BATPLANE WINGS AWAY IN THE SKY!
WELL, I GUESS WE'RE NOT NEEDED HERE ANYMORE!
ALL RIGHT, MEN! LET'S GET THE RATS!
WELL, I GUESS THAT JUST ABOUT FINISHES THE PUPPET MASTER!
JUST ABOUT! ONE OF THOSE FELLOWS MUST HAVE HAD SHARP NAILS! SCRATCHED MY FACE!!
IGNORANT OF THE "THOUGHT" SERUM, THE BATMAN ATTACHES NO IMPORTANCE TO THE SCRATCH AND DOES NOT REALIZE HIS IMPENDING DANGER!
ONE HIRELING ESCAPES TO REPORT TO THE PUPPET MASTER!
.. AND, MASTER, BEFORE HE COULD STOP ME I SCRATCHED HIM WITH THE NEEDLE!
THE BATMAN! SCRATCHED HIM, YOU SAY? GOOD! I'LL FIX THAT MEDDLER ONCE AND FOR ALL!
WITH DEFT FINGERS THE MADMAN BEGINS TO FASHION A PUPPET IN THE FORM OF A FAMILIAR FIGURE...

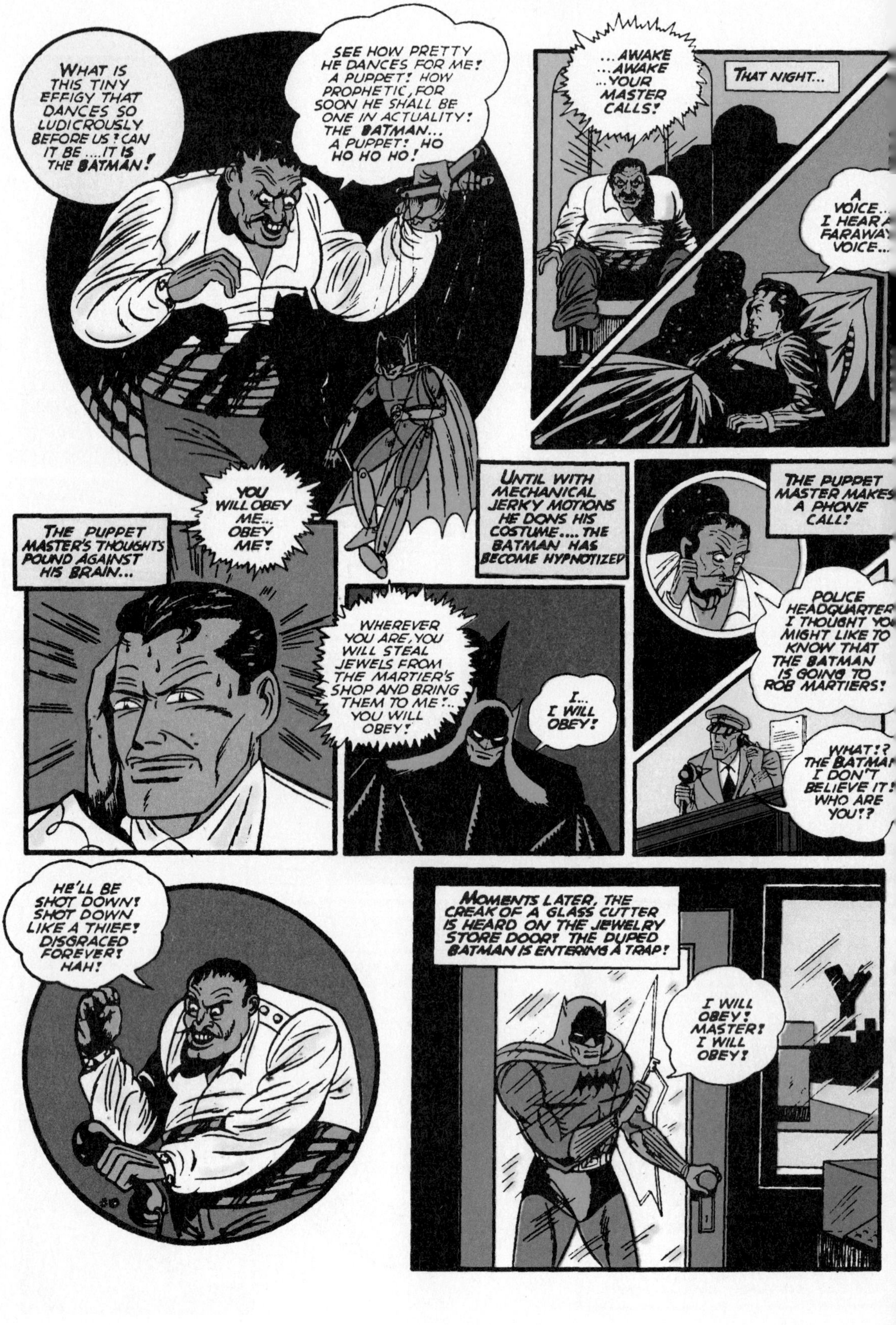
WHAT IS THIS TINY EFFIGY THAT DANCES SO LUDICROUSLY BEFORE US? CAN IT BE ....IT IS THE BATMAN!
SEE HOW PRETTY HE DANCES FOR ME! A PUPPET! HOW PROPHETIC, FOR SOON HE SHALL BE ONE IN ACTUALITY! THE BATMAN... A PUPPET! HO HO HO HO!
THAT NIGHT...
...AWAKE ...AWAKE ...YOUR MASTER CALLS!
A VOICE... I HEAR A FARAWAY VOICE...
THE PUPPET MASTER'S THOUGHTS POUND AGAINST HIS BRAIN...
YOU WILL OBEY ME... OBEY ME!
UNTIL WITH MECHANICAL JERKY MOTIONS HE DONS HIS COSTUME.... THE BATMAN HAS BECOME HYPNOTIZED
WHEREVER YOU ARE, YOU WILL STEAL JEWELS FROM THE MARTIER'S SHOP AND BRING THEM TO ME!... YOU WILL OBEY!
I... I WILL OBEY!
THE PUPPET MASTER MAKES A PHONE CALL!
POLICE HEADQUARTERS I THOUGHT YOU MIGHT LIKE TO KNOW THAT THE BATMAN IS GOING TO ROB MARTIERS!
WHAT!? THE BATMAN I DON'T BELIEVE IT! WHO ARE YOU!?
HE'LL BE SHOT DOWN! SHOT DOWN LIKE A THIEF! DISGRACED FOREVER! HAH!
MOMENTS LATER, THE CREAK OF A GLASS CUTTER IS HEARD ON THE JEWELRY STORE DOOR! THE DUPED BATMAN IS ENTERING A TRAP!
I WILL OBEY! MASTER! I WILL OBEY!

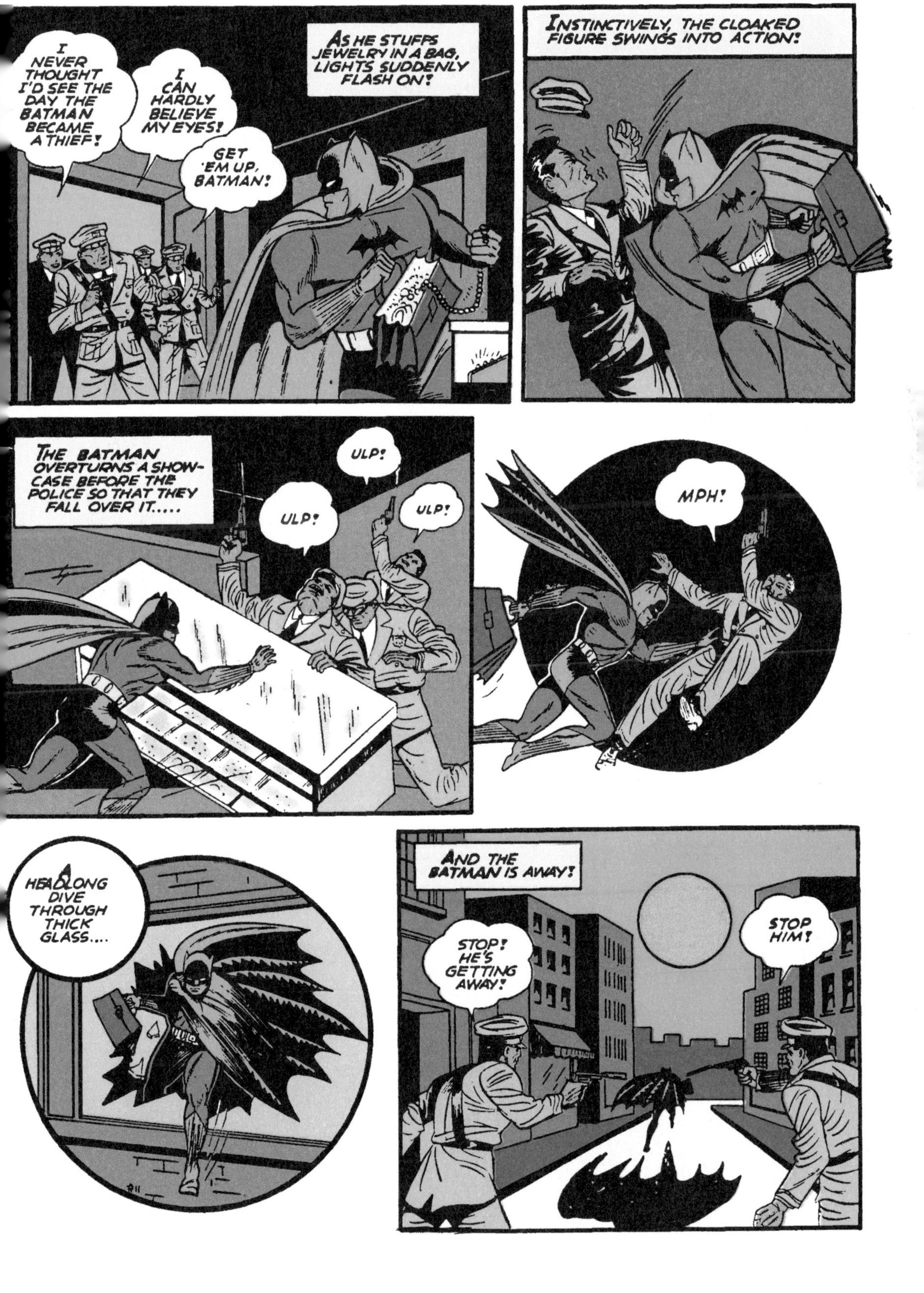
AS HE STUFFS JEWELRY IN A BAG, LIGHTS SUDDENLY FLASH ON!
I NEVER THOUGHT I'D SEE THE DAY THE BATMAN BECAME A THIEF!
I CAN HARDLY BELIEVE MY EYES!
GET 'EM UP, BATMAN!
INSTINCTIVELY, THE CLOAKED FIGURE SWINGS INTO ACTION!
THE BATMAN OVERTURNS A SHOW-CASE BEFORE THE POLICE SO THAT THEY FALL OVER IT.....
ULP!
ULP!
ULP!
MPH!
A HEADLONG DIVE THROUGH THICK GLASS....
AND THE BATMAN IS AWAY!
STOP! HE'S GETTING AWAY!
STOP HIM!

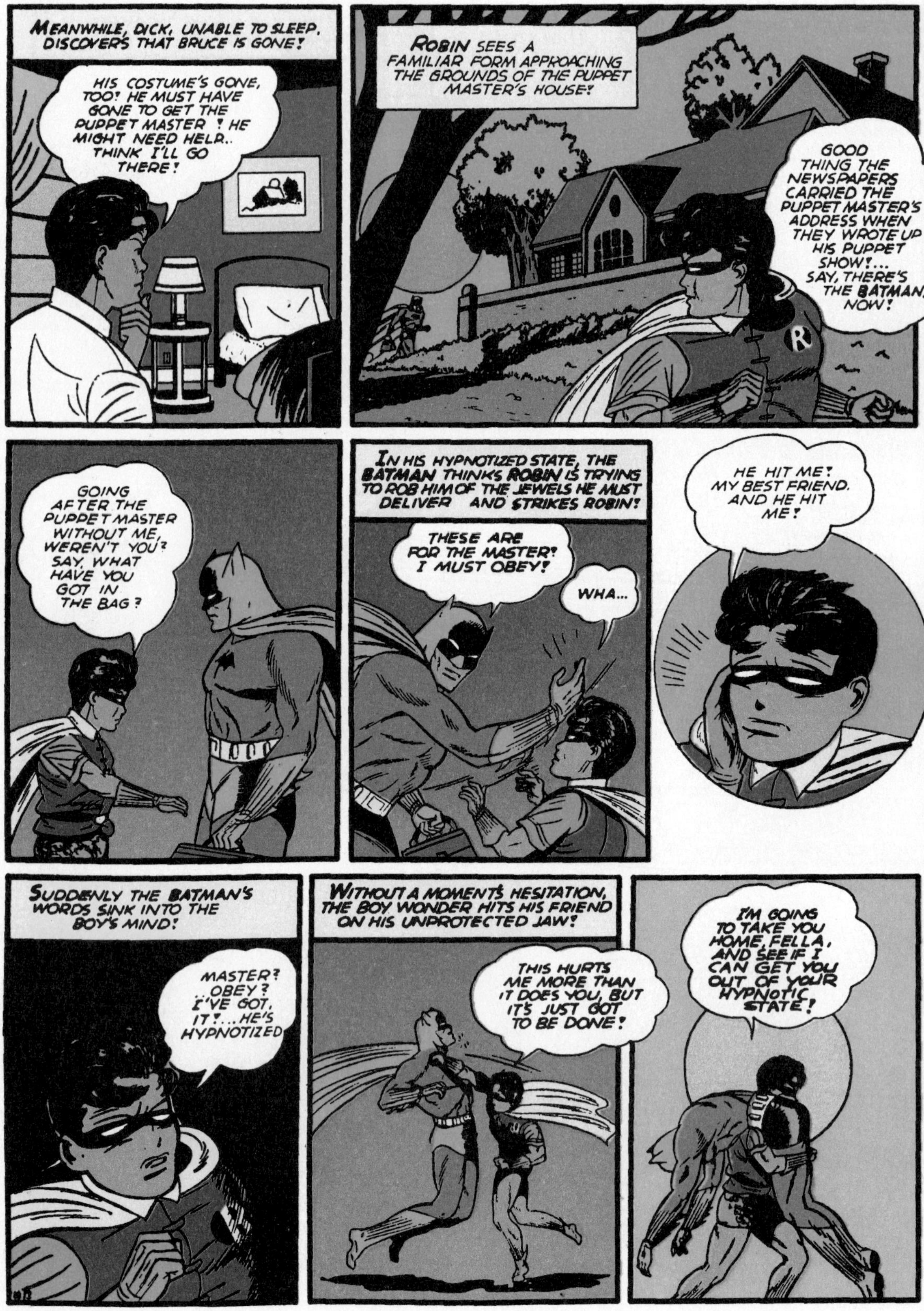
MEANWHILE, DICK, UNABLE TO SLEEP, DISCOVERS THAT BRUCE IS GONE!
HIS COSTUME'S GONE, TOO! HE MUST HAVE GONE TO GET THE PUPPET MASTER ! HE MIGHT NEED HELP.. THINK I'LL GO THERE!
ROBIN SEES A FAMILIAR FORM APPROACHING THE GROUNDS OF THE PUPPET MASTER'S HOUSE!
GOOD THING THE NEWSPAPERS CARRIED THE PUPPET MASTER'S ADDRESS WHEN THEY WROTE UP HIS PUPPET SHOW!... SAY, THERE'S THE BATMAN, NOW!
GOING AFTER THE PUPPET MASTER WITHOUT ME, WEREN'T YOU? SAY, WHAT HAVE YOU GOT IN THE BAG?
IN HIS HYPNOTIZED STATE, THE BATMAN THINKS ROBIN IS TRYING TO ROB HIM OF THE JEWELS HE MUST DELIVER AND STRIKES ROBIN!
THESE ARE FOR THE MASTER! I MUST OBEY!
WHA...
HE HIT ME! MY BEST FRIEND. AND HE HIT ME!
SUDDENLY THE BATMAN'S WORDS SINK INTO THE BOY'S MIND!
MASTER? ..OBEY? I'VE GOT IT!...HE'S HYPNOTIZED
WITHOUT A MOMENT'S HESITATION, THE BOY WONDER HITS HIS FRIEND ON HIS UNPROTECTED JAW!
THIS HURTS ME MORE THAN IT DOES YOU, BUT IT'S JUST GOT TO BE DONE!
I'M GOING TO TAKE YOU HOME, FELLA, AND SEE IF I CAN GET YOU OUT OF YOUR HYPNOTIC STATE!

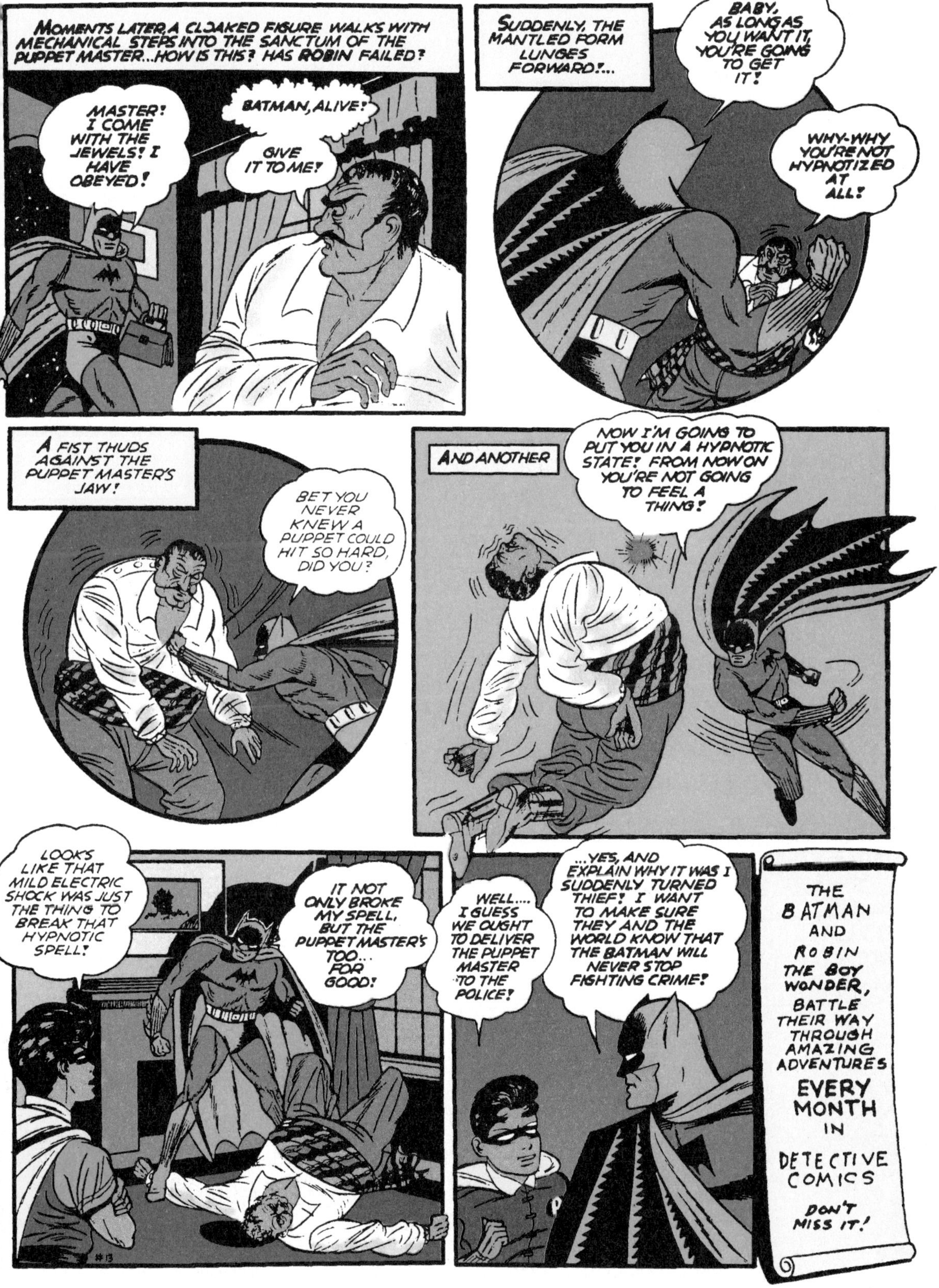
MOMENTS LATER A CLOAKED FIGURE WALKS WITH MECHANICAL STEPS INTO THE SANCTUM OF THE PUPPET MASTER...HOW IS THIS? HAS ROBIN FAILED?
MASTER! I COME WITH THE JEWELS! I HAVE OBEYED!
BATMAN, ALIVE?
GIVE IT TO ME!
SUDDENLY, THE MANTLED FORM LUNGES FORWARD!...
BABY, AS LONG AS YOU WANT IT, YOU'RE GOING TO GET IT!
WHY-WHY YOU'RE NOT HYPNOTIZED AT ALL!
A FIST THUDS AGAINST THE PUPPET MASTER'S JAW!
BET YOU NEVER KNEW A PUPPET COULD HIT SO HARD, DID YOU?
AND ANOTHER
NOW I'M GOING TO PUT YOU IN A HYPNOTIC STATE! FROM NOW ON YOU'RE NOT GOING TO FEEL A THING!
LOOKS LIKE THAT MILD ELECTRIC SHOCK WAS JUST THE THING TO BREAK THAT HYPNOTIC SPELL!
IT NOT ONLY BROKE MY SPELL, BUT THE PUPPET MASTER'S TOO... FOR GOOD!
WELL.... I GUESS WE OUGHT TO DELIVER THE PUPPET MASTER TO THE POLICE!
...YES, AND EXPLAIN WHY IT WAS I SUDDENLY TURNED THIEF! I WANT TO MAKE SURE THEY AND THE WORLD KNOW THAT THE BATMAN WILL NEVER STOP FIGHTING CRIME!
THE BATMAN AND ROBIN THE BOY WONDER, BATTLE THEIR WAY THROUGH AMAZING ADVENTURES EVERY MONTH IN DETECTIVE COMICS
DON'T MISS IT!

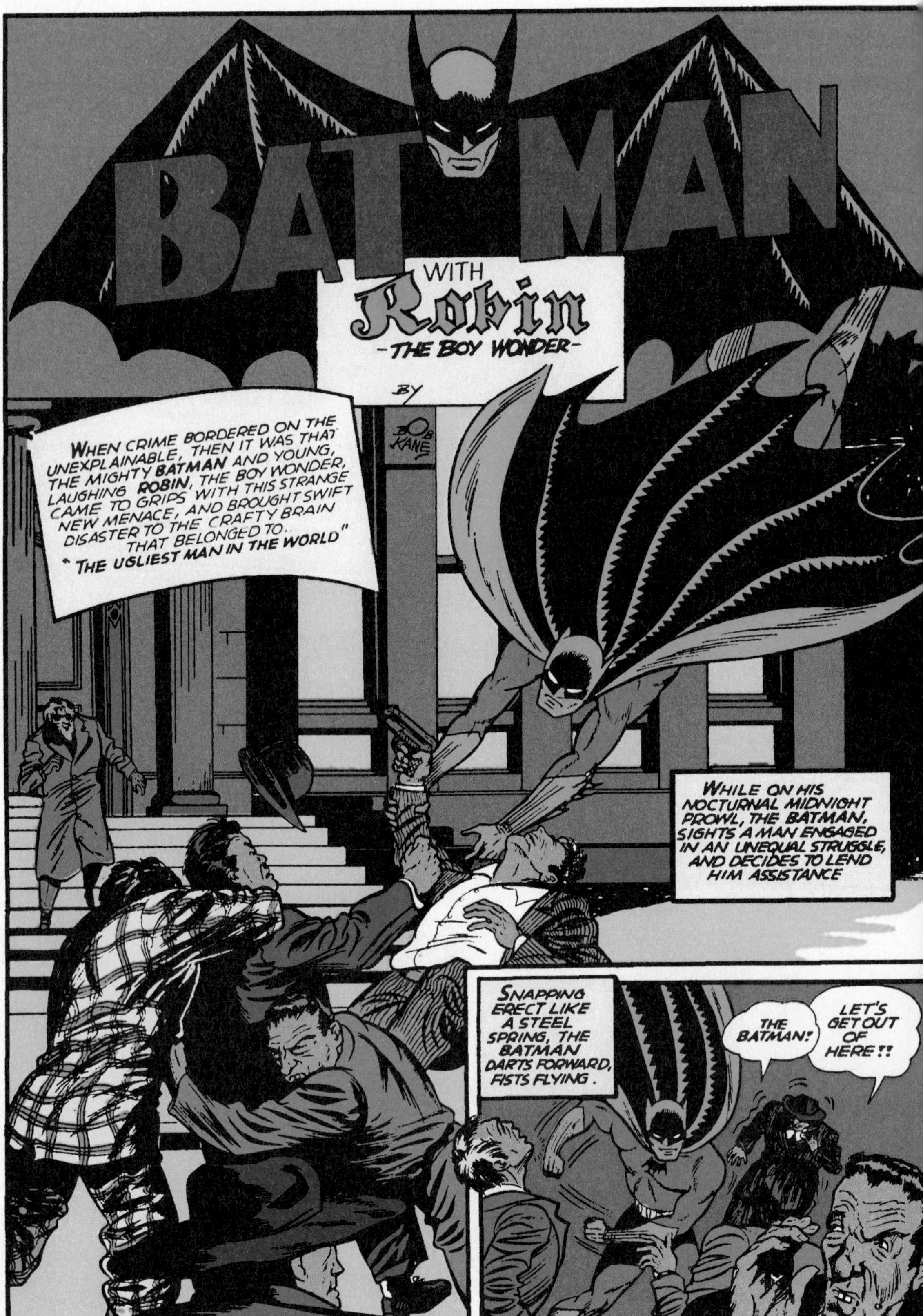
BATMAN
WITH Robin
-THE BOY WONDER-
BY BOB KANE
WHEN CRIME BORDERED ON THE UNEXPLAINABLE, THEN IT WAS THAT THE MIGHTY BATMAN AND YOUNG, LAUGHING ROBIN, THE BOY WONDER, CAME TO GRIPS WITH THIS STRANGE NEW MENACE, AND BROUGHT SWIFT DISASTER TO THE CRAFTY BRAIN THAT BELONGED TO.. "THE UGLIEST MAN IN THE WORLD"
WHILE ON HIS NOCTURNAL MIDNIGHT PROWL, THE BATMAN, SIGHTS A MAN ENGAGED IN AN UNEQUAL STRUGGLE, AND DECIDES TO LEND HIM ASSISTANCE
#1
SNAPPING ERECT LIKE A STEEL SPRING, THE BATMAN DARTS FORWARD, FISTS FLYING.
THE BATMAN!
LET'S GET OUT OF HERE!!

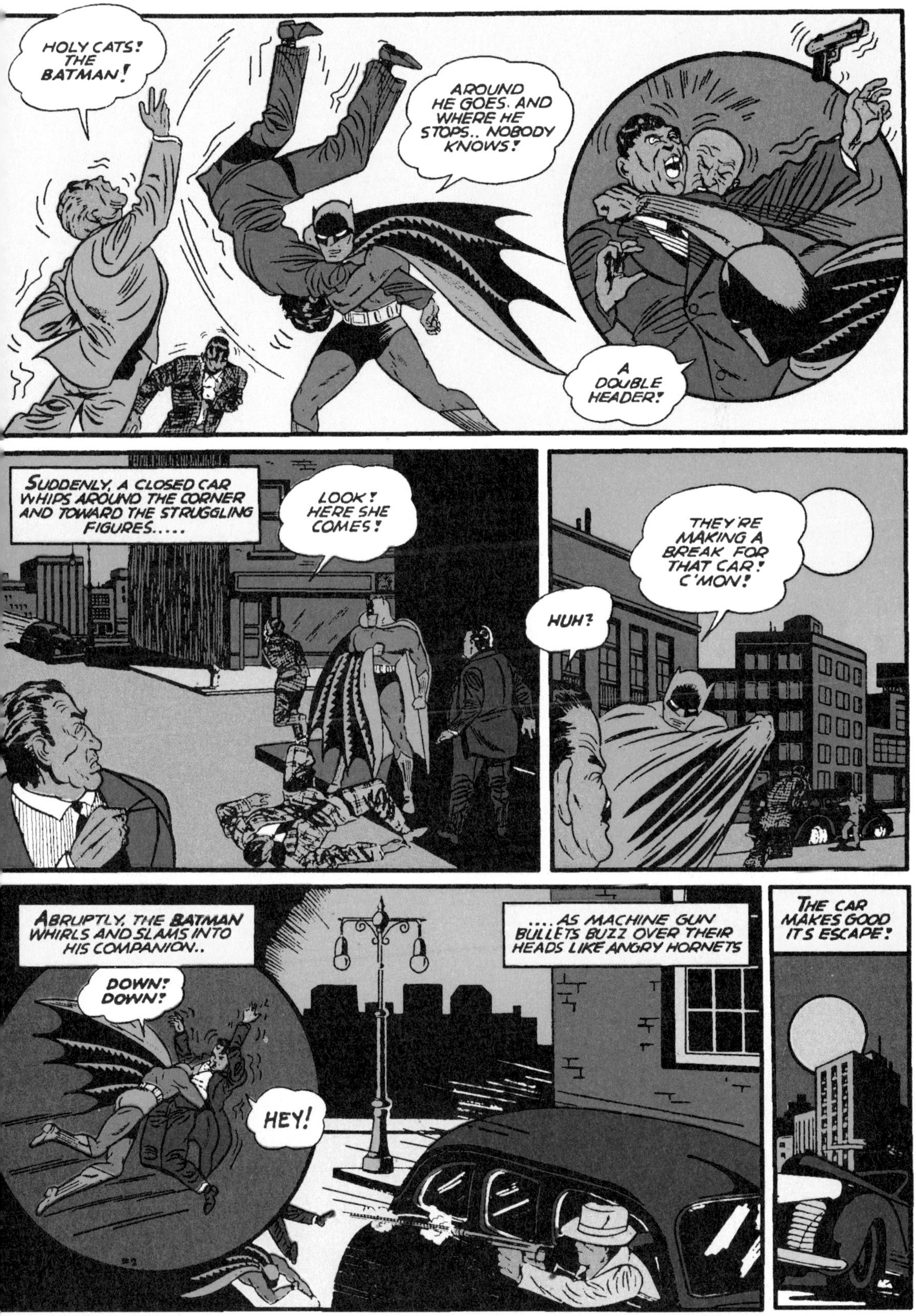
HOLY CATS! THE BATMAN!
AROUND HE GOES. AND WHERE HE STOPS.. NOBODY KNOWS!
A DOUBLE HEADER!
SUDDENLY, A CLOSED CAR WHIPS AROUND THE CORNER AND TOWARD THE STRUGGLING FIGURES.....
LOOK! HERE SHE COMES!
THEY'RE MAKING A BREAK FOR THAT CAR! C'MON!
HUH?
ABRUPTLY, THE BATMAN WHIRLS AND SLAMS INTO HIS COMPANION..
DOWN! DOWN!
HEY!
....AS MACHINE GUN BULLETS BUZZ OVER THEIR HEADS LIKE ANGRY HORNETS
THE CAR MAKES GOOD ITS ESCAPE!

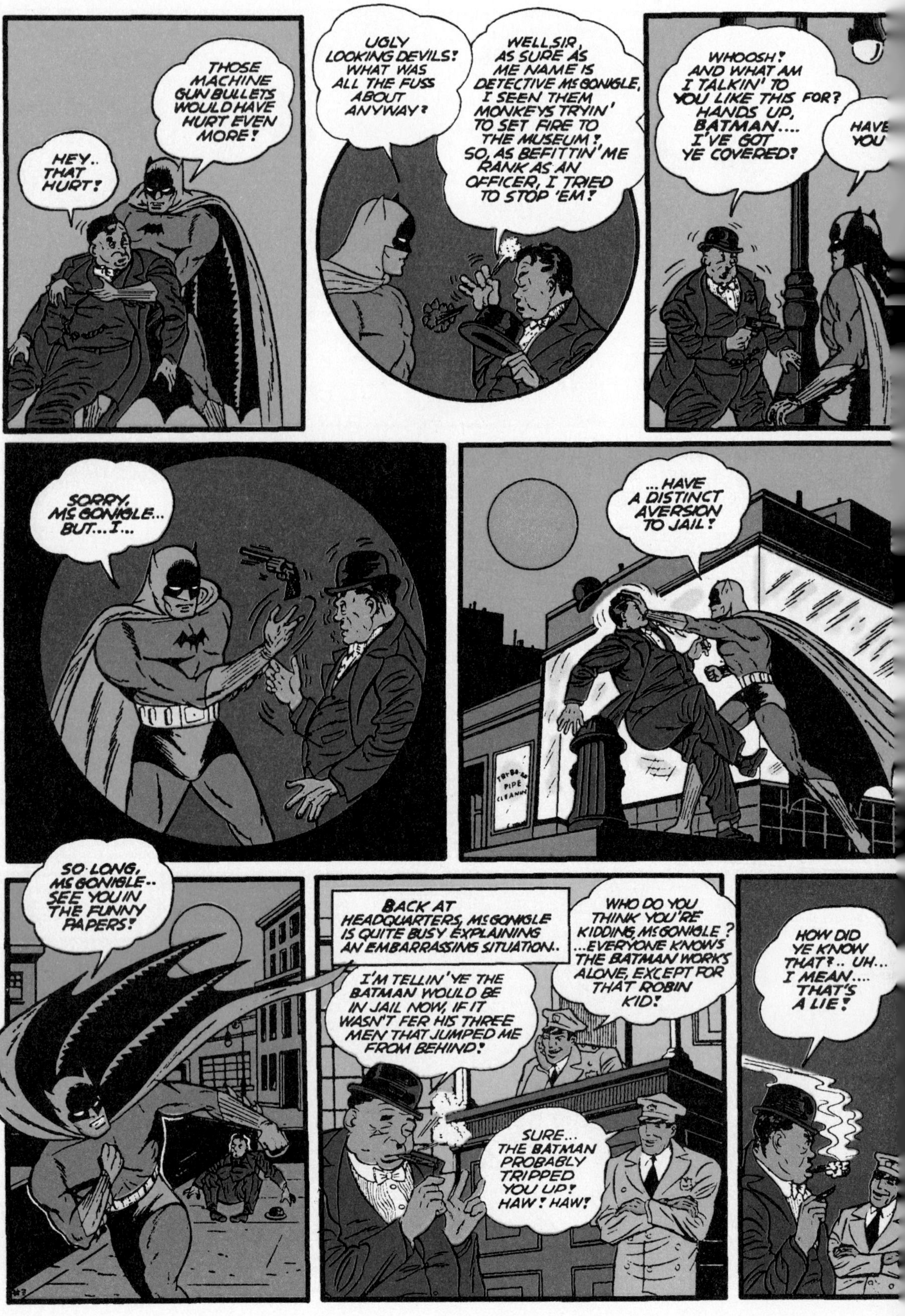
HEY.. THAT HURT!
THOSE MACHINE GUN BULLETS WOULD HAVE HURT EVEN MORE!
UGLY LOOKING DEVILS! WHAT WAS ALL THE FUSS ABOUT ANYWAY?
WELL SIR, AS SURE AS ME NAME IS DETECTIVE McGONIGLE, I SEEN THEM MONKEYS TRYIN' TO SET FIRE TO THE MUSEUM! SO, AS BEFITTIN' ME RANK AS AN OFFICER, I TRIED TO STOP 'EM!
WHOOSH! AND WHAT AM I TALKIN' TO YOU LIKE THIS FOR? HANDS UP, BATMAN.... I'VE GOT YE COVERED!
HAVE YOU
SORRY, McGONIGLE... BUT...I...
...HAVE A DISTINCT AVERSION TO JAIL!
SO LONG, McGONIGLE.. SEE YOU IN THE FUNNY PAPERS!
BACK AT HEADQUARTERS, McGONIGLE IS QUITE BUSY EXPLAINING AN EMBARRASSING SITUATION..
I'M TELLIN' YE THE BATMAN WOULD BE IN JAIL NOW, IF IT WASN'T FER HIS THREE MEN THAT JUMPED ME FROM BEHIND!
WHO DO YOU THINK YOU'RE KIDDING, McGONIGLE? ...EVERYONE KNOWS THE BATMAN WORKS ALONE, EXCEPT FOR THAT ROBIN KID!
SURE... THE BATMAN PROBABLY TRIPPED YOU UP! HAW! HAW!
HOW DID YE KNOW THAT?.. UH... I MEAN.... THAT'S A LIE!

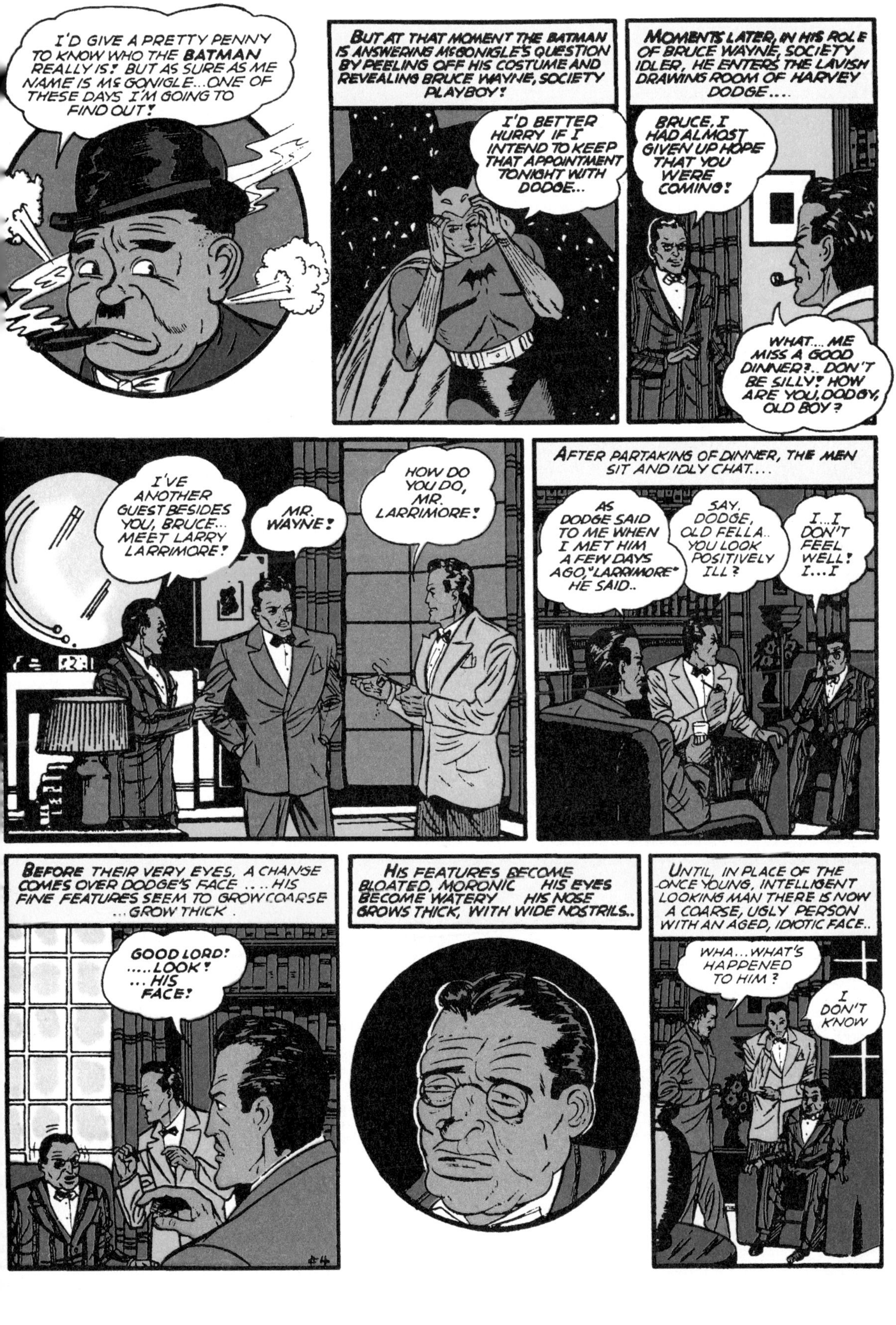
I'D GIVE A PRETTY PENNY TO KNOW WHO THE BATMAN REALLY IS! BUT AS SURE AS ME NAME IS MCGONIGLE...ONE OF THESE DAYS I'M GOING TO FIND OUT!
BUT AT THAT MOMENT THE BATMAN IS ANSWERING MCGONIGLE'S QUESTION BY PEELING OFF HIS COSTUME AND REVEALING BRUCE WAYNE, SOCIETY PLAYBOY!
I'D BETTER HURRY IF I INTEND TO KEEP THAT APPOINTMENT TONIGHT WITH DODGE...
MOMENTS LATER, IN HIS ROLE OF BRUCE WAYNE, SOCIETY IDLER, HE ENTERS THE LAVISH DRAWING ROOM OF HARVEY DODGE....
BRUCE, I HAD ALMOST GIVEN UP HOPE THAT YOU WERE COMING!
WHAT.... ME MISS A GOOD DINNER?.. DON'T BE SILLY! HOW ARE YOU, DODGY, OLD BOY?
I'VE ANOTHER GUEST BESIDES YOU, BRUCE... MEET LARRY LARRIMORE!
MR. WAYNE!
HOW DO YOU DO, MR. LARRIMORE!
AFTER PARTAKING OF DINNER, THE MEN SIT AND IDLY CHAT....
AS DODGE SAID TO ME WHEN I MET HIM A FEW DAYS AGO, "LARRIMORE" HE SAID..
SAY, DODGE, OLD FELLA.. YOU LOOK POSITIVELY ILL?
I...I DON'T FEEL WELL! I...I
BEFORE THEIR VERY EYES, A CHANGE COMES OVER DODGE'S FACE ....HIS FINE FEATURES SEEM TO GROW COARSE ...GROW THICK.
GOOD LORD! .....LOOK! ... HIS FACE!
HIS FEATURES BECOME BLOATED, MORONIC HIS EYES BECOME WATERY HIS NOSE GROWS THICK, WITH WIDE NOSTRILS..
UNTIL, IN PLACE OF THE ONCE YOUNG, INTELLIGENT LOOKING MAN THERE IS NOW A COARSE, UGLY PERSON WITH AN AGED, IDIOTIC FACE..
WHA...WHAT'S HAPPENED TO HIM?
I DON'T KNOW

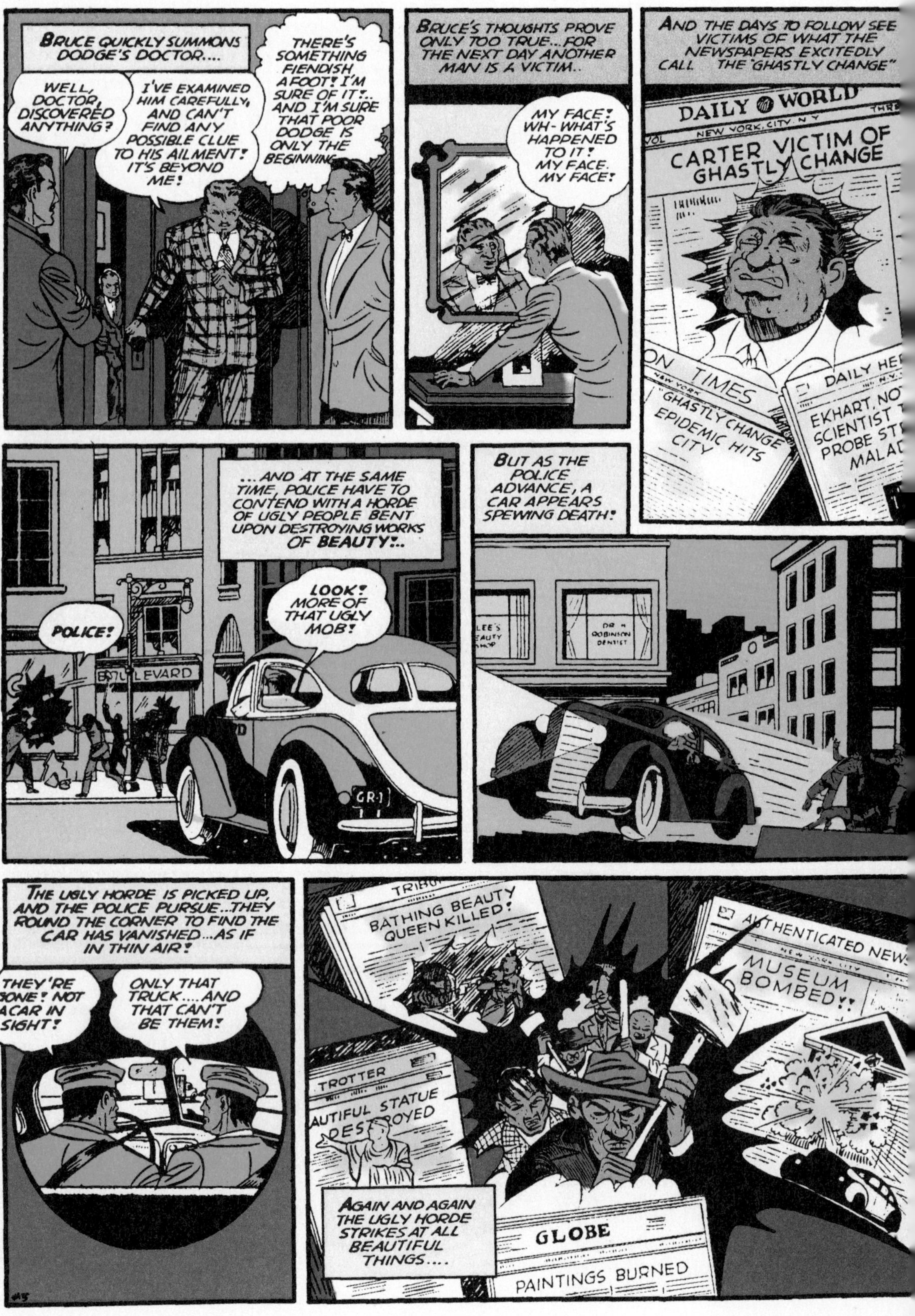
BRUCE QUICKLY SUMMONS DODGE'S DOCTOR....
WELL, DOCTOR, DISCOVERED ANYTHING?
I'VE EXAMINED HIM CAREFULLY, AND CAN'T FIND ANY POSSIBLE CLUE TO HIS AILMENT! IT'S BEYOND ME!
THERE'S SOMETHING FIENDISH AFOOT! I'M SURE OF IT!.. AND I'M SURE THAT POOR DODGE IS ONLY THE BEGINNING..
BRUCE'S THOUGHTS PROVE ONLY TOO TRUE...FOR THE NEXT DAY ANOTHER MAN IS A VICTIM..
MY FACE! WH-WHAT'S HAPPENED TO IT! MY FACE. MY FACE!
AND THE DAYS TO FOLLOW SEE VICTIMS OF WHAT THE NEWSPAPERS EXCITEDLY CALL THE "GHASTLY CHANGE"
DAILY WORLD
NEW YORK CITY N.Y.
CARTER VICTIM OF GHASTLY CHANGE
TIMES
"GHASTLY CHANGE" EPIDEMIC HITS CITY
DAILY HE
EKHART, NOT SCIENTIST PROBE ST MALAD
...AND AT THE SAME TIME, POLICE HAVE TO CONTEND WITH A HORDE OF UGLY PEOPLE BENT UPON DESTROYING WORKS OF BEAUTY!..
POLICE!
LOOK! MORE OF THAT UGLY MOB!
BOULEVARD
GR-1
BUT AS THE POLICE ADVANCE, A CAR APPEARS SPEWING DEATH!
LEE'S BEAUTY SHOP
DR H ROBINSON DENTIST
THE UGLY HORDE IS PICKED UP, AND THE POLICE PURSUE...THEY ROUND THE CORNER TO FIND THE CAR HAS VANISHED...AS IF IN THIN AIR!
THEY'RE GONE! NOT A CAR IN SIGHT!
ONLY THAT TRUCK....AND THAT CAN'T BE THEM!
BATHING BEAUTY QUEEN KILLED!
AUTHENTICATED NEWS
MUSEUM BOMBED!!
TROTTER
AUTIFUL STATUE DESTROYED
AGAIN AND AGAIN THE UGLY HORDE STRIKES AT ALL BEAUTIFUL THINGS....
GLOBE
PAINTINGS BURNED

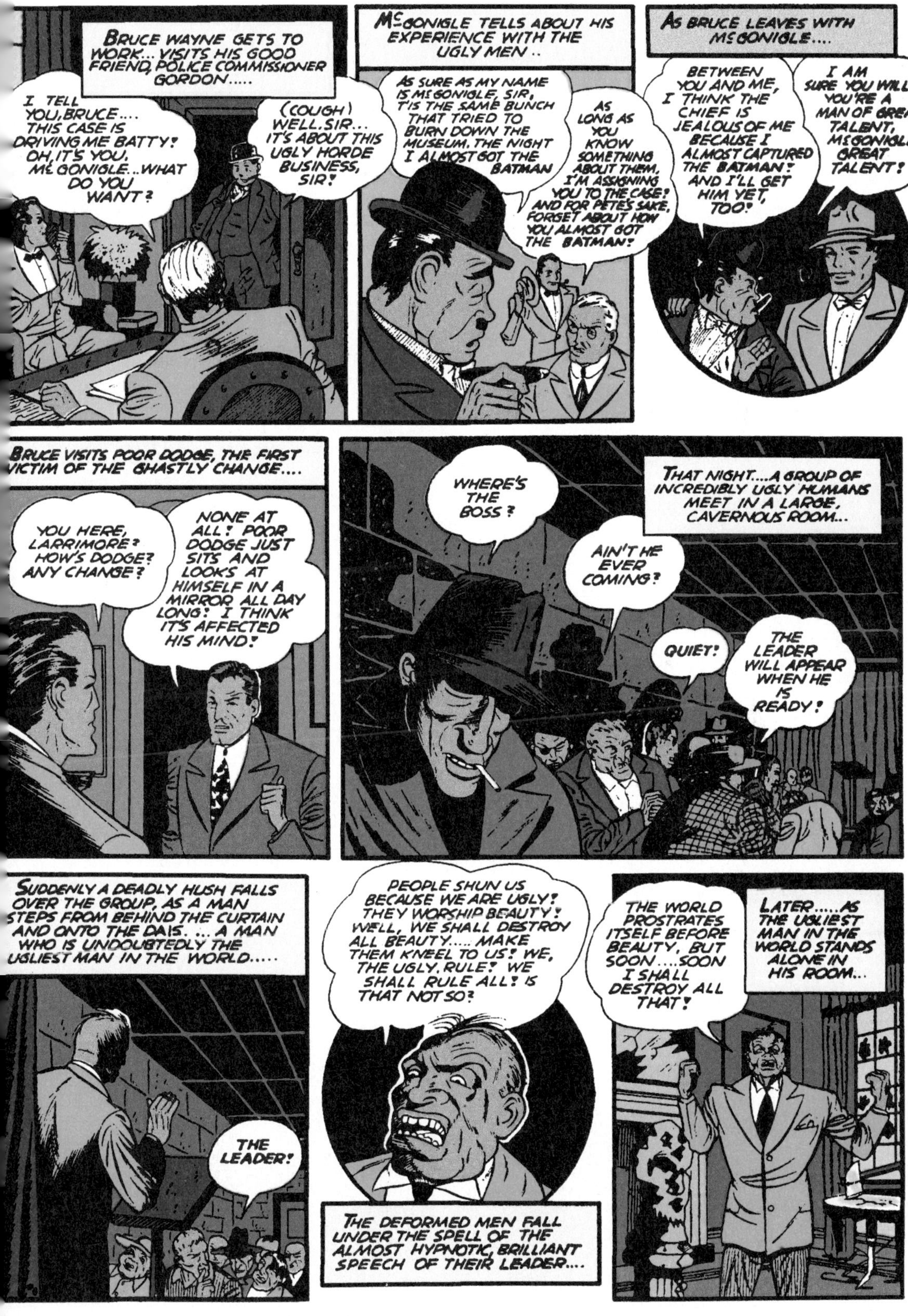
BRUCE WAYNE GETS TO WORK... VISITS HIS GOOD FRIEND, POLICE COMMISSIONER GORDON.....
I TELL YOU, BRUCE.... THIS CASE IS DRIVING ME BATTY! OH, IT'S YOU, MCGONIGLE...WHAT DO YOU WANT?
(COUGH) WELL, SIR... IT'S ABOUT THIS UGLY HORDE BUSINESS, SIR!
MCGONIGLE TELLS ABOUT HIS EXPERIENCE WITH THE UGLY MEN..
AS SURE AS MY NAME IS MCGONIGLE, SIR, T'IS THE SAME BUNCH THAT TRIED TO BURN DOWN THE MUSEUM, THE NIGHT I ALMOST GOT THE BATMAN
AS LONG AS YOU KNOW SOMETHING ABOUT THEM, I'M ASSIGNING YOU TO THE CASE! AND FOR PETE'S SAKE, FORGET ABOUT HOW YOU ALMOST GOT THE BATMAN!
AS BRUCE LEAVES WITH MCGONIGLE....
BETWEEN YOU AND ME, I THINK THE CHIEF IS JEALOUS OF ME BECAUSE I ALMOST CAPTURED THE BATMAN! AND I'LL GET HIM YET, TOO!
I AM SURE YOU WILL! YOU'RE A MAN OF GREAT TALENT, MCGONIGLE.. GREAT TALENT!
BRUCE VISITS POOR DODGE, THE FIRST VICTIM OF THE GHASTLY CHANGE....
YOU HERE, LARRIMORE? HOW'S DODGE? ANY CHANGE?
NONE AT ALL! POOR DODGE JUST SITS AND LOOKS AT HIMSELF IN A MIRROR ALL DAY LONG! I THINK IT'S AFFECTED HIS MIND!
THAT NIGHT....A GROUP OF INCREDIBLY UGLY HUMANS MEET IN A LARGE, CAVERNOUS ROOM...
WHERE'S THE BOSS?
AIN'T HE EVER COMING?
QUIET!
THE LEADER WILL APPEAR WHEN HE IS READY!
SUDDENLY A DEADLY HUSH FALLS OVER THE GROUP, AS A MAN STEPS FROM BEHIND THE CURTAIN AND ONTO THE DAIS.... A MAN WHO IS UNDOUBTEDLY THE UGLIEST MAN IN THE WORLD.....
THE LEADER!
PEOPLE SHUN US BECAUSE WE ARE UGLY! THEY WORSHIP BEAUTY! WELL, WE SHALL DESTROY ALL BEAUTY..... MAKE THEM KNEEL TO US! WE, THE UGLY, RULE! WE SHALL RULE ALL! IS THAT NOT SO?
THE DEFORMED MEN FALL UNDER THE SPELL OF THE ALMOST HYPNOTIC, BRILLIANT SPEECH OF THEIR LEADER....
LATER.....AS THE UGLIEST MAN IN THE WORLD STANDS ALONE IN HIS ROOM...
THE WORLD PROSTRATES ITSELF BEFORE BEAUTY, BUT SOON....SOON I SHALL DESTROY ALL THAT!

SEIZING A KNIFE, HE BEGINS TO HACK AND SLASH AT A BEAUTIFUL PAINTING, LAUGHING ALL THE WHILE LIKE A MADMAN!

HA HA! THIS IS WHAT I SHALL DO TO ALL PRETTY THINGS! HA HA HA! GOOD-BYE, BEAUTY! HA HA HA!

WHILE AT THAT MOMENT, BRUCE WAYNE READS AN INTERESTING ITEM ALOUD TO DICK GRAYSON... WHO IS IN REALITY... ROBIN, THE BOY WONDER....

...AND SO, FEARING THE INVADING COUNTRY WILL APPROPRIATE THIS GREAT ART TREASURE, BORAVIA HAS SENT IT TO THE UNITED STATES. IT WILL BE UNLOADED TONIGHT, AT PIER 3, FROM THE SHIP!

BRUCE, I CAN ALMOST READ YOUR MIND!

YOU THINK THIS UGLY HORDE WILL TRY TO DESTROY THIS STATUE AS IT'S UNLOADED?

THIS STATUE IS A HANDSOME ONE. FIGURE IT OUT FOR YOURSELF!

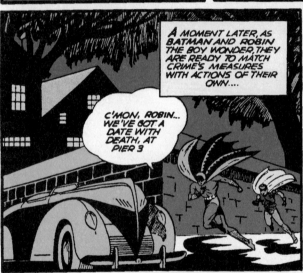

A MOMENT LATER, AS BATMAN AND ROBIN THE BOY WONDER, THEY ARE READY TO MATCH CRIME'S MEASURES WITH ACTIONS OF THEIR OWN....

C'MON, ROBIN... WE'VE GOT A DATE WITH DEATH, AT PIER 3!

AT PIER 3, THE UGLY HORDE DESCENDS UPON THE GUARDS IN OVERWHELMING NUMBERS....

BUT TWO RASH MORTALS RACE TOWARD THE DREADFUL SCENE, READY TO OFFER BATTLE....THEY ARE.... BATMAN AND ROBIN!

BATMAN!

LOOK!

BEFORE WE'RE THROUGH WITH YOU, YOU'LL KNOW YOU'VE BEEN IN A FIGHT!

LIKE TWO PROJECTILES, THEY BORE INTO THE HORDE, SENDING THEM SPRAWLING!

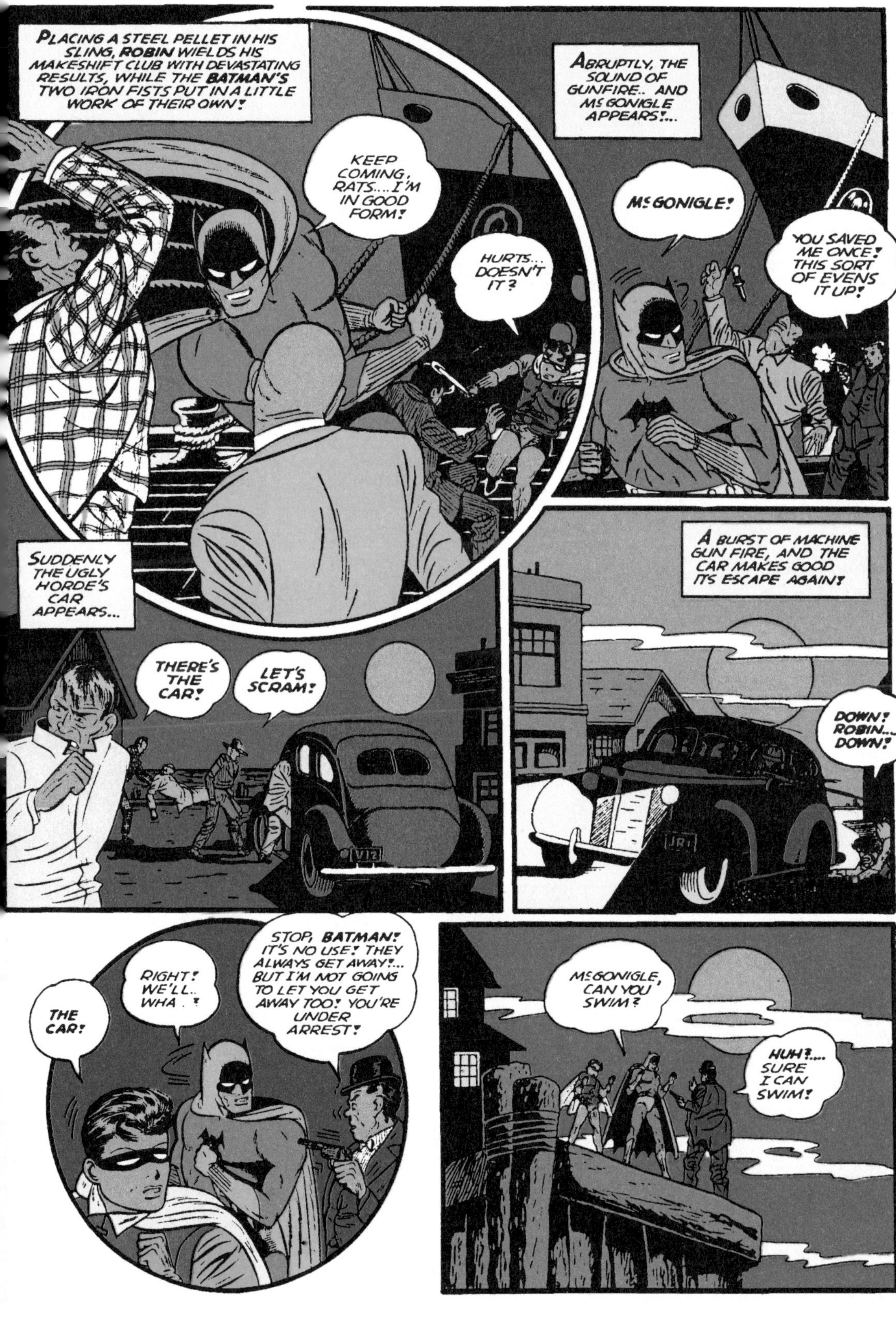
PLACING A STEEL PELLET IN HIS SLING, ROBIN WIELDS HIS MAKESHIFT CLUB WITH DEVASTATING RESULTS, WHILE THE BATMAN'S TWO IRON FISTS PUT IN A LITTLE WORK OF THEIR OWN!
KEEP COMING, RATS.... I'M IN GOOD FORM!
HURTS... DOESN'T IT?
ABRUPTLY, THE SOUND OF GUNFIRE.. AND MCGONIGLE APPEARS!...
MCGONIGLE!
YOU SAVED ME ONCE! THIS SORT OF EVENS IT UP!
SUDDENLY THE UGLY HORDE'S CAR APPEARS...
THERE'S THE CAR!
LET'S SCRAM!
A BURST OF MACHINE GUN FIRE, AND THE CAR MAKES GOOD ITS ESCAPE AGAIN!
DOWN! ROBIN... DOWN!
THE CAR!
RIGHT! WE'LL.. WHA..!
STOP, BATMAN! IT'S NO USE! THEY ALWAYS GET AWAY!... BUT I'M NOT GOING TO LET YOU GET AWAY TOO! YOU'RE UNDER ARREST!
MCGONIGLE, CAN YOU SWIM?
HUH?.... SURE I CAN SWIM!

THAT'S ALL I WANTED TO KNOW!

WHA..?

C'MON, ROBIN.... MAYBE WE CAN STILL CATCH THEM!

I'M RIGHT BEHIND YOU!

(SPLUTTE GLU... UGLUG (SPLUTTE

BUT WHEN THE *BATMAN* AND *ROBIN* ROUND THE CORNER....

THE STREETS DESERTED EXCEPT FOR THAT TRUCK! NOW WHAT DO WE DO?

NOT A SIGN OF THEM!

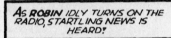

AS *ROBIN* IDLY TURNS ON THE RADIO, STARTLING NEWS IS HEARD!

AND DOCTOR EKHART FEELS SURE HE HAS AT LAST DISCOVERED THE CAUSE OF THE "GHASTLY CHANGE" AND AN ANTIDOTE FOR IT!

KNOW WHAT THAT MEANS, ROBIN?

LISTEN!

THAT MEANS THAT EKHART'S LIFE IS IN DANGER! WHOEVER IS BEHIND THIS "GHASTLY CHANGE" WILL TRY TO KILL HIM! I HOPE WE'RE NOT TOO LATE!

MOMENTS LATER AS THE CAR SCREECHES TO A HALT OUTSIDE THE HOME OF DOCTOR EKHART.

THOSE DEVILS ARE HERE ALREADY! THEY WORK FAST! C'MON!

HELP!

WHAT'S THAT!

THE DOOR! THEY MUST HAVE LOCKED IT!

GET OUT MY WAY, ROBIN... I'M GOING THROUGH!

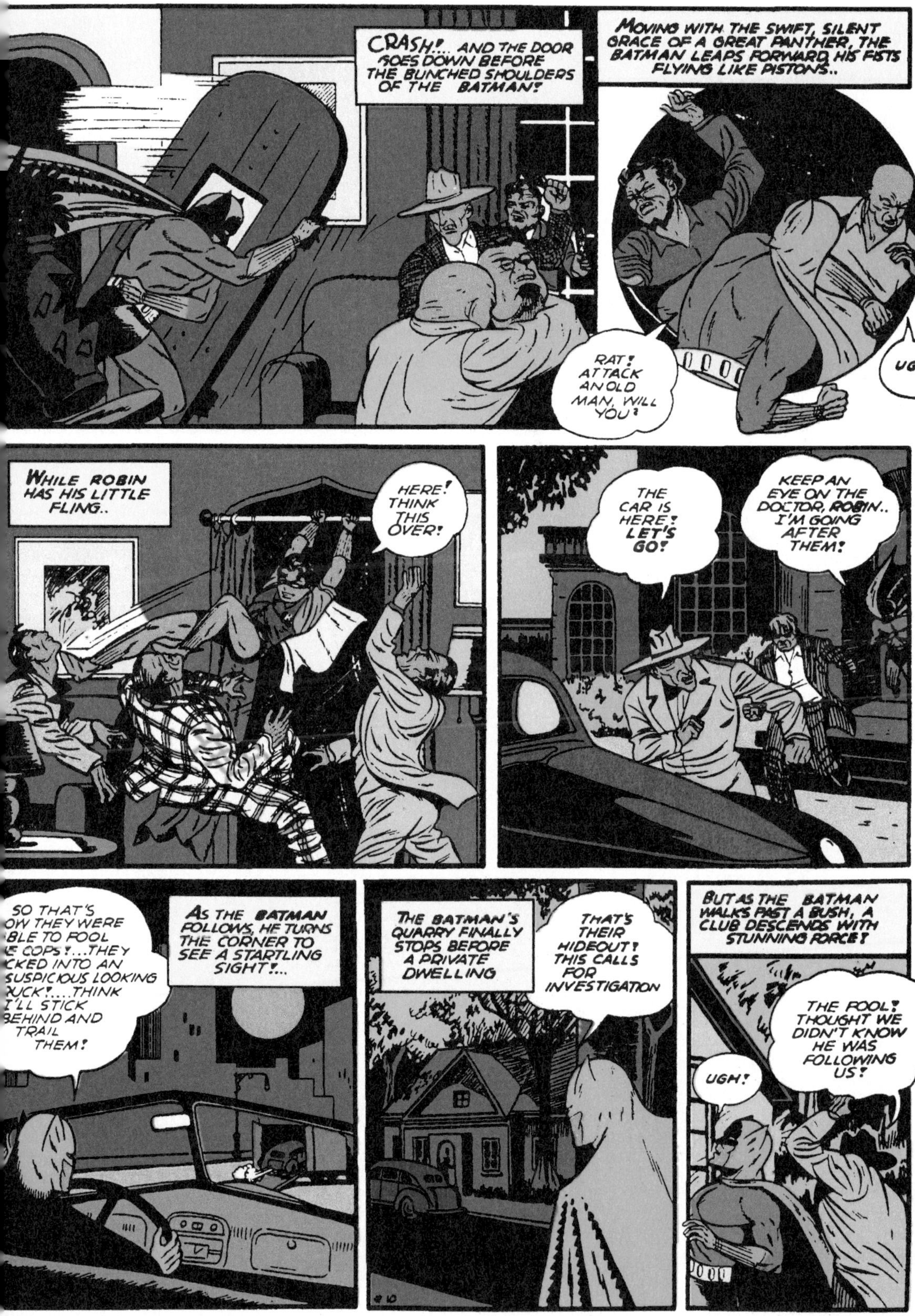
CRASH!... AND THE DOOR GOES DOWN BEFORE THE BUNCHED SHOULDERS OF THE BATMAN!
MOVING WITH THE SWIFT, SILENT GRACE OF A GREAT PANTHER, THE BATMAN LEAPS FORWARD, HIS FISTS FLYING LIKE PISTONS..
RAT! ATTACK AN OLD MAN, WILL YOU?
UGH!
WHILE ROBIN HAS HIS LITTLE FLING..
HERE! THINK THIS OVER!
THE CAR IS HERE! LET'S GO!
KEEP AN EYE ON THE DOCTOR, ROBIN.. I'M GOING AFTER THEM!
SO THAT'S OW THEY WERE BLE TO FOOL E COPS!...THEY CKED INTO AN SUSPICIOUS LOOKING RUCK!....THINK I'LL STICK BEHIND AND TRAIL THEM!
AS THE BATMAN FOLLOWS, HE TURNS THE CORNER TO SEE A STARTLING SIGHT!...
THE BATMAN'S QUARRY FINALLY STOPS BEFORE A PRIVATE DWELLING
THAT'S THEIR HIDEOUT! THIS CALLS FOR INVESTIGATION
BUT AS THE BATMAN WALKS PAST A BUSH, A CLUB DESCENDS WITH STUNNING FORCE!
UGH!
THE FOOL! THOUGHT WE DIDN'T KNOW HE WAS FOLLOWING US!

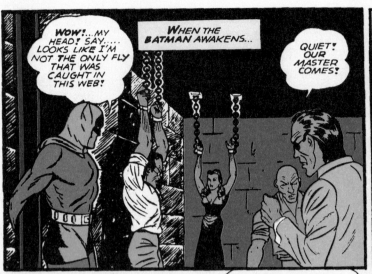

WOW!...MY HEAD! SAY..... LOOKS LIKE I'M NOT THE ONLY FLY THAT WAS CAUGHT IN THIS WEB!

WHEN THE BATMAN AWAKENS...

QUIET! OUR MASTER COMES!

THROUGH THE DOOR STEPS A MAN... THAT MAN.....

OUR LEADER?

LARRIMORE

SLOWLY FINGERS PEEL OFF A RUBBEROID MASK AND REVEAL UNDERNEATH THE FEATURES OF THE UGLIEST MAN IN THE WORLD!

JOHN TYLER AND MRS. TYLER! MY GUESTS.. I BID YOU WELCOME! UNFORTUNATELY I HAD NO ENTERTAINMENT PREPARED, SO TO DIVERT YOU, I WILL TELL A STORY ..A VERY INTERESTING STORY!

"IT BEGINS WHEN A YOUNG MAN WAS BEING INITIATED INTO A COLLEGE FRATERNITY ..."

WHAT HAVE YOU GOT THERE, TYLER?

IT'S A HYPO NEEDLE FILLED WITH A LOT OF DRUGS I MIXED TOGETHER HAPHAZARDLY. I'LL PRETEND TO INJECT IT INTO CARLSON!

BUT AS TYLER APPROACHED HIS "VICTIM" THE INJECTION BECAME REALITY AS ANOTHER ACCIDENTLY JOSTLED AGAINST HIM."

WATCH IT!

THE NEEDLE!...IT'S GONE INTO CARLSON!

"AT FIRST THERE WAS NO IMMEDIATE EFFECT, BUT A FEW DAYS LATER CARLSON AWOKE ONE MORNING TO FIND HIS HANDSOME FACE HAD CHANGED OVERNIGHT!"

MY FACE!.....WHAT'S HAPPENED TO IT? IT'S UGLY! HIDEOUS!

"NO REMEDY COULD BE FOUND, FOR THE CHEMICALS HAD BEEN MIXED HAPHAZARDLY... AND CARLSON FOUND HIMSELF SHUNNED.. EVEN BY HIS FIANCEE ... "

CAN'T YOU SEE?...I..I.. CAN'T MARRY YOU NOW! I JUST CAN'T!

SO MY FACE IS REPULSIVE TO YOU! EVEN TO YOU, WHO I THOUGH LOVE ME!

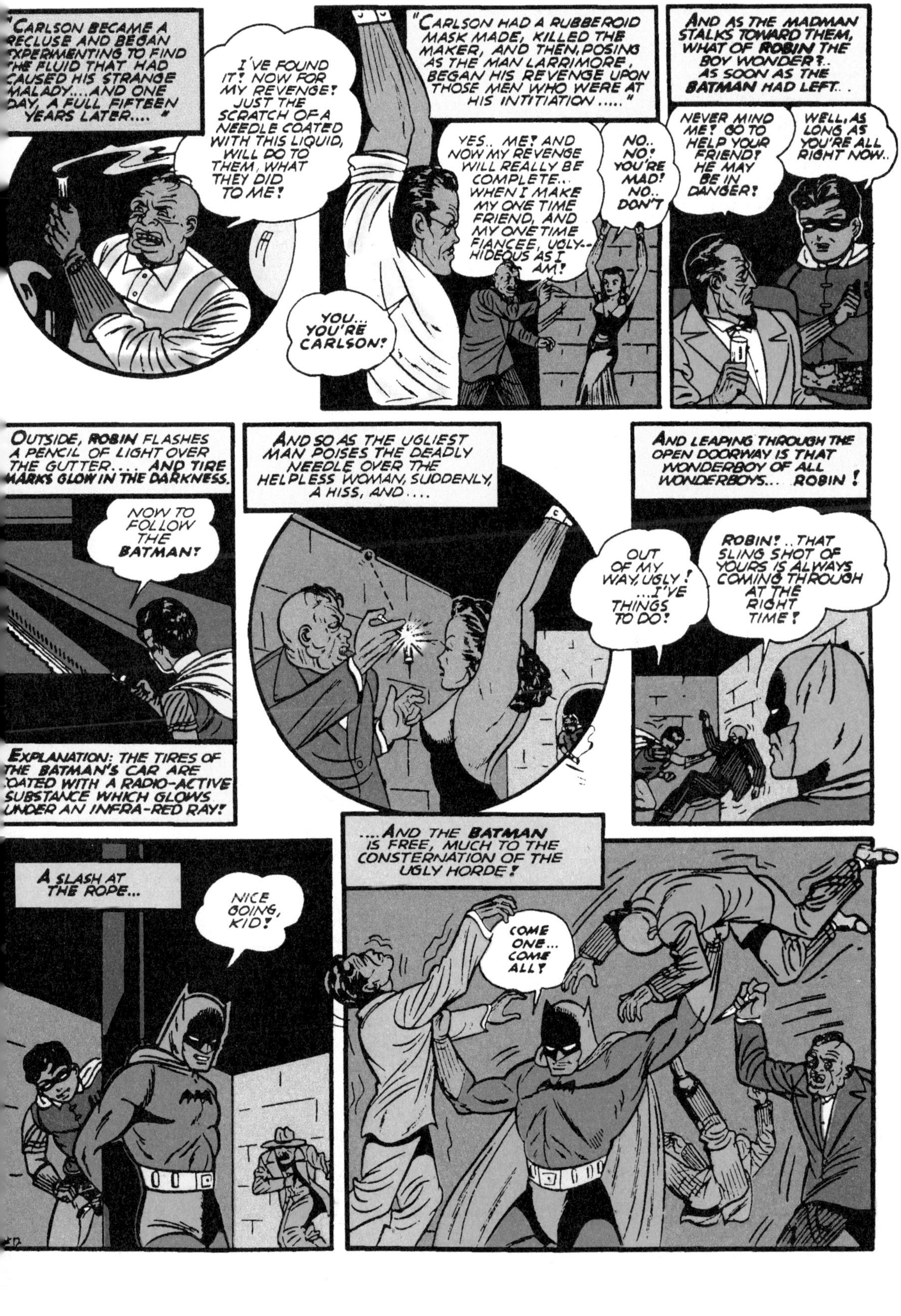
"CARLSON BECAME A RECLUSE AND BEGAN EXPERIMENTING TO FIND THE FLUID THAT HAD CAUSED HIS STRANGE MALADY.... AND ONE DAY, A FULL FIFTEEN YEARS LATER.... "
I'VE FOUND IT! NOW FOR MY REVENGE! JUST THE SCRATCH OF A NEEDLE COATED WITH THIS LIQUID, WILL DO TO THEM, WHAT THEY DID TO ME!
"CARLSON HAD A RUBBEROID MASK MADE, KILLED THE MAKER, AND THEN, POSING AS THE MAN LARRIMORE, BEGAN HIS REVENGE UPON THOSE MEN WHO WERE AT HIS INTITIATION ....."
YOU... YOU'RE CARLSON!
YES.. ME! AND NOW MY REVENGE WILL REALLY BE COMPLETE.. WHEN I MAKE MY ONE TIME FRIEND, AND MY ONE TIME FIANCEE, UGLY-- HIDEOUS AS I AM!
NO.. NO! YOU'RE MAD! NO.. DON'T
AND AS THE MADMAN STALKS TOWARD THEM, WHAT OF ROBIN THE BOY WONDER?.. AS SOON AS THE BATMAN HAD LEFT.. .
NEVER MIND ME! GO TO HELP YOUR FRIEND! HE MAY BE IN DANGER!
WELL, AS LONG AS YOU'RE ALL RIGHT NOW..
OUTSIDE, ROBIN FLASHES A PENCIL OF LIGHT OVER THE GUTTER.... AND TIRE MARKS GLOW IN THE DARKNESS.
NOW TO FOLLOW THE BATMAN!
EXPLANATION: THE TIRES OF THE BATMAN'S CAR ARE COATED WITH A RADIO-ACTIVE SUBSTANCE WHICH GLOWS UNDER AN INFRA-RED RAY!
AND SO AS THE UGLIEST MAN POISES THE DEADLY NEEDLE OVER THE HELPLESS WOMAN, SUDDENLY, A HISS, AND....
AND LEAPING THROUGH THE OPEN DOORWAY IS THAT WONDERBOY OF ALL WONDERBOYS... ROBIN!
OUT OF MY WAY, UGLY! ...I'VE THINGS TO DO!
ROBIN! ..THAT SLING SHOT OF YOURS IS ALWAYS COMING THROUGH AT THE RIGHT TIME!
A SLASH AT THE ROPE...
NICE GOING, KID!
....AND THE BATMAN IS FREE, MUCH TO THE CONSTERNATION OF THE UGLY HORDE!
COME ONE... COME ALL!

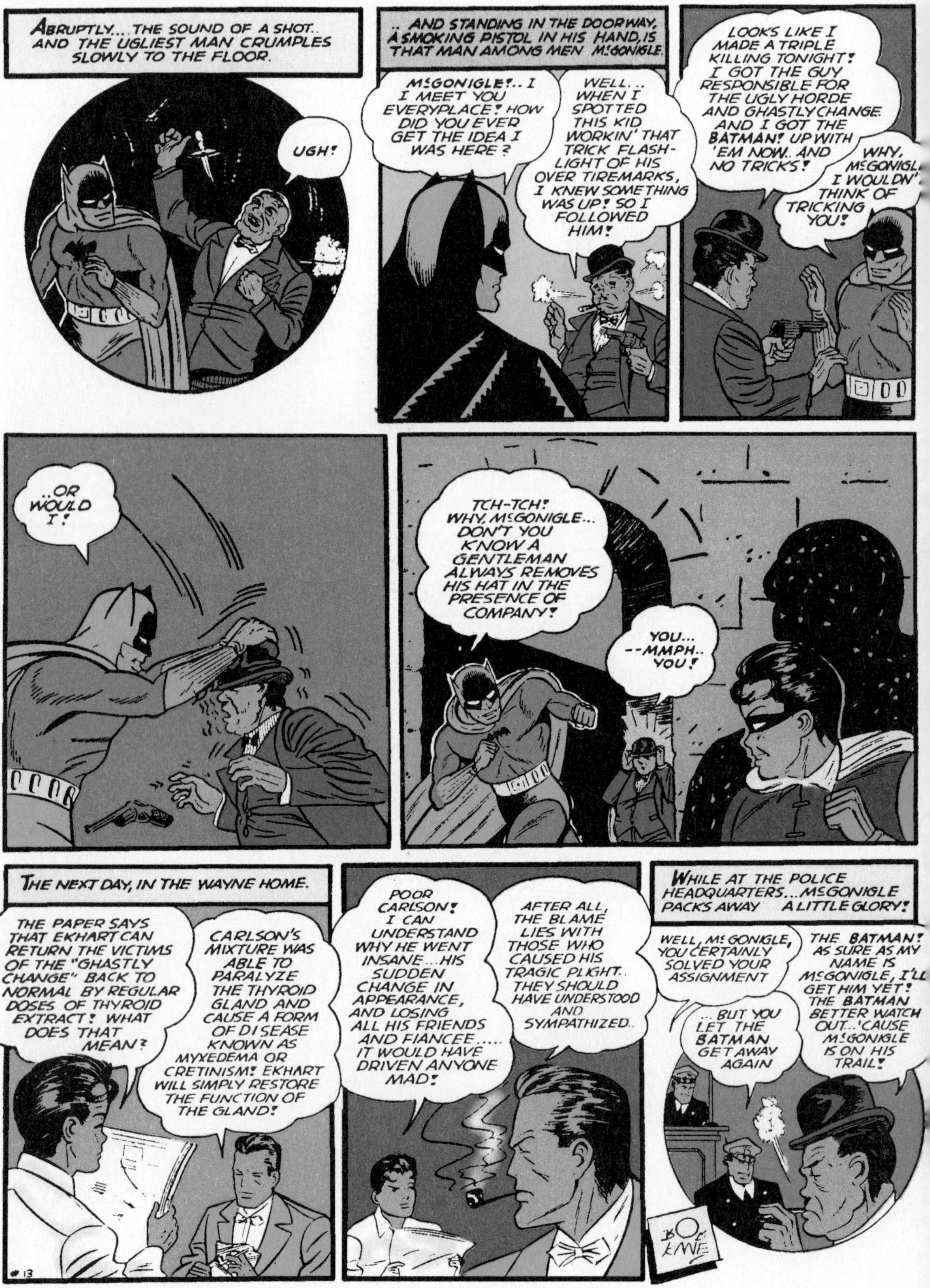
ABRUPTLY.... THE SOUND OF A SHOT.. AND THE UGLIEST MAN CRUMPLES SLOWLY TO THE FLOOR.
UGH!
.. AND STANDING IN THE DOORWAY, A SMOKING PISTOL IN HIS HAND, IS THAT MAN AMONG MEN McGONIGLE.
McGONIGLE!.. I I MEET YOU EVERYPLACE! HOW DID YOU EVER GET THE IDEA I WAS HERE?
WELL... WHEN I SPOTTED THIS KID WORKIN' THAT TRICK FLASH-LIGHT OF HIS OVER TIREMARKS, I KNEW SOMETHING WAS UP! SO I FOLLOWED HIM!
LOOKS LIKE I MADE A TRIPLE KILLING TONIGHT! I GOT THE GUY RESPONSIBLE FOR THE UGLY HORDE AND GHASTLY CHANGE. AND I GOT THE BATMAN! UP WITH 'EM NOW.. AND NO TRICKS!
WHY, McGONIGLE I WOULDN' THINK OF TRICKING YOU!
..OR WOULD I!
TCH-TCH! WHY, McGONIGLE... DON'T YOU KNOW A GENTLEMAN ALWAYS REMOVES HIS HAT IN THE PRESENCE OF COMPANY!
YOU... --MMPH.. YOU!
THE NEXT DAY, IN THE WAYNE HOME.
THE PAPER SAYS THAT EKHART CAN RETURN THE VICTIMS OF THE "GHASTLY CHANGE" BACK TO NORMAL BY REGULAR DOSES OF THYROID EXTRACT! WHAT DOES THAT MEAN?
CARLSON'S MIXTURE WAS ABLE TO PARALYZE THE THYROID GLAND AND CAUSE A FORM OF DISEASE KNOWN AS MYXEDEMA OR CRETINISM! EKHART WILL SIMPLY RESTORE THE FUNCTION OF THE GLAND!
POOR CARLSON! I CAN UNDERSTAND WHY HE WENT INSANE...HIS SUDDEN CHANGE IN APPEARANCE, AND LOSING ALL HIS FRIENDS AND FIANCEE..... IT WOULD HAVE DRIVEN ANYONE MAD!
AFTER ALL, THE BLAME LIES WITH THOSE WHO CAUSED HIS TRAGIC PLIGHT.. THEY SHOULD HAVE UNDERSTOOD AND SYMPATHIZED..
WHILE AT THE POLICE HEADQUARTERS...McGONIGLE PACKS AWAY A LITTLE GLORY!
WELL, McGONIGLE, YOU CERTAINLY SOLVED YOUR ASSIGNMENT
... BUT YOU LET THE BATMAN GET AWAY AGAIN
THE BATMAN! AS SURE AS MY NAME IS McGONIGLE, I'LL GET HIM YET! THE BATMAN BETTER WATCH OUT...'CAUSE McGONIGLE IS ON HIS TRAIL!
#13
BOB KANE

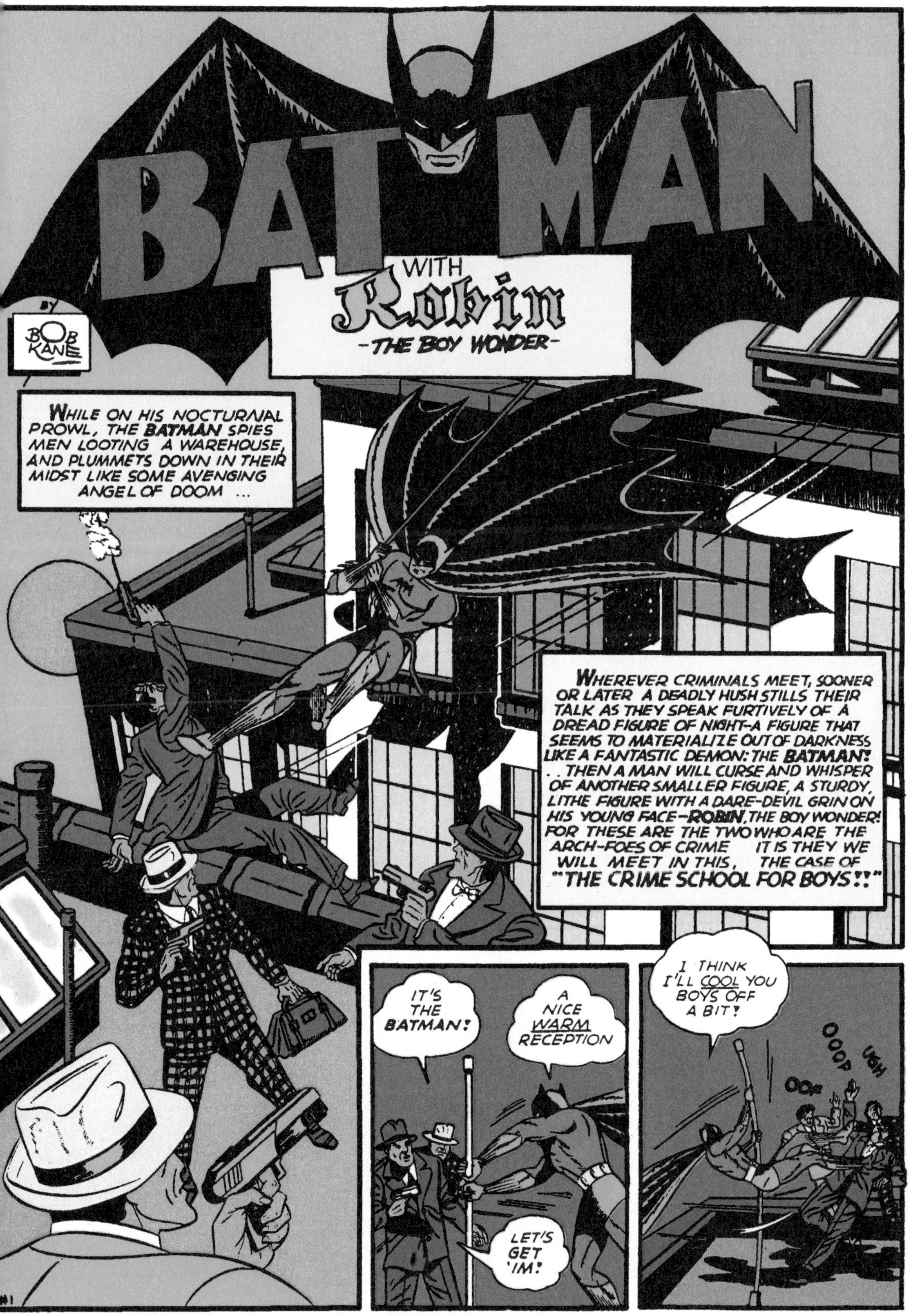
BATMAN
WITH Robin
-THE BOY WONDER-
BY BOB KANE
WHILE ON HIS NOCTURNAL PROWL, THE BATMAN SPIES MEN LOOTING A WAREHOUSE, AND PLUMMETS DOWN IN THEIR MIDST LIKE SOME AVENGING ANGEL OF DOOM ...
WHEREVER CRIMINALS MEET, SOONER OR LATER A DEADLY HUSH STILLS THEIR TALK AS THEY SPEAK FURTIVELY OF A DREAD FIGURE OF NIGHT-A FIGURE THAT SEEMS TO MATERIALIZE OUT OF DARKNESS LIKE A FANTASTIC DEMON: THE BATMAN! . . THEN A MAN WILL CURSE AND WHISPER OF ANOTHER SMALLER FIGURE, A STURDY, LITHE FIGURE WITH A DARE-DEVIL GRIN ON HIS YOUNG FACE-ROBIN, THE BOY WONDER! FOR THESE ARE THE TWO WHO ARE THE ARCH-FOES OF CRIME IT IS THEY WE WILL MEET IN THIS, THE CASE OF "THE CRIME SCHOOL FOR BOYS!!"
#1
IT'S THE BATMAN!
A NICE WARM RECEPTION
LET'S GET 'IM!
I THINK I'LL COOL YOU BOYS OFF A BIT!
OOOP
UGH
OOF

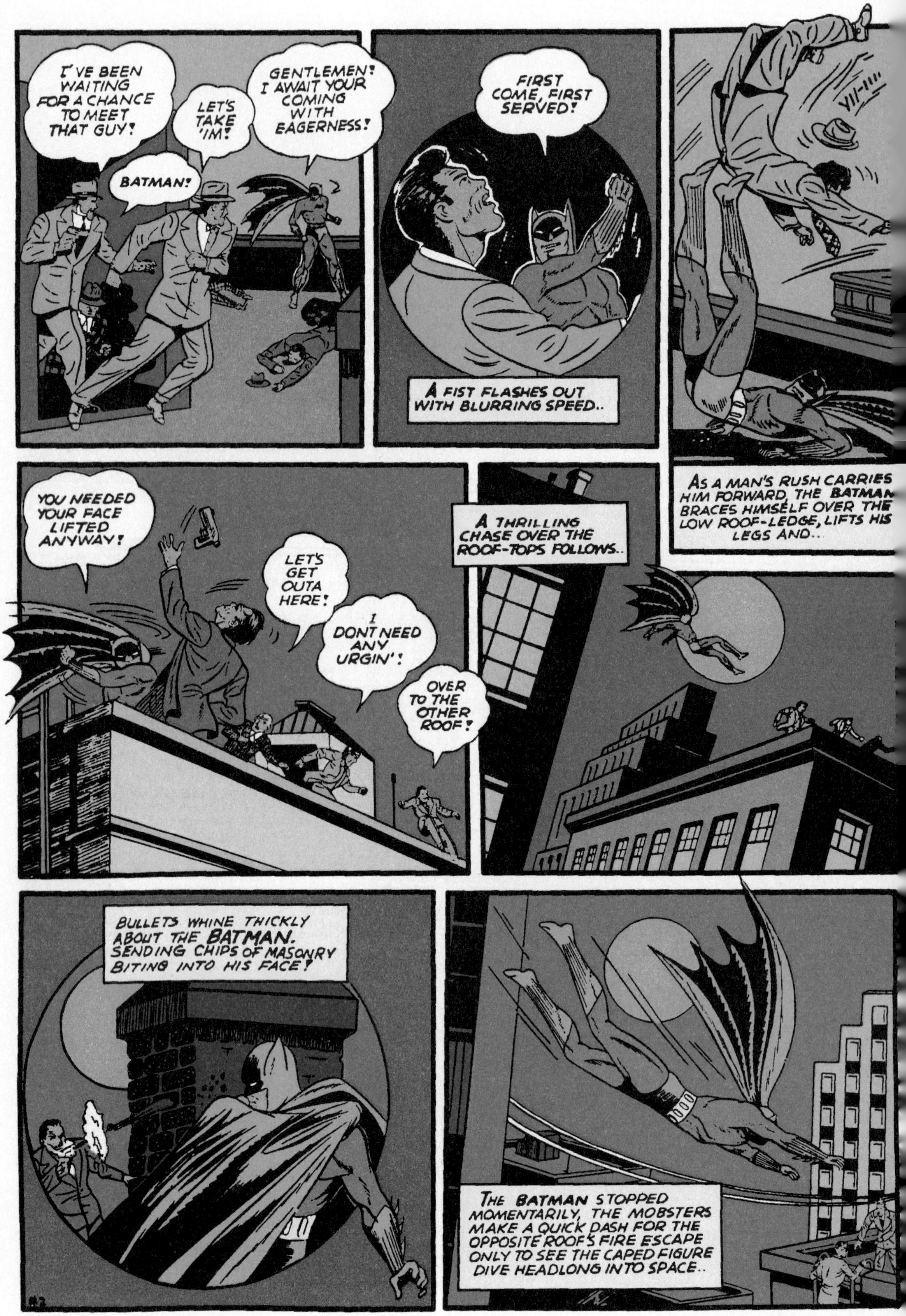

I'VE BEEN WAITING FOR A CHANCE TO MEET THAT GUY!
LET'S TAKE 'IM!
GENTLEMEN! I AWAIT YOUR COMING WITH EAGERNESS!
BATMAN!
FIRST COME, FIRST SERVED!
A FIST FLASHES OUT WITH BLURRING SPEED..
YII-III!
AS A MAN'S RUSH CARRIES HIM FORWARD, THE BATMAN BRACES HIMSELF OVER THE LOW ROOF-LEDGE, LIFTS HIS LEGS AND...
YOU NEEDED YOUR FACE LIFTED ANYWAY!
LET'S GET OUTA HERE!
I DONT NEED ANY URGIN'!
OVER TO THE OTHER ROOF!
A THRILLING CHASE OVER THE ROOF-TOPS FOLLOWS..
BULLETS WHINE THICKLY ABOUT THE BATMAN. SENDING CHIPS OF MASONRY BITING INTO HIS FACE!
THE BATMAN STOPPED MOMENTARILY, THE MOBSTERS MAKE A QUICK DASH FOR THE OPPOSITE ROOF'S FIRE ESCAPE ONLY TO SEE THE CAPED FIGURE DIVE HEADLONG INTO SPACE..

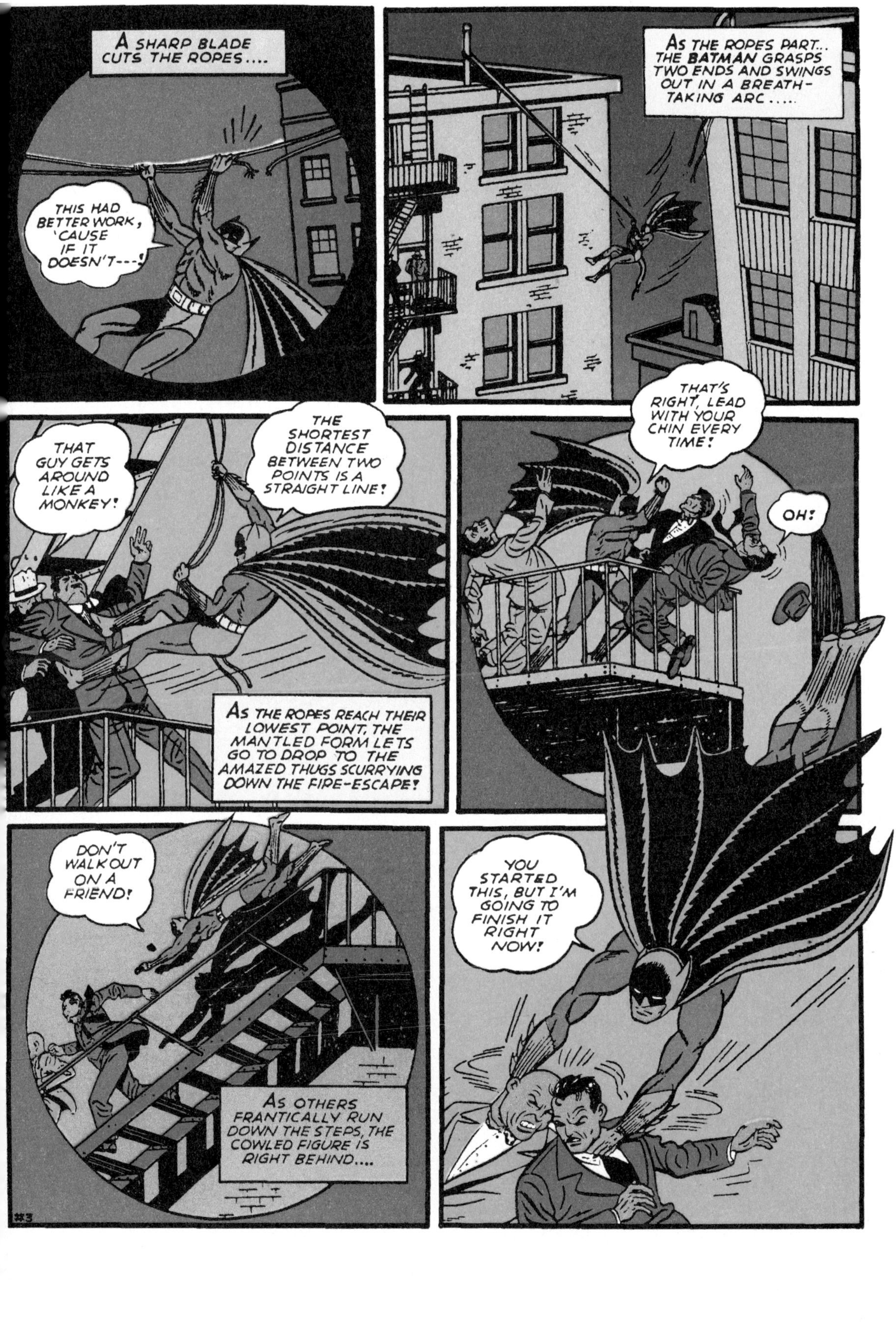
A SHARP BLADE CUTS THE ROPES....
THIS HAD BETTER WORK, 'CAUSE IF IT DOESN'T---!
AS THE ROPES PART... THE BATMAN GRASPS TWO ENDS AND SWINGS OUT IN A BREATH-TAKING ARC.....
THAT GUY GETS AROUND LIKE A MONKEY!
THE SHORTEST DISTANCE BETWEEN TWO POINTS IS A STRAIGHT LINE!
AS THE ROPES REACH THEIR LOWEST POINT, THE MANTLED FORM LETS GO TO DROP TO THE AMAZED THUGS SCURRYING DOWN THE FIRE-ESCAPE!
THAT'S RIGHT, LEAD WITH YOUR CHIN EVERY TIME!
OH!
DON'T WALK OUT ON A FRIEND!
AS OTHERS FRANTICALLY RUN DOWN THE STEPS, THE COWLED FIGURE IS RIGHT BEHIND....
YOU STARTED THIS, BUT I'M GOING TO FINISH IT RIGHT NOW!

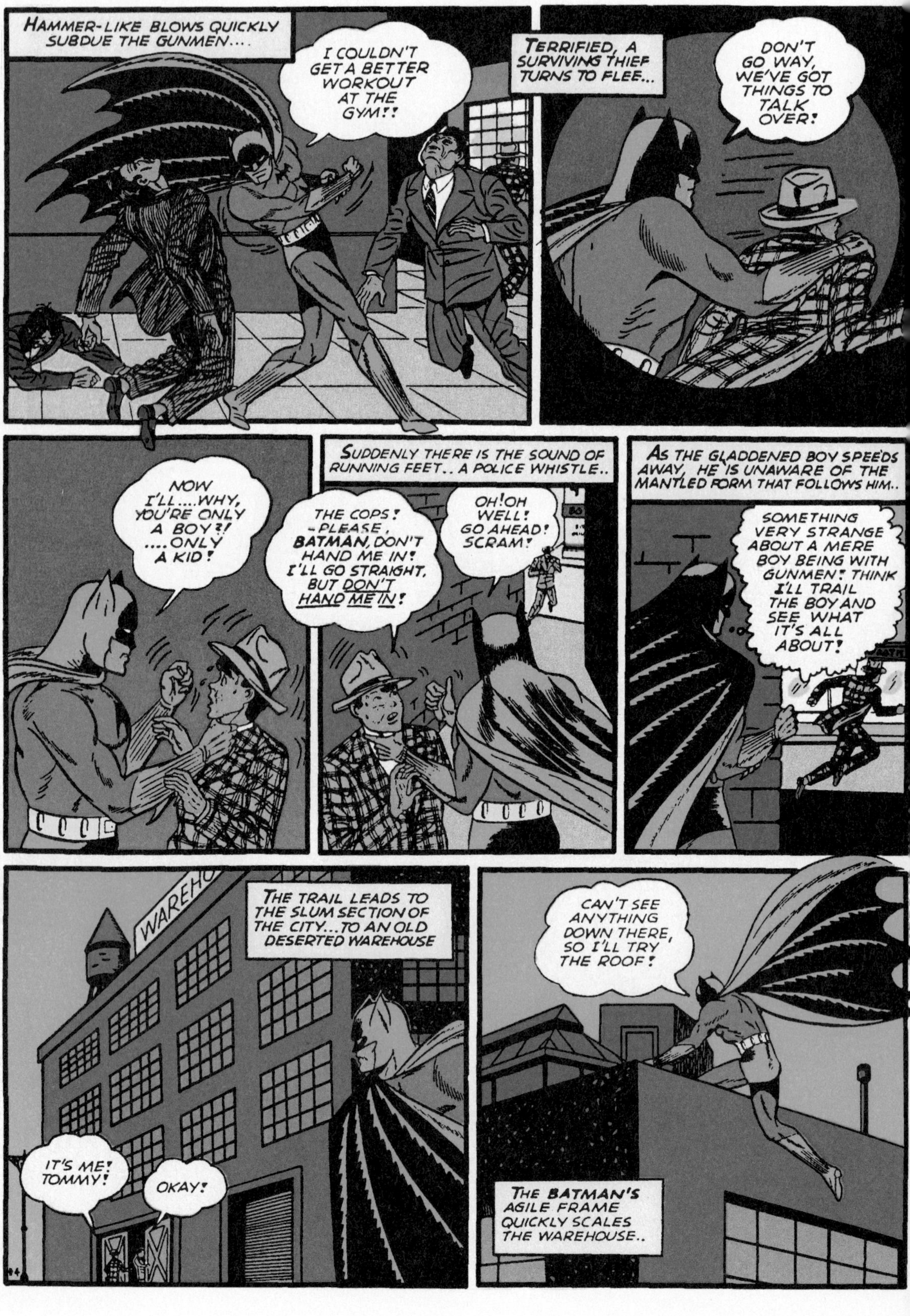
HAMMER-LIKE BLOWS QUICKLY SUBDUE THE GUNMEN....
I COULDN'T GET A BETTER WORKOUT AT THE GYM!!
TERRIFIED, A SURVIVING THIEF TURNS TO FLEE...
DON'T GO WAY, WE'VE GOT THINGS TO TALK OVER!
NOW I'LL....WHY, YOU'RE ONLY A BOY?! ....ONLY A KID!
SUDDENLY THERE IS THE SOUND OF RUNNING FEET.. A POLICE WHISTLE..
THE COPS! -PLEASE, BATMAN, DON'T HAND ME IN! I'LL GO STRAIGHT, BUT DON'T HAND ME IN!
OH!OH WELL! GO AHEAD! SCRAM!
AS THE GLADDENED BOY SPEEDS AWAY, HE IS UNAWARE OF THE MANTLED FORM THAT FOLLOWS HIM..
SOMETHING VERY STRANGE ABOUT A MERE BOY BEING WITH GUNMEN! THINK I'LL TRAIL THE BOY AND SEE WHAT IT'S ALL ABOUT!
WAREHO
THE TRAIL LEADS TO THE SLUM SECTION OF THE CITY...TO AN OLD DESERTED WAREHOUSE
IT'S ME! TOMMY!
OKAY!
CAN'T SEE ANYTHING DOWN THERE, SO I'LL TRY THE ROOF!
THE BATMAN'S AGILE FRAME QUICKLY SCALES THE WAREHOUSE..

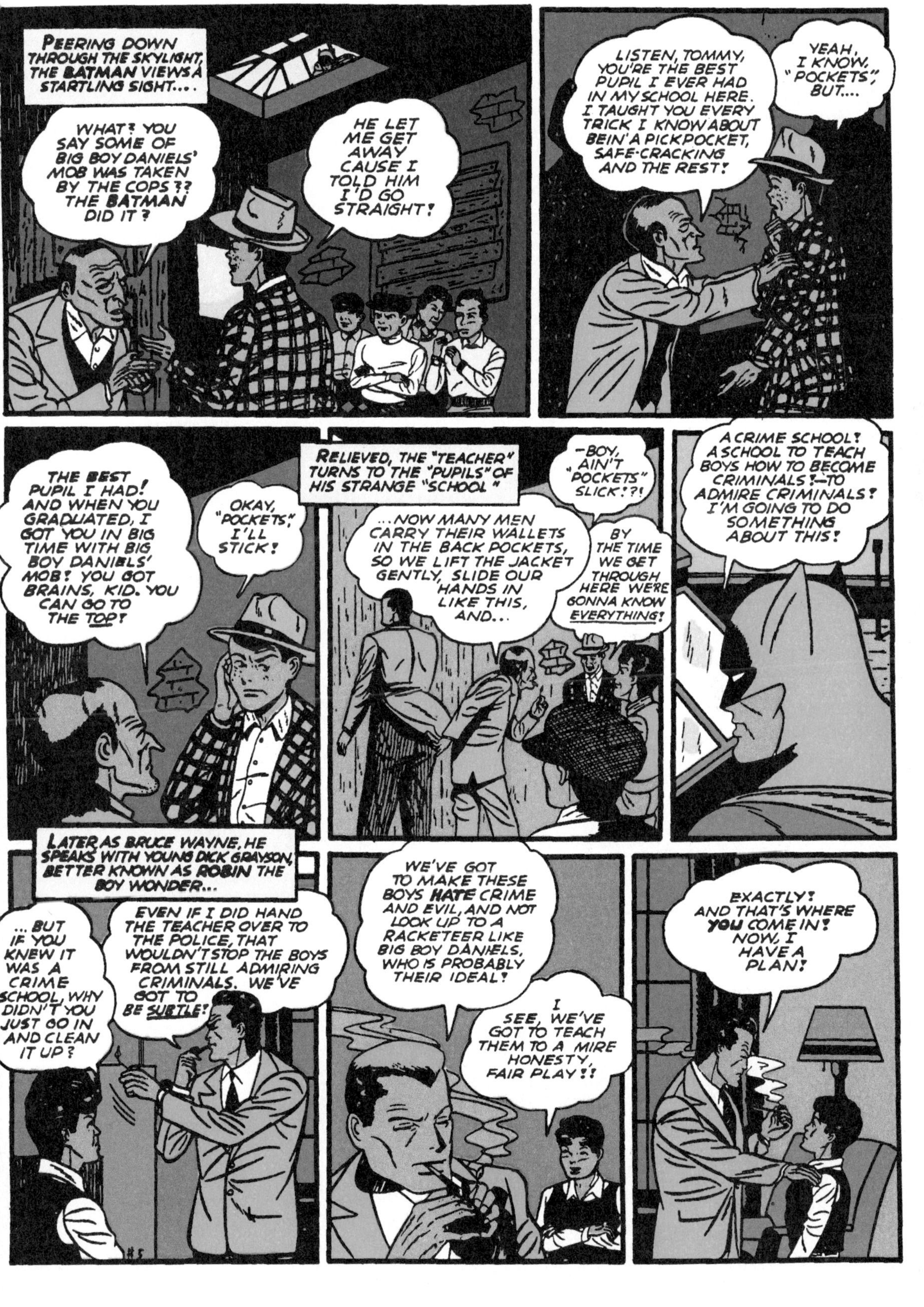
PEERING DOWN THROUGH THE SKYLIGHT, THE BATMAN VIEWS A STARTLING SIGHT....
WHAT? YOU SAY SOME OF BIG BOY DANIELS' MOB WAS TAKEN BY THE COPS?? THE BATMAN DID IT?
HE LET ME GET AWAY CAUSE I TOLD HIM I'D GO STRAIGHT!
LISTEN, TOMMY, YOU'RE THE BEST PUPIL I EVER HAD IN MY SCHOOL HERE. I TAUGHT YOU EVERY TRICK I KNOW ABOUT BEIN' A PICKPOCKET, SAFE-CRACKING AND THE REST!
YEAH, I KNOW, "POCKETS", BUT....
THE BEST PUPIL I HAD! AND WHEN YOU GRADUATED, I GOT YOU IN BIG TIME WITH BIG BOY DANIELS' MOB! YOU GOT BRAINS, KID. YOU CAN GO TO THE TOP!
OKAY, "POCKETS", I'LL STICK!
RELIEVED, THE "TEACHER" TURNS TO THE "PUPILS" OF HIS STRANGE "SCHOOL"
...NOW MANY MEN CARRY THEIR WALLETS IN THE BACK POCKETS, SO WE LIFT THE JACKET GENTLY, SLIDE OUR HANDS IN LIKE THIS, AND...
—BOY, AIN'T "POCKETS" SLICK!?!
BY THE TIME WE GET THROUGH HERE WE'RE GONNA KNOW EVERYTHING!
A CRIME SCHOOL! A SCHOOL TO TEACH BOYS HOW TO BECOME CRIMINALS!—TO ADMIRE CRIMINALS! I'M GOING TO DO SOMETHING ABOUT THIS!
LATER AS BRUCE WAYNE, HE SPEAKS WITH YOUNG DICK GRAYSON, BETTER KNOWN AS ROBIN THE BOY WONDER...
...BUT IF YOU KNEW IT WAS A CRIME SCHOOL, WHY DIDN'T YOU JUST GO IN AND CLEAN IT UP?
EVEN IF I DID HAND THE TEACHER OVER TO THE POLICE, THAT WOULDN'T STOP THE BOYS FROM STILL ADMIRING CRIMINALS. WE'VE GOT TO BE SUBTLE!
WE'VE GOT TO MAKE THESE BOYS HATE CRIME AND EVIL, AND NOT LOOK UP TO A RACKETEER LIKE BIG BOY DANIELS, WHO IS PROBABLY THEIR IDEAL!
I SEE, WE'VE GOT TO TEACH THEM TO A MIRE HONESTY, FAIR PLAY!!
EXACTLY! AND THAT'S WHERE YOU COME IN! NOW, I HAVE A PLAN!

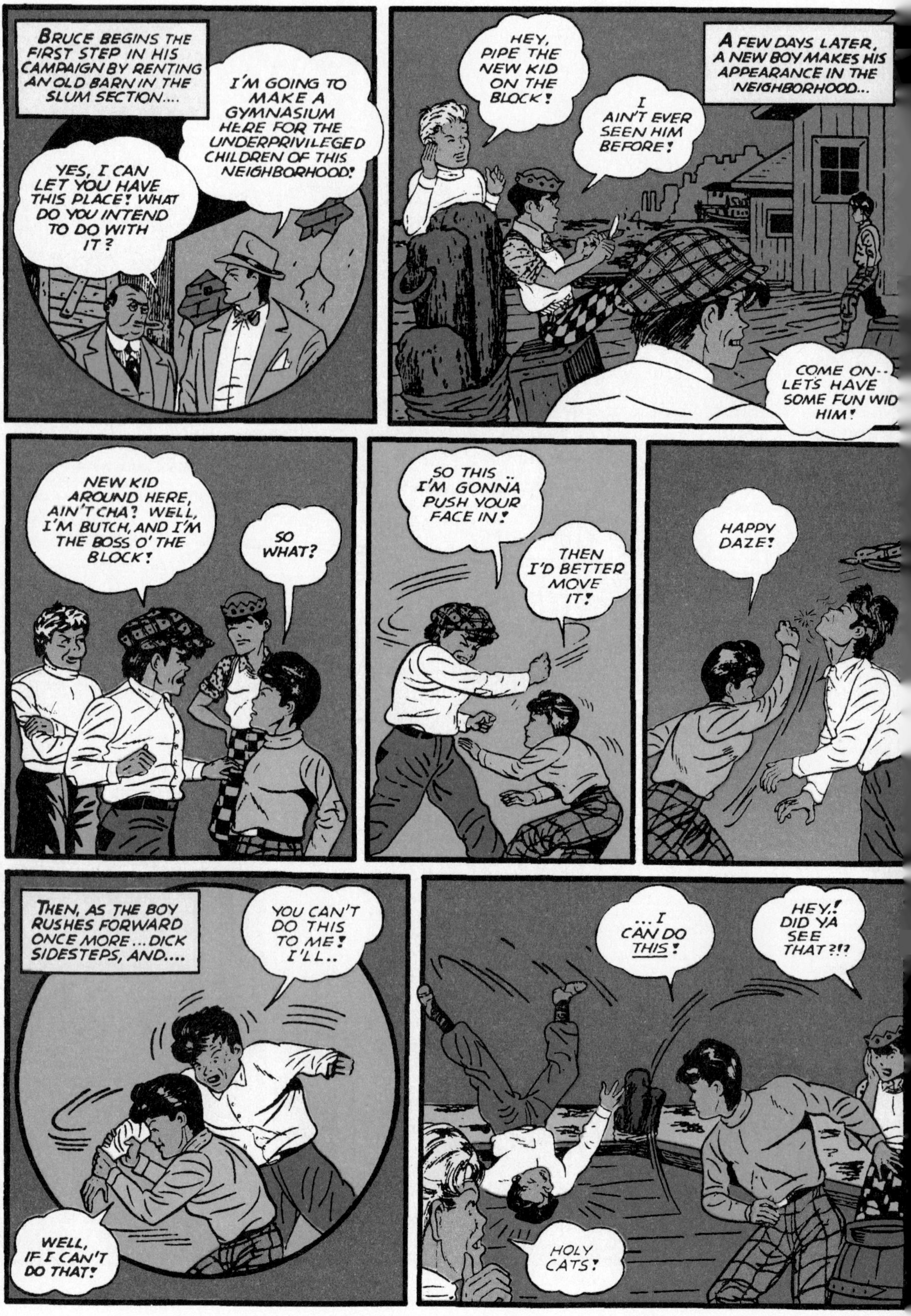
BRUCE BEGINS THE FIRST STEP IN HIS CAMPAIGN BY RENTING AN OLD BARN IN THE SLUM SECTION....
YES, I CAN LET YOU HAVE THIS PLACE! WHAT DO YOU INTEND TO DO WITH IT?
I'M GOING TO MAKE A GYMNASIUM HERE FOR THE UNDERPRIVILEGED CHILDREN OF THIS NEIGHBORHOOD!
A FEW DAYS LATER, A NEW BOY MAKES HIS APPEARANCE IN THE NEIGHBORHOOD...
HEY, PIPE THE NEW KID ON THE BLOCK!
I AIN'T EVER SEEN HIM BEFORE!
COME ON-- LET'S HAVE SOME FUN WID HIM!
NEW KID AROUND HERE, AIN'T CHA? WELL, I'M BUTCH, AND I'M THE BOSS O' THE BLOCK!
SO WHAT?
SO THIS .. I'M GONNA PUSH YOUR FACE IN!
THEN I'D BETTER MOVE IT!
HAPPY DAZE!
THEN, AS THE BOY RUSHES FORWARD ONCE MORE... DICK SIDESTEPS, AND....
YOU CAN'T DO THIS TO ME! I'LL..
WELL, IF I CAN'T DO THAT!
...I CAN DO THIS!
HEY.! DID YA SEE THAT?!?
HOLY CATS!

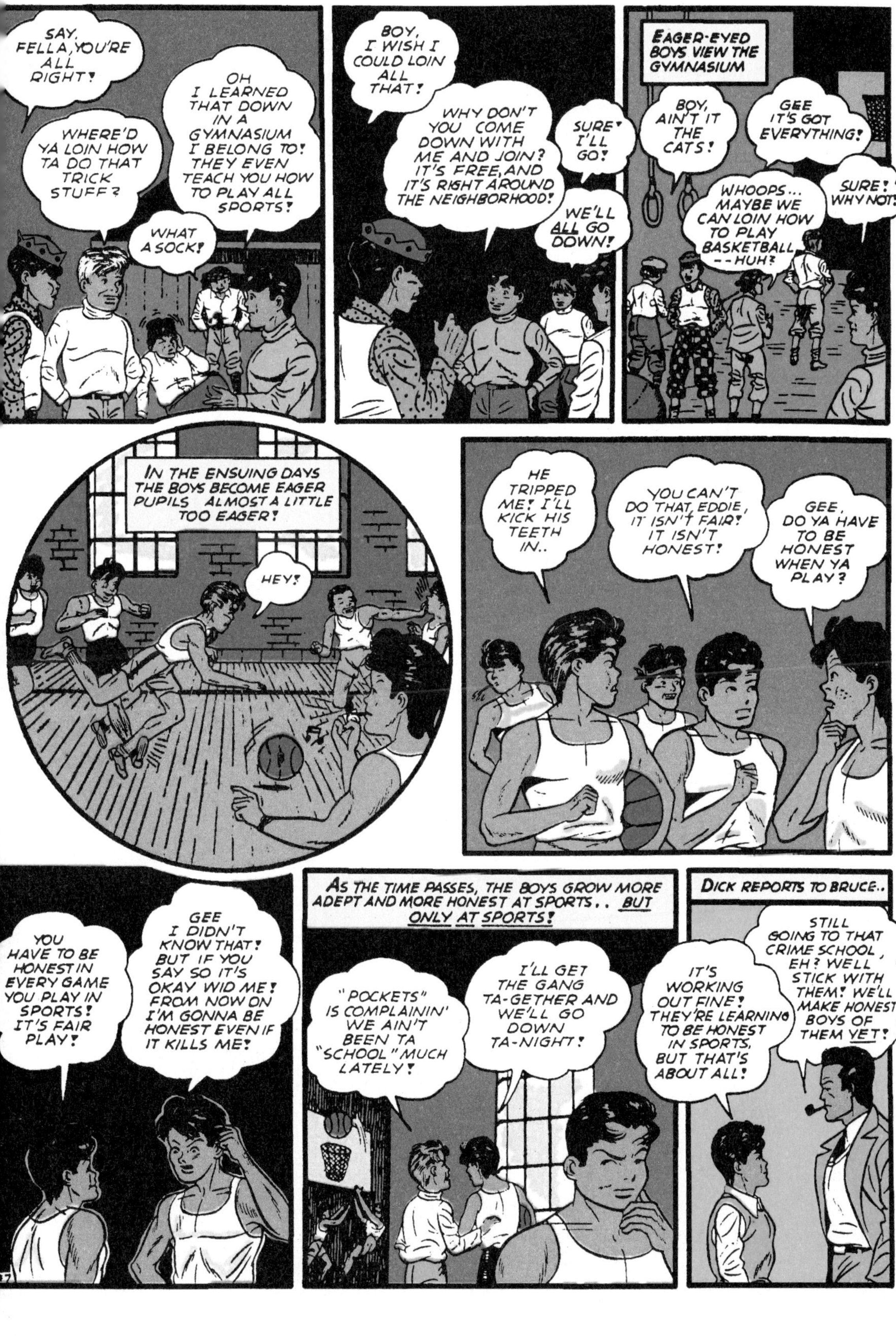
SAY, FELLA, YOU'RE ALL RIGHT!
WHERE'D YA LOIN HOW TA DO THAT TRICK STUFF?
OH I LEARNED THAT DOWN IN A GYMNASIUM I BELONG TO! THEY EVEN TEACH YOU HOW TO PLAY ALL SPORTS!
WHAT A SOCK!
BOY, I WISH I COULD LOIN ALL THAT!
WHY DON'T YOU COME DOWN WITH ME AND JOIN? IT'S FREE, AND IT'S RIGHT AROUND THE NEIGHBORHOOD!
SURE! I'LL GO!
WE'LL ALL GO DOWN!
EAGER-EYED BOYS VIEW THE GYMNASIUM
BOY, AIN'T IT THE CATS!
GEE IT'S GOT EVERYTHING!
WHOOPS... MAYBE WE CAN LOIN HOW TO PLAY BASKETBALL --HUH?
SURE! WHY NOT!
IN THE ENSUING DAYS THE BOYS BECOME EAGER PUPILS ALMOST A LITTLE TOO EAGER!
HEY!
HE TRIPPED ME! I'LL KICK HIS TEETH IN..
YOU CAN'T DO THAT, EDDIE, IT ISN'T FAIR! IT ISN'T HONEST!
GEE, DO YA HAVE TO BE HONEST WHEN YA PLAY?
YOU HAVE TO BE HONEST IN EVERY GAME YOU PLAY IN SPORTS! IT'S FAIR PLAY!
GEE I DIDN'T KNOW THAT! BUT IF YOU SAY SO IT'S OKAY WID ME! FROM NOW ON I'M GONNA BE HONEST EVEN IF IT KILLS ME!
AS THE TIME PASSES, THE BOYS GROW MORE ADEPT AND MORE HONEST AT SPORTS.. BUT ONLY AT SPORTS!
"POCKETS" IS COMPLAININ' WE AIN'T BEEN TA "SCHOOL" MUCH LATELY!
I'LL GET THE GANG TA-GETHER AND WE'LL GO DOWN TA-NIGHT!
DICK REPORTS TO BRUCE..
IT'S WORKING OUT FINE! THEY'RE LEARNING TO BE HONEST IN SPORTS. BUT THAT'S ABOUT ALL!
STILL GOING TO THAT CRIME SCHOOL, EH? WELL STICK WITH THEM! WE'LL MAKE HONEST BOYS OF THEM YET!

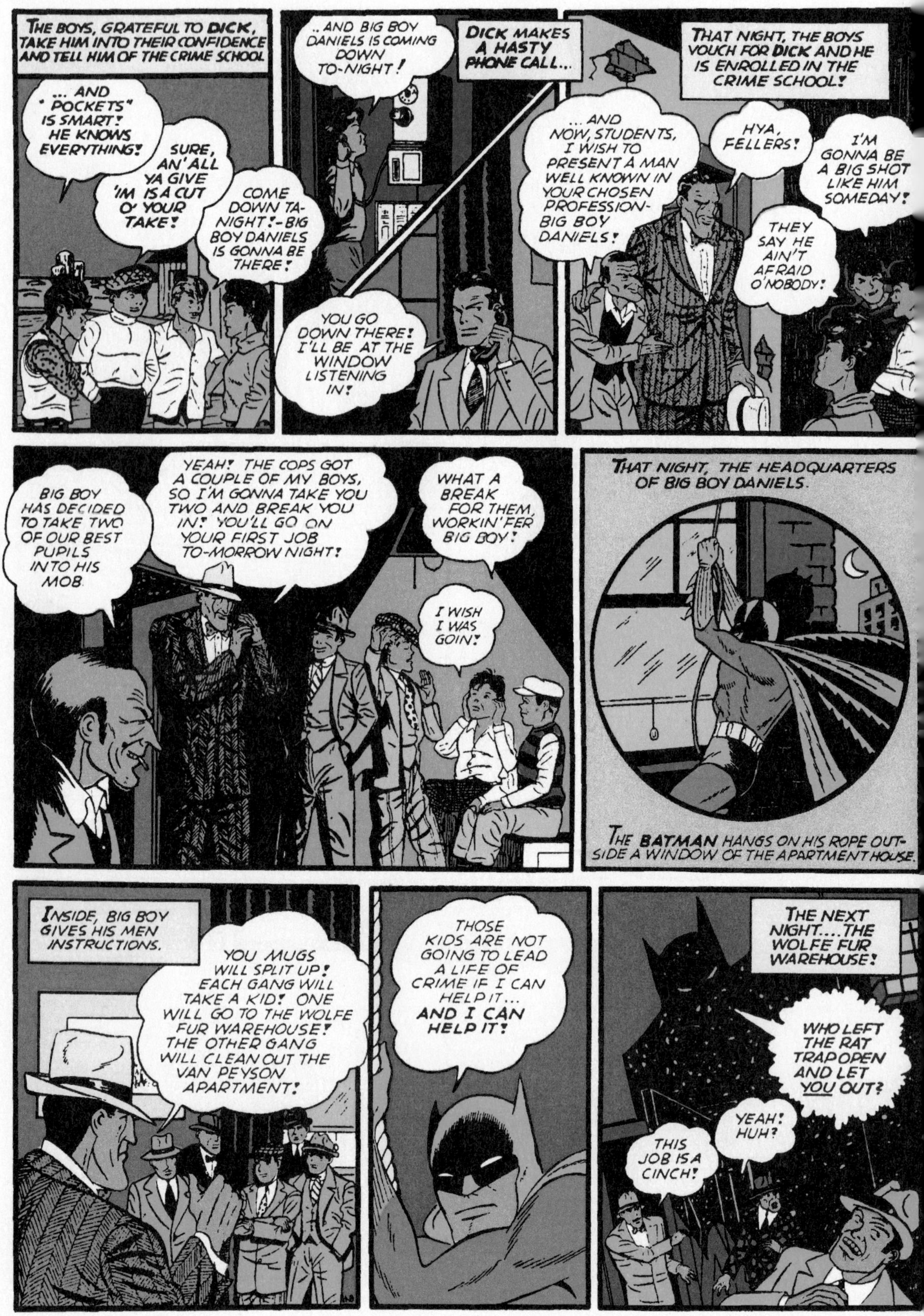
THE BOYS, GRATEFUL TO DICK, TAKE HIM INTO THEIR CONFIDENCE AND TELL HIM OF THE CRIME SCHOOL
... AND "POCKETS" IS SMART! HE KNOWS EVERYTHING!
SURE, AN' ALL YA GIVE 'IM IS A CUT O' YOUR TAKE!
COME DOWN TA-NIGHT! - BIG BOY DANIELS IS GONNA BE THERE!
..AND BIG BOY DANIELS IS COMING DOWN TO-NIGHT!
DICK MAKES A HASTY PHONE CALL...
YOU GO DOWN THERE! I'LL BE AT THE WINDOW LISTENING IN!
THAT NIGHT, THE BOYS VOUCH FOR DICK AND HE IS ENROLLED IN THE CRIME SCHOOL!
... AND NOW, STUDENTS, I WISH TO PRESENT A MAN WELL KNOWN IN YOUR CHOSEN PROFESSION- BIG BOY DANIELS!
HYA, FELLERS!
I'M GONNA BE A BIG SHOT LIKE HIM SOMEDAY!
THEY SAY HE AIN'T AFRAID O'NOBODY!
BIG BOY HAS DECIDED TO TAKE TWO OF OUR BEST PUPILS INTO HIS MOB.
YEAH! THE COPS GOT A COUPLE OF MY BOYS, SO I'M GONNA TAKE YOU TWO AND BREAK YOU IN! YOU'LL GO ON YOUR FIRST JOB TO-MORROW NIGHT!
WHAT A BREAK FOR THEM, WORKIN' FER BIG BOY!
I WISH I WAS GOIN!
THAT NIGHT, THE HEADQUARTERS OF BIG BOY DANIELS.
THE BATMAN HANGS ON HIS ROPE OUTSIDE A WINDOW OF THE APARTMENT HOUSE.
INSIDE, BIG BOY GIVES HIS MEN INSTRUCTIONS.
YOU MUGS WILL SPLIT UP! EACH GANG WILL TAKE A KID! ONE WILL GO TO THE WOLFE FUR WAREHOUSE! THE OTHER GANG WILL CLEAN OUT THE VAN PEYSON APARTMENT!
THOSE KIDS ARE NOT GOING TO LEAD A LIFE OF CRIME IF I CAN HELP IT... AND I CAN HELP IT!
THE NEXT NIGHT.... THE WOLFE FUR WAREHOUSE!
WHO LEFT THE RAT TRAP OPEN AND LET YOU OUT?
YEAH! HUH?
THIS JOB IS A CINCH!

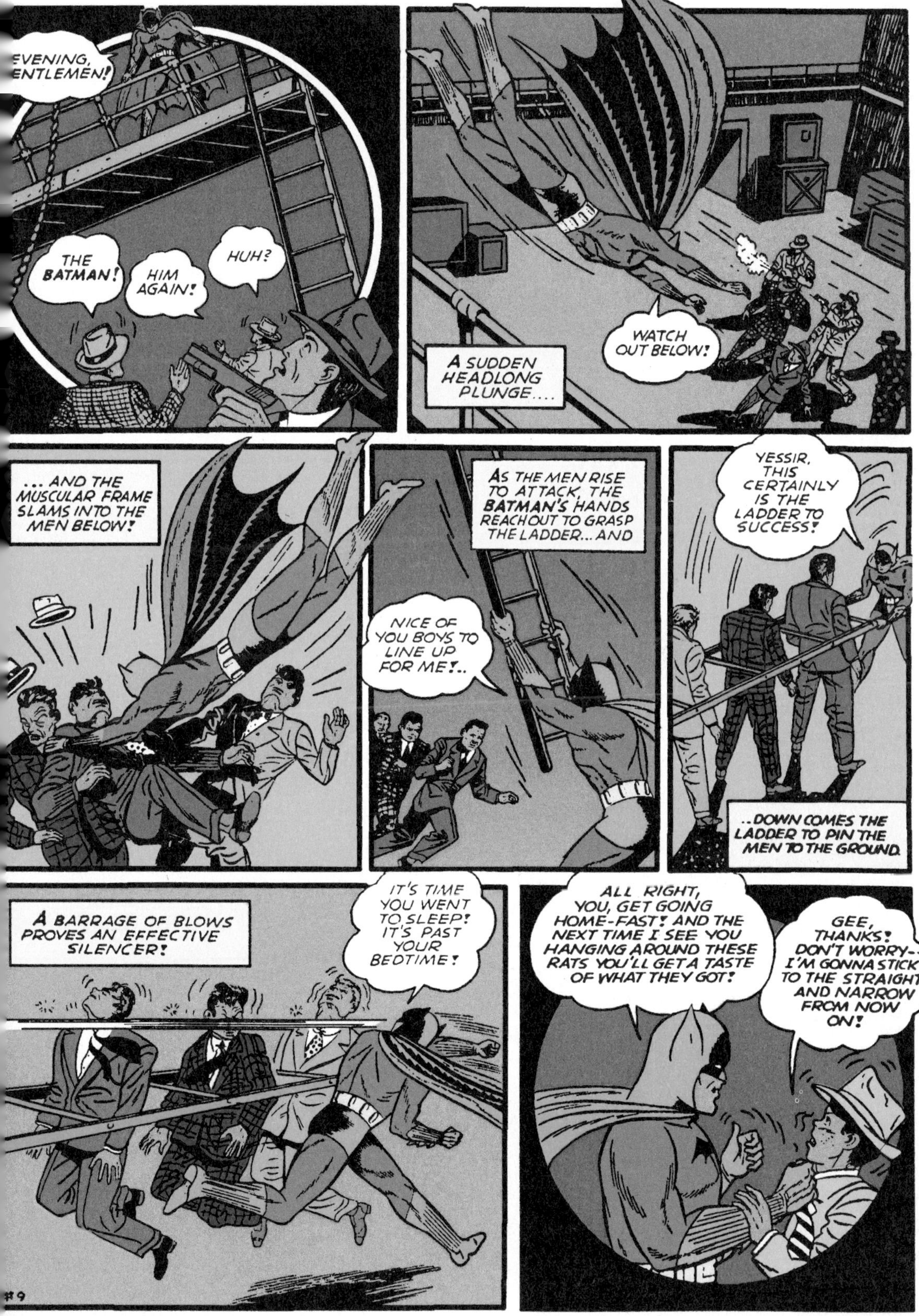
EVENING, ENTLEMEN!
THE BATMAN!
HIM AGAIN!
HUH?
A SUDDEN HEADLONG PLUNGE....
WATCH OUT BELOW!
... AND THE MUSCULAR FRAME SLAMS INTO THE MEN BELOW!
AS THE MEN RISE TO ATTACK, THE BATMAN'S HANDS REACH OUT TO GRASP THE LADDER... AND
NICE OF YOU BOYS TO LINE UP FOR ME!..
YESSIR, THIS CERTAINLY IS THE LADDER TO SUCCESS!
..DOWN COMES THE LADDER TO PIN THE MEN TO THE GROUND.
A BARRAGE OF BLOWS PROVES AN EFFECTIVE SILENCER!
IT'S TIME YOU WENT TO SLEEP! IT'S PAST YOUR BEDTIME!
ALL RIGHT, YOU, GET GOING HOME-FAST! AND THE NEXT TIME I SEE YOU HANGING AROUND THESE RATS YOU'LL GET A TASTE OF WHAT THEY GOT!
GEE, THANKS! DON'T WORRY-- I'M GONNA STICK TO THE STRAIGHT AND NARROW FROM NOW ON!
#9

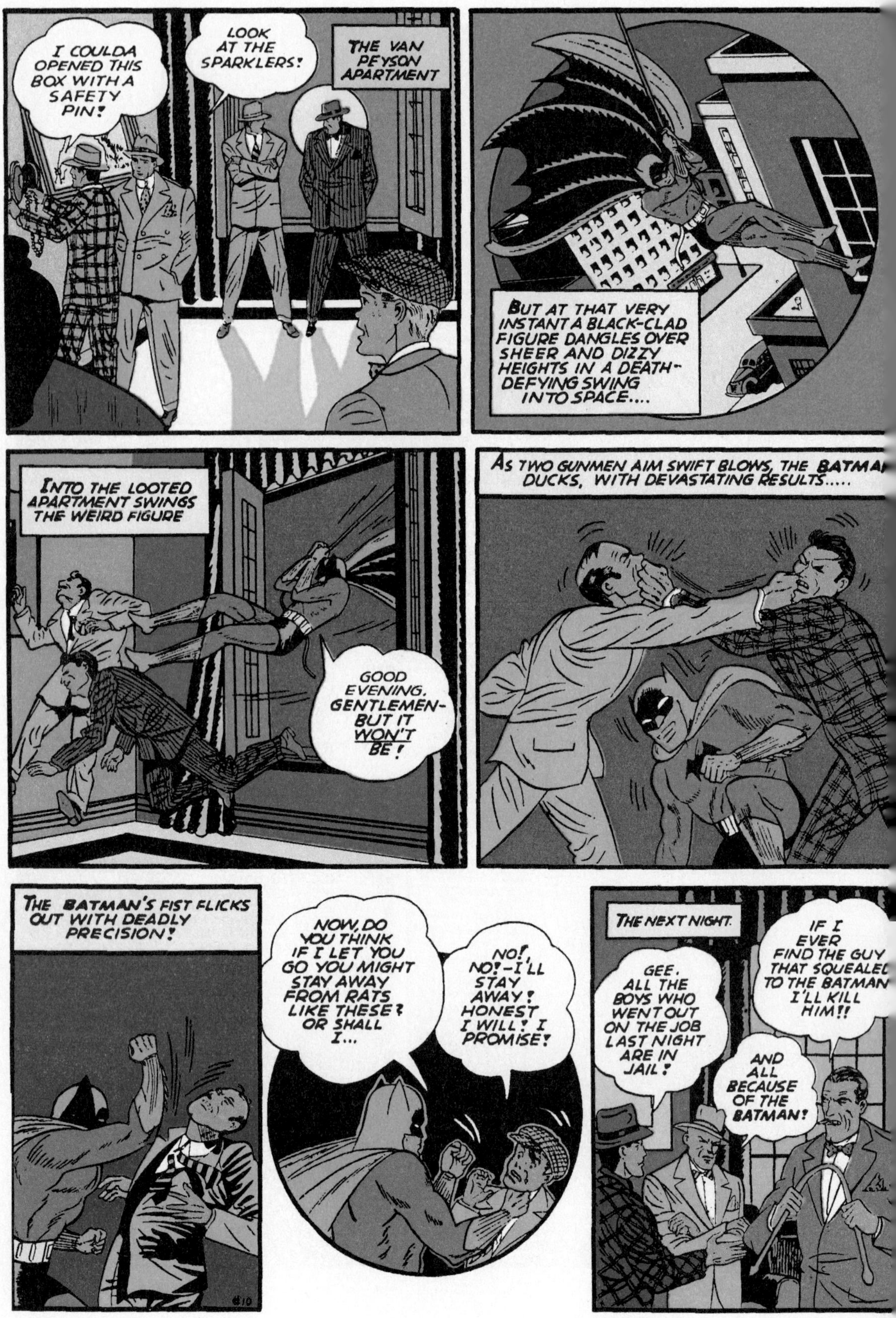

THE VAN PEYSON APARTMENT
I COULDA OPENED THIS BOX WITH A SAFETY PIN!
LOOK AT THE SPARKLERS!
BUT AT THAT VERY INSTANT A BLACK-CLAD FIGURE DANGLES OVER SHEER AND DIZZY HEIGHTS IN A DEATH-DEFYING SWING INTO SPACE....
INTO THE LOOTED APARTMENT SWINGS THE WEIRD FIGURE
GOOD EVENING, GENTLEMEN- BUT IT WON'T BE!
AS TWO GUNMEN AIM SWIFT BLOWS, THE BATMAN DUCKS, WITH DEVASTATING RESULTS.....
THE BATMAN'S FIST FLICKS OUT WITH DEADLY PRECISION!
NOW, DO YOU THINK IF I LET YOU GO YOU MIGHT STAY AWAY FROM RATS LIKE THESE? OR SHALL I...
NO!, NO!-I'LL STAY AWAY! HONEST I WILL! I PROMISE!
THE NEXT NIGHT.
GEE. ALL THE BOYS WHO WENT OUT ON THE JOB LAST NIGHT ARE IN JAIL!
IF I EVER FIND THE GUY THAT SQUEALED TO THE BATMAN I'LL KILL HIM!!
AND ALL BECAUSE OF THE BATMAN!

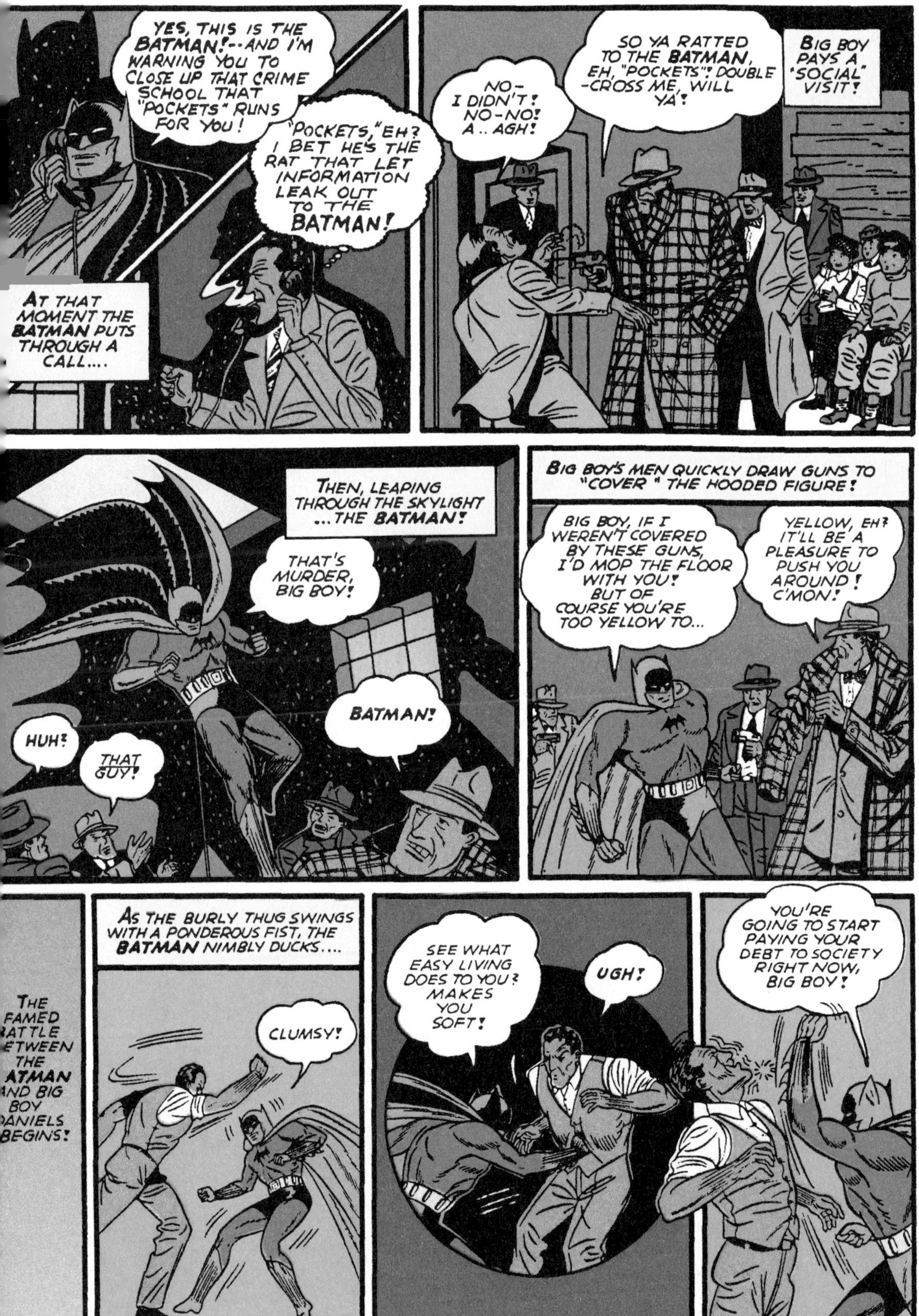
YES, THIS IS THE BATMAN!--AND I'M WARNING YOU TO CLOSE UP THAT CRIME SCHOOL THAT "POCKETS" RUNS FOR YOU!
"POCKETS," EH? I BET HE'S THE RAT THAT LET INFORMATION LEAK OUT TO THE BATMAN!
AT THAT MOMENT THE BATMAN PUTS THROUGH A CALL....
BIG BOY PAYS A "SOCIAL" VISIT!
SO YA RATTED TO THE BATMAN, EH, "POCKETS"! DOUBLE-CROSS ME, WILL YA!
NO-I DIDN'T! NO-NO! A.. AGH!
THEN, LEAPING THROUGH THE SKYLIGHT ...THE BATMAN!
THAT'S MURDER, BIG BOY!
BATMAN!
HUH?
THAT GUY!
BIG BOY'S MEN QUICKLY DRAW GUNS TO "COVER" THE HOODED FIGURE!
BIG BOY, IF I WEREN'T COVERED BY THESE GUNS, I'D MOP THE FLOOR WITH YOU! BUT OF COURSE YOU'RE TOO YELLOW TO...
YELLOW, EH? IT'LL BE A PLEASURE TO PUSH YOU AROUND! C'MON!
THE FAMED BATTLE BETWEEN THE BATMAN AND BIG BOY DANIELS BEGINS!
AS THE BURLY THUG SWINGS WITH A PONDEROUS FIST, THE BATMAN NIMBLY DUCKS....
CLUMSY!
SEE WHAT EASY LIVING DOES TO YOU? MAKES YOU SOFT!
UGH!
YOU'RE GOING TO START PAYING YOUR DEBT TO SOCIETY RIGHT NOW, BIG BOY!

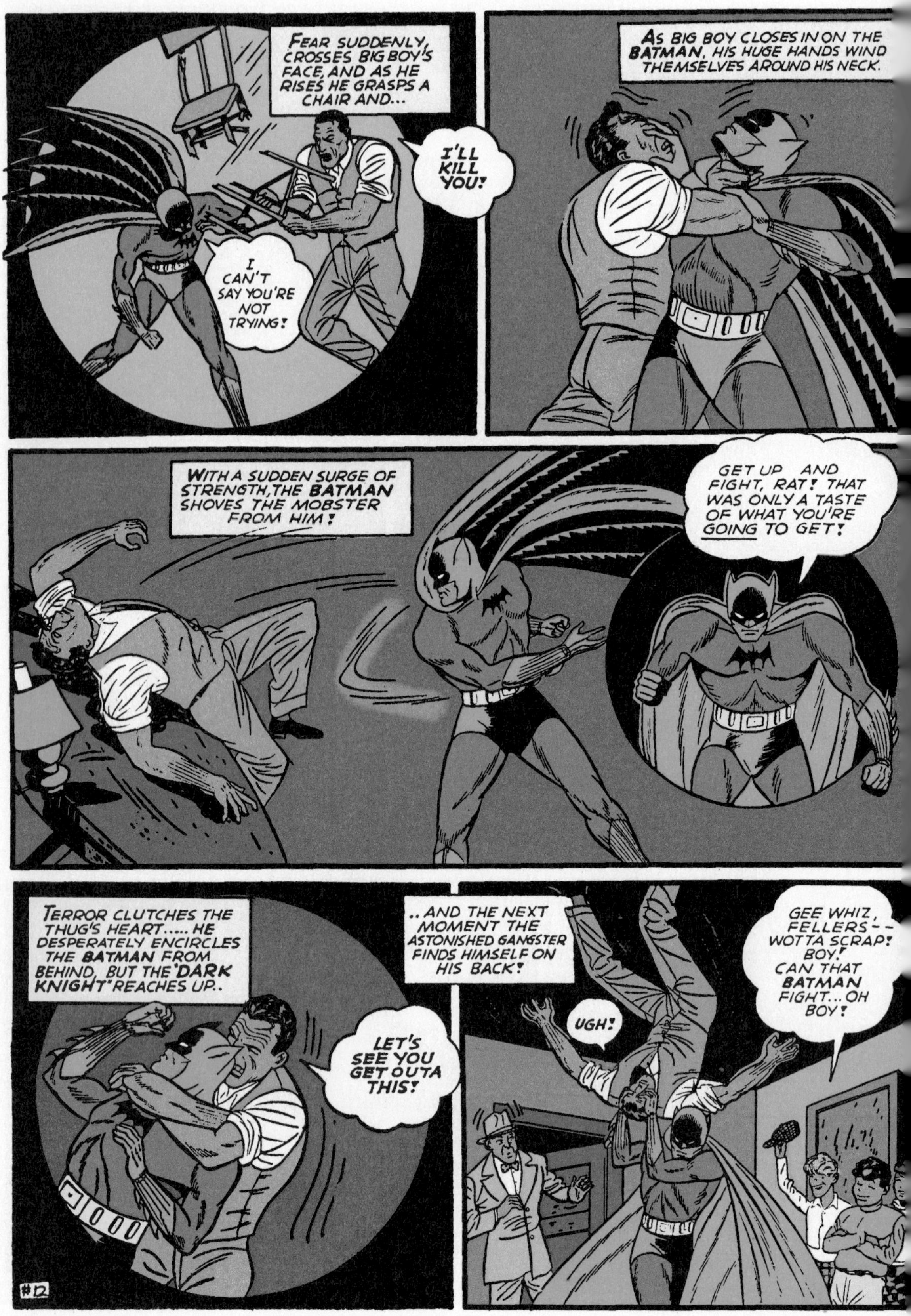

FEAR SUDDENLY CROSSES BIG BOY'S FACE, AND AS HE RISES HE GRASPS A CHAIR AND...
I'LL KILL YOU!
I CAN'T SAY YOU'RE NOT TRYING!
AS BIG BOY CLOSES IN ON THE BATMAN, HIS HUGE HANDS WIND THEMSELVES AROUND HIS NECK.
WITH A SUDDEN SURGE OF STRENGTH, THE BATMAN SHOVES THE MOBSTER FROM HIM!
GET UP AND FIGHT, RAT! THAT WAS ONLY A TASTE OF WHAT YOU'RE GOING TO GET!
TERROR CLUTCHES THE THUG'S HEART..... HE DESPERATELY ENCIRCLES THE BATMAN FROM BEHIND, BUT THE "DARK KNIGHT" REACHES UP..
LET'S SEE YOU GET OUTA THIS!
#12
..AND THE NEXT MOMENT THE ASTONISHED GANGSTER FINDS HIMSELF ON HIS BACK!
UGH!
GEE WHIZ, FELLERS-- WOTTA SCRAP! BOY! CAN THAT BATMAN FIGHT... OH BOY!

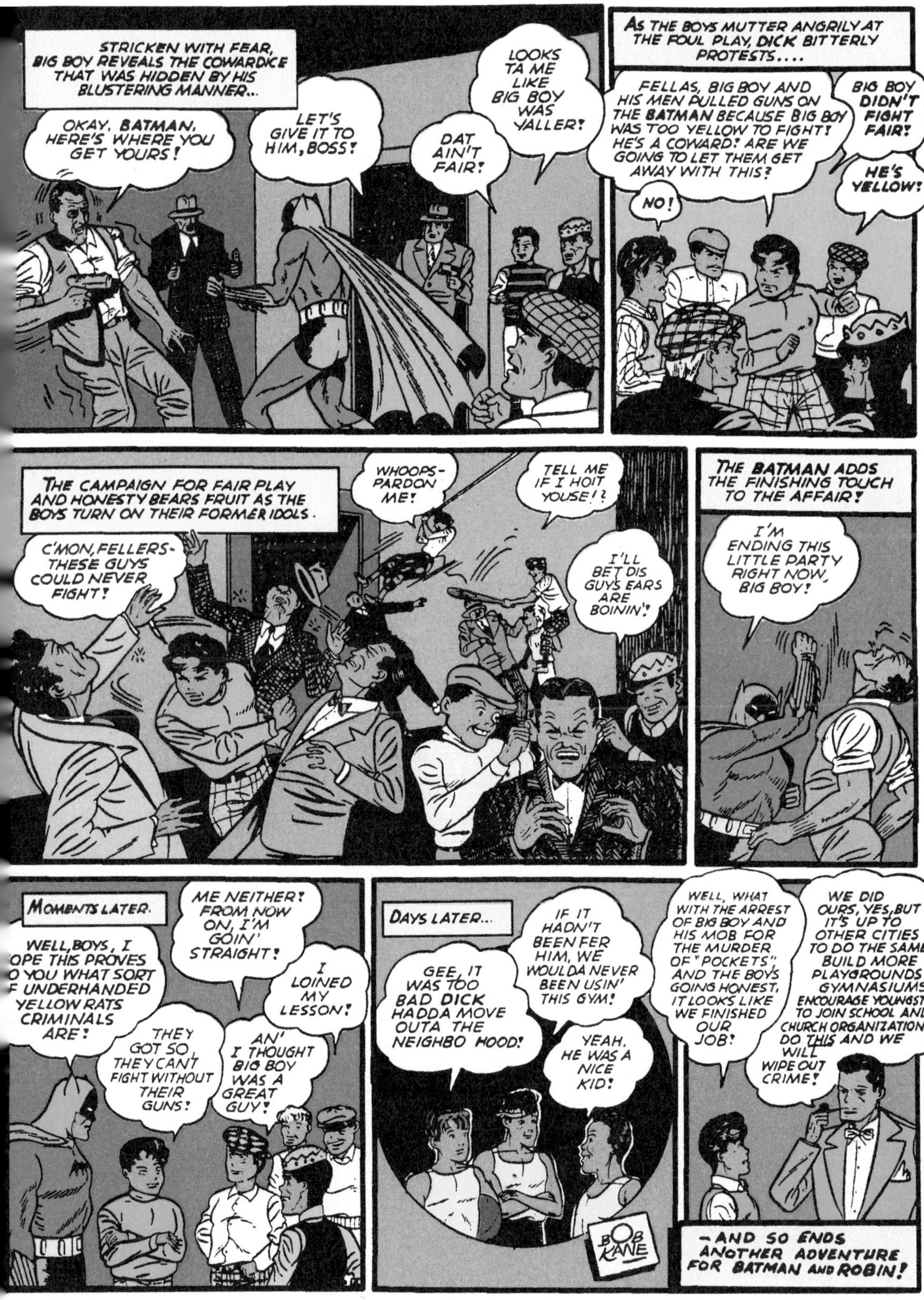
STRICKEN WITH FEAR, BIG BOY REVEALS THE COWARDICE THAT WAS HIDDEN BY HIS BLUSTERING MANNER...
OKAY, BATMAN, HERE'S WHERE YOU GET YOURS!
LET'S GIVE IT TO HIM, BOSS!
DAT AIN'T FAIR!
LOOKS TA ME LIKE BIG BOY WAS YALLER!
AS THE BOYS MUTTER ANGRILY AT THE FOUL PLAY, DICK BITTERLY PROTESTS....
FELLAS, BIG BOY AND HIS MEN PULLED GUNS ON THE BATMAN BECAUSE BIG BOY WAS TOO YELLOW TO FIGHT! HE'S A COWARD! ARE WE GOING TO LET THEM GET AWAY WITH THIS?
BIG BOY DIDN'T FIGHT FAIR!
HE'S YELLOW!
NO!
THE CAMPAIGN FOR FAIR PLAY AND HONESTY BEARS FRUIT AS THE BOYS TURN ON THEIR FORMER IDOLS.
WHOOPS-PARDON ME!
TELL ME IF I HOIT YOUSE!?
C'MON, FELLERS-THESE GUYS COULD NEVER FIGHT!
I'LL BET DIS GUY'S EARS ARE BOININ'!
THE BATMAN ADDS THE FINISHING TOUCH TO THE AFFAIR!
I'M ENDING THIS LITTLE PARTY RIGHT NOW, BIG BOY!
MOMENTS LATER.
WELL, BOYS, I
OPE THIS PROVES
O YOU WHAT SORT
F UNDERHANDED YELLOW RATS CRIMINALS ARE!
ME NEITHER! FROM NOW ON, I'M GOIN' STRAIGHT!
I LOINED MY LESSON!
THEY GOT SO, THEY CAN'T FIGHT WITHOUT THEIR GUNS!
AN' I THOUGHT BIG BOY WAS A GREAT GUY!
DAYS LATER...
GEE, IT WAS TOO BAD DICK HADDA MOVE OUTA THE NEIGHBO HOOD!
IF IT HADN'T BEEN FER HIM, WE WOULDA NEVER BEEN USIN' THIS GYM!
YEAH, HE WAS A NICE KID!
BOB KANE
WELL, WHAT WITH THE ARREST OF BIG BOY AND HIS MOB FOR THE MURDER OF "POCKETS", AND THE BOYS GOING HONEST, IT LOOKS LIKE WE FINISHED OUR JOB!
WE DID OURS, YES, BUT IT'S UP TO OTHER CITIES TO DO THE SAME BUILD MORE PLAYGROUNDS, GYMNASIUMS-ENCOURAGE YOUNGSTERS TO JOIN SCHOOL AND CHURCH ORGANIZATIONS DO THIS AND WE WILL WIPE OUT CRIME!
-AND SO ENDS ANOTHER ADVENTURE FOR BATMAN AND ROBIN!

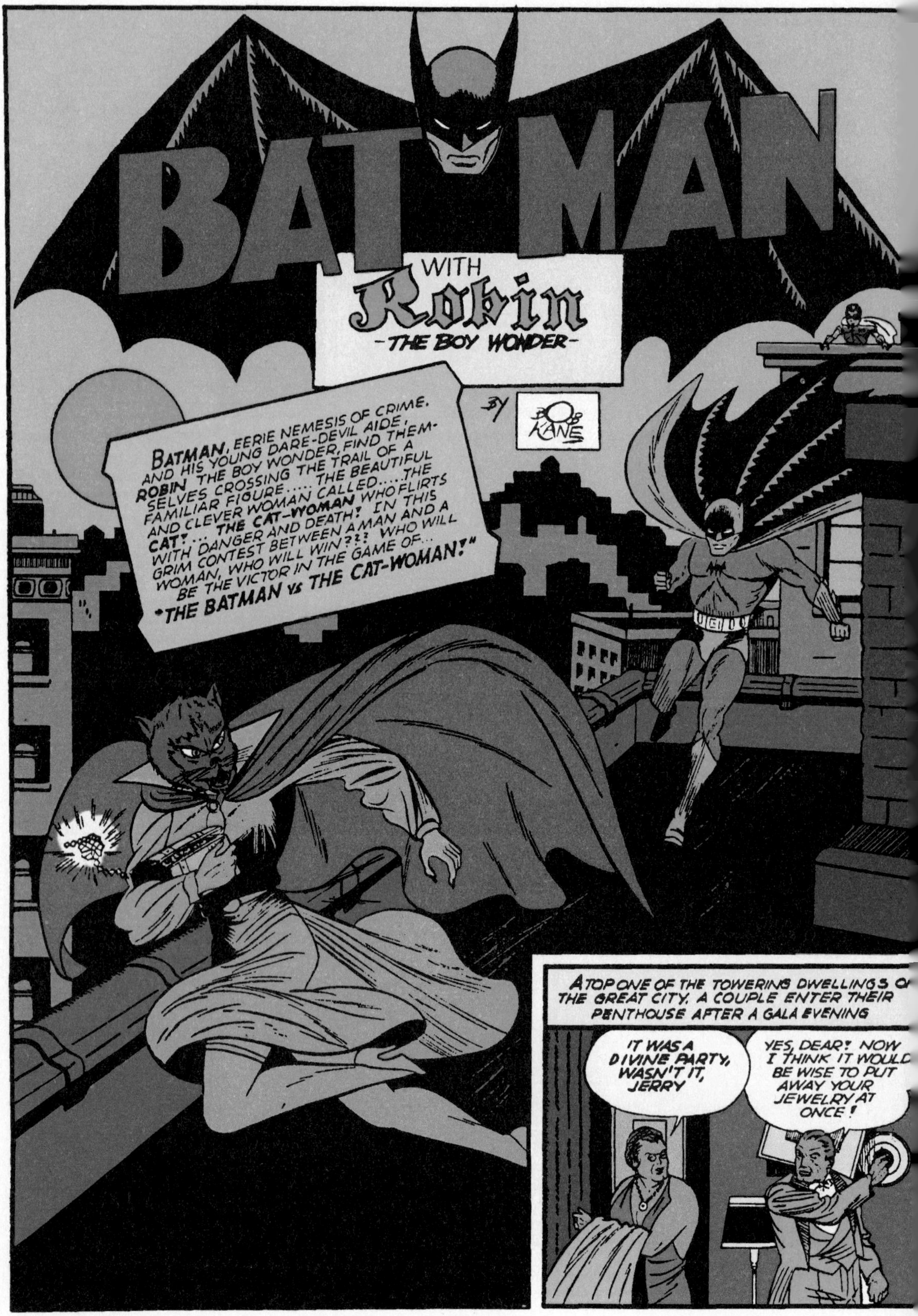
BATMAN
WITH Robin
-THE BOY WONDER-
BY BOB KANE
BATMAN, EERIE NEMESIS OF CRIME, AND HIS YOUNG DARE-DEVIL AIDE, ROBIN THE BOY WONDER, FIND THEMSELVES CROSSING THE TRAIL OF A FAMILIAR FIGURE..... THE BEAUTIFUL AND CLEVER WOMAN CALLED.....THE CAT!... THE CAT-WOMAN WHO FLIRTS WITH DANGER AND DEATH! IN THIS GRIM CONTEST BETWEEN A MAN AND A WOMAN, WHO WILL WIN?!? WHO WILL BE THE VICTOR IN THE GAME OF...
"THE BATMAN vs THE CAT-WOMAN!"
ATOP ONE OF THE TOWERING DWELLINGS OF THE GREAT CITY, A COUPLE ENTER THEIR PENTHOUSE AFTER A GALA EVENING
IT WAS A DIVINE PARTY, WASN'T IT, JERRY
YES, DEAR! NOW I THINK IT WOULD BE WISE TO PUT AWAY YOUR JEWELRY AT ONCE!

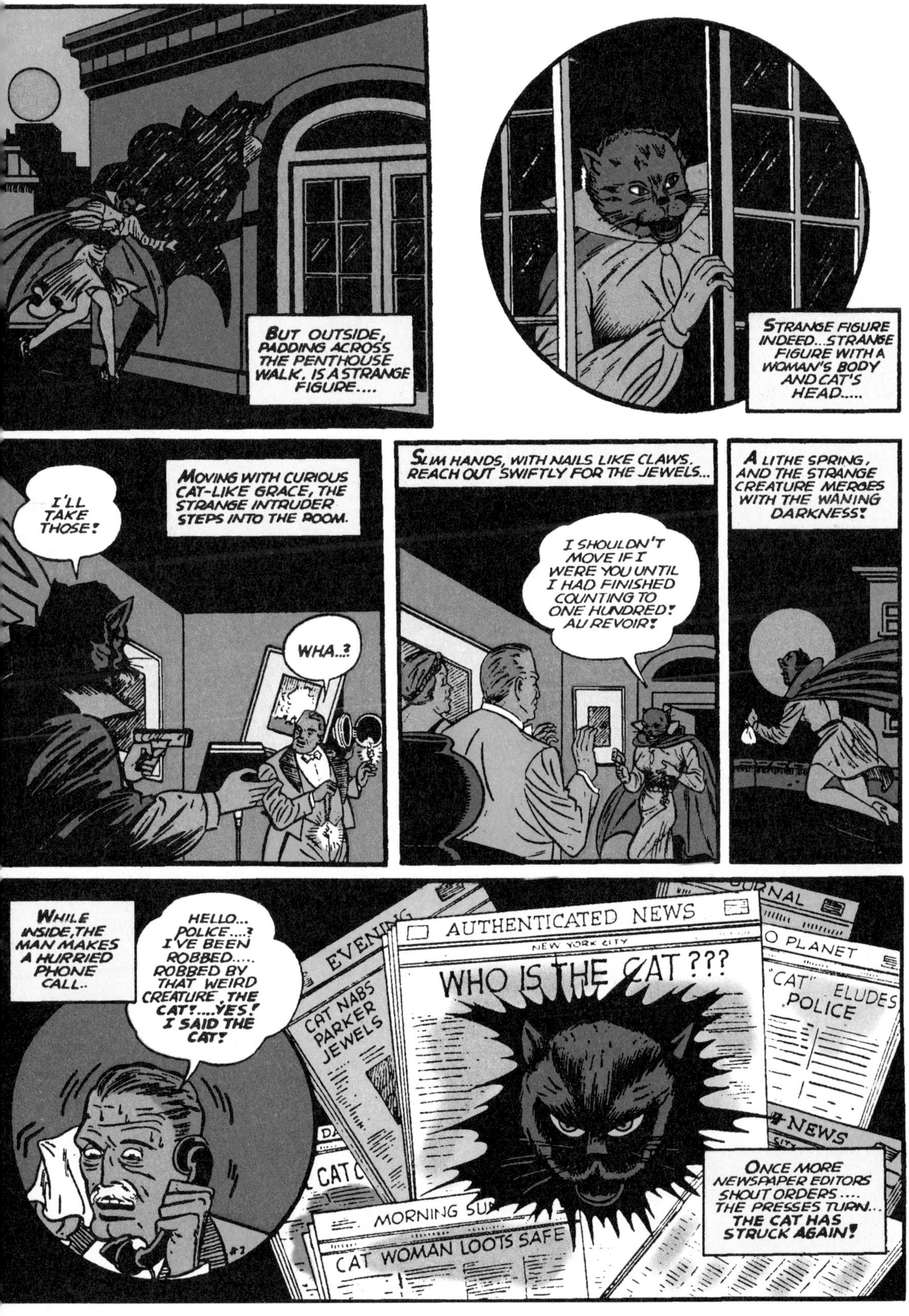
BUT OUTSIDE, PADDING ACROSS THE PENTHOUSE WALK, IS A STRANGE FIGURE....
STRANGE FIGURE INDEED...STRANGE FIGURE WITH A WOMAN'S BODY AND CAT'S HEAD.....
MOVING WITH CURIOUS CAT-LIKE GRACE, THE STRANGE INTRUDER STEPS INTO THE ROOM.
I'LL TAKE THOSE!
WHA..?
SLIM HANDS, WITH NAILS LIKE CLAWS, REACH OUT SWIFTLY FOR THE JEWELS...
I SHOULDN'T MOVE IF I WERE YOU UNTIL I HAD FINISHED COUNTING TO ONE HUNDRED! AU REVOIR!
A LITHE SPRING, AND THE STRANGE CREATURE MERGES WITH THE WANING DARKNESS!
WHILE INSIDE, THE MAN MAKES A HURRIED PHONE CALL..
HELLO... POLICE....? I'VE BEEN ROBBED..... ROBBED BY THAT WEIRD CREATURE, THE CAT!...YES! I SAID THE CAT!
AUTHENTICATED NEWS
NEW YORK CITY
WHO IS THE CAT???
EVENING
CAT NABS PARKER JEWELS
O PLANET
"CAT" ELUDES POLICE
NEWS
MORNING SU
CAT WOMAN LOOTS SAFE
ONCE MORE NEWSPAPER EDITORS SHOUT ORDERS.... THE PRESSES TURN... THE CAT HAS STRUCK AGAIN!

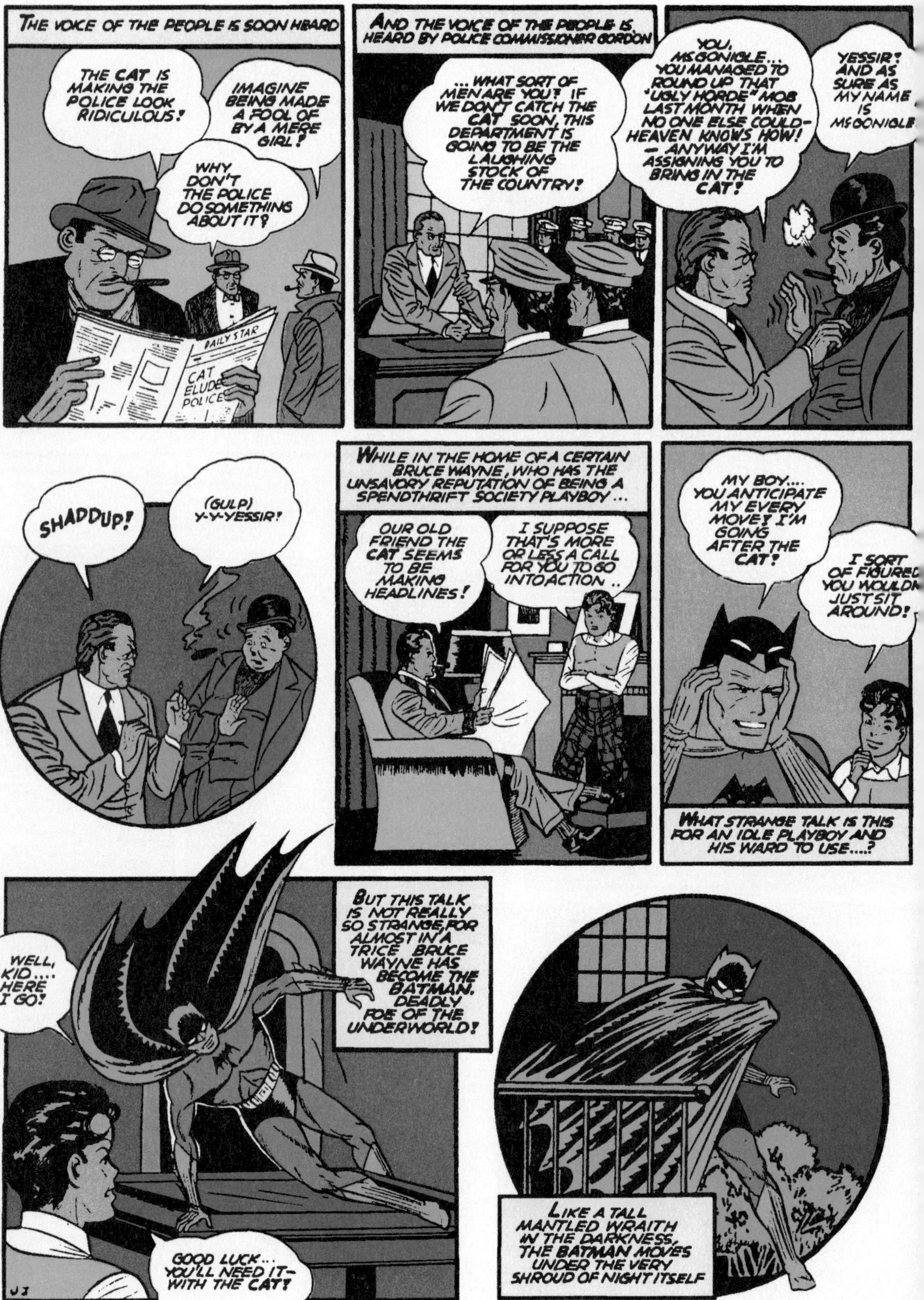

THE VOICE OF THE PEOPLE IS SOON HEARD
THE CAT IS MAKING THE POLICE LOOK RIDICULOUS!
IMAGINE BEING MADE A FOOL OF BY A MERE GIRL!
WHY DON'T THE POLICE DO SOMETHING ABOUT IT?
DAILY STAR
CAT ELUDES POLICE
AND THE VOICE OF THE PEOPLE IS HEARD BY POLICE COMMISSIONER GORDON
... WHAT SORT OF MEN ARE YOU? IF WE DON'T CATCH THE CAT SOON, THIS DEPARTMENT IS GOING TO BE THE LAUGHING STOCK OF THE COUNTRY!
YOU, McGONIGLE... YOU MANAGED TO ROUND UP THAT "UGLY HORDE" MOB LAST MONTH WHEN NO ONE ELSE COULD-HEAVEN KNOWS HOW! — ANYWAY I'M ASSIGNING YOU TO BRING IN THE CAT!
YESSIR! AND AS SURE AS MY NAME IS McGONIGLE
SHADDUP!
(GULP) Y-Y-YESSIR!
WHILE IN THE HOME OF A CERTAIN BRUCE WAYNE, WHO HAS THE UNSAVORY REPUTATION OF BEING A SPENDTHRIFT SOCIETY PLAYBOY ...
OUR OLD FRIEND THE CAT SEEMS TO BE MAKING HEADLINES!
I SUPPOSE THAT'S MORE OR LESS A CALL FOR YOU TO GO INTO ACTION ..
MY BOY.... YOU ANTICIPATE MY EVERY MOVE! I'M GOING AFTER THE CAT!
I SORT OF FIGURED YOU WOULDN'T JUST SIT AROUND!
WHAT STRANGE TALK IS THIS FOR AN IDLE PLAYBOY AND HIS WARD TO USE....?
WELL, KID.... HERE I GO!
BUT THIS TALK IS NOT REALLY SO STRANGE, FOR ALMOST IN A TRICE BRUCE WAYNE HAS BECOME THE BATMAN. DEADLY FOE OF THE UNDERWORLD!
GOOD LUCK... YOU'LL NEED IT-WITH THE CAT!
LIKE A TALL MANTLED WRAITH IN THE DARKNESS, THE BATMAN MOVES UNDER THE VERY SHROUD OF NIGHT ITSELF

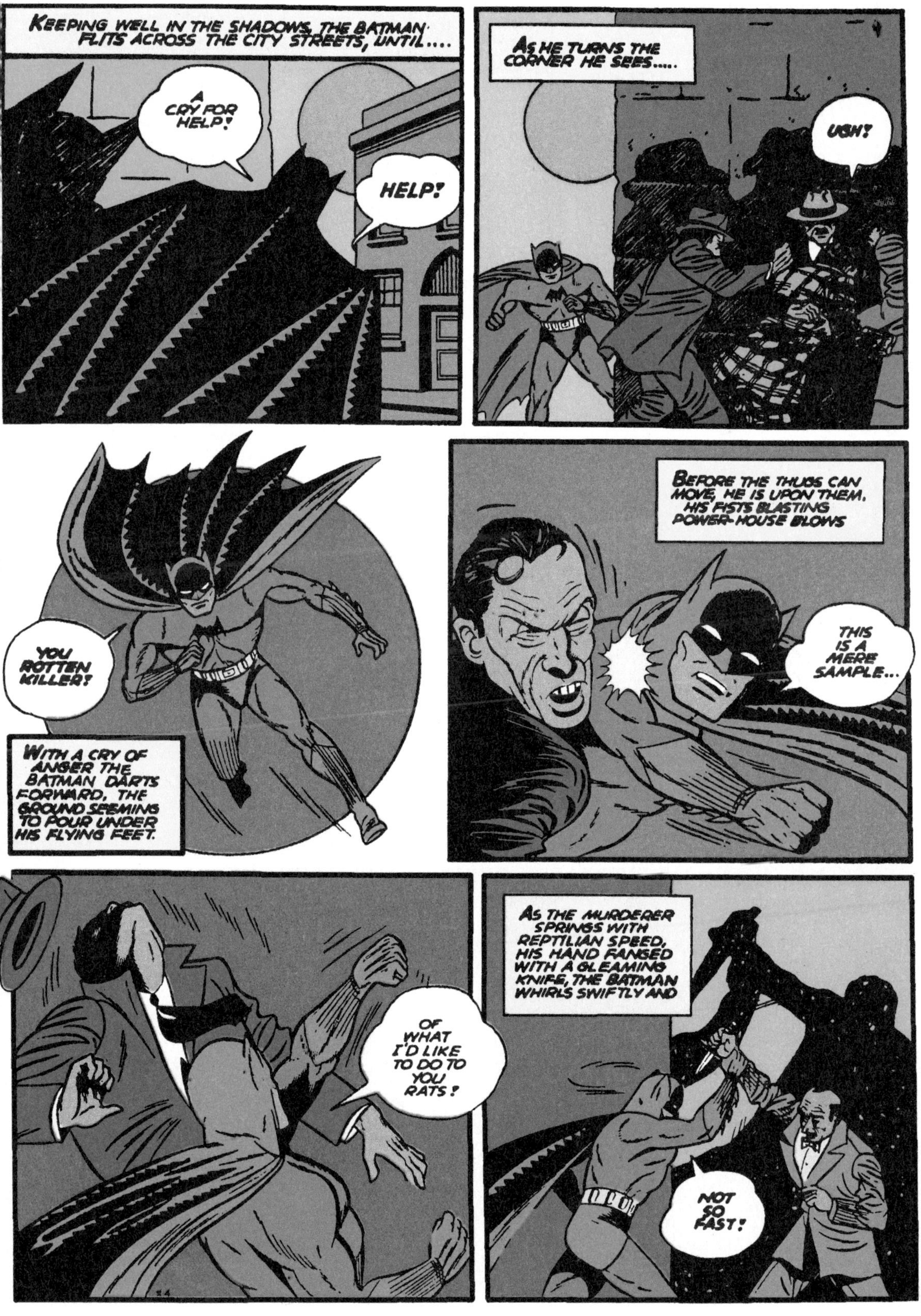

KEEPING WELL IN THE SHADOWS, THE BATMAN FLITS ACROSS THE CITY STREETS, UNTIL....
A CRY FOR HELP!
HELP!
AS HE TURNS THE CORNER HE SEES.....
UGH!
YOU ROTTEN KILLER!
WITH A CRY OF ANGER THE BATMAN DARTS FORWARD, THE GROUND SEEMING TO POUR UNDER HIS FLYING FEET.
BEFORE THE THUGS CAN MOVE, HE IS UPON THEM, HIS FISTS BLASTING POWER-HOUSE BLOWS
THIS IS A MERE SAMPLE...
OF WHAT I'D LIKE TO DO TO YOU RATS!
AS THE MURDERER SPRINGS WITH REPTILIAN SPEED, HIS HAND FANGED WITH A GLEAMING KNIFE, THE BATMAN WHIRLS SWIFTLY AND
NOT SO FAST!

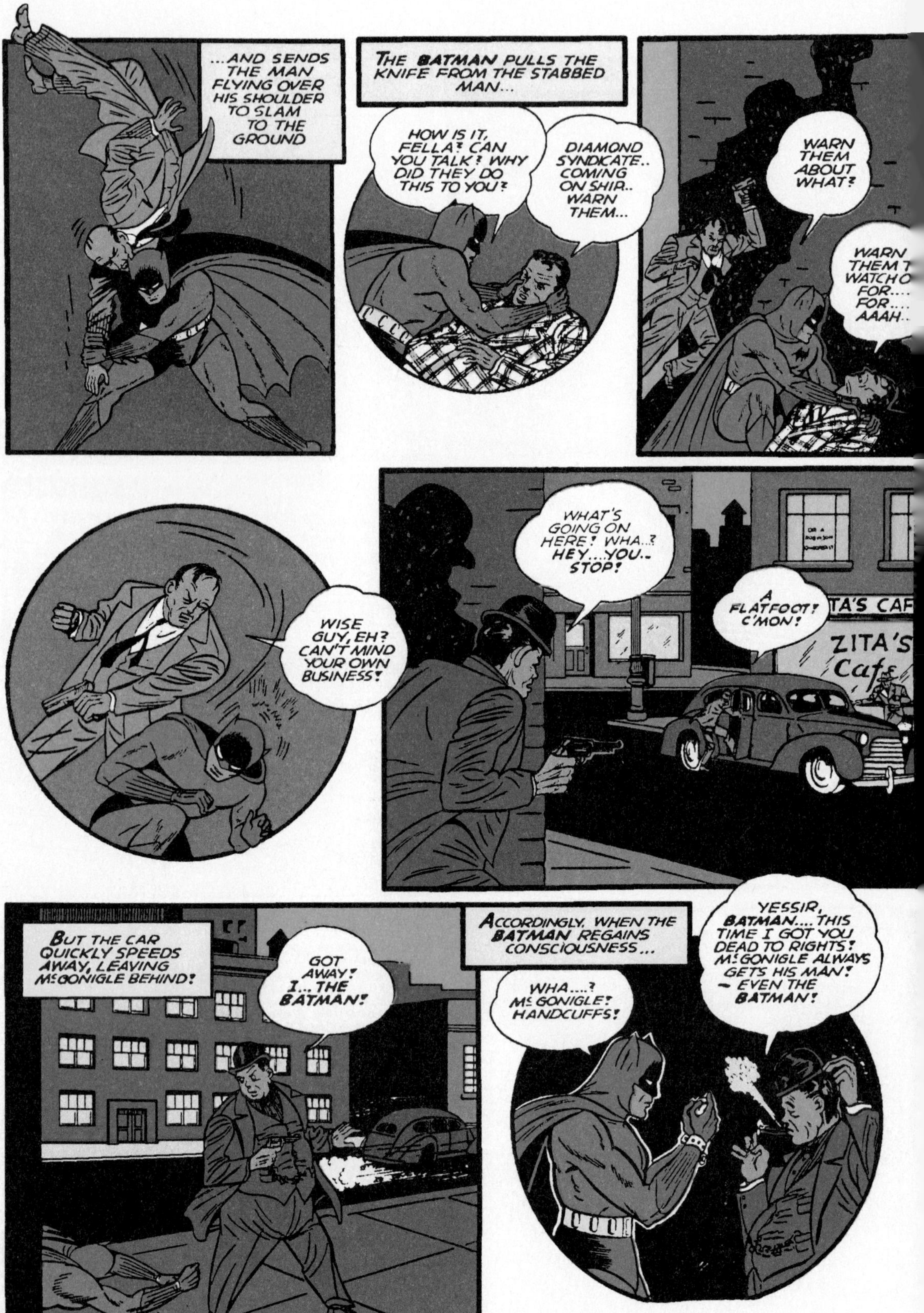
...AND SENDS THE MAN FLYING OVER HIS SHOULDER TO SLAM TO THE GROUND
THE BATMAN PULLS THE KNIFE FROM THE STABBED MAN...
HOW IS IT, FELLA? CAN YOU TALK? WHY DID THEY DO THIS TO YOU?
DIAMOND SYNDICATE.. COMING ON SHIP.. WARN THEM...
WARN THEM ABOUT WHAT?
WARN THEM T WATCH O FOR.... FOR.... AAAH...
WISE GUY, EH? CAN'T MIND YOUR OWN BUSINESS?
WHAT'S GOING ON HERE? WHA...? HEY...YOU.. STOP!
A FLATFOOT! C'MON!
TA'S CAF
ZITA'S Cafe
BUT THE CAR QUICKLY SPEEDS AWAY, LEAVING McGONIGLE BEHIND!
GOT AWAY! I...THE BATMAN!
ACCORDINGLY, WHEN THE BATMAN REGAINS CONSCIOUSNESS...
WHA....? McGONIGLE? HANDCUFFS!
YESSIR, BATMAN.... THIS TIME I GOT YOU DEAD TO RIGHTS! McGONIGLE ALWAYS GETS HIS MAN! - EVEN THE BATMAN!

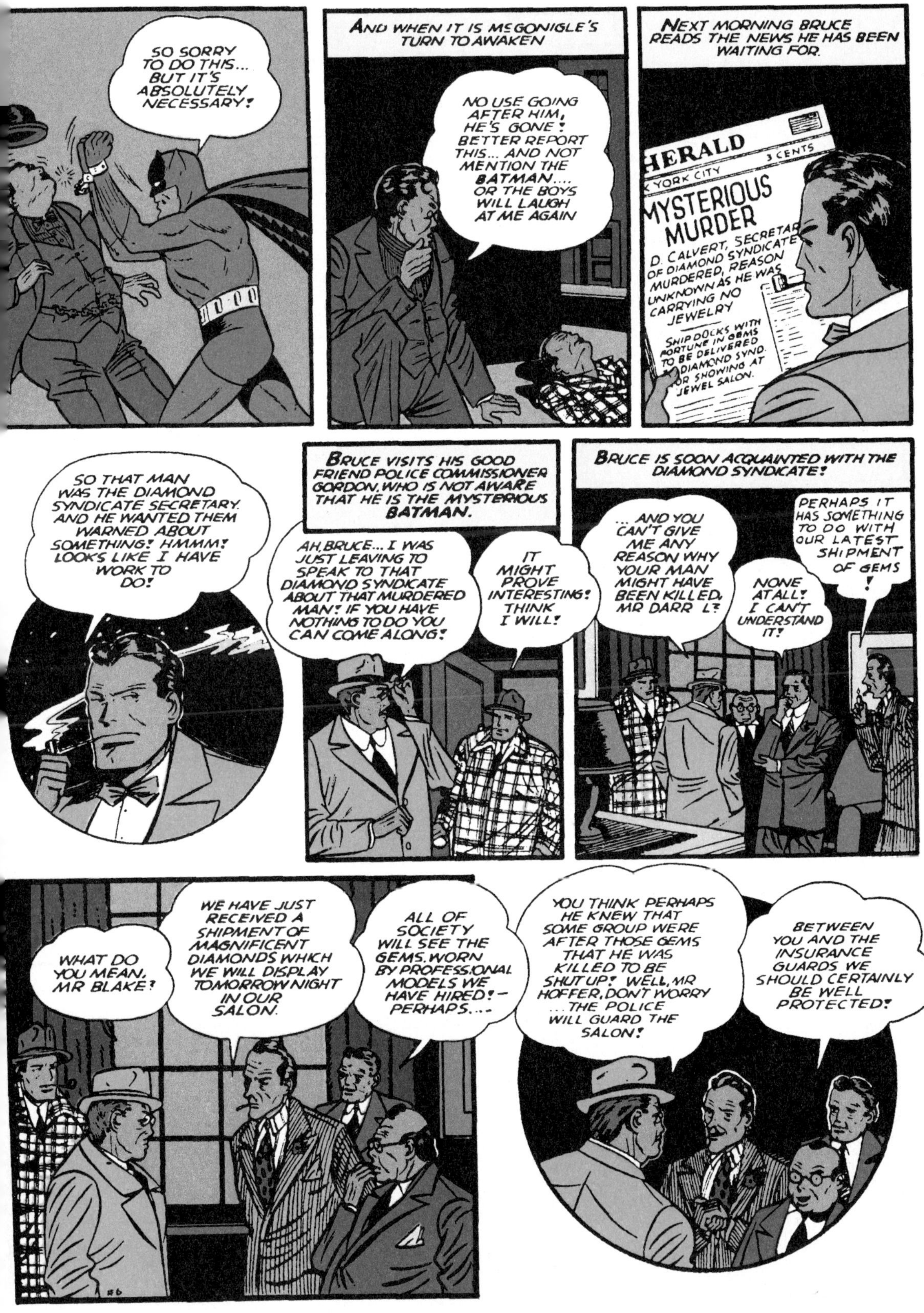

SO SORRY TO DO THIS... BUT IT'S ABSOLUTELY NECESSARY!
AND WHEN IT IS McGONIGLE'S TURN TO AWAKEN
NO USE GOING AFTER HIM, HE'S GONE! BETTER REPORT THIS... AND NOT MENTION THE BATMAN.... OR THE BOYS WILL LAUGH AT ME AGAIN
NEXT MORNING BRUCE READS THE NEWS HE HAS BEEN WAITING FOR.
HERALD
3 CENTS
K YORK CITY
MYSTERIOUS MURDER
D. CALVERT, SECRETAR OF DIAMOND SYNDICATE MURDERED, REASON UNKNOWN AS HE WAS CARRYING NO JEWELRY
SHIP DOCKS WITH FORTUNE IN GEMS TO BE DELIVERED O DIAMOND SYND. OR SHOWING AT JEWEL SALON.
SO THAT MAN WAS THE DIAMOND SYNDICATE SECRETARY. AND HE WANTED THEM WARNED ABOUT SOMETHING! HMMM! LOOKS LIKE I HAVE WORK TO DO!
BRUCE VISITS HIS GOOD FRIEND POLICE COMMISSIONER GORDON, WHO IS NOT AWARE THAT HE IS THE MYSTERIOUS BATMAN.
AH, BRUCE... I WAS JUST LEAVING TO SPEAK TO THAT DIAMOND SYNDICATE ABOUT THAT MURDERED MAN! IF YOU HAVE NOTHING TO DO YOU CAN COME ALONG!
IT MIGHT PROVE INTERESTING! THINK I WILL!
BRUCE IS SOON ACQUAINTED WITH THE DIAMOND SYNDICATE!
...AND YOU CAN'T GIVE ME ANY REASON WHY YOUR MAN MIGHT HAVE BEEN KILLED, MR DARR L?
NONE AT ALL! I CAN'T UNDERSTAND IT!
PERHAPS IT HAS SOMETHING TO DO WITH OUR LATEST SHIPMENT OF GEMS!
WHAT DO YOU MEAN, MR BLAKE?
WE HAVE JUST RECEIVED A SHIPMENT OF MAGNIFICENT DIAMONDS WHICH WE WILL DISPLAY TOMORROW NIGHT IN OUR SALON.
ALL OF SOCIETY WILL SEE THE GEMS, WORN BY PROFESSIONAL MODELS WE HAVE HIRED! — PERHAPS....
YOU THINK PERHAPS HE KNEW THAT SOME GROUP WERE AFTER THOSE GEMS THAT HE WAS KILLED TO BE SHUT UP! WELL, MR HOFFER, DON'T WORRY ...THE POLICE WILL GUARD THE SALON!
BETWEEN YOU AND THE INSURANCE GUARDS WE SHOULD CERTAINLY BE WELL PROTECTED!

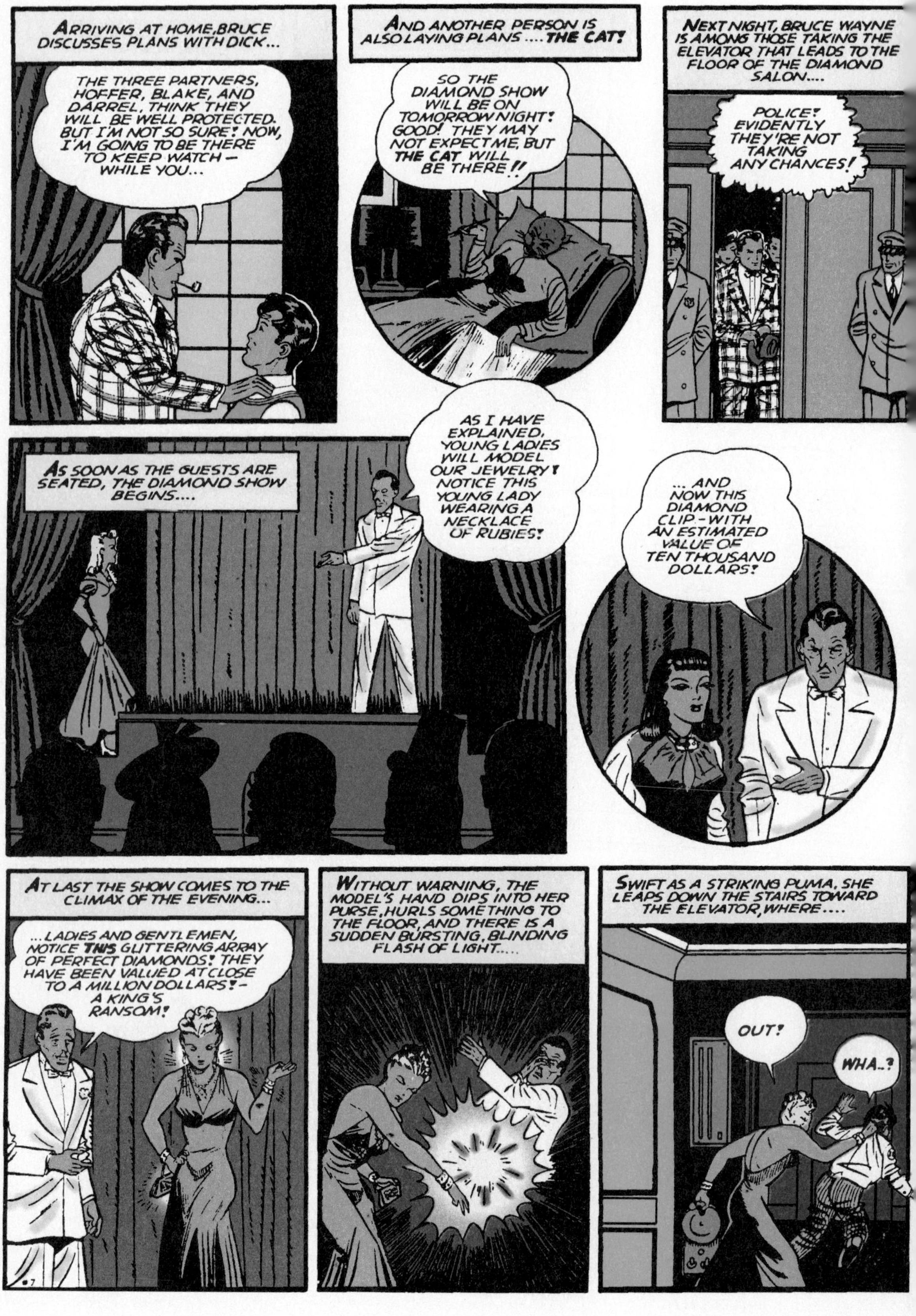
ARRIVING AT HOME, BRUCE DISCUSSES PLANS WITH DICK...
THE THREE PARTNERS, HOFFER, BLAKE, AND DARREL, THINK THEY WILL BE WELL PROTECTED. BUT I'M NOT SO SURE! NOW, I'M GOING TO BE THERE TO KEEP WATCH — WHILE YOU...
AND ANOTHER PERSON IS ALSO LAYING PLANS .... THE CAT!
SO THE DIAMOND SHOW WILL BE ON TOMORROW NIGHT! GOOD! THEY MAY NOT EXPECT ME, BUT THE CAT WILL BE THERE!!
NEXT NIGHT, BRUCE WAYNE IS AMONG THOSE TAKING THE ELEVATOR THAT LEADS TO THE FLOOR OF THE DIAMOND SALON....
POLICE! EVIDENTLY THEY'RE NOT TAKING ANY CHANCES!
AS SOON AS THE GUESTS ARE SEATED, THE DIAMOND SHOW BEGINS....
AS I HAVE EXPLAINED, YOUNG LADIES WILL MODEL OUR JEWELRY! NOTICE THIS YOUNG LADY WEARING A NECKLACE OF RUBIES!
... AND NOW THIS DIAMOND CLIP - WITH AN ESTIMATED VALUE OF TEN THOUSAND DOLLARS!
AT LAST THE SHOW COMES TO THE CLIMAX OF THE EVENING...
... LADIES AND GENTLEMEN, NOTICE THIS GLITTERING ARRAY OF PERFECT DIAMONDS! THEY HAVE BEEN VALUED AT CLOSE TO A MILLION DOLLARS! - A KING'S RANSOM!
WITHOUT WARNING, THE MODEL'S HAND DIPS INTO HER PURSE, HURLS SOMETHING TO THE FLOOR, AND THERE IS A SUDDEN BURSTING, BLINDING FLASH OF LIGHT....
SWIFT AS A STRIKING PUMA, SHE LEAPS DOWN THE STAIRS TOWARD THE ELEVATOR, WHERE....
OUT!
WHA..?

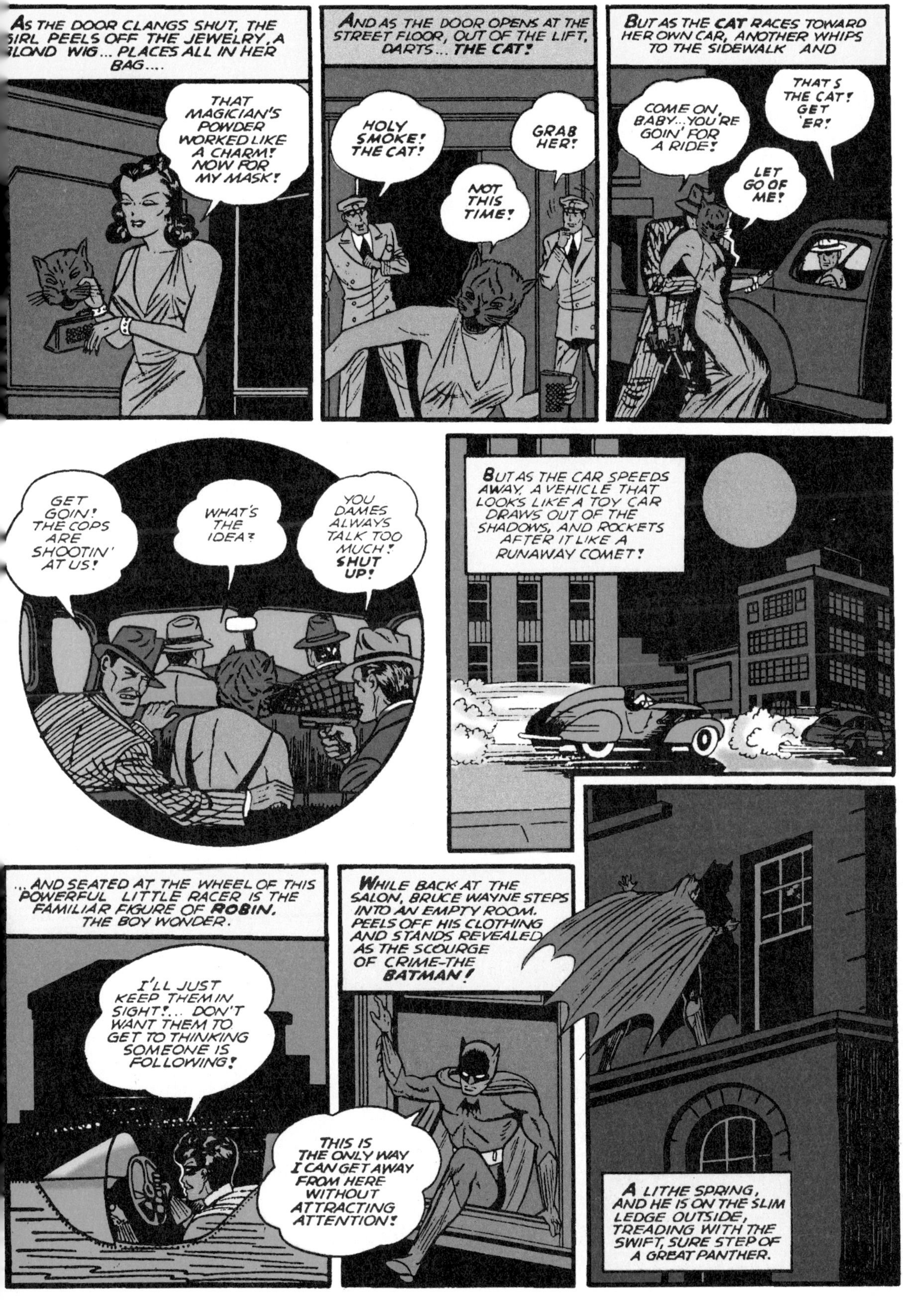
As the door clangs shut, the girl peels off the jewelry, a blond wig... places all in her bag....
That magician's powder worked like a charm! Now for my mask!
And as the door opens at the street floor, out of the lift, darts... the Cat!
Holy smoke! The Cat!
Grab her!
Not this time!
But as the Cat races toward her own car, another whips to the sidewalk and
Come on, baby... you're goin' for a ride!
That's the Cat! Get 'er!
Let go of me!
Get goin'! The cops are shootin' at us!
What's the idea?
You dames always talk too much! Shut up!
But as the car speeds away, a vehicle that looks like a toy car draws out of the shadows, and rockets after it like a runaway comet!
...And seated at the wheel of this powerful little racer is the familiar figure of Robin, the Boy Wonder.
I'll just keep them in sight!... Don't want them to get to thinking someone is following!
While back at the salon, Bruce Wayne steps into an empty room. Peels off his clothing and stands revealed as the scourge of crime-the Batman!
This is the only way I can get away from here without attracting attention!
A lithe spring, and he is on the slim ledge outside, treading with the swift, sure step of a great panther.

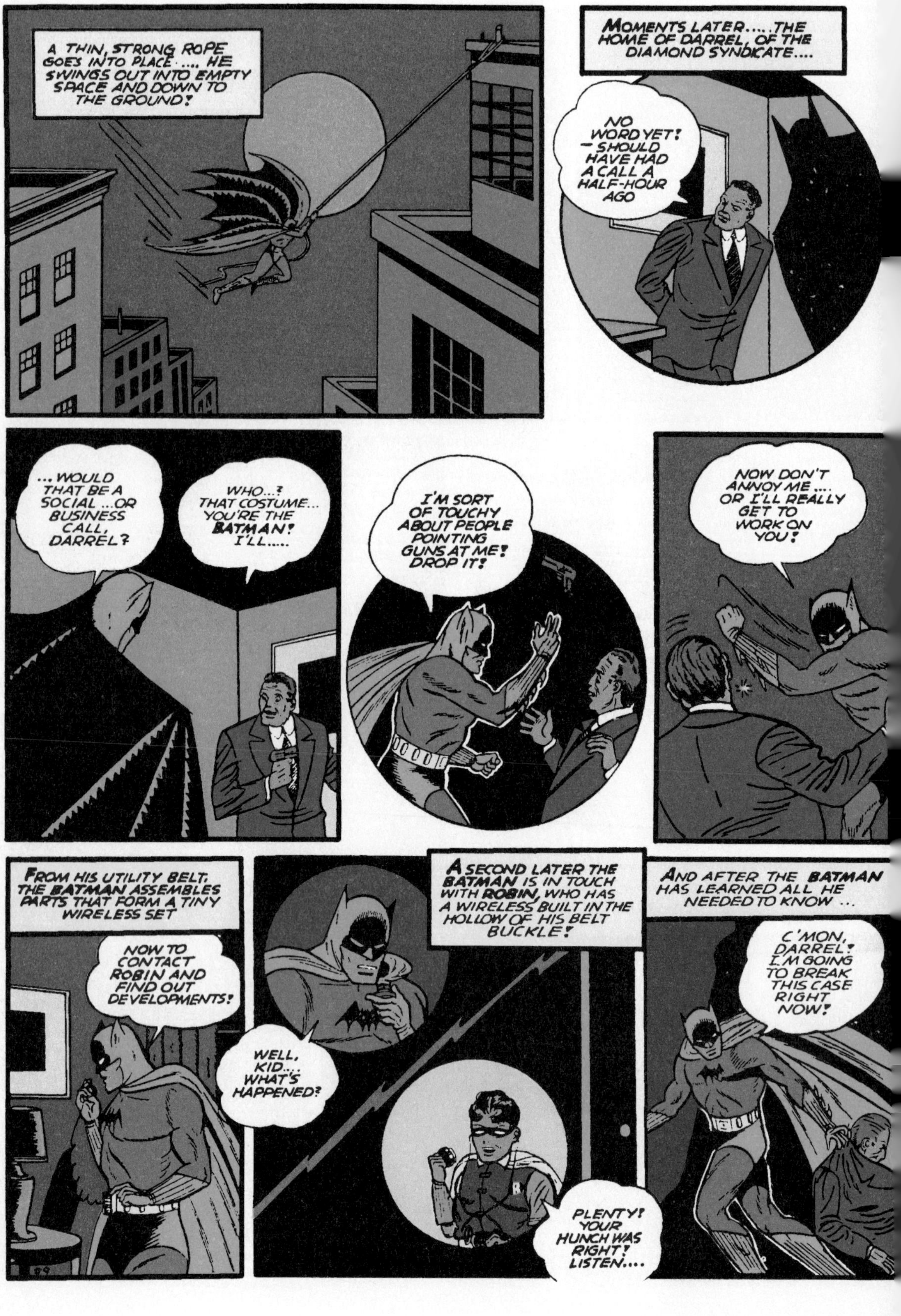
A THIN, STRONG ROPE GOES INTO PLACE.... HE SWINGS OUT INTO EMPTY SPACE AND DOWN TO THE GROUND!
MOMENTS LATER.....THE HOME OF DARREL, OF THE DIAMOND SYNDICATE....
NO WORD YET! — SHOULD HAVE HAD A CALL A HALF-HOUR AGO
...WOULD THAT BE A SOCIAL ...OR BUSINESS CALL, DARREL?
WHO...? THAT COSTUME... YOU'RE THE BATMAN! I'LL.....
I'M SORT OF TOUCHY ABOUT PEOPLE POINTING GUNS AT ME! DROP IT!
NOW DON'T ANNOY ME.... OR I'LL REALLY GET TO WORK ON YOU!
FROM HIS UTILITY BELT, THE BATMAN ASSEMBLES PARTS THAT FORM A TINY WIRELESS SET
NOW TO CONTACT ROBIN AND FIND OUT DEVELOPMENTS!
A SECOND LATER THE BATMAN IS IN TOUCH WITH ROBIN, WHO HAS A WIRELESS BUILT IN THE HOLLOW OF HIS BELT BUCKLE!
WELL, KID... WHAT'S HAPPENED?
PLENTY! YOUR HUNCH WAS RIGHT! LISTEN....
AND AFTER THE BATMAN HAS LEARNED ALL HE NEEDED TO KNOW ...
C'MON, DARREL! I'M GOING TO BREAK THIS CASE RIGHT NOW!

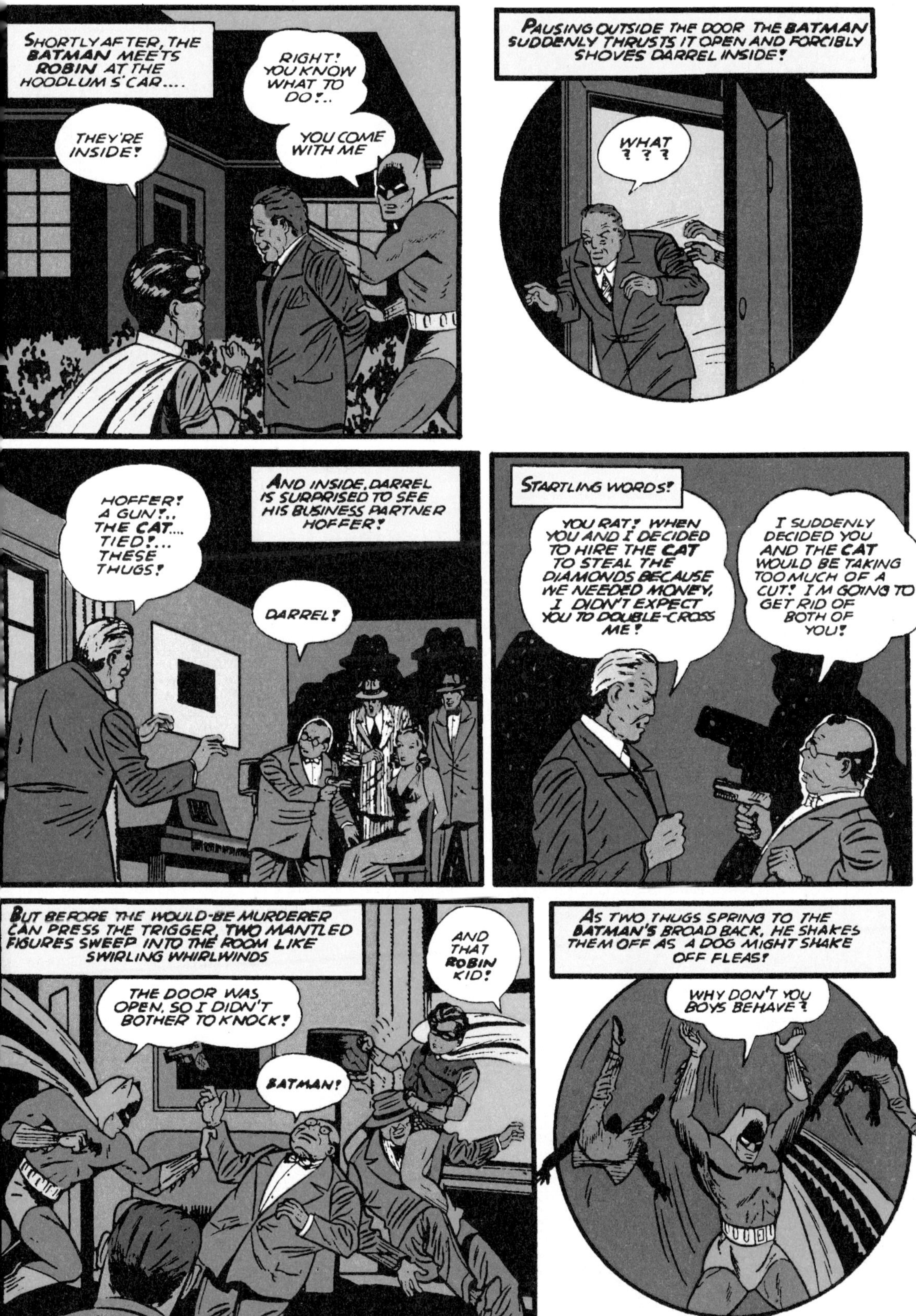
SHORTLY AFTER, THE BATMAN MEETS ROBIN AT THE HOODLUM'S CAR....
RIGHT! YOU KNOW WHAT TO DO!..
THEY'RE INSIDE!
YOU COME WITH ME
PAUSING OUTSIDE THE DOOR THE BATMAN SUDDENLY THRUSTS IT OPEN AND FORCIBLY SHOVES DARREL INSIDE!
WHAT ???
AND INSIDE, DARREL IS SURPRISED TO SEE HIS BUSINESS PARTNER HOFFER!
HOFFER! A GUN!.. THE CAT... TIED!... THESE THUGS!
DARREL!
STARTLING WORDS!
YOU RAT! WHEN YOU AND I DECIDED TO HIRE THE CAT TO STEAL THE DIAMONDS BECAUSE WE NEEDED MONEY, I DIDN'T EXPECT YOU TO DOUBLE-CROSS ME!
I SUDDENLY DECIDED YOU AND THE CAT WOULD BE TAKING TOO MUCH OF A CUT! I'M GOING TO GET RID OF BOTH OF YOU!
BUT BEFORE THE WOULD-BE MURDERER CAN PRESS THE TRIGGER, TWO MANTLED FIGURES SWEEP INTO THE ROOM LIKE SWIRLING WHIRLWINDS
THE DOOR WAS OPEN, SO I DIDN'T BOTHER TO KNOCK!
AND THAT ROBIN KID!
BATMAN!
AS TWO THUGS SPRING TO THE BATMAN'S BROAD BACK, HE SHAKES THEM OFF AS A DOG MIGHT SHAKE OFF FLEAS!
WHY DON'T YOU BOYS BEHAVE?

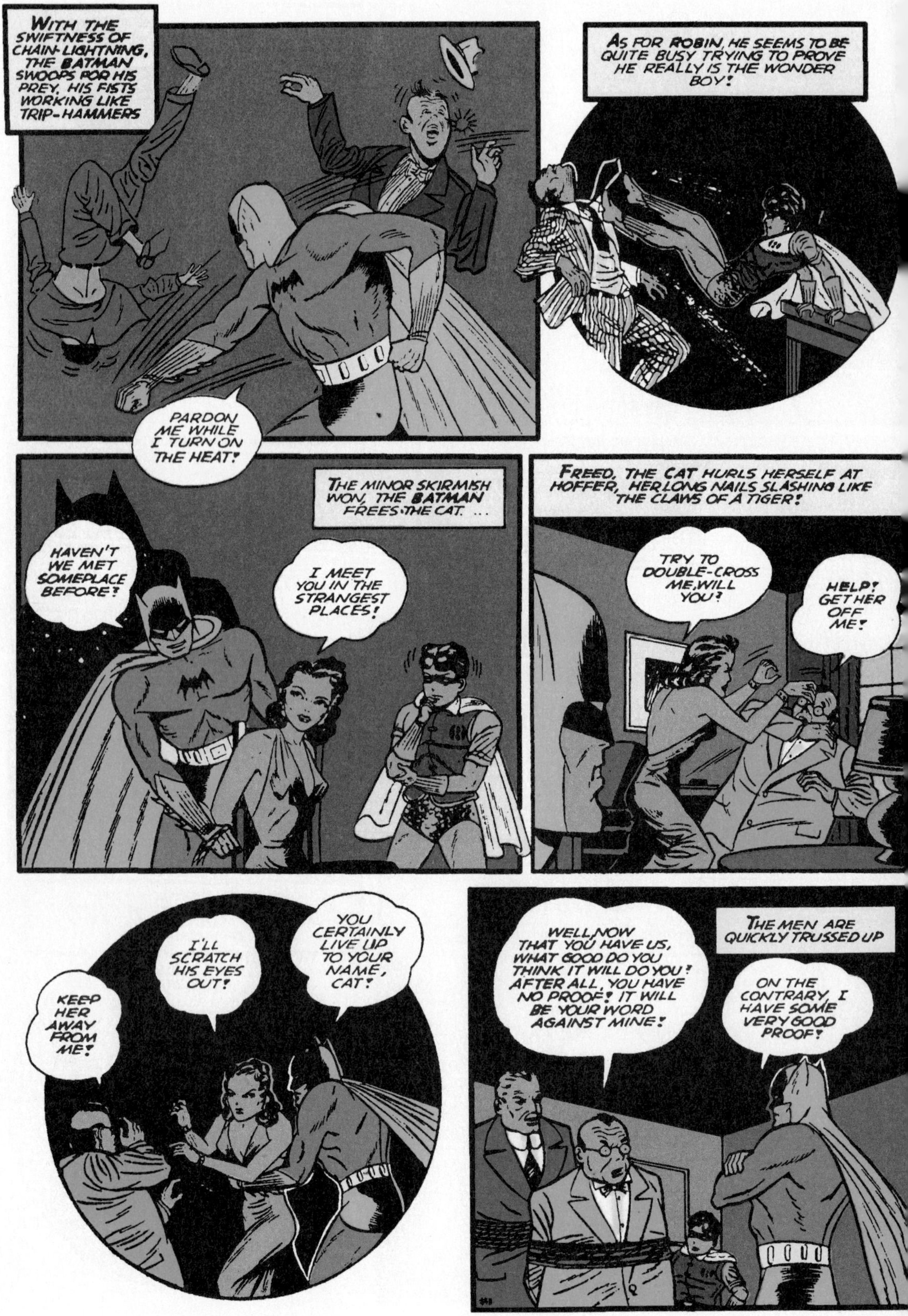
WITH THE SWIFTNESS OF CHAIN-LIGHTNING, THE BATMAN SWOOPS FOR HIS PREY, HIS FISTS WORKING LIKE TRIP-HAMMERS
PARDON ME WHILE I TURN ON THE HEAT!
AS FOR ROBIN, HE SEEMS TO BE QUITE BUSY TRYING TO PROVE HE REALLY IS THE WONDER BOY!
THE MINOR SKIRMISH WON, THE BATMAN FREES THE CAT. ...
HAVEN'T WE MET SOMEPLACE BEFORE?
I MEET YOU IN THE STRANGEST PLACES!
FREED, THE CAT HURLS HERSELF AT HOFFER, HER LONG NAILS SLASHING LIKE THE CLAWS OF A TIGER!
TRY TO DOUBLE-CROSS ME, WILL YOU?
HELP! GET HER OFF ME!
KEEP HER AWAY FROM ME!
I'LL SCRATCH HIS EYES OUT!
YOU CERTAINLY LIVE UP TO YOUR NAME, CAT!
THE MEN ARE QUICKLY TRUSSED UP
WELL, NOW THAT YOU HAVE US, WHAT GOOD DO YOU THINK IT WILL DO YOU? AFTER ALL, YOU HAVE NO PROOF! IT WILL BE YOUR WORD AGAINST MINE!
ON THE CONTRARY, I HAVE SOME VERY GOOD PROOF!

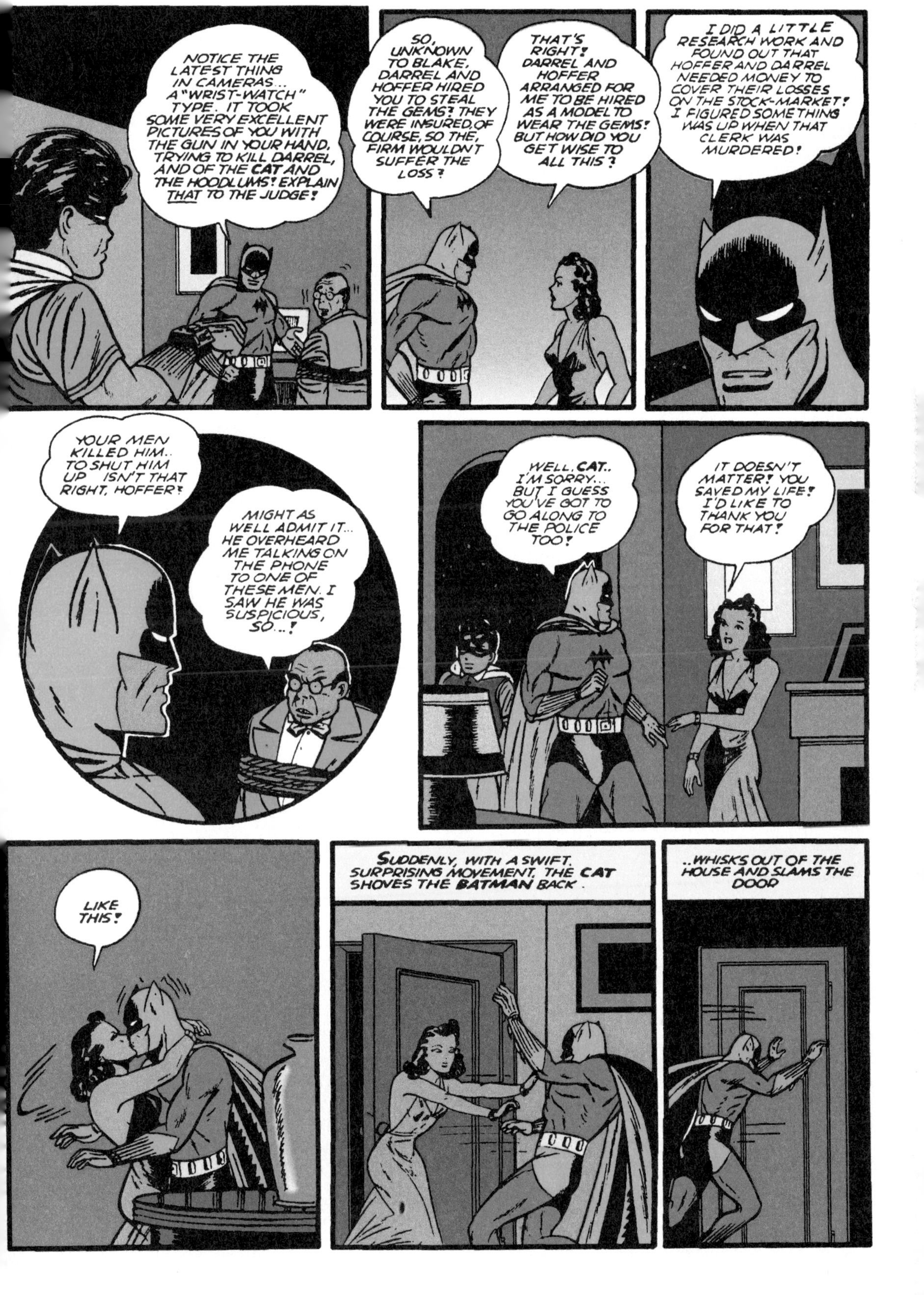
NOTICE THE LATEST THING IN CAMERAS... A "WRIST-WATCH" TYPE. IT TOOK SOME VERY EXCELLENT PICTURES OF YOU WITH THE GUN IN YOUR HAND, TRYING TO KILL DARREL, AND OF THE CAT AND THE HOODLUMS! EXPLAIN THAT TO THE JUDGE!
SO, UNKNOWN TO BLAKE, DARREL AND HOFFER HIRED YOU TO STEAL THE GEMS? THEY WERE INSURED, OF COURSE, SO THE FIRM WOULDN'T SUFFER THE LOSS?
THAT'S RIGHT! DARREL AND HOFFER ARRANGED FOR ME TO BE HIRED AS A MODEL TO WEAR THE GEMS! BUT HOW DID YOU GET WISE TO ALL THIS?
I DID A LITTLE RESEARCH WORK AND FOUND OUT THAT HOFFER AND DARREL NEEDED MONEY TO COVER THEIR LOSSES ON THE STOCK-MARKET! I FIGURED SOMETHING WAS UP WHEN THAT CLERK WAS MURDERED!
YOUR MEN KILLED HIM.. TO SHUT HIM UP ISN'T THAT RIGHT, HOFFER?
MIGHT AS WELL ADMIT IT... HE OVERHEARD ME TALKING ON THE PHONE TO ONE OF THESE MEN. I SAW HE WAS SUSPICIOUS, SO...!
WELL, CAT.. I'M SORRY... BUT I GUESS YOU'VE GOT TO GO ALONG TO THE POLICE TOO!
IT DOESN'T MATTER! YOU SAVED MY LIFE! I'D LIKE TO THANK YOU FOR THAT!
LIKE THIS!
SUDDENLY, WITH A SWIFT, SURPRISING MOVEMENT, THE CAT SHOVES THE BATMAN BACK.
..WHISKS OUT OF THE HOUSE AND SLAMS THE DOOR

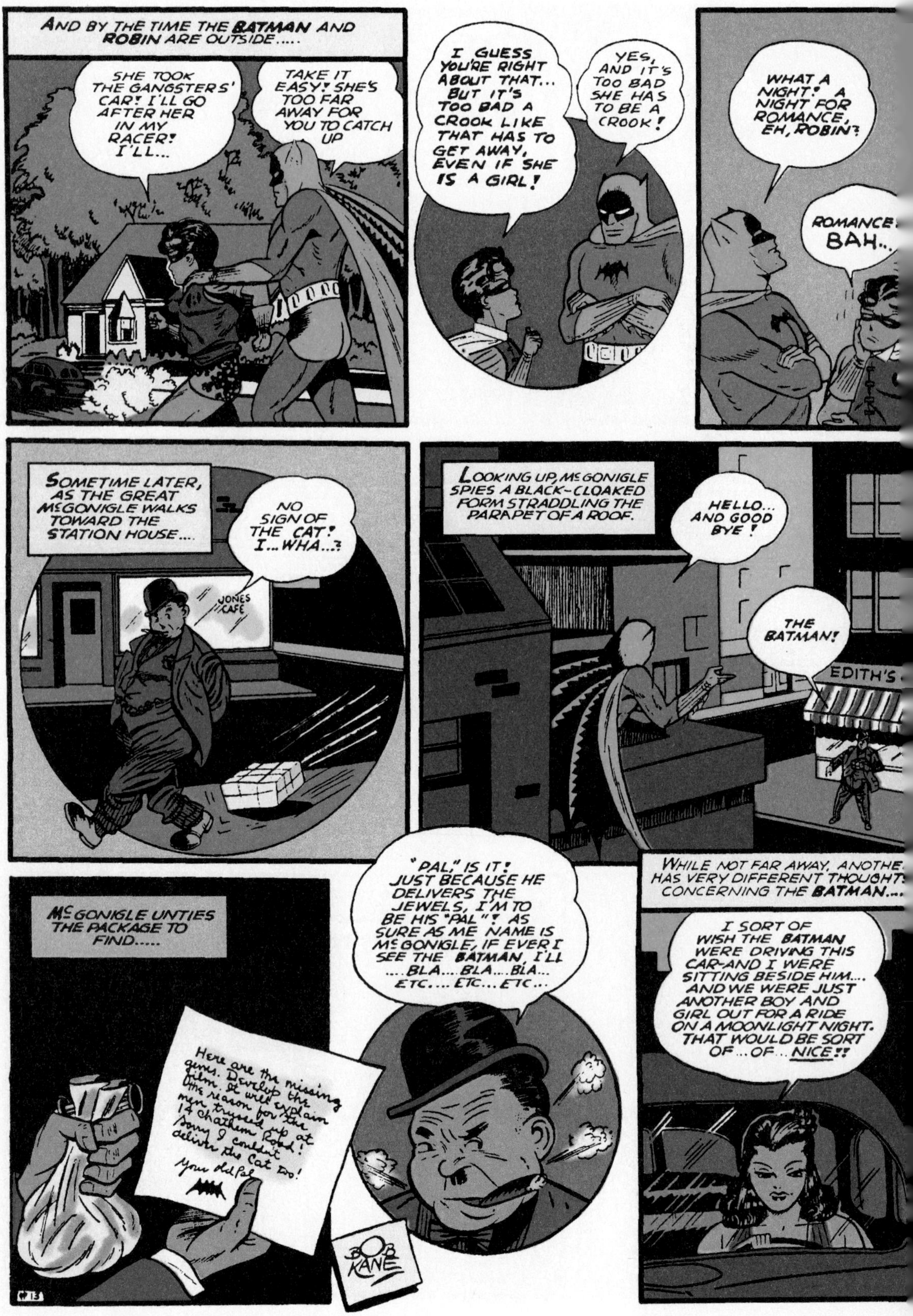
AND BY THE TIME THE BATMAN AND ROBIN ARE OUTSIDE.....
SHE TOOK THE GANGSTERS' CAR! I'LL GO AFTER HER IN MY RACER! I'LL...
TAKE IT EASY! SHE'S TOO FAR AWAY FOR YOU TO CATCH UP
I GUESS YOU'RE RIGHT ABOUT THAT... BUT IT'S TOO BAD A CROOK LIKE THAT HAS TO GET AWAY, EVEN IF SHE IS A GIRL!
YES, AND IT'S TOO BAD SHE HAS TO BE A CROOK!
WHAT A NIGHT! A NIGHT FOR ROMANCE, EH, ROBIN?
ROMANCE! BAH...
SOMETIME LATER, AS THE GREAT McGONIGLE WALKS TOWARD THE STATION HOUSE....
NO SIGN OF THE CAT! I...WHA...?
JONES CAFE
LOOKING UP, McGONIGLE SPIES A BLACK-CLOAKED FORM STRADDLING THE PARAPET OF A ROOF.
HELLO... AND GOOD BYE!
THE BATMAN!
EDITH'S
McGONIGLE UNTIES THE PACKAGE TO FIND.....
Here are the missing gems. Develop the film. It will explain the reason for the men trussed up at 14 Chatham Road! Sorry I couldn't deliver the Cat too! Your old Pal
"PAL," IS IT! JUST BECAUSE HE DELIVERS THE JEWELS, I'M TO BE HIS "PAL"! AS SURE AS ME NAME IS McGONIGLE, IF EVER I SEE THE BATMAN, I'LL ....BLA....BLA....BLA... ETC.... ETC... ETC...
BOB KANE
WHILE NOT FAR AWAY, ANOTHER HAS VERY DIFFERENT THOUGHTS CONCERNING THE BATMAN....
I SORT OF WISH THE BATMAN WERE DRIVING THIS CAR-AND I WERE SITTING BESIDE HIM.... AND WE WERE JUST ANOTHER BOY AND GIRL OUT FOR A RIDE ON A MOONLIGHT NIGHT. THAT WOULD BE SORT OF...OF... NICE!!

The BATMAN SAYS:

HELLO, Readers! Now that you've read all these new adventures of mine and Robin's, I'd like to talk right AT you for a minute or so.

I think Robin and I make it pretty clear that WE HATE CRIME AND CRIMINALS! There's nothing we like better than to crack down on the distasteful denizens of the underworld. Why? Because we're proud of being AMERICANS—and we know there's no place in this great country of ours for lawbreakers!

That phrase, "CRIME DOESN'T PAY," has been used over and over again to the point where I hesitate to repeat it. But remember this: IT'S JUST AS TRUE NOW AS IT EVER WAS—AND THAT'S PLENTY TRUE!

Sure, it may seem that lawbreakers DO get away with breaking the law. Some may get away with it longer than others. But in the end, every crook gets what's coming to him—and that means plenty of trouble with the law!

Robin and I hope that our adventures may help to "put over" that fact. We'd like to feel that our efforts may help every youngster to grow up into an honest, useful citizen.

It depends on YOU and YOU and YOU. You've got to govern your own lives so that they can be worthwhile, fruitful lives—not lives wasted in prison, or even thrown away altogether before the ready guns of the law-enforcement agents who duty it is to guard those of us who are honest from those of us who are not. And not only must you guide your OWN life in the proper channels—you must also strive to be a good influence on the lives of others.

If you do all this, if you are definitely on the side of Law and Order, then Robin and I salute you and are glad to number you among our friends!

....and what the BATMAN says goes DOUBLE for me!

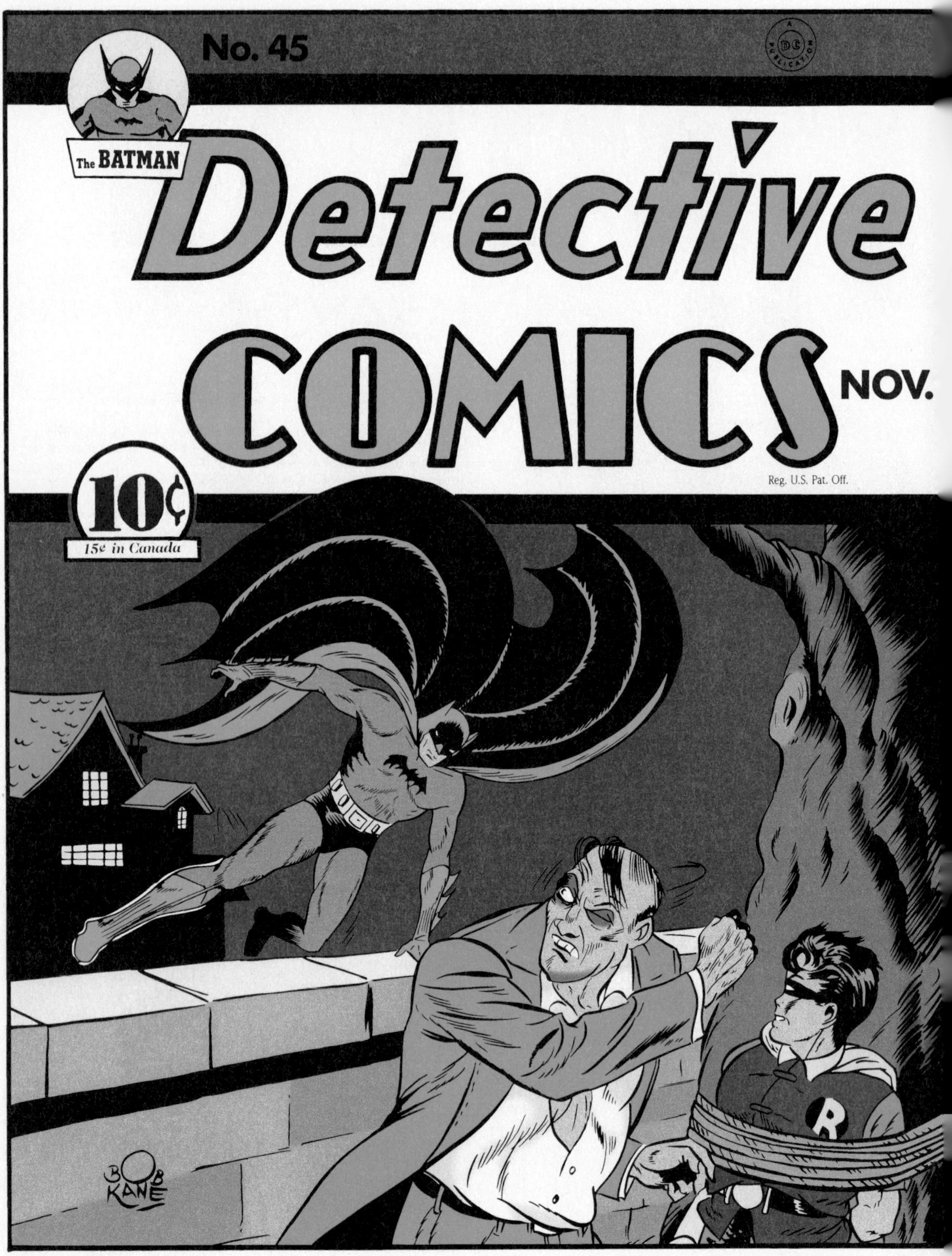
No. 45
The BATMAN
A DC PUBLICATION
Detective COMICS
NOV.
10¢
15¢ in Canada
Reg. U.S. Pat. Off.
BOB KANE

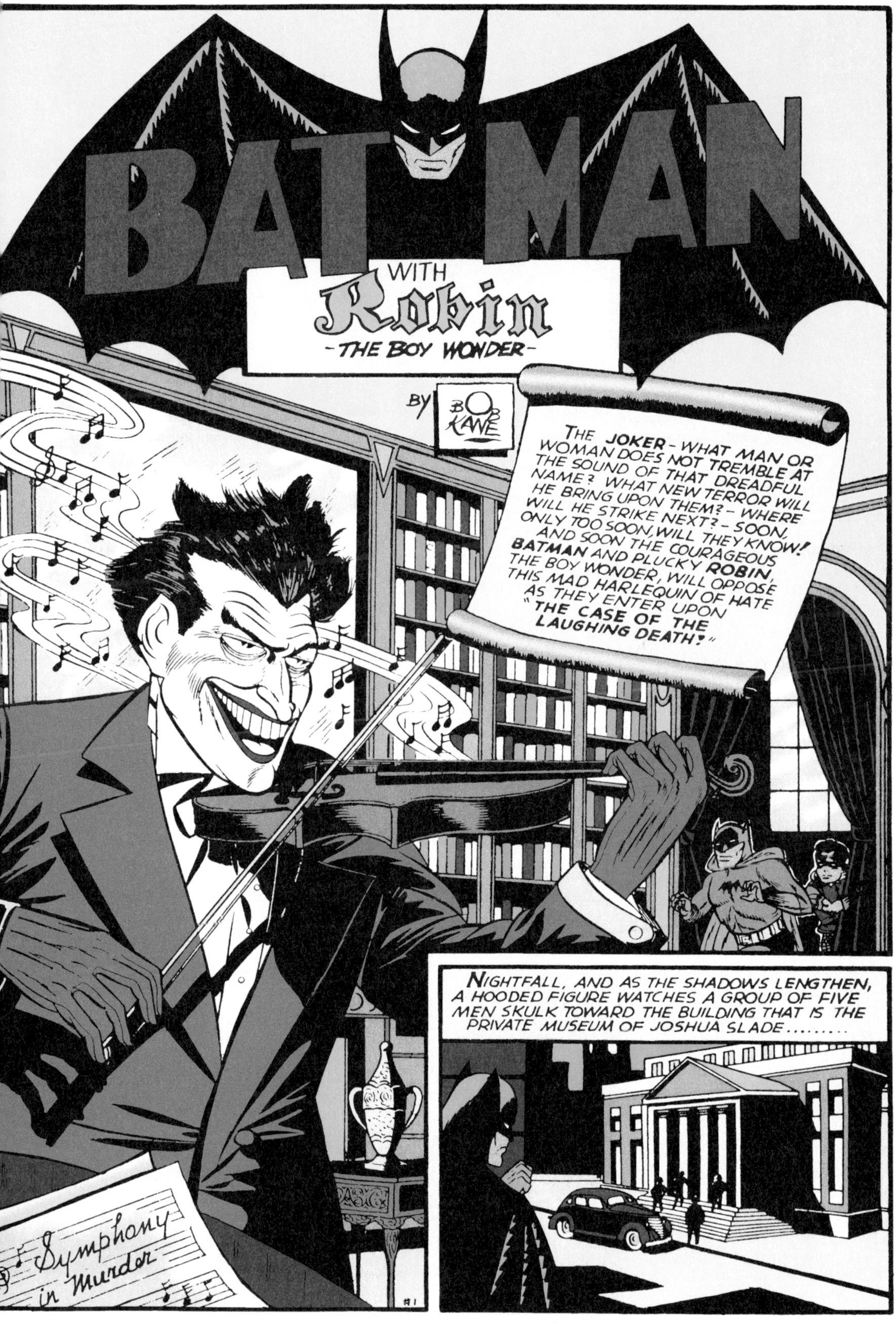
BATMAN
WITH
Robin
-THE BOY WONDER-
BY BOB KANE
THE JOKER - WHAT MAN OR WOMAN DOES NOT TREMBLE AT THE SOUND OF THAT DREADFUL NAME? WHAT NEW TERROR WILL HE BRING UPON THEM? - WHERE WILL HE STRIKE NEXT? - SOON, ONLY TOO SOON, WILL THEY KNOW! AND SOON THE COURAGEOUS BATMAN AND PLUCKY ROBIN, THE BOY WONDER, WILL OPPOSE THIS MAD HARLEQUIN OF HATE AS THEY ENTER UPON "THE CASE OF THE LAUGHING DEATH!"
Symphony in Murder
#1
NIGHTFALL, AND AS THE SHADOWS LENGTHEN, A HOODED FIGURE WATCHES A GROUP OF FIVE MEN SKULK TOWARD THE BUILDING THAT IS THE PRIVATE MUSEUM OF JOSHUA SLADE........

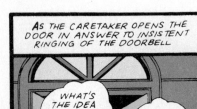

AS THE CARETAKER OPENS THE DOOR IN ANSWER TO INSISTENT RINGING OF THE DOORBELL

WHAT'S THE IDEA OF... ...UGH!

THAT GOT 'IM!

SWIFTLY, THE COWLED FIGURE OF THE 'BATMAN' GOES INTO ACTION

I FELT THERE WAS SOMETHING SUSPICIOUS ABOUT THEIR ACTIONS, AND NOW I KNOW IT!

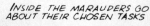

INSIDE THE MARAUDERS GO ABOUT THEIR CHOSEN TASKS

OKAY, BOYS, LET'S GET TO WORK! FRANKIE, YOU TAKE CARE O' THE BURGLAR ALARM!

THIS JOB IS GONNA BE A CINCH!

SORRY, GENTLEMEN! BUT I DON'T THINK YOU'RE GOING TO DO MUCH OF YOUR WORK TO-NIGHT!

THEN LIKE A DARK THUNDER CLOUD, THE BATMAN STORMS INTO THE ROOM!

THE BATMAN!

NO GUNS! IT MIGHT DRAW THE COPS! CLUB 'IM DOWN!

AS THE DESPERATE THUGS RACE TOWARD HIM, THE BATMAN SEIZES A LANCE.....

HAVEN'T DONE THIS SINCE MY COLLEGE DAYS, BUT...

IT SEEMS I HAVEN'T FORGOTTEN HOW TO POLE-VAULT!

WHAT TH'

HUH?

AND STREAKING FORWARD, PLUNGES THE POINT INTO THE FLOOR --- AND VAULTS OVER THE ASTOUNDED GANGSTERS!

AS HIS LITHE BODY CLIMBS UPWARD, THE BATMAN RELEASES HIS HOLD UPON THE LANCE AND REACHES FOR THE CHANDELIER.

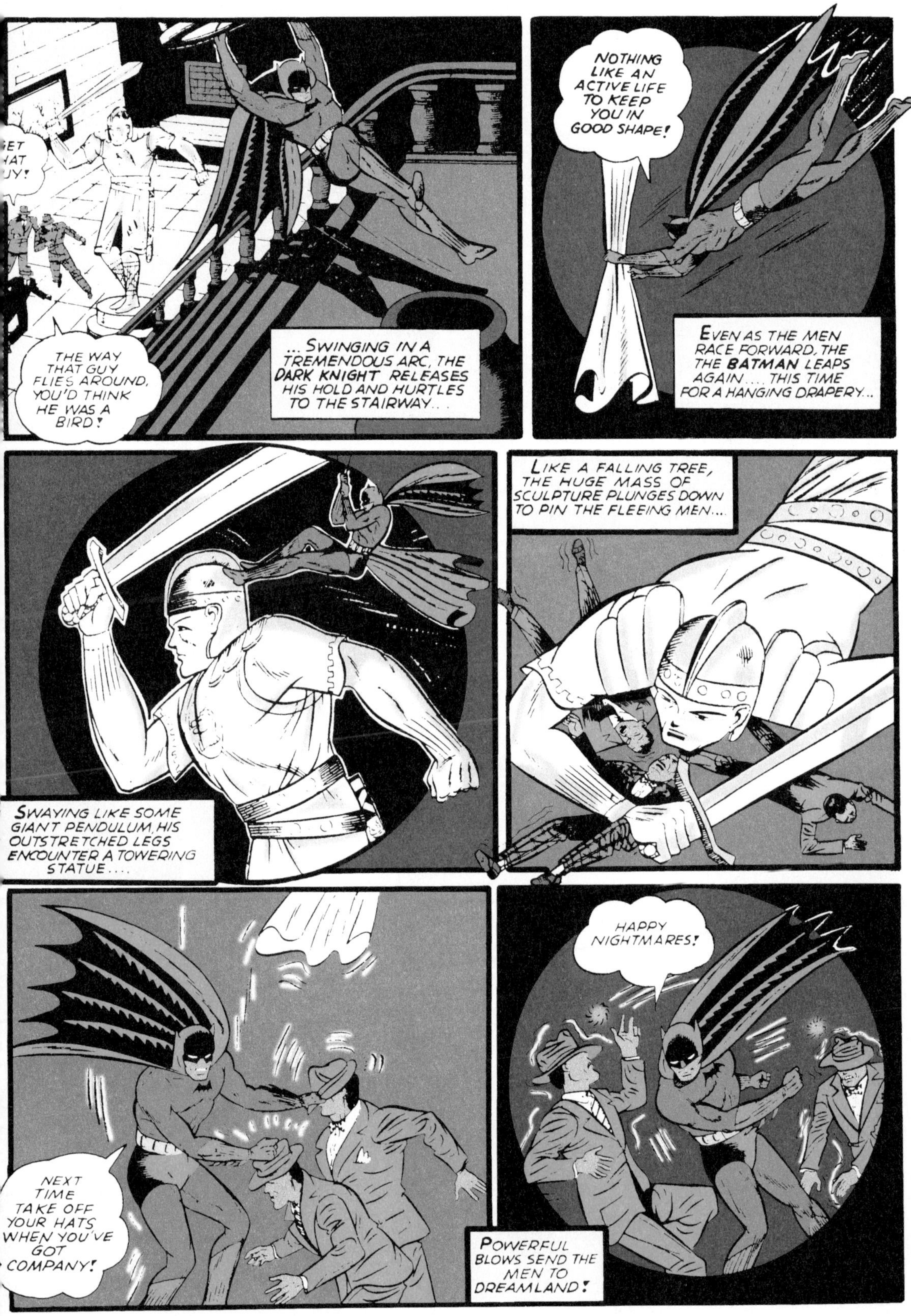
ET
HAT
UY!
THE WAY THAT GUY FLIES AROUND, YOU'D THINK HE WAS A BIRD!
... SWINGING IN A TREMENDOUS ARC, THE DARK KNIGHT RELEASES HIS HOLD AND HURTLES TO THE STAIRWAY...
NOTHING LIKE AN ACTIVE LIFE TO KEEP YOU IN GOOD SHAPE!
EVEN AS THE MEN RACE FORWARD, THE THE BATMAN LEAPS AGAIN.... THIS TIME FOR A HANGING DRAPERY...
SWAYING LIKE SOME GIANT PENDULUM, HIS OUTSTRETCHED LEGS ENCOUNTER A TOWERING STATUE....
LIKE A FALLING TREE, THE HUGE MASS OF SCULPTURE PLUNGES DOWN TO PIN THE FLEEING MEN...
NEXT TIME TAKE OFF YOUR HATS WHEN YOU'VE GOT COMPANY!
HAPPY NIGHTMARES!
POWERFUL BLOWS SEND THE MEN TO DREAMLAND!

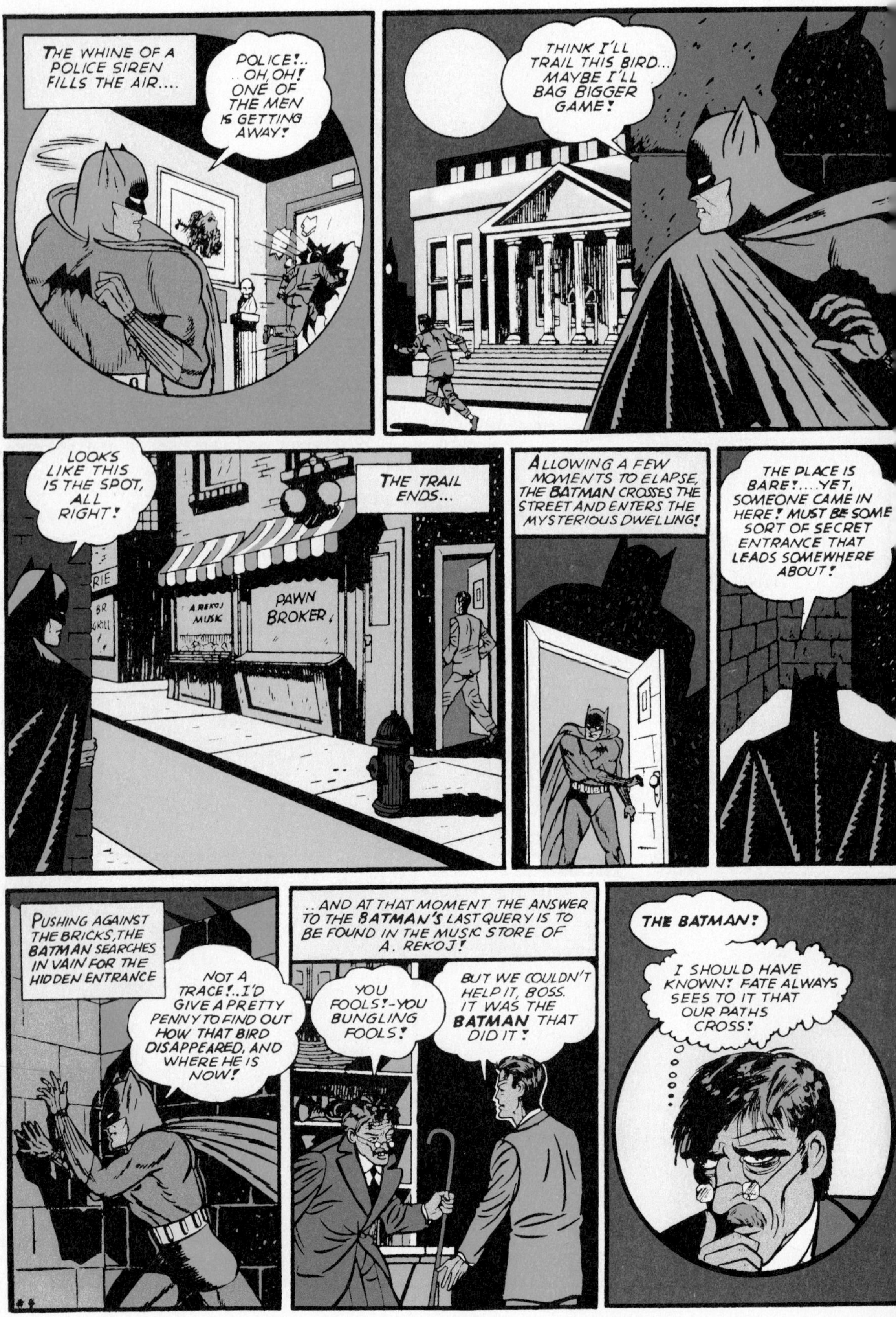

THE WHINE OF A POLICE SIREN FILLS THE AIR....
POLICE!.. ..OH, OH! ONE OF THE MEN IS GETTING AWAY!
THINK I'LL TRAIL THIS BIRD... MAYBE I'LL BAG BIGGER GAME!
LOOKS LIKE THIS IS THE SPOT, ALL RIGHT!
THE TRAIL ENDS...
A. REKOJ MUSIC
PAWN BROKER
ALLOWING A FEW MOMENTS TO ELAPSE, THE BATMAN CROSSES THE STREET AND ENTERS THE MYSTERIOUS DWELLING!
THE PLACE IS BARE!....YET, SOMEONE CAME IN HERE! MUST BE SOME SORT OF SECRET ENTRANCE THAT LEADS SOMEWHERE ABOUT!
PUSHING AGAINST THE BRICKS, THE BATMAN SEARCHES IN VAIN FOR THE HIDDEN ENTRANCE
NOT A TRACE!..I'D GIVE A PRETTY PENNY TO FIND OUT HOW THAT BIRD DISAPPEARED, AND WHERE HE IS NOW!
..AND AT THAT MOMENT THE ANSWER TO THE BATMAN'S LAST QUERY IS TO BE FOUND IN THE MUSIC STORE OF A. REKOJ!
YOU FOOLS!-YOU BUNGLING FOOLS!
BUT WE COULDN'T HELP IT, BOSS. IT WAS THE BATMAN THAT DID IT!
THE BATMAN!
I SHOULD HAVE KNOWN! FATE ALWAYS SEES TO IT THAT OUR PATHS CROSS!

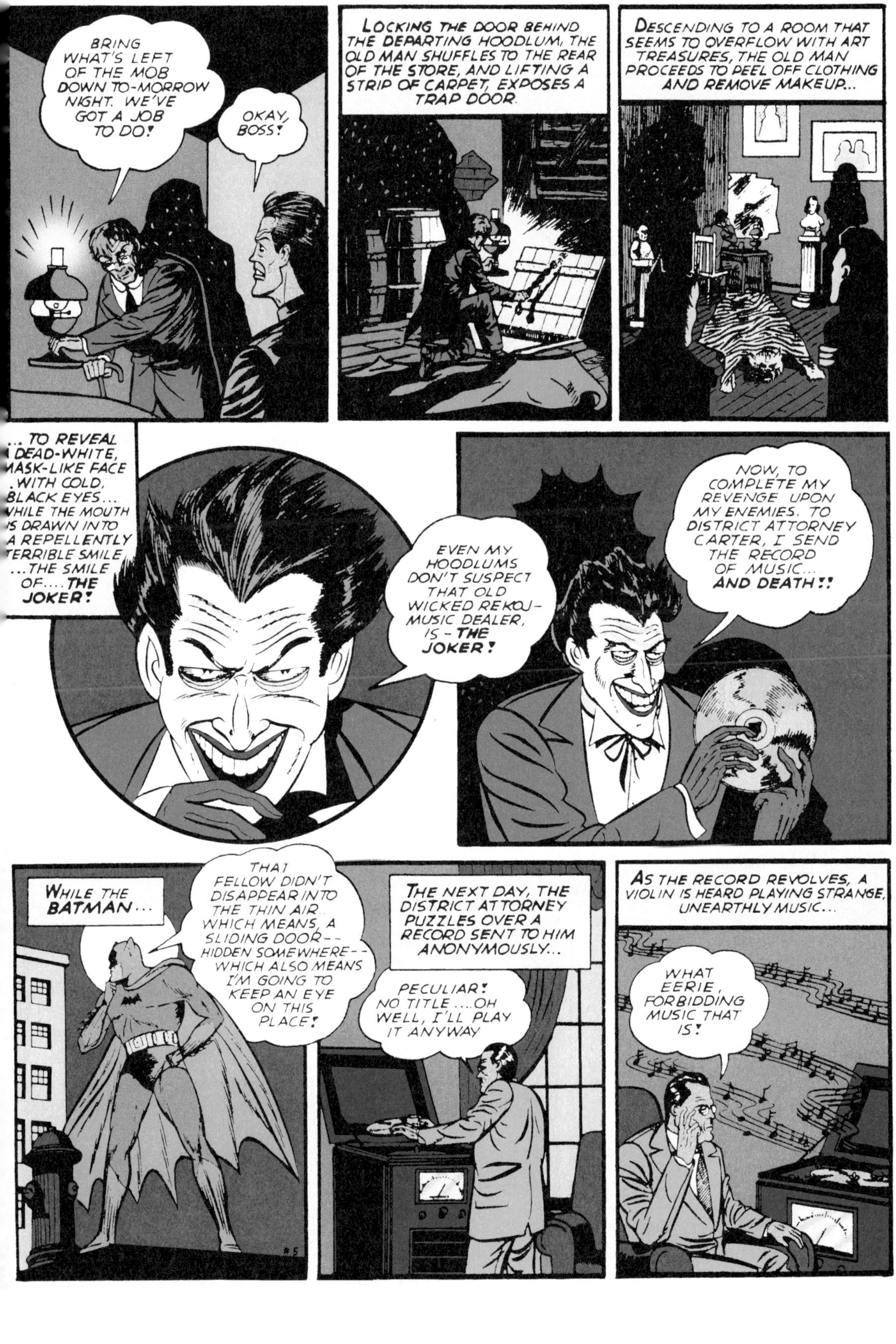
BRING WHAT'S LEFT OF THE MOB DOWN TO-MORROW NIGHT. WE'VE GOT A JOB TO DO!
OKAY, BOSS!
LOCKING THE DOOR BEHIND THE DEPARTING HOODLUM, THE OLD MAN SHUFFLES TO THE REAR OF THE STORE, AND LIFTING A STRIP OF CARPET, EXPOSES A TRAP DOOR.
DESCENDING TO A ROOM THAT SEEMS TO OVERFLOW WITH ART TREASURES, THE OLD MAN PROCEEDS TO PEEL OFF CLOTHING AND REMOVE MAKEUP...
...TO REVEAL DEAD-WHITE, MASK-LIKE FACE WITH COLD, BLACK EYES... WHILE THE MOUTH IS DRAWN INTO A REPELLENTLY TERRIBLE SMILE ...THE SMILE OF.... THE JOKER!
EVEN MY HOODLUMS DON'T SUSPECT THAT OLD WICKED REKOJ- MUSIC DEALER, IS - THE JOKER!
NOW, TO COMPLETE MY REVENGE UPON MY ENEMIES. TO DISTRICT ATTORNEY CARTER, I SEND THE RECORD OF MUSIC... AND DEATH!!
WHILE THE BATMAN...
THAT FELLOW DIDN'T DISAPPEAR INTO THE THIN AIR.. WHICH MEANS, A SLIDING DOOR-- HIDDEN SOMEWHERE-- WHICH ALSO MEANS I'M GOING TO KEEP AN EYE ON THIS PLACE!
THE NEXT DAY, THE DISTRICT ATTORNEY PUZZLES OVER A RECORD SENT TO HIM ANONYMOUSLY...
PECULIAR! NO TITLE....OH WELL, I'LL PLAY IT ANYWAY
AS THE RECORD REVOLVES, A VIOLIN IS HEARD PLAYING STRANGE, UNEARTHLY MUSIC...
WHAT EERIE, FORBIDDING MUSIC THAT IS!

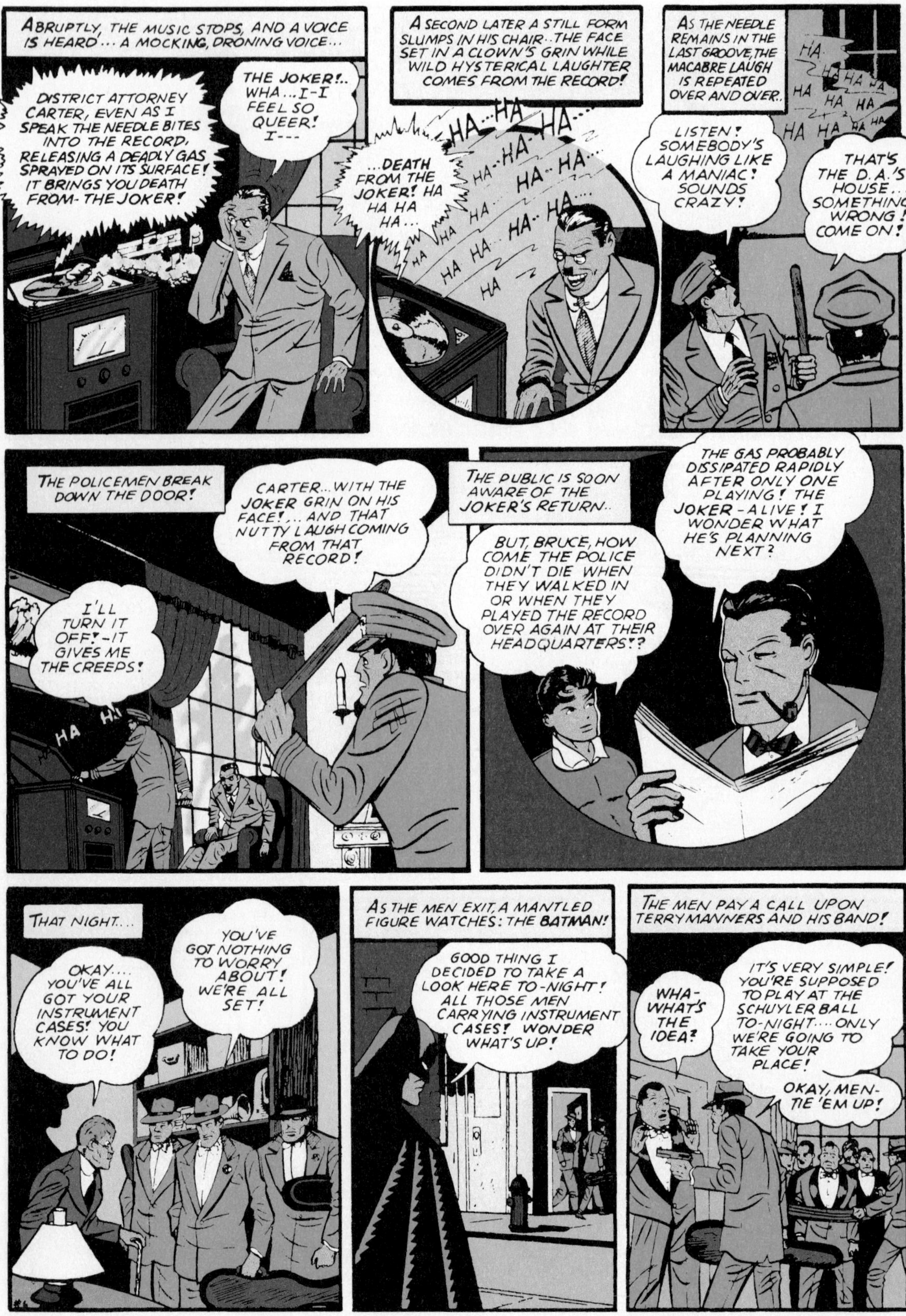
ABRUPTLY, THE MUSIC STOPS, AND A VOICE IS HEARD... A MOCKING, DRONING VOICE...
DISTRICT ATTORNEY CARTER, EVEN AS I SPEAK THE NEEDLE BITES INTO THE RECORD, RELEASING A DEADLY GAS SPRAYED ON ITS SURFACE! IT BRINGS YOU DEATH FROM- THE JOKER!
THE JOKER!.. WHA...I-I FEEL SO QUEER! I---
A SECOND LATER A STILL FORM SLUMPS IN HIS CHAIR..THE FACE SET IN A CLOWN'S GRIN WHILE WILD HYSTERICAL LAUGHTER COMES FROM THE RECORD!
...DEATH FROM THE JOKER! HA HA HA HA...
HA-HA-HA... HA-HA-HA... HA-HA-HA...
AS THE NEEDLE REMAINS IN THE LAST GROOVE, THE MACABRE LAUGH IS REPEATED OVER AND OVER..
LISTEN! SOMEBODY'S LAUGHING LIKE A MANIAC! SOUNDS CRAZY!
THAT'S THE D. A.'S HOUSE... SOMETHING'S WRONG! COME ON!
THE POLICEMEN BREAK DOWN THE DOOR!
CARTER...WITH THE JOKER GRIN ON HIS FACE!...AND THAT NUTTY LAUGH COMING FROM THAT RECORD!
I'LL TURN IT OFF! -IT GIVES ME THE CREEPS!
THE PUBLIC IS SOON AWARE OF THE JOKER'S RETURN..
BUT, BRUCE, HOW COME THE POLICE DIDN'T DIE WHEN THEY WALKED IN OR WHEN THEY PLAYED THE RECORD OVER AGAIN AT THEIR HEADQUARTERS!?
THE GAS PROBABLY DISSIPATED RAPIDLY AFTER ONLY ONE PLAYING! THE JOKER - ALIVE! I WONDER WHAT HE'S PLANNING NEXT?
THAT NIGHT...
OKAY.... YOU'VE ALL GOT YOUR INSTRUMENT CASES! YOU KNOW WHAT TO DO!
YOU'VE GOT NOTHING TO WORRY ABOUT! WE'RE ALL SET!
AS THE MEN EXIT, A MANTLED FIGURE WATCHES: THE BATMAN!
GOOD THING I DECIDED TO TAKE A LOOK HERE TO-NIGHT! ALL THOSE MEN CARRYING INSTRUMENT CASES! WONDER WHAT'S UP!
THE MEN PAY A CALL UPON TERRY MANNERS AND HIS BAND!
WHA- WHAT'S THE IDEA?
IT'S VERY SIMPLE! YOU'RE SUPPOSED TO PLAY AT THE SCHUYLER BALL TO-NIGHT.... ONLY WE'RE GOING TO TAKE YOUR PLACE!
OKAY, MEN- TIE 'EM UP!

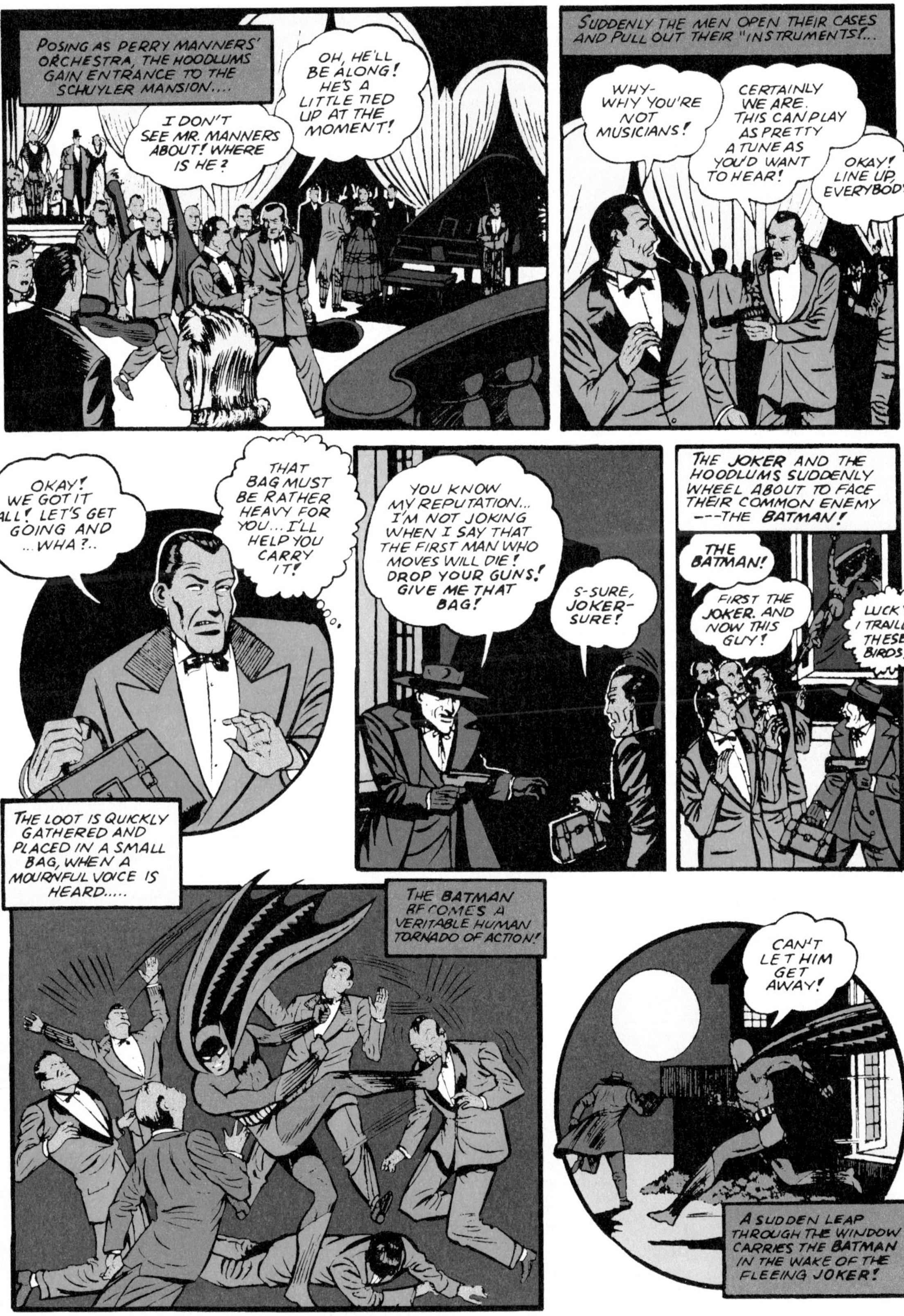
POSING AS PERRY MANNERS' ORCHESTRA, THE HOODLUMS GAIN ENTRANCE TO THE SCHUYLER MANSION....
I DON'T SEE MR. MANNERS ABOUT! WHERE IS HE?
OH, HE'LL BE ALONG! HE'S A LITTLE TIED UP AT THE MOMENT!
SUDDENLY THE MEN OPEN THEIR CASES AND PULL OUT THEIR "INSTRUMENTS!"...
WHY-WHY YOU'RE NOT MUSICIANS!
CERTAINLY WE ARE. THIS CAN PLAY AS PRETTY A TUNE AS YOU'D WANT TO HEAR!
OKAY! LINE UP, EVERYBODY!
OKAY! WE GOT IT ALL! LET'S GET GOING AND ...WHA?..
THAT BAG MUST BE RATHER HEAVY FOR YOU... I'LL HELP YOU CARRY IT!
THE LOOT IS QUICKLY GATHERED AND PLACED IN A SMALL BAG, WHEN A MOURNFUL VOICE IS HEARD.....
YOU KNOW MY REPUTATION... I'M NOT JOKING WHEN I SAY THAT THE FIRST MAN WHO MOVES WILL DIE! DROP YOUR GUNS! GIVE ME THAT BAG!
S-SURE, JOKER-SURE!
THE JOKER AND THE HOODLUMS SUDDENLY WHEEL ABOUT TO FACE THEIR COMMON ENEMY ---THE BATMAN!
THE BATMAN!
FIRST THE JOKER. AND NOW THIS GUY!
LUCKY I TRAILED THESE BIRDS!
THE BATMAN BECOMES A VERITABLE HUMAN TORNADO OF ACTION!
CAN'T LET HIM GET AWAY!
A SUDDEN LEAP THROUGH THE WINDOW CARRIES THE BATMAN IN THE WAKE OF THE FLEEING JOKER!

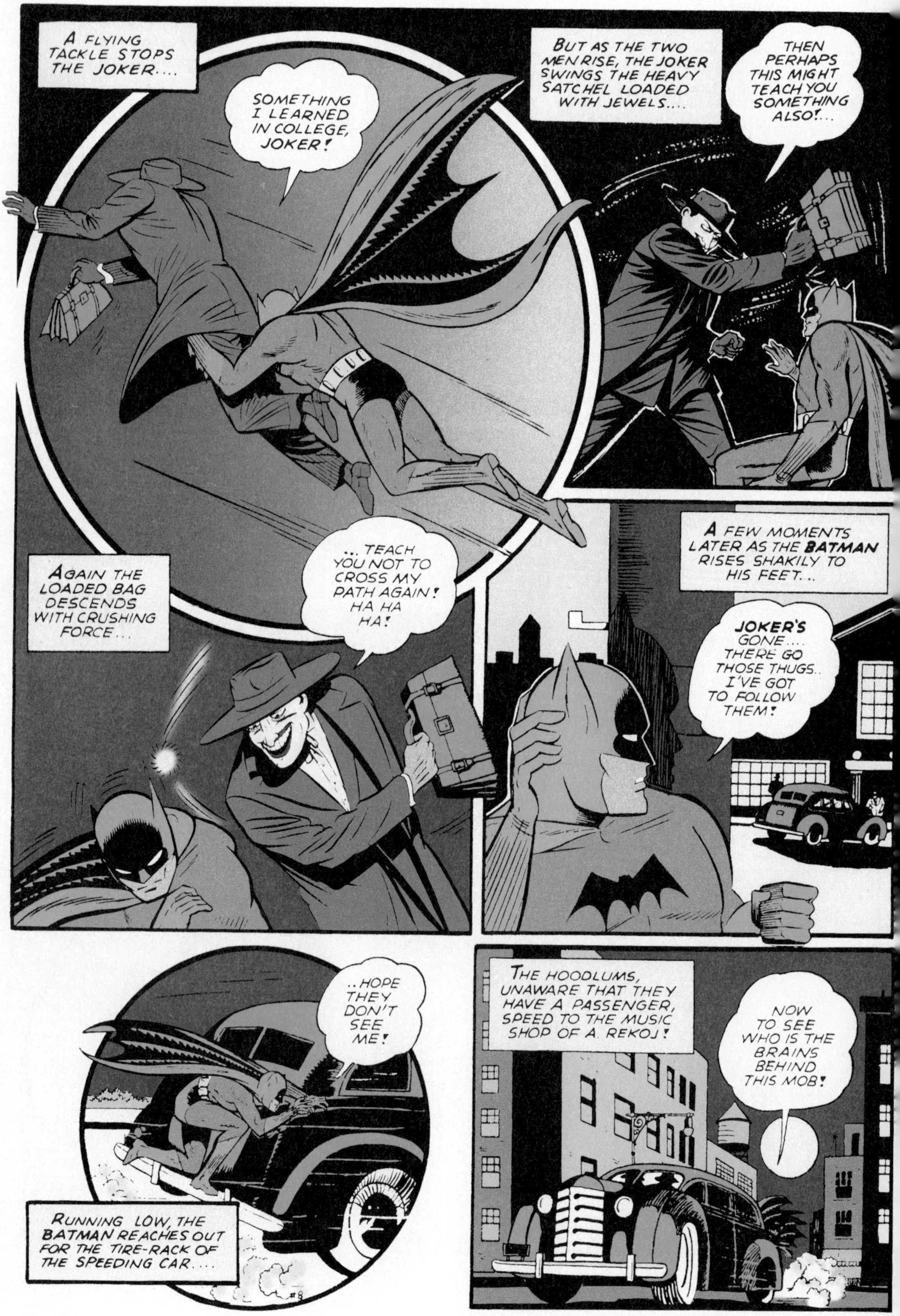
A FLYING TACKLE STOPS THE JOKER....
SOMETHING I LEARNED IN COLLEGE, JOKER!
BUT AS THE TWO MEN RISE, THE JOKER SWINGS THE HEAVY SATCHEL LOADED WITH JEWELS....
THEN PERHAPS THIS MIGHT TEACH YOU SOMETHING ALSO!...
AGAIN THE LOADED BAG DESCENDS WITH CRUSHING FORCE...
... TEACH YOU NOT TO CROSS MY PATH AGAIN! HA HA HA!
A FEW MOMENTS LATER AS THE BATMAN RISES SHAKILY TO HIS FEET...
JOKER'S GONE.... THERE GO THOSE THUGS.. I'VE GOT TO FOLLOW THEM!
..HOPE THEY DON'T SEE ME!
RUNNING LOW, THE BATMAN REACHES OUT FOR THE TIRE-RACK OF THE SPEEDING CAR....
THE HOODLUMS, UNAWARE THAT THEY HAVE A PASSENGER, SPEED TO THE MUSIC SHOP OF A. REKOJ!
NOW TO SEE WHO IS THE BRAINS BEHIND THIS MOB!

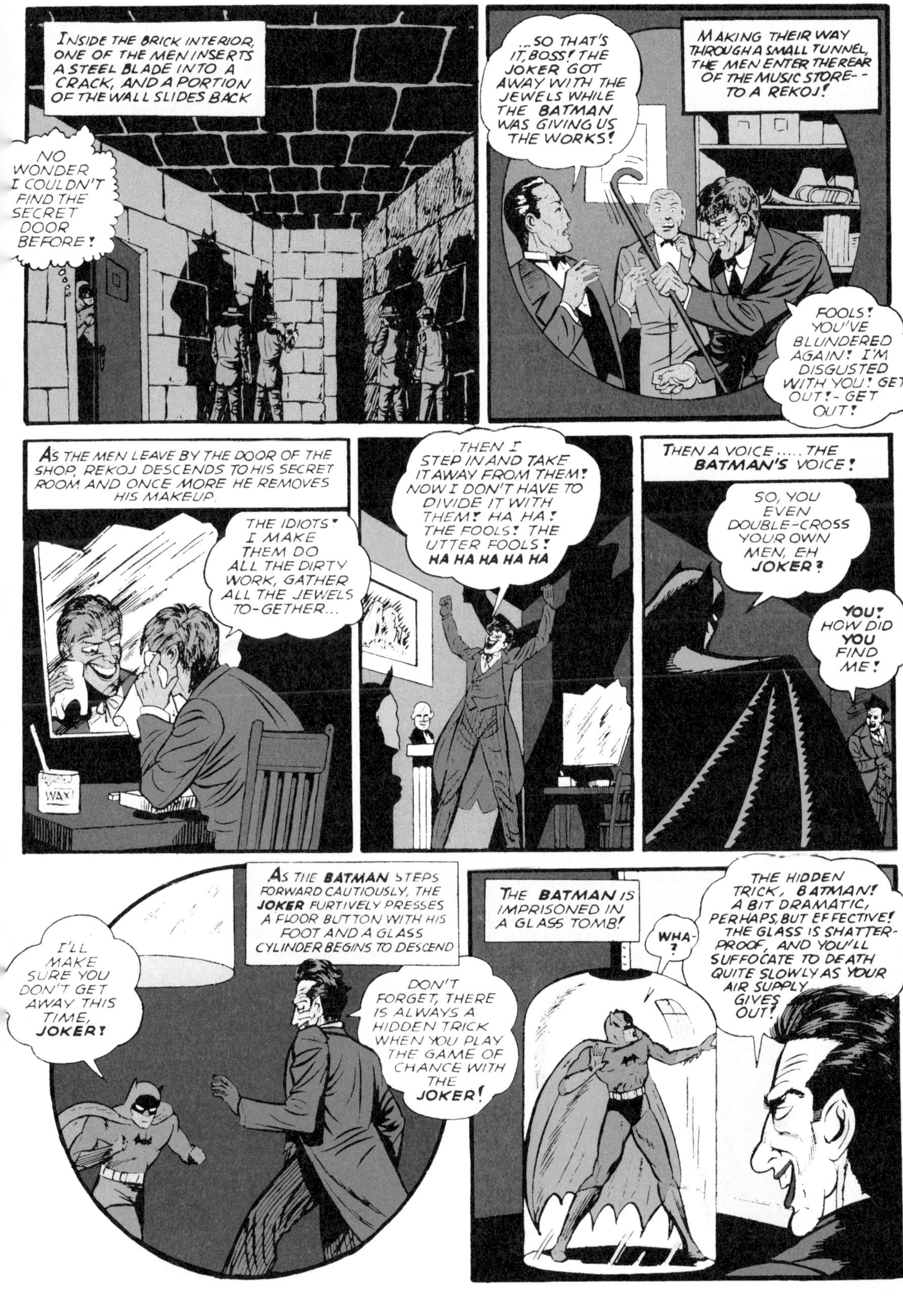
INSIDE THE BRICK INTERIOR, ONE OF THE MEN INSERTS A STEEL BLADE INTO A CRACK, AND A PORTION OF THE WALL SLIDES BACK
NO WONDER I COULDN'T FIND THE SECRET DOOR BEFORE!
MAKING THEIR WAY THROUGH A SMALL TUNNEL, THE MEN ENTER THE REAR OF THE MUSIC STORE-- TO A REKOJ!
...SO THAT'S IT, BOSS! THE JOKER GOT AWAY WITH THE JEWELS WHILE THE BATMAN WAS GIVING US THE WORKS!
FOOLS! YOU'VE BLUNDERED AGAIN! I'M DISGUSTED WITH YOU! GET OUT!- GET OUT!
AS THE MEN LEAVE BY THE DOOR OF THE SHOP, REKOJ DESCENDS TO HIS SECRET ROOM AND ONCE MORE HE REMOVES HIS MAKEUP.
THE IDIOTS! I MAKE THEM DO ALL THE DIRTY WORK, GATHER ALL THE JEWELS TO-GETHER...
WAX
...THEN I STEP IN AND TAKE IT AWAY FROM THEM! NOW I DON'T HAVE TO DIVIDE IT WITH THEM! HA HA! THE FOOLS! THE UTTER FOOLS! HA HA HA HA HA
THEN A VOICE..... THE BATMAN'S VOICE!
SO, YOU EVEN DOUBLE-CROSS YOUR OWN MEN, EH JOKER?
YOU! HOW DID YOU FIND ME!
AS THE BATMAN STEPS FORWARD CAUTIOUSLY, THE JOKER FURTIVELY PRESSES A FLOOR BUTTON WITH HIS FOOT AND A GLASS CYLINDER BEGINS TO DESCEND
I'LL MAKE SURE YOU DON'T GET AWAY THIS TIME, JOKER!
DON'T FORGET, THERE IS ALWAYS A HIDDEN TRICK WHEN YOU PLAY THE GAME OF CHANCE WITH THE JOKER!
THE BATMAN IS IMPRISONED IN A GLASS TOMB!
WHA-?
THE HIDDEN TRICK, BATMAN! A BIT DRAMATIC, PERHAPS, BUT EFFECTIVE! THE GLASS IS SHATTER-PROOF, AND YOU'LL SUFFOCATE TO DEATH QUITE SLOWLY AS YOUR AIR SUPPLY GIVES OUT!

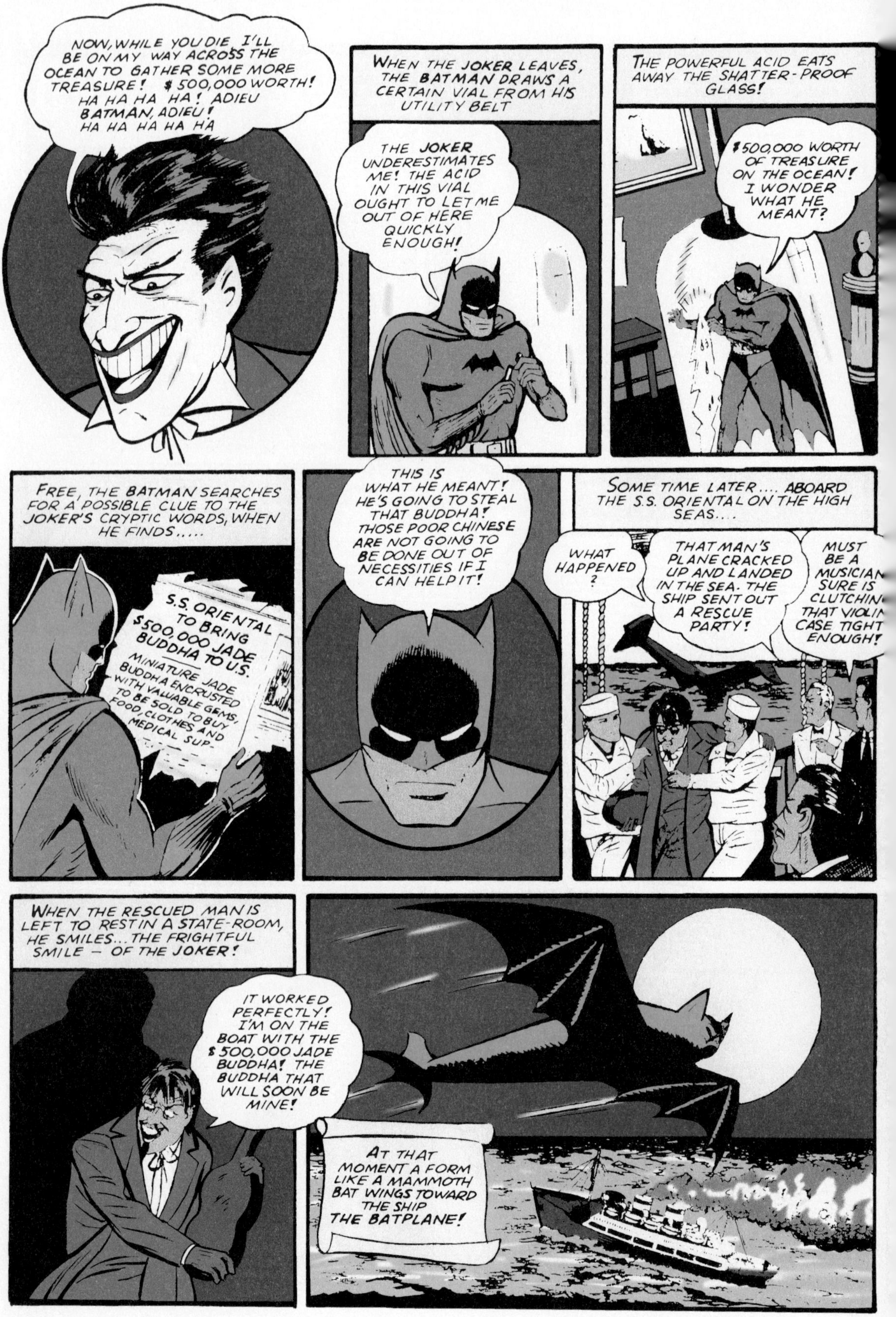
NOW, WHILE YOU DIE I'LL BE ON MY WAY ACROSS THE OCEAN TO GATHER SOME MORE TREASURE! $500,000 WORTH! HA HA HA HA! ADIEU BATMAN, ADIEU! HA HA HA HA HA
WHEN THE JOKER LEAVES, THE BATMAN DRAWS A CERTAIN VIAL FROM HIS UTILITY BELT
THE JOKER UNDERESTIMATES ME! THE ACID IN THIS VIAL OUGHT TO LET ME OUT OF HERE QUICKLY ENOUGH!
THE POWERFUL ACID EATS AWAY THE SHATTER-PROOF GLASS!
$500,000 WORTH OF TREASURE ON THE OCEAN! I WONDER WHAT HE MEANT?
FREE, THE BATMAN SEARCHES FOR A POSSIBLE CLUE TO THE JOKER'S CRYPTIC WORDS, WHEN HE FINDS.....
S.S. ORIENTAL TO BRING $500,000 JADE BUDDHA TO U.S.
MINIATURE JADE BUDDHA ENCRUSTED WITH VALUABLE GEMS, TO BE SOLD TO BUY FOOD, CLOTHES AND MEDICAL SUP-
THIS IS WHAT HE MEANT! HE'S GOING TO STEAL THAT BUDDHA! THOSE POOR CHINESE ARE NOT GOING TO BE DONE OUT OF NECESSITIES IF I CAN HELP IT!
SOME TIME LATER.... ABOARD THE S.S. ORIENTAL ON THE HIGH SEAS....
WHAT HAPPENED?
THAT MAN'S PLANE CRACKED UP AND LANDED IN THE SEA. THE SHIP SENT OUT A RESCUE PARTY!
MUST BE A MUSICIAN SURE IS CLUTCHIN THAT VIOLI CASE TIGHT ENOUGH!
WHEN THE RESCUED MAN IS LEFT TO REST IN A STATE-ROOM, HE SMILES... THE FRIGHTFUL SMILE – OF THE JOKER!
IT WORKED PERFECTLY! I'M ON THE BOAT WITH THE $500,000 JADE BUDDHA! THE BUDDHA THAT WILL SOON BE MINE!
AT THAT MOMENT A FORM LIKE A MAMMOTH BAT WINGS TOWARD THE SHIP THE BATPLANE!

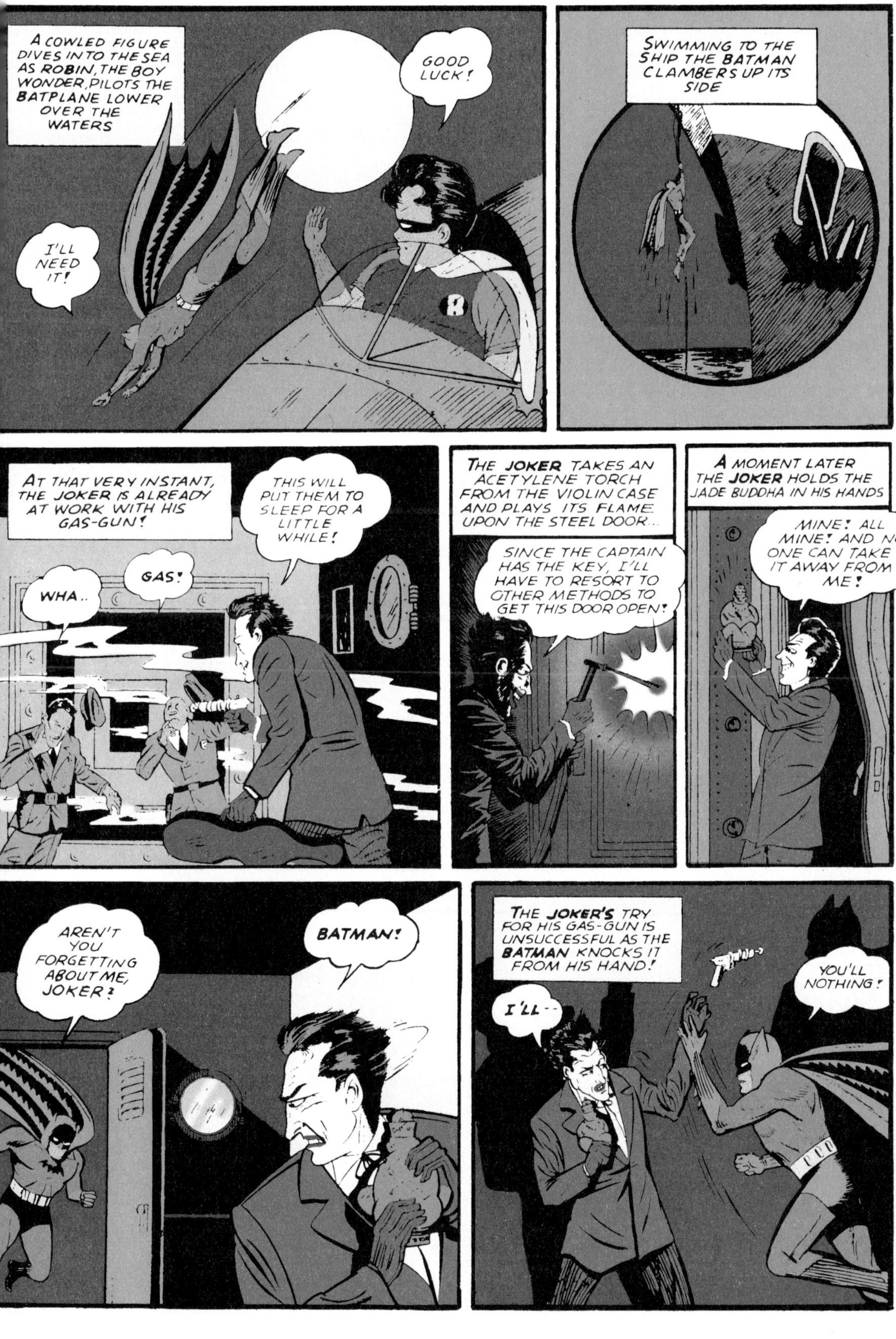
A COWLED FIGURE DIVES INTO THE SEA AS ROBIN, THE BOY WONDER, PILOTS THE BATPLANE LOWER OVER THE WATERS
GOOD LUCK!
I'LL NEED IT!
SWIMMING TO THE SHIP THE BATMAN CLAMBERS UP ITS SIDE
AT THAT VERY INSTANT, THE JOKER IS ALREADY AT WORK WITH HIS GAS-GUN!
THIS WILL PUT THEM TO SLEEP FOR A LITTLE WHILE!
WHA..
GAS!
THE JOKER TAKES AN ACETYLENE TORCH FROM THE VIOLIN CASE AND PLAYS ITS FLAME UPON THE STEEL DOOR...
SINCE THE CAPTAIN HAS THE KEY, I'LL HAVE TO RESORT TO OTHER METHODS TO GET THIS DOOR OPEN!
A MOMENT LATER THE JOKER HOLDS THE JADE BUDDHA IN HIS HANDS
MINE! ALL MINE! AND NO ONE CAN TAKE IT AWAY FROM ME!
AREN'T YOU FORGETTING ABOUT ME, JOKER?
BATMAN!
THE JOKER'S TRY FOR HIS GAS-GUN IS UNSUCCESSFUL AS THE BATMAN KNOCKS IT FROM HIS HAND!
I'LL--
YOU'LL NOTHING!

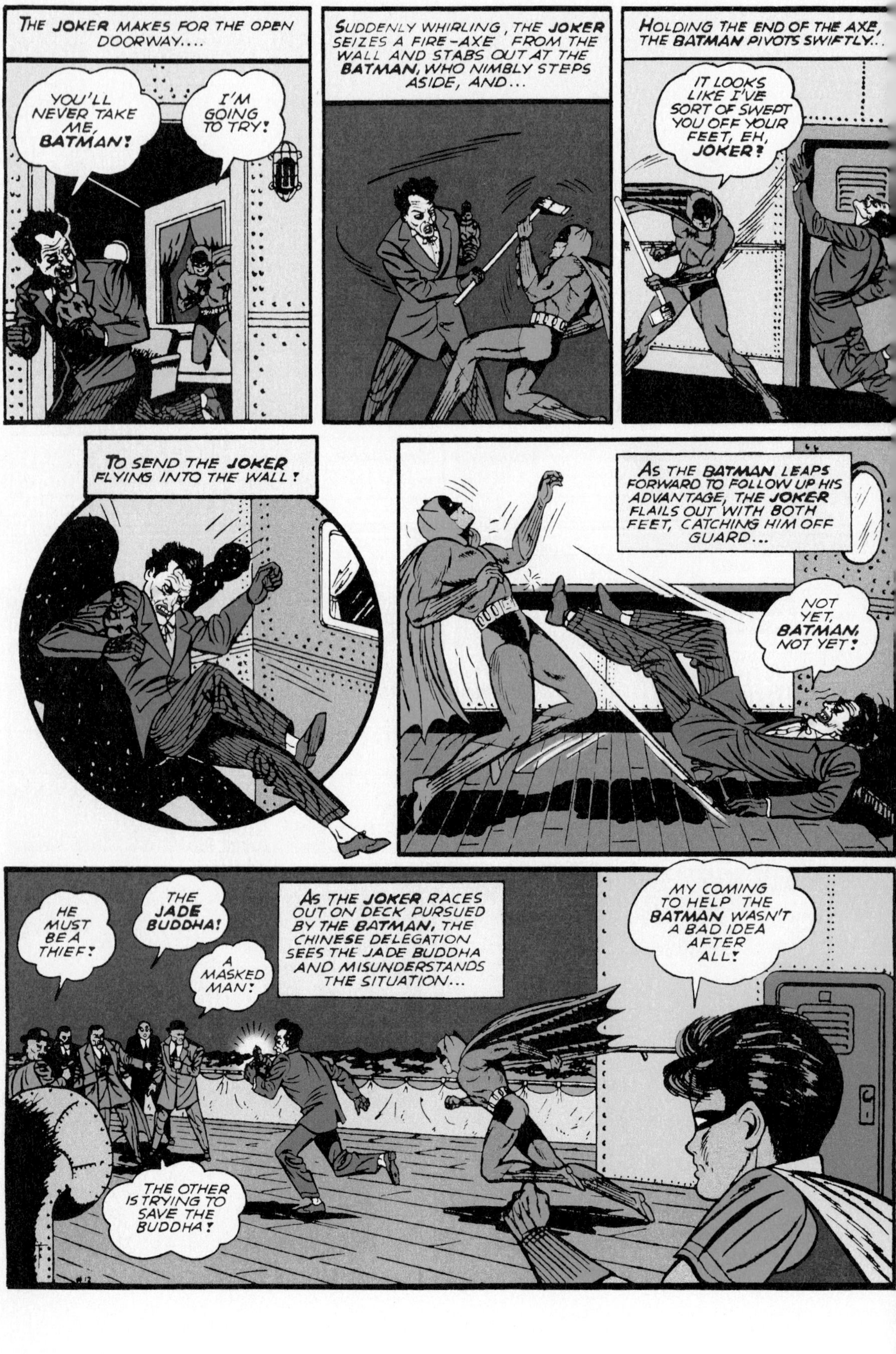
THE JOKER MAKES FOR THE OPEN DOORWAY....
YOU'LL NEVER TAKE ME, BATMAN!
I'M GOING TO TRY!
SUDDENLY WHIRLING, THE JOKER SEIZES A FIRE-AXE FROM THE WALL AND STABS OUT AT THE BATMAN, WHO NIMBLY STEPS ASIDE, AND...
HOLDING THE END OF THE AXE, THE BATMAN PIVOTS SWIFTLY...
IT LOOKS LIKE I'VE SORT OF SWEPT YOU OFF YOUR FEET, EH, JOKER?
TO SEND THE JOKER FLYING INTO THE WALL!
AS THE BATMAN LEAPS FORWARD TO FOLLOW UP HIS ADVANTAGE, THE JOKER FLAILS OUT WITH BOTH FEET, CATCHING HIM OFF GUARD...
NOT YET, BATMAN, NOT YET!
HE MUST BE A THIEF!
THE JADE BUDDHA!
A MASKED MAN!
AS THE JOKER RACES OUT ON DECK PURSUED BY THE BATMAN, THE CHINESE DELEGATION SEES THE JADE BUDDHA AND MISUNDERSTANDS THE SITUATION...
MY COMING TO HELP THE BATMAN WASN'T A BAD IDEA AFTER ALL!
THE OTHER IS TRYING TO SAVE THE BUDDHA!

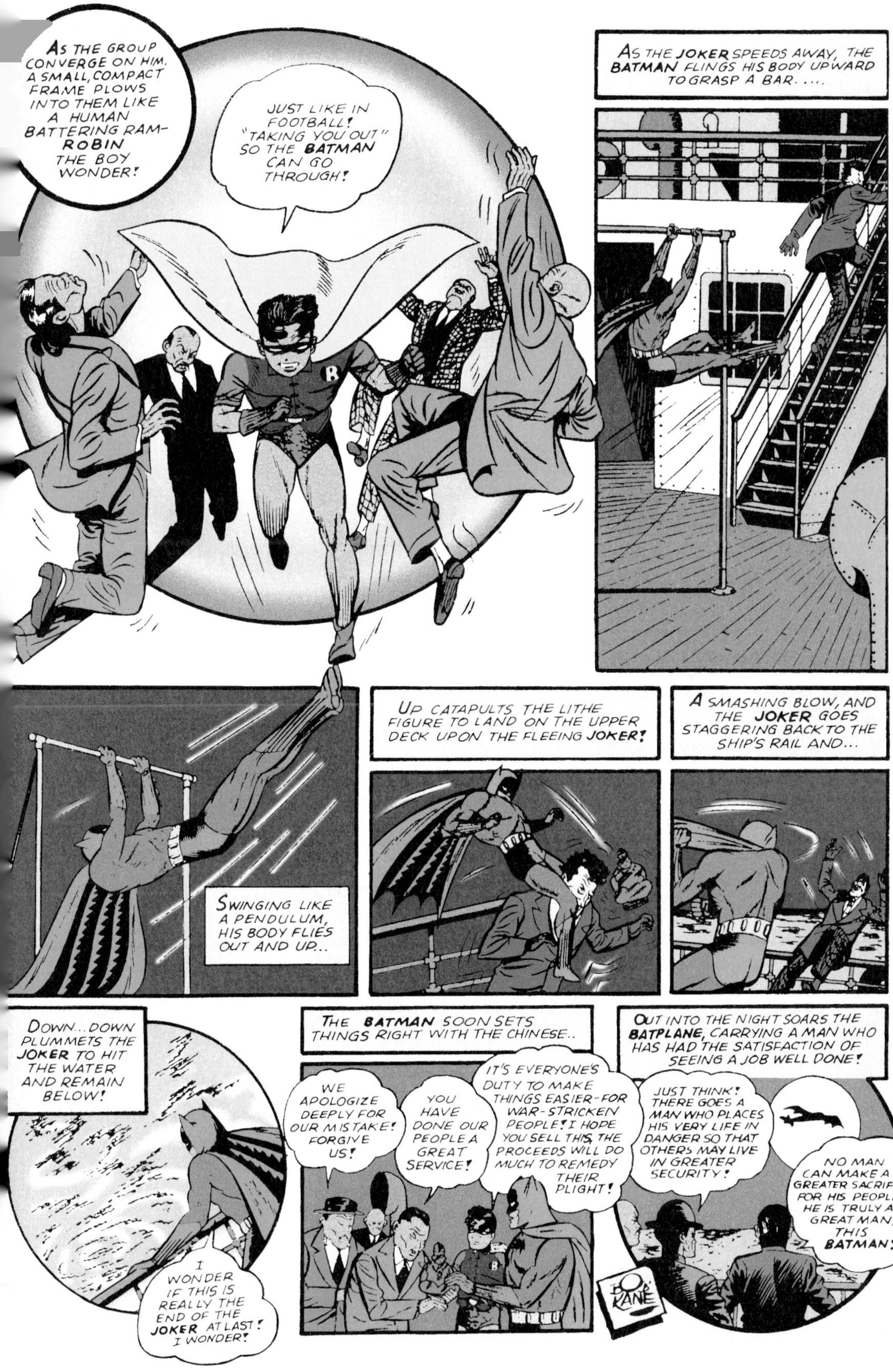

AS THE GROUP CONVERGE ON HIM, A SMALL, COMPACT FRAME PLOWS INTO THEM LIKE A HUMAN BATTERING RAM- ROBIN THE BOY WONDER!
JUST LIKE IN FOOTBALL! "TAKING YOU OUT" SO THE BATMAN CAN GO THROUGH!
AS THE JOKER SPEEDS AWAY, THE BATMAN FLINGS HIS BODY UPWARD TO GRASP A BAR.....
SWINGING LIKE A PENDULUM, HIS BODY FLIES OUT AND UP...
UP CATAPULTS THE LITHE FIGURE TO LAND ON THE UPPER DECK UPON THE FLEEING JOKER!
A SMASHING BLOW, AND THE JOKER GOES STAGGERING BACK TO THE SHIP'S RAIL AND...
DOWN...DOWN PLUMMETS THE JOKER TO HIT THE WATER AND REMAIN BELOW!
I WONDER IF THIS IS REALLY THE END OF THE JOKER AT LAST! I WONDER!
THE BATMAN SOON SETS THINGS RIGHT WITH THE CHINESE..
WE APOLOGIZE DEEPLY FOR OUR MISTAKE! FORGIVE US!
YOU HAVE DONE OUR PEOPLE A GREAT SERVICE!
IT'S EVERYONE'S DUTY TO MAKE THINGS EASIER-FOR WAR-STRICKEN PEOPLE! I HOPE YOU SELL THIS, THE PROCEEDS WILL DO MUCH TO REMEDY THEIR PLIGHT!
OUT INTO THE NIGHT SOARS THE BATPLANE, CARRYING A MAN WHO HAS HAD THE SATISFACTION OF SEEING A JOB WELL DONE!
JUST THINK! THERE GOES A MAN WHO PLACES HIS VERY LIFE IN DANGER SO THAT OTHERS MAY LIVE IN GREATER SECURITY!
NO MAN CAN MAKE A GREATER SACRIFICE FOR HIS PEOPLE! HE IS TRULY A GREAT MAN, THIS BATMAN!
BOB KANE

BIOGRAPHIES

BOB KANE

Robert Kahn was born on October 24, 1916, in the Bronx, and at age 18 legally changed his name to Kane. In 1936, this self-proclaimed "compulsive doodleholic" pencilled and inked his first comic book work, *Hiram Hick*. By 1938 he was selling humorous filler stories to DC Comics, including "Professor Doolittle" and "Ginger Snap."

Kane met writer Bill Finger at a party in 1938, and they soon were collaborating on comic book submissions. Their most famous effort, Batman, first appeared in DETECTIVE COMICS #27 (May 1939). As Batman's popularity demanded additional output, Kane kept up the pace by adding assistants and dropping non-Batman assignments. He discontinued his comic book efforts in mid-1943 to pencil the daily *Batman and Robin* newspaper strip. After the strip's 1946 demise, Kane returned to illustrating Batman's comic book adventures and, with the help of several ghosts, remained involved with comics until his retirement in 1968.

The success of the *Batman* television series brought Kane and his art back into the public eye in 1966. He was subsequently featured in various one-man art shows at galleries and museums nationwide and released a number of limited-edition lithographs. He served as a consultant on the 1989 *Batman* feature film and its sequels. His autobiography, *Batman and Me*, was published in 1989, and in 1996 he was inducted into the Eisner Awards Hall of Fame. Kane died on November 3, 1998.

BILL FINGER

William Finger was born on February 8, 1914. He met cartoonist Bob Kane at a party in 1938, and, soonafter, they began collaborating on several adventure strips. Within a year, Batman appeared. Finger's fondness for pulp fiction and movies influenced his plots and writing style for comic books. He worked on many other DC characters and titles, scripted some of the 1940s daily and Sunday *Batman and Robin* newspaper strip continuities, and wrote for Quality, Fawcett and Timely.

Bill Finger was one of the true innovative talents and legendary figures of the comics industry. He collaborated with Bob Kane on the creation of Batman and scripted the first two episodes of the Dark Knight's appearances in DETECTIVE COMICS. Finger went on to write features for many publishers, including Plastic Man (for Quality Comics), Green Lantern, Wildcat, Vigilante, Johnny Quick, Superman, Superboy, Blackhawk, Tomahawk, Robin, Challengers of the Unknown, Batman (in the comics and in the syndicated newspaper strip), as well as Captain America and All Winners Comics (for Timely). He also wrote for radio and television, contributing scripts to *Mark Trail, 77 Sunset Strip, The Roaring Twenties, Hawaiian Eye*, and, naturally enough, two episodes of *Batman* TV program in 1966. He also wrote television commercials and one feature film, the 1969 cult film *The Green Slime*. Finger was still writing for DC Comics at the time of his death in 1974.

GARDNER FOX

Born in 1911 in Brooklyn, New York, Gardner Fox was probably the single most imaginative and productive writer in the Golden Age of comics. In the 1940s, he created or co-created dozens of long-running features for DC Comics, including the Flash, Hawkman, the Sandman, and Doctor Fate, as well as penning most of the adventures of comics' first super-team, the Justice Society of America. He was also the second person to script Batman, beginning with the Dark Knight Detective's third story. For other companies over the years Fox also wrote Skyman, the Face, Jet Powers, Dr. Strange, Doc Savage and many others—including *Crom the Barbarian*, the first sword-and-sorcery series in comics. Following the revival in the late 1950s of the superhero genre, Fox assembled Earth's Mightiest Heroes once more and scripted an unbroken 65-issue run of JUSTICE LEAGUE OF AMERICA. Though he produced thousands of other scripts and wrote over 100 books, it is perhaps this body of work for which he is best known. Fox passed away in 1986.

SHELDON MOLDOFF

Born in 1920, Sheldon Moldoff broke into comics by assisting Bob Kane on Batman—a collaboration that would last, on and off, for almost two decades. Following his work on the Dark Knight, Moldoff soon got assignments of his own from DC, including "The Black Pirate" in ACTION COMICS and "The Hawkman" in FLASH COMICS, both collaborations with writer Gardner Fox. In time, Moldoff became one of the company's most prolific artists.

After serving in World War II, Moldoff returned to work for former All-American publisher M.C. Gaines, who had parted company with DC to create the new E.C. comics line. As E.C.'s horror comics wound down in the mid-1950s, Moldoff reunited with Bob Kane to draw most of the Batman stories credited to Kane between 1954 and 1967. He also worked with Kane on his early 1960s cartoon takeoff on Batman, *Courageous Cat and Minute Mouse*, and inked quite a few stories and covers for DC. Moldoff remained a popular and frequent convention guest until his death in 2012.

JERRY ROBINSON

It was around October 1939 when a 17-year-old Jerry Robinson began assisting Bob Kane. Robinson worked on *Rusty and His Pals* and *Clip Carson, Soldier of Fortune* in addition to lettering and inking backgrounds on Batman. Within three years, he was completely pencilling, lettering, inking and coloring certain stories and covers for BATMAN and DETECTIVE COMICS. His contributions to Robin and the Joker proved to be significant events in Batman's history.

Robinson's credits are many and diverse. They include advertising work and comic book art for Vigilante, Johnny Quick and the Black Terror, as well as illustrations for science fiction, crime, war, Western and other genres. He created and illustrated various syndicated newspaper features (including *Jet Scott*) and he taught and lectured on graphic journalism at the School of Visual Arts and The New School in New York City. Robinson is the only past president of both the Association of American Editorial Cartoonists and the National Cartoonists Society, and he was awarded three Reubens by the NCS. He also served as the President and Editorial Director of the Cartoonists & Writers Syndicate and on the board of directors of the International Museum of Cartoon Art. In addition to writing several books and illustrating more than 30 others, he produced the syndicated political cartoon *Life With Robinson* for many years and curated museum and gallery exhibitions of cartoon art in the U.S. and around the world. In 2004 Robinson was inducted into the Eisner Awards Hall of Fame. He passed away on December 11, 2011.

GEORGE ROUSSOS

Born in August of 1920, George Roussos was 19 years old when he was hired by Jerry Robinson to assist on Batman. Roussos started on May 30, 1940, inking backgrounds and handling lettering. His first work appeared in BATMAN #2 (Summer 1940), and he became a mainstay on the character until 1944, when he left the DC bullpen to freelance.

Roussos pencilled, inked and colored Airwave, as well as inking Superman, Johnny Quick, Vigilante, the Star-Spangled Kid and many other DC heroes.

From the late 1940s and into the 1950s, Roussos worked freelance for a number of comic book publishers, including Harvey, Hillman, Avon, Ziff-Davis, Fiction House, E.C., Timely, Prize and Pines. In 1963 he began inking stories for Marvel (sometimes using the name George Bell), ultimately leaving DC around 1970 to work fulltime as Marvel's cover colorist. Other efforts included work on syndicated newspaper strips and in advertising. Roussos remained in the comics industry well into the 1990s. He passed away on February 19, 2000.